WEST ACADEMIC PUBLISHING'S EMERITUS ADVISORY BOARD

WEST ACADEMIC PUBLISHING'S LAW SCHOOL ADVISORY BOARD

CONFLICT OF LAWS

CASES—COMMENTS—QUESTIONS

Eleventh Edition

■ ■ ■

Herma Hill Kay
Late Barbara Nachtrieb Armstrong Professor of Law
and Former Dean of the School of Law
University of California Berkeley

Larry Kramer
President, William and Flora Hewlett Foundation
and Dean Emeritus, Stanford Law School

Kermit Roosevelt
David Berger Professor for the Administration of Justice
University of Pennsylvania

David L. Franklin
Assistant Professor of Law
DePaul University

AMERICAN CASEBOOK SERIES®

WEST ACADEMIC PUBLISHING

444 Cedar Street, Suite 700
St. Paul, MN 55101
1-877-888-1330

Printed in the United States of America

ISBN: 978-1-63659-469-9

To Herma—
scholar, teacher, friend

PREFACE

Law comes from many sources. In an ideal world, the authority of these sources would be clearly defined and neatly demarcated, so that no event or occurrence was ever subject to control by more than one law maker or law enforcer. But such is not our world. The power of different bodies to make or administer law is often unclear and, even when clear, frequently overlaps. Conflicts arise, and a way is needed to resolve them. This, broadly speaking, is the subject matter of "conflict of laws."

The classic conflict-of-laws problem—classic at least in the sense of being the problem most thought about and discussed—involves a choice of law between or among states. In the United States, for example, a transaction or occurrence may have contacts with more than one state: the parties may live or action may be taken in different places. When this is so, and a dispute arises, whose law should govern? That inquiry, in turn, may be broken down into at least three further questions: (1) What are the limits of each state's power to regulate? (2) Acting within those limits, has more than one state sought to apply its law to the particular dispute? (3) If so, how should we choose among them? The first question is one of fundamental or constitutional law, ordinarily resolved in interstate disputes by reference to the United States Constitution. The latter two questions, in contrast, involve matters of policy that are decided by examining the relevant state or federal law. As the materials in this book illustrate, the states and Congress have used many different methods to identify and resolve choice-of-law problems.

Choice of law is not the only situation in which judges or policymakers must sort out overlapping exercises of authority. It is, however, the situation that has received the most careful scrutiny. Studying choice of law is thus useful not merely for its own sake, but also to understand other types of conflicts. The organization of the book reflects this conception. Part I focuses on choice of law; it is designed to teach students the law in this area but also to get them thinking more generally about techniques for resolving conflicts among lawmaking or policymaking entities. Part II then presents additional contexts in which the activities of more than one authority may overlap and be inconsistent. By comparing the basic choice-of-law model to solutions developed in other areas, we believe students will develop a better understanding of both choice of law and these other areas.

Part I consists of the first three chapters, which present choice of law as both a policy and a constitutional problem. The first two chapters address the policy question. Chapter 1 lays out the old learning. Choice of law has been thoroughly reexamined in the last sixty years, but it is premature to abandon the teaching of traditional theories. Analytically, one cannot fully understand the new learning except in light of the old. Moreover, even apart from jurisprudential considerations, judicial rejection of the traditional approach is by no means unanimous, and the careful lawyer must still be prepared to argue this theory in support of his or her case.

Chapter 2 explores modern departures from the traditional approach. The chapter emphasizes four approaches in particular: party autonomy, interest analysis, the "better law" approach, and the Second Restatement. Time and judicial practice have shown these to be the most viable modern alternatives. In addition, we include a short introductory section on statutory solutions as well as a concluding section on the draft Third Restatement, which aims to achieve a workable blend of the traditional approach's rule-based approach and the Second Restatement's focus on state policies and state interests.

In this edition, we have revised and updated the materials on party autonomy, complex litigation, and conflicts on the Internet as the law in those areas continues to evolve. One problem facing a teacher of conflicts is how to give students a sense of the field's relevance. Most choice-of-law doctrine developed in cases dealing with guest statutes, interspousal immunity, spendthrift provisions, and other matters unlikely to stir the modern imagination. Many of these cases must be retained, because they still contain the best and clearest explanations of the law (though we have ruthlessly pruned the materials to eliminate redundancy). But too large a dose of such problems risks leaving students feeling that choice of law is arcane, unimportant, even a bit silly. In fact, choice of law is—or can by a good lawyer be made—central to practically any case, and choice-of-law problems are critical in our interdependent modern world. We emphasize this point throughout the book, but the materials on complex litigation and the Internet especially are intended to focus attention on the centrality of choice of law to some of today's most pressing legal issues.

Chapter 3 turns to the problem of constitutional limits on choice of law. Essential to any regime in which more than one lawmaking authority exists is a process for defining the outer boundaries of each lawmaker's power; this process determines the field within which the policy debate takes place. Among states of the United States, limits on sovereign authority are framed as constitutional questions, mainly questions of due process, full faith and credit, and privileges and immunities. Generally speaking, these clauses reflect concern for interstate relations and for fairness to individuals, issues the Supreme Court has dealt with in several fascinating lines of cases. Chapter 3 presents these cases in a manner designed to allow teachers simultaneously to explore three distinct themes: the doctrine as it has actually developed; the complex substantive issues raised in thinking about limits on sovereignty; and the institutional difficulties faced in designing these limits. New sections in this edition reflect recent developments concerning the dormant Commerce Clause's extraterritoriality doctrine and the issue of interstate sovereign immunity.

Part II consists of the final five chapters. As noted above, Chapters 4 through 8 examine other conflicts among lawmakers or law enforcers. Our choice of topics by no means exhausts the possibilities, and we invite readers to think of additional contexts in which the basic choice-of-law model applies or helps to clarify analysis. We have selected what we believe are the most salient and illuminating problems. Some of these raise policy questions of constitutional limits more closely related to the material covered in Chapter 3.

Constitutional questions, for example, are the focus of Chapter 4, which deals with adjudicatory jurisdiction. States enact laws to define the particular cases or controversies that the state's lawmakers want their courts to hear. Choices made by different states may come into conflict if a case falls within the jurisdiction-granting provisions of more than one state. Here, too, deciding which state's courts should hear the case presents both a policy question and a constitutional question. In contrast to "ordinary" choice of law, however, many states have made the policy question moot by adopting statutes that assert power to the full extent permitted by the Constitution. As a result, and also because courts generally exercise jurisdiction over any case within their statutory power, the case law has focused primarily on constitutional limits. Chapter 4 examines the extent to which constitutional constraints on adjudicatory jurisdiction are (or should be seen as) analogous to the constraints on choice of law discussed in Chapter 3. This edition contains several new cases in the area of specific jurisdiction.

Chapter 5 deals with recognition of judgments. It is relatively unchanged, although it has been updated to reflect important developments since the last edition. Chapter 6 covers selected problems of family law. It has been revised and updated to include recent decisions, and although the Supreme Court has eliminated interstate variation on the question of same-sex marriage, same-sex divorce and adoption continue to present difficult issues, which are addressed at length in this chapter.

Chapter 7 turns to conflicts between state and federal law. Many teachers mistakenly assume that there are no real conflicts here because the supremacy clause of the United States Constitution directs that federal law shall govern. But difficult questions respecting the permissible scope of federal law remain, and the mere fact that Congress can impose federal law does not mean either that it has done so or that it should. Choosing between state and federal law in cases involving both thus presents difficult and interesting questions of constitutional law and federal policy. This edition contains a distinct section on preemption, but as in previous editions we have chosen to examine only a few of the problems here: federal question jurisdiction, the *Erie* doctrine, federal common law, and the applicability of federal law in state courts. Note, however, that many other aspects of federal jurisdiction—such as separation of powers, sovereign immunity, abstention, and habeas corpus—could just as profitably be examined in choice-of-law terms.

Finally, Chapter 8 deals with international conflicts. There is growing interest in this area among students and teachers, and for good reason. International law is rapidly emerging as the most exciting field of law today. The growth of the European Community, the collapse of the Soviet Union, the spread of democratic institutions around the world, the strengthening of international organizations like the United Nations and WTO, the growth of human rights treaties and conventions, and a variety of other developments highlight the importance of international law and make it essential to pay more attention to our relations with other countries. Conflict of laws, which is, after all, essentially devoted to the problem of facilitating governance by more than one sovereign, obviously has a significant role to play in understanding and shaping these developments.

Chapter 8 exposes students to the core set of issues needed to understand the place of conflict-of-laws analysis in international law. Section 1 deals with the extent to which international law imposes constraints on legislative jurisdiction analogous to those imposed on the states by the Constitution. The section then turns to the problem of making choices within those limits, using the Supreme Court's decisions in *Morrison*, *RJR Nabisco*, and *Hoffman La-Roche* to illuminate the issue. The geographic scope of constitutional rights is also discussed through the lens of the *Verdugo-Urquidez*, *Boumediene*, and *Hernandez* cases. New questions about the application of constitutional rights to detainees at Guantanamo Bay in the wake of *Boumediene* are also explored.

Section 2 contrasts the approach taken in American courts with that developed in Europe; we focus on Europe not because what happens there is intrinsically more important than what happens elsewhere in the world, but because other nations have for the most part simply copied the European model. It includes the recent European codifications, Rome I and II. Section 3 turns to the problem of public international law in the form of the act-of-state doctrine. Finally, the chapter closes with a section on recognition of judgments. The materials are organized to facilitate comparison with domestic choice of law: To what extent are the methods and techniques developed in Part I applicable to international conflicts? Structurally, the problems seem identical. But variations in law and culture are much greater in the international arena, while the constraining force of community is weaker. Exploring how these differences matter (if at all) is fascinating and worthwhile.

The editorial practices followed in the book require brief explanations. In general we have reprinted cases rather fully in a desire to provide class material that retains the texture of the originals, but we have not carried this approach so far as to preserve passages that are repetitious or irrelevant. Authorities cited in principal cases have been ruthlessly edited, and only those citations that build an understanding of the course as a whole or that a curious student might want to examine have been preserved. Similarly, the notes after the cases do not attempt to double as a treatise, since exhaustive citation to the cases and secondary literature would interfere with our primary goal of fostering discussion. We have discussed and cited all the materials that we think a careful instructor or diligent student might want to examine for class purposes.

Omissions from principal cases or quoted materials are indicated in all instances. Periods (. . .) signal the omission of words or sentences; asterisks (* * *) are used to indicated the omission of citations to cases or other authorities. Periods rather than asterisks are used when words containing substantive content have been omitted even if a citation was contained in the omitted passage. Most of the footnotes in principal cases and quoted materials have been discarded. Those footnotes which have been included retain their original number. Our own infrequent footnotes may be readily distinguished.

Professor Franklin has borne principal responsibility for this revision.

L.K.
K.R.
D.F.

ACKNOWLEDGMENTS

We gratefully acknowledge the permission extended by the following authors, publishers, and organizations to reprint excerpts from the works indicated: William F. Baxter, *Choice of Law and the Federal System*, 16 Stan.L.Rev. 1 (1963); David F. Cavers, The Choice-of-Law Process (University of Michigan Press, 1965); Albert A. Ehrenzweig, A Treatise on Conflict of Laws (West Publishing Co., 1962); Henry J. Friendly, *In Praise of Erie—And of the New Federal Common Law*, 39 N.Y.U.L.Rev 383 (1964); Alfred Hill, *The Erie Doctrine and the Constitution*, 53 Nw.U.L.Rev 427 (1958); Robert A. Leflar, *Conflicts Law: More on Choice-Influencing Considerations*, 54 Calif.L.Rev. 1584 (1966); Lawrence Lessig, Code and Other Laws of Cyberspace (Basic Books 1999); von Mehren, The *Renvoi and Its Relations to Various Approached to the Choice-of-Law Problem*, in XXth Century Comparative and Conflicts Law (American Assn. for Comparative Study of Law, 1962); von Mehren & Donald T. Trautman, *Jurisdiction to Adjudicate: A Suggested Analysis*, 79 Harv.L.Rev. 1121 (1966); von Mehren & Trautman, The Law of Multistate Problems (Little, Brown & Co., 1965); Monrad Paulsen and Michael Sovern, *"Public Policy" in the Conflict of Laws*, 56 Colum.L.Rev. 969 (1956); Mathias Reimann, Conflict of Laws in Western Europe: A Guide Through the Jungle (Transnational Publishers, Inc. 1995); Rheinstein, *How to Review a Festschrift*, 11 Am.J.Comp.L. 632 (1962); Willis L.M. Reese, *Power of Parties to Choose Law Governing Their Contract*, 54 Proc.Am.Soc.Int'l L. 49 (1960); Reese and Johnson, *The Scope of Full Faith and Credit to Judgments*, 49 Colum.L.Rev. 153 (1949); Terrance Sandalow, *Henry v. Mississippi and the Adequate State Ground*, 1965 Sup.Ct.Rev. 187. In each of the foregoing instances, permission has been received from both the author and copyright owner.

In other instances, in which the author is deceased, we are grateful for permission granted by the copyright owner: Harvard University Press (Cook, The Logical and Legal Bases of Conflicts of Laws); The University of Chicago Law Review (B. Currie, *Full Faith and Credit to Foreign Land Decrees*, 21 U.Chi.L.Rev. 620; Duke University Press (B. Currie, Selected Essays on the Conflict of Laws); Columbia Law Review (Jackson, *Full Faith and Credit—The Lawyer's Clause of the Constitution*, 45 Colum.L.Rev. 1); Yale Law Journal Co. (B. Currie and Schreter, *Unconstitutional Discrimination in the Conflict of Law: Privileges and Immunities*, 69 Yale L.J. 1323); Yale University Press (Lorenzen, Selected Articles on the Conflict of Laws); Harvard Law Review (Morgan, *Choice of Law Governing Proof*, 58 Harv.L.Rev. 153); Foundation Press (Stumberg, Conflict of Laws).

We are especially indebted to the University of Michigan Press and to Duke University Press for permission to reprint substantial portions of the work of David F. Cavers and Brainerd Currie.

SUMMARY OF CONTENTS

TABLE OF CONTENTS

PART 2. OTHER APPLICATIONS

TABLE OF CASES

The principal cases are in bold type.

TABLE OF AUTHORITIES

CONFLICT OF LAWS

CASES—COMMENTS—QUESTIONS

Eleventh Edition

PART 1

CHOICE OF LAW: THE BASIC MODEL

▪ ▪ ▪

CHAPTER 1

THE TRADITIONAL APPROACH TO CHOICE OF LAW

■ ■ ■

SECTION 1. TRADITIONAL THEORY: A SURVEY OF JURISDICTION-SELECTING RULES

A Short History of Choice of Law

Disputes involving what are typically thought of as "choice of law" problems can arise in two settings: cases with facts connected to different jurisdictions, and cases involving enactments of different lawmakers within a single jurisdiction. In England, choice-of-law principles developed slowly in both contexts.[1] After the Norman Conquest, the royal courts purported to administer a single common law of the land, preventing recognition of conflicts within England. And English courts held as early as 1280 that they lacked power to entertain suits involving foreign acts or transactions. Consequently, there was no basis for developing an international law of conflicts either.

The same was not true on the Continent, where the need to apply different bodies of general and local law was a legacy of the Roman Empire. By the 12th century, jurists in medieval French and Italian universities had begun to develop principles for choosing among competing laws. These scholars were called "statutists" after their approach, which was based on the assumption that conflict of laws was essentially a problem of statutory interpretation. The statutists divided enactments into two categories: real and personal. As David Cavers explains, "[t]he real statute applied only within the territory of the city whose law it was. The personal statutes followed the city's citizenry wherever they might go. In time, this simple scheme failed to satisfy the intricacies of life and scholarship. As a consequence, a third class of statutes was identified—as you can guess, this was known as 'mixed.' . . . The trouble was that neither judges nor scholars could agree upon which statute was personal, which was real, and what

---

[1] The discussion in this section is drawn primarily from Sack, *Conflict of Laws in the History of English Law*, in 3 Law: A Century of Progress 1835–1935 342 (1937), reprinted in AALS, Selected Readings on the Conflict of Laws 1 (1956) [hereinafter AALS Readings]; and Yntema, *The Historic Bases of Private International Law*, 2 Am.J.Comp.L. 297 (1953), reprinted in AALS Readings at 30.

should be done with those that were mixed." D. Cavers, The Choice-of-Law Process 2 (1965).

Despite this increasing complexity, the choice of law system devised by the statutists functioned reasonably well so long as Europe remained politically unified. As the hold of the Papacy and Holy Roman Empire weakened, however, independent nation-states emerged, and with these came the demand for a better accounting of why courts should not always just apply their own law. In the 16th century, a group of Dutch scholars repudiated the work of the statutists and developed an alternative approach to choice of law based on the principle of territoriality. The most influential of these scholars was Ulrich Huber, whose major work on the functioning of nation-states included a chapter entitled "On the Conflict of Different Laws in Different States." According to Huber:

> It often happens that transactions entered into in one place have force and effect in a different country or are judicially decided upon in another place. It is well known, furthermore, that . . . the laws of the different nations disagree in many respects. . . For the purpose of solving the subtlety of this most intricate question, we shall lay down three maxims which being conceded as they should be everywhere will smooth our way for the solution of the remaining questions.
>
> They are these:
>
> (1) The laws of each state have force within the limits of that government and bind all subject to it, but not beyond.
>
> (2) All persons within the limits of a government, whether they live there permanently or temporarily, are deemed to be subjects thereof.
>
> (3) Sovereigns will so act by way of comity that rights acquired within the limits of a government retain their force everywhere so far as they do not cause prejudice to the power or rights of such government or of its subjects.
>
> [A]lthough the laws of one nation can have no force directly within another, yet nothing could be more inconvenient to commerce and to international usage than that transactions valid by the law of one place should be rendered of no effect elsewhere on account of a difference in the law. . .
>
> On the other hand, transactions and acts done in violation of the law of that place [where done], since they are invalid from the beginning, cannot be valid anywhere; and this is true not only as regards persons having their domicile in the place of the contract, but also as regards those who are there for the time being.

Ulrich Huber, *De Conflictu Legum Diversarum in Diversis Imperiis,* Vol. II, Book I, title iii of Praelectiones Juris Romani et Hodierni (1689), translated in E. Lorenzen, Selected Articles on the Conflict of Laws 163–66 (1947).

Events in England, meanwhile, were not entirely static, and subsequent developments made it impossible to avoid the problem of conflict of laws forever. Most important, burgeoning international trade and commerce gave rise to demand for a forum in which English citizens could settle disputes involving foreign or partly foreign transactions. At first, these pressures were relieved by the development of independent courts enforcing distinct bodies of law, the most important of which was the admiralty court. Early conflicts problems were thus resolved at the jurisdictional level, as competing courts jockeyed for power to hear and apply "their" law to the cases.

During this same period, the jury evolved from a body of witnesses called to give evidence into an impartial fact-finder. This change made it possible for courts to entertain suits based on events occurring elsewhere, opening the way for recognition of "transitory" causes of action. By the end of the 16th century, suits based on events occurring in other parts of England were common, and by the early 17th century, common law courts had begun to entertain actions involving events outside England. At first the courts held steadfastly to the principle that they would apply only the common law. But this limitation proved inconvenient for merchants and traders, who frequently operated under international rules of trade and needed to know that these rules would be enforced. The English courts solved this problem by simply declaring the "law merchant" and the rules of public international law to be part of the common law.

The courts were more reluctant to go further and decide cases under the municipal law of another nation. The first step entailed judicial recognition of an obligation to enforce foreign *judgments* validly rendered. Not until the middle of the 18th century, however, did common law judges begin to apply the *laws* of other nations. The doctrine was first openly formulated in 1775. In *Holman v. Johnson,* 1 Cowper 341, 344 (1775), Lord Mansfield extended the incorporation theory used earlier to explain the application of international law, observing that "Every action tried here must be tried by the law of England, but the law of England says that in a variety of circumstances . . . the laws of the country where the cause of action arose shall govern."

As part of the common law, rules governing choice of law developed haphazardly, on a case-by-case basis. These precedents quickly made their way to the American colonies, which faced an abundance of conflicts problems due to their dependence on international and interstate trade, and, increasingly, interstate differences over slavery. The first commentator to offer a satisfying explanation of these decisions was

Justice Joseph Story, who published the first edition of his Commentaries on the Conflict of Laws in 1834. Story looked to the Continent and borrowed Huber's three maxims, using them to organize and explain the seemingly chaotic common-law precedents. The effort was spectacularly successful. According to Ernest Lorenzen, Story's Commentaries "were without question the most remarkable and outstanding work on the conflict of laws which had appeared since the thirteenth century in any country and in any language. . . In the United States and England, Story is revered today as the father of the conflict of laws." E. Lorenzen, Selected Articles on the Conflict of Laws at 193–94, 203.

Story's approach was subsequently modified by Professor Joseph Beale, who urged replacing the principle of comity with a notion of "vested rights." (These issues are explored in the materials that follow.) Beale's theory was then endorsed from the bench by Justice Holmes, see *Slater v. Mexican Nat'l R.R.*, 194 U.S. 120, 126 (1904), and Beale was subsequently made Reporter for the American Law Institute's influential Restatement of the Law of Conflict of Laws. Beale's work was subjected to criticism from the start—including a withering critique by legal realists such as Walter Wheeler Cook, Ernest Lorenzen, and David Cavers. Yet despite academic criticism, Beale's theory was universally adopted (though not always followed) by courts in the United States for at least the first half of the 20th century.

In the late 1950s and early 1960s, Brainerd Currie wrote a series of influential articles, most of which were published collectively in a 1963 volume titled Selected Essays on the Conflict of Laws. Building on the earlier work of Cook, Cavers, and Lorenzen, Currie developed a comprehensive alternative approach to choice of law known as "governmental interest analysis." Like Beale before him, Currie was criticized from the start. But Currie's work nevertheless inspired a substantial rethinking of conflict of laws, evidenced by the proliferation of new approaches that began to appear in law reviews and judicial opinions in the mid-1960s. In 1971, after nearly 20 years of work, the American Law Institute published a Restatement (Second) of Conflict of Laws. Reflecting an uneasy compromise between new and old, the Second Restatement retains many of the traditional rules but situates them in a flexible, policy-oriented framework. The Second Restatement approach has since become the most widely used tool for resolving choice of law questions.

We will consider these modern approaches to choice of law in Chapter 2. But first we must understand the "traditional approach" to which these other approaches were a response and which is still used in many states. For most judges and commentators, the traditional approach is synonymous with Beale's territorial "vested rights" approach, which thus forms the real starting point for understanding choice of law.

ALABAMA GREAT SOUTHERN R.R. CO. V. CARROLL

97 Ala. 126, 11 So. 803 (1892).

MCCLELLAN, J. The plaintiff, W.D. Carroll, is, and was at the time of entering into the service of the defendant, the Alabama Great Southern Railroad Company, and at the time of being injured in that service, a citizen of Alabama. The defendant is an Alabama corporation, operating a railroad extending from Chattanooga, in the state of Tennessee, through Alabama to Meridian, in the state of Mississippi. At the time of the casualty complained of plaintiff was in the service of the defendant in the capacity of brakeman on freight trains running from Birmingham, Ala., to Meridian, Miss., under a contract which was made in the state of Alabama. The injury was caused by the breaking of a link between two cars in a freight train which was proceeding from Birmingham to Meridian. The point at which the link broke and the injury was suffered was in the state of Mississippi. The evidence tended to show that the link which broke was a defective link, and that it was in a defective condition when the train left Birmingham. . . It was shown to be the duty of certain employees of defendant stationed along its line to inspect the links attached to cars to be put in trains, or forming the couplings between cars in trains at Chattanooga, Birmingham, and some points between Birmingham and the place where this link broke, and also that it was the duty of the conductor of freight trains, and the other train men, to maintain such inspection as occasion afforded throughout the runs or trips of such trains; and the evidence affords ground for inference that there was a negligent omission on the part of such employees to perform this duty, or, if performed, the failure to discover the defect in, and to remove, this link was the result of negligence. . .

This was the negligence, not of the master, the defendant, but of fellow servants of the plaintiff, for which at common law the defendant is not liable. . .

It is, however, further contended that the plaintiff, if his evidence be believed, has made out a case for the recovery sought under the employers' liability act of Alabama, it being clearly shown that there is no such or similar law of force in the state of Mississippi. Considering this position in the abstract,—that is, disassociated from the facts of this particular case, which are supposed to exert an important influence upon it,—there cannot be two opinions as to its being unsound and untenable. So looked at, we do not understand appellee's counsel even to deny either the proposition or its application to this case,—that there can be no recovery in one state for injuries to the person sustained in another, unless the infliction of the injuries is actionable under the law of the state in which they were received. Certainly this is the well-established rule of law, subject, in some jurisdictions, to the qualification that the infliction of the injuries would also support an action in the state where the suit is brought had they been received within that state. * * *

But it is claimed that the facts of this case take it out of the general rule which the authorities cited above abundantly support, and authorize the courts of Alabama to subject the defendant to the payment of damages under section 2590 of the Code, although the injuries counted on were sustained in Mississippi under circumstances which involved no liability on the defendant by the laws of that state. This insistence is, in the first instance, based on that aspect of the evidence which goes to show that the negligence which produced the casualty transpired in Alabama, and the theory that, wherever the consequences of that negligence manifested itself, a recovery can be had in Alabama. We are referred to no authority in support of this proposition, and exhaustive investigation on our part has failed to disclose any. There are at least two well-considered cases against it. . .

It is admitted, or at least cannot be denied, that negligence of duty unproductive of damnifying results will not authorize or support a recovery. Up to the time this train passed out of Alabama no injury had resulted. For all that occurred in Alabama, therefore, no cause of action whatever arose. The fact which created the right to sue,—the injury,—without which confessedly no action would lie anywhere, transpired in the state of Mississippi. It was in that state, therefore, necessarily that the cause of action, if any, arose; and whether a cause of action arose and existed at all, or not, must in all reason be determined by the law which obtained at the time and place when and where the fact which is relied on to justify a recovery transpired. Section 2590 of the Code of Alabama had no efficacy beyond the lines of Alabama. It cannot be allowed to operate upon facts occurring in another state, so as to evolve out of them rights and liabilities which do not exist under the law of that state, which is of course paramount in the premises. . . Section 2590 of the Code, in other words, is to be interpreted in the light of universally recognized principles of private, international, or interstate law, as if its operation had been expressly limited to this state, and as if its first line read as follows: "When a personal injury is received in Alabama by a servant or employe," etc. The negligent infliction of an injury here, under statutory circumstances, creates a right of action here, which, being transitory, may be enforced in any other state or country the comity of which admits of it; but for an injury inflicted elsewhere than in Alabama our statute gives no right of recovery, and the aggrieved party must look to the local law to ascertain what his rights are. Under that law this plaintiff had no cause of action, as we have seen, and hence he has no rights which our courts can enforce. . . We have not been inattentive to the suggestions of counsel in this connection, which are based upon that rule of the statutory and common criminal law under which a murderer is punishable where the fatal blow is delivered, regardless of the place where death ensues. *Green v. State,* 66 Ala. 40. This principle is patently without application here. There would be some analogy if the plaintiff had been stricken in Alabama, and suffered in Mississippi, which is not the fact. There is, however, an analogy which is afforded by the criminal law, but which points away from the conclusion appellee's counsel desires us to reach. This is found in that well-established doctrine of criminal law that where the unlawful act is committed in one jurisdiction or state, and takes effect—produces the result which it is the purpose of the law to prevent, or, it having ensued, punish for—in another jurisdiction or state, the crime is deemed to have been committed and is punished in that jurisdiction or state in which the result is manifested, and not where the act was committed. * * *

Another consideration, . . . it is insisted, entitles this plaintiff to recover here under the employers' liability act for an injury inflicted beyond the territorial operation of that act. This is claimed upon the fact that at the time plaintiff was injured he was in the discharge of duties which rested on him by the terms of a contract between him and the defendant, which had been entered into in Alabama, and hence was an Alabama contract, in connection with the facts that plaintiff was and is a citizen of this state, and the defendant is an Alabama corporation. These latter facts—of citizenship and domicile, respectively, of plaintiff and defendant—are of no importance in this connection, it seems to us, further than this: they may tend to show that the contract was made here, which is not controverted, and, if the plaintiff has a cause of action at all, he, by reason of them, may prosecute it in our courts. They have no bearing on the primary question of the existence of a cause of action, and, as that is the question before us, we need not further advert to the fact of plaintiff's citizenship or defendant's domicile.

The [plaintiff's] theory is that the employers' liability act became a part of this contract, that the duties and liabilities which it prescribes became contractual duties and liabilities or duties and liabilities springing out of the contract, and that these duties attended upon the execution whenever its performance was required, in Mississippi as well as in Alabama, and that the liability prescribed for a failure to perform any of such duties attached upon such failure and consequent injury wherever it occurred, and was enforceable here, because imposed by an Alabama contract, notwithstanding the remission of duty and the resulting injury occurred in Mississippi, under whose laws no liability was incurred by such remission. . . If this argument is sound, and it is sound if the duties and liabilities prescribed by the act can be said to be contractual duties and obligations at all, it would lead to conclusions, the possibility of which has not hitherto been suggested by any court or law writer, and which, to say the least, would be astounding to the profession. . .

[T]he duties and liabilities incident to the relation between the plaintiff and the defendant, which are involved in this case, are not imposed by, and do not rest in or spring from, the contract between the parties. The only office of the contract, under section 2590 of the Code, is the establishment of a relation between them,—that of master and servant; and it is upon that relation, that incident or consequence of the contract, and not upon the rights of the parties under the contract, that our statute operates. The law is not concerned with the contractual stipulations, except in so far as to determine from them that the relation upon which it is to operate exists. Finding this relation, the statute imposes certain duties and liabilities on the parties to it, wholly regardless of the stipulations of the contract as to the rights of the parties under it, and, it may be, in the teeth of such stipulations. It is the purpose of the statute, and must be the limit of its operation, to govern persons standing in the relation of master and servants to each other, in respect of their conduct in certain particulars within the state of Alabama. Mississippi has the same right to establish governmental rules for such persons within her borders as Alabama, and she has established rules which are different from those of our law; and the conduct of such persons towards each other is, when its legality is brought in question, to be adjudged by the rules of the one or the other state, as it falls territorially within the one or the other. . .

For the error in refusing to instruct the jury to find for the defendant, if they believed the evidence, the judgment is reversed, and the cause will be remanded.

Traditional Choice of Law Theory

(1) Why should a court ever apply foreign law? To an Alabama judge Alabama law is the most familiar; to an Alabama policymaker it is the most just. Why shouldn't an Alabama court apply Alabama law in every case? And if the *Carroll* case was not governed by Alabama law, why should the Alabama court have heard it at all?

(2) One problem with allowing the forum always to apply its own law is that the applicable law, and hence the outcome, would differ according to where the action was brought. Traditional choice-of-law thinking, however, placed a high value on uniformity of result, predictability, and the discouragement of forum-shopping. Judge Herbert Goodrich, for example, argued that:

> Fairness demands that once one's rights and liabilities are settled under the law, those same rights and liabilities shall be the measure of legal obligation everywhere. . . It is not alone for the people who get into a lawsuit that we need to have our law of

Conflict of Laws in certain terms. Of far more importance are the thousands of persons who seek to avoid litigation by a careful compliance with the law which is to govern their conduct. They should be able to know what rule of law is to govern them and have reasonable confidence that this rule of law will be the measure of their rights and obligations whenever and wherever the question may subsequently arise.

Goodrich, *Public Policy in the Law of Conflicts,* 36 W.Va.L.Q. 156, 165, 167 (1930).

Professor Max Rheinstein emphasized the importance of protecting the reasonable expectations of the parties:

> Except where other higher aspirations interfere, expectations must be relied upon, and one of those expectations is that we ought not to be subjected to punishment, liability or other legal detriment for conduct which we had good reason to believe would not subject us to such troubles. It is in this order of ideas that we find the *raison d'être* of the condemnation of *ex post facto* laws as well as of that branch of the legal order with which we are concerned here, *viz.* choice of law [and contracts, estoppel, and stare decisis]. . . It is *not* suggested here that the policy of protecting justified expectations is the *only* explanation of the fact that domestic courts occasionally apply a foreign law. . . [But] the policy of protecting justified expectations plays a prominent role.

Rheinstein, *The Place of Wrong: A Study in the Method of Case Law,* 19 Tul.L.Rev. 4, 22–23 (1944).

How important are these considerations really? Can you imagine cases in which they could be outweighed by competing concerns?

(3) Uniformity, predictability, and the protection of expectations may suggest that the same law should be applied in *Carroll* regardless of where the action is brought, but do they tell us why that law should be the law of Mississippi? Alabama and Mississippi seem to have a stronger claim to apply their law in *Carroll* than, say, Georgia, but can you explain why? Suppose the plaintiff lived in Georgia. Would that justify applying Georgia law? Suppose it was his second cousin who lived there: now what result? What if the plaintiff's wife and children lived in Georgia and counted on the plaintiff for support? Would your answer change if the plaintiff had died and it was a wrongful death action?

(4) Huber's territorial theory for choosing the applicable law (p. 4 supra), which underlies the *Carroll* opinion, was restated by Justice Story in his Commentaries on the Conflict of Laws (2d ed. 1841):

> § 18. I. The first and most general maxim or proposition is . . . that every nation possesses an exclusive sovereignty and

> jurisdiction within its own territory. The direct consequence of this rule is, that the laws of every state affect, and bind directly all property, whether real or personal, within its territory; and all persons, who are resident within it, whether natural born subjects, or aliens; and also all contracts made, and acts done within it. A state may, therefore, regulate the manner and circumstances, under which property, whether real, or personal, or in action, within it, shall be held, transmitted, bequeathed, transferred, or enforced; the condition, capacity, and state, of all persons within it; the validity of contracts, and other acts, done within it; the resulting rights and duties growing out of these contracts and acts; and the remedies, and modes of administering justice in all cases calling for the interposition of its tribunals to protect, and vindicate, and secure the wholesome agency of its own laws within its own domains. . .
>
> § 20. II. Another maxim, or proposition, is, that no state or nation can, by its laws, directly affect, or bind property out of its own territory, or bind persons not resident therein, whether they are natural born subjects, or others. This is a natural consequence of the first proposition; for it would be wholly incompatible with the equality and exclusiveness of the sovereignty of all nations, that any one nation should be at liberty to regulate either persons or things not within its own territory. It would be equivalent to a declaration, that the sovereignty over a territory was never exclusive in any nation, but only concurrent with that of all nations; that each could legislate for all, and none for itself; and that all might establish rules, which none were bound to obey. . .

Is there any justification for the territorial principle apart from naked power? Is power an acceptable basis for the allocation of lawmaking competence within a federal system?

(5) Suppose in *Carroll* that it was Mississippi that had abolished the fellow-servant rule and Alabama that had preserved it. Plaintiff could then recover under Mississippi but not Alabama law. Wouldn't the threat of liability for injuries in Mississippi force the Alabama railroad to alter its conduct in Alabama? Is this an avoidable consequence?

The *Carroll* court suggests that the Alabama statute must be read "as if its operation had been expressly limited to this state." Do you think that this is what the legislature intended? Why wouldn't it be appropriate for Alabama to award damages to any Alabama resident who is negligently injured anywhere in the world? To anyone who is negligently injured anywhere by an Alabama resident? To the plaintiff in *Carroll*? (In 1928, the Alabama legislature amended the statute to specify that it applied to out-of-state injuries as long as the employment contract was formed in Alabama. See Ala. Code § 7540 (1928).)

(6) Justice Story says in § 20 that "it would be wholly incompatible with the equality and exclusiveness of the sovereignty of all nations, that any one nation should be at liberty to regulate either persons or things not within its own territory." Isn't that exactly what Mississippi does if its law must be used in Alabama courts? How can we reconcile the principle of exclusive territorial sovereignty with the goal of having courts in every state apply the same law in a particular case?

Borrowing an argument from Huber, Story explained a court's willingness to apply foreign law on the basis of policy rather than power:

> § 23. III. From these two maxims or propositions, there flows a third, and that is, that whatever force and obligation the laws of one country have in another, depend solely upon the laws, and municipal regulations of the latter, that is to say, upon its own proper jurisprudence and polity, and upon its own express or tacit consent. A state may prohibit the operation of all foreign laws, and the rights growing out of them, within its own territories. It may prohibit some foreign laws, and it may admit the operation of others. . . When its own code speaks positively on the subject, it must be obeyed by all persons, who are within the reach of its sovereignty. When its customary, unwritten, or common law speaks directly on the subject, it is equally to be obeyed; for it has an equal obligation with its positive code. When both are silent, then, and then only, can the question properly arise, what law is to govern in the absence of any clear declaration of the sovereign will. . .
>
> § 38. There is, then, not only no impropriety in the use of the phrase, "comity of nations," but it is the most appropriate phrase to express the true foundation and extent of the obligation of the laws of one nation within the territories of another. It is derived altogether from the voluntary consent of the latter; and it is inadmissible, when it is contrary to its known policy, or prejudicial to its interests. . .

Does this reasoning offer guidance to an Alabama court trying to decide whether to apply Mississippi law? How should a court distinguish between foreign laws that are contrary to local policy, and those that are merely different? (This issue is discussed further in the context of the public policy exception in Section 2, infra.)

If the effect of foreign law depends on the voluntary consent of the forum, it might seem unlikely that forum courts will apply foreign law that differs from their own when sensitive issues are involved. In dealing with the issue of slavery, however, American courts in the pre-Civil War era for a time followed a compromise approach under which slaves brought temporarily into free states or territories did not thereby acquire liberty, but those who stayed for an indefinite time did. The compromise eventually broke down as courts in both slave and free states began to adopt more extreme positions and deny any effect to foreign law. The Missouri Supreme Court's opinion in *Dred Scott v. Emerson*, 15 Mo. 576 (1852), a precursor to the famous United States Supreme Court case, is an example of such a decision. Is this a failure of conflicts law?

(7) What concerns might lead to dissatisfaction with a "comity"-based system for conflict of laws? Rejecting Story's comity argument, Professor Beale explained the application of foreign law on the basis of a theory of "vested rights":

> Law being a general rule to govern future transactions, its method of creating rights is to provide that upon the happening of a certain event a right shall accrue. The creation of a right is therefore conditioned upon the happening of an event. . . When a right has been created by law, this right itself becomes a fact. . . A right having been created by the appropriate law, the recognition of its existence should follow everywhere. Thus, an act valid where done cannot be called into question anywhere.

1 J. Beale, Treatise on the Conflict of Laws § 73 at 105 (1916). The classic judicial formulation of the vested rights doctrine came from Justice Holmes: "The theory of the foreign suit is that, although the act complained of was subject to no law having force in the forum, it gave rise to an obligation, an *obligatio*, which like other obligations, follows the person, and may be enforced wherever the person may be found." *Slater v. Mexican Nat'l R.R.*, 194 U.S. 120, 126 (1904).

Does vested rights theory help us in determining whether Mississippi law was, in Beale's terms, the "appropriate" law in *Carroll*?

(8) No other aspect of the traditional approach to choice of law has been criticized as much as the principle of vested rights.[2] Is it so clear that the vested rights idea was wrong? Doesn't the legal system rest on the principle that laws establish relationships or obligations that courts ought to enforce? Or did Beale and Holmes have something else in mind?

Beale's chief critics came from the ranks of the legal realists, who argued that choice of law could be better explained by what came to be known as "local law" theory. As Walter Wheeler Cook explained:

> [T]he forum, when confronted by a case involving foreign elements, always applies its own law to the case, but in so doing

---

[2] See, e.g., W.W. Cook, The Logical and Legal Bases of the Conflict of Laws chs. 1–3 (1942); E. Lorenzen, Selected Articles on the Conflict of Laws chs. 1–8 (1947); L. Brilmayer, Conflict of Laws: Foundations and Future Directions ch. 1 (1991).

> adopts and enforces as its own law a rule of decision identical, or at least highly similar, . . . to a rule of decision found in the system of law in force in another state or country with which some or all of the foreign elements are connected. . . The forum thus enforces not a foreign right but a right created by its own law.

W.W. Cook, The Logical and Legal Bases of the Conflict of Laws 20–21 (1942). How does this refute the argument for vested rights? See also E. Lorenzen, Selected Articles on the Conflict of Laws at 11: "Nothing can be gained by hiding the truth and making it appear that certain rules govern in the nature of things. . . [T]he adoption of the one rule or the other depends entirely upon considerations of policy which each sovereign state must determine for itself."

Local law theory has its modern fans, who interpret it to mean that the forum should always apply its own law. See Cox, *Razing Conflicts Facades to Build Better Jurisdiction Theory: The Foundation—There is No Law but Forum Law,* 28 Valparaiso U.L. Rev. 1 (1993). Does this seem like a good approach to take?

(9) Regardless of their heated arguments over the theories of comity, vested rights, and local law, adherents of the traditional learning essentially agreed on the territorial principle: The governing substantive rule was derived from the law of the place where the relevant events had occurred.

The Place of Wrong

(1) Proceeding on the territorial premise that "[e]ach state has legislative jurisdiction [i.e. authority] to determine the legal effect of acts done or events caused within its territory" (§ 377, comment a), § 384 of the 1934 Restatement predictably provided that the existence of a cause of action for tort depended upon the law of "the place of wrong." Additional sections specified in what seems over-abundant detail the particular issues governed by the law of the place of wrong. Does it make sense to assume that the same state's law should decide every issue in a tort case? The application of different states' laws to different issues in the same case is called dépeçage and is generally disfavored at common law. See pp. 267–272, infra.

(2) The place-of-wrong rule is easy enough to apply when the relevant events all occur in a single state. But how should one determine the place of wrong in a case like *Carroll,* with events spanning state boundaries? Does anything in the territorial theory help us to decide, for example, whether a tort occurs where the injury is suffered rather than where the negligent act is committed?

Like the court in *Carroll,* the Restatement generally resolved questions of this nature by focusing upon the last event: "The place of wrong is in the state where the last event necessary to make an actor liable for an alleged tort takes place" (§ 377). The reason, according to Judge Goodrich, is that "[t]he plaintiff does not sue the defendant for the latter's negligence, but because the negligence has caused the plaintiff harm. The tort is complete only when the harm takes place, for this is the last event necessary to make the actor liable for the tort." H. Goodrich, Handbook of the Conflict of Laws § 93 (3d ed. 1949). But there would have been no tort without negligence either; so why is one element more significant than another when each is equally essential to the cause of action? See Kramer, *Vestiges of Beale: Extraterritorial Application of American Law,* 1991 Sup.Ct.Rev. 179, 190 n. 36: "The last event test is arbitrary because there is no claim unless all the elements are established. A tort may be *consummated* where the last act occurs, but it is *being committed* from the first to the last act and thus 'occurs' at all these places."

Doesn't *Carroll* permit Mississippi to determine the legal effect of Alabama negligence, contrary to the cardinal principle of the territorial theory? Would application of Alabama law be equally offensive by permitting Alabama to determine the legal effect of a Mississippi injury? Does the territorial theory provide any answers to problems in which relevant facts occur in more than one state?

(3) There are two interesting exceptions to the Restatement's last-event test in the tort field. If the law of the place of wrong depends upon "the application of a standard of care," that standard should be taken from the law of the "place of the actor's conduct," § 380(2); and a person required, forbidden, or privileged to act under the law of the "place of acting" should not be held liable for consequences in another state, § 382. What is the reason for these exceptions? And how can they be prevented from swallowing the rule?

(4) David Cavers once observed that because "deduction from territorial postulates could indicate only one jurisdiction as a source of law in a given case, the content of that law would be logically irrelevant." Cavers, *A Critique of the Choice-of-Law Problem,* 47 Harv.L.Rev. 173, 178 (1933). For this reason the traditional rules are sometimes called "jurisdiction-selecting" rules. Is the content of the respective laws important in developing rules for choosing the applicable law? Should it be?

(5) Where is the place of wrong—and what should be the result—in the following cases?

(a) The defendant's dog strays from its home in Massachusetts and bites the plaintiff in New Hampshire. Massachusetts imposes absolute liability on the owner of a dog; New Hampshire follows the dangerous propensity ("one free bite") approach. See *Le Forest v. Tolman,* 117 Mass. 109 (1875).

(b) An employee of a Massachusetts corporation takes a company car and negligently injures the plaintiff in New Hampshire. Massachusetts imposes strict liability on the employer for an employee's negligence; New Hampshire requires negligence on the part of the employer. Is there any reason to treat this case differently from the last one? See *Scheer v. Rockne Motors Corp.,* 68 F.2d 942, 944 (2d Cir.1934) (L. Hand, J.): "It is clear that the defendant did not give him authority to go to Canada merely by giving him the car. Unless more than that was shown, the law of Ontario could not reach the defendant; the charge gave it extraterritorial effect." The same rule is found in § 387 of the Restatement. What happened to the principle that the critical question is where the injury occurred?

(c) The plaintiff in *Carroll,* injured in Mississippi by the Alabama negligence of a fellow servant, is removed to a hospital in Georgia, where he dies. An action for wrongful death is brought on behalf of surviving relatives. Georgia and Alabama have abolished the fellow-servant rule; Mississippi has not. See Restatement of Conflict of Laws § 377, Note (1934):

> 1. Except in the case of harm from poison, when a person sustains bodily harm, the place of wrong is the place where the harmful force takes effect upon the body. . . The person harmed may thereafter go into another state and die from the injury. . . The place where this last event happens is . . . immaterial. The question is only where did the force impinge upon his body.

Why should that be, in light of the Restatement's usual rule? In case of poison, the same note tells us, "the place of injury is where the deleterious substance takes effect." Thus, if a train passenger eats poisoned candy in Michigan, falls ill in Indiana, and dies in Illinois, Indiana law will govern. How does one justify that rule?

(6) Kathy Keeton, an editor of Penthouse Magazine, lives and works in New York. Hustler Magazine, a competitor of Penthouse, publishes and distributes in all 50 states several cartoons that Keeton alleges libel her. Keeton sues in New Hampshire, her only connection with that state being that Penthouse, like Hustler, is sold there. Where is the place of the wrong?

The 1934 Restatement (§ 377 Rule 5) tells us that "[w]here harm is done to the reputation of a person, the place of wrong is where the defamatory statement is communicated." Does that mean Keeton has 50 separate causes of action under 50 different laws? See *Brewster v. Boston Herald-Traveler Corp.,* 188 F.Supp. 565, 577 (D.Mass.1960): The plaintiff "is entitled to have his claims for recovery treated not globally but severally, state by state." In *Keeton* the court held that all damages from the multistate libel must be sought in a single action under the "single publication rule" but left open the question whether damages would be determined under one law or many. *Keeton v. Hustler Magazine, Inc.,* 131 N.H. 6, 549 A.2d 1187, 1189–90 (1988).

If one law is to govern the entire proceeding, which law should it be? Would it make sense to apply the law of New Hampshire? See *Dale System, Inc. v. Time, Inc.,* 116 F.Supp. 527, 530 (D.Conn.1953), where the court applied the law of the plaintiff's home state on the ground that "in cases of multi-state libel generally, the greatest harm to repute will occur in the state of domicile." Is this conclusion consistent with the territorial theory? With Rule 5 of § 377?

In *Bernstein v. National Broadcasting Co.,* 129 F.Supp. 817, 826 (D.D.C.1955), the court held that a cause of action for invasion of privacy depended on the law of the jurisdiction where the "plaintiff was when his feelings were wounded." Is the place of wrong different in privacy cases than in defamation cases?

(7) During the 1960s Monsanto, Dow, and other chemical companies manufactured a herbicide known as Agent Orange, which the armed forces used in Vietnam to destroy enemy crops and to clear roads and communications lines. In the mid-1970s Vietnam veterans and their children began to file suits alleging that exposure to Agent Orange had brought about a variety of diseases and injuries, including chloracne, liver damage, birth defects, and cancer. How does one determine the place of the wrong in such a case? See *In re Agent Orange Product Liability Litigation,* 580 F.Supp. 690 (E.D.N.Y.1984).

Difficult choice-of-law issues pervade the litigation of toxic tort claims. How are judges to identify the place of injury with respect to products to which victims have been exposed over a prolonged period, and that have dangers which remain latent for many years or cause harm to the children of the persons exposed? Does it make sense to determine the legal consequences in such cases by searching for the place where the deleterious substance takes effect?

(8) How well does the place of wrong rule fulfill its purpose of generating uniform, predictable results? See Richman & Riley, *The First Restatement of Conflict of Laws on the Twenty-Fifth Anniversary of Its Successor: Contemporary Practice in Traditional Courts,* 56 Md. L. Rev. 1196 (1997). In *Spinozzi v. ITT Sheraton Corp.,* 174 F.3d 842 (7th Cir.1999), Judge Posner defended the place of injury rule on party expectations grounds:

> Most people affected as victims or as injurers by accidents and other injury-causing events are residents of the jurisdiction in which the event takes place. So if law can be assumed to be generally responsive to the values and preferences of the people who live in the community that formulated the law, the law of the

> place of the accident can be expected to reflect the values and preferences of the people most likely to be involved in accidents—can be expected, in other words, to be responsive and responsible law, law that internalizes the costs and benefits of the people affected by it.

Is this persuasive? Even granting Judge Posner's premise about the values reflected in law, why should that law be applied when parties come from outside the community? And why should these sorts of expectations matter anyway? If most people expect their tort law to provide for strict liability, should a court ignore negligence rules adopted on policy grounds? Why, in other words, should party expectations as to choice of law be given more normative weight than party expectations as to any other law?

If you do not like the place-of-injury rule, what would you substitute for it? Why?

MILLIKEN V. PRATT

125 Mass. 374 (1878).

The plaintiffs are partners doing business in Portland, Maine, under the firm name of Deering, Milliken & Co. The defendant is and has been since 1850, the wife of Daniel Pratt, and both have always resided in Massachusetts. In 1870, Daniel, who was then doing business in Massachusetts, applied to the plaintiffs at Portland for credit, and they required of him, as a condition of granting the same, a guaranty from the defendant to the amount of five hundred dollars, and accordingly he procured from his wife the following instrument:

> "Portland, January 29, 1870. In consideration of one dollar paid by Deering, Milliken & Co., receipt of which is hereby acknowledged, I guarantee the payment to them by Daniel Pratt of the sum of five hundred dollars, from time to time as he may want—this to be a continuing guaranty. Sarah A. Pratt."

This instrument was executed by the defendant two or three days after its date, at her home in Massachusetts, and there delivered by her to her husband, who sent it by mail from Massachusetts to the plaintiffs in Portland; and the plaintiffs received it from the post office in Portland early in February, 1870.

The plaintiffs subsequently sold and delivered goods to Daniel from time to time until October 7, 1871, and charged the same to him, and, if competent, it may be taken to be true, that in so doing they relied upon the guaranty. Between February, 1870, and September 1, 1871, they sold and delivered goods to him on credit to an amount largely exceeding $500, which were fully settled and paid for by him. This action is brought for goods sold from September 1, 1871, to October 7, 1871, inclusive, amounting to $860.12, upon which he paid $300, leaving a balance due of $560.12. The one dollar mentioned in the guaranty was not paid, and the only consideration moving to the defendant therefor was the giving of credit by the plaintiffs to her husband. Some of the goods were selected personally by Daniel at the plaintiffs' store in Portland, others were ordered by letters mailed by Daniel from Massachusetts to the plaintiffs at Portland, and all were sent by the plaintiffs by express from Portland to Daniel in Massachusetts, who paid all express charges. . .

Payment was duly demanded of the defendant before the date of the writ, and was refused by her.

The Superior Court ordered judgment for the defendant; and the plaintiffs appealed to this court.

GRAY, C.J. The general rule is that the validity of a contract is to be determined by the law of the state in which it is made; if it is valid there, it is deemed valid everywhere, and will sustain an action in the courts of a state whose laws do not permit such a contract. *Scudder v. Union National Bank*, 91 U.S. 406. Even a contract expressly prohibited by the statutes of the state in which the suit is brought, if not in itself immoral, is not necessarily nor usually deemed so invalid that the comity of the state, as administered by its courts, will refuse to entertain an action on such a contract made by one of its own citizens abroad in a state the laws of which permit it. * * *

If the contract is completed in another state, it makes no difference in principle whether the citizen of this state goes in person, or sends an agent, or writes a letter, across the boundary line between the two states. . . So if a person residing in this state signs and transmits, either by a messenger or through the post-office, to a person in another state, a written contract, which requires no special forms or solemnities in its execution, and no signature of the person to whom it is addressed, and is assented to and acted on by him there, the contract is made there, just as if the writer personally took the executed contract into the other state, or wrote and signed it there; and it is no objection to the maintenance of an action thereon here, that such a contract is prohibited by the law of this Commonwealth. * * *

The guaranty, bearing date of Portland, in the State of Maine, was executed by the defendant, a married woman, having her home in this Commonwealth, as collateral security for the liability of her husband for goods sold by the plaintiffs to him, and was sent by her through him by mail to the plaintiffs at Portland. The sales of the goods ordered by him from the plaintiffs at Portland, and there delivered by them to him in person, or to a carrier for him, were made in the State of Maine. * * * The contract between the defendant and the plaintiffs was complete when the guaranty had been received and acted on by them at Portland, and not before. * * * It must therefore be treated as made and to be performed in the State of Maine.

The law of Maine authorized a married woman to bind herself by any contract as if she was unmarried. St. of Maine of 1866, c. 52, *Mayo v. Hutchinson,* 57 Maine 546. The law of Massachusetts, as then existing, did not allow her to enter into a contract as surety or for the accommodation of her husband or of any third person. Gen.Sts. c. 108, § 3. *Nourse v. Henshaw,* 123 Mass. 96. Since the making of the contract sued on, and before the bringing of this action, the law of this Commonwealth has been changed, so as to enable married women to make such contracts. St.1874, c. 184. * * *

The question therefore is, whether a contract made in another state by a married woman domiciled here, which a married woman was not at the time capable of making under the law of this Commonwealth, but was then allowed by the law of that state to make, and which she could now lawfully make in this Commonwealth, will sustain an action against her in our courts.

It has been often stated by commentators that the law of the domicil, regulating the capacity of a person, accompanies and governs the person everywhere. But this statement, in modern times at least, is subject to many qualifications; and the opinions of foreign jurists upon the subject . . . are too varying and contradictory to control the general current of the English and American authorities in favor of holding that a contract, which by the law of the place is recognized as lawfully made by a capable person, is valid everywhere, although the person would not, under the law of his domicil, be deemed capable of making it. . .

Mr. Justice Story, in his Commentaries on the Conflict of Laws, after elaborate consideration of the authorities, arrives at the conclusion that . . . "although foreign jurists generally hold that the law of the domicil ought to govern in regard to the capacity of persons to contract; yet the common law holds a different doctrine, namely, that the *lex loci contractus* is to govern." Story Confl. §§ 103, 241. . .

In *Pearl v. Hansborough,* 9 Humph. 426, the rule was carried so far as to hold that where a married woman domiciled with her husband in the State of Mississippi, by the law of which a purchase by a married woman was valid and the property purchased went to her separate use, bought personal property in Tennessee, by the law of which married women were incapable of contracting, the contract of purchase was void and could not be enforced in Tennessee. Some authorities, on the other hand, would uphold a contract made by a party capable by the law of his domicil, though incapable by the law of the place of the contract. * * * But that alternative is not here presented. . .

The principal reasons on which continental jurists have maintained that personal laws of the domicil, affecting the status and capacity of all inhabitants of a particular class, bind them wherever they may go, appear to have been that each state has the rightful power of regulating the status and condition of its subjects, and, being best acquainted with the circumstances of climate, race, character, manners and customs, can best judge at what age young persons may begin to act for themselves, and whether and how far married women may act independently of their husbands; that laws limiting the capacity of infants or of married women are intended for their protection, and cannot therefore be dispensed with by their agreement; that all civilized states recognize the incapacity of infants and married women; and that a person, dealing with either, ordinarily has notice, by the apparent age or sex, that the person is likely to be of a class whom the laws protect, and is thus put upon inquiry how far, by the law of the domicil of the person, the protection extends.

On the other hand, it is only by the comity of other states that laws can operate beyond the limit of the state that makes them. In the great majority of cases, especially in this country, where it is so common to travel, or to transact business through agents, or to correspond by letter, from one state to another, it is more just, as well as more convenient, to have regard to the law of the place of the contract, as a uniform rule operating on all contracts of the same kind, and which the contracting parties may be presumed to have in contemplation when making their contracts, than to require them at their peril to know the domicil of those with whom they deal, and to ascertain the law of that domicil, however remote, which in many cases could not be done without such delay as would greatly cripple the power of contracting abroad at all. . .

It is possible also that in a state where the common law prevailed in full force, by which a married woman was deemed incapable of binding herself by any contract whatever, it might be inferred that such an utter incapacity, lasting throughout the joint lives of husband and wife, must be considered as so fixed by the settled policy of the state, for the protection of its own citizens, that it could not be held by the courts of that state to yield to the law of another state in which she might undertake to contract.

But it is not true at the present day that all civilized states recognize the absolute incapacity of married women to make contracts. The tendency of modern legislation is to enlarge their capacity in this respect, and in many states they have nearly or quite the same powers as if unmarried. In Massachusetts, even at the time of the making of the contract in question, a married woman was vested by statute with a very extensive power to carry on business by herself, and to bind herself by contracts with regard to her own property, business and earnings; and before the bringing of the present action, the power had been extended so as to include the making of all kinds of contracts, with any person but her husband, as if she were unmarried. There is therefore no reason of public policy which should prevent the maintenance of this action.

Judgments for the plaintiffs.

The Place of Contracting

(1) Restatement of Conflict of Laws § 332 (1934), provides:

Law Governing Validity of Contract. The law of the place of contracting determines the validity and effect of a promise with respect to

(a) capacity to make the contract;

(b) the necessary form, if any, in which the promise must be made;

(c) the mutual assent or consideration, if any, required to make a promise binding;

(d) any other requirements for making a promise binding;

(e) fraud, illegality, or any other circumstances which make a promise void or voidable;

(f) except as stated in § 358, the nature and extent of the duty for the performance of which a party becomes bound;

(g) the time when and the place where the promise is by its terms to be performed;

(h) the absolute or conditional character of the promise.

Section 358 provides:

Law Governing Performance. The duty for the performance of which a party to a contract is bound will be discharged by compliance with the law of the place of performance of the promise with respect to

(a) the manner of performance;

(b) the time and locality of performance;

(c) the person or persons by whom or to whom performance shall be made or rendered;

(d) the sufficiency of performance;

(e) excuse for non-performance.

Does this mean that more than one state's law will be applied in contract cases? How often is this likely to be the case?

(2) To Professor Beale, the place-of-making rule was as obvious as the laws of nature: "The question whether a contract is valid . . . can on general principles be determined by no other law than that . . . of the place of contracting. If the law at that place annexes an obligation to the acts of the parties, the promisee has a legal right which no other law has power to take away. . . If on the other hand the law of the place where the agreement is made annexes no legal obligation to it, there is no other law which has power to do so." Beale, *What Law Governs the Validity of a Contract,* 23 Harv.L.Rev. 260, 270–71 (1910).

Moreover, said Beale, the rule was not only "sound theoretically" but also "most practical in operation," for two reasons: First, "there is no uncertainty in the application of the rule. There can only be one place in which a contract is made, and what that place is can never be subject to great or serious doubt. . ." Second, "it is easiest for the parties to follow. . . Parties do not in fact, in most cases, know what the law is under which they act, . . . [but if] their business is so important that they wish to be sure that they are proceeding in accordance with the law, they will be almost certain to consult counsel. Neither party is likely to go back to his own state and there take advice. While, therefore, a party cannot be presumed to know the law of [the place where he acts], he can very properly be called upon to consult counsel there." Beale, 23 Harv.L.Rev. at 271–272. Are these considerations persuasive?

(3) Where is a contract made? In his treatise, Professor Beale defined "place of contracting" as "the place in which the final act was done which made the promise or promises binding," and he said that this must necessarily be determined by the law of the forum. 2 J. Beale, A Treatise on the Conflict of Laws 1045, 1046 (1935). The 1934 Restatement, for which Beale served as Reporter, modified this terminology, referring instead to the "principal event necessary to make a contract":

> § 311. *Place of Contracting.* The law of the forum decides as a preliminary question by the law of which state questions arising concerning the formation of a contract are to be determined, and this state is, in the Restatement of this Subject, called the "place of contracting."
>
> *Comment [to § 311]*: . . .
>
> (d) *Determination of "place of contracting."* Under its Conflict of Laws rules, in determining the place of contracting, the forum ascertains the place in which, under the general law of Contracts, the principal event necessary to make a contract occurs. The forum at this stage of the investigation does not seek to ascertain whether there is a contract. It examines the facts of the transaction in question only so far as is necessary to determine the place of the principal event, if any, which, under the general

> law of Contracts, would result in a contract. Then, and not until then, does the forum refer to the law of such state to ascertain if, under the law, there is a contract, although of course there normally will be a contract unless the local law of Contracts of the state to which reference is thus made differs from the general law of Contracts as understood at the forum. . .

Subsequent provisions specified the place of contracting "under the general law of contracts in a number of important situations":

> § 312. *Formal Contract.* Except as stated in § 313 [dealing with renewal of formal contracts], when a formal contract becomes effective on delivery the place of contracting is where the delivery is made.
>
> § 323. *Informal Unilateral Contract.* In the case of an informal unilateral contract, the place of contracting is where the event takes place which makes the promise binding.
>
> § 325. *Informal Bilateral Contract.* In the case of an informal bilateral contract, the place of contracting is where the second promise is made in consideration of the first promise.
>
> § 326. *Acceptance Sent From One State to Another.* When an offer for a bilateral contract is made in one state and an acceptance is sent from another state to the first state in an authorized manner the place of contracting is as follows:
>
> (a) if the acceptance is sent by an agent of the acceptor, the place of contracting is the state where the agent delivers it;
>
> (b) if the acceptance is sent by any other means, the place of contracting is the state from which the acceptance is sent.

The Comment to § 326 sets forth the Restatement's position on determining the place of contracting where the acceptance is communicated in various ways. Where acceptance is authorized to be sent by mail, the place of contracting is where the acceptance is mailed; where acceptance is authorized by telegraph, the place of contracting is the place at which the message of acceptance is received by the telegraph company for transmission; where acceptance by telephone is authorized, the place of contracting is where the acceptor speaks his acceptance; and finally, where a contract is formed by spoken word between two parties standing on opposite sides of a state boundary (how frequently does that occur?), the place of contracting is the place from which the acceptor speaks his acceptance. Comment e provides, however, that the rule of § 326 does not apply to an offer that stipulates that actual communication of consent to the offeror is required to constitute acceptance. In this case the Comment provides that the place of contracting is the place at which the acceptance is received in accord with the provisions of the offer.

(4) Who made the offer in *Milliken v. Pratt*? Was it an offer for a unilateral or for a bilateral contract? When and where was it accepted? Would the result have been the same if the seller had delivered the goods personally to the buyer in Massachusetts?

(5) Mrs. Pratt, in Massachusetts, telephones Milliken in Maine and says "I'll give you $10 for a barrel of flour." Milliken says "Sold." Where is the contract made? Suppose Mrs. Pratt calls up and asks, "How much is flour?" Milliken replies "I will sell you a barrel for ten dollars." Mrs. Pratt says "Sold." Same result? If not, is the disparity required by the territorial theory? Is it acceptable in the light of the Restatement's supposed concern for protecting the parties' justified expectations? See 2 E. Rabel, The Conflict of Laws: A Comparative Study 461–62 (2d ed. 1958): "The uncertainty included in the principle of *lex loci contractus* is sometimes welcomed by the courts. When a proposal is sent from one state to another, or an agent intervenes in transmitting an order . . . prepared here and sent there for approval and signature . . .—a court may sometimes manage an equitable decision . . . by purposefully locating the place of contracting in the desirable jurisdiction."

(6) Suppose the laws in *Milliken* were reversed, so that Maine barred married women from acting as surety for their husbands while Massachusetts allowed them to do so. Would it still make sense to apply the law of Maine?

(7) Davis, in Michigan, mails an offer to Peters, in Indiana, inviting Peters to do construction work on a building owned by Davis in Michigan. In Michigan an offer is revocable until accepted, while in Indiana a written offer must be kept open for a reasonable period of time. Peters sues Davis, alleging that he mailed his acceptance of the offer within a week of the time it arrived. Davis alleges that she withdrew the offer the day after it arrived. If Indiana law applies, there is a contract and Peters wins; if Michigan law applies, there is no contract and Davis is entitled to judgment.

(a) Where is the place of contract? The majority rule for substantive purposes is that an offer is accepted and a contract made upon dispatch of the acceptance by the offeree. *Adams v. Lindsell,* 1 Barn. & Ald. 681 (K.B.1818). What if Indiana has rejected the dispatch rule and its law says that a contract is not made until the acceptance is received? Should a rule designed to determine *when* a contract is concluded also determine *where* a contract is made?

(b) Suppose Peters brings his lawsuit in Wisconsin. How is the Wisconsin court to decide where the contract was made? The Restatement says that this determination is made according to the law of the forum. But why should Wisconsin law determine where a contract with no connections to Wisconsin was made?

(c) If the place of contracting is determined by forum law, but states may have different rules about where this is, will the Restatement provide uniform or predictable results? Recall comment d to § 311, which provides that the forum should determine where the "principal event" necessary to make a contract occurred according to "the general law of Contracts." Does this solve the problem? (Hint: if forum law determines the place of contract, why include §§ 312–331 telling readers where a contract was made in different situations?) Does resort to "the general law of Contracts" make matters better or worse?

(d) Is this problem unique to contract cases? Where, for example, is the place of injury in an action for loss of consortium? Is that a factual question or a legal one?

(8) Suppose that in the previous hypothetical both parties agree that the contract was made in Indiana. Davis and Peters get into a dispute about whether Davis must pay in cash or can give Peters a note. Whose law applies? Is this a question of "the nature and extent of the duty for performance," governed by § 332 and the law of the place of contracting? Or is it a question of the "manner" or "sufficiency" of performance, governed by § 358 and the law of the place of performance? Consider comment b to § 358:

> [T]here is no logical line which separates questions of the obligation of contract, which is determined by the law of the place of contracting, from questions of performance, determined by the law of the place of performance. There is, however, a practical line which is drawn in every case by the particular circumstances thereof. When the application of the law of the place of contracting would extend to the determination of the minute details of the manner, method, time and sufficiency of performance so that it would be an unreasonable regulation of acts in the place of performance, the law of the place of contracting will cease to control and the law of the place of performance will be applied. On the other hand, when the application of the law of the place of performance would extend to a regulation of the substance of the obligation to which the parties purported to bind themselves so that it would unreasonably determine the effect of an agreement made in the place of contracting, the law of the place of performance will give way to the law of the place of contracting.

How are courts supposed to draw this line? How much uncertainty does this add to the administration of contract cases?

(9) If the place-of-contracting rule were more certain, would you object to it? Consider the case of two New York businessmen who conclude a sale of New York property while vacationing in Florida—or on the high seas. Consider the case of the New York gamblers who go to Puerto Rico to make a contract illegal in New York. Is there something wrong with the entire territorial principle?

IN RE BARRIE'S ESTATE

240 Iowa 431, 35 N.W.2d 658 (1949).

[Mary E. Barrie, a resident of Sterling, Illinois, executed a will in 1928 which left her property, including 160 acres of land in Iowa, to the First Presbyterian Church of Sterling and to three other named beneficiaries. Ms. Barrie died in 1944 and the 1928 will was offered for probate in Whiteside County, Illinois. Although duly signed and properly witnessed, the instrument, when found after Ms. Barrie's death, had the word "void" written across its face, on its cover, and upon the envelope containing it. The Illinois Supreme Court, finding that the instrument had been revoked by cancellation within the meaning of an Illinois statute, refused to admit it to probate. Ms. Barrie's property located in Illinois was distributed to relatives who were her heirs under the Illinois law of intestate succession.]

HAYS, JUSTICE. . . Thereafter the instrument was offered for probate in Tama County, Iowa, by [the First Presbyterian Church]. . . [D]ecedent's heirs at law filed objections based upon the judgment of the Illinois Supreme Court, to the effect that the said last will and testament had been revoked. Objectors assert that this judgment is conclusive upon the Iowa Courts. Proponent's motion to strike said objections, for the reason that they do not constitute a valid basis for denying probate, being overruled by the trial court, this appeal was taken. . .

No question is raised as to the due execution of the instrument, either under the Illinois or the Iowa Statutes. No question is raised as to the testamentary capacity of decedent, nor is it claimed by the objectors that there has been a revocation under the Iowa statute, Section 633.10, Code of 1946. . .

Upon the general question as to the validity, operation, effect, etc., of a will by which property is devised, there are certain well established and generally recognized rules, and which definitely differentiate between movable (personal) and immovable (real) property. We are only concerned with immovables, in the instant case. The general rule as stated in Story, *Conflict of Laws,* 8th Ed., p. 652, is, "The doctrine is clearly established at the common law, that the law of the place where the property (speaking of real immovable property) is located is to govern as to capacity or incapacity of the testator, the forms and solemnities to give the will or testament its due attestation and effect." . . . Upon the specific question as to revocation of a will, Beale, *Conflict of Laws,* Vol. 3, p. 972 states, "The revocation of a will is governed by the law of the state of situs of the land." Restatement of the Law, *Conflict of Laws,* Section 250, says, "The effectiveness of an intended revocation of a will of an interest in land is determined by the law of the state where the land is." Under the above stated rule, Iowa courts are free to place their construction, interpretation, and sanction upon the will of a non-resident of the state who dies owning real property within the state. . .

Does a different rule pertain where instead of being admitted to probate in the domicile state, probate is denied? We think not. It is generally held that the full faith and credit provision of the Federal Constitution, Section 1, Article 4, does not render foreign decrees of probate conclusive as to the validity of a will, as respects real property situated in a state other than the one in which the decree was rendered, nor does the doctrine of res adjudicata or estoppel by judgment apply. . .

We deem it to be immaterial to the deciding of this appeal whether the thing which constituted the revocation was by operation of law, the act done being incidental thereto, (such as a marriage when the law makes same a revocation of a prior will), or whether the act was done for the express purpose of revoking, as assumed in the instant case. . . To hold that an act which constitutes a revocation in one state is a revocation in another state where under the law the act does not constitute a revocation, is contrary to the general rule, which is stated in 57 Am.Jur.Wills, Sec. 493, to be, "Where a statute prescribes the method and acts by which a will may be revoked, no acts other than those mentioned in the statute are to operate as a revocation, no matter how clearly appears the purpose of the testator to revoke his will and his belief that such purpose has been accomplished." * * * That the acts held to be a revocation in Illinois, do not constitute such in Iowa, see Sec. 633.10, Code of 1946; *Blackett v. Ziegler,* 153 Iowa 344, 133 N.W. 901 [requiring either destruction of a will or its cancellation witnessed by two persons].

Sec. 633.49, Code of 1946, provides: "A last will and testament executed without this state, in the mode prescribed by the law, either of the place where executed or of the testator's domicile, shall be deemed to be legally executed, and shall be of the same force and effect as if executed in the mode prescribed by the laws of this state, provided said last will and testament is in writing and subscribed by the testator."

This statute has not been before this court, so far as the writer of this opinion can find. It is clearly a modification of the common law and should not be extended to include matters not clearly included therein. It specifically deals with the formalities in the execution of the will, and nothing more. No question of execution is here involved. That the legislature might have waived the common law rule, as applicable to revocations as well as to the formal execution, as it has done, cannot be denied. However the legislature has not seen fit to do so. * * * The statute is not applicable. . .

We hold that the Illinois judgment denying probate to the will in question is not conclusive and binding upon the courts of this state, in so far as the disposition of the Iowa real estate is concerned. That the objections filed to the petition do not constitute a basis for denying probate of the will and the appellant's motion to strike should have been sustained.

Reversed and remanded.

[Three dissenting justices argued that the historical distinctions between devises of real estate and bequests of personalty had largely disappeared; that Iowa, by determining the validity of a will by reference to the law of the place of execution or of the testator's domicile, had abandoned the situs rule; and, more specifically, that section 633.49 should be interpreted to cover formalities relating to revocation as well as those pertaining to execution.]

The Situs of Property

(1) *In re Barrie's Estate* deals with the effect to be given a foreign judgment as well as foreign law. Although the usual rule is that a court must give a judgment of another state the same effect it would be given in the state where the judgment was rendered, the Iowa court was applying traditional principles in refusing to give the Illinois decision any effect insofar as it dealt with land in Iowa. See Chapter 5, infra, at pp. 599–609.

(2) Not surprisingly, the territorial theory places great emphasis on the law of the place where property is situated, especially in the case of "immovable" as contrasted with "movable" property. For the most part these categories correspond to the usual notions of real and personal property. But certain interests in land that are ordinarily treated as personalty—most notably leaseholds—are classified as "immovables" for purposes of conflict of laws.

Cases involving interests in immovables are traditionally governed by the law of the situs. Sections 214–254 of the 1934 Restatement applied the situs rule to a broad range of issues respecting immovable property, including the creation of original title, the validity and effect of a subsequent transfer, the creation of incumbrances or subsidiary interests, and the legal effect of such events as marriage or death. See generally R. Leflar, The Law of Conflict of Laws 270 (1959).

(3) Why is such preeminence given to the law of the situs? An early draft of the Second Restatement, which adheres rigidly to the situs rule for immovable property, succinctly stated three reasons:

> First, land and things attached to the land are within the exclusive control of the state in which they are situated, and the officials of that state are the only ones who can lawfully deal with them physically. Since interests in immovables cannot be affected without the consent of the state of the situs, it is natural that the latter's law should be applied by the courts of other states. The second reason is that immovables are of greatest concern to the state in which they are situated; it is therefore proper that the law of this state should be applied to them. The third reason is to be found in the demands of certainty and convenience. . .

Restatement (Second) of Conflict of Laws § 214 (Introductory Note) (Tent.Draft No. 5, April 24, 1959). Note also the ease with which the situs rule can ordinarily be applied: The location of land, unlike the place where a contract is made, is rarely a matter of controversy.

(4) How persuasive are these arguments? Don't courts have ways to compel parties to obey judgments respecting land without having control of the property itself? Is it so clear that Iowa was the state with the "greatest concern" for the question of revocation in *Barrie's Estate*? Are uniformity and predictability more important here than in contract or tort cases? Docs the need for a reliable recording system justify the Restatement's broad situs rule in the case of land?

Are there objections to the situs rule even as applied to land? Note that in *Barrie's Estate* uniformity and certainty in the application of Iowa law to Iowa land were achieved only at the price of disuniformity and uncertainty in the application of Illinois law to the wills of Illinois citizens.

(5) Many questions pertaining to movable property are similarly governed by the law of the situs under traditional theory. See the 1934 Restatement at §§ 255–310. In *Cammell v. Sewell,* 5 Hurl. & N. 728 (Ex.Ch.1860), a firm of English underwriters insured a cargo being shipped aboard a Prussian vessel from Russia to England. Shifting cargo forced the ship to put ashore in Norway, where it was driven against rocks and damaged beyond repair. Unable to complete the journey, the captain arranged to have the cargo sold at auction; it was purchased by one Clausen, who eventually resold to the defendants. The cargo was subsequently shipped to London and there sold by the defendants. The underwriters, having paid the original consignees for their loss, brought suit to recover the cargo or its value. The trial judge held for the defendants. On appeal, the court affirmed, explaining:

> We think that the law on this subject was correctly stated by the Lord Chief Baron . . . in the Court below, where he says "if personal property is disposed of in a manner binding according to the law of the country where it is, that disposition is binding everywhere." And we do not think that it makes any difference

> that the goods were wrecked, and not intended to be sent to the country where they were sold. . .
>
> [O]n the evidence before us, we cannot treat Clausen otherwise than as an innocent purchaser, and as the law of Norway appears to us . . . to give title to an innocent purchaser, we think that the property vested in him, and in the defendants as sub-purchasers from him, and that, having once vested, it did not become divested by its being subsequently brought to this country. . .

(6) Two recurring difficulties arise in applying the situs rule to movable property.

(a) Movable property does not always remain in one place. At what time should its location be determined? Suppose that an Illinois manufacturer sells a steam shovel to a Massachusetts contractor on credit, retaining a chattel mortgage as security. The contractor uses the shovel in New Hampshire, becomes insolvent, and sells it there to a bona fide purchaser. When the shovel is later taken to Vermont, it is repossessed by the seller. Should the seller's rights be determined by the law of the situs at the time of the original sale, of the sale to the innocent third party, or of repossession? See *Shanahan v. George B. Landers Constr. Co.*, 266 F.2d 400 (1st Cir.1959) (applying the law of the place of repossession, which was also the residence of the original purchaser). Doesn't the power justification offered for the situs rule in note (3) suggest that the critical factor should be the location of property at the time of litigation? Why might an advocate of the traditional approach shy away from this conclusion?

(b) Once one determines the relevant moment, it is usually easy enough to decide where a steam shovel or a barrel of flour was at that time. But the situs rule applies to intangible property as well. Is an insurance policy, a bank account, or a share of stock located where the piece of paper representing the property is found? Where the insured or the insurer, the debtor or the creditor, the shareholder or the corporation resides?

Apart from these difficulties of administration, does it make sense to apply the situs rule to movable property?

(7) There are a number of important exceptions to the traditional rule that matters respecting interests in movable property are governed by the law of the situs. Succession to movables, for example, is controlled by the law of the decedent's domicile. See, e.g., Restatement of Conflict of Laws (1934) § 303 (intestate succession), § 306 (testamentary succession), § 284 (testamentary powers of appointment), § 295 (validity of testamentary trust). Similarly, the rights of spouses in one another's movable property are determined by domiciliary rather than situs law. E.g., § 290 (ownership of movables acquired during marriage).

What is the reason for these exceptions? Are they consistent with the territorial principle? Professor Beale insisted that the situs state always had power to apply its own law but that it deferred to the state of domicile on matters of succession and marital rights so that the entire estate could be distributed as a unit. 2 J. Beale, A Treatise on the Conflict of Laws 1029–30 (1935). Why doesn't this argument apply to the distribution of land?

WHITE V. TENNANT

31 W.Va. 790, 8 S.E. 596 (1888).

SNYDER, J. This is a suit brought December, 1886, in the circuit court of Monongalia county by William L. White and others against Emrod Tennant, administrator of Michael White, deceased, and Lucinda White, the widow of said Michael White, to set aside the settlement and distribution made by the administrator of the personal estate of said decedent, and have the same settled and distributed according to the laws of the state of Pennsylvania, which state it is claimed was the domicile of said decedent at the time of his death. The plaintiffs are the brothers and sisters of the decedent, who died in this state intestate. On October 28, 1887, the court entered a decree dismissing the plaintiffs' bill, and they have appealed.

The sole question presented for our determination is whether the said Michael White, at the time of his death, in May, 1885, had his legal domicile in this state or in the state of Pennsylvania. It is admitted to be the settled law that the law of the state in which the decedent had his domicile at the time of his death will control the succession and distribution of his personal estate. Before referring to the facts proved in this cause, we shall endeavor to determine what in law is meant by "domicile." Dr. Wharton says: " 'Domicile' is a residence acquired as a final abode. To constitute it there must be (1) residence, actual or inchoate; (2) the non-existence of any intention to make a domicile elsewhere." Whart.Confl.Law, § 21. . . Two things must concur to establish domicile,—the fact of residence, and the intention of remaining. These two must exist, or must have existed, in combination. There must have been an actual residence. The character of the residence is of no importance; and, if domicile has once existed, mere temporary absence will not destroy it, however long continued. * * * The original domicile continues until it is fairly changed for another. It is a legal maxim that every person must have a domicile somewhere; and he can have but one at a time for the same purpose. From this it follows that one domicile cannot be lost or extinguished until another is acquired. * * * When one domicile is definitely abandoned, and a new one selected and entered upon, length of time is not important; one day will be sufficient, provided the *animus* exists. Even when the point of destination is not reached, domicile may shift *in itinere,* if the abandonment of the old domicile, and the setting out for the new, are plainly shown. . .

[Michael White had lived all his life in West Virginia, where he owned a farm. Pursuant to an agreement with his mother and brothers and sisters, Michael sold his West Virginia farm and agreed to occupy a house on a forty-acre tract in Pennsylvania, just across the state line from West Virginia. This tract was part of a larger family farm, the main part of which, including the mansion-house, was in West Virginia. On the morning of April 2, 1885, Michael and his wife, with their possessions and stock, left their former home in West Virginia and started for the Pennsylvania house "with the declared intent and purpose of making the Pennsylvania house his home that evening." Arriving at the Pennsylvania house about sundown, they found it damp and uncomfortable, and, his wife complaining of feeling ill, Michael accepted the invitation of his brothers and sisters to spend the night in the mansion-house in West Virginia. Before going to the mansion-house, Michael unloaded his household goods at the Pennsylvania house and turned loose his livestock. Michael's wife, it transpired, had typhoid fever, and Michael stayed at the mansion-house to care for her, going daily to the Pennsylvania farm to care for his stock. Two weeks later, Michael was attacked with typhoid fever and, shortly thereafter, died intestate in the West Virginia mansion-house. Michael's wife recovered and his estate was administered in West Virginia by defendant Tennant, her father.]

The administrator settled his accounts before a commissioner of said county, and distributed the estate according to the laws of West Virginia; that is, by paying over to the widow the whole personal estate remaining after the payment of the debts of the decedent. It is admitted that if the distribution had been according to the laws of the state of Pennsylvania the wife would have been entitled to the one-half only of said estate, and the plaintiffs would have been entitled to the other half. As the law of the state in which the decedent had his domicile at the time of his death must govern the distribution of his estate, the important question is, where, according to the foregoing facts, was the domicile of Michael at the time of his death? It is unquestionable that prior to the 2nd day of April, 1885, his domicile was and had always been in the state of West Virginia. Did he on that day or at any subsequent day, change his domicile to the state of Pennsylvania? . . .

The facts in this case conclusively prove that Michael White, the decedent, abandoned his residence in West Virginia with the intention and purpose not only of not returning to it, but for the expressed purpose of making a fixed place in the state of Pennsylvania his home for an indefinite time. This fact is shown by all the circumstances, as well as by his declarations and acts. . . When he left his former home, without any intention of returning, and in pursuance of that intention did in fact move with his family and effects to his new home with the intention of making it his residence for an indefinite time, it is my opinion that when he and his wife arrived at his new home it became *eo instanti* his domicile, and that his leaving there, under the circumstances he did, with the intention of returning the next day, did not change the fact. By the concurrence of his intention to make the Pennsylvania house his permanent residence with the fact that he had actually abandoned his former residence, and moved to and put his goods in the new one, made the latter his domicile. He . . . must of necessity have a domicile somewhere. If he did not have one in Pennsylvania, where did he have one? His leaving the Pennsylvania house after he had moved to it with his family and goods, to spend the night, did not revive his domicile at his former residence on Day's Run, because he had sold that, and left it without any purpose of returning there. By going from his new home to the house of his relatives to spend the night he certainly did not make the house thus visited his domicile; therefore, unless the Pennsylvania house was, on the evening of April 2, 1885, his domicile, he was in the anomalous position of being without a domicile anywhere, which, as we have seen, is a legal impossibility; and that house having become his domicile, there is nothing in this case to show that he ever did in fact change or intend to change it, or to establish a domicile elsewhere.

It follows, therefore, that that house remained his domicile up to and at the time of his death; and, that house being in the state of Pennsylvania, the laws of that state must control the distribution of his personal estate, notwithstanding the fact that he died in the state of West Virginia. For these reasons the decree of the circuit court must be reversed, and the cause must be remanded to that court to be there further proceeded in according to the principles announced in this opinion, and the rules of courts of equity.

JOHNSON, P., and GREEN and WOODS, JJ., concurred.

Domicile

(1) The function of domicile in choice of law is summarized in the Second Restatement, § 11 comment c (1971):

> A man may go to many different states during his lifetime. Yet it is desirable that some of his legal interests should at all times be determined by a single law . . . particularly in matters where continuity of application of the same law is important, as family law and decedents' estates.

The range of topics to which this reasoning has been applied is extremely diverse, including such matters as the validity of a marriage or divorce, the legitimacy of a child, succession to personal property (as in *White v.*

Tennant), voter qualifications, taxation, welfare benefits, and amenability to service of process.

(2) What is domicile? Thirty-three sections of the First Restatement defined it (§§ 9–41). Everyone had a domicile, and nobody had more than one (§ 11). A legitimate child took its father's domicile at birth, an illegitimate child its mother's (§ 14). A wife took her husband's domicile (§ 27), but she could acquire a separate domicile by living apart from him if she was not guilty of desertion (§ 28).

The Second Restatement generally takes a similar approach to domicile, requiring physical presence and intent to remain, but makes an effort to eliminate disparities in the treatment of husbands and wives. As noted above, for example, the First Restatement allowed a wife who lived apart from her husband to acquire a separate domicile only if she was not guilty of desertion. In a caveat, the Institute "expresse[d] no opinion" on the continuing validity of the common law rule that a wife guilty of desertion may not acquire a separate domicile. First Restatement at 51. In recognition of subsequent caselaw, the Second Restatement took the bold position that "[i]f there has been an actual rupture of marital relations, [the wife] may acquire a separate domicile of her own even though she was the party at fault. And she may likewise do so if for any reason she is living apart from her husband even though her relations with him are wholly amicable." § 21 comment d. Apparently worried that even this small change might stir controversy, the Reporter assured readers that the problem would seldom arise:

> In the vast majority of situations, husband and wife will have but a single home and this home will be in the place of their domicil. Only in rare situations will the wife have close ties . . . with a state which is not the state of the husband's domicil. Even in such situations, the wife will usually regard the husband's home as her own because he is the head of the family and because she will wish her home to be the same as his. These natural feelings on the part of the wife may also be buttressed by an awareness of the advantages of having a single law govern the interests of each member of the family unit.

Id. at comment b. In 1988, the Institute revised these provisions once more "to reflect modern times and modern mores." The title of § 21 was changed from "Domicil of Wife" to "Domicil of Married Persons," and it was moved from the section dealing with infants and incompetents to the section dealing with change of domicile generally. Comment b was rewritten. It no longer talks about how the wife will naturally want her home to be the same as her husband, but instead says that "the husband and wife will usually regard the same place as their home" and that "[t]hese natural feelings on the part of the spouses may also be buttressed by an awareness of the advantages of having a single law" govern the interests of the family. How likely is it, by the way, that couples consider choice of law in making decisions about whether to live together or not?

The draft Third Restatement continues the basic approach of the Second Restatement, stating that "[a] natural person's domicile is the place where the person's life is centered and the person is physically present." Restatement (Third) of Conflict of Laws, Tentative Draft. No. 2 (2021) § 2.03. The "center" of a person's life is to be determined by "objective evidence of the person's domestic, familial, social, religious, economic, professional, and civic activities." *Id.* Intent to remain is no longer part of the black letter of the Restatement, but "the question whether a person's life is centered in a particular place is informed by a person's intentions, which are determined by a holistic evaluation of objective facts, conduct, and personal statements." *Id.* § 2.03 comment d.

(3) In order to change domicile, the 1934 Restatement declared, "a person must establish a dwelling-place with the intention of making it his home. . . The fact of physical presence at a dwelling-place and the intention to make it a home must concur; if they do so, even for a moment, the change of domicil takes place" (§ 15). Were these conditions satisfied in *White v. Tennant*? How about in the following variations:

(a) After starting for his Pennsylvania farmhouse with a wagon full of belongings and an intention to live in Pennsylvania forever, but before crossing the state line, Michael White is run over by a train. Where is his domicile? According to the Second Restatement, § 16 comment a, "[p]hysical presence in a particular area is essential for the acquisition in that area of a domicile of choice." Statements that even a moment's presence is enough, however, "should not be taken literally. At least for most purposes, a person will not have a sufficient relationship to a place to warrant holding that place to be his domicile unless he has been there for a time at least" (§ 16 comment b).

(b) What if Michael sent his wife ahead to establish a home on the Pennsylvania property and then died before arriving? The cases conflict. Compare *Bangs v. Inhabitants of Brewster,* 111 Mass. 382 (1873), and *Lea v. Lea,* 18 N.J. 1, 112 A.2d 540 (1955) (both finding a change of domicile), with *McIntosh v. Maricopa County,* 73 Ariz. 366, 241 P.2d 801 (1952) (contra). The First Restatement said that a husband could not change his domicile without going there himself (§ 16, comments a and b); the Second Restatement, in contrast, provides that "the wife's presence . . . may, at least on occasion, serve as a substitute" (§ 16, comment c).

(c) What if Michael died after taking a room in a Pittsburgh hotel while looking for a permanent home in the metropolitan area? *Winans v. Winans,* 205 Mass. 388, 91 N.E. 394 (1910), held that there was a change of domicile. If so, and if there are several counties in the metropolitan area, in which county is Michael domiciled? Is it logical to conclude, with both Restatements, that he is domiciled in Pennsylvania but not in any county? See First Restatement § 16, comment d; Second Restatement § 11, comment p (1988 Revisions).

(d) What if Michael's new home straddled the border between West Virginia and Pennsylvania? The First Restatement says in § 25 that the occupant is domiciled in "the territorial division in which the preponderant part of his dwelling-house is situated"; if there is no preponderance, the "principal entrance" is determinative. Some decisions prefer the place where the person sleeps. See 1 J. Beale, A Treatise on the Conflict of Laws § 25.1 (1935).

(4) Where is the domicile of a law student who left her parents in New York to attend school in Chicago? Of a soldier who lived in Maine until he was drafted and stationed in Texas? Of a convict who lived in Seattle until he was sent to the federal penitentiary in Leavenworth, Kansas?

The First Restatement's answer to the last two cases was simple and clear: "A person cannot acquire a domicil of choice by any act done under legal or physical compulsion" (§ 21). Why not?

Later decisions reflect a weakening of the old Restatement rule. In *Stifel v. Hopkins,* 477 F.2d 1116, 1124–25 (6th Cir. 1973), a federal prisoner serving a life sentence in Pennsylvania, but who had lived in Ohio before his conviction, was treated as a Pennsylvanian for purposes of diversity jurisdiction: "[T]he prisoner, like the serviceman or the Cabinet official, should not be precluded from showing that he has developed the intention to be domiciled at the place to which he has been forced to remove. . . We ought to be hesitant to define a cognizable class of citizens out of access to the federal courts. . ."

The Second Restatement took account of the new trend in 1986 with a well-placed adverb in § 17 (our italics): "A person does not *usually* acquire a domicil of choice by his presence in a place under physical or legal compulsion." In the draft Third Restatement, the adverb is gone again:

"A natural person's domicile does not change because that person is compelled to be present in a place." Restatement (Third) of Conflict of Laws, Tentative Draft No. 2 (2021) § 2.07. The new Restatement recognizes, however, that prisoners "may adopt the place of confinement as their domicile by voluntarily taking action to make that place the center of their lives." *Id.* § 2.07 comment b.

(5) Does it make sense to apply the same concept of domicile to such disparate matters as divorce jurisdiction, income taxation, and the validity of a will? When the First Restatement was under discussion, Walter Wheeler Cook took the position that the meaning of domicile depended upon the context in which it was used:

> The court has a concrete problem to solve. It is trying to decide whether the courts of the state should grant a divorce on constructive service; whether the man is sufficiently connected with the state to make that a reasonable thing to do. It may be reasonable to do that, but not reasonable to apply the same concept in the case involving the validity of the provisions of a will. . . I do not believe that you can determine the exact scope of any legal concept unless you know what you are trying to do with it.

3 ALI, Proceedings 226–28 (1925).

Professor Cook lost the immediate battle, and some courts continue to argue for a unitary concept of domicile. E.g., *Toll v. Moreno,* 284 Md. 425, 397 A.2d 1009 (1979) ("Regardless of some views expressed by commentators, in Maryland . . . the meaning and basic principles for determining domicile do not vary depending on the context.") But such expressions are becoming increasingly rare, and Professor Cook's arguments are now widely accepted. See, e.g., *Galva Foundry Co. v. Heiden,* 924 F.2d 729 (7th Cir. 1991) (Posner, J.) ("Domicile is not a thing, like a rabbit or a carrot, but a legal conclusion. . . And in drawing legal conclusions, it is always helpful to have in mind the purpose for which the conclusion is being drawn.")

The draft Third Restatement embodies this change of attitude, stating that "[a] natural person has only one domicile at a time for the purpose of deciding a particular conflict-of-laws issue," Restatement (Third) of Conflict of Laws, Tentative Draft No. 2 (2021), § 2.03, while noting that "a person might be found domiciled in one State for one purpose and domiciled in another State for another purpose," *id.* § 2.03 comment f.

(6) "Domicile" and "residence" are confusing companions. "Domicile" is a judicial concept, only rarely found in statutes. "Residence" is a layperson's term and the one most frequently employed by legislators. Judges have the last word, however, and in interpreting the term "residence" they appear to exercise good sense in shaping its meaning depending upon the function for which the term is employed. A statute allowing substituted service of process on "residents" absent from the state will usually be interpreted as synonymous with domicile. Jurisdiction to divorce a "resident" often requires both more and less than domicile: the plaintiff must establish a continuity of physical presence for a prescribed period of a kind not required of "domicile" (cf. *White v. Tennant*); but expressions of intent are likely to be taken at face value. For other purposes, such as eligibility for schooling, "residence" often means physical presence without any requirement of an indefinite intention to remain. Thus a minor who is staying for a year or so with his grandparents is entitled to free education from the local school district. See generally Reese

& Green, *That Elusive Word, "Residence,"* 6 Vand.L.Rev. 561 (1953). Finally, both "residence" and "domicile" should be distinguished from nationality, which is used for choice-of-law purposes in some European countries, and from "habitual residence," a term used in many foreign laws, treaties, and international agreements such as the Hague Convention on the Civil Aspects of International Child Abduction, discussed infra Chapter 6, Section 2.B.

Miscellaneous Traditional Rules

(1) "Except as stated in §§ 131 and 132," said § 121 of the First Restatement, "a marriage is valid everywhere if the requirements of the marriage law of the state where the contract of marriage takes place are complied with." Section 131, in wishy-washy terms quite uncharacteristic of the First Restatement, provided that the law of the place of celebration governed the period during which marriage was prohibited following a divorce "unless . . . the statute which forbids the parties to marry is interpreted as being applicable to the marriage of domiciliaries in another state. . ." Section 132 listed situations in which the validity of a marriage celebrated elsewhere would be governed by the law of "the domicil of either party": polygamous marriage, incestuous marriage, and "marriage of a domiciliary which a statute at the domicil makes void even though celebrated in another state."

In the light of these exceptions, what was left of the general rule stated in § 121? The comments to the above sections attempted to rationalize the rules stated with the territorial theory by distinguishing between the contract of marriage and the status of marriage. The validity of the marriage contract was governed by the law of the place where the promises were exchanged; but the status conferred on the parties was governed, "like all domestic status, by the law of the domicil or domiciles of the parties." § 121, comment d. In an effort to reduce the potential conflict between the state of the ceremony and the state of the newlyweds' domicile, the First Restatement endorsed the 1912 Uniform Marriage Evasion Act, a measure designed to ensure that couples who left their home state to seek more permissive marriage laws elsewhere would not succeed in having the foreign marriage recognized when they returned home. § 132, comment e. The Act was adopted only in five states. One of them, however, was Massachusetts, the first state to recognize same-sex marriage. See *Goodridge v. Department of Public Health*, 440 Mass. 309, 798 N.E.2d 941 (2003). Once Massachusetts began issuing marriage licenses to same-sex couples domiciled there while denying them to similar couples domiciled elsewhere, a perfect conflict-of-laws storm was set in motion. Professor Joanna L. Grossman sets the problem in historical perspective and sorts out the analytical difficulties in *Fear and Loathing in Massachusetts: Same-Sex Marriage and Some Lessons From the History of Marriage and Divorce,* 14 Boston Univ. Pub. Int. L.J. 87 (2004). The problem of interstate variation with respect to same-sex marriage was resolved by the Supreme Court in *Obergefell v. Hodges*, 576 U.S. 644 (2015), which held that same-sex couples may exercise the fundamental right to marry in all states.

(2) Should a distinction be drawn between the *validity* of a marriage and its incidents or *effects*? Suppose a foreign sheik dies intestate leaving a bank account in California and, back home, four wives who are considered as such by his domicile. Are the "wives" entitled to whatever share the marital domicile gives them? Or should California consider them as concubines who are not entitled to inherit? See *In re Dalip Singh Bir's Estate,* 83 Cal.App.2d 256, 188 P.2d 499 (1948), where the court ordered distribution to the wives. Would the same result be reached if Dalip Singh Bir came to California to live, bringing his wives with him, and California authorities prosecuted him for illegal cohabitation?

(3) The legitimacy of a child at birth, according to the First Restatement, was determined by the law of the state in which the parent whose relationship is in issue was domiciled when the child was born, § 138; whether a subsequent act has legitimated a child was determined by the law of the state in which the acting parent was domiciled when the act was done, § 140. The status of adoption, § 142, could be created by the state of the child's domicile or, if there was jurisdiction over any person having custody of the child, by the state of domicile of the adopting parents. Custody of legitimate children at birth was determined by the law of the state where the father was domiciled; the state in which the child was domiciled might thereafter change the right to custody, §§ 144–46, and any state "into which the child comes" might take custody from an unfit guardian, § 148. "The status of guardian and ward," says § 149, "is created and terminated by the state of the domicil of the ward."

Interestingly, the Second Restatement basically retains the same rules with respect to marriage and legitimacy, but simply drops the question of custody altogether. Conflict-of-laws problems regarding child custody are considered in Chapter 6, infra.

(4) Many matters affecting corporations were referred by the 1934 Restatement to the law of the state of incorporation. E.g., whether an association has been incorporated, and the effects of an unsuccessful attempt to incorporate, § 155; the status and rights of shareholders, §§ 182–83; the liability of shareholders for assessments to pay corporate debts, § 185. With respect to certain "internal" corporate affairs this principle was carried further, resulting in an exercise of "judicial discretion" to refuse jurisdiction over cases involving foreign corporations. See §§ 191–202 and Scope Note to Topic 5. On the other hand the power of a corporation was subject to limitation by the law of the state in which it sought to act as well as by that of the state of incorporation, §§ 156, 165, and as to acts not ultra vires "the effect of an act directed to be done by a foreign corporation is governed by the law of the state where it is done." § 166. Do you suppose there is any difficulty in applying these rules? Are they subject to other objections?

(5) The general principle that matters of "procedure" are governed by the law of the forum state is considered at pp. 52–65, infra.

(6) The omission from this chapter of choice-of-law rules for criminal law, workers' compensation, and divorce is not without significance. These are areas in which rules respecting judicial jurisdiction have performed most of the work elsewhere left to choice-of-law rules. The crucial determination in the application of criminal laws is whether the court has jurisdiction; if it has, it applies its own criminal law. Although this does not exclude interpretive problems of the territorial scope of criminal law (e.g., did the legislature intend to prohibit acts done elsewhere?), or the use of another state's felony conviction in applying the forum's "three strikes" law (see People v. Washington, 210 Cal.App.4th 1042, 1044, 148 Cal. Rptr. 3d 748, 750 (2012) (counting defendant's prior Illinois conviction for battery with personal infliction of great bodily harm as a "strike" because "the term 'great bodily harm' under Illinois law is synonymous with 'great bodily injury' under California law")), the court does not concern itself with the distinct question whether it should apply foreign law. Similarly, the special tribunals and procedures provided for workers' compensation (as well as some other modern regulatory legislation) tend to exclude any consideration of foreign law. And the vagaries of divorce, a field where the choice-of-law process has been notably absent, are so special that they will receive detailed consideration in Chapter 6, infra.

Is there any common ground that explains why the choice-of-law process is largely excluded from criminal law, workers' compensation, and divorce? See von Mehren & Trautman, The Law of Multistate Problems 84–90 (1965).

SECTION 2. TRADITIONAL PRACTICE: A SURVEY OF ESCAPE DEVICES

A. CHARACTERIZATION

If there is one choice-of-law rule for contract cases and another for torts, there must be some way to determine whether the problem before the court is one of contract or tort. This problem of categorization, commonly known as "characterization," is by no means peculiar to conflict of laws. But conflicts presents especially difficult questions in this regard because every case involves at least two different bodies of law, each of which may use the same or similar concepts to mean different things. The nature of traditional choice-of-law rules exacerbated these difficulties: The rules were relatively few in number, they were applicable to legal categories of enormous breadth (e.g., "contracts" or "torts"), and they were brought into play by connecting factors drawn from domestic law situations (e.g., the "place of making" of a contract). Characterization problems thus pervaded the traditional choice of law system and often gave rise to conflicting results, as the following cases demonstrate.

LEVY V. DANIELS' U-DRIVE AUTO RENTING CO.

108 Conn. 333, 143 A. 163 (1928).

WHEELER, C.J. The complaint alleged these facts: The defendant, Daniels' U-Drive Auto Renting Company, Incorporated, rented in Hartford to Sack an automobile, which he operated, and in which Levy, the plaintiff [a resident of Hartford], was a passenger. During the time the automobile was rented and operated, the defendant renting company was subject to section 21 of chapter 195 of the Public Acts of Connecticut, 1925, which provides:

> "Any person renting or leasing to another any motor vehicle owned by him shall be liable for any damage to any person or property caused by the operation of such motor vehicle while so rented or leased."

While the plaintiff was a passenger, Sack brought the car to a stop on the main highway at Longmeadow, Mass., and negligently allowed it to stand directly in the path of automobiles proceeding southerly in the same direction his automobile was headed, without giving sufficient warning to automobiles approaching from his rear, and without having a tail light in operation, and when, due to inclement weather, the visibility was reduced to an exceedingly low degree. At this time the defendant Maginn negligently ran into and upon the rear end of the car Sack was operating, and threw plaintiff forcibly forward, causing him serious injuries. The specific acts of Maginn's negligence are set up at length in the complaint; it is not essential at this time to recite them. The plaintiff suffered his severe injuries in consequence of the concurrent negligence of both defendants.

The defendant demurred to the complaint upon several grounds, upon only one of which the trial court rested its decision; namely, that the liability of the defendant must be determined by the law of Massachusetts, which did not impose upon persons renting automobiles any such obligation as the Connecticut act did. . .

It is the defendant's contention in support of this ground of demurrer that the action set forth in the complaint is one of tort, and, since Massachusetts has no statute like, or substantially like, the Connecticut act, it must be determined by the common law of that state, under which the plaintiff must prove, to prevail, the negligence of the defendant in renting a defective motor vehicle and in failing to disclose the defect. If this were the true theory of the complaint, the conclusion thus reached must have followed. "The locus delicti determined the existence of the cause of action." * * * Under the law of Massachusetts, the plaintiff concededly would have a cause of action against Sack and Maginn for their tortious conduct in the operation of the cars they were driving. The plaintiff concedes the correctness of this. His counsel, however, construe the complaint as one in its nature contractual. The act makes him who rents or leases any motor vehicle to another liable for any damage to any person or property caused by the operation of the motor vehicle while so rented or leased. Liability for "damage caused by the operation of such motor vehicle" means caused by its tortious operation. This was undoubtedly the legislative intent; otherwise the act would be invalid. The plaintiff concedes this to be the true construction of these words, and the defendant acquiesces in this construction.

The complaint alleges a tortious operation of the automobile rented to Sack by the defendant, causing the injuries to the plaintiff as alleged, and constituting an action ex delicto. The statute gives, in terms, the injured person a right of action against the defendant which rented the automobile to Sack, though the injury occurred in Massachusetts. It was a right which the statute gave directly, not derivatively, to the injured person as a consequence of the contract of hiring. The purpose of the statute was not primarily to give the injured person a right of recovery against the tortious operator of the car, but to protect the safety of the traffic upon highways by providing an incentive to him who rented motor vehicles to rent them to competent and careful operators, by making him liable for damage resulting from the tortious operation of the rented vehicles. The common law would not hold the defendant liable upon the facts recited in the complaint for the negligence of Sack in the operation of this automobile. * * * The rental of motor vehicles to any but competent and careful operators, or to persons of unknown responsibility, would be liable to result in injury to the public upon or near highways, and this imminent danger justified, as a reasonable exercise of the police power, this statute, which requires all who engage in this business to become responsible for any injury inflicted upon the public by the tortious operation of the rented motor vehicle. . .

The statute made the liability of the person renting motor vehicles a part of every contract of hiring a motor vehicle in Connecticut. . . A liability arising out of a contract depends upon the law of the place of contract, "unless the contract is to be performed or to have its beneficial operation and effect elsewhere, or it is made with reference to the law of another place." . . .

If the liability of this defendant under this statute is contractual, no question can arise as to the plaintiff's right to enforce this contract, provided the obligation imposed upon this defendant was for the "direct, sole and exclusive benefit" of the plaintiff. The contract was made in Connecticut; at the instant of its making the statute made a part of the contract of hiring the liability of the defendant which the plaintiff seeks to enforce. The law inserted in the contract this provision. The statute did not create the liability; it imposed it in case the defendant voluntarily rented the automobile. Whether the defendant entered into this contract of hiring was his own voluntary act; if he did he must accept the condition upon which the law permitted the making of the contract. The contract was for the "direct, sole, and exclusive benefit" of the plaintiff, who is alleged to have been injured through the tortious operation of the automobile rented by the defendant to Sack. The right of the plaintiff as a beneficiary of this contract to maintain this action is no longer an open question in this state. * * * The contract was made for him and every other member of the public. That the beneficiary was undetermined because each of the public was a beneficiary is of no consequence. His injury determines his identity and right of action. * * * The assent of the beneficiary, if required, is manifested in his action upon the contract. The demurrer should have been overruled. . .

HAUMSCHILD V. CONTINENTAL CAS. CO.

7 Wis.2d 130, 95 N.W.2d 814 (1959).

[Ms. Haumschild sued her former husband and his insurer for personal injuries sustained through his negligence in a California automobile accident. At the time of the accident, Mr. and Ms. Haumschild were still married and were domiciled in Wisconsin. The trial court dismissed the action on the ground that spouses could not sue one another in tort under California law. Ms. Haumschild appealed.]

CURRIE, JUSTICE. This appeal presents a conflict of laws problem with respect to interspousal liability for tort growing out of an automobile accident. Which law controls, that of the state of the forum, the state of the place of wrong, or the state of domicile? Wisconsin is both the state of the forum and of the domicile while California is the state where the alleged wrong was committed. Under Wisconsin law a wife may sue her husband in tort. Under California law she cannot. * * *

This court was first faced with this question in *Buckeye v. Buckeye,* 1931, 203 Wis. 248, 234 N.W. 342. In that case Wisconsin was the state of the forum and domicile, while Illinois was the state of the place of wrong. It was there held that the law governing the creation and extent of tort liability is that of the place where the tort was committed, citing Goodrich, Conflict of Laws (1st ed.), p. 188. From this premise it was further held that interspousal immunity from tort liability necessarily is governed by the law of the place of injury. . .

The principle enunciated in the *Buckeye* case and followed in subsequent Wisconsin cases, that the law of the place of wrong controls as to whether one spouse is immune from suit in tort by the other, is the prevailing view in the majority of jurisdictions in this country. . . However, criticism of the rule of the *Buckeye* case, by legal writers, some of them recognized authorities in the field of conflict of laws, and recent decisions by the courts of California, New Jersey, and Pennsylvania, have caused us to re-examine the question afresh.

[The court discussed the writings of Walter Wheeler Cook, Max Rheinstein, Ernst Rabel, and Alan Ford.]

The first case to break the ice and flatly hold that the law of domicile should be applied in determining whether there existed an immunity from suit for tort based upon family relationship is *Emery v. Emery,* 1955, 45 Cal.2d 421, 289 P.2d 218. In that case two unemancipated minor sisters sued their unemancipated minor brother and their father to recover for injuries sustained in an automobile accident that occurred in the state of Idaho, the complaint alleging wilful misconduct in order to come within the provisions of the Idaho "guest" statute. All parties were domiciled in California. The opinion by Mr. Justice Traynor recognized that the California court, in passing on the question of whether an unemancipated minor child may sue the parent or an unemancipated brother, had a choice to apply the law of the place of wrong, of the forum, or of the domicile. It was held that the immunity issue was not a question of tort but one of capacity to sue and be sued, and rejected the law of the place of injury as "both fortuitous and irrelevant." . . .

". . . We think that disabilities to sue and immunities from suit because of a family relationship are more properly determined by reference to the law of the state of the family domicile. That state has the primary responsibility for establishing and regulating the incidents of the family relationship and it is the only state in which the parties can, by participation in the legislative processes, effect a change in those incidents. Moreover, it is undesirable that the rights, duties, disabilities, and immunities conferred or imposed by the family relationship should constantly change as members of the family cross state boundaries during temporary absences from their home." . . .

The two reasons most often advanced for the common law rule, that one spouse may not sue the other, are the ancient concept that husband and wife constitute in law but one person, and that to permit such suits will be to foment family discord and strife. The Married Women's Acts of the various states have effectively destroyed the "one person" concept thereby leaving as the other remaining reason for the immunity the objective of preventing family discord. This is also the justification usually advanced for denying an unemancipated child the capacity to sue a parent, brother or sister. Clearly this policy reason for denying the capacity to sue more properly lies within the sphere of family law, where domicile usually controls the law to be applied, than it does tort law, where the place of injury generally determines the substantive law which will govern. . .

We are convinced that, from both the standpoint of public policy and logic, the proper solution of the conflict of laws problem, in cases similar to the instant action, is to hold that the law of the domicile is the one that ought to be applied in determining any issue of incapacity to sue based upon family relationship. . .

While the appellant's counsel did not request that we overrule *Buckeye v. Buckeye,* supra, and the subsequent Wisconsin cases dealing with this particular conflict of laws problem, he did specifically seek to have this court apply California's conflict of laws principle, that the law of the domicile is determinative of interspousal capacity to sue, to this particular case. However, to do so would violate the well recognized principle of conflict of laws that, where the substantive law of another state is applied, there necessarily must be excluded such foreign state's law of conflict of laws. Restatement, *Conflict of Laws,* p. 11, sec. 7(b). . .

Judgment reversed and cause remanded for further proceedings not inconsistent with this opinion.

Characterization as a Rational Process

(1) Section 387 of the 1934 Restatement characterized vicarious liability as a tort question: "When a person authorizes another to act for him in any state and the other does so act, whether he is liable for the torts of the other is determined by the law of the place of the wrong." This provision was applied in *Venuto v. Robinson,* 118 F.2d 679 (3d Cir. 1941). Robinson, the owner-operator of a truck, agreed in North Carolina to lease his equipment to Ross Motor Lines and to take a load of goods for Ross from North Carolina to New England. While making this trip, Robinson collided with another vehicle in New Jersey, killing several people. Citing § 387, Judge Goodrich applied New Jersey law, under which Ross was vicariously liable for Robinson's negligence, even though their contract was made in North Carolina. Recall also *Alabama Great Southern R.R. v. Carroll,* supra p. 7, in which the plaintiff argued that an Alabama statute making employers liable for the acts of fellow-employees was incorporated into the employment contract. There, too, the court rejected a contract characterization, holding that the statute created a tort liability that acted upon an employment relationship.

Is there any way to reconcile these decisions with *Levy v. Daniels' U-Drive*? Which of the three cases—*Daniels' U-Drive, Carroll,* or *Venuto*—seems most consistent with traditional choice-of-law theory? Which requires the greatest stretch to reach its result? Which reaches the soundest result? Does this suggest anything about the nature of the characterization process?

(2) How persuasive are the court's reasons in *Haumschild* for concluding that interspousal immunity was a matter of domestic relations rather than tort? Is it so clear that California law should not apply? Would your answer be the same if the laws were reversed, so that California allowed suits between spouses and Wisconsin did not?

(3) How should the following cases be characterized?

(a) *Preine v. Freeman,* 112 F.Supp. 257 (E.D.Va. 1953). Injured in an automobile accident in Virginia, the plaintiffs had released two of five alleged joint tortfeasors from liability by contracts made in Colorado or New York. Virginia, but not Colorado or New York, provided that a release of one tortfeasor discharged them all. The court applied Virginia law:

> The construction and validity of a release are governed by the law of the place where it is executed . . . ; but [its] validity . . . as a defense in an action in tort is governed by the law of the place of injury.

Why?

(b) *Caldwell v. Gore,* 175 La. 501, 143 So. 387 (1932). The defendant erected a dam on Louisiana property, obstructing the flow of water from the plaintiff's adjacent land in Arkansas. Under Louisiana law "the lower estate owes a natural easement or servitude to the upper estate to receive all the natural drainage thereof," so the obstruction was unlawful. Under Arkansas law, drainage could be obstructed "if this is done reasonably, for proper objects, and with due care as regards adjacent property." The court applied Louisiana law: "By permitting this, no greater hardship is imposed upon the owner of the servient estate than if both estates were situated in Louisiana."

Was the issue one of tort or property? If property, did it concern the right of drainage appurtenant to Arkansas land or the right to build in Louisiana?

(c) *Swank v. Hufnagle,* 111 Ind. 453, 12 N.E. 303 (1887). To secure her husband's debt, an Ohio woman executed in Ohio a promissory note and a mortgage on land in Indiana. Ohio permitted wives to act as surety for their husbands; Indiana did not. In an action upon the "note and mortgage," the court applied Indiana law and denied the creditor relief: "The validity of the mortgage of real property is to be determined by the law of the place where the property is situated."

Similar facts were presented in *Burr v. Beckler,* 264 Ill. 230, 106 N.E. 206 (1914), except that the laws were reversed (i.e., the place where the contract was made created the contract disability). The Supreme Court of Illinois applied the law of the place of contracting to deny the creditor relief. According to this court, the validity of the note was a contract question, and the mortgage was merely "incidental" to the note. In a case identical to *Burr,* the Supreme Court of Florida adopted still another solution. An Alabama woman tried to secure a debt of her husband by executing a promissory note and a mortgage on her separate land in Florida. The Florida court held the note invalid while enforcing the mortgage. "It does not follow," the court said, "that because Mrs. Thomson is not bound by the note it is for that reason totally void. It still remains a valid obligation of her husband which she can in this State secure by a mortgage of her separate statutory property. . ." *Thomson v. Kyle,* 39 Fla. 582, 23 So. 12 (1897). Which of these three approaches was right?

(d) *Cutts v. Najdrowski,* 123 N.J.Eq. 481, 198 A. 885 (1938). Leon Najdrowski, a resident of New Jersey, held an account in a New York bank that was designated "Leon Najdrowski, in trust for Joseph Najdrowski." After Leon's death, Joseph closed the account and took the money. Leon's administratrix sued, alleging that the money belonged to the estate. Did Leon attempt to make an inter vivos gift, the validity of which is governed under traditional choice-of-law rules by the law of the situs? Or was this a testamentary gift, governed by the law of decedent's domicile?

The chancellor held that the gift was testamentary under New Jersey law and found for the plaintiff on the ground that it failed to comply with the New Jersey statute of wills. On appeal, this decision was overturned. Under New York law, Leon had created an inter vivos trust that was revocable at will. The appellate court therefore concluded that New York law should be applied to determine its validity. Whose law determines whether the trust was testamentary or inter vivos? How is this determination to be made?

(4) The traditional theory has surprisingly little to say on the subject of characterization. The 1934 Restatement resolved a number of troublesome characterization problems for anyone who cared to follow its advice, but it gave no guidance on how to characterize issues that were not dealt with explicitly. Beale's three-volume treatise was similarly reticent; the subject of characterization was not even listed in his index.[3]

[3] Recall Kipling's Painted Jaguar, who complained that his mother had told him that if he found a tortoise he should scoop it out of its shell and that if he found a hedgehog he should hold it under water, but that she had not told him how to tell which was a hedgehog and which a tortoise.

(5) Courts sometimes try to resolve the problem by adopting for choice-of-law purposes a characterization that has been employed in another context. Is this appropriate?

Suppose, for example, that before the decision in *Levy v. Daniels' U-Drive* the Connecticut court had held in a case without foreign complications that actions under the owner-consent statute were governed by the statute of limitations for tort cases rather than for contract cases. Are the considerations that might have led to this conclusion relevant to the question of characterization for choice of law? See W.W. Cook, The Logical and Legal Bases of the Conflict of Laws 159 (1942):

> The tendency to assume that a word which appears in two or more legal rules, and so in connection with more than one purpose, has and should have precisely the same scope in all of them runs all through legal discussions. It has all the tenacity of original sin and must constantly be guarded against.

Cf. the discussion of domicile, pp. 33–40 supra.

(6) Lawyers often decide whether a case falls within one rule or another by asking about their purposes. Do the purposes of the place-of-wrong and place-of-contracting rules help to determine whether an issue such as the car owner's liability in *Daniels' U-Drive* should be characterized as one of tort rather than contract? Here are Beale's reasons for these two basic rules, 2 J. Beale, A Treatise on the Conflict of Laws 1086, 1288 (1935):

> If the law of the place where the parties act refuses legal validity to their acts, it is impossible to see on what principle some other law may nevertheless give their acts validity. . . Any attempt to make the law of the place of performance govern the act of contracting is an attempt to give to that law extraterritorial effect.
>
> It is impossible for a plaintiff to recover in tort unless he has been given by some law a cause of action in tort; and this cause of action can be given only by the law of the place where the tort was committed.

Does that help? What about the policy of uniformity, or of protecting legitimate expectations?

Should the plaintiff be permitted to determine by his or her pleadings which characterization will be employed? Should the plaintiff be able to argue in the alternative? How are characterization questions handled in purely domestic cases? How is a judge acting in complete good faith and trying to do the "right" thing supposed to choose the proper law?

(7) Some writers have accused the courts of manipulating the characterization process in order to apply a law they prefer on the merits. In this connection Professor Leflar described a revealing series of Arkansas decisions respecting the applicability of an Arkansas statute providing damages for mental anguish caused by failure to deliver a telegram. In *Western Union Telegraph Co. v. Griffin,* 92 Ark. 219, 122 S.W. 489 (1909), a wire was sent from Arkansas to Mississippi; since the contract had been made in Arkansas, the court applied Arkansas law and granted relief. In *Western Union Telegraph Co. v. Chilton,* 100 Ark. 296, 140 S.W. 26 (1911), the wire was sent from Missouri to Arkansas; since the tort had occurred in Arkansas, the court applied Arkansas law and granted relief. Leflar cited six additional cases, decided within less than a decade, all managing to apply Arkansas law by choosing whichever characterization was necessary for the occasion. See R. Leflar, The Law of Conflict of Laws 95 (1962).

(8) Is there any excuse for such behavior? Commenting favorably on the much-criticized decision in *Daniels' U-Drive,* Professor Stumberg seemed actually to applaud insincerity:

> [A] decision like that [in *Daniels'*] cannot be lightly dismissed without considering the soundness of the result, regardless of the method whereby it was reached. . . A theory of quasi-contract was employed as a rationalizing device. . .
>
> Measured by the standard which has been most frequently applied by American courts in torts cases, the decision is unsound. It may, however, be undesirable always to apply the usual standard. In the instant case the State of Connecticut had sufficient interest in the business of renting cars there to warrant application of its own law. If its social policy is in fact one with respect to the business of renting cars, its courts would be justified in placing emphasis upon the fact that the car was rented in Connecticut rather than upon the fact that the injury occurred in Massachusetts.

Stumberg, Principles of Conflict of Laws 202–03 & n. 84 (3d ed. 1963). What would happen to certainty and predictability if this approach were widely adopted? Wouldn't plaintiffs be tempted to shop for a forum willing to indulge a favorable "social policy"?

(9) Should a court characterize the case as a whole, the particular statute or law that is involved, or the legal problem with which that statute or law deals? Note the efforts in *Daniels'* and in *Haumschild* to determine whether or not the law in question served a "tort law" purpose. The 1934 Restatement, on the other hand, generally characterized the case as a whole: e.g., the law of the place of injury determined all the issues involved in deciding whether a "tort" was committed. Why?

B. SUBSTANCE OR PROCEDURE?

GRANT V. MCAULIFFE

41 Cal.2d 859, 264 P.2d 944 (1953).

TRAYNOR, JUSTICE. [Three Californians, including Grant, were injured in Arizona when the car in which they were riding collided with a car driven by Pullen, also a Californian. Pullen died several weeks later, and McAuliffe was appointed administrator of his estate by a California court. Grant and the other two occupants of the car with which Pullen collided brought suit against Pullen's estate to recover for their injuries. The trial court granted defendant's motion to dismiss, relying on Arizona law, under which a tort action which has not been commenced prior to the death of the tortfeasor must be abated. Under California law, causes of action for negligent torts survive the death of the tortfeasor and can be maintained against the administrator or executor of the estate.]

Thus, the answer to the question whether the causes of action against Pullen survived and are maintainable against his estate depends on whether Arizona or California law applies. In actions on torts occurring abroad, the courts of this state determine the substantive matters inherent in the cause of action by adopting as their own the law of the place where the tortious acts occurred, unless it is contrary to the public policy of this state. . . But the forum does not adopt as its own the procedural law of the place where the tortious acts occur. It must, therefore, be determined whether survival of causes of action is procedural or substantive for conflict of laws purposes.

This question is one of first impression in this state. The precedents in other jurisdictions are conflicting. In many cases it has been held that the survival of a cause of action is a matter of substance and that the law of the place where the tortious acts occurred must be applied to determine the question. * * * The Restatement of the Conflict of Laws, section 390, is in accord. It should be noted, however, that the majority of the foregoing cases were decided after drafts of the Restatement were first circulated in 1929. Before that time, it appears that the weight of authority was that survival of causes of action is procedural and governed by the domestic law of the forum. * * * Many of the cases, decided both before and after the Restatement, holding that survival is substantive and must be determined by the law of the place where the tortious acts occurred, confused the problems involved in survival of causes of action with those involved in causes of action for wrongful death. . . A cause of action for wrongful death is statutory. It is a new cause of action vested in the widow or next of kin, and arises on the death of the injured person. Before his death, the injured person himself has a separate and distinct cause of action and, if it survives, the same cause of action can be enforced by the personal representative of the deceased against the tortfeasor. The survival statutes do not create a new cause of action, as do the wrongful death statutes. . . They merely prevent the abatement of the cause of action of the injured person, and provide for its enforcement by or against the personal representative of the deceased. They are analogous to statutes of limitation, which are procedural for conflict of laws purposes and are governed by the domestic law of the forum. *Biewend v. Biewend,* 17 Cal.2d 108, 114, 109 P.2d 701. Thus, a cause of action arising in another state, by the laws of which an action cannot be maintained thereon because of lapse of time, can be enforced in California by a citizen of this state, if he has held the cause of action from the time it accrued. * * *

Defendant contends, however, that the characterization of survival of causes of action as substantive or procedural is foreclosed by *Cort v. Steen,* 36 Cal.2d 437, 442, 224 P.2d 723, where it was held that the California survival statutes were substantive and therefore did not apply retroactively. The problem in the present proceeding, however, is not whether the survival statutes apply retroactively, but whether they are substantive or procedural for purposes of conflict of laws. " 'Substance' and 'procedure,' . . . are not legal concepts of invariant content" * * * and a statute or other rule of law will be characterized as substantive or procedural according to the nature of the problem for which a characterization must be made. . .

Since we find no compelling weight of authority for either alternative, we are free to make a choice on the merits. We have concluded that survival of causes of action should be governed by the law of the forum. Survival is not an essential part of the cause of action itself but relates to the procedures available for the enforcement of the legal claim for damages. Basically the question is one of the administration of decedents' estates, which is a purely local proceeding. The problem here is whether the causes of action that these plaintiffs had against Pullen before his death survive as liabilities of his estate. Section 573 of the Probate Code provides that "all actions founded . . . upon any liability for physical injury, death or injury to property, may be maintained by and against executors and administrators in all cases in which the cause of action . . . is one which may not abate upon the death of their respective testators or intestates. . ." Civil Code section 956 provides that "A thing in action arising out of a wrong which results in physical injury to the person . . . shall not abate by reason of the death of the wrongdoer . . . ," and causes of action for damage to property are maintainable against executors and administrators under section 574 of the Probate Code. * * * Decedent's estate is located in this state, and letters of administration were issued to defendant by the courts of this state. The responsibilities of defendant, as administrator of Pullen's estate, for injuries inflicted by Pullen before his death are governed by the laws of this state. This approach has been followed in a number of well-reasoned cases. * * * It retains control of the administration of estates by the local legislature, and avoids the problems involved in determining the administrator's amenability to suit under the laws of other states. The common law doctrine *actio personalis moritur cum persona* had its origin in a penal concept of tort liability. * * * Today, tort liabilities of the sort involved in these actions are regarded as compensatory. When, as in the present case, all of the parties were residents of this state, and the estate of the deceased tortfeasor is being administered in this state, plaintiffs' right to prosecute their causes of action is governed by the laws of this state relating to administration of estates.

The orders granting defendant's motions to abate are reversed, and the causes remanded for further proceedings. . .

SCHAUER, JUSTICE. I dissent. In *Cort v. Steen* (1950), 36 Cal.2d 437, 442, 224 P.2d 723, this court held that under the doctrine of nonsurvivability the abatement of an action by the death of the injured person through the tort feasor's act or otherwise, or by the death of the tort feasor, abates the wrong as well; that the effect of a survival statute is to create a right or cause of action rather than to either continue an existing right or revive or extend a remedy theretofore accrued for the redress of an existing wrong; and that consequently a survival statute enacted after death of the tort feasor did not apply to the tort or cause of action involved. . .

[E]ven more regrettable than the failure to either follow or unequivocally overrule the cited cases is the character of the "rule" which is now promulgated: the majority assert that henceforth "a statute or other rule of law will be characterized as substantive or procedural according to the nature of the problem for which a characterization must be made," thus suggesting that the court will no longer be bound to consistent enforcement or uniform application of "a statute or other rule of law" but will instead apply one "rule" or another as the untrammelled whimsy of the majority may from time to time dictate, "according to the nature of the problem" as they view it in a given case. This concept of the majority strikes deeply at what has been our proud boast that ours was a government of laws rather than of men. . .

The Substance-Procedure Distinction

(1) In a sense, the substance-procedure distinction is merely a straightforward characterization problem. It warrants separate treatment for at least two reasons. First, it comes up very often; indeed, every case in which foreign law is applied presents this problem. Second, unlike other characterization problems, the substance-procedure distinction is dealt with explicitly and has been extensively analyzed. Consider the following provisions from the 1934 Restatement:

> § 584. *Determination of Whether Question Is One of Procedure.* The court at the forum determines according to its own Conflict of Laws rule whether a given question is one of substance or procedure.
>
> § 585. *What Law Governs Procedure.* All matters of procedure are governed by the law of the forum.
>
> § 592. *Procedure in Court.* The law of the forum governs all matters of pleading and the conduct of proceedings in court.
>
> § 594. *Mode of Trial.* The law of the forum determines whether an issue of fact shall be tried by the court or by a jury.
>
> § 595. *Proof of Facts.* (1) The law of the forum governs the proof in court of a fact alleged. (2) The law of the forum governs presumptions and inferences to be drawn from evidence.
>
> § 596. *Witnesses.* The law of the forum determines the competency and the credibility of witnesses.
>
> § 597. *Evidence.* The law of the forum determines the admissibility of a particular piece of evidence.
>
> § 603. *Statute of Limitations of Forum.* If action is barred by the statute of limitations of the forum, no action can be maintained though action is not barred in the state where the cause of action arose.
>
> § 604. *Foreign Statute of Limitations.* If action is not barred by the statute of limitations of the forum, an action can be maintained, though action is barred in the state where the cause of action arose.
>
> § 605. *Time Limitations on Cause of Action.* If by the law of the state which has created a right of action, it is made a condition of the right that it shall expire after a certain period of limitation has elapsed, no action begun after the period has elapsed can be maintained in any state.
>
> § 606. *Limitation of Amount Recoverable.* If a statute of the forum limits the amount which in any action of a certain class may be recovered in its courts, no greater amount can be recovered though under the law of the state which created the cause of action, a greater recovery would be justified or required.

Chapter 6 of Restatement (Second) §§ 122–44 (1971) covers much of the same ground.

(2) Can you state the general principle underlying these rules? How, in other words, should a court decide whether a rule not specifically covered in the Restatement deals with substance or procedure? In *Levy v. Steiger*, 233 Mass. 600, 124 N.E. 477 (1919), a tort case involving a question of the burden of proof, the court stated the test as follows: "It is elementary that the law of the place where the injury was received determines whether a right of action exists, and that the law of the place where the action is brought regulates the remedy and its incidents, such as pleading, evidence, and practice." Is a right/remedy distinction more useful than a distinction between substance and procedure? Is the test purely a matter of form?

The Introductory Note to Chapter 12 of the 1934 Restatement offers the following explanation for the rule that forum law governs matters of procedure:

> One of the chief ends secured by a rational system of Conflict of Laws rules is that the rights and duties of parties arising from a legal situation shall not be substantially varied because of the forum in which an action is brought to settle disputed questions arising out of the situation. . .
>
> If theoretically complete uniformity of right and duty were to be attained, a court having before it a case in which reference to the foreign rule of law had been appropriately made, would apply the foreign law to furnish the rule of decision for both the existence of the right or duty, and those things ordinarily thought of by lawyers as the means by which the prevailing party could, by that law, compel the other to perform the legal duty found to exist. . .
>
> Such all-inclusive reference to the foreign law is never made. The difficulties involved would be very great; so great as to be impossible in many instances. A heavy burden would be thrown upon the courts of the forum and the orderly administration of justice there would be hampered and delayed. A limitation upon the scope of the reference to the foreign law is thus necessary. Such limitation excludes those phases of the case which make administration of the foreign law by the local tribunal impracticable, inconvenient, or violative of local policy. In these instances, the local rules at the forum are applied and are classified as matters of procedure (see § 585). . .

Professor Beale elaborated this point in his treatise, adding that matters were classified as substantive or procedural according to whether or not they satisfied the reasons for applying the law of the forum: "If the practical convenience to the court in adopting the local rule of law is great, and the effect of so doing upon the rights of the parties is negligible, the law of the forum will be held to be controlling. If the situation is reversed the rule of the foreign law will be adopted." 3 J. Beale, A Treatise on the Conflict of Laws 1600 (1935). But are the black-letter rules of the 1934 Restatement consistent with this explanation?

(3) Walter Wheeler Cook, in a classic treatment of the substance-procedure distinction, offered the following test for distinguishing "substance" from "procedure":

> In determining the legal consequences of certain conduct or events it has seemed reasonable to apply "foreign substantive law" because of some factual connection of the situation with the foreign state; but on the other hand it would obviously be quite inconvenient for the court of the forum, though not unfair to the litigants concerned, to take over all the machinery of the foreign court for the "enforcement," as we say, of the "substantive rights." If we admit that the "substantive" shades off by imperceptible degrees into the "procedural," and that the "line" between them does not "exist," to be discovered merely by logic and analysis, but is rather to be drawn so as best to carry out our purpose, we see that the problem resolves itself substantially into this: How far can the court of the forum go in applying the rules taken from the foreign system of law without unduly hindering or inconveniencing itself?
>
> Against the inconvenience involved in learning the foreign rule is the fact that so closely are "procedure" and "substance" connected that in many cases a refusal to accept the foreign rule as to a matter falling into the doubtful class will defeat the policy involved in following the foreign substantive law. Clearly a decision on this basis might place the line at a somewhat different point from where it might be drawn when the purpose is that involved in [cases involving other problems, such as the constitutionality of retroactive legislation].

W.W. Cook, The Logical and Legal Bases of the Conflict of Laws 154, 166 (1942).

How would Professor Cook's approach work in practice? Can you name a procedural rule that is unduly difficult to apply? Doesn't the problem arise from the inconvenience of having to apply *all* the rules of a foreign jurisdiction? Is there something to be said for a formal approach over a functional one, after all?

(4) How does the test proposed by Professor Cook apply to the survival problem? Is it inconvenient for the forum to discover the foreign survival rule? Is it determinative of the result? What is to be said for the court's suggestion in *Grant v. McAuliffe* that the survival question was one respecting the administration of estates?

(5) The immediate reaction to *Grant v. McAuliffe* was generally critical. Professor Sumner took an especially hostile position: The *Grant* decision, based upon an "erroneous" characterization or an "improper" choice of law, was so "outrageous" that it probably violated the due process, full faith and credit, and privileges and immunities clauses of the Federal Constitution. The procedural classification of survival was "definitely against the overwhelming weight of authority in the United States." "[T]he only conclusion to be reached respecting the *Grant* case is that an erroneous determination was made or that the court was greatly influenced by the 'sympathy' factors in the case." Sumner, *Choice of Law Governing Survival of Actions,* 9 Hastings L.J. 128, 130–31, 136–37 (1958). But isn't Justice Traynor right that California's survival rule merely extends the right to recover in a way that is indistinguishable from a long statute of limitations (and that Arizona's abatement rule bars the action in a way that is analogous to a short one)? Put another way, because in form the abatement and survival rules affect only the remedy, what is the basis for classifying them as "substantive"? If the answer is that these rules have substantive purposes, what does that say about the general process of characterizing matters as substantive or procedural?

Assume that the purpose of California's survival rule is substantive. Does it then seem improper to apply it on the facts of *Grant v. McAuliffe*? What does *that* say about the general process of characterizing matters as substantive or procedural?

(6) A similar, and equally notorious, use of the substance-procedure distinction is found in *Kilberg v. Northeast Airlines, Inc.,* 9 N.Y.2d 34, 211 N.Y.S.2d 133, 172 N.E.2d 526 (1961). A New York man bought a ticket in New York from Northeast Airlines, a Massachusetts corporation, to fly from New York City to Massachusetts. The plane crashed in Massachusetts, and the decedent's estate sued for wrongful death. Massachusetts limited recovery in wrongful death actions to $15,000. The New York court acknowledged that Massachusetts law should apply as the place of the wrong, but said it was troubled by the damages limitation:

> Modern conditions make it unjust and anomalous to subject the traveling citizen of this State to the varying laws of other States through and over which they move... Our courts should if possible provide protection for our own State's people against unfair and anachronistic treatment of the lawsuits which result from these disasters. There is available, we find, a way of accomplishing this conformably to our State's public policy and without doing violence to the accepted pattern of conflict of law rules.

That way, it turned out, was really two ways: First, the court said, a damages ceiling is "so completely contrary to our public policy that we should refuse to apply that part of the Massachusetts law." (The "public policy" exception is considered infra pp. 74–84.) Second, and "equally pertinent," a damages limitation

> pertains to the remedy, rather than the right . . . [and] does not strictly affect the rule of damages, but rather the extent of damages; and that extent, as limited or unlimited, does not enter into any definition of the right enforced, or the cause of action permitted to be prosecuted.

How does this analysis square with the general approach of the First Restatement? Section 606 uncharacteristically treats the characterization of damage limitations as "a question of interpretation": a forum limitation applies even in a case based on foreign law if the limitation is general, but not if it qualifies only a particular forum cause of action; similarly, the court should apply a limitation imposed by the state where a cause of action arose if that limitation is "a qualification of the cause of action." First Restatement § 606 comments a, b. How should *Kilberg* be decided under these provisions? Is the decision sound?

In *Davenport v. Webb,* 11 N.Y.2d 392, 230 N.Y.S.2d 17, 183 N.E.2d 902 (1962), the court retracted the "procedural" basis of the *Kilberg* decision, stating that *Kilberg* "must be held merely to express this State's strong policy with respect to *limitations* in wrongful death actions."

BOURNIAS V. ATLANTIC MARITIME CO., LTD.

220 F.2d 152 (2d Cir.1955).

HARLAN, CIRCUIT JUDGE. Libelant, a seaman, was employed on respondents' vessel at the time she was changed from Panamanian to Honduran registry. As originally filed the libel contained two causes of action. The first was based on several Articles of the Panama Labor Code, under which the libelant claimed an extra three-months' wages payable to seamen upon change of registry, and other amounts for vacation, overtime and holiday pay. The second was for penalties under 46 U.S.C.A. § 596 for failure to pay these amounts promptly.

The respondents filed exceptive allegations asserting, *inter alia,* that the action was barred by the one-year statute of limitations contained in Article 623 of the Panama Labor Code. . .[T]he question of whether the action was barred by lapse of time was set down for a separate hearing.

At this hearing the Court held that the defense of laches, which was treated by Court and counsel as going only to the claim for advances, had not been substantiated, but that the Panama statute of limitations did bar the claims under the Panama Labor Code, and that in consequence the claim for penalties must also fail *pro tanto*. . .

Article 623 of the Labor Code of Panama, applicable to Articles 127, 154, 166 and 170 of the Code, upon which the libelant based his first cause of action, reads:

> "Actions and rights arising from labor contracts not enumerated in Article 621 shall prescribe [i.e., shall be barred by the Statute of Limitations] in a year from the happening of the events from which arise or are derived the said actions and rights."

The libelant's employment terminated on December 27, 1950, and since his libel was not filed until December 29, 1952, his first cause of action would be barred by Article 623 if it is controlling in this action.

In actions where the rights of the parties are grounded upon the law of jurisdictions other than the forum, it is a well-settled conflict-of-laws rule that the forum will apply the foreign substantive law, but will follow its own rules of procedure. Restatement of Conflict of Laws § 585; Beale, *Conflict of Laws* § 584.1 (1935); Stumberg, *Conflict of Laws* 134 et seq. (2d ed. 1951). While it might be desirable, in order to eliminate "forum-shopping," for the forum to apply the entire foreign law, substantive and procedural—or at least as much of the procedural law as might significantly affect the choice of forum, it has been recognized that to do so involves an unreasonable burden on the judicial machinery of the forum, see Restatement of Conflict of Laws, Introductory Note to Chapter 12, and perhaps more significantly, on the local lawyers involved, see Ailes, Substance and Procedure in the Conflict of Laws, 39 Mich.L.Rev. 392, 416 (1941). Consequently, for at least some questions the law applied is that of the forum, with which the lawyers and judges are more familiar, and which can be administered more conveniently. . .

The general rule appears established that for the purpose of deciding whether to apply local law or foreign law, statutes of limitations are classified as "procedural." Stumberg, *Conflict of Laws* 147 (1951); Lorenzen, The Statute of Limitation and the Conflict of Laws, 28 Yale L.J. 492 (1919). Hence the law of the forum controls. * * * This rule has been criticized as inconsistent with the rationale expressed above, since the foreign statute, unlike evidentiary and procedural details, is generally readily discovered and applied, and a difference in periods of limitation would often be expected to influence the choice of forum. Lorenzen, supra; Stumberg, op. cit., supra. The rule is in fact an accident of history. * * * And although it may perhaps be explained as a device for giving effect to strong local policies on limitations, this explanation would not satisfy the objections of its critics. Lorenzen, supra. Be all this as it may, this general rule is firmly embedded in our law.

But as might be expected, some legislatures and courts, perhaps recognizing that in light of the rationale of the underlying conflict-of-laws doctrine it is anomalous to classify across-the-board statutes of limitation as "procedural," have created exceptions to the rule so categorizing such statutes. A legislative example are the so-called "borrowing statutes" which require the courts of the forum to apply the statute of limitations of another jurisdiction, often that where the cause of action arose, when the forum's statute has been tolled. See Note, Legislation Governing the Applicability of Foreign Statutes of Limitation, 35 Col.L.Rev. 762 (1935). A court-made exception, and the one with which we are concerned here, is that where the foreign statute of limitations is regarded as barring the foreign right sued upon, and not merely the remedy, it will be treated as conditioning that right and will be enforced by our courts as part of the foreign "substantive" law. See Beale, *Conflict of Laws* §§ 604.3, 605.1 (1935) . Such exceptions operate *pro tanto* to give the result which commentators have advocated.

It is not always easy to determine whether a foreign statute of limitations should be regarded as "substantive" or "procedural," for the tests applied by the courts are far from precise. In *The Harrisburg,* 1886, 119 U.S. 199, the Supreme Court held "substantive" a limitation period contained in a wrongful death statute, emphasizing that "the liability and the remedy are created by the same statutes, and the limitations of the remedy are therefore to be treated as limitations of the right," 119 U.S. at 214. It now appears settled that limitation periods in wrongful death statutes will be regarded as "substantive." Restatement of Conflict of Laws § 397. And the rule of *The Harrisburg* has been stated to apply not merely to rights to sue for wrongful death, but to any statute-created right unknown to the common law. * * * The rule was also carried a step further in *Davis v. Mills,* 1904, 194 U.S. 451. Suggesting that in the instances where courts have found some statutes of limitation to be "substantive" they were seeking a "reasonable distinction" for escaping from the anomaly of the rule that limitations are generally to be regarded as "procedural," Mr. Justice Holmes continued, "The common case [where limitations are treated as 'substantive'] is where a statute creates a new liability, and in the same section or in the same act limits the time within which it can be enforced, whether using words of condition or not. *The Harrisburg,* 119 U.S. 199. But the fact that the limitation is contained in the same section or the same statute is material only as bearing on construction. It is merely a ground for saying that the limitation goes to the right created, and accompanies the obligation everywhere. The same conclusion would be reached if the limitation was in a different statute, provided it was directed to the newly created liability so specifically as to warrant saying that it qualified the right." . . .

Two other approaches to the problem were suggested in our opinion in *Wood & Selick, Inc. v. Compagnie Generale Transatlantique,* 2 Cir., 1930, 43 F.2d 941. First, that the foreign law might be examined to see if the defense possessed the attributes which the forum would classify as "procedural" or "substantive"; that is, for example, whether the defense need be pleaded, as a "substantive" period of limitations need not be in this country. Second, the foreign law might be examined to see if the operation of limitation completely extinguished the right, in which case limitation would be regarded as "substantive." Still other tests are suggested by *Goodwin v. Townsend,* 3 Cir., 1952, 197 F.2d 970—namely, whether the foreign limitation is regarded as "procedural" or "substantive" by the courts of the foreign state concerned, and possibly whether the limitation is cast in language commonly regarded as "procedural."

Which, then, of these various tests should be applied here? It appears to us that it should be the one which *Davis v. Mills,* 1904, 194 U.S. 451, suggests for use where the right and its limitation period are contained in separate statutes, viz.: Was the limitation "directed to the newly created liability so *specifically* as to warrant saying that it qualified the right"? 194 U.S. at page 454, italics supplied. To be sure *Davis* was concerned with the statute of limitations of a sister state (Montana), but there is nothing in Mr. Justice Holmes' opinion to suggest that the application of the test there laid down is limited to that type of case. And where, as here, we are dealing with a statute of limitations of a foreign country, and it is not clear on the face of the statute that its purpose was to limit the enforceability, outside as well as within the foreign country concerned, of the substantive rights to which the statute pertains, we think that as a yardstick for determining whether that was the purpose this test is the most satisfactory one. It does not lead American courts into the necessity of examining into the unfamiliar peculiarities and refinements of different foreign legal systems, and where the question concerns the applicability of a code provision of a civil law country, this test seems more appropriate than any of the others.

Even though the limitation period here is contained in the same statute as enacts the right sought to be enforced, *The Harrisburg,* supra, still, as noted later, because of the breadth of the Panama Labor Code, as contrasted with the limited scope of the statute involved in *The Harrisburg,* the limitation period should not automatically be regarded as "substantive." Nor would it be appropriate to make this case turn on the fact that the right sued upon was unknown at common law . . . when we are dealing with the statutes of a country where the common law does not exist. And we do not think that it should matter whether the foreign court has interpreted its statute as being "procedural" or "substantive" for some other purpose, which may have happened in *Goodwin,* supra, or whether the foreign practice requires that limitation be pleaded, *Wood & Selick,* supra. . . We conclude, therefore, that the "specificity" test is the proper one to be applied in a case of this type, without deciding, of course, whether the same test would also be controlling in cases involving domestic or other kinds of foreign statutes of limitations.

Applying that test here it appears to us that the libelant is entitled to succeed, for the respondents have failed to satisfy us that the Panamanian period of limitation in question was specifically aimed against the particular rights which the libelant seeks to enforce. The Panama Labor Code is a statute having broad objectives, viz.: "The present Code regulates the relations between capital and labor, placing them on a basis of social justice, so that, without injuring any of the parties, there may be guaranteed for labor the necessary conditions for a normal life and to capital an equitable return for its investment." In pursuance of these objectives the Code gives laborers various rights against their employers. Article 623 establishes the period of limitation for *all* such rights, except certain ones which are enumerated in Article 621. And there is nothing in the record to indicate that the Panamanian legislature gave special consideration to the impact of Article 623 upon the particular rights sought to be enforced here, as distinguished from the other rights to which that Article is also applicable. . .

Statutes of Limitations and Other Problems

(1) In the *Bournias* case a Panamanian seaman was allowed to recover from a Panamanian shipowner under the Panama Labor Code even though a Panama court would have denied a recovery. What justification can there be for this? Is it not apparent that the reason that justifies the forum's application of its own procedure—the burden of ascertaining foreign law on matters unlikely to affect the outcome of litigation—is inapplicable to statutes of limitation?

(2) What purposes are served by statutes of limitations? Such limitations are sometimes said to be designed to free defendants from having to worry about litigation and to allow them to release assets held in reserve. At other times, statutes of limitations are justified as a means of allocating judicial resources by pruning old claims based on stale evidence from the docket. Does consideration of these purposes help to characterize statutes of limitations as "substantive" or "procedural"? If so, how is the court to decide which purpose underlies any state's particular statute of limitations? What if both purposes are present?

Suppose that the laws in *Bournias* were reversed: Panama barred the action after three years, while the forum's statute of limitations would bar it after one. How should the case be decided? Why?

(3) The Uniform Conflict of Laws-Limitations Act, promulgated in 1982, provides that a state's decision to apply the substantive law of another state will carry with it that state's limitation period as well. See 12 Uniform Laws Annotated 158, § 2(a) (1996). Does the Act do anything more than require that statutes of limitation be characterized as substantive rather than procedural? Will this mechanical change produce better results than the earlier procedural characterization? Would it have changed the result in *Bournias*?

A 1988 amendment to the Second Restatement provides that, unless "exceptional circumstances" exist, the forum (1) will apply its own statute of limitations barring the claim; and (2) will apply its own statute of limitations permitting the claim, unless the limitation period of the state whose law will otherwise govern the merits bars the action. Restatement (Second) of Conflict of Laws § 142 (Supp.1988). Is this approach better or worse than the approach of the Uniform Act? Why should the court apply a forum statute of limitations that is *shorter* than the limitation period of the state whose law will govern the merits, but not one that is *longer*?

Prompted partly by these reform efforts and partly by the more general choice-of-law revolution discussed in Chapter 2, many courts have abandoned the traditional procedural characterization of statutes of limitation. As of 2019, only 28 states automatically treat statutes of limitation as procedural. See Symeonides, *Choice of Law in the American Courts in 2019,* 68 Am.J.Comp.L. 235, 296 (2020). Is this a good or a bad thing? How should the problem of limitations periods be handled?

(4) In *Marie v. Garrison,* 13 Abb.N.Cas. 210 (N.Y.Super.Ct.1883), the plaintiff sued for breach of an oral contract made in Missouri. The defendant argued that the agreement failed to comply with the Statute of Frauds in both states. The court nevertheless enforced the contract. The New York statute provided that specified contracts "shall be void" unless in writing. According to the referee:

> I regard the word "void" as a word of substance, and not as a mere word of procedure. In that view, the [New York] statute cannot, by accepted rules under the "Conflict of Laws," be applied to contracts made in other States, and accordingly not to the present case.

In contrast, the Missouri statute said only that "no action shall be brought" on an oral contract. According to the referee, this meant that "the remedy in Missouri only is affected by these words." Therefore, "whether tested by the law of New York or Missouri, [this agreement] does not trench upon any provision of the Statute of Frauds."

Is it a fair summary of this decision to say that the court enforced an agreement that was unenforceable under the laws of the only two states whose laws could conceivably apply? If so, hasn't the entire system gone haywire? Or is the problem simply that the particular interpretations offered here are implausible? How should the case be decided, and why?

(5) Should the parol evidence rule be held substantive or procedural? See 3 J. Beale, A Treatise on the Conflict of Laws § 599.1 (1935): "That the so-called parol evidence rule is in reality a rule of substance rather than a rule of evidence has frequently been pointed out by the courts." Accord, Restatement Conflict of Laws § 599 (1934).

(6) What about the burden of proof? See *Levy v. Steiger,* 233 Mass. 600, 124 N.E. 477 (1919), applying the law of the forum to conclude that the defendant had the burden of proving contributory negligence. In *Sampson v. Channell,* 110 F.2d 754, 756–58 (1st Cir.1940), the court held that state law governed the question of burden of proof in a federal diversity action under *Erie R.R. v. Tompkins,* but it followed *Levy* in applying the law of the forum state rather than that of the place of wrong. Can the two parts of the *Sampson* opinion stand together?

C. RENVOI

IN RE SCHNEIDER'S ESTATE

198 Misc. 1017, 96 N.Y.S.2d 652 (Sur.Ct.N.Y.Co.1950).
Adhered to on reargument, 198 Misc. 1017, 100 N.Y.S.2d 371.

FRANKENTHALER, SURROGATE. This case presents a novel question in this State in the realm of the conflict of laws. Deceased, a naturalized American citizen of Swiss origin, died domiciled in New York County, leaving as an asset of his estate certain real property located in Switzerland. In his will he attempted to dispose of his property, including the parcel of Swiss realty, in a manner which is said to be contrary to the provisions of Swiss internal law. That law confers upon one's legitimate heirs a so-called *legitime,* i.e., a right to specified fractions of a decedent's property, which right cannot be divested by testamentary act. The precise issue, therefore, is whether this deceased had the power to dispose of the realty in the manner here attempted.

Ordinarily, the courts of a country not the situs of an immovable are without jurisdiction to adjudicate questions pertaining to the ownership of that property. * * * Actions concerning realty are properly litigable only before the courts of the situs. However, in this case the administratrix appointed prior to the probate of the will has liquidated the foreign realty and transmitted the proceeds to this State. She is now accounting for the assets of the estate including the fund representing that realty. As a consequence this court is called upon to direct the administration and distribution of the substituted fund and to determine the property rights therein. * * * In doing so, however, reference must be made to the law of the situs, as the question of whether the fund shall be distributed to the devisee of the realty under the terms of the will is dependent upon the validity of the original devise thereof, * * * which must be determined under the law of the situs of the land itself. * * *

The court is confronted at the outset with the preliminary question as to the meaning of the term "law of the situs"—whether it means only the internal or municipal law of the country in which the property is situated or whether it also includes the conflict of laws rules to which the courts of that jurisdiction would resort in making the same determination. If the latter is the proper construction to be placed upon that term, then this court must, in effect, place itself in the position of the foreign court and decide the matter as would that court in an identical case.

The meaning of the term "law of the situs" can be ascertained best from a consideration of the reasons underlying the existence of the rule which requires the application thereof. The primary reason for its existence lies in the fact that the law-making and law-enforcing agencies of the country in which land is situated have exclusive control over such land. * * * As only the courts of that country are ultimately capable of rendering enforceable judgments affecting the land, the legislative authorities thereof have the exclusive power to promulgate the law which shall regulate its ownership and transfer. When the land itself formed the estate asset upon which the will was intended to operate, the power of [the] sovereign to enforce such laws created rights therein between the parties in interest. If an instrument which was intended to transfer that land did not meet the standards set by that law or violated some provision thereof regarding the land, the courts had the physical power to deny it effect and enforce instead the rights decreed by the law of that country or the law of any other country which the law-making agencies deemed appropriate in a particular case.

Hence, the rights which were created in that land are those which existed under the whole law of the situs and as would be enforced by those courts which normally would possess exclusive judicial jurisdiction. Griswold, Renvoi Revisited, 51 Harvard L.R. 1165, 1186; cf. Schreiber, The Doctrine of Renvoi in Anglo-American Law, 31 Harvard L.R. 523, 559. If another court, in this case our own, is thrust into a position where it is obliged to adjudicate the same questions concerning title to that land, or a substitute therefor, it should be guided by the methods which would be employed in the country of situs. The purely fortuitous transfer of the problem to the courts of another state by virtue of a postmortuary conversion of the land, effected for the purpose of administering the entire estate in the country of domicile, ought not to alter the character of the legal relations which existed with respect to the land at the date of death and which continued to exist until its sale. Consequently, this court, in making a determination of ownership, must ascertain the body of local law to which the courts of the situs would refer if the matter were brought before them.

It has been urged, however, that a reference to the conflict of laws rules of the situs may involve an application of the principle of *renvoi,* and if so it would place the court in a perpetually-enclosed circle from which it could never emerge and that it would never find a suitable body of substantive rules to apply to the particular case. See Schreiber, op.cit. supra; *Matter of Tallmadge,* 109 Misc. 696, 181 N.Y.S. 336, and authorities cited. This objection is based upon the assumption that if the forum must look to the whole law of the situs, and that law refers the matter to the law of the domicile, this latter reference must be considered to be the whole law of the latter country also, which would refer the matter back to the law of the situs, which process would continue without end. That reasoning is based upon a false premise, for as has been said by Dean Griswold, Renvoi Revisited, op.cit. supra, p. 1190: "Recognition of the foreign conflict of laws rule will not lead us into an endless chain of references if it is clear for any reason that the particular foreign conflicts rule (or any rule along the line of reference) is one which refers to the internal law alone. . ." * * *

The precise question here considered, namely whether there shall be a reference to the entire law of the situs to determine the ownership of the proceeds of foreign realty, is one of first impression in this State. Nevertheless, the above stated principles, together with the rule enunciated in the Restatement of the Conflict of Laws, in the English authorities on the subject and in analogous cases in courts of this State and others, require us to accept it as a part of our law and to hold that a reference to the law of the situs necessarily entails a reference to the whole law of that country, including its conflict of laws rules.

The rule as formulated in the Restatement is as follows: "Section 8. *Rule in Question of Title to Land or Divorce.* (1) All questions of title to land are decided in accordance with the law of the state where the land is, including the Conflict of Laws rules of that state. (2) All questions concerning the validity of a decree of divorce are decided in accordance with the law of the domicile of the parties, including the Conflict of Laws rules of that state." In all other cases the Restatement rejects the *renvoi* principle and provides that where a reference is made to foreign law that law should be held to mean only the internal law of the foreign country. Section 7; cf. Note, A Distinction in the Renvoi Doctrine, 35 Harvard L.R. 454. . .

The broad assertion in *Matter of Tallmadge* [109 Misc. 696, 181 N.Y.S. 336] that the *renvoi* principle is not applicable in New York is not in accord with the earlier or later cases. The precise limits of its applicability are as yet undefined. Cf. Rabel, *Conflict of Laws: A Comparative Study,* p. 71 et seq. It may be that in some fields the underlying policies of our law will require its rejection and a direct reference to foreign internal law. Thus far it has been found applicable in the realm of divorce, * * * and in the use of foreign borrowing statutes. * * * Other states have applied it to sustain the validity of a marriage, *Lando v. Lando,* 112 Minn. 257, 127 N.W. 1125, to determine the rule for distribution of the proceeds of a wrongful death action, *Hartley v. Hartley,* 71 Kan. 691, 81 P. 505, to decide the applicability of foreign exemption statutes, *Faris v. Tennant,* 194 Ind. 506, 141 N.E. 784, and to determine the capacity of a party to enter into contractual relations. *University of Chicago v. Dater,* 277 Mich. 658, 270 N.W. 175. The rule of the Restatement, section 8, subdivision 1, and the English decisions, as well as the persuasive analogy of the above cases require the court to hold it equally applicable to the question presented in this case, i.e., to the determination of title to a fund representing foreign immovables.

Thus it is now necessary to ascertain the whole of the applicable Swiss law and apply it to this case. . .[T]he expert witnesses summoned by the respective parties are in agreement that the Swiss internal law would apply to the real and personal estate of a Swiss citizen domiciled in Switzerland, and that the laws of the country of domicile would, under the Swiss theory of unity of succession, apply to all of the Swiss property belonging to a foreign national.

The experts disagreed, however, upon the ultimate question in this case, i.e., the Swiss rule applicable to the distribution of the Swiss realty of a person of *hybrid* nationality domiciled not in Switzerland but in the country of his second citizenship. Under Swiss law the decedent herein was vested with dual nationality. The law of that country provides that a citizen, in order to divest himself of the cloak of citizenship must formally renounce his allegiance in the manner prescribed by statute. Such formal act of renunciation was not performed by the decedent. . .

The court has carefully examined the authorities and materials submitted by the experts and has formed its conclusion upon the basis of those authorities. None of the cases submitted involved the precise facts here presented. They rather present guides, signs and close analogies. From these indicia, however, the court concludes that the Swiss law would refer a matter such as this to the New York internal law, under which law the will is a valid disposition of the testator's property. The testamentary power of this decedent would not be curtailed by the *legitime*. . .

Consequently, the court holds that the testamentary plan envisaged by the testator and set out in his will is valid, even in its application to the Swiss realty. The proceeds of that realty must therefore be distributed pursuant to the directions contained in the will. . .

The Renvoi Problem

(1) Renvoi has a vocabulary all its own. Choice-of-law rules may refer either to a state's "internal" law—the law that would be applied to a purely domestic case without multistate contacts—or to its "whole" law—the law that state would apply to the multistate case actually presented, by reference to its own choice-of-law rules. If the forum state refuses to consider the choice-of-law rules of the state to which it refers, it is said to "reject" the renvoi; if it follows the foreign choice-of-law rule, it is said to "accept" the renvoi. If the renvoi is accepted and the state whose choice-of-law rules are examined refers the case back to the law of the forum state, there is said to be "remission"; if it refers to a third state, a "transmission." Finally, the renvoi is said to be "partial" if the foreign choice-of-law rule is found to refer to the internal law of a state and "total" if the foreign reference is also to whole law.

Few issues in choice of law have attracted as much attention as the renvoi, which has been the subject of innumerable law review articles and other commentary. In part, this may be because the renvoi problem forces courts and commentators to explain what it means to apply another state's law: "To solve the problem of the renvoi, in other words, one must understand what exactly it means to 'choose' a foreign law." Kramer, *Return of the Renvoi,* 66 N.Y.U. L. Rev. 979, 983 (1991).

(2) Should courts accept or reject the renvoi? The majority of American commentators—including not only Joseph Beale, but also his chief critics, Walter Wheeler Cook and Ernest Lorenzen—concluded that the forum should ignore foreign choice-of-law rules. But powerful voices—including Erwin Griswold, Herbert Goodrich, and Ernst Rabel—took the opposite position. Which view is more consistent with territorial theory?

According to Beale:

> The vice in the decisions [accepting the renvoi] results from the assumption that the foreign law has legal force in a decision of the case; whereas . . . the only Conflict-of-Laws rule that can possibly be applied is the law of the forum and the foreign law is called in simply for furnishing a factual rule [to fix the parties' vested rights]. The rule of the foreign law adopted by the law of the forum is [the substantive rule], not the Conflict of Laws rule.

1 J. Beale, A Treatise on the Conflict of Laws 56–57 (1935). Does this answer the question or beg it? If foreign courts, applying their own choice-of-law rules, would conclude that no rights have vested under their law, can a territorialist forum ignore that conclusion? And doesn't the renvoi, if accepted, become part of the forum's choice-of-law rules?

Cook countered with the realist claim that a right vests under the law of a particular state only if that state's courts would recognize and enforce it. It follows, he argued, that a court following the vested rights approach "is compelled to study the decisions of [foreign courts] upon the conflict of laws." See W.W. Cook, The Logical and Legal Bases of the Conflict of Laws 19–20 (1942). But rather than urging acceptance of the renvoi, Cook took this point as a reason to reject the notion of vested rights entirely. Cook and Lorenzen argued instead that the forum is always free to determine under its own law what rights the parties should have and that sometimes, for reasons of policy or expediency, the forum chooses to make its law conform to that of another state. It follows, they reasoned, that the renvoi should be rejected: if the forum deems the presence of some contact in a foreign state to require the application of a substantive rule resembling that state's law, the matter should end there; the fact that the foreign state directs its courts to apply a different law is irrelevant. Id. at 239–51; see Roosevelt, *Resolving Renvoi: The Bewitchment of Our Intelligence by Means of Language*, 80 Notre Dame L. Rev. 1842–49 (2005). Indeed, Professor Lorenzen went so far as to suggest that allowing another state to dictate the applicable law is "nothing less than an abdication of sovereignty." Lorenzen, *The* Renvoi *Theory and the Application of Foreign Law*, 10 Colum.L.Rev. 190, 205 (1910). Is this argument less question-begging than Beale's? Isn't the entire point of choice of law to identify circumstances in which foreign law should be given authority to determine the result? Why shouldn't the forum include the other state's choice-of-law rules when it modifies its law to resemble that of another state?

Advocates of accepting the renvoi were hardly more successful in defending their position. Dean Griswold and Ernst Rabel, for example, maintained that courts should accept the renvoi because the rights provided by another state are by definition the rights that would be provided by courts in that state. 1 E. Rabel, The Conflict of Laws: A Comparative Study 79 (2d ed. 1958); Griswold, *Renvoi Revisited,* 51 Harv.L.Rev. 1165, 1183–87 (1938). But what if the court refers to foreign law because, as Cook and Lorenzen assumed, some connection to another state makes it more just to determine the parties' rights under the other state's internal law? How can we decide which of these views is correct? See Kramer, *Return of the Renvoi,* 66 N.Y.U. L. Rev. at 991–92, suggesting that this question cannot be resolved "without some further refinement in the underlying theory." What might that refinement be?

(3) If the theoretical debate is inconclusive, can we resolve the renvoi problem on grounds of practicality?

One practical difficulty associated with renvoi is illustrated by the *Schneider* case. The forum must inform itself not only of foreign internal law and foreign conflicts rules but perhaps also of foreign rules about renvoi. This is problem enough if the law referred to is that of another of the United States; if a foreign nation is involved, and especially if the materials are in a foreign language, there may be real difficulties in discovering and understanding the relevant materials. And since the precise question may have arisen in neither jurisdiction, the court's task may be to determine what the Swiss courts would think that the New York courts would think on an issue about which neither has thought. Cf. *Nolan v. Transocean Air Lines,* 276 F.2d 280, 281 (2d Cir.1960) (Friendly, J.).

Distinguished commentators have asserted that there is reason to believe that in the *Schneider* case the Surrogate misinterpreted Swiss law.

Professor Falconbridge argues that: "The New York court . . . misconstrued the relevant conflict rule of Swiss law (finding a reference by that rule to the law of the domicil, when there was no such reference in the circumstances of the case) and failed completely to consider whether in any event Swiss law would have accepted a reference back to Swiss law, and in the result applied domestic New York law although a Swiss court would have applied domestic Swiss law." Falconbridge, *Renvoi in New York and Elsewhere,* 6 Vand.L.Rev. 708, 730–31 (1953).

(4) A more serious objection, often encountered, is that if every state accepted the renvoi, no case could ever be decided. Each state would direct the case back to the other state's whole law, locking the court in an endless cycle of references back and forth; in Dean Griswold's words, "Alphonse and Gaston would never get through the door." Griswold, 51 Harv.L.Rev. at 1169. Other critics offered their own colorful descriptions—a "logical 'cabinet of mirrors,' " a "*circulus inextrabilis,*" a game of "lawn tennis,"—and argued that this phenomenon rendered the renvoi unworkable. See id. at 1167, n. 8.

Professor Rabel responded that if uniform acceptance of the renvoi leads to an endless cycle, "it stands to reason that it cannot be applied in the *same* manner by the two antagonistic groups." 1 E. Rabel, The Conflict of Laws at 82. If some states follow a situs rule in cases of succession to real property, while other states apply the law of the decedent's nationality, courts can avoid the endless cycle by incorporating the renvoi into only one of the competing rules. Id. at 83. But how should courts decide which rule? Consider also Professor Lorenzen's comment: "Personally I cannot approve a doctrine which is workable only if the other country rejects it." E. Lorenzen, Selected Articles on the Conflict of Laws 127 (1947).

Dean Griswold made a different response. Noting first that the problem arises only if both states accept the renvoi, he suggested that since few states do so, the endless cycle will "in practice [be] an extremely rare apparition." Griswold, 51 Harv.L.Rev. at 1192. In those cases, Griswold continued, the forum should simply accept the reference back and apply its own internal law—not because logic dictates, but because we must resolve the case and this answer is as good as any:

> If we get into a situation where there is an endless series of references, there is no logical reason for stopping after the second reference [or accepting the renvoi]; it would be just as "logical" to stop after the third reference or the seventeenth. But by the same token, it is no more "logical" to stop after the first reference [or reject the renvoi]. It may or may not be expedient to stop there for one reason or another, but a solution reached on this ground cannot be accorded the accolade of logic.

Id. at 1192–93. Is Griswold's first point that courts need not fear adopting the renvoi because its adoption will not be widespread? And which way does Griswold's second response cut? If no stopping point is less arbitrary than any other, why not just reject the renvoi and forget the whole problem?

(5) Proponents of the renvoi advocated its adoption on the ground that it was useful for achieving uniform results. Critics were quick to point out the obvious fallacy in this claim: the renvoi will not produce uniformity if it is applied in the same way by both the forum and the foreign state. In *Schneider,* for example, if both states accepted the renvoi, the New York court would apply Swiss law and the Swiss court would apply New York law. Is it a sufficient answer that *selective* use of the renvoi will further the goals of uniformity and predictability? Compare Griswold, 51 Harv.L.Rev., *passim* (advocating selective use) with Kramer, 66 N.Y.U. L. Rev. at 996 (arguing that selective use makes results less uniform and predictable).

(6) The 1934 Restatement generally directed courts to ignore foreign choice-of-law rules. Restatement of Conflict of Laws § 7 (1934). Two exceptions, however, were contained in § 8: questions of "title of land" and "the validity of a decree of divorce" were controlled by the law of the situs of land, or of the domicile of the parties, respectively, "including the Conflict of Laws rules of that state."

The *Schneider* case falls within one of these exceptions. Indeed, it parallels the classic situation in which renvoi was first developed by a common-law court. *In re Annesley,* [1926] Ch. 692, concerned the distribution of movable property on the death of a British subject domiciled in France. The English rule determined succession to movables by reference to the law of the decedent's domicile at death; France followed the nationality principle. But an earlier French decision indicated that a French court would refer to the whole law of England, whose choice-of-law rule referred back to France; the French court would break the circle by accepting the reference back and applying French internal law. See *Forgo's Case,* 10 Clunet 64 (1883). Had the English court in *Annesley* also employed a partial renvoi, it would have applied English internal law, and the outcome would have depended upon where suit was brought. To escape this difficulty the court applied a total renvoi, deciding the case as a French court would have decided it in accord with French internal law.

If the renvoi is incompatible with the traditional approach, what justification is there for the exception relating to land title and divorce decrees? It isn't really an exception, said Beale:

> It is not in any sense an adoption of the foreign law as operative in the cases enumerated. The answer that would be given to the question at issue is accepted in fact only without regard to any reason which the foreign tribunal might have or any legal

> considerations applicable. Because of the paramount social importance of treating the existence of marriage, for instance, in the same way in all states, the law of the forum attempts to bring about a warranty of such treatment by providing in its law for a decision of the question in the way that the law which in its opinion is the proper law would determine it; not because of any effect given to that law but simply as the rule adopted by the law of the forum for the determination of such problems. The same argument applies to a determination of the title of foreign land; it being essential to the protection of the interests of all parties that such a title should be determined everywhere as the state of situs would determine it since that state alone must have the final authority.

1 J. Beale, A Treatise on the Conflict of Laws 57 (1935). Since uniformity was essential to Beale in the entire field of choice of law, why don't these same considerations support a broader use of renvoi? In particular, shouldn't renvoi be extended to questions relating to movable property, as in *Annesley,* since the power rationale is satisfied by deciding the case as the situs state would?

(7) Recall *Haumschild v. Continental Casualty Co.,* 7 Wis.2d 130, 95 N.W.2d 814 (1959), supra p. 45. Justice Fairchild concurred. "I would dispose of the case," he explained

> upon the theory that [as the place of injury] California law governs the existence of the alleged cause of action and that in California the immunity question cannot be decided by resort to the law of torts but rather the law of status.

95 N.W.2d at 822. Is this resolution of the case by using the renvoi better or worse than the majority's characterization strategy? What are the relative advantages and disadvantages of each solution for this case? For other cases?

(8) Section 8(2) of the Second Restatement recognizes renvoi whenever "the objective of the particular choice-of-law rule is that the forum reach the same result on the very facts involved as would the courts of another state." Professor Ehrenzweig, who was a friend neither of renvoi nor of the Second Restatement, stated that "[t]his test is unacceptable analytically, since it is, of course, met always and never." A. Ehrenzweig, Private International Law 142 (1967). Comment h to § 8 attempts to clear the matter up by stating that its test "will usually be [met] when the other state clearly has the dominant interest in the issue to be decided and its interest would be furthered by having the issue decided in the way that its courts would have done." The two examples given are the validity and effect of a transfer of interests in land and the succession to interests in movables in a decedent's estate.

(9) Although the renvoi has not found widespread use in American courts, it was given a boost by the United States Supreme Court in *Richards v. United States,* 369 U.S. 1 (1962). The Federal Tort Claims Act, 28 U.S.C. § 1346(b), subjects the United States to tort liability "under circumstances where the United States, if a private person, would be liable to the claimant in accordance with the law of the place where the act or omission occurred." The Court held that this referred to the whole law of the place where the defendant acted: To apply the internal law of that state would often result in treating the Government unlike a private person similarly situated, both because the traditional rule looks to the place of injury and because state courts increasingly depart from the traditional rule. The implications and consequences of this decision are critically analyzed in Shapiro, *Choice of Law Under the Federal Tort Claims Act:* Richards *and* Renvoi *Revisited,* 70 N.Car.L.Rev. 641 (1992).

(10) The treatment of renvoi in other countries is diverse. Traditional systems tend to reject it. See, e.g., Greek Civ. Code, Article 32; Spanish Civil Code, Article 12(2). Some codifications do likewise, see, e.g., U.K. codification § 9(5); Quebec Civil Code Article 3080, as does Article 15 of the European Union's Convention on the Law Applicable to Contractual Obligations. Other countries' modern codifications accept the renvoi, e.g., Austria (Federal Statute of 15 June 1978 on Private International Law, § 5) and Germany (Intro. Law to the Civil Code, Part III, Article 4). In a case dealing with succession to land in Japan, the Japanese Supreme Court looked to the decedent's national law, that of China, but then accepted a reference back to Japanese law. The decision is translated at 38 Japanese Ann. Int'l Law 142 (1995).

D. PUBLIC POLICY, PENAL LAWS, AND TAX CLAIMS

LOUCKS V. STANDARD OIL CO. OF NEW YORK

224 N.Y. 99, 120 N.E. 198 (1918).

CARDOZO, J. The action is brought to recover damages for injuries resulting in death. The plaintiffs are the administrators of the estate of Everett A. Loucks. Their intestate, while traveling on a highway in the state of Massachusetts, was run down and killed through the negligence of the defendant's servants then engaged in its business. He left a wife and two children, residents of New York. A statute of Massachusetts (R.L. c. 171, § 2, as amended by L.1907, c. 375) provides that:

> "If a person or corporation by his or its negligence, or by the negligence of his or its agents or servants while engaged in his or its business, causes the death of a person who is in the exercise of due care, and not in his or its employment or service, he or it shall be liable in damages in the sum of not less than $500, nor more

than $10,000, to be assessed with reference to the degree of his or its culpability, or . . . that of his or its . . . servants, to be recovered in an action of tort commenced within two years after the injury which caused the death, by the executor or administrator of the deceased, one-half thereof to the use of the widow and one-half to the use of the children of the deceased, or, if there are no children, the whole to the use of the widow, or if there is no widow, the whole to the use of the next of kin."

The question is whether a right of action under that statute may be enforced in our courts.

[The court first considered and rejected the argument that it should not enforce the Massachusetts law because it was "penal" in nature; this discussion is considered below at p. 85.]

Another question remains. Even though the statute is not penal, it differs from our own. We must determine whether the difference is a sufficient reason for declining jurisdiction. A tort committed in one state creates a right of action that may be sued upon in another unless public policy forbids. That is the generally accepted rule in the United States. * * * It is not the rule in every jurisdiction where the common law prevails. In England it has been held that the foreign tort must be also one by English law * * * which then becomes the source and measure of the resulting cause of action. * * * That is certainly not the rule with us. But there are some decisions in death cases which suggest a compromise. They say that jurisdiction will be refused unless the statutes of the two states are substantially the same. . .The question is whether the enforcement of a right of action for tort under the statutes of another state is to be conditioned upon the existence of a kindred statute here. Support for the restriction is supposed to be found in four cases in the court:. . . [The court discussed the New York cases.]

A foreign statute is not law in this state, but it gives rise to an obligation, which, if transitory, "follows the person and may be enforced wherever the person may be found." * * * *Cuba R.R. Co. v. Crosby*, 222 U.S. 473, 478. "No law can exist as such except the law of the land; but . . . it is a principle of every civilized law that vested rights shall be protected." Beale, supra, § 51. The plaintiff owns something, and we help him to get it. * * * We do this unless some sound reason of public policy makes it unwise for us to lend our aid. "The law of the forum is material only as setting a limit of policy beyond which such obligations will not be enforced there." *Cuba R.R. Co. v. Crosby*, supra. Sometimes we refuse to act where all the parties are nonresidents. * * * That restriction need not detain us; in this case all are residents. If aid is to be withheld here, it must be because the cause of action in its nature offends our sense of justice or menaces the public welfare. * * *

Our own scheme of legislation may be different. We may even have no legislation on the subject. That is not enough to show that public policy forbids us to enforce the foreign right. A right of action is property. If a foreign statute gives the right, the mere fact that we do not give a like right is no reason for refusing to help the plaintiff in getting what belongs to him. We are not so provincial as to say that every solution of a problem is wrong because we deal with it otherwise at home. Similarity of legislation has indeed this importance; its presence shows beyond question that the foreign statute does not offend the local policy. But its absence does not prove the contrary. It is not to be exalted into an indispensable condition.

The misleading word "comity" has been responsible for much of the trouble. It has been fertile in suggesting a discretion unregulated by general principles. Beale, *Conflict of Laws,* § 71. The sovereign in its discretion may refuse its aid to the foreign right. * * * From this it has been an easy step to the conclusion that a like freedom of choice has been confided to the courts. But that, of course, is a false view. * * * The courts are not free to refuse to enforce a foreign right at the pleasure of the judges, to suit the individual notion of expediency or fairness. They do not close their doors, unless help would violate some fundamental principle of justice, some prevalent conception of good morals, some deep-rooted tradition of the common weal.

This test applied, there is nothing in the Massachusetts statute that outrages the public policy of New York. We have a statute which gives a civil remedy where death is caused in our own state. We have thought it so important that we have now imbedded it in the Constitution. Const. art. 1, § 18. The fundamental policy is that there shall be some atonement for the wrong. Through the defendant's negligence, a resident of New York has been killed in Massachusetts. He has left a widow and children, who are also residents. The law of Massachusetts gives them a recompense for his death. It cannot be that public policy forbids our courts to help in collecting what belongs to them. We cannot give them the same judgment that our law would give if the wrong had been done here. Very likely we cannot give them as much. But that is no reason for refusing to give them what we can. We shall not make things better by sending them to another state, where the defendant may not be found, and where suit may be impossible. Nor is there anything to shock our sense of justice in the possibility of a punitive recovery. The penalty is not extravagant. . . It varies between moderate limits according to the defendant's guilt. We shall not feel the pricks of conscience, if the offender pays the survivors in proportion to the measure of his offense.

We have no public policy that prohibits exemplary damages or civil penalties. We give them for many wrongs. To exclude all penal actions would be to wipe out the distinction between the penalties of public justice and the remedies of private law. Finally, there are no difficulties of procedure that stand in the way. . . The case is not one where special remedies established by the foreign law are incapable of adequate enforcement except in the home tribunals. * * *

We hold, then, that public policy does not prohibit the assumption of jurisdiction by our courts and that this being so, mere differences of remedy do not count. . . We must apply the same rules that are applicable to other torts; and the tendency of those rules today is toward a larger comity, if we must cling to the traditional term. * * * The fundamental public policy is perceived to be that rights lawfully vested shall be everywhere maintained. At least, that is so among the states of the Union. * * * There is a growing conviction that only exceptional circumstances should lead one of the states to refuse to enforce a right acquired in another. The test of similarity has been abandoned [in Massachusetts]. If it has ever been accepted here, we think it should be abandoned now.

The judgment of the Appellate Division should be reversed, and the order of the Special Term affirmed, with costs in the Appellate Division and in this court.

MERTZ V. MERTZ

271 N.Y. 466, 3 N.E.2d 597 (1936).

Action by Emmy Mertz against Fred Mertz. From a judgment of the Appellate Division, First Department * * *, which affirmed a judgment of the Special Term * * * dismissing the complaint, plaintiff appeals.

LEHMAN, JUDGE.

The plaintiff has brought an action in this state against her husband to recover damages for personal injuries which, she alleges, she sustained in the state of Connecticut through her husband's negligent operation of an automobile, owned and controlled by him. Under the law of New York the rule is well established that a husband is not liable to his wife for personal injuries caused by his negligence. * * * The complaint alleges that under the law of the state of Connecticut a husband is liable for such injuries. The parties are residents of the state of New York. The problem presented upon this appeal is whether a wife residing here may resort to the courts of this state to enforce liability for a wrong committed outside of the state, though under the laws of this state a husband is immune from such liability. . .

The Legislature of Connecticut has chosen to remove the common law disability. There a wife may maintain an action against her husband for damages caused by his wrong, and no exception has been engrafted there upon the general rule that "illegality established, liability ensues." . . . The courts of the state of New York are not concerned with the wisdom of the law of Connecticut or of the internal policy back of that law. They must enforce a transitory cause of action arising elsewhere, unless enforcement is contrary to the law of this state. So we have said, "The courts are not free to refuse to enforce a foreign right at the pleasure of the judges, to suit the individual notion of expediency or fairness. They do not close their doors unless help would violate some fundamental principle of justice, some prevalent conception of good morals, some deep-rooted tradition of the common weal." Loucks v. Standard Oil Co. of New York, 224 N.Y. 99, 111 * * *.

"The term 'public policy' is frequently used in a very vague, loose or inaccurate sense. The courts have often found it necessary to define its juridical meaning, and have held that a state can have no public policy except what is to be found in its Constitution and laws. * * * Therefore, when we speak of the public policy of the state, we mean the law of the state, whether found in the Constitution, the statutes or judicial records." People v. Hawkins, 157 N.Y. 1, 12, 51 N.E. 257, 260 * * *. There is nothing in the opinion in Loucks v. Standard Oil Co. of New York, supra, which could indicate that in the field of conflict of laws the "juridical meaning" of the vague concept of public policy is different.

In that case the administrator of a resident of this state who was killed in Massachusetts sued here to recover the damages caused by his death. . . This court held only that in such case the courts may not read into the law a limitation created by a supposed public policy, founded on its own notion of expediency and justice. It did not hold that the courts might disregard a limitation, contained in the law of the state, established by authority and tradition, because the court could not discern a sound public policy back of the law.

The law of the forum determines the jurisdiction of the courts, the capacity of parties to sue or to be sued, the remedies which are available to suitors and the procedure of the courts. Where a party seeks in this state enforcement of a cause of action created by foreign law, he can avail himself only of the remedies provided by our law, and is subject to the general limitations which are part of our law. . . The law of this state attaches to the marriage status a reciprocal disability which precludes a suit by one spouse against the other for personal injuries. It recognizes the wrong, but denies remedy for such wrong by attaching to the person of the spouse a disability to sue. No other state can, outside of its own territorial limits, remove that disability or provide by its law a remedy available in our courts which our law denies to other suitors. So we said in Herzog v. Stern, 264 N.Y. 379, 191 N.E. 23. A disability to sue which arises solely from the marital status and which has no relation to a definition of wrong or the quality of an act from which liability would otherwise spring may perhaps be an anachronistic survivor of a common-law rule. Even then the courts should not transform an anachrony into an anomaly, and a disability to sue attached by our law to the person of a wife becomes an anomaly if another state can confer upon a wife, even though residing here, capacity to sue in our courts upon a cause of action arising there.

The judgment should be affirmed, with costs.

CROUCH, JUDGE (dissenting). . .

The public policy concept is a vague and variable phenomenon. When we find it necessary, in a general way, to embody it in words, we are apt to . . . say that when we use the term "we mean the law of the state, whether found in the Constitution, the statutes or judicial records." We go further, sometimes, and in explanation say that the law so found evidences "the will of the Legislature," * * * and so, perhaps, represents an inarticulate public opinion on the specific matter involved. In that broad sense it may be true to say that back of every law there is something which is conventionally referred to as public policy. Obviously, however, the bulk of public policy, so defined, relates to "minor morals of expediency and debatable questions of internal policy." Hence the difference between our own public policy and that of our sister states is for the most part disregarded by our own law of conflict of laws. . . The "strong public policy," which alone serves to prevent the enforcement of foreign rights, must have relation to something which "in its nature offends our sense of justice or menaces the public welfare." Loucks v. Standard Oil Co. of New York * * *.

It may be freely conceded that back of the New York rule which withholds from the wife the right to sue the husband for personal injuries is a public policy of the kind which is back of every other rule of law. But neither in the history of the rule nor in its operation is there anything to indicate that that policy is founded upon a definite view—or even upon some vague feeling—that justice or the public welfare would be affected by a contrary rule. . . It is enough to say that the rule exists merely as a product of judicial interpretation, is vestigial in character, and embodies no tenable policy of morals or of social welfare. To urge that it survives because it is an aid to conjugal peace disregards reality. Conjugal peace would be as seriously jarred by an action for breach of contract, or on a promissory note, or for an injury to property, real or personal, all of which the law permits, as by one for personal injury. In short, even though we assume that there is some shadowy element of policy back of the rule, it should give way to "the controlling public policy * * * that the courts of each State shall give effect to all valid causes of action created by the laws of another State except possibly in extreme cases." Hubbs, J., in Herzog v. Stern, 264 N.Y. 379, 191 N.E. 23, 26. . .

HOLZER V. DEUTSCHE REICHSBAHN-GESELLSCHAFT ET. AL.

277 N.Y. 474, 14 N.E.2d 798 (1938).

PER CURIAM.

The complaint alleges two causes of action arising out of a contract between plaintiff, a German national, and Schenker & Co., a German corporation, for services to be performed by plaintiff for three years from January 1, 1932, in Germany and in other locations outside this state. Defendants, German corporations, controlled either through stock ownership or otherwise, the transportation system known as Schenker & Co.

Both causes of action allege that the contract provides that "in the event the plaintiff should die or become unable, without fault on his part, to serve during the period of the contract the defendants would pay to him or his heirs the sum of 120,000 marks, in discharge of their obligations under the hiring aforesaid."

The first cause of action alleges that on June 21, 1933, defendants discharged plaintiff as of October 31, 1933, upon the sole ground that he is a Jew and that as the result of such discharge he was damaged in a sum upwards of $50,000.

The second cause of action alleges that in April, 1933, the German government incarcerated plaintiff in prison and in a concentration camp for about six months, that his imprisonment was not brought about by any act or fault of plaintiff but solely by reason of the policy of the government which required the elimination of all persons of Jewish blood from leading commercial, industrial, and transportation enterprises, that as a result "plaintiff became unable, without any fault on his part, to continue his services from the month of April 1933," and has been damaged in the sum of $50,000.

The second separate defense of defendant Deutsche Reichsbahn-Gesellschaft alleges that the contract of hiring was made and was to be performed in Germany, was terminated in Germany and is governed by the laws of Germany, that subsequent to April 7, 1933, the government of Germany adopted and promulgated certain laws, decrees, and orders which required persons of non-Aryan descent, of whom plaintiff is one, to be retired.

The Special Term granted plaintiff's motion to strike out this defense, the Appellate Division affirmed and certified these questions: "(1) Is the second separate defense contained in the answer of the defendant, Deutsche Reichsbahn-Gesellschaft, sufficient in law upon the face thereof? (2) Does the complaint herein state facts sufficient to constitute a cause of action?"

The courts of this state are empowered to entertain jurisdiction of actions between citizens of foreign countries or other states of this Union based upon contracts between nonresidents to be performed outside this state. * * * Under the decisions of this court and of the Supreme Court of the United States, the law of the country or state where the contract was made and was to be performed by citizens of that country or state governs. * * * "Every sovereign State is bound to respect the independence of every other sovereign State, and the courts of one country will not sit in judgment on the acts of the government of another done within its own territory." Oetjen v. Central Leather Co., 246 U.S. 297, 303, 38 S.Ct. 309, 311, 62 L.Ed. 726. In the Dougherty Case, 266 N.Y. 71, at page 90, 193 N.E. 897, 903, we have held: "It cannot be against the public policy of this State to hold nationals to the contracts which they have made in their own country to be performed there according to the laws of that country."

Therefore, in respect to the first cause of action, we are bound to decide, as a matter of pleading, that the complaint does not state facts sufficient to constitute a cause of action and that the second separate defense of the answer is sufficient in law upon its face. Defendants did not breach their contract with plaintiff. They were forced by operation of law to discharge him.

[The court reversed the dismissal of the second cause of action, however, holding that it could not say as a matter of law that the provision of the contract requiring defendant to pay if plaintiff should "become unable" to work was limited to physical illness rather than applying "to any factor which might prevent his service."]

Public Policy

(1) Is the public policy exception consistent with the premises of the First Restatement? Section 612 did indeed recognize the doctrine, precluding suits "upon a cause of action created in another state the enforcement of which is contrary to the strong public policy of the forum." This provision is preserved in Restatement (Second) of Conflict of Laws § 90 (1971). How can a court refuse to enforce foreign law just because it strongly disagrees with it? Is public policy a sort of clean hands doctrine for judges? See Paulsen & Sovern, *"Public Policy" in the Conflict of Laws*, 56 Colum.L.Rev. 969, 980 (1956): "Our courts properly should deny effect to a foreign contract of slavery or an agreement to subvert the governmental processes of a friendly foreign government. In a world in which despotic governments exist, our courts should not become the handmaiden of tyrants." Can you reconcile this argument with the theory of vested rights? What about the other objectives of the traditional approach, such as uniformity, certainty, and protecting reasonable expectations?

(2) According to Professor Weintraub, Judge Cardozo's formulation in *Loucks* is "[t]he classic definition of public policy as a valid reason for closing the forum to suit. . ." R. Weintraub, Commentary on the Conflict of Laws 121 (6th ed. 2010). We have, however, seen previous references to the public policy exception. Recall, for example, *Kilberg v. Northeast Airlines*, 9 N.Y.2d 34, 211 N.Y.S.2d 133, 172 N.E.2d 526 (1961), supra p. 58, in which the court refused to enforce a damages limitation in the Massachusetts wrongful death statute on public policy grounds. Does *Kilberg* overrule *Loucks,* which enforced an earlier version of the same law?

Is either *Mertz* or *Holzer* consistent with the *Loucks* standard?

(3) *Mertz* and *Holzer* were decided within two years by the same court, after a change in membership of only a single judge (the dissenter in *Mertz*). Can you distinguish the cases? It seems safe to say (does it not?) that the difference is *not* that Connecticut's interspousal immunity violated "some fundamental principle of justice, some prevalent conception of good morals," whereas Hitler's Nuremberg laws did not. Are there other ways to reconcile the results? One possible distinction is that *Mertz* involved the law of a sister state while *Holzer* involved the law of another nation. Should that matter? Aren't courts more likely to need the public policy exception when it comes to the laws of other nations, which may have greatly different cultures and values?

(4) What is the res judicata effect of a dismissal on public-policy grounds? Given Cardozo's explanation of the exception, what should it be?

Suppose that, after the *Mertz* decision, the New York husband and wife return to Connecticut, where an attorney representing Ms. Mertz serves the cooperative Mr. Mertz with process. When Mr. Mertz's insurer appears to "defend" him, what effect must the Connecticut court give to the prior New York judgment? Would application of the public policy exception in *Holzer* have had a different res judicata consequence?

Such questions as these led Justice Brandeis to distinguish sharply between the rejection on public policy grounds of a foreign cause of action and of a foreign defense:

> A State may, on occasion, decline to enforce a foreign cause of action. In so doing, it merely denies a remedy, leaving unimpaired the plaintiff's substantive right, so that he is free to enforce it elsewhere. But to refuse to give effect to a substantive defense under the applicable law of another State . . . subjects the defendant to irremediable liability. This may not be done.

Bradford Elec. Light Co. v. Clapper, 286 U.S. 145, 160 (1932). In such cases as *Kilberg* this possible distinction was ignored. Should it have been? Does it explain the results in *Mertz* and *Holzer*?

(5) Consider Professor Nussbaum's evaluation of the public policy exception:

> In general, however, a foreign law which in itself is repugnant to the forum will be accorded recognition where the repercussion of that law upon the forum is remote and unharmful. Although the forum abhors polygamy, it will, nevertheless, recognize the legitimacy of a child born abroad in a polygamous marriage entered into and valid abroad. All depends on the circumstances, or, more precisely, on the importance of the "contacts" of the case with the territory of the forum. Only an actual, strong and adverse interest of the forum will prompt the court to refuse the application of the foreign law that would govern under general conflict of laws rules. This is the doctrine of the "relativity" of public policy. . .
>
> Courts all over the world act, on the whole, in accord with the relativity principle. . . Using the traditional technique of the common law, the English and American courts have succeeded in building up, without misleading formulas, a flexible and intrinsically sound public policy doctrine, to which the relativity of public policy is a matter of course.

Nussbaum, *Public Policy and the Political Crisis in the Conflict of Laws,* 49 Yale L.J. 1027 (1940), *reprinted in* AALS Readings at 220, 223. Given the cases we've seen—*Loucks, Kilberg, Mertz,* and *Holzer*—do you agree? Does this explain the results in *Mertz* and *Holzer*?

(6) After these decisions, would you expect a New York court to enforce a New Yorker's foreign gambling debt when New York makes gambling illegal and allows losing gamblers to recover their losses in a civil action? See *Intercontinental Hotels Corp. v. Golden,* 15 N.Y.2d 9, 254 N.Y.S.2d 527, 203 N.E.2d 210 (1964) (enforcing foreign law). How about a foreign statute allowing an injured person to bring a direct action against an alleged tortfeasor's insurer when New York prohibits such actions and says that revealing the fact of insurance to the jury is reversible error? See *Oltarsh v. Aetna Ins. Co.,* 15 N.Y.2d 111, 256 N.Y.S.2d 577, 204 N.E.2d 622 (1965) (allowing a New Yorker injured elsewhere to bring such an action).

(7) Professors Paulsen and Sovern, in their illuminating article *"Public Policy" in the Conflict of Laws,* 56 Colum.L.Rev. 969, 980–81, 1016 (1956), agree that courts use the public policy exception in cases with close forum connections, but do not agree that the resulting doctrine is "intrinsically sound":

> The overwhelming number of cases which have rejected foreign law on public policy grounds are cases with which the forum had some important connection. . .The common invocation of the public policy argument to defeat a foreign claim is a denial that foreign law should govern at all and an assertion of the forum's right to have its law applied to the transaction because of the forum's relationship to it. . .
>
> The most troublesome use of public policy comes when it is employed as a cloak for the selection of local law to govern a transaction having important local contacts. Resort to the concept is beguilingly easy and does not demand the hard thinking which the careful formulation of narrower, more realistic, choice of law rules would require. . .We urge that courts take a second look and ask, "In what sense are we applying the public policy doctrine?" If judges honestly put the question whether the foreign law is barbarous in its provisions or frightfully unjust in the particular case, few cases will provide an affirmative answer. If a judge sees that, in a given case, public policy doctrine substitutes for choice of law, he should address himself directly to questions concerning choice of law policy. What are the most important contacts with respect to the matter at hand? Will the reference to local law be made only in the forum state so that it achieves a result not obtainable in other possible places of trial? Should a broadly-stated choice of law rule, supposedly applicable to the problem at hand, be narrowed to take into account the significance of differences in detail?
>
> The principal vice of the public policy concepts is that they provide a substitute for analysis. The concepts stand in the way of careful thought, of discriminating distinctions, and of true policy development in the conflict of laws.

That sounds fine, but what would it mean in practice? Won't the result of following this advice be hopelessly ad-hoc decisionmaking? Or is that what we had anyway under the guise of public policy?

Penal Laws

(1) The First Restatement provided in § 611 that "[n]o action can be maintained to recover a penalty the right to which is given by the law of another state." See also Restatement (Second) of Conflict of Laws § 89 (1971) (no action will be entertained on "a foreign penal cause of action"). This so-called penal-law exception has its roots in Chief Justice Marshall's unsupported dictum that "the courts of no country execute the penal laws of another." *The Antelope,* 23 U.S. (10 Wheat.) 66, 123 (1825). Why not? Isn't this inconsistent with the basic objectives of the traditional system—uniformity, protecting expectations, and territorial sovereignty? Or is it all right if the case is simply dismissed, leaving the plaintiff to sue elsewhere?

(2) What constitutes a "penal" statute? In addition to its public policy argument, the defendant in *Loucks v. Standard Oil Co. of New York* also claimed that the Massachusetts wrongful death statute was penal. The court disagreed. Judge Cardozo explained:

> Penal in one sense the statute indisputably is. The damages are not limited to compensation; they are proportioned to the offender's guilt. A minimum recovery of $500 is allowed in every case. But the question is not whether the statute is penal in some sense. The question is whether it is penal within the rules of private international law. A statute penal in that sense is one that awards a penalty to the state, or to a public officer in its behalf, or to a member of the public, suing in the interest of the whole community to redress a public wrong. *Huntington v. Attrill,* 146 U.S. 657, 668; *Huntington v. Attrill,* [1903] A.C. 150, 156; * * * The purpose must be, not reparation to one aggrieved, but vindication of the public justice. . .
>
> We think the better reason is with those cases which hold that the [Massachusetts] statute is not penal in the international sense. . . It is true that the offender is punished, but the purpose of the punishment is reparation to those aggrieved by his offense. *Com. v. B. & A.R.R. Co.,* 121 Mass. 36, 37; *Com. v. Eastern R.R. Co.,* 5 Gray (Mass.) 473, 474. The common law did not give a cause of action to surviving relatives. * * * In the light of modern legislation, its rule is an anachronism. Nearly everywhere, the principle is now embodied in statute that the next of kin are wronged by the killing of their kinsman. The family becomes a legal unit, invested with rights of its own, invested with an interest in the continued life of its members, much as it was in primitive law. * * * The damages may be compensatory or punitive according to the statutory scheme. * * * In either case the plaintiffs have a grievance above and beyond any that belongs to them as members of the body politic. They sue to redress an outrage peculiar to themselves.

(3) Can you tell from this discussion which laws are "penal" and which are not? Criminal laws obviously qualify. See Restatement of Conflict of Laws § 427 (1934) ("no state will punish a violation of the criminal law of another state"). As *Loucks* makes clear, however, the penal-law exception also includes at least some civil laws. According to the 1934 Restatement, § 611 comment a, "[a] penalty . . . is a sum of money exacted as punishment for a civil wrong as distinguished from compensation for the loss suffered by the injured party." Examples include a penalty payable to an informer, a penal sum named in a bond, and punitive damages "when action is brought in a state which does not award such damages on the ground that to do so would be to impose a penalty." On the other hand, liabilities imposed for wrongful death or for a corporate director's misconduct "are not penalties because the money satisfies a pre-existing claim or right. . ." See also *Huntington v. Attrill,* 146 U.S. 657, 683 (1892), where Maryland was required to enforce a New York judgment based on a statute making corporate directors personally liable for certain debts of the corporation. According to the Court, the test of whether a statute is penal is "not by what name the statute is called by the legislature or courts of the State in which it was passed, but whether it appears to the tribunal which is called upon to enforce it to be, in its essential character and effect, a punishment of an offence against the public. . ." Can you draw this line?

(4) Are provisions for double or treble damages penal? See, e.g., *Chavarria v. Superior Court,* 40 Cal.App.3d 1073, 115 Cal.Rptr. 549 (1974), holding that a provision of the California Labor Code imposing double damages for fraudulent misrepresentations in hiring migrant workers was not penal because it "grants a civil remedy to a private person" rather than "a penalty to the state."

In *Newman v. Piggie Park Enterprises, Inc.,* 390 U.S. 400, 402 (1968) (per curiam), the Supreme Court noted that civil rights laws often create private remedies to ensure adequate enforcement, so that a plaintiff who obtains relief "does so not only for himself alone but also as a 'private attorney general,' vindicating a policy . . . of the highest priority." Are the civil rights laws of one state unenforceable in another?

(5) A related provision in the 1934 Restatement states that "[n]o action can be maintained on a right created by the law of a foreign state as a method of furthering its own governmental interests." Restatement of Conflict of Laws § 610 (1934). What does this refer to? The comments cite criminal laws, tax laws (considered below at pp. 87–89), and laws requiring someone to provide financial support in order to "reliev[e] the public burden." Interestingly, claims brought by the state against a private person for breach of contract or for a tort do not qualify as rights created to promote "governmental interests" of the state.

(6) Why should one state, especially in a federal system, refuse to assist another in the enforcement of penal or other laws designed to further "governmental interests"? See the famous explanation given by Judge Learned Hand in *Moore v. Mitchell,* 30 F.2d 600, 604 (2d Cir.1929) (concurring opinion), aff'd on other grounds, 281 U.S. 18 (1930):

> Even in the case of ordinary municipal liabilities, a court will not recognize those arising in a foreign state, if they run counter to

> the "settled public policy" of its own. Thus a scrutiny of the liability is necessarily always in reserve, and the possibility that it will be found not to accord with the policy of the domestic state. This is not a troublesome or delicate inquiry when the question arises between private persons, but it takes on quite another face when it concerns the relations between the foreign state and its own citizens or even those who may be temporarily within its borders. To pass upon the provisions for the public order of another state is, or at any rate should be, beyond the powers of a court; it involves the relations between the states themselves, with which courts are incompetent to deal, and which are intrusted to other authorities. It may commit the domestic state to a position which would seriously embarrass its neighbor.

Professor Leflar considered these and other arguments against enforcing foreign penal claims and concluded that "the absolute exclusion of extrastate claims on account of their penal or governmental nature should be limited to those by which enforcement of the criminal law as such is sought." Leflar, *Extrastate Enforcement of Penal and Governmental Claims,* 46 Harv.L.Rev. 193, 225 (1932). Are the arguments against enforcement persuasive even in criminal cases? Is the case against enforcing foreign criminal laws strengthened by the availability of extradition under Article IV of the Constitution, or by the discretionary element common in sentencing? Enforcement of the criminal laws of another sovereign is not unknown in the United States; compare 28 U.S.C. §§ 1442, 1443, permitting removal to the federal courts of criminal prosecutions against federal officers and in certain civil-rights cases, because of the danger that state courts may impair federal rights beyond the repairing capacity of Supreme Court review. Do any of the arguments against foreign criminal prosecutions apply to civil claims involving a punitive element, such as a claim for punitive damages?

Tax Laws

(1) A final exception to the recognition of foreign causes of action is the rule that one state will not enforce the revenue laws of another. There was no separate provision to this effect in the First Restatement, but tax laws were mentioned as a type of law that should not be enforced because they furthered a foreign state's "own governmental interests." Restatement of Conflict of Laws § 610 comment c (1934). In fact, the status of this exception was more precarious than that of the related exception for penal laws. According to the court in *Oklahoma ex rel. Oklahoma Tax Comm'n v. Neely,* 225 Ark. 230, 282 S.W.2d 150 (1955), the rule against enforcing foreign revenue laws was based on dicta from two eighteenth-century

English cases and was not unequivocally applied by an American court of last resort until 1921. See *State of Colorado v. Harbeck,* 232 N.Y. 71, 133 N.E. 357 (1921).

(2) What is the justification for refusing to enforce foreign tax laws? Learned Hand urged the same explanation as for penal laws. Revenue laws, he said, "affect a state in matters as vital to its existence as its criminal laws." *Moore v. Mitchell,* 30 F.2d at 604, supra p. 86, note (6). These and other arguments for the exception were criticized in *State ex rel. Oklahoma Tax Comm'n v. Rodgers,* 238 Mo.App. 1115, 193 S.W.2d 919 (1946), in which a Missouri court enforced an Oklahoma tax claim. Drawing heavily on Professor Leflar's article, supra note (6), the court reasoned that, unlike an attempt to enforce a penal law, a tax claim could not interfere with the prerogatives of the foreign state "for the obvious reason that the foreign state is the one that wants to sue." In addition, the court argued, interstate complications were more likely to result from the exclusion of tax claims than from their acceptance; concerns about retribution were irrelevant since "tax laws are not passed to punish people"; and factors of trial inconvenience and expense were no more significant in tax cases than in other transitory civil actions. 238 Mo.App. at 1127–28, 193 S.W.2d at 927. In *Neely,* where an Arkansas court similarly enforced an Oklahoma tax claim, the court cited Professor Leflar in adding that the rule against enforcing foreign revenue laws "encourages willful, dishonest tax evasion" and "offers a legally respectable asylum to the tax dodger." 282 S.W.2d at 152.

(3) *Neely* and *Rodgers* reflected a strong trend in the case law to abandon the exception for tax laws. See also *City of Detroit v. Gould,* 12 Ill.2d 297, 146 N.E.2d 61 (1957). In other states, judicial reluctance to enforce foreign tax and governmental claims has been overcome by legislation. More than half the states have adopted statutes requiring their courts to entertain such actions on a reciprocal basis—that is, provided that the state whose claim is to be enforced extends a like privilege to the forum state.

The case for enforcement of foreign tax claims was further strengthened by *Milwaukee County v. M.E. White Co.,* 296 U.S. 268 (1935), which held that the full faith and credit clause required an Illinois court to enforce a Wisconsin *judgment* for unpaid Wisconsin taxes. As the Court acknowledged, special considerations apply to the enforcement of judgments (see Chapter 5, infra), but much of the Court's reasoning could easily be transplanted to a case like *Neely* or *Rodgers:* "In the circumstances here disclosed no state can be said to have a legitimate policy against payment of its neighbor's taxes. . ." 296 U.S. at 277.

(4) Some statutes, including most notably the Racketeer Influenced and Corrupt Organizations act (RICO), include as an element of the offense or cause of action the violation of another law. If this other law is a foreign tax law, does a RICO action amount to forbidden enforcement of that law? In *Pasquantino v. United States*, 544 U.S. 349 (2005), the Supreme Court resolved a split among the circuits by answering the question in the negative—at least with respect to criminal actions brought by the United States. *Pasquantino* upheld a conviction for wire fraud, where the fraud consisted of evasion of Canadian taxes due on imported liquor. The Court also vacated and remanded for reconsideration in light of *Pasquantino* a Second Circuit decision that had dismissed a civil RICO suit brought by the European Community against tobacco manufacturers, where the alleged predicate offense was violation of tax laws by smuggling cigarettes into the plaintiffs' territories. On remand, the Second Circuit reinstated its earlier decision, asserting that the involvement of the U.S. government as plaintiff in *Pasquantino* made a decisive difference. See *European Community v. RJR Nabisco, Inc.*, 424 F.3d 175 (2d Cir. 2005). On review of a later iteration of the *RJR Nabisco* litigation, the Supreme Court left this holding undisturbed. *RJR Nabisco, Inc. v. European Community*, 579 U.S. 325, 333 n.4 (2016).

SECTION 3. PLEADING AND PROVING FOREIGN LAW

WALTON V. ARABIAN AMERICAN OIL CO.

233 F.2d 541 (2d Cir.1956).

Before FRANK, LUMBARD and WATERMAN, CIRCUIT JUDGES.

FRANK, CIRCUIT JUDGE. Plaintiff is a citizen and resident of Arkansas, who, while temporarily in Saudi Arabia, was seriously injured when an automobile he was driving collided with a truck owned by defendant, driven by one of defendant's employees. Defendant is a corporation incorporated in Delaware, licensed to do business in New York, and engaged in extensive business activities in Saudi Arabia. Plaintiff's complaint did not allege pertinent Saudi Arabian "law," nor at the trial did he prove or offer to prove it. Defendant did not, in its answer, allege such "law," and defendant did not prove or offer to prove it. There was evidence from which it might have been inferred, reasonably, that, under well-established New York decisions, defendant was negligent and therefore liable to plaintiff. The trial judge, saying he would not take judicial notice of Saudi Arabian "law," directed a verdict in favor of the defendant and gave judgment against the plaintiff.

1. As jurisdiction here rests on diversity of citizenship, we must apply the New York rules of conflict of laws. It is well settled by the New York decisions that the "substantive law" applicable to an alleged tort is the "law" of the place where the alleged tort occurred. See, e.g., *Conklin v.*

Canadian-Colonial Airways, Inc., 266 N.Y. 244, 248, 194 N.E. 692. This is the federal doctrine; see, e.g., *Slater v. Mexican National Railroad Co.,* 194 U.S. 120; *Cuba R. Co. v. Crosby,* 222 U.S. 473. This doctrine is often said to be based on the notion that to hold otherwise would be to interfere with the authority of the foreign sovereign. . .

2. The general federal rule is that the "law" of a foreign country is a fact which must be proved. However, under Fed.Rules Civ.Proc. rule 43(a), 28 U.S.C.A., a federal court must receive evidence if it is admissible according to the rules of evidence of the state in which the court sits. At first glance, then, it may seem that the judge erred in refusing to take judicial notice of Saudi Arabian "law" in the light of New York Civil Practice Act, § 344–a. In *Siegelman v. Cunard White Star,* 2 Cir., 221 F.2d 189, 196–197, applying that statute, we took judicial notice of English "law" which had been neither pleaded nor proved. Our decision, in that respect, has been criticized; but it may be justified on the ground that an American court can easily comprehend, and therefore, under the statute, take judicial notice of, English decisions, like those of any state in the United States.[9] However, where, as here, comprehension of foreign "law" is, to say the least, not easy, then, according to the somewhat narrow interpretation of the New York statute by the New York courts a court "abuses" its discretion under that statute perhaps if it takes judicial notice of foreign "law" when it is not pleaded, and surely does so unless the party, who would otherwise have had the burden of proving that "law," has in some way adequately assisted the court in judicially learning it.

3. Plaintiff, however, argues thus: The instant case involves such rudimentary tort principles, that the judge, absent a contrary showing, should have presumed that those principles are recognized in Saudi Arabia; therefore the burden of showing the contrary was on the defendant, which did not discharge that burden. But we do not agree that the applicable tort principles, necessary to establish plaintiff's claim, are "rudimentary": In countries where the common law does not prevail, our doctrines relative to negligence, and to a master's liability for his servant's acts, may well not exist or be vastly different. Consequently, here plaintiff had the burden of showing, to the trial court's satisfaction, Saudi Arabian "law."

This conclusion seems unjust for this reason: Both the parties are Americans. The plaintiff was but a transient in Saudi Arabia when the

[9] [A]n American court may go astray even in taking judicial notice of English "law." The similarity in language may be deceptive by concealing significant differences. Indeed, just because the English language appears the same as the American language (although it is not), an American may understand the former less adequately than he understands German or French, which is more obviously "foreign" and different. * * *

Moreover, the taken-for-granted, unexpressed, background assumptions of English judges and lawyers differ from the unspoken assumptions of American judges and lawyers, and thus may well induce serious misunderstandings. . . .

accident occurred and has not been there since that time. The defendant company engages in extensive business operations there, and is therefore in a far better position to obtain information concerning the "law" of that country. But, under the New York decisions which we must follow, plaintiff had the burden. As he did not discharge it, a majority of the court holds that the judge correctly gave judgment for the defendant.

4. In argument, plaintiff's counsel asserted that Saudi Arabia has "no law or legal system," and no courts open to plaintiff, but only a dictatorial monarch who decides according to his whim whether a claim like plaintiff's shall be redressed, i.e., that Saudi Arabia is, in effect, "uncivilized." According to Holmes, J. * * * the *lex loci* does not apply "where a tort is committed in an uncivilized country" or in one "having no law that civilized countries would recognize as adequate." If such were the case here, we think the New York courts would apply (and therefore we should) the substantive "law" of the country which is most closely connected with the parties and their conduct—in this case, American "law." But plaintiff has offered no data showing that Saudi Arabia is thus "uncivilized." We are loath to and will not believe it, absent such a showing.

5. The complaint in this action was filed on May 10, 1949. . . At [pre-trial] hearings the question of proving Saudi Arabian law was discussed. When the case came on for trial on November 7, 1953 Judge Bicks indicated that in his view the burden was on the plaintiff to prove the foreign "law". When the plaintiff's counsel said that he was not prepared to prove the "law" of Saudi Arabia, Judge Bicks proposed that the case be adjourned long enough to allow the plaintiff to prepare such proof. It was agreed that the case be put over for two days to enable the plaintiff to decide whether to request an adjournment for that purpose.

When the hearing resumed on November 9, plaintiff's counsel unequivocally took the position that he did not wish to prove the foreign "law" and wanted no adjournment. He chose to rely on the applicability of New York "law." To that end he proposed that he proceed to present his case in order to make a record for appeal. The plaintiff's evidence as to liability was presented and on a proper motion the judge dismissed the complaint. He specifically ruled that he would not take judicial notice of the "law" of Saudi Arabia and that the plaintiff's failure to prove that "law" required dismissal.

Since the plaintiff deliberately refrained from establishing an essential element of his case, the complaint was properly dismissed. The majority of the court thinks that, for the following reasons, it is inappropriate to remand the case so that the plaintiff may have another chance: He had abundant opportunity to supply the missing element and chose not to avail himself of it. . .[I]t would have been an abuse of discretion under the New York cases to take notice of the foreign "law" here. The judgment of dismissal must therefore be affirmed.

The writer of the opinion thinks we should remand for this reason: Apparently neither the trial judge nor the parties were aware of New York Civil Practice Act, § 344–a; consequently, in the interests of justice, we should remand with directions to permit the parties, if they so desire, to present material which may assist the trial judge to ascertain the applicable "law" of Saudi Arabia.[16]

Affirmed.

Notice and Proof of Foreign Law

(1) A forum that undertakes to apply foreign law must have some mechanism, preferably a convenient and accurate one, for ascertaining the content of the relevant foreign rules. Common-law courts treated foreign law as a matter of fact to be pleaded and proved by the party whose cause of action or defense depended upon foreign law. See 3 J. Beale, A Treatise on the Conflict of Laws § 621.2 (1935). Treating foreign law as a question of fact has some important consequences: (1) Foreign law must be pleaded like other facts. (2) Foreign law must be proved in conformity with the law of evidence (usually requiring direct and cross-examination of a properly qualified expert). (3) The issue as to foreign law is decided by the trier of fact (usually the jury). And (4) the finding of the trier of fact is subject only to very limited appellate review.

Given the inconvenience of establishing foreign law this way, why should we treat foreign law as a fact? Why not adhere to the usual division of labor in litigation, which leaves legal questions to the judge after briefing and argument from the parties? According to Professor Beale, "a court neither will nor can apply any law to the case before it other than the law of the forum. It must necessarily follow that foreign law, in so far as it is in

---

[16] Or that it has no "civilized" legal system; see point 4 of the text, supra.

Nussbaum, 3 Am.J. of Comp.Law (1954) 60, 63–64—criticizing *Usatorre v. The Victoria,* 2 Cir., 172 F.2d 434 points to an important fact: the prohibitive expense to a party of modest financial means in obtaining an expert to explain foreign "law." Subsequently (pp. 66–67), Nussbaum suggests that the trial judge call his own expert; the judge, says Nussbaum, would require the parties to advance the expert's fee, or, "if this is not feasible, the court (hence eventually the losing party), may be charged with the fee as part of the court's business." But, as matters now stand, this solution is not feasible: In a federal criminal case, a trial judge may call upon his own expert whom the government will pay; see Criminal Rule 28, 18 U.S.C.A. However, in a civil case (at any rate, one to which the government is not a party) the government has no authority to pay an expert; and the use of the device of taxing the expert's fee as part of the costs to the losing party may be beyond the judge's power (absent a statute); in any event, the expert will go unpaid if the losing party has not the funds to pay such costs.

any way material to the issue, must operate not as law but as fact." Id. § 621.1. Is that explanation satisfactory? Can you do better?

(2) One modern solution to the problem is found in statutes authorizing courts to take judicial notice of foreign law. Article IV of the Uniform Interstate and International Procedure Act is illustrative of such provisions:

> **Article IV. Determination of Foreign Law.**
>
> Section 4.01. [Notice.] A party who intends to raise an issue concerning the law of any jurisdiction or governmental unit thereof outside this state shall give notice in his pleadings or other reasonable written notice.
>
> Section 4.02. [Materials to be Considered.] In determining the laws of any jurisdiction or governmental unit thereof outside this state, the court may consider any relevant material or source, including testimony, whether or not submitted by a party or admissible under the rules of evidence.
>
> Section 4.03. [Court Decision and Review.] The court, not jury, shall determine the law of any governmental unit outside this state and its determination shall be subject to review on appeal as a ruling on a question of law.

See also Fed.R.Civ.Proc. 44.1, which adopts substantially identical provisions for establishing the law of foreign nations.

Not all statutes are this broad. American courts are generally authorized to take notice of the law of *sister states,* but authorization for courts to notice the law of *foreign countries* is not universal, and even where recognized is usually discretionary rather than mandatory.

(3) Do statutes authorizing judicial notice of foreign law solve the problem? By treating foreign law as a question of law, these provisions permit the matter to be presented in briefs, resolved by the judge, and reviewed on appeal. But what about the requirement that foreign law be pleaded or otherwise formally noticed? Do liberal rules for amending the pleadings alleviate this concern?

Some difficulties remain even with the adoption of a mechanism that puts foreign law on an equal footing with other legal questions. Determining the content of foreign law may still be difficult and expensive, especially if the law is that of a foreign country. Who should bear these burdens? What mechanisms are there for allocating the costs between the parties?

Even when the foreign state is one of the United States, determining its law may be difficult if the question is one of first impression or the precedents conflict. More than thirty states authorize certification of the disputed question to an appropriate court of the other state in such a case, most of them on the basis of the Uniform Certification of Questions Law, 12 U.L.A. 49 (1975). One problem with this procedure is that typically only appellate courts are authorized to make the request; another is that certification itself can be costly and causes delay.

(4) What should a court do when, as in *Walton,* no one establishes the content of foreign law? Does a judicial notice provision like that quoted in note (2) answer the question? Was the court in *Walton* right to dismiss?

Some courts faced with this problem have adopted a presumption that foreign law is identical to that of the forum, unless the contrary is shown. In *Louknitsky v. Louknitsky,* 123 Cal.App.2d 406, 266 P.2d 910 (1954), for example, the court indulged in the dubious presumption that Chinese marital-property law was the same as that of California. Variants of this approach limit the presumption to "rudimentary principles of justice" followed in all "civilized" countries, or to the common law of the forum unmodified by its statutes. The latter approach may have the disadvantage of applying a law that is in force nowhere in the world, while the former is somewhat plastic: Is *respondeat superior,* which was essential to recovery against the tortfeasor's employer in *Walton,* a "rudimentary" principle of justice?

(5) Disapproving all these solutions, Professor Brainerd Currie argued that, if foreign law was not established, the "normal and natural" thing for a court to do was to apply its own law because no one had shown why it should be displaced. A party who wants the benefit of foreign law, Currie urged, should be required to plead it—just as he or she would have to plead such domestic rules as res judicata or the statute of limitations. B. Currie, Selected Essays on the Conflict of Laws 9, 46–48, 74 (1963).

But what if the defendant moves to dismiss for failure to state a claim? Isn't it then up to the plaintiff to persuade the court that some law gives him a right to recovery on the facts alleged? New York law surely gives no rights to an Arkansas citizen injured by a Delaware corporation in Saudi Arabia. So if the plaintiff does not convince the court that some foreign law gives him a right to relief, hasn't he failed to state a claim upon which relief can be granted? See Kramer, *Interest Analysis and the Presumption of Forum Law,* 56 U.Chi.L.Rev. 1301 (1989) (arguing that this is how the sufficiency of a claim is handled in wholly domestic cases and that the same procedures work just as well in multistate cases). Does this analysis explain the outcome in *Walton*?

Currie conceded that it would be inappropriate to apply a New York *speed limit* to a case like *Walton,* even in the absence of proof of Saudi Arabian law. "It should be sufficient for the defendant simply to point out that the New York rule was not intended to apply, and cannot reasonably be applied, outside New York." But he thought this reasoning did not extend to the question whether a Delaware corporation should be liable for injuries caused by its driver's negligence in Saudi Arabia:

> No conflict of interest among states being apparent, justice between the parties becomes the sole consideration. And where should the New York court look for a rule of decision that will do justice between the parties but to the body of principle and experience which has served that purpose . . . for the people of New York in their domestic affairs?

Selected Essays on the Conflict of Laws at 64–65.

Doesn't this suggestion offend the first principle of the territorial theory? Even if one rejects territoriality, how can it be "normal and natural" for an Arkansas plaintiff injured in Saudi Arabia to recover damages from a Delaware defendant under New York law? See Kramer, *More Notes on Methods and Objectives in the Conflict of Laws,* 24 Cornell Int'l L.J. 245, 255 (1991): "The proposition seems inconsistent with our most fundamental intuitions about law—that its function is to regulate human action and its consequences. One would think that the applicable law ought to have *something* to do with the real world events that gave rise to a dispute."

CHAPTER 2

MODERN APPROACHES TO CHOICE OF LAW

■ ■ ■

SECTION 1. STATUTORY SOLUTIONS

One possible solution to the choice-of-law dilemma is legislation. Oregon and Louisiana have enacted codifications. See Nafziger, *The Louisiana and Oregon Codifications of Choice-of-Law Rules in Context*, 58 Am. J. Comp. L. 165 (2010). But state legislatures cannot enact a comprehensive choice-of-law code without confronting the same difficulties as judges or the drafters of a Restatement. A more modest approach might call for the legislature to attach custom-made choice-of-law rules to particular statutes. Would this provide a complete solution? What if states adopt different or overlapping rules? A number of state statutes contain "localizing provisions" requiring the application of the enacting state's law notwithstanding choice-of-law clauses in consumer, employment, franchise, or insurance contracts. For an argument that these enactments constitute codified choice-of-law rules, see Symeonides, Codifying Choice Of Law Around The World: An International Comparative Analysis 294–99 (2015). But such provisions are relatively rare, and most legislation is enacted without any consideration of multistate situations. The following notes describe some of the more prominent legislative efforts to resolve choice-of-law problems. As you read them, ask yourself how useful such efforts ultimately seem likely to be.

(1) *Foreign Executed Wills.* The problem of succession is especially difficult in a migratory society like that of the United States. Traditional choice-of-law rules can create substantial problems if an American dies owning property located in several states. As we have seen, the validity of a will is governed as to movable property by the law of the domicile at death and as to immovable property by the law of each situs. Restatement of Conflict of Laws §§ 249, 306 (1934). If the will complied with testamentary formalities in the state where the decedent was domiciled when it was executed, but does not satisfy the corresponding requirements of the state of domicile at the time of death or of the situs of immovables, the will is invalid and the testator's intentions are frustrated. The importance of this problem gave rise to legislative reform many years ago, and today most American states have statutes that validate wills executed outside the state of administration. Section 2–506 of the Uniform Probate Code is illustrative:

> A written will is valid if executed in compliance with [this Code] or if its execution complies with the law at the time of execution of the place where the will is executed, or of the law of the place where at the time of execution or at the time of death the testator is domiciled, has a place of abode or is a national.

Interpretive problems remain. First, it is unclear whose law determines such preliminary issues as domicile, nationality, place of execution, and place of abode. Second, the statutes are limited to matters relating to the "execution" of a will, leaving differences among states on matters of revocation to the common law. Third, even as to matters of execution, it is unclear whether the statute applies only to formalities or whether it includes substantive issues like the rule against perpetuities and forced shares. See generally Schoenblum, *Multijurisdictional Estates and Article II of the Uniform Probate Code,* 55 Albany L.Rev. 1291 (1992).

(2) *The Uniform Commercial Code.* The most litigated statutory choice-of-law provisions are those of the UCC. The basic rule is stated in § 1–301:

> **Territorial Applicability; Parties' Power to Choose Applicable Law.**
>
> (a) Except as otherwise provided in this section, when a transaction bears a reasonable relation to this state and also to another state or nation the parties may agree that the law either of this state or of such other state or nation shall govern their rights and duties.
>
> (b) In the absence of an agreement effective under subsection (a), and except as provided in subsection (c), [the Uniform Commercial Code] applies to transactions bearing an appropriate relation to this state.

Allowing the parties to choose an applicable law for consensual transactions is considered in greater detail in Section 2. The UCC qualifies this approach in § 1–301(c), however, by listing provisions from other parts of the Code and providing that if one of these specifies the applicable law, the parties' agreement is only effective "to the extent permitted by the law so specified." The most important such provision is § 9–301, which subjects questions relating to the perfection or non-perfection of a security interest to the law of the jurisdiction where the collateral is located. § 9–301(2). Other subsections recognize exceptions to this rule. The only way fully to appreciate the incredible complexity of these provisions is to try to make sense of them. Professor Weintraub discusses many of the problems in R. Weintraub, Commentary on the Conflict of Laws 635–51 (6th ed. 2010).

(a) One problem with the UCC's mix of rules is that the court must still characterize issues to select the appropriate choice-of-law provision.

Unfortunately, the UCC does not furnish any better tools for completing this process than the First Restatement. *Skinner v. Tober Foreign Motors, Inc.*, 345 Mass. 429, 187 N.E.2d 669 (1963), is illustrative. Plaintiffs, of Connecticut, bought an airplane from defendant, a Massachusetts corporation. The original contract called for payments of $200 per month, but the parties agreed orally to reduce these payments to $100 for the first year. After five months, the defendant reneged and demanded payment according to the original schedule. The plaintiffs refused and defendant repossessed the airplane. Plaintiffs sued, and defendant argued that the modification was invalid for lack of consideration. Because the Massachusetts version of the Code then in force required no additional consideration for agreements modifying a contract, defendant argued that Connecticut law applied. Defendant relied on a provision of § 9–103 (as it then stood) subjecting questions respecting the "validity and perfection" of a security interest in mobile goods to the law of the debtor's chief place of business. The court rejected this argument on the ground that the case "involves the duties of the parties under the primary obligation; neither party contests the validity or perfection of the security interest." The court therefore applied Massachusetts law under § 1–105(1), finding that the contract bore "an appropriate relation" to Massachusetts and that the parties had not made a contrary choice.

According to Professor Gilmore, *Skinner*'s characterization of a purchase money transaction as part sale (governed by § 1–105) and part security (governed by § 9–103) is "bad law" because all questions pertaining to security interests should be governed by Article 9. I G. Gilmore, Security Interests in Personal Property § 10.8 at 319, n. 5 (1965). Professor Weintraub, in contrast, deplored the "many puzzles" complicating choice of law in the UCC but concluded that *Skinner* selected "the better of two unsatisfactory Code approaches to choice of law." R. Weintraub, Commentary on the Conflict of Laws 476 (3d ed. 1986). Who is right? The 1972 amendments to the UCC endorsed the result in *Skinner*, and subsequent developments (including the abandonment of the Article 9 provisions in every state) have eliminated the problem.

(b) The story behind UCC § 1–301 is more complicated than it might seem. The initial UCC choice-of-law provision was § 1–105, substantively identical to current § 1–301. In 2001, the American Law Institute replaced it with a provision (the first § 1–301) that, subject to some exceptions to protect consumers, allowed parties to choose the law governing their transaction regardless of whether the transaction bore a reasonable relation to the state whose law was chosen. This greater emphasis on party autonomy reflected the trend among academics. See, e.g., O'Hara & Ribstein, The Law Market (2009). But when states enacted the new version of the UCC, they uniformly rejected the new choice-of-law provision. (The Virgin Islands was the only U.S. jurisdiction to adopt it.) Faced with this reaction, the ALI approved an official reversion to the old choice-of-law provision in 2008. Does it surprise you that states were less enthusiastic about party autonomy than law professors?

(3) *No-Fault Insurance.* Shortcomings in existing automobile claims systems have led many states to adopt "no-fault" insurance plans. The plans vary enormously in detail, but typically cover loss regardless of fault while eliminating negligence claims for injuries suffered in traffic accidents. In a notable departure from the usual legislative indifference to conflict of laws, virtually all of the state no-fault insurance plans contain provisions delimiting their scope in multistate situations. Two states (New York and Utah) cover only injuries occurring within the state; most other states extend coverage to specified persons injured outside the state. North Dakota, for example, provides no-fault coverage to the insured and to members of his or her family who are injured "in the United States or its possessions or in Canada. . ." N.D.Cent.Code § 26.1–41–06 (2008).

Half the states enacted some variant of no-fault insurance between 1970 and 1975, although some states have since repealed those laws. With the nation thus divided, opportunities for conflict of laws problems abound. Worse, the bewildering variety of plans means that potential conflicts may also arise between no-fault states. Two efforts were undertaken to provide uniformity: the Commissioners on Uniform State Laws promulgated the Uniform Motor Vehicle Accident Reparations Act in 1972, and Congress considered but failed to adopt a National No-Fault Motor Vehicle Insurance Act (see S. 354 and H.R. 19000, 94th Congress). Both acts propose statutory choice-of-law rules for multistate situations—the Uniform Act opting for a territorial approach while the federal act chose the law of the victim's domicile. Unfortunately, neither proposal addresses conflicts between fault and no-fault states, because both assume nationwide scope for some form of no-fault insurance. In any event, almost no one has adopted the Uniform Act, and there is little momentum for enacting the federal legislation.

(4) *Borrowing Statutes.* One of the oldest statutory choice-of-law provisions is the so-called borrowing statute, which directs the forum to dismiss claims under foreign statutes of limitations in appropriate circumstances. About three-fourths of the states have such provisions. See Prefatory Note to Uniform Conflict of Laws—Limitations Act, 12 U.L.A. 54 (Supp.1989). The Illinois statute is illustrative:

> When a cause of action has arisen in a state or territory out of this state, or in a foreign country, and, by the laws thereof, an action thereon cannot be maintained by reason of the lapse of time, an action thereon shall not be maintained in this state.

735 ILCS 5/13–210 (2016). Professor Ester collected judicial opinions reflecting a remarkable range of views on the purpose of such provisions, including docket clearing, avoiding forum shopping, and even such unlikely

explanations as encouraging commerce and immigration or fulfilling an implied intent of the parties to a contract. Ester, *Borrowing Statutes of Limitations and Conflict of Laws,* 15 U.Fla.L.Rev. 33, 40–41 (1962). Should borrowing statutes be viewed more straightforwardly as an attempt to reverse the traditional choice-of-law rule that statutes of limitations are procedural? Professor Ester thinks so:

> [A]s a matter of policy, there is no sound reason why an obligee should be entitled to recover in the forum if his action has been fully barred by the law of the state in which it arose. . . If the right of action has been extinguished, this defense should accompany defendant to each jurisdiction in which he might subsequently reside.

Id.

Many borrowing statutes apply only to cases in which the plaintiff, or sometimes both parties, is not a forum resident. Does that complicate the argument that they are about characterization?

A surprising number of difficult interpretive problems have arisen with respect to borrowing statutes. Consider the following:

(a) Whose statute of limitations should the forum apply? Several borrowing statutes refer to the state in which the defendant resided at one time or another, but most refer to the state in which a cause of action "arose," "accrued," or "originated." These terms have proved difficult to interpret. The Uniform Conflict of Laws-Limitations Act, promulgated in 1982, solves the problem by directing the forum to apply the limitations period of the law chosen to govern the merits of the case. This is consistent with the idea that the purpose of a borrowing statute is to recharacterize the limitations question as substantive, but it means that the limitations period applicable to a given case will vary from state to state depending on what approach the forum uses for choice of law. Is this a serious objection?

(b) How should a borrowing statute be applied to a claim that would be barred by the forum's own statute of limitations? According to the great weight of authority, "the statute of limitations of the forum provides an ultimate limitation upon the period within which suit may be brought in its courts." *Conner v. Spencer,* 304 F.2d 485 (9th Cir.1962). Consistent with these results, the 1988 amendments to § 142 of the Second Restatement provide that the forum will apply its own statute of limitations barring a claim "unless the exceptional circumstances of the case make such a result unreasonable." (Comment f illustrates such circumstances with a case in which "through no fault of the plaintiff an alternative forum is not available.") The Uniform Conflict of Laws-Limitations Act, in contrast, directs the forum to apply the limitations law of the state whose law governs the merits even if it permits an action that the forum would otherwise bar. Which approach is better? Professor Leflar, a member of the committee that drafted the Uniform Act, criticized an approach that always applies the shorter limitations period on the ground that it fails adequately to take "concerns of justice" into account and seeks only to simplify the judicial task. Leflar, *The New Conflicts-Limitation Act,* 35 Mercer L.Rev. 461, 465 (1984). Might the forum have other reasons to apply its own shorter statute of limitations?

(c) Closely related to borrowing statutes are "tolling statutes," which suspend the running of a statute of limitations against out-of-state defendants. Tolling statutes were enacted to ensure that plaintiffs would not be deprived of a reasonable opportunity to sue because a time bar ran while the defendant was beyond the reach of service of process.

Interpreting tolling statutes and borrowing statutes together can be difficult. Thus, when a borrowing statute makes foreign limitations law applicable, is the reference only to the limitation period of the foreign state or are its tolling provisions also included? The usual view, reflected in both the Uniform Act and the Second Restatement, is that tolling provisions are included. This may, however, lead to some strange results. In *West v. Theis,* 15 Idaho 167, 96 P. 932 (1908), the defendant gave the plaintiff several promissory notes in Kansas, but left the state without repaying before the Kansas statute of limitations ran against the plaintiff. The defendant then moved to Washington and later to Idaho, where (eighteen years after the notes were executed) the plaintiff's estate finally brought suit. The court held that the action was not barred. Although the defendant had lived in Washington longer than the period of its statute of limitations, Idaho's borrowing statute referred to the law of the place where an action "has arisen," and the court interpreted this to mean the state where the contract was made or to be performed—i.e., Kansas. The claim was not barred under Kansas law, however, because the defendant left Kansas before its statute of limitations expired, and no further time had elapsed under Kansas's tolling statute. Finally, the claim was not barred by Idaho law because Idaho's tolling statute allowed the limitations period to run only when the defendant was in the state, and this defendant had been present for less than the time allowed. Has the widespread adoption of long-arm statutes subjecting absent defendants to personal jurisdiction in cases connected with the forum eliminated this problem? Has it obviated the need for tolling statutes?

A related problem is whether the reference to another state's limitations law includes the other state's borrowing statute. What would have happened in *West v. Theis,* for example, if the Kansas borrowing statute referred to the statute of limitations of any state in which the defendant had resided since leaving Kansas? Should the Idaho court have held that the plaintiff's claim was barred under the Washington statute of limitations referred to by the Kansas borrowing statute? Compare *Holmes v. Hengen,* 41 Misc. 521, 85 N.Y.S. 35 (Sup.Ct.1903) (yes), with *Hobbs v. Firestone Tire & Rubber Co.,* 195 F.Supp. 56 (N.D.Ind.1961) (no).

(d) What is the effect of a borrowing statute on a contract governed by the UCC? In *Bridge Prods., Inc. v. Quantum Chem. Corp.,* 1990 WL 19968 (N.D.Ill.1990), Bridge Products (a Delaware corporation) bought manufacturing assets, including property located in Virginia, from Quantum's predecessor in interest. The contract provided that Delaware law should govern and required Quantum to indemnify Bridge Products for preexisting defects. Virginia authorities required Bridge Products to clean up environmental contamination on the Virginia property, and Bridge Products sued Quantum in Illinois seeking indemnification. Quantum raised a limitations defense under Delaware law. The court upheld the validity of the choice-of-law clause, but said that it did not apply because statutes of limitations were procedural "and therefore not subject to the application of foreign law." The court then referred to the Illinois borrowing statute, which led it to Virginia law, which (the court held) barred the claim. See also *McMahon v. Pennsylvania Life Ins. Co.,* 891 F.2d 1251 (7th Cir.1989) (ignoring the contractual choice of law on the ground that the forum borrowing statute required the court to apply the shortest statute of limitations). How should this problem be analyzed?

(5) The European Union has adopted two fairly comprehensive choice-of-law regulations, Rome I, governing contracts, and Rome II, governing torts. They are excerpted and discussed infra Chapter 8, Section 2.

SECTION 2. PARTY AUTONOMY AND THE RULE OF VALIDATION

PRITCHARD V. NORTON

106 U.S. 124 (1882).

In Error to the Circuit Court of the United States for the District of Louisiana.

[Pritchard, a Louisiana citizen, signed an appeal bond on behalf of a railroad against which a Louisiana trial court had rendered judgment. Subsequently, Norton, a New York citizen, and McComb, a Delaware citizen, executed and delivered to Pritchard in New York a bond of indemnity in which Norton and McComb undertook to indemnify Pritchard against all loss or damage arising from the bond. The railroad's appeal was unsuccessful, and Pritchard was required to pay the judgment. Pritchard's executrix then sued Norton on the indemnity agreement. The defense was that, since McComb and Norton had not requested Pritchard to become a surety, the bond of indemnity lacked consideration and was therefore void under New York law.]

MR. JUSTICE MATTHEWS, after stating the case, delivered the opinion of the court.

It is claimed on behalf of the plaintiff in error that by the law of Louisiana the pre-existing liability of Pritchard as surety for the railroad company would be a valid consideration to support the promise of indemnity, notwithstanding Pritchard's liability had been incurred without any previous request from the defendant below. This claim is not controverted, and is fully supported by the citations from the Civil Code of Louisiana of 1870, arts. 1893–1960, and the decisions of the supreme court of that state. . .

The single question presented by the record, therefore, is whether the law of New York, or that of Louisiana, defines and fixes the rights and obligations of the parties. . . The argument in support of the judgment . . . is that New York is the place of the contract, both because it was executed and delivered there, and because no other place of performance being either designated or necessarily implied, it was to be performed there. . .

[The Court first considered and rejected an argument that the requirement of consideration was procedural and hence governed by the law of the forum.]

The phrase *lex loci contractus* is used, in a double sense, to mean, sometimes, the law of the place where a contract is entered into; sometimes, that of the place of its performance. And when it is employed to describe the law of the seat of the obligation, it is, on that account, confusing. The law we are in search of, which is to decide upon the nature, interpretation, and validity of the engagement in question, is that which the parties have, either expressly or presumptively, incorporated into their contract as constituting its obligation. It has never been better described than it was incidentally by Chief Justice Marshall in *Wayman v. Southard,* 10 Wheat. 1, 48, where he defined it as a principle of universal law—"the principle that in every forum a contract is governed by the law with a view to which it was made." The same idea had been expressed by Lord Mansfield in *Robinson v. Bland,* 2 Burr. 1077. "The law of the place," he said, "can never be the rule where the transaction is entered into with an express view to the law of another country, as the rule by which it is to be governed." . . .

It is upon this ground that the presumption rests that the contract is to be performed at the place where it is made, and to be governed by its laws, there being nothing in its terms, or in the explanatory circumstances of its execution, inconsistent with that intention. So, Phillimore says, . . . "As all the foregoing rules rest upon the presumption that the obligor has voluntarily submitted himself to a particular local law, that presumption may be rebutted, either by an express declaration to the contrary, or by the fact that the obligation is illegal by that particular law, though legal by another. The parties cannot be presumed to have contemplated a law which would defeat their engagements." This rule, if universally applicable,—which perhaps it is not, . . . would be decisive of the present controversy, as conclusive of the question of the application of the law of Louisiana, by which alone the undertaking of the obligor can be upheld. At all events, it is a circumstance highly persuasive in its character of the presumed intention of the parties, and entitled to prevail, unless controlled by more express and positive proofs of a contrary intent. . .

If now we examine the terms of the bond of indemnity, and the situation and relation of the parties, we shall find conclusive corroboration of the presumption that the obligation was entered into in view of the laws of Louisiana.

The antecedent liability of Pritchard, as surety for the railroad company on the appeal bond, was confessedly contracted in that state, according to its laws, and it was there alone that it could be performed and discharged. Its undertaking was that Pritchard should, in certain contingencies, satisfy a judgment of its courts. That could be done only within its territory and according to its laws. The condition of the obligation, which is the basis of this action, is that McComb and Norton, the obligors, shall hold harmless and fully indemnify Pritchard against all loss or damage arising from his liability as surety on the appeal bond. A judgment was, in fact, rendered against him on it in Louisiana. There was but one way in which the obligors in the indemnity bond could perfectly satisfy its warranty. That was, the moment the judgment was rendered against Pritchard on the appeal bond, to come forward in his stead, and, by payment, to extinguish it. He was entitled to demand this before any payment by himself, and to require that the fund should be forthcoming at the place where otherwise he could be required to pay it. Even if it should be thought that Pritchard was bound to pay the judgment recovered against himself, before his right of recourse accrued upon the bond of indemnity, nevertheless he was entitled to be reimbursed the amount of his advance at the same place where he had been required to make it. So that it is clear, beyond any doubt, that the obligation of the indemnity was to be fulfilled in Louisiana, and, consequently, is subject, in all matters affecting its construction and validity, to the law of that locality. . .

We do not hesitate, therefore, to decide that the bond of indemnity sued on was entered into with a view to the law of Louisiana as the place for the fulfillment of its obligation; and that the question of its validity, as depending on the character and sufficiency of the consideration, should be determined by the law of Louisiana, and not that of New York.

For error in its rulings on this point, consequently, the judgment of the circuit court is reversed, with directions to grant a new trial. New trial ordered.

SIEGELMAN V. CUNARD WHITE STAR LTD.

221 F.2d 189 (2d Cir.1955).

Before CLARK, CHIEF JUDGE, and FRANK and HARLAN, CIRCUIT JUDGES.

HARLAN, CIRCUIT JUDGE. [Siegelman, in his own right and as administrator of his wife's estate, brought suit to recover for injuries suffered by his wife aboard Cunard's vessel, the Queen Elizabeth, during a voyage from New York to Cherbourg. The steamship ticket, which had been purchased in New York, provided that actions must be brought within one year of the day of injury (clause 10); that an agent could not waive conditions of the ticket except in a writing signed by designated officials (clause 11); and that "all questions arising on this contract ticket shall be decided according to English law with reference to which this contract is made" (clause 20).* In a conversation with Siegelman's attorney eleven months after the accident, Cunard's New York claim agent, one Swaine, offered $800 in settlement of the passenger's claim. The attorney agreed to inform his client of the offer, but indicated that he would also institute suit against Cunard to prevent the bar of the one-year limitation provision in the ticket. Swaine replied that the prospect of early agreement made filing a complaint unnecessary and that Cunard's offer would remain open. No complaint was filed and no settlement was reached before the one-year period expired. Three months later, Cunard's offer was revoked. Eleven months later Siegelman brought this action, which was dismissed in the lower court for the reason that the one-year limitation period had run and that defendant's agent had no authority to waive the provision.]

[W]e must decide what law applies to the validity and interpretation of certain provisions of the "Contract Ticket," and to the effect of Swaine's conduct upon Cunard's right to resort to the one-year limitation period in the contract. . .

[W]e construe the contract as establishing the intention of the parties that English law should govern both the interpretation and validity of its terms. And we think it clear that the federal conflicts rule will give effect to the parties' intention that English law is to be applied to the *interpretation* of the contract. Stipulating the governing law for this purpose is much like stipulating that words of the contract have the meanings given in a particular dictionary. * * * On the other hand, there is

* The Contract Ticket . . . was a large sheet of light green paper, about 13 inches long and 11 inches wide. On the back were certain notices to passengers, relating to baggage, time of collection of ticket, location of the company's piers and offices, etc. On the front was printed in black Cunard's promise to provide specified transportation, in this case from New York to Cherbourg, subject to certain exceptions, and to 22 "terms and conditions," also printed in black. Printed in red in heavier type was a notice directing the attention of passengers to these "terms and conditions." Also printed in red, and in capital letters, was a statement that "it is mutually agreed that this contract ticket is issued by the Company and accepted by the passenger on the following terms and conditions." . . .

much doubt that parties can stipulate the law by which the *validity* of their contract is to be judged. Beale, Conflict of Laws § 332.2 (1935). To permit parties to stipulate the law which should govern the validity of their agreement would afford them an artificial device for avoiding the policies of the state which would otherwise regulate the permissibility of their agreement. It may also be said that to give effect to the parties' stipulation would permit them to do a legislative act, for they rather than the governing law would be making their agreement into an enforceable obligation. And it may be further argued that since courts have not always been ready to give effect to the parties' stipulation, no real uniformity is achieved by following their wishes. * * *

Here, of course, the question is neither one of interpretation nor one of validity, but instead involves the circumstances under which parties may be said to have partially rescinded their agreements or to be barred from enforcing them. The question is, however, more closely akin to a question of validity. Nevertheless, we see no harm in letting the parties' intention control. * * * Instead of viewing the parties as usurping the legislative function, it seems more realistic to regard them as relieving the courts of the problem of resolving a question of conflict of laws. Their course might be expected to reduce litigation, and is to be commended as much as good draftsmanship which relieves courts of problems of resolving ambiguities. To say that there may be no reduction in litigation because courts may not honor the provision is to reason backwards. A tendency toward certainty in commercial transactions should be encouraged by the courts. Furthermore, in England, where much of the litigation on these contracts might be expected to arise, the parties' stipulation would probably be respected. * * *

Where the law of the parties' intention has been permitted to govern the validity of contracts, it has often been said (1) that the choice of law must be *bona fide,* and (2) that the law chosen must be that of a jurisdiction having some relation to the agreement, generally either the place of making or the place of performance. The second of these conditions is obviously satisfied here. The fact that a conflicts question is presented in the absence of a stipulation is some indication that the first condition is also satisfied. Furthermore, there does not appear to be an attempt here to evade American policy. We have no statute indicating a policy contrary to England's on this subject. * * * And there is no suggestion that English law is oppressive to passengers. We regard the primary purpose of making English law govern here as being not to substitute English for American policies, but rather on the one hand, to achieve uniformity of result, which is often hailed as the chief objective of the conflict of laws, and on the other hand, to simplify administration of the contracts in question. Cunard's employees need be trained in only one set of legal rules.

This is not to suggest that English and American policies on this subject are identical. Any difference in law reflects some difference in policy. Consequently, to the extent English and American policies may differ on this question, we would consider that the parties may choose to have the English policies apply. But we express no opinion on what result would follow if we had stronger policies at stake, or if the parties had attempted a feigned rather than a genuine solution of the conflicts problem. . .

Finally we come to the substantive question whether Swaine's conduct prevents Cunard from successfully invoking the contractual limitation period as a defense. . .

[The court held that, under English law, even if Swaine was authorized to waive periods of limitation, no waiver or estoppel was present. English law required an express promise or a misrepresentation of fact, not merely a misrepresentation of intention, to raise an estoppel. Finally, even if Swaine's conduct had tolled the limitation, the period would have begun to run again when Cunard withdrew its offer, and the action would still be barred.]

Affirmed.

FRANK, CIRCUIT JUDGE (dissenting). This case presents an important question relative to the rights of American passengers traveling from American ports on English vessels. Here a ticket, covering a voyage from New York to Cherbourg, was purchased by an American in New York. . . Disregarding for the moment clause 20 of the ticket (referring to "English law"), I think it clear that, under federal and New York decisions, the defendant waived (or is estopped to assert) the one-year provision (clause 10) and thereby completely abandoned it. . .

My colleagues, in holding that there was no waiver or estoppel, rely principally on [an] English decision and on clause 20 which reads: "All questions arising on this contract ticket shall be decided according to English Law with reference to which this contract is made."

[Judge Frank argued that the language of clause 20 referring to questions "on this contract" was ambiguous with respect to waiving the contract's provisions and that this question of interpretation should be decided according to American law: "to consult 'English law,' in interpreting an American contract ambiguously referring to 'English law,' would indeed be a pulling-yourself-up-by-your-own-bootstraps device." Judge Frank then concluded that English law did not govern the waiver question because clause 20 referred to the whole law of England rather than merely to its internal law.]

I call attention to another factor which, while unnecessary to my conclusion, I think supports it: The ticket is what has been called a "contract of adhesion" or a "take-it-or-leave-it" contract. In such a standardized or mass-production agreement, with one-sided control of its terms, when the one party has no real bargaining power, the usual contract rules, based on the idea of "freedom of contract," cannot be applied rationally. For such a contract is "sold not bought." The one party dictates its provisions; the other has no more choice in fixing those terms than he has about the weather. . .

All this has special pertinence here: A party, like the passenger here, having no real choice about the matter, cannot in fairness be said to have joined in a "choice of law" merely because the carrier has inserted a provision that some particular foreign "law" shall govern; therefore it would seem that that party should not be bound by such a provision. I shall not elaborate this point, since it is amply discussed in a recent excellent article, Ehrenzweig, "*Adhesion Contracts in The Conflict of Laws,*" 53 Colum.L.Rev. 1072 (1953), where most of the authorities are cited and considered.

I grant that, in this context, I am stressing the need to do justice in particular instances. I do so unashamedly. For it is generally agreed that the decisions of conflict-of-laws cases by mechanized rules, without regard to particularized justice, cannot be defended on the ground that they have promoted certainty and uniformity, since such results have not been thus achieved. Several wise commentators have urged that the element of justice should have a dominating influence. [A footnote cited articles by Cavers and others.]

[A concluding portion of Judge Frank's dissenting opinion argued that the majority had misinterpreted the English law of estoppel by waiver.]

Alternative Choice-of-Law Rules for Contracts

(1) Complete the following sentence: "Louisiana law was held applicable in *Pritchard v. Norton* because. . ."

(2) As *Pritchard v. Norton* indicates, the idea that the applicable law in a contract case may have something to do with the intentions of the parties is hardly new. Both the common law as it developed in England and the civil law as it developed on the Continent generally allowed parties great freedom to choose the law that governed their contract. See G. Cheshire & P. North, Private International Law 552–53 (13th ed. 1999); 2 E. Rabel, The Conflict of Laws: A Comparative Study 359–431 (2d ed. 1960). Justice Story also favored party autonomy in a roundabout fashion:

> Generally speaking, the validity of a contract is to be decided by the law of the place where it is made, unless it is to be performed in another country. . . But where the contract is, either expressly or tacitly, to be performed in any other place, there the

> general rule is in conformity to the presumed intention of the parties that the contract, as to its validity, nature, obligation, and interpretation, is to be governed by the law of the place of performance.

J. Story, Commentaries on the Conflict of Laws §§ 242, 280 (8th ed. 1883). Professor Beale (naturally) objected, protesting that party autonomy "involves permission to the parties to do a legislative act" and thereby frees them "at their pleasure . . . from the power of the law which would otherwise apply to their acts." Beale, *What Law Governs the Validity of a Contract,* 23 Harv.L.Rev. 260, 260–61 (1910). A majority of American jurisdictions followed Beale's lead and adopted jurisdiction-selecting rules like those discussed in Chapter 1. Yet decisions giving effect to the law chosen by the parties made persistent appearances even during the heyday of vested rights. In 1935, Beale wrote that "eleven states, and perhaps ten more, adopt the *lex loci contractus;* seven states and perhaps two more adopt the *lex loci solutionis* [i.e., the place of performance]; eight states and perhaps four more (with fourteen others, and perhaps two more yet in usury cases), adopt the law intended by the parties." 2 J. Beale, A Treatise on the Conflict of Laws 1173 (1935).

(3) Many of the First Restatement's critics favored allowing parties to select a law to govern the validity of their contract. E.g., W.W. Cook, The Logical and Legal Bases of the Conflict of Laws 389–432 (1942); Rheinstein, Book Review, 15 U.Chi.L.Rev. 478 (1948); Yntema, *Contract and Conflict of Laws: "Autonomy" in Choice of Law in the United States,* 1 N.Y.L.F. 46 (1955). See 2 Rabel, The Conflict of Laws: A Comparative Study 359–431 (2d ed. 1958), for extensive discussion of the literature. The party-autonomy rule is central to the treatment of consensual transactions in Restatement (Second) of Conflict of Laws (1971):

> **§ 187. *Law of the State Chosen by the Parties.***
>
> (1) The law of the state chosen by the parties to govern their contractual rights and duties will be applied if the particular issue is one which the parties could have resolved by an explicit provision in their agreement directed to that issue.
>
> (2) The law of the state chosen by the parties to govern their contractual rights and duties will be applied, even if the particular issue is one which the parties could not have resolved by an explicit provision in their agreement directed to that issue, unless either
>
> > (a) the chosen state has no substantial relationship to the parties or the transaction and there is no other reasonable basis for the parties' choice, or
> >
> > (b) application of the law of the chosen state would be contrary to a fundamental policy of a state which has a materially

greater interest than the chosen state in the determination of the particular issue and which, under the rule of § 188, would be the state of the applicable law in the absence of an effective choice of law by the parties.

(3) In the absence of a contrary indication of intention, the reference is to the local law of the state of the chosen law.

In the absence of an effective party choice, the Second Restatement resorts in § 188 to the law of the state having the "most significant relationship" to the parties and the transaction. This formulation will be discussed in Section 5, infra. Subsequent provisions of the Second Restatement particularize these general rules and make the parties' choice of governing law controlling on matters other than validity.

(4) Note the distinction, discussed in *Siegelman,* between matters of interpretation and matters of validity. Subsection (1) of § 187 of the Second Restatement deals with the former: it allows incorporation by reference to foreign law to spell out what the parties could otherwise have drafted for themselves. Is there any reason to object to the parties selecting foreign law as a shorthand method of defining terms?

How about matters that lie beyond the contractual power of the parties, such as issues of capacity (infancy, incompetency, etc.), formalities (statute of frauds), or substantive validity (illegality, consideration, etc.)? Subsection (2) of § 187 of the Second Restatement permits the parties to choose a governing law (subject to the stated exceptions) even if they lack the power to draft the applicable provision themselves. As we have seen, supra note (2), Professor Beale objected that this allowed the parties to "do a legislative act." Learned Hand elaborated the objection in *E. Gerli & Co. v. Cunard S.S. Co.,* 48 F.2d 115, 117 (2d Cir.1931):

> People cannot by agreement substitute the law of another place; they may of course incorporate any provisions they wish into their agreements—a statute like anything else—and when they do, courts will try to make sense out of the whole, so far as they can. But an agreement is not a contract, except as the law says it shall be, and to try to make it one is to pull on one's bootstraps. Some law must impose the obligation, and the parties have nothing whatever to do with that; no more than with whether their acts are torts or crimes.

Professor Reese found the objection spurious:

> The forum must decide in each case what law shall be applied to determine the validity of a contract and the rights created thereby. There is nothing to prevent the forum from adopting a choice-of-law rule that the governing law shall, in the ordinary case, be that chosen by the parties. When the forum adopts such

> a rule, the chosen law is applied not because the parties are legislators but simply because this is the result required by the choice-of-law rule of the forum.

Reese, *Power of Parties to Choose Law Governing Their Contract,* 54 Proc.Am.Soc'y Int'l L. 49, 51 (1960).

(5) The fact that a state *may* adopt a choice-of-law rule permitting the parties to pick the law that will determine questions of validity doesn't prove that it *should.* Professor Singer argues that party autonomy in choice of law runs counter to the modern trend of restricting contractual freedom: "From reading conflicts scholarship, one would have no idea that . . . the goal of contract law in the twentieth century has moved steadily away from freedom of contract to the regulation of contract as a means of protecting the weaker party against unequal bargaining power and promoting social justice." Singer, *Real Conflicts,* 69 B.U.L.Rev. 1, 75–76 (1989). Professor Kramer responds that this argument is overstated because the changes have been at the margins and freedom of contract remains the dominant policy in most states. Kramer, *Return of the Renvoi,* 66 N.Y.U. L. Rev. 979, 1030–31 & n. 164 (1991). But even if Kramer is right (is he?), why does it follow that a state should permit party autonomy to undermine those restrictions on contractual freedom that it has adopted? See Cheatham, *Review of Rabel, The Conflict of Laws: A Comparative Study,* 48 Colum.L.Rev. 1267, 1268–69 (1948):

> [T]he intention of the parties may well be dominant with [respect to] . . . matters . . . which the parties had the power to determine for themselves. . . It is a different thing, especially when the parties are of unequal bargaining power, to seek to escape from protective rules which prevent the making of a contract at all.

Could a married woman in a case like *Milliken v. Pratt,* supra p. 19, contract not to be protected by the Massachusetts incapacity rule? Then why should she be permitted to reach the same result by contracting to be governed by foreign law?

Here is Professor Reese's answer:

> [T]here are at least two important reasons why the parties should be given this power of choice. First and foremost, this is the only practical device for bringing certainty and predictability into the area of multi-state contracts. Likewise, to the extent that the parties can and do choose the governing law, the court is spared the pains of decision. This is not an insignificant consideration in an area such as contracts, where choice of the governing law may present many difficulties.

Reese, 54 Proc.Am.Soc'y Int'l L. at 51–52. Has Reese adequately justified party autonomy? Wouldn't any other rule equally serve these purposes if it was sufficiently clear and easy to apply? See Ribstein, *Choosing Law By Contract,* 18 J. Corp. L. 245 (1993) (economic analysis arguing that there are strong efficiency-based reasons for enforcing choice-of-law clauses, such as facilitating exit from inefficient mandatory terms, promoting interjurisdictional competition, furthering development of efficient standard form terms, resolving problems of multiple state regulation, and reducing uncertainty).

(6) Even the Second Restatement does not give parties unrestricted freedom to select the governing law. Thus, responding in part to concerns like those expressed by Professors Singer and Cheatham, § 187(2)(a) requires that the state whose law is chosen have a "substantial relationship" to the parties or transaction or that there be some other "reasonable basis" for the choice.

If it is desirable for reasons of certainty and predictability to give effect to the parties' choice of law, why should their choice be restricted to a state with which the contract has a "substantial relationship"? And what kinds of relationships are "substantial"? In a spectacular example of shopping for a favorable law, several banks, led by Citibank, relocated their credit card operations to South Dakota during the 1980s to get the benefit of that state's lenient usury law. Did South Dakota thereby obtain a "substantial relationship" to all of Citibank's credit card contracts? What if, without relocating, Citibank simply opened a branch office in South Dakota for the processing of credit card applications? What if a contract between two New Yorkers to be performed in New York is signed in South Dakota in the hope of avoiding New York's usury law?

Under what circumstances may the parties under § 187 select the law of a state that has no connection with the contract? Comment f gives the example of parties contracting in a country whose legal system is unfamiliar to them and relatively immature. In this situation there is a "reasonable basis" for the choice of an unrelated law "on the ground that [the parties] know it well and that it is sufficiently developed." Does that mean that New York or English law is always appropriate?

Section 187(2)(b) further restricts party autonomy, prohibiting the choice of a law that is contrary to a "fundamental policy" of the state whose law would otherwise apply. What does that mean? Restatement (Second) of Conflict of Laws § 187 explains in comment g:

> To be "fundamental," a policy must in any event be a substantial one. Except perhaps in the case of contracts relating to wills, a policy of this sort will rarely be found in a requirement, such as the statute of frauds, that relates to formalities. . . Nor is such policy likely to be represented by a rule tending to become obsolete, such as a rule concerned with the capacity of married women . . . , or by general rules of contract law, such as those

> concerned with the need for consideration. . . On the other hand, a fundamental policy may be embodied in a statute which makes one or more kinds of contracts illegal or which is designed to protect a person against the oppressive use of superior bargaining power. . . To be "fundamental" within the meaning of the present rule, a policy need not be as strong as would be required to justify the forum in refusing to entertain suit upon a foreign cause of action.

Do you agree with the comment's conclusions as to which policies are "fundamental"? What does this exception do to the arguments of certainty and ease of application that underlie the party autonomy rule?

(7) Professor Juenger espouses a more extreme form of party autonomy, criticizing scholars on both sides of the existing debate for assuming that the applicable law must emanate from a sovereign state. According to Juenger, parties should be free to select rules that reflect commercial practice and the "best law," without regard for the desires of any particular sovereign or sovereigns. He supports this version of party autonomy by citing the old "law merchant," a body of "transcendental" principles used in the early modern era. Observing that a modern "law merchant" has already begun to emerge in transnational cases through the use of international arbitration, he urges states to abandon outdated ideas of sovereignty and to permit parties to make their own law. Juenger, *American Conflicts Scholarship and the New Law Merchant,* 28 Vand.J.Transnat'l L. 487 (1995). See also O'Hara & Ribstein, The Law Market (2009) (arguing for broad party autonomy). Does this make sense? Can you reconcile such an approach with modern understandings of law and of when or why parties are allowed to develop their own substantive rules? By allowing some room for party autonomy, have states forfeited their sovereignty?

Something like Juenger's approach found expression in the ALI's unsuccessful revision to the UCC, discussed in Section 1 of this chapter. Why do you think enacting states rejected it? For commentary, see *The Internationalization of Contractual Conflicts Law,* 28 Vand.J.Transnat'l L. 421 (1995) (including an appendix with an exchange of letters between Professors Juenger and Kramer); Woodward, *Contractual Choice of Law: Legislative Choice in an Era of Party Autonomy,* 54 S.M.U. L. Rev. 697 (2001) (discussing proposed UCC revisions).

(8) What happens if the parties fail to choose an applicable law? At one point in its rather confusing opinion, the *Pritchard* Court implies that whichever law upholds the contract governs, quoting Phillimore to the effect that parties to a contract "cannot be presumed to have contemplated a law that would defeat their engagements." This approach is illustrated in *Seeman v. Philadelphia Warehouse Co.,* 274 U.S. 403 (1927). The

Warehouse Co. lent money or credit by giving borrowers a note payable to its order; in return, the borrower had to repay the note with interest and an additional 3% "commission." The Warehouse Co. sued to recover a quantity of canned salmon that had been pledged as security for one of its notes. The defendant, an innocent purchaser from the original debtor, defended on the ground that the note had been issued in New York and that its terms were usurious under New York law. The court of appeals found that the contract had been made in Pennsylvania, where it was lawful. The Supreme Court held that the question where the note was issued was "immaterial" because "a policy of upholding contractual obligations assumed in good faith" required application of the law permitting the higher interest rate.

The Second Restatement endorses this approach in usury cases, providing in § 203 that:

> The validity of a contract will be sustained against the charge of usury if it provides for a rate of interest that is permissible in a state to which the contract has a substantial relationship and is not greatly in excess of the rate permitted by the general usury law of the state of the otherwise applicable law under the rule of § 188.

Note that this provision is an exception to the usual Second Restatement rule that, in the absence of an effective choice by the parties, the court should apply the law of the state with the "most significant relationship." See supra note (3).

(9) Does the principle underlying the usury cases have broader significance? According to the Second Restatement, the usury rule rests on the belief that "the parties will expect on entering a contract that the provisions of the contract will be binding upon them." Restatement (Second) of Conflict of Laws § 203 comment b (1971). A number of commentators point out that this assumption is generally applicable and argue that, rather than party autonomy, courts should adopt a "rule of validation" and apply whichever law upholds a contract (subject to exceptions like those that limit party autonomy). See, e.g., A. Ehrenzweig, A Treatise on the Conflict of Laws 465–90 (1962); R. Weintraub, Commentary on the Conflict of Laws § 7.4 (4th ed. 2001); Lorenzen, *Validity and Effects of Contracts in the Conflict of Laws,* 30 Yale L.J. 655, 673 (1921). Professor Weintraub explains:

> The party autonomy rule . . . reflects a legitimate concern for facilitating the planning of interstate and international commercial transactions. This purpose is also served by a rebuttable presumption that the contract will be valid under the local law of any contact state provided that the validating policies underlying that law will be advanced by application to the

> transaction in issue. This presumption gives the parties the benefits that they would receive under a party autonomy rule except a rule . . . which permits a choice of the law of an unconnected jurisdiction to validate. The presumption of validity does not limit the search for validating law to a single state named in a choice-of-law clause and focuses on a policy that all states share—making commercial transactions convenient and reliable by enforcing commercial contracts in the absence of compelling countervailing considerations articulated in a particular invalidating rule.

R. Weintraub, Commentary on the Conflict of Laws 542 (6th ed. 2010).

(10) Apart from statutes validating foreign executed wills, see supra pp. 97–98, the rule of validation is seldom used. Does the rule of validation ever make sense when it leads to a law different from that chosen by the parties in their contract? The implicit assumption must be that the choice of an invalidating law is inadvertent. Is that always true? Is it true often enough to justify this rule? Consider the following:

> Certainly there are cases where it makes sense to assume that the parties did not mean to choose an invalidating law. The assumption seems reasonable, for example, when the ground for holding the agreement unenforceable was apparent when the contract was made, such as a failure to comply with proper formalities. But this will not always be the case. The parties' mistake may have been in adding the substantive provision that renders the contract invalid under the chosen law. Boilerplate, after all, is not limited to choice of law clauses. Moreover, the assumption that the choice of an invalidating law was inadvertent makes no sense at all when the dispute turns on facts that were not apparent when the contract was made, such as cases concerning the invalidity of an oral modification. On the contrary, a law that precludes enforcement may be precisely what the parties bargained for in such cases.
>
> Thus, there is no a priori reason to conclude that the rule of validation reflects the parties' "true" intentions better than the choice made explicitly in the contract. The court could engage in case-by-case analysis to determine when the choice of an invalidating law was deliberate. But that would defeat the chief reason for adopting either of these rules, which is to provide certainty and predictability. For just this reason, the usual approach to interpreting contracts is to take the parties at their (written) word, and that seems the correct approach here as well. If the parties' choice does inadvertently defeat their contract, they have only themselves to blame.

> On the other hand, the intuition behind the rule of validation—that parties ordinarily intend to make enforceable agreements—makes sense when there is nothing in the contract to the contrary.

Kramer, *Rethinking Choice of Law,* 90 Colum.L.Rev. 277, 332 (1990). Does this argument exaggerate the likelihood that an invalidating choice of law was deliberate? Even if it does, are you convinced that a state that embraces a policy against enforcement of a specific kind of agreement should resolve choice-of-law problems in favor of a general policy of upholding private arrangements?

(11) Party autonomy has become increasingly popular as a solution to choice-of-law problems in consensual transactions. The principle was given a boost by a series of Supreme Court decisions upholding contractual choice-of-forum provisions. In *M/S Bremen v. Zapata Off-Shore Co.,* 407 U.S. 1 (1972), and *Scherk v. Alberto-Culver Co.,* 417 U.S. 506 (1974), the Court enforced choice-of-forum clauses that were the result of arms-length bargaining, arguing that this would help to achieve predictability in international business transactions. But does the Court's most recent decision in this field suggest that it may be possible to have too much of a good thing? In *Carnival Cruise Lines, Inc. v. Shute,* 499 U.S. 585 (1991), the Shutes purchased tickets in their home state of Washington for an excursion on a cruise ship operated by the defendant. The ticket provided that all disputes arising out of the contract would be litigated in Florida, where the defendant's headquarters was located. Ms. Shute was injured, and the Shutes brought suit in Washington. The Supreme Court enforced the forum selection clause and ordered the suit dismissed: although the contract was not subject to negotiation, the choice-of-forum clause served several desirable ends, such as limiting the fora in which the defendant would have to litigate, making clear in advance where litigation would occur, and reducing the fares to passengers. Florida was not a "remote alien forum," and the inconvenience to the Shutes in having to litigate there was not intolerable. Id. at 592–94.

Several efforts have been made to codify the principle of party autonomy. In addition to the UCC provisions discussed supra pp. 98–100, the American Law Institute has suggested this approach in the context of mass contract actions. ALI, Complex Litigation: Statutory Recommendations and Analysis, § 6.02 (1994). Several states have provided by statute that parties to transactions whose value exceeds a certain threshold may select their law regardless of whether the transaction bears a reasonable relation to the state. See, e.g., N.Y. Gen. Oblig. L. § 5–1401. Outside the contract area, the Second Restatement adopts party autonomy to determine the law governing the validity of testamentary and inter vivos trusts in movables. Restatement (Second) of Conflict of Laws §§ 269–270 (1971).

Consider whether the following three cases strike the right balance between the principle of party autonomy and the policies of the relevant states.

WYATT V. FULRATH

16 N.Y.2d 169, 264 N.Y.S.2d 233, 211 N.E.2d 637 (1965).

BERGAN, JUDGE. The Duke and Duchess of Arion were nationals and domiciliaries of Spain. Neither of them had ever been in New York, but through a long period of political uncertainty in Spain, from 1919 to the end of the Civil War, they sent cash and securities to New York for safekeeping and investment.

Under the law of Spain this was the community property of the spouses. Substantial parts of it were placed with the New York custodians in joint accounts. In establishing or in continuing these accounts, the husband and wife either expressly agreed in writing that the New York law of survivorship would apply or agreed to a written form of survivorship account conformable to New York law.

The husband died in November, 1957; the wife in March, 1959. After the husband's death the wife took control of the property in New York and undertook to dispose of it by a will executed according to New York law and affecting property in New York. . .

This action is by plaintiff as an ancillary administrator in New York of the husband against defendant as executor of the wife's will to establish a claim of title to one half of the property which at the time of the husband's death was held in custody accounts under sole or joint names of the spouses by banks in New York. . . The total value of the property in New York is about $2,275,000. . .

The main issue in the case is whether the law of Spain should be applied to the property placed in New York during the lives of the spouses, in which event only half of the property would have gone to the wife at her husband's death, or the law of New York, in which event all of such jointly held property would have gone to her as survivor. . .

The agreements giving full title to the survivor in the joint accounts were executed either in Spain, or if not there at least not in New York, and were, in any event, executed by persons who were domiciliaries and citizens of Spain. Usually rights flowing from this kind of legal act are governed by the law of the domiciliary jurisdiction * * *.

It is abundantly established in the record that the law of Spain would have prevented either spouse in the circumstances shown here from agreeing that community property go entirely to the survivor on the death of either; but half would go to the survivor and at least two thirds of the remaining half would pass to the heirs of the deceased spouse. Dispositions of property in violation of this prohibition are shown to be void according to Spanish law. . .

But New York has the right to say as a matter of public policy whether it will apply its own rules to property in New York of foreigners who choose to place it here for custody or investment, and to honor or not the formal agreements or suggestions of such owners by which New York law would apply to the property they place here. * * *

It seems preferable that as to property which foreign owners are able to get here physically, and concerning which they request New York law to apply to their respective rights, when it actually gets here, that we should recognize their physical and legal submission of the property to our laws, even though under the laws of their own country a different method of fixing such rights would be pursued. . .

Thus we would at once honor their intentional resort to the protection of our laws and their recognition of the general stability of our Government which may well be deemed inter-related things.

Such a law of conflicts choice seems to be suggested by *Hutchison v. Ross* (262 N.Y. 381, 187 N.E. 65 [1933]) although there are some differences between that case and this. . .

Still the case suggests a direction to our present public policy and, in the course of an examination of great depth into the conflicts problem, Judge Lehman noted: "Physical presence in one jurisdiction is a fact; the maxim [*mobilia sequuntur personam*, or movables follow the person] is only a juristic formula which cannot destroy the fact. . . When the owner of personal property authorizes its removal from his domicile or acquires property elsewhere, he must be deemed to know that his property comes under the protection of, and subject to, the laws of the jurisdiction to which it has been removed, and that appeal may be made to the courts of that jurisdiction for the determination of conflicting rights in such property" (supra, pp. 388–389, 187 N.E. p. 68).

[The court concluded that defendant, the Duchess's executor, was entitled to property, including joint accounts and her separate property, which was transferred to New York during the Duke's lifetime. The court then discussed the treatment of funds transferred from London to New York by the Duchess after her husband's death, and concluded that the disposition of these funds should be governed by English law. With this modification, the lower court was affirmed.]

DESMOND, CHIEF JUDGE (dissenting). Resolution of the dispute as to this property (or any part of it) by any law other than that of Spain, the matrimonial domicile, is utterly incompatible with historic and settled conflict of laws principles and is not justifiable on any ground. No policy ground exists for upsetting the uniform rules and no precedent commands such a result. . .

The majority of this court is throwing overboard not one but three of the oldest and strongest conflict rules: first, that with exceptions not pertinent here the law of the domicile of the owner governs as to the devolution of personal property * * *; second, that the law of the matrimonial domicile controls as to the property and contract rights of husband and wife *inter se* * * *; and third, that whether such personalty is separate or community property is determined by the law of the matrimonial domicile. . .

The directly controlling case in this court is *Matter of Mesa y Hernandez's Estate,* 172 App.Div. 467, 159 N.Y.S. 59, affd. 219 N.Y. 566, 114 N.E. 1069. In *Mesa* the New York courts, in a transfer tax proceeding, had to adjudicate the claim of the widow to a half ownership under the laws of Cuba, the matrimonial domicile (which has a community or property law like that of Spain), of personalty in custody of New York banks. A unanimous Appellate Division, affirmed without opinion by this court, held that "the law of matrimonial domicile governed, not only as to all the rights of the parties to their property in that place, but also as to all personal property everywhere, upon the principle that movables have no situs, or rather that they accompany the person everywhere, while as to immovable property the law *rei sitae* prevails." . . .

Hutchison v. Ross has only the most superficial resemblance to the situation now being examined. Among other differences, the *Hutchison* case dealt with the validity of a conveyance whereas here there was the merest deposit of property for safekeeping in New York—that is, a bailment without change of title. . . *Hutchison v. Ross* involved a situation where not only had title passed to a trustee but application of the foreign law would have destroyed rights of third parties created and acquired in good faith and which merited protection. . .

If the intent of the parties to apply New York law is to control, there was undisputed proof in the *Hutchison* case of such intent, whereas in ours there is no real proof at all. The signing by the Duke and Duchess in Spain of routine joint-account-for-custody agreements on forms supplied by the New York banks is not substantial proof that these people (who had no apparent reason for so doing) were attempting to abrogate as to these items of property the ancient community laws of their country. . . The court below mentioned the difficulties which New York banks would encounter if they had to comply with the laws of other jurisdictions. Such inconvenience there may be, but surely it does not justify repeal of the basic rules without any felt necessity for such abrogation and with no real proof that even the parties themselves ever intended such a result.

MINISTERS AND MISSIONARIES BENEFIT BOARD V. SNOW

26 N.Y.3d 466, 45 N.E.3d 917, 25 N.Y.S.3d 21 (2015).

[Ministers and Missionaries Benefit Board (MMBB), a New York not-for-profit corporation, administered a retirement plan and a death benefit plan. Clark Flesher was enrolled in both plans. He named his then-wife, LeAnn Snow, as his primary beneficiary and her father, Leon Snow, as the contingent beneficiary. Both plans stated that they "shall be governed by and construed in accordance with the laws of the State of New York."

After divorcing, Flesher moved to Colorado in 2010 and died there in 2011. A Colorado court admitted his will to probate. Despite the divorce, Flesher never changed his beneficiary designations. Because MMBB was unsure to whom the plan benefits should be paid after Flesher's death, it filed a federal interpleader action. The New York Court of Appeals took the case on a certified question.]

Stein, J. The retirement and death benefit plans here each state that they "shall be governed by and construed in accordance with the laws of the State of New York." The . . . certified question essentially asks us how to interpret the phrase "laws of . . . New York" in those contractual provisions.

We begin with the basic premises that courts will generally enforce choice-of-law clauses and that contracts should be interpreted so as to effectuate the parties' intent. In a case based on New York law, the United States Supreme Court held that a choice-of-law provision in a contract "may reasonably be read as merely a substitute for the conflict-of-laws analysis that otherwise would determine what law to apply to disputes arising out of the contractual relationship." *Mastrobuono v. Shearson Lehman Hutton, Inc.*, 514 U.S. 52, 59 (1995). Thus, the parties here agree that, pursuant to the choice-of-law provisions in the MMBB plans, the contracts will be governed only by New York's substantive law, not by New York's common-law conflict-of-laws rules.

Nevertheless, we must decide whether the New York law to be applied includes a New York statutory choice-of-law directive, such as EPTL 3–5.1(b)(2). That statute provides that "[t]he intrinsic validity, effect, revocation or alteration of a testamentary disposition of personal property, and the manner in which such property devolves when not disposed of by will, are determined by the law of the jurisdiction in which the decedent was domiciled at death." The question is whether section 3–5.1(b)(2) should be characterized as part of New York's substantive or "local law," which the contracting parties intended to apply, or whether it is simply a conflict-of-laws rule, which they did not intend to apply. The answer to this question is crucial here because the recipients of the MMBB plan benefits will be different depending on whether courts apply the law of New York or the law of Colorado.

[Under] New York's purely substantive law, Flesher's designation of LeAnn Snow as a beneficiary of the plans was revoked upon their divorce in 2008, while the designation of Leon Snow as contingent beneficiary remained in effect. . . In contrast, the relevant Colorado statute provides that a divorce acts to revoke any dispositions or appointments by the divorced person to his or her former spouse and to relatives of the former spouse (*see* Colo Rev Stat § 15–11–804[2]). . . . Because Leon Snow, as the father of LeAnn Snow, falls within the definition of a "[r]elative of the divorced individual's former spouse" in relation to Flesher, under Colorado law, the divorce revoked the designations of both LeAnn Snow and Leon Snow as beneficiaries of the MMBB plans.

The Second Circuit concluded that this case presented a close question based, in part, on this Court's recent decision in *IRB-Brasil Resseguros, S.A.*, 20 N.Y.3d 310, 958 N.Y.S.2d 689, 982 N.E.2d 609. There, we decided that the need for a conflict-of-laws analysis is obviated by a contract, made pursuant to General Obligations Law § 5–1401, that contains a New York choice-of-law clause. . . . We reasoned that, "[t]o find . . . that courts must engage in a conflict-of-laws analysis despite the parties' plainly expressed desire to apply New York law would frustrate the Legislature's purpose of encouraging a predictable contractual choice of New York commercial law and, crucially, of eliminating uncertainty regarding the governing law." Significantly, this Court noted that the Restatement (Second) of Conflict of Laws § 187(3) supports the same result. Section 187(3) provides that, in the absence of an expressed contrary intention, references to the law of a state chosen by the parties means the "local law" of that state, which is defined elsewhere in the Restatement as the chosen state's "body of standards, principles and rules, *exclusive* of its rules of Conflict of Laws, which the courts of that state apply in the decision of controversies brought before them" (emphasis added). . . .

Although *IRB* concerned only common-law conflict-of-laws principles, whereas EPTL 3–5.1(b)(2) is a statutory choice-of-law directive, the latter is merely a codification of a longstanding common-law conflict-of-laws principle, eventually placed within the EPTL because it corresponds to that general area of law. . . . Although codification may be an indication that the legislature attaches some importance to the rule, EPTL 3–5.1(b)(2) nevertheless remains, in its essence, a conflict-of-laws rule, rather than a statement of substantive law. . . .

While *IRB* does not entirely answer the current question because that case does not address the applicability of a statutory choice-of-law directive, logic dictates that, by including a choice-of-law provision in their contracts, the parties intended for only New York substantive law to apply. A contrary interpretation is conceivable. However, we should apply the most reasonable interpretation of the contract language that effectuates the parties' intended and expressed choice of law. To do otherwise—by applying New York's statutory conflict-of-laws principles, even if doing so results in the application of the substantive law of another state—would contravene the primary purpose of including a choice-of-law provision in a contract—namely, to avoid a conflict-of-laws analysis and its associated time and expense. Such an interpretation would also interfere with, and ignore, the parties' intent, contrary to the basic tenets of contract interpretation. . . .

Therefore, we hold that, when parties include a choice-of-law provision in a contract, they intend that the law of the chosen state—and no other state—will be applied. In such a situation, the chosen state's substantive law—but not its common-law conflict-of-laws principles or statutory choice-of-law directives—is to be applied, unless the parties expressly indicate otherwise.

ABDUS-SALAAM, J. (dissenting), [joined by RIVERA, J.]. When is a duly enacted law of the State of New York not part of "the laws of the State of New York"? One would think that the answer is never. But the majority disagrees. In the majority's estimation, a law passed by New York elected representatives is not part of the "laws of the State of New York" if those legislators modeled the statute on a common-law rule specifying a particular jurisdiction's laws as controlling the disposition of a person's property upon death. . . .

The principle that a contractual governing-law provision generally precludes a common-law choice-of-law analysis has never been extended to eliminate the application of a statutory choice-of-law directive, which otherwise would be the applicable local and substantive law of the State (*see* Restatement [Second] of Conflict of Laws § 4[1]). In fact, as we explained in *IRB-Brasil Resseguros, S.A.*, the parties' choice of New York law does not remove a contract from the ambit of "[l]ocal law," and because such local law includes New York's substantive "body of standards, principles and rules," New York statutory standards, principles and rules logically govern a contract that deems the State's law to be controlling.

In that vein, there is ample authority demonstrating that a New York statute embodies the State's substantive policy, which we cannot readily presume to have been cast aside by a contractual governing-law provision. New York courts have held that where a conflict arises between the provisions of a statute and the terms of a contract, the statute typically controls because it is the binding substantive policy determination of the legislature, though a statutory right may be waived expressly or by unequivocal and necessary implication. Additional authority for a statute's role as the substantive local law of a state can be found in the Restatement (Second) of Conflict of Laws, which declares that "[a] court, subject to constitutional restrictions, *will follow* a statutory directive of its own state on choice of law" (Restatement [Second] of Conflict of Laws § 6[1] [emphasis added]). Thus, unlike the common-law conflict rules at issue in *IRB-Brasil Resseguros, S.A.* and similar cases, statutory rules make up the substantive law of the state and cannot be easily or presumptively dispensed with by contrary provisions of a contract; indeed, in some instances, it is impossible for contracting parties to avoid the application of a state statute, even where they clearly and expressly agree to do so. It follows that, where, as here, the parties have agreed to apply the substantive law of New York, they presumably have agreed to eliminate common-law choice-of-law rules that are inconsistent with their definitive choice of law under the contract, but they have not clearly manifested an intent to waive application of statutory choice-of-law directives such as EPTL 3–5.1(b)(2), which form part of the very substantive law that the parties have opted to apply. . . .

COTTER V. LYFT, INC.

60 F.Supp.3d 1059 (N.D. Cal. 2014).

CHHABRIA, DISTRICT JUDGE. Patrick Cotter and Alejandra Maciel, two former drivers for Lyft, Inc., bring this putative nationwide class action against Lyft under California's wage and hour laws. Specifically, the plaintiffs allege that: (i) California law requires Lyft to treat all drivers throughout the nation as employees rather than independent contractors; and (ii) because Lyft classifies and pays these drivers as independent contractors, it is depriving them of California's minimum wage, along with other rights that California law confers upon employees. . . .

The plaintiffs argue that California's connection with the claims brought on behalf of the drivers who work in other states is sufficient to justify application of California wage and hour law to those claims. In particular, the plaintiffs allege that Lyft's principal place of business is in California, that its decision to classify drivers as independent contractors was made in California, and that its decision to implement the "administrative fee" that the plaintiffs challenge was made in California. They contend that because of these connections, California wage and hour laws can potentially apply to work performed by drivers exclusively in other states, and the only thing that might bar the application of those laws is if they if conflict with the law of the drivers' home states. Therefore, the plaintiffs argue, they may bring claims on behalf of a nationwide class under California law unless Lyft demonstrates that another state has a greater interest in applying its own law. And the plaintiffs contend that because California's laws are more worker-protective than those of other states, Lyft will be unable to show that the other states have a greater interest in applying their own laws.

There are several problems with this argument. As a preliminary matter, the plaintiffs are wrong that California's wage and hour laws are the most worker-protective. Washington and Oregon, for example, both have higher minimum wages than California. Therefore, pursuit of claims under California law on behalf of people in those states appears against their interest. Moreover, even if California law were most protective of workers, each state has the right (subject to federal law, of course) to regulate the work performed within its own borders without regard to another state's approach to regulating the employer-employee relationship. But most importantly, by jumping straight to a conflict of laws analysis, the plaintiffs skip an important analytical step. A court conducts a conflict of laws analysis only where the laws of multiple states could conceivably apply to the same claim. Where only one state's law applies, no such analysis is necessary. And as explained below, the California wage and hour laws asserted here simply do not apply to employees who work exclusively in another state. Therefore, regardless of the connection between Lyft and California, Lyft drivers who worked in other states cannot bring claims under California's wage and hour statutes.

State statutes are presumed not to have extraterritorial effect. *See, e.g., North Alaska Salmon Co. v. Pillsbury,* 174 Cal. 1 (1916). . . . In *North Alaska Salmon Co.,* the California Supreme Court considered whether a worker injured outside of California could seek compensation under the state's workers' compensation statute. . . . The statute contained nothing about "the place of injury," nor did it contain any other "language from which the intention to extend [its] operation . . . beyond the territorial limits of the state [could] be inferred." *Id.* at 4–5. Therefore, the Court held, the statute was limited to injuries that occurred within California.

More recently, California's Supreme Court has explained that an employee may be understood to be a "wage earner of California," and therefore subject to the state's wage orders, if the "employee resides in California, receives pay in California, and works exclusively, or principally, in California." *Tidewater Marine W., Inc. v. Bradshaw,* 927 P.2d 296 (1996). The Court left open the possibility that the state's wage orders—and, presumably, other labor provisions—"may" be enforced outside of California "in limited circumstances, such as when California residents working for a California employer travel temporarily outside the state during the course of the normal workday but return to California at the end of the day." *Id.* But there is no hint that the wage and hour laws could apply to people who work exclusively in other states.

And in *Sullivan v. Oracle Corp.,* 254 P.3d 237 (2011), the California Supreme Court considered and rejected an argument similar to the one the plaintiffs make here—that because the company was based in California and because decisions about the workers' employment status were made in California, California law should govern the employer-employee relationship. Rather than focusing on the location of the company or its decisionmakers, the Court focused on the location of the work. The Court held that the California Labor Code applies to overtime work "performed in California," but that California law did not, at least on the facts of that case, "apply to overtime work performed outside California for a California-based employer by out-of-state plaintiffs."

Beyond these cases, the idea that the wage and hour provisions do not apply to people who perform work exclusively in other states finds support in the provisions themselves. For example, the California Labor Code directs the Industrial Welfare Commission "to ascertain the wages paid to all employees *in this state,* to ascertain the hours and conditions of labor and employment in the various occupations, trades, and industries in which employees are employed *in this state,* and to investigate the health, safety, and welfare of those employees." Cal. Lab. Code § 1173 (emphasis added). And "[o]ne of the functions of the Department of Industrial Relations is to foster, promote, and develop the welfare of the *wage earners of California.*" *Id.* § 50.5 (emphasis added). Conversely, where the legislature has intended a Labor Code provision to apply to a broader range of people, it has said so explicitly. The current workers' compensation statute, for example, applies to certain accidents that occur "outside of this state" and characterizes this application as "extraterritorial." Cal. Lab. Code § 3600.5.

Here, the plaintiffs propose to represent class members who are residents of other states, who drive for Lyft exclusively in those states, and who apparently never set foot in California in furtherance of their work with the company. The California wage and hour laws at issue here do not create a cause of action for people who fit this description, even if they work for a California-based company that makes all employment-related decisions in California.

The opposite conclusion would raise serious constitutional concerns. "The Commerce Clause . . . precludes the application of a state statute to commerce that takes place wholly outside of the State's borders, whether or not the commerce has effects within the State." *Edgar v. MITE Corp.,* 457 U.S. 624, 642–43 (1982); *see also Healy v. Beer Inst., Inc.,* 491 U.S. 324, 336 (1989) ("[A] statute that directly controls commerce occurring wholly outside the boundaries of a State exceeds the inherent limits of the enacting State's authority and is invalid. The critical inquiry is whether the practical effect of the regulation is to control conduct beyond the boundaries of the State."). The compensation of nonresidents who work exclusively outside the state would seem to constitute "commerce that takes place wholly outside of [California's] borders." Whether California may constitutionally regulate this compensation is therefore, at best, a difficult question. Although the wage and hour laws themselves are clear that they do not apply to work performed exclusively outside the state, these constitutional concerns cement that conclusion.

The plaintiffs argue that even if California does not directly provide a statutory cause of action for drivers outside the state, these drivers may bring claims under the state's Labor Code because the contract between Lyft and its drivers contains a California choice of law provision. That provision states: "This agreement shall be governed by the laws of the State of California without regard to choice-of-law principles."

This argument conflates statutory claims that exist independent of the contract with claims that arise from the agreement itself. California's labor laws "are part of a broad regulatory policy defining the obligations" of employers "*without regard to* the substance of [their] contractual obligations." *Narayan v. EGL, Inc.*, 616 F.3d 895, 897 (9th Cir. 2010) (emphasis added); *see also id.* ("[S]tatutes enacted to confer special benefits on workers are designed to defeat rather than implement contractual arrangements."). Although the agreement "will likely be used as evidence" to support their statutory claims, their "claims do not arise out of the contract, involve the interpretation of any contract terms, or otherwise require there to be a contract" in the first place. *Narayan,* 616 F.3d at 899. The choice of law provision governing the agreement is therefore inapplicable to the plaintiffs' wage and hour claims.

Even if the choice of law provision were intended to confer upon out-of-state drivers a cause of action for violation of California's wage and hour laws, it could not do so. An employee cannot create by contract a cause of action that California law does not provide. "When a law contains geographical limitations on its application, . . . courts will not apply it to parties falling outside those limitations, even if the parties stipulate that the law should apply." *Gravquick A/S v. Trimble Navigation Int'l Ltd.,* 323 F.3d 1219, 1223 (9th Cir. 2003). California wage and hour law contains such a limitation: It does not apply extraterritorially. Parties cannot, by contract, extend its reach.

The Ninth Circuit's decision in *Gravquick* is not to the contrary. In that case, the parties entered into a distribution contract that was to "be governed and construed under the laws of the State of California." When the defendant—a California manufacturer—refused to renew the agreement, the plaintiff—a Danish distributor—sued, alleging that the refusal violated the California Equipment Dealer's Act. Although the parties agreed that their distribution agreement fell "within the literal terms" of the Act, they disagreed about whether the statute "contains unstated geographical limitations that," despite the choice of law provision, would "prevent its application" to non-California distributors. *See id.* at 1222. The Ninth Circuit held that it did not. Therefore, the Court reasoned, the California choice of law provision could be applied to govern the plaintiff's claims.

Thus, as with their argument that the mere connection between Lyft and California allows the application of California law to work performed elsewhere, the plaintiffs skip a preliminary analytical step in arguing that the choice of law provision should apply here. When companies from different states enter into a distribution agreement where goods are transported between states, they may, to avoid future confusion, specify which state's law applies to the transaction, since both laws could potentially apply. And in this case, it made sense for the parties to identify which state's law applies to interpretation of the contract itself, because the parties who entered into that contract are from different states (Lyft being from California and the driver being from elsewhere), meaning that the contract law of either state could apply. But with respect to the employer-employee relationship relating to work performed exclusively in one state, only the law of that state can apply, which means a choice of law provision has no application in this context.

This is not to say the drivers could never have entered into a contract with Lyft that would have imposed substantive obligations similar to the ones California imposes for work performed inside its borders. For example, there would presumably be nothing wrong with a contractual provision that stated, "Lyft agrees to pay its drivers an amount equal to California's minimum wage" (at least where the relevant drivers work in a jurisdiction with a lower minimum wage than California's). Lyft would then have a contractual obligation to pay its drivers that amount. But it would be a contractual obligation, not a statutory one, and failure to pay the prescribed amount would give rise to a breach of contract claim. In this case the parties did not adopt contractual provisions borrowing California's substantive rules regarding wages and the employer-employee relationship. Instead, even if the plaintiffs were correct about the intended meaning of the choice of law provision, the most that can be said is that the parties attempted to give the drivers the ability to sue Lyft under California wage and hour law. But because California's wage and hour provisions do not create a cause of action for work performed exclusively outside the state, and because parties cannot create a cause of action under the wage and hour statutes where none exists, the plaintiffs cannot seek to enforce those provisions on behalf of a nationwide class.

---

(1) In *Wyatt*, which is more important to the court's conclusion that New York's law applies, the fact that the Duke and Duchess apparently chose New York law, or the brute fact that their property is now in New York? As to the former, is it significant that the parties seem to have simply established a "survivorship account conformable to New York law" on a boilerplate form provided by a New York bank—a type of account that Spanish law prohibits? As to the latter, why should the physical presence of the property in New York be enough to overcome Spain's interest in disposing of its domiciliaries' assets? Should the court have assessed the relative strength of the states' interests?

(2) In 1966, shortly after the *Wyatt* decision, New York adopted Estates, Powers and Trusts Law § 3–5.1. Section h provides that when a testator domiciled outside the state "elects to have the disposition of his property situated in this state governed by the laws of this state," the validity of that choice is to be decided under New York internal law. In *Estate of Renard*, 56 N.Y.2d 973, 453 N.Y.S.2d 625, 439 N.E.2d 341 (1982), the Court of Appeals affirmed without opinion a decision of the Surrogate's Court (reported at 108 Misc.2d 31, 437 N.Y.S.2d 860) holding that a woman who had lived in New York for 30 years but died domiciled in France could select New York law to govern the descent of bank and brokerage accounts located in New York, thereby depriving her son of the one-half forced share granted him by French law. While reading EPTL § 3–5.1(h) as a blanket authorization of the selection of New York internal law to govern the descent of New York property, the Surrogate also reasoned that New York had the "paramount interest" based on decedent's long New York residence and the fact that the son was not a French resident. Chief Judge Cooke dissented from the Court of Appeals judgment. Is there any connection between the party autonomy rationale and the analysis of the different jurisdictions' interests?

(3) The 1966 amendments to EPTL § 3–5.1 are also at issue in *Ministers and Missionaries*. What is the basis for the majority's conclusion that § 3–5.1(b)(2) is "merely a codification of a longstanding common-law conflict-of-laws principle"? The dissent undertook a lengthy analysis of the text and legislative history of the 1966 amendments, concluding that § 3–5.1 "is not a reflexive or inconsequential repetition of a common-law conflict principle that might be readily waived sub silentio by parties to a contract, but instead represents the legislature's considered judgment to keep some aspects of the common law constant while simultaneously modifying others." 26 N.Y.3d 466, 486 (Abdus-Salaam, J., dissenting). The dissenting judge also cites the Second Restatement's directive, in § 6(1), that a "court, subject to constitutional restrictions, will follow a statutory directive of its own state on choice of law"—but is she selling short the same Restatement's § 187, which gives the parties broad autonomy to choose the governing law?

The majority reasons that MMBB would want certainty and predictability in benefit distribution, rather than having its contracts enforced in different ways depending on where its policyholders—many of whom are itinerant ministers and missionaries—might relocate. By contrast, the dissent notes that "the parties to a death benefit contract would ordinarily expect that, regardless of which state's law they choose, they will be subject to the rule that the law of the state of domicile determines the recipients of personal property upon the owner's death." 26 N.Y.3d 466, 487 (Abdus-Salaam, J., dissenting). Which side is right? Or are these concerns about the parties' expectations misplaced, given that they explicitly chose New York law?

(4) The question whether the parties' reference to "the laws of the State of New York" includes that state's choice-of-law rules is a version of the renvoi problem. For more on this problem, see infra Section 6.B.

(5) The draft Third Restatement cites *Cotter v. Lyft, Inc.*, among other cases, for the proposition that "the parties' selection of a state's law does not allow them to extend that law beyond its specified scope." Restatement (Third) of Conflict of Laws, Tentative Draft No. 2, Reporters' Notes at 33 (2021). The basic issue here is whether a limit on the geographic scope of a statute is part of its content, akin to a limit to employers with 15 or more employees, or whether it is a choice-of-law rule that can be overridden by party choice (and ignored by the courts of other states). Were you persuaded by that California's wage and hour laws do not reach out-of-state drivers, even if the parties choose to submit to them? Is there a meaningful difference for purposes of this case between a contract that says "This agreement shall be governed by the laws of the State of California without regard to choice-of-law principles" and one that says "Lyft agrees to pay its drivers an amount equal to California's minimum wage"? It is true, as the court points out, that the former gives rise to a statutory claim and the latter to a contract claim, but once the parties have chosen California law, should the viability of the statutory claim be limited by a presumption against extraterritorial effect? Would recognizing a statutory claim entitle parties to invoke state administrative enforcement mechanisms and give them access to specialized tribunals? (Would a contract selecting federal law create federal question jurisdiction?) How would *Cotter* be decided under § 187 of the Second Restatement?

(6) The European Union has also favored party autonomy for contracts in the Rome I Regulations and for tort liability in the Rome II Conventions; for a discussion of these enactments, see infra Chapter 8, Section 2.

SECTION 3. INTEREST ANALYSIS

A. INTRODUCTION

CHESNY V. MAREK

720 F.2d 474 (7th Cir.1983).

POSNER, CIRCUIT JUDGE. Rule 68 of the Federal Rules of Civil Procedure allows a defendant, up to 10 days before the trial begins, to "serve upon the adverse party an offer to allow judgment to be taken against him for the money or property or to the effect specified in his offer, with costs then accrued." If the offer is rejected and "the judgment finally obtained by the offeree is not more favorable than the offer, the offeree must pay the costs incurred after the making of the offer." Little known and little used * * *, Rule 68 has attracted attention recently as part of a broader interest in limiting the number of federal trials at a time of rising costs of litigation and unprecedented federal caseloads.

This case, a civil rights suit under 42 U.S.C. § 1983, involves the interplay between Rule 68 and statutes that allow a prevailing plaintiff to get his attorney's fees reimbursed by the defendant, specifically the Civil Rights Attorney's Fees Awards Act of 1976, 42 U.S.C. § 1988. The Act provides that in a civil rights case the district "court, in its discretion, may allow the prevailing party . . . a reasonable attorney's fee as part of the costs." Though no explicit distinction is made between plaintiffs and defendants, the Supreme Court has interpreted the statute as creating a presumption in favor of awarding fees to a prevailing plaintiff, * * * but as not allowing a prevailing defendant to get his attorney's fees reimbursed unless the suit was frivolous * * *.

The defendants in this case made a timely Rule 68 offer "for a sum, including costs now accrued and attorney's fees, of ONE HUNDRED THOUSAND ($100,000) DOLLARS." We must decide whether an offer that included attorney's fees is valid under the rule, and if so whether the rejection of a valid Rule 68 offer more favorable than the judgment the plaintiff finally obtains prevents the plaintiff from getting an award of attorney's fees for any work done after the offer was made. . .

It is undisputed that if the offer was valid and more favorable than the judgment, the plaintiff cannot recover any of the usual taxable costs—filing fees and the like (see 28 U.S.C. § 1920)—that accrued after the offer was made; but these we are told are no more than $1000. The dispute is over whether "costs" in Rule 68 includes attorney's fees where a statute allows attorney's fees to be taxed as costs recoverable by the prevailing party.

The district court's conclusion that it does rests on the following rather mechanical linking up of Rule 68 and section 1988. Since this is a civil rights case, since Rule 68 refers to costs, and since section 1988 allows attorney's fees to be taxed as costs in civil rights cases, Rule 68 costs must include any section 1988 attorney's fees that might be awarded to the prevailing plaintiff. If, therefore, the plaintiff rejects a valid Rule 68 offer and later gets a less favorable judgment, he cannot make the defendant pay him any of his attorney's fees that accrued after the date of the offer.

This approach, though in a sense logical, puts Rule 68 into conflict with the policy behind section 1988. Section 1988 was intended to encourage the bringing of meritorious civil rights actions, such as the present action, which resulted in a judgment for the plaintiff of $60,000 for the death of his decedent at the hands of the three police officers who are the defendants. * * * The effectiveness of section 1988 would be reduced if the rejection of a Rule 68 offer that turned out to be more favorable than the judgment the plaintiff eventually received prevented the plaintiff from getting any award of legal fees that accrued after the date of the offer. That would mean in this case that the plaintiff's lawyers would have either to collect an additional fee from the plaintiff, thus reducing his net recovery from the jury's $60,000 damage award, or to swallow the time they put in on the trial. Either way, the next time they are faced with a similar offer they will have to think very hard before rejecting it even if they consider it inadequate, knowing that rejection could cost themselves or their client a lot if it turned out to be a mistake.

Placing civil rights plaintiffs and counsel in this predicament cuts against the grain of section 1988. " '[P]rivate attorneys general' should not be deterred from bringing good faith actions to vindicate the fundamental rights here involved by the prospect of having to pay their opponent's counsel fees should they lose." S.Rep. No. 1011, *supra* at 5, U.S.Code Cong. & Admin.News 1976, p. 5912. By the same token they should not be deterred from bringing good faith actions to vindicate fundamental rights by the prospect of sacrificing all claims to attorney's fees for legal work at the trial if they win, merely because on the eve of trial they turned down what turned out to be a more favorable settlement offer. * * * Moreover, since 10 days before trial is merely the deadline for the offer, if it were made right after the complaint was filed it might deter the plaintiff's lawyers from conducting any pretrial discovery.

The Rules Enabling Act, now 28 U.S.C. § 2072, provides that the Federal Rules of Civil Procedure "shall not abridge, enlarge or modify any substantive right. . ." Although no rule has ever been invalidated under this provision, * * * rules have sometimes been interpreted or their domain of application narrowed to avoid abridging substantive rights. . . Although the right to attorney's fees created by section 1988 is in one sense not "substantive" but "procedural," because it governs the relations between the parties to a lawsuit, in another sense it is more "substantive" than "procedural." It does not make the litigation process more accurate and efficient for both parties; even more clearly than the statute of limitations, * * * it is designed instead to achieve a substantive objective—compliance with the civil rights laws. This makes it more like a right to receive punitive damages (universally regarded as a substantive right) than like a right to take depositions. But no doubt the right is better described as both substantive and procedural, or as substantive for some purposes and procedural for others. * * * For present purposes it is substantive. When Congress authorized the Supreme Court to make rules of procedure for civil cases it did not authorize the Court to alter substantive policies (that is the force of the "shall not abridge" clause), such as those that underlie the right to attorney's fees created by section 1988, call that right what you will. But that is what the Court would (unwittingly) have been doing when it promulgated Rule 68 if the district court's interpretation of the rule were upheld. And the Rules Enabling Act to one side, section 1988 of its own force prevents us from reading "costs" in Rule 68 to include attorney's fees. The legislators who enacted section 1988 would not have wanted its effectiveness blunted because of a little known rule of court promulgated almost 40 years earlier. . .

We thus affirm the fee award insofar as it gave the plaintiff $32,000 for his fees and costs incurred up to the date of the award, but we reverse insofar as the district court denied the plaintiff any award of fees for services beyond that date and we remand the case to the district court to determine a reasonable attorney's fee for those services.

Affirmed in part, reversed in part, and remanded.

MAREK V. CHESNY

473 U.S. 1 (1985).

CHIEF JUSTICE BURGER delivered the opinion of the Court.

We granted certiorari to decide whether attorney's fees incurred by a plaintiff subsequent to an offer of settlement under Federal Rule of Civil Procedure 68 must be paid by the defendant under 42 U.S.C. § 1988, when the plaintiff recovers a judgment less than the offer. . .

[The] question we address is whether the term "costs" in Rule 68 includes attorney's fees awardable under 42 U.S.C. § 1988. [The Court noted that when Rule 68 was adopted in 1938 there were a number of exceptions to the "American rule" that each side must pay its own attorney's fees, most in federal statutes directing courts to award attorney's fees as part of the costs in particular cases.]

The authors of Federal Rule of Civil Procedure 68 were fully aware of these exceptions to the American Rule. The Advisory Committee's Note to Rule 54(d), * * * contains an extensive list of the federal statutes which allowed for costs in particular cases; of the 35 "statutes as to costs" set forth in the final paragraph of the Note, no fewer than 11 allowed for attorney's fees as part of costs. Against this background of varying definitions of "costs," the drafters of Rule 68 did not define the term; nor is there any explanation whatever as to its intended meaning in the history of the Rule.

In this setting, given the importance of "costs" to the Rule, it is very unlikely that this omission was mere oversight; on the contrary, the most reasonable inference is that the term "costs" in Rule 68 was intended to refer to all costs properly awardable under the relevant substantive statute or other authority. In other words, all costs properly awardable in an action are to be considered within the scope of Rule 68 "costs." Thus, absent congressional expressions to the contrary, where the underlying statute defines "costs" to include attorney's fees, we are satisfied such fees are to be included as costs for purposes of Rule 68. * * *

Here respondent sued under 42 U.S.C. § 1983. Pursuant to ... 42 U.S.C. § 1988, a prevailing party in a § 1983 action may be awarded attorney's fees "as part of the costs." Since Congress expressly included attorney's fees as "costs" available to a plaintiff in a § 1983 suit, such fees are subject to the cost-shifting provision of Rule 68. This "plain meaning" interpretation of the interplay between Rule 68 and § 1988 is the only construction that gives meaning to each word in both Rule 68 and § 1988.

Unlike the Court of Appeals, we do not believe that this "plain meaning" construction of the statute and the Rule will frustrate Congress' objective in § 1988 of ensuring that civil rights plaintiffs obtain " 'effective access to the judicial process.' " * * * Merely subjecting civil rights plaintiffs to the settlement provision of Rule 68 does not curtail their access to the courts, or significantly deter them from bringing suit. Application of Rule 68 will serve as a disincentive for the plaintiff's attorney to continue litigation after the defendant makes a settlement offer. There is no evidence, however, that Congress, in considering § 1988, had any thought that civil rights claims were to be on any different footing from other civil claims insofar as settlement is concerned. Indeed, Congress made clear its concern that civil rights plaintiffs not be penalized for "helping to lessen docket congestion" by settling their cases out of court. * * *

Moreover, Rule 68's policy of encouraging settlements is neutral, favoring neither plaintiffs nor defendants; it expresses a clear policy of favoring settlement of all lawsuits. Civil rights plaintiffs—along with other plaintiffs—who reject an offer more favorable than what is thereafter recovered at trial will not recover attorney's fees for services performed after the offer is rejected. But, since the Rule is neutral, many civil rights plaintiffs will benefit from the offers of settlement encouraged by Rule 68. Some plaintiffs will receive compensation in settlement where, on trial, they might not have recovered, or would have recovered less than what was offered. And, even for those who would prevail at trial, settlement will provide them with compensation at an earlier date without the burdens, stress, and time of litigation. In short, settlements rather than litigation will serve the interests of plaintiffs as well as defendants.

To be sure, application of Rule 68 will require plaintiffs to "think very hard" about whether continued litigation is worthwhile; that is precisely what Rule 68 contemplates. This effect of Rule 68, however, is in no sense inconsistent with the congressional policies underlying § 1983 and § 1988. Section 1988 authorizes courts to award only "reasonable" attorney's fees to prevailing parties. * * * In a case where a rejected settlement offer exceeds the ultimate recovery, the plaintiff—although technically the prevailing party—has not received any monetary benefits from the postoffer services of his attorney. This case presents a good example: the $139,692 in postoffer legal services resulted in a recovery $8,000 less than petitioners' settlement offer. Given Congress' focus on the success achieved, we are not persuaded that shifting the postoffer costs to respondent in these circumstances would in any sense thwart its intent under § 1988.

Rather than "cutting against the grain" of § 1988, as the Court of Appeals held, we are convinced that applying Rule 68 in the context of a § 1983 action is consistent with the policies and objectives of § 1988. Section 1988 encourages plaintiffs to bring meritorious civil rights suits; Rule 68 simply encourages settlements. There is nothing incompatible in these two objectives. . .

The judgment of the Court of Appeals is reversed.

[JUSTICES POWELL and REHNQUIST concurred.]

[JUSTICE BRENNAN, with whom JUSTICE MARSHALL and JUSTICE BLACKMUN joined, dissented.]

The Domestic Choice-of-Law Process

(1) Why are these opinions included in a Conflict of Laws casebook? Is there a conflict of laws in *Marek*? How do you decide?

(2) P from New York is injured in a car accident in New York. P sues D, also from New York, alleging that D's negligence was the proximate cause of the accident and requesting $50,000 in damages. So far, there is no conflict of laws. Suppose D answers that P was contributorily negligent. Is there a conflict? Suppose P alleges that the accident took place on the ramp onto I-80, seeking recovery under a New York statute allowing treble damages for accidents "on an interstate highway." What would D argue? Is there a conflict of laws? Suppose D answers that he is a police officer who was acting in the course of duty and that New York limits recovery to $10,000 in such circumstances. Now is there a conflict of laws? How would you decide this last case?

(3) How does Judge Posner resolve the conflict in *Marek*? How does Chief Justice Burger do it? Are you persuaded by his "plain language" argument? Does the Supreme Court's decision depend on this argument? Who do you think has the more persuasive account of the policy behind § 1988? (Legislative history of the Civil Rights Act of 1991 explicitly disapproves of *Marek*, and Congress amended Title VII to provide for the award of fees and costs separately. See 42 U.S.C.A. § 2000e–5(g)(2)(b).)

(4) Consider the following problems:

(a) Plaintiff brings an action under the Sherman Antitrust Act challenging a New York Stock Exchange rule that fixes rates. Price fixing is ordinarily a *per se* violation of the antitrust laws. The exchange defends its rule on the ground that it is permitted by § 19(b) of the Securities Exchange Act. What result? See *Gordon v. New York Stock Exchange,* 422 U.S. 659 (1975) (Securities Exchange Act applies).

(b) The Indian Reorganization Act of 1934 gives an employment preference to qualified Native Americans seeking employment in the Bureau of Indian Affairs. Non-Indian employees challenge the preference under the Equal Employment Opportunity Act of 1972 (which extends Title VII of the Civil Rights Act to public employment). What result? See *Morton v. Mancari,* 417 U.S. 535 (1974) (Indian Reorganization Act applies).

(c) A securities investor sues his broker for failing to disclose material information required by the Securities Act of 1933. The broker moves to dismiss on the ground that the sales agreement requires submitting the dispute to arbitration. Section 3 of the Federal Arbitration Act requires federal courts to enforce such agreements. The plaintiff argues that the arbitration provision is unenforceable under § 14 of the Securities Act, which makes void "[a]ny condition, stipulation, or provision binding any person acquiring any security to waive compliance with any provision" of the Securities Act. What result? Compare *Wilko v. Swan,* 346 U.S. 427 (1953) (Securities Act applies), with *Rodriguez v. Shearson/American Express, Inc.,* 490 U.S. 477 (1989) (overruling *Wilko*).

(5) To what extent is the reasoning process used to identify and resolve domestic conflicts applicable in multistate disputes? Keep this question in mind as you read the following lengthy excerpt.

BRAINERD CURRIE, MARRIED WOMEN'S CONTRACTS: A STUDY IN CONFLICT-OF-LAWS METHOD

25 U.Chi.L.Rev. 227 (1958), reprinted in B. Currie, Selected Essays on the Conflict of Laws ch. 2 (1963).

In 1870 Mrs. Pratt, at her home in Massachusetts, executed a guaranty of her husband's credit in favor of a partnership doing business in Portland, Maine. She delivered the instrument to her husband, who mailed it to the firm in Maine. In reliance on the guaranty, and in response to orders placed by Mr. Pratt, the partnership delivered goods to Mr. Pratt, either in person or by common carrier "for him," Mr. Pratt paying the shipping charges. Upon default, the partners sued Mrs. Pratt in Massachusetts on the guaranty. According to a Maine statute enacted in 1866, a married woman was competent to bind herself by contract as if she were unmarried. According to the law of Massachusetts at the time of the transaction, a married woman could not bind herself by contract as surety or for the accommodation of her husband or of any third person.

Reversing a judgment for the defendant, Mr. Justice Gray, for the Supreme Judicial Court of Massachusetts, announced that "[t]he general rule is that the validity of a contract is to be determined by the law of the state in which it is made. . ." Treating the instrument executed by Mrs. Pratt as an offer for a unilateral contract, and concluding that the offer was accepted when and where the offeree delivered goods to the buyer or to a carrier for him, which was in Maine, the court concluded that Maine law governed and gave the contract validity. . .

Before we begin our discussion of *Milliken v. Pratt,* I should like to change one of the facts. It is evident from the opinion of the court . . . that the change in the Massachusetts law between the time of the transaction and the filing of the suit had a material influence on the decision. . . I should therefore like to assume that, shortly prior to 1870, a bill was introduced in the Massachusetts General Assembly for the enactment of a law similar to that enacted in Maine in 1866, removing the contractual disabilities of married women; that the issue was fully debated; that the proposal was defeated by a decisive though by no means overwhelming majority; and that the explicit reason for its defeat was the only one even remotely intelligible in modern times: that (in the judgment of the majority of the General Assembly) married women as a class are a peculiarly susceptible lot, prone to make improvident promises, especially under the influence of their husbands. We thus assume that by its negative action the General Assembly in effect gave deliberate approval to the existing rule: that no contract whereby any married woman might undertake to assume liability as a surety should subject her to judgment in any court.

Lawgivers, legislative and judicial, are accustomed to speak in terms of unqualified generality. Apart from the imperatives, the words most inevitably found in rules of law are words like "all," "every," "no," "any," and "whoever." . . . [I]n a great many cases it is quite obvious that the lawgivers do not mean all that they say. Suppose, for example, that we could buttonhole in the statehouse corridor the personification of the Massachusetts General Assembly and ask, "Now, really, do you mean to say that, if a married woman living in Maine should execute in Maine a guaranty of her husband's obligation to a Maine creditor, a Maine court could not or should not enter judgment on the guaranty against her?" There is no doubt at all what the startled, condescending reply would be: "Certainly not. What Maine courts do in actions between Maine parties arising out of Maine transactions is no affair of mine. Massachusetts problems are more than enough to keep me busy, thank you."

The important reason why lawgivers speak in such extravagantly general terms is that they ordinarily give no thought to the phenomena that would suggest the need for qualification. When the Massachusetts legislature addresses itself to the problem of married women as sureties, the undeveloped image in its mind is that of Massachusetts married women, husbands, creditors, transactions, courts, and judgments. In the history of Anglo-American law the domestic case has been normal, the conflict-of-laws case marginal. Probably this is still true, despite the much-publicized mobility of modern society. . .

Marginal or not, however, the conflict-of-laws case must be dealt with when it arises, if not before; and between the wholly domestic case visualized by the Massachusetts legislature and the wholly foreign case posed by our impertinent question lies an unimagined range of mixed configurations, each of them, however rare in actual occurrence, a conflict-of-laws case by definition. It may be interesting and even instructive to enumerate these cases in detail. . .

[I]n a case like *Milliken v. Pratt* there are just four factors that may be significant for our purposes:

1. The domicile, or nationality, or residence, or place of business of the creditor;

2. The domicile, or nationality, or residence of the married woman;

3. The place of the transaction, i.e., the place where the contract is made, or possibly the place where it is to be performed;

4. The place where the action is brought. . .

In such a case as *Milliken v. Pratt,* then, there are four factors of possible significance for the conflict of laws, each of which may be either domestic or foreign (to Massachusetts). There are therefore sixteen possible combinations—sixteen different cases that may arise. One of these is the purely domestic case, and one is purely foreign. That leaves fourteen conflict-of-laws cases. . .

Table 1

	Factors				
Case No.	**Residence of the creditor**	**Residence of the married woman**	**Place of contracting**	**Forum**	
1	D	D	D	D	All factors domestic (1)
2	F	D	D	D	One foreign factor (4)
3	D	F	D	D	
4	D	D	F	D	

Table 1

	Factors				
Case No.	Residence of the creditor	Residence of the married woman	Place of contracting	Forum	
5	D	D	D	F	
6	F	F	D	D	Two foreign factors (6)
7	D	F	F	D	
8	D	D	F	F	
9	F	D	D	F	
10	F	D	F	D	
11	D	F	D	F	
12	F	F	F	D	Three foreign factors (4)
13	F	F	D	F	
14	F	D	F	F	
15	D	F	F	F	
16	F	F	F	F	All factors foreign (1)

If we were to place this array before our personification of the Massachusetts General Assembly, asking that he point out just which of the fourteen mixed cases the Massachusetts rule is intended to govern, and why, we should almost certainly meet with impatience and rebuff. Most likely, the reply would be that such questions belong to the realm of conflict of laws, and are for the courts to determine. This does not mean that legislatures, when they are disposed to specify how their laws shall apply to cases involving foreign factors, refrain from doing so out of deference to the courts. It simply means, in this case, that the legislature has not thought about the matter, and does not want to think about it.

Left thus to our own devices, we may inquire what policy can reasonably be attributed to the legislature, and how it can best be effectuated by the courts in their handling of mixed cases. . .

It is surely not a difficult matter to formulate the legislative policy in this case. . . Massachusetts, in common with all other American states and many foreign countries, believes in freedom of contract, in the security of commercial transactions, in vindicating the reasonable expectations of promisees. It also believes, however, that married women constitute a class requiring special protection. It has therefore subordinated its policy of security of transactions to its policy of protecting married women. More specifically, it has subordinated the interests of creditors to the interest of this particular, favored class of debtors. . . [A]lthough the decision runs counter to the interests of powerful constituents, the legislature decides in favor of protecting married women.

What married women? Why, those with whose welfare Massachusetts is concerned, of course—i.e., Massachusetts married women. In 1866 Maine emancipated (its) married women. Is Massachusetts declaring that decision erroneous, attempting to alter its effect? Certainly not. Given a slightly different configuration of the little causes that determine the outcome of the legislative process, Massachusetts might have decided the same way. Who can say that Maine, or Massachusetts for that matter, was wrong? All that happened was that in each state the legislature weighed competing considerations, with different results. Well, each to his own. Let Maine go feminist and modern; as for Massachusetts, it will stick to the old ways—for Massachusetts women. Never mind, for the time being, exactly what we mean by "Massachusetts" married women—whether citizens, domiciliaries, residents. For the sake of convenience, until we must decide that question, let us say that it is *residence* in Massachusetts that defines the ambit of the state's protective policy. . .

So far, nothing that we have said provides any basis for a suggestion that the place where the contract is made has anything whatever to do with the policy of the Massachusetts legislature. Yet Mr. Justice Gray tells us that "[t]he general rule is that the validity of a contract is to be determined by the law of the state in which it is made. . ." Unless we have been very much mistaken in the foregoing formulation of the Massachusetts policy, the legislature was concerned with *people*—primarily Massachusetts married women—and the effects of their being induced to sign certain documents. What possible difference can it make where the document is signed? What effect will such a general rule have upon the Massachusetts policy? . . .

Assume a quite selfish state, concerned only with promoting its own interests; a state, if you please, blind to consequences, and interested only in short-run "gains." Such a state might be expected to apply its law disabling married women, or to desire its application: (a) to every case in which both parties reside in the state . . . since it has decided to subordinate the interests of domestic creditors to the interests of domestic married women; and, a fortiori, (b) to all cases in which the married woman is domestic and the creditor foreign . . .—in short, to all cases in which the married woman is a local resident, regardless of the creditor's residence. Such a state would not be expected to apply its law to any case in which the creditor is a local resident and the married woman a foreigner. . . It would be indifferent, and would cheerfully apply the foreign law, to the cases in which neither party is a local resident. . . The question is not, for the moment, whether such an attitude would be shocking, or unwise, or unjust, or unconstitutional. The question is whether it would be rational; and the answer is that it *would*—in the sense that, in the short run, without considering how other states or higher authority might react, the state would in this manner be doing all it could to maximize its own interests. . .

[The author then discusses each of the fourteen hypothetical variants of *Milliken* that present conflicts problems. In three situations litigated in Massachusetts (Cases 2, 3, and 6), because the contract is made in Massachusetts, the traditional rule would point to Massachusetts law. This makes sense, says Currie, when the woman is from Massachusetts and the creditor from Maine (Case 2): "It protects Massachusetts married women" at the expense of "Maine's interest in the security of transactions"; and "if one state's policy must yield, should not the court prefer the policy of its own state?" When the facts are inverted, however, so that the creditor is from Massachusetts and the woman from Maine (Case 3), applying Massachusetts law "makes no sense whatever": "It does not advance the interest of Massachusetts in protecting Massachusetts married women, for the defendant is not a resident of Massachusetts" and "it subverts the interest of Massachusetts in the security of transactions, to the detriment of a Massachusetts creditor," without serving any interest of Maine. Nor does the Massachusetts law reflect a policy "relating to the administration of her courts" such as "when the state believes that certain types of claims consume the time of courts without adequate social justification, or tend to the corruption of judicial processes": "[N]o one suggests that the Massachusetts rule as to a married woman's capacity is 'procedural.' " Applying Massachusetts law to a contract made between two Maine residents in Massachusetts (Case 6) makes no sense either: "Massachusetts is merely meddling. . . [I]t subverts Maine's legitimate interest in the security of transactions where Maine creditors are concerned, without advancing any state's interest in protecting married women."

[The interests of each state are the same, Currie continues, if in each variant the contract is made or the suit brought in Maine. Massachusetts' traditional application of Maine law in a case like *Milliken* itself (a Massachusetts woman contracting with a Maine creditor in Maine—Case 10) should not be too hastily condemned: "Where the interest of a foreign state is substantial and legitimate, as here, there may well be, among civilized states, reasons for relaxing the uncompromising attitude of selfishness and requiring legitimate local policy to yield. . . [But] Massachusetts' position in this case is quite inconsistent with its position in Case No. 2 . . . [the case differing only in that the contract was made in

Massachusetts,] where, faced with the identical conflict of interests, Massachusetts reached the conclusion that the foreign policy must yield. If Massachusetts . . . is acting upon altruistic or farsighted considerations that we have not yet discovered, she does not do so consistently."

[Finally when two Massachusetts people have contracted in Maine (Case 4), "the position taken by Massachusetts seems incredibly perverse. No state other than Massachusetts has any interest in the matter. . . The result . . . is to defeat Massachusetts' own preferred policy of protecting its married women, without advancing any policy whatever."

[Summarizing the entire series of fourteen cases (see Table 6), the author concludes that the place-of-making rule produces desirable results in only six of the fourteen cases (four cases in which the interests of the two states do not conflict and two cases in which the domestic interests are advanced at the expense of the foreign interest). On the other hand, "perverse" results are produced in six other cases, by subverting the interest of one of the states without advancing the interest of the other. In the remaining two cases, the foreign interest is advanced at the expense of the domestic interest. Similarly perverse results are produced if the fourteen possible cases are analyzed from the viewpoint of Maine (i.e., of a state which has emancipated its married women).]

Table 6

I	Domestic interest advanced without detriment to foreign interests	Case No. 5	(D D D F)	(3)
		Case No. 7	(D F F D)	
		Case No. 15	(D F F F)	
II	Foreign interest advanced without detriment to domestic interests	Case No. 12	(F F F D)	(1)
III	Domestic interest advanced at expense of foreign interests	Case No. 2	(F D D D)	(2)
		Case No. 9	(F D D F)	
IV	Foreign interest advanced at expense of domestic interests	Case No. 10	(F D F D)	(2)
		Case No. 14	(F D F F)	
V	Foreign interest subverted with no advancement of domestic interests	Case No. 6	(F F D D)	(2)
		Case No. 13	(F F D F)	
VI	Domestic interest subverted without advancement of foreign interests	Case No. 3	(D F D D)	(4)
		Case No. 11	(D F D F)	
		Case No. 4	(D D F D)	
		Case No. 8	(D D F F)	

The utility of a rule that operates so capriciously must certainly be suspect. That such a rule should have been announced and followed at all seems almost incredible. In fact, as everyone knows, it has not been followed consistently. When the indicated result is absurd and is perceived to be so, there are means of escaping it. The connecting factor—the place of contracting—is not always intractable and reexamination of the facts may lead to its relocation. In the cases [in which the domestic interest would otherwise be subverted] . . . , applicability of the foreign law may be conceded and the result avoided by invoking "local public policy". . . Alternative choice-of-law rules are available (law of the place of performance, law intended by the parties, law giving validity to the contract, law of the place having the most substantial connection). Fortified with knowledge of the availability of these devices, the uninitiated reader might well ask whether any court would actually reach such results as are indicated. . .

It may be doubted that Mr. Justice Gray would have done so. Like an Alpinist ascending an unknown slope, he left inconspicuous little handholds to facilitate his retreat if the route should lead to danger.[32] Let there be no doubt, however, that courts actually do reach the results that seem so indefensible. Bad law makes hard cases. The hypnotic power of the idea of territorial jurisdiction and vested rights is not to be underestimated. . .

We need not pause to inquire *why* courts behave in such strange ways. The history of conflict-of-laws theory makes that plain enough. The question is whether there is any rational justification for their continuing to do so, now that the infirmities of the traditional method are so well understood.

The most forceful affirmative defense that can be made for the traditional method is that it leads to uniformity of result, regardless of the state in which the action is brought. This, given the assumptions of the method, is undeniably true. It is also undeniably true that uniformity of result should be one of the primary objectives of a rational system of conflict of laws. According to the rule that the law of the place of making governs, any given case is decided in the same way irrespective of the state in which the action is brought. That is to say, this is the result if both states (a) characterize the problem in the same way, as one involving the validity of a contract, and (b) apply the rule that the law of the place of making governs (rather than some alternative rule), and (c) locate the connecting factor (the place of making) in the same way, and (d) do not invoke any second-line defenses, such as local public policy. This is a long list of "ifs," and we are well aware that the discipline of the system is not always

[32] He stated that the rule was the "general" rule, implying the possibility of exceptions. He stated that a contract valid by the law of the place of making was valid everywhere, but did not state the converse proposition. He noted that the contract was not only made but to be performed in Maine. He also left open the possibility that some significance might be attached to the fact that the guaranty bore "date of Portland." * * *

sufficient to maintain adherence to all of the necessary conditions when the result is perceived to be anomalous. The ideal of uniformity of result is, therefore, to some extent illusory. But assume that the necessary conditions are all observed, and the ideal uniformity results. Is the achievement worth the cost at which it was attained? The cost, be it remembered, is that in six of the fourteen possible cases the interests of one state are defeated without advancement of the interests of the other, and that in two additional cases the interests of the forum are made to yield to foreign interests. In only four cases are the interests of one state advanced without impairment of a foreign interest. In two cases the interests of the forum are given preference over foreign interests. This seems an extravagant price to pay for uniformity of result—the more so since the attainment of that goal is in fact problematical. We are moved to recognize again that uniformity of result, while it is a basic and ever-present desideratum in conflict-of-laws cases, is one that should at times be made to yield to stronger considerations. . .

[Another] excuse for adhering to the capricious rule that exalts the law of the place of making is that no acceptable substitute has been found. Though purely negative, this defense is a formidable one and doubtless constitutes, at least in modern times, an important reason for the endurance of the system.

The available alternative rules for choice of law are not satisfactory substitutes. The place of performance would be quite as irrelevant in the context of the *Pratt* problem as the place of making. This is not to say that the place of performance is always irrelevant; a contract to dance naked in the streets of Rome can hardly be considered without reference to Roman law. It is difficult to perceive any connection, however, between the law of the place where payment is to be made and the capacity of a married woman to contract. The rule that the law intended by the parties shall govern (in so far as it is not a pure fiction, totally incapable of explaining the choice) accords to the incapacitated party the power to contract out of her disability—a privilege she may be assumed not to enjoy in a purely domestic case; and the result is pro tanto the subversion of the interest of the state to which she belongs. Similarly, a rule permitting the selection of the law of any state having a connection (in terms of the given factors) with the case, so long as that law gives validity to the contract, must to some extent impair the apparent interest of a state that has, and has asserted, an interest in protecting the incapacitated party. The rule that points to the law of the state having the most real or substantial connection with the case seems an amorphous substitute for the analysis that must go into any satisfactory handling of this difficult problem. . .

The final alternative, or set of alternatives, is offered by the high-minded, transcendent, and form-free counsels of those who tell us that the choice should be of "the more effective and more useful law," or of the law that fulfills the demands of justice in the particular situation, or of the law that fulfills the "needs and interests of the community," or of the law that produces acceptable results. . . The inescapable fact remains that [these approaches] have proved ineffective. . . This cardinal disappointment is due in part to the intractable character of the problem itself. It is due in part to the fact that the proffered solutions undoubtedly beg the question; for the original question, at least—i.e., the question as it stood prior to the erection by the territorialists of a structure of false questions—was precisely: What is the just result? It is due in part to the fact that the approach attributes to courts a freedom and a competence that they do not possess; for courts are committed to the administration of justice under law, and the constraint of that commitment is not lightly to be thrown off simply because the law in question may seem to the court old-fashioned, unwise, unjust, or misguided.

[Concern for "just" disposition of the individual case assumes] a proposition that cannot with comfort be stated baldly. Baldly stated, the proposition is: In a domestic case, a judge has little choice but to apply the law of his state, no matter how silly or misguided he may think it is or how regrettable the results it produces. In a conflicts case, on the other hand, there is such a great deal of looseness in the joints of the apparatus and such a lack of any clear mandate as to how to proceed that there is available to the judge for the taking a freedom that he should employ with a will, in order to frustrate, in this limited but satisfying area of opportunity, all that is archaic and foolish in the law.

I think it is clear that we cannot accept any conflict-of-laws method that proceeds on such premises. In the context of the contractual capacity of married women the suggestion seems innocuous and almost palatable, since practically everyone will agree, nowadays, that the law imposing incapacity did more harm than good. Transferred to the context of live issues of policy, however, the suggestion is an alarming one. It is simply not the business of courts to substitute their judgment for that of the legislature. The content of the law to be applied must be inquired into, to be sure, and one of the grievous faults of the traditional system is its treatment of that content as immaterial. But the inquiry should be in aid of a determination of the scope of legislative policy and of the ways in which that policy is to be implemented, not an instrument for undermining that policy. . .

The fourteen possible conflict-of-laws cases that have been enumerated fall into two classes. The ten cases in the larger class present *no real conflicts problem*. The four cases in the smaller class present real problems, but they are problems that *cannot be solved* by any science or method of conflict-of-laws. Recognition of these blunt facts provides a basis—so far as I can see, the only basis—for progress toward a more satisfactory method of dealing with the cases.

[The "false conflict" cases, such as those in which both creditor and married woman are from the same state] do not involve conflicting interests of the respective states. It is perfectly clear what the result should be in each. Either state, though approaching the case with no other purpose than to advance its own interests, would reach that result... In each of these cases, the result that Massachusetts would reach if it ignored conventional choice-of-law rules and simply consulted its own interest coincides with that which Maine would reach if it adopted the same attitude. These are the cases in which application of the law of the place of making advances the interest of one state without impairing any interest of the other (in which the result is clearly satisfactory) plus the cases in which the interest of one state is defeated without advancing any interest of the other (in which the result is clearly unsatisfactory).

The [four] cases in the smaller class are the cases in which advancement of the interest of one state results in subordination or impairment of the interest of the other. Each state has a policy, expressed in its law, and each state has a legitimate interest, because of its relationship to one of the parties, in applying its law and policy to the determination of the case...

The plain truth is that the apparatus designed for the handling of real problems of conflict of laws generates problems where none existed before, and more often than not disposes of those false problems unsatisfactorily; at the same time, it provides no more than the illusion of a solution for the real problems. Where the legitimate interests of two states are in genuine conflict, the system does not reconcile them, nor determine which is more important, nor even permit the state in position to do so to pursue its own interest. It simply strikes down the one interest or the other, indiscriminately, arbitrarily, on the basis of fortuitous and irrelevant circumstances. Ultimately, the survival of such a system can be attributed only to the fact that few people care very much whether such matters are handled intelligently or not, so long as they are more or less expeditiously disposed of.

If this analysis is sound, the situation could be improved at least to the extent of eliminating the false problems that constitute the greater part of the array, together with the unfortunate results that follow in a majority of them...

[There follows a complicated discussion of whether denying the protection of Massachusetts law to nonresident wives is an unconstitutional discrimination.

[The author then turns to the "true conflict" situation in which a Massachusetts married woman has dealt with a Maine creditor.] Paradoxically, the problem is insoluble with the resources of conflict-of-laws law precisely because it is a true problem of conflict of interests, which is presumably the type of problem for which the system of conflict of laws was devised. Maine is committed to a policy of security of transactions, and has a legitimate interest in enforcing that policy where Maine creditors are concerned. Massachusetts is committed to a policy of protecting married women, and has a legitimate interest in enforcing that policy where Massachusetts married women are concerned. The policies are here in direct conflict. Who is to say which is the more important, or the more deserving, or the more enlightened? Not even the United States Supreme Court is in a position to do so. Certainly it is not for the courts of one state to sacrifice local policy because they feel that it is relatively old-fashioned or misguided. The legislature might do so; it might conceivably direct that its protective law should not apply to cases in which the local married woman is sued by a foreign creditor; but in such apparent favoritism to foreign as distinguished from domestic creditors it would be destroying the problem, not solving it. In the process it might remove the disability altogether.

A Massachusetts court, lacking legislative guidance, might tentatively take a similar position with some justification. It might reason: Certainly our law expresses a policy for the protection of married women, and there is no doubt that that policy is to be enforced in the domestic situation. But how far is it to be carried? When a local creditor deals with a local married woman, he is "presumed to know the law," or at least he cannot be heard to assert that he did not know it. But how is it when a Massachusetts woman deals with a businessman in another state, where the law imposes no such disability, who is accustomed to dealing with married women as persons sui juris? Isn't it a bit unfair to "presume" that he knows our law, or to impose on him the burden of ascertaining it? Are we really so deeply concerned about our married women as to want the protective policy pushed that far? Perhaps it should be applied only where both parties are local residents.

This would be a rational position. It is a recognition of the fact that local policy is relatively weak, and suitable only for home consumption. It is a solution—but, again, one for a case that does not present a true problem of conflicting interests. It will not serve when local policy is strong, or is thought to be strong. The legislature, if it disagrees with the court's estimate of the force of the policy, can direct that its law be applied where the married woman is a local resident and the creditor a nonresident, and we will be back where we started.

There is no conceivable choice-of-law rule that will solve the problem, even though both states adopt it and consistently apply it. The rule that the law of the place of making governs (which ought to be discarded, in the first place, because of the bad results it produces in the majority of the false-problem cases), will advance domestic policy at the expense of foreign in just half of the cases, since the place where a contract is made appears to be a matter of pure chance; in the other half, it will advance foreign policy at the expense of domestic. The rule that the law of the married woman's domicile governs (which eliminates the irrational results in the false-problem cases) will always advance the protective interest at the expense of the common interest in security of transactions. There is no apparent warrant for such an arbitrary preference of the one policy over the other; indeed, the result would be quite reactionary in terms of the modern consensus as to the unwisdom of such protective policies. . .

The sensible and clearly constitutional thing for any court to do, confronted with a true conflict of interests, is to apply its own law. In this way it can be sure at least that it is consistently advancing the policy of its own state. It should apply its own law, not because of any notion or pretense that the problem is one relating to procedure, but simply because a court should never apply any other law except when there is a good reason for doing so. That so doing will promote the interests of a foreign state at the expense of the interests of the forum state is not a good reason. Nor is the fact that such deference may lead to a conjectural uniformity of results among the different forums a good reason, when the price for that uniformity is either the indiscriminate impairment of local policy in half of the cases or the consistent yielding of local policy to the policy of a foreign state. . .

[W]here the creditor is a resident of Maine and the married woman a resident of Massachusetts, we should adopt for each state the principle that its own law will be applied. . . The result, unhappily for the quest for uniformity, will depend upon the forum. That is not a satisfactory result, but, the ideal being unattainable, it is the one that makes the best sense; it is better than chasing rainbows. . .

It will be said that this is a "give-it-up" philosophy. Of course it is. A give-it-up attitude is constructive when it appears that the task is impossible of accomplishment with the resources that are available. . . It would be constructive if legal scholars were to give up the attempt to construct systems for choice of law—an attempt that cannot result in the satisfactory resolution of true conflicts of interest between states, and that is very likely to result in the creation of problems that do not otherwise exist, and that are badly resolved by the system. It would be constructive if the energies thus released were directed to the solution of the true problems by other means, for by the use of other means [interstate agreement or congressional implementation of the Full Faith and Credit Clause] they may be solved. . .

Brainerd Currie's "Governmental Interest Analysis"

(1) It is difficult to overstate the importance of Brainerd Currie's contribution to modern conflict-of-laws thinking. Writing in the late 1950s and early 1960s, Currie published a series of articles that revitalized and revolutionized the field. The article excerpted above and a companion piece analyzing *Grant v. McAuliffe* in a similar fashion are the most important of these writings. Most of Currie's major articles, which remain the starting point for contemporary choice-of-law scholarship, are collected in B. Currie, Selected Essays on the Conflict of Laws (1963).

While Currie's status among academics is clear, measuring his influence in the courts is more difficult. On the one hand, few courts purport actually to apply "interest analysis" in the form Currie advocated. See Symeonides, *Choice of Law in the American Courts in 2019: Twenty-Third Annual Survey,* 68 Am. J. Comp. L. 235, 258–59 (2020) (2 states for tort, none for contracts). On the other hand, many courts that claim to follow the Second Restatement's "most significant relationship" test (discussed in the next section) apply it in a way that is indistinguishable from straightforward interest analysis. See Kramer, *Choice of Law in the American Courts in 1990: Trends and Developments,* 39 Am.J.Comp.L. 465, 487–89 (1991). More important, other modern approaches all build on Currie—most accepting his analysis of "false conflicts" while proposing alternatives to always applying forum law in "true conflict" situations. Currie's precise methodology has thus had less influence than his general reasoning and approach, which provide the basis for modern thinking on choice of law.

(2) Currie's central insight is that the process of determining whether a state's law applies in a particular multistate case "is essentially the familiar one of construction or interpretation." B. Currie, Selected Essays at 178. A complaint is filed alleging certain facts and claiming a right to relief. Whether the plaintiff is entitled to the relief sought depends on whether some rule of law so provides—something the court determines by interpreting and applying the laws proffered by the parties. According to interest analysis, this same process should be followed in multistate cases, only instead of asking questions like whether the plaintiff must prove that the defendant was negligent or not acting within the scope of employment, we ask questions concerning spatial elements of a claim, like whether the plaintiff must prove that he or she is from the state or that the accident occurred there.

Currie assumes that the court should make the determination of applicability by examining a law's purposes. Resort to purposive interpretation places Currie squarely within the "legal process" school of thought that was dominant at the time he was writing. See H. Hart & A. Sacks, The Legal Process: Basic Problems in the Making and Application of Law 1377–80 (William N. Eskridge & Philip P. Frickey, eds. 1994). But does this approach to interpretation still make sense? In the decades since Currie wrote, an increasing number of state courts have adopted a textualist approach to statutory interpretation. See Abbe R. Gluck, *The States as Laboratories of Statutory Interpretation: Methodological Consensus and the New Modified Textualism*, 119 Yale L. J. 1750 (2010). If a Massachusetts law says that "no married woman shall act as surety," shouldn't the court follow its plain language and decline to enforce any such contract without regard to the woman's residence? See *INS v. Cardoza-Fonseca,* 480 U.S. 421, 452 (1987) (Scalia, J., concurring in judgment) (if the language of a statute is clear, that language must be given effect—at least in the absence of a patent absurdity). Can the force of the textualist argument be reduced by the observation that the statute says nothing about how to resolve conflicts with sister-state law? And even if we reject a plain language approach to interpretation, does it follow that "purposivism" of the type advocated by Currie is the best alternative?[4]

(3) Sixty years of vigorous academic debate have produced many refinements in the method originally proposed by Currie. Consequently, rather than focus on Currie in particular, the remainder of this section explores the approach that seems to follow from his basic insight, using Currie together with supporters and critics to understand its strengths and weaknesses. There is, however, an enormous literature devoted specifically to Brainerd Currie's writings. The most important critiques include L. Brilmayer, Conflict of Laws: Foundations and Future Directions ch. 2 (2d ed. 1995); Brilmayer, *Interest Analysis and the Myth of Legislative Intent,* 78 Mich.L.Rev. 392 (1978); T. de Boer, Beyond Lex Loci Delicti pt. II (1987); Ely, *Choice of Law and the State's Interest in Protecting Its Own,* 23 Wm. & Mary L.Rev. 173 (1981); Hill, *Governmental Interest and the Conflict of Laws—A Reply to Professor Currie,* 27 U.Chi.L.Rev. 463 (1960); Juenger, *A Critique of Interest Analysis,* 32 Am.J.Comp.L. 1 (1984); Korn, *The Choice-of-Law Revolution: A Critique,* 83 Colum.L.Rev. 772 (1983); Laycock, *Equal Citizens of Equal and Territorial States: The Constitutional Foundations of Choice of Law,* 92 Colum.L.Rev. 249 (1992). The most comprehensive defense of Currie is H. Kay, *A Defense of Currie's Governmental Interest Analysis,* 215 Recueil des cours (1989-III). Other significant responses to

---

[4] There are terminological differences among those who, in common with Currie, view the court's task as one of choosing between competing rules of law by reference to the purposes of those laws viewed in light of the particular facts. Currie spoke of "interests," "policies," and the "ordinary processes of construction and interpretation." Cavers thought "construction" a misleading term and preferred to speak of "purposes" instead of "policies." D. Cavers, The Choice-of-Law Process 88–102 (1965). Von Mehren and Trautman invent a whole new vocabulary: contacts become "relating elements," the interested state becomes the "concerned jurisdiction," and the interest analysis becomes a "functional" one. A. T. von Mehren & D. Trautman, The Law of Multistate Problems 76–79, 102–25 (1965). Arguments like these are not very fruitful, however. Call the process whatever you like; many scholars today—though certainly not all of them—argue that the first step in a choice of law case should be to determine, in light of their underlying purposes, which states' laws should be read to apply.

critics include Posnak, *Choice of Law: Interest Analysis and Its "New Crits"*, 36 Am.J.Comp.L. 681 (1988); Posnak, *Choice of Law—Interest Analysis: They Still Don't Get It,* 40 Wayne L. Rev. 1121 (1994); Sedler, *Interest Analysis and the Forum Preference in the Conflict of Laws: A Response to the 'New Critics',* 34 Mercer L.Rev. 593 (1983); Weintraub, *A Defense of Interest Analysis in the Conflict of Laws and the Use of that Analysis in Products Liability,* 46 Ohio St.L.J. 493 (1985).

There is a fascinating roundtable discussion of Currie among a group of the nation's leading conflicts scholars, together with a series of responsive comments and articles, in *Choice of Law: How It Ought to Be,* 48 Mercer L. Rev. 623–916 (1997).

B. IDENTIFYING FALSE CONFLICTS

TOOKER V. LOPEZ

24 N.Y.2d 569, 301 N.Y.S.2d 519, 249 N.E.2d 394 (1969).

KEATING, JUDGE. On October 16, 1964, Catharina Tooker, a 20-year-old coed at Michigan State University, was killed when the Japanese sports car in which she was a passenger overturned after the driver had lost control of the vehicle while attempting to pass another car. The accident also took the life of the driver of the vehicle, Marcia Lopez, and seriously injured another passenger, Susan Silk. The two girls were classmates of Catharina Tooker at Michigan State University and lived in the same dormitory. They were en route from the University to Detroit, Michigan, to spend the week-end.

Catharina Tooker and Marcia Lopez were both New York domiciliaries. The automobile which Miss Lopez was driving belonged to her father who resided in New York, where the sports car he had given his daughter was registered and insured.

This action for wrongful death was commenced by Oliver P. Tooker, Jr., the father of Catharina Tooker, as the administrator of her estate. The defendant asserted as an affirmative defense the Michigan "guest statute," * * * which permits recovery by guests only by showing willful misconduct or gross negligence of the driver. The plaintiff moved to dismiss the affirmative defense on the ground that under the governing choice-of-law rules it was New York law rather than Michigan law which applied. . . [The lower court] felt "constrained" by the holding in Dym v. Gordon, 16 N.Y.2d 120, 262 N.Y.S.2d 463, 209 N.E.2d 792 (1965), to apply the Michigan guest statute.

We are presented here with a choice-of-law problem which we have had occasion to consider in several cases since our decision in Babcock v. Jackson rejected the traditional rule which looked invariably to the law of the place of the wrong. Unfortunately, as we recently had occasion to observe, our decisions subsequent to rejection of the *lex loci delictus* rule "have lacked a precise consistency" * * *. This case gives us the opportunity to resolve those inconsistencies in a class of cases which have been particularly troublesome. . .

In Babcock v. Jackson the plaintiff was injured when an automobile in which she was a passenger crashed into a stone wall during a weekend trip with her neighbors to Ontario, Canada. The plaintiff as well as her neighbors, who owned and operated the vehicle, were New York domiciliaries and the car was registered and insured in the State. Upon her return to New York the plaintiff commenced an action to recover for her personal injuries. The Ontario "guest statute", which prohibited suits by guests against negligent hosts, was asserted as a defense.

This court rejected unequivocally the traditional *lex loci delictus* rule and refused to apply Ontario law. We noted that the traditional rule placed controlling reliance upon one fact which had absolutely no relation to the purpose of the ostensibly conflicting laws and thus resulted in decisions which often frustrated the interests and policies of the State in which the accident had taken place as well as our own State.

We thus observed that the purpose of the Ontario guest statute was "to prevent the fraudulent assertion of claims by passengers, in collusion with the drivers, against insurance companies" (Survey of Canadian Legislation, 1 U. Toronto L.J. 358, 366) and that, "quite obviously, the fraudulent claims intended to be prevented by the statute are those asserted against Ontario defendants and their insurance carriers, not New York defendants and their insurance carriers. Whether New York defendants are imposed upon or their insurers defrauded by a New York plaintiff is scarcely a valid legislative concern of Ontario simply because the accident occurred there, any more so than if the accident had happened in some other jurisdiction." . . .

The issue before us, as Judge Fuld pointed out, was "not whether the defendant offended against a rule of the road prescribed by Ontario for motorists generally or whether he violated some standard of conduct imposed by the jurisdiction, but rather whether the plaintiff, because she was a guest in the defendant's automobile, is barred from recovering damages for a wrong concededly committed." As to that issue we concluded it was New York which had the only interest. "New York's policy of requiring a tort-feasor to compensate his guest for injuries caused by his negligence cannot be doubted * * * and our courts have neither reason nor warrant for departing from that policy simply because the accident, solely affecting New York residents and arising out of the operation of a New York based automobile, happened beyond its borders. Per contra, Ontario has no conceivable interest in denying a remedy to a New York guest against his New York host for injuries suffered in Ontario by reason of conduct which was tortious under Ontario law." (12 N.Y.2d p. 482, 240 N.Y.S.2d p. 750, 191 N.E.2d p. 284.)

Babcock v. Jackson was followed by Dym v. Gordon, * * *. There, the plaintiff and defendant were both New York domiciliaries who were taking courses at the University of Colorado during the summer of 1959. The plaintiff and defendant became acquainted at school and on one occasion, while a passenger in a car driven by the defendant, plaintiff was injured when the automobile collided with another vehicle.

Upon her return to New York, the plaintiff commenced an action to recover for her personal injuries. Again, a "guest statute" defense, predicated this time on Colorado law, was asserted. The Colorado statute, less severe in its effect than that of Ontario, permitted a guest to recover upon showing of gross negligence. . .

[W]e concluded that the purpose of this guest statute was not only to prevent fraudulent claims against Colorado insurers, but was intended as well to grant injured parties in other cars priority over the "ungrateful guest" in the assets of the negligent driver. Since the case, in fact, involved another vehicle and injured third parties, we concluded that Colorado, unlike Ontario in Babcock v. Jackson, had an interest in the application of its law. Faced with a true conflict of laws, a closely divided court determined that Colorado law ought to govern since the parties had resided in that State for so prolonged a period of time and there, therefore, seemed no unfairness in subjecting them to the law of Colorado.

The primary point of division in Dym v. Gordon focused . . . upon the construction placed on the Colorado guest statute which, upon reflection, we conclude was mistaken.

The teleological argument advanced by some (see Cavers, Choice-of-Law Process, p. 298) that the guest statute was intended to assure the priority of injured nonguests in the assets of a negligent host, in addition to the prevention of fraudulent claims, overlooks not only the statutory history but the fact that the statute permits recovery by guests who can establish that the accident was due to the gross negligence of the driver. If the purpose of the statute is to protect the rights of the injured "nonguest", as opposed to the owner or his insurance carrier, we fail to perceive any rational basis for predicating that protection on the degree of negligence which the guest is able to establish. The only justification for discrimination between injured guests which can withstand logical as well as constitutional scrutiny * * * is that the legitimate purpose of the statute—prevention of fraudulent claims against local insurers or the protection of local automobile owners—is furthered by increasing the guest's burden of proof. This purpose can never be vindicated when the insurer is a New York carrier and the defendant is sued in the courts of this State. Under such circumstances, the jurisdiction enacting such a guest statute has absolutely no interest in the application of its law. . .

Viewed in the light of the foregoing discussion, the instant case is one of the simplest in the choice-of-law area. If the facts are examined in light of the policy considerations which underlie the ostensibly conflicting laws it is clear that New York has the only real interest in whether recovery should be granted and that the application of Michigan law "would defeat a legitimate interest of the forum State without serving a legitimate interest of any other State" * * *.

The policy of this State with respect to all those injured in automobile accidents is reflected in the legislative declaration which prefaces New York's compulsory insurance law: "The legislature is concerned over the rising toll of motor vehicle accidents and the suffering and loss thereby inflicted. The legislature determines that it is a matter of grave concern that motorists shall be financially able to respond in damages for their negligent acts, so that innocent victims of motor vehicle accidents may be recompensed for the injury and financial loss inflicted upon them" * * *.

Neither this declaration of policy nor the standard required provisions for an auto liability insurance policy make any distinction between guests, pedestrians or other insured parties.

New York's "grave concern" in affording recovery for the injuries suffered by Catharina Tooker, a New York domiciliary, and the loss suffered by her family as a result of her wrongful death, is evident merely in stating the policy which our law reflects. On the other hand, Michigan has no interest in whether a New York plaintiff is denied recovery against a New York defendant where the car is insured here.[1] The fact that the deceased guest and driver were in Michigan for an extended period of time is plainly irrelevant. Indeed, the Legislature, in requiring that insurance policies cover liability for injuries regardless of where the accident takes place, * * * has evinced commendable concern not only for residents of this State, but residents of other States who may be injured as a result of the activities of New York residents. . .

The argument that the choice of law in tort cases should be governed by the fictional expectation of the parties has been rejected unequivocally by this court. ". . . 'Though our nation is divided into fifty-one separate legal systems, our people act most [of] the time as if they lived in a single one. . . [They suffer from a] chronic failure to take account of differences in state laws'." . . . It is for this reason that "[f]ew speculations are more slippery than assessing the expectations of parties as to the laws applicable to their

1 The Michigan courts have suggested that the purpose of their guest statute is to protect the owner of the vehicle. . . .

activities, and especially is this true where the expectations relate to the law of torts."

Moreover, when the Legislature has chosen to compel an owner of an automobile to provide a fund for recovery for those who will be injured, and thus taken the element of choice and expectation out of the question, it seems unreasonable to look to that factor as a basis for a choice of law. And, even if we were to engage in such fictions as the expectations of the parties, it seems only fair to infer that the owner of the vehicle by purchasing a New York insurance policy which provided for the specific liability "intended to protect [the] passenger against negligent injury, as well as to secure indemnity for liability, in whatever state an accident might occur." * * *

Choice-of-law decisions in guest statute cases, the dissent suggests, ought to turn on whether or not it was "adventitious" that the passenger was in a car registered and insured in New York as opposed to the jurisdiction in which the relationship is seated and has its purpose.

The dissent is, of course, correct that it was "adventitious" that Miss Tooker was a guest in an automobile registered and insured in New York. For all we know, her decision to go to Michigan State University as opposed to New York University may have been "adventitious". Indeed, her decision to go to Detroit on the weekend in question instead of staying on campus and studying may equally have been "adventitious". The fact is, however, that Miss Tooker went to Michigan State University; that she decided to go to Detroit on October 16, 1964; that she was a passenger in a vehicle registered and insured in New York; and that as a result of all these "adventitious" occurrences, she is dead and we have a case to decide. Why we should be concerned with what might have been is unclear.

The only reason suggested by the dissent is that such a rule is "a simple rule easy to apply with a high degree of certainty". We cannot agree that this is so. But even if we did, we would reject the rule for the same reason we rejected the *lex loci delictus* rule which this description more aptly fits. To state the matter simply, we are concerned with rational and just rules and not merely simple rules. . .

Applying the choice-of-law rule which we have adopted, it is not an "implicit consequence" that the Michigan passenger injured along with Miss Lopez should be denied recovery. Under the reasoning adopted here, it is not at all clear that Michigan law would govern * * *. We do not, however, find it necessary or desirable to conclusively resolve a question which is not now before us. It suffices to note that any anomaly resulting from the application of Michigan law to bar an action brought by Miss Silk is "the implicit consequence" of a federal system which, at a time when we have truly become one nation, permits a citizen of one State to recover for injuries sustained in an automobile accident and denies a citizen of another

State the right to recover for injuries sustained in a similar accident. The anomaly does not arise from any choice-of-law rule.

Indeed, the rule advanced by the dissent, unlike the rule we have adopted, will only foster rather than alleviate such anomalies. Thus, suppose in Babcock v. Jackson the driver of the vehicle had picked up a hitchhiker in Ontario who was injured along with his guest, Miss Babcock. . . Under the rule advanced by the dissent, Ontario law would clearly apply to govern the right of the "Ontario" guest since it was purely "adventitious" that [she was] in a New York car rather than an Ontario car. On the other hand, the same rule would permit recovery by the "New York" guest since it was not "adventitious" that [she] should have been in a New York vehicle at the time. . .

[It is also argued] that the choice-of-law rule articulated in our recent decisions merely amounts to a rule which will always result in the application of New York law—"a domiciliary conceptualism that rested on a vested right accruing from the fact of domicile" * * *. This argument ignores the fact that our decisions since Babcock v. Jackson have not always resulted in the application of the law of New York and have, indeed, indicated proper recognition and respect for the legitimate concerns of other jurisdictions and the real expectations of the parties. As we recently observed, "[w]e must recognize that, in addition to the interest in affording the plaintiff full recovery, there may be other more general considerations which should concern 'a justice-dispensing court in a modern American state.' . . . Among other considerations are the 'fairness' of applying our law where a nonresident or even a resident has patterned his conduct upon the law of the jurisdiction in which he was acting . . . as well as the possible interest of a sister State in providing the remedy for injuries sustained as a result of conduct undertaken within its borders." (Miller v. Miller * * *.)

The order of the Appellate Division should be reversed, with costs, and the order of Special Term reinstated.

FULD, CHIEF JUDGE (concurring). . .

Babcock and the decisions it heralded place in our hands an instrument not confined to the rare and unusual situation. Rather, they comprise a sound foundation for a set of basic principles which the practicing lawyer, as well as the conflicts scholar, may be able to wield with good results. They have helped us uncover the underlying values and policies which are operative in this area of the law. Now that these values and policies have been revealed, we may proceed to the next stage in the evolution of the law—the formulation of a few rules of general applicability, promising a fair level of predictability. Although no rule may be found or framed to guarantee a satisfying result in every case, we cannot hope to deal justly with the legion of multi-state highway accident cases by regarding each case as one of a kind and unique. We should attempt, as has been suggested, to avoid "both unreasonable rules and an unruly reasonableness that is destructive of many of the values of law and that loses sight of the need for coordinating a multi-state system". * * *

Without attempting too much, I believe that we may accept the following principles as sound for situations involving guest statutes in conflicts settings:

1. When the guest-passenger and the host-driver are domiciled in the same state, and the car is there registered, the law of that state should control and determine the standard of care which the host owes to his guest.

2. When the driver's conduct occurred in the state of his domicile and that state does not cast him in liability for that conduct, he should not be held liable by reason of the fact that liability would be imposed upon him under the tort law of the state of the victim's domicile. Conversely, when the guest was injured in the state of his own domicile and its law permits recovery, the driver who has come into that state should not—in the absence of special circumstances—be permitted to interpose the law of his state as a defense.

3. In other situations, when the passenger and the driver are domiciled in different states, the rule is necessarily less categorical. Normally, the applicable rule of decision will be that of the state where the accident occurred but not if it can be shown that displacing that normally applicable rule will advance the relevant substantive law purposes without impairing the smooth working of the multi-state system or producing great uncertainty for litigants. * * *

Guidelines of the sort suggested will not always be easy of application, nor will they furnish guidance to litigants and lower courts in all cases. They are proffered as a beginning, not as an end, to the problems of sound and fair adjudication in the troubled world of the automobile guest statute.

Since, in the case before us, the guest-passenger and the host-driver were both domiciled in this State and the automobile was here registered, we look to New York law to determine the standard of care to be applied between those parties.

BREITEL, JUDGE (dissenting). . .

What [*Babcock* and subsequent cases] . . . established, and very rightly so, was that when the territory in which the accident occurs is wholly adventitious to the relationship or status among the parties, that factor should not determine the applicable law. In each of these cases the seat and purpose of the relationship was established to be elsewhere than where the accident occurred. It was the place of the accident that could be changed without changing or affecting the other relationships. In short, except in a rather minimal way, the conduct of the parties was not affected by the place where the accident occurred. It was, therefore, adventitious.

The converse occurred in this case. The incidental registration and ownership of the car, and the domicile of these Michigan students, did not influence their conduct or the establishment or nature of the relationship among them. Regardless of these facts they would undoubtedly have entered into the same relationship, made the same trip, and behaved the same way. These facts were, therefore, extrinsic or adventitious.

On this view, Dym v. Gordon * * * was soundly decided, and this case, which is even stronger on its intrinsic facts because of the young women's being students in residence, as that term is used in the academic world, should be decided the same way. . .

There are truly difficult cases where the division between the significant and adventitious facts is elusive. This case is hardly such a one. The trouble with overextending the successive and changing rationales from Auten v. Auten in the contract field, through the *Babcock* case and its progeny, is to introduce the very uncertainty and chaotic unpredictability that the extremist critics of any change from the *lex loci* rules predicted. It is not necessary to fulfill the worst of those predictions if one significant factor is recalled.

In modern theories in the field of conflicts, the analysts have generally posited, or in fact assumed, as a significant factor the place where the transaction occurred * * *. What has happened of course, is that lip service is paid to the factor of place, and promptly ignored thereafter, if the forum prefers its own policy preconceptions and especially if it requires denial of recovery to a plaintiff in a tort case. . .

Intra-mural speculation on the policies of other States has obvious limitations because of restricted information and wisdom. It is difficult enough to interpret the statutes and decisional rules of one's own State. To be sure, there is no total escape from considering the policies of other States. But this necessity should not be extended to produce anomalies of results out of the same accident, with unpredictability, and lack of consistency in determinations. Thus, it is hard to accept the implicit consequence that Miss Silk, the Michigan resident injured in the accident, should not be able to recover in Michigan (and presumably in New York) but a recovery can be had for her deceased fellow-passenger in the very same accident. . .

If the trend continues uninterruptedly, the shift to a personal law approach in conflicts law, especially in the torts field, will continue apace (see Cavers, Choice-of-Law Process, pp. 150–156). Apart from the fact that such a development is not logically consistent with Anglo-American jurisprudence, it would create a sharp division between intra-national conflicts rules and extra-national conflicts rules. It is most unlikely that such a development would be recognized elsewhere. Inevitably, the goals of uniformity, let alone predictability, in conflict rules would be frustrated, and the arbitrary results produced by forum-selection would be proliferated beyond tolerable limits.

SCHULTZ V. BOY SCOUTS OF AMERICA, INC.

65 N.Y.2d 189, 491 N.Y.S.2d 90, 480 N.E.2d 679 (1985).

SIMONS, J. [Plaintiffs, Richard and Margaret Schultz, residents of New Jersey, sued defendants Boy Scouts of America, Inc., Franciscan Brothers of the Poor, Inc., the Pine Creek Reservation, and various individuals to recover damages for personal injuries to themselves and their two sons, Richard and Cristopher, and for Cristopher's wrongful death by suicide. The injuries arose from the sexual molestation of the two boys, then aged 11 and 13, by defendant Edmond Coakeley, the Franciscan Brother who was their classroom teacher at the Assumption School in Emerson, New Jersey, and who was also the Scoutmaster of their Boy Scout troop. The sexual molestation of both boys commenced on scouting trips to the Pine Creek Reservation in upstate New York, and continued, as to Cristopher, after their return to New Jersey. Cristopher committed suicide, allegedly as the result of distress resulting from the molestation, in New Jersey. The theory of recovery against the Boy Scouts and Franciscan Brothers was that they were negligent in the hiring and supervision of Coakley. New Jersey recognizes charitable immunity; New York does not. A New Jersey court had earlier determined that plaintiffs' claims were barred in a separate action against the Roman Catholic Archdiocese of Newark, which operated the school their sons attended. See *Schultz v. Roman Catholic Archdiocese,* 95 N.J. 530, 472 A.2d 531 (1984). The majority treated defendant Boy Scouts of America as a New Jersey domiciliary because its national headquarters was in that state at the time the molestation occurred. It added that Boy Scouts' "change of domicile after the commission of the wrongs from New Jersey to Texas, which no longer recognizes the doctrine of charitable immunity * * * provides New York with no greater interest in this action than it would have without the change." Defendant Franciscan Brothers was incorporated in Ohio and was treated as domiciled there. Ohio law recognized charitable immunity in general, but imposed liability on charities in actions based on negligence in hiring and supervising employees. The court noted "[f]or this reason, no doubt, defendant Franciscan Brothers does not claim Ohio law governs and the choice is between the law of New York and the law of New Jersey."]

II . . .

B

Historically, choice-of-law conflicts in tort actions have been resolved by applying the law of the place of the wrong. In *Babcock v. Jackson,* * * * we departed from traditional doctrine, however, and refused to invariably apply the rule of *lex loci delicti* to determine the availability of relief for commission of a tort. In doing so, we applied New York law to an action involving New York parties in which recovery was sought for injuries received in an automobile accident in Ontario, Canada. . .

The analysis was flexible and to the extent that it may have placed too much emphasis on contact-counting without specifying the relative significance of those contacts, the necessary refinements were added in later decisions of this court. In four of the five subsequent tort cases presenting the same *Babcock*-style fact pattern of common New York domiciliaries and a foreign locus having loss-distribution rules in conflict with those of New York we reached results consistent with *Babcock* and applied New York law. . . In each of the five cases, however, the court rejected the indiscriminate grouping of contacts, which in *Babcock* had been a consideration coequal to interest analysis, because it bore no reasonable relation to the underlying policies of conflicting rules of recovery in tort actions * * *. Interest analysis became the relevant analytical approach to choice of law in tort actions in New York. "[T]he law of the jurisdiction having the greatest interest in the litigation will be applied and * * * the [only] facts or contacts which obtain significance in defining State interests are those which relate to the purpose of the particular law in conflict" (*Miller v. Miller, supra,* at pp. 15–16, 290 N.Y.S.2d 734, 237 N.E.2d 877 * * *). Under this formulation, the significant contacts are, almost exclusively, the parties' domiciles and the locus of the tort * * *.

Thus, under present rules, most of the nondomicile and nonlocus contacts relied on in *Babcock v. Jackson (supra),* such as where the guest-host relationship arose and where the journey was to begin and end, are no longer controlling in tort actions involving guest statutes * * *. Both *Tooker* and *Neumeier* [*v. Kuehner,* noted at p. 215, infra] continued to place some importance on where the automobile involved was insured * * *, but this is not inconsistent with the present rule because usually a defendant host's automobile will be insured in the State of his domicile and also because it reflects a recognition that the insurer, rather than the individually named defendant, is often "the real party in interest" * * *. Insofar as issues of liability insurance might also be relevant in a case such as the one before us involving charitable immunity, the record provides no relevant information on the subject.

These decisions also establish that the relative interests of the domicile and locus jurisdictions in having their laws apply will depend on the particular tort issue in conflict in the case. Thus, when the conflicting rules involve the appropriate standards of conduct, rules of the road, for example, the law of the place of the tort "will usually have a predominant, if not exclusive, concern" * * * because the locus jurisdiction's interests in protecting the reasonable expectations of the parties who relied on it to govern their primary conduct and in the admonitory effect that applying its law will have on similar conduct in the future assume critical importance and outweigh any interests of the common-domicile jurisdiction * * *. Conversely, when the jurisdictions' conflicting rules relate to allocating losses that result from admittedly tortious conduct, as they do here, rules such as those limiting damages in wrongful death actions, vicarious liability rules, or immunities from suit, considerations of the State's admonitory interest and party reliance are less important. Under those circumstances, the locus jurisdiction has at best a minimal interest in determining the right of recovery or the extent of the remedy in an action by a foreign domiciliary for injuries resulting from the conduct of a codomiciliary that was tortious under the laws of both jurisdictions * * *. Analysis then favors the jurisdiction of common domicile because of its interest in enforcing the decisions of both parties to accept both the benefits and the burdens of identifying with that jurisdiction and to submit themselves to its authority.[2]

These considerations made the need for change in the *lex loci delicti* rule obvious in *Babcock,* but the validity of this interest analysis is more clearly demonstrated in the split domicile case of *Neumeier v. Kuehner,* 31 N.Y.2d 121, 335 N.Y.S.2d 64, 286 N.E.2d 454, *supra.* In *Neumeier* we applied Ontario's guest statute in an action on behalf of an Ontario decedent against a New York defendant at least in part because the Ontario statute, which contained reciprocal benefits and burdens depending on one's status as either host or guest, was "obviously addressed" to Ontario domiciliaries such as plaintiff's decedent (*id.,* at pp. 125–126, 335 N.Y.S.2d 64, 286 N.E.2d 454). In *Babcock* New York had an important interest in protecting its own residents injured in a foreign State against unfair or anachronistic statutes of that State but it had no similar interest in *Neumeier* in protecting a guest domiciled in Ontario and injured there.

C

As to defendant Boy Scouts, this case is but a slight variation of our *Babcock* line of decisions and differs from them on only two grounds: (1) the issue involved is charitable immunity rather than a guest statute, and (2) it presents a fact pattern which one commentator has characterized as a "reverse" *Babcock* case because New York is the place of the tort rather than the jurisdiction of the parties' common domicile (*see,* Korn, The Choice-of-Law Revolution: A Critique, 83 Colum.L.Rev. 772, 789).

[2] New York's rule holding charities liable for their tortious acts, or its rule of nonimmunity as the dissent characterizes it, is also a loss-allocating rule, just as New Jersey's charitable immunity statute is.

Although most of our major choice-of-law decisions after *Babcock* involved foreign guest statutes in actions for personal injuries, we have not so limited them, but have applied the *Babcock* reasoning to other tort issues as well * * *. Nor is there any logical basis for distinguishing guest statutes from other loss-distributing rules because they all share the characteristic of being postevent remedial rules designed to allocate the burden of losses resulting from tortious conduct in which the jurisdiction of the parties' common domicile has a paramount interest. There is even less reason for distinguishing *Babcock* here where the conflicting rules involve the defense of charitable immunity. . .

Thus, if this were a straight *Babcock* fact pattern, rather than the reverse, we would . . . apply the law of the parties' common domicile. Because this case presents the first case for our review in which New York is the forum-locus rather than the parties' common domicile, however, we consider the reasons most often advanced for applying the law of the forum-locus and those supporting application of the law of the common domicile.

The three reasons most often urged in support of applying the law of the forum-locus in cases such as this are: (1) to protect medical creditors who provided services to injured parties in the locus State, (2) to prevent injured tort victims from becoming public wards in the locus State and (3) the deterrent effect application of locus law has on future tort-feasors in the locus State (*see,* Comments on Babcock v. Jackson, A Recent Development in Conflict of Laws, 63 Colum.L.Rev. 1212, 1222–1226, 1237–1238; Korn, *supra,* at 841, 962). The first two reasons share common weaknesses. First, in the abstract, neither reason necessarily requires application of the locus jurisdiction's law, but rather invariably mandates application of the law of the jurisdiction that would either allow recovery or allow the greater recovery * * *. They are subject to criticism, therefore, as being biased in favor of recovery. Second, on the facts of this case neither reason is relevant since the record contains no evidence that there are New York medical creditors or that plaintiffs are or will likely become wards of this State. Finally, although it is conceivable that application of New York's law in this case would have some deterrent effect on future tortious conduct in this State, New York's deterrent interest is considerably less because none of the parties is a resident and the rule in conflict is loss-allocating rather than conduct-regulating.

Conversely, there are persuasive reasons for consistently applying the law of the parties' common domicile. First, it significantly reduces forum-shopping opportunities, because the same law will be applied by the common-domicile and locus jurisdictions, the two most likely forums. Second, it rebuts charges that the forum-locus is biased in favor of its own laws and in favor of rules permitting recovery. Third, the concepts of mutuality and reciprocity support consistent application of the common-domicile law. In any given case, one person could be either plaintiff or defendant and one State could be either the parties' common domicile or the locus, and yet the applicable law would not change depending on their status. Finally, it produces a rule that is easy to apply and brings a modicum of predictability and certainty to an area of the law needing both.

As to defendant Franciscan Brothers, . . . because the parties are domiciled in different jurisdictions with conflicting loss-distribution rules and the locus of the tort is New York, . . . the law of the place of the tort will normally apply, unless displacing it " 'will advance the relevant substantive law purposes without impairing the smooth working of the multi-state system or producing great uncertainty for litigants' " (*Neumeier v. Kuehner, supra,* 31 N.Y.2d at p. 128, 335 N.Y.S.2d 64, 286 N.E.2d 454). For the same reasons stated in our analysis of the action against defendant Boy Scouts, application of the law of New Jersey in plaintiffs' action against defendant Franciscan Brothers would further that State's interest in enforcing the decision of its domiciliaries to accept the burdens as well as the benefits of that State's loss-distribution tort rules and its interest in promoting the continuation and expansion of defendant's charitable activities in that State. Conversely, although application of New Jersey's law may not affirmatively advance the substantive law purposes of New York, it will not frustrate those interests because New York has no significant interest in applying its own law to this dispute. Finally, application of New Jersey law will enhance "the smooth working of the multi-state system" by actually reducing the incentive for forum shopping and it will provide certainty for the litigants whose only reasonable expectation surely would have been that the law of the jurisdiction where plaintiffs are domiciled and defendant sends its teachers would apply, not the law of New York where the parties had only isolated and infrequent contacts as a result of Coakeley's position as Boy Scout leader. Thus, we conclude that defendant Franciscan Brothers has met its burden of demonstrating that the law of New Jersey, rather than the law of New York, should govern plaintiffs' action against it. . .

Accordingly, the order of the Appellate Division should be affirmed, with costs.

JASEN, JUDGE (dissenting).

I respectfully dissent. In my view, the majority overstates the significance of New Jersey's interests in having its law apply in this case and understates the interests of New York. While I agree with much of the majority's general exposition of the rules governing conflicts of law, nevertheless I believe that its application of these rules to the facts of this case and the resulting analysis are uneven. . .

New Jersey's interests, denominated by the majority as loss-distribution, are hardly pressing under the circumstances. While it is true that laws providing for charitable immunity typically are intended to serve the purpose of protecting and promoting the charities incorporated within a state's jurisdiction, that function is virtually irrelevant in this case. Presently, neither corporate defendant is a resident of New Jersey. . .

Consequently, because the majority cannot in actuality rely upon New Jersey's interest in protecting resident charities—into which category neither corporate defendant now falls—the decision today is, in effect, predicated almost exclusively upon the plaintiffs' New Jersey domicile. What emerges from the majority's holding is an entirely untoward rule that nonresident plaintiffs are somehow less entitled to the protections of this State's law while they are within our borders. Besides smacking of arbitrary and injudicious discrimination against guests in this State and before our courts * * *, such a position, without more, has severely limited, if any, validity in resolving conflicts questions. * * * This is especially so where, as here, the defendants' contacts with the foreign State are insignificant for the purposes of interest analysis while, at the same time, the parties' contacts with New York are so clear and direct, and the resulting interests of this State so strong.

There can be no question that this State has a paramount interest in preventing and protecting against injurious misconduct within its borders. This interest is particularly vital and compelling where, as here, the tortious misconduct involves sexual abuse and exploitation of children, regardless of the residency of the victims and the tort-feasors. . .

As the majority stresses, a charitable immunity law such as New Jersey's typically serves a loss-distribution purpose reflecting a legislative paternalism toward resident charities. But that is obviously not true with regard to a rule, such as New York's, which denies charitable immunity. Consequently, it is mistaken to adjudge the propriety of applying the latter law by giving weight only to the interests served by the former. . . A closer attention to the specific policy purposes of New York's charitable nonimmunity rule is essential to a more appropriate resolution of the conflict. . .

[T]here can be little doubt that New York has an interest in insuring that justice be done to nonresidents who have come to this State and suffered serious injuries herein. There is no cogent reason to deem that interest any weaker whether such guests are here for the purpose of conducting business or personal affairs, or, as in this case, have chosen to spend their vacation in New York. * * * Likewise, it cannot be denied that this State has a strong legitimate interest in deterring serious tortious misconduct, including the kind of reprehensible malfeasance that has victimized the nonresident infant plaintiffs in this case. Indeed, this deterrence function of tort law, whether it be in the form of imposing liability or denying immunity, is a substantial interest of the locus state which is almost universally acknowledged by both commentators and the courts to be a prominent factor deserving significant consideration in the resolution of conflicts problems. * * * While the majority mentions New York's interest in deterrence, it dismisses that interest in short fashion by referring to the "rule in conflict" as being "loss-allocating rather than conduct-regulating." * * * Of course, there is not one but two rules at issue, and the majority's characterization is accurate only with regard to New Jersey's law granting immunity, not with regard to New York's rule denying the same. * * *

False Conflicts

(1) *Babcock v. Jackson,* 12 N.Y.2d 473, 240 N.Y.S.2d 743, 191 N.E.2d 279 (1963), discussed in *Tooker,* is widely credited as the first case explicitly to reject the traditional approach and embrace the modern "revolution" in choice of law. In *Tooker,* Judge Keating interprets *Babcock* as a straightforward application of interest analysis to a false conflict. At various points in the *Babcock* opinion itself, however, the court appears also to endorse the "center of gravity" approach of *Auten v. Auten,* infra p. 263, and the "most significant relationship" test of the Second Restatement, infra p. 241—leading Currie to observe that *Babcock* "contains items of comfort for almost every critic of the traditional system." Currie, *Comments on Babcock v. Jackson, A Recent Development in Conflict of Laws,* 63 Colum.L.Rev. 1212, 1235 (1963).

(2) The process of interpretation used by courts employing interest analysis has two components: (a) ascertaining the purpose that led to the adoption of a law in wholly domestic cases, and (b) determining which contacts bring a multistate case within that purpose. Underlying both steps is the assumption that a law should be interpreted and applied in a way that advances its purpose. See Kramer, *Rethinking Choice of Law,* 90 Colum.L.Rev. 277, 299 (1990) (describing the second component as a presumption that a law applies only when its domestic purpose is advanced in the state). Each component has been criticized.

(a) *Ascertaining purposes.* Early critics of interest analysis focused on the difficulty of identifying the policies underlying the relevant laws. Professor Reese, for example, argued that the uncertainty involved in ascertaining policies would facilitate "judicial masquerading." He continued:

> [A] pure interests approach will require a court to decide each case on an ad hoc basis, since the court is required in every case to ascertain the purpose, or purposes of each of the potentially applicable local law rules in order to determine which of the rules to apply. And, theoretically at least, a determination that a

> statute of one state has a given purpose cannot properly be considered precedent in a case involving an identically worded statute of another state, since, as the guest-passenger statutes indicate, it is entirely possible for two identically worded statutes to have been enacted for different purposes. . . Such a system can be expected to cast an intolerable burden upon the over-worked trial courts. It can also be expected to lead to a constant stream of appeals, since there would usually be a good possibility that the appellate court would find that a given rule embodies a different policy than did the trial court. . .

Reese, *Chief Judge Fuld and Choice of Law,* 71 Colum.L.Rev. 548, 559–60 (1971). Professor Rheinstein echoed these sentiments, questioning whether the court was supposed to determine the purposes of other states' laws "by expert witnesses, or by its own scrutiny of the contents, history and background of these laws, or by its own impressions obtained through a general look at the local law in connection with the choice of law rules," and concluding that "[l]ittle imagination is required to see that . . . consistent attention to local law policies is practically unworkable." Rheinstein, *How to Review a Festschrift,* 11 Am.J.Comp.L. 632, 663 (1962).

Other critics of interest analysis argue that the attribution of purposes is invariably fictitious and unrealistic. Professor Brilmayer illustrates the point with the married women's contract disability from *Milliken.* Conceding that one purpose of such a law may be to protect married women from overreaching, Brilmayer reasons that the legislature presumably was also aware of, and approved, the deterrent effects such a statute would have. "Treating married women's contract statutes as protective rather than regulatory," she concludes, "is arbitrary—they are both." Brilmayer suggests that similar arguments can be made for most laws, the implication being that determinations of a law's purpose reflect arbitrary judicial or academic preferences that are "reminiscent of the Bealean system's arbitrary process of characterization. . ." Brilmayer, *Interest Analysis and the Myth of Legislative Intent,* 78 Mich.L.Rev. 392, 405 (1980). Professor Singer adds that because multiple purposes can plausibly be attributed to most laws, false conflicts are exceedingly rare. To the extent that courts purport to find false conflicts, Singer says, it is because judges ignore or assume away inconvenient arguments:

> [Interest analysis] gives the courts an impetus to resolve the case by finding a false conflict if they can; otherwise, the court will appear to be trampling on the interests of one state or another. . . False conflict analysis, on the other hand, makes the problem appear to go away. . . This set of incentives to search for false conflicts causes the courts both to oversimplify the interests at stake in choice-of-law cases and to overlook obvious interests which do exist.

Singer, *Facing Real Conflicts,* 24 Cornell Int'l L.J. 197, 219–20 (1991).

Are these criticisms of interest analysis or of interpretation generally? See *NLRB v. Hearst Publications, Inc.,* 322 U.S. 111, 124 (1944), where the Supreme Court declared, as it often has, that a statute "must be read in the light of the mischief to be corrected and the end to be attained." Isn't this how a court would go about interpreting foreign law once it has determined, under any choice-of-law theory, that foreign law applies?[5]

(b) *Determining what contacts are relevant.* What led Professor Currie to the conclusion that "of course" the protective policy behind the married women's disability in *Milliken v. Pratt* was designed solely for Massachusetts women? A number of commentators have criticized this line of reasoning as parochial and self-serving. See Brilmayer, 78 Mich.L.Rev. at 408–17; Ely, *Choice of Law and the State's Interest in Protecting Its Own,* 23 Wm. & Mary L.Rev. 173, 192–99 (1981); Laycock, *Equality and the Citizens of Sister States,* 15 Fla.St.U.L.Rev. 431, 446 (1987). Is it? "If the state were being parochial," Professor Kramer protested, "it would apply its own law whenever the Constitution permitted it to do so. By presuming that the law applies only when this advances the law's underlying domestic purpose, the court leaves room for the laws of other states in cases implicating their underlying purposes." Kramer, 90 Colum.L.Rev. at 302. "A state does not disprove its brazen desire to favor residents," retorted Professor Laycock, "by deferring in cases where it has no opportunity to favor a resident. I will believe that one state is deferring to others when deference imposes costs as well as benefits." Laycock, *Equal Citizens of Equal and Territorial States,* 92 Colum.L.Rev. 249, 284 (1992).

If our task is to determine what the law means, is it any objection that the result is parochial? Wouldn't you expect a state to favor its own citizens? Then isn't it troublesome to discover that, when legislatures do address choice-of-law questions, they often opt for traditional territorial rules? See Brilmayer, 78 Mich.L.Rev. at 424–29. Does this datum cast doubt on the basic principle that the purpose of a law is relevant in determining its reach? Or does it cast doubt on idea that states are as selfish as Currie suggested? Other than promoting the policies behind a law, what goals might a legislature pursue in addressing a choice-of-law question?

(3) Consider *Tooker* and *Schultz* in light of the criticisms just noted. What is the purpose of a guest statute? *Tooker* says that such laws protect insurance rates by preventing guests and hosts from colluding to defraud insurers. How does the court know this? What sources should it examine?

[5] What is a court to do if it decides that a particular rule (such as one for determining when a contract has been concluded by correspondence) reflects no substantive preference but only the need for a clear rule? Does Currie's suggestion that "the ideal rule" for such cases would be to "pick the state first in alphabetical order" (Selected Essays at 609) show that there is something wrong with interest analysis itself?

In *Neumeier v. Kuehner,* 31 N.Y.2d 121, 124, 335 N.Y.S.2d 64, 286 N.E.2d 454, 455 (1972), Chief Judge Fuld asserted that "[f]urther research . . . has revealed the distinct possibility that one purpose, and perhaps the only purpose, of [Ontario's guest] statute was to protect owners and drivers against suits by ungrateful guests." He relies on an article by Professor Reese which, in turn, relies on Professor Trautman's recounting of a "rumor . . . that the Premier of Ontario was receptive to the guest statute because he personally had suffered the ingratitude of a pair of hitch-hikers who had sued him successfully." Trautman, *Two Views on Kell v. Henderson: A Comment,* 67 Colum.L.Rev. 465, 470 (1967). Is this proper authority? Does the uncertainty reflected in cases like *Tooker, Dym,* and *Neumeier* lend credence to the criticisms made above? Assuming the purpose of Ontario's guest statute is to protect insurance rates, what contacts trigger its applicability: the driver's residence, the insurer's place of incorporation, the place where the car is registered, or something else? What if the purpose is to prevent suits by ungrateful guests? Does applicability then turn on where the guest is from, where the driver is from, where the ride began, where the accident occurred, or what? Can the law reflect both purposes?

In *Schultz,* why does New Jersey have an interest in protecting Boy Scouts, which is now domiciled in Texas? Should the court look at the contacts as they exist at the time of the incident or at the time of the lawsuit? Why does New Jersey have an interest in protecting Franciscan Brothers, which is domiciled in Ohio? Would New Jersey protect a local charity that did all its good work out-of-state? And what is New Jersey's interest in "enforcing the decision of its domiciliaries to accept the burdens as well as the benefits of that State's loss-distribution tort rules"—an interest in denying recovery to the New Jersey plaintiffs regardless of where the defendant is domiciled?

Twenty-three years after *Schultz,* the New Jersey Supreme Court declined to apply New Jersey's Charitable Immunity Act [CIA] to an action by a mentally disabled New Jersey resident seeking damages from a New Jersey charity for injuries she suffered at a summer camp the charity operated in Pennsylvania resulting from sexual abuse by a fellow-camper. In reaching the result in *P.V. ex rel. T.V. v. Camp Jaycee,* 197 N.J. 132, 962 A.2d 453 (2008), a 4–3 majority gave little weight to the common domicile of the parties or to plaintiff's status as a beneficiary of the defendant charity. Instead, it found Pennsylvania's interest in regulating the conduct of parties within its borders weightier, observing that "although the parties legitimately might have expected that Camp Jaycee's activities *in New Jersey* were immune under the CIA, they should not have expected to carry that immunity into another state." Id., 197 N.J. at 154, 962 A.2d at 467 (italics in original). In the process, the majority changed its approach to choice of law, abandoning governmental interest analysis in tort cases in favor of the Second Restatement (discussed in Section 5, infra). The three dissenters charged that the majority was less concerned with conflict-of-laws methodology than it was with accomplishing what the New Jersey Legislature had repeatedly refused to do: eliminate (or at least limit to in-state activities) the doctrine of charitable immunity. Does this mean that Judge Jasen had it right in his *Schultz* dissent?

The court's handling of New York's interests in *Schultz* is also provocative. Do you agree that one purpose of New York's tort recovery rules is to protect local medical creditors? Have you ever seen this consideration discussed in ordinary domestic cases? Judge Simons dismisses this interest because it "invariably mandates application of the law . . . that would allow recovery or allow the greater recovery." Is that right? If California allowed still greater damages, would New York have an interest in applying California law? The court also dismisses New York's interest in deterrence. Are you persuaded? What is the precedential effect of this interpretation? Can you state the holding of the case?

(4) Is interest analysis just a complicated way of saying that a domiciliary principle should replace territoriality as the governing rule for choice of law? See Corr, *Interest Analysis and Choice of Law: The Dubious Dominance of Domicile,* 1983 Utah L.Rev. 651. Is interest analysis merely a means of applying forum law to help local parties win lawsuits? Professor Ely contends that under interest analysis a state is only interested in helping its own citizens and, conversely, that it can have no interest in causing a local party to lose. Ely, 23 Wm. & Mary L.Rev. at 196. Is either proposition true? Many critics think so. See, e.g., Laycock, 92 Colum.L.Rev. at 274–77; Korn, *The Choice-of-Law Revolution: A Critique,* 83 Colum.L.Rev. 772, 898 (1983). Professor Brilmayer offers the following illustration: Anderson from State A makes a contract with Becker from State B; the contract does not satisfy A's statute of frauds but is binding under the law of B.

> The contract could be either valid or invalid since A's "interest" in having its statute of frauds apply depends upon which party is seeking to enforce the contract. If Anderson is suing Becker, then A has no interest in supplying a protective defense. If, on the other hand, Becker is suing Anderson, State A will have an interest in asserting its statute of frauds on his behalf.

Brilmayer, 78 Mich.L.Rev. at 408. Do you agree with this analysis? Do you agree that it shows the impropriety of interest analysis?

(5) Does interest analysis wrongly ignore concerns other than state interests, such as discouraging forum shopping or fairness to a party who would not expect a particular law to apply? See Brilmayer, *Rights, Fairness, and Choice of Law,* 98 Yale L.J. 1277 (1989); Singer, *Real Conflicts,* 69 B.U.L.Rev. 1, 47–74 (1989); Hill, *Governmental Interest Analysis and the Conflict of Laws: A Reply to Professor Currie,* 27

U.Chi.L.Rev. 463, 488–89 (1960). But why should a state's law ever apply if the contacts are such that applying it does not further the law's underlying domestic policy?

(6) Was Professor Cavers correct in concluding that a false conflict existed whenever "both laws are the same or would yield the same result"? D. Cavers, The Choice-of-Law Process 89 (1965). Suppose a contract fails to satisfy the statute of frauds of both the forum and the state where the parties are from and the contract was made. Does it follow that the contract is unenforceable? What if the forum's statute of frauds is designed only to protect residents from liability on promises they never made, and that of the locus state only to prevent perjury in its courts? Cf. *Marie v. Garrison,* supra p. 64.

C. THE "UNPROVIDED-FOR" CASE

ERWIN V. THOMAS

264 Or. 454, 506 P.2d 494 (1973).

HOLMAN, JUSTICE. [Erwin, a Washington resident, was injured in Washington by Thomas, an Oregon resident. Erwin's wife sued Thomas in Oregon for loss of consortium; she appeals from a judgment dismissing her action. Washington follows the common law rule that a wife cannot sue for loss of consortium (though a husband can); Oregon has abrogated that rule by statute and allows both spouses to sue.]

[B]efore engaging in the mysteries of the solution of an actual conflict, we must make certain that we have a conflict of consequence which requires a choice. All authorities agree that there is such a thing as a false conflict which requires no choice.

Where, in the particular factual context, the interests and policies of one state are involved and those of the other are not (or, if they are, they are involved in only a minor way), reason would seem to dictate that the law of the state whose policies and interests are vitally involved should apply; or, if those of neither state are vitally involved, that the law of the forum should apply. It may well be that determining what interests or policies are behind the law of a particular state is far from an exact science and is something about which there can be legitimate disagreement; but, on the other hand, it is the kind of an exercise, for better or for worse, which courts do every day and, therefore, feel secure in doing. If such a claimed conflict can be so disposed of, whether it is called false or not, the disposition certainly seems preferable to wandering off into the jungle with a compass which everyone but its maker says is defective.

Let us examine the interests involved in the present case. Washington has decided that the rights of a married woman whose husband is injured are not sufficiently important to cause the negligent defendant who is responsible for the injury to pay the wife for her loss. It has weighed the matter in favor of protection of defendants. No Washington defendant is going to have to respond for damages in the present case, since the defendant is an Oregonian. Washington has little concern whether other states require non-Washingtonians to respond to such claims. Washington policy cannot be offended if the court of another state affords rights to a Washington woman which Washington does not afford, so long as a Washington defendant is not required to respond. The state of Washington appears to have no material or urgent policy or interest which would be offended by applying Oregon law.

On the other hand, what is Oregon's interest? Oregon, obviously, is protective of the rights of married women and believes that they should be allowed to recover for negligently inflicted loss of consortium. However, it is stretching the imagination more than a trifle to conceive that the Oregon Legislature was concerned about the rights of all the nonresident married women in the nation whose husbands would be injured outside of the state of Oregon. Even if Oregon were so concerned, it would offend no substantial Washington interest.

It is apparent, therefore, that neither state has a vital interest in the outcome of this litigation and there can be no conceivable material conflict of policies or interests if an Oregon court does what comes naturally and applies Oregon law. Professor Currie expresses it thusly:

> ". . . The closest approximation to the renvoi problem that will be encountered under the suggested method is the case in which neither state has an interest in the application of its law and policy; in that event, the forum would apply its own law simply on the ground that that is the more convenient disposition. . ." B. Currie, Notes on Methods and Objectives in the Conflict of Laws, Selected Essays on the Conflict of Laws 184 (Footnote omitted) (1963).

An examination of the writings of those scholars who believe that an actual controversy exists in a situation similar to the present indicates, without an exception, they would reach the same result as we do, by either different or partially different reasoning.

The next question is whether our decision in *Casey v. Manson Constr. Co.,* 247 Or. 274, 428 P.2d 898 (1967), is incompatible with our disposition of the present case. In *Casey,* which adopted and applied Restatement, Second, Conflict of Laws, an actual conflict existed. An Oregon wife brought a loss of consortium action because of an injury to her husband, also an Oregon resident, which was negligently inflicted in Washington by a Washington resident. We there held that Washington defendants should not be required to accommodate themselves to the law of the state of residence of any traveler whom they might injure in Washington; that under the given circumstances, Washington's interest in the matter, which was protective of Washington defendants, was paramount to Oregon's interest in having its resident recover for her loss; and that Washington's relationship was the more significant and Washington law applied.

Our confidence in any set body of rules as an all-encompassing and readily applicable means of solution to conflict cases is not so great that we desire to undertake the application of such rules except in those situations where the policies and interests of the respective states are in substantial opposition. We see no such conflict here, and, therefore, find it unnecessary to resort to any such set of rules. We are little concerned whether we are presented with a false conflict or with an actual conflict capable of solution by resorting to our analysis of the interests and policies of the respective states. Where such policies and interests can be identified with a fair degree of assurance and there appears to be no substantial conflict, we do not believe it is necessary to have recourse to the "contacts" of Section 145(2) of Restatement, Second, Conflict of Laws.

The judgment of the trial court is reversed and the case is remanded for further proceedings.

BRYSON, JUSTICE (dissenting). . .

Regardless of whether we follow the [Second] Restatement . . . or the law of the place of the wrong, I do not believe we can or should bestow Oregon statutory rights for women on women of the state of Washington. . .

Obviously the plaintiff could not bring this action in her state, Washington, but the majority opinion holds that by merely stepping over the state boundary into Oregon she is then bestowed with the right given wives who are residents of the state of Oregon, which includes the right of action for loss of consortium of her husband.

There is definitely a conflict in the policy of the states of Washington and Oregon regarding the right to bring an action for loss of consortium.

I would affirm.

The "Unprovided-For Case"

(1) According to interest analysis, the proper resolution of a choice-of-law case depends on the configuration of state policies. In analyzing *Milliken v. Pratt,* Brainerd Currie discussed two possible configurations: only one state may be interested, in which case there is a false conflict and the court should apply that state's law; or more than one state may be interested, in which case there is a "true conflict" and resolution becomes more difficult. (True conflicts are considered in the next section.) There is, however, a third possibility: no state may be interested. Currie discovered this phenomenon in his article analyzing *Grant v. McAuliffe,* supra p. 52. As you will recall, three Californians, one of whom was Grant, were injured in Arizona when their car collided with a car driven by Pullen, who was also from California. Pullen died from his injuries, and McAuliffe was appointed administrator of his estate. Grant brought an action in California against Pullen's estate. Arizona followed the common-law rule that a tort action abates if it is not commenced before the death of the tortfeasor; California had abrogated this rule by statute. According to Currie, *Grant* itself presented a false conflict. (Can you explain why?) The "unprovided-for" case turned up in Currie's discussion of a hypothetical variant of *Grant* in which a plaintiff from Arizona was injured in Arizona and sued the estate of a deceased California tortfeasor. Currie's analysis was forthright:

> Application of Arizona law impairs no interest of California. The injured person was not a resident and was not injured there. On the other hand, that result advances no interest of Arizona. Though the injured person is both a resident of Arizona and is injured there, Arizona has no policy of compensation for him. If California law were applied instead, California interests would be neither advanced nor impaired; nor would those of Arizona.
>
> This is the "unprovided case" in a very special sense. Neither state cares what happens. . . While the laws of California and Arizona on the subject of survival of personal injury actions are different, the policies expressed in those laws are not in conflict here. It may be that the laws of neither state, nor of both states together, purport to dispose of the entire universe of possible cases. Identical laws do not necessarily mean identical policies, and different laws do not necessarily mean conflicting policies, when it is remembered that the scope of policy is limited by the legitimate interests of the respective states.

Currie, Selected Essays on the Conflict of Laws 152–53 (1963).

(2) Following Currie's reasoning, was *Erwin v. Thomas* an unprovided-for case? The court treats Washington's rule that wives cannot recover damages for loss of consortium as a defendant-protecting exception to the general rule favoring recovery. Prosser and Keeton explain that a husband could recover for loss of consortium at common law because the defendant's negligence deprived him of services his wife owed by law; a wife could not make the same claim, however, because her husband did not owe her similar services. W. Keeton, D. Dobbs, R. Keeton & D. Owen, Prosser and Keeton on the Law of Torts 931–32 (5th ed. 1984). Does this affect your analysis?

Consider also *Neumeier v. Kuehner,* 31 N.Y.2d 121, 335 N.Y.S.2d 64, 286 N.E.2d 454 (1972), in which an Ontario guest riding with a New York owner-operator was killed in a car accident in Ontario. Ontario has a guest statute; New York does not. Would Currie call this an unprovided-for case? Does Ontario have an interest in applying its guest statute? Does New York have an interest in allowing recovery?

(3) Although little notice was taken of the "unprovided-for case" at the time of its disclosure, Currie rather mildly observed that "[t]raditionalists may stand aghast at this anomaly, and take it as proof of the unsoundness of the analysis." Currie, Selected Essays at 152. This prediction was right on the money. Dean Ely made the unprovided-for case a central feature of his critique, and Professor Brilmayer cited it as a "substantial practical failing" of interest analysis. Ely, *Choice of Law and the State's Interest in Protecting Its Own,* 23 Wm. & Mary L.Rev. 173 (1981); L. Brilmayer et al., An Introduction to Jurisdiction in the American Federal System 240 (1986). Even supporters of interest analysis found the unprovided-for case troubling. Professor Sedler, for example, observed that "it is the unprovided-for case that has given the courts the most difficulty in practice." Sedler, *The Governmental Interest Approach to Choice of Law: An Analysis and a Reformulation,* 25 UCLA L.Rev. 181, 190 (1977). The strongest reaction came from Professor Aaron Twerski, who wrote that any choice-of-law method that produces unprovided-for cases deserves "the strongest ridicule." Twerski, *Neumeier v. Kuehner: Where Are the Emperor's Clothes?*, 1 Hofstra L.Rev. 104, 107 (1973). According to Twerski, the unprovided-for case reveals why interest analysis is intellectually bankrupt:

> In evaluating interests Currie and his academic followers placed tremendous emphasis on the *interest of the domicile state of the parties in granting or denying recovery.* For example, whenever plaintiff hailed from a state granting recovery and defendant was domiciled in a state denying recovery the interest analysts claimed that there was an irreconcilable conflict. After all doesn't the domicile state of one party want him to recover and the domicile state of the other party seek to deny recovery? There was rarely any attempt to view the policies behind these rules in broader perspective. . .
>
> In an unprovided for case like *Neumeier* we face a situation where there are no domiciliary interests to protect on the part of the contact states. New York has no domiciliary interests to protect by its pro-compensation rule since the plaintiff is not a New Yorker. Ontario has no domiciliary interests to protect by its anti-compensation rule because the defendant is not an Ontario domiciliary. Thus, the entire structure of interest analysis crumbled. Having defined the interests as domiciliary oriented when you run out of domiciliaries to protect you run out of interests. The emperor indeed stands naked for all to see.

Id. at 107–08.

(4) How should a forum committed to interest analysis go about deciding an "unprovided-for case"? Professor Currie listed four possibilities: (a) apply the law that appears to the judge to be "more enlightened and humane"; (b) selfishly apply the law that aids the litigant who is a local resident; (c) reach the same result as in (b) by applying a more sophisticated rule treating foreign claimants as they would be treated in their home states; and (d) apply the law of the forum. Currie rejected the first solution as beyond judicial competence and the second and third solutions as constitutionally infirm. He advocated applying forum law "simply on the basis that this is the rational and convenient way to try a lawsuit when no good purpose is to be served by putting the parties to the expense and the court to the trouble of ascertaining the foreign law." B. Currie, Selected Essays at 153–56.[6]

Other adherents of interest analysis have offered different solutions. Professor Cavers suggested that the forum adhere to its own self-restricting interpretation and "apply the law of the other state, even though that law doesn't want to be applied." D. Cavers, The Choice-of-Law Process (1965). Is this sensible? Would Cavers be willing to rephrase it as "enforce the rights created by the law of the other state, even though that law doesn't create any rights"? Is that a fair paraphrase? See Roosevelt, *Resolving Renvoi: The Bewitchment of Our Intelligence by Means of Language*, 80 Notre Dame L. Rev. 1821, 1855–64 (2005).

Professor Posnak recommends resolving unprovided-for cases by applying the "better law." Posnak, *Choice of Law: A Very Well-Curried Leflar Approach,* 34 Mercer L. Rev. 731, 777–83 (1983). Professor Weintraub suggests that the court "re-examine" the state interests to find an additional policy that will be advanced by applying the law of one of the states. R. Weintraub, Commentary on the Conflict of Laws 459 (6th ed. 2010). Professor Sedler offers a more acceptable analysis. Commenting on *Neumeier,* supra note (2), he suggests that both New York and Ontario have a common policy of compensating injured automobile accident victims. To be sure, Ontario has "put aside this compensatory policy where the victim was a passenger in the car of the driver," but it has no interest in applying this exception where the defendant's car is not registered or insured in Ontario. According to Sedler, "this means that the only state

---

[6] This is consistent with Currie's analysis of the burden of raising foreign law, discussed in connection with *Walton v. Arabian American Oil Co.,* supra pp. 94–95. According to Currie, forum law provides the natural background rule until another state is affirmatively shown to have an interest. In the absence of such an interest—either because none exists or because neither of the parties has shown that one exists—the court should simply apply its own law. Does such a presumption make any more sense in this context than in *Walton*? Would a court in the purely domestic context presume that some statute created a cause of action in every case unless the defendant could show otherwise? See Kramer, *Interest Analysis and the Presumption of Forum Law,* 56 U.Chi.L.Rev. 1301 (1989).

interested in protecting the defendant and his insurer does not do so, and the common policy of both states in allowing victims to recover from negligent drivers should prevail, causing the court to disallow the defense." Sedler, *Interstate Accidents and the Unprovided For Case: Reflections on Neumeier v. Kuehner,* 1 Hofstra L.Rev. 125, 138 (1973).

Has Sedler found a satisfactory resolution to the unprovided-for case? What does it mean to allow recovery under "the common policy of both states"? Whose *law* should be applied? Should the court apply the law that reflects the common policy (New York), or should it simply ignore the "exception" and allow recovery under Ontario law? Does it matter? How would Sedler resolve a case like *Erwin v. Thomas*? Don't the conflicting laws in that case simply reflect different policies, making it impossible to characterize either as an exception to a shared general policy?

(5) Professor Kramer concludes that this whole debate rests on a fallacy in the way interests have been analyzed and that there is no such thing as an unprovided-for case. Kramer, *The Myth of the "Unprovided-For" Case,* 75 Va.L.Rev. 1045 (1989). The mistake is to think about a state's interest by reference to how the state would decide a wholly domestic case, rather than by reference to the particular multistate case before the court. In *Neumeier,* for example, Kramer agrees that an Ontario plaintiff injured in Ontario cannot recover under New York law, because New York confers a right to recover only on plaintiffs from New York (furthering a compensatory interest) or on plaintiffs injured there (furthering a deterrence interest). For just these reasons, however, Kramer notes that the plaintiff *can* assert a right to recover under Ontario law, for Ontario presumably allows tort damages to further the same interests. Other commentators assume that Ontario has an interest in protecting defendants because of its guest statute. But while this might be true in a wholly domestic case, Ontario presumably enacted the guest statute to protect Ontario insurance rates and this defendant is from New York. Therefore, Ontario's guest statute does not apply, the case is a false conflict, and the plaintiff recovers under Ontario law.

Can the same analysis be used to resolve Currie's hypothetical variant of *Grant v. McAuliffe,* supra note (1)? How does it suggest deciding *Erwin v. Thomas*? Kramer concludes that the *Grant* hypothetical is also a false conflict and that *Erwin* is simply a case in which the plaintiff fails to state a claim upon which relief can be granted. Id. at 1048–64. Can every so-called unprovided-for case be resolved in a similarly noncontroversial fashion? In the *Neumeier* fact pattern, is it discriminatory to construe Ontario's guest statute not to protect a defendant simply because the defendant was not its domiciliary?

D. RESOLVING TRUE CONFLICTS

LILIENTHAL V. KAUFMAN

239 Or. 1, 395 P.2d 543 (1964).

DENECKE, JUSTICE. This is an action to collect two promissory notes. The defense is that the defendant maker has previously been declared a spendthrift by an Oregon court and placed under a guardianship and that the guardian has declared the obligations void. The plaintiff's counter is that the notes were executed and delivered in California, that the law of California does not recognize the disability of a spendthrift, and that the Oregon court is bound to apply the law of the place of the making of the contract. The trial court rejected plaintiff's argument and held for the defendant.

This same defendant spendthrift was the prevailing party in our recent decision in *Olshen v. Kaufman,* 235 Or. 423, 385 P.2d 161 (1963). In that case the spendthrift and the plaintiff, an Oregon resident, had gone into a joint venture to purchase binoculars for resale. For this purpose plaintiff had advanced moneys to the spendthrift. The spendthrift had repaid plaintiff by his personal check for the amount advanced and for plaintiff's share of the profits of such venture. The check had not been paid because the spendthrift had had insufficient funds in his account. The action was for the unpaid balance of the check.

The evidence in that case showed that the plaintiff had been unaware that Kaufman was under a spendthrift guardianship. The guardian testified that he knew Kaufman was engaging in some business and had bank accounts and that he had admonished him to cease these practices; but he could not control the spendthrift.

The statute applicable in that case and in this one is ORS 126.335:

> "After the appointment of a guardian for the spendthrift, all contracts, except for necessaries, and all gifts, sales and transfers of real or personal estate made by such spendthrift thereafter and before the termination of the guardianship are voidable." (Repealed 1961, ch. 344, § 109, now ORS 126.280).

We held in that case that the voiding of the contract by the guardian precluded recovery by the plaintiff and that the spendthrift and the guardian were not estopped to deny the validity of plaintiff's claim. Plaintiff does not seek to overturn the principle of that decision but contends it has no application because the law of California governs, and under California law the plaintiff's claim is valid.

The facts here are identical to those in *Olshen v. Kaufman,* supra, except for the California locale for portions of the transaction. The notes were for the repayment of advances to finance another joint venture to sell binoculars. The plaintiff was unaware that defendant had been declared a spendthrift and placed under guardianship. The guardian, upon demand for payment by the plaintiff, declared the notes void. The issue is solely one involving the principles of conflict of laws. . .

Before entering the choice-of-law area of the general field of conflict of laws, we must determine whether the laws of the states having a connection with the controversy are in conflict. Defendant did not expressly concede that under the law of California the defendant's obligation would be enforceable, but his counsel did state that if this proceeding were in the courts of California, the plaintiff probably would recover. We agree. . .

[The court then discussed several possible approaches to resolving the choice of law problem—the place of the contract rule, the place of performance rule, and the rule of validation—all of which suggested that California law should govern.]

Thus far all signs have pointed to applying the law of California and holding the contract enforceable. There is, however, an obstacle to cross before this end can be logically reached. In *Olshen v. Kaufman,* supra, we decided that the law of Oregon, at least as applied to persons domiciled in Oregon contracting in Oregon for performance in Oregon, is that spendthrifts' contracts are voidable. Are the choice-of-law principles of conflict of laws so superior that they overcome this principle of Oregon law?

To answer this question we must determine, upon some basis, whether the interests of Oregon are so basic and important that we should not apply California law despite its several intimate connections with the transaction. The traditional method used by this court and most others is framed in the terminology of "public policy." The court decides whether or not the public policy of the forum is so strong that the law of the forum must prevail although another jurisdiction, with different laws, has more and closer contacts with the transaction. Included in "public policy" we must consider the economic and social interests of Oregon. When these factors are included in a consideration of whether the law of the forum should be applied this traditional approach is very similar to that advocated by many legal scholars. This latter theory is "that choice-of-law rules should rationally advance the policies or interests of the several states (or of the nations in the world community)." Hill, Governmental Interest and the Conflict of Laws—A Reply to Professor Currie, 27 U.Chi.L.Rev. 463 (1960); Currie, Selected Essays on the Conflict of Laws, 64–72 (1963), reprint from 58 Col.L.Rev. 964 (1958).

[The court then rejected an approach based on the common-law public policy doctrine because of "the lack of any even remotely objective standards [for] deciding what is the fundamental law forming a cornerstone of the forum's jurisprudence."]

However, as previously stated, if we include in our search for the public policy of the forum a consideration of the various interests that the forum has in this litigation, we are guided by more definite criteria. In addition to the interests of the forum, we should consider the interests of the other jurisdictions which have some connection with the transaction.

Some of the interests of Oregon in this litigation are set forth in *Olshen v. Kaufman,* supra. The spendthrift's family which is to be protected by the establishment of the guardianship is presumably an Oregon family. The public authority which may be charged with the expense of supporting the spendthrift or his family, if he is permitted to go unrestrained upon his wasteful way, will probably be an Oregon public authority. These, obviously, are interests of some substance.

Oregon has other interests and policies regarding this matter which were not necessary to discuss in *Olshen.* As previously stated, Oregon, as well as all other states, has a strong policy favoring the validity and enforceability of contracts. This policy applies whether the contract is made and to be performed in Oregon or elsewhere.

The defendant's conduct,—borrowing money with the belief that the repayment of such loan could be avoided—is a species of fraud. Oregon and all other states have a strong policy of protecting innocent persons from fraud. "The law . . . is intended as a protection to even the foolishly credulous, as against the machinations of the designedly wicked." *Johnson v. Cofer,* 204 Or. 142, 150, 281 P.2d 981, 985 (1955).

It is in Oregon's commercial interest to encourage citizens of other states to conduct business with Oregonians. If Oregonians acquire a reputation for not honoring their agreements, commercial intercourse with Oregonians will be discouraged. If there are Oregon laws, somewhat unique to Oregon, which permit an Oregonian to escape his otherwise binding obligations, persons may well avoid commercial dealings with Oregonians.

The substance of these commercial considerations, however, is deflated by the recollection that the Oregon Legislature has determined, despite the weight of these considerations, that a spendthrift's contracts are voidable.

California's most direct interest in this transaction is having its citizen creditor paid. As previously noted, California's policy is that any creditor, in California or otherwise, should be paid even though the debtor is a spendthrift. California probably has another, although more intangible, interest involved. It is presumably to every state's benefit to have the reputation of being a jurisdiction in which contracts can be made and performance be promised with the certain knowledge that such contracts will be enforced. Both of these interests, particularly the former, are also of substance.

We have, then, two jurisdictions, each with several close connections with the transaction, and each with a substantial interest, which will be served or thwarted, depending upon which law is applied. The interests of neither jurisdiction are clearly more important than those of the other. We are of the opinion that in such a case the public policy of Oregon should prevail and the law of Oregon should be applied; we should apply that choice-of-law rule which will "advance the policies or interests of" Oregon. * * *

Courts are instruments of state policy. The Oregon Legislature has adopted a policy to avoid possible hardship to an Oregon family of a spendthrift and to avoid possible expenditure of Oregon public funds which might occur if the spendthrift is required to pay his obligations. In litigation Oregon courts are the appropriate instrument to enforce this policy. The mechanical application of choice-of-law rules would be the only apparent reason for an Oregon court advancing the interests of California over the equally valid interests of Oregon. The present principles of conflict of laws are not favorable to such mechanical application.

We hold that the spendthrift law of Oregon is applicable and the plaintiff cannot recover.

Judgment affirmed.

O'CONNELL, JUSTICE (specially concurring). . .

In the *Olshen* case we had to choose between two competing policies; on one hand the policy of protecting the interest of persons dealing with spendthrifts which, broadly, may be described as the interest in the security of transactions, and on the other hand the policy of protecting the interests of the spendthrift, his family and the county. It was decided that the Oregon Legislature adopted the latter policy in preference to the former. . .

To distinguish the *Olshen* case it would be necessary to assume that although the legislature intended to protect the interest of the spendthrift, his family and the county when local creditors were harmed, the same protection was not intended where the transaction adversely affected foreign creditors. I see no basis for making that assumption. There is no reason to believe that our legislature intended to protect California creditors to a greater extent than our own.

GOODWIN, JUSTICE (dissenting). I am unable to agree with the conclusion of the majority. . .

[The dissenting opinion argued that the court should adopt an approach like that found in the Second Restatement, concluding as follows:]

In the case before us, I believe that the policy of both states, Oregon and California, in favor of enforcing contracts, has been lost sight of in favor of a questionable policy in Oregon which gives special privileges to the rare spendthrift for whom a guardian has been appointed.

The majority view in the case at bar strikes me as a step backward toward the balkanization of the law of contracts. *Olshen v. Kaufman,* 235 Or. 423, 385 P.2d 161 (1963), held that there was a policy in this state to help keep spendthrifts out of the almshouse. I can see nothing, however, in Oregon's policy toward spendthrifts that warrants its extension to permit the taking of captives from other states down the road to insolvency.

I would enforce the contract.

The Law of the Forum

(1) With cases such as *Lilienthal* we reach the point at which proponents of a functional or interest analysis begin to shout at one another in earnest. Why was Professor Currie so adamant that in a true-conflict case a court of each interested state should apply its own law? In his discussion of *Milliken v. Pratt,* supra p. 19, Currie defended this recommendation on the ground that the tools of choice-of-law analysis afforded no preferable solution, adding that by applying forum law the court "can be sure at least that it is consistently advancing the policy of its own state." Currie later supplemented this argument in *Notes on Methods and Objectives in the Conflict of Laws,* 1959 Duke L.J. 171, 176–77 (reprinted in B. Currie, Selected Essays on the Conflict of Laws 177, 182 (1963)):

> I know that courts make law, and that in the process they "weigh conflicting interests" and draw upon all sorts of "norms" to inform and justify their action. . . But assessment of the respective values of the competing legitimate interests of two sovereign states, in order to determine which is to prevail, is a political function of a very high order . . . that should not be committed to courts in a democracy. It is a function that the courts cannot perform effectively, for they lack the necessary resources. Not even a very ponderous Brandeis brief could marshal the relevant considerations in choosing, for example, between the interest of the state of employment and that of the state of injury in matters concerning workmen's compensation. This is a job for a legislative committee, and determining the policy to be formulated on the basis of the information assembled is a job for a competent legislative body.

Don't courts balance competing interests all the time in common-law and constitutional litigation? In what sense are they less equipped for the task, or is it less democratic for them to do so, in a multistate case?

Was Currie looking for laws prescribing choice-of-law rules, or making substantive policy choices? See Gottesman, *Draining the Dismal Swamp: The Case for Federal Choice of Law Statutes,* 80 Geo.L.J. 1 (1991). Which do you think is more likely?

For a case study, consider the question of the vicarious liability of car rental agencies for injuries caused by the negligence of their customers, familiar from *Levy v. Daniels' U-Drive*, supra p. 42. In 2005, 19 U.S. jurisdictions imposed such liability. See *Cates v. Creamer*, 431 F.3d 456 (5th Cir. 2005). Car rental agencies from no-liability states were held liable based on injuries occurring in pro-liability jurisdictions, or involving plaintiffs from pro-liability states, sometimes in circumstances in which their home courts would not have applied the pro-liability law. See, e.g., *Budget Rent-A-Car System, Inc. v. Chappell*, 407 F.3d 166 (3d Cir. 2005) (applying New York law to hold a Michigan rental agency liable for a one-car accident in Pennsylvania injuring the New York passenger of a car rented in Michigan). When Congress acted, it wiped out this vicarious liability entirely. See 49 U.S.C. § 30106 (2005).

(2) What happens when a true-conflict case is brought in a third state that has no interest of its own? Arguing that cases of this sort rarely occurred, Currie urged that they be dismissed whenever practicable on grounds of forum non conveniens. If all else failed, he finally suggested, the forum should either select the "more enlightened and humane" law or apply its own—provided that it coincided with that of one of the interested states. Currie, *The Disinterested Third State,* 28 L. & Contemp. Probs. 754, 765–69, 775–80 (1963).

Is either of these proposals acceptable? Recall Currie's fervent denunciation of a choice of the "better law" in any other true-conflict situation, supra p. 181. And isn't application of the law of a disinterested state contrary to the most basic principle of his analysis? But what would you do about it? Throw out the baby too?

(3) Consider also *Western Air Lines, Inc. v. Sobieski,* 191 Cal.App.2d 399, 12 Cal.Rptr. 719 (1961). Western, a Delaware corporation with its principal place of business in California, sought to eliminate from its charter a provision allowing cumulative voting for directors. California required cumulative voting; Delaware merely permitted it. The California Commissioner of Corporations disallowed the change on the ground that it would be "unfair" to California shareholders, who owned some 30% of Western's stock. The court of appeals upheld the Commissioner's decision, reasoning that otherwise the corporation, "by the device of amending [its] charter," could "destroy the rights which the state of California has deemed worthy of protection by the enactment of the Corporate Securities Act." Was there a true conflict in this case? Was the case correctly decided? Do your answers depend on the amount of business Western did in California or Delaware? What interest did Delaware have as the state of incorporation?

Suppose that Delaware, instead of being indifferent to cumulative voting, had actually *forbidden* it. Notice how much more serious the conflict would have been. Ordinarily one can live with conflicting laws by complying with whichever is more stringent, but here one state would require what the other forbade. Consequently, Western could not do business in both states. Is it tolerable for each state to apply its own law in *this* situation?

(4) The suggestion that the forum always apply its own law in true conflict cases has generally been rejected by both courts and commentators. Hill, *The Judicial Function in Choice of Law,* 85 Colum.L.Rev. 1585, 1592–93 (1985). It has had a few supporters, however. Professor Sedler observed that if the forum has a real interest, the court is likely to apply forum law "regardless of its purported approach to choice of law." Therefore, he concluded, it might as well be open about it. More important, Sedler asserted that applying forum law produces the most "functionally sound and fair results." Sedler, *Interest Analysis and Forum Preference in the Conflict of Laws: A Response to the 'New Critics',* 34 Mercer L.Rev. 593, 595 (1983) (citing Sedler, *Reflections on Conflict-of-Laws Methodology,* 32 Hastings L.J. 1628 (1981)). What is the basis for this conclusion? Professor Weinberg explains that "forum preference vindicates widely shared policy concerns" because plaintiffs shop for a favorable forum and "what the plaintiff seeks in the general run of cases is precisely the vindication of policies all states share: compensation for injury, deterrence of wrongdoing, and enforcement of agreements." Weinberg, *On Departing From Forum Law,* 35 Mercer L.Rev. 595, 599 (1984). Consequently, applying forum law will usually result in application of the "better" law. If the forum believes that the law of a sister state is preferable, "the cleaner, more direct approach would be to make a change in local law." Id. at 601. See also Singer, *Facing Real Conflicts,* 24 Cornell Int'l L.J. 197, 198–206 (1991) (defending a rebuttable presumption of forum law). Are these arguments persuasive? How well do they explain the result in *Lilienthal*? If, in the particular case, the foreign state would not afford compensation, seek to deter, or enforce an agreement, how does applying contrary forum law further that state's interests?

(5) Does applying the law of the forum in true conflicts discriminate unfairly against nonresidents? Professor Laycock offers the following example to show that it does: Mary from Maryland and Del from Delaware occasionally go out together. One night, with Mary driving, they have an accident and Del is hurt. Another night, with Del driving, they have a second accident and Mary is hurt. They file claims against each other in Delaware. Delaware has a guest statute; Maryland does not. Del wins both claims. Del's claim against Mary is a false conflict: Maryland has not protected her and Delaware has no interest in applying its guest statute to do so. Mary's claim against Del, in contrast, is a true conflict, and Delaware will therefore apply its guest statute to protect Del. "The bottom line," Laycock concludes, "is that Mary has to pay Del, but Del need not pay Mary" even though their claims are mirror-images. Laycock, *Equal Citizens of Equal and Territorial States: The Constitutional Foundations of Choice of Law,* 92 Colum.L.Rev. 249, 276 (1992). Is that right? Is it fair or rational? How about Professor Weinberg's response that the nonresident is distinguishable from the resident precisely because he or she is a nonresident? The real source of discrimination, Weinberg urges, is the unequal treatment of similarly situated residents if the forum *departs* from forum law. Weinberg, 35 Mercer L.Rev. at 596–97.

(6) Resolving true conflicts by applying forum law obviously encourages forum shopping. How serious a problem is this? The range of views is surprisingly diverse. Currie, you may recall, downplayed the importance of forum shopping, particularly if preventing it required sacrificing substantive policy. But since at least one state's policy must be sacrificed in a true conflict, shouldn't we at least try to minimize forum shopping? See Baxter, *Choice of Law and the Federal System,* 16 Stan.L.Rev. 1, 9–10 (1963) (noting that forum shopping encourages parties to sue in inconvenient places and produces needless jurisdictional disputes). Is preventing forum shopping incompatible with promoting a state's substantive policies? Recall Professor Weinberg's novel argument, supra note (4), that forum shopping is actually beneficial because it advances shared pro-plaintiff policies. At the opposite end of the spectrum, Professor Dane reasoned that a law-of-the-forum solution is inconsistent with the rule of law because it repudiates the idea that laws reflect norms that exist apart from their enforcement. Dane, *Vested Rights, "Vestedness," and Choice of Law,* 96 Yale L.J. 1191 (1987). Jurisprudential questions about the nature of law aside, doesn't a forum-law solution make it impossible to know what law will apply until after one acts, and to that extent isn't it inconsistent with the notice requirement of due process? See D. Cavers, The Choice-of-Law Process 22–23 (1965). Finally, consider Professor Kramer's observation that "[t]he assumption that it is unfair to allow plaintiffs to [forum shop] presupposes a 'correct' or 'fair' baseline defining how often the plaintiff's choice ought to prevail. . . Why are defendants entitled to anything other than the most unfavorable of the laws that can constitutionally be applied? Indeed, why is it not unfair to deprive plaintiffs of the benefit of the most favorable law that may constitutionally be applied?" Kramer, *Rethinking Choice of Law,* 90 Colum.L.Rev. 277, 313 n. 117 (1990). Kramer says that he shares the intuition that it is unfair to give plaintiffs a free choice but that he is loath to rely on an intuition that he cannot satisfactorily defend. What is the defense?

Can we evaluate the problem of forum shopping without empirical data? How frequently does forum shopping occur? Who engages in it? Do factors other than choice of law bear on where suit is filed? What factors, and how important are they? Most parties probably consult local attorneys. How many of these attorneys are willing to file suit and litigate in another state? How many have regular referral arrangements? How many simply file at home and hope for the best? Thanks to empirical legal scholarship, we know more about these questions than we used to (particularly in specialized fields like bankruptcy), but a great deal of work remains to be done. For empirical studies, see, e.g., Lynn M. LoPucki & William C. Whitford, *Venue Choice and Forum Shopping in the Bankruptcy Reorganization of Large, Publicly Held Companies*, 1991 Wis. L. Rev. 11 (1991); Samir D. Parikh, *Modern Forum Shopping in Bankruptcy*, 46 Conn. L. Rev. 159 (2013); Christopher A. Whytock, *The Evolving Forum Shopping System*, 96 Cornell L. Rev. 481 (2011).

(7) Was Currie correct to say, supra note (1), that by applying forum law in true conflicts the court "can be sure at least that it is consistently advancing the policy of its own state"? Critics argue that a preference for forum law gives insufficient emphasis to "a whole range of policies and values . . . relating to effective and harmonious intercourse and relations between and among communities. . ." A. T. von Mehren, *Recent Trends in Choice-of-Law Methodology,* 60 Cornell L.Rev. 927, 938 (1975). These policies, generally referred to as "multistate policies" in the literature, include such matters as uniformity, predictability and evenhandedness, comity toward other states, and facilitating multistate activity. See Singer, *Real Conflicts,* 69 B.U.L.Rev. 1, 47–74 (1989); Hill, *Governmental Interest and the Conflict of Laws—A Reply To Professor Currie,* 27 U.Chi.L.Rev. 463, 487–89 (1960). But how do these considerations figure in the decision of concrete cases? How and when should they be applied? How much weight do they deserve as against the more specific policies of the forum's otherwise applicable domestic rule?

Apart from multistate policies, does always applying forum law assure advancement of the domestic policies underlying a state's laws? What if every state follows this prescription? See Kramer, *Return of the Renvoi,* 66 N.Y.U. L. Rev. 979, 1016 (1991) ("From a purely selfish and parochial standpoint, it may still be advantageous for the forum to defer to foreign law in order to encourage other states to do the same"); L. Brilmayer, Conflict of Laws: Foundations and Future Directions 75, 82 (1991) ("One ought at least to consider the possibility that maximization of long-range interests would require cooperating with other states"). But see Weinberg, *Against Comity,* 80 Geo.L.J. 53 (1991) ("in implementation, [reciprocal comity] is discriminatory and substantively damaging to the rule of law").

(8) Wasn't the court in *Lilienthal* right that "courts are instruments of state policy"? Does that mean that separation of powers requires an Oregon court to obey the dictates of the Oregon legislature provided they are not unconstitutional? That an Oregon court has an obligation to apply Oregon statutes in every case they are construed to reach? That *Lilienthal* was rightly decided after all?

(9) If you think the court was wrong not to balance the competing interests in *Lilienthal,* which state had the dominant interest in that case? In *Milliken v. Pratt*? In *Western Air Lines v. Sobieski*? Why?

BERNKRANT V. FOWLER

55 Cal.2d 588, 12 Cal.Rptr. 266, 360 P.2d 906 (1961).

TRAYNOR, JUSTICE. [The plaintiffs, Louis, Florence, and Alfred Bernkrant, residents of Nevada, owed John Granrud $24,000, representing the unpaid balance on the purchase of a Nevada apartment building. The trial court found that in 1954 Granrud orally stated to the plaintiffs, at a meeting in Las Vegas, that he would "make a sporting proposition and provide in his Will that any debt at the time of his death would be forgiven and cancelled in exchange for a partial payment and refinancing" of this debt. The requested refinancing, which cost the plaintiff approximately $800 in out-of-pocket expenses, reduced the debt by a little over $13,000 and enabled Granrud to purchase a trailer park in Las Vegas.

[Less than a year and a half after the refinancing, Granrud died. His will neither forgave the debt nor directed the cancellation of the plaintiffs' notes. They sued Granrud's executrix, Dorothy Fowler, in the Superior Court of Los Angeles County to compel cancellation and a reconveyance of the property, which had been effectively mortgaged to secure the debt. The trial court held that the action was barred by the statutes of frauds of both Nevada and California; the District Court of Appeal upheld the lower court with respect to the California statute of frauds, and the plaintiffs took the case to the Supreme Court.]

Subdivision 6 of section 1624 of the [California] Civil Code provides that "An agreement which by its terms is not to be performed during the lifetime of the promisor, or an agreement to devise or bequeath any property, or to make any provision for any person by will" is "invalid, unless the same, or some note or memorandum thereof, is in writing, and subscribed by the party to be charged or by his agent." * * * Plaintiffs concede that in the absence of an estoppel, the contract in this case would be invalid under this provision if it is subject thereto. They contend, however, that only the Nevada statute of frauds is applicable and point out that the Nevada statute has no counterpart to subdivision 6. Defendant contends that the California statute of frauds is applicable, and that if it is not, the Nevada statute of frauds covering real property transactions invalidates the contract.

We have found no Nevada case in point. We believe, however, that Nevada would follow the general rule in other jurisdictions, that an oral agreement providing for the discharge of an obligation to pay money secured by an interest in real property is not within the real property provision of the statute of frauds, on the ground that the termination of the security interest is merely incidental to and follows by operation of law from the discharge of the principal obligation. * * *

We are therefore confronted with a contract that is valid under the law of Nevada but invalid under the California statute of frauds if that statute is applicable. We have no doubt that California's interest in protecting estates being probated here from false claims based on alleged oral contracts to make wills is constitutionally sufficient to justify the Legislature's making our statute of frauds applicable to all such contracts sought to be enforced against such estates. * * * The Legislature, however, is ordinarily concerned with enacting laws to govern purely local transactions, and it has not spelled out the extent to which the statute of frauds is to apply to a contract having substantial contacts with another state. Accordingly, we must determine its scope in the light of applicable principles of the law of conflict of laws. See *People v. One 1953 Ford Victoria,* 48 Cal.2d 595, 598–599, 311 P.2d 480; 2 Corbin on Contracts, p. 67; Currie, Married Women's Contracts, 25 U.Chi.L.Rev. 227, 230–231; Cheatham and Reese, Choice of the Applicable Law, 52 Col.L.Rev. 959, 961.

In the present case plaintiffs were residents of Nevada, the contract was made in Nevada, and plaintiffs performed it there. If Granrud was a resident of Nevada at the time the contract was made, the California statute of frauds, in the absence of a plain legislative direction to the contrary, could not reasonably be interpreted as applying to the contract even though Granrud subsequently moved to California and died here. * * * The basic policy of upholding the expectations of the parties by enforcing contracts valid under the only law apparently applicable would preclude an interpretation of our statute of frauds that would make it apply to and thus invalidate the contract because Granrud moved to California and died here. Such a case would be analogous to *People v. One 1953 Ford Victoria,* 48 Cal.2d 595, 311 P.2d 480, where we held that a Texas mortgagee of an automobile mortgaged in Texas did not forfeit his interest when the automobile was subsequently used to transport narcotics in California although he had failed to make the character investigation of the mortgagor required by California law. A mortgagee entering into a purely local transaction in another state could not reasonably be expected to take cognizance of the law of all the other jurisdictions where the property might possibly be taken, and accordingly, the California statute requiring an investigation to protect his interest could not reasonably be interpreted to apply to such out of state mortgagees. Another analogy is found in the holding that the statute of frauds did not apply to contracts to make wills entered into before the statute was enacted (*Rogers v. Schlotterback,* 167 Cal. 35, 45, 138 P. 728). Just as parties to local transactions cannot be expected to take cognizance of the law of other jurisdictions, they cannot be expected to anticipate a change in the local statute of frauds. Protection of rights growing out of valid contracts precludes interpreting the general language of the statute of frauds to destroy such rights whether the possible applicability of the statute arises from the movement of one or more of the parties across state lines or subsequent enactment of the statute. See Currie and Schreter, Unconstitutional Discrimination in the Conflict of Laws: Privileges and Immunities, 69 Yale L.J. 1323, 1334.

In the present case, however, there is no finding as to where Granrud was domiciled at the time the contract was made. Since he had a bank account in California at that time and died a resident here less than two years later it may be that he was domiciled here when the contract was made. Even if he was, the result should be the same. The contract was made in Nevada and performed by plaintiffs there, and it involved the refinancing of obligations arising from the sale of Nevada land and secured by interests therein. Nevada has a substantial interest in the contract and in protecting the rights of its residents who are parties thereto, and its policy is that the contract is valid and enforceable. California's policy is also to enforce lawful contracts. That policy, however, must be subordinated in the case of any contract that does not meet the requirements of an applicable statute of frauds. In determining whether the contract herein is subject to the California statute of frauds, we must consider both the policy to protect the reasonable expectations of the parties and the policy of the statute of frauds. See Cheatham and Reese, Choice of the Applicable Law, 52 Col.L.Rev. 959, 978–980. It is true that if Granrud was domiciled here at the time the contract was made, plaintiffs may have been alerted to the possibility that the California statute of frauds might apply. Since California, however, would have no interest in applying its own statute of frauds unless Granrud remained here until his death, plaintiffs were not bound to know that California's statute might ultimately be invoked against them. Unless they could rely on their own law, they would have to look to the laws of all of the jurisdictions to which Granrud might move regardless of where he was domiciled when the contract was made. We conclude, therefore, that the contract herein does not fall within our statute of frauds. * * * Since there is thus no conflict between the law of California and the law of Nevada, we can give effect to the common policy of both states to enforce lawful contracts and sustain Nevada's interest in protecting its residents and their reasonable expectations growing out of a transaction substantially related to that state without subordinating any legitimate interest of this state.

The judgment is reversed.

Moderate and Restrained Interpretation

(1) Responding to critics who attacked interest analysis as excessively parochial, Professor Currie stated:

> [A]nalysis may at first indicate an apparent conflict of interests; specifically, it may be clear that *if* the forum were to assert an interest in the application of its policy, it would be constitutionally justified in doing so. But no principle dictates that a state exploit every possible conflict, or exert to the outermost limit its constitutional power. On the contrary, to assert a conflict between the interests of the forum and the foreign state is a serious matter; the mere fact that a suggested broad conception of a local interest will create conflict with that of a foreign state is a sound reason why the conception should be re-examined, with a view to a more moderate and restrained interpretation both of the policy and of the circumstances in which it must be applied to effectuate the forum's legitimate purpose.

Currie, *The Disinterested Third State,* 28 L. & Contemp.Probs. 754, 757 (1963). Currie cited *Bernkrant* as a "brilliant" example of this kind of analysis. Id. Professor Cavers commented that such "moderate and restrained" interpretation is "essentially the same" as balancing state interests. Cavers, *The Changing Choice of Law Process and the Federal Courts,* 28 L. & Contemp.Probs. 732, 734 n. 9 (1963). Do you agree? Is balancing or weighing competing interests the only way to resolve a true conflict?

(2) Why, exactly, did Justice Traynor decide to subordinate (or, if you like, to construe away) California's interest in *Bernkrant*? Is his reasoning satisfactory? Could a Nevada court have resolved the case through this technique?[7]

Is *Bernkrant* a false conflict or a true conflict that the court managed to resolve? Does anything turn on these labels?

(3) Reconsider *Lilienthal v. Kaufman,* supra p. 177, in light of *Bernkrant.* Could the Oregon court have applied California law using the same reasoning? Should it have done so? Would the force of the argument

---

[7] Professor Cavers later wrote that Nevada had a Dead Man's Statute that would presumably have blocked enforcement of the oral contract if the action had been brought there. Cavers, *Oral Contracts to Provide By Will and the Choice-of-Law Process: Some Notes on Bernkrant,* in Perspectives of Law—Essays for Austin Wakeman Scott 38 (1964). Justice Traynor, writing after he left the bench, disputed Cavers' conclusion. Traynor, *War and Peace in the Conflict of Laws,* 25 Int'l & Comp.L.Q. 121, 134 (1976).

be dissipated if Lilienthal had advanced the money to Kaufman without inquiring about Kaufman's credit or competence? In an informal interview, Lilienthal claimed that two Portland banks said Kaufman's credit was good and made no mention of a spendthrift declaration. If these non-record facts are true, does Oregon's application of its own law affront your sense of justice?

Reconsider also *Schultz v. Boy Scouts of America, Inc.*, supra p. 159. Did the court there actually resolve a true conflict by giving a restrained interpretation to New York law in finding no deterrent interest?

(4) How many true conflicts can be avoided by the process used in *Bernkrant*? How often will party expectations provide a basis for interpreting a state's law narrowly? Are there other principles that may similarly be employed to resolve or avoid true conflicts?

(5) Does this approach to handling true conflicts adequately take multistate policies into account? Does it adequately protect domestic policies? What about problems like predictability, uniformity, and forum shopping? Is there a better way to address these concerns?

BERNHARD V. HARRAH'S CLUB

16 Cal.3d 313, 128 Cal.Rptr. 215, 546 P.2d 719 (1976).

SULLIVAN, JUSTICE. . .

On July 24, 1971, Fern and Philip Myers, in response to defendant's advertisements and solicitations, drove from their California residence to defendant's gambling and drinking club in Nevada, where they stayed until the early morning hours of July 25, 1971. During their stay, the Myers were served numerous alcoholic beverages by defendant's employees, progressively reaching a point of obvious intoxication rendering them incapable of safely driving a car. Nonetheless defendant continued to serve and furnish the Myers alcoholic beverages.

While still in this intoxicated state, the Myers drove their car back to California. Proceeding in a northeasterly direction on Highway 49, near Nevada City, California, the Myers' car, driven negligently by a still intoxicated Fern Myers, drifted across the center line into the lane of oncoming traffic and collided head-on with plaintiff Richard A. Bernhard, a resident of California, who was then driving his motorcycle along said highway. As a result of the collision plaintiff suffered severe injuries. Defendant's sale and furnishing of alcoholic beverages to the Myers, who were intoxicated to the point of being unable to drive safely, was negligent and was the proximate cause of the plaintiff's injuries in the ensuing automobile accident in California for which plaintiff prayed $100,000 in damages.

Defendant filed a general demurrer to the first amended complaint. In essence it was grounded on the following contentions: that Nevada law denies recovery against a tavern keeper by a third person for injuries proximately caused by the former by selling or furnishing alcoholic beverages to an intoxicated patron who inflicts the injuries on the latter; that Nevada law governed since the alleged tort was committed by defendant in Nevada; and that section 25602 of the California Business and Professions Code which established the duty necessary for liability under our decision in *Vesely v. Sager* (1971) 5 Cal.3d 153, 95 Cal.Rptr. 623, 486 P.2d 151, was inapplicable to a Nevada tavern. The trial court sustained the demurrer without leave to amend and entered a judgment of dismissal. This appeal followed.

We face a problem in the choice of law governing a tort action. As we have made clear on other occasions, we no longer adhere to the rule that the law of the place of the wrong is applicable in a California forum regardless of the issues before the court. * * * Rather we have adopted in its place a rule requiring an analysis of the respective interests of the states involved—the objective of which is "to determine the law that most appropriately applies to the issue involved." * * *

The issue involved in the case at bench is the civil liability of defendant tavern keeper to plaintiff, a third person, for injuries allegedly caused by the former by selling and furnishing alcoholic beverages in Nevada to intoxicated patrons who subsequently injured plaintiff in California. Two states are involved: (1) California—the place of plaintiff's residence and domicile, the place where he was injured, and the forum; and (2) Nevada—the place of defendant's residence and the place of the wrong.

We observe at the start that the laws of the two states—California and Nevada—applicable to the issue involved are not identical. California imposes liability on tavern keepers in this state for conduct such as here alleged. In *Vesely v. Sager*, supra, 5 Cal.3d 153, 166, 95 Cal.Rptr. 623, 632, 486 P.2d 151, 160, this court rejected the contention that "civil liability for tavern keepers should be left to future legislative action. . . First, liability has been denied in cases such as the one before us solely because of the judicially created rule that the furnishing of alcoholic beverages is not the proximate cause of injuries resulting from intoxication. As demonstrated, supra, this rule is patently unsound and totally inconsistent with the principles of proximate cause established in other areas of negligence law. . . Second, the Legislature has expressed its intention in this area with the adoption of Evidence Code section 669, and Business and Professions Code section 25602. . . It is clear that Business and Professions Code section 25602 [making it a misdemeanor to sell to an obviously intoxicated person] is a statute to which this presumption [of negligence, Evidence Code section 669] applies and that the policy expressed in the statute is to promote the safety of the people of California. . ." Nevada on the other hand refuses to impose such liability. In *Hamm v. Carson City Nugget, Inc.* (1969) 85 Nev. 99, 450 P.2d 358, 359, the court held it would create neither common law liability nor liability based on the criminal statute banning sale of alcoholic beverages to a person who is drunk, because "if civil liability is to be imposed, it should be accomplished by legislative act after appropriate surveys, hearings, and investigations to ascertain the need for it and the expected consequences to follow." It is noteworthy that in *Hamm* the Nevada court in relying on the common law rule denying liability cited our decision in *Cole v. Rush* (1955) 45 Cal.2d 345, 289 P.2d 450, later overruled by us in *Vesely* to the extent that it was inconsistent with that decision. . .

Defendant contends that Nevada has a definite interest in having its rule of decision applied in this case in order to protect its resident tavern keepers like defendant from being subjected to a civil liability which Nevada has not imposed either by legislative enactment or decisional law. It is urged that in *Hamm v. Carson City Nugget,* supra, 85 Nev. 99, 450 P.2d 358, 359, the Supreme Court of Nevada clearly delineated the policy underlying denial of civil liability of tavern keepers who sell to obviously intoxicated patrons: ". . . extending liability . . . would subject the tavern owner to ruinous exposure every time he poured a drink and would multiply litigation endlessly in a claim-conscious society. Every liquor vendor visited by the patron who became intoxicated would be a likely defendant in subsequent litigation flowing from the patron's wrongful conduct. . ." Accordingly defendant argues that the Nevada rule of decision is the appropriate one for the forum to apply.

Plaintiff on the other hand points out that California also has an interest in applying its own rule of decision to the case at bench. California imposes on tavern keepers civil liability to third parties injured by persons to whom the tavern keeper has sold alcoholic beverages when they are obviously intoxicated "for the purpose of protecting members of the general public from injuries to person and damage to property resulting from the excessive use of intoxicating liquor." (*Vesely v. Sager,* supra, 5 Cal.3d 153, 165, 95 Cal.Rptr. 623, 631, 486 P.2d 151, 159.) California, it is urged, has a special interest in affording this protection to all California residents injured in California.

Thus, since the case at bench involves a California resident (plaintiff) injured in this state by intoxicated drivers and a Nevada resident tavern keeper (defendant) which served alcoholic beverages to them in Nevada, it is clear that each state has an interest in the application of its respective law of liability and nonliability. It goes without saying that these interests conflict. Therefore, unlike *Reich v. Purcell,* 67 Cal.2d 551, 63 Cal.Rptr. 31, 432 P.2d 727, and *Hurtado v. Superior Court,* 11 Cal.3d 574, 114 Cal.Rptr. 106, 522 P.2d 666, where we were faced with "false conflicts," in the instant case for the first time since applying a governmental interest analysis as a choice of law doctrine in *Reich,* we are confronted with a "true" conflicts case. We must therefore determine the appropriate rule of decision in a controversy where each of the states involved has a legitimate but conflicting interest in applying its own law in respect to the civil liability of tavern keepers.

The search for the proper resolution of a true conflicts case, while proceeding within orthodox parameters of governmental interest analysis, has generated much scholarly examination and discussion. The father of the governmental interest approach, Professor Brainerd Currie, originally took the position that in a true conflicts situation the law of the forum should always be applied. (Currie, *Selected Essays on the Conflict of Laws* (1963) p. 184.) However, upon further reflection, Currie suggested that when under the governmental interest approach a preliminary analysis reveals an apparent conflict of interest upon the forum's assertion of its own rule of decision, the forum should reexamine its policy to determine if a more restrained interpretation of it is more appropriate. . . This process of reexamination requires identification of a "real interest as opposed to a hypothetical interest" on the part of the forum (Sedler, Value of Principled Preferences, 49 Texas L.Rev. 224) and can be approached under principles of "comparative impairment." (Baxter, Choice of Law and the Federal Systems, supra, 16 Stan.L.Rev. 1–22; Horowitz, The Law of Choice of Law in California—A Restatement, supra, 21 UCLA L.Rev. 719, 748–758.)

Once this preliminary analysis has identified a true conflict of the governmental interests involved as applied to the parties under the particular circumstances of the case, the "comparative impairment" approach to the resolution of such conflict seeks to determine which state's interests would be more impaired if its policy were subordinated to the policy of the other state. This analysis proceeds on the principle that true conflicts should be resolved by applying the law of the state whose interest would be the more impaired if its law were not applied. Exponents of this process of analysis emphasize that it is very different from a weighing process. The court does not " 'weigh' the conflicting governmental interests in the sense of determining which conflicting law manifested the 'better' or the 'worthier' social policy on the specific issue. . . [The process] can accurately be described as . . . accommodation of conflicting state policies, as a problem of allocating domains of law-making power in multi-state contexts—limitations on the reach of state policies as distinguished from evaluating the wisdom of those policies. . ." Horowitz, The Law of Choice of Law in California—A Restatement, supra, 21 UCLA L.Rev. 719, 753; see also Baxter, Choice of Law and the Federal System, supra, 16 Stan.L.Rev. 1, 18–19.) . . .

Although the concept and nomenclature of this methodology may have received fuller recognition at a later time, it is noteworthy that the core of its rationale was applied by Justice Traynor in his opinion for this court in

People v. One 1953 Ford Victoria (1957) 48 Cal.2d 595, 311 P.2d 480. There in a proceeding to forfeit an automobile for unlawful transportation of narcotics we dealt with the question whether a chattel mortgage of the vehicle given in Texas and, admittedly valid in both that state and this, succumbed to the forfeiture proceedings. Applicable California statutes made clear that they did not contemplate the forfeiture of the interest of an innocent mortgagee, that is a person "whose interest was created after a reasonable investigation of the moral responsibility, character, and reputation of the purchaser, and without any knowledge that the vehicle was being, or was to be, used for the purpose charged. . ." Texas had no similar statute; nor had the mortgagee, though proving that the mortgage was bona fide, also proved that he had made the above reasonable investigation of the mortgagor.

It was clear that Texas had an interest in seeing that valid security interests created upon the lawful purchase of automobiles in Texas be enforceable and recognized. California had an interest in controlling the transportation of narcotics. Each interest was at stake in the case, since the chattel mortgage had been validly created in Texas and the car was used to transport narcotics in California. The crucial question confronting the court was whether the "reasonable investigation" required by statute of a California mortgagee applied to the Texas mortgagee. Employing what was in substance a "comparative impairment" approach, the court answered the question in the negative.

> "It is contended that a holding that the 'reasonable investigation' requirement is not applicable to respondent will subvert the enforcement of California's narcotics laws. We are not persuaded that such dire consequences will ensue. The state may still forfeit the interest of the wrongdoer. It has done so in this case. Moreover, the legislature has made plain its purpose not to forfeit the interests of innocent mortgagees. It has not made plain that 'reasonable investigation' of the purchaser is such an essential element of innocence that it must be made by an out-of-state mortgagee although such mortgagee could not reasonably be expected to make such investigation." (*Id.* 48 Cal.2d at p. 599, 311 P.2d at p. 482.)

Mindful of the above principles governing our choice of law, we proceed to reexamine the California policy underlying the imposition of civil liability upon tavern keepers. At its broadest limits this policy would afford protection to all persons injured in California by intoxicated persons who have been sold or furnished alcoholic beverages while intoxicated regardless of where such beverages were sold or furnished. Such a broad policy would naturally embrace situations where the intoxicated actor had been provided with liquor by out-of-state tavern keepers. Although the State of Nevada does not impose such *civil* liability on its tavern keepers, nevertheless they are subject to *criminal* penalties under a statute making it unlawful to sell or give intoxicating liquor to any person who is drunk or known to be an habitual drunkard. (See Nev.Rev.Stats. 202.100; see *Hamm v. Carson City Nugget, Inc.,* supra, 85 Nev. 99, 450 P.2d 358.)

We need not, and accordingly do not here determine the outer limits to which California's policy should be extended, for it appears clear to us that it must encompass defendant, who as alleged in the complaint, "advertis[es] for and otherwise solicit[s] in California the business of California residents at defendant Harrah's Club Nevada drinking and gambling establishments, knowing and expecting said California residents, in response to said advertising and solicitation, to use the public highways of the State of California in going and coming from defendant Harrah's Club Nevada drinking and gambling establishments." Defendant by the course of its chosen commercial practice has put itself at the heart of California's regulatory interest, namely to prevent tavern keepers from selling alcoholic beverages to obviously intoxicated persons who are likely to act in California in the intoxicated state. It seems clear that California cannot reasonably effectuate its policy if it does not extend its regulation to include out-of-state tavern keepers such as defendant who regularly and purposely sell intoxicating beverages to California residents in places and under conditions in which it is reasonably certain these residents will return to California and act therein while still in an intoxicated state. California's interest would be very significantly impaired if its policy were not applied to defendant.

Since the act of selling alcoholic beverages to obviously intoxicated persons is already proscribed in Nevada, the application of California's rule of civil liability would not impose an entirely new duty requiring the ability to distinguish between California residents and other patrons. Rather the imposition of such liability involves an increased economic exposure, which, at least for businesses which actively solicit extensive California patronage, is a foreseeable and coverable business expense. Moreover, Nevada's interest in protecting its tavern keepers from civil liability of a boundless and unrestricted nature will not be significantly impaired when as in the instant case liability is imposed only on those tavern keepers who actively solicit California business.

Therefore, upon reexamining the policy underlying California's rule of decision and giving such policy a more restrained interpretation for the purpose of this case pursuant to the principles of the law of choice of law discussed above, we conclude that California has an important and abiding interest in applying its rule of decision to the case at bench, that the policy of this state would be more significantly impaired if such rule were not applied and that the trial court erred in not applying California law.

Defendant argues, however, that even if California law is applied, the demurrer was nonetheless properly sustained because the tavern keeper's duty stated in *Vesely v. Sager,* supra, 5 Cal.3d 153, 95 Cal.Rptr. 623, 486 P.2d 151, is based on Business and Professions Code section 25602, which is a criminal statute and thus without extraterritorial effect. . .

It is also clear, as defendant's argument points out, that since, unlike the California vendor in *Vesely,* defendant was a Nevada resident which furnished the alcoholic beverage to the Myers in that state, the above California statute had no extraterritorial effect and that civil liability could not be posited on defendant's violation of a California criminal law. We recognize, therefore, that we cannot make the same determination as quoted above with respect to defendant that we made with respect to the defendant vendor in *Vesely.*

However, our decision in *Vesely* was much broader than defendant would have it. There, at the very outset of our opinion, we declared that the traditional common law rule denying recovery on the ground that the furnishing of alcoholic beverage is not the proximate cause of the injuries inflicted on a third person by an intoxicated individual "is patently unsound." (5 Cal.3d at p. 157, 95 Cal.Rptr. 623, 486 P.2d 151.)

In sum, our opinion in *Vesely* struck down the old common law rule of nonliability constructed on the basis that the consumption, not the sale, of alcoholic beverages was the proximate cause of the injuries inflicted by the intoxicated person. Although we chose to impose liability on the *Vesely* defendant on the basis of his violating the applicable statute, the clear import of our decision was that there was no bar to civil liability under modern negligence law. Certainly, we said nothing in *Vesely* indicative of an intention to retain the former rule that an action at common law does not lie. The fact then, that in the case at bench, section 25602 of the Business and Professions Code is not applicable to this defendant in Nevada so as to warrant the imposition of civil liability on the basis of its violation, does not preclude recovery on the basis of negligence apart from the statute. Pertinent here is our observation in *Rowland v. Christian* (1968) 69 Cal.2d 108, 118–119, 70 Cal.Rptr. 97, 104, 443 P.2d 561, 568: "It bears repetition that the basic policy of this state set forth by the Legislature in section 1714 of the Civil Code is that everyone is responsible for an injury caused to another by his want of ordinary care or skill in the management of his property."

The judgment is reversed and the cause is remanded to the trial court with directions to overrule the demurrer and to allow defendant a reasonable time within which to answer.

Comparative Impairment and Policy-Selecting Rules

(1) The principle of comparative impairment, so far adopted only in California, was developed by Professor William Baxter in his article *Choice of Law and the Federal System,* 16 Stan.L.Rev. 1 (1963). Discussing a situation in which State X's negligence rule comes into conflict with State Y's rule imposing strict liability for distributing adulterated food products, Baxter considers "the course of discussion that would occur if the lawmakers of X and Y assembled for interstate negotiations on the scope of application of their inconsistent rules":

> Each group at the outset might unreasonably demand application of its law in every situation having any contact with its state. But as each became aware that the other had roughly equal bargaining power and tactical skill, the usual fruits of negotiation would emerge: each would cautiously give up what it wanted less to obtain what it wanted more, each side's perception of its own self-interest and of the other's objectives would sharpen, and the final agreement would approximate maximum utility to each. In the course of negotiations the participants would realize the basis of this particular conflict of law: the lawmakers had allocated differently certain costs of civilized society. X lawmakers were more favorably disposed to food processors than were Y lawmakers; Y lawmakers, comparatively speaking, favored consumers. Neither group was oblivious to the welfare of the category of persons it had, in the immediate context, treated less favorably: Y lawmakers afforded legal protection to food processors in other contexts, and X lawmakers protected consumers—even vis-a-vis food processors—where negligence was shown. But that each had reached different comparative judgments regarding product liability is evident. And from that conclusion, the paramount negotiating objective of each becomes clear: the same value judgment that dictated the respective internal rules of law now dictates the choice-of-law objective. X lawmakers want X law to apply in cases involving X food processors, and Y lawmakers want Y law to apply in cases involving Y consumers. Because the objective of Y is not necessarily inconsistent with that of X, negotiating progress can be made. X is willing to relinquish to the Y sphere of influence cases not involving X processors in exchange for bringing within its legal control cases involving X processors; Y takes a similar position with respect to Y consumers. . .
>
> The cases disposed of by the above points of agreement are those Professor Currie has called false conflicts cases. . . The same analysis by which Currie distinguishes real from false conflicts

> cases can resolve real conflicts cases. The question "Will the social objective underlying the X rule be furthered by the application of the rule in cases like the present one?" need not necessarily be answered "Yes" or "No"; the answer will often be, "Yes, to some extent." The extent to which the purpose underlying a rule will be furthered by application or impaired by nonapplication to cases of a particular category may be regarded as the measure of the rule's pertinence and of the state's interest in the rule's application to cases within the category. Normative resolution of real conflicts cases is possible where one of the assertedly applicable rules is more pertinent to the case than the competing rule.

Baxter went on to illustrate this point with a different hypothetical:

> Suppose a State Y resident, while driving a truck on State X highways in violation of the X speed limit, causes injury to another resident of Y, and X but not Y attaches a per se negligence subrule to violations of its speed limits. Y lawmakers have a superior claim to control loss-distribution rights and duties between the Y residents involved. Although no X resident is involved, the fact that the proscribed conduct took place in X cannot be dismissed as irrelevant. The objective of the X lawmakers in passing the speed limit and one of their objectives in establishing the per se subrule was to create a condition of safety for the principal users of the state's highways, X residents. The application of X's per se rule in a case involving only Y residents is not totally unrelated to that objective: effectuation of the regulatory purpose of the per se rule depends on deterrence, which depends on expectation of the rule's application. . .
>
> If the Y driver causes injury to an X resident while driving in X at a speed in excess of the X speed limit, X's per se rule should be applied. X has an interest in implementing its regulatory provision, and its interest in the application of its loss-distribution rule offsets Y's corresponding loss-distribution interest. If an X driver causes injury to a Y resident while driving at excessive speed within X, the X per se rule should also be applied. X has an interest in implementing its regulatory provision, and again the respective loss-distribution factors offset one another.
>
> If these conclusions are accepted, it seems to follow in the original per se rule hypothetical case involving only Y parties that X's per se rule ought not to be applied. There, X's regulatory interest stands alone in opposition to Y's loss-distribution interest. The suggestion is not that some rough parity in the number of instances allocated to each state is to be achieved; rather, it is that the X regulatory interest will not be impaired

significantly if it is subordinated in the comparatively rare instances involving two nonresidents, who are residents of a state or states that reject the per se subrule. Conduct on X highways will not be affected by knowledge of Y residents that the X per se rule will not be applied to them if the person they injure happens to be a co-citizen. To the extent that the objective of the per se rule is loss-distribution rather than regulation, X has no legitimate interest in the rule's application because neither party is identified with X. . .

The preceding group of hypothetical situations illustrates several propositions. First, in choice-of-law cases there are two distinct types of governmental objectives, internal and external. The internal objectives are those underlying each state's resolution of conflicting private interests. These objectives inhere in a case even if the fact situation is wholly localized to a single state. In a usury case, for example, the competing private interests of commercial freedom and protection of economically weak borrowers are present even if the case is wholly internal to either State X or State Y. External objectives are introduced when a transaction affects persons identified with different states. They are the objectives of each state to make effective, in all situations involving persons as to whom it has responsibility for legal ordering, that resolution of contending private interests the state has made for local purposes. In each real conflicts case the external objective of one state must be subordinated. The choice problem posed is that of allocating spheres of lawmaking control.

The second proposition the hypothetical situations illustrate is that one can articulate and apply a normative principle to determine which external objective to subordinate. The principle is to subordinate, in the particular case, the external objective of the state whose internal objective will be least impaired in general scope and impact by subordination in cases like the one at hand.

Implicit in the principle is an assertion that a court can and should go beyond a determination whether a state has *any* governmental interest in the application of its internal law—that a court can and should determine which state's internal objective will be least impaired by subordination in cases like the one before it. This determination is very different in kind from the weighing process often referred to by similar rubrics, but the two are often confused. . .

[Resolving true conflicts by applying forum law is subject to the same objection as] that which Currie and others have used to discredit the mechanical choice-of-law system expounded by

> Professor Beale and the first *Restatement*: [always applying forum law], like the *Restatement* system, will, in Currie's delightfully apt phraseology, "casually defeat now the one and now the other policy, depending upon a purely fortuitous circumstance." Under [the forum law] proposal, the fortuitous circumstance is the act of forum selection by the plaintiff. It is fortuitous because it has no greater normative content than the conceptual signposts of the *Restatement*. Indeed, with respect to real conflicts cases, the mechanical system of the *Restatement* must be preferred, for it affords the utility inherent in primary predictability and avoids the costs of predictable nonuniformity.
>
> The comparative-impairment principle is advocated because, without sacrificing primary predictability, it invokes the normative criterion of implementing state policies. The principle seems to me vulnerable to attack only on the ground of uncertainty—that it is so vacuous in content and uncertain in application as to be inappropriate for adjudicative administration. Professor Currie seems to invoke a part of this uncertainty objection when he states that courts should not attempt to weigh the comparative external objectives because they are not equipped to discover the facts upon which resolution must turn. Neither this part of the objection . . . nor the more general objection seems to me to be persuasive.

16 Stan.L.Rev. at 7–8, 12–13, 17–20. Why is a model of interstate negotiations appropriate in thinking about the resolution of true conflicts? If actual negotiations were held, do you think the participants would produce an agreement resembling Baxter's principle of comparative impairment? Is this what existing treaties and international conventions look like?

(2) What is the relationship between Baxter's comparative impairment principle and Currie's "moderate and restrained" interpretation? Did Justice Sullivan get it right in *Bernhard*? See Kay, *The Use of Comparative Impairment to Resolve True Conflicts: An Evaluation of the California Experience,* 68 Calif.L.Rev. 577, 583–84 (1980) (arguing that Sullivan's fusion of these approaches fundamentally misconstrues both Currie and Baxter). Isn't *People v. One 1953 Ford Victoria* (discussed in *Bernhard*) merely a replica of *Bernkrant v. Fowler,* supra p. 186? Is *Bernhard* itself merely *Bernkrant*'s restrained interpretation applied to another state's law?

Baxter says that comparative impairment analysis differs from balancing state interests. How? Can we decide that one state's interest would be more seriously impaired than another's without deciding how great the interests are in the first place? And if we could, would comparative impairment necessarily "approximate maximum utility"? Isn't Baxter simply asking whether the glass is more than half full instead of less than half empty?

(3) How persuasive are Baxter's own illustrations? In the case of two Y residents who have an accident in X, Baxter would apply Y law because accidents in X between citizens of Y are rare enough that applying Y law in such cases will only marginally impair X's policy of deterrence. But why is it not true for the very same reason that if X law is applied Y's loss-distribution policy will also be impaired only marginally? What is the basis for Baxter's confident assertion that the (incremental) impairment of Y's loss-distribution policy is greater than the (incremental) impairment of X's deterrence policy? Aren't we comparing apples and oranges? How does one measure the impairment of a regulatory policy of deterrence against that of a distributive policy for allocating losses?

Consider also the case in which a Y driver injures an X resident in X. According to Baxter, X's per se negligence rule should apply because "X has an interest in implementing its regulatory provision, and its interest in the application of its loss-distribution rule offsets Y's corresponding loss-distribution interest." But what if Y is more deeply committed to its loss-distribution policy than X? Is Baxter just counting up interests?

(4) How well does the comparative impairment principle work in practice? Was Baxter's analysis correctly applied in *Bernhard*? Since Nevada's gambling business depends so heavily on out-of-state patronage, won't its interest in protecting local casinos be severely impaired if it must apply the regulatory laws of other states? How would you decide the case?[8] Was Baxter too quick to dismiss the charge of uncertainty (and hence unpredictability)?

Consider also *Offshore Rental Co. v. Continental Oil Co.*, 22 Cal.3d 157, 148 Cal.Rptr. 867, 583 P.2d 721 (1978). Plaintiff, a California corporation, sent its vice-president, Howard Kaylor, from his office in Texas to a meeting at defendant's facilities in Louisiana, where Kaylor was injured through the negligence of defendant's employees. After Kaylor was compensated for his injury, plaintiff brought an action in California for damages caused by the loss of services of this "key" employee. California Civil Code § 49 prohibited "[a]ny injury to a servant which affects his ability to serve his master," and the court assumed "for purposes of analysis" that this provision created a cause of action for injuring employees of corporations; a recent Louisiana case, in contrast, had held that a corporate plaintiff had no cause of action under an analogous statute. Assuming the existence of a true conflict without examining the

[8] The California Supreme Court's opinion, by the way, failed to reflect that the Nevada criminal statute construed in *Hamm* had been repealed in 1973. Thus, the suggestion that applying California law "would not impose an entirely new duty requiring the ability to distinguish between California residents and other patrons" is inaccurate. Does this change the outcome?

content of the different laws, the California Supreme Court reasoned that impairment depended on how strongly a state's policy is held, which in turn depends on the law's "current vitality." The court held:

> Applying the comparative impairment principle to the present case, we first probe the history and current status of the laws before us. The majority of common law states that have considered the matter do not sanction actions for harm to business employees, recognizing that even if injury to the master-servant relationship were at one time the basis for an action at common law, the radical change in the nature of that relationship since medieval times nullifies any right by a modern corporate employer to recover for negligent injury to his employees. . .
>
> Indeed California itself has exhibited little concern in applying section 49 to the employer-employee relationship: despite the provisions of the antique statute, no California court has heretofore squarely held that California law provides an action for harm to business employees, and no California court has recently considered the issue at all. If, as we have assumed, section 49 does provide an action for harm to key corporate employees, in Professor Freund's words the section constitutes a law "archaic and isolated in the context of the laws of the federal union." We therefore conclude that the trial judge in the present case correctly applied Louisiana, rather than California, law, since California's interest in the application of its unusual and outmoded statute is comparatively less strong than Louisiana's corollary interest, so lately expressed, in its "prevalent and progressive" law. . .
>
> Furthermore, in connection with our search for the proper law to apply based on the "maximum attainment of underlying purposes by all governmental entities," we note the realistic fact that insurance is available to guard against the exigencies of the present case. . . The present plaintiff, a business corporation, . . . could have obtained protection against the occurrence of injury to its corporate vice-president by purchasing key-employee insurance, certainly a reasonable and foreseeable business expense. . .
>
> Although it is equally true that defendant is a business corporation able to calculate the risks of potential tort liability and to plan accordingly, because defendant's operations in Louisiana presumably involved dealing with key employees of companies incorporated in diverse states defendant would most reasonably have anticipated a need for the protection of premises' liability insurance based on Louisiana law. Accordingly, under these

> circumstances we conclude that the burden of obtaining insurance for the loss at issue here is most properly borne by the plaintiff corporation. . .
>
> [W]e have determined that the California statute has historically been of minimal importance in the fabric of California law, and that the Louisiana courts have recently interpreted their analogous Louisiana statute narrowly in light of that statute's obsolescence. We do not believe that California's interests in the application of its law to the present case are so compelling as to prevent an accommodation to the stronger, more current interest of Louisiana.

22 Cal.3d at 167–69, 583 P.2d at 727–29. How persuasive is the court's discussion of insurance and expectations? Couldn't the court have avoided the conflict by doing what the Louisiana court did and interpreting § 49 narrowly? Why didn't it do so? Is the court's analysis what Baxter had in mind or did it simply apply what it regarded as the better law?

Was there a true conflict in *Offshore Rental*? Since the court did not bother to examine the content of California's local policy, how can you decide? What sense does it make to assume without deciding that there is a choice-of-law problem? See Kay, 68 Cal. L. Rev. at 604–06.[9]

Does *Offshore Rental* expand the factors to be considered when applying Baxter's comparative impairment technique? Note the court's reliance upon Professor Freund's article as justification for considering the current vitality of local policy in the choice-of-law process. Would either Currie or Baxter have assented to this formulation? Baxter himself cited the very passage quoted by the court from Freund as an example of the type of super-value judgment that comparative impairment analysis would avoid. See Baxter, 16 Stan.L.Rev. at n. 39.

Several commentators have examined the cases employing comparative impairment analysis and concluded that it creates more problems than it solves. See, e.g., Kay, *The Use of Comparative Impairment to Resolve True Conflicts: An Evaluation of the California Experience,* 68 Cal. L. Rev. 577 (1980); Kanowitz, *Comparative Impairment and Better Law: Grand Illusions in the Conflict of Laws,* 30 Hastings L.J. 255 (1978); Note, *After* Hurtado *and* Bernhard*: Interest Analysis and the Search for a Consistent Theory for Choice-of-Law Cases,* 29 Stan.L.Rev. 127 (1976).

[9] Seven years after it decided *Offshore Rental,* the California Supreme Court finally got around to deciding whether the California statute created a domestic cause of action on behalf of a corporation for injuries to a key employee. Not surprisingly, it concluded that the doctrine is "obsolete, archaic and outmoded and that, as an instrument of social policy, it has no relevance to present-day employer-employee relations." *I.J. Weinrot & Son, Inc. v. Jackson,* 40 Cal.3d 327, 340, 220 Cal.Rptr. 103, 708 P.2d 682, 691 (1985). Does this mean that *Offshore Rental* didn't even present a choice of law problem, let alone a true conflict?

(5) In *Kearney v. Salomon Smith Barney, Inc.*, 39 Cal.4th 95, 137 P.3d 914, 45 Cal.Rptr.3d 730 (2006), the California Supreme Court confronted a conflict between a California law requiring the consent of all parties before a telephone conversation could be recorded and a Georgia law which allowed recording with the consent of one participant. (Employees at the Atlanta branch of Salomon Smith Barney had recorded conversations with clients in California without their knowledge or consent.) Writing for a unanimous court, Chief Justice George concluded that the case presented a true conflict and proceeded to apply the comparative impairment analysis set forth in *Bernhard and Offshore Rental.* He pointedly refrained, however, from endorsing *Offshore Rental*'s search for whether one of the conflicting laws was "archaic and isolated in the context of the laws of the federal union," noting only that the California law, although in the minority, was not "ancient." 39 Cal.4th at 124–125, 583 P.2d at 934 (citing *Offshore Rental,* 22 Cal.3d at 167–168, 583 P.2d at 721). The court decided that California's interest would be more impaired and therefore applied California law.

The decision invokes several different concepts of impairment. First, there is quantitative impairment. "[W]ith respect to businesses in Georgia that record telephone calls," the court observed, "California law would apply only to those telephone calls that are made to or received from California, not to all telephone calls to and from such Georgia businesses." Second, there is qualitative impairment. California's interest in protecting privacy is "strong and continuing," the Court observes, because courts have enforced the privacy law and the legislature has continued to add protections. 39 Cal.4th at 124–125, 137 P.3d at 934–935. Georgia's interests may or may not be as strong and continuing, but they are less impaired qualitatively. For one thing, "because California law, with regard to the particular matter here at issue, is more protective of privacy interests than the comparable Georgia privacy statute, the application of California law would not violate any privacy interest protected by Georgia law." For another, California law "prohibits only the *secret* or *undisclosed* recording of telephone conversations [and thus] if a Georgia business discloses at the outset of a call made to or received from a California customer that the call is being recorded" California law will not impose liability. "Accordingly, to the extent Georgia law is intended to protect the right of a business to record conversations when it has a legitimate business justification for doing so, the application of California law to telephone calls between a Georgia business and its California clients or customers would not defeat that interest." 39 Cal.4th at 126–127, 137 P.3d at 936.

Is the quantitative assessment valid, or should we ask only what the degree of impairment is when it exists? (And couldn't the court just as well have said that with respect to California residents, Georgia law would apply only to calls made to or from Georgia?) For qualitative impairment, is the court suggesting that a more protective law will always be more impaired? *Butler v. Adoption Media, LLC*, 486 F.Supp.2d 1022 (N.D. Cal. 2007), suggests this may be the case. There, a California same-sex couple seeking to adopt a child tried to use the services of a website, operated from Arizona by Arizona domiciliaries, that allowed prospective adoptive parents to post profiles in hopes of contacting mothers who might give up a child for adoption. The website refused their posting on the grounds that the service was limited to heterosexual married couples. The California couple sued under the California Civil Rights Act, alleging discrimination based on marital status and sexual orientation. Relying on *Kearney*, the court concluded that California's interests would be more impaired, offering as one of several reasons that applying California law would "not violate any right protected by Arizona law." Id. at 1053.

The *Kearney* court admits that applying California law will impinge on a Georgia "business's ability *secretly* to record its customers' telephone calls. . ." But, the court said, "we believe that, particularly as applied to a business's blanket policy of routinely recording telephone calls to and from California customers, this consequence would represent only a relatively minor impairment of Georgia's interests." 39 Cal.4th at 128, 137 P.3d at 936. Later it added that:

> because this case does not involve the isolated recording of a personal telephone call by an out-of-state individual in a nonbusiness setting, or the recording of a phone call by an out-of-state business that has a reasonable, individualized basis for believing that a particular caller is engaged in criminal or wrongful conduct, we have no occasion to determine how the comparative impairment analysis would apply in those or other comparable settings.

39 Cal.4th at 131 n.18, 137 P.3d at 939 n.18. How fact- and case-specific should choice-of-law analysis be?

Last, the court decided that "in order to accommodate Georgia's interest in protecting persons who acted in Georgia in reasonable reliance on Georgia law from being subjected to liability on the basis of such action" it would not allow recovery of damages for past recordings. 39 Cal.4th at 128, 137 P.3d at 937. Is this adding a temporal dimension to choice of law?

(6) Chief Justice George, the author of *Kearney*, wrote a second unanimous opinion on comparative impairment in *McCann v. Foster Wheeler LLC*, 225 P.3d 516, 48 Cal.4th 68 (2010). *McCann* involved a plaintiff diagnosed with mesothelioma suing a defendant who designed and installed a boiler that plaintiff observed being treated with an application of asbestos insulation over a two-week period in Oklahoma in 1957. At the time, he lived and worked in Oklahoma. He was diagnosed in 2005 with mesothelioma in California, where he had lived and worked since 1975. *McCann* presented a conflict between the statute of repose in Oklahoma, which cut off the personal injury liability of a designer or constructor of "an improvement to real property" in Oklahoma 10 years after completion, and the longer California statute of limitations, which allowed suit within one year after the plaintiff first suffered disability from asbestos and knew or reasonably should have known that the disability was caused by exposure to asbestos. The Supreme Court held that Oklahoma's interest in providing a reasonable assurance of protection to businesses operating within the state would be severely impaired if plaintiffs could revive their claims by moving (deliberately or not) to a state with a more lenient limitations period. By contrast, California's interest in compensating Californians would be only minimally impaired by denying recovery for out-of-state torts barred by foreign limitations periods. The Court called this a "restrained view" of California's interest. Will interests created by post-event changes of domicile tend to be less impaired? Is *McCann* similar to *Bernkrant*?

(7) Professor Kramer has sought to reinterpret and modify comparative impairment analysis. According to Kramer, Currie's original proposal to resolve true conflicts by applying forum law assumed that such cases were zero-sum, i.e., that the gain to one state from having its policy advanced was matched by the other state's identical loss. The insight behind comparative impairment is that, while this may be true for any particular case, it is not true for the entire set of true conflicts. Rather, each state presumably cares more about some true conflicts than others because some true conflicts affect more important purposes of the state's laws or affect these purposes in more important ways. Choice of law is thus a variable-sum game in which some solutions advance state interests better than others by calling for the application of each state's laws in more of the cases that state cares about most. Baxter's comparative impairment principle attempts to make these trade-offs and in this way to maximize the extent to which each state realizes its objectives in multistate cases.

The problem is that identifying which state has the greater stake on a case-by-case basis is too complex and difficult for judges in practice. Therefore, Kramer proposes instead to develop and apply a set of "policy-selecting rules" that direct courts to apply the law that reflects a generally shared policy or policy preference—regardless of whose law that is in the particular case. In this way, Kramer argues, all states may systematically advance their more important interests better than with a forum preference or case-by-case analysis. Kramer claims that a rule-based approach will also be superior in advancing multistate policies, because preventing forum shopping, achieving uniformity and predictability, and facilitating multistate activity all depend on parties being able to know the applicable law in advance. Finally, Kramer observes that maximizing state interests requires reciprocity inasmuch as each state's forbearance from applying its own law must be repaid by the reciprocal forbearance of other states in other cases, and he argues that states can better coordinate their handling of cases and monitor each other with a system of articulated rules for reference. See Kramer, *Rethinking Choice of Law,* 90 Colum.L.Rev. 277, 311–44 (1990); Kramer, *Return of the Renvoi,* 66 N.Y.U. L. Rev. 979, 1015–28 (1991); Kramer, *More Notes on Methods and Objectives in the Conflict of Laws,* 24 Cornell Int'l L.J. 245, 271–77 (1991).

According to Kramer, such rules need not be based on value judgments about which policies are normatively superior, but rather should turn on shared policies or policy preferences reflected in existing laws. He offers several strategies for developing appropriate rules. First, we can identify situations in which both states prefer one type of policy over another. If courts in both states then apply the law reflecting this preferred policy—regardless of whose law it is in the particular case—both states should benefit over time. For example, Kramer argues that states generally prefer substantive to procedural policies because the "ultimate purpose of procedural law . . . is to implement substantive law" and because "when conflicts between substantive and procedural policies arise in wholly domestic cases, courts typically favor the substantive rule." 66 N.Y.U. L. Rev. at 1020–21. Therefore, he proposes a rule providing that "in a conflict between one state's procedural policy and another state's substantive policy, the court should apply the law reflecting the substantive policy." Kramer explains:

> The forum sacrifices its procedural policies in favor of another state's substantive policies, but gains by having its substantive policies similarly preferred when they conflict with [a foreign state's] procedural rules in cases outside the forum. Hence, in addition to the increased certainty and reduced forum shopping associated with rules generally, this particular rule systematically advances the more important [substantive] policies of both states.

Id. at 1021. In contexts where it is not possible as an empirical matter to say that one type of policy is preferred in both states, Kramer suggests trying to identify a "shared third policy" around which to construct a tiebreaking rule: "Because the conflicting interests underlying specific laws will presumably balance out over time and many cases, choosing the law that consistently advances the shared policy again yields a marginal benefit to both states." Id. Kramer illustrates this strategy with a rule calling for courts to apply the law on which parties actually relied, which (he reasons) advances a shared third policy of fairness.

Is this an improvement over Baxter? In addition to the rules described above, Kramer provides several further illustrations, explaining that these are meant to invite debate rather than to provide an exhaustive system for deciding cases. 90 Colum.L.Rev. at 319–38. He proposes applying the law chosen by the parties in contract cases, or, if no choice is made, applying whichever law validates the agreement; and he argues that "[w]here one of two conflicting laws is obsolete (i.e., inconsistent with prevailing legal and social norms in the state that enacted it), the other law should be applied." 90 Colum.L.Rev. at 329–36. Do such rules satisfy Kramer's own requirements? Do they make choice of law more predictable? What if more than one rule is potentially applicable in the same case? More important, how likely is it that courts can develop such rules, and what are they supposed to do in the meantime? Can you think of rules that satisfy Kramer's criteria? How should a case like *Bernhard* be decided? How about *Offshore*? What are the prospects for developing and adopting a comprehensive system of policy-selecting rules through the legislative process? See Kramer, *On the Need for a Uniform Choice of Law Code,* 89 Mich.L.Rev. 2134 (1991). Both Kramer's general approach and his specific examples arc criticized in Weinberg, *Against Comity,* 80 Geo.L.J. 53 (1991). Conversely, Professors Allen and O'Hara make very much the same argument as Kramer (except for putting greater emphasis on predictability) in urging that Baxter's approach supports resuscitating the First Restatement, with some slight modifications in the rules. Allen & O'Hara, *Second Generation Law and Economics of Conflict of Laws: Baxter's Comparative Impairment and Beyond,* 51 Stan. L. Rev. 1011 (1999).

EDWARDS V. ERIE COACH LINES COMPANY

17 N.Y.3d 306, 952 N.E.2d 1033, 929 N.Y.S.2d 41 (2011).

READ, J.

Near Geneseo, New York on January 19, 2005 a charter bus carrying members of an Ontario women's hockey team plowed into the rear end of a tractor-trailer parked on the shoulder of the highway. Three bus passengers and the tractor driver died; several bus passengers were seriously hurt. We are called upon to decide the choice-of-law issue presented by these six lawsuits, which were brought to recover damages for wrongful death and/or personal injuries.

I.

Nearly a half-century ago, in *Babcock v. Jackson,* 12 N.Y.2d 473, 240 N.Y.S.2d 743, 191 N.E.2d 279 (1963), we abandoned what had long been our choice-of-law rule whereby the law of the place of the tort invariably governed. Because "in nearly all such cases, the conduct causing injury and the injury itself occurred in the same jurisdiction" * * * this rule offered "the advantages of certainty, ease of application and predictability," but at the expense of "the interest which [other] jurisdictions . . . [might] have in the resolution of particular issues". * * *

To "accomodat[e] the competing interests in tort cases with multi-State contacts," we adopted the "center of gravity" or "grouping of contacts" approach, which gave the "controlling effect to the law of the jurisdiction which, because of its relationship or contact with the occurrence or the parties, ha[d] the greatest concern with the specific issue raised in the litigation" * * * This new method of analysis, however, was limited to competing loss-allocation—not conduct-regulating—rules.[1] As we explained in *Babcock,*

> "[w]here the defendant's exercise of due care in the operation of his automobile is in issue, the jurisdiction in which the allegedly wrongful conduct occurred will usually have a predominant, if not exclusive, concern. In such a case, it is appropriate to look to the law of the place of the tort so as to give effect to that jurisdiction's interest in regulating conduct within its borders, and it would he almost unthinkable to seek the applicable rule in the law of some other place".* * *

The facts of *Babcock* illustrate how "grouping of contacts" worked. In that case, a New York passenger in a car operated by a New York driver was injured in an automobile accident that occurred in Ontario during a weekend trip to Canada. We noted that the trip began and was to end in New York, where the car was garaged, licensed and insured, and where the driver-passenger relationship arose. * * * The "guest" passenger sued the "host" driver in New York for negligence. At the time, the Ontario guest statute barred the passenger from recovering damages from the driver, while New York law did not.

Looking to the "grouping of contacts," we decided that New York—not Ontario, the place of the tort—possessed "the dominant contacts and the superior claim for application of its law" as to whether the passenger should "recover[ ] for damages for a wrong concededly committed" * * * We commented that, in this context,

> "[a]lthough the rightness or wrongness of [the driver's] conduct may depend upon the law of the particular jurisdiction through which the automobile passes, the rights and liabilities of the parties which stem from their guest-host relationship should remain constant and not vary and shift as the automobile proceeds from place to place. Indeed, such a result . . . accords with the interests of the host in procuring liability insurance adequate under the applicable law, and the interests of his insurer in reasonable calculability of the premium" * * *.

---

[1] Loss-allocation rules "prohibit, assign, or limit liability *after the tort occurs,*" whereas conduct-regulating rules "have the prophylactic effect of governing conduct to prevent injuries from occurring" in the first place. * * *

Over time, the "grouping of contacts" approach put into place by *Babcock* evolved into a more explicit "interest analysis." This method of deciding choice-of-law issues "reject[ed] a quantitative grouping of contacts" because "[c]ontacts obtain significance only to the extent that they relate to the policies and purposes sought to be vindicated by the conflicting laws" * * *.

We refined our "interest analysis" so as "to assure a greater degree of predictability and uniformity" in *Neumeier v. Kuehner,* 31 N.Y.2d 121, 127, 335 N.Y.S.2d 64, 286 N.E.2d 454 (1972), a case where a domiciliary of Ontario was killed when the automobile in which he was a passenger collided with a train in Ontario. The vehicle was owned and driven by a resident of New York, who was also killed in the accident. The passenger's wife and administratrix, a citizen of Canada and a domiciliary of Ontario, brought an action for wrongful death in New York against the driver's estate and the railway company, both of which interposed affirmative defenses involving the Ontario guest statute. . .

Neumeier set up a three-rule framework for resolving choice of law in conflicts settings involving guest statutes, which by definition allocate losses after the tort occurs rather than regulate primary conduct. Under the first *Neumeier* rule, when the driver and passenger are domiciled in the same state, and the vehicle is registered there, the law of their shared jurisdiction controls * * * The second rule addresses the situation where the driver and the passenger are domiciled in different states, and the law of the place where the accident occurred favors its domiciliary. When the driver's conduct occurs in the state where he is domiciled, which would not impose liability, that state's law applies. Conversely, if the law of the place where the accident occurred permits the injured passenger to recover, then the driver, "in the absence of special circumstances," may not interpose a conflicting law of his state as a defense. * * * [In essence, the second Neumeier rule adopts a "place of injury" test for true-conflict guest statute cases.]

"In other situations, when the passenger and the driver are domiciled in different states, the rule is necessarily less categorical." * * * Thus, under the third *Neumeier* rule, the law of the state where the accident occurred governs unless "it can be shown that displacing that normally applicable rule will advance the relevant substantive law purposes without impairing the smooth working of the multi-state system or producing great uncertainty for litigants."

Since the passenger in *Neumeier* was domiciled in Ontario, where the guest statute did not allow recovery, and the driver in New York, the third rule—the law of the place of the tort (i.e., Ontario)—would normally control. We saw no reason to apply the third rule's proviso since the wife "failed to show that [New York's] connection with the controversy was sufficient to justify displacing" lex loci delicti, the law of the place of the wrong. * * * The wife did not show that ignoring Ontario's guest statute in a case "involv[ing] an Ontario-domiciled guest at the expense of a New Yorker . . . further[ed] the substantive law purposes of New York"; and "failure to apply Ontario's law would impair . . . the smooth working of the multi-state system [and] produce great uncertainty for litigants by sanctioning forum shopping and thereby allowing a party to select a forum [countenancing] a larger recovery than [that party's] own domicile". * * *

We have routinely applied the *Neumeier* framework to conflicts in loss-allocation situations not involving guest statutes. [For example, *Schultz v. Boy Scouts of America*, supra p. 159.]

II.

[The bus driver, his employer, and the company that leased the bus (the "bus defendants") are Ontario domiciliaries, as are (or were) all the injured and deceased passengers. The tractor-trailer driver, his employer, and the companies that hired the trailer (the "trailer defendants") are (or were) Pennsylvania domiciliaries.] The injured passengers and the representatives of those who died (collectively, plaintiffs) filed multiple wrongful death and personal injury lawsuits in Supreme Court.

These split-domicile lawsuits presented an obvious choice-of-law issue because Ontario caps noneconomic damages where negligence causes catastrophic personal injury, while New York does not cap such damages in a no-fault case involving serious injury. [The trial court, performing a single analysis for both the bus and the trailer defendants, decided that Ontario law governed as to the damages cap.]

Citing the third *Neumeier* rule, the judge stated, without elaboration, that "[a]pplying Ontario loss allocation laws [would] not impair the smooth working of the multi-state system, and [would] advance the relevant substantive law purposes of the jurisdiction having the most significant connections to the allocation of loss"; and that Ontario "clearly [had] the predominant interest[ ] in applying its loss allocation laws to its citizens, whereas New York [had] no such interest."

[The Appellate division conducted a separate choice-of-law analysis for each group of defendants.] With respect to the bus defendants, the court looked to the first *Neumeier* rule, which directs that the law of the parties' common domicile—here, Ontario—governs. The court observed that applying the law of a shared domicile reduced the risk of forum shopping; rebutted the charge of local bias; and served "the concepts of mutuality and reciprocity," which are "support[ed by the] consistent application of the common domicile law" * * *

As between plaintiffs and the trailer defendants, the Appellate Division applied the third *Neumeier* rule, which prefers the law of the place of the tort. Invoking the proviso to the third rule, the court decided, however, that Ontario law should govern, reasoning that "while applying Ontario law '[might] not affirmatively advance the substantive law purposes of New York, it [would] not frustrate those interests because New York has no significant interest in applying its own law to this dispute' " * * * The court also commented that New York law created great uncertainty for the litigants because the trailer defendants were only 10% liable for the accident pursuant to the parties' [earlier] settlement. If the trailer defendants' exposure to noneconomic damages was unlimited while the bus defendants' liability for this item of damages was capped, the trailer defendants might end up paying far more than their stipulated share. [Neither court considered Pennsylvania law because no party requested it.]

For the reasons that follow, we [reverse] with respect to the trailer defendants.

III.

. . .[P]laintiffs press for what they call a "single, joint *Neumeier* analysis" in cases, such as this one, with multiple tortfeasors. As a result, the . . . plaintiffs argue, the trial judge "properly analyzed both sets of Defendants—those related to the bus and those related to the tractor trailer—together," although he reached the wrong conclusion. In our view, however, the correct way to conduct a choice-of-law analysis is to consider each plaintiff vis-à-vis each defendant, which is essentially the approach taken by the Appellate Division. More to the point, this is the path we ourselves have already traveled: in *Schultz,* the plaintiffs likewise demanded judgment, jointly and severally, against multiple defendants, and we applied the *Neumeier* rules separately in relation to the New Jersey-domiciled Boy Scouts and the Ohio-domiciled Franciscan Brothers. The rules in the *Neumeier* framework, in fact, by their very nature call for a plaintiff-by-defendant inquiry.[10]

Here, the Ontario cap controls any award of noneconomic damages against the bus defendants because they share an Ontario domicile with plaintiffs. We described the relevant choice-of-law principle and its rationale in *Cooney v. Osgood Machinery, Inc.*, 81 N.Y.2d 66, 595 N.Y.S.2d 919, 612 N.E.2d 277 (1993):

---

[10] The dissent opines that "[a]pplying a single *Neumeier* analysis to jointly and severally liable defendants and having them subject to the same laws would further the goals of predictability and uniformity". * * * Making multiple defendants ultimately subject to the same loss-allocation rules might make management of a case simpler for the courts and the parties. A "single . . . analysis," however, would not guarantee "predictability and uniformity." For one thing, under this approach the choice of law for loss allocation in a multi-state, multi-tortfeasor case would depend on which potential defendants a plaintiff chose to sue. The fact is, when we departed from *lex loci delicti* in *Babcock,* we knowingly sacrificed a degree of certainty so as to honor our sister states' interests in enforcing their own loss-allocation rules with respect to their own domiciliaries.* * *

> "Under the first *Neumeier* rule, when [the plaintiff and the defendant] share a common domicile, that law should control. Indeed, when both parties are from the same jurisdiction, there is often little reason to apply another jurisdiction's loss allocation rules. The domiciliary jurisdiction, which has weighed the competing considerations underlying the loss allocation rule at issue, has the greater 'interest in enforcing the decisions of both parties to accept both the benefits and the burdens of identifying with that jurisdiction and to submit themselves to its authority' . . . Moreover, this rule reduces opportunities for forum shopping because the same law will apply whether the suit is brought in the locus jurisdiction or in the common domicile, the two most likely forums." * * *

We had earlier made the same point at least as forcefully in *Schultz,* where we stressed that "the locus jurisdiction has *at best a minimal interest* in determining the right of recovery or the extent of the remedy in an action by a foreign domiciliary for injuries resulting from the conduct of a codomiciliary that was tortious under the laws of both jurisdictions". . .

In sum, Ontario has weighed the interests of tortfeasors and their victims in cases of catastrophic personal injury, and has elected to safeguard its domiciliaries from large awards for nonpecuniary damages. In lawsuits brought in New York by Ontario-domiciled plaintiffs against Ontario-domiciled defendants, New York courts should respect Ontario's decision, which differs from but certainly does not offend New York's public policy. * * *

Finally, we look to the third *Neumeier* rule to decide whether the Ontario cap controls with respect to the trailer defendants. Critically, the third rule establishes the place of the tort—here, New York—as the "normally applicable" choice in a conflicts situation such as this one, where the domicile of plaintiffs, the domicile of the trailer defendants and the place of the tort are different. Initially, the fact that the trailer defendants declined to advocate for Pennsylvania law does not permit them to take advantage of the Ontario cap. To rule otherwise would only encourage a kind of forum shopping.

[T]here is no cause to contemplate a jurisdiction other than New York, the place where the conduct causing injuries and the injuries themselves occurred. The trailer defendants did not ask Supreme Court to consider the law of their domicile, Pennsylvania, and they had no contacts whatsoever with Ontario other than the happenstance that plaintiffs and the bus defendants were domiciled there. . .

CIPARICK, J. (dissenting in part).

Because I believe that a single analysis pursuant to *Neumeier v. Kuehner,* 31 N.Y.2d 121, 335 N.Y.S.2d 64, 286 N.E.2d 454 (1972) should be applied where nondomiciliary defendants are jointly and severally liable to nondomiciliary plaintiffs in a tort action arising out of a single incident within the State of New York, and that under such an analysis New York law should apply to all defendants for purposes of uniformity and predictability, I respectfully dissent.

In this matter, all plaintiffs and the bus defendants are domiciliaries of Ontario whereas the tractor-trailer defendants are domiciled in Pennsylvania. The majority opines that each defendant should be analyzed separately under the *Neumeier* rules relying on *Schultz v. Boy Scouts of Am.*, 65 N.Y.2d 189, 491 N.Y.S.2d 90, 480 N.E.2d 679 (1985). * * * In applying a separate *Neumeier* analysis to each defendant, the majority determines that Ontario law should apply to the bus defendants, while New York law should apply to the tractor-trailer defendants. I disagree.

While the facts in *Schultz* lent themselves to a separate analysis for each defendant, the facts in this case do not justify such an analysis. The plaintiffs in *Schultz* alleged that the two defendants, the Boy Scouts of America and the Brothers of the Poor of St. Francis, had each negligently hired and supervised the same sexually abusive employee. The alleged sexual abuse occurred while the plaintiffs' sons were at a Boy Scout camp in New York and continued at a school in New Jersey. The tortious activities in *Schultz* took place over varied periods of time and in different locations. Moreover, there was no relationship between the defendants' actions other than the fact that they employed the same alleged bad actor. Because the torts were distinct acts occurring at different times, it was appropriate for us to perform a separate choice-of-law analysis.

In contrast, in the instant case, the causes of action arise from a single incident in New York—the collision of the bus into the parked tractor-trailer—and the liability of the defendants is interrelated. * * *

Furthermore, a separate *Neumeier* analysis for differently domiciled defendants creates additional unpredictability and lack of uniformity in litigation that arises from a single incident. The purpose of the *Neumeier* rules is to "assure a greater degree of predictability and uniformity, on the basis of our present knowledge and experience." * * * Applying a single *Neumeier* analysis to jointly and severally liable defendants and having them subject to the same laws would further the goals of predictability and uniformity. In fact, this case illustrates the potential for grossly inequitable results when different laws are applied to defendants who are jointly and severally liable. Here, during a jury trial on liability, defendants entered into a stipulation whereby they agreed that they are 100% jointly and severally liable to plaintiffs and further agreed to apportion such liability between themselves at 90% to the bus defendants and the remaining 10% to the tractor-trailer defendants. The majority allows for a situation whereby the tractor-trailer defendants may end up paying more than the bus defendants because of the cap applied on noneconomic tort awards by Ontario—a patently absurd result. Therefore, to further the goal of predictability and uniformity, this matter should be analyzed under a single *Neumeier* analysis.

In analyzing this matter under a single *Neumeier* analysis, it is clear that, because plaintiffs and defendants are differently domiciled, the law of the site of the tort—here New York—should apply as set forth in the third *Neumeier* rule. Moreover, the exception to the third *Neumeier* rule does not apply to these facts. . .

[T]he exception to the third *Neumeier* rule should only apply when a state other than the forum-locus state has a "greate[r] interest in the litigation" * * *

Here, it is uncontroverted that both defendants are commercial enterprises that perform significant business in the State of New York and more significantly are frequent users of New York's highways in pursuit of their business. New York has a strong interest in the conduct of business enterprises on its highways and in properly compensating the victims of torts, whether New York or foreign domiciliaries, committed by business enterprises on its highways.

Thus, in determining which forum has the greatest interest in this litigation, it is clear that it is New York. Not only does New York have a strong interest in regulating the conduct of commercial vehicles on its highways, it also has an even stronger interest in having commercial vehicles that use its highways maintain insurance to compensate victims of torts committed by said vehicles. In contrast, Ontario's primary interest in having its law applied and capping nonpecuniary losses is to keep motor vehicle insurance costs low. * * * That interest, however, need not extend to commercial vehicles operating outside of Ontario and subject to the loss-allocation laws of those states.

Finally, because New York is "the only State with which [all] parties have purposefully associated themselves" * * * and availed themselves of New York highways for profit and tourism, applying New York law is entirely appropriate in this matter.

Accordingly, I would reverse the order of the Appellate Division.

The New York Approach

(1) While New York started the modern choice-of-law "revolution" in *Babcock v. Jackson*, 12 N.Y.2d 473, 240 N.Y.S.2d 743, 191 N.E.2d 279 (1963), since then it has fumbled around for a consistent approach to the problem. As noted above, p. 165, *Babcock* itself appeared to endorse a variety of different theories, leading to considerable confusion in subsequent cases. *Tooker v. Lopez*, 24 N.Y.2d 569, 301 N.Y.S.2d 519, 249 N.E.2d 394 (1969), sought to settle this confusion by adopting a straightforward form of interest analysis, but Chief Judge Fuld laid the groundwork for further changes in a concurring opinion in which he argued that the court had enough experience to adopt three new rules for guest statute cases. See supra, p. 156. Fuld persuaded a majority of the court to adopt these rules in *Neumeier v. Kuehner*, 31 N.Y.2d 121, 335 N.Y.S.2d 64, 286 N.E.2d 454 (1972). *Schultz v. Boy Scouts of America*, 65 N.Y.2d 189, 491 N.Y.S.2d 90, 480 N.E.2d 679 (1985), included references to the *Neumeier* rules in its analysis of state interests, thus suggesting that the rules might apply outside the area of guest statutes. And after *Schultz*, many lower courts in New York began to use *Neumeier*'s rules as a general solution for multistate tort cases.

Neumeier analysis begins by distinguishing between laws that are "conduct-regulating" and laws that are "loss-allocating." When a conflict involves conduct-regulating laws, the court explains, the law of the jurisdiction where the tort occurred will generally apply. The *Neumeier* rules come into play only if there is a conflict between laws that allocate loss after a tort has occurred. Is this distinction useful? How is it to be drawn? Does the distinction turn on the *form* of a rule (*i.e.*, whether the rule "regulates primary conduct" or is a "postevent remedial rule")? If so, isn't it nonsense? See Twerski, *A Sheep in Wolf's Clothing: Territorialism in the Guise of Interest Analysis in* Cooney v. Osgood Machinery, Inc., 59 Brooklyn L. Rev. 1351, 1358–59 (1994) (criticizing *Schultz*'s effort to label charitable immunities as loss-allocating because the debate about tort immunities is over whether they encourage lax standards and negligent conduct).

If not based on form, how should the distinction between conduct-regulating and loss-allocating rules be drawn? Twerski seems to assume that it should turn on the *purpose* of a rule (a proposition that would be endorsed by any interest analyst). But if we look at purposes, won't the distinction become unmanageable—at least if it's to be used for the suggested gatekeeping role? The problem, of course, is that many rules serve both conduct-regulating and loss-allocating functions. Take, for example, the charitable immunity at issue in *Schultz*. This certainly allocates loss, but it might also logically be presumed to have an effect on conduct by making charities less careful. In fact, its purpose is to affect conduct by encouraging charities to perform good works without fear of liability. And what about cases that feature damages caps, like *Edwards*, or immunities, like *Schultz*, where one state's conduct-regulating rule comes into conflict with another state's loss-allocating rule?

In *Padula v. Lilarn Properties Corp.*, 84 N.Y.2d 519, 620 N.Y.S.2d 310, 644 N.E.2d 1001 (1994), a New York domiciliary fell from a scaffold while working at a construction site in Massachusetts. Sections 240 and 241 of New York's labor law impose strict liability on the owner of a scaffold if it fails to meet certain specifications; Massachusetts applies ordinary tort rules of negligence. Recognizing that §§ 240 and 241 are both loss-allocating and conduct-regulating, the Court nonetheless held that Massachusetts law should apply because these provisions "are primarily conduct-regulating." Is this a useful way to resolve cases involving laws that embody both functions? (Incidentally, what is the effect on conduct of the choice between strict liability and negligence? See Posner, Economic Analysis of Law 180–182 (5th ed. 1998).)

After reviewing the efforts of New York courts to distinguish between conduct-regulating and loss-allocating rules, Peter Hay and Robert Ellis conclude that the distinction "creates more trouble than it is worth." They recommend using the *Neumeier* rules in all tort cases. Hay & Ellis, *Bridging the Gap Between Rules and Approaches in Tort Choice of Law in the United States: A Survey of the Current Case Law*, 27 Int'l Lawyer 369, 382 (1993). Patrick Borchers concludes that the task of distinguishing between loss-allocating and conduct-regulating rules "is not hopeless, although the Court of Appeals is doing a good job of making it appear so." Borchers, *The Return of Territoriality to New York's Conflicts Law:* Padula v. Lilarn Properties Corp., 58 Albany L. Rev. 775, 784 (1995). He says to ask whether the difference between conflicting laws is one that is likely to generate territory-based expectations; if so, the laws should be treated as conduct-regulating.

(2) What is your evaluation of the *Neumeier* rules? What assumptions underlie them? Do the rules reflect a consistent or rational set of policies?

(a) The first *Neumeier* rule says to apply the law of the parties' common domicile (if there is one)—apparently on the assumption that such cases are false conflicts. This was true in *Babcock* and *Tooker*, but is it always true? What about a so-called reverse-*Babcock* case (in which the state where the injury occurred has the pro-recovery rule)? See Simson, 56 Albany L. Rev. at 921: "Under the interest analysis approach, a court could sensibly decide that if the tortious conduct occurred in a state with a nonimmunity (or vicarious liability or unlimited damages) law having a substantial conduct-regulating purpose, that state has an interest in the application of its law despite the parties' common domicile outside the state." Wasn't this, in fact, the case in *Schultz*?

(b) Under the second rule, the law of the place of injury should apply if the place of injury is the defendant's home state and its law protects defendants, or if the place of injury is the plaintiff's home state and its law protects plaintiffs. Why? Chief Judge Fuld did not explain or justify the rules, simply asserting that experience showed that they were "sound for situations involving guest statute conflicts." *Neumeier*, 286 N.E.2d at 457;

Tooker, 249 N.E.2d at 405. In *Cooney*, relying on Professor Korn's meticulous analysis of New York caselaw in *The Choice-of-Law Revolution: A Critique*, 83 Colum. L. Rev. 722 (1983), Chief Judge Kaye says to assume that state interests are equal in true conflict cases and break the tie with a place of injury rule because "that is the only State with which both parties have purposefully associated themselves in a significant way." Are you persuaded? She adds that the place of injury is a "neutral factor, rebutting an inference that the forum State is merely protecting its own domiciliary or favoring its own law" and that it was the "traditional choice of law crucible." Now are you persuaded? How would you rate *Neumeier*'s second rule in comparison to other solutions (such as forum preference, comparative impairment, or moderate and restrained interpretation) to true conflicts?

(c) The third rule provides that the law of the place of injury should govern any remaining cases, with a proviso that a different law may be applied if it "will advance the relevant substantive law purposes without impairing the smooth working of the multistate system or producing great uncertainty for the litigants." This rule will apply in two situations: unprovided-for cases, and true conflicts where the injury occurs in neither party's home state. Its justification is presumably the same as for the second rule. Does the idea of a territorial tiebreak make equal sense for these two kinds of case? And what about the proviso? How is a judge to decide when to depart from the place-of-injury rule, particularly since questions of uncertainty and of the "smooth working of the multistate system" are largely dependent on how often courts depart from the rule? And how is a court supposed to weigh substantive law purposes against effects on the multistate system or uncertainty for litigants? Would you expect departures to be more common in the true conflict or the unprovided-for variant of the third rule?

Justice Ciparick's dissent in *Edwards* asserts that the exception should apply only when a state other than the place of injury has a greater interest. If we take this seriously, it suggests that courts should invoke the exception primarily in true conflicts where the injury occurs in a third state, presumably to avoid applying the law of a disinterested state when other states are interested. See, e.g., *Gilbert v. Seton Hall University*, 332 F.3d 105 (2d Cir. 2003) (invoking exception to apply New Jersey law to suit by Connecticut student against New Jersey university based on injury in New York). Is this use of the exception unobjectionable in principle? Is it likely that its use will be confined to such cases in practice? See, e.g., *Schultz*, supra p. 159 (applying New Jersey law to Ohio defendant Franciscan Brothers); *Stevens v. Shields*, 131 Misc.2d 145, 499 N.Y.S.2d 351 (Sup. Ct. 1986) (applying Florida law to impose vicarious liability on the parents of a Florida minor who had an accident in New York on the ground that New York had no interest in protecting these nonresidents from liability).

Hay & Ellis collect additional cases and conclude that the exception in *Neumeier*'s third rule

> potentially provides an avenue for the disregard of the basic rules. . . All rule-based approaches to choice of law do, of course, need an ultimate escape (corrective) device, as the European experience in contracts choice-of-law unification also teaches. There, however, the tradition has been more rule oriented. The question, therefore, is to what extent U.S. courts can resist the temptation to start the analysis with the broadly phrased exception rather than with the narrowly drawn rule?

Hay & Ellis, 27 Int'l Lawyer at 379–80 & nn. 46–47.

(3) Other commentators, downplaying the importance of the third rule's proviso, have observed that the *Neumeier* rules amount to little more than an exception to the traditional place of injury rule for cases in which the parties share a common domicile. See Korn, 83 Colum. L. Rev. at 799; Borchers, *Conflicts Pragmatism*, 56 Albany L. Rev. 883, 909 n. 201 (1993). Is this an accurate assessment? If so, are the rules an improvement?

(4) The dissent in *Edwards* suggests that courts should do a single analysis for all defendants. Does this make any sense? It also concludes that New York has the greater interest than Ontario with respect to the application of a loss-allocating rule between two Ontario domiciliaries. If that is so (is it?), is there any point in distinguishing between loss-allocating and conduct-regulating rules?

(5) What, if anything, do *Neumeier* and *Edwards* have to say about how New York courts will—or should—handle non-tort cases? In *In re Allstate Insurance Co. (Stolarz)*, 81 N.Y.2d 219, 597 N.Y.S.2d 904, 613 N.E.2d 936 (1993), the Court of Appeals addressed a dispute over the meaning of an insurance contract. Writing for the court, Chief Judge Kaye explained that the *Neumeier* rules are designed to accommodate the significant government interests present in tort cases.

> By contrast, contract cases often involve only the *private* economic interests of the parties, and analysis of the public policy underlying the conflicting contract laws may be inappropriate to resolution of the dispute. It may even be difficult to identify the competing "policies" at stake, because the laws may differ only slightly, and evolve through the incremental process of common-law adjudication as a response to the facts presented.
>
> The "center of gravity" or "grouping of contacts" choice of law theory applied in contract cases (*see, e.g., Auten v. Auten*, 308 N.Y. 155, 124 N.E.2d 99 (1954) [discussed infra, p. 263]) enables the

> court to identify which law to apply without entering the difficult, and sometimes inappropriate, policy thicket. Under this approach, the spectrum of significant contacts—rather than a single possibly fortuitous event—may be considered (*see*, Restatement [Second] of Conflict of Laws § 188[2]). Critical to a sound analysis, however, is selecting the contacts that obtain significance in the particular contract dispute. As we have noted, the traditional choice of law factors should be given "heavy weight" in a grouping of contacts analysis * * *.

613 N.E.2d at 939. Under this test, the court held, New Jersey law governed:

> When the significant contacts are considered in light of the reality that this is a contract case, not a tort, it is plain that this dispute overwhelmingly centers on New Jersey. The Restatement, for example, enumerates five generally significant contacts in a contract case: the place of contracting, negotiation and performance; the location of the subject matter of the contract; and the domicile of the contracting parties (*see* Restatement [Second] of Conflict of Laws 188[2]).
>
> Indisputably, New Jersey is the place where the contract was negotiated and made. The parties to the contract are both New Jersey entities. The subject matter of the contract, a vehicle, does not have a fixed location but is registered in New Jersey. Thus, four of the five factors identified in the Restatement plainly point to New Jersey law. (The fifth factor, place of performance, is immaterial here because there is no issue as to performance.)

Id. at 940. Where is the concern for predictability and uniformity that motivated the adoption of rules in *Neumeier*? If these considerations were important to justify formulating rules for tort cases, why not in contract cases as well (where the need for certainty is greatest)?

The court in *Stolarz* proved reluctant to abandon interest analysis altogether. Hence, before analyzing the "grouping of contacts," Chief Judge Kaye acknowledged that "[t]here are, of course, instances where the policies underlying conflicting laws in a contract dispute are readily identifiable and reflect strong governmental interests, and therefore should be considered." Id. at 939. And based on that understanding, the court preceded its conclusion that New Jersey was the "center of gravity" with a finding that New Jersey law applied under interest analysis:

> The [New York] State interest . . . is that consumers purchasing insurance in this State should not be deceived by misleading policy limits. That interest, however, is irrelevant where, as here, the policy is sold in New Jersey by a New Jersey insurance company to a New Jersey insured, and the clause is written to

> conform to a New Jersey statute. Indeed, while Stolarz (by virtue of her use of the car) is an additional insured under the policy, she is not a party to the contract * * *, nor did she pay the premiums—her New Jersey employer did. Thus, New York has no governmental interest in applying its law to this dispute and New Jersey law must be applied * * *.

Id. at 939–40.

After *Edwards* and *Stolarz*, what is the New York approach to conflict of laws?

Principles of Preference

(1) Professor David Cavers took a somewhat different approach to developing rules for true conflicts. According to Cavers, "We may have to accept the adequately articulated *ad hoc* decision as an interim substitute, but we should persevere in the search for rules or principles which would determine when the law of a state which served one purpose should be preferred to the law of another state which served a different purpose." D. Cavers, The Choice-of-Law Process 121–22 (1965). Cavers attempted to develop seven such rules, which he called "principles of preference," to use in resolving true conflicts. With respect to tort actions, for example, Cavers's first principle provides that the law of the state of injury should apply if it is more protective of plaintiffs than the law of the states in which the defendant resides or acted. Cavers reasoned that the regulatory scheme of the state of injury "would be impaired if a person who enters the territory of a state were not subject to its laws requiring conformity to legally prescribed health and safety standards." At the same time, the defendant should not be allowed to enter the state and enjoy whatever benefits it provides while avoiding concomitant burdens, and, if the defendant has caused harm from without "then, save perhaps where the physical or legal consequences of his action were not foreseeable, it is equally fair to hold him to the standards of the state into which he sent whatever harmful agent . . . caused the injury." Id. at 139–45.

Cavers's second principle of preference, a corollary of the first, provides that the law of the state where a defendant acted and caused injury should apply if it is less protective than the law of the plaintiff's home state: "By entering the state or nation, the visitor has exposed himself to the risks of the territory and should not expect to subject persons living there to a financial hazard that their law had not created." Id. at 146–47. Other principles deal with cases in which one state imposes "special controls" over particular conduct within its borders, such as blasting or the sale of liquor (apply that state's law) and cases in which the parties have established a relationship of some sort such as the purchase of an airplane ticket in *Kilberg v. Northeast Airlines, Inc.,* supra p. 58 (apply the law of the "seat" of this relationship if it protects the plaintiff more than the law of the state of injury).

With respect to contract actions, Cavers suggested applying the protective law of a state if the party protected was from that state and the affected transaction was centered there. "When the seller or lender is selling or lending to customers who have sought him out in his own home market," however, as in *Milliken v. Pratt,* "the case for allowing him the benefit of those laws would ordinarily be a strong one." Id. at 189. In other contract cases, Cavers agreed that the court should follow "the express (or reasonably inferable) intention of the parties" as to the applicable law. Id. at 194.

Cavers emphasized that the principles he discusses were not meant to constitute a complete choice-of-law system. Can you develop other principles based on Cavers's reasoning? What underlying theory motivates these proposals?

(2) Cavers's principles of preference played a central role in *Cipolla v. Shaposka,* 439 Pa. 563, 267 A.2d 854 (1970), another in the dreary and seemingly endless line of guest statute cases that courts have used to develop modern choice-of-law theory. Cipolla, of Pennsylvania, went to school in Delaware with Shaposka, of Delaware. Cipolla was injured in Delaware while being driven home from school by Shaposka. Delaware but not Pennsylvania had a guest statute barring the claim. The court found that the case presented a true conflict based on Pennsylvania's interest in compensating its injured resident and Delaware's interest in protecting its host (and his insurer) from liability. The court applied Delaware law, citing Cavers's second principle and explaining that "it seems only fair to permit a defendant to rely on his home state law when he is acting within that state." Why is it unfair to allow plaintiff to recover under Pennsylvania law? Is "fairness" the basis for Cavers's principles? How constructive is that likely to be in resolving true conflicts?

(3) In discussing the origin of his proposals, Cavers observed:

> As I have reviewed the principles I have formulated and the facts that have seemed to me significant as connecting links, I have found in my thinking what I suspect some of you will consider a territorialist bias. Today the tendency is to lean in the opposite direction. An inquiry into the purposes of conflicting laws—and the formulation of principles of preference necessitates that inquiry—leads naturally to an emphasis on the persons on whom the laws have their impact when, at least, it is mainly the interests of the parties to a relationship or a controversy that appears to be at stake. It becomes easy in such situations for one

> to ascribe to the state or states with which those persons are connected a paternalistic concern for them, wherever they may be, thereby rendering the place of their actions "fortuitous" and even irrelevant to the process of choice. . .
>
> [I] believe that there are circumstances where the citizen may properly, if metaphorically, be considered to carry a law of his state about with him. However, I also agree with Judge Wyzanski that "departures from the territorial view of torts ought not to be lightly undertaken," and I would not confine his admonition to the law of torts. Our states and nations are territorially organized; the legal order that each has created impinges on actions and affairs which, in a very high proportion of all instances, are wholly domestic to the state where they take place. To withdraw like actions and affairs from the reach of domestic law because the persons participating in them are not domestic to the state causes a wrench away from customary attitudes toward law that may lead the disadvantaged party to "regard the distinction as involving a personal discrimination against him rather than as a step toward comity between states," to quote Judge Wyzanski once more.

D. Cavers, The Choice-of-Law Process 134–35. Is Cavers's territoriality the same as Beale's or Story's? In explaining why he reverted to territoriality in true conflict cases, Cavers referred to "customary attitudes" toward law. Was he suggesting that people consciously rely on the law of the state where they act, or was his concern that people may be surprised after the fact if this law is not applied? How powerful is the latter concern? Either way, isn't the argument circular because these expectations are themselves merely a product of our past emphasis on territoriality? To paraphrase Holmes, should we stick with a practice for no better reason than that it has been followed since the time of Henry IV?

(4) A few scholars have enthusiastically endorsed a return to territoriality. Professor Twerski argued that territoriality is as basic as nature itself. If the stars suddenly disappeared, he observed, we would be upset because "we have a right to believe in the regularity of nature." Twerski, *Enlightened Territorialism and Professor Cavers—The Pennsylvania Method,* 9 Duquesne L.Rev. 373, 382 (1971). So, too, for law:

> Law is no stranger to human activity. If we live in a world of nature—we also live in a world of law. A Delaware driver, on a trip in Delaware, expects Delaware law to apply. He may be driving a Pennsylvania guest to his home in Pennsylvania but his expectation prior and subsequent to any accident is that whatever the Delaware law may be it will apply to him. It is immaterial

> whether it affects his conduct. People have a right to expect a regularity and rhythm from the law.

Id. Professor Laycock, in contrast, emphasizes the importance of being able quickly and easily to determine the applicable law so that law can serve its chief function as "enforcer of strongly held norms":

> No set of choice-of-law rules has yet achieved a high degree of predictability in hard cases, but only territorial rules offer any hope. When the applicable law depends on the forum in which litigation is eventually conducted, it is impossible in principle to know which law will govern my conduct. It is only a little better for the applicable law to depend on the residence of strangers. I can know the residence of the few people with whom I have continuing relationships, but not of the thousands of people with whom I share highways or have casual transactions. So if the governing law may depend on the residence of the person with whom I come to have a dispute, it is impossible in principle to know which law governs my conduct.
>
> By contrast, I can be in only one place at a time, and I can always know where I am. . . Unlike approaches based on forum or domicile, these territorial approaches make it possible in principle to identify the applicable law and obey it.

Laycock, *Equal Citizens of Equal and Territorial States: The Constitutional Foundations of Choice of Law*, 92 Colum.L.Rev. 249, 319 (1992). Are these arguments more persuasive than the one made by Cavers? How would you translate them into specific solutions for choice of law?

SECTION 4. THE BETTER LAW

R.A. LEFLAR, CONFLICTS LAW: MORE ON CHOICE-INFLUENCING CONSIDERATIONS

54 Cal.L.Rev. 1584, 1585–88 (1966).

In the minds of all the commentators [on choice of law] there has always been a continuing urge to focus upon the true reasons that underlie choice-of-law adjudication: the basic choice-influencing considerations that actually lead, or should lead, the courts to one result or another in particular cases or types of cases. . . What remained after [their] studies was a need to reduce the choice-influencing considerations to a manageably compact form, a form in which it is realistically practical to make use of them in the day-to-day process of deciding conflicts cases. An effort to do this has produced a tentative list of five major choice-influencing considerations, within which all or most of the factors that ordinarily affect choice-of-law decisions can be incorporated.

If this tentative summarization is reasonably complete, it can serve as a guide in the actual determination of choice-of-law questions. By using it, courts can replace with statements of real reasons the mechanical rules and circuitously devised approaches which have appeared in the language of conflicts opinions, too often as cover-ups for the real reason that underlay the decisions. Results in cases will not often be changed by setting out in opinions real choice-influencing considerations instead of mechanical rules. This is because the real reasons have probably been there all along, whether they were stated or not. Understanding of the decisions, by students, by lawyers, and by other judges will, however, be immeasurably facilitated if the relevant considerations are clearly identified and openly employed. In addition results will occasionally be different. . .

A short restatement of the five summarized considerations is given here. . .

A. Predictability of Results

Uniformity of results, regardless of forum, has always been a major goal in choice-of-law theory. Achievement of this goal would enable parties entering into a consensual transaction to plan it with reference to a body of law that would give them the results they desired. As a result, their transactions would normally be validated and their justified expectations thus protected. This would further the broad social policies of most forum states by sustaining legal arrangements in which parties have in good faith engaged themselves. At the same time it would discourage "forum shopping."

B. Maintenance of Interstate and International Order

Both nations and states within a nation are interested in facilitating the orderly legal control of transactions that in any fashion cross their boundary lines. Smooth conduct of affairs between the peoples of different nations is essential to modern civilization; the easy movement of persons and things—free social and economic commerce—between states in a federal nation is essential to the very existence of the federation. There must be a minimum of mutual interference with claims or aspirations to sovereignty. No forum whose concern with a set of facts is negligible should claim priority for its law over the law of a state which has a clearly superior concern with the facts; nor should any state's choice-of-law system be based upon deliberate across-the-board "forum preference." Encouragement of that measure of interstate and international intercourse which is in keeping with the interests of the forum state and its people has always been a prime function of conflicts law.

C. Simplification of the Judicial Task

Courts do not like to do things the hard way if an easier way serves the ends of justice substantially as well. It would be utterly impractical for a court hearing a case brought on extrastate facts to apply the whole body of procedural law of the place where the facts occurred, and not much would be gained by doing so. Courts therefore use their own procedural rules. There are, however, some outcome-determinative rules, at times classified as procedural, which are so simple that one state's rule can be used as easily as another's so that the substance-procedure dichotomy is not sensibly applicable to them. Purely mechanical rules for choice of substantive law are also easy for courts to apply, but other considerations may outweigh simplification of the judicial task where such rules are involved. Ease in judicial performance is ordinarily not of first importance among the choice-influencing considerations, but it is important in some choices.

D. *Advancement of the Forum's Governmental Interests*

If a forum state has a genuine concern with the facts in a given case, a concern discoverable from its strongly felt social or legal policy, it is reasonable to expect the state's courts to act in accordance with that concern. This refers to legitimate concerns, not just to the local occurrence of some facts, or to the local existence of some rule of law that could constitutionally be applied to the facts. A state's governmental interests in the choice-of-law sense need not coincide with its rules of local law, especially if the local rules, whether statutory or judge-made, are old or out of tune with the times. A state's total governmental interests in a case is to be discovered from all the considerations that properly motivate the state in its law-making and law-administering tasks, viewed as of the time when the question is presented. So viewed, the circumstances may show that the forum is truly interested in applying its own law to a set of facts. If they do show this that conclusion becomes a major choice-influencing consideration.

E. *Application of the Better Rule of Law*

The better rule of law is the most controversial of the considerations, yet a potent one. If choice of law were purely a jurisdiction-selecting process, with courts first deciding which state's law should govern and checking afterward to see what that state's law was, this consideration would not be present. Everyone knows that this is not what courts do, nor what they should do. Judges know from the beginning between which rules of law, and not just which states, they are choosing. A state's "governmental interest" in a set of facts can be analyzed only by reference to the content of the competing rules of law. Choice of law is not wholly a choice between laws as distinguished from a choice between jurisdictions, but partly it is.

A judge's natural feeling that his own state's law is better than that of other states to some extent explains forum preference. Of course the local law is sometimes not better, and most judges are perfectly capable of realizing this. The inclination of any reasonable court will be to prefer rules of law which make good socio-economic sense for the time when the court speaks, whether they be its own or another state's rules. The law's legitimate concerns with "justice in the individual case," sometimes spoken of as a choice-of-law objective, and with that "protection of justified expectations of the parties" which often corresponds with Ehrenzweig's "basic rule of validation," are furthered by deliberate preference for the better rule of law. The preference is objective, not subjective. It has to do with preferred law, not preferred parties. It is "result selective" only in the same sense that in any non-conflicts case a determination of what the law is (presumably the "better law," if there was argument about the law) controls the results of litigation. In conflicts cases, just as in other cases, courts have always taken the content of competing rules into account, but they have too often used characterization, renvoi, multiple-choice rules or the like as manipulative devices to cover up what they were really doing, when there was no need at all for any cover-up.

MILKOVICH V. SAARI

295 Minn. 155, 203 N.W.2d 408 (1973).

TODD, JUSTICE. [In this automobile guest case a group of Ontario residents set out from Ontario to shop and attend a play in Duluth, Minnesota. The host, defendant Saari, garaged, registered and insured her automobile in Ontario, which has a guest statute requiring proof of gross negligence. The guest, plaintiff Milkovich, was injured when the car, then being driven by a codefendant, left the road in Minnesota, which does not have a guest statute; she was hospitalized in Duluth for about six weeks and then returned to her home in Ontario. The complaint did not allege gross negligence and defendants, relying on Ontario law, appeal from the denial of their motion to dismiss.]

[The court discussed the abandonment of the traditional place of injury rule in *Babcock v. Jackson,* supra p. 159, and the difficulties experienced by the New York court in subsequent cases dealing with different fact situations.]

Finally, the New York court was confronted with the exact factual situation we have in this case. In *Kell v. Henderson,* 47 Misc.2d 992, 263 N.Y.S.2d 647 (1965), affirmed, 26 A.D.2d 595, 270 N.Y.S.2d 552 (1966), . . . the plaintiff, a minor child, in the company of the two defendants, a mother and son, set out from Ontario, Canada, to tour nearby New York. The plaintiff and the defendants were all residents of Ontario. The car was garaged in Ontario and insured in Ontario. While being driven in New York by the defendant son, the car went out of control and careened off the highway, striking a bridge and injuring Miss Kell. The defendants in that case argued that under the *Babcock* decision the most significant interests were in Ontario and not New York and therefore the plaintiff could not recover by reason of the Ontario guest statute. The New York Supreme Court, after pointing out that the state had significant interests by reason of its traffic vehicle regulations, its public policy regarding guest statutes, and the fact that its laws applied to residents and nonresidents equally, stated[:]

"The conflict-of-laws doctrine enunciated in *Babcock* recognizes that we no longer mechanically turn to the common-law rule of *lex loci delicti* in tort cases. The courts now have adopted a rule of choice of law in a conflict situation which looks to reason and justice in its selection of which law is to apply and which fits the needs of today's changing world where frequent travel is the rule, rather than the exception." . . .

While New York was experiencing its difficulties in the changing field of conflict of laws, a [case] . . . arose in . . . New Hampshire, which allowed its learned Mr. Chief Justice Kenison to enunciate a doctrine which has been followed by many courts throughout the country, including our own Minnesota court. In *Clark v. Clark,* 107 N.H. 351, 222 A.2d 205 (1966) [another guest statute case], Mr. Chief Justice Kenison traced the history and difficulty of the lex loci rule. He then proceeded to adopt [Professor Robert Leflar's] five basic "choice-influencing considerations": (a) Predictability of results; (b) maintenance of interstate and international order; (c) simplification of the judicial task; (d) advancement of the forum's governmental interests; and (e) application of the better rule of law.

The court pointed out that the first three tests caused very few problems. Predictability of results can be overlooked since basically this test relates to consensual transactions where people should know in advance what law will govern their act. Obviously, no one plans to have an accident, and, except for the remote possibility of forum shopping, this test is of little import in an automobile accident case. As to the second consideration, the court found little trouble since under this heading no more is called for than that the court apply the law of no state which does not have substantial connection with the total facts and the particular issue being litigated. The third point, simplification of the judicial task, poses no problem since the courts are fully capable of administering the law of another forum if called upon to do so.

The court observed that in selecting the law of a particular case the last two considerations carry most weight. In the case before it, the court found adequate governmental interest in applying its state's law and concluded that the New Hampshire law was unquestionably the better law and should be applied. . .

[Minnesota adopted the same approach] in *Schneider v. Nichols,* 280 Minn. 139, 158 N.W.2d 254 (1968). . . [O]ur court quoted with approval the choice-influencing considerations laid down by Mr. Chief Justice Kenison in *Clark v. Clark,* supra, and also quoted his statement regarding guest statutes * * *:

> ". . . No American state has newly adopted a guest statute for many years. Courts of states which did adopt them are today construing them much more narrowly, evidencing their dissatisfaction with them. . . Though still on the books, they contradict the spirit of the times. . . Unless other considerations demand it, we should not go out of our way to enforce such a law of another state as against the better law of our own state." . . .

As we indicated earlier in this opinion, the New York case of *Kell v. Henderson,* supra, is on "all fours" with the facts of this case. Professor Leflar, whose original article provided the groundwork for the opinion of Mr. Chief Justice Kenison in *Clark v. Clark,* supra, which is the foundation of the approach our court has taken in these matters, had occasion to comment on the effect of *Kell v. Henderson,* supra, in an article entitled, Conflicts Law: More on Choice-Influencing Considerations, 54 Calif.L.Rev. 1584. Professor Leflar set forth the fact situation of the *Kell* case. He then proceeded to analyze the decision in the light of these choice-influencing considerations. He pointed out that predictability was irrelevant since automobile accidents are seldom planned, and that, since the accident occurred in New York, that state was an appropriate jurisdiction in which to try the lawsuit. He further pointed out that neither international order nor ease of judicial administration had much bearing on the case.

On the consideration of governmental interest, Professor Leflar found adequate support for the decision rendered by the New York court. In so doing, he rejected the concept of the practical interest of the state in the supervision and safety of its state highways since the rule in question, unlike rules of the road and definitions of negligence, does not bear upon vehicle operation as such. Instead, he pointed out that the factor to be considered is the relevant effect the New York rule has on the duty of host to guest and the danger of collusion between them to defraud the host's insurer. New York's interest in applying its own law rather than Ontario law on these issues, he found to be based primarily on its status as a justice-administering state. In that status, it is strongly concerned with seeing that persons who come into the New York courts to litigate controversies with substantial New York connections have these cases determined according to rules consistent with New York concepts of justice, or at least not inconsistent with them. That will be as true for nondomiciliary litigants as for domiciliaries. This interest will not manifest itself clearly if the out-of-state rule does not run contrary to some strong socio-legal policy of the forum, but it will become a major consideration if there is such a strong opposing local policy.

Professor Leflar then pointed out that this consideration leads to preference for what is regarded as the better rule of law, that New York has such a preference, and that it is a vigorous one. He concluded that the combination of the last two items, governmental interest and better rule of law, called for the application of New York law. His statements and reasoning apply equally to the facts of this case and lead to the conclusion that Minnesota should apply its better rule of law and should allow plaintiff to proceed with her action. . .

In *Conklin v. Horner,* 38 Wis.2d 468, 157 N.W.2d 579 (1968), the Wisconsin court was confronted with a fact situation again exactly on all fours with our situation. There the court, speaking through Mr. Justice Heffernan, adopted the better-rule approach which we have adopted here and, in a well-reasoned opinion, arrived at the same conclusion that this court has. In the Wisconsin case, the litigants were all residents of the State of Illinois; the automobile in question was licensed and garaged in Illinois; the trip originated in Illinois with the intent and purpose to return to Illinois; and the insurance policy was issued in the State of Illinois. Illinois has a guest statute; Wisconsin does not. The court [said]:

> ". . . in *Wilcox v. Wilcox* (1965), 26 Wis.2d 617, 133 N.W.2d 408, . . . we abandoned the choice-of-law rule of lex loci delicti and adopted in its stead . . . the general approach of *Babcock v. Jackson*. . . . We emphasized that what we adopted was not a rule, but a method of analysis that permitted dissection of the jural bundle constituting a tort and its environment to determine what elements therein were relevant to a reasonable choice of law.
>
> "When the *Wilcox* case is so viewed, it is apparent that we cannot conclude that, when one set of facts leads logically to the law of the forum, the reverse, or the apparent reverse, of these facts will lead to the opposite conclusion. We, too, adopt this concept that what the court is considering is a methodology and not a rule."

The Wisconsin court then proceeded to adopt the choice-influencing considerations [approach and] . . . concluded that the Wisconsin law was the better law to apply under the circumstances. . .

We have already noted the relative unimportance of predictability of results to tort actions. Similarly, the simplification of the judicial task need not concern us to any great extent since we have no doubt our judicial system could in the appropriate case apply the guest statute rule of gross negligence as readily as our common-law rule. Interstate and international relations are maintained without harm where, as here, the forum state has a substantial connection with the facts and issues involved. This requirement is amply met by the fact that the accident occurred in

Minnesota, as well as by the fact that plaintiff was hospitalized for well over a month in the state.

The compelling factors in this case are the advancement of the forum's governmental interests and the application of the better law. While there may be more deterrent effect in our common-law rule of liability as opposed to the guest statute requirement of gross negligence, the main governmental interest involved is that of any "justice-administering state." Leflar, Conflicts Law: More on Choice-Influencing Considerations, 54 Calif.L.Rev. 1584, 1594. In that posture, we are concerned that our courts not be called upon to determine issues under rules which, however accepted they may be in other states, are inconsistent with our own concept of fairness and equity. We might also note that persons injured in automobile accidents occurring within our borders can reasonably be expected to require treatment in our medical facilities, both public and private . . . with a consequent governmental interest that injured persons not be denied recovery on the basis of doctrines foreign to Minnesota.

In our search for the better rule, we are firmly convinced of the superiority of the common-law rule of liability to that of the Ontario guest statute. We can find little reason for the strict limitation of a host's liability to his guest beyond the fear of collusive suits and the vague disapproval of a guest "biting the hand that feeds him." Neither rationale is persuasive. We are convinced the judicial system can uncover collusive suits without such overinclusive rules, and we do not find any discomfort in the prospect of a guest suing his host for injuries suffered through the host's simple negligence.

Accordingly, we hold that Minnesota law should be applied to this lawsuit.

PETERSON, JUSTICE (dissenting). . .

The "choice-influencing factor" in the majority opinion is simply that Minnesota law is "better law" because, unlike Ontario law, this state has no guest statute. Notwithstanding our undoubted preference for this forum's standard of liability, I am not persuaded that decision should turn on that factor alone. We may assume that these Canadian citizens have concurred in the rule of law of their own government as just, so the law of this American forum is not for them the "better" standard of justice. The litigation, indeed, was first initiated by plaintiff in the courts of Ontario and was later commenced in Minnesota as an act of forum shopping.

Our own cases, of course, do not compel such a decision. Two cases from other jurisdictions that are "on all fours" are not persuasive. The New York case of *Kell v. Henderson* * * * is not the decision of that state's highest court and, in addition, is at odds with the later case of *Arbuthnot v. Allbright,* 35 A.D.2d 315, 316 N.Y.S.2d 391 (1970). The Wisconsin case of *Conklin v. Horner* * * * is a final expression of its highest court, based upon a well-written majority opinion of Mr. Justice Heffernan. I nevertheless am more persuaded by the dissenting opinion of two justices. Mr. Chief Justice Hallows, in dissent, appropriately observed that the so-called "methodology of analysis" is really little more than a mechanical application of the law of the forum. As he wrote * * *: "If we are going to be consistent only in applying the law of the forum, then we are merely giving lip service to the new 'significant contacts' rule."

JEPSON V. GENERAL CASUALTY CO. OF WISCONSIN

513 N.W.2d 467 (Minn.1994).

PAGE, JUSTICE. [Jepson was injured in Arizona while a passenger in a real estate agent's car. Though he had moved to Arizona by the time suit was filed, Jepson lived in Minnesota near the North Dakota border at the time of the accident. Jepson settled with the driver of the other car and also received benefits from the driver's insurer. Jepson subsequently brought an action for a declaratory judgment in Minnesota seeking benefits under an insurance policy his North Dakota business had purchased from the defendant. The policy covered seven vehicles, six of which were registered in North Dakota, one in Indiana. It had been purchased through a Minnesota agency on behalf of Jepson, his wife, and two North Dakota corporations. The policy charged North Dakota rates, and the premiums were paid by one of the North Dakota corporations. Minnesota rates were substantially higher, and testimony suggested that the policy would not have been purchased at the higher Minnesota rates. Plaintiff argued that the benefits allowed under the policy for each vehicle should be "stacked." At the time of the accident, stacking was permitted under Minnesota but not North Dakota law. The lower courts applied Minnesota law.]

Having concluded that there is a conflict between Minnesota and North Dakota law and that either may be constitutionally applied, we next look to the five choice influencing factors set out in *Milkovich v. Saari,* 295 Minn. 155, 203 N.W.2d 408 (1973). They are: (1) predictability of result; (2) maintenance of interstate and international order; (3) simplification of the judicial task; (4) advancement of the forum's governmental interest; and (5) application of the better rule of law. . . These factors were not intended to spawn the evolution of set mechanical rules but instead to prompt courts to carefully and critically consider each new fact situation and explain in a straight-forward manner their choice of law. * * * The lower courts need to wrestle with each situation anew. While prior opinions may be helpful to a court's deliberations, the court's obligation is to be true to the method rather than to seek superficial factual analogies between cases and import wholesale the choice of law analysis contained therein.

The trial court determined that the first factor, predictability, was not of great importance and the court of appeals agreed. General Casualty, however, contends that predictability is essential to insurance contracts and argues it reasonably expected its obligations to be governed by the law of the state where the contract was issued and where the insured property was generally located—North Dakota. The Jepsons argue that predictability of result favors Minnesota law because the policy was sold through a Minnesota agency, the Jepsons resided in Minnesota, and the policy covered at least two vehicles that were regularly driven from Minnesota residences to Jepson's place of business in Fargo.

This case involves the coverage an insurance policy provides for injuries suffered in an accident, and so has aspects of both contract and tort. Predictability of result as it relates to the tort aspect of a case is not of great importance in situations such as the one presented here because of the unplanned nature of automobile accidents. * * * Predictability of result is of value in analyzing the contract aspects of a case. While where an accident occurs is unimportant, the obligations the insurer has to the insured at that time are important. The heart of the bargain between the insurer and the insured is the coverage the insured purchased. The parties enter into the insurance contract with the expectation that, should a dispute arise, the legal system will endeavor to give each side the benefit of their bargain. To the extent the choice of law in this case contributes to giving the parties the benefit of their bargain, it enhances the predictability of the parties' contractual arrangements.

Although the accident occurred in Arizona, nothing was planned or done by either of the parties with regard to the insurance contract that was in any way directed to that state. In considering the bargain between Jepson and General Casualty, we note it was based on a number of factors that could only reflect a mutual expectation that they had negotiated a North Dakota contract. The insurance policy covered named insureds at a North Dakota address and North Dakota registered and titled vehicles. The premium charges for the coverage were calculated at North Dakota rates. These circumstances suggest what the parties' reasonable expectations should have been at the time of contracting. Perhaps the parties might have predicted that, had Jepson been injured in one of the vehicles in Minnesota, Minnesota law might be applied. It is unlikely that parties would have predicted Minnesota law would apply in such circumstances as occurred here, that is, where Jepson was injured while riding in another person's vehicle in a state other than Minnesota or North Dakota.

Differences among the states in their laws and in their choice of law methods make predicting what law will apply to a case an uncertain exercise. It is, however, desirable for the courts of the different states to reach similar conclusions on the choice of law in a given dispute. We think it unlikely most other courts would apply Minnesota law on the facts before us. The factor of preserving the parties' justified expectations and enhancing the predictability of what state's law will govern in a contractual dispute points away from the application of Minnesota law.

In discussing the second factor, the maintenance of interstate order, we are primarily concerned with whether the application of Minnesota law would manifest disrespect for North Dakota's sovereignty or impede the interstate movement of people and goods. An aspect of this concern is to maintain a coherent legal system in which the courts of different states strive to sustain, rather than subvert, each other's interests in areas where their own interests are less strong. * * * By approaching choice of law questions with these considerations in mind, the opportunities for forum shopping may be kept within reasonable bounds. . .

If the law of North Dakota promised Jepson a greater recovery than Minnesota, we doubt very much that he would be litigating this coverage dispute in our courts. People who purposefully seek advantages offered by another state ought not be allowed to avoid the burdens associated with their choice. We find evidence that Jepson is forum shopping in bringing this suit in our state's courts because he commenced, although settling prior to filing suit, litigation in North Dakota to secure no fault benefits payable under North Dakota law. Minnesota does not have an interest in encouraging forum shopping, particularly where we would be sending a message to those people living on our borders to take advantage of the benefits our neighboring states offer in terms of lower insurance rates, lower vehicle registration fees, and sales tax, and then, if they are injured, take advantage of Minnesota's greater willingness to compensate tort victims. Minnesota does not have an interest in encouraging that conduct. . .

Unlike the trial court and court of appeals, we find that the maintenance of interstate order weighs in favor of applying North Dakota law. North Dakota has the authority to regulate the terms of insurance for vehicle licensed and titled in that state. We interfere with the sovereignty of a sister state when we make our law available for people who seek Minnesota benefits while burdening the North Dakota insurance rate base and regulatory system.

The third factor, simplification of the judicial task, is not a significant factor in this case because the law of either state could be applied without difficulty.

The fourth choice influencing factor is which choice of law most advances a significant interest of the forum. General Casualty argues that Minnesota has no legitimate interest in applying its law, especially since Jepson no longer resides in Minnesota. Jepson believed that because he was a domiciliary of Minnesota at the time of the accident, and more generally because he is a tort victim, it is in Minnesota's interest to apply its law.

Minnesota places great value in compensating tort victims. . . But, however significant Minnesota's interest in the compensation of tort victims, we have other interests which in situations like this one are in conflict with the value we place on victim compensation. For example, we also believe that people should get the benefit of the contract they enter into, nothing less and nothing more. Were the only choice-influencing consideration in this case our governmental interest, we might side with Jepson. On the facts of this case, however, our choice is influenced more by our analyses of predictability and maintenance of the interstate order than it is by our governmental interest in compensating a tort victim.

The final choice influencing factor to consider is whether, in an objective sense, North Dakota or Minnesota has the better rule of law. At the time of Jepson's accident, Minnesota law would not enforce the anti-stacking provision in the insurance policy while North Dakota would. In 1985, the legislature amended the law to prohibit stacking. * * * General Casualty claims that to allow stacking cannot be considered the better rule of law precisely because Minnesota has banned stacking. As authority for this point, General Casualty relies on *Stenzel v. State Farm Mutual Automobile Insurance Company,* 379 N.W.2d 674 (Minn.App.1986), where the court of appeals reasoned that the 1985 amendment prohibiting stacking should be regarded as the better rule of law: "[n]ow that the legislature has spoken, we must follow its assessment of the 'better rule.' " Jepson counters that he is entitled to the benefit of the law that existed at the time of his injury. He relies on *Wille v. Farm Bureau Mutual Insurance Company,* 432 N.W.2d 784 (Minn.App.1988), where the court of appeals concluded the 1985 amendment prohibiting stacking did not require it to enforce anti-stacking provisions that violated Minnesota policy when the insurance contract was made.

The trial court found, and the court of appeals apparently agreed, that Minnesota's treatment of stacking at the time of the accident is the better rule of law. On our reading of the cases and briefs, however, neither *Stenzel* nor *Wille,* nor the parties offer a compelling explanation of exactly why stacking or anti-stacking is a better rule. *Stenzel* wrongly asserts that, because the legislature prohibited stacking, we must find it to be the better rule of law. * * * If that were true, forum law would always be the better law and this step in our choice of law analysis would be meaningless. *Wille* simply states that because stacking provides greater compensation, it is a better rule. * * *

Leflar intended the better rule of law to be the rule that makes "good socio-economic sense for the time when the court speaks." * * * We disagree with the views expressed in *Stenzel* and *Wille,* as well as by the parties, as to which is the better rule of law. From our present day vantage point, neither the law Minnesota had then, nor the law we have now, is clearly better. Sometimes different laws are neither better nor worse in an objective way, just different. Because we do not find either stacking or anti-stacking to be a better rule in the sense Leflar intended, this consideration does not influence our choice of law.

We hold that North Dakota law applies to Jepson's stacking claim. So deciding, the issue of how many vehicles may be stacked under the policy is moot.

Choice-Influencing Considerations and the Better Law

(1) Are Leflar's "choice-influencing considerations" merely a variation of the seven factors that make up the Second Restatement's "most significant relationship" test? How does Leflar's approach differ from that of the Second Restatement?

Leflar illustrated his method by working through a number of hypothetical situations (many based on real cases). See Leflar, *Choice-Influencing Considerations in Conflicts Law,* 41 N.Y.U.L.Rev. 267, 310–24 (1966) (12 cases); Leflar, *Conflicts Law: More on Choice-Influencing Considerations,* 54 Cal.L.Rev. 1584, 1588–98 (1966) (6 cases). A number of patterns emerge in these illustrations. Two of the factors—predictability of results and simplification of the judicial task—are important only in cases involving, respectively, consensual transactions and questions of procedure. Maintenance of the interstate or international order, in the meantime, turns out to be false conflict analysis: a disinterested state should not apply its law out of respect for the interests of other, interested states or nations. The remaining non-false conflicts are decided under the final two considerations. The fourth consideration—advancing the forum's governmental interests—looks at first like Currie's original proposal to apply forum law, but Leflar says that this refers to a state's "total" governmental interest, including its interest as a "justice administering state," which need not coincide with its domestic law. Rather, at least absent a strong expression of forum interest, the court should do justice by applying the better rule of law. The fourth and fifth considerations thus operate together to resolve most true conflicts according to the "better law."

Is Leflar's approach just interest analysis with a better-law inquiry to resolve true conflicts? Does this accurately describe the reasoning and result in *Milkovich*? (Is *Milkovich* a true or a false conflict? If *Tooker v. Lopez,* supra p. 151, was a false conflict, why is a reversal of the law-fact pattern also not a false conflict? Cf. *Schultz v. Boy Scouts of America, Inc.,* supra p. 159.)

(2) Is *Jepson* consistent with *Milkovich*? Justice Page begins by announcing that prior opinions "may be helpful," but that "the court's obligation is to be true to the method rather than to seek superficial factual analogies." But is the same method being applied? Which opinion seems truer to Leflar's approach? Which is more persuasive? See Pielmeier, *Some Hope for Choice of Law in Minnesota,* 18 Hamline L. Rev. 8 (1994) (criticizing Minnesota decisions and noting that *Jepson* "raises the hope . . . that thoughtful analysis will become the order of the day.")

(3) A number of commentators, including Leflar, suggest that judicial use of the "better law" approach will usually lead to the application of forum law. According to Leflar, "The idea that the forum's own law is the best in the world . . . is unfortunately but understandably still current among some members of our high courts." Leflar, 41 N.Y.U.L.Rev. at 298. See also Singer, *Facing Real Conflicts,* 24 Cornell Int'l L.J. 197, 199 (1991). Do you believe this? Are you biased toward your home state's law? If anything, isn't it more likely that judges will use the freedom afforded by the better law approach to avoid domestic law they dislike? For what it is worth, the "evidence" to support this assertion is conclusory and anecdotal and ignores the fact that in a fair number of the cases another state's law was found to be "better." See, e.g., *Tillett v. J.I. Case Co.,* 756 F.2d 591 (7th Cir.1985); *Bigelow v. Halloran,* 313 N.W.2d 10 (Minn.1981); *LaBounty v. American Ins. Co.,* 122 N.H. 738, 451 A.2d 161 (1982); *Hunker v. Royal Indem. Co.,* 57 Wis.2d 588, 204 N.W.2d 897 (1973). Moreover, two empirical studies suggest that courts employing the better law approach are no more likely to favor forum law than courts employing other modern approaches—though all these approaches lead to forum law more frequently than the traditional rules. See Solimine, *An Economic and Empirical Analysis of Choice of Law,* 24 Ga.L.Rev. 49 (1989); Borchers, *The Choice-of-Law Revolution: An Empirical Study,* 49 Wash. & Lee L.Rev. 357 (1992).

(4) Leflar thought that states should not automatically assume that forum law was better:

> [A conscientious conclusion], after intelligent comparison, that its local rules of law are wiser, sounder, and better calculated to serve the total ends of justice under law in the controversy before it than are the competing rules of the other state . . . is to be respected. But it does not amount to an automatic preference for local law, nor is an automatic preference justifiable.

Leflar, 41 N.Y.U.L.Rev. at 298–99. Why not? Brainerd Currie, no fan of allowing courts to make this sort of inquiry, acknowledged that there might be a few situations in which state interests provided no answer and justice between the parties became the paramount consideration. When this was the case, however, Currie had no doubt about what law to apply: "where should the . . . court look for a rule that will do justice between the parties but to the body of principle and experience which has served that purpose, as well as the ends of governmental policy, for the people of [the state] in their domestic affairs?" B. Currie, Selected Essays on the Conflict of Laws 65 (1963).

If the "better law" is not forum law, then what is it? How is a judge to decide? What reasons does the *Milkovich* court give for its conclusion that Ontario's guest statute is "worse" than Minnesota's law permitting recovery? What reasons would you give? Is this a purely subjective reaction, or are there objective elements to the analysis? Is it important that a law is out of line with what other states are doing? Why? What about innovations? Should courts consider whether a law is over-or under-inclusive in achieving its stated ends?

(5) Is it legitimate for courts to undertake this sort of inquiry? As Leflar points out, when laws conflict or are unclear in wholly domestic cases, courts routinely consider which law or interpretation is better. Why should multistate cases be different? Consider the following responses:

> It is not for us to consider which is the better law when the policy making body of the state has spoken. . . Appellant believes the Wisconsin rule is the better law. When he asks us to apply it to this case in which all significant relationships are with the State of Iowa, he is in effect asking us to ignore all other considerations. . . Such a rule would eliminate the necessity for determining which state has the strongest interest in the particular issue. The result reached in this manner might have no more relevancy to the interests of the state with the most significant relationships than the result reached by applying the law of the place of their injury.

Fuerste v. Bemis, 156 N.W.2d 831, 834 (Iowa 1968).

> [I]t makes no sense to talk about which law is "better" or "more just"—not because such decisions are better left to legislators, but because the very notion of a "more just" law is contrary to a fundamental premise of the federal system. The whole problem in a true conflict is that different states have made different judgments about what is just, and it is axiomatic that, *except* as constrained by the Constitution, states are coequal sovereigns entitled to make their own value judgments. Each state is free to define its own version of the "just" result, and no general law limits or controls any state's power in this regard (something I had thought settled by *Erie Railroad v. Tompkins*). True conflicts thus present competing but equally legitimate versions of what is just in a particular case, and each state—by definition—has an equal claim to have its law applied, its policy implemented, and its version of the just result vindicated.

Kramer, *Return of the Renvoi,* 66 N.Y.U. L. Rev. 979, 1019 (1991). Do these passages make the same or different points? Do they effectively refute

Leflar's point that, once equipoise is reached, it makes sense to turn to normative considerations in choosing?

(6) Professor Friedrich Juenger stakes out a bolder position than Leflar in favor of a better law approach. According to Juenger, there have historically only ever been three kinds of approaches to multistate and multinational problems: (1) "unilateralist approaches," of which interest analysis is the foremost example, which purport to resolve multistate disputes by ascertaining the intended scope of potentially applicable local substantive rules; (2) "multilateralist approaches," exemplified by the First and Second Restatements, which select among local laws based on some kind of multilateral policy or policies; and (3) "the substantive law approach," which holds that multistate disputes are not governed by any state's or nation's local law, but should be decided under substantive rules formulated specially for these transactions. F. Juenger, Choice of Law and Multistate Justice 45–46 (1993). The problem with the first two categories, Juenger argues, is that both attempt to resolve multistate problems by employing domestic rules that were not formulated or designed for cross-boundary transactions. Unilateral approaches fail because they myopically ask how far laws reach in cases that go beyond what they were designed to do. Multilateral approaches similarly founder by searching vainly for reasons to select among laws that are irrelevant because they were not designed for the case at hand. The proper solution, Juenger insists, is for judges to decide multistate cases free from the constraints of sovereignty by "devising teleological choice-of-law rules that promote those substantive policies that merit supranational recognition." Id. at 190. Fashioning enlightened substantive rules for multistate situations, Juenger argues, has numerous advantages. Among other things, it will "simplify and rationalize the foreign law problem" while giving judges "a welcome measure of creative freedom" to decide cases in the most just manner. Id. at 191–94.

Is the way to achieve "justice" in multistate or multinational cases to liberate judges to make up whatever law they think is best? What is the standard for measuring whether a result is "just"? Once we free judges from the "constraints" of sovereignty, what is the source of their authority? Juenger justifies the authority of a "transcendental" body of law by observing that such law has a long historical pedigree—stretching as far back as ancient Rome and as far forward from there as the 19th century. Is that an adequate justification? What concept or theory of law is at work here?

(7) While Leflar reaches the better law inquiry almost by default, and Juenger by a sense that ordinary principles of legal interpretation are inapplicable in a multistate setting, Professor Joseph Singer argues that the better law is the only appropriate criterion for resolving choice-of-law problems. According to Singer, modern conflicts scholars have betrayed the premise of policy analysis by formalizing it with simplifying assumptions:

> They argue that compensatory policies in both contract and tort law favor widely shared goals of compensating plaintiffs, deterring wrongful conduct, and promoting reliance on agreements. But how do they know this? They have engaged in formalism by identifying these policies as "shared" or "basic" or "emerging" or "prevalent" or "better," without confronting the conflicting values and policy arguments that are faced by those who debate the substantive content of the law. They have formalized state interests by often ignoring moral interests and interests in liberty.

Singer, *Real Conflicts,* 69 B.U.L.Rev. 1, 75 (1989). Because "[c]onflicts cases raise fundamental questions about the substantive norms governing social relationships among neighboring political communities," Singer maintains, such problems can *only* be resolved by directly confronting the pertinent value and policy choices. Id. This means doing what courts do when confronted with similar value choices in wholly domestic cases: choosing which of the competing substantive laws is best as a matter of social policy and justice.

Ordinarily, Singer explains, the forum should prefer its own law, though examining forum law in a multistate context may lead the court to reinterpret or change it. The presumption of forum law may be rebutted, moreover, if (a) necessary to protect the justified expectations of a party, or (b) applying forum law "will significantly interfere with the ability of another state to constitute itself as a normative and political community." Id. at 85. See also Singer, *A Pragmatic Approach to Conflicts,* 70 B.U.L.Rev. 731 (1990); Singer, *Facing Real Conflicts,* 24 Cornell Int'l L.J. 197 (1991). Does Singer's justification for focusing on the "better law" answer the objections raised above? Do courts in wholly domestic cases engage in the sort of analysis Singer recommends? Does this approach seem workable?

(8) Leflar's choice-influencing considerations have been used in Arkansas, New Hampshire, Rhode Island, and Wisconsin as well as Minnesota. See Symeonides, *Choice of Law in the American Courts in 2019: Thirty-Third Annual Survey,* 65 Am.J.Comp.L. 235, 258–259 (2020). They have also been applied to provisions other than guest statutes. See, e.g., *Tillett v. J.I. Case Co.,* 756 F.2d 591 (7th Cir.1985) (wrongful death); *DeRemer v. Pacific Intermountain Express Co.,* 353 N.W.2d 694 (Minn.Ct.App.1984) (comparative negligence); *Barrett v. Foster Grant Co.,* 450 F.2d 1146 (1st Cir.1971) (vicarious liability). A few courts and commentators use Leflar's "better law" considerations in combination with other choice-of-law approaches. See, e.g., *Bushkin Assocs., Inc. v. Raytheon,* 393 Mass. 622, 473 N.E.2d 662 (1985) (with Second Restatement).

SECTION 5. THE SECOND RESTATEMENT

Restatement (Second) of Conflict of Laws (1971)

§ 6. *Choice-of-Law Principles*

(1) A court, subject to constitutional restrictions, will follow a statutory directive of its own state on choice of law.

(2) When there is no such directive, the factors relevant to the choice of the applicable rule of law include

(a) the needs of the interstate and international systems,

(b) the relevant policies of the forum,

(c) the relevant policies of other interested states and the relative interests of those states in the determination of the particular issue,

(d) the protection of justified expectations,

(e) the basic policies underlying the particular field of law,

(f) certainty, predictability and uniformity of result, and

(g) ease in the determination and application of the law to be applied.

§ 145. *The General Principle in Tort Cases*

(1) The rights and liabilities of the parties with respect to an issue in tort are determined by the local law of the state which, with respect to that issue, has the most significant relationship to the occurrence and the parties under the principles stated in § 6.

(2) Contacts to be taken into account in applying the principles of § 6 to determine the law applicable to an issue include:

(a) the place where the injury occurred,

(b) the place where the conduct causing the injury occurred,

(c) the domicil, residence, nationality, place of incorporation and place of business of the parties, and

(d) the place where the relationship, if any, between the parties is centered.

These contacts are to be evaluated according to their relative importance with respect to the particular issue.

§ 186. *Applicable Law in Contract Cases*

Issues in contract are determined by the law chosen by the parties in accordance with the rule of § 187 [allowing the parties to choose the applicable law and reproduced at p. 110, supra] and otherwise by the law selected in accordance with the rule of § 188.

§ 188. *Law Governing Contract Issues in Absence of Effective Choice by the Parties*

(1) The rights and duties of the parties with respect to an issue in contract are determined by the local law of the state which, with respect to that issue, has the most significant relationship to the transaction and the parties under the principles stated in § 6.

(2) In the absence of an effective choice of law by the parties (see § 187) the contacts to be taken into account in applying the principles of § 6 to determine the law applicable to an issue include:

(a) the place of contracting,

(b) the place of negotiation of the contract,

(c) the place of performance,

(d) the location of the subject matter of the contract, and

(e) the domicil, residence, nationality, place of incorporation and place of business of the parties.

These contacts are to be evaluated according to their relative importance with respect to the particular issue.

(3) If the place of negotiating the contract and the place of performance are in the same state, the local law of this state will usually be applied, except as otherwise provided in §§ 189–199 and 203.

The Second Restatement

(1) By the early 1950s, mounting dissatisfaction with Beale's Restatement led the American Law Institute to make a second effort to restate the law of conflicts. Because the field was evolving rapidly during these years, achieving consensus was difficult, and more than seventeen years passed before the project was completed (1953–1971). In the meantime, what started as a modest update in response to criticisms of the traditional rules as too broad and inflexible turned into a radically different approach to choice of law. Early drafts of the Second Restatement attempted to refine the rules by making them narrower and somewhat more flexible. But critics and commentators attacked the whole notion of jurisdiction-selecting rules, arguing that any solution to choice of law must begin with the policies embodied in the competing laws and reflect the play of those policies in particular situations. Over time, the commitment to jurisdiction-selecting rules was compromised by a grudging and finally a more wholehearted acceptance of policy analysis. The final step in this process came in 1967, when the predecessor to § 6 was first incorporated in the proposed Second Restatement.

In some ways, § 6 was a predictable response to the perceived flaws of the traditional rules. Critics had identified a variety of concerns that these rules failed to take into account, and § 6 offers a kind of "laundry list" response that enables the court to consider all of them when appropriate. An approach along these lines had previously been suggested by Judge Fuld of the New York Court of Appeals, advocating what he called the "center of gravity" theory: "Under this theory, the courts, instead of regarding as conclusive the parties' intention or the place of making or performance, lay emphasis rather upon the law of the place 'which has the most significant contacts with the matter in dispute.' " *Auten v. Auten,* 308 N.Y. 155, 124 N.E.2d 99 (1954). The particular considerations enumerated in § 6, however, were drawn from an article by the Second Restatement's Reporter, Professor Willis Reese, *Conflict of Laws and the Restatement Second,* 28 Law & Contemp. Probs. 679 (1963), which itself drew on a still earlier piece, Cheatham & Reese, *Choice of the Applicable Law,* 52 Colum.L.Rev. 959 (1952). According to the restaters, "this mode of treatment leaves the answer to specific problems very much at large" and "reduces certitude," but its greater flexibility "accord[s] sensitivity in judgment to important values that were formerly ignored." Restatement (Second) of Conflict of Laws vii-viii (1971) (Introduction by H. Wechsler).

(2) The Second Restatement says that the factors listed in § 6 are not exclusive and are not listed in the order of their relative importance. And "some of them will point in different directions in all but the simplest case." The weight to be given a particular factor will vary depending on the context:

> So, for example, the policy in favor of effectuating the relevant policies of the state of dominant interest is given predominant weight in the rule that transfers of interests in land are governed by the law that would be applied by the courts of the situs (see §§ 223–243). On the other hand, the policies in favor of protecting the justified expectations of the parties and of effectuating the basic policy underlying the particular field of law come to the fore in the rule that, subject to certain limitations, the parties can choose the law to govern their contract (see § 187) and in the rules which provide, subject to certain limitations, for the application of a law which will uphold the validity of a trust of movables (see §§ 269–270) or the validity of a contract against the charge of commercial usury (see § 203). Similarly, the policy favoring uniformity of result comes to the fore in the rule that succession to interests in movables is governed by the law that would be

> applied by the courts of the state where the decedent was domiciled at the time of his death (see §§ 260 and 263).

Restatement (Second) of Conflict of Laws § 6, comment c (1971).

With respect to factor (b), "the relevant policies of the forum," the Second Restatement comments:

> Every rule of law, whether embodied in a statute or in a common law rule, was designed to achieve one or more purposes. A court should have regard for these purposes in determining whether to apply its own rule or the rule of another state in the decision of a particular issue. If the purposes sought to be achieved by a local statute or common law rule would be furthered by its application to out-of-state facts, this is a weighty reason why such application should be made. On the other hand, the court is under no compulsion to apply the statute or rule to such out-of-state facts since the originating legislature or court had no ascertainable intentions on the subject. The court must decide for itself whether the purposes sought to be achieved by a local statute or rule should be furthered at the expense of the other choice-of-law factors mentioned in this Subsection.

Id., § 6, comment e.

Factor (d), "the protection of justified expectations," is "an important value in all fields of the law, including choice of law".

> Generally speaking, it would be unfair and improper to hold a person liable under the local law of one state when he had justifiably molded his conduct to conform to the requirements of another state. Also, it is in part because of this factor that the parties are free within broad limits to choose the law to govern the validity of their contract (see § 187) and that the courts seek to apply a law that will sustain the validity of a trust of movables (see §§ 269–270).
>
> There are occasions, particularly in the area of negligence, when the parties act without giving thought to the legal consequences of their conduct or to the law that may be applied. In such situations, the parties have no justified expectations to protect, and this factor can play no part in the decision of a choice-of-law question.

Id., comment g.

> "Certainty, predictability and uniformity of result", the concerns identified in factor (f), are important values in all areas of the law. To the extent that they are attained in choice of law, forum shopping will be discouraged. These values can, however, be

> purchased at too great a price. In a rapidly developing area, such as choice of law, it is often more important that good rules be developed than that predictability and uniformity of result should be assured through continued adherence to existing rules. Predictability and uniformity of result are of particular importance in areas where the parties are likely to give advance thought to the legal consequences of their transactions.

Id., comment i.

(3) The Second Restatement does not, however, abandon rules entirely. On the contrary, it contains a great many rules. But these are reduced to presumptions that identify the state most likely to have the "most significant relationship" in a given situation. For example, while § 145 tells the court in a tort case to apply the law of the state with "the most significant relationship" as determined under § 6, subsequent provisions indicate which state this will "usually" be for some 25 different issues. Section 156 is typical:

> **§ 156.** *Tortious Character of Conduct*
>
> (1) The law selected by application of the rule of § 145 determines whether the actor's conduct was tortious.
>
> (2) The applicable law will usually be the local law of the state where the injury occurred.

Ten more provisions identify the state whose law should govern particular torts, in each case qualified by a reminder that some other state could have a more significant relationship. For example, § 149 states:

> In an action for defamation, the local law of the state where the publication occurs determines the rights and liabilities of the parties, . . . unless, with respect to the particular issue, some other state has a more significant relationship under the principles stated in § 6 to the occurrence and the parties, in which event the local law of the other state will be applied.

Generally speaking, then, the Second Restatement contemplates a two-step process in which the court (1) chooses a presumptively applicable law under the appropriate jurisdiction-selecting rule, and (2) tests this choice against the principles of § 6 in light of relevant contacts identified by general provisions like § 145 (torts) and § 188 (contracts). Adding further confusion, the first step may sometimes collapse into the second one, because some of the presumptive rules refer back to the general provisions without more. Section 161, for example, provides simply that "The law selected by the application of § 145 determines what defenses to the plaintiff's claim may be stated on the merits." Similar treatment is accorded to questions concerning an actor's duty or privilege to act (§ 163), survival (§ 167), charitable immunity (§ 168), the effect of a release or covenant not to sue (§ 170), the measure of damages (§ 171), the right to contribution (§ 173), and vicarious liability (§ 174). Why should there be a presumptive reference for some issues but not others? Why should there be a presumptive reference at all?

(4) The claim that the Second Restatement's presumptive rules reflect a more refined consideration of policies is somewhat deceptive given how often the rules replicate the First Restatement. This is particularly true of the chapter on torts, where almost every reference is to the law of the place of injury. There are a few changes, of course. Section 169, for example, says that questions of intra-family immunity should usually be governed by the law of the parties' domicile, reflecting the reasoning of cases like *Haumschild v. Continental Cas. Co.,* supra p. 45. But even Professor Leflar, who helped write the chapter, expressed dissatisfaction because "the old Restatement's 'place of the injury' rule hovers like a ghost over the entire chapter." Leflar, *The Torts Provisions of the Restatement (Second),* 72 Colum.L.Rev. 267, 269 (1972).

Note also that because the rules are organized in terms of subject-matter categories, characterization remains a problem. Unlike its predecessor, the Second Restatement at least acknowledges the problem, providing in § 7 that questions of characterization "are determined in accordance with the law of the forum." How helpful is that?

(5) How well do you think the Second Restatement is likely to work? Consider the following cases:

PHILLIPS V. GENERAL MOTORS CORP.

298 Mont. 438, 995 P.2d 1002 (2000).

JUSTICE JIM REGNIER delivered the opinion of the Court. . .

FACTUAL BACKGROUND . . .

The vehicle which is the subject of this action was a 1985 Chevrolet pickup. The vehicle was originally sold by General Motors in North Carolina. Darrell Byrd subsequently purchased the pickup in or about February 1995 from Mike's Wholesale Cars in Newton, North Carolina. In doing so, he supplied a North Carolina address. The 1985 Chevrolet pickup truck was designed, tested, manufactured, and distributed by General Motors. The subject vehicle had fuel tanks mounted outside the frame rail.

On December 22, 1997, Darrell Byrd was driving with his family in the 1985 Chevrolet pickup truck from their home near Fortine, Montana, where Darrell Byrd was employed and where Timothy and Samuel Byrd attended school. The purpose of the trip was to spend Christmas vacation with family in North Carolina. The Byrds were domiciled in Montana before and at the time of the 1997 accident.

The wreck and fire which form the basis of this action occurred on December 22, 1997, on Interstate 70 near Russell, Kansas. A 1997 International semi-tractor trailer driven by Betty J. Kendall collided with the subject 1985 Chevrolet pickup truck driven by Darrell Byrd. A fire ensued. Darrell, Angela, and Timothy Byrd died. Samuel Byrd sustained personal injuries which required emergency treatment and hospitalization.

Before and at the time of the 1997 accident, Samuel, Timothy, Darrell, and Angela Byrd were Montana residents. The deceased, Darrell and Angela Byrd, were respectively the father and mother of the deceased, Timothy Byrd. Timothy was 13 years of age at the time of his death. Samuel Byrd, who survived the accident is also the son of the deceased, Darrell and Angela Byrd, and was 11 years old at the time of the 1997 accident.

Plaintiff Alvin Phillips is the legal guardian of Samuel Byrd and the personal representative of the estates of Angela Byrd, Darrell Byrd, and Timothy Byrd. Alvin Phillips resides in Newton, North Carolina. Samuel Byrd presently resides in North Carolina. Probate proceedings for the Estates of Timothy, Angela, and Darrell Byrd are filed with and pending in the Montana Nineteenth Judicial District Court, Lincoln County, Montana.

In these product liability cases, in which Plaintiffs raise claims of negligence and strict liability, Plaintiffs seek compensatory and punitive damages related to the deaths of Darrell, Angela, and Timothy Byrd and the personal injuries sustained by Samuel Byrd. General Motors denies all liability.

[Suit was filed in the United States District Court for the District of Montana, which certified three questions to the state supreme court pursuant to Mont. R. Civ. Proc. 44.] According to the District Court's Order, the parties disagree about the substantive law that should be applied to this case. . . Montana does not have a statutory provision governing choice of law nor has this Court reached a choice of law issue in a case involving conflicting tort rules. * * * Absent a definitive determination of Montana's choice of law rule in tort cases, federal judges for the District of Montana have applied the "most significant relationship" test of the Restatement (Second) of Conflict of Laws. * * *

The District Court observed that the instant case raised significant policy questions involving Montana's choice of law rules, that choice of law questions in tort cases are frequent in diversity litigation in federal court, and that it would be helpful in resolving this case and others to have a definitive determination of what the Montana choice of law rule is.

QUESTION ONE

Whether, in a personal injury/product liability/wrongful death action, where there is a potential conflict of laws, Montana will follow the Restatement (Second) of Conflict of Laws, including the "most significant relationship" test set forth in §§ 146 and 6, in the determination of which state's substantive law to apply?

The traditional choice of law rule, known as *lex loci delicti commissi* (or the law of place where the wrong was committed), provides that the infliction of injury is actionable under the law of the state in which it was received. *See Alabama Great S. R.R. Co. v. Carroll* (Ala.1892), 97 Ala. 126, 11 So. 803, 805. . . The theoretical basis for the traditional rule was the "vested rights" theory propounded by Joseph H. Beale. The theory explained the forum's use of foreign legal rules in terms of the creation and enforcement of vested rights. According to Professor Beale's theory, the only law that can operate in a foreign territory is the law of the foreign sovereign. When an event occurred in a foreign territory (an injury caused by a defective product, for example), and under the laws of that territory that event gave rise to a right (damages), a right "vested" under that territory's law. The role of the forum court was simply to enforce the right which had vested in the foreign territory according to that territory's law. Crucial to this theory was a determination of where and when a right vested, because the law in place where the right vested would control the existence and content of the right. As evidenced by the decision in *Carroll,* courts have held that for tort claims a right vested where and when an injury occurred. * * *

Traditional practice depends on a few broad, single-contact, jurisdiction-selecting rules. Traditionalist courts find the location of the last event necessary for a right to vest and apply the law of that location. As a result, courts following the traditional approach often choose the law of a state with no interest in the resolution of the dispute, like the choice of Mississippi law in *Carroll.* * * *

The traditional rule has largely been justified on the basis of the practical advantages that it offers: certainty, predictability, and forum neutrality. * * * However, problems inherent in its application as well as escape devices used to avoid results perceived to be arbitrary or unfair have greatly diminished the advantages the traditional rule supposedly provides. For example, the explicit public policy exception to the *lex loci* rule allows courts to avoid the law of the place of injury by concluding that it violates the public policy of the forum. Use of the public policy escape device by *lex loci* courts continues today. . .

The traditional rule also no longer affords consistency and predictability across jurisdictions. While some jurisdictions still cling to the traditional rule, the vast majority of states have rejected it. At the end of

1998, only 11 states still adhered to the *lex loci* rule, and their continued adherence is questionable. *See* Symeon C. Symeonides, *Choice of Law in the American Courts in 1998: Twelfth Annual Survey,* 47 Am.J.Comp.L. 327, 331. Professor Symeonides observes:

> As the century draws to a close, the traditional theory in tort and contract conflicts in the United States finds itself in a very precarious state. This assessment is based not simply on the relatively low number of states that still adhere to that theory, but also on the shallowness of their commitment to it. Although the degree of commitment varies from state to state, it is fair to say that very few of these states are philosophically committed to the traditional theory. . . More often, these rules remain in place only because [a] court is able to find a way to evade them by using one of the traditional escapes, such as characterization, substance versus procedure, renvoi, or, more often, the [public policy] exception.

Symeonides, *supra,* at 345.

The Restatement (Second) of Conflict of Laws largely abandoned the traditional rule in favor of an approach which seeks to apply the law of the state with the "most significant relationship to the occurrence and the parties." Restatement (Second) of Conflict of Laws § 145(1) (1971) (hereinafter "Restatement (Second)"). In adopting a policy analysis approach, the drafters noted that "[e]xperience has shown that the last event rule does not always work well. Situations arise where the state of the last event (place of injury) bears only a slight relationship to the occurrence and the parties with respect to the particular issue." Restatement (Second), Introductory Note to Ch. 7, at 412.

In abandoning the *lex loci* rule in favor of the most significant relationship test, one court observed:

> The majority of courts which have considered the question have abandoned the lex loci rule in favor of a more flexible approach which permits analysis of the policies and interests underlying the particular issue before the court. Additionally, the commentators are overwhelmingly opposed to its retention and, although they disagree as to a substitute approach, all advocate a method which allows Courts to focus on the policies underlying the conflicting laws . . . and the governmental interests which would be advanced by their application.

In re Air Crash Disaster at Boston, Mass. on July 31, 1973 (D.Mass.1975), 399 F.Supp. 1106, 1110.

In determining the choice of law rules for contract disputes, we adopted the approach contained in the Restatement (Second) of Conflict of

Laws. *See Casarotto v. Lombardi* (1994), 268 Mont. 369, 886 P.2d 931, *rev'd sub nom. on other grounds, Doctor's Assocs., Inc. v. Casarotto* (1996), 517 U.S. 681, *reaff'd on reh'g, Casarotto v. Lombardi* (1995), 274 Mont. 3, 901 P.2d 596. We see no reason to have one choice of law approach for contracts and another for torts. For the reasons set forth above, we now hereby adopt the "most significant relationship" approach to determine the applicable substantive law for issues of tort.

QUESTION TWO

Given the facts of this case, which state's law applies to plaintiff's various tort and damages claims under Montana's choice of law rules?

The Byrds claim that under the most significant relationship test Montana law applies. General Motors contends that under this same test, the law of Kansas applies. We agree with the Byrds.

At the outset, we note that many appellate courts that have analyzed the most significant relationship test have done so in a fairly conclusory fashion. Although the analysis that follows appears somewhat tedious, our attempt is to comply with the procedures set forth in the Restatement (Second) of Conflict of Laws. We also raise an additional caveat. Any analysis under the Restatement approach is necessarily driven by the unique facts, issues, applicable law, and jurisdictions implicated in a particular case.

A. Relevant Restatement Provisions.

[The court set out in their entirety sections 6 and 145, supra pp. 241.]

The Restatement also has more specific sections relating to personal injury and wrongful death actions. Sections 146 and 175 provide that the rights and liabilities of the parties are to be determined in accordance with the law of the state where the injury occurred unless, with respect to a particular issue, another state has a more significant relationship. Whether another state has a more significant relationship is determined under § 145(2). We further note that issues such as the tortious character of conduct, available defenses, contributory fault, and damages are all to be determined by applying the most significant relationship rule of § 145. See, e.g., Restatement (Second) §§ 156 ("Tortious Character of Conduct"), 157 ("Standard of Care"), 161 ("Defenses"), 164 ("Contributory Fault"), and 171 ("Damages").

B. Most Significant Relationship Analysis.

Under the Restatement (Second) approach, the local law of the place of injury, Kansas, is presumptively applicable in a product liability and wrongful death action unless, with respect to a particular issue, a different state has a more significant relationship. See Restatement (Second) §§ 146 and 175. In order to determine whether a state other than the place of injury has a more significant relationship, the contacts listed under § 145(2) "are to be taken into account in applying the principles of § 6." Restatement (Second) § 145(2). Accordingly, we shall address each of the factors enumerated under § 6(2), taking into account, when appropriate, the contacts of § 145(2).

1. Needs of the Interstate and International System.

The first factor we must consider under § 6(2) is the needs of the interstate and international system. Restatement (Second) § 6(2)(a). The drafters stated,

> Choice-of-law rules, among other things, should seek to further harmonious relations between states and to facilitate commercial intercourse between them. In formulating rules of choice of law, a state should have regard for the needs and policies of other states and of the community of states. Rules of choice of law formulated with regard for such needs and policies are likely to commend themselves to other states and to be adopted by these states.

Restatement § 6 cmt. d.

On the facts of this case, this factor does not point toward the importance of applying any particular state's law. Rather, this factor supports the application of the Restatement approach, namely the law of the state with the most significant relationship to an issue. We believe the Restatement approach fosters harmonious relationship between states by respecting the substantive law of other states when those states have a greater interest in the determination of a particular issue litigated in a foreign jurisdiction. The Restatement approach is preferable, in our view, to the traditional *lex loci* rule which applies the law of the place of the accident which may be fortuitous in tort actions. We further conclude that there is no need to evaluate the contacts listed in § 145 with regard to this issue.

2. The Policies of Interested States.

The second and third factors we must consider are the relevant policies of the forum state and other interested states. See Restatement (Second) § 6(2)(b) and (c). In the case *sub judice*, these are the most important factors in our analysis. . . This principle requires us to consider whether applying the law of a state with a relevant contact would further the purpose that law was designed to achieve. Upon consideration of this principle, it is clear that Montana has the more significant relationship to the issues raised by this dispute for the reasons set forth below.

a. Place of Injury.

As noted above, in product liability and wrongful death actions, the law of the place of injury is presumptively applicable unless another state has a more significant relationship. * * * The injury here occurred in Kansas. Kansas law provides for a cause of action against a manufacturer whose product causes harm as a result of its defective design. *See* Kan. Stat. Ann. § 60–3302. The purpose of a state's product liability statute is to regulate the sale of products in that state and to prevent injuries incurred by that state's residents due to defective products.* * * Any conduct the state of Kansas may have been attempting to regulate through § 60–3302 could not be implicated by the facts of this case as it involves neither a sale in Kansas nor an injury to a Kansas resident.

Kansas law provides for multiple defenses to a product liability claim. For example, Kansas law bars recovery for injuries occurring after "the time during which the product would be normally likely to perform or be stored in a safe manner." * * * Kansas law also allows a party defending a product liability claim to assert that the injury causing aspect of the product was in compliance with the regulatory standards relating to design or performance at the time of manufacture. * * * Once again, the overriding purpose of Kansas's product liability laws is to establish the level of safety of products sold either in Kansas or to a Kansas resident. Clearly, these rules regarding defenses were not enacted in order to grant a defense to a manufacturer when a non-Kansas resident is injured by a product not purchased in Kansas.

Under Kansas law, an award of damages for product liability may be diminished in proportion to the amount of negligence attributed to the plaintiff or decedent. * * * General Motors asserts that the issue of comparative negligence turns upon conduct that occurred in Kansas and therefore Kansas law should apply because Kansas has an interest in regulating conduct which occurred within its borders. However, the record before us does not contain the substance of General Motors' allegations regarding the Byrds' allegedly negligent conduct. Therefore, there is no evidence that General Motors' allegations concerning the comparative negligence of the Byrds are limited to conduct occurring solely within Kansas.

Moreover, even if General Motors' allegations concerned conduct occurring solely in Kansas, the Kansas Supreme Court did not extend Kansas's comparative negligence statute to product liability causes of action in order to regulate conduct occurring in Kansas. In concluding that the comparative negligence statute applied to product liability actions, the Kansas Supreme Court stated:

> *Comparative liability provides a system for allocating responsibility* for an injury while still serving the social policy of not allowing a manufacturer or seller to escape liability for defective products merely because of slight culpability on the part of the product user in bringing about the injury.

[*Kennedy v. City of Sawyer,* 618 P.2d 788, 796 (Kan.1980) (emphasis added).]

It is clear from the *Kennedy* decision that the Kansas Supreme Court extended Kansas's comparative negligence standard to product liability cases in order to "allocate responsibility for an injury" due to a defective product, disallowing defenses such as "assumption of the risk," "product misuse," or "unreasonable use" from completely precluding recovery under Kansas product liability law. * * * Kansas has no interest in allocating responsibility for the injuries suffered by Montana residents and caused by a product purchased in North Carolina. Again, the purpose of a state's product liability laws is to protect and provide compensation to its residents and regulate the sale of products within its borders. * * *

Kansas law limits the total amount recoverable for "noneconomic loss" in a personal injury action to $250,000, and limits "nonpecuniary" damages in wrongful death actions to $100,000. * * * [These provisions were] enacted in an effort to alleviate a perceived crisis in the availability and affordability of liability insurance. * * * The purpose of these limitations would be furthered if any damage award issued would affect the availability or affordability of liability insurance for Kansas residents. The purpose of these limitations would not be furthered by applying them to the instance case because an award of damages against General Motors which exceeded Kansas's statutory damage limitations would not affect the availability or affordability of liability insurance for Kansas residents.

Lastly, Kansas law allows for punitive damages, but limits them to the lesser of $5 million or the defendant's highest gross annual income earned during any one of the five years immediately before the act for which such damages are awarded. * * * The purpose of the availability and extent of punitive damage awards is to punish or deter conduct deemed wrongful when the availability of a cause of action and compensatory damages are considered an insufficient punishment or deterrence. * * * Accordingly, the purpose of Kansas's punitive damage provisions would only be furthered on a particular set of facts if it had an interest in punishing or deterring the conduct at issue. As noted above, the purpose of Kansas's cause of action for product liability would not be furthered by its application to these facts because the pickup was not sold in Kansas nor were the Byrds Kansas residents. Correspondingly, this case does not involve conduct which Kansas was attempting to punish or deter through its punitive damages provisions.

b. Place of Conduct.

The Byrds purchased the vehicle in North Carolina. General Motors has made a general assertion that North Carolina might have an interest in having its law applied, but has not briefed us on which North Carolina laws might be applicable. Accordingly, our discussion will be somewhat general in nature. General Motors has argued that North Carolina has an interest because General Motors initially sold the truck in North Carolina, the Byrds subsequently purchased the truck in North Carolina, and the Byrds may have been North Carolina residents when they made this purchase.

The fact that the Byrds purchased the truck in North Carolina while residing there indicates that one of the purposes of North Carolina product liability law—the regulation of products sold within its borders—might be implicated by the facts of this case. However, we think it significant that a North Carolina court would not apply North Carolina law to these facts, even if the Byrds had remained in North Carolina; North Carolina still adheres to the traditional place of injury rule in tort cases. * * * On the facts of this case, a North Carolina court would apply the law of Kansas because they still adhere to the "vested rights" theory that any right created by an injury is solely a product of the law of the territory in which that injury occurred. * * * Accordingly, the scope of North Carolina product liability law does not include causes of action for products purchased in North Carolina by North Carolina residents which cause injury outside of North Carolina. This belies the significance of North Carolina's interest in having its law applied. We note, however, that the place of purchase may have had greater significance if North Carolina followed the Restatement's approach rather than the traditional place of injury rule.

General Motors asserts that Michigan has an interest in regulating conduct occurring in Michigan. We note that evidence of where the pickup truck was designed and manufactured is not in the record nor has General Motors briefed us on the content of the precise laws which it claims might be applicable to these facts. However, we do not believe that the purpose of any potentially applicable Michigan product liability law would be to regulate the design and manufacture of products within its borders.* * * The purpose of product liability law is to regulate in-state sales or sales to residents and to set the level of compensation when residents are injured. * * *

Significantly, Michigan courts have recognized that it would not further the purpose of Michigan product liability law to apply it to a similar set of facts. Michigan courts have not applied Michigan law under similar circumstances because Michigan has little interest in applying its law when its only contact with the dispute is the location of the manufacturer. * * *

Other courts have observed that applying the law of the place of manufacture would be unfair because it would tend to leave victims under compensated as states wishing to attract and hold manufacturing companies would raise the threshold of liability and reduce compensation. * * * We agree that stressing the importance of the place of manufacture for choice of law purposes in a product liability case would be unfair. The conclusion that the place of manufacture is a relatively unimportant factor in a product liability case is obvious when we consider a hypothetical case in which all of the relevant contacts are in the forum state except the location of the manufacturer (most likely the fact pattern for the vast majority of product liability cases). Applying the law of the place of manufacture to that case simply because the product was manufactured out-of-state would allow a state with a high concentration of industry to capture all of the benefits of a high threshold of liability and a low level of compensation. Specifically, the manufacturing state could enjoy the benefits associated with liability laws which favored manufacturers in order to attract and retain manufacturing firms and encourage business within its borders while placing the costs of its legislative decision, in the form of less tort compensation, on the shoulders of nonresidents injured by its manufacturers' products. This seems inherently unfair.

c. Residence of Parties.

The Plaintiffs were residents of Montana at the time they were injured. Unlike the laws of the other states with relevant contacts under § 145(2), the purposes sought to be achieved by Montana's product liability laws would be furthered by their application to this set of facts. One of the central purposes of Montana's product liability scheme is to prevent injuries to Montana residents caused by defectively designed products. In contrast to Kansas, Montana has a direct interest in the application of its product liability laws because its residents were injured in this accident. Montana adopted a strict liability standard in order to afford *"maximum protection for consumers against dangerous defects in manufactured products with the focus on the condition of the product, and not on the manufacturer's conduct or knowledge." See Sternhagen v. Dow Co.* (1997), 282 Mont. 168, 176, 935 P.2d 1139, 1144 (emphasis added).

As is clear from *Sternhagen,* the focus of Montana law is not only on the regulation of products sold in Montana, but also on providing the maximum protection and compensation to Montana residents with the focus on the condition of the product and not on the conduct of the manufacturer. Applying Montana's provisions guaranteeing strict liability and full compensation to a cause of action involving a Montana domiciliary injured by a defective product would further the purposes of Montana law by insuring that the costs to Montana residents due to injuries from defective products are fully borne by the responsible parties. It will also have the salutary effect of deterring future sales of defective products in Montana and encouraging manufacturers to warn Montana residents about defects in their products as quickly and as thoroughly as possible.

Likewise, the purposes of Montana's laws regarding the availability and extent of punitive damages in product liability actions would also be furthered by their application to these facts. This is because, as described more fully above, punitive damages serve to punish and deter conduct deemed wrongful—in this case, placing a defective product into the stream of commerce which subsequently injured a Montana resident. * * *

Lastly, we must address whether the purpose underlying Montana's rules governing product liability would be furthered by their application in this case despite the fact that Samuel Byrd is no longer a Montana domiciliary. We believe that the application of Montana law to an injury received by a Montana domiciliary would further the purpose of that law regardless of the post-accident residency of the plaintiff. As discussed previously, the purpose of Montana product liability law is to regulate product sales in Montana and to compensate injured Montana [citizens]. Clearly, that concern arises as soon as a product is either sold in Montana or causes injury to a Montana resident. Consequently, the relevant residence of the plaintiff is the residence at the time of injury.

We note that the only reason Samuel Byrd is currently residing in North Carolina is because his parents died in the accident which forms the basis of the Plaintiffs' claims. The guarantee of full compensation for Montana residents who suffer injuries due to defective products certainly will not turn on such fortuitous circumstances as a postaccident move caused by the allegedly wrongful conduct of a defendant.

d. The place where the relationship, if any, between the parties is centered.

It doesn't appear that there is a place where the relationship, if any, between General Motors and the Byrds is centered. As one court described in similar circumstances:

> [P]roducts liability arises out of the most casual "relationship" imaginable, the one-time purchase and sale of the product, and the plaintiff, as here, may have had no connection with it. The only "relationship" between the parties here is that of injured victim and alleged tortfeasor.
>
> * * *

In sum, upon an analysis of the principle requiring us to consider the policies of interested states, it appears that Montana, as the domicile of the Byrds, has a significant relationship to the issues raised by this dispute. This is because, in general, the purpose of a state's product liability law is to regulate purchases made within its borders and to protect and compensate its residents. The policies underlying Montana product liability law would be furthered on these facts because the Byrds were Montana domiciliaries at the time they were injured. The policies underlying Kansas and Michigan law would not be furthered by their application to these facts because the product was not sold in either state, nor were the Plaintiffs domiciled in either state at the time they were injured. The purposes underlying North Carolina product liability law would not be furthered on these facts because, under North Carolina's vested rights approach to conflict of laws, North Carolina would apply the law of the jurisdiction where the injury occurred, whatever that law may be.

3. Justified Expectations.

Although we are to consider the justified expectations of the parties, tort cases generally do not involve justified expectations. Particularly in the area of negligence, when parties act without giving thought to the legal consequences of their conduct or to the law to be applied, they have no justified expectations. See Restatement (Second) § 6 cmt. g.

Automobile manufacturers do presumably give advance thought to the legal consequences of their conduct when designing and manufacturing their products. However, we note that the law of any state could potentially apply in a product liability action involving an automobile. For example, because North Carolina employs the traditional place of injury rule for choice of law purposes, if a North Carolina resident receives an injury from a defective vehicle while driving out-of-state, the law of the place of injury would govern that dispute. * * * Accordingly, any expectation General Motors had that the law of North Carolina would govern a product liability suit involving a pickup truck it sold in North Carolina would not be justified. Furthermore, as noted by the court in *Ness*, automobiles are moveable and frequently resold and the maintenance of a product liability action does not require privity. * * * For example, the pickup could have been subsequently resold by the initial purchaser in a state which does not adhere to the traditional *lex loci* rule. Therefore, any expectation General Motors had that a dispute concerning this pickup truck would be governed by North Carolina's place of injury rule would not be justified.

4. Basic Policies Underlying Particular Field of Law.

We must also consider the relevant contacts in regard to the basic policies underlying the particular field of law. *See* Restatement (Second) § 6(2)(e). The drafters state that:

> This factor is of particular importance in situations where the policies of the interested states are largely the same but there are nevertheless minor differences between their relevant local law rules. In such instances, there is good reason for the court to apply the local law of the state which will best achieve the basic policy, or policies, underlying the particular field of law involved.

Restatement (Second) § 6(2) cmt. h.

This is not a case in which the policies of interested states are basically the same except for minor differences in their local rules. For example, although under Kansas and Montana law, manufacturers of defective products are strictly liable for injuries, North Carolina law does not permit strict liability in tort in product liability actions. * * * Instead, it appears that the various interested states have reached different conclusions concerning the right level of compensation and deterrence for injuries caused by defective products. Therefore, we need go no further in addressing this contact.

5. Certainty, Predictability, Uniformity, Ease.

We are also instructed to give consideration to the certainty, predictability and uniformity of result as well as the ease in the determination and application of the law to be applied. *See* Restatement (Second) § 6(2)(f) and (g). The comments state:

> Predictability and uniformity of result are of particular importance in areas where parties are likely to give advance thought to the legal consequences of their transactions. It is partly on account of these factors that the parties are permitted within broad limits to choose the law that will determine the validity and effect of their contract. . .

Restatement (Second) § 6(2) cmt. i.

A consideration of this principle does not indicate that any one state has a more significant relationship than any other. Applying the law of the place of injury would not increase certainty or predictability any more than applying the law of the plaintiff's residence at the time of accident.

C. Conclusion.

Under the most significant relationship approach of the Restatement (Second), the local law of the place of injury, Kansas, governs the rights and liabilities of the parties to a product liability and wrongful death action unless, with respect to a particular issue, a different state has a more significant relationship. * * * In order to determine whether a state other than the place of injury has a more significant relationship, the contacts listed under § 145(2) must be analyzed in relation to the principles enumerated under § 6(2). However, the principles of § 6(2) need not be given equal consideration in each case. Varying weight must be given to a particular factor, or group of factors, in different areas of choice of law. *See* Restatement (Second) § 6 cmt. c. On the facts before us, we give most weight to the principles requiring us to consider the relevant policies of interested states. Restatement (Second) § 6(2)(b) and (c). The other principles do not indicate the significance of any one contact.

Upon an analysis of the policies of interested states, it appears that the purposes of both Montana and North Carolina product liability law would presumably be furthered by their application to these facts. The place of purchase has an interest in regulating the safety of products sold within its borders; the place of the plaintiff's residence has an interest in deterring injuries to its residents and setting the level of compensation. Significantly, however, North Carolina would not apply its own law to these facts, even if the Byrds had been North Carolina residents at the time of injury.

The purpose behind Montana product liability laws is clearly implicated by these facts. The following factors all point toward applying Montana law: the Byrds resided in Montana at the time of the accident, General Motors does business in Montana, Montana has a direct interest in preventing defective products from causing injuries to Montana residents as well as punishing and deterring manufacturers whose products injure Montana residents, and finally Montana is interested in fully compensating Montana residents. All of these factors would be furthered by applying Montana product liability, defenses, damages, and wrongful death statutes to the facts of this case.

QUESTION THREE

Does Montana recognize a "public policy" exception that would require application of Montana law even where Montana's choice of law rules dictate application of the laws of another state, and would such an exception apply in this case?

For choice of law purposes, the public policy of a state is simply the rules, as expressed in its legislative enactments and judicial decisions, that it uses to decide controversies.* * * The purpose of a choice of law rule is to resolve conflicts between competing policies. Considerations of public policy are expressly subsumed within the most significant relationship approach. * * * In order to determine which state has the more significant relationship, the public policies of all interested states must be considered. A "public policy" exception to the most significant relationship test would be redundant.

Accordingly, in answer to the questions certified, we adopt the Restatement (Second) of Conflict of Laws for tort actions. Under the analysis contained in the Restatement (Second), we conclude that given the facts as presented in the District Court's Order, the laws of Montana apply. Lastly, considerations of public policy are accounted for under the analysis contained in the Restatement (Second) of Conflict of Laws.

WOOD BROS. HOMES, INC. V. WALKER ADJUSTMENT BUREAU

198 Colo. 444, 601 P.2d 1369 (1979).

HODGES, CHIEF JUSTICE.

Plaintiff-respondent, Walker Adjustment Bureau (Walker), brought suit in Colorado against defendant-petitioner, Wood Bros. Homes, Inc.

(Wood), to recover on a contract between Walker's assignor, Fred Gagnon, and Wood. The trial court granted Wood's motion for summary judgment, ruling that under Colorado choice of law rules New Mexico law applied, and barred the action. In *Walker Adjustment Bureau v. Wood Bros. Homes, Inc.*, 41 Colo.App. 26, 582 P.2d 1059 (1978), the court of appeals reversed the trial court's judgment, holding that under the traditional conflict of law rules or the Restatement (Second) of Conflict of Laws (*Restatement (Second)*) the law of Colorado applied and the contract was enforceable. We granted certiorari and now reverse the judgment of the court of appeals.

Fred Gagnon, a resident of California, contracted with Wood, a Delaware corporation having its principal place of business in Colorado, to perform rough carpentry work on a Wood's apartment complex in Albuquerque, New Mexico. Contract negotiations took place in California, Colorado, and New Mexico. Gagnon commenced work on the project before August 22, 1972, the date the contract was signed in Colorado.

Shortly after Gagnon commenced work, New Mexico officials ordered construction halted because he had not obtained a New Mexico contractor's license. The New Mexico Construction Industries Licensing Act prohibits any person from engaging in the business of a contractor without first obtaining a license from the appropriate state commission. * * * Wood promptly cancelled Gagnon's contract and refused to pay him, although Wood did pay approximately $27,000 to employees of Gagnon for the work they had completed. Walker, as Gagnon's assignee, then brought suit in Colorado seeking recovery against Wood on either a contract or quantum meruit theory.

I.

The first issue is whether an unlicensed New Mexico contractor can recover either damages for breach of a construction contract to be performed in New Mexico or in quantum meruit for the value of services performed. Application of Colorado law would result in Wood being liable as there is no impediment to enforceability of the contract. Applying New Mexico law, however, the converse is true. N.M.Stat.Ann. section 67–35–33 (now section 60–13–30) provides:

> "No contractor shall act as agent or bring or maintain any action in any court of the state for the collection of compensation for the performance of any act for which a license is required by the Construction Industries Licensing Act without alleging and proving that such contractor was a duly licensed contractor at the time the alleged cause of action arose."[1]

[1] The courts of New Mexico have consistently interpreted this section to preclude recovery by an unlicensed contractor in both contract and quantum meruit actions. Without an allegation and proof of a contractor's license, New Mexico law treats the complaint as invalid and the court as without jurisdiction to hear the matter. * * *

It is thus necessary to determine which law applies to resolve this issue.

Under the traditional conflict of laws rule for contract actions, the law of the place of execution governs questions regarding the formation of the contract, while the law of the place of performance governs issues relating to the performance of the contract. * * * This rule, however, has frequently proven unduly inflexible, leading to harsh and unjust results. Courts have often been forced to employ a multitude of escape devices to reach an equitable result. Therefore the traditional choice of law rules no longer provide the predictability and uniformity which were considered their primary virtues. See *First National Bank v. Rostek,* 182 Colo. 437, 514 P.2d 314 (1973). . .

Where a conflict of laws question is raised, the objective of the *Restatement (Second)* is to locate the state having the "most significant relationship" to the particular issue. In analyzing which state has the most significant relationship, the principles set forth in *Restatement (Second)* sections 6 and 188 are to be taken into account. Once the state having the most significant relationship is identified, the law of that state is then applied to resolve the particular issue.

In addition to the general principles set forth in sections 6 and 188, several sections of Chapter 8 (Contracts) of the *Restatement (Second)* apply to specific types of contracts. Section 196 applies to contracts for the rendition of services. It provides:

> "The validity of a contract for the rendition of services and the rights created thereby are determined, in the absence of an effective choice of law by the parties, by the local law of the state where the contract requires that the services, or a major portion of the services, be rendered, unless, with respect to the particular issue, some other state has a more significant relationship under the principles stated in § 6 to the transaction and the parties, in which event the local law of the other state will be applied."

The effect of section 196 is to create a presumption that the state where services are to be performed is the state having the most significant relationship to the issue of the validity of the contract. The presumption is not conclusive. If another state has a more significant relationship, then the law of that state will be applied.

The court of appeals held that under the *Restatement (Second)* Colorado would be the state having the most significant relationship because of the "rule of validation." We disagree.

Colorado's interest in the validation of agreements and protection of the parties' expectations is a central policy underlying the law of contracts.

See *Restatement (Second)* section 6, comment (2)(h) (1971). While this interest is strong, it does not necessarily supersede all others.

The New Mexico Construction Industries Licensing Act provides a comprehensive and mandatory system of licensing for persons engaged in construction work in New Mexico. The act is designed to protect New Mexico citizens against "substandard or hazardous construction . . . and by providing protection against the fiscal irresponsibility of persons engaged in construction occupations or trades. . ." N.M.Stat.Ann. section 67–35–4 (now section 60–13–4). Potential contractors must present evidence of financial responsibility, demonstrate a familiarity with building regulations, submit proof of registration with the tax office, pass an examination, and must not have engaged illegally in the contracting business in New Mexico within the past year. Those who build without a license are subject to a criminal sanction and are expressly barred from obtaining judicial enforcement of their contract or from recovery for the value of services performed.

In this situation the value of protecting the parties' contractual expectations is outweighed by New Mexico's interest in applying its invalidating rule. *A fortiori,* the presumption of section 196 that New Mexico law applies has not been rebutted. The law of New Mexico applies to resolve this issue, and as discussed above, the action is consequently barred. This conclusion is in accord with *Restatement (Second)* section 202(2) (1971) which provides: "When performance is illegal in the place of performance, the contract will usually be denied enforcement."

II.

The second issue before us is whether Wood should be estopped from asserting that Gagnon was an unlicensed contractor in New Mexico. The court of appeals determined that under Colorado law Wood was estopped because it knew Gagnon did not have a New Mexico contractor's license and had indicated to Gagnon that he could work under its general contractor's license.

Assuming *arguendo* that Colorado has an interest in the resolution of this issue and that a conflict exists between the results of applying Colorado and New Mexico law, the state having the most significant relationship to resolution of this issue must be located. For the reasons set forth above, New Mexico's interest clearly preponderates, and therefore is the state having the most significant relationship to this issue.

Since under New Mexico law estoppel cannot be founded on an illegal contract, a defendant cannot be estopped from asserting a plaintiff's nonconformance with the licensing requirement of the New Mexico Construction Industries Licensing Act. *Kaiser v. Thomson,* 55 N.M. 270, 232 P.2d 142 (1951). Therefore Wood cannot be estopped from asserting Gagnon's failure to have a New Mexico contractor's license.

Accordingly, the judgment of the court of appeals is reversed.

Using the Second Restatement

(1) What do you make of the Montana Supreme Court's attempt to apply the Second Restatement in *Phillips*? Which of the factors listed in § 6 do the work here? Which, if any, of the factors listed in § 6 ought to have counted for more? Is this just interest analysis under another guise? Do you think this case to be atypical?

Do you agree with the court in *Phillips* that modern choice-of-law approaches render the public policy exception obsolete? In *Cooney v. Osgood Machinery, Inc.*, 81 N.Y.2d 66, 79, 595 N.Y.S.2d 919, 612 N.E.2d 277 (1993), the New York Court of Appeals—after noting how the exception was sometimes used as a cover for interest analysis—suggested instead that "[i]n view of modern choice of law doctrine, resort to the public policy exception should be reserved for those foreign laws that are truly obnoxious." Who is right here?

The court in *Wood* gives precedence to New Mexico's interest in applying its invalidating rule (factor (c) of § 6). The lower court, in contrast, reasoned that applying Colorado law and enforcing the contract was supported by factor (d) (protecting justified expectations), factor (f) (certainty, predictability, and uniformity), and factor (g) (ease in determining the law to be applied). Why does New Mexico's interest outweigh these considerations? What role in the analysis is played by the contacts listed in § 188? Should New Mexico law also govern the question of estoppel?

(2) Some of the difficulties in identifying the state with the "most significant relationship" should have been apparent from New York's experience with the "center of gravity" approach mentioned supra p. 219. In *Auten v. Auten,* 308 N.Y. 155, 124 N.E.2d 99 (1954), an English couple separated, and the husband moved to New York. The wife travelled to New York, where they executed an agreement obligating the husband to provide child support. He stopped paying, and she brought an action in England but failed to pursue it. Later she brought another action to enforce the separation agreement in New York. The husband defended on the ground that her earlier suit operated to repudiate their contract. This was a valid defense under New York law, but not under the law of England. Looking for the "center of gravity," Judge Fuld concluded that contacts like the place of making or performance were "entirely fortuitous" in the case before him: "It is still England, as the jurisdiction of marital domicile and the place where the wife and children were to be, that has the greatest concern in defining and regulating the rights and duties existing under the [separation] agreement."

Seven years later the court decided *Haag v. Barnes,* 9 N.Y.2d 554, 216 N.Y.S.2d 65, 175 N.E.2d 441 (1961). Barnes, an Illinois lawyer, hired Haag, a New York secretary, to work for him on frequent trips to New York. They began a sexual relationship, and Haag became pregnant. She travelled to Illinois, where the child was born, and they executed a contract there under which Barnes agreed to provide $275 per month in child support in exchange for a release from any further obligation. Haag subsequently sued to increase these payments, and Barnes offered their agreement in defense. The contract was valid under Illinois law, but New York required an independent judicial determination that adequate provision had been made for the child. In another opinion by Judge Fuld the court applied Illinois law, this time explaining that the fact that mother and child lived in New York was entitled to little weight. Instead, the court relied heavily on the fact that the contract had been made in Illinois and included a clause stating that Illinois law would govern, noting that "even if the parties' intention and the place of the making of the contract are not given decisive effect, they are nevertheless to be given heavy weight in determining which jurisdiction 'has the most significant contacts with the matter in dispute.' *Auten v. Auten.*"

Thus, in both *Auten* and *Haag* a woman left with responsibility for offspring a man shared in creating negotiated a support agreement at the man's home base and returned home to raise her family and receive payments. Despite these similarities, the "center of gravity" turned out to be her home in *Auten* and his home in *Haag*. Can this be justified in choice-of-law terms?

The center of gravity approach asked the court to choose a law based on an overall evaluation of contacts without providing a mechanism to assign these contacts weight or priority. Section 6 of the Second Restatement is supposed to fill this gap. Does it? Can you articulate the theory underlying the "most significant relationship" test? What exactly is the judge looking for?

(3) The presumptive rules of the Second Restatement are supposed to facilitate analysis under § 6. Do they succeed? Isn't § 6 analysis always required, if only to make sure that no other state has a more significant relationship than the state identified by the rules? Do the presumptive rules simplify this analysis? The Restatement explains that the rules set forth "the choice of law the courts will 'usually' make in given situations. The formulations are cast as empirical appraisals rather than purported rules to indicate how far the statements may be subject to reevaluation in a concrete instance in light of the more general and open-ended norm [in § 6]." Restatement (Second) of Conflict of Laws viii (1971). Of what use is the presumption if it has no normative basis and the judge cannot know whether it fits a particular case without doing a full § 6 analysis anyway?

In practice, the difficulty of deciding how much weight to give the presumptive rules has led courts to treat them in one of two ways. Most courts pay lip service to the rules but make their own evaluation under § 6. See Borchers, *Courts and the Second Conflicts Restatement: Some Observations and an Empirical Note,* 56 Md. L. Rev. 1232 (1997). For these courts, the rules serve little purpose other than to provide a convenient first or last paragraph in an opinion. Both principal cases above are in this category. In *Wood,* for example, the court ignored the rules in explaining why New Mexico law applied under § 6, adding as an afterthought that "*A fortiori,* the presumption of § 196 that New Mexico law applies has not been rebutted." For many of these courts, moreover, analysis under § 6 looks an awful lot like interest analysis: as in *Phillips,* the other factors are mentioned, but the outcome is determined by the court's examination of state interests. See, e.g., *NL Indus. v. Commercial Union Ins. Co.,* 65 F.3d 314 (3d Cir.1995); *General Ceramics Inc. v. Firemen's Fund Ins. Co.,* 66 F.3d 647 (3d Cir.1995). Other courts essentially end their analysis with the rules: little or no attention is paid to § 6, and instead the court makes the presumption effectively irrebuttable. For these courts the Second Restatement is little more than an updated version of the First. See, e.g., *Leksi, Inc. v. Federal Ins. Co.,* 736 F.Supp. 1331 (D.N.J.1990); *Trailways, Inc. v. Clark,* 794 S.W.2d 479 (Tex.Ct.App.1990); *In re Marriage of Adams,* 133 Ill.2d 437, 141 Ill.Dec. 448, 551 N.E.2d 635 (1990).

A particularly egregious example of the latter is *Spinozzi v. ITT Sheraton Corp.,* 174 F.3d 842 (7th Cir.1999). Plaintiff, a citizen of Illinois, was injured while staying at defendant's hotel in Mexico. Applying Illinois choice of law, which meant the Second Restatement, the trial court found Mexican law applicable and dismissed his claim. The court of appeals affirmed. Noting that the modern search for flexibility had "led, alas, to standards that were nebulous, such as the 'most significant relationship' test of the Second Restatement that is orthodox in Illinois," Judge Posner noted with relief that "[o]ften, however, the simple old rules can be glimpsed through modernity's fog, though spectrally thinned to presumptions." Although obliged to apply state law under *Klaxon Co. v. Stentor Elec. Mfg. Co.,* 313 U.S. 487 (1941), infra p. 888, the court of appeals all but ignored the Second Restatement and Illinois law and wrote an opinion meant to justify the old place of injury rule on party expectations grounds.

(4) Many judges find the Second Restatement an attractive alternative to the first one. Getting an exact count is difficult because state courts are not always clear about the approach they use and because they sometimes mix approaches or use different approaches for different types of cases. The growth seems to have slowed in recent decades, although

Wyoming adopted the Second Restatement for both contracts and torts in 2017. See *Elworthy v. First Tennessee Bank,* 391 P.3 1113 (Wyo. 2017). Compare Symeonides, *Choice of Law in the American Courts in 1997,* 46 Am.J.Comp.L. 233, 266 (1998) (25 states use Second Restatement for contracts, 21 for torts) with Symeonides, *Choice of Law in the American Courts in 2019: Thirty-Third Annual Survey,* 68 Am.J.Comp.L. 235, 258–59 (2020) (24 states use Second Restatement for contracts, 25 for torts). The Second Restatement is by far the most widely used alternative to the traditional choice-of-law rules.

The Second Restatement's reception by academics has been as hostile as its reception by judges has been favorable. To be sure, a few scholars have praised its flexible, open-ended analysis. See, e.g., Morris, *Law and Reason Triumphant, or How Not to Review a Restatement,* 21 Am.J.Comp.L. 322 (1973). Most, however, are critical. Beginning long before it was approved, see, e.g., Ehrenzweig, *The Second Conflicts Restatement: A Last Appeal for Its Withdrawal,* 113 U.Pa.L.Rev. 1230 (1965); Weintraub, *The Contracts Proposal of the Second Restatement of the Conflict of Laws,* 46 Iowa L.Rev. 713 (1961), complaints about the Second Restatement have only increased with experience. See, e.g., Laycock, *Equal Citizens of Equal and Territorial States: The Constitutional Foundations of Choice of Law,* 92 Colum.L.Rev. 249, 253 (1992) ("Trying to be all things to all people, it produced mush"); Kramer, *Choice of Law in the American Courts in 1990: Trends and Developments,* 39 Am.J.Comp.L. 465, 466, 486–89 (1991) ("one needs to read a lot of opinions in a single sitting fully to appreciate just how badly the Second Restatement works in practice," and it is "time to abandon this dead-end project in order to channel judges in more productive directions"); Singer, *Real Conflicts,* 69 B.U.L.Rev. 1, 77 (1989) ("silence regarding the priority of [§ 6] policies mystifies rather than clarifies"); Shayman, *The Vicissitudes of Choice of Law: The* Restatement *(First, Second) and Interest Analysis,* 45 Buff. L. Rev. 329, 357–64 (1997) ("Because the second *Restatement* tries to be so much and do so much, it is rife with inconsistency, incongruence, and incoherence.").

What accounts for the wide discrepancy between judicial and academic reaction? See Reynolds, *Legal Process and Choice of Law,* 56 Md. L. Rev. 1371, 1394–1410 (1997) (arguing that judges find most academic writing on conflicts turgid and incomprehensible while desiring the flexibility and elasticity the Second Restatement gives them).

SECTION 6. PROBLEMS OLD AND NEW

A. DÉPEÇAGE

AN IMAGINARY CASE: ADAMS V. KNICKERBOCKER NATURE SOC'Y, INC.

David F. Cavers, The Choice-of-Law Process 19, 34–43 (1965).

[In his 1965 book, The Choice-of-Law Process, Professor David Cavers reviewed contemporary approaches to choice of law by constructing a series of five hypothetical cases and a hypothetical court of five judges to decide them. The court consisted of Professors Cavers, Currie, Reese, Rheinstein, and Dean Griswold. Cavers drafted opinions reflecting the different views of these "judges" on each of the five cases. The opinions were later shown to the respective authors, who suggested changes or rewrote them. What follows is an excerpt from Cavers's third hypothetical case.]

Adams is a dues-paying member of the Society (hereafter called "Knickerbocker"). Knickerbocker is a nonprofit corporation organized under the laws of the State of New York to promote nature study. Its principal office is in New York City, but it maintains a summer camp for adult nature lovers in New York's Adirondacks. In 1961 Andrew Adams, a New York domiciliary and botanist, enrolled for a two-week session. He was taken in a camp truck with fellow-campers to visit Mount Greylock, tallest peak in the Berkshires in Massachusetts. . .

On the trip to Mount Greylock, the Knickerbocker truck broke down in Massachusetts ten miles from the destination, and an accommodating farmer offered to rent the Knickerbocker representative an old truck of his for use while the Knickerbocker truck was being repaired. When the farmer explained that he had not registered his truck that year, the Knickerbocker representative said, "Oh, we'll chance it." [While driving the truck, the Knickerbocker driver backed into Adams under circumstances where no negligence could be shown. New York, but not Massachusetts, permits tort actions against charitable corporations; Massachusetts, but not New York, considers the driver of an unregistered motor vehicle an "outlaw on the highways," liable without fault. The plaintiff, Adams, brings his action against the New York charitable corporation, Knickerbocker, in a New York court; he appeals from a summary judgment for the defendant.]

Judge Griswold . . . voted to uphold the decision below on immunity grounds but also expressed the opinion that, but for the defendant's immunity, the Massachusetts law governing unregistered vehicles would have been applicable. His belief that the same state's law should govern both issues led him to remark, "I cannot refrain from observing the paradox which would have been produced had a majority been ready to follow Judge Cavers in denying defendant the immunity which Massachusetts law would confer while giving plaintiff the benefit of the Massachusetts strict liability rule. If all the facts of this case had been in New York, plaintiff would have lost for failure to prove negligence. If all the facts of this case had been in Massachusetts, plaintiff would have lost because of the Massachusetts charitable immunity rule. Now, by reason of the division of the facts of the case between the two states, Judge Cavers would perform the miracle of creating a cause of action where none existed in either state. If this represents justice, then so does the principle: 'Heads I win; tails you lose.' " . . .

Judge Currie, after having been led again by his governmental interest analysis to apply New York law to the immunity issue, addressed himself to the question whether it would be proper to give effect to what would appear to be the clear interest of Massachusetts in imposing a civil sanction on this violation of the control which it exercises over vehicles on its highways through its vehicle registration law. He decided that it would not be proper. His opinion on the point follows:

CURRIE, J. ". . . Agreeing as I must with Judge Griswold that the result reached by Judge Cavers in applying both the New York law denying charitable immunity and the Massachusetts law of strict liability for unregistered vehicles is paradoxical, I would affirm the judgment for the defendant.

"True it is that choice of law must proceed on an issue-by-issue basis; but modern conflict-of-laws analysis can make no more serious mistake than to indulge in an unprincipled eclecticism, picking and choosing from among the available laws in order to reach a result that cannot be squared with the interests of any of the related states. Issue-by-issue analysis should not result in the cumulation of negative policies to produce a result not contemplated by the law of either state. . .

"Unlike Judge Cavers, I do not find distressingly paradoxical the results even of such cases as *Marie v. Garrison* and *Scheer v. Rockne Motors,* cited by him, where the courts reach results at variance with the identical laws of the states concerned. Their results might be reached, if with some difficulty, by a fair approximation of the governmental-interest analysis. A plaintiff's claim may fall between two stools and be governed by the common law rather than by the statute of either state.

"In our case, however, the problem is different. While Massachusetts has a policy of deterring the operation of unlicensed vehicles, it does not extend that policy to charities. . . While New York has a policy of requiring compensation for its injured residents, it has no policy of imposing liability in the absence of negligence. To impose liability on this New York corporation, which has been free from fault, simply in order to carry out a nonexistent Massachusetts policy of deterrence, seems to me entirely unjustified. . .

"It is one thing to fall between two stools; it is quite another to put together half a donkey and half a camel, and then ride to victory on the synthetic hybrid."[8] . . .

[Judge Cavers voted to hold the defendant liable under the Massachusetts strict liability rule while denying it the Massachusetts charitable immunity. He] addressed himself to the characterization by Judges Griswold and Currie of the result he would reach as "paradoxical" in permitting the plaintiff to recover in a two-state case when he would fail if the accident had been localized in either state.

CAVERS, J. "I find nothing paradoxical in the differing results to which Judge Griswold points. That a paradox may seem to exist is due to our habituation to choice-of-law thinking that requires us to choose between legal systems rather than between specific conflicting rules. Otherwise, we should think it natural enough that a two-state case involving two distinct policy problems should not always have the same result as a one-state case involving the same problems. * * * Where both states have the same policies on the problem at issue then I agree it would be paradoxical, to put it mildly, for a two-state case to produce a different result than the same case in either state. Yet traditional conflicts thinking has permitted such results. *Marie v. Garrison*, 13 Abb.N.C. 210 (N.Y.1883) * * *

"Judge Currie's joinder in the charge of paradox cannot be laid to addiction to jurisdiction-selecting rules, and I agree with him that, when laws are chosen on an issue-by-issue basis, care must be taken not to combine rules in such fashion as to work injustice. . .

"What characterizes the case where it is improper to join rules drawn from two states to produce a cause of action that would be recognized as a domestic cause in neither state is the fact that the rules thus combined are closely related in purpose—the 'built-in' statute of limitations being an example. . .

"What Judge Currie has done in the principal case is to insist that two rules, unrelated in policy, be drawn from a single source. Massachusetts' policy of granting immunity to charitable corporations has no relation to its policy of imposing strict liability on drivers of unregistered vehicles. Massachusetts excepts its charities from that rule just as it excepts them from all its rules imposing liability for tort. The fact that the liability is strict introduces no distinguishing element. Must a New York court refuse to impose liability for tortious conduct in Massachusetts on a New York charitable corporation unless it can be shown that the defendant would have been liable under the New York law of torts? If so, then we are letting the Massachusetts immunity rule in by the back door. Yet I had supposed that most of us were agreed that the state of injury had no reasonable basis

---

[8] This opinion represents a condensation of a draft opinion prepared by Professor Currie. . . .

for injecting its immunity rule into a case in which the charity's state of incorporation and principal activities had done away with the immunity doctrine.

"As I see it, New York has given to its charities just the same status with respect to vicarious liability for their servants' conduct as it has given to any other legal entity of its creation. The policy embodied in that action is not delimited by New York views as to the basis of tort liability or by the views of other states as to the status of their charities. The New York charitable corporation in Massachusetts should be held answerable to Massachusetts law governing conduct there."

Dépeçage in the Courts

(1) Dépeçage—a French word for carving up or dismembering an animal—stands for a simple phenomenon in choice of law: applying the rules of different states to determine different issues. When a case presents more than one choice-of-law issue and each is analyzed separately, situations arise in which it is claimed that the law of one state should govern one issue and that of another a second. This was done routinely on some issues even under the traditional approach, such as the application of the forum's law to "procedure" and another state's law to "substance." Under modern approaches, won't resort to dépeçage be the rule rather than the exception? See Reese, *Dépeçage: A Common Phenomenon in Choice of Law,* 73 Colum.L.Rev. 58, 59 (1973). The Second Restatement instructs courts to perform their analysis on an issue-by-issue basis (see, e.g. § 145(1)) but does not explain how to decide what constitutes a single "issue." Is that a problem?

(2) What limits, if any, should there be on the use of dépeçage? In *Adams v. Knickerbocker,* "Judge" Currie observes that "[i]ssue-by-issue analysis should not result in the cumulation of negative policies to produce a result not contemplated by the law of either state." But it was he (among others) who pointed out that these laws were not written with multistate situations in mind. B. Currie, Selected Essays on the Conflict of Laws 82 (1963). (Indeed, Cavers initially drafted a "Currie" opinion allowing Adams to recover under Massachusetts law, only to have Currie reject it upon inspection.) Why should results contemplated for wholly domestic cases affect the result in a multistate case? Recall Kramer's analysis of the unprovided-for case, supra p. 176. "Judge" Cavers disagrees with Currie on this point. What does he say? Who is right?

(3) *Maryland Cas. Co. v. Jacek,* 156 F.Supp. 43 (D.N.J.1957), was a suit by a Maryland insurer for a declaratory judgment determining its liability under an automobile liability insurance policy it had issued in New

Jersey to defendant. Jacek had driven the car, with his wife as passenger, into New York, where she was injured. Under New Jersey law, where the Jaceks were domiciled, spousal immunity in tort was recognized. In New York, spousal immunity had been abolished. The same law that enabled spouses to sue one another provided, however, that a spouse who was successfully sued would not be entitled to coverage from his or her liability insurer unless an express provision covering injuries to the spouse was included in the policy. No such provision appeared in Mr. Jacek's policy; under New Jersey law, however, the insurer was liable for any sums the insured might become legally obligated to pay. Thus, had the case been entirely domestic to either state, the plaintiff insurer would have been entitled to a declaration of non-liability: in New Jersey because Mrs. Jacek could not have sued her husband and so could not have created a legal obligation on which the insurer would have been liable; in New York because, although she could have recovered from her husband, he would not have been able to recover from the insurer.

Following the traditional choice-of-law analysis, which was at that time the law in New Jersey, the court applied the law of New Jersey, the place of making, to the contract, and the law of New York, the place of wrong, to the tort—thus permitting the insurer to be held liable even though it could not have been so held in a purely domestic case in either state.

Was *Jacek* a proper case for the use of dépeçage? Professor Peter Westen, then a law student, found the result "grotesque":

> But it is grotesque *not* because the court reached an outcome different from any which New York or New Jersey alone would have provided, but rather because it split and combined issues improperly. . . . New Jersey has avoided [the danger of collusion] by proscribing such suits altogether. New York, on the other hand, permits suit but minimizes the danger of collusion by interpreting insurance policies strictly. The *Jacek* court ignored the protective measures of each state by treating the immunity issue separately from the insurance issue. In doing so, it subverted New Jersey policy of preventing collusion against insurance companies without serving any New York policy of providing compensation for injured spouses.

Comment, *False Conflicts,* 55 Cal.L.Rev. 74, 114–15 (1967).

Professor Reese, on the other hand, thought the decision was correct:

> A contrary result might well have disappointed the legitimate expectations of the husband. The policy, according to its terms, insured him without qualification against any liability he might incur through the negligent operation of the automobile. And he did incur such liability to his wife under New York law, which was

> the law made applicable by the New Jersey choice-of-law rule. . . . [The] court gave effect to the choice-of-law policy favoring protection of the expectation of the parties, and it is by no means clear that the respective purposes of the relevant state rules were seriously distorted if indeed they were distorted at all.

Reese, 73 Colum.L.Rev. at 67–68.

Is Westen or Reese right about *Jacek*? Does their dispute help you to understand what limits there ought to be on dépeçage? According to one commentator, dépeçage is inappropriate when rules which are related in purpose are separated and combined with rules of other states; to avoid this problem, "the process of construction and interpretation of conflicting domestic rules should not be confined to a single rule, but rather must include consideration of the rule in its legal context." Wilde, *Dépeçage in the Choice of Tort Law,* 41 S.C. L. Rev. 329, 354, 359 (1968). What does that mean in actual practice? What, for example, should the parties or the court have done in *Jacek*? How about in *Adams v. Knickerbocker*?

B. RENVOI

PFAU V. TRENT ALUMINUM CO.

55 N.J. 511, 263 A.2d 129 (1970).

PROCTOR, JUSTICE. This appeal presents a conflict of laws problem regarding a host's liability to his guest for negligence arising out of an automobile accident. Plaintiff, a Connecticut domiciliary, was injured in Iowa while a passenger in an automobile driven by a New Jersey domiciliary and owned by a New Jersey corporation. Iowa has a guest statute which provides that a host-driver is not liable to his passenger-guest for ordinary negligence. The defendants pleaded, *inter alia,* the Iowa guest statute as a defense. . .

The facts pertinent to this appeal are undisputed. Plaintiff, Steven Pfau, a domiciliary of Connecticut, was a student at Parsons College in Iowa, and the defendant, Bruce Trent, a domiciliary of New Jersey, was a student at the same college. The boys met for the first time at Parsons.

Following the Easter vacation in 1966, the defendant, Bruce Trent, drove the automobile involved in the accident back to Iowa for his use at college. The automobile was registered in New Jersey in the name of the Trent Aluminum Company, a New Jersey corporation owned by Bruce's father. Bruce was using the car with the owner-corporation's consent. The vehicle was insured in New Jersey by a New Jersey carrier.

About a month after Bruce's return to college and several days before the accident, he agreed to drive the plaintiff to Columbia, Missouri, for a weekend visit. They never reached their destination. Shortly after leaving

Parsons on April 22, 1966, and while still in Iowa, Bruce failed to negotiate a curve and the car he was operating collided with an oncoming vehicle. . . The sole question presented by this appeal is whether the Iowa guest statute is applicable to this action.

In Mellk v. Sarahson, 49 N.J. 226, 229 A.2d 625 (1967), this Court abandoned the old *lex loci delicti* rule for determining choice of law in tort cases . . . and adopted the governmental interest analysis approach. . .

In order to determine whether the Iowa guest statute should apply to this case, we must first examine its purposes as articulated by the Iowa courts. . . These purposes are: "to cut down litigation arising from the commendable unselfish practice of sharing with others transportation in one's vehicle and protect the Good Samaritan from claims based on negligence by those invited to ride as a courtesy," Rainsbarger v. Shepherd, 254 Iowa 486, 492, 118 N.W.2d 41, 44, 1 A.L.R.3d 1074 (1962); to prevent ingratitude by guests, Knutson v. Lurie, 217 Iowa 192, 195, 251 N.W. 147, 149 (1933); to prevent suits by hitchhikers, id.; "to prevent collusion suits by friends and relatives resulting in excessively high insurance rates," Hardwick v. Bublitz, 253 Iowa 49, 54, 111 N.W.2d 309, 312 (1961).

The above policies expressed by the Iowa courts would not appear to be relevant to the present matter. [The court followed *Tooker v. Lopez,* supra p. 151, and excluded in turn each of the possible Iowa policies as inapplicable to a Connecticut plaintiff and a New Jersey defendant in a New Jersey car.]

It would appear that Connecticut's substantive law allowing a guest to recover for his host's ordinary negligence would give it a significant interest in having that law applied to this case. Defendants argue, however, that if we apply Connecticut's substantive law, we should apply its choice-of-law rule as well. In other words, they contend Connecticut's interest in its domiciliaries is identified not only by its substantive law, but by its choice-of-law rule. Connecticut adheres to *lex loci delicti* and according to its decisions would most likely apply the substantive law of Iowa in this case. * * * Defendants contend that plaintiff should not be allowed to recover when he could not do so in either Iowa where the accident occurred or in Connecticut where he is domiciled. We cannot agree for two reasons. First, it is not definite that plaintiff would be unable to recover in either of those states.[4] More importantly, however, we see no reason for applying Connecticut's choice-of-law rule. To do so would frustrate the very goals of governmental-interest analysis. Connecticut's choice-of-law rule does not identify that state's interest in the matter. *Lex loci delicti* was born in an

---

[4] [I]t is possible that Connecticut would avoid applying the Iowa guest statute to these facts. If, as defendants urge, we should look to Connecticut's whole law, i.e., both its substantive law and its choice-of-law rule, why should not Connecticut look to Iowa's whole law if suit were brought in Connecticut? If it did look to Iowa's whole law, Connecticut might well be led back to its own substantive law. * * *

effort to achieve simplicity and uniformity, and does not relate to a state's interest in having its law applied to given issues in a tort case. . .

We conclude that since Iowa has no interest in this litigation, and since the substantive laws of Connecticut and New Jersey are the same, this case presents a false conflict and the Connecticut plaintiff should have the right to maintain an action for ordinary negligence in our courts. . .

For the reasons expressed the order of the Appellate Division is reversed and the order of the trial court striking the separate defense of the Iowa guest statute is reinstated.

Renvoi and Interest Analysis

(1) Why shouldn't a forum committed to an interest-based approach refer to the choice-of-law rules of other interested states? In *Pfau,* for example, suppose that Iowa still followed the First Restatement and would apply its own law under the place of wrong rule. How can the New Jersey court say that Iowa has no interest? The court follows Iowa decisions respecting the policies underlying Iowa's guest statute. Why is it not similarly bound to respect Iowa decisions regarding the statute's territorial scope? And if Connecticut would apply Iowa law, how can the court say that it furthers Connecticut's interests to apply Connecticut law?

To put the point more strongly, if Connecticut courts would say that Connecticut law does not apply extraterritorially (and thus creates no rights or liabilities pertaining to the accident in Iowa), can a New Jersey court finding such rights or liabilities really claim to be applying Connecticut law? Professor Roosevelt argues that in such a case the New Jersey court would not be applying Connecticut law, or would be applying such a knowingly distorted version as to violate the Full Faith and Credit Clause of the Constitution. See Roosevelt, *Resolving Renvoi: The Bewitchment of Our Intelligence by Means of Language,* 80 Notre Dame L. Rev. 1821, 1855–64 (2005). Is that a plausible claim? Does it depend on whether choice-of-law rules are substantive or procedural? What would the consequences be?

(2) Most interest analysts agree with the court in *Pfau* that under interest analysis the renvoi question disappears. Making the suggestion "with some trepidation," Brainerd Currie wrote:

> it seems clear that the problem of the renvoi would have no place at all in the analysis that has been suggested. Foreign law would be applied only when the court has determined that the foreign state has a legitimate interest in the application of its law and policy to the case at bar and that the forum has none. Hence, there

> can be no question of applying anything other than the internal law of the foreign state.

B. Currie, Selected Essays on the Conflict of Laws 184 (1963). Currie's analysis was only preliminary, however, and in a later essay he found a limited role for foreign choice-of-law rules. According to Currie, if two states have the same choice-of-law rule, a disinterested forum called upon to decide a true conflict between their laws may use their choice-of-law rule to resolve the conflict. Currie, *The Disinterested Third State,* 28 L. & Contemp. Probs. 754, 781–82 (1963). Unfortunately, Currie's views were only tentative, and he failed to explain why foreign choice-of-law rules should be used in this situation but not others. Currie's position seems to be that foreign rules are not essential to defining state interests but may be consulted if this helps to resolve a difficult problem (like a true conflict in a disinterested forum).

A majority of other commentators have reached essentially the same conclusion: foreign choice-of-law rules can be informative, but they are not binding and need not be considered unless the forum finds this useful in resolving a difficult case. T. de Boer, Beyond Lex Loci Delicti 125–39 (1987). Suppose, for example, that analysis of the relevant interests reveals a true conflict, but the other interested state still follows the First Restatement and would not apply its own law. In such cases, most interest analysts will invoke the foreign choice-of-law rule to say that the other state has renounced its interest, thereby converting the true conflict into a false one.

The key thing to note is that this use of renvoi is purely tactical: foreign choice-of-law rules have no mandatory role under interest analysis. Moreover, the prevailing view among interest analysts is that it is preferable to ignore foreign choice-of-law rules, especially if they are of the jurisdiction-selecting variety.

(3) Interest analysts have offered two explanations of why foreign choice-of-law rules can, and usually should, be ignored. According to some, state interests are defined *objectively*. The fact that a state says it is interested does not make it so. Rather, a state is interested only if (and when) the forum determines that applying its law advances one of the state's legitimate domestic policies. Professor Peter Westen expressed this view in his student note:

> [I]f the forum decides that a foreign state is interested in a case by looking to that state's conflicts law, it subordinates its own choice of law rule to that of a foreign state, however archaic the latter may be. To do so frustrates the very goals of governmental-interest analysis. Instead, as Currie himself admitted, the forum should assume final responsibility for deciding whether another state is properly interested in the facts at issue. The forum ultimately makes such a finding not by asking whether—in light

> of forum policy—that declared interest seems reasonable. Ultimately, the forum imputes those policies to a foreign law which it could conceive a rational foreign court adopting, were that foreign court deciding the case at hand.

Comment, *False Conflicts,* 55 Cal.L.Rev. 74, 85 (1967). See also Kay, *Comment on Reich v. Purcell,* 15 UCLA L. Rev. 584, 589 n. 31 (1968) ("The mere fact that Ohio might mistakenly fail to recognize her own interests need not prevent California from recognizing her interests on her behalf . . .").

A second view treats state interests as defined *subjectively* by a state's own declaration of interests, but holds that generalized choice-of-law rules do not reflect the state's views on the subject. Professor Weintraub, for example, reasons that a state committed to interest analysis may ignore another state's adherence to the First Restatement because

> a territorially-oriented conflicts rule, by its nature, selects a geographical location as the source of the applicable law without first requiring inquiry into either the content of that law or that law's underlying policies. . . [A] court cannot reasonably read [such a] choice-of-law rule as a functional decision [about state interests].

R. Weintraub, Commentary on the Conflict of Laws 107 (6th ed. 2010). Professor von Mehren expresses a similar view in his oft-cited discussion of the "modern" renvoi problem:

> [A] court today cannot accept choice-of-law rules at their face value. Until the policies animating the other jurisdiction's relevant domestic rules have been analyzed and compared with the thinking underlying its connected choice-of-law rules, these choice-of-law rules do not provide guidance for a court that adopts a functional approach.

A. T. von Mehren, *The Renvoi and Its Relation to Various Approaches to the Choice-of-Law Problem,* in XXth Century Comparative and Conflicts Law 380, 391 (1961). Things will be different, von Mehren adds, once all states have adopted functional approaches to choice of law:

> In such a system, [choice of law] rules would be relatively particularized and nuanced; they should state fairly precisely whether the jurisdiction wishes to regulate a given issue at all, and, if so, under what conditions. . . Choice-of-law rules based on a functional analysis should thus go far in clarifying the question whether a true conflict exists. And, in those situations in which a true conflict does exist, the choice of law rules will help . . . to define that conflict precisely and will suggest each jurisdiction's dominant concern or concerns. In sum, considerable significance

> could then be properly assigned to each jurisdiction's choice-of-law rule.

Id. at 393–94. Professor von Mehren clearly believes that old-fashioned jurisdiction-selecting rules can be ignored. But what status does he assign to choice-of-law rules based on functional analysis? Is examining these rules mandatory or are they merely advisory or informational?

Which of these rationales does the court in *Pfau* rely on?

(4) Are you persuaded that foreign choice-of-law rules can be ignored? Which explanation is more persuasive and why? Not all commentators agree that the renvoi has no place in modern choice-of-law thinking. Professor Brilmayer, for example, notes that "[i]f we take seriously the idea [central to interest analysis] that conflict of laws is really an extension of substantive law, then it would seem that the forum ought to treat the other state's determination regarding the territorial scope of its statute with the same deference as it treats the other state's determination of what [its substantive law is]." Brilmayer, *The Other State's Interests,* 24 Cornell Int'l L.J. 233, 241 (1991); see also L. Brilmayer, Conflict of Laws: Foundations and Future Directions 105–109 (2d ed. 1995). Professor Kramer explains why this requires rejecting both explanations offered by interest analysts:

> [B]ecause choice of law is a process of interpreting laws to determine their applicability on the facts of a particular case, the forum can never ignore other states' choice-of-law systems—whether these consist of ad hoc decisions, functional rules, or jurisdiction-selecting rules of the First Restatement variety. . . A state's approach to choice of law *by definition* establishes the state's rules of interpretation for questions of extraterritorial scope. This is true even if the approach is not self-consciously adopted with this in mind, for the very function of choice-of-law rules is to define the applicability of the state's substantive law in multistate cases. A state may, for example, reject Currie's notion that the object of choice of law is to implement domestic policies, adhering to the First Restatement on the ground that it furthers uniformity and predictability. Misguided or not, by this decision the state chooses to circumscribe the applicability of its laws according to these rules. The rules thus define the state's "interests" in the only sense in which that concept is meaningful, and they should be respected by courts in other states.
>
> Given this conclusion, both explanations offered by interest analysts for ignoring foreign choice-of-law rules must be rejected. The first explanation—that interests are defined objectively—is inconsistent with the premise that choice of law is a process of interpreting the relevant laws. In interpreting another state's

> laws, the court is asking whether that state has conferred a right, not whether the forum or an interest analyst thinks it should. . .
>
> [The second explanation—that jurisdiction-selecting rules say nothing about state interests—is similarly untenable.] To be sure, these rules operate on the basis of assumptions about what state lawmakers can and cannot regulate and the importance of goals like uniformity and predictability. But that hardly makes them irrelevant from an interpretive perspective. Like it or not, and however foolish they may seem, traditional choice-of-law rules are intended directly to limit the scope and meaning of substantive law. This makes them "interpretive" in the relevant sense: they reflect a state's decisions about how far to extend local law in multistate cases. It follows that if the question is whether a state's law applies in a particular case, one must take the state's choice-of-law rules into account. By substituting their own view of proper interpretation, interest analysts betray their own fundamental premise.

Kramer, *Return of the Renvoi,* 66 N.Y.U. L. Rev. 979, 1005, 1011–12 (1991). Do you agree with this analysis? What bearing, if any, does a desire to limit a law's spatial application have on its substantive policy? Is Kramer talking about interpretation or interstate harmony? Or are these concepts related?

(5) How is the court supposed to use another state's choice-of-law rules? Noting that interest analysis requires a first step to determine whether there is a conflict and a second step to resolve whatever conflicts are discovered, Kramer explains:

> Each of the two steps . . . corresponds to one of two purposes served by choice-of-law rules. First, choice-of-law rules define the scope of a state's law and in this way determine when a conflict exists. Second, choice-of-law rules define the circumstances in which a state may forgo enforcing its otherwise applicable law and in this way determine how a true conflict should be resolved. Both these purposes must necessarily be satisfied one way or another under any approach to choice of law.
>
> [T]he proper treatment of foreign choice-of-law rules depends on which purpose is being served. To the extent that foreign choice-of-law rules serve the first purpose—defining the scope of foreign law—they are fully determinative and ought simply to be followed. This follows from [the analysis of] how choice of law is a process of interpretation and how each state's rules of interpretation are part of the state's positive law. Matters are more complex, however, when choice-of-law rules serve the second purpose—that of resolving true conflicts. In this guise, the rules do more than interpret the scope of a state's law: they purport to

> identify a resolution that is best for other states as well. No state's rule has a privileged status from this multilateral perspective. Accordingly, while the forum should consider whether the foreign state's rule produces a better multistate accommodation of interests, if the forum remains convinced that its rule is better, it should adhere to that rule.

Kramer, 66 N.Y.U. L. Rev. at 1028–29. How is this different from von Mehren's approach? How should the analysis work if the other state uses the Second Restatement? Leflar's "better law" approach? The First Restatement? How would Kramer have decided *Pfau*? Suppose that *Pfau* was brought in Iowa and that Iowa used interest analysis while Connecticut followed the First Restatement; Iowa would then apply Connecticut law while Connecticut would apply Iowa law. Now what should the court do? See id. at 1029–43. Cf. *Hamilton v. Accu-Tek,* 47 F. Supp. 2d 330, 338–46 (E.D.N.Y.1999) (taking foreign choice-of-law rules into account in analyzing conflict under New York's version of interest analysis).

Building on Kramer's analysis, Roosevelt argues that if each state would decide at the first step (i.e., as a matter of scope) that its law does not apply, the proper conclusion is simply that the plaintiff cannot state a claim. That each state's choice-of-law approach might suggest that the other state's law should apply makes no difference. See Roosevelt, 80 Notre Dame L. Rev. at 1880–87. Rather than an endless cycle, that is, such a situation is simply an unprovided-for case. (Recall the discussion at p. 176, supra.) Are you convinced? Is *Pfau* such a case?

(6) In *American Motorists Ins. Co. v. ARTRA Group, Inc.*, 338 Md. 560, 659 A.2d 1295 (1995), a dispute arose between the Sherwin-Williams Co. and the ARTRA Group over responsibility for cleaning up a hazardous waste site in Maryland. ARTRA requested its insurer, American Motorists, to assume responsibility for the litigation and to indemnify it. American Motorists refused, relying on a "pollution exclusion" clause in the contract; it sued for a declaratory judgment in Maryland state court. The trial court ruled in favor of American Motorists, but was reversed on appeal. The Maryland Court of Appeals restored the trial court's judgment. In the course of its opinion, the Maryland Court considered but declined to abandon the traditional *lex loci contractus* rule. Noting that the contract was made in Illinois and that an Illinois court would apply Maryland law, the court borrowed from more modern approaches in analyzing the resulting renvoi problem:

> Where the forum would apply the law of the foreign jurisdiction and the foreign jurisdiction would apply the law of the forum, it would seem that the balance should tip in favor of the jurisdiction with the most significant contacts or, if not to the jurisdiction with

the most significant contacts, then for ease of application and to prevent forum shopping, the law of the forum should be applied. In the instant case, Maryland is apparently the jurisdiction with the most significant contacts as well as the forum. Maryland courts should, in applying Illinois law, apply Illinois' most significant relationship choice-of-law rule and follow the law an Illinois court would follow if the case was instituted in Illinois—Maryland law. Thus, whether suit was filed in Maryland or Illinois, Maryland law would govern the contract.

In our situation, there may not even be a real "conflict." In the absence of some reason to apply foreign law, Maryland courts would ordinarily apply Maryland substantive law, and there is no reason to apply the substantive law of a foreign state if that foreign state recognizes that Maryland has the most significant interest in the issues and that Maryland substantive law ought to be applied to the contract issues. . .

It is axiomatic that Maryland law is Maryland law because our courts and legislature believe the rules of substantive law we apply are the best of the available alternatives. From this fundamental principle, it is safe to assume our courts would prefer to follow Maryland law unless there is some good reason why Maryland law should yield to the law of a foreign jurisdiction. Our own substantive law is not only more familiar to and easier for Maryland judges to apply, but there has been a legislative or judicial determination that it is preferable to the available alternatives. Sometimes, however, there are good reasons why our courts should, and do, apply the law of a foreign jurisdiction. First, if Maryland does not defer to other states when they have a significant interest, they might not defer to Maryland when we have significant interest. Second, we should discourage forum shopping and strive for some uniformity and predictability in resolving conflict of law issues regardless of where suit is filed. For simplicity, predictability, and uniformity in contract law, Maryland courts have, as have a majority of other state courts, followed the rule of *lex loci contractus* and have applied the substantive law of the place of contracting. In declining to apply Maryland law to a contract made in another state, we do so not because we deem the law of the other state preferable to Maryland law, but because our preference for Maryland law is outweighed by considerations of simplicity, predictability and uniformity. Where, however, the place of contracting applies Maryland law, then simplicity, predictability, and uniformity would be better achieved if Maryland courts followed the conflict of law rule of the place of contracting and apply Maryland law. In that case, there would be uniformity in choice of law regardless of in which jurisdiction suit was filed, and where, as in the instant case, suit was filed in Maryland, then Maryland courts would be applying Maryland law.

The limited renvoi exception which we adopt today will allow Maryland courts to avoid the irony of applying the law of a foreign jurisdiction when that jurisdiction's conflict of law rules would apply Maryland law. Under this exception, Maryland courts should apply Maryland substantive law to contracts entered into in foreign states' jurisdictions in spite of the doctrine of *lex loci contractus* when:

1) Maryland has the most significant relationship, or, at least, a substantial relationship with respect to the contract issue presented; and

2) The state where the contract was entered into would not apply its own substantive law, but instead would apply Maryland substantive law to the issue before the court.

Our holding that Maryland's adherence to *lex loci contractus* must yield to a test such as Restatement (Second) Conflict of Laws § 188 when the place of contracting would apply Maryland law pursuant to that test is not a total jettisoning of lex loci contractus. We do note, however, that there appears to be growing support for substituting an approach such as Restatement (Second) Conflict of Laws § 188 for the more traditional approach of *lex loci contractus* in light of modern technology. . . We are not yet, however, ready to jettison *lex loci contractus* except in those instances already noted. *Lex loci contractus* is still the law in the majority of jurisdictions, although there is a significant modern erosion of the rule. If that erosion continues, however, this Court may, in the proper case, have to reevaluate what the best choice-of-law rules ought to be to achieve simplicity, predictability, and uniformity.

American Motorists, 659 A.2d at 1302–05. The court went on to find that, under Maryland law, American Motorists was entitled to the relief it sought.

Would renvoi apply if the contacts from *American Motorists* were reversed, i.e., if the injury occurred in another state and the insurance contract was executed in Maryland? Would that depend on the other state's choice-of-law rules? *See Erie Ins. Exchange v. Heffernan*, 925 A.2d 636, 652–53, 399 Md. 598 (2007) (distinguishing *American Motorists* and applying *lex loci delicti* under these circumstances).

(7) The Second Restatement generally rejects renvoi, except for cases in which the objective of its choice-of-law rule is that the forum reach the same result as the courts of another state. See § 8. It does, however, see a role for foreign choice-of-law rules on resolving true conflicts. The existence and intensity of a state interest, comment k to § 8 provides, "can sometimes be obtained from an examination of that state's choice-of-law decisions."

The draft Third Restatement defines "internal law" as "a state's law exclusive of its choice-of-law rules. It is the body of law which the courts of that state apply when they have selected their own law as the rule of decision for one or more issues." Restatement (Third) of Conflict of Laws, Preliminary Draft No. 7 (2021), § 1.03(1). The comments then specify that "[i]nternal law excludes rules that select the law of one state rather than another" and conclude that determinations of geographic scope "are included within the category of internal law because they do not select the law of one state rather than another but simply determine the content of a state's law." *Id.* comment a, c. In short, specifications of the geographic scope of state law are not treated as choice-of-law rules. Do these definitions have implications for renvoi? For fuller discussion of the Third Restatement, see infra Section 7.

C. RULES VERSUS STANDARDS

PAUL V. NATIONAL LIFE

177 W.Va. 427, 352 S.E.2d 550 (1986).

NEELY, JUSTICE. In September of 1977, Eliza Vickers and Aloha Jane Paul, both West Virginia residents, took a weekend trip to Indiana. The two women were involved in a one-car collision on Interstate 65 in Indiana when Ms. Vickers lost control of the car. That collision took both women's lives. The administrator of Mrs. Paul's estate brought a wrongful death action against Ms. Vickers' estate and the National Life Accident Company in the Circuit Court of Kanawha County. Upon completion of discovery, the defendants below moved for summary judgment. Defendants' motion contended that: (1) the Indiana guest statute, which grants to a gratuitous host immunity from liability for the injury or death of a passenger unless that host was guilty of willful and wanton misconduct at the time of the accident, was applicable; and (2) that the record was devoid of any evidence of willful or wanton misconduct on the part of Ms. Vickers. By order dated 29 October 1984, the Circuit Court of Kanawha County entered summary judgment for the defendants below. The order of the circuit court held that our conflicts doctrine of lex loci delicti required that the law of the place of the injury, namely, Indiana, apply to the case, and that the record contained no evidence of willful or wanton misconduct on the part of Ms. Vickers. It is from this order that the plaintiffs below appeal.

The sole question presented in this case is whether the law of Indiana or of West Virginia shall apply. The appellees urge us to adhere to our traditional conflicts doctrine of lex loci delicti, while the appellants urge us to reject our traditional doctrine and to adopt one of the "modern" approaches to conflicts questions. Although we stand by lex loci delicti as our general conflicts rule, we nevertheless reverse the judgment of the court below.

I

Unlike other areas of the law, such as contracts, torts and property, "conflicts of law" as a body of common law is of relatively recent origin. Professor Dicey has written that he knew of no decisions in England considering conflicts of law points before the accession of James I, and it is generally acknowledged that the first authoritative work on conflicts did not appear until the publication of Joseph Story's Conflict of Laws in 1834. Accordingly, no conflicts of law doctrine has ever had any credible pretense to being "natural law" emergent from the murky mist of medieval mysticism. Indeed, the mention of conflicts of law and the jus naturale in the same breath would evoke a powerful guffaw in even the sternest scholastic. In our post-Realist legal world, it is the received wisdom that judges, like their counterparts in the legislative branch, are political agents embodying social policy in law. Nowhere is this received wisdom more accurate than in the domain of conflict of laws.

Conflicts of law has become a veritable playpen for judicial policymakers. The last twenty years have seen a remarkable shift from the doctrine of lex loci delicti to more "modern" doctrines, such as the more flexible, manipulable [Second] Restatement "center of gravity" test. Of the twenty-five landmark cases cited by appellants in which a state supreme court rejected lex loci delicti and adopted one of the modern approaches, the great majority of them involved the application to an automobile accident case of a foreign state's guest statute, doctrine of interspousal or intrafamily immunity, or doctrine of contributory negligence. All but one of these landmark cases was decided in the decade between 1963 and 1973, when many jurisdictions still retained guest statutes, the doctrine of interspousal immunity, and the doctrine of contributory negligence. However, in the years since 1970, these statutes and doctrines have all but disappeared from the American legal landscape. . .

Thus nearly half of the state supreme courts of this country have wrought a radical transformation of their procedural law of conflicts in order to sidestep perceived substantive evils, only to discover later that those evils had been exorcised from American law by other means. Now these courts are saddled with a cumbersome and unwieldy body of conflicts law that creates confusion, uncertainty and inconsistency, as well as complication of the judicial task. This approach has been like that of the misguided physician who treated a case of dandruff with nitric acid, only to discover later that the malady could have been remedied with medicated shampoo. Neither the doctor nor the patient need have lost his head.

The Restatement approach has been criticized for its indeterminate language and lack of concrete guidelines. . . Section 6 of the *Restatement* lists the following factors as important choice of law considerations in all areas of law.

> (a) The needs of the interstate and international systems;
>
> (b) The relevant policies of the forum;
>
> (c) The relevant policies of other interested states and relative interest of those states in the determination of the particular issue;
>
> (d) The protection of justified expectations;
>
> (e) The basic policies underlying the particular field of law;
>
> (f) Certainty, predictability, and uniformity of results; and
>
> (g) Ease in the determination and application of the law to be applied.

As Javolenus once said to Julian, *res ipsa loquitur*. The appellant cites with approval the description of the Restatement approach set forth in Conklin v. Horner, 38 Wis.2d 468, 473, 157 N.W.2d 579, 581 (1968):

> We emphasized that what we adopted was not a rule, but a method of analysis that permitted dissection of the jural bundle constituting a tort and its environment to determine what elements therein were relevant to a reasonable choice of law.

That sounds pretty intellectual, but we still prefer a rule. The lesson of history is that methods of analysis that permit dissection of the jural bundle constituting a tort and its environment produce protracted litigation and voluminous, inscrutable appellate opinions, while rules get cases settled quickly and cheaply. . .

II

The appellant urges us in the alternative to adopt the "choice-influencing considerations approach" set forth by Professor Leflar in "Choice-Influencing Considerations and Conflicts of Law", 41 N.Y.U. L. Rev. 267 (1966). Professor Leflar has narrowed the list of considerations in conflicts cases to five:

(1) Predictability of results;

(2) Maintenance of interstate or international order;

(3) Simplification of the judicial task;

(4) Advancement of the forum's governmental interests;

(5) Application of the better rule of law.

Professor Leflar's approach has been adopted in the guest statute context in the landmark cases of Clark v. Clark, Milkovich v. Saari, and Conklin v. Horner. In practice the cases tend to focus more on the fourth and fifth considerations than the first three, and the upshot is that the courts of New Hampshire, Minnesota and Wisconsin simply will not apply guest statutes. This seems to us a perfectly intelligible and sensible bright-line rule. However, it seems unnecessary to scrap an entire body of law and dress this rule up in a newfangled five-factor costume when the same concerns can be addressed and the same result achieved through judicious employment of the traditional public policy exception to lex loci delicti.

Lex loci delicti has long been the cornerstone of our conflict of laws doctrine. The consistency, predictability, and ease of application provided by the traditional doctrine are not to be discarded lightly, and we are not persuaded that we should discard them today. The appellant contends that the various exceptions that have been engrafted onto the traditional rule have made it manipulable and have undermined the predictability and uniformity that were considered its primary virtues. There is certainly some truth in this, and we generally eschew the more strained escape devices employed to avoid the sometimes harsh effects of the traditional rule. Nevertheless, we remain convinced that the traditional rule, for all of its faults, remains superior to any of its modern competitors. Moreover, if we are going to manipulate conflicts doctrine in order to achieve substantive results, we might as well manipulate something we understand. Having mastered marble, we decline an apprenticeship in bronze. We therefore reaffirm our adherence to the doctrine of lex loci delicti today.

However, we have long recognized that comity does not require the application of the substantive law of a foreign state when that law contravenes the public policy of this State. West Virginia has never had an automobile guest passenger statute. It is the strong public policy of this State that persons injured by the negligence of another should be able to recover in tort. . . Today we declare that automobile guest passenger statutes violate the strong public policy of this State in favor of compensating persons injured by the negligence of others. Accordingly, we will no longer enforce the automobile guest passenger statutes of foreign jurisdictions in our courts.

For the foregoing reasons, the order of the circuit granting summary judgment in favor of the appellees is hereby, vacated, and the cause remanded for further proceedings not inconsistent with this opinion.

Good Rules, Bad Rules, or No Rules?

(1) *Paul* is not the only decision to reject the Second Restatement in strong terms. In *Dowis v. Mud Slingers*, the Georgia Supreme Court announced its continued adherence to *lex loci delicti*, quoting academic assessments of the Second Restatement as "dominating the field while bewildering its users" and of conflicts theory as "chaos," "a total disaster," and "gibberish." 621 S.E.2d 413, 417, 418 n.8 (Ga. 2005) (citations omitted). "Utilizing a rule in the area of conflict of laws," the court went on, "can serve the ends of justice because it furnishes the judicial machinery by which like situations are adjudged equally." Id. at 419. Do you agree with these assessments?

Even if *Paul* is right about Leflar and the Second Restatement, is the First Restatement the best or only alternative? What exactly is the court's beef? If the concern is predictability, how can it justify resort to the common law public policy exception? Is the court simply angry with what it sees as the intellectual pretensions of academic commentators? Was there really no need for change outside the areas of guest statutes, interspousal immunity, and contributory negligence, or has the court confused the fact that change first occurred in these areas with the need for change itself?

Justice Neely suggests that he is adopting a clear and simple rule: West Virginia courts will no longer enforce guest statutes. But in a footnote, he notes that they *would* enforce a state's guest statute in a suit between two domiciliaries of that state. 352 S.E.2d at 556 n.14. Does this suggest that he should have chosen a different rule—perhaps that in common domicile cases, the enforceability of a guest statute should be governed by the law of shared domicile? Isn't that rule the product of the modern analysis he deplores?

(2) Several other courts have likewise rejected modern approaches to choice of law, albeit usually in less colorful terms. See, e.g., *Cunningham v. Feinberg*, 107 A.3d 1194, 1211 n.23 (Md. 2015) (declining to abandon *lex loci contractus* and expressing satisfaction "with the level of simplicity, predictability, and uniformity provided by the doctrine."). In *Cunningham*, the court declined to apply *lex loci contractus* because the claim did "not involve the validity, enforceability, interpretation, or construction of the employment contract." *Id.* at 1197. Beyond that, in what the court itself described as "a nifty bit of considered dicta," *id.* at 1201, the court opined that it would not have enforced *lex loci contractus* even if it applied, on public policy grounds. Recall also *American Motorists*, supra pp. 279–281, in which the same court avoided *lex loci contractus* through a "limited renvoi exception." Do you think the Maryland court is satisfied with the traditional rules in part because it knows it has the power to escape them in particular cases?

Along similar lines, consider *Coon v. Medical Center, Inc.*, 797 S.E.2d 828 (Ga. 2017). In a tragic act of negligence, a Georgia hospital released the body of the wrong stillborn baby to a grieving Alabama mother. The court concluded that Alabama was the place of injury but applied Georgia law, which barred recovery because the plaintiff did not suffer physical impact or pecuniary loss. Rather than renounce *lex loci delicti* or rely on a public policy exception, the Georgia court simply declared that in cases governed by the common law Georgia law always applies. Even when another state's common-law rule is superior, the court reasoned, "we may adopt that position and apply it to the case at hand. In that instance, however, this Court would still be applying our conclusion regarding the common law, and the same rule would apply in future Georgia cases with no out-of-state element." *Id.* at 834. What on earth is this? A Georgia version of Walter Wheeler Cook's local law theory, supra pp. 14–15? A wholesale rejection of *Erie Railroad v. Tompkins* (which, the court derisively implies, is "steeped in relativist theories of legal realism," *id.*)? Do cases like *Paul*, *Cunningham*, and *Coon* suggests that some courts adhere to the traditional approach while sacrificing its supposed virtues of uniformity and predictability?

(3) In 1972, fresh from his labors as Reporter for the Second Restatement, Professor Reese wrote, "The principal question in choice of law today is whether we should have rules or an approach." Reese, *Choice of Law: Rules or Approach?*, 57 Cornell L.Rev. 315, 315 (1972). Professor Herma Hill Kay commented in 1989 that "it seems clear that there is still no consensus on the fundamental question that Willis Reese posed nearly 20 years ago," H. Kay, *A Defense of Currie's Governmental Interest Analysis*, 215 Recueil des cours 197 (1989-III), and the question remains in the forefront of choice of law. Of course, the choice between rules and standards is not unique to conflicts, but is pervasive throughout the law. Advocates of a rule-based approach to legal analysis maintain that law in a free society means adherence to precepts fixed and announced beforehand to limit the arbitrary exercise of authority, make it possible to plan one's affairs, and minimize the costs of administration. Scalia, *The Rule of Law as a Law of Rules,* 56 U.Chi.L.Rev. 1175 (1989). Proponents of discretionary analysis, in contrast, emphasize achieving substantive justice: rules, they note, are invariably overinclusive and/or underinclusive and therefore inevitably yield unfair or inappropriate results. Moreover, all systems of rules have gaps, glitches, or conflicts, and leave their precise domain uncertain anyway. See generally M. Kelman, A Guide to Critical Legal Studies 40–54 (1987); F. Schauer, Playing By the Rules (1992).

There is, of course, no answer to the rules versus standards question that is "right" for all areas of law. Instead, different solutions will be appropriate in different contexts. What is the proper balance in choice of law? How do the concerns identified above play out in this context?

(4) A number of commentators, especially those writing in the early years of the choice-of-law "revolution," opposed choice-of-law rules on principle. They argued that such rules too often lead to arbitrary results and that the solutions produced on a case-by-case basis would be clear enough to achieve the ends sought by rules-advocates. According to Professor Hancock:

> Simple, comprehensive formulae are actually more a hindrance than a useful guide because they distract the judge's attention from the real problems of ascertaining policy and policy range. . . [T]he traditionalist is quite right when he complains that abandonment of the rigid old formulae may lead to some increase in litigation. However, when the policy-directed construction analysis is better understood than it is today, the correct decision for many cases will be fairly obvious and there will be no need to litigate them.

Hancock, *Torts Problems in Conflict of Laws Resolved by Statutory Construction: The* Halley *and Other Older Cases Revisited,* 18 U.Toronto L.J. 331, 350 (1968).

Deploring the uncertainty that followed the revolution in choice of law, other commentators have concluded that rules of some sort are necessary. See, e.g., D. Cavers, The Choice-of-Law Process (1965); R. Weintraub, Commentary on the Conflict of Laws (6th ed. 2010); Gottesman, *Draining the Dismal Swamp: The Case for Federal Choice of Law Statutes,* 80 Geo.L.J. 1, 11–16 (1991); Rosenberg, *The Comeback of Choice-of-Law Rules,* 81 Colum.L.Rev. 946, 946 (1981); Sedler, *Rules of Choice of Law Versus Choice-of-Law Rules: Judicial Method in Conflicts Torts Cases,* 44 Tenn.L.Rev. 975 (1977). As Professor Reese explained:

> [T]he fact that a choice of law rule . . . would lead on some rare occasion to the application of the law of a state which is not that of greatest concern, or would result in the disregard of other multistate or local law policies, is not an adequate reason why the rule should not be applied on that occasion. Perfection is not for this world. The advantages which good rules bring are worth the price of an occasional doubtful result.

Reese, 57 Cornell L.Rev. at 322. The question, of course, is whether the "doubtful results" will be only occasional. Professor Kramer maintains that they will be no more frequent than with case-by-case analysis:

> [W]hile the choices made by the First Restatement rules were often arbitrary, ad hoc decisionmaking has not led to any noticeable improvement. The reason is simple: even if one might in theory articulate case-specific distinctions to resolve true conflicts, these distinctions are too fine for courts to draw in practice. Asking courts to engage in case-by-case analysis is

asking them to look for something that, if it exists at all, is beyond their ability to detect.

Kramer, *Rethinking Choice of Law,* 90 Colum.L.Rev. 277, 321 (1990). According to Kramer, the best we can hope for is rough generalization, so that a well designed system of rules may be equally effective in realizing substantive results while also providing the pragmatic benefits of rules. Kramer, *On the Need for a Uniform Choice of Law Code,* 89 Mich.L.Rev. 2134, 2136–46 (1991); L. Brilmayer, Conflict of Laws: Foundations and Future Directions 179–89 (1991).

(5) Which assessment is more persuasive? Have we had enough time and experience to decide? Doesn't your answer depend on the particular rules or approach in question? We have seen systems of both types. Approaches eschewing rules range from the open-ended balancing of Leflar's "better law" and § 6 of the Second Restatement to the more structured analyses of Currie and Baxter. Rule-based systems include the fixed rules of the First Restatement and the presumptive rules in the body of the Second Restatement. Finally, we have considered intermediate approaches that mix rules and ad hoc analysis, such as the proposals of Cavers and Kramer. How well do the rule-based systems work? How unpredictable are the ad hoc approaches? Are they all equally good or bad?

Professor Roosevelt suggested that the supposed tradeoff between rules and standards is illusory. What we care about, he argued, is not the form of a system but how well it satisfies two distinct sets of goals: first, delivering sensible answers when applied correctly, and second, simplicity, predictability, uniformity, and ease of application. While we often associate standards with the first set of goals and rules with the second, this is not a necessary connection, and well-drafted rules can improve a system on both dimensions. Roosevelt, *Certainty and Flexibility in the Conflict of Laws,* in Private International Law: Contemporary Challenges and Continuing Relevance (Franco Ferrari & Diego Fernandez Arroyo, eds.) (2019).

Could you do better? Professor von Mehren addressed the problem of formulating effective choice-of-law rules and concluded that the task is a herculean one. A. T. von Mehren, *Recent Trends in Choice-of-Law Methodology,* 60 Cornell L.Rev. 927, 946 (1975). His conclusion is supported by the number of commentators who make the argument for rules but put off until another day the effort to specify what these rules might be. A few commentators have made partial efforts to develop alternative choice-of-law rules, however. In addition to Cavers and Kramer, see R. Weintraub, Commentary on the Conflict of Laws (6th ed. 2010) (developing rules based on "functional analysis"); Laycock, *Equal Citizens of Equal and Territorial States: The Constitutional Foundations of Choice of Law,* 92 Colum.L.Rev. 249, 322–31 (1992) (rejecting interest-based approaches for territoriality and proposing territorial rules more "sophisticated" than those of the First Restatement); Symeonides, *Problems and Dilemmas in Codifying Choice of Law for Torts: The Louisiana Experience in Comparative Perspective,* 38 Am.J.Comp.L. 431 (1990) (discussing the process of developing "open-ended," "content-oriented" choice-of-law rules). In addition, several foreign nations and the European Union have formulated choice-of-law codes that, to varying degrees, incorporate modern conflicts thinking. See, e.g., Rep. No. 58, Australia Law Reform Comm'n: Choice of Law (1992); Regulation (EC) 593/2008 on the law applicable to contractual obligations (Rome I); Regulation (EC) 864/2007 on the law applicable to non-contractual obligations (Rome II). Rome I and II are excerpted and discussed infra Chapter 8, Section 2. The Third Restatement attempts to survey outcomes under modern approaches and synthesize them into rules. Do you think this is possible?

Or is this all much ado about nothing? Professor Singer argued that the debate over rules versus discretion is itself a "false conflict" that distracts our attention from more fundamental issues. Singer, *Real Conflicts,* 69 B.U.L.Rev. 1, 7–23 (1989). According to Singer, the difference between rules and standards is "much less significant than is commonly supposed" because "whatever method we adopt in the real world will necessarily combine rules and standards." A rule-based system will require standards because all choice-of-law rule systems create characterization problems, because rules inevitably contain gaps and ambiguities, because judges always find ways to modify rules in light of contemporary notions of social justice, and because exceptions develop to supplement the basic rules. By the same token, an approach to conflicts based entirely on standards will nevertheless generate rules because the process of making analogies and deciding like cases alike will lead to rule-like patterns of decision. Therefore, Singer concludes, "the choice between rules and standards can only be made sensibly in the context of particular social conflicts and particular legal questions. . . [T]he real question is how to balance substantively the competing interests of the parties when their dispute emerges out of a social context that includes contacts with several states with different policies." Id. at 23. Singer is content to tackle this problem on a case-by-case basis, trusting to the ordinary legal process to generate rule-like patterns for the courts and the parties. But don't differences in degree or the stage of analysis at which one makes a commitment to rules matter?

D. COMPLEX LITIGATION

IN RE AIR CRASH DISASTER NEAR CHICAGO, ILLINOIS ON MAY 25, 1979

644 F.2d 594 (7th Cir.1981).

Before SPRECHER, BAUER and CUDAHY, CIRCUIT JUDGES.

SPRECHER, CIRCUIT JUDGE.

This case presents complex conflicts-of-law questions regarding the allowance of punitive damages in wrongful death actions arising out of an air crash disaster. The law of the place of the disaster, the law of the place of manufacturer of the airplane, and the law of the primary place of business of the airline do not allow punitive damages; but, the law of the primary place of business of the manufacturer of the airplane and the law of the place of maintenance of the airline do allow punitive damages. We find that, under each of the applicable state choice-of-law rules, punitive damages cannot be allowed against either the manufacturer or the airline.

I

The stark facts of the tragedy resulting in this litigation are undisputed. On May 25, 1979, a DC-10 jet airplane, designed and built by McDonnell Douglas Corporation ("MDC"), operated by American Airlines ("American") was scheduled to fly from Chicago, Illinois to Los Angeles, California as American's Flight 191. Shortly after takeoff from O'Hare International Airport, however, the plane lost an engine and crashed in the immediate vicinity of the airport. All two hundred seventy-one persons aboard the plane, and two persons on the ground, were killed.

Now there are one hundred eighteen wrongful death actions arising out of the crash. These cases were originally filed in Illinois, California, New York, Michigan, Hawaii, and Puerto Rico.[1] Many of the complaints allege wrongful death counts which request awards of punitive as well as compensatory damages. The plaintiffs and their decedents are and were residents of California, Connecticut, Hawaii, Illinois, Indiana, Massachusetts, Michigan, New Jersey, New York, Vermont, Puerto Rico, Japan, the Netherlands, and Saudi Arabia.

The defendants in these cases are MDC and American. MDC is a Maryland corporation having its principal place of business, now and at the time of the accident, in Missouri. The plaintiffs contend MDC's conduct in the design and manufacture of the DC-10 was egregious. That alleged misconduct occurred in California. American is a Delaware corporation. American's place of business prior to 1979 was New York. During 1979,

[1] The cases have been transferred to the Northern District of Illinois for pretrial purposes by order of the Judicial Panel on Multidistrict Litigation.

American moved its principal place of business to Texas. Some plaintiffs contend that, on the date of the crash, American's principal place of business was in Texas, but American contends that its principal place of business on that date was New York. The plaintiffs contend that American's conduct regarding the maintenance of the DC-10 was egregious. That alleged misconduct occurred in Oklahoma, site of American's maintenance base.

Both defendants moved in district court to strike the claims for punitive damages on the ground that such claims failed to state legally sufficient claims for relief. The parties disputed many issues: whether certain states allowed punitive damages, the choice-of-law theories to be used regarding certain states, and the results of the application of the choice-of-law theories which were used.

Using the choice-of-law rules of each state where these actions had originally been filed, the district court arrived at the following results. Under the Illinois "most significant relationship" test, the district court found that the law of the state of the principal place of business should prevail with regard to the issue of punitive damages. Finding that New York was American's principal place of business at the time of the crash and does not allow punitive damages, and that Missouri, MDC's principal place of business, does allow the equivalent of punitive damages, the court allowed the motions to strike punitive damage claims against American but not against MDC.

Under the California "comparative impairment" test, the district court held that the policies of the state of the principal place of business would be impaired more than the policies of the state of misconduct if those policies were not applied. Thus, the court allowed the motion to strike punitive damage claims with regard to American but not with regard to MDC. The district court reached the same result with regard to the actions filed in New York, Michigan, Puerto Rico, and Hawaii.

Although generally agreeing with the district court regarding which states allow punitive damages and the choice-of-law theories to be used, we reach a different result in applying those theories. For the reasons discussed below, we find that the motions to strike claims of punitive damages should be granted with regard to both MDC and American.

II

At the outset, we must first determine whether we confront "real" rather than "apparent" conflicts between the laws to be applied. This requires a determination, first, of the law regarding punitive damages in the relevant states: Illinois, Missouri, California, Oklahoma, New York, Texas and Hawaii. After this determination, it will then be necessary to determine the conflict-of-law theories of the forum states and to apply those theories. [The court examined the content of the substantive laws of these various states.]

In summary, we find that the "line-up" of the states involved regarding the issue of punitive damages is as follows: Illinois, place of the injury, does not allow punitive damages. Missouri, MDC's principal place of business, does allow punitive damages, but California, place of MDC's conduct, does not. New York, one principal place of business of American, does not allow punitive damages while Texas, another principal place of business of American, does. Oklahoma, the place of American's conduct, does allow punitive damages. . .

IV

We now confront the actual conflicts issues among the various states. It is not disputed that, since federal jurisdiction is based on diversity of citizenship, the choice-of-law rules to be used are those choice-of-law rules of the states where the actions were originally filed. *Klaxon Co. v. Stentor Electric Mfg. Co.*, 313 U.S. 487 (1941); *Van Dusen v. Barrack,* 376 U.S. 612 (1964); * * * We will consider the law of each state in turn. We emphasize at the outset that the tests to be used, although containing significant differences, mandate an analytical inquiry which is basically the same. As Professor Leflar has stated:

> [I]t appears that the various scholarly views concerning choice of law, developed during the last couple of decades, are being accepted by the courts as though they constituted one somewhat multi-faceted approach to the subject. Essentially, they are consistent with each other. Any one of them is likely to produce about the same result on a given set of facts as will another. . . The point to be emphasized is that the modern decisions, regardless of exact language, are substantially consistent with each other.

Leflar, *American Conflicts Law,* § 109, p. 218 (3d ed. 1977).

In general, we must attempt to determine which, if any, of the states having some relationship to the parties or to the crash has the most significant interest in the application of its own substantive law to the merits of the punitive damage issue. The application of choice-of-law rules is not a mechanical process of cranking various factors through a formula. Critical to conflicts analysis is the notion that we must examine the choice-of-law rules not with regard to various states' interests in general, but precisely, with regard to each state's interest in the specific question of punitive damages. Thus, we approve the concept of "depecage": the process of applying rules of different states on the basis of the precise issue involved. . .

V

We begin with the actions filed in Illinois. The Illinois courts apply the "most significant relationship" test of the Restatement (Second) of Conflict of Laws ("Restatement (Second)") to determine the applicable law in wrongful death actions. This test incorporates a presumption that the local law of the state where the injury occurred should govern, unless another state has a "more significant relationship" to the occurrence or to the parties. [The court cited and described Restatement (Second) Conflict of Laws §§ 6, 145, supra p. 241.]

A

Turning to defendant MDC, the precise issue, of course, is which state's law regarding the availability of punitive damages should apply. The states having contacts to be taken into account are: Illinois, place of injury; California, place of MDC's alleged misconduct; Missouri, MDC's principal place of business; and, if it can be determined, the states where the relationship between the parties is centered.

It is unclear where the relationship of the parties is "centered". As the district court noted, most of the Illinois actions involve Illinois decedents who purchased their tickets in Illinois for a flight which began in Illinois. But the flight was to California. Surely the importance of the place of destination of a journey is just as great as the importance of the place of departure. This issue need not detain us, however, because neither California nor Illinois allows punitive damages.

We next turn to the interests of the states of domicile of the plaintiffs. The domiciliary states do not have an interest in disallowing punitive damages because the decision to disallow such damages is obviously designed to protect the interest of resident defendants, not to effectuate the interest of the domiciliary states in the welfare of plaintiffs. * * *

Nor do the domiciliary states have an interest in imposing punitive damages on the defendants. The legitimate interests of these states, after all, are limited to assuring that the plaintiffs are adequately compensated for their injuries and that the proceeds of any award are distributed to the appropriate beneficiaries. * * * Those interests are fully served by applying the law of the plaintiffs' domiciles as to issues involving the measure of compensatory damages (insofar as that law would enhance the plaintiffs' recovery) and the distribution of any award. Once the plaintiffs are made whole by recovery of the full measure of compensatory damages to which they are entitled under the law of their domiciles, the interests of those states are satisfied.

We thus return to the interests of the three relevant states, Illinois, California, and Missouri. Illinois and California do not allow punitive damages but Missouri does. If the interests of these three states were to be weighed equally, the tally would be two-to-one against allowing punitive damages. But the process of weighing states' interests requires more than merely tabulating the states pro and con. We must examine the precise interest of each state with regard to the purpose of punitive damages.

The purposes underlying the allowance of punitive damages, as the district court noted, are punishment of the defendant and deterrence of future wrongdoing. The purpose underlying the disallowance of punitive damages is protection of defendants from excessive financial liability. Two states which very definitely have an interest in punishment or protection are California and Missouri, the states in which, respectively, the conduct occurred and the principal place of business is located. Both states have an obvious interest in preventing future misconduct; both states have an obvious interest in protecting businesses located or acting within its borders. Illinois, the place of injury, also has an interest in the punitive damages question; its interest will be discussed after the discussion of Missouri's and California's interests.

MDC's wrongful conduct here complained of involved the design and manufacture of the DC-10. Because the corporate headquarters of MDC is located in Missouri, Missouri has an obvious interest in deterring wrongful conduct in such design and manufacture, even if the actual work was performed in California. To find otherwise would be to gut the very concept of corporate accountability. Moreover, to say that Missouri has no interest in the imposition of punitive damages as defendants do would encourage rampant subterfuge and confusion. For example, many corporations have corporate headquarters in one state and far-flung operations in many others. If courts held that the place of "conduct" had the critical interest in punitive damages and that the place of corporate headquarters had no interest in punitive damages, then litigation would center around exactly where activities and decisions occurred. The practical effect of such a holding would be to require extensive examinations of numerous employees and to require complex investigations into the precise locations of many areas of corporate decision. Corporations seeking to avoid potential punitive damages would be encouraged to structure decisions so that no specific locus for a major decision could ever be proved to have occurred in a "punitive" state. . .

California, place of MDC's conduct in manufacture and design of the DC-10, also has a strong interest in the issue of punitive damages. California, as does every state, has a substantial interest in the economic health of corporations which do business within its borders. It derives substantial sales and income taxes, as well as other revenues, directly and indirectly from a corporation's activities within the state. Indeed, California's interest is strong with regard to a rule disallowing punitive damages because such a rule protects the economic well-being of the corporations and therefore enhances the economic well-being of the state.

Moreover, the rule may have been a factor in various corporations' decisions to move to California.

The district court concluded that where, with regard to punitive damages, the law of the principal place of business conflicted with the law of the place of misconduct, the former should prevail. The court reasoned that responsibility for corporate conduct should be uniform, regardless of where individual instances of that conduct took place. But the district court's analysis only looked at the purpose behind the decision to allow punitive damages. As we have discussed, both the decision to allow punitive damages and the decision to disallow punitive damages must be accorded great respect.

Thus, we find that the balance on the scales of significant contacts is even: we cannot say that either California or Missouri has a "greater" interest in the decision whether to allow punitive damages against MDC. This situation involves a total and genuine conflict: one jurisdiction allows punitive damages, the other does not. There does not seem to be any way to arrive at a "moderate and restrained" interpretation of either policy so as to avoid a true conflict.

With the scales evenly balanced, we now turn to the interest of Illinois, the place of injury. The old rule in many jurisdictions, developed from torts other than air crashes, was that where there was nothing fortuitous about the fact that the injury occurred in a given state, great weight would be given to the law of the place of injury. But air crash disasters often present situations where the place of injury is largely fortuitous. * * * That the injury in our case occurred in Illinois can only be described as fortuitous. Had the DC-10's engine fallen off later, the injury might have occurred in one of any number of states. Because the place of injury is much more fortuitous than the place of misconduct or the principal place of business, its interest in and ability to control behavior by deterrence or punishment, or to protect defendants from liability, is lower than that of the place of misconduct or principal place of business. Also, merely as the place of injury, Illinois would not have strong interests in protecting nonresident defendants from excessive financial liability.

But the fact that the interest of the place of injury is less than the interest of the principal place of business and the interest of the place of alleged misconduct does not mean that Illinois has no interest in the punitive damages question. Illinois has very strong interests in not suffering air crash disasters and also in promoting airplane safety. . . Also, in this case Illinois is more than merely the place of injury. As noted before, many of the other contacts of significance were in Illinois. With regard to the actions filed in Illinois, all but two of the decedents resided in Illinois. As the home of O'Hare International Airport, one of the world's busiest airports, Illinois certainly has strong interests in encouraging air transportation corporations to do business in the state. . .

As noted earlier, Illinois' choice-of-law law gives presumptive importance to the place of injury. The law of the place of injury is to be supplanted only when another state has a more significant relationship than the place of injury. Restatement (Second) § 175. Although either California or Missouri, taken separately, would have a greater interest than Illinois, the fact that the laws of these states are in absolute conflict indicates that neither state has an interest greater than the other's. Thus, in terms of a principled basis upon which a choice can be made, neither state has a "more significant interest" than Illinois. Since neither California nor Missouri can be chosen on a principled basis, the application of the "most significant relationship" test leads to the use of Illinois law.

Finally, application of Illinois law comports with the general criteria of the Restatement (Second) which emphasize certainty, predictability, uniformity of result, and ease in the determination and application of the law to be applied.[25] In this case, it is important to resolve the conflict between states by a principled means. Determining that all other factors being equal, the law of the place of injury shall be used, provides a principled means of decision which also creates certainty.

Future defendants cannot predict, of course, where airplane disasters will occur. But air transportation companies will now be on notice that, under the "most significant relationship" test, when there is a true conflict between laws of states having equal interests in the issue of punitive damages, and when the place of injury has a strong interest in air safety and in protection of air transportation corporations, the law of the place of injury will apply. Our result also comports with the Restatement (Second)'s principle that choice-of-law rules should be relatively simple and easy to apply. * * * We conclude, therefore, that under the "most significant relationship" test, the law of Illinois should apply. For the above reasons, we grant MDC's motion to strike punitive damages claims.

B

We now apply the Illinois "most significant relationship" test to American. . . As discussed with regard to MDC, the place of injury is Illinois

[25] The Restatement (Second) also lists other policies including the needs of the interstate system, the policies of the forum and other interested states, the protection of justified expectations, and the basic policies underlying the particular field of law. * * * These other principles are not helpful in the resolution of this issue because their application can cut either way. Neither a decision for nor a decision against punitive damages will make the interstate system work better or worse. The relevant policies of the forum, as we have seen, are countered by the relevant policies of Missouri. "Justified expectations" are not an issue because MDC's corporate headquarters are in Missouri. MDC does not argue, nor reasonably could it, that it somehow justifiably expected it would not be held to Missouri law for its corporate decisions. Finally, the basic policies underlying the field of punitive damages are in conflict. Each state legislature weighs the balance of deterring wrongful conduct or protecting defendants from excessive liability and then makes its decision accordingly.

and the place where the relationship between the parties is centered is either Illinois or California. Neither of these states allows punitive damages. The place of American's alleged misconduct is Oklahoma, site of its maintenance base, which does allow punitive damages.

The place of American's principal place of business for purposes of this analysis is disputed. [After extensive discussion, the court ruled that the relevant jurisdiction was the principal place of business on the date of the accident and that in the case of American this was New York.]

We now turn to the specific conflict of laws regarding American. Oklahoma, the place of American's alleged misconduct does allow punitive damages, but New York, American's principal place of business does not. Just as we concluded with regard to MDC, we conclude that the place of conduct and the principal place of business each have strong interests in having its law applied to the punitive damages question; we are unable to say that one state's interest is greater than the other. Thus, we follow the same analysis used above in concluding that, under the "most significant relationship" test, when the interests of the states of alleged misconduct and primary place of business are equal and in a true and total conflict, the law of the place of injury is to be used.

Again, we emphasize that this result in no way signifies a return to the mechanical, wooden law of lex loci delicti. Rather, it emphasizes the fact that there must be some principled method of decision when the standard "interest analysis" of conflicts law cannot settle the question. Moreover, as discussed above, the choice of Illinois law is particularly appropriate here. Illinois has strong interests in both protection of airline corporations and in the deterrence of wrongful conduct by those corporations. Therefore, we affirm the district court's decision to strike the claims for punitive damages against American with regard to the actions filed in Illinois.

VI

We now turn to the actions filed in California. California follows the "comparative impairment" approach to choice-of-law questions. * * * The resolution of conflicts under this test is as follows. First, the respective laws of interested states are examined to ensure that there is an apparent conflict. * * * There is such a conflict with regard to both MDC and American because, in both situations, the law of the place of alleged misconduct differs from the law of the principal place of business.

Second, when an apparent conflict is found to exist, the court reexamines the applicable laws and circumstances to see if a "moderate and restrained interpretation" of both the policy and the circumstances reveals that only one state has a legitimate interest in the application of its policy. * * * But as discussed with regard to the actions filed in Illinois, both the principal place of business and the place of alleged misconduct have strong interests in the protection of defendants and the deterrence of wrongful conduct. We see no restrained or moderate interpretation of either state's policy which can resolve this conflict.

When, as here, the reexamination of an apparent conflict reveals no way in which the conflict can be resolved by a restrained or moderate interpretation, the conflict is indeed a "true" conflict. The comparative impairment analysis "proceeds on the principle that true conflicts should be resolved by applying the law of the state whose interest would be the more impaired if its law were not applied." * * * This approach does not involve the court in "weighing" the conflicting governmental interests in the sense of determining which law represents "better" social policies. Such an approach would vitiate the policies of federalism which, within constitutional limits, allow states to determine their own policies as they wish. * * * Rather, the process used by the comparative impairment approach is " 'essentially a process of allocating respective spheres of lawmaking influence.' " * * * This process of allocation involves several steps. First, of course, the states with relevant interests must be identified.

As discussed in relation to the Illinois "most significant relationship" test, the principal place of business and the place of alleged misconduct have strong and equal relevant interests. These states have the interests of deterrence of misconduct or protection of local corporations, as discussed above. Illinois, the state in which the injury occurred, also has an important interest in the application of its law because it is a state in which both the policies of protection of airline corporations and deterrence of misconduct are peculiarly important. Also as discussed with regard to the Illinois test, the domiciliary states of the plaintiffs and their representatives do not have significant interests in the punitive damages question.

The comparative impairment theory requires that the court attempt to determine the relative commitment by each interested state to the law involved. * * * This examination of relative commitment examines two factors: (1) the current status of a statute and the intensity of interest with which it is held; and (2) the "comparative pertinence" of the statute: the "fit" between the purpose of the legislature and the situation in the case at hand; * * *.

A

Applying California's "comparative impairment" analysis to MDC, we begin with Missouri. We look first to the current status of its interest in the application of its punitive damages law. . . [W]e find that Missouri permits recovery in death cases for "aggravating circumstances" when there has been a showing of "wilful misconduct, wantonness, recklessness, or a want of care indicative of indifference to consequences." * * *

Recovery for "aggravating circumstances" has been permitted, and the provision has been maintained in the statute through many amendments, the most recent ones being in 1978 and 1979. * * * When a statutory provision that has received judicial construction is reenacted, it is presumed that the intention of the legislature was to adopt the construction given by the court. * * * Thus, the current status of Missouri's interest in the application of its punitive damages statute seems strong. . .

We look, second, to the "comparative pertinence" of Missouri's punitive damages rule to this case, involving a corporation headquartered in Missouri. That is, we look to the "fit" between the purpose of Missouri's legislation and the facts here. The general purposes of allowing punitive damages are punishment of defendants and deterrence of future wrongful conduct. Those purposes are pertinent to the facts of this case. If the claims for punitive damages are allowed and are proven at trial, damage awards against MDC will be larger, perhaps significantly larger, than they would be if the claims are not allowed. Such an increase will certainly be felt by MDC to be "punishment". Similarly, such awards could be expected to deter future wrongful conduct, of the type alleged in this case, both by MDC and by other corporations based in Missouri. . .

Thus, the application of the "comparative impairment" test to Missouri produces the following results. Missouri has a strong current interest in its punitive damages law; there is a solid "fit" between the purpose of that law and its application to a Missouri-based corporation such as MDC; but, there is some slippage in that "fit" in the sense that Missouri can theoretically achieve at least some of the purposes of its law by [imposing criminal sanctions].

We now examine California's interest under the comparative impairment test. First, we consider the current status of its policy against allowing punitive damages in wrongful death cases. Case law indicates that California seems to have a strong commitment to its policy of denying punitive damages in wrongful death cases. . .

In addition to case law, the refusal of the California legislature to change the law also indicates that California has a strong commitment to its no-punitive-damages rule for wrongful death cases. Although plaintiffs set forth historical and policy arguments designed to show that California has no commitment to its policy against allowance of punitive damages, these arguments have not been persuasive with the California legislature. That legislature failed to amend California's wrongful death statute to include punitive damages after attention had been drawn to that omission. . .

Second, we now examine the "comparative pertinence" of California's legislation to the facts of this case. First, if California's no-punitive-damages rule is used in this case, the purpose of that rule, protection of defendants from excessive financial liability, will certainly be achieved. If punitive damages are disallowed, damages cannot be assessed beyond the award for compensatory damages.

The second aspect of the "comparative pertinence" test is whether the state can achieve its policy by means other than enforcement of the statute in question. The allowance of insurance is an alternative means of vindication of a state's protective policy... California law permits defendants to insure against punitive damages.

Having applied the "comparative impairment" test to California, we arrive at the following results. California has a strong current interest in its policy disallowing punitive damages; there is a solid "fit" between the purposes of that policy and its application to a corporation engaging in conduct in California; but, there is some slippage in that "fit" in the sense that at least some of the purposes of California's policy of financial protection theoretically can be achieved by other means, such as insurance.

Thus, the application of California's "comparative impairment" analysis to the states with the greatest interest in application of their laws reveals that both states have strong commitments to their respective policies. Both policies are clearly pertinent to the issue in this case: Missouri would wish to punish MDC, a Missouri-based corporation, for any wrongdoing related to the DC-10 crash; California would want to shield MDC, a corporation doing business in California, from excessive liability regarding any wrongdoing committed in California related to the DC-10 crash. We do not regard the fact that, in each state, there is a theoretical possibility that the state can vindicate its policy by, respectively, the criminal sanction or the availability of insurance, as significant enough to outweigh each state's interest in application of its respective policy. Moreover, to the extent that these theoretical possibilities do exist, they cancel each other out. Thus, we are unable to say that either state's interest would be impaired less by the failure to apply its policy.

We now turn to the place of injury, Illinois. As discussed above, Illinois does have significant interests under the facts of this case. Under the comparative impairment test, we first consider the current status of the Illinois policy disallowing punitive damages. This policy . . . is strongly held. The rule against punitive damages in wrongful death cases was recently affirmed...

The second aspect of a state's commitment to its policy involves the "comparative pertinence" of the state's policy to the facts of the case. Here, the "fit" between the purpose of the Illinois rule and our facts is strong. The purpose of the no-punitive-damages rule is to protect defendants from excessive liability. If Illinois law is applied, MDC, a company which designs airplanes which fly from and over Illinois, will be protected from excessive liability related to a crash that occurred in Illinois. Perhaps merely as the fortuitous place of an injury alone, Illinois might not have a special interest in protecting this corporation, headquartered in Missouri, which performed its alleged misconduct in California. But . . . Illinois was severely affected by this major disaster and Illinois also has strong interests in the protection of airplane-related industries. Because Illinois does have unique interests in both the awarding and the denial of punitive damages, the decision of its legislature to deny punitive damages must be given special attention. For these reasons, then, we find that, all other factors being equal, the interests of Illinois tip the scales against the allowance of punitive damages.

The use of Illinois' interests as the deciding factor regarding the substantive question of punitive damages also comports with principles of certainty and uniformity. Our result under current California choice-of-law law is consistent with our result under Illinois choice-of-law law, which requires the adoption of the law of the place of injury, unless another state has a greater interest in the application of its law. Although California choice-of-law law does not require this result, nothing in our approach is inconsistent with California law. . .

B

We now consider the punitive damage claims sought against American, with regard to the actions filed in California. [The court performed the same analysis except that it looked to New York law as the principal place of American's business, and to Oklahoma law, as the place of its alleged misconduct.]

Regarding American, then, we are now confronted with virtually the same situation as with regard to the California actions filed against MDC. There is a true and equal conflict between the punitive damage rules of the principal place of business and of the place of alleged misconduct. Each state's interest would be equally impaired if the rule of the other state were used. The only difference between the analysis regarding MDC and the analysis regarding American is that it seems clear that insurance may be sold to cover punitive damages in California, but it is not clear that such insurance may be sold in New York. But even if the sale of such insurance is not allowed in New York, we do not deem this factor to be strong enough to tip the scales in favor of the application of New York Law.

As we did in the analysis regarding MDC, we now turn to the state with the next strongest relevant interest, Illinois. For the reasons discussed with regard to the claims against MDC, it seems proper that Illinois law, which does not allow punitive damages, should be the deciding factor. For the foregoing reasons, therefore, we hold that, with regard to the actions filed in California, the motions to strike punitive damage claims against American are granted.

VII

We turn now to the actions filed in New York. Although the New York Court of Appeals has characterized its choice-of-law approach in varying terms, that Court has applied a relatively consistent rule. That rule was formulated in *Babcock v. Jackson,* 12 N.Y.2d 473 (1963). In *Babcock,* the court specifically rejected the rule of lex loci delicti and announced a rule it viewed as equivalent to the Restatement (Second)'s "most significant relationship" test. The court stated that the law to be applied should be that of the state with "the greatest concern with the specific issue." 12 N.Y.2d at 481. The *Babcock* rule has been followed in * * *, *Tooker v. Lopez,* 24 N.Y.2d 569 (1969), and *Neumeier v. Kuehner,* 31 N.Y.2d 121 (1972).

Because the New York test is the functional equivalent of the Restatement (Second) test, the Illinois test, the conflicts analysis with regard to New York law is the same as the conflicts analysis with regard to Illinois. Thus, for the reasons discussed with regard to Illinois law, we grant the motion to strike New York punitive damage claims against both MDC and American.

VIII

We turn now to the actions filed in Michigan. For many years, Michigan had followed the traditional rule that the substantive law of the place of injury governed all issues in tort actions. * * * In recent years, however, the Michigan courts' adherence to this lex loci delicti rule has weakened. Although it is now clear that Michigan Courts have rejected automatic application of the rule of lex loci delicti, it is not clear what the new choice-of-law law is.

In *Sweeney v. Sweeney,* 402 Mich. 234, 262 N.W.2d 625 (1978), the Michigan Supreme Court declared that the lex loci delicti rule would not be applied when to do so would frustrate Michigan public policy. In discussing exceptions to the lex loci delicti rule, the *Sweeney* court cited approvingly the case of *Branyan v. Alpena Flying Service, Inc.,* 65 Mich.App. 1, 236 N.W.2d 739 (1975). The *Branyan* case held that the lex loci delicti rule did not apply to airplane accidents and concluded that the "most significant relationship" test should be used to resolve conflicts questions regarding such accidents 236 N.W.2d at 742.[46] Thus, it appears that under Michigan law, a court would attempt to determine which state

[46] The *Branyan* court stated:

> We agree with [the] line of authority that the strict lex loci delicti rule should be abandoned in favor of the more flexible rule which permits analysis of the policies and interests underlying the particular issue before the court. More particularly, we think that considerations of public policy and analysis of the respective interests of the jurisdictions involved should accompany the judicial decision-making process in these types of conflict-of-laws cases, and that the rule of lex loci delicti should no longer serve to automatically determine which body of law should govern.

236 N.W.2d at 742–43.

had the most significant relationship to the parties or to the occurrence such that its law should be applied. But if that test did not resolve the question, because of Michigan's strong history of following the lex loci delicti rule, and because the *Sweeney* court declined to completely abandon that rule, we conclude that the Michigan court would then consider the law of the place of injury to be determinative.

Since, in this case, the place of conduct and the principal place of business have equal interests in the application of their laws, we conclude a Michigan court would resolve this matter by applying the law of the place of injury, Illinois, because of Michigan's strong history of following the lex loci delicti rule. Thus, we grant the motions to strike punitive damage claims against both defendants with regard to the actions filed in Michigan.

IX

As the district court determined, Puerto Rico applies the lex loci delicti test to tort actions. * * * The law of the place of injury, Illinois, does not permit punitive damages in wrongful death actions. Moreover, denying punitive damages here does not frustrate the public policy of Puerto Rico, since Puerto Rico does not allow punitive damages in tort actions. * * * Therefore, the district court's grant of the motions to strike punitive damage claims against both MDC and American is affirmed.

X

Finally, we turn to Hawaii. Neither the parties nor the district court have been able to identify the choice-of-law law of Hawaii. . . The inability to determine the governing choice-of-law law does not justify placing the burden on one of the parties to disprove the possibility that a choice-of-law rule would impose liability on it. We conclude that where the choice-of-law law cannot be determined, absent an affirmative showing to the contrary, the court should presume that the forum would apply its own law. . .

Hawaii's law regarding punitive damages is disputed. The Hawaii Wrongful Death Act, Haw.Rev.Stat. § 663–3 (1976 Repl.), authorizes the recovery of "such damages . . . as under the circumstances shall be deemed fair and just compensation, with reference to the pecuniary injury and loss of love and affection, including" itemized elements of loss. The statute makes no reference to punitive damages. [The court went on to conclude that the law of Hawaii does not allow the recovery of punitive damages.]

Having determined that Hawaii law does not authorize punitive damages in wrongful death cases, we must now consider whether the application of that law would "not meet the needs of the case or would not be in the interest of justice." Restatement (Second) § 136, Comment h, at 378. Since we have denied the availability of punitive damages with regard to each other state in which actions have been filed, we do not find that the application of Hawaii law would fail to meet the needs of the case or would not be in the interest of justice. In addition, we have found that the use of two modern choice-of-law theories, as well as the old rule of lex loci delicti, all lead to the same result in this case. We see no reason why the result with regard to the Hawaii plaintiffs should be different, especially since Hawaii does not allow punitive damages. For these reasons, we grant the motions to strike Hawaii punitive damage claims against both defendants.

XI

In conclusion, we agree with the district court's comments on the problems involved in determining choice-of-law issues in airplane crash cases. Airline corporations and airplane manufacturers are subject to uniform federal regulation in almost every aspect of their operations, except their liability in tort. . . Along with the district court, we conclude that it is clearly in the interests of passengers, airline corporations, airplane manufacturers, and state and federal governments, that airline tort liability be regulated by federal law. Of course, we are well aware of the fact that it is up to Congress, and not the courts, to create the needed uniform law.

For the foregoing reasons, the orders of the district court in denying the motions to strike punitive damage claims against MDC are reversed, while its orders granting such motions with regard to American are affirmed. . .

IN RE "AGENT ORANGE" PRODUCT LIABILITY LITIGATION, 580 F.Supp. 690 (E.D.N.Y.1984). More than two million Vietnam war veterans and members of their families sued for injuries allegedly caused by exposure to herbicides used by the United States Army during the war; because the Federal government was immune, the plaintiffs sued the companies that produced and sold the herbicides. Separate lawsuits filed throughout the United States were transferred to New York for pretrial proceedings under 28 U.S.C. § 1405. The court certified a class comprising the claimants in nearly 600 of these actions; the claimants in 400 additional actions opted out of the class, but the court transferred their cases to itself under 28 U.S.C. § 1404 and consolidated them for trial with the class action. In an earlier phase of the litigation, the court had ruled that the plaintiffs' claims were governed by federal common law, but the Second Circuit reversed, holding that "there is [no] identifiable federal policy at stake in this litigation that warrants the creation of federal common law rules." *In re "Agent Orange" Product Liability Litigation,* 635 F.2d 987, 993 (2d Cir.1980). The court was thus required to adjudicate the case using state law. Moreover, because class certification does not affect the law applicable to any individual claim, the Court had to follow *Klaxon* and *Van Dusen* and apply the choice-of-law rules of the original transferor courts.

Chief Judge Weinstein began his analysis by emphasizing that, no matter where the plaintiffs lived or had filed suit, it was "obviously sensible" to treat "members of this nation's armed forces and their families in essentially the same way for any injuries suffered in a national war fought on foreign soil." Like the court in *Air Crash,* he claimed that "[m]odern approaches" to choice of law, "although differing in their formulations, mandate an analytical inquiry which is essentially the same." With that in mind, he proceeded to examine the applicable law under the Second Restatement, interest analysis, Leflar's choice-influencing considerations, the traditional rules, and a lex fori approach. Under any of these methods, he concluded, a court would reach the same result—applying not its own law or the law of any state, but rather a new "national-consensus law" formulated just for this case. Speaking of the Second Restatement, for example, Chief Judge Weinstein noted the large number of different states with relevant contacts under §§ 6 and 145. He then explained:

> Having analyzed, under Restatement § 6(2)(b), the relevant policies of the various [original] forum states, it is suggested that we select the law of one of those fora to be applied to one or more of the substantive issues in this litigation. Yet it has already been pointed out that considering only the defendants' principal places of business and manufacture and principal contracts relevant to the conduct causing the injury, we count more than twenty jurisdictions. If to these jurisdictions are added the states and countries which bear much of the expense of caring for the service people, spouses and children who need public assistance, the number of jurisdictions far exceeds fifty. This complexity is compounded by the fact that at least three of the foreign countries involved—Canada, Australia and New Zealand—are themselves federal republics with federal-state issues not unlike our own.
>
> [A] state court passing on the claims of an individual or a group of veterans might well recognize the unfairness in treating differently legally identical claims involving servicemen who fought a difficult foreign war shoulder-to-shoulder and were exposed to virtually identical risks. . . Similarly, it would make little sense to have a serviceman's recovery (or that of a spouse or child) in this suit depend on the fortuity of where he manifested his injuries or where he filed suit.
>
> It quickly becomes apparent that it is impossible through sensible application of Restatement (Second) choice of law doctrine or analysis to identify the interest of any one state as being sufficiently greater than that of any others to a degree sufficient to justify the application of that state's law in resolving the issues in this litigation. Any narrow and mechanical state

> choice of law system simply collapses under the weight of the multiplicity of contacts, policies and unarticulated or conflicting state interests in this unique case. A state court, therefore, because of its inability to identify and select any other state's law to be applied as the rule of decision and because of the need for uniformity across the country, would seek to divine what the national rule of decision with regard to product liability law would be so that such law would appropriately reflect the national and international characteristics of this case. By contrast, the application of an individual state's law rather than a federal law or a national consensus law would be irrational and unfair.

Turning to governmental interest analysis, Chief Judge Weinstein explained:

> What was said above in connection with the discussion of the Restatement approach applies to an analysis of the application of the governmental interest analysis. It makes no difference whether this litigation poses a false conflict or a true conflict. There is no rational method by which a state could choose one state's law to govern some or all of the issues in the case and a state would look to a single national common law.

The better law approach was easy. After listing the five choice-influencing considerations discussed by Leflar, supra pp. 224–227, the Chief Judge observed that all but the "better law" factor were also part of the Second Restatement test and pointed to the application of a national consensus law for reasons explained in connection with that approach. As for the better law, he continued, "[t]his last factor calls into play the notion of the national law as the 'more progressive' law and possibly provides further support for the application of federal common law."

One might have thought that the traditional rules or a *lex fori* approach would not leave much room to resolve the choice-of-law dilemma by resort to national consensus law; but Chief Judge Weinstein thought otherwise. With respect to states that still follow the traditional rule, he argued:

> The fact that a state uses the lex loci approach in most cases does not mean that it is immune to arguments based on the relative interests of jurisdictions. . . The [uniformity] rationale given by state courts for adhering to the lex loci approach does not apply here. . . When the choice is between forum law and a federal or national consensus law as distinguished from a choice between forum law and a sister state's law, that danger of "inconstancy" does not exist.

As for states that might prefer simply to apply forum law:

> There is no need to fall back on this alternative of desperation. * * * First, state law has not considered the complex question of a war contractor's liability to soldiers injured by toxic chemicals subject to federal regulation while engaged in combat and serving abroad. Second, a state with only a tangential connection to the litigation which has the choice of applying a far more relevant federal or national consensus common law will not apply a body of law to a case merely because the law happens to be that of the forum.

The court concluded its analysis by scolding Congress for failing to address the Agent Orange problem and by appealing to the uniqueness of the case as justification for its unusual analysis:

> The overwhelming need for a uniform approach and a single substantive standard is obvious. Normally we would expect Congress to recognize this and provide a federal statute which would be all encompassing or which would leave lacunae to be filled by the federal courts directly or through absorption of state law. Although it could do so under its commerce or war powers, Congress has not enacted such a statute.
>
> Given a failure of the legislature and the executive, the federal courts could be expected to step in by creating federal common law to cover a national problem. But the Second Circuit has blocked that route by denying that federal substantive law controls of its own force. * * * Thus, under *Klaxon,* we look to the states to accomplish the sound result. As a federal court we sit as a surrogate for the state courts, attempting to predict how pragmatic and wise state judges would address the problem. . .
>
> Once it is conceded, as we think it must be, that each of the jurisdictions involved would appreciate the overwhelming need for uniformity, to what single state's law could any state look to as controlling? Given the plethora of states and nations with contacts and the impossibility without a full trial of even knowing where the allegedly offending dioxin was produced, it becomes apparent that no acceptable test can point to any single state. Thus, the law is driven in this most unusual case to either federal or national consensus substantive law as the only workable approach. . .
>
> That neither New York nor, as far as we have ascertained, any state has had a case such as this one before us does not permit our throwing up our hands and refusing to decide the question. Perhaps it would have been better if certification rules permitted posing the conflicts question to the more than half-a-hundred

jurisdictions involved. But no such procedure is presently in place. * * * In the meantime, this court must ascertain the living state law as best it can. . .

For the reasons noted, it is likely that each of the states would look to a federal or a national consensus law of manufacturer's liability, government contract defense and punitive damages. What is the nature of the national consensus or federal law is a subject for another memorandum.

Choice of Law in Mass Actions

(1) Mass tort and other complex cases present the most important and difficult challenge to the litigation system today. Such actions arise in a variety of contexts and forms. The earliest cases were single-event torts, such as environmental disasters, airplane crashes, or the collapse of a skywalk in the Kansas City Hyatt Regency Hotel. Victims in such cases typically number in the hundreds, though an explosion at the Union Carbide plant in Bhopal, India, killed more than 2,000 people and injured more than 200,000. More recently, courts have had to struggle with dispersed torts involving the exposure of thousands or tens of thousands of plaintiffs to some harmful agent in a variety of settings over an extended period of time. In addition to *Agent Orange,* complex litigation has arisen over injuries allegedly caused by Vioxx, DES, Bendectin, the Dalkon Shield, breast implants, and other drugs or medical supplies. Some 700,000 asbestos claimants have filed cases, with thousands still pending in multidistrict litigation. Tobacco litigation, too, proliferated until a master settlement agreement was reached in November 1998. A similar story has unfolded with respect to opioids, with thousands of actions by states, municipalities, and tribal nations against pharmaceutical companies combined in multidistrict litigation in federal court. Finally, there are mass contract actions, such as cases involving allegations of nationwide securities fraud. Such mass actions strain every resource and institution of the legal system, and choice of law is no exception. Yet the choice-of-law problems, which (as *Air Crash* and *Agent Orange* make clear) can be a nightmare, are invariably central to these cases.

(2) How persuasive is Judge Sprecher's handling of the choice-of-law issues in *Air Crash*? Do you agree that the various choice-of-law approaches are all "basically the same"? Are conflicts scholars who fight bitterly about the differences among approaches wasting their time or quibbling about aesthetic qualities? Are you surprised to discover that all the different choice-of-law approaches produced the same result? Before you answer that question, consider the following:

(a) *Illinois claims.* Did the court apply the Second Restatement approach to the claims filed in Illinois, or did it apply interest analysis? How persuasive is its analysis of the interests? Do you agree that the plaintiffs' home states have no interest in either awarding or denying punitive damages? Do you agree that because the two most interested states have opposing rules the correct solution is to apply the law of some third, concededly less-interested state?

(b) *California claims.* Did the court fairly apply the comparative impairment test? If the states with the greatest interests are the defendants' home states and the states where the conduct took place, how is it possible to conclude that the law of the place of injury will suffer greater impairment if not applied?

(c) *New York claims.* Do you agree that the New York test articulated in *Babcock,* supra p. 208, *Tooker,* supra p. 151, and *Neumeier,* supra p. 210, is "the functional equivalent of the Restatement (Second) test"? How do you think a New York court would analyze the choice-of-law issue if the suit of one of the New York plaintiffs were before it?

(d) *Michigan claims.* Choice-of-law scholars have classified Michigan as a "lex fori" state with regard to tort claims. See Symeonides, *Choice of Law in the American Courts in 2019: Twenty-Third Annual Survey,* 68 Am. J. Comp. L. 235, 258–59 (2020). The Michigan Supreme Court has stated that Michigan follows interest analysis with a presumption of forum law, making it perhaps the closest adherent to Brainerd Currie's original vision. See *Sutherland v. Kennington Truck Service,* 454 Mich. 274, 286, 562 N.W.2d 466, 471 (1997). The Seventh Circuit concluded, however, that Michigan was a Second Restatement state because the Michigan Supreme Court in *Sweeney* had "cited approvingly" the opinion of the Michigan intermediate appellate court in *Branyan,* which had supposedly resolved a multistate tort using the most significant relationship test. Professor Kramer calls this interpretation of Michigan law a "grotesque distortion." Kramer, *Choice of Law in Complex Litigation,* 71 N.Y.U. L. Rev. 547, 559 (1996).

(3) Did Chief Judge Weinstein do better in *Agent Orange*? What exactly is the difference between federal common law, which the Second Circuit found inappropriate, and Weinstein's "national consensus law"? Do you agree that state courts would create such a law? Doesn't Weinstein's argument depend on these courts being faced with the very same class action, and isn't the appropriate question what the courts of origin would do if the separate claims were dispersed? What do you think the state courts would do were that the case?

Because Weinstein's ruling was interlocutory, no appeal could be taken under the final judgment rule. (As discussed in note 9, class certification decisions are now, at the circuit court's discretion, subject to immediate review under Federal Rule of Civil Procedure 23(f).) The defendants therefore sought relief by way of writ of mandamus. Applying the stricter standard applicable to such writs, the Second Circuit declined to grant relief. "While we will not disclaim considerable skepticism as to the existence of a 'national substantive rule,' " the court explained, "we note Chief Judge Weinstein's declared intention to create subclasses as dictated by variations in state law. Given the unique aspects of this case arguably creating the need for a single dispositive trial on the common issues [of fact], we cannot say that the use of subclasses corresponding to variations in state law is a palpable error remediable by mandamus." *In re Diamond Shamrock Chemicals Co.,* 725 F.2d 858, 861 (2d Cir.1984). In fact, Chief Judge Weinstein declared no such intention, though Judge Winter may have been giving Weinstein a hint about what to do in formulating the details of his national consensus law.

As it turned out, the court never had to deal with the problem. Faced with uncertainty over the applicable law, and under considerable pressure from the judge, the lawyers settled *Agent Orange* on the eve of the trial. In a subsequent appeal on other issues, the Second Circuit reiterated its skepticism regarding the choice-of-law solution. Calling Weinstein's approach "bold and imaginative," the court nonetheless observed:

> in light of our prior holding that federal common law does not govern plaintiffs' claims, every jurisdiction would be free to render its own choice of law decision, and common experience suggests that the intellectual power of Chief Judge Weinstein's analysis alone would not be enough to prevent widespread disagreement.

In re "Agent Orange" Product Liability Litigation, 818 F.2d 145, 165 (2d Cir.1987). Because the parties settled, however, any error in this regard was treated as harmless. But wasn't Weinstein's resolution of the choice-of-law issue critical in leading to the settlement and dictating its terms? In *In re Air Crash Disaster at Sioux City,* 734 F.Supp. 1425 (N.D.Ill.1990), eighteen cases from ten states were consolidated for pretrial purposes. The plaintiffs declined to brief the choice-of-law issues regarding punitive damages on the ground that it was premature and that individual plaintiffs should be permitted to litigate the question after the cases were remanded to the courts in which they were originally filed. Judge Conlon disagreed (and ruled anyway):

> The choice of law question regarding punitive damages should be resolved as early as possible. First and foremost, this determination may facilitate settlement negotiations and thus enable victims of the crash to be compensated expeditiously. [The availability or applicable standard for recovering punitive damages may] differ from state to state. Consequently, the settlement value of an individual claim is difficult to measure

> without first determining whether punitive damages are available and, where available, the standard for recovery. Once the choice of law question is resolved, some plaintiffs may choose to forego lengthy and expensive discovery and accept defendants' offer. . .

Id. at 1429–30. For a fascinating (if overly apologetic) account of the *Agent Orange* case, see P. Schuck, Agent Orange on Trial (enlarged ed. 1987).

(4) One striking feature of both *Air Crash* and *Agent Orange* is the lengths to which the courts go—the extent to which they are willing to bend ordinary choice-of-law rules—to ensure that one law only is selected to govern all the claims on any given issue. Many other courts have done the same, using a variety of irregular techniques to justify their decisions. See James A.R. Nafziger, *Choice of Law in Air Crash Disaster Cases: Complex Litigation Rules and the Common Law,* 54 La. L. Rev. 1001, 1015–84 (1994) (describing results and analysis in 62 cases decided between 1975 and 1993); Kramer, *Choice of Law in Complex Litigation,* 71 N.Y.U. L. Rev. at 552–55 (surveying techniques courts use to find only one law applicable in complex cases). Why do you think this is the case?

(5) Equally striking is the unwillingness of most courts to admit that they are treating the choice-of-law issues in complex cases differently than they would treat the same or similar issues in ordinary litigation. *Agent Orange* is an unusual exception here, and most opinions read more like *Air Crash* instead. Academic commentators tend to be less reticent in advocating change, and many have made proposals for special rules to handle complex cases. Professor Juenger, for example, recommended resolving mass disaster cases with a rule of alternative reference that selects the best substantive law; he would direct the court to examine the law of the place of conduct, of injury, and of each party's home, and "as to each issue" choose from these "the most suitable rule of decision." Juenger, *Mass Disasters and the Conflict of Laws,* 1989 U.Ill.L.Rev. 105, 126. Professor Weintraub, in contrast, wanted the parties to select an applicable law: he would apply the law of the plaintiff's "habitual residence" if either party chooses it; if not, he would give first the plaintiff and then the defendant a choice among the law of defendant's principal place of business, the place of sale or acquisition, or the place of manufacture or design. Weintraub, *Methods for Resolving Conflict-of-Laws Problems in Mass Tort Litigation,* 1989 U.Ill.L.Rev. 129, 148.

The most thoughtful and well-developed proposal is found in the American Law Institute's Complex Litigation: Statutory Recommendations and Analysis (1994). Drafted principally by Professor Mary Kay Kane, the proposal sets forth six rules for mass tort and contract actions. With respect to torts, for example, § 6.01 provides that the court's objective should be to apply, "to the extent feasible, a single state's law to all similar tort claims being asserted against a defendant," with an option to divide the actions into subgroups to facilitate consolidated treatment. In determining which state's law should apply, the ALI calls for the court to consider (1) the place or places of injury; (2) the place or places of the conduct causing the injury; and (3) the principal places of business or habitual residences of the plaintiffs and defendants. If more than one state is interested, the court should apply, in order of preference, (1) the law of the place of injury and the place of the conduct causing the injury, if they are the same state; (2) the law of the state where all parties have a habitual residence or principal place of business, if any; or (3) the law of the state where all of the plaintiffs have a habitual residence or principal place of business, if it was the place of injury. If none of these solutions is available, the law of the state where the conduct causing the injury occurred governs. American Law Institute, Complex Litigation: Statutory Recommendations and Analysis § 6 (1994).

Is this proposal better suited for single-event or dispersed torts? What result under this provision in *Air Crash*? In *Agent Orange*? How would you characterize the ALI approach? Is it interest analysis or a variation on the Second Restatement?

(6) *Agent Orange* is a dispersed tort, whereas *Air Crash* is a single event. Should single-event torts be handled differently? In 2002, Congress passed the Multiparty, Multiforum Trial Jurisdiction Act, codified at 28 U.S.C. § 1369. The Act grants federal courts jurisdiction over actions resulting from a single accident that causes at least 75 deaths on the basis of "minimal diversity" rather than the "complete diversity" ordinarily required under 28 U.S.C. § 1332. "Minimal diversity" is satisfied if any two adverse parties are citizens of different states, or if one party is a state citizen and an adverse party is foreign. Despite (or because of?) extensive congressional debates over the appropriate choice-of-law rules for such cases, the Act does not provide one. It does, however, have an exception based in part on choice-of-law factors: district courts are directed to "abstain from hearing" cases in which "the substantial majority of all plaintiffs are citizens of a single State of which the primary defendants are also citizens; and the claims asserted will be governed primarily by the laws of that State."

(7) Most academic proposals for handling choice of law in complex litigation aim to select a single law to govern all of the claims on any given issue. The reasons typically given for this objective are (1) that it is unfair to apply different laws to different victims, (2) that applying one law reduces the likelihood of inconsistent results, and (3) that applying many laws will unduly complicate consolidated treatment in a single proceeding.

Are these justifications persuasive? According to Professors Sedler and Twerski, there is nothing "unfair" about applying different laws to different victims, which is simply a product of having a federal system:

> It is irrelevant that the parties were victims in the same "mass tort." The "mass" nature of the tort has nothing to do with the consequences of that tort for the individual victims and with the interest of the victims' home state. . . The consequences of this "mass tort" will be felt by the victims in their home states, and it is the law of their respective home states that should determine the amount of damages they will each recover for this "mass tort."

Sedler & Twerski, *The Case Against All Encompassing Federal Mass Tort Legislation: Sacrifice Without Gain,* 73 Marquette L.Rev. 76, 89–90 (1989).

This leaves the argument that, without a single law, it will be difficult or impossible to adjudicate complex cases. See Cabraser, *Just Choose: The Jurisprudential Necessity to Select a Single Governing Law for Mass Claims Arising from Nationally Marketed Consumer Goods and Services,* 14 Roger Williams L.Rev. 29 (2009). How appropriate or weighty ought that consideration to be? After all, choice of law is not some minor, threshold procedural matter unrelated to the merits. Choice of law is part of the process by which we define the parties' rights—the very paradigm of what we mean by "substantive." That being so, why should the applicable law change just because claims that would otherwise have been litigated individually have been consolidated for joint treatment? Consider the following observation:

> If choice of law is substantive (in the sense that it defines the parties' rights), then courts should not alter choice-of-law rules for complex cases. The reasoning is straightforward. We start with claims that everyone concedes would otherwise be adjudicated under different laws. We combine these claims, whether through transfer and consolidation or by certifying a class, on the ground that we can adjudicate the parties' rights more effectively and efficiently in one big proceeding. So far, so good. Then, having constructed this proceeding, we are told we must change the parties' rights to facilitate the consolidated adjudication. And that makes no sense. If the reason for consolidating is to make adjudication of the parties' rights more efficient and effective, then the fact of consolidation itself cannot justify changing those rights. To let it do so is truly to let the tail wag the dog.

Kramer, *Choice of Law in Complex Litigation,* 71 N.Y.U. L. Rev. at 572. Is there *any* sense in which class or consolidated treatment changes, or should change, the nature of the parties' substantive rights? Is a class more than an aggregation of individual claims? See *Phillips Petroleum Co. v. Shutts,* 472 U.S. 797 (1985), infra p. 383 (rejecting the argument that aggregation justifies changing constitutional limits on choice of law); David Shapiro, *The Class as Party and Client,* 73 Notre Dame L. Rev. 913 (1998) (arguing for a "class as entity" model); *In re Bridgestone/Firestone,* 288 F.3d 1012,

1020 (7th Cir. 2002) (arguing that a single action with a single law follows a "central planning model" that "suppresses information that is vital to accurate resolution").

(8) In the 1990s, courts began to reject arguments that ordinary choice-of-law rules could be altered or bent in order to apply a single law in complex cases. See, e.g., *Georgine v. Amchem Prods., Inc.*, 83 F.3d 610, 627, 630 (3d Cir. 1996), *aff'd*, 521 U.S. 591 (1997); *Castano v. Am. Tobacco Co.*, 84 F.3d 734, 741–42 (5th Cir. 1996); *In re Rhone-Poulenc Rorer Inc.*, 51 F.3d 1293, 1304 (7th Cir. 1995).

In 1998, Federal Rule of Civil Procedure 23(f) was adopted, allowing an immediate appeal, at the circuit court's discretion, from decisions certifying class actions. As the Advisory Committee notes indicate, Rule 23(f) embodies the recognition that certification decisions frequently ended litigation as a practical matter: most defendants settled if the class was certified, and most plaintiffs gave up if it was not. Federal circuit courts have used Rule 23(f) to expand the trend towards decertification.

And in 2005, Congress passed the Class Action Fairness Act ("CAFA"), codified at various section of title 28 of the U.S. Code. The Act grants federal courts jurisdiction, subject to some exceptions, over class actions based on state law where the amount in controversy exceeds $5 million in the aggregate and minimal diversity exists. It also makes it easier for defendants to remove such cases to federal court. CAFA does not contain any choice-of-law provision, and the Senate voted down a proposed amendment that would have prevented federal courts from refusing to certify a class on the grounds that the plaintiffs' claims would be governed by more than one state's law.

In the wake of these developments, commentators have concluded that nationwide class actions based on state law are now virtually uncertifiable under Rule 23(b)(3) because variations in state law mean that common questions of law do not predominate and trial management is too difficult. See Bradt, *The Shortest Distance: Direct Filing and Choice of Law in Multistate Litigation*, 88 Notre Dame L. Rev. 759, 781 (2012); Linda Silberman, *The Role of Choice of Law in National Class Actions*, 156 U. Pa. L. Rev. 2001, 2009 (2008).

(9) The difficulty of obtaining class certification has led plaintiffs in complex cases to shift *en masse* to federal multidistrict litigation (MDL). To cite just one example, the MDL involving claims by U.S. service members for hearing damage allegedly caused by 3M's combat earplugs now includes more than 200,000 cases. *In re 3M Combat Arms Earplug Products Liability Litigation*, No. 19–md–2885 (N.D. Fla.). The federal MDL statute authorizes the Judicial Panel on Multidistrict Litigation to transfer civil actions from different districts to "any district for coordinated or consolidated pretrial proceedings" as long as the cases feature "one or more common questions of fact" and the transfer serves "the convenience of parties and witnesses and will promote the just and efficient conduct of such actions." 28 U.S.C. § 1407(a). The transferee court has wide authority over pretrial matters, including dispositive motions, but may not retain jurisdiction over transferred cases for trial. *Lexecon, Inc. v. Milberg, Weiss, Bershad, Hynes & Lerach,* 523 U.S. 26 (1998). In practice, however, a transfer back to the transferor court for trial rarely happens, as the MDL process is aimed from the start at producing a global settlement. To this end, the transferee court often conducts representative or "bellwether" trials, which are voluntary proceedings designed to inform settlement negotiations by indicating the value of the remaining lawsuits in the MDL. See generally Gluck & Burch, *MDL Revolution,* 96 N.Y.U. L. Rev. 1 (2021).

Despite being consolidated for pretrial purposes, the cases in an MDL retain their individual character; unlike in a class action, common issues need not predominate. In particular, as Judge Sprecher explains in *In re Air Crash,* the transferee court must apply the same law that the transferor court would apply. *Van Dusen v. Barrack,* 376 U.S. 612 (1964). This means that the transferee court will apply the choice-of-law rules of the transferor court, which in turn will be the choice-of-law rules of the state in which the transferor court sits. *Klaxon Co. v. Stentor Elec. Mfg. Co.*, 313 U.S. 487, 496 (1941).

Some commentators blame the difficulties encountered with choice of law in complex litigation on *Klaxon* and *Van Dusen.* Even if Congress will not enact a uniform federal choice-of-law statute, they argue, overruling *Klaxon* and *Van Dusen* would help solve the problem by enabling federal courts to develop a federal common law of choice of law. See, e.g., Lowenfeld, *Mass Torts and the Conflict of Laws: The Airline Disaster,* 1989 U.Ill.L.Rev. 157, 163–65; Mullinex, *Class Resolution of the Mass Tort Case: A Proposed Federal Procedure Act,* 64 Tex.L.Rev. 1039, 1077–79 (1986). Is this the answer? Consider the following comment:

> [T]he federal common law approach has several distinct disadvantages. Not only will uncertainty and a lack of uniformity continue, at least until the courts determine what the standards should be, but also there is no assurance that a single federal standard will ever evolve. Rather, just as the states have had difficulty in reaching agreement in various substantive contexts as to what choice of law standard seems most appropriate, it is likely that variations will develop among the federal circuits. . . To expect the Supreme Court to review two or three cases a year to resolve choice of law differences between the circuits and provide some certainty seems totally unrealistic.

ALI, Complex Litigation: Statutory Recommendations and Analysis ch. 6, Intro. Note at 314.

For discussion of *Klaxon* and *Van Dusen* as well as the choice-of-law issues presented by MDL proceedings, see infra Chapter 7, pp. 888–895.

(10) Is it really true, as Professor Silberman has asserted, that the choice-of-law problem is (or ought to be) a "virtually insuperable obstacle to certification"? Silberman, *The Role of Choice of Law in National Class Actions*, 156 U. Pa. L. Rev. at 2009. Not necessarily, says Professor Kramer:

> First, while in theory all fifty states could have different laws, in practice there are seldom more than two or three rules on any given question, each adopted by many states. Consequently, there will seldom be more than a few conflicts in any particular case. Second, the number of different approaches to choice of law is also limited; indeed, three-fourths of the states use either the First or Second Restatement. Therefore, even when conflicts arise, many states will agree on the applicable law, and the court can dispose of claims by grouping these states together. Finally, if there are subclasses of litigants whose claims are governed by different laws, the court can divide them into a few appropriate categories and analyze them sequentially. This should be easy in bench trials, while in jury cases the court can use special verdicts to facilitate the process.

Kramer, *Choice of Law in the American Courts in 1990: Trends and Developments,* 39 Am.J.Comp.L. 465, 475 (1991).

Is application of the defendant's home law a possible solution? Consider a case in which plaintiffs nationwide seek to bring a products liability class action and invoke the law of the defendant's principal place of business, where the products were designed and manufactured. Their home states' laws, if materially different, will be either more plaintiff-friendly or more defendant-friendly. As to the more plaintiff-friendly states, the plaintiffs could argue, the issue is really an election of remedies, not a conflict of laws. And as to the more defendant-friendly states, the plaintiffs can argue that such states have no interest in protecting the out-of-state manufacturer and limiting the recovery available to their domiciliaries.

Consider the *Asbestos School* litigation: In 1983, a state-law action was filed on behalf of 30,000 public and private schools and school districts throughout the nation against virtually the entire asbestos industry. In 1984, the district court certified a nationwide class for punitive and compensatory damages, noting that as to the duty to warn 51 of 54 relevant jurisdictions applied § 388 of the Second Restatement of Torts, and as to strict liability 47 jurisdictions had adopted strict liability theories. In addition, the plaintiffs agreed that the most stringent tests of liability would apply. Finally, the court observed that subclasses could be created to account for variances pursuant to Rule 23(c)(4). *In re Asbestos School*

Litigation, 104 F.R.D. 422, 434 (E.D. Pa. 1984). The Third Circuit affirmed this part of the decision, though not before noting "some doubt" about manageability. *In re School Asbestos Litigation,* 789 F.2d 996, 1010 (3d Cir. 1986).

How realistic is it to think that courts can do this sort of thing in other complex cases? *Asbestos School* involved only property-damage claims. Is it likely that there will be so few differences among the laws of different states when we move to realm of personal injuries? In *Georgine v. Amchem Prods., Inc.*, 83 F.3d 610, 627 n. 13 (3d Cir. 1996), *aff'd*, 521 U.S. 591 (1997), a nationwide asbestos class action for personal injury claims, the Third Circuit refused to allow a settlement class to be certified, distinguishing *Asbestos School* because, in that case, "[c]lass counsel made a credible argument that the applicable law of the different states could be broken down into approximately four patterns. . . Of course, this case could not be broken into anywhere near that small a number of patterns." Do you agree?

(11) Limitations periods are another pervasive problem in complex litigation. Should a single statute of limitations be applied to every claim? Whose? Interestingly, after considering a variety of options, the ALI beat a partial retreat from its proposal to apply one law, reasoning that it would be unfair to dismiss the claims of parties who could have sued in the state where they originally filed. Section 6.04 directs courts to apply the limitations law of the state whose law is selected to govern the action, "except that any claim that was timely where filed but is not under the law chosen pursuant to this section will be deemed timely. . ." Such claims may, however, be remanded for individual determination "upon application of any party." ALI, Complex Litigation: Statutory Recommendations and Analysis ch. 6.

(12) Professor Lowenfeld concludes that the task of finding a uniform choice-of-law solution to the mass accident problem is "quite hopeless": "Having thought about this question for close to three decades, I give up." 1989 U.Ill.L.Rev. at 170. He recommends creating federal substantive law to govern such cases. What odds would you give for the enactment of such legislation? And would it help in cases involving contacts with foreign countries?

E. CONFLICTS ON THE INTERNET

LAWRENCE LESSIG, CODE AND OTHER LAWS OF CYBERSPACE

190–94, 196–98 (1999).

[A]s conflicts among laws from outside a single sovereign . . . grow in number and significance, a problem emerges. People have never really been subject to the laws of only one sovereign. Behavior across borders, or behavior that had effects across borders, has always risked running afoul of competing rules. As the integration of international life has increased, so have these conflicts. Behavior has effects in many places; how many places legitimately have a claim to regulate in these spaces? How, in other words, could it be just that a single act is subject to the control of many sovereigns?

Cyberspace has exploded this . . . debate. What was once the exception will become the rule. Behavior was once governed ordinarily within one jurisdiction, or within two coordinating jurisdictions. Now it will systematically be governed within multiple, noncoordinating jurisdictions. How can law handle this?

This question has produced a ferocious argument between two extremes. At one end is the work of David Post and David Johnson. Johnson and Post argue that the multiplicity of jurisdictions in which your behavior is subject to regulation (since anything you do in cyberspace has an effect in every other context) should mean that much behavior is presumptively not subject to regulation anywhere. Anywhere, that is, save cyberspace. The inconsistency of any other solution, they argue, would be absurd. Rather than embracing the absurd, we should embrace something far more sensible: life in cyberspace, as Milan Kundera might put it, is life elsewhere.

At the other extreme is the work of scholars such as Jack Goldsmith, who claims there is nothing new here. For many years the law has worked through these conflicts of authority. Cyberspace may increase the incidence of these conflicts, but it does not change their nature. Old structures may have to be molded to fit this new form, but the pattern of the old will suffice.

While both sides embrace partial truths, in my view both are mistaken. It is true, as Johnson and Post argue, that there is something new here. But what is new is not a difference in kind, only a difference in degree. And it is true, as Goldsmith argues, that we have always had disputes of this form. But we have not had conflicts at this level of actor. We have not had a time when we could say that people are actually living in two places at once, with no principle of supremacy between them. This is the challenge that we will face in the future.

This duality is a problem because the legal tools we have used to resolve these questions before were not designed to deal with conflicts among citizens. They were designed to deal with conflicts among institutions, or relatively sophisticated actors. They are rules made for business interacting with business, or businesses interacting with governments. They were not designed for disputes between citizens.

Jessica Litman makes an analogous point in her work on copyright. For much of the last century, Litman argues, copyright has worked fairly well as a compromise between publishers and authors. It is a law that has largely been applied to institutions. Individuals were essentially outside copyright's purview since individuals didn't really "publish."

The Internet, of course, changes all this. Now everyone is a publisher. And Litman argues (convincingly, in my view) that copyright's rules do not necessarily work well when applied to individuals. More precisely, the ideal rules for individuals would not necessarily be the ideal rules for institutions. The rules of copyright need to be reformed to make them better suited to a world where individuals are publishers.

The same is true of conflicts between sovereigns. The rules for dealing with these conflicts work well when the parties are repeat players—corporations that must do business in two places. These people can take steps to conform their behavior to the limited range of contexts in which they live, and the existing rules help them to that end. But it does not follow (as it does not follow in the context of copyright) that the same mix of rules would work best in a world where anyone could be multinational.

The solution to this change will not come from insisting either that everything is the same or that everything is different. It will take more work than that. When a large number of citizens live in two different places, and when one of those places is not solely within the jurisdiction of a particular sovereign, then what kinds of claims should one sovereign be able to make on others, and what kinds of claims can these sovereigns make on cyberspace?

Imagine a nation with a well-developed balance of rights built into its law of contract. These rights protect consumers in some cases; they set the terms for business relationships in others. Some of these rights are default, in the sense that the parties could agree to change them. But some are mandatory for a certain class of contractor or for a certain kind of contract. . .

These rules of contract law would be effective in real space to define the rights of one individual making a claim against another. The enforcement of any contract in this space would be subject to these rules.

Enter cyberspace, where the architecture of interaction, or the architecture of a particular cyberspace, determines a host of rules about contracts. These rules—about how an offer is accepted, when it is effective, how it can be canceled, what terms must be bargained for, whether terms are enforceable, whether there must be a written agreement, and so on—may or may not be consistent with the contract rules of a particular jurisdiction. But a citizen from a particular jurisdiction can not enter into an agreement subject to these terms. These terms governing the agreements are the effective rules of contract for that particular agreement, and if they are inconsistent with the rules of the local jurisdiction from which the person comes, then so much the worse for the local rules. The terms of the contract are those agreed to in the text of the agreement, or implicit in the architecture that regulates dealings about the agreement.

One might say this is nothing new. One might say, following Goldsmith, that people have always been able to enter into international agreements. These agreements have always implied a choice of law, and the law chosen may or may not be consistent with local law. If it is inconsistent, then there are restrictions on a local jurisdiction's ability to enforce it against a local citizen. So the same structure would constrain in this context.

But this analytical similarity should not obscure a substantive difference. Again, international agreements for the most part are agreements between sophisticated actors. Before cyberspace, ordinary consumers were not international actors. We can assume that sophisticated actors are able to defend themselves against rules inconsistent with their interest, or with the requirements of their local jurisdictions. Consumers, individuals, and ordinary cyber-contractors are not in the same position. When people lack the competence or advice to negotiate effectively, the effect is to shift control over such agreements from local courts and administration to whatever rule is built into the code. Thus, local governments lose control over the rules and the effective rule-maker shifts to cyberspace.

Another example pushes the public law dimension of this conflict more strongly. Think again about copyright law. The law of copyright establishes a set of rights that individuals have against the copyright owner. . . [F]or convenience, we can lump [these rights together] under the label "fair use." There is some controversy in the United States about the extent to which fair use rights can legitimately be modified by contract. In an important opinion, Judge Easterbrook of the 7th Circuit Court of Appeals said, in effect, that these rights can plainly be modified through contract. Thus, if you buy a piece of copyrighted work and promise to waive your rights of fair use, that promise, on this theory, can be held against you.

Easterbrook's conclusion might well make sense in real space, where there are real costs to contracting. In real space these costs prevent most copyrighted material from being wrapped in these anti-fair use agreements. The cost of real-space contracting creates a balance, tilting the result toward the protection of fair use.

But in cyberspace—especially when we consider the international dimensions to cyberspace—this balance is again skewed. If it becomes one of the rules of the space to click away fair use rights, then the balance of property and fair use so important to copyright's very design becomes skewed. Again, the architecture, and the rules it makes possible, conflict with real-space regimes. Once again, real-space sovereigns must decide how far they will allow this conflict to reach. . .

To the extent that architectures in cyberspace are the rules that affect behavior, the space is sovereign. In the sense that any set of normative commitments is sovereign, cyberspace is sovereign. But this sovereignty produces perpetual competition. The rules that govern cyberspace may be different from those that govern real space. As the rules that govern real space compete, cyberspace increasingly wins out. It is the norms, the freedom, the rules, and the law of the place that in an increasingly large range of cases govern the norms, the freedom, the rules, and the law of people also living here.

There is little question about how real-space sovereigns will respond to this. They will come to see that the power of another sovereign is wired into their telephones, and they will struggle (as the United States has done with hackers) as the rules and norms of this other sovereign affect the behavior of their citizens in their space. They have the tools at their disposal to resist the architecture of the Net to protect their regulatory power.

LICRA ET UEJF V. YAHOO! INC.

(Tribunal de Grande Instance de Paris, May 22, 2000).

[Yahoo! Inc. owns Yahoo.com, a website which includes a page marked "auctions" that offers items for sale including, among other things, Nazi relics, insignia, emblems, flags, and other objects. Yahoo.com also offers links to other pages on which various Nazi texts are sold, including *Mein Kampf* and *The Protocols of the Elders of Zion*. These same links include "Holocaust revisionist" material, such as aerial photos supposedly "proving" that no gas chambers ever existed. The Union des Etudiants Juifs de France (Jewish Students' Union of France, or UEJF) and the Ligue Contre le Racisme et l'Antisemitisme (League Against Racism and Antisemitism, or LICRA) sued Yahoo, alleging violations of article R.645–1 of the French Penal Code. They sought damages, an order commanding Yahoo to cease making this material available in France, and various other forms of specific relief.]

[Opinion delivered by the CHIEF JUSTICE.]

. . . Whereas it is not challenged that surfers who call up Yahoo.com from French territory may, directly or via the link offered by Yahoo.fr, see on their screens the pages, services and sites to which Yahoo.com gives access, in particular the auction service (Auctions) lodged by Geocities.com, the lodging service of Yahoo! Inc., in particular in its declension relating to Nazi objects;

Whereas the exposition for the purpose of sale of Nazi objects constitutes a violation of French law (article R.645–2 of the Criminal Code) as well as an offence against the collective memory of a country profoundly wounded by the atrocities committed by and in the name of a the Nazi criminal enterprise against its citizens and most importantly against its citizens of the Jewish religion;

Whereas while permitting the visualization in France of these objects and eventual participation of a surfer in France in such an exposition/sale, Yahoo! Inc. thus has committed a wrong on the territory of France, a wrong, the unintentional nature of which is apparent, but which is the cause of harm to the LICRA as well as the UEJF, which both have the mission of pursuing in France any and all forms of banalization of Nazism, regardless of the fact that the litigious activity is marginal in relation with the entire business of the auction sales service offered on its site Yahoo.com . . . ;

Whereas Yahoo! Inc. claims that it is technically impossible to control access to its auction service or any other service, and that therefore it cannot prohibit any surfer from France from visualizing same on his screen;

Whereas it wishes nevertheless to emphasize that it warns all visitors against any uses of its services for purposes that are "worthy of reprobation for whatsoever reason," such as for purposes of racial or ethnic discrimination;

But whereas Yahoo! Inc. is in a position to identify the geographical origin of the site which is coming to visit, based on the IP address of the caller, which should therefore enable it to prohibit surfers from France, by whatever means are appropriate, from accessing the services and sites the visualization of which on a screen set up in France . . . would be likely to be qualified in France as a crime and/or constitute a manifestly illegal nuisance within the meaning of articles 808 and 809 of New Code of Civil Procedure, which is manifestly the case of the exhibition of uniforms, insignia, emblems reminiscent of those worn or exhibited by the Nazis;

Whereas as regards surfers who navigate through sites which guarantee them anonymity, Yahoo! Inc. has fewer means of control except, for example, through refusing systematically access to such sites to all visitors who [do] not disclose their geographical origin;

Whereas the real difficulties encountered by Yahoo do not constitute insurmountable obstacles;

That [Yahoo] will therefore be ordered to take any and all measures of such kind as to dissuade and make impossible any consultations by surfers calling from France to sites and services [that] infringe upon the internal public order of France, especially the site selling Nazi objects;

Whereas there may usefully be a debate about the nature of such measures within the confines of these proceedings;

That Yahoo will be given two months to enable it to formulate proposals of technical measures likely to lead to a settlement of this dispute;

Whereas, as regards Yahoo France, it bears mentioning that its site Yahoo.fr does not itself offer surfers calling from France access to the sites or series the title and/or the contents of which constitute infractions of French law; that therefore, it does not provide access to the site or services for auction sales of Nazi objects;

But whereas it offers surfers a link to Yahoo.com entitled "further research on Yahoo.com," without any particular warning;

Or whereas, knowing what are the contents of the services offered by Yahoo.com, and in this case the service of auction sales including . . . the sale of Nazi objects, it behooves it to warn surfers, by a banner, prior to the surfer's entry into the Yahoo.com site, that should the result of his search on Yahoo.com . . . point toward sites, pages or forums the title and/or contents of which constitute a violation of French law . . . , it must interrupt the consultation of the site in question lest it incur the sanctions stipulated by French law or answer to legal actions which might be initiated against it; . . .

That whereas on the other hand, it is appropriate to apply the provisions of 700 of the New Code of Civil Procedure in favor of the plaintiffs;

NOW THEREFORE

At a public audience and rendering its judgment in first instance, after having heard all the parties, the Court:

* * *

Orders Yahoo! Inc. to take such measures as will dissuade and render impossible any and all consultation on Yahoo.com of the auction service for Nazi objects as well as any other site or service which makes apologies of Nazism or questions of the existence of Nazi crimes;

Orders Yahoo France to warn any and all surfers consulting Yahoo.fr [that they may access material that is illegal under French law, and to the extent such access occurs] it must interrupt the consultation of the relevant site lest it incur the sanctions stipulated by French law or answer to actions initiated against it;

Orders [a further hearing at] which Yahoo! Inc. shall submit the measures which it intends to implement to end the harm and the nuisance suffered by the plaintiffs and to prevent any new incidents of nuisance.

Finds Yahoo! Inc. liable to pay to the LICRA an amount of 10,000 Francs [approximately $1300] on the basis of article 700 of the New Code of Civil Procedure;

Finds Yahoo! Inc. and Yahoo France liable to pay to the UEJF an amount of 10,000 Francs on the basis of article 700 of the New Code of Civil Procedure;

Declares that no further measures are appropriate at this juncture;

Awards the costs of LICRA's action to be borne by Yahoo! Inc. and those of the UEJF by Yahoo! Inc. and Yahoo France.*

YAHOO!, INC. V. LA LIGUE CONTRE LE RACISME ET L'ANTISEMITISME, 169 F.Supp.2d 1181 (N.D. Cal. 2001). Following the French judgment, Yahoo! Inc. posted on Yahoo.fr a warning to French citizens that searches might lead them to items prohibited by Article R-645-1 and that viewing such items might subject them to liability. It also amended the auction policy of Yahoo.com to prohibit individuals from auctioning

> [a]ny item that promotes, glorifies, or is directly associated with groups or individuals known principally for hateful or violent positions or acts, such as Nazis or the Ku Klux Klan. Official government-issue stamps and coins are not prohibited under this policy. Expressive media, such as books and films, may be subject to more permissive standards as determined by Yahoo! in its sole discretion.

Nonetheless, prohibited items continued to appear on the Yahoo.com auction site. Yahoo subsequently brought suit in federal district court seeking a declaratory judgment that the French order could not be enforced in the United States. Yahoo argued that because it was technologically incapable of preventing French citizens from accessing Yahoo.com, it could not block their access to prohibited items without excluding the items from Yahoo.com entirely, something the First Amendment guaranteed that it could not be required to do. Judge Fogel began by framing the issues:

> This case is *not* about the moral acceptability of promoting the symbols or propaganda of Nazism. . .
>
> Nor is this case about the right of France or any other nation to determine its own law and social policies. A basic function of a sovereign state is to determine by law what forms of speech and conduct are acceptable within its borders. In this instance, as a nation whose citizens suffered the effects of Nazism in ways that are incomprehensible to most Americans, France clearly has the

* The court issued a further opinion on August 11, 2000, concluding that it still lacked sufficient information to evaluate whether, as Yahoo claimed, the technological means to block access to prohibited sites did not yet exist. The court appointed a panel of specialists to investigate the matter.

right to enact and enforce laws such as those relied upon by the French Court here. * * *

What *is* at issue here is whether it is consistent with the Constitution and laws of the United States for another nation to regulate speech by a United States resident within the United States on the basis that such speech can be accessed by Internet users in that nation. In a world in which ideas and information transcend borders and the Internet in particular renders the physical distance between speaker and audience virtually meaningless, the implications of this question go far beyond the facts of this case. The modern world is home to widely varied cultures with radically divergent value systems. There is little doubt that Internet users in the United States routinely engage in speech that violates, for example, China's laws against religious expression, the laws of various nations against advocacy of gender equality or homosexuality, or even the United Kingdom's restrictions on freedom of the press. If the government or another party in one of these sovereign nations were to seek enforcement of such laws against Yahoo! or another U.S.-based Internet service provider, what principles should guide the court's analysis?

The Court has stated that it must and will decide this case in accordance with the Constitution and laws of the United States. It recognizes that in so doing, it necessarily adopts certain value judgments embedded in those enactments, including the fundamental judgment expressed in the First Amendment that it is preferable to permit the non-violent expression of offensive viewpoints rather than to impose viewpoint-based governmental regulation upon speech. The government and people of France have made a different judgment based upon their own experience. In undertaking its inquiry as to the proper application of the laws of the United States, the Court intends no disrespect for that judgment or for the experience that has informed it.

Judge Fogel next reasoned that because an American law similar to the French law would violate the First Amendment, a United States court was constitutionally prohibited from enforcing a judgment based on that law. He then considered the matter from the perspective of comity.

No legal judgment has any effect, of its own force, beyond the limits of the sovereignty from which its authority is derived. * * * The extent to which the United States, or any state, honors the judicial decrees of foreign nations is a matter of choice, governed by "the comity of nations." * * * United States courts generally recognize foreign judgments and decrees unless enforcement would be prejudicial or contrary to the country's interests.

> As discussed previously, the French order's content and viewpoint-based regulation of the web pages and auction site on Yahoo.com, while entitled to great deference as an articulation of French law, clearly would be inconsistent with the First Amendment if mandated by a court in the United States. What makes this case uniquely challenging is that the Internet in effect allows one to speak in more than one place at the same time. Although France has the sovereign right to regulate what speech is permissible in France, this Court may not enforce a foreign order that violates the protections of the United States Constitution by chilling protected speech that occurs simultaneously within our borders. . . The reason for limiting comity in this area is sound. "The protection to free speech and the press embodied in [the First] amendment would be seriously jeopardized by the entry of foreign [ ] judgments granted pursuant to standards deemed appropriate in [another country] but considered antithetical to the protections afforded the press by the U.S. Constitution." * * * Absent a body of law that establishes international standards with respect to speech on the Internet and an appropriate treaty or legislation addressing enforcement of such standards to speech originating within the United States, the principle of comity is outweighed by the Court's obligation to uphold the First Amendment.

On appeal, a panel of the Ninth Circuit vacated the district court decision on the grounds that the court lacked personal jurisdiction over LICRA. See Yahoo! Inc. v. LICRA, 379 F.3d 1120 (9th Cir. 2004). In February 2005, the Ninth Circuit granted en banc review and vacated the panel opinion. See Yahoo! Inc. v. LICRA, 399 F.3d 1010 (9th Cir. 2005). Finally, in January 2006, the en banc court issued a decision. See Yahoo! Inc. v. LICRA, 433 F.3d 1199 (9th Cir. 2006). Of the eleven judges on the en banc court, eight found that personal jurisdiction existed and three did not. But three of the eight judges finding personal jurisdiction believed the case did not meet prudential ripeness standards, in large part because of uncertainty about whether Yahoo!'s compliance measures eliminated the threat of enforcement of the French judgment and about the effect on U.S. Internet users of any further measures Yahoo! might be ordered to take. Six judges thus voted to dismiss the case without prejudice, and the court did so.

(For a fuller exploration of the conflicts problems presented by personal jurisdiction and recognition of judgments, see Chapters 4 and 5 respectively.)

GOOGLE INC. V. EQUUSTEK SOLUTIONS INC.

2017 SCC 34 (28 June 2017).
Supreme Court of Canada.

ABELLA J.

The issue in this appeal is whether Google can be ordered, pending a trial, to globally de-index the websites of a company which, in breach of several court orders, is using those websites to unlawfully sell the intellectual property of another company. The answer turns on classic interlocutory injunction jurisprudence: is there a serious issue to be tried; would irreparable harm result if the injunction were not granted; and does the balance of convenience favour granting or refusing the injunction. Ultimately, the question is whether granting the injunction would be just and equitable in all the circumstances of the case.

Background

Equustek Solutions Inc. is a small technology company in British Columbia. It manufactures networking devices that allow complex industrial equipment made by one manufacturer to communicate with complex industrial equipment made by another manufacturer.

[Equustek] claimed that Datalink, while acting as a distributor of Equustek's products, began to re-label one of the products and pass it off as its own. Datalink also acquired confidential information and trade secrets belonging to Equustek, using them to design and manufacture a competing product, the GW1000. Any orders for Equustek's product were filled with the GW1000. When Equustek discovered this in 2011, it terminated the distribution agreement it had with Datalink and demanded that Datalink delete all references to Equustek's products and trademarks on its websites. . .

Despite [several] court orders prohibiting the sale of inventory and the use of Equustek's intellectual property, Datalink continues to carry on its business from an unknown location, selling its impugned product on its websites to customers all over the world.

Not knowing where Datalink or its suppliers were, and finding itself unable to have the websites removed by the websites' hosting companies, Equustek approached Google in September 2012 and requested that it de-index the Datalink websites. Google refused. Equustek then brought court proceedings seeking an order requiring Google to do so.

When it was served with the application materials, Google asked Equustek to obtain a court order prohibiting Datalink from carrying on business on the Internet. Google told Equustek it would comply with such an order by removing specific webpages. Pursuant to its internal policy, Google only voluntarily de-indexes individual webpages, not entire websites. Equustek agreed to try this approach. . . .

Equustek soon discovered that de-indexing webpages but not entire websites was ineffective since Datalink simply moved the objectionable content to new pages within its websites, circumventing the court orders.

Google had limited the de-indexing to those searches that were conducted on google.ca. . . . Internet users with Canadian Internet Protocol addresses are directed to "google.ca" when performing online searches. But users can also access different Google websites directed at other countries by using the specific Uniform Resource Locator, or URL, for those sites. That means that someone in Vancouver, for example, can access the Google search engine as though he or she were in another country simply by typing in that country's Google URL. Potential Canadian customers could, as a result, find Datalink's websites even if they were blocked on google.ca. Given that the majority of the sales of Datalink's GW1000 were to purchasers outside of Canada, Google's de-indexing did not have the necessary protective effect.

Equustek therefore sought an interlocutory injunction to enjoin Google from displaying any part of the Datalink websites on any of its search results worldwide. . . . For the following reasons, . . . the test for granting an interlocutory injunction against Google has been met in this case.

Analysis

. . . Google does not dispute that there is a serious claim. Nor does it dispute that Equustek is suffering irreparable harm as a result of Datalink's ongoing sale of the GW1000 through the Internet. And it acknowledges . . . that it inadvertently facilitates the harm through its search engine which leads purchasers directly to the Datalink websites.

Google argues, however, that the injunction issued against it is not necessary to prevent that irreparable harm, and that it is not effective in so doing. Moreover, it argues that as a non-party, it should be immune from the injunction. As for the balance of convenience, it challenges the propriety and necessity of the extraterritorial reach of such an order, and raises freedom of expression concerns that it says should have tipped the balance against granting the order. . .

Google's first argument is, in essence, that non-parties cannot be the subject of an interlocutory injunction. With respect, this is contrary to the jurisprudence. Not only can injunctive relief be ordered against someone who is not a party to the underlying lawsuit, the contours of the test are not changed. . .

In other words, where a non-party violates a court order, there is a principled basis for treating the non-party as if it had been bound by the order. The non-party's obligation arises "not because [it] is bound by the injunction by being a party to the cause, but because [it] is conducting [itself] so as to obstruct the course of justice." . . .

Google's next argument is the impropriety of issuing an interlocutory injunction with extraterritorial effect. But this too contradicts the existing jurisprudence.

The British Columbia courts in these proceedings concluded that because Google carried on business in the province through its advertising and search operations, this was sufficient to establish the existence of *in personam* and territorial jurisdiction. Google does not challenge those findings. It challenges instead the global reach of the resulting order. Google suggests that if any injunction is to be granted, it should be limited to Canada (or google.ca) alone.

When a court has *in personam* jurisdiction, and where it is necessary to ensure the injunction's effectiveness, it can grant an injunction enjoining that person's conduct anywhere in the world. * * *

[The trial judge] explained why Equustek's request that the order have worldwide effect was necessary as follows:

> The majority of GW1000 sales occur outside Canada. Thus, quite apart from the practical problem of endless website iterations, the option Google proposes is not equivalent to the order now sought which would compel Google to remove the [Datalink] websites from all search results generated by any of Google's websites worldwide. I therefore conclude that [Equustek does] not have an out-of-court remedy available to [it]. . . [T]o be effective, even within Canada, Google must block search results on all of its websites.

. . . The problem in this case is occurring online and globally. The Internet has no borders—its natural habitat is global. The only way to ensure that the interlocutory injunction attained its objective was to have it apply where Google operates—globally. . . [The] majority of Datalink's sales take place outside Canada. If the injunction were restricted to Canada alone or to google.ca, as Google suggests it should have been, the remedy would be deprived of its intended ability to prevent irreparable harm. Purchasers outside Canada could easily continue purchasing from Datalink's websites, and Canadian purchasers could easily find Datalink's websites even if those websites were de-indexed on google.ca. Google would still be facilitating Datalink's breach of the court's order which had prohibited it from carrying on business on the Internet. There is no equity in ordering an interlocutory injunction which has no realistic prospect of preventing irreparable harm. . .

Nor does the injunction's worldwide effect tip the balance of convenience in Google's favour. The order does not require that Google take any steps around the world, it requires it to take steps only where its search engine is controlled. This is something Google has acknowledged it can do—and does—with relative ease. There is therefore no harm to Google which can be placed on its "inconvenience" scale arising from the global reach of the order.

Google's argument that a global injunction violates international comity because it is possible that the order could not have been obtained in a foreign jurisdiction, or that to comply with it would result in Google violating the laws of that jurisdiction is, with respect, theoretical. As [the trial judge] noted, "Google acknowledges that most countries will likely recognize intellectual property rights and view the selling of pirated products as a legal wrong".

And while it is always important to pay respectful attention to freedom of expression concerns, particularly when dealing with the core values of another country, I do not see freedom of expression issues being engaged in any way that tips the balance of convenience towards Google in this case.

. . . If Google has evidence that complying with such an injunction would require it to violate the laws of another jurisdiction, including interfering with freedom of expression, it is always free to apply to the British Columbia courts to vary the interlocutory order accordingly. To date, Google has made no such application.

In the absence of an evidentiary foundation, and given Google's right to seek a rectifying order, it hardly seems equitable to deny Equustek the extraterritorial scope it needs to make the remedy effective, or even to put the onus on it to demonstrate, country by country, where such an order is legally permissible. We are dealing with the Internet after all, and the balance of convenience test has to take full account of its inevitable extraterritorial reach when injunctive relief is being sought against an entity like Google.

This is not an order to remove speech that, on its face, engages freedom of expression values, it is an order to de-index websites that are in violation of several court orders. We have not, to date, accepted that freedom of expression requires the facilitation of the unlawful sale of goods.

And I have trouble seeing how this interferes with what Google refers to as its content neutral character. The injunction does not require Google to monitor content on the Internet, nor is it a finding of any sort of liability against Google for facilitating access to the impugned websites. As for the balance of convenience, the only obligation the interlocutory injunction creates is for Google to de-index the Datalink websites. . . Even if it could be said that the injunction engages freedom of expression issues, this is far outweighed by the need to prevent the irreparable harm that would result from Google's facilitating Datalink's breach of court orders.

Google did not suggest that it would be inconvenienced in any material way, or would incur any significant expense, in de-indexing the Datalink websites. It acknowledges, fairly, that it can, and often does, exactly what is being asked of it in this case, that is, alter search results. It does so to avoid generating links to child pornography and websites containing "hate speech". It also complies with notices it receives under the US *Digital Millennium Copyright Act*, Pub. L. No. 105–304, 112 Stat. 2680 (1998) to de-index content from its search results that allegedly infringes copyright, and removes websites that are subject to court orders. . .

Datalink and its representatives have ignored all previous court orders made against them, have left British Columbia, and continue to operate their business from unknown locations outside Canada. Equustek has made efforts to locate Datalink with limited success. Datalink is only able to survive—at the expense of Equustek's survival—on Google's search engine which directs potential customers to its websites. In other words, Google is how Datalink has been able to continue harming Equustek in defiance of several court orders.

This does not make Google liable for this harm. It does, however, make Google the determinative player in allowing the harm to occur. On balance, therefore, since the interlocutory injunction is the only effective way to mitigate the harm to Equustek pending the resolution of the underlying litigation, the only way, in fact, to preserve Equustek itself pending the resolution of the underlying litigation, and since any countervailing harm to Google is minimal to non-existent, the interlocutory injunction should be upheld.

CÔTÉ and ROWE JJ. [dissenting].

[Equustek] seek a novel form of equitable relief—an effectively permanent injunction, against an innocent third party, that requires court supervision, has not been shown to be effective, and for which alternative remedies are available. Our response calls for judicial restraint. While the court had jurisdiction to issue the . . . order against Google Inc. * * *, in our view it should have refrained from doing so. The authority to grant equitable remedies has always been constrained by doctrine and practice. In our view, the Google Order slipped too easily from these constraints. . .

The most that can be said is that the Google Order might reduce the harm to Equustek which Fenlon J. found "Google is inadvertently facilitating" * * *. But it has not been shown that the Google Order is effective in doing so. As Google points out, Datalink's websites can be found using other search engines, links from other sites, bookmarks, email, social media, printed material, word-of-mouth, or other indirect means. Datalink's websites are open for business on the Internet whether Google searches list them or not. In our view, this lack of effectiveness suggests restraint in granting the Google Order.

Moreover, the quest for elusive effectiveness led to the Google Order having worldwide effect. This effect should be taken into consideration as a factor in exercising discretion. . . [T]erritorial limitations to equitable jurisdiction are "to some extent determined by reference to questions of effectiveness and of comity" * * *. While the worldwide effect of the Google Order does not make it more effective, it could raise concerns regarding comity. . .

Highlighting the lack of effectiveness are the alternatives available to Equustek. An equitable remedy is not required unless there is no other appropriate remedy at law * * *. In our view, Equustek has an alternative remedy in law. Datalink has assets in France. . . [The] Court of Appeal for British Columbia urged Equustek to pursue a remedy in French courts: "At present, it appears that the proposed defendants reside in France . . . . The information before the Court is that French courts will assume jurisdiction and entertain an application to freeze the assets in that country" * * *. We see no reason why Equustek cannot do what the Court of Appeal urged it to do. Equustek could also pursue injunctive relief against the ISPs. . . In addition, Equustek could initiate contempt proceedings in France or in any other jurisdiction with a link to the illegal websites. . .

Conflict of Laws and the Internet

(1) The development of new technologies—the railroad, the airplane, the telegraph, the telephone, and so on—invariably and predictably puts a strain on choice of law. By increasing the feasibility and velocity of acting across geographical boundaries, such improvements in transportation and communications technology multiply conflict situations in ways that may pressure existing forms of legal regulation. But how to adapt? What do we do with all the law developed to regulate transportation in a world of horses after the railroad has been invented? Can we modify existing rules to conform to the peculiarities of a new technology, or must we radically reconceive our whole approach? Claims that the Internet is producing a revolution in human interaction have become commonplace—though there have also been notable rebuttals—and an enormous amount of ink has been spilled (and bits transmitted) discussing how to regulate virtual interactions.

Do *LICRA v. Yahoo* and *Google v. Equustek* raise distinctive questions because they involve the Internet? Are existing principles (including choice-of-law rules or approaches) adequate to resolve these questions? Why or why not? (You might want to revisit some of these issues after you've read about recognition and enforcement of judgments in Chapter 5, infra.)

Did the French judgment in *LICRA et UELF v. Yahoo* give French law extraterritorial effect? Did the district court's decision in *Yahoo v. LICRA* give the First Amendment extraterritorial effect? If so, was this impermissible? Was the Ninth Circuit panel right to conclude that LICRA had not done enough to subject itself to personal jurisdiction in California? (The jurisdiction of courts is explored in Chapter 4, infra.)

Was it realistic for Google to argue that the Canadian court should have ordered it to de-list Datalink's websites only on google.ca? Only for Canadian users? Does the Supreme Court of Canada's broader remedy effectively give worldwide effect to Canadian law?

The Canadian Supreme Court doubted that this dispute between two tech companies over trade secrets would generate international conflicts. If Google feared that complying with the injunction would require it to violate another country's laws, the court said, it could seek modification of the injunction. But is that the right inquiry? What if an American court determined, as in the Yahoo case, that it would violate the First Amendment for it to enforce the Google injunction? And what if, say, a Turkish court cited *Google v. Equustek* as the basis for requiring Google or Facebook to silence critics of the Turkish president worldwide by making their criticisms essentially impossible to find online?

(2) If the commercial dispute in *Google v. Equustek* seems far removed from freedom-of-speech concerns, consider the "right to be forgotten." In *Google Spain SL v. Agencia Española de Protección de Datos*, Case C–131/12 (May 13, 2014), the Court of Justice of the European Union (ECJ) held that Internet search engine operators must consider requests by individuals to remove links containing personal information from their search results if the information is inaccurate, inadequate, irrelevant, or excessive. *Id.* ¶ 93. Google has since reviewed more than 1.5 million webpages in response to requests for de-listing, granting nearly half of them. In 2016, Google announced that it would use geolocation signals such as IP addresses to ensure that de-listed search results could not be accessed from the country of the person who requested their removal. That wasn't good enough for the French data protection agency, CNIL, which fined Google €100,000 for its refusal to de-list the offending links worldwide. Google appealed, and in September 2019 the ECJ arrived at a middle ground, holding that search engine operators do not have to de-list worldwide but must do so on the versions of their search engines corresponding to the EU member nations. *Google LLC v. CNIL*, Case C–507/17 (September 24, 2019). If the ECJ had ordered worldwide de-listing and Google sought a declaration from a U.S. court that such an order violated the First Amendment as applied to U.S. users, what result?

(3) Consider the following choice-of-law issues raised by the Internet.

(a) *Defamation.*

Dow Jones publishes periodicals including The Wall Street Journal, Barron's, and the Dow Jones Newswire. The October 29, 2000 issue of Barron's online edition contained an article that made allegedly defamatory references to Joseph Gutnick, an Australian businessman and philanthropist. Gutnick brought a defamation suit in Australia, seeking damages under Australian law for injury to his reputation in Australia.

Australia follows lex loci delicti. Dow Jones, seeking the protection of the First Amendment, argued that the alleged tort was committed in New Jersey, the physical location of the servers on which the article was hosted. The High Court of Australia held that publication occurred where the article was downloaded, as did damage, and that Australian law should apply. *Gutnick v. Dow Jones*, [2002] HCA 56 (High Court of Australia, 2002). How worried should Dow Jones have been about an Australian judgment? (The case was settled for $440,000.) Would an individual blogger have more to worry about?

Following high-profile UK judgments against American authors, Congress in 2010 enacted the creatively named Securing the Protection of our Enduring and Established Constitutional Heritage (SPEECH) Act. The SPEECH Act provides that U.S. courts may not recognize foreign defamation judgments unless (a) the defamation law applied by the foreign court provided at least as much protection for freedom of speech and press as the First Amendment and the law of the State in which the U.S. court is located; or (b) the party opposing recognition or enforcement of the foreign judgment would have been found liable for defamation by a domestic court. 28 U.S.C. § 4102(a)(1). Does this seem like a good solution?

(b) *Internet domain names.*

In 1995, Dale Mayberry, a resident of Virginia, registered "rl.com," a domain name that eventually proved to be of interest to Ralph Lauren among others. Later, through a series of purchases, a California citizen named John Laxton gained control of the domain name, claiming that Mayberry had let his registration expire. Mayberry sued Laxton in California district court, alleging state-law causes of action including conversion and unfair competition. Under California law, domain names are intangible personal property; under Virginia law, according to Laxton, they were governed by contract law.

Applying California's choice-of-law rules, the Ninth Circuit held that the case was a false conflict and that California substantive law applied. *CRS Recovery, Inc. v. Laxton*, 600 F.3d 1138 (9th Cir. 2010). Even if Virginia courts rejected the treatment of domain names as property, "Virginia is concerned with protecting Virginia residents who purchase domain names *from* property claims, not *from asserting* property claims. Yet the defendant-purchaser, Laxton, is from California, not Virginia." Id. at 1143. Meanwhile, "California's policy in treating domain names as property is . . . accurately characterized as protecting the rightful holders of domain names, encouraging investment in and development of that property"—even if the plaintiff is not a Californian. Id. at 1144. Finally, because the alleged tortious conduct occurred in California, that state had a deterrent interest. Id.

The court concluded with a more general observation about choice of law in domain name litigation:

> Holding otherwise would encourage a race to the bottom, allowing purchasers of potentially disputed domain names, as well as cybersquatters, to reside or operate in states where intangible property is provided little or no protection from potentially tortious conversion. Such a situation could vitiate the intangible property rights of the true holders of such property notwithstanding states' well-intentioned efforts to protect these intellectual property interests.

Did the court read Virginia's interests too narrowly? Why is California interested in protecting nondomiciliaries if Virginia isn't? Can the place of the tortious conduct be identified here? In its passage about the need to avoid a "race to the bottom," is the court just weighing the competing states' interests? Or is it performing a kind of comparative impairment analysis? Finally, did the fact that the fact pattern involved the Internet change anything, or was this a garden variety conflicts case? For critical commentary on *CRS Recovery*, see Andrews & Newman, *Personal Jurisdiction and Choice of Law in the Cloud*, 73 Md. L. Rev. 313, 376–81 (2013).

(c) *Pornography and community standards.*

Whether something is "obscene" depends in part on whether the average person, "applying contemporary community standards" would find that the work appeals to "the prurient interest" and is "patently offensive." *Miller v. California,* 413 U.S. 15, 30–34 (1973). But whose community standards apply to material on the Internet? In *United States v. Thomas,* 74 F.3d 701, 711 (6th Cir.1996), the court said "[i]ssues regarding which community's standards are to be applied are tied to those involving venue . . . and obscenity is determined by the standards of the community where the trial takes place." Should prosecutors be allowed to forum-shop by downloading material in communities with restrictive standards (an Old Order Amish village?) and bringing prosecutions there?

In *American Civil Liberties Union v. Reno*, 217 F.3d 162 (3d Cir. 2000), the Third Circuit said no. The Child Online Protection Act ("COPA") prohibited individuals from making material "harmful to minors" available to minors on the World Wide Web. The "harmful to minors" standard essentially follows the *Miller* obscenity test but applies each factor with respect to minors, in practice allowing the government somewhat greater leeway. But like the *Miller* test it requires application of contemporary community standards. The court concluded that the impossibility of screening website visitors by geography, and the possibility of prosecutorial forum-shopping, meant that Web material was effectively subjected to the standards of the most restrictive community, and that COPA was unconstitutionally overbroad for that reason alone. Do you agree?

The Supreme Court did not. Finding the overbreadth not sufficiently substantial, it vacated the Third Circuit's opinion in *Ashcroft v. ACLU*, 535 U.S. 564 (2002). The ACLU eventually prevailed on the theory that less restrictive alternatives such as filtering software were available. See *Ashcroft v. ACLU*, 542 U.S. 656 (2004).

(d) *Trademark and unfair competition.*

In *Silverlit Toys Manufactory, Ltd. v. Absolute Toy Marketing, Inc.*, 2007 WL 521239 (N.D. Cal.), a Hong Kong toy manufacturer brought an action in a California federal district court against a Utah corporation that operated an online toy shopping website, alleging that the defendant was marketing and distributing remote control toy helicopters throughout the United States, including in California, that were similar to the plaintiff's products. Most of the claims were governed by federal copyright and trademark law. As to the remaining state-law claims for common-law trademark and trade name infringement, unfair competition, and common-law passing off and disparagement, the court concluded that, "[a]s with many cases involving the internet, no jurisdiction has a particularly strong connection to this case. The marketing and sale of goods over the internet occurred on a national scale. Therefore, the alleged injury occurred wherever a consumer bought a product." Id. at *11. And in denying the defendant's motion for transfer to a district court in Utah, the court reasoned that "[b]ecause internet cases affect all jurisdictions, Utah law is not applicable in this case" and California law applied.

Why should a Hong Kong plaintiff get the benefit of California law simply by filing there? Is the court effectively adopting a *lex fori* approach for Internet cases? Can you do better?

Does the Internet Change Everything?

(1) As Professor Lessig explains in the excerpt that opens this subsection, a basic question hovers over all of these materials: Does the Internet fundamentally alter—or even uproot—the entire landscape of conflicts? Consider the following views:

(a) In an influential early article, Professors Johnson and Post criticize the impulse to choose among the laws of geographically defined sovereign states:

> Because events on the Net occur everywhere but nowhere in particular, are engaged in by online personae who are both "real"

> (possessing reputations, able to perform services, and deploy intellectual assets) and "intangible" (not necessarily or traceably tied to any particular person in the physical sense), and concern "things" (messages, databases, standing relationships) that are not necessarily separated from one another by any physical boundaries, no physical jurisdiction has a more compelling claim than any other to subject these events exclusively to its laws.

Johnson & Post, *Law And Borders—The Rise of Law in Cyberspace,* 48 Stan. L. Rev. 1367, 1379 (1996). To similar effect, the court in *ACLU v. Reno*, 217 F.3d 162, 169 (3d Cir. 2000), memorably opined that the Internet "negates geometry . . . it is fundamentally and profoundly anti-spatial. You cannot say where it is or describe its memorable shape and proportions or tell a stranger how to get there. But you can find things in it without knowing where they are. The [Internet] is ambient—nowhere in particular and everywhere at once." (citation omitted). Is this description accurate as applied to *Yahoo* or the other situations presented above?

Johnson and Post argue that geographic boundaries generally make sense for law only because (1) sovereignty and statehood are defined in terms of *power* over physical space; (2) physical space is where the *effects* of behavior are typically felt; (3) as a matter of *legitimacy*, "[w]e generally accept the notion that the persons within a geographically defined border are the ultimate source of law-making authority for activities within that border"; and (4) parties need *notice* of the applicable law, and geographical boundaries "are generally well-equipped to serve this signpost function." Id. at 1369–70. The Internet, they say, subverts all four premises, and should be conceived "as a distinct 'place' for purposes of legal analysis by recognizing a legally significant border between Cyberspace and the 'real world.' " Id. at 1378. Rules governing the behavior that takes place on the Internet, they continue, can be expected to emerge naturally, as online users and service providers bring order to anarchy and find meaningful ways to accomplish their ends and govern themselves. Id. at 1387–91.

But what should we do when conflicts arise between local territorial laws and the "law" created by net users? "The doctrine of 'comity,' " they answer, "as well as principles applied when delegating authority to self-regulatory organizations provide us with guidance for reconciling such disputes." Id. at 1391.

Should state and federal governments just delegate this sort of broad lawmaking authority to private lawmaking bodies? Can they do so? See Metzger, *Privatization as Delegation,* 103 Colum. L. Rev. 1367 (2003) (discussing constitutional problems with delegating too much unsupervised authority to private agencies). Even if it can be done, and even if users of cyberspace do develop their own rules, how useful is the conflict resolution principle offered by Johnson and Post?

For a more modern, and somewhat more modest, version of Johnson and Post's argument, see Daskal, *The Un-Territoriality of Data*, 125 Yale L. J. 326 (2015), which argues that "data's mobility, divisibility, location independence, intermingling, and third party control" undercuts the law's often dispositive focus on where events occur in the physical world. *Id.* at 366.

(b) Professor Goldsmith disputes Johnson's and Post's basic claim that cyberspace is a unique place that cannot be governed by existing choice-of-law doctrine:

> The internet is not, as many suggest, a separate place removed from our world. Like the telephone, the telegraph, and the smoke signal, the Internet is a medium through which people in real space in one jurisdiction communicate with people in real space in another jurisdiction. [A] nation's prerogative to control events within its territory entails the power to regulate the local effects of extraterritorial acts. When a person abroad uses the Internet to produce harmful local effects, the local sovereign is justified in regulating these local effects.

Goldsmith, *The Internet and the Abiding Significance of Territorial Sovereignty*, 5 Ind. J. Global Legal Stud. 475, 476–77 (1998). With this as his starting point, Goldsmith challenges every element of the Johnson and Post position. By mistakenly assuming that what happens on the Internet has no effects beyond the Internet, he argues, Johnson and Post miss the very reason for preserving national regulation: "Cyberspace users solicit and deliver kiddie porn, launder money, sexually harass, defraud, and so on. It is these and many other real-space costs—costs that cyberspace communities cannot effectively internalize—that national regulatory regimes worry about and aim to regulate." Goldsmith, *Against Cyberanarchy,* 65 U. Chi. L. Rev. at 1199, 1242 (1998). He argues as well that filtering and identification technologies such as geolocation make it possible to reduce potential "spillover" effects from allowing one country to regulate Internet use; at the very least, these problems are no worse than or different from similar problems imposed by regulating pollution, securities trading, or antitrust activity. Id. at 1240–42.

Cyberspace transactions, Goldsmith concludes, "do not inherently warrant any more deference by national regulators, and are not significantly less resistant to the tools of conflict of laws, than other transnational transactions." Id. at 1201. To be sure, he concedes, the problem of choosing a single law can be complex, particularly when contacts with multiple jurisdictions make it difficult to pinpoint the exact location where an event occurred. But these sorts of problems inhere in all sorts of transnational conflicts, such as mass torts or contracts; they are neither unique nor particularly exacerbated when it comes to cyberspace.

Moreover, while territorial criteria may prove difficult to apply to the Internet, domicile and its cognates, such as principal place of business, habitual residence, can be used. Id. at 1236. For an updated statement of Goldsmith's thesis, illustrated by historical case studies and further technological developments, see Goldsmith & Wu, Who Controls the Internet: Illusions of a Borderless World (2006).

To what extent does the argument depend upon a particular technological balance of power between governments and those they seek to regulate? Can we expect this to stabilize, or is an oscillating cycle (or an "arms race") the more likely pattern? (Consider the history of music filesharing and the various legal and technological weapons deployed by both sides.) Who is responsible for assuring that the architecture of the Internet facilitates governmental regulation? And even assuming we can make digital space replicate real space or facilitate traditional forms of real space regulation, is it so obviously clear that we should do so?

For a more recent version of the Goldsmith thesis, see Woods, *Against Data Exceptionalism*, 68 Stan. L. Rev. 729 (2016), which argues that, "[c]ontrary to prevailing wisdom, jurisdiction over cloud-based data has nearly everything to do with territoriality—it requires an inquiry into the location of the data, the domicile of the data controller, the location of the crime, the citizenship of the victim, and/or the citizenship of the perpetrator. . . . [C]onflict[ ] of laws casebooks are filled with such disputes, and the fact that the subject of the dispute is Internet data changes very little as a conceptual matter." Id. at 735.

(c) Without going so far as Johnson and Post, Professor Yochai Benkler criticizes Goldsmith for failing to appreciate how technological solutions like filtering or identification may, in fact, still fail to solve or even exacerbate problems. Goldsmith, he observes, assumes that organizations subject to regulation by multiple jurisdictions can protect themselves by requiring users to identify their country of origin. In order to implement this technological solution, however, "a multi-jurisdictional actor must reconfigure its relationships with *all* its users, regardless of national origin, in order to exclude those users from contact with those who would subject it to regulation. Pervasive adoption of such strategies by multi-jurisdictional actors will, in turn, pervasively alter the relationships of users to information they seek." Benkler, *Internet Regulation: A Case Study in the Problem of Unilateralism,* 11 Eur. J. Int'l L. 171, 174 (2000). Benkler illustrates his point with the following example:

> One might imagine that nation A abhors pornography, while nation B cherishes privacy and its implementing mode of communication—anonymity. The effect of an information provider's adaptation to the regulation of A by seeking identification from all users everywhere is to negate the

possibility of the implementation of state B's public policy of facilitating anonymous communication.

Id. How serious is this problem? Is it what is happening in *Yahoo*? In *Equustek*? Is it unique to the Internet? Do conflict-of-laws solutions require the complete elimination of extraterritorial effects to be acceptable? See Goldsmith, 5 Ind. J. Global Legal Stud. at 488–89 ("spillover" effects are inevitable and have long been accepted).

(d) In the excerpt you read above, Professor Lessig suggests that both sides in this debate are exaggerating: while some form of government regulation is both possible and appropriate, he says, existing choice-of-law rules are inadequate because "the legal tools we have used to resolve these questions before were not designed to deal with conflicts among citizens. They were designed to deal with conflicts among institutions, or relatively sophisticated actors." Based on the materials you have studied in Chapters 1 and 2, is this an accurate characterization? Is Lessig's analogy to copyright law (and the power of the Internet to make everyone a publisher) an appropriate one for choice of law?

(2) To what extent does the ability of existing choice-of-law tools to handle cyberspace turn on which approach one uses? Are some choice-of-law approaches more or less useful? How should *Yahoo* or *Equustek* be resolved under the First Restatement? The Second Restatement? Interest analysis? Professor Goldsmith seems to concede that the traditional approach, with its reliance on identifying the situs of particular events, may not work in cyberspace. See also Y. Benkler, Rules of the Road for the Information Superhighway: Electronic Communications and the Law 625 (1996) ("Courts applying traditional doctrines . . . will find themselves entangled in a variety of questions for which their physical-space-based conceptual framework will leave them unprepared.") Does that mean that states adhering to the traditional approach must change their views after all? The problem is by no means unimportant, as most countries outside the United States still use some form of jurisdiction-selecting rules that depend on specifying where some event took place.

Professor Benkler also agrees with Goldsmith that "American courts applying the contemporary American approach are likely to find electronic transactions not significantly different from any other transaction, because it is an approach that already focuses on the interests of people and societies, not on places." Id. Is that right? (What is "the" contemporary American approach anyway?)

(3) As fascinating as these theoretical debates may be, does the Internet really pose a serious *practical* problem for choice of law? Professor Swire argues that it doesn't, outside of a few areas such as intellectual property and defamation law. Several mechanisms, he argues,

> have reduced the possibility of incessant choice-of-law disputes down to [a] handful of cases. Four significant filters exist before a court must choose among conflicting national laws: technology's ability to trump law; lack of jurisdiction over defendants; the harmonization of diverse laws; and the existence of self-regulatory and other systems that suppress choice-of-law conflicts for transactions. For . . . business sales to consumers over the Internet[,] this last filter has proven decisive in avoiding choice-of-law conflicts.

Swire, *Elephants and Mice Revisited: Law and Choice of Law on the Internet*, 153 U. Pa. L. Rev. 1975, 1976 (2005). Are you convinced?

SECTION 7. THE THIRD RESTATEMENT

RESTATEMENT (THIRD) OF CONFLICT OF LAWS (2021)

Tentative Draft No. 2—Introduction (xix–xxi).

The early American understanding of choice of law, and the position taken by the American Law Institute's first Restatement, was territorial. A single act or event was used to localize legal transactions such as torts or contracts, and the state within whose borders that act or even occurred was selected as the state whose law would govern. This approach was thought to follow from the nature of law.

The territorial principle came under sustained attack, beginning around the publication of the first Restatement in 1935. Judges and scholars argued that consideration of the policies behind states' laws showed that the answers provided by the territorial system were often arbitrary, frustrating the policies of states whose law was not selected while not advancing the policies of those whose law was selected.

Analysis in terms of state policies suggested that using a single territorial factor to select the governing law was a mistake. Instead, the choice-of-law revolution suggested that multiple connecting factors might be relevant. These included not just territorial connecting factors—like the place of conduct or injury, or of the formation of a contract—but also personal connecting factors, like the domicile of the parties. Importantly, these contacts would not have the same weight for every issue or every legal rule a state might enact: instead, they would have greater or lesser weight depending on the issue under consideration or the policies behind a state's law. Sometimes territorial factors would be more significant than personal ones, and sometimes the reverse.

The Restatement Second of the Conflict of Laws, begun in 1953 but not completed until 1971, started out as a relatively modest attempt to modify the rigid rules of the first Restatement to incorporate the more recent insights. By the time the project ended, though, its Reporter had decided that more sweeping change was needed and that choice of law in many areas was not ripe for restatement in the form of rules. "[T[he difficulties and complexities involved," the second Restatement noted, "have as yet prevented the courts from formulating a precise rule, or series of rules, which provide a satisfactory accommodation of the underlying factors in all of the situations which may arise." Restatement of the Law, Second, Conflict of Laws § 6, Comment *c*. Instead, the second Restatement ended up with an open-ended multifactor balancing approach that offered a nonexhaustive list of six principles to take into account in deciding any choice of law question. The Reporter's hope was that judicial practice in applying this approach would converge in particular categories of cases, producing decisions that could be restated in the form of rules.

Almost 50 years later, we have a large sample of cases applying the second Restatement and other modern approaches. We are happy to report that in most circumstances, the convergence the drafters of the second Restatement hoped for has occurred. There are recognizable patterns of judicial decisions that can be captured in the form of rules.

Writing such rules is the primary goal of this [third] Restatement. We have two ancillary goals. First, we hope to produce a more user-friendly document than the second Restatement. We seek to be more explicit and transparent about the theoretical framework within which the third Restatement operates, about how its rules were derived, and about how to use them. To that end, we include an introductory section on choice of law . . . which restates the methodology of modern choice of law, before proceeding to the specific rules. We will also include explicit instruction on how to use the Restatement, and on when exceptional and unforeseen circumstances may justify departure from its rules.

Second, we hope to make choice of law intelligible in terms of ordinary legal concepts. Choice of law is often seen as a forbiddingly esoteric subject, with its own specialized concepts and vocabulary. Beginning in the 1950s, some scholars urged that this exceptionalism was unnecessary, and that modern choice of law could largely be described as ordinary legal analysis. Our survey of modern methodology suggests that this is correct: modern choice of law can be described in ordinary legal vocabulary as a two-step process. The first step is to determine whether the facts of the case fall within the scope of the relevant states' laws: to determine whether those laws grant the parties rights or impose obligations. This is ordinary legal analysis: as the second Restatement put it, a law's "range of application . . . can sometimes be ascertained by a process of interpretation and construction." Restatement of the Law, Second, of Conflict of Laws § 6, Comment *b*. The second step is to resolve any conflicts between rights under different states' laws.

---

(1) *Origins.* In 2014, the American Law Institute began work on a Third Restatement, still in draft form, with Kermit Roosevelt as Reporter and Laura Little and Chris Whytock as Associate Reporters. What one thinks a Third Restatement should do is likely influenced by several factors. What does one value, in terms of individual choice-of-law decisions and a choice-of-law system more generally? What lessons does one draw from the First Restatement, the choice-of-law revolution, and the Second Restatement? And what, fundamentally, does one think is going on in a choice-of-law decision? Roosevelt suggests that the Third Restatement can be understood as based on answers to these questions.

First, our choice-of-law desiderata can be separated into two categories, which we can call "right answer values" and "systemic values." Right answer values relate to outcomes a system directs in particular cases: they suggest that the choice of law should be reasonable in terms of the policies of the relevant states, their relative interests in the issue, and the expectations of the parties—roughly, factors (b), (c), and (d) of the Second Restatement's § 6. While we might assume that a system that generates perfectly correct answers exists in theory, in practice we will probably have to be content with something less than perfect or undisputed accuracy. Different people might differ about the relevant right answer factors (some might include the basic policies of the field of law, or even the better law) and about how to weigh them in particular cases. Still, even in the face of moderate disagreement, we can distinguish different systems in terms of how close they get to delivering the right answer to choice-of-law questions. As far as modern methodologies go, the way to promote right answer values is generally to choose a law by considering the state interests at stake in a particular decision or category of decisions—the significance of state policies, as affected by particular contacts, is the major insight of the choice-of-law revolution.

Systemic values relate to the operation of the choice-of-law system more generally (that is, not just in terms of the answers it delivers if correctly applied). They have more to do with the form of the system than with the outcomes it delivers, and they suggest primarily that the system should be simple and easy to apply—roughly, factors (f) and (g) of § 6. Such a system will be predictable for parties planning their out-of-court conduct and for parties engaged in litigation. It will reduce the workload of lawyers and judges and the cost of litigating choice-of-law issues. It will also allow judges to apply it correctly and uniformly—something that has proved quite difficult both with more sophisticated systems like comparative impairment and more flexible systems like the Second Restatement. The way to promote right answer values, generally, is to have a rule-based system.

We often think of right answer values and systemic values as existing in tension with each other, a point explored in the rules vs. standards debate (infra Section 6.C). Standards, we might suppose, promote right answer values at the expense of systemic ones, while rules do the reverse.

But that oversimplifies things. Yes, there probably is a genuine and inevitable tradeoff between rules and standards—one choice-of-law system cannot be both more rule-based and more standard-based than another. But there is no necessary tradeoff between right answer and systemic values. It is possible for one system to improve over another on both dimensions. In fact, it is possible to understand the history of American choice of law not as an oscillation back and forth along a one dimensional rules vs. standards line but as an attempt to improve the system in terms of both of these values. That version of the story also points towards a particular understanding of the goals of the Third Restatement.

Here is the story. The First Restatement had rules. These promoted systemic values, though perhaps not as well as is generally believed. (The mammoth First Restatement was significantly more complicated than the simple lex loci rules, and its complexity reduced uniformity and predictability even when judges were only trying to apply it faithfully.) But because they were derived from the metaphysical principle of territoriality, rather than a consideration of state policies, those rules sometimes delivered results that seemed arbitrary in terms of those policies.

Judges could see that these results were arbitrary, but the First Restatement gave them no way to explain why one result was arbitrary and another sensible, or to reach sensible results while following its rules. Driven to reach sensible results anyway, they resorted to escape devices. The opportunistic use of such doctrines as characterization and renvoi allowed judges to reach sensible answers more frequently, but it further reduced uniformity, predictability, and ease of application.

Willis Reese, drafting the Second Restatement, realized that the first step in reform was to figure out why the sensible answers were sensible. The way to achieve that, he believed, was to give judges a nonexhaustive list of relevant considerations and turn them loose to make decisions and explain them candidly. That, fundamentally, is what the Second Restatement does, at least when § 6 guides the analysis. (In some areas, where Reese believed that sensible rules could be identified, the Second Restatement provides more direction.)

If this understanding of the Second Restatement is accurate, it was never intended as an intrinsically desirable methodology that could last indefinitely. (Reese himself called it a "transitional" document.) Rather, it was intended to generate the raw materials from which future Reporters could draft appropriate rules. As Reese put it in *Conflict of Laws and the Restatement, Second*, 28 Law & Contemp. Probs. 679, 699 (1963), "more definite and precise rules can be stated after more experience has accumulated. That will be the task of future Restatements."

The task for the Reporters of the Third Restatement is thus to survey the outcomes reached under the Second Restatement and other modern approaches to see when they can be captured in appropriate rules. Decisions in a particular category of cases (loss-allocating tort issues featuring common domicile, for instance) might converge on a particular answer (law of common domicile). In such circumstances, capturing this agreed-upon right answer in a simple rule ("for loss-allocating issues in common domicile cases, select the law of common domicile") will advance both right answer and systemic values.

If decisions in a category of cases do not converge, there are two possibilities. First, it might be that the category has not been defined with sufficient precision, and a different definition will reveal convergence. In that situation, the Reporters should refine the definition. Second, it might be that the relevant question is just a hard one, with strong arguments on both sides. (True conflicts with cross-border torts can be hard, and sometimes it is not clear whether an issue should be characterized as loss-allocating or conduct-regulating.) In that situation, it may be best just to write a rule that picks one side anyway. The cost in terms of right answers will, by hypothesis, be slight: with strong arguments on both sides, if the rule gets some cases "wrong," they will not be very wrong. The benefits in terms of systemic factors will be substantial: rather than a hard and unpredictable issue, courts and parties will have a clear and simple rule.

The last question is how to describe all of this. What is going on when a court decides a choice-of-law issue? Saying something about this, the Reporters believe, is helpful to users of the Third Restatement because it allows them to understand how the rules were derived, what they are intended to achieve, and when they might misfire, making resort to an exception appropriate.

Here the Third Restatement, following Currie and Kramer, tries to assimilate choice-of-law to ordinary legal analysis. Choice of law, the Third Restatement suggests, is a matter of determining what rights the parties have and what happens if those rights conflict. See generally Kramer, *Rethinking Choice of Law*, 90 Colum L. Rev. 277 (1990). This is what courts do in domestic cases, and the same model can work in multistate cases.

From this perspective, choice of law can be described in ordinary legal vocabulary as a two-step process. First, a court must figure out what rights the parties have—whether they come within the scope of the laws they invoke. Statutes sometimes specify their scope in domestic cases—for instance, employment discrimination laws might impose obligations only on employers with more than 15 employees. If they do not, courts interpret them to determine whether a party has a right in a marginal case.

Similarly, statutes sometimes specify their scope in multistate cases—for instance, wage and hour laws might give claims only for work performed within a state. If they do not, courts interpret them to determine whether a party has a right in a marginal case.

Second, if both parties have rights and those rights conflict, courts must resolve the conflict. In the domestic case, this is done via rules that establish a hierarchy of laws: the federal Constitution is superior to federal statutes, which are superior to state constitutions, which are superior to state laws, and so on. In multistate cases, courts come up with rules of priority that accommodate the relative interests of the relevant states based on the nature of the issue and the distribution of contacts. "If the issue is one of loss-allocation and the parties share a common domicile, the law of the common domicile gets priority over the law of the place of injury" is an example of such a rule.

Do you agree that choice-of-law cases present fundamentally the same issues as domestic ones? Is it helpful to describe choice of law in ordinary legal terms? Is this the same thing as interest analysis?

(2) *Content.* Consistent with the above description, drafts of the Third Restatement provide rules to govern specific categories of cases or issues. In torts, for instance, the draft largely reproduces the *Neumeier* rules. It divides issues into questions of loss-allocation and conduct-regulation, explaining that the distinction is between issues for which personal connecting factors like domicile are more important and those for which territorial connecting factors, like the location of conduct and/or injury are more important.

Loss-allocating issues include intra-family immunities, charitable immunity, damages limitations, joint and several liability, contribution and indemnity among tortfeasors, comparative and contributory negligence, survival of actions, guest statutes, and workers' compensation immunities. Conduct-regulating issues include standards of conduct or safety, whether conduct is tortious, strict liability, punitive damages, the existence of a duty to the plaintiff, the scope of liability, duty or privilege to act, defenses that negate wrongfulness, and requirements for liability. Do these characterizations seem correct?

The draft then provides a set of rules based on the type of issue and the distribution of connecting factors. For conduct-regulating issues, if conduct and injury occur in the same state, that state's law governs. If they occur in different states, the law of the state of conduct governs, unless the plaintiff shows that the location of injury was foreseeable, in which case the law of the state of injury governs. (Because the plaintiff need not attempt such a showing and the defendant is not given the opportunity to make it, this effectively allows the plaintiff to choose the governing law in such cases. Does that rule make sense?)

For loss-allocating issues, if both parties share a domicile, domiciliary law governs. If the parties do not share a domicile, and conduct and injury occur in the same state, that state's law governs. The Comments to the relevant rule suggest that if the state of conduct and injury is not one party's domicile, and its law on the loss-allocating issue is not the same as either domiciliary state's, it may be appropriate to use an exception and select one of the domiciliary laws, especially if each party is favored by the law of their domicile. (Compare the exception to the third *Neumeier* rule.)

If parties do not share a domicile and conduct and injury occur in different states, the law of the state of conduct governs unless the plaintiff shows that the location of the injury was foreseeable.

Do these rules seem adequate to resolve most tort questions in a simple and sensible way? The draft also provides special rules for some claims or issues where other factors are relevant. A special rule for products liability, for instance, takes account of the place of first sale.

In contracts, the draft Third Restatement largely follows the Second Restatement with respect to contracts with choice-of-law clauses. It provides that the parties may select any state's law to govern an issue they could have resolved by explicit agreement, and the law of any state with a substantial relationship to the parties or transaction to govern an issue they could not have resolved by explicit agreement, unless that law is contrary to a fundamental policy of the state whose law would otherwise govern. (The difference here is that the Third Restatement test, for simplicity's sake, invalidates the parties' choice without a determination that the state whose law would otherwise govern has a "materially greater interest.") For contracts without choice-of-law clauses, the Third Restatement, based on a survey of decisions under the Second Restatement and other modern approaches, offers rules based first on subject matter (personal services contracts vs. sales of goods, for instance) and then formation and performance (if negotiation and performance occur in the same state, select that state's law). The (hopefully small!) remainder of contracts are remitted to an open-ended balancing analysis similar to that of the Second Restatement.

(3) *Issues and Applications.* Debate about the draft Third Restatement has centered mostly on three issues. First, there has been debate about the overarching framework and the attempt to describe choice of law in the vocabulary of ordinary legal analysis. Is it correct to describe modern choice of law as a two-step process involving the steps of determining scope and, if necessary, assigning priority? Is it helpful? For commentary, see Brilmayer & Listwa, *Change and Continuity in the Draft Restatement (Third) of Conflict of Laws: One Step Forward and Two Steps Back?*, 128 YALE L.J.F. 266 (2018); Roosevelt & Jones, *The Draft*

Restatement (Third) of Conflict of Laws: A Response to Brilmayer & Listwa, 28 YALE L.J.F. 293 (2018).

Second, there has been debate over a narrower issue within the two-step framework: whether states have the authority to determine the scope of their law. If, for instance, a state wage-and-hour statute provides that it creates a cause of action under certain circumstances "for work performed in this state," may another state's court use that law to create a cause of action for work performed outside the state? If we assimilate choice of law to ordinary legal analysis, the answer appears to be no—states are authoritative as to the content of their law, *i.e.*, to whom it grants rights and under what circumstances. If we think of choice of law as its own special field of law, courts and scholars have more freedom. (Does this just recapitulate the debate within interest analysis about whether interests are objective or subjective?)

This issue is likely of relatively minor practical significance; to use our example, both existing decisions and the draft Third Restatement tend to select the law of the state where the work was performed anyway. A different version of the same question arises with somewhat more frequency in the context of choice-of-law clauses: what if the parties select a law whose scope excludes them? (What if, for instance, a California-based employer enters into a contract with an employee working in Arizona and selects California law to govern the contract? Would the employee have rights under a territorially limited California wage-and-hour law?)

The draft Third Restatement provides that parties cannot extend the scope of a state law, so they cannot give themselves statutory rights that the legislature seeks to withhold. They can, however, incorporate the content of that law if the issue is one that they could have resolved by explicit provision. (Is that the right test? Why should such issues not be submitted to the "substantial relationship and not contrary to a fundamental policy of state whose law would otherwise govern" test?) Critics suggest that limits on scope are simply choice-of-law rules that parties can override via a choice-of-law clause. Would this produce any troubling consequences? For cases discussing these issues, see, e.g., *Cromeens, Holloman, Sibert, Inc. v. AB Volvo*, 349 F.3d 376, 387–90 (7th Cir. 2003); *Cotter v. Lyft, Inc.*, supra p. 124.

Third, there has been debate about the categories of loss allocation and conduct regulation. Critics suggest that the categories are incoherent and impossible to separate, because all rules have both conduct-regulating and loss-allocating effects and purposes. Is that true? If so, is it a fatal objection? Is it even relevant? The main achievement of the past seventy years of choice-of-law theory has been to recognize that there are some issues for which personal connecting factors, such as domicile, are more important and others for which territorial connecting factors, such as the place of conduct and/or injury, are more important. Is there a better way to describe these categories than by using a distinction that exists already in the decisions? Is this distinction circular?

To get a sense of how the Third Restatement would work in practice, consider how it would resolve some of the cases discussed earlier in the book. How do *Carroll*, *Levy*, *Haumschild*, *Grant*, *Mertz*, *Tooker*, and *Schultz* come out? (Should *Schultz* come out that way?) Do other cases pose more difficult challenges?

CHAPTER 3

THE CONSTITUTION AND CHOICE OF LAW

■ ■ ■

SECTION 1. THE LIMITS OF LEGISLATIVE JURISDICTION

A. DUE PROCESS

HOME INS. CO. V. DICK

281 U.S. 397 (1930).

MR. JUSTICE BRANDEIS delivered the opinion of the Court.

Dick, a citizen of Texas, brought this action in a court of that state against Compania General Anglo-Mexicana de Seguros, S.A., a Mexican corporation, to recover on a policy of fire insurance for the total loss of a tug. Jurisdiction was asserted in rem through garnishment, by ancillary writs issued against The Home Insurance Company and Franklin Fire Insurance Company, which reinsured, by contracts with the Mexican corporation, parts of the risk which it had assumed. The garnishees are New York corporations. . .

Their defense rests upon the following facts: This suit was not commenced till more than one year after the date of the loss. The policy provided: "It is understood and agreed that no judicial suit or demand shall be entered before any tribunal for the collection of any claim under this policy, unless such suits or demands are filed within one year counted as from the date on which such damage occurs." This provision was in accord with the Mexican law to which the policy was expressly made subject. It was issued by the Mexican company in Mexico to one Bonner, of Tampico, Mexico, and was there duly assigned to Dick prior to the loss. It covered the vessel only in certain Mexican waters. The premium was paid in Mexico; and the loss was "payable in the City of Mexico in current funds of the United States of Mexico, or their equivalent elsewhere." At the time the policy was issued, when it was assigned to him, and until after the loss, Dick actually resided in Mexico, although his permanent residence was in Texas. The contracts of reinsurance were effected by correspondence between the Mexican company in Mexico and the New York companies in New York. Nothing thereunder was to be done, or was in fact done, in Texas.

In the trial court, the garnishees contended that, since the insurance contract was made and was to be performed in Mexico, and the one-year provision was valid by its laws, Dick's failure to sue within one year after accrual of the alleged cause of action was a complete defense to the suit on the policy; that this failure also relieved the garnishees of any obligation as reinsurers, the same defense being open to them, * * *; and that they, consequently, owed no debt to the Mexican company subject to garnishment. To this defense, Dick demurred, on the ground that article 5545 of the Texas Revised Civil Statutes (1925) provides: "No person, firm, corporation, association or combination of whatsoever kind shall enter into any stipulation, contract, or agreement, by reason whereof the time in which to sue thereon is limited to a shorter period than two years. And no stipulation, contract, or agreement for any such shorter limitation in which to sue shall ever be valid in this State."

The trial court sustained Dick's contention and entered judgment against the garnishees. On appeal, both in the Court of Civil Appeals * * * and in the Supreme Court of the state * * *, the garnishees asserted that, as construed and applied, the Texas statute violated the due process clause of the Fourteenth Amendment and the contract clause. Both courts treated the policy provision as equivalent to a foreign statute of limitation; held that article 5545 related to the remedy available in Texas courts; concluded that it was validly applicable to the case at bar; and affirmed the judgment of the trial court. The garnishees appealed to this Court on the ground that the statute, as construed and applied, violated their rights under the Federal Constitution. . .

First. Dick contends that this Court lacks jurisdiction of the action, because the errors assigned involve only questions of local law and of conflict of laws. The argument is that, while a provision requiring notice of loss within a fixed period is substantive because it is a condition precedent to the existence of the cause of action, the provision for liability only in case suit is brought within the year is not substantive because it relates only to the remedy after accrual of the cause of action; that while the validity, interpretation and performance of the substantive provisions of a contract are determined by the law of the place where it is made and is to be performed, matters which relate only to the remedy are unquestionably governed by the lex fori; and that even if the Texas court erred in holding the statute applicable to this contract, the error is one of state law or of the interpretation of the contract, and is not reviewable here.

The contention is unsound. There is no dispute as to the meaning of the provision in the policy. It is that the insurer shall not be liable unless suit is brought within one year of the loss. Whether the provision be interpreted as making the commencement of a suit within the year a condition precedent to the existence of a cause of action, or as making failure to sue within the year a breach of a condition subsequent which extinguishes the cause of action, is not of legal significance here. Nor are we concerned with the question whether the provision is properly described as relating to remedy or to substance. However characterized, it is an express term in the contract of the parties by which the right of the insured and the correlative obligation of the insurer are defined. If effect is given to the clause, Dick cannot recover from the Mexican corporation and the garnishees cannot be compelled to pay. If, on the other hand, the statute is applied to the contract, it admittedly abrogates a contractual right and imposes liability, although the parties have agreed that there should be none.

The statute is not simply one of limitation. It does not merely fix the time in which the aid of the Texas courts may be invoked. Nor does it govern only the remedies available in the Texas courts. It deals with the powers and capacities of persons and corporations. It expressly prohibits the making of certain contracts. As construed, it also directs the disregard in Texas of contractual rights and obligations wherever created and assumed; and it commands the enforcement of obligations in excess of those contracted for. Therefore, the objection that, as applied to contracts made and to be performed outside of Texas, the statute violates the Federal Constitution, raises federal questions of substance; and the existence of the Federal claim is not disproved by saying that the statute, or the one-year provision in the policy, relates to the remedy and not to the substance. . .

Second. The Texas statute as here construed and applied deprives the garnishees of property without due process of law. A state may, of course, prohibit and declare invalid the making of certain contracts within its borders. Ordinarily, it may prohibit performance within its borders, even of contracts validly made elsewhere, if they are required to be performed within the state and their performance would violate its laws. But, in the case at bar, nothing in any way relating to the policy sued on, or to the contracts of reinsurance, was ever done or required to be done in Texas. All acts relating to the making of the policy were done in Mexico. All in relation to the making of the contracts of reinsurance were done there or in New York. And, likewise, all things in regard to performance were to be done outside of Texas. Neither the Texas laws nor the Texas courts were invoked for any purpose, except by Dick in the bringing of this suit. The fact that Dick's permanent residence was in Texas is without significance. At all times here material, he was physically present and acting in Mexico. Texas was, therefore, without power to affect the terms of contracts so made. Its attempt to impose a greater obligation than that agreed upon and to seize property in payment of the imposed obligation violates the guaranty against deprivation of property without due process of law. * * * *New York Life Ins. Co. v. Dodge,* 246 U.S. 357 * * *.

The cases relied upon, in which it was held that a state may lengthen its statute of limitations, are not in point. * * * In those cases, the parties had not stipulated a time limit for the enforcement of their obligations. It is true that a state may extend the time within which suit may be brought in its own courts, if in doing so, it violates no agreement of the parties. And, in the absence of a contractual provision, the local statute of limitation may be applied to a right created in another jurisdiction even where the remedy in the latter is barred.[7] In such cases, the rights and obligations of the parties are not varied. When, however, the parties have expressly agreed upon a time limit on their obligation, a statute which invalidates the agreement and directs enforcement of the contract after the time has expired increases their obligation and imposes a burden not contracted for.

It is true also that a state is not bound to provide remedies and procedure to suit the wishes of individual litigants. It may prescribe the kind of remedies to be available in its courts and dictate the practice and procedure to be followed in pursuing those remedies. Contractual provisions relating to these matters, even if valid where made, are often disregarded by the court of the forum, pursuant to statute or otherwise. But the Texas statute deals neither with the kind of remedy available nor with the mode in which it is to be pursued. It purports to create rights and obligations. It may not validly affect contracts which are neither made nor are to be performed in Texas.

Third. Dick urges that article 5545 of the Texas law is a declaration of its public policy; and that a state may properly refuse to recognize foreign rights which violate its declared policy. Doubtless, a state may prohibit the enjoyment by persons within its borders of rights acquired elsewhere which violate its laws or public policy; and, under some circumstances, it may refuse to aid in the enforcement of such rights. * * * But the Mexican corporation never was in Texas; and neither it nor the garnishees invoked the aid of the Texas courts or the Texas laws. The Mexican corporation was not before the court. The garnishees were brought in by compulsory process. Neither has asked favors. They ask only to be let alone. We need not consider how far the state may go in imposing restrictions on the conduct of its own residents, and of foreign corporations which have received permission to do business within its borders; or how far it may go in refusing to lend the aid of its courts to the enforcement of rights acquired outside its borders. It may not abrogate the rights of parties beyond its borders having no relation to anything done or to be done within them.

Fourth. Finally, it is urged that the Federal Constitution does not require the states to recognize and protect rights derived from the laws of foreign countries—that as to them the full faith and credit clause has no application. * * * The claims here asserted are not based upon the full faith and credit clause. * * * They rest upon the Fourteenth Amendment. Its protection extends to aliens. Moreover, the parties in interest here are

---

7 Whether a distinction is to be drawn between statutes of limitation which extinguish or limit the right and those which merely bar the remedy, we need not now determine. * * *

American companies. The defense asserted is based on the provision of the policy and on their contracts of reinsurance. The courts of the state confused this defense with that based on the Mexican Code. They held that even if the effect of the foreign statute was to extinguish the right, Dick's removal to Texas prior to the bar of the foreign statute removed the cause of action from Mexico, and subjected it to the Texas statute of limitation. And they applied the same rule to the provision in the policy. Whether or not that is a sufficient answer to the defense based on the foreign law, we may not consider; for no issue under the full faith and credit clause was raised. But in Texas, as elsewhere, the contract was subject to its own limitations. . .

Reversed.

Due Process and Choice of Law

(1) The Due Process Clause provides that no state shall "deprive any person of life, liberty, or property, without due process of law. . ." What does this have to do with choice of law? What interests or concerns does due process protect? How, if at all, does the fact that *Dick* is a multistate case affect the due process analysis? Recall that during this same period the Court also employed due process in other contexts to limit extraterritorial assertions of state power. E.g., *Pennoyer v. Neff,* infra p. 440 (personal jurisdiction); *Union Refrigerator Transit Co. v. Kentucky,* 199 U.S. 194 (1905) (taxation); *Allgeyer v. Louisiana,* 165 U.S. 578 (1897) (contract law).

Is the Court in *Dick* simply constitutionalizing the place of contract rule? If so, couldn't it have said so more simply and clearly than this?

(2) Consider the earlier case of *New York Life Ins. Co. v. Dodge,* 246 U.S. 357 (1918). A Missouri resident purchased insurance from a New York insurance company at its office in Missouri. The insured subsequently mailed from Missouri an application for a loan from the insurance company on the security of his policy. The application was accepted by return mail from New York. The insured defaulted on the loan. In accordance with the terms of the loan agreement and with New York law, the company therefore cancelled the policy and applied its reserve value to pay off the outstanding debt. The insured died, and his widow sued to collect on the policy. The Missouri court applied Missouri law—which forbade cancellation of an insurance policy under such circumstances—and ordered the company to make payment. The Supreme Court reversed. Writing for the Court, Justice McReynolds said:

> Considering the circumstances recited above, we think competent parties consummated the loan contract now relied upon in New York, where it was to be performed. And, moreover, that it is one

> of a kind which ordinarily no state by direct action may prohibit a citizen within her borders from making outside of them. . . To hold otherwise would permit destruction of the right—often of great value—freely to borrow money upon a policy from the issuing company at its home office, and would, moreover, sanction the impairment of that liberty of contract guaranteed to all by the Fourteenth Amendment.

Justice Brandeis dissented. Arguing first that the loan contract was made in Missouri, he added:

> Even if the rules ordinarily applied in determining the place of a contract required this court to hold, as a matter of general law, that the loan agreement was made in New York, it would not necessarily follow that the Missouri statute was unconstitutional, because it prohibited giving effect in part to the loan agreement. There is no constitutional limitation by virtue of which a statute enacted by a state in the exercise of the police power is necessarily void, if, in its operation, contracts made in another state may be affected. . . The test of constitutionality to be applied here is that commonly applied when the validity of a statute limiting the right of contract is questioned, namely: Is the subject-matter within the reasonable scope of regulation? Is the end legitimate? Are the means appropriate to the end sought to be obtained? If so, the act must be sustained, unless the court is satisfied that it is clearly an arbitrary and unnecessary interference with the right of the individual to his personal liberty. Here the subject is insurance; a subject long recognized as being within the sphere of regulation of contracts. The specific end to be attained was the protection of the net value of insurance policies by prohibiting provisions for forfeiture; an incident of the insurance contract long recognized as requiring regulation. The means adopted was to prescribe the limits within which the parties might agree to dispose of the net value of the policy otherwise than by commutation into extended insurance; a means commonly adopted in nonforfeiture laws, only the specific limitation in question being unusual. The insurance policy sought to be protected was a contract made within the state, between a citizen of the state and a foreign corporation also resident or present there. The protection was to be afforded while the parties so remained subject to the jurisdiction of the state. The protection was accomplished by refusing to permit the courts of the state to give to acts done within it by such residents (Dodge did no act elsewhere) the effect of nullifying in part that nonforfeiture provision which the legislature deemed necessary for the welfare of the citizens of the state and for their protection against acts of insuring corporations. The statute does not

invalidate any part of the loan; it leaves intact the ordinary remedies for collecting debts. The statute merely prohibits satisfying a part of the debt out of the reserve in a manner deemed by the legislature destructive of the protection devised against forfeiture. . .

Wasn't *Dick* easy after *Dodge*? Was the *Dodge* Court constitutionalizing the place of contracting rule? Does Brandeis's rationale in *Dick* differ from that of the majority in *Dodge*? Can you reconcile his votes in the two cases?

(3) Four years after *Dick,* the Supreme Court decided *Hartford Acc. & Indem. Co. v. Delta & Pine Land Co.,* 292 U.S. 143 (1934). Delta, a corporation doing business in both Mississippi and Tennessee, entered into an insurance contract in Tennessee. The insurer agreed to pay Delta for pecuniary losses suffered due to defalcation by any employee "in any position, anywhere." Delta's treasurer stole $2,700 from its Mississippi office, and Delta sued the insurer in Mississippi to recover under the policy. The insurance company argued that Delta had failed to file its claim within 15 months after the loss, as required by the policy. Delta responded that, under Mississippi law, such limitations were invalid. Applying Mississippi law, the court ordered the insurance company to pay. The Supreme Court reversed:

> The Mississippi statutes . . . deprive the appellant of due process of law. A state may limit or prohibit the making of certain contracts within its own territory * * *; but it cannot extend the effect of its laws beyond its borders so as to destroy or impair the right of citizens of other states to make a contract not operative within its jurisdiction, and lawful where made. * * * Nor may it in an action based upon such a contract enlarge the obligations of the parties to accord with every local statutory policy solely upon the ground that one of the parties is its own citizen. *Home Insurance Co. v. Dick,* 281 U.S. 397, 407–8.
>
> It is urged, however, that in this case the interest insured was in Mississippi when the obligation to indemnify the appellee matured, and it was appellant's duty to make payment there; and these facts justify the state in enlarging the appellant's obligation beyond that stipulated in the bond, to accord with local public policy. . . It is true the bond contemplated that the employee whose faithfulness was guaranteed might be in any state. He was in fact in Mississippi at the date of loss, as were both obligor and obligee. The contract being a Tennessee contract and lawful in that state, could Mississippi, without deprivation of due process, enlarge the appellant's obligations by reason of the state's alleged interest in the transaction? We think not. Conceding that

> ordinarily a state may prohibit performance within its borders even of a contract validly made elsewhere, if the performance would violate its laws (*Home Insurance Co. v. Dick*), it may not, on grounds of policy, ignore a right which has lawfully vested elsewhere, if, as here, the interest of the forum has but slight connection with the substance of the contract obligations. Here performance at most involved only the casual payment of money in Mississippi. In such a case the question ought to be regarded as a domestic one to be settled by the law of the state where the contract was made. A legislative policy which attempts to draw to the state of the forum control over the obligations of contracts elsewhere validly consummated and to convert them for all purposes into contracts of the forum regardless of the relative importance of the interests of the forum as contrasted with those created at the place of the contract, conflicts with the guaranties of the Fourteenth Amendment. * * * *Home Insurance Co. v. Dick.*

The decision in *Delta & Pine* was unanimous. Is the Court's rationale more consistent with the rationale in *Dick* or in *Dodge*? Which case do the facts more closely resemble? Why does Brandeis join the majority here instead of dissenting as in *Dodge*?

(4) What is the nature of the protection afforded by the due process clause in these cases? Can you state the test? In the paragraph of the *Dick* opinion beginning "Third," Justice Brandeis notes that the defendants were never in Texas and never "asked favors" from the state other than "to be let alone." Is this argument different from his earlier argument that applying Texas law violates due process because the transaction had no connection to Texas?

(5) The Court notes that Dick was residing in Mexico when he acquired the policy but that his permanent residence was in Texas. Why isn't it sufficient to apply Texas law that the plaintiff is a Texas domiciliary? See Rosenberger, *Who Was Dick? Constitutional Limitations on Choice of Law,* 1998 Utah L. Rev. 37.

B. FULL FAITH AND CREDIT

BRADFORD ELECTRIC LIGHT CO. V. CLAPPER

286 U.S. 145 (1932).

[Clapper, a resident of Vermont, worked for Bradford Elec. Co., a Vermont corporation with its principal place of business in Vermont. Bradford had lines extending into New Hampshire, and Clapper was sent there to replace some fuses. He was accidentally electrocuted, and his estate administrator brought a common law action in New Hampshire alleging that Bradford's negligence caused the death. Under New

Hampshire law, an injured employee could elect either to accept compensation under the state's workers' compensation law or to bring a common law tort action. Vermont's workers' compensation act, in contrast, provided the exclusive remedy for an injured employee unless "prior to the accident an express statement to the contrary shall have been made, in writing, by one of the parties." The Vermont act expressly stated that it applied to injuries outside the state. Neither Clapper nor Bradford had filed a statement electing to forgo the protection of Vermont's workers' compensation act. The court applied New Hampshire law, and a jury awarded the plaintiff $4,000. Bradford appealed, arguing that the full faith and credit clause required the New Hampshire court to recognize a defense based on Vermont law. The Supreme Court agreed.]

MR. JUSTICE BRANDEIS delivered the opinion of the Court. . .

By requiring that, under the circumstances here presented, full faith and credit be given to the public act of Vermont, the Federal Constitution prevents the employee or his representative from asserting in New Hampshire rights which would be denied him in the State of his residence and employment. A Vermont court could have enjoined Leon Clapper from suing the Company in New Hampshire, to recover damages for an injury suffered there, just as it would have denied him the right to recover such damages in Vermont. * * * The rights created by the Vermont Act are entitled to like protection when set up in New Hampshire by way of defense to the action brought there. If this were not so, and the employee or his representative were free to disregard the law of Vermont and his contract, the effectiveness of the Vermont Act would be gravely impaired. For the purpose of that Act, as of the workmen's compensation laws of most other States, is to provide, in respect to persons residing and businesses located in the State, not only for employees a remedy which is both expeditious and independent of proof of fault, but also for employers a liability which is limited and determinate. * * *

[I]t is urged that the provision of the Vermont statute which forbids resort to common law remedies for injuries incurred in the course of employment is contrary to the public policy of New Hampshire; that the full faith and credit clause does not require New Hampshire to enforce an act of another State which is obnoxious to its public policy; and that a federal court sitting in that State may, therefore, decline to do so. * * * It is true that the full faith and credit clause does not require the enforcement of every right conferred by a statute of another State. There is room for some play of conflicting policies. Thus, a plaintiff suing in New Hampshire on a statutory cause of action arising in Vermont might be denied relief because the forum fails to provide a court with jurisdiction of the controversy, * * * or because it fails to provide procedure appropriate to its determination, * * * or because the enforcement of the right conferred would be obnoxious to the public policy of the forum, * * * or because the liability imposed is deemed a penal one * * *. But the Company is in a position different from that of a plaintiff who seeks to enforce a cause of action conferred by the laws of another State. The right which it claims should be given effect is set up by way of defense to an asserted liability; and to a defense different considerations apply. Compare *Home Ins. Co. v. Dick,* 281 U.S. 397, 407, 408. A State may, on occasion, decline to enforce a foreign cause of action. In so doing, it merely denies a remedy, leaving unimpaired the plaintiff's substantive right, so that he is free to enforce it elsewhere. But to refuse to give effect to a substantive defense under the applicable law of another State, as under the circumstances here presented, subjects the defendant to irremediable liability. This may not be done.

Moreover, there is no adequate basis for the lower court's conclusion that to deny recovery would be obnoxious to the public policy of New Hampshire. No decision of the state court has been cited indicating that recognition of the Vermont statute would be regarded in New Hampshire as prejudicial to the interests of its citizens. In support of the contention that the provision of the Vermont Act is contrary to the New Hampshire policy, it is urged that New Hampshire's compensation law is unique among workmen's compensation acts in that it permits the injured employee to elect, subsequent to injury, whether to bring a suit based upon negligence or to avail himself of the remedy provided by the Act; and that the legislature of New Hampshire has steadily refused to withdraw this privilege. But the mere fact that the Vermont legislation does not conform to that of New Hampshire does not establish that it would be obnoxious to the latter's public policy to give effect to the Vermont statute in cases involving only the rights of residents of that State incident to the relation of employer and employee created there. * * * Nor does sufficient reason appear why it should be so regarded. The interest of New Hampshire was only casual. Leon Clapper was not a resident there. He was not continuously employed there. So far as appears, he had no dependent there. It is difficult to see how the State's interest would be subserved, under such circumstances, by burdening its courts with this litigation.

ALASKA PACKERS ASSOC. V. INDUSTRIAL ACC. COMM'N

294 U.S. 532 (1935).

MR. JUSTICE STONE delivered the opinion of the Court.

This is an appeal under § 237 of the Judicial Code from a judgment of the Supreme Court of California, * * * upholding an award of compensation, by the state Industrial Accident Commission, to appellee Palma, against appellant, his employer, and holding that the award does not infringe prohibitions of the Federal Constitution. The award was made in conformity to the statutes of California, where the contract of employment was entered into, rather than those of Alaska, where the injury occurred.

On May 13, 1932, Palma, a non-resident alien, and appellant, doing business in California, executed at San Francisco a written contract of employment. Palma agreed to work for appellant in Alaska during the salmon canning season; the appellant agreed to transport him to Alaska and, at the end of the season, to return him to San Francisco where he was to be paid his stipulated wages, less advances. The contract recited that appellant had elected to be bound by the Alaska Workmen's Compensation Law and stipulated that the parties should be subject to and bound by the provisions of that statute. Section 58 of the California Workmen's Compensation Act was then in force, which provides: "The commission shall have jurisdiction over all controversies arising out of injuries suffered without the territorial limits of this state in those cases where the injured employee is a resident of this state at the time of the injury and the contract of hire was made in this State, . . . ".

At that time the California Supreme Court had held in *Quong Ham Wah Co. v. Industrial Accident Comm'n,* 184 Cal. 26, 36–44, 192 Pac. 1021 (writ of error dismissed, 255 U.S. 445), that this section was applicable to non-residents of California, since the privileges and immunities clause of the Federal Constitution prevented giving any effect to the requirement that the employee be a resident. The California Workmen's Compensation Act also provides, § 27(a): "No contract, rule or regulation shall exempt the employer from liability for the compensation fixed by this act, . . . ".

In August, 1932, after his return from Alaska to California, the employee applied for and later received an award by the California Commission in compensation for injuries received by him in the course of his employment in Alaska. On petition for review by the state supreme court, appellant assailed the California statute, as he does here, as invalid under the due process and the full faith and credit clauses of the Federal Constitution. Insofar as the California statute denies validity to the agreement that the parties should be bound by the Alaska Workmen's Compensation Act, and attempts to give a remedy for injuries suffered by a non-resident employee without the state, it is challenged as a denial of due process. Petitioner also insists that as the Alaska statute affords, in Alaska, an exclusive remedy for the injury which occurred there, the California courts denied full faith and credit to the Alaska statute by refusing to recognize it as a defense to the application for an award under the California statute. [The California Supreme Court refused to set the award aside.]

[The Court first rejected petitioner's due process argument, concluding that "we cannot say that [the California Workmen's Compensation Act], as applied, lacked a rational basis or involved any arbitrary or unreasonable exercise of state power."]

2. Even though the compensation acts of either jurisdiction may, consistently with due process, be applied in either, the question remains whether the California court has failed to accord full faith and credit to the Alaska statute in refusing to allow it as a defense to the award of the California Commission. Appellant contends that as the provisions of the Alaska statute conflict with those of the California statutes, the full faith and credit clause . . . compel[s] recognition of the Alaska statute as a defense to the proceedings before the California Commission. . .

In the case of statutes, the extra-state effect of which Congress has not prescribed, where the policy of one state statute comes into conflict with that of another, the necessity of some accommodation of the conflicting interests of the two states is . . . apparent. A rigid and literal enforcement of the full faith and credit clause, without regard to the statute of the forum, would lead to the absurd result that, wherever the conflict arises, the statute of each state must be enforced in the courts of the other, but cannot be in its own. Unless by force of that clause a greater effect is thus to be given to a state statute abroad than the clause permits it to have at home, it is unavoidable that this Court determine for itself the extent to which the statute of one state may qualify or deny rights asserted under the statute of another. . .

Prima facie every state is entitled to enforce in its own courts its own statutes, lawfully enacted. One who challenges that right, because of the force given to a conflicting statute of another state by the full faith and credit clause, assumes the burden of showing, upon some rational basis, that of the conflicting interests involved those of the foreign state are superior to those of the forum. It follows that not every statute of another state will override a conflicting statute of the forum by virtue of the full faith and credit clause; that the statute of a state may sometimes override the conflicting statute of another, both at home and abroad; and, again, that the two conflicting statutes may each prevail over the other at home, although given no extraterritorial effect in the state of the other.

This was fully recognized by this Court in *Bradford Electric Light Co. v. Clapper*. There, upon an appraisal of the governmental interests of the two states, Vermont and New Hampshire, it was held that the Compensation Act of Vermont, where the status of employer and employee was established, should prevail over the conflicting statute of New Hampshire, where the injury occurred and the suit was brought. In reaching that conclusion, weight was given to the following circumstances: that liability under the Vermont Act was an incident of the status of employer and employee created within Vermont, and as such continued in New Hampshire where the injury occurred; that it was a substitute for a tort action, which was permitted by the statute of New Hampshire; that the Vermont statute expressly provided that it should extend to injuries occurring without the state and was interpreted to preclude recovery by proceedings both in any other state; and that there was no adequate basis for saying that the compulsory recognition of the Vermont statute by the courts of New Hampshire would be obnoxious to the public policy of that state.

If, for the reasons given, the Vermont statute was held to override the New Hampshire statute in the courts of New Hampshire, it is hardly to be supposed that the Constitution would require it to be given any less effect in Vermont, even though the New Hampshire statute were set up as a defense to proceedings there. Similarly, in the present case, only if it appears that, in the conflict of interests which have found expression in the conflicting statutes, the interest of Alaska is superior to that of California, is there rational basis for denying to the courts of California the right to apply the laws of their own state. While in *Bradford Electric Light Co. v. Clapper,* it did not appear that the subordination of the New Hampshire statute to that of Vermont, by compulsion of the full faith and credit clause, would be obnoxious to the policy of New Hampshire, the Supreme Court of California has declared it to be contrary to the policy of the State to give effect to the provisions of the Alaska statute and that they conflict with its own statutes.

There are only two differences material for present purposes, between the facts of the *Clapper* case and those presented in this case: the employee here is not a resident of the place in which the employment was begun, and the employment was wholly to be performed in the jurisdiction in which the injury arose. Whether these differences, with a third—that the Vermont statute was intended to preclude resort to any other remedy even without the state—are, when taken with the differences between the New Hampshire and Alaska compensation laws, sufficient ground for withholding or denying any effect of the California statute in Alaska, we need not now inquire. But it is clear that they do not lessen the interest of California in enforcing its compensation act within the state, or give any added weight to the interest of Alaska in having its statute enforced in California. We need not repeat what we have already said of the peculiar concern of California in providing a remedy for those in the situation of the present employee. Its interest is sufficient to justify its legislation and is greater than that of Alaska, of which the employee was never a resident and to which he may never return. Nor should the fact that the employment was wholly to be performed in Alaska, although temporary in character, lead to any different result. It neither diminishes the interest of California in giving a remedy to the employee, who is a member of a class in the protection of which the state has an especial interest, nor does it enlarge the interest of Alaska whose temporary relationship with the employee has been severed.

The interest of Alaska is not shown to be superior to that of California. No persuasive reason is shown for denying to California the right to enforce its own laws in its own courts, and in the circumstances the full faith and credit clause does not require that the statutes of Alaska be given that effect.

PACIFIC EMPLOYERS INS. CO. V. INDUSTRIAL ACC. COMM'N

306 U.S. 493 (1939).

MR. JUSTICE STONE delivered the opinion of the Court.

The question is whether the full faith and credit which the Constitution requires to be given to a Massachusetts workmen's compensation statute precludes California from applying its own workmen's compensation act in the case of an injury suffered by a Massachusetts employee of a Massachusetts employer while in California in the course of his employment. . .

The injured employee, a resident of Massachusetts, was regularly employed there under written contract in the laboratories of the Dewey & Almy Chemical Company as a chemical engineer and research chemist. In September, 1935, in the usual course of his employment he was sent by his employer to its branch factory in California to act temporarily as a technical adviser in the effort to improve the quality of one of the employer's products manufactured there. Upon completion of the assignment he expected to return to the employer's Massachusetts place of business, and while in California he remained subject to the general direction and control of the employer's Massachusetts office, from which his compensation was paid. . .

The California Commission directed petitioner to pay the compensation prescribed by the California Act, including the amounts of lien claims filed in the proceeding for medical, hospital and nursing services and certain further amounts necessary for such services in the future.

By the applicable Massachusetts statute, §§ 24, 26, c. 152, Mass.Gen.Laws (Ter.Ed.1932), an employee of a person insured under the Act, as was the employer in this case, is deemed to waive his "right of action at common law or under the law of any other jurisdiction" to recover for personal injuries unless he shall have given appropriate notice to the employer in writing that he elects to retain such rights. Section 26 directs that without the notice his right to recover be restricted to the compensation provided by the Act for injuries received in the course of his employment, "whether within or without the commonwealth." [No such notice was given here.]

Petitioner, which as insurance carrier has assumed the liability of the employer under the California Act, relies on the provisions of the Massachusetts Act that the compensation shall be that prescribed for injuries suffered in the course of the employment, whether within or without the state. It insists that since the contract of employment was entered into in Massachusetts and the employer consented to be bound by the Massachusetts Act, that, and not the California statute, fixes the employee's right to compensation whether the injuries were received within or without the state, and that the Massachusetts statute is constitutionally entitled to full faith and credit in the courts of California.

We may assume that these provisions are controlling upon the parties in Massachusetts, and that since they are applicable to a Massachusetts contract of employment between a Massachusetts employer and employee, they do not infringe due process. *Bradford Electric Light Co. v. Clapper*, 286 U.S. 145, 156, et seq. Similarly the constitutionality of the provisions of the California statute awarding compensation for injuries to an employee occurring within its borders, and for injuries as well occurring elsewhere, when the contract of employment was entered into within the state, is not open to question. *Alaska Packers Association v. Industrial Accident Comm.*, 294 U.S. 532 * * *.

While in the circumstances now presented, either state, if its system for administering workmen's compensation permitted, would be free to adopt and enforce the remedy provided by the statute of the other, here each has provided for itself an exclusive remedy for a liability which it was constitutionally authorized to impose. But neither is bound, apart from the compulsion of the full faith and credit clause, to enforce the laws of the other, *Milwaukee County v. White Co.*, 296 U.S. 268, 272; and the law of neither can by its own force determine the choice of law to be applied in the other. . .

To the extent that California is required to give full faith and credit to the conflicting Massachusetts statute it must be denied the right to apply in its own courts its own statute, constitutionally enacted in pursuance of its policy to provide compensation for employees injured in their employment within the state. It must withhold the remedy given by its own statute to its residents by way of compensation for medical, hospital and nursing services rendered to the injured employee, and it must remit him to Massachusetts to secure the administrative remedy which that state has provided. We cannot say that the full faith and credit clause goes so far.

While the purpose of that provision was to preserve rights acquired or confirmed under the public acts and judicial proceedings of one state by requiring recognition of their validity in other states, the very nature of the federal union of states, to which are reserved some of the attributes of sovereignty, precludes resort to the full faith and credit clause as the means for compelling a state to substitute the statutes of other states for its own statutes dealing with a subject matter concerning which it is competent to legislate. As was pointed out in *Alaska Packers Association v. Industrial Accident Comm.*, * * *: "A rigid and literal enforcement of the full faith and credit clause, without regard to the statute of the forum, would lead to the absurd result that, wherever the conflict arises, the statute of each state must be enforced in the courts of the other, but cannot be in its own." And in cases like the present it would create an impasse which would often leave the employee remediless. Full faith and credit would deny to California the right to apply its own remedy, and its administrative machinery may well not be adapted to giving the remedy afforded by Massachusetts. Similarly, the full faith and credit demanded for the California Act would deny to Massachusetts the right to apply its own remedy, and its Department of Industrial Accidents may well be without statutory authority to afford the remedy provided by the California statute.

It has often been recognized by this Court that there are some limitations upon the extent to which a state may be required by the full faith and credit clause to enforce even the judgment of another state in contravention of its own statutes or policy. * * * And in the case of statutes, the extra-state effect of which Congress has not prescribed, as it may under the constitutional provision, we think the conclusion is unavoidable that the full faith and credit clause does not require one state to substitute for its own statute, applicable to persons and events within it, the conflicting statute of another state, even though that statute is of controlling force in the courts of the state of its enactment with respect to the same persons and events.

This Court must determine for itself how far the full faith and credit clause compels the qualification or denial of rights asserted under the laws of one state, that of the forum, by the statute of another state. See *Alaska Packers Association v. Industrial Accident Comm.*, * * *. But there would seem to be little room for the exercise of that function when the statute of the forum is the expression of domestic policy, in terms declared to be exclusive in its application to persons and events within the state. Although Massachusetts has an interest in safeguarding the compensation of Massachusetts employees while temporarily abroad in the course of their employment, and may adopt that policy for itself, that could hardly be thought to support an application of the full faith and credit clause which would override the constitutional authority of another state to legislate for the bodily safety and economic protection of employees injured within it. Few matters could be deemed more appropriately the concern of the state in which the injury occurs or more completely within its power. Considerations of less weight led to the conclusion, in *Alaska Packers*

Association v. Industrial Accident Comm., supra, that the full faith and credit clause did not require California to give effect to the Alaska Compensation Act in preference to its own. There this Court sustained the award by California of the compensation provided by its own statute for employees where the contract of employment was made within the state, although the injury occurred in Alaska, whose statute also provided compensation for the injury. Decision was rested explicitly upon the grounds that the full faith and credit exacted for the statute of one state does not necessarily preclude another state from enforcing in its own courts its own conflicting statute having no extra-territorial operation forbidden by the Fourteenth Amendment, and that no persuasive reason was shown for denying that right.

Bradford Electric Light Co. v. Clapper, supra, on which petitioner relies, fully recognized this limitation on the full faith and credit clause. It was there held that a federal court in New Hampshire, in a suit brought against a Vermont employer by his Vermont employee to recover for an injury suffered in the course of his employment while temporarily in New Hampshire, was bound to apply the Vermont Compensation Act rather than the provision of the New Hampshire Compensation Act which permitted the employee, at his election, to enforce his common law remedy. But the Court was careful to point out that there was nothing in the New Hampshire statute, the decisions of its courts, or in the circumstances of the case, to suggest that reliance on the provisions of the Vermont statute, as a defense to the New Hampshire suit, was obnoxious to the policy of New Hampshire. The *Clapper* case cannot be said to have decided more than that a state statute applicable to employer and employee within the state, which by its terms provides compensation for the employee if he is injured in the course of his employment while temporarily in another state, will be given full faith and credit in the latter when not obnoxious to its policy. * * *

Here, California legislation not only conflicts with that of Massachusetts providing compensation for the Massachusetts employee if injured within the state of California, but it expressly provides, for the guidance of its own commission and courts, that "No contract, rule or regulation shall exempt the employer from liability for the compensation fixed by this act." The Supreme Court of California has declared in its opinion in this case that it is the policy of the state, as expressed in its Constitution and Compensation Act, to apply its own provisions for compensation, to the exclusion of all others, and that "It would be obnoxious to that policy to deny persons who have been injured in this state the right to apply for compensation when to do so might require physicians and hospitals to go to another state to collect charges for medical care and treatment given to such persons."

Full faith and credit does not here enable one state to legislate for the other or to project its laws across state lines so as to preclude the other from prescribing for itself the legal consequences of acts within it.

Affirmed.

State Interests and the Constitution

(1) Why didn't the defendant in *Clapper* argue that applying New Hampshire law violated due process? Why couldn't New Hampshire apply its law as the state where the injury occurred? (Recall the *Carroll* case from Chapter 1.)

In *Alaska Packers,* the state court followed *Clapper* and applied the law of the place of contract. Why did the Court bother to hear this case only to affirm that decision? Was the fact that suit in *Alaska Packers* was brought in the state of contract significant in the grant of certiorari?

Alaska Packers reserves the question whether the state of injury could apply its law, the issue presented in *Pacific Employers.* Hadn't *Clapper* already decided that question? Does the Court in *Pacific Employers* do a persuasive job distinguishing the case? Does *Pacific Employers* overrule *Clapper*?

(2) Although a principal focus of the full faith and credit clause was to require recognition of judgments, it seems clear that "public Acts" means statutes. Statements to this effect were made on the floor of the Convention, the First Congress so understood it, and the Supreme Court has long held this to be the case. See Laycock, *Equal Citizens of Equal and Territorial States: The Constitutional Foundations of Choice of Law,* 92 Colum.L.Rev. 249, 290 (1992) (citing authorities). Decisional law is not expressly mentioned, and some scholars have assumed that it was not included. See, e.g., W.W. Cook, The Logical and Legal Bases of the Conflict of Laws 105 (1942). The modern view recognizes that common law is within the policy of the clause, however, and treats it as such—though there is uncertainty as to whether judicial decisions are "Records," "Judicial Proceedings," or even "public Acts." See Laycock, 92 Colum.L.Rev. at 290 (citing authorities).

A 1790 statute implementing the full faith and credit clause provided for *proof* of acts, records, and judicial proceedings, but unaccountably omitted any reference to acts when it came to the question of *credit*: "And the said records and judicial proceedings . . . shall have such faith and credit given to them in every court within the United States, as they have by law or usage in the courts of the state from whence [they are] taken." Act of May 26, 1790, 1 Stat. 122. The 1948 revision remedied this omission by inserting the word "Acts." 28 U.S.C. § 1738. Is it surprising that this statute has not figured prominently in the decisions? Does it mean anything at all? For an argument that the early history of the statute indicates that the Full Faith and Credit Clause was designed to give Congress broad authority to declare the substantive effect of sister-state records, see Stephen E. Sachs, *Full Faith and Credit in the Early Congress*, 95 Va. L. Rev. 1201 (2009).

(3) *Alaska Packers* adopts a balancing approach to full faith and credit. *Pacific Employers* weakens this, holding that an interested state can always apply its law notwithstanding the interest of any other state. What was wrong with balancing? Doesn't *Pacific Employers* water down the protection of the clause too much? According to Justice Jackson, the full faith and credit clause was designed "to federalize the separate and independent state legal systems by the overriding principle of reciprocal recognition. . . It was placed foremost among those measures which would guard the new political and economic union against the disintegrating influence of provincialism in jurisprudence. . ." Jackson, *Full Faith and Credit—The Lawyer's Clause of the Constitution,* 45 Colum.L.Rev. 1, 17 (1945). It follows, Jackson concludes, that federal courts must police the choice-of-law process:

> That the Supreme Court should impose uniformity in choice-of-law problems is a prospect comforting to none, least of all to a member of that body. I have not paid any exaggerated tribute to its performance thus far in this complex field. But the available courses from which our choice may be made seem to me limited. One is that we will leave choice of law in all cases to the local policy of the state. This seems to me to be at odds with the implication of our federal system that the mutual limits of the states' powers are defined by the Constitution. It also seems productive of confusion, for it means that the choice among conflicting substantive rules depends only upon which state happens to have the last word. . . A second course is that we will adopt no rule, permit a good deal of overlapping and confusion, but interfere now and then, without imparting to the bar any reason by which the one or the other course is to be guided or predicted. This seems to me about where our present decisions leave us. Third, we may candidly recognize that choice-of-law questions, when properly raised ought to and do present constitutional questions under the full faith and credit clause which the Court may properly decide and as to which it ought at least to mark out reasonably narrow limits of permissible variation in areas where there is confusion. . .
>
> Certainly the personal preferences of the Justices among the conflicting state policies is not a permissible basis of determining

> which shall prevail in a case. But only a singularly balanced mind could weigh relative state interests in such subject matter except by resort to what are likely to be strong preferences in sociology, economics, governmental theory, and politics. There are no judicial standards of valuation of such imponderables. . . But, even if we could appraise or compare relative local interests, we must lift these questions above the control of local interest and must govern conflict in these cases by the wider considerations arising out of the federal order. How to determine when these require the law of the forum to give way to that of another state seems to me an unsettled question. I cannot regard the "balance of interest" test used in the compensation cases as more than a tentative and inadequate answer. . . I doubt that the position can long be maintained that the reach of a state's power is a by-product of an interest. The ultimate answer, it seems to me, will have to be based on considerations of state relations to each other and to the federal system.

Id. at 26–28. Professor Laycock agrees, arguing that the full faith and credit clause presupposes that only one law can be applied to any case, and that therefore the federal courts must impose uniform choice-of-law rules in the absence of congressional action. Laycock, 92 Colum.L.Rev. at 296–97, 331–36. See also Baxter, *Choice of Law and the Federal System,* 16 Stan.L.Rev. 1, 25–42 (1963); Cardozo, *Choosing and Declaring State Law,* 55 Nw.U.L.Rev. 419, 432–35 (1960).

Does the full faith and credit clause presuppose that there is a single right answer to the question of which law should apply? Professor Roosevelt agrees with Laycock that "full faith and credit" means that states must treat the laws of other states as equal to their own, but concludes that this simply means that they must have some nondiscriminatory reason, such as a belief that their interest is greater, for applying their own law rather than foreign law. See Roosevelt, *The Myth of Choice of Law: Rethinking Conflicts,* 97 Mich. L. Rev. 2448, 2528–29 (1999). He suggests that the sincerity of such a belief could be tested by examining how a state handles "mirror-image" cases, in which the relevant contacts are arrayed in opposite fashion. (Recall Laycock's example of Mary and Del, supra pp. 183–184.) Applying forum law to both of a pair of mirror image cases indicates a full faith and credit violation. Is this an appealing understanding of the clause? Could it be enforced in practice?

Professor Cheatham conceded that federal control over choice of law would promote uniformity and reduce provincialism, but he questioned the resulting "diminution of state power" and thought the endeavor premature because "[c]onflict of laws is a fairly young subject in the common law, with many of its basic ideas still vague and unformulated." Cheatham, *Federal*

Control of Conflict of Laws, 6 Vand.L.Rev. 581, 588 (1953). Have the intervening years done away with Cheatham's objections?

The second sentence of the full faith and credit clause provides "And the Congress may by general Laws prescribe the manner in which such Acts, Records and Proceedings shall be proved, and the Effect thereof." U.S. Const., Art. IV, § 1. Does this provision preclude courts from using the full faith and credit clause to limit state choice of law? Does it support the Supreme Court's decision to minimize judicial interference and leave federal regulation of choice of law to Congress in the first instance? See B. Currie, Selected Essays on the Conflict of Laws 272–73 (1963) (arguing that courts are not equipped politically or institutionally to resolve conflicts and that "the Constitution specifically confers that function upon Congress"). Or does the effects clause have exactly the opposite implication: that courts can make federal common law safe in the knowledge that Congress can override any serious mistakes?

(4) How should the Court determine whether a state has a constitutionally sufficient interest to justify application of its law? Does a generalized interest in the well-being of the plaintiff or the regulation of the defendant suffice, or must the state have an interest in the application of its actual law to the particular point in issue? Is the process of defining interests the same for constitutional as for state law purposes? Should it be? Can a state's declaration that it has an interest be determinative of the constitutional question? If not, then what defines the limits? See Brilmayer, *Methods and Objectives in the Conflict of Laws: A Challenge,* 35 Mercer L.Rev. 555, 558 (1984); H. Kay, *A Defense of Currie's Governmental Interest Analysis,* 215 Recueil des cours 136–45 (1989-III).

Consider *Carroll v. Lanza,* 349 U.S. 408 (1955). Carroll, a resident of Missouri employed by a Missouri subcontractor, was injured while working in Arkansas; he was taken back to Missouri for treatment. Carroll received compensation under the Missouri workers' compensation act, which stated that it provided an exclusive remedy. Arkansas, in contrast, preserved an employee's remedy against third parties, defined to include general contractors. Carroll therefore sued the general contractor, Lanza, in Arkansas. The Court relied on *Pacific Employers* in upholding an award of damages:

> [Arkansas'] interests are large and considerable and are to be weighed not only in the light of the facts of this case but by the kind of situation presented. For we write not only for this case and this day alone, but for this type of case. The State where the tort occurs certainly has a concern in the problems following in the wake of the injury. The problems of medical care and of possible dependents are among these, as *Pacific Employers* emphasizes. A State that legislates concerning them is exercising traditional

> powers of sovereignty. * * * Arkansas therefore has a legitimate interest in opening her courts to suits of this nature, even though in this case Carroll's injuries may have cast no burden on her or on her institutions.

What does the fact that Arkansas interests might be affected in another case of the same type but with different facts have to do with this case?

(5) One apparently glaring exception to the approach announced in *Pacific Employers* is *Order of United Commercial Travelers v. Wolfe,* 331 U.S. 586 (1947). An Ohio association sold life insurance to a South Dakota member; the policy required that claims be filed within six months of his death. A South Dakota court applied its own law to invalidate the time limitation, and the Supreme Court reversed under the full faith and credit clause. After waxing eloquent on the unique relationship among members of a fraternal benefit society, Justice Burton explained:

> [T]his Court has consistently upheld, on the basis of evaluated public policy, the law of the state of incorporation of a fraternal benefit society as the law that should control the validity of the terms of membership in that corporation. The weight of public policy behind the general statute of South Dakota, which seeks to avoid certain provisions in ordinary statutes, does not equal that which makes necessary the recognition of the same terms of membership for members of fraternal benefit societies wherever their beneficiaries may be.

Can you reconcile this decision with *Pacific Employers*? Are there some contexts in which more intrusive judicial intervention may safely be attempted? Would you, for instance, support extending the rule of *Wolfe* more generally to questions respecting the internal structure or organization of corporations? See Shreve, *Choice of Law and the Forgiving Constitution,* 71 Ind. L.J. 271 (1996) (arguing that Supreme Court passivity has costs but that more intrusive intervention is hard to justify short of wholesale creation of a federal choice-of-law regime); Suggs, *Business Combination Antitakeover Statutes,* 56 Ohio St. L.J. 1097 (1995) (arguing that the "internal affairs" doctrine for corporations should be constitutionalized).

C. CONVERGENCE

ALLSTATE INS. CO. V. HAGUE

449 U.S. 302 (1981).

JUSTICE BRENNAN announced the judgment of the Court and an opinion in which JUSTICE WHITE, JUSTICE MARSHALL, and JUSTICE BLACKMUN join.

This Court granted certiorari to determine whether the Due Process Clause of the Fourteenth Amendment or the Full Faith and Credit Clause of Art. 4, § 1, of the United States Constitution bars the Minnesota Supreme Court's choice of substantive Minnesota law to govern the effect of a provision in an insurance policy issued to respondent's decedent. 444 U.S. 1070 (1980).

I

Respondent's late husband, Ralph Hague, died of injuries suffered when a motorcycle on which he was a passenger was struck from behind by an automobile. The accident occurred in Pierce County, Wis., which is immediately across the Minnesota border from Red Wing, Minn. The operators of both vehicles were Wisconsin residents, as was the decedent who, at the time of the accident, resided with respondent in Hager City, Wis., which is one and one-half miles from Red Wing. Mr. Hague had been employed in Red Wing for the 15 years immediately preceding his death and had commuted daily from Wisconsin to his place of employment.

Neither the operator of the motorcycle nor the operator of the automobile carried valid insurance. However, the decedent held a policy issued by petitioner Allstate Insurance Company covering three automobiles owned by him and containing an uninsured motorist clause insuring him against loss incurred from accidents with uninsured motorists. The uninsured motorist coverage was limited to $15,000 for each automobile.

After the accident, but prior to the initiation of this lawsuit, respondent moved to Red Wing. Subsequently, she married a Minnesota resident and established residence with her new husband in Savage, Minn. At approximately the same time, a Minnesota Registrar of Probate appointed respondent personal representative of her deceased husband's estate. Following her appointment, she brought this action in Minnesota District Court seeking a declaration under Minnesota law that the $15,000 uninsured motorist coverage on each of her late husband's three automobiles could be "stacked" to provide total coverage of $45,000. Petitioner defended on the ground that whether the three uninsured motorist coverages could be stacked should be determined by Wisconsin law, since the insurance policy was delivered in Wisconsin, the accident occurred in Wisconsin, and all persons involved were Wisconsin residents at the time of the accident.

The Minnesota District Court disagreed. Interpreting Wisconsin law to disallow stacking, the court concluded that Minnesota's choice-of-law rules required the application of Minnesota law permitting stacking. The court refused to apply Wisconsin law as "inimical to the public policy of Minnesota" and granted summary judgment for respondent.

The Minnesota Supreme Court, sitting en banc, affirmed the District Court. The court, also interpreting Wisconsin law to prohibit stacking, applied Minnesota law after analyzing the relevant Minnesota contacts and interests within the analytical framework developed by Professor Leflar. . . Although stating that the Minnesota contacts might not be, "in themselves, sufficient to mandate application of [Minnesota] law," 289 N.W.2d 43, 49 (1978), under the first four factors, the court concluded that the fifth factor—application of the better rule of law—favored selection of Minnesota law. The court emphasized that a majority of States allow stacking and that legal decisions allowing stacking "are fairly recent and well considered in light of current uses of automobiles." Id., at 49. In addition, the court found the Minnesota rule superior to Wisconsin's "because it requires the cost of accidents with uninsured motorists to be spread more broadly through insurance premiums than does the Wisconsin rule." Ibid. Finally, after rehearing en banc, the court buttressed its initial opinion by indicating "that contracts of insurance on motor vehicles are in a class by themselves" since an insurance company "knows the automobile is a movable item which will be driven from state to state." 289 N.W.2d 49, 50 (1979). From this premise the court concluded that application of Minnesota law was "not so arbitrary and unreasonable as to violate due process." Ibid.

II

In deciding constitutional choice-of-law questions, whether under the Due Process Clause or the Full Faith and Credit Clause,[10] this Court has traditionally examined the contacts of the State, whose law was applied, with the parties and with the occurrence or transaction giving rise to the litigation. See *Clay II,* supra, 377 U.S., at 183. In order to ensure that the choice of law is neither arbitrary nor fundamentally unfair, see *Alaska Packers Assn. v. Industrial Accident Commission,* 294 U.S. 532, 542 (1935), the Court has invalidated the choice of law of a State which has had no

[10] This Court has taken a similar approach in deciding choice-of-law cases under both the Due Process Clause and the Full Faith and Credit Clause. In each instance, the Court has examined the relevant contacts and resulting interests of the State whose law was applied. See, e.g., *Nevada v. Hall,* 440 U.S. 410, 424 (1979). Although at one time the Court required a more exacting standard under the Full Faith and Credit Clause than under the Due Process Clause for evaluating the constitutionality of choice-of-law decisions, see *Alaska Packers Assn. v. Industrial Accident Comm'n,* 294 U.S. 532, 549–550 (1935) (interest of State whose law was applied was no less than interest of State whose law was rejected), the Court has since abandoned the weighing of interests requirement. *Carroll v. Lanza,* 349 U.S. 408 (1955); see *Nevada v. Hall,* supra; Weintraub, Due Process and Full Faith and Credit Limitations on a State's Choice of Law, 44 Iowa L.Rev. 449 (1959). Different considerations are of course at issue when full faith and credit is to be accorded to acts, records and proceedings outside the choice-of-law area, such as in the case of sister state court judgments.

significant contact or significant aggregation of contacts, creating state interests, with the parties and the occurrence or transaction.[11]

Two instructive examples of such invalidation are *Home Insurance Company v. Dick,* 281 U.S. 397 (1930), and *John Hancock Mutual Life Insurance Co. v. Yates,* 299 U.S. 178 (1936). . .

Dick and *Yates* stand for the proposition that if a State has only an insignificant contact with the parties and the occurrence or transaction, application of its law is unconstitutional. *Dick* concluded that nominal residence—standing alone—was inadequate; *Yates* held that a postoccurrence change of residence to the forum State—standing alone—was insufficient to justify application of forum law. Although instructive as extreme examples of selection of forum law, neither *Dick* nor *Yates* governs this case. For in contrast to those decisions, here the Minnesota contacts with the parties and the occurrence are obviously significant. . .

The lesson from *Dick* and *Yates,* which found insufficient forum contacts to apply forum law, and from *Alaska Packers* [and other cases], which found adequate contacts to sustain the choice of forum law, is that for a State's substantive law to be selected in a constitutionally permissible manner, that State must have a significant contact or significant aggregation of contacts, creating state interests, such that choice of its law is neither arbitrary nor fundamentally unfair. Application of this principle to the facts of this case persuades us that the Minnesota Supreme Court's choice of its own law did not offend the Federal Constitution.

III

Minnesota has three contacts with the parties and the occurrence giving rise to the litigation. In the aggregate, these contacts permit selection by the Minnesota Supreme Court of Minnesota law allowing the stacking of Mr. Hague's uninsured motorist coverages.

First, and for our purposes a very important contact, Mr. Hague was a member of Minnesota's workforce, having been employed by a Red Wing, Minn., enterprise for the 15 years preceding his death. While employment status may implicate a state interest less substantial than does resident status, that interest is nevertheless important. The State of employment has police power responsibilities towards the nonresident employee that

---

[11] Prior to the advent of interest analysis in the state courts as the "dominant mode of analysis in modern choice of law theory," * * * the prevailing choice of law methodology focused on the jurisdiction where a particular event occurred. . . .

Hartford Accident and Indemnity Co. v. Delta & Pine Land Co., 292 U.S. 143 (1934), can, perhaps, best be explained as an example of that period. . . .

That case, however, has scant relevance for today. It implied a choice-of-law analysis which, for all intents and purposes, gave an isolated event—the writing of the bond in Tennessee—controlling constitutional significance, even though there might have been contacts with another State (there Mississippi) which would make application of its law neither unfair nor unexpected. * * *

are analogous, if somewhat less profound, than towards residents. Thus, such employees use state services and amenities and may call upon state facilities in appropriate circumstances.

In addition, Mr. Hague commuted to work in Minnesota, . . . and was presumably covered by his uninsured motorist coverage during the commute. The State's interest in its commuting nonresident employees reflects a state concern for the safety and well-being of its workforce and the concomitant effect on Minnesota employers.

That Mr. Hague was not killed while commuting to work or while in Minnesota does not dictate a different result. To hold that the Minnesota Supreme Court's choice of Minnesota law violated the Constitution for that reason would require too narrow a view of Minnesota's relationship with the parties and the occurrence giving rise to the litigation. An automobile accident need not occur within a particular jurisdiction for that jurisdiction to be connected to the occurrence. Similarly, the occurrence of a crash fatal to a Minnesota employee in another State is a Minnesota contact. If Mr. Hague had only been injured and missed work for a few weeks, the effect on the Minnesota employer would have been palpable and Minnesota's interest in having its employee made whole would be evident. Mr. Hague's death affects Minnesota's interest still more acutely, even though Mr. Hague will not return to the Minnesota workforce. Minnesota's workforce is surely affected by the level of protection the State extends to it, either directly or indirectly. Vindication of the rights of the estate of a Minnesota employee, therefore, is an important state concern.

Second, Allstate was at all times present and doing business in Minnesota.[23] By virtue of its presence, Allstate can hardly claim unfamiliarity with the laws of the host jurisdiction and surprise that the state courts might apply forum law to litigation in which the company is involved. "Particularly since the company was licensed to do business in [the forum], it must have known it might be sued there, and that [the forum] courts would feel bound by [forum] law."[24] *Clay v. Sun Insurance*

---

[23] The Court has recognized that examination of a State's contacts may result in divergent conclusions for jurisdiction and choice-of-law purposes. See *Kulko v. Superior Court,* 436 U.S. 84, 98 (1978) (no jurisdiction in California but California law "arguably might" apply); *Shaffer v. Heitner,* supra, 433 U.S., at 215 (no jurisdiction in Delaware, although Delaware interest "may support the application of Delaware law"); cf. *Hanson v. Denckla,* 357 U.S. 235, 254, and n. 27 (1958) (no jurisdiction in Florida; the "issue is personal jurisdiction, not choice of law," an issue which the Court found no need to decide). Nevertheless, "both inquiries 'are often closely related and to a substantial degree depend upon similar considerations.' " 433 U.S., at 224–225 (Brennan, J., concurring in part and dissenting in part). Here, of course, jurisdiction in the Minnesota courts is unquestioned, a factor not without significance in assessing the constitutionality of Minnesota's choice of its own substantive law. * * *

[24] There is no element of unfair surprise or frustration of legitimate expectations as a result of Minnesota's choice of its law. Because Allstate was doing business in Minnesota and was undoubtedly aware that Mr. Hague was a Minnesota employee, it had to have anticipated that Minnesota law might apply to an accident in which Mr. Hague was involved. . . . Indeed, Allstate specifically anticipated that Mr. Hague might suffer an accident either in Minnesota or elsewhere in the United States, outside of Wisconsin, since the policy it issued offered continental

Office Limited, 363 U.S. 207, 221 (1960) (Black, J., dissenting). Moreover, Allstate's presence in Minnesota gave Minnesota an interest in regulating the company's insurance obligations insofar as they affected both a Minnesota resident and court appointed representative—respondent—and a longstanding member of Minnesota's workforce—Mr. Hague. * * *

Third, respondent became a Minnesota resident prior to institution of this litigation. The stipulated facts reveal that she first settled in Red Wing, Minn., the town in which her late husband had worked. She subsequently moved to Savage, Minn., after marrying a Minnesota resident who operated an automobile service station in Bloomington, Minn. Her move to Savage occurred "almost concurrently," 289 N.W.2d, at 45, with the initiation of the instant case. There is no suggestion that Mrs. Hague moved to Minnesota in anticipation of this litigation or for the purpose of finding a legal climate especially hospitable to her claim.[28] The stipulated facts, sparse as they are, negate any such inference.

While *John Hancock Mutual Life Insurance Company v. Yates,* supra, held that a postoccurrence change of residence to the forum State was insufficient in and of itself to confer power on the forum State to choose its law, that case did not hold that such a change of residence was irrelevant. Here, of course, respondent's bona fide residence in Minnesota was not the sole contact Minnesota had with this litigation. And in connection with her residence in Minnesota, respondent was appointed personal representative of Mr. Hague's estate by the Registrar of Probate for the County of Goodhue, Minn. Respondent's residence and subsequent appointment in Minnesota as personal representative of her late husband's estate constitute a Minnesota contact which gives Minnesota an interest in respondent's recovery, an interest which the court below identified as full compensation for "resident accident victims" to keep them "off welfare rolls" and able "to meet financial obligations." 289 N.W.2d, at 49.

In sum, Minnesota had a significant aggregation[29] of contacts with the parties and the occurrence, creating state interests, such that application of its law was neither arbitrary nor fundamentally unfair. Accordingly, the choice of Minnesota law by the Minnesota Supreme Court did not violate the Due Process Clause or the Full Faith and Credit Clause.

Affirmed.

---

coverage. . . . At the same time, Allstate did not seek to control construction of the contract since the policy contained no choice-of-law clause dictating application of Wisconsin law. . . .

[28] The dissent suggests that considering respondent's postoccurrence change of residence as one of the Minnesota contacts will encourage forum shopping. This overlooks the fact that her change of residence was bona fide and not motivated by litigation considerations.

[29] We express no view whether the first two contacts, either together or separately, would have sufficed to sustain the choice of Minnesota law made by the Minnesota Supreme Court.

JUSTICE STEWART took no part in the consideration or decision of this case.

JUSTICE STEVENS, concurring in the judgment.

As I view this unusual case—in which neither precedent nor constitutional language provides sure guidance—two separate questions must be answered. First, does the Full Faith and Credit Clause *require* Minnesota, the forum State, to apply Wisconsin law? Second, does the Due Process Clause of the Fourteenth Amendment *prevent* Minnesota from applying its own law? The first inquiry implicates the federal interest in ensuring that Minnesota respect the sovereignty of the State of Wisconsin; the second implicates the litigants' interest in a fair adjudication of their rights.

I realize that both this Court's analysis of choice-of-law questions and scholarly criticism of those decisions have treated these two inquiries as though they were indistinguishable. Nevertheless, I am persuaded that the two constitutional provisions protect different interests and that proper analysis requires separate consideration of each.

I

The Full Faith and Credit Clause is one of several provisions in the Federal Constitution designed to transform the several States from independent sovereignties into a single, unified Nation. * * * The Full Faith and Credit Clause implements this design by directing that a State, when acting as the forum for litigation having multistate aspects or implications, respect the legitimate interests of other States and avoid infringement upon their sovereignty. The Clause does not, however, rigidly require the forum State to apply foreign law whenever another State has a valid interest in the litigation. * * * On the contrary, in view of the fact that the forum State is also a sovereign in its own right, in appropriate cases it may attach paramount importance to its own legitimate interests. Accordingly, the fact that a choice-of-law decision may be unsound as a matter of conflicts law does not necessarily implicate the federal concerns embodied in the Full Faith and Credit Clause. Rather, in my opinion, the Clause should not invalidate a state court's choice of forum law unless that choice threatens the federal interest in national unity by unjustifiably infringing upon the legitimate interests of another State.

In this case, I think the Minnesota courts' decision to apply Minnesota law was plainly unsound as a matter of normal conflicts law. Both the execution of the insurance contract and the accident giving rise to the litigation took place in Wisconsin. Moreover, when both of those events occurred, the plaintiff, the decedent, and the operators of both vehicles were all residents of Wisconsin. Nevertheless, I do not believe that any threat to national unity or Wisconsin's sovereignty ensues from allowing the substantive question presented by this case to be determined by the law of another State.

The question on the merits is one of interpreting the meaning of the insurance contract. Neither the contract itself, nor anything else in the record, reflects any express understanding of the parties with respect to what law would be applied or with respect to whether the separate uninsured motorist coverage for each of the decedent's three cars could be "stacked." Since the policy provided coverage for accidents that might occur in other States, it was obvious to the parties at the time of contracting that it might give rise to the application of the law of States other than Wisconsin. Therefore, while Wisconsin may have an interest in ensuring that contracts formed in Wisconsin in reliance upon Wisconsin law are interpreted in accordance with that law, that interest is not implicated in this case.

Petitioner has failed to establish that Minnesota's refusal to apply Wisconsin law poses any direct or indirect threat to Wisconsin's sovereignty. In the absence of any such threat, I find it unnecessary to evaluate the forum State's interest in the litigation in order to reach the conclusion that the Full Faith and Credit Clause does not require the Minnesota courts to apply Wisconsin law to the question of contract interpretation presented in this case.

II

It may be assumed that a choice-of-law decision would violate the Due Process Clause if it were totally arbitrary or if it were fundamentally unfair to either litigant. I question whether a judge's decision to apply the law of his own State could ever be described as wholly irrational. For judges are presumably familiar with their own state law and may find it difficult and time consuming to discover and apply correctly the law of another State. The forum State's interest in the fair and efficient administration of justice is therefore sufficient, in my judgment, to attach a presumption of validity to a forum State's decision to apply its own law to a dispute over which it has jurisdiction.

The forum State's interest in the efficient operation of its judicial system is clearly not sufficient, however, to justify the application of a rule of law that is fundamentally unfair to one of the litigants. Arguably, a litigant could demonstrate such unfairness in a variety of ways. Concern about the fairness of the forum's choice of its own rule might arise if that rule favored residents over nonresidents, if it represented a dramatic departure from the rule that obtains in most American jurisdictions, or if the rule itself was unfair on its face or as applied.

The application of an otherwise acceptable rule of law may result in unfairness to the litigants if, in engaging in the activity which is the subject of the litigation, they could not reasonably have anticipated that their actions would later be judged by this rule of law. A choice-of-law decision that frustrates the justifiable expectations of the parties can be fundamentally unfair. This desire to prevent unfair surprise to a litigant has been the central concern in this Court's review of choice-of-law decisions under the Due Process Clause.

Neither the "stacking" rule itself, nor Minnesota's application of that rule to these litigants, raises any serious question of fairness. As the plurality observes, "[s]tacking was the rule in most States at the time the policy was issued." Moreover, the rule is consistent with the economics of a contractual relationship in which the policyholder paid three separate premiums for insurance coverage for three automobiles, including a separate premium for each uninsured motorist coverage. Nor am I persuaded that the decision of the Minnesota courts to apply the "stacking" rule in this case can be said to violate due process because that decision frustrates the reasonable expectations of the contracting parties.

Contracting parties can, of course, make their expectations explicit by providing in their contract either that the law of a particular jurisdiction shall govern questions of contract interpretation, or that a particular substantive rule, for instance "stacking," shall or shall not apply.[20] . . .

In this case, no express indication of the parties' expectations is available. The insurance policy provided coverage for accidents throughout the United States; thus, at the time of contracting, the parties certainly could have anticipated that the law of States other than Wisconsin would govern particular claims arising under the policy. By virtue of doing business in Minnesota, Allstate was aware that it could be sued in the Minnesota courts; Allstate also presumably was aware that Minnesota law, as well as the law of most States, permitted "stacking." Nothing in the record requires that a different inference be drawn. Therefore, the decision of the Minnesota courts to apply the law of the forum in this case does not frustrate the reasonable expectations of the contracting parties, and I can find no fundamental unfairness in that decision requiring the attention of this Court.

In terms of fundamental fairness, it seems to me that two factors relied upon by the plurality—the plaintiff's post-accident move to Minnesota and the decedent's Minnesota employment—are either irrelevant to or possibly even tend to undermine the plurality's conclusion. When the expectations of the parties at the time of contracting are the central due process concern, as they are in this case, an unanticipated post-accident occurrence is clearly irrelevant for due process purposes. The fact that the plaintiff

[20] . . .While such express provisions are obviously relevant, they are not always dispositive. In *Clay v. Sun Insurance Office, Ltd.*, 377 U.S. 179 (1964), the Court allowed the lower court's choice of forum law to override an express contractual limitations period. The Court emphasized the fact that the insurer had issued the insurance policy with the knowledge that it would cover the insured property wherever it was taken. . . .

became a resident of the forum State after the accident surely cannot justify a ruling in her favor that would not be made if the plaintiff were a nonresident. Similarly, while the fact that the decedent regularly drove into Minnesota might be relevant to the expectations of the contracting parties, the fact that he did so because he was employed in Minnesota adds nothing to the due process analysis. The choice-of-law decision of the Minnesota courts is consistent with due process because it does not result in unfairness to either litigant, not because Minnesota now has an interest in the plaintiff as resident or formerly had an interest in the decedent as employee. . .

JUSTICE POWELL, with whom the CHIEF JUSTICE and JUSTICE REHNQUIST join, dissenting.

My disagreement with the plurality is narrow. I accept with few reservations Part II of the plurality opinion, which sets forth the basic principles that guide us in reviewing state choice-of-law decisions under the Constitution. The Court should invalidate a forum State's decision to apply its own law only when there are no significant contacts between the State and the litigation. . .

To assess the sufficiency of asserted contacts between the forum and the litigation, the Court must determine if the contacts form a reasonable link between the litigation and a state policy. In short, examination of contacts addresses whether "the state has an interest in the application of its policy in this instance." . . .

A contact, or a pattern of contacts, satisfies the Constitution when it protects the litigants from being unfairly surprised if the forum State applies its own law, and when the application of the forum's law reasonably can be understood to further a legitimate public policy of the forum State.

II . . .

I would agree that no reasonable expectations of the parties were frustrated. The risk insured by petitioner was not geographically limited. See *Clay v. Sun Ins. Office, Ltd.*, supra, 377 U.S., at 182. The close proximity of Hager City, Wis. to Minnesota, and the fact that Hague commuted daily to Red Wing, Minn., for many years should have led the insurer to realize that there was a reasonable probability that the risk would materialize in Minnesota. . .

The more doubtful question in this case is whether application of Minnesota's substantive law reasonably furthers a legitimate state interest. The plurality attempts to give substance to the tenuous contacts between Minnesota and this litigation. Upon examination, however, these contacts are either trivial or irrelevant to the furthering of any public policy of Minnesota.

First, the post-accident residence of the plaintiff-beneficiary is constitutionally irrelevant to the choice-of-law question. *John Hancock Mut. Life Ins. Co. v. Yates,* supra. . .

This rule is sound. If a plaintiff could choose the substantive rules to be applied to an action by moving to a hospitable forum, the invitation to forum shopping would be irresistible. Moreover, it would permit the defendant's reasonable expectations at the time the cause of action accrues to be frustrated, because it would permit the choice-of-law question to turn on a post-accrual circumstance. Finally, post-accrual residence has nothing to do with facts to which the forum State proposes to apply its rule; it is unrelated to the substantive legal issues presented by the litigation.

Second, the plurality finds it significant that the insurer does business in the forum State. . . The State does have a legitimate interest in regulating the practices of such an insurer. But this argument proves too much. The insurer here does business in all 50 States. The forum State has no interest in regulating that conduct of the insurer unrelated to property, persons or contracts executed within the forum State. . .

Third, the plurality emphasizes particularly that the insured worked in the forum State.[5] . . . The fact that the insured was a nonresident employee in the forum State provides a significant contact for the furtherance of some local policies. See, e.g., *Pacific Ins. Co. v. Industrial Accident Comm'n,* supra (forum State's interest in compensating workers for employment-related injuries occurring within the State); *Alaska Packers Assn. v. Industrial Accident Comm'n,* 294 U.S. 532, 549 (1935) (forum State's interest in compensating the employment-related injuries of a worker hired in the State). The insured's place of employment is not, however, significant in this case. Neither the nature of the insurance policy, the events related to the accident, nor the immediate question of stacking coverage are in any way affected or implicated by the insured's employment status. The plurality's opinion is understandably vague in explaining how trebling the benefits to be paid to the estate of a nonresident employee furthers any substantial state interest relating to employment. Minnesota does not wish its workers to die in automobile accidents, but permitting stacking will not further this interest. The substantive issue here is solely one of compensation, and whether the compensation provided by this policy is increased or not will have no relation to the State's employment policies or police power. See n. 5, supra.

---

[5] The plurality exacts double service from this fact, by finding a separate contact in that the insured commuted daily to his job. This is merely a repetition of the facts that the insured lived in Wisconsin and worked in Minnesota. The State does have an interest in the safety of motorists who use its roads. This interest is not limited to employees, but extends to all nonresident motorists on its highways. This safety interest, however, cannot encompass, either in logic or in any practical sense, the determination whether a nonresident's estate can stack benefit coverage in a policy written in another State regarding an accident that occurred on another State's roads. . . .

Neither taken separately nor in the aggregate do the contacts asserted by the plurality today indicate that Minnesota's application of its substantive rule in this case will further any legitimate state interest. The plurality focuses only on physical contacts *vel non,* and in doing so pays scant attention to the more fundamental reasons why our precedents require reasonable policy-related contacts in choice-of-law cases. Therefore, I dissent.

PHILLIPS PETROLEUM CO. V. SHUTTS

472 U.S. 797 (1985).

JUSTICE REHNQUIST delivered the opinion of the Court.

[During the 1970s, Phillips Petroleum leased mineral rights from some 30,000 individuals. Under these leases, Phillips agreed to pay a percentage "royalty" of its profits from sales of oil and gas. At various times during this period, Phillips raised prices. Price increases required approval from the FPC (now FERC). The agency would give tentative approval when the new rates were filed, subject to further study before final approval was given. During the interim, Phillips could charge the higher prices, but if the rates were not approved it would have to refund the difference. Higher prices meant higher royalties to the lessors. Concerned that it might have to refund this money, Phillips did not pay these until after final approval. When it did pay the additional royalties, Phillips did not include interest for the period during which the rates were only tentative.

In an earlier decision the Kansas Supreme Court had held equitable principles required Phillips to pay such interest. The present suit was brought for similar relief on behalf of royalty owners residing in all 50 states and possessing interests in land located in 11 states, including Kansas. Phillips is a Delaware corporation having its principal place of business in Oklahoma.]

III

The Kansas courts applied Kansas contract and Kansas equity law to every claim in this case, notwithstanding that over 99% of the gas leases and some 97% of the plaintiffs in the case had no apparent connection to the State of Kansas except for this lawsuit. Petitioner protested that the Kansas courts should apply the laws of the States where the leases were located, or at least apply Texas and Oklahoma law because so many of the leases came from those States. The Kansas courts disregarded this contention and found petitioner liable for interest on the suspended royalties as a matter of Kansas law, and set the interest rates under Kansas equity principles.

Petitioner contends that total application of Kansas substantive law violated the constitutional limitations on choice of law mandated by the

Due Process Clause of the Fourteenth Amendment and the Full Faith and Credit Clause of Article IV, § 1. We must first determine whether Kansas law conflicts in any material way with any other law which could apply. There can be no injury in applying Kansas law if it is not in conflict with that of any other jurisdiction connected to this suit. . .

The conflicts on the applicable interest rates, alone—which we do not think can be labeled "false conflicts" without a more thoroughgoing treatment than was accorded them by the Supreme Court of Kansas—certainly amounted to millions of dollars in liability. We think that the Supreme Court of Kansas erred in deciding on the basis that it did that the application of its laws to all claims would be constitutional. . .

The plurality in *Allstate* noted that a particular set of facts giving rise to litigation could justify, constitutionally, the application of more than one jurisdiction's laws. The plurality recognized, however, that the Due Process Clause and the Full Faith and Credit Clause provided modest restrictions on the application of forum law. These restrictions required "that for a State's substantive law to be selected in a constitutionally permissible manner, that State must have a significant contact or significant aggregation of contacts, creating state interests, such that choice of its law is neither arbitrary nor fundamentally unfair." The dissenting Justices were in substantial agreement with this principle. . .

Petitioner owns property and conducts substantial business in the State, so Kansas certainly has an interest in regulating petitioner's conduct in Kansas. 235 Kan., at 210, 679 P.2d, at 1174. Moreover, oil and gas extraction is an important business to Kansas, and although only a few leases in issue are located in Kansas, hundreds of Kansas plaintiffs were affected by petitioner's suspension of royalties; thus the court held that the State has a real interest in protecting "the rights of these royalty owners both as individual residents of [Kansas] and as members of this particular class of plaintiffs." *Id.,* at 211–212, 679 P.2d, at 1174. The Kansas Supreme Court pointed out that Kansas courts are quite familiar with this type of lawsuit, and "[t]he plaintiff class members have indicated their desire to have this action determined under the laws of Kansas." *Id.,* at 211, 222, 679 P.2d, at 1174, 1181. Finally, the Kansas court buttressed its use of Kansas law by stating that this lawsuit was analogous to a suit against a "common fund" located in Kansas. *Id.,* at 201, 211–212, 679 P.2d, at 1168, 1174.

We do not lightly discount this description of Kansas' contacts with this litigation and its interest in applying its law. There is, however, no "common fund" located in Kansas that would require or support the application of only Kansas law to all these claims. * * * As the Kansas court noted, petitioner commingled the suspended royalties with its general corporate accounts. 235 Kan. 201, 679 P.2d, at 1168. There is no specific identifiable res in Kansas, nor is there any limited amount which may be depleted before every plaintiff is compensated. Only by somehow aggregating all the separate claims in this case could a "common fund" in any sense be created, and the term becomes all but meaningless when used in such an expansive sense.

We also give little credence to the idea that Kansas law should apply to all claims because the plaintiffs, by failing to opt out, evinced their desire to be bound by Kansas law. Even if one could say that the plaintiffs "consented" to the application of Kansas law by not opting out, plaintiff's desire for forum law is rarely, if ever controlling. In most cases the plaintiff shows his obvious wish for forum law by filing there. "If a plaintiff could choose the substantive rules to be applied to an action . . . the invitation to forum shopping would be irresistible." *Allstate,* 449 U.S., at 337 (opinion of Powell, J.). Even if a plaintiff evidences his desire for forum law by moving to the forum, we have generally accorded such a move little or no significance. *John Hancock Mut. Life Ins. Co. v. Yates,* 299 U.S. 178, 182 (1936); *Home Ins. Co. v. Dick,* 281 U.S. 397, 408 (1930). In *Allstate* the plaintiff's move to the forum was only relevant because it was unrelated and prior to the litigation. 449 U.S., at 318–319, 101 S.Ct., at 643. Thus the plaintiffs' desire for Kansas law, manifested by their participation in this Kansas lawsuit, bears little relevance.

The Supreme Court of Kansas in its opinion in this case expressed the view that by reason of the fact that it was adjudicating a nationwide class action, it had much greater latitude in applying its own law to the transactions in question than might otherwise be the case:

> "The general rule is that the law of the forum applies unless it is expressly shown that a different law governs, and in case of doubt, the law of the forum is preferred... Where a state court determines it has jurisdiction over a nationwide class action and procedural due process guarantees of notice and adequate representation are present, we believe the law of the forum should be applied unless compelling reasons exist for applying a different law... Compelling reasons do not exist to require this court to look to other state laws to determine the rights of the parties involved in this lawsuit." 235 Kan., at 221–222, 679 P.2d, at 1181.

We think that this is something of a "bootstrap" argument. The Kansas class-action statute, like those of most other jurisdictions, requires that there be "common issues of law or fact." But while a state may, for the reasons we have previously stated, assume jurisdiction over the claims of plaintiffs whose principal contacts are with other States, it may not use this assumption of jurisdiction as an added weight in the scale when considering the permissible constitutional limits on choice of substantive law. It may not take a transaction with little or no relationship to the forum and apply the law of the forum in order to satisfy the procedural requirement that there be a "common question of law." The issue of personal jurisdiction over plaintiffs in a class action is entirely distinct from the question of the constitutional limitations on choice of law; the latter calculus is not altered by the fact that it may be more difficult or more burdensome to comply with the constitutional limitations because of the large number of transactions which the State proposes to adjudicate and which have little connection with the forum.

Kansas must have a "significant contact or aggregation of contacts" to the claims asserted by each member of the plaintiff class, contacts "creating state interests" in order to ensure that the choice of Kansas law is not arbitrary or unfair. *Allstate, supra,* 449 U.S., at 312–313. Given Kansas' lack of "interest" in claims unrelated to that State, and the substantive conflict with jurisdictions such as Texas, we conclude that application of Kansas law to every claim in this case is sufficiently arbitrary and unfair as to exceed constitutional limits.

When considering fairness in this context, an important element is the expectation of the parties. See *Allstate, supra,* 449 U.S., at 333, 101 S.Ct., at 650 (opinion of Powell, J.). There is no indication that when the leases involving land and royalty owners outside of Kansas were executed, the parties had any idea that Kansas law would control. Neither the Due Process Clause nor the Full Faith and Credit Clause requires Kansas "to substitute for its own [laws], applicable to persons and events within it, the conflicting statute of another state," *Pacific Employers Insurance Co. v. Industrial Accident Comm'n,* 306 U.S. 493, 502 (1939), but Kansas "may not abrogate the rights of parties beyond its borders having no relation to anything done or to be done within them." *Home Insurance Co. v. Dick, supra,* 281 U.S., at 410.

Here the Supreme Court of Kansas took the view that in a nationwide class action where procedural due process guarantees of notice and adequate representation were met, "the laws of the forum should be applied unless compelling reasons exist for applying a different law." 235 Kan. at 221, 679 P.2d at 1181. Whatever practical reasons may have commended this rule to the Supreme Court of Kansas, for the reasons already stated we do not believe that it is consistent with the decisions of this Court. We make no effort to determine for ourselves which law must apply to the various transactions involved in this lawsuit, and we reaffirm our observation in *Allstate* that in many situations a state court may be free to apply one of several choices of law. But the constitutional limitations laid down in cases such as *Allstate* and *Home Insurance Co. v. Dick, supra,* must be respected even in a nationwide class action.

We therefore affirm the judgment of the Supreme Court of Kansas insofar as it upheld the jurisdiction of the Kansas courts over the plaintiff class members in this case, and reverse its judgment insofar as it held that Kansas law was applicable to all of the transactions which it sought to adjudicate. We remand the case to that Court for further proceedings not inconsistent with this opinion.

JUSTICE POWELL took no part in the decision of this case.

JUSTICE STEVENS, concurring in part and dissenting in part. . .

As the Court recognizes, there "can be no [constitutional] injury in applying Kansas law if it is not in conflict with that of any other jurisdiction connected to this suit." * * * A fair reading of the Kansas Supreme Court's opinion in light of its earlier opinion in *Shutts v. Phillips Petroleum Co.*, 222 Kan. 527, 567 P.2d 1292 (1977), cert. denied, 434 U.S. 1068 (1978) (hereinafter *Shutts I*), reveals that the Kansas court has examined the laws of connected jurisdictions and has correctly concluded that there is no "direct" or "substantive" conflict between the law applied by Kansas and the laws of those other States. * * * Kansas has merely developed general common law principles to accommodate the novel facts of this litigation—other State courts either agree with Kansas or have not yet addressed precisely similar claims. Consequently, I conclude that the Full Faith and Credit Clause of the Constitution did not require Kansas to apply the law of any other State, and the Fourteenth Amendment's Due Process Clause did not prevent Kansas from applying its own law in this case. . .

Minimum Contacts and Choice of Law

(1) *Hague* and *Shutts* equate the constitutional protections of due process and full faith and credit. The process of merging analysis under these clauses began in *Watson v. Employers Liab. Assur. Corp.*, 348 U.S. 66 (1954). Watson, a citizen of Louisiana, was injured while using a hair-waving product manufactured by the Toni Co., an Illinois subsidiary of the Gillette Safety Razor Co., which had its headquarters in Massachusetts. Watson sued their insurer in Louisiana, relying on that state's direct action statute. The insurance policy, which was negotiated and issued in Massachusetts and Illinois, contained a clause—valid in both those states—prohibiting direct actions against the insurer until after Toni's liability had been determined. Applying Louisiana law, the Court refused to enforce this provision, and the insurer appealed on due process and full faith and credit grounds. In explaining why there was no due process violation, the Court noted that the modern practice of conducting business throughout the United States required businesses to recognize that more than one law might apply to the same transaction. This was such a transaction:

> Although this insurance contract was issued in Massachusetts, it was to protect Gillette and its Illinois subsidiary against damages on account of personal injuries that might be suffered by users of Toni Home Permanents anywhere in the United States, its territories, or in Canada.

Louisiana in particular had an interest in applying its direct action statute because the injured plaintiff was one of its citizens:

> [M]odern transportation and business methods have made it more difficult to serve process on wrongdoers who live or do business in other states. In this case, efforts to serve the Gillette company were answered by a motion to dismiss on the ground that Gillette had no Louisiana agent on whom process could be served. If this motion is granted, Mrs. Watson, but for the direct action law, could not get her case tried without going to Massachusetts or Illinois although she lives in Louisiana and her claim is for injuries from a product bought and used there.

The Court observed that "[w]hat we have said above goes far toward answering the Full Faith and Credit Clause contention," because, given Louisiana's interest, that clause "does not require Louisiana to subordinate its direct action provisions to Massachusetts contract rules."

Watson was followed in *Clay v. Sun Ins. Office, Ltd.*, 377 U.S. 179 (1964). Clay, a citizen of Illinois, purchased personal property insurance from a British insurer doing business in Illinois, Florida, and several other states. A few months after purchasing the policy, Clay moved to Florida, where two years later he suffered a loss. The insurance company moved to dismiss Clay's action, citing a provision in the contract that required suit to be brought within 12 months. Florida law instead provided a five-year statute of limitations, and the Florida Supreme Court stated that this law would displace the contract limitation. This time the Supreme Court merged the analysis of due process and full faith and credit, treating them together and finding "no difficulty whatever with either the Full Faith and Credit Clause or the Due Process Clause." As in *Watson,* Florida had an interest because the plaintiff was a resident. Quoting an earlier opinion by Justice Black in the same case, the Court then explained why, given that interest, applying forum law was permissible:

> Insurance companies, like other contractors, do not confine their contractual activities and obligations within state boundaries. They sell to customers who are promised protection in States far away from the place where the contract is made. In this very case the policy was sold to Clay with knowledge that he could take his property anywhere in the world he saw fit without losing the protection of his insurance. In fact, his contract was described on its face as a "Personal Property Floater Policy (World Wide)." The

contract did not even attempt to provide that the law of Illinois would govern when suits were filed anywhere else in the country.

Were *Watson* and *Clay* correctly decided? Can you distinguish these cases from *Home Ins. Co. v. Dick*? Why should it matter that coverage is extended to losses that might occur in many places?

(2) Do the full faith and credit clause and the due process clause protect distinct concerns? So long as we examine all the interests identified as important under either of these clauses, why should the matter of constitutional labeling trouble us?

Does the plurality in *Hague* take all these concerns into account? Justice Brennan observes that a state may apply its law if it has a sufficient "aggregation of contacts," but he does little to clarify what makes a contact significant for these purposes. How are the relevant constitutional concerns satisfied by the contacts discussed in the plurality opinion? Why, for instance, is the fact that Hague worked in Minnesota significant in *this* case? Why is the fact that Allstate does business in Minnesota relevant when the transaction at issue had nothing to do with that business? Why does it matter that plaintiff now lives in Minnesota? Justice Brennan distinguishes *Yates* on the ground that a post-occurrence change of residence is insufficient "standing alone." But what does this contact add? What do the other two contacts add? What, in other words, are we looking for when we examine a state's contacts?

With the notable exception of Professor Leflar, conflicts scholars have made a cottage industry of criticizing the plurality opinion in *Hague*. See, e.g., *Symposium: Choice of Law Theory After* Allstate Insurance Co. v. Hague, 10 Hofstra L.Rev. 1 (1981); Weinberg, *Choice of Law and Minimal Scrutiny,* 49 U.Chi.L.Rev. 440 (1982).

(3) The plurality opinion in *Hague* may be confused, but is the outcome incorrect? The due process cases establish that a state must have contacts such that the defendant is not unfairly surprised by the application of its law. As in *Clay* and *Watson* (and unlike in *Dick*), this concern is satisfied by the fact that Allstate extended coverage to accidents in Minnesota. Indeed, this case is *easier* than *Clay* because Allstate knew when it issued the policy that Hague worked in Minnesota and drove there every day, making apparent the possible application of Minnesota law to these insurance policies. To be sure, *this particular* accident did not occur in Minnesota, but why should that matter in terms of the law governing a contract covering potential losses in many places? The full faith and credit cases, in the meantime, establish that a state must also have contacts that give it an interest in applying its law. This concern is met by the plaintiff's present residence in Minnesota. The fact that the state's interest results from the plaintiff's post-occurrence move might create a problem of unfair surprise were her residence relied on to satisfy the due process concern.

But, as just noted, there are other contacts that satisfy this constitutional concern (unlike in *Dick* and *Yates*). And *Clay* had already made clear that the unfair surprise concern and the state interest concern can be satisfied independently by different contacts: in that case, the unfair surprise element was satisfied by the extension of insurance coverage to Florida, while the state interest element was satisfied by Clay's residence in Florida at the time of the lawsuit. Isn't *Hague,* in fact, indistinguishable from *Clay,* since the fact that the loss occurred in Florida was not significant in that case?

(4) Is it imaginable that Minnesota courts would have applied Wisconsin law in a mirror-image case involving an accident between two Minnesotans, occurring in Minnesota, on the grounds that one of them commuted to work in Wisconsin and the plaintiff moved to Wisconsin after the accident? If not, does that suggest that Minnesota has given Wisconsin law something less than full faith and credit? See Roosevelt, 97 Mich. L. Rev. at 2514. Justice Stevens argues in *Hague* that the full faith and credit clause is violated only if the application of forum law "threatens the federal interest in national unity by unjustifiably infringing upon the legitimate interests of another State." What does that mean? According to Stevens, Wisconsin's interests are not threatened because the parties did not make their contract in reliance on Wisconsin law. Why are Wisconsin's "legitimate interests" limited to contracts in which the parties rely on Wisconsin law? What does party reliance have to do with national unity? Can you reconcile this position with Justice Stevens's statement in footnote 20 that express choice-of-law provisions "are not always dispositive"?

(5) Coming after *Hague,* is *Shutts* surprising? Does it signify a retreat from *Hague*? The Court holds that Kansas law cannot be applied to leases on land that is neither in Kansas nor owned by someone from Kansas. Is this because Kansas has no interest? What is wrong with the argument that Kansas has a procedural interest in applying Kansas law to facilitate the efficient adjudication of a large class action? Is this a phony interest, or is the Court retreating from *Pacific Employers* and holding that such procedural interests must yield to the substantive interests of other states? Isn't the real problem in *Shutts* that the defendant is unfairly surprised by the application of Kansas law to leases having no connection to Kansas?

(6) Suppose that on remand in *Shutts* the defendant argues that many of the claims are time-barred. Kansas has a five-year statute of limitations—longer than that of any other state. The Kansas court holds that limitations questions are "procedural" and therefore that forum law may be applied to all the claims. What result on appeal? What conceivable "procedural" interest does Kansas have in affording *more* time to out-of-state claimants? Since limitations are at least partly substantive in purpose, isn't Kansas undermining the interests of other states for no legitimate reason? In any event, didn't *Shutts* hold that such procedural interests must yield to the substantive interests of other states?

This is what actually happened, and (believe it or not) the Supreme Court upheld the decision of the Kansas court to apply the Kansas statute of limitations. *Sun Oil Co. v. Wortman*, 486 U.S. 717 (1988). Writing for the Court, Justice Scalia explained that limitations questions were treated as procedural (and thus governed by forum law) when the Constitution was adopted. Therefore, he reasoned, this characterization remained constitutional today. Defendant argued that subsequent developments required the Court to update the rule, to which Justice Scalia responded:

> We cannot imagine what would be the basis for such an updating. [T]he words "substantive" and "procedural" themselves (besides not appearing in the Full Faith and Credit Clause) do not have a precise content, even (indeed especially) as their usage has evolved. And if one consults the purpose of their usage in the full-faith-and-credit context, that purpose is quite simply to give both the forum State and other interested States the legislative jurisdiction to which they are entitled. If we abandon the currently applied, traditional notions of such entitlement we would embark upon the enterprise of constitutionalizing choice-of-law rules, with no compass to guide us beyond our own perceptions of what seems desirable. There is no more reason to consider recharacterizing statutes of limitations as substantive under the Full Faith and Credit Clause than there is to consider recharacterizing a host of other matters generally treated as procedural under conflicts law, and hence generally regarded as within the forum State's legislative jurisdiction. *See,* e.g., Restatement (Second) of Conflict of Laws § 131 (remedies available), § 133 (placement of burden of proof), § 134 (burden of production), § 135 (sufficiency of the evidence), § 139 (privileges) (1971).

Noting that the protections of due process and full faith and credit are identical in this area, the Court relied on the same reasoning to dismiss defendant's due process claim.

What is one to make of this opinion? One of its more pernicious consequences emerged two years later, in *Ferens v. John Deere Co.*, 494 U.S. 516 (1990). Plaintiff, a Pennsylvania resident, was injured in Pennsylvania while using farm machinery manufactured by defendant, a Delaware corporation with its principal place of business in Illinois. Having waited longer than Pennsylvania's two-year statute of limitations to sue, plaintiff brought suit in Mississippi, which has a six-year period; jurisdiction was based on the fact that Deere did business in Mississippi. Plaintiff moved to transfer the case to Pennsylvania under 28 U.S.C.

§ 1404(a), which allows transfer for "the convenience of parties and witnesses." Under *Van Dusen v. Barrack,* 376 U.S. 612 (1964), the transferor court must apply the law that would have been applied by the court where the case was originally filed. While finding that a Mississippi court would apply its own statute of limitations, the Pennsylvania court refused to do the same. The Supreme Court reversed—allowing the plaintiff, in effect, to stop off in Mississippi and pick up a long statute of limitations on his way to the court in Pennsylvania. Justice Scalia dissented.

D. THE COMMERCE CLAUSE AND EXTRATERRITORIALITY

ASSOCIATION FOR ACCESSIBLE MEDICINES V. FROSH

887 F.3d 664 (4th Cir. 2018).

THACKER, CIRCUIT JUDGE:

. . . In response to reports of price gouging by pharmaceutical manufacturers in the sale of certain prescription medications, Maryland's legislature passed HB 631. . . . The Act prohibits "[a] manufacturer or wholesale distributor" from "engag[ing] in price gouging in the sale of an essential off-patent or generic drug." Md. Code Ann., Health—General § 2–802(a). The Act defines "price gouging" as "an unconscionable increase in the price of a prescription drug." *Id.* § 2–801(c). "Unconscionable increase" is further defined as an increase that "[i]s excessive and not justified by the cost of producing the drug or the cost of appropriate expansion of access to the drug to promote public health" and "[r]esults in consumers . . . having no meaningful choice about whether to purchase the drug at an excessive price" due to the drug's "importance . . . to their health" and "[i]nsufficient competition in the market." *Id.* § 2–801(f). . . . A manufacturer or wholesale distributor determined to be in violation of the Act may face a number of legal consequences, including a civil penalty of $10,000 per violation or an action to enjoin the sale of the medication at the increased price.

AAM is a voluntary organization with a membership that consists of prescription drug manufacturers and wholesale distributors and other entities in the pharmaceutical industry. AAM's member-manufacturers, only one of which is based in Maryland, typically sell their products to wholesale pharmaceutical distributors, *none of which are based in Maryland.* The vast majority of these sales occur outside Maryland's borders. . . .

Among other claims, AAM asserts that the Act violates the dormant commerce clause. . . Implicit in the constitutional allocation of the "Power . . . To regulate Commerce . . . among the several States," U.S. Const. art. I, § 8, cl. 3, to the federal government is a corollary "constraint on the power of the States to enact legislation that interferes with or burdens interstate commerce." This doctrine, known as the "dormant" commerce clause, "is driven by concern about economic protectionism" and seeks to prevent state "regulatory measures designed to benefit in-state economic interests by burdening out-of-state competitors."

The principle against extraterritoriality as it relates to the dormant commerce clause is derived from the notion that "a State may not regulate commerce occurring wholly outside of its borders." The principle "reflect[s] the Constitution's special concern both with the maintenance of a national economic union unfettered by state-imposed limitations on interstate commerce and with the autonomy of the individual States within their respective spheres." A state law violates the extraterritoriality principle if it either expressly applies to out-of-state commerce or has that "practical effect," regardless of the legislature's intent.

One of the earliest cases to address the extraterritoriality principle as it relates to the dormant commerce clause is *Baldwin v. G.A.F. Seelig, Inc.*, 294 U.S. 511 (1935). The New York law at issue in *Baldwin* required milk dealers to pay a minimum amount to milk producers, even when the milk was purchased outside New York. The parties agreed that "New York ha[d] no power to project its legislation into Vermont by regulating the price to be paid in that state for milk acquired there." *Id.* at 521. In holding that the law violated the dormant commerce clause, the Supreme Court observed that the law essentially operated as a duty on milk produced in other states and therefore unlawfully burdened interstate commerce. *See id.* at 521–22.

A plurality of the Court expounded on this concept nearly half a century later in *Edgar v. MITE Corp.*, 457 U.S. 624 (1982) (plurality opinion). The Illinois law challenged in *Edgar* required "any takeover offer for the shares of a target company [to] be registered with the Secretary of State" if Illinois shareholders owned at least 10% of the company or if the company was organized under Illinois law or headquartered in the state, among other conditions. *Id.* at 626–27. . . . The plurality held that the Illinois law violated the dormant commerce clause by "directly regulat[ing] transactions which take place across state lines, even if wholly outside the State of Illinois" because it permitted the Illinois Secretary of State to reject a tender offer even as to those shares not owned by Illinois shareholders. *Id.* at 641–42. In other words, the law granted the Illinois Secretary of State the ability to intervene in transactions between an out-of-state acquiring company and out-of-state shareholders of the target company when neither the acquiring company nor the target company's shareholders had connections to Illinois.

The Court favorably referenced both *Baldwin* and *Edgar* in *Brown-Forman Distillers Corp. v. New York State Liquor Authority*, 476 U.S. 573

(1986). The New York law struck down in *Brown-Forman* "requir[ed] distillers to affirm that they will make no sales anywhere in the United States at a price lower than the posted price in New York," which prohibited the distillers from lowering their prices in other states. *Id.* at 579–80. The Court noted that the law regulated commerce in other states by controlling liquor prices in those states, which would "effectively force [the distiller] to abandon its promotional allowance program in States in which that program is legal, or force those other States to alter their own regulatory schemes in order to permit [the distiller] to lower its New York prices without violating the affirmation laws of those States." *Id.* at 583–84. As a result, the law was invalid. *See id.* at 584.

Just three years later, the Supreme Court considered a similar Connecticut law in *Healy v. Beer Institute*, 491 U.S. 324 (1989). The law, which was aimed at preventing Connecticut residents from crossing state lines to purchase cheaper beer, required beer producers to affirm that their Connecticut prices were, "at the moment of posting, no higher than the prices at which those products are sold in the bordering States." *Id.* at 326. From its "cases concerning the extraterritorial effects of state economic regulation," *id.* at 336, the Supreme Court outlined the principle against extraterritoriality:

> 1) A state statute may not regulate "commerce that takes place wholly outside of the State's borders, whether or not the commerce has effects within the State." *Id.* at 336. . . .
>
> 2) "A statute that directly controls commerce occurring wholly outside the [legislating state's] boundaries . . . is invalid regardless of whether the statute's extraterritorial reach was intended by the legislature." *Id.* . . .
>
> 3) In evaluating a statute's "practical effect," the Court considers "not only . . . the consequences of the statute itself, but also . . . how the challenged statute may interact with the legitimate regulatory regimes of other States and what effect would arise if
>
> . . . every[ ] State adopted similar legislation." *Id.* at 336. . . .

Applying these three directives, the Court invalidated the Connecticut law due to its "undeniable effect of controlling commercial activity occurring wholly outside the boundary of the State." *Id.* at 337. . . .

Maryland asserts that in *Pharmaceutical Research & Manufacturers of America v. Walsh*, 538 U.S. 644, 669 (2003), the Supreme Court limited the principle against extraterritoriality in the dormant commerce clause context to price affirmation statutes. The Maine law at issue in *Walsh* established a program through which the state would "attempt to negotiate rebates with drug manufacturers to fund the reduced price for drugs offered to [program] participants." *Id.* at 649. . . . The Supreme Court concluded that "[t]he rule that was applied in *Baldwin* and *Healy*" did not apply to the rebate program because "unlike price control or price affirmation statutes, [the program] does not regulate the price of any out-of-state transaction, either by its express terms or by its inevitable effect." *Id.*

Maryland's reading of this language, while adopted by two of our sister circuits, is too narrow. The Supreme Court's statement does not suggest that "[t]he rule that was applied in *Baldwin* and *Healy*" applies *exclusively* to "price control or price affirmation statutes." . . . The Maine program challenged in *Walsh* directly affected only transactions in Maine and did not impact the prices drug manufacturers could charge elsewhere. Further, the Illinois statute at issue in *Edgar*, which permitted the Secretary of State to block the takeover of a target company with certain connections to Illinois, clearly was not a price control or price affirmation statute, but the Court nonetheless concluded that it ran afoul of the principle against extraterritoriality. We therefore reject Maryland's argument that *Walsh* limited the extraterritoriality principle only to price affirmation statutes.

. . . We agree with AAM that the district court erroneously upheld the Act under the dormant commerce clause. First, the Act is not triggered by any conduct that takes place within Maryland. Second, even if it were, the Act controls the prices of transactions that occur outside the state. Finally, the Act, if similarly enacted by other states, would impose a significant burden on interstate commerce involving prescription drugs. All of these factors combine to create a violation of the dormant commerce clause.

In reaching its conclusion, the district court emphasized that the Act's provisions "are triggered only when there is a drug . . . made available for sale *within* the state." J.A. 486 (emphasis in original). . . . [But] the Act's plain language allows Maryland to enforce the Act against parties to a transaction that did not result in a single pill being shipped to Maryland. Specifically, the Act prohibits "price gouging in the sale of an essential off-patent or generic drug." "Essential off-patent or generic drug" is defined, in part, as a drug "[t]hat is made available for sale in [Maryland]." This "made available for sale" language does not limit the Act's application to sales that actually occur within Maryland, nor does it restrict the Act's operation to the context of a resale transaction with a Maryland consumer. Indeed, Maryland acknowledges that the Act is intended to reach sales upstream from consumer retail sales. Such "upstream" sales would occur almost exclusively outside Maryland. . . .

Even if the Act did require a nexus to an actual sale in Maryland, it is nonetheless invalid because it still controls the price of transactions that occur wholly outside the state. The Act, by its own terms, is not fixated on the price the Maryland consumer ultimately pays for the drug. Instead, the lawfulness of a price increase is measured according to the price the manufacturer or wholesaler charges *in the initial sale of the drug. . . .* Significantly, the retailers that sell the drug directly to the consumer cannot be held liable under the Act; only "[a] manufacturer or wholesale distributor" is prohibited from "engag[ing] in price gouging." This structure makes clear that the conduct the Act targets is the upstream pricing and sale of prescription drugs, and the parties agree that nearly all of these transactions occur outside Maryland.

Therefore, the Act effectively seeks to compel manufacturers and wholesalers to act in accordance with Maryland law outside of Maryland. This it cannot do.

More importantly, the Act is effectively a price control statute that instructs manufacturers and wholesale distributors as to the prices they are permitted to charge in transactions that do not take place in Maryland. This is precisely the conduct the rule that was applied in *Baldwin* and *Healy* aims to prevent. We acknowledge that the Act does not establish a price schedule for prescription drugs, nor does it aim to tie the prices charged for prescription drugs in Maryland to the prices at which those drugs are sold in other states. But like the laws struck down in *Healy* and *Brown-Forman*, the Act attempts to dictate the price that may be charged elsewhere for a good. Any legitimate effects the Act may have in Maryland are insufficient to protect the law from invalidation. . . .

The Act's significant scope is further illuminated by the burden similar legislation would place on interstate commerce. Because the Act targets wholesale rather than retail pricing, an analogous restriction imposed by a state other than Maryland has the potential to subject prescription drug manufacturers to conflicting state requirements. And the Act's relatively subjective definition of what constitutes an unlawful price increase only exacerbates the problem. If multiple states enacted this type of legislation, then a manufacturer may consummate a transaction in a state where the transaction is fully permissible, yet still be subject to an enforcement action in another state (such as Maryland) wholly unrelated to the transaction.

In upholding the Act, the district court referred to this conundrum as a "practical problem" and suggested that prescription drug manufacturers could simply modify their distribution systems to track the shipments of drugs bound for Maryland and isolate those drugs in order to comply with the Act. . . . But the Act requires manufacturers and wholesale distributors to do more than alter their distribution channels. It sets prescription drug prices in a way that "interfere[s] with the natural function of the interstate market" by superseding market forces that dictate the price of a good. If Maryland compels manufacturers to sell prescription drugs in the initial transaction at a particular price, but another state imposes a different price, then manufacturers could not comply with both laws in a single transaction. . . . The potential for "the kind of competing and interlocking local economic regulation that the Commerce Clause was meant to preclude" is therefore both real and significant. *Healy*, 491 U.S. at 337. We are thus pressed to invalidate the Act.

WYNN, CIRCUIT JUDGE, dissenting:

. . . Because pre-enforcement constitutional challenges to state statutes—like AAM's dormant Commerce Clause challenge—are disfavored, and because the State repeatedly has represented that HB 631's reach does not extend to generic drugs that are not later sold in Maryland, principles of federalism and judicial restraint dictate that we construe the statute's reach as not extending to any stream of commerce that does not end in Maryland. . . . Because HB 631 regulates, at most, sales of essential generic drugs in streams of commerce that end in Maryland, AAM's Commerce Clause challenge is without merit. . . .

AAM does not argue that HB 631 implicates either of [the] concerns underlying the Supreme Court's modern dormant Commerce Cause jurisprudence: discrimination against interstate commerce or favoring in-state economic interests over out-of-state economic interests. Rather, AAM contends—and the majority opinion agrees—that HB 631 violates the "extraterritoriality doctrine."

The extraterritoriality doctrine—a judge-made doctrine which states that a State may not regulate "commerce occurring wholly outside [its] boundaries," *Healy*, 491 U.S. at 336—has been characterized by our sister circuits as the "the most dormant" of the Supreme Court's dormant Commerce Clause jurisprudence, *Energy & Envtl. Legal Inst. v. Epel* (*EELI*), 793 F.3d 1169, 1172 (10th Cir. 2015) (GORSUCH, J.).

Not only have courts questioned the extraterritoriality doctrine's continuing vitality, judges and commentators also have questioned the constitutional rationale underlying the doctrine, in light of new and expanded modes of interstate commerce, changes to the Supreme Court's interpretation of the Commerce Clause, and the availability of potentially more appropriate constitutional provisions, like the Due Process Clause, to ensure that States do not unduly extend their regulatory authority beyond their borders. *See* Brandon P. Denning, *Extraterritoriality and the Dormant Commerce Clause: A Doctrinal Post-Mortem*, 73 La. L. Rev. 979, 998 (2013); Jack L. Goldsmith & Alan O. Sykes, *The Internet and the Dormant Commerce Clause*, 110 Yale L.J. 785, 788–90, 806 (2001). . . .

[None] of the three dormant Commerce Clause cases upon which the majority opinion relies—*Baldwin*, *Healy*, and *Brown-Forman*—holds that a nondiscriminatory State law regulating an upstream transaction in a stream of transactions that ends in the State—like HB 631—constitutes an unconstitutional regulation of "wholly" out-of-state "commerce." Rather, each of the three cases turns on the principle concerns animating the

Supreme Court's dormant Commerce Clause jurisprudence: economic protectionism, discrimination against interstate commerce, and State regulation of a stream of transactions that never crosses through the State's borders. . . .

As then-Judge, now-Justice Gorsuch explained after closely analyzing the Court's opinions in *Baldwin*, *Brown-Forman*, and *Healy*, "[i]n all three cases, then, the Court . . . faced (1) a price control or price affirmation regulation, (2) linking in-state prices to those charged elsewhere, with (3) the effect of raising costs for out-of-state consumers or rival businesses." *EELI*, 793 F.3d at 1172–73. . . . The extraterritoriality doctrine, therefore, as explicated in *Baldwin*, *Brown-Forman*, and *Healy*, applies "*only* [to] price control or price affirmation statutes that link in-state prices with those charged elsewhere and discriminate against out-of-staters." *Id.* at 1174 (emphasis added).

Here, HB 631 is not a price affirmation statute, nor does it link in-state prices to out-of-state prices. HB 631 also does not dictate the prices that manufacturers or distributors charge to downstream purchasers in States other than Maryland. Additionally, it is undisputed that HB 631 does not favor in-state interests at the expense of out-of-state interests—it subjects out-of-state and in-state manufacturers and distributors to the same unconscionability limitation. And it is undisputed that HB 631 does not discriminate against interstate commerce—manufacturers and distributors remain free to engage in interstate commerce, they just may not charge unconscionable prices for essential generic drugs later sold to Maryland consumers. HB 631, therefore, does not violate the extraterritoriality doctrine, as that doctrine was applied in *Baldwin*, *Brown-Forman*, and *Healy*. . . .

According to the majority opinion, HB 631 poses a risk of subjecting manufacturers to "the kind of competing and interlocking local regulation that the Commerce Clause was meant to preclude" because "[i]f Maryland compels manufacturers to sell prescription drugs in the initial transaction at a particular price, but another state imposes a different price, then manufacturers could not comply with both laws in a single transaction." This contention is wrong as a matter of both fact and law.

As a matter of fact, HB 631 does not "compel manufacturers to sell prescription drugs . . . *at a particular price*." Rather, it forbids manufacturers from imposing an "unconscionable" price increase for essential generic drugs. Generic drug manufacturers, therefore, retain broad discretion to set prices for essential generic drugs and to increase the prices of such drugs, even if another state adopted a similar law. . . . [T]here would seem to be no obstacle to a generic drug manufacturer entering into a single contract with a distributor for an essential generic drug, under which the manufacturer imposes a conscience-shocking price increase for those pills the distributor resells outside of Maryland and a non-conscience-shocking price increase for the pills the distributor resells in Maryland. . .

The majority opinion's assertion that HB 631 violates the dormant Commerce Clause because it "interferes with the natural function of the interstate market by superseding market forces that dictate the price of a good" fares no better. As a matter of fact, the market at issue—like many markets for health care goods and services—is not one that "natural[ly] function[s]." On the contrary, the essential generic drugs at issue in this case present classic examples of market failure. The "business model" detailed in the Senate Report—which HB 631 targets—shows that the generic drug manufacturers that imposed conscience-shocking price increases exploited patients who were at a gross disadvantage in terms of bargaining power. . . .

At the end of the day, AAM argues—and the majority opinion concludes—that, absent federal regulation, its members are *constitutionally entitled* to impose conscience-shocking price increases on Maryland consumers, so long as AAM's members sell their essential generic drugs to Maryland consumers through out-of-state intermediaries. But "[t]he Constitution does not secure to any one liberty to conduct his business in such fashion as to inflict injury upon the public at large, or upon any substantial group of the people." *Nebbia v. New York*, 291 U.S. 502, 538–39 (1934). And the dormant Commerce Clause is not a "roving license" for federal courts to strike down non-discriminatory state consumer protection laws, like HB 631. Accordingly, I respectfully dissent from the majority opinion's conclusion that HB 631 violates the extraterritoriality doctrine.

---

(1) The Commerce Clause is a grant of authority to Congress "[t]o regulate Commerce . . . among the several States." U.S. Const. art. I, § 8, cl. 3. But at least since *Cooley v. Board of Wardens*, 53 U.S. 299 (1852), the clause has also been interpreted as a limitation on state regulatory power. Most of the Supreme Court's modern cases under the so-called "dormant Commerce Clause" have enforced two kinds of limitations. First, state laws that discriminate against interstate commerce by favoring in-state economic interests over out-of-state ones are virtually *per se* unconstitutional, unless there is no other means to advance a legitimate local purpose. See, *e.g.*, *Philadelphia v. New Jersey*, 437 U.S. 617, 624 (1978); *Maine v. Taylor*, 477 U.S. 131, 138 (1986). Second, state laws that impose incidental burdens on interstate commerce are invalid if "the burden imposed on [interstate] commerce is clearly excessive in relation to the putative local benefits." *Pike v. Bruce Church, Inc.*, 397 U.S. 137, 142 (1970).

Association for Accessible Medicines and the cases it discusses involve a third and lesser-known strand of dormant Commerce Clause jurisprudence: the extraterritoriality principle. In its strongest form the extraterritoriality rule holds that a State may not regulate "commerce that takes place wholly outside of the State's borders, whether or not the commerce has effects within the State." *Healy v. Beer Inst., Inc.*, 491 U.S. 324, 336 (1989) (citation omitted).

(2) Does the extraterritoriality principle, as applied in *Association for Accessible Medicines*, constitutionalize a form of Beale-style territorialism? If so, how can it be reconciled with *Hague*'s formulation that a state may apply its own law so long as there is a "significant contact or significant aggregation of contacts, creating state interests"? Do the effects of price gouging in Maryland not give that state an adequate interest in applying its law?

Or can a law satisfy the Due Process and Full Faith and Credit clauses and yet still violate the Commerce Clause? Judge Posner thought the answer was yes, in a case invalidating, as applied to an Illinois car title lender, an Indiana statute requiring lenders to obtain a license in Indiana if they advertise or solicit loans in that state:

> [I]f the presence of an interest that might support state jurisdiction without violating the due process clause of the Fourteenth Amendment dissolved the constitutional objection to extraterritorial regulation, there wouldn't be much left of *Healy* and its cognates. Connecticut had an interest in the price of beer to its residents, but that didn't save its statute from being held to violate the commerce clause. . . . The concerns behind the due process and commerce clauses are different. The former protects persons from unreasonable burdens imposed by government, including extraterritorial regulation that is disproportionate to the governmental interest. The latter protects interstate commerce from being impeded by extraterritorial regulation. And imposing a state's law on transactions in another state has a greater extraterritorial effect (and greater effect on commerce) than the state's applying its own law to suits in its courts.

Midwest Title Loans v. Mills, 593 F.3d 660, 668 (7th Cir. 2010).

(3) Perhaps the extraterritoriality principle can be squared with *Hague* insofar as it only bars states from regulating commerce that takes place *wholly* outside their borders. But does the relevant price gouging in *Association for Accessible Medicines* really occur *wholly* outside of Maryland? Does the Commerce Clause provide any criteria for making that determination?

Or are the extraterritoriality cases different from the *Alaska Packers/ Hague/Shutts* cases because the latter involve facial challenges to the scope of state *legislative* jurisdiction whereas the former involve as-applied challenges to state *courts'* choice of forum law? Why should that distinction make a constitutional difference? See Florey, *State Courts, State Territory, State Power: Reflections on the Extraterritoriality Principle in Choice of Law and Legislation*, 84 Notre Dame L. Rev. 1057, 1113–18 (2009) (arguing that legislative jurisdiction issues and choice-of-law issues should generally be governed by the same constitutional standard).

(4) What is the significance of the Fourth Circuit's observation that, if other states passed similar laws, this could "subject prescription drug manufacturers to conflicting state requirements"? Doesn't the entire field of choice of law presume that states will often impose conflicting legal rules? Generally speaking, corporations that operate in multiple states should expect to be faced with multiple sets of regulations. Does the court help its argument by asserting that Maryland's law "interferes with the natural function of the interstate market"? Some commentators have argued that the concern about inconsistent regulations ought to be addressed, not through an extraterritoriality principle, but through the balancing test that applies under conventional Commerce Clause analysis to state laws that impose incidental burdens on interstate commerce. See *Pike v. Bruce Church, Inc.*, supra note (1); Goldsmith & Sykes, *The Internet and the Dormant Commerce Clause*, 110 Yale L.J. at 806–08.

(5) Why should extraterritoriality be a concern of the Commerce Clause to begin with? The dormant Commerce Clause's limitation on state regulatory power is generally viewed as a bulwark against protectionism and discrimination. But the Fourth Circuit seems to admit that Maryland's price-gouging statute suffers from neither of these faults. By contrast, for instance, the plurality in *Healy* noted that the Connecticut price affirmation statute discriminated against interstate brewers and shippers, providing an independent basis for its invalidation. 491 U.S. at 341. Moreover, some instances of extraterritorial legislation might not be regulations of interstate commerce at all; presumably, Oklahoma cannot regulate how close to a Texas school one may carry a gun. Cf. *United States v. Lopez*, 514 U.S. 549 (1995). And the dormant Commerce Clause is unique among constitutional limitations in that Congress has the power to authorize what would otherwise be invalid state action. See *Southern Pacific Co. v. Arizona ex rel. Sullivan*, 325 U. S. 761, 769 (1945). If territoriality is truly a structural limitation on state legislative jurisdiction, why should Congress have the power to waive it? In light of all this, shouldn't we agree with Professor Regan that "extraterritoriality is not a dormant commerce clause problem"? Regan, *Siamese Essays: (i)* CTS Corp. v. Dynamics Corp. of America *and Dormant Commerce Clause Doctrine; (II) Extraterritorial State Legislation*, 85 Mich. L. Rev. 1865, 1873 (1987).

(6) As Judge Wynn's dissent notes, the extraterritoriality doctrine has come in for its share of academic and judicial criticism. Writing in 2013, Professor Denning pronounced a "post-mortem" on the doctrine, arguing that the Supreme Court in *Walsh* effectively limited its reach to price affirmation statutes of the type at issue in *Baldwin*, *Brown-Forman*, and *Healy*. Denning, *Extraterritoriality and the Dormant Commerce Clause*, 73 La. L. Rev. at 990–94. Several circuits have read the doctrine narrowly along similar lines. Thus, for example, in upholding a California statute banning *foie gras* against a Commerce Clause challenge brought by out-of-state duck farmers, the Ninth Circuit concluded that "*Healy* and *Baldwin* are not applicable to a statute that does not dictate the price of a product and does not tie the price of its in-state products to out-of-state prices." *Assoc. des Eleveurs de Canards et d'Oies du Quebec v. Harris*, 729 F.3d 937, 951 (9th Cir. 2013) (citation omitted). In a later case involving California's ban on the sale of pork meat from animals inhumanely confined, the Ninth Circuit retreated from the proposition that the extraterritoriality principle was limited to price-control and price affirmation laws, but upheld the law despite its considerable upstream effects because it formally regulated sales in California. *Nat'l Pork Producers Council v. Ross*, 6 F.4th 1021, 1027–31 (9th Cir. 2021). Certiorari was granted on March 28, 2022.

The lower courts have been divided about how aggressively to apply the extraterritoriality doctrine in the context of state regulations of the Internet. In *American Booksellers Foundation v. Dean*, 342 F.3d 96, 102–04 (2d Cir. 2003), the Second Circuit invalidated Vermont's statute regulating sexually explicit content on the Internet as a violation of the Commerce Clause, finding it "likely that the internet will soon be seen as falling within the class of subjects that are protected from State regulation because they "imperatively demand[ ] a single uniform rule." *Id.* at 104 (quoting *Cooley v. Bd. of Wardens*, 53 U.S. 299, 319 (1851)). But see, *e.g.*, *People v. Garelick*, 74 Cal. Rptr. 3d 815, 825 (Ct. App. 2008) (upholding, against Commerce Clause challenge, California's statute criminalizing electronic distribution of pornographic material to minors).

The Second Circuit's prediction that the Internet might soon be deemed beyond the authority of state law was dealt a serious blow by the Supreme Court's decision in *South Dakota v. Wayfair, Inc.*, 138 S. Ct. 2080 (2018). Overruling half a century of dormant Commerce Clause precedent, the Court held that states may assess sales tax on Internet transactions even when the seller lacks a physical presence in the state. The fact that the sale is consummated in-state, the Court reasoned, provides the taxing state with a sufficient nexus to the transaction. *Id.* at 2092–93. Moreover, advances in technology have rendered the physical presence requirement obsolete, while software makes it comparatively easy for sellers to calculate their sales tax obligations in each state. *Id.* at 2095, 2098. Does *Wayfair* also suggest that the Court takes a dim view of the concern about conflicting state requirements that was central to the Fourth Circuit's reasoning in *Association for Accessible Medicines*?

(7) The Supreme Court has dabbled in a different version of territorialism, this time under the auspices of the Due Process Clause, in cases involving the imposition of punitive damages. In *BMW of North America, Inc. v. Gore*, 517 U.S. 559 (1996), the Court held that an Alabama jury award of $2 million in punitive damages for a faulty presale paint job violated the Due Process Clause. In an opinion by Justice Scalia, the Court began by noting that "a State may protect its citizens by prohibiting deceptive trade practices and by requiring automobile distributors to disclose presale repairs that affect the value of a new car." *Id.* at 568–69. But then, citing *Healy* and *Edgar v. MITE Corp.*, the Court stated that "one State's power to impose burdens on the interstate market for automobiles is not only subordinate to the federal power over interstate commerce, but is also constrained by the need to respect the interests of other States." *Id.* at 571 (citations omitted). The Court concluded (*id.* at 572–73):

> We think it follows from these principles of state sovereignty and comity that a State may not impose economic sanctions on violators of its laws with the intent of changing the tortfeasors' lawful conduct in other States. . . . Alabama does not . . . have the power to punish BMW for conduct that was lawful where it occurred and that had no impact on Alabama or its residents. Nor may Alabama impose sanctions on BMW in order to deter conduct that is lawful in other jurisdictions.

Seven years later, in *State Farm Mut. Auto. Ins. Co. v. Campbell*, 538 U.S. 408 (2003), the Court again invalidated a punitive damage award, in this case a Utah award against an insurer that had refused to settle a claim. Reaffirming *Gore*, the Court stated that "as a general rule, . . . a State [does not] have a legitimate concern in imposing punitive damages to punish a defendant for unlawful acts committed outside of the State's jurisdiction." *Id.* at 421. The Court then confusingly added, with a citation to *Phillips Petroleum Co. v. Shutts*, "Any proper adjudication of conduct that occurred outside Utah to other persons would require their inclusion, and, to those parties, the Utah courts, in the usual case, would need to apply the laws of their relevant jurisdiction." *Id.* at 421–22.

Do *Gore* and *State Farm* suggest a return to a strong form of territorialism in which only the state where the legally relevant act took place has the power to regulate it? Justice Scalia's reference in *Gore* to "conduct that was lawful where it occurred" could have been written by Joseph Beale, couldn't it? (On the other hand, the rest of that sentence concedes that Alabama may regulate conduct that has an "impact on Alabama or its residents.") Thus far, these cases have not had much effect beyond the context of punitive damages. Perhaps that is because the Court views punitive damages as similar to criminal punishments, which are generally governed by a stricter principle against extraterritoriality. See Catherine M. Sharkey, *Punitive Damages as Societal Damages*, 113 Yale L.J. 347, 431 (2003).

(8) What, if anything, does the Contracts Clause of Art. I, § 10 have to do with choice of law? Compare *Ogden v. Saunders,* 25 U.S. (12 Wheat.) 213, 233 (1827) (Marshall, C.J., dissenting) (explaining that *McMillan v. McNeill,* 17 U.S. (4 Wheat.) 209 (1819), held that the Contracts Clause was infringed by application of a preexisting insolvency law to a contract "made in a different state, by persons residing in that state, and consequently without any view to" the law in question), with *Watson v. Employers Liab. Assur. Corp.,* supra p. 387 (rejecting a similar contention "since the direct action provisions became effective before this insurance contract was made").

E. INTERSTATE SOVEREIGN IMMUNITY

Does the *Hague* plurality's analysis apply in cases where a state or one of its officers or agencies is a party? Does Stevens's full faith and credit test apply instead? No fewer than four cases pitting the states of Nevada and California against one another have explored these questions.

In *Nevada v. Hall,* 440 U.S. 410 (1979), a state official from Nevada drove to California and, in the course of his employment, injured a citizen of California. The injured party sued the State of Nevada in a California court. While California had waived sovereign immunity for such suits, Nevada restricted awards against the state to $25,000. The California court refused to apply this Nevada law and the jury awarded the plaintiff $1,150,000. What result under Stevens's test? Can you think of a case *more* likely to "threaten the federal interest in national unity"? The Court in *Nevada v. Hall* upheld the award. Who do you think wrote the opinion? In a footnote, Justice Stevens explained that the award "poses no substantial threat to our constitutional system of cooperative federalism" because "[s]uits involving traffic accidents occurring outside of Nevada could hardly interfere with Nevada's capacity to fulfill its own sovereign responsibilities." True enough, but how about multimillion-dollar damage awards?

The Court expanded on *Nevada v. Hall* in *Franchise Tax Board v. Hyatt,* 538 U.S. 488 (2003) ("*Hyatt I*"). Gilbert Hyatt filed a California tax return representing that he had ceased to reside in California and become a Nevada resident. The California Franchise Tax Board conducted an audit, ultimately rejecting Hyatt's claim of changed residence. During the audit, Hyatt alleged, the Tax Board committed numerous torts against him, including invasion of privacy, outrageous conduct, abuse of process, fraud, and negligent misrepresentation. He sued in a Nevada court; the

Tax Board defended on the basis of a California statute giving it absolute immunity for actions taken in the course of tax collection. The analogous Nevada statute does not immunize state agencies for intentional torts, and the Nevada Supreme Court allowed the intentional tort claims to proceed.

A unanimous Supreme Court affirmed. Justice O'Connor's opinion first acknowledged the Court's failure to find a satisfactory method of balancing state interests in Full Faith and Credit cases:

> We have, in the past, appraised and balanced state interests when invoking the Full Faith and Credit Clause to resolve conflicts between overlapping laws of coordinate States. [See *Clapper*]. This balancing approach quickly proved unsatisfactory. [Compare *Alaska Packers* with *Pacific Employers.*] . . . In light of this experience, we abandoned the balancing-of-interests approach to conflicts of law under the Full Faith and Credit Clause. [See *Hague.*] We have recognized, instead, that "it is frequently the case under the Full Faith and Credit Clause that a court can lawfully apply either the law of one State or the contrary law of another."

Acknowledging the Court's abandonment of balancing, the Tax Board suggested that a new rule was needed to protect core state sovereignty interests. The Court declined the invitation, observing that the rule would effectively require the Court to hold that California's sovereign interest exceeded that of Nevada. Concluding that *Hyatt* was not a case like *Hughes v. Fetter*, infra p. 414, "in which a State has exhibited a 'policy of hostility to the public Acts' of a sister state," the Court pointed out that "[t]he Nevada Supreme Court sensitively applied principles of comity with a healthy regard for California's sovereign status, relying on the contours of Nevada's own sovereign immunity from suit as a benchmark for its analysis." It concluded, "Without a rudder to steer us, we decline to embark on the constitutional course of balancing coordinate States' competing sovereign interests to resolve conflicts of laws under the Full Faith and Credit Clause."

After remand, the case went to trial, and Hyatt was awarded almost $500 million in damages and fees. The Nevada Supreme Court affirmed $1 million of the damages award, despite the fact that Nevada statutes would impose a $50,000 limit in a similar suit against its own officials.

The Court vacated that judgment in *Franchise Tax Board v. Hyatt*, 578 U.S. 171 (2016) ("*Hyatt II*"). In *Hyatt II*, an eight-member Court divided equally on the question whether the Nevada courts lacked jurisdiction to entertain the action, thus ensuring *Nevada v. Hall*'s survival (for the moment) by the narrowest possible margin. An opinion by Justice Breyer for a six-justice majority went on, however, to hold that the Full Faith and Credit Clause prohibited Nevada from awarding greater damages against

California agencies under Nevada law than it could award against Nevada agencies in similar circumstances:

> The Nevada decision before us embodies a critical departure from its earlier approach. Nevada has not applied the principles of Nevada law ordinarily applicable to suits against Nevada's own agencies. Rather, it has applied a special rule of law applicable only in lawsuits against its sister States, such as California. With respect to damages awards greater than $50,000, the ordinary principles of Nevada law do not "conflic[t]" with California law, for both laws would grant immunity. *Carroll v. Lanza.*
>
> But that is not so in respect to Nevada's special rule. That rule, allowing damages awards greater than $50,000, is not only "opposed" to California law, it is also inconsistent with the general principles of Nevada immunity law. . . . [Viewed] through a full faith and credit lens, a State that disregards its own ordinary legal principles on this ground is hostile to another State. A constitutional rule that would permit this kind of discriminatory hostility is likely to cause chaotic interference by some States into the internal, legislative affairs of others. . . In our view, Nevada's rule lacks the "healthy regard for California's sovereign status" that was the hallmark of its earlier decision, and it reflects a constitutionally impermissible "policy of hostility to the public Acts of a sister State." [*Hyatt I.*]

Chief Justice Roberts, joined by Justice Thomas, dissented: "The majority's approach is nowhere to be found in the Full Faith and Credit Clause. Where the Clause applies, it expressly requires a State to give full faith and credit to another State's laws. If the majority is correct that Nevada has no sufficient policy justification for applying Nevada immunity law, then California law applies. And under California law, the Board is entitled to *full* immunity. Or, if Nevada has a sufficient policy reason to apply its own law, then Nevada law applies, and the Board is subject to *full* liability."

On remand, the Nevada Supreme Court ordered that damages be limited according to the Nevada cap. Unsatisfied, the Board sought certiorari a third time, resulting in the following closely divided decision.

FRANCHISE TAX BOARD OF CALIFORNIA V. HYATT

139 S.Ct. 1485 (2019).

JUSTICE THOMAS delivered the opinion of the Court.

This case, now before us for the third time, requires us to decide whether the Constitution permits a State to be sued by a private party without its consent in the courts of a different State. We hold that it does not and overrule our decision to the contrary in *Nevada v. Hall*, 440 U.S. 410 (1979). . . .

Nevada v. Hall is contrary to our constitutional design and the understanding of sovereign immunity shared by the States that ratified the Constitution. *Stare decisis* does not compel continued adherence to this erroneous precedent. We therefore overrule *Hall* and hold that States retain their sovereign immunity from private suits brought in the courts of other States.

Hall held that the Constitution does not bar private suits against a State in the courts of another State. The opinion conceded that States were immune from such actions at the time of the founding, but it nonetheless concluded that nothing "implicit in the Constitution" requires States "to adhere to the sovereign-immunity doctrine as it prevailed when the Constitution was adopted." Instead, the Court concluded that the Founders assumed that "prevailing notions of comity would provide adequate protection against the unlikely prospect of an attempt by the courts of one State to assert jurisdiction over another." The Court's view rested primarily on the idea that the States maintained sovereign immunity vis-à-vis each other in the same way that foreign nations do, meaning that immunity is available only if the forum State "voluntar[ily]" decides "to respect the dignity of the [defendant State] as a matter of comity." . . .

Hall's determination that the Constitution does not contemplate sovereign immunity for each State in a sister State's courts misreads the historical record and misapprehends the "implicit ordering of relationships within the federal system necessary to make the Constitution a workable governing charter and to give each provision within that document the full effect intended by the Framers." *Id.*, at 433 (Rehnquist, J., dissenting). . . . [A]lthough the Constitution assumes that the States retain their sovereign immunity except as otherwise provided, it also fundamentally adjusts the States' relationship with each other and curtails their ability, as sovereigns, to decline to recognize each other's immunity.

After independence, the States considered themselves fully sovereign nations. . . . "An integral component" of the States' sovereignty was "their immunity from private suits." As Alexander Hamilton explained:

> "It is inherent in the nature of sovereignty not to be amenable to the suit of an individual without its consent. This is the general sense and the general practice of mankind; and the exemption, as one of the attributes of sovereignty, is now enjoyed by the government of every State in the Union." The Federalist No. 81, at 487 (emphasis deleted).

[The] founding generation thus took as given that States could not be haled involuntarily before each other's courts. This understanding is perhaps best illustrated by preratification examples. In 1781, a creditor named Simon Nathan tried to recover a debt that Virginia allegedly owed him by attaching some of its property in Philadelphia. James Madison and other Virginia delegates to the Confederation Congress responded by sending a communiqué to Pennsylvania requesting that its executive branch have the action dismissed. As Madison framed it, the Commonwealth's property could not be attached by process issuing from a court of "any other State in the Union." . . . Similarly, a Pennsylvania Admiralty Court that very same year dismissed a libel action against a South Carolina warship, brought by its crew to recover unpaid wages. The court reasoned that the vessel was owned by a "sovereign independent state."

The Founders were well aware of the international-law immunity principles behind these cases. Federalists and Antifederalists alike agreed in their preratification debates that States could not be sued in the courts of other States. . . . In short, at the time of the founding, it was well settled that States were immune under both the common law and the law of nations. The Constitution's use of the term "States" reflects both of these kinds of traditional immunity. And the States retained these aspects of sovereignty, "except as altered by the plan of the Convention or certain constitutional Amendments." *Alden v. Maine*, 527 U.S. 706, 713 (1999).

One constitutional provision that abrogated certain aspects of this traditional immunity was Article III, which provided a neutral federal forum in which the States agreed to be amenable to suits brought by other States. Art. III, § 2. . . . The States, in ratifying the Constitution, similarly surrendered a portion of their immunity by consenting to suits brought against them by the United States in federal courts. "While that jurisdiction is not conferred by the Constitution in express words, it is inherent in the constitutional plan." Given that "all jurisdiction implies superiority of power," the only forums in which the States have consented to suits by one another and by the Federal Government are Article III courts.

The Antifederalists worried that Article III went even further by extending the federal judicial power over controversies "between a State and Citizens of another State." They suggested that this provision implicitly waived the States' sovereign immunity against *private* suits in federal courts. But "[t]he leading advocates of the Constitution assured the people in no uncertain terms" that this reading was incorrect [citing Madison, Marshall, and Hamilton]. . . .

Not long after the founding, however, the Antifederalists' fears were realized. In *Chisholm v. Georgia*, 2 Dall. 419, 1 L.Ed. 440 (1793), the Court held that Article III allowed the very suits that the "Madison-Marshall-Hamilton triumvirate" insisted it did not. That decision precipitated an immediate "furor" and "uproar" across the country. Congress and the

States accordingly acted swiftly to remedy the Court's blunder by drafting and ratifying the Eleventh Amendment.[2]

The Eleventh Amendment confirmed that the Constitution was not meant to "rais[e] up" any suits against the States that were "anomalous and unheard of when the Constitution was adopted." *Hans v. Louisiana*, 134 U.S. 1, 18 (1890). Although the terms of that Amendment address only "the specific provisions of the Constitution that had raised concerns during the ratification debates and formed the basis of the *Chisholm* decision," the "natural inference" from its speedy adoption is that "the Constitution was understood, in light of its history and structure, to preserve the States' traditional immunity from private suits." The "sovereign immunity of the States," we have said, "neither derives from, nor is limited by, the terms of the Eleventh Amendment." *Alden*, 527 U.S. at 713. Consistent with this understanding of state sovereign immunity, this Court has held that the Constitution bars suits against nonconsenting States in a wide range of cases.

Despite this historical evidence that interstate sovereign immunity is preserved in the constitutional design, Hyatt insists that such immunity exists only as a "matter of comity" and can be disregarded by the forum State. He reasons that, before the Constitution was ratified, the States had the power of fully independent nations to deny immunity to fellow sovereigns; thus, the States must retain that power today with respect to each other because "nothing in the Constitution or formation of the Union altered that balance among the still-sovereign states." . . .

The problem with Hyatt's argument is that the Constitution affirmatively altered the relationships between the States, so that they no longer relate to each other solely as foreign sovereigns. Each State's equal dignity and sovereignty under the Constitution implies certain constitutional "limitation[s] on the sovereignty of all of its sister States." *World-Wide Volkswagen Corp. v. Woodson*, 444 U.S. 286, 293 (1980). One such limitation is the inability of one State to hale another into its courts without the latter's consent. The Constitution does not merely allow States to afford each other immunity as a matter of comity; it embeds interstate sovereign immunity within the constitutional design. Numerous provisions reflect this reality.

To begin, Article I divests the States of the traditional diplomatic and military tools that foreign sovereigns possess. Specifically, the States can no longer prevent or remedy departures from customary international law because the Constitution deprives them of the independent power to lay

---

[2] The Eleventh Amendment provides: "The Judicial power of the United States shall not be construed to extend to any suit in law or equity, commenced or prosecuted against one of the United States by Citizens of another State, or by Citizens or Subjects of any Foreign State."

imposts or duties on imports and exports, to enter into treaties or compacts, and to wage war.

Article IV also imposes duties on the States not required by international law. The Court's Full Faith and Credit Clause precedents, for example, demand that state-court judgments be accorded full effect in other States and preclude States from "adopt[ing] any policy of hostility to the public Acts" of other States. *Hyatt II*, 136 S.Ct., at 1281; see Art. IV, § 1. States must also afford citizens of each State "all Privileges and Immunities of Citizens in the several States" and honor extradition requests upon "Demand of the executive Authority of the State" from which the fugitive fled. Art. IV, § 2. Foreign sovereigns cannot demand these kinds of reciprocal responsibilities absent consent or compact. But the Constitution imposes them as part of its transformation of the States from a loose league of friendship into a perpetual Union based on the "fundamental principle of *equal* sovereignty among the States." *Shelby County v. Holder*, 570 U.S. 529, 544 (2013).

The Constitution also reflects implicit alterations to the States' relationships with each other, confirming that they are no longer fully independent nations. For example, States may not supply rules of decision governing "disputes implicating the[ir] conflicting rights." *Texas Industries, Inc. v. Radcliff Materials, Inc.*, 451 U.S. 630, 641 (1981). Thus, no State can apply its own law to interstate disputes over borders, water rights, or the interpretation of interstate compacts. . . . Some subjects that were decided by pure "political power" before ratification now turn on federal "rules of law."

Interstate sovereign immunity is similarly integral to the structure of the Constitution. Like a dispute over borders or water rights, a State's assertion of compulsory judicial process over another State involves a direct conflict between sovereigns. The Constitution implicitly strips States of any power they once had to refuse each other sovereign immunity, just as it denies them the power to resolve border disputes by political means. Interstate immunity, in other words, is "implied as an essential component of federalism." *Hall*, 440 U.S. at 430–431 (Blackmun, J., dissenting).

Hyatt argues that we should find no right to sovereign immunity in another State's courts because no constitutional provision explicitly grants that immunity. But this is precisely the type of "ahistorical literalism" that we have rejected when "interpreting the scope of the States' sovereign immunity since the discredited decision in *Chisholm*." In light of our constitutional structure, the historical understanding of state immunity, and the swift enactment of the Eleventh Amendment after the Court departed from this understanding in *Chisholm*, "[i]t is not rational to suppose that the sovereign power should be dragged before a court." Elliot's Debates 555 (Marshall). Indeed, the spirited historical debate over Article

III courts and the immediate reaction to *Chisholm* make little sense if the Eleventh Amendment were the only source of sovereign immunity and private suits against the States could already be brought in "partial, local tribunals." Elliot's Debates 532 (Madison). Nor would the Founders have objected so strenuously to a neutral federal forum for private suits against States if they were open to a State being sued in a different State's courts. Hyatt's view thus inverts the Founders' concerns about state-court parochialism.

Moreover, Hyatt's ahistorical literalism proves too much. There are many other constitutional doctrines that are not spelled out in the Constitution but are nevertheless implicit in its structure and supported by historical practice—including, for example, judicial review, intergovernmental tax immunity, executive privilege, executive immunity, and the President's removal power. Like these doctrines, the States' sovereign immunity is a historically rooted principle embedded in the text and structure of the Constitution.

With the historical record and precedent against him, Hyatt defends *Hall* on the basis of *stare decisis*. But *stare decisis* is "not an inexorable command," and we have held that it is "at its weakest when we interpret the Constitution because our interpretation can be altered only by constitutional amendment." . . .

We have already explained that *Hall* failed to account for the historical understanding of state sovereign immunity and that it failed to consider how the deprivation of traditional diplomatic tools reordered the States' relationships with one another. We have also demonstrated that *Hall* stands as an outlier in our sovereign-immunity jurisprudence, particularly when compared to more recent decisions. . . .

[We] acknowledge that some plaintiffs, such as Hyatt, have relied on *Hall* by suing sovereign States. Because of our decision to overrule *Hall*, Hyatt unfortunately will suffer the loss of two decades of litigation expenses and a final judgment against the Board for its egregious conduct. But in virtually every case that overrules a controlling precedent, the party relying on that precedent will incur the loss of litigation expenses and a favorable decision below. Those case-specific costs are not among the reliance interests that would persuade us to adhere to an incorrect resolution of an important constitutional question. . . .

JUSTICE BREYER, with whom JUSTICE GINSBURG, JUSTICE SOTOMAYOR, and JUSTICE KAGAN join, dissenting.

Can a private citizen sue one State in the courts of another? Normally the answer to this question is no, because the State where the suit is brought will choose to grant its sister States immunity. But the question here is whether the Federal Constitution *requires* each State to grant its sister States immunity, or whether the Constitution instead *permits* a State to grant or deny its sister States immunity as it chooses. . . .

The majority asserts that before ratification "it was well settled that States were immune under both the common law and the law of nations." The majority thus maintains that States were exempt from suit in each other's courts.

But the question in *Hall* concerned the *basis* for that exemption. Did one sovereign have an absolute right to an exemption from the jurisdiction of the courts of another, or was that exemption a customary matter, a matter of consent that a sovereign might withdraw? As to that question, nothing in the majority's opinion casts doubt on *Hall's* conclusion that States—like foreign nations—were accorded immunity as a matter of consent rather than absolute right. . . .

The majority next argues that "the Constitution affirmatively altered the relationships between the States" by giving them immunity that they did not possess when they were fully independent. The majority thus maintains that, whatever the nature of state immunity before ratification, the Constitution accorded States an absolute immunity that they did not previously possess.

The most obvious problem with this argument is that no provision of the Constitution gives States absolute immunity in each other's courts. The majority does not attempt to situate its newfound constitutional immunity in any provision of the Constitution itself. Instead, the majority maintains that a State's immunity in other States' courts is "implicit" in the Constitution, "embed[ded] . . . within the constitutional design," and reflected in "the plan of the Convention." . . .

But . . . concepts like the "constitutional design" and "plan of the Convention" are "highly abstract, making them difficult to apply"—at least absent support in "considerations of history, of constitutional purpose, or of related consequence." Such concepts "invite differing interpretations at least as much as do the Constitution's own broad liberty-protecting phrases" such as "due process" and "liberty," and "they suffer the additional disadvantage that they do not actually appear anywhere in the Constitution."

At any rate, I can find nothing in the "plan of the Convention" or elsewhere to suggest that the Constitution converted what had been the customary practice of extending immunity by consent into an absolute federal requirement that no State could withdraw. None of the majority's arguments indicates that the Constitution accomplished any such transformation.

The majority argues that the Constitution sought to preserve States' "equal dignity and sovereignty." That is true, but tells us nothing useful here. When a citizen brings suit against one State in the courts of another, both States have strong sovereignty-based interests. In contrast to a State's power to assert sovereign immunity in its own courts, sovereignty interests here lie on both sides of the constitutional equation.

The majority also says—also correctly—that the Constitution demanded that States give up certain sovereign rights that they would have retained had they remained independent nations. From there the majority infers that the Constitution must have implicitly given States immunity in each other's courts to provide protection that they gave up when they entered the Federal Union. . . . But where the Constitution alters the authority of States vis-à-vis other States, it tends to do so explicitly. . . .

Nor does there seem to be any need to create implicit constitutional protections for States. As the history of this case shows, the Constitution's express provisions seem adequate to prohibit one State from treating its sister States unfairly—even if the State permits suits against its sister States in its courts [citing *Hyatt II*]. . . .

Why would the Framers, silently and without any evident reason, have transformed sovereign immunity from a permissive immunity predicated on comity and consent into an absolute immunity that States must accord one another? The Court in *Hall* could identify no such reason. Nor can I.

---

(1) In *Nevada v. Hall* and the first two installments of the *Hyatt* saga, the Court posed the question of interstate sovereign immunity from the perspective of constitutional limitations on choice of law: Does the Full Faith and Credit Clause require the forum state to apply the sovereign immunity law of the defendant state? *Hall* and *Hyatt I* answered this question with a resounding "no," while *Hyatt II* took a more nuanced approach, requiring the forum to treat officers or agencies of a sister state no worse than it would treat officers or agencies of the forum. (What full faith and credit principle necessitated this result? Wasn't Chief Justice Roberts right to complain, in his *Hyatt II* dissent, that the majority was being a bit too Solomonic? See if your answer changes—or your confusion grows—after you read *Hughes v. Fetter*, infra Section 2.)

By contrast, *Hyatt III* does not approach the question from the perspective of choice of law or full faith and credit at all. Instead, drawing upon its Eleventh Amendment jurisprudence, the Court holds that the obligation to respect state sovereign immunity is simply one of the backdrop principles against which the Constitution as a whole was enacted. Does the Court attempt to supply any textual basis for this principle? Are you confident, having read *Hyatt III*, that the Court has a methodology for identifying other such background principles? Is sovereign immunity unique because of the distinctive threat posed to state prerogatives when it is vitiated? Why aren't those prerogatives adequately protected by the antidiscrimination rule of *Hyatt II*?

(2) The Court cites, as another instance where the Constitution presupposes a lack of state power, the states' inability to resolve disputes over borders or water rights. Which way does this example cut? Isn't it telling that this power lies instead with Congress and the Supreme Court? By parity of reasoning, perhaps the federal courts should have exclusive jurisdiction over cases between citizens of one state and the government of another—but of course, these are the very cases the Eleventh Amendment ousts from federal court. (By the way, how does the Supreme Court have appellate jurisdiction over Hyatt's suit? Could Nevada have sued California on Hyatt's behalf under the Court's *original* jurisdiction?)

Were you persuaded by Justice Thomas's reasoning that, since citizen-versus-sister-state cases don't belong in federal court because of the Eleventh Amendment, *a fortiori* they don't belong in state court either? *Alden v. Maine* held that Congress ordinarily may not abrogate state sovereign immunity in state courts, but why can't *states* do so? What happened to the Tenth Amendment's guarantee that all powers not granted to the federal government are retained by the states?

(3) If *Hyatt III* had come out the other way and Nevada were not required to respect California's sovereign immunity *law*, would California be required to recognize the resulting Nevada *judgment*? To sharpen the issue: assume the Franchise Tax Board had refused to appear in Nevada state court on sovereign immunity grounds and had suffered a default judgment. Could that judgment be levied against it in California? As you will learn infra Chapter 5, courts are generally obliged by the Full Faith and Credit Clause to recognize sister-state judgments—*unless* the judgment was issued by a court that lacked jurisdiction over the parties. If states are not amenable to jurisdiction without their consent, then perhaps full faith and credit would not be owed to judgments that rested on the abrogation of sister-state sovereign immunity. *Cf.* Sachs, *Pennoyer Was Right*, 95 Tex. L. Rev. 1249, 1276 (2017).

SECTION 2. THE OBLIGATION TO PROVIDE A FORUM

HUGHES V. FETTER

341 U.S. 609 (1951).

MR. JUSTICE BLACK delivered the opinion of the Court.

Basing his complaint on the Illinois wrongful death statute, appellant administrator brought this action in the Wisconsin state court to recover damages for the death of Harold Hughes, who was fatally injured in an automobile accident in Illinois. The allegedly negligent driver and an insurance company were named as defendants. On their motion the trial court entered summary judgment "dismissing the complaint on the merits." It held that a Wisconsin statute, which creates a right of action only for deaths caused in that state, establishes a local public policy against Wisconsin's entertaining suits brought under the wrongful death acts of other states.[2] The Wisconsin Supreme Court affirmed, notwithstanding the contention that the local statute so construed violated the Full Faith and Credit Clause of Art. IV, § 1 of the Constitution. . .

We are called upon to decide the narrow question whether Wisconsin, over the objection raised, can close the doors of its courts to the cause of action created by the Illinois wrongful death act. Prior decisions have established that the Illinois statute is a "public act" within the provision of Art. IV, § 1 that "Full Faith and Credit shall be given in each State to the public Acts . . . of every other State." It is also settled that Wisconsin cannot escape this constitutional obligation to enforce the rights and duties validly created under the laws of other states by the simple device of removing jurisdiction from courts otherwise competent. We have recognized, however, that full faith and credit does not automatically compel a forum state to subordinate its own statutory policy to a conflicting public act of another state; rather, it is for this Court to choose in each case between the competing public policies involved. The clash of interests in cases of this type has usually been described as a conflict between the public policies of two or more states.[8] The more basic conflict involved in the present appeal, however, is as follows: On the one hand is the strong unifying principle embodied in the Full Faith and Credit Clause looking toward maximum enforcement in each state of the obligations or rights created or recognized by the statutes of sister states;[9] on the other hand is the policy of Wisconsin, as interpreted by its highest court, against permitting Wisconsin courts to entertain this wrongful death action.[10]

---

2 Wis.Stat., 1949, § 331.03. This section contains language typically found in wrongful death acts but concludes as follows: "provided, that such action shall be brought for a death caused in this state."

8 See, e.g., *Alaska Packers Ass'n v. Industrial Accident Commission*, 294 U.S. 532, 547–550.

9 This clause "altered the status of the several states as independent foreign sovereignties, each free to ignore rights and obligations created under the laws or established by the judicial proceedings of the others, by making each an integral part of a single nation. . . ." *Magnolia Petroleum Co. v. Hunt*, 320 U.S. 430, 439 * * *.

10 The present case is not one where Wisconsin, having entertained appellant's lawsuit, chose to apply its own instead of Illinois' statute to measure the substantive rights involved. This distinguishes the present case from those where we have said that "Prima facie every state is entitled to enforce in its own courts its own statutes, lawfully enacted." *Alaska Packers Ass'n v. Industrial Acc. Commission*, 294 U.S. 532, 547 * * *.

We hold that Wisconsin's policy must give way. The state has no real feeling of antagonism against wrongful death suits in general.[11] To the contrary, a forum is regularly provided for cases of this nature, the exclusionary rule extending only so far as to bar actions for death not caused locally. The Wisconsin policy, moreover, cannot be considered as an application of the forum non conveniens doctrine, whatever effect that doctrine might be given if its use resulted in denying enforcement to public acts of other states. Even if we assume that Wisconsin could refuse, by reason of particular circumstances, to hear foreign controversies to which nonresidents were parties, the present case is not one lacking a close relationship with the state. For not only were appellant, the decedent and the individual defendant all residents of Wisconsin, but also appellant was appointed administrator and the corporate defendant was created under Wisconsin laws. We also think it relevant, although not crucial here, that Wisconsin may well be the only jurisdiction in which service could be had as an original matter on the insurance company defendant. And while in the present case jurisdiction over the individual defendant apparently could be had in Illinois by substituted service, in other cases Wisconsin's exclusionary statute might amount to a deprivation of all opportunity to enforce valid death claims created by another state.

Under these circumstances, we conclude that Wisconsin's statutory policy which excludes this Illinois cause of action is forbidden by the national policy of the Full Faith and Credit Clause. The judgment is reversed and the cause is remanded to the Supreme Court of Wisconsin for proceedings not inconsistent with this opinion.

MR. JUSTICE FRANKFURTER, whom MR. JUSTICE REED, MR. JUSTICE JACKSON, and MR. JUSTICE MINTON join, dissenting. . .

In the field of commercial law—where certainty is of high importance—we have often imposed a rather rigid rule that a State must defer to the law of the State of incorporation, or to the law of the place of contract. . . In cases involving workmen's compensation, there is also a pre-existing relationship between the employer and employee that makes certainty of result desirable. The possible interest of the forum in protecting the workman, however, has made this Court reluctant to impose rigid rules. . .

In the tort action before us, there is little reason to impose a "state of vassalage" on the forum. The liability here imposed does not rest on a pre-existing relationship between the plaintiff and defendant. There is consequently no need for fixed rules which would enable parties, at the time they enter into a transaction, to predict its consequences. . .

[11] It may well be that the wrongful death acts of Wisconsin and Illinois contain different provisions in regard to such matters as maximum recovery and disposition of the proceeds of suit. Such differences, however, are generally considered unimportant * * *.

This Court should certainly not require that the forum deny its own law and follow the tort law of another State where there is a reasonable basis for the forum to close its courts to the foreign cause of action... Wisconsin may be willing to grant a right of action where witnesses will be available in Wisconsin and the courts are acquainted with a detailed local statute and cases construing it. It may not wish to subject residents to suit where out-of-state witnesses will be difficult to bring before the court, and where the court will be faced with the alternative of applying a complex foreign statute—perhaps inconsistent with that of Wisconsin on important issues—or fitting the statute to the Wisconsin pattern. The legislature may well feel that it is better to allow the courts of the State where the accident occurred to construe and apply its own statute, and that the exceptional case where the defendant cannot be served in the State where the accident occurred does not warrant a general statute allowing suit in the Wisconsin courts. The various wrongful death statutes are inconsistent on such issues as beneficiaries, the party who may bring suit, limitations on liability, comparative negligence, and the measure of damages. * * * The measure of damages and the relation of wrongful death actions to actions for injury surviving death have raised extremely complicated problems, even for a court applying the familiar statute of its own State. * * * These diversities reasonably suggest application by local judges versed in them...

In the present case, the decedent, the plaintiff, and the individual defendant were residents of Wisconsin. The corporate defendant was created under Wisconsin law. The suit was brought in the Wisconsin courts. No reason is apparent—and none is vouchsafed in the opinion of the Court—why the interest of Illinois is so great that it can force the courts of Wisconsin to grant relief in defiance of their own law.

Finally, it may be noted that there is no conflict here in the policies underlying the statute of Wisconsin and that of Illinois. The Illinois wrongful death statute has a proviso that "no action shall be brought or prosecuted in this State to recover damages for a death occurring outside of this State where a right of action for such death exists under the laws of the place where such death occurred and service of process in such suit may be had upon the defendant in such place." Smith-Hurd's Ill.Ann.Stat., 1936, c. 70, § 2. The opinion of the Court concedes that "jurisdiction over the individual defendant apparently could be had in Illinois by substituted service." Smith-Hurd's Ill.Ann.Stat., 1950, c. 95½, § 23. Thus, in the converse of the case at bar—if Hughes had been killed in Wisconsin and suit had been brought in Illinois—the Illinois courts would apparently have dismissed the suit. There is no need to be "more Roman than the Romans."

The "Equal Protection" Component of Full Faith and Credit

(1) What is the principle for which *Hughes* stands? In footnote 10, the Court says that Wisconsin could have applied its own wrongful death statute "to measure the substantive rights involved." The Wisconsin statute, quoted in footnote 2 of the Court's opinion, limited recovery to deaths in Wisconsin. Because the death in *Hughes* occurred in Illinois, then, applying Wisconsin law would have resulted in dismissal for failure to state a claim upon which relief can be granted. What is the difference between this and what the Wisconsin court actually did? Put another way, what is the difference between a Wisconsin law that limits recovery to accidents in Wisconsin and one that limits recovery to actions based on Wisconsin law?

Or does the reference to "substantive rights" in footnote 10 imply a belief that the limitation to deaths in Wisconsin is "procedural"? Was the Court assuming, in other words, that the Wisconsin court could have disregarded this limitation and applied the substantive provisions of its law to measure liability? But what makes the limitation "procedural"? And even if it is, why should that matter? What about cases like *Pacific Employers,* which held that the Full Faith and Credit Clause does not compel a state to subordinate its policies to the policies of other states? Is *Hughes* performing the balancing of interests that *Pacific Employers* renounces? What rudder is guiding this balancing? See B. Currie, Selected Essays on the Conflict of Laws 294 (1963).

(2) Compare *Broderick v. Rosner,* 294 U.S. 629 (1935). New York enacted legislation to pierce the corporate veil and make bank stockholders personally liable for a share of the bank's debts. The New York Superintendent of Banks brought an action in New Jersey to recover unpaid assessments levied against 557 New Jersey stockholders of a failed New York bank. His suit was dismissed under a New Jersey statute requiring such actions to be brought in the form of an equitable accounting in which the corporation, its officers, stockholders, debtors, and creditors were all necessary parties. Because of limitations on joinder and on the court's power to exercise personal jurisdiction over out-of-state parties, bringing such an action was a practical and legal impossibility. Justice Brandeis held that the full faith and credit clause compelled New Jersey to entertain the suit regardless of its statute:

> A State may adopt such system of courts and form of remedy as it sees fit. It may in appropriate cases apply the doctrine of *forum non conveniens.* * * * But it may not, under the guise of merely affecting the remedy, deny the enforcement of claims otherwise within the protection of the full faith and credit clause, when its courts have general jurisdiction of the subject matter and the parties. * * *

The most logical policy behind the New Jersey rule was to limit the liability of New Jersey stockholders. According to Justice Brandeis, such a justification still violated full faith and credit:

> Obviously, recognition could not be accorded to a local policy of New Jersey, if there really were one, of enabling all residents of the State to escape from the performance of a voluntarily assumed statutory obligation, consistent with morality, to contribute to the payment of the depositors of a bank of another State of which they were stockholder.

Why not? How is the New Jersey statute different from laws that invalidate usurious agreements, disable minors from making contracts, or limit the time in which suit can be brought? Is the New Jersey policy anything other than the traditional one of encouraging investment by allowing shareholders to limit their liability? (Note that New Jersey did not impose liability on shareholders in domestic corporations either.) According to Currie, while New Jersey could enforce a policy of limited liability, it could not draft a statute concealing this policy and expect the Court to recognize it:

> *Broderick* . . . presents the following situation: New York had expressly declared a policy of protecting the creditors of banks by imposing personal liability on stockholders. It had a clear interest in the application of the policy to a New York bank, both for the security of local depositors and to enhance the credit of the bank in general. New Jersey had declared no conflicting policy of protecting its residents, as stockholders, against such liability. Neither had it suggested any reason relating to the administration of its courts why actions to enforce such liability should not be brought in New Jersey. It had only pretended a concern for the procedural aspects of such actions. . . In such circumstances, New York having a legitimate governmental interest in the application of its policy and New Jersey having none, the Court quite properly held that New Jersey must entertain the action. . .

B. Currie, Selected Essays at 347. Can it similarly be said that in *Hughes* Wisconsin failed to assert any interest in the matter and therefore was required to defer to the law of the state that had?

The problem with this explanation is that laws seldom declare their policies forthrightly. Indeed, one of the courts' primary tasks in statutory interpretation is to articulate and clarify a law's underlying policies. The usual rule, moreover, is to accord the legislature a great deal of deference and uphold its enactment if a rational policy can be inferred. In *Hughes,* for example, Justice Frankfurter offers several justifications for Wisconsin's decision not to hear claims based on foreign law, such as the difficulty in bringing evidence and witnesses before the court. Surely these are legitimate: similar policies could, for example, be the basis for the state's decision to limit the right to recover to accidents in Wisconsin. That being so, why does the full faith and credit clause require Wisconsin to yield its law and policy to the law and policy of Illinois? Is *Hughes* inconsistent with *Pacific Employers*? Or does the full faith and credit clause impose restrictions on the *means* a state uses to pursue even ends that are legitimate under *Pacific Employers,* allowing the state to enforce its own substantive law but not simply to refuse to enforce foreign law? Is this what Justice Black means when he says that *Hughes* is not like the usual "clash of public policies of two or more states"? How does such a principle advance the purpose of the full faith and credit clause? According to Professor Kramer:

> [T]o understand *Hughes,* we should distinguish between two kinds of laws: those that promote a state's objectives by defining the parties' substantive rights in particular ways, and those that promote a state's objectives by withholding from state courts the power to entertain claims based on other states' laws. Most laws are of the former type, like Wisconsin's wrongful death statute limiting recovery to deaths occurring in Wisconsin. When it comes to the applicability of such laws, the Full Faith and Credit Clause has little to say. States may define substantive rights differently, and so long as the forum has a legitimate interest—so long, in other words, as we are dealing with the usual "conflict between the public policies of two or more states"—the forum may apply its law notwithstanding any other state's competing interest.
>
> Laws of the second type, which can be described as discriminating against other states' laws, are different. A state that chooses to promote even legitimate objectives by directing its courts not to entertain claims based on other states' laws generates "a more basic conflict"—not just between its policy and that of another state, but between its policy and what Justice Black says is "the strong unifying principle embodied in the Full Faith and Credit Clause looking toward maximum enforcement in each state of the obligations or rights created or recognized by the statutes of sister states." And because this *means* of advancing state objectives is so directly at odds with the primary objective of the Full Faith and Credit Clause, a state that uses it will have its discriminatory law subjected to heightened constitutional scrutiny.

Kramer, *Same-Sex Marriage, Conflict of Laws, and the Unconstitutional Public Policy Exception,* 106 Yale L.J. 1965, 1983–84 (1997). Is this a plausible reading of *Hughes*?

Can similar reasoning explain *Broderick*? Is it fair to say that New Jersey was simply attempting to do by subterfuge what Wisconsin did openly in *Hughes*?

(3) How strict is heightened scrutiny under *Hughes v. Fetter*? Does the common-law public policy doctrine violate the full faith and credit clause? The Court has never suggested such a thing, and several earlier cases recognize the doctrine. See, e.g., *Klaxon Co. v. Stentor Elec. Mfg. Co.,* 313 U.S. 487 (1941); *Griffin v. McCoach,* 313 U.S. 498 (1941). But if a state cannot decline to enforce foreign law for reasons like those advanced in Justice Frankfurter's *Hughes* dissent, how can it decline to do so on the ground that it finds this law offensive or repugnant? Should it matter whether, in invoking public policy, the forum *could* constitutionally assert an interest in applying forum law? Should it matter whether, after invoking public policy, the forum applies its own law or dismisses for want of jurisdiction? In *Hughes,* Justice Black emphasizes that the Wisconsin court dismissed the complaint "on the merits." Do you think the result would have been different if the court instead declined to exercise jurisdiction and dismissed without prejudice? See Kramer, *Same-Sex Marriage,* 106 Yale L.J. at 1985–92.

How about the doctrine of *forum non conveniens*? *Hughes* and *Broderick* both affirm the legitimacy of this doctrine, but why isn't this an unconstitutional refusal to enforce a foreign claim? Is it that dismissal for *forum non conveniens* is not on the merits? Or is it that while the Wisconsin rule struck down in *Hughes* applied to any claim based on foreign law, *forum non conveniens* permits a more refined analysis in which only cases that are truly inconvenient will be dismissed?

How about statutes of limitations? In *Wells v. Simonds Abrasive Co.,* 345 U.S. 514 (1953), plaintiff's decedent was killed in Alabama while using a grinding wheel manufactured by defendant. More than one but less than two years later, plaintiff filed an action in Pennsylvania. While recognizing that plaintiff's claim was governed by Alabama law, which allowed two years to bring an action, the court applied the one-year Pennsylvania statute of limitations and dismissed. The Supreme Court affirmed. Can you reconcile this result with *Hughes*? The Court might have relied on the fact that the defendant was a Pennsylvania company, but its analysis assumes that Pennsylvania has no substantive interest and that the state court applied local limitations law on procedural grounds. According to the Court, "the crucial factor" in *Hughes* was that "the forum laid an uneven hand on causes of action arising within and without the forum state. Causes of action arising in sister states were discriminated against. Here Pennsylvania applies her one-year limitation to all wrongful death actions wherever they may arise." Is *Hughes* just an anti-discrimination principle?

Or are all these questions rendered moot by the decision in *Sun Oil Co. v. Wortman,* 486 U.S. 717 (1988), supra p. 391, which upholds the constitutionality of practices that were in existence when the relevant constitutional provision was adopted and are still followed?

(4) Apart from the possible implications of *Wortman* with respect to traditional practices, is the following a correct statement of the law? A state may not "discriminate" against foreign law by refusing to enforce it unless the state (a) has a sufficient justification and (b) tailors the discrimination to fit that justification. The fact that the state has a substantive interest and applies its own substantive law always satisfies these requirements. Concern for the conduct of litigation in the state's courts may constitute an adequate justification. But if the mechanism chosen to further this interest is overbroad, it will be struck down. The law in *Hughes* was thus found unconstitutional because it treated every claim based on foreign law as inconvenient, while *forum non conveniens* is permissible because it furthers the state's legitimate interests in a way that is narrowly tailored to prevent undue discrimination. On this view, is the public policy doctrine constitutional or not?

How carefully should the Court scrutinize a state's procedural justifications? Is the real difference between the majority and dissenting opinions in *Hughes* that Frankfurter applies rational basis scrutiny while Black applies some sort of heightened scrutiny?

TENNESSEE COAL, IRON & R.R. CO. V. GEORGE

233 U.S. 354 (1914).

MR. JUSTICE LAMAR delivered the opinion of the court:

Wiley George, the defendant in error, was an engineer employed by the Tennessee Coal, Iron & Railroad Company at its steel plant in Jefferson County, Alabama. While he was under a locomotive repairing the brakes, a defective throttle allowed steam to leak into the cylinder, causing the engine to move forward automatically in consequence of which he was seriously injured. He brought suit by attachment, in the city court of Atlanta, Georgia, founding his action on § 3910 of the Alabama Code, which makes the master liable to the employee when the injury is "caused by reason of any defect in the condition of the ways, works, machinery, or plant connected with or used in the business of the master or employer."

The defendant filed a plea in abatement in which it was set out that § 6115 of that Code also provided that "all actions under § 3910 must be brought in a court of competent jurisdiction within the state of Alabama, and not elsewhere." The defendant thereupon prayed that the action be abated because "to continue said case of said statutory cause of action given by the statutes of Alabama, and restricted by said statutes to the courts of Alabama, would be a denial so far as the rights of this defendant are concerned of full faith and credit to said public acts of the state of Alabama in the state of Georgia, contrary to the provisions of art. 4, § 1 of the Constitution of the United States." A demurrer to the plea in abatement was sustained and the judgment for the plaintiff thereafter entered was affirmed by the court of appeals. The case was then brought to this court. . .

There are many cases where right and remedy are so united that the right cannot be enforced except in the manner and before the tribunal designated by the act. For the rule is well settled that "where the provision for the liability is coupled with a provision for a special remedy, that remedy, and that alone, must be employed." * * *

But that rule has no application to a case arising under the Alabama Code relating to suits for injuries caused by defective machinery. For, whether the statute be treated as prohibiting certain defenses, as removing common-law restrictions, or as imposing upon the master a new and larger liability, it is in either event evident that the place of bringing the suit is not part of the cause of action,—the right and the remedy are not so inseparably united as to make the right dependent upon its being enforced in a particular tribunal. The cause of action is transitory and like any other transitory action can be enforced "in any court of competent jurisdiction within the state of Alabama. . ." But the owner of the defective machinery causing the injury may have removed from the state, and it would be a deprivation of a fixed right if the plaintiff could not sue the defendant in Alabama because he had left the state, nor sue him where the defendant or his property could be found because the statute did not permit a suit elsewhere than in Alabama. The injured plaintiff may likewise have moved from Alabama, and for that, or other reason may have found it to his interest to bring suit by attachment or in personam in a state other than where the injury was inflicted.

The courts of the sister state, trying the case, would be bound to give full faith and credit to all those substantial provisions of the statute which inhered in the cause of action, or which name conditions on which the right to sue depend. But venue is no part of the right; and a state cannot create a transitory cause of action and at the same time destroy the right to sue on that transitory cause of action in any court having jurisdiction. That jurisdiction is to be determined by the law of the court's creation, and cannot be defeated by the extraterritorial operation of a statute of another state, even though it created the right of action.

The case here is controlled by the decision of this court in *Atchison, T. & S.F.R. Co. v. Sowers,* 213 U.S. 55, 59, 70, where the New Mexico statute, giving a right of action for personal injuries, and providing that suits should be brought after certain form of notice in a particular district, was preceded by the recital that "it has become customary for persons claiming damages for personal injuries received in this territory to institute and maintain suits for the recovery thereof in other states and territories, to the increased cost and annoyance and manifest injury and oppression of the business interests of this territory and in derogation of the dignity of the courts thereof." Despite this statement of the public policy of the territory, the judgment obtained by the plaintiff in Texas was affirmed by this court. . .

It is claimed, however, that the decision in the *Sowers* case is not in point because the plaintiff was there seeking to enforce a common-law liability, while here he is asserting a new and statutory cause of action. But that distinction marks no difference between the two cases because in New Mexico common-law liability is statutory liability—the adopting statute (Comp.Laws, § 1823) providing that "the common law as recognized in the United States of America shall be the rule of practice and decision."

The decision in the *Sowers* Case, however, was not put upon the fact that the suit was based on a common-law liability. The court there announced the general rule that a transitory cause of action can be maintained in another state even though the statute creating the cause of action provides that the action must be brought in local domestic courts.

In the present case the Georgia court gave full faith and credit to the Alabama act and its judgment is affirmed.

MR. JUSTICE HOLMES dissents.

State Power to Keep Litigation at Home

(1) What is the policy behind Alabama's provision requiring suit to be brought in Alabama? Suppose the purpose is to ensure proper administration of Alabama law or to minimize harassment and expense by keeping litigation connected primarily with Alabama at home. Are these legitimate interests under the full faith and credit clause? If so, what interest does Georgia have in entertaining the action and infringing these Alabama policies?

Does *George* stand for the proposition that the full faith and credit clause establishes an independent federal policy favoring transitory causes of action? *Could* the Georgia court have enforced the Alabama limitation and dismissed, or would that have violated the principle of *Hughes v. Fetter*? What if, in *Hughes,* Illinois law had provided that the wrongful death statute could only be enforced in Illinois courts? Would the Wisconsin court have been required to hear the case against the wishes of both states?

(2) Should Georgia be free to accept only so much of Alabama law as it wants? In *Pearson v. Northeast Airlines, Inc.,* 309 F.2d 553 (2d Cir.1962) (en banc), a New Yorker was killed when a flight from New York crashed in Massachusetts. Relying on a state-court decision in another case arising from the same accident, the trial judge found that, while plaintiff's right to recover derived from Massachusetts law, the accompanying Massachusetts damages limitation would not apply. See *Kilberg v. Northeast Airlines, Inc.*, 9 N.Y.2d 34, 211 N.Y.S.2d 133, 172 N.E.2d 526 (1961). The Second Circuit rejected constitutional challenges to this determination. Writing for the dissenters, Judge Friendly conceded that New York could have made its wrongful death statute applicable in its entirety. But, he said, that did not justify what the court did:

> It does not follow that when New York looks to a statute of a sister state as the source of a claim . . . , the Constitution allows it to decline . . . "to give full faith and credit to all those substantial provisions of the statute which inhered in the cause of action or which name conditions on which the right to sue depend[s]."

According to Judge Friendly, it was improper for New York to express its interest by displacing only parts of Massachusetts law because requiring lawmakers "to speculate that other states may take what is liked and reject what is disliked . . . might well discourage or prevent enactments otherwise deemed desirable." Is that persuasive?

(3) In *Crider v. Zurich Ins. Co.*, 380 U.S. 39 (1965), an Alabama resident was injured in Alabama while working there for a Georgia corporation. The Alabama court awarded a remedy under the Georgia Workers' Compensation Act despite a provision of that act confiding its enforcement exclusively to the Georgia Compensation Board. Citing *Pacific Employers* and *Carroll v. Lanza,* supra p. 371, Justice Douglas argued that Alabama could choose to enforce its interest in providing recovery for residents injured within its borders by following Georgia law. The dictum in *George* requiring respect for "a provision for a special remedy" such as the administrative one in workers' compensation cases, he added, had been "eroded by the line of cases beginning with *Alaska Packers* and *Pacific Employers*."

Does this mean that *Pearson* was rightly decided? Does it mean that a *disinterested* forum (like the Georgia court in *George*) could also have ignored a provision for exclusive enforcement by a special administrative board?

On remand from the Supreme Court decision in *Crider,* the Court of Appeals adhered to its previous position that the Alabama court's judgment should not be enforced, on the ground that Alabama law rather than the Full Faith and Credit Clause required respect for the localizing provision. *Crider v. Zurich Ins. Co.*, 348 F.2d 211 (5th Cir.1965). In light of *George* and *Hughes,* did Alabama have constitutional power to *refuse* jurisdiction?

(4) *Weaver v. Alabama Great Southern R. Co.*, 200 Ala. 432, 76 So. 364 (1917). Injured in an Alabama grade-crossing accident, an Alabama resident sued an Alabama corporation in Georgia. An Alabama court enjoined the Georgia action on the ground that it had been brought in an attempt to avoid the Alabama rule that failure to stop, look, and listen at the crossing was conclusive of contributory negligence—Georgia leaving the question, even in cases based on foreign law, to the jury. Such an injunction, as the Alabama court said, had been held not to violate the full faith and credit clause in *Cole v. Cunningham,* 133 U.S. 107 (1890). The *George* case, "upon which appellant strongly relies, merely holds that an Alabama statute cannot, while creating a transitory cause of action, deny to the courts of other states the right to entertain a suit for its enforcement. It does not even refer to the case of *Cole v. Cunningham* * * *, and has no sort of bearing on the present case." 200 Ala. at 436, 76 So. at 368. See also *James v. Grand Trunk Western Ry.,* 14 Ill.2d 356, 152 N.E.2d 858 (1958) (dictum), infra p. 615, reaffirming *Cole* as applied to an injunction against suing in another state in violation of a statute restricting venue under the circumstances to the county where the plaintiff resided but holding that the injunction need not be respected by the court in which the action was brought. How in the world can these decisions be reconciled with *George*? The answer is not that *George* is no longer good law; the Supreme Court reaffirmed it in 2006. See *Marshall v. Marshall,* 547 U.S. 293 (2006).

SECTION 3. UNCONSTITUTIONAL DISCRIMINATION IN CHOICE OF LAW

SUPREME COURT OF NEW HAMPSHIRE V. PIPER

470 U.S. 274 (1985).

JUSTICE POWELL delivered the opinion of the Court.

The Rules of the Supreme Court of New Hampshire limit bar admission to state residents. We here consider whether this restriction violates the Privileges and Immunities Clause of the United States Constitution, Art. IV, § 2.

I

A

Kathryn Piper lives in Lower Waterford, Vermont, about 400 yards from the New Hampshire border. In 1979, she applied to take the February 1980 New Hampshire bar examination. . .

On May 7, 1980, Piper requested from the Clerk of the New Hampshire Supreme Court a dispensation from the residency requirement. Although she had a "possible job" with a lawyer in Littleton, New Hampshire, Piper stated that becoming a resident of New Hampshire would be inconvenient. Her house in Vermont was secured by a mortgage with a favorable interest rate, and she and her husband recently had become parents. According to

Piper, these "problems peculiar to [her] situation . . . warrant[ed] that an exception be made." . . .

On May 13, 1980, the Clerk informed Piper that her request had been denied. . .

II

A

Article IV, § 2 of the Constitution provides that the "citizens of each State shall be entitled to all Privileges and Immunities of Citizens in the several States."[6] This clause was intended to "fuse into one Nation a collection of independent, sovereign States." *Toomer v. Witsell,* 334 U.S. 385, 395 (1948). Recognizing this purpose, we have held that it is "[o]nly with respect to those 'privileges' and 'immunities' bearing on the vitality of the nation as a single entity" that a State must accord residents and nonresidents equal treatment. *Baldwin v. Montana Fish & Game Comm'n, supra,* at 383. In *Baldwin,* for example, we concluded that a State may charge a nonresident more than it charges a resident for the same elk-hunting license. Because elk-hunting is "recreation" rather than a "means of livelihood," we found that the right to a hunting license was not "fundamental" to the promotion of interstate harmony. 436 U.S., at 388.

Derived, like the Commerce Clause, from the fourth of the Articles of Confederation,[7] the Privileges and Immunities Clause was intended to create a national economic union.[8] It is therefore not surprising that this Court repeatedly has found that "one of the privileges which the Clause guarantees to citizens of State A is that of doing business in State B on terms of substantial equality with the citizens of that State." *Toomer v. Witsell, supra,* 334 U.S., at 396. In *Ward v. Maryland,* 12 Wall. 418 (1871), the Court invalidated a statute under which nonresidents were required to pay $300 per year for a license to trade in goods not manufactured in Maryland, while resident traders paid a fee varying from $12 to $150. Similarly, in *Toomer, supra,* the Court held that nonresident fishermen

---

6 Under this Clause, the terms "citizen" and "resident" are used interchangeably. See *Austin v. New Hampshire,* 420 U.S. 656, 662, n. 8 (1975). Under the Fourteenth Amendment, of course, "[a]ll persons born or naturalized in the United States . . . are citizens . . . of the State wherein they reside."

7 Article IV of the Articles of Confederation provided:

"The better to secure and perpetuate mutual friendship and intercourse among the people of the different States in this Union, the free inhabitants of each of these States . . . shall be entitled to all privileges and immunities of free citizens in the several States; and the people of each State shall have free ingress and regress to and from any other State, and shall enjoy therein all the privileges of trade and commerce, subject to the same duties, impositions and restrictions as the inhabitants thereof. . . . "

Charles Pinckney, who drafted the Privileges and Immunities Clause, stated that it was "formed exactly upon the principles of the 4th article of the present Confederation." 3 M. Farrand, Records of the Federal Convention of 1787, at 112 (1911).

8 This Court has recognized the "mutually reinforcing relationship" between the Commerce Clause and the Privileges and Immunities Clause. *Hicklin v. Orbeck,* 437 U.S. 518, 531 (1978).

could not be required to pay a license fee of $2,500 for each shrimp boat owned when residents were charged only $25 per boat. Finally, in *Hicklin v. Orbeck,* 437 U.S. 518 (1978), we found violative of the Privileges and Immunities Clause a statute containing a resident hiring preference for all employment related to the development of the State's oil and gas resources.

There is nothing in *Ward, Toomer,* or *Hicklin* suggesting that the practice of law should not be viewed as a "privilege" under Article IV, § 2.[10] Like the occupations considered in our earlier cases, the practice of law is important to the national economy. As the Court noted in *Goldfarb,* the "activities of lawyers play an important part in commercial intercourse." *Goldfarb v. Virginia State Bar,* 421 U.S. 773, 788.

The lawyer's role in the national economy is not the only reason that the opportunity to practice law should be considered a "fundamental right." We believe that the legal profession has a noncommercial role and duty that reinforce the view that the practice of law falls within the ambit of the Privileges and Immunities Clause.[11] Out-of-state lawyers may—and often do—represent persons who raise unpopular federal claims. In some cases, representation by nonresident counsel may be the only means available for the vindication of federal rights. See *Leis v. Flynt,* 439 U.S., at 450, 99 S.Ct., at 704 (Stevens, J., dissenting). The lawyer who champions unpopular causes surely is as important to the "maintenance or well-being of the Union," *Baldwin,* as was the shrimp fisherman in *Toomer, supra,* or the pipeline worker in *Hicklin.*

B

The State asserts that the Privileges and Immunities Clause should be held inapplicable to the practice of law because a lawyer's activities are "bound up with the exercise of judicial power and the administration of justice." Its contention is based on the premise that the lawyer is an "officer of the court," who "exercises state power on a daily basis." The State

---

[10] In *Corfield v. Coryell,* 6 F.Cas. 546 (No. 3,230) (CCED Pa.1825), Justice Bushrod Washington, sitting as Circuit Justice, stated that the "fundamental rights" protected by the Clause included:

> "The right of a citizen of one state to pass through, or to reside in any other state, for purposes of trade, agriculture, professional pursuits, or otherwise; to claim the benefit of the writ of habeas corpus; to institute and maintain actions of any kind in the courts of the state; to take, hold and dispose of property, either real or personal. . ." *Id.,* at 552.

Thus in this initial interpretation of the Clause, "professional pursuits," such as the practice of law, were said to be protected.

The "natural rights" theory that underlay *Corfield* was discarded long ago. *Hague v. CIO,* 307 U.S. 496, 511 (1939) (opinion of Roberts, J.); see *Paul v. Virginia,* 8 Wall. 168 (1869). Nevertheless, we have noted that those privileges on Justice Washington's list would still be protected by the Clause. *Baldwin v. Montana Fish & Game Comm'n,* 436 U.S. 371, 387 (1978).

[11] The Court has never held that the Privileges and Immunities Clause protects only economic interests. See *Doe v. Bolton,* 410 U.S. 179 (1973) (Georgia statute permitting only residents to secure abortions found violative of the Privileges and Immunities Clause).

concludes that if it cannot exclude nonresidents from the bar, its ability to function as a sovereign political body will be threatened.[13]

Lawyers do enjoy a "broad monopoly . . . to do things other citizens may not lawfully do." *In re Griffiths,* 413 U.S. 717, 731 (1973). We do not believe, however, that the practice of law involves an "exercise of state power" justifying New Hampshire's residency requirement. In *In re Griffiths, supra,* we held that the State could not exclude an alien from the bar on the ground that a lawyer is an " 'officer of the Court who' . . . is entrusted with the 'exercise of actual governmental power.' " *Id.,* at 728 (quoting Brief for Appellee in *In re Griffiths,* O.T.1972, No. 71–1336, p. 5). We concluded that a lawyer is not an "officer" within the ordinary meaning of that word. 413 U.S., at 728. He " 'makes his own decisions, follows his own best judgment, collects his own fees and runs his own business.' " *Id.,* at 729 (quoting *Cammer v. United States,* 350 U.S. 399, 405 (1956)). Moreover, we held that the state powers entrusted to lawyers do not "involve matters of state policy or acts of such unique responsibility that they should be entrusted only to citizens." *Id.,* at 724, 93 S.Ct., at 2856.

Because, under *Griffiths,* a lawyer is not an "officer" of the State in any political sense, there is no reason for New Hampshire to exclude from its bar nonresidents. We therefore conclude that the right to practice law is protected by the Privileges and Immunities Clause.

III

The conclusion that Rule 42 deprives nonresidents of a protected privilege does not end our inquiry. The Court has stated that "[l]ike many other constitutional provisions, the privileges and immunities clause is not an absolute." *Toomer v. Witsell,* 334 U.S., at 396, see *United Building & Construction Trades Council v. Mayor & Council of Camden,* 465 U.S. 208, 222 (1984). The Clause does not preclude discrimination against nonresidents where: (i) there is a substantial reason for the difference in treatment; and (ii) the discrimination practiced against nonresidents bears a substantial relationship to the State's objective. *Ibid.* In deciding whether the discrimination bears a close or substantial relationship to the State's objective, the Court has considered the availability of less restrictive means.

The Supreme Court of New Hampshire offers several justifications for its refusal to admit nonresidents to the bar. It asserts that nonresident members would be less likely: (i) to become, and remain, familiar with local

---

[13] We recognize that without certain residency requirements the State "would cease to be the separate political communit[y] that history and the constitutional text make plain w[as] contemplated." Simson, Discrimination Against Nonresidents and the Privileges and Immunities Clause of Article IV, 128 U.Pa.L.Rev. 379, 387 (1979). A State may restrict to its residents, for example, both the right to vote, see *Dunn v. Blumstein,* 405 U.S. 330, 343, 344 (1972), and the right to hold state elective office. *Baldwin v. Montana Fish & Game Comm'n, supra,* 436 U.S., at 383.

rules and procedures; (ii) to behave ethically; (iii) to be available for court proceedings; and (iv) to do *pro bono* and other volunteer work in the State.[18] We find that none of these reasons meets the test of "substantiality," and that the means chosen do not bear the necessary relationship to the State's objectives.

There is no evidence to support the State's claim that nonresidents might be less likely to keep abreast of local rules and procedures. Nor may we assume that a nonresident lawyer—any more than a resident—would disserve his clients by failing to familiarize himself with the rules. As a practical matter, we think that unless a lawyer has, or anticipates, a considerable practice in the New Hampshire courts, he would be unlikely to take the bar examination and pay the annual dues of $125.

We also find the State's second justification to be without merit, for there is no reason to believe that a nonresident lawyer will conduct his practice in a dishonest manner. The nonresident lawyer's professional duty and interest in his reputation should provide the same incentive to maintain high ethical standards as they do for resident lawyers. A lawyer will be concerned with his reputation in any community where he practices, regardless of where he may live. Furthermore, a nonresident lawyer may be disciplined for unethical conduct. The Supreme Court of New Hampshire has the authority to discipline all members of the bar, regardless of where they reside. See N.H.S.Ct.Rule 37.

There is more merit to the State's assertion that a nonresident member of the bar at times would be unavailable for court proceedings. In the course of litigation, pretrial hearings on various matters often are held on short notice. At times a court will need to confer immediately with counsel. Even the most conscientious lawyer residing in a distant State may find himself unable to appear in court for an unscheduled hearing or proceeding. Nevertheless, we do not believe that this type of problem justifies the exclusion of nonresidents from the state bar. One may assume that a high percentage of nonresident lawyers willing to take the state bar examination and pay the annual dues will reside in places reasonably convenient to New Hampshire. Furthermore, in those cases where the nonresident counsel will be unavailable on short notice, the State can protect its interests through less restrictive means. The trial court, by rule or as an exercise of discretion, may require any lawyer who resides at a great distance to retain a local attorney who will be available for unscheduled meetings and hearings.

---

[18] A former president of the American Bar Association has suggested another possible reason for the rule: "Many of the states that have erected fences against out-of-state lawyers have done so primarily to protect their own lawyers from professional competition." Smith, Time for a National Practice of Law Act, 64 A.B.A.J. 557 (1978). This reason is not "substantial." The Privileges and Immunities Clause was designed primarily to prevent such economic protectionism.

The final reason advanced by the State is that nonresident members of its bar would be disinclined to do their share of *pro bono* and volunteer work. Perhaps this is true to a limited extent, particularly where the member resides in a distant location. We think it is reasonable to believe, however, that most lawyers who become members of a state bar will endeavor to perform their share of these services. This sort of participation, of course, would serve the professional interest of a lawyer who practices in the State. Furthermore, a nonresident bar member, like the resident member, could be required to represent indigents and perhaps to participate in formal legal-aid work.

In summary, the State neither advances a "substantial reason" for its discrimination against nonresident applicants to the bar, nor demonstrates that the discrimination practiced bears a close relationship to its proffered objectives.

IV

We conclude that New Hampshire's bar residency requirement violates Art. IV, § 2, of the United States Constitution. The nonresident's interest in practicing law is a "privilege" protected by the Clause. Although the lawyer is "an officer of the court," he does not hold a position that can be entrusted only to a "full-fledged member of the political community." A State may discriminate against nonresidents only where its reasons are "substantial," and the difference in treatment bears a close or substantial relation to those reasons. No such showing has been made in this case. Accordingly, we affirm the judgment of the Court of Appeals.

It is so ordered.

[JUSTICE WHITE concurred in the result. JUSTICE REHNQUIST, dissenting largely on the basis of the role played by lawyers in "New Hampshire's self-governance," objected more generally to the majority's "less restrictive means analysis"]:

> I believe the challenge of a "less restrictive means" should be overcome if merely a legitimate reason exists for not pursuing that path. And in any event courts should not play the game the Court has played here—independently scrutinizing each asserted state interest to see if it could devise a better way than the State to accomplish that goal.

Unconstitutional Discrimination in Choice of Law

(1) The effect upon conflict of laws of Article IV's guarantee that citizens of other states shall be given the privileges and immunities of citizens in each state (not to be confused with the Fourteenth Amendment's protection of the privileges and immunities of *national* citizenship) was largely avoided by the application of traditional choice-of-law rules commonly phrased without regard to the parties' home. The emergence of interest analysis, with its recognition of residence and domicile as an important determinant of state interests, thus has the potential to increase the importance of the Privileges and Immunities Clause in limiting discriminatory application of choice-of-law rules.

Initially, the Privileges and Immunities Clause remained obscured by two limitations on its scope. One limitation was that the Clause prevented discrimination only against *citizens,* not against *residents* of other states. *Piper* put this limitation to rest in footnote 6, completing a line of cases suggesting that the terms "citizen" and "resident" are interchangeable for these purposes. The second limitation, originating in Justice Washington's opinion while riding circuit in *Corfield v. Coryell,* was that the protected privileges were only those which are "fundamental" in some sense. *Piper* reaffirms this limitation. Is there any justification for it? See Laycock, *Equal Citizens of Equal and Territorial States: The Constitutional Foundations of Choice of Law,* 92 Colum.L.Rev. 249, 261–66 (1992) (arguing that there is not).

(2) Can you tell from *Piper* which interests will be held protected? Cf., e.g., *Morris v. Crown Equipment Corp.*, 219 W.Va. 347, 633 S.E.2d 292 (W.Va. 2006) (access to courts is fundamental); *Lee v. Minner*, 458 F.3d 194 (3d Cir. 2006) (state freedom of information act rights are fundamental), *abrogated by McBurney v. Young,* 569 U.S. 221 (2013) (restriction of state FOIA rights to citizens is constitutional because nonprotectionist); *Ostrager v. State Bd. of Control,* 99 Cal.App.3d 1, 160 Cal.Rptr. 317 (1979) (crime victim compensation is not fundamental). According to Dean Ely, "the cases we are talking about [in choice of law] involve . . . questions such as whether a given state's guest statute or contractual immunity is to be applied in a given case, and therefore whether the defendant will or will not be held liable. . . [I]t is not likely to be suggested that such decisions implicate rights so unimportant that they can be dismissed as beyond the coverage of the Privileges and Immunities Clause." Ely, *Choice of Law and the State's Interest in Protecting Its Own,* 23 Wm. & Mary L.Rev. 173, 182–83 (1981). Do you agree?

(3) Can you square the use of residence or domicile in interest analysis as a basis for limiting the scope of a state's laws with the Privileges and Immunities Clause? Relying on *Austin v. New Hampshire,* 420 U.S. 656 (1975), Dean Ely answers no. In *Austin,* the Supreme Court held unconstitutional a New Hampshire tax imposed only on nonresident employees. The state argued that the tax was permissible because nonresidents were not taxed at a rate higher than that at which they would have been taxed by their home state. The Court rejected this justification, explaining that it "cannot be squared with the underlying policy of comity to which the Privileges and Immunities Clause commits us." According to Ely, the holding in *Austin:*

> undercuts the entire methodology [of interest analysis] by indicating that whenever a state would claim an interest in enforcing its protective policy on the ground that the party its law would protect is a local resident—and that much is common to all "interest" or "functional" analyses—it is obligated by the United States Constitution to claim a similar interest in protecting out-of-staters, irrespective of what their home states' law provides. That . . . spells the end of "interest analysis" in any recognizable sense of the term and insists instead that we direct our choice-of-law references to that state which will most often bear the strongest relations to the issue in question—relation, however, not being defined in terms of who lives where.

Ely, 23 Wm. & Mary L.Rev. at 187. Professor Laycock agrees, arguing that this conclusion is compelled by the language and purpose of the privileges and immunities clause, and asserting that "[i]f legislatures acted generally on Currie's view that they owe nothing to the citizens of sister states, the Union would be destroyed." Laycock, 92 Colum.L.Rev. at 275. See also L. Tribe, American Constitutional Law 1268 n. 88 (3d ed. 2000).

Noting (as did the Court in *Piper*) that the command of the Privileges and Immunities Clause is not absolute and that the Clause forbids treating nonresidents differently only when "there is no substantial reason for the discrimination," Currie and Schreter argue that interest analysis is constitutional. A state may be interested because a party is a resident and therefore lack this interest when the party is a nonresident—which means that applying the state's law would violate the Due Process and Full Faith and Credit Clauses. "The constitutional limits of a state's power constitute a reasonable basis for classification," Currie and Schreter argue, and therefore "if it is established that a state, by applying its law, will violate the Due Process Clause or the Full Faith and Credit Clause, its failure so to apply its law cannot be a violation of the Privileges and Immunities Clause." B. Currie, Selected Essays on the Conflict of Laws 473–86 (1963).

The argument can be stated more generally. Under interest analysis, a state that is interested in applying its law because a party is a resident withholds the protection of that law from a nonresident in the interest of comity: to leave room for the law of the nonresident's home state. Furthering comity this way constitutes a "substantial reason" for differential treatment under *Piper,* and withholding the protection of forum law in order to apply that other state's law is exactly tailored to further this interest. See Kramer, *The Myth of the "Unprovided-For" Case,* 75 Va.L.Rev. 1045, 1065–68 (1989). On this view, *Austin v. New Hampshire* is correctly decided because New Hampshire had no similar reason for imposing higher taxes on nonresidents and was simply gouging them for extra revenue. Id. at 1068–69. Can *Austin* be fit within the *Piper* framework this way? See *Lunding v. New York Tax Appeals Tribunal,* 522 U.S. 287 (1998) (interpreting *Austin* to permit tax discrimination when there is a "substantial justification" but striking down on privileges and immunities grounds a New York law that denied only non-residents an income tax deduction for alimony because the state's justifications were inadequate).

The problem with this justification is that it begins by accepting the definition of interests used in the due process/full faith and credit context, in particular the acceptance of residence or domicile. By doing so it begs the question, for the opposite result would be reached if analysis began at the other end: If citizenship is an unreasonable basis for classification, it cannot be a violation of the Full Faith and Credit or Due Process Clauses to extend a law to citizens of other states. In other words, if we assume that one clause cannot require what the other forbids, the "reasonableness" of interest-based approaches for constitutional purposes will depend on which clause one looks at first. See also Gergen, *Equality and the Conflict of Laws,* 73 Iowa L.Rev. 893, 902–05 (1988): "Arguments that the interest-based or territorial approach unfairly treats people unequally usually derive entirely from the author's views on the merits of a territorial or a personal order. The debate is really over two different forms of inequality, each of which is arbitrary in its own way."

(4) If both approaches beg the question, how are we to choose? Currie and Schreter make their choice on the basis of authority, for (as we saw in Sections 1 and 2 of this chapter) there is a substantial body of Supreme Court precedent recognizing residence and domicile as a legitimate basis for a state's interest under the Due Process and Full Faith and Credit Clauses. See also *Conner v. Elliott,* 59 U.S. (18 How.) 591, 594 (1855) (Louisiana does not violate the Privileges and Immunities Clause by withholding the benefit of its community property law from couples whose marital domicile is not Louisiana because "it is deemed proper not to interfere, by Louisiana laws, with the relations of married persons out of that state"); *Sosna v. Iowa,* 419 U.S. 393, 407 (1975) (Iowa's one-year durational residency requirement does not impermissibly discriminate against out-of-staters because it furthers the state's interest "in avoiding officious intermeddling in matters in which another State has a paramount interest"). Laycock, in contrast, makes the opposite choice based on his reading of the language and structure of the Constitution. Laycock, 92 Colum.L.Rev. at 266–88.

Which interpretation makes more sense in terms of the policies underlying these clauses? The Currie and Schreter interpretation preserves a wider scope for states to exercise legislative jurisdiction by allowing *both* residency-based and territorial justifications to limit a state's laws. Doesn't it also do a better job furthering the ultimate purpose of both the Privileges and Immunities Clause and the Full Faith and Credit Clause, which is to reduce interstate friction? See David Currie's argument in discussing in *Connor v. Elliot,* supra, that reading the Privileges and Immunities Clause to require "a state with lenient marriage or divorce laws to provide a haven for those hoping to circumvent the more restrictive rules of their own states would convert a provision designed to forestall interstate friction into a tool for exacerbating it." D. Currie, The Constitution in the Supreme Court: The First Hundred Years 241 (1985). See also D. Currie, Comments on *Reich v. Purcell,* 15 UCLA L. Rev. 595, 602 (1968). Under Laycock's and Ely's approach, what happens to the concern, paramount in the Full Faith and Credit Clause cases, that states should not meddle in affairs which are none of their concern?

Laycock and Ely seem to assume that withholding from out-of-staters rights they do not enjoy under their home states' laws does *not* further comity or reduce interstate friction. Do you think that states would rather have their residents restricted to the rights those states give, or allowed to enjoy all the rights accorded to residents of the states into which they travel? Does it depend on the rights at issue? On whether the suit is between two out-of-staters or between an out-of-stater and a local? Do these questions boil down to whether the non-forum state has an interest in the application of its law?

(5) Does it follow that every application of interest analysis is constitutional? At the conclusion of their analysis, Currie and Schreter offer the following statement of the principle of the Privileges and Immunities Clause:

> [W]hen the law of a state provides benefits for its residents generally, the same benefits should be extended to citizens of other states unless there is some substantial reason, in addition to the fact that the governmental interests of the state do not require extension of the benefit to foreigners, for limiting the benefit to residents.

B. Currie, Selected Essays at 508. On this view, it is permissible for a state to define a conflict as false and apply nonforum law to accommodate the interest of another state. Similarly, the state can sacrifice a forum interest and apply nonforum law for the same reason in a true conflict case. (Bear in mind, however, that the forum may resolve true conflicts by applying forum law, in which case there is no discrimination and so no privileges and immunities question at all.) What about the cases we called "unprovided for" in Chapter 2? Recall, for example, *Erwin v. Thomas,* supra p. 170, in which a Washington plaintiff sued an Oregon defendant for loss of consortium resulting from her husband's injury in Washington; Oregon but not Washington permitted plaintiff to recover, though Washington's failure to allow recovery did not reflect an affirmative policy of disabling plaintiff-wives from receiving compensation for loss of consortium. That being so, what justification does Oregon have for denying this Washington plaintiff the benefit of its law allowing recovery? Does the Constitution *require* Oregon to award this plaintiff damages simply because she managed to get jurisdiction in Oregon? Suppose she sued in California, which also allowed recovery? Compare Kramer, 75 Va.L.Rev. at 1072–74 (recovery is required) with B. Currie, Selected Essays at 505 (recovery is not required if plaintiff seeks the benefit of a forum law that creates an exception to a general policy shared by both states and the plaintiff's home state recognizes no similar exception).

(6) The Supreme Court has never departed from its holding in *Blake v. McClung,* 172 U.S. 239 (1898), that corporations are not "citizens" within the Privileges and Immunities Clause. Nor does the clause protect aliens or American citizens who are not citizens of any state. To the rescue comes the Equal Protection Clause of the Fourteenth Amendment, which refers to "persons" instead of citizens and therefore (?) has been held to include corporations, *Pembina Consolidated Silver Mining and Milling Co. v. Pennsylvania,* 125 U.S. 181 (1888), as well as real people who are not state citizens.

The Equal Protection Clause, according to Currie and Schreter, is relevant in two ways to choice of law. First, it has a function akin to that of the Privileges and Immunities Clause, of preventing discrimination against "foreigners" of various types, not all of whom are within the Privileges and Immunities Clause, and in that sphere the test of the reasonableness of the distinction appears to be the same under both clauses. B. Currie, Selected Essays at 536–72. Second, the Equal Protection Clause forbids unreasonable distinctions between citizens of the state whose law is in issue. Specifically, this suggests that some traditional choice-of-law rules, such as those referring to the place of a wrong or of making a contract, may be unconstitutional when applied to deny relief in a case between two local people merely because a connecting factor occurred outside the state. B. Currie, Selected Essays at 572–83 (arguing that *Hughes v. Fetter*, supra p. 414, should have been decided on equal protection grounds). Would you expect the Court to apply a very high level of scrutiny in such cases under the equal protection clause? Then why did it do so in *Piper*?

(7) Although interest analysis has been used by courts for more than 50 years, no court in that time has ever held a choice-of-law decision unconstitutional under either the Privileges and Immunities Clause or the Equal Protection Clause. Does that surprise you? See Gergen, 73 Iowa L.Rev. at 915–16 (arguing that, in practice, courts using interest-based approaches are not excessively parochial).

PART 2

OTHER APPLICATIONS

CHAPTER 4

JURISDICTION OF COURTS

■ ■ ■

Introductory Note

Choice of law is usually limited to the problem dealt with in the first three chapters: overlap or conflict among laws designed to provide substantive rules of decision. But many other situations pose the same or similar problems. Indeed, the analytic models developed in the first three chapters may be useful in any context in which policies or objectives of more than one lawmaking authority overlap or are inconsistent. The remaining chapters explore a number of such problems, though our choices by no means exhaust the possibilities.

Chapter 4 deals with "adjudicatory" or "judicial" jurisdiction over the parties: where may a plaintiff sue a defendant? States enact laws that define the particular cases or controversies the state's lawmakers want its courts to hear. As with any law, the cases chosen were presumably selected for a reason—to advance some policy of the state. Consequently, the choices made by different states may come into conflict if a case falls within the jurisdiction-granting provisions of more than one state. As with any choice-of-law problem, two issues must be faced to resolve such conflicts: (1) what are the permissible constitutional limits of state power to assert jurisdiction (the question dealt with in Chapter 3), and (2) when more than one state may hear a case, how do we decide which state should do so (the question dealt with in Chapters 1 and 2)? A court with power to exercise jurisdiction may decide that it is more appropriate for another state's courts to hear a case (i.e., for that state's law respecting adjudicatory jurisdiction to apply) and may therefore dismiss and require the plaintiff to go elsewhere.

In contrast to "ordinary" choice of law, many states have made the second question moot in the context of adjudicatory jurisdiction by adopting statutes that assert power to the full extent permitted by the Constitution. As a result, the caselaw has focused primarily on the constitutional limits of adjudicatory jurisdiction. Statutory questions remain, however, and in reading the materials below, you should pay attention to the questions involved in interpreting the relevant statutes.

The problem of defining constitutional limits on adjudicatory jurisdiction can be seen as merely an example of the more general problem dealt with in Chapter 3: what contacts or connections must a state have with a particular dispute to apply its law (here its law permitting courts to exercise jurisdiction)? If one state applies its law respecting jurisdiction, other states cannot. (Recall the cases discussed supra pp. 425–425 involving whether a state can require claims under its workers' compensation laws to be heard only by that state's administrative board.) Are there constraints on adjudicatory jurisdiction analogous to the sovereignty and federalism concerns found in cases like *Alaska Packers* and *Pacific Employers*? How do the fairness considerations embodied in the Due Process Clause play themselves out in this context? Although courts have not made an explicit connection between jurisdiction and choice of law, in working through the materials below, consider whether understanding adjudicatory jurisdiction as a choice-of-law problem helps clarify the analysis.

There are, at the same time, important interactions between jurisdiction and choice of law: because states use different approaches to choice of law, the choice of a forum may significantly affect the law applied. This opens up a variety of strategic considerations that may affect how parties approach the early stages of litigation. Keep these considerations in mind as well, and consider whether the constitutional constraints on adjudicatory jurisdiction should be molded to limit this impact on the applicable law.

SECTION 1. SPECIFIC JURISDICTION

The Evolution of Due Process

(1) For a long time, the area of judicial jurisdiction was ruled unambiguously by *Pennoyer v. Neff,* 95 U.S. 714 (1877). While living in Oregon, Neff hired Mitchell to perform some legal services. Neff failed to pay, and Mitchell sued to recover the debt, approximately $300, in an Oregon state court. Because Neff had moved to California and Mitchell did not know his whereabouts, Mitchell served Neff constructively by publication in an Oregon newspaper; it is unclear whether Neff received actual notice of the lawsuit. Neff failed to appear, and the Oregon court entered a default judgment against him. Mitchell executed the judgment by getting the sheriff to seize and sell property owned by Neff in Oregon. Mitchell then purchased the property at the sheriff's sale and resold it (earning a $14,500 profit) to Pennoyer. Neff sued Pennoyer in Oregon federal court, claiming title to the land under his original deed. Pennoyer set up the sheriff's deed as a defense. Neff argued that Pennoyer's deed was invalid because the sale was based on a judgment rendered by a court that lacked jurisdiction over him. The Supreme Court agreed:

> And that [Neff's arguments] are sound would seem to follow from two well established principles of public law respecting the jurisdiction of an independent State over persons and property. . . One of these principles is, that every State possesses exclusive jurisdiction and sovereignty over persons and property within its territory. . . The other principle of public law referred to follows from the one mentioned; that is, that no State can exercise direct jurisdiction and authority over persons and property without its territory. * * * The several States are of equal dignity and authority, and the independence of one implies the exclusion of power from all others. And so it is laid down by jurists, as an elementary principle, that the laws of one State have no operation outside its territory, except so far as is allowed by comity; and that no tribunal established by it can extend its process beyond that territory so as to subject either persons or property to its decisions. . .
>
> So the State, through its tribunals, may subject property within its limits owned by non-residents to the payment of the demand of its own citizens against them; and the exercise of this jurisdiction in no respect infringes upon the sovereignty of the State where the owners are domiciled. . .
>
> Substituted service by publication, or in any other authorized form, may be sufficient to inform parties of the object of proceedings taken where property is once brought under the control of the court by seizure or some equivalent act. . . In other words, such service may answer in all actions which are substantially proceedings *in rem*. But where the entire object of the action is to determine the personal rights and obligations of the defendants, that is, where [as in this case] suit is merely *in personam*, constructive service in this form upon a non-resident is ineffectual for any purpose. Process from the tribunals of one State cannot run into another State, and summon parties there domiciled to leave its territory and respond to proceedings against them. Publication of process or notice within the State where the tribunal sits cannot create any greater obligation upon the non-resident to appear.

Pennoyer argued that since Neff had property in the state that could be the basis for an action *in rem*, it should not matter whether that property was attached before or after the judgment. The Court responded:

> But the answer to this position has already been given in the statement, that the jurisdiction of the court to inquire into and determine [the defendant's] obligations at all is only incidental to its jurisdiction over the property. . . If the judgment be previously

> void, it will not become valid by the subsequent discovery of property of the defendant, or by his subsequent acquisition of it.

Because the question presented was what effect to give Mitchell's judgment against Neff, the Court could have stopped at this point, holding that a judgment rendered without jurisdiction was not entitled to full faith and credit. Instead, the Court added an important dictum announcing that the principles in the opinion were embodied in the Due Process Clause.

(2) What has due process to do with the problem of locating the place of trial? The distinct question of notice and opportunity to defend, so often confused with personal jurisdiction because both are commonly dealt with under the single rubric of service of process, is plainly a component of the notion of a fair trial. If the defendant is not notified of the proceedings, he has no opportunity to defend himself, and he is deprived of his property or liberty without due process. See *Mullane v. Central Hanover Bank,* 339 U.S. 306 (1950). But the Court had something quite different in mind in *Pennoyer,* for it made clear that jurisdiction could not have been obtained by mailing notice to the defendant in California.

Why not? The *Pennoyer* opinion made no effort to relate the limitation to the idea that due process guarantees a fair trial; rather it reflects the traditional notion of territoriality (reflected in choice of law in the work of Story and Beale) that Oregon simply had no power over persons outside its borders. In an international context the absence of the defendant might make the judgment unenforceable, and that might be reason enough for the court to refuse to entertain the action; but why does it follow that the court lacks power to do so? What application does this principle have when the defendant owns property in the forum state? More fundamentally, what place have these arguments about physical power in a federation whose members can be required to respect one another's judgments under the Full Faith and Credit Clause? See Kurland, *The Supreme Court, the Due Process Clause and the In Personam Jurisdiction of State Courts,* 25 U.Chi.L.Rev. 569, 585–86 (1958). And, once again, what has any of this to do with due process?

(3) Even at its inception, there were exceptions to the *Pennoyer* doctrine that seem difficult to reconcile with its strict territorial premises. One problem was extraterritorial effects: an Oregon court that awards Mitchell title to Neff's property in Oregon necessarily affects Neff in California; and, conversely, a California court that makes this award affects property supposedly under the exclusive control of Oregon. The Court's response to this seeming inconsistency was a very unsatisfying declaration that "[t]o any influence exerted in this way by a State affecting persons resident or property situated elsewhere, no objection can justly be taken." 95 U.S. at 723. In addition, the opinion in *Pennoyer* recognized other exceptions, such as the power of a state to determine the status of a nonresident toward one of its citizens (as in divorce) and to condition the grant of a corporate charter or license to do business on consent to receive service of process in the state. Id. at 734–35. There was also language in *Pennoyer* suggesting that a state could exercise jurisdiction over domiciliaries who were not present in the state—an exception that was later explicitly endorsed in *Blackmer v. United States,* 284 U.S. 421 (1932) (service in a foreign nation), and *Milliken v. Meyer,* 311 U.S. 457 (1940) (service in another state). Modern developments created pressure for further exceptions to the rule against extraterritorial service. The most famous example is *Hess v. Pawloski,* 274 U.S. 352 (1927), in which the Court upheld a statute providing that anyone who used the state's roads was deemed to consent to service of process for resulting accidents.

(4) *Pennoyer* was formally abandoned in *International Shoe Co. v. Washington,* 326 U.S. 310 (1945). Corporations presented a particularly tricky problem under the *Pennoyer* framework, for it is difficult to determine when a fictional entity is "present" in the state to be served. Earlier cases relied either on the implied consent theory approved in *Pennoyer* or on the legal fiction that, by engaging in a sufficient amount of activity in the state, a corporation becomes present in the same sense as a natural person. In *International Shoe,* the state of Washington sued a foreign corporation to recover taxes on commissions paid to the company's Washington salesmen. The company had no Washington office, and orders transmitted by its Washington salesmen were filled outside the state. Service was made on one of the company's Washington salesmen and by registered mail to its St. Louis office. In upholding jurisdiction, the Court (per Stone, C.J.) flatly rejected the old learning:

> [N]ow that the capias ad respondendum has given way to personal service of summons or other form of notice, due process requires only that in order to subject a defendant to a judgment in personam, if he be not present within the territory of the forum, he have certain minimum contacts with it such that the maintenance of the suit does not offend "traditional notions of fair play and substantial justice." . . .
>
> It is evident that the criteria by which we mark the boundary line between those activities which justify the subjection of a corporation to suit, and those which do not, cannot be made simply mechanical or quantitative. The test is not merely, as has sometimes been suggested, whether the activity, which the corporation has seen fit to procure through its agents in another state, is a little more or a little less. * * * Whether due process is satisfied must depend rather upon the quality and nature of the activity in relation to the fair and orderly administration of the laws which it was the purpose of the due process clause to insure. That clause does not contemplate that a state may make a binding

> judgment in personam against an individual or corporate defendant with which the state has no contacts, ties, or relations. * * *
>
> But to the extent that a corporation exercises the privilege of conducting activities within a state, it enjoys the benefits and protections of the laws of that state. The exercise of that privilege may give rise to obligations; and, so far as those obligations arise out of or are connected with the activities within the state, a procedure which requires the corporation to respond to a suit brought to enforce them can, in most instances, hardly be said to be undue. . .

The Court went on to uphold jurisdiction:

> Applying these standards, the activities carried on in behalf of appellant in the State of Washington . . . were systematic and continuous throughout the years in question. They resulted in a large volume of interstate business, in the course of which appellant received the benefits and protection of the laws of the state, including the right to resort to the courts. . . The obligation which is here sued upon arose out of those very activities. It is evident that these operations establish sufficient contacts or ties with the state of the forum to make it reasonable and just according to our traditional conception of fair play and substantial justice to permit the state to enforce the obligations which appellant has incurred there.

Justice Black, in a separate opinion, argued that the due-process objection was frivolous: "There is a strong emotional appeal in the words 'fair play,' 'justice,' and 'reasonableness.' But they were not chosen by those who wrote the original Constitution or the Fourteenth Amendment. . ."

(5) *International Shoe* abandons the notion that power to adjudicate depends solely on the defendant's relation to the state at the time when the court asserts its authority. Instead, judicial jurisdiction is made to turn on the defendant's contacts with the state, past and present, in relation to what the state wants to do (make the defendant litigate there) and why. Note that the opinion was written by the Justice who crafted *Alaska Packers* and *Pacific Employers.* Unlike those decisions, however, *International Shoe* is a due process case, decided under the fair-trial guarantee of that clause. Why, exactly, is it unfair to subject a person to suit in a state with which he lacks, in the influential words of *International Shoe,* "minimum contacts"? Is it because of the cost and inconvenience of defending in a remote forum? Then why would due process permit a resident of Texarkana, Texas, to be sued 900 miles away in El Paso but not across town in Texarkana, Arkansas? And why has the Supreme Court said that the Due Process Clause of the Fifth Amendment does not prevent

Congress from providing nationwide service of process for the federal courts? *Mississippi Pub. Corp. v. Murphree,* 326 U.S. 438, 442 (1946) (dictum). Is "unfairness" just a new name for state sovereignty? Might the unfairness have something to do with choice of law?

Can you state the implications of *International Shoe* for: (a) jurisdiction over corporations? (b) service of process rules? (c) jurisdiction over natural persons? Does the new theory only expand jurisdiction, or does it also invalidate assertions of jurisdiction that would have been permitted under *Pennoyer*?

(6) The difficult problem since *International Shoe* has been to give content to the rather vague tests of "minimum contacts" and "fundamental fairness." Until 1977 the most important efforts in this direction were two Supreme Court cases decided in the late 1950s, which must be studied if the more recent decisions are to be understood.

The first was *McGee v. International Life Ins. Co.*, 355 U.S. 220 (1957). A California resident had been insured by a company whose obligations were assumed by another insurer with its principal place of business in Texas. The Texas company had neither office nor agents in California; it mailed the insured an offer to continue his coverage, and all later transactions between them were conducted by mail. There was no evidence that the Texas company did any other business or had any other contacts in California. California's jurisdiction in a suit to recover on the policy was upheld (per Black, J.) on the basis of *International Shoe*:

> It is sufficient for purposes of due process that the suit was based on a contract which had substantial connection with [California]. * * * The contract was delivered in California, the premiums were mailed from there and the insured was a resident of that State when he died. It cannot be denied that California has a manifest interest in providing effective means of redress for its residents when their insurers refuse to pay claims. These residents would be at a severe disadvantage if they were forced to follow the insurance company to a distant State in order to hold it legally accountable. When claims were small or moderate individual claimants frequently could not afford the cost of bringing an action in a foreign forum—thus in effect making the company judgment proof. Often the crucial witnesses—as here on the company's defense of suicide—will be found in the insured's locality. Of course there may be inconvenience to the insurer if it is held amenable to suit in California where it had this contract but certainly nothing which amounts to a denial of due process.

355 U.S. at 223. After *International Shoe,* was the result in *McGee* surprising? What interests or concerns did the Court look for in deciding whether the contacts are adequate? Notice how little the Court said about

the *defendant's* contacts with California. Would you have upheld jurisdiction in *McGee*?

(7) The second important decision giving content to *International Shoe* was *Hanson v. Denckla*, 357 U.S. 235 (1958). While living in Pennsylvania, Donner created a trust, naming a Delaware bank as trustee and reserving a power of appointment as to the disposition of the residue at her death. She subsequently moved to Florida, where she designated the children of her daughter Elizabeth (one of whom was Hanson) to receive the trust assets. Donner died in Florida, and her other daughters (one of whom was Denckla) sued the granddaughters and the Delaware bank in Florida. They argued that the trust was invalid and that the trust assets should pass to them under the residuary clause of Donner's will. In the meantime, Hanson brought suit against Denckla in Delaware to resolve the same issue. The Florida case came to judgment first, and the Florida court held the trust invalid. Denckla argued to the Delaware court that this judgment was res judicata. The Delaware court disagreed, reasoning that the Delaware bank, as trustee, was an indispensable party and that Florida had no jurisdiction over it. The Delaware court then upheld the trust and awarded the assets to Hanson. The inconsistent judgments were taken to the Supreme Court, which agreed that Florida lacked jurisdiction over the Delaware bank:

> [I]t is a mistake to assume that [*International Shoe*] heralds the eventual demise of all restrictions on the personal jurisdiction of the state courts. * * * Those restrictions are more than a guarantee of immunity from inconvenient or distant litigation. They are a consequence of territorial limitations on the power of the respective States. However minimal the burden of defending in a foreign tribunal, a defendant may not be called upon to do so unless he has had the "minimal contacts" with that State that are a prerequisite to its exercise of power over him. * * *
>
> We fail to find such contacts in the circumstances of this case. The defendant trust company has no office in Florida, and transacts no business there. None of the trust assets has ever been held or administered in Florida, and the record discloses no solicitation of business in that State either in person or by mail. * * *
>
> The cause of action in this case is not one that arises out of an act done or transaction consummated in the forum State. In that respect, it differs from *McGee v. International Life Ins. Co.*, 355 U.S. 220, and the cases there cited. . . In contrast, this action involves the validity of an agreement that was entered without any connection with the forum State. The agreement was executed in Delaware by a trust company incorporated in that

> State and a settlor domiciled in Pennsylvania. The first relationship Florida had to the agreement was years later when the settlor became domiciled there, and the trustee remitted the trust income to her in that State. From Florida Mrs. Donner carried on several bits of trust administration that may be compared to the mailing of premiums in *McGee.* But the record discloses no instance in which the *trustee* performed any acts in Florida that bear the same relationship to the agreement as the solicitation in *McGee.* Consequently, this suit cannot be said to be one to enforce an obligation that arose from a privilege the defendant exercised in Florida. * * * This case is also different from *McGee* in that there the State had enacted special legislation * * * to exercise what *McGee* called its "manifest interest" in providing effective redress for citizens who had been injured by nonresidents engaged in an activity that the State treats as exceptional and subjects to special regulation. * * *
>
> The execution in Florida of the powers of appointment under which the beneficiaries and appointees claim does not give Florida a substantial connection with the contract on which this suit is based. It is the validity of the trust agreement, not the appointment, that is at issue here. For the purpose of applying its rule that the validity of a trust is determined by the law of the State of its creation, Florida ruled that the appointment amounted to a "republication" of the original trust instrument in Florida. For choice-of-law purposes such a ruling may be justified, but we think it an insubstantial connection with the trust agreement for purposes of determining the question of personal jurisdiction over a nonresident defendant. The unilateral activity of those who claim some relationship with a nonresident defendant cannot satisfy the requirement of contact with the forum State. The application of that rule will vary with the quality and nature of the defendant's activity, but it is essential in each case that there be some act by which the defendant purposefully avails itself of the privilege of conducting activities within the forum State, thus invoking the benefits and protections of its laws. * * * The settlor's execution in Florida of her power of appointment cannot remedy the absence of such an act in this case.

357 U.S. at 251–54.

McGee and *Hanson* came only a year apart. Can they be reconciled on their facts? Taken together, do they state a coherent theory of personal jurisdiction? Does *Hanson* displace the test developed in *McGee* or add something to it? What? See D. Currie, *The Growth of the Long Arm: Eight*

Years of Extended Jurisdiction in Illinois, 1963 U.Ill.L.F. 533, 548–50. Would you have upheld jurisdiction in *Hanson*?

(8) Jurisdiction had been based in *Hess v. Pawloski,* supra p. 443, on a statute applicable only to nonresident motorists, and in *McGee* on a statute reaching only foreign insurers. Encouraged by *International Shoe* and *McGee,* many states adopted general "long-arm" statutes extending the principle of the nonresident-motorist and insurer statutes to other cases in which the events in suit, or some of them, occurred within the forum state. The prototype for many similar statutes was Ill.Rev.Stat. c. 110, § 17 (now ¶ 2–209), first enacted in 1955:

> (1) Any person, whether or not a citizen or resident of this State, who in person or through an agent does any of the acts hereinafter enumerated, thereby submits said person, and, if an individual, his personal representative, to the jurisdiction of the courts of this State as to any cause of action arising from the doing of any of said acts:
>
> (a) The transaction of any business within this State;
>
> (b) The commission of a tortious act within this State;
>
> (c) The ownership, use, or possession of any real estate situated in this State;
>
> (d) Contracting to insure any person, property or risk located within this State at the time of contracting.
>
> (2) Service of process upon any person who is subject to the jurisdiction of the courts of this State, as provided in this section, may be made by personally serving the summons upon the defendant outside this State, as provided in this Act, with the same force and effect as though summons had been personally served within this State.
>
> (3) Only causes of action arising from acts enumerated herein may be asserted against a defendant in an action in which jurisdiction over him is based upon this section.
>
> (4) Nothing herein contained limits or affects the right to serve any process in any other manner now or hereafter provided by law.

Courts frequently interpret these statutes as if they assert jurisdiction to the constitutional limit, and other legislatures have simply chosen to do so explicitly. E.g., Cal.Code Civ.Proc. § 410.10: "A court of this state may exercise jurisdiction on any basis not inconsistent with the constitution of this state or of the United States." Is this a responsible way to legislate? See Cheatham, *Conflict of Laws: Some Developments and Some Questions,* 25 Ark.L.Rev. 9, 25 (1971): "To say that a law does not violate the due process clause is to say the least possible good about it. Due process is manifestly not a fair or wise test of the competence of a court over a defendant."

(9) After *McGee,* there was little doubt that a state could validly exercise jurisdiction whenever the defendant was sued for an act committed while he or she was physically present in the forum state. The more challenging question was the extent to which a state might exercise long-arm jurisdiction over persons who had never entered the state at all, but whose activities elsewhere had caused harm there. *McGee* was such a case, and jurisdiction was upheld. So, too, was *Ohio v. Wyandotte Chem. Corp.*, 401 U.S. 493 (1971), in which the Supreme Court refused to entertain an original nuisance action brought by the state against Canadian manufacturers who had allegedly caused injury in Ohio by dumping mercury into Lake Erie on the ground that such a claim could be adjudicated in the Ohio state courts. How far did the principle extend? For example, could the insurance company in *McGee* have brought an action in Texas for a declaration that it was not liable to the California beneficiary? The following cases may help to answer these questions.

WORLD-WIDE VOLKSWAGEN CORP. V. WOODSON

444 U.S. 286 (1980).

MR. JUSTICE WHITE delivered the opinion of the Court.

The issue before us is whether, consistently with the Due Process Clause of the Fourteenth Amendment, an Oklahoma court may exercise *in personam* jurisdiction over a nonresident automobile retailer and its wholesale distributor in a products liability action, when the defendants' only connection with Oklahoma is the fact that an automobile sold in New York to New York residents became involved in an accident in Oklahoma.

I

Respondents Harry and Kay Robinson purchased a new Audi automobile from petitioner Seaway Volkswagen, Inc. (Seaway) in Massena, N.Y., in 1976. The following year the Robinson family, who resided in New York, left that State for a new home in Arizona. As they passed through the State of Oklahoma, another car struck their Audi in the rear, causing a fire which severely burned Kay Robinson and her two children.

The Robinsons subsequently brought a products liability action in the District Court for Creek County, Okla., claiming that their injuries resulted from defective design and placement of the Audi's gas tank and fuel system. They joined as defendants the automobile's manufacturer, Audi NSU Auto Union Aktiengesellschaft (Audi); its importer, Volkswagen of America, Inc. (Volkswagen); its regional distributor, petitioner World-Wide Volkswagen Corporation (World-Wide); and its retail dealer, petitioner Seaway. Seaway and World-Wide entered special appearances,[3] claiming that Oklahoma's exercise of jurisdiction over them would offend the limitations on the State's jurisdiction imposed by the Due Process Clause of the Fourteenth Amendment.

The facts presented to the District Court showed that World-Wide is incorporated and has its business office in New York. It distributes vehicles, parts and accessories, under contract with Volkswagen, to retail dealers in New York, New Jersey, and Connecticut. Seaway, one of these retail dealers, is incorporated and has its place of business in New York. Insofar as the record reveals, Seaway and World-Wide are fully independent corporations whose relations with each other and with Volkswagen and Audi are contractual only. Respondents adduced no evidence that either World-Wide or Seaway does any business in Oklahoma, ships or sells any products to or in that State, has an agent to receive process there, or purchases advertisements in any media calculated to reach Oklahoma. In fact, as respondents' counsel conceded at oral argument there was no showing that any automobile sold by World-Wide or Seaway has ever entered Oklahoma with the single exception of the vehicle involved in the present case.

Despite the apparent paucity of contacts between petitioners and Oklahoma, the District Court rejected their constitutional claim and reaffirmed that ruling in denying petitioners' motion for reconsideration. Petitioners then sought a writ of prohibition in the Supreme Court of Oklahoma to restrain the District Judge, respondent Charles S. Woodson, from exercising *in personam* jurisdiction over them. They renewed their contention that because they had no "minimal contacts" with the State of Oklahoma, the actions of the District Judge were in violation of their rights under the Due Process Clause.

The Supreme Court of Oklahoma denied the writ, 585 P.2d 351 (1978), holding that personal jurisdiction over petitioners was authorized by Oklahoma's "Long-Arm" Statute, Okla.Stat., Tit. 12, § 1701.03(a)(4) (1961). Although the Court noted that the proper approach was to test jurisdiction against both statutory and constitutional standards, its analysis did not distinguish these questions, probably because § 1701.03(a)(4) has been interpreted as conferring jurisdiction to the limits permitted by the United States Constitution. The Court's rationale was contained in the following paragraph, 585 P.2d, at 354:

> "In the case before us, the product being sold and distributed by the petitioners is by its very design and purpose so mobile that petitioners can foresee its possible use in Oklahoma. This is

3 Volkswagen also entered a special appearance in the District Court, but unlike World-Wide and Seaway did not seek review in the Supreme Court of Oklahoma and is not a petitioner here. Both Volkswagen and Audi remain as defendants in the litigation pending before the District Court in Oklahoma.

especially true of the distributor, who has the exclusive right to distribute such automobile [*sic*] in New York, New Jersey and Connecticut. The evidence presented below demonstrated that goods sold and distributed by the petitioners were used in the State of Oklahoma, and under the facts we believe it reasonable to infer, given the retail value of the automobile, that the petitioners derive substantial income from automobiles which from time to time are used in the State of Oklahoma. This being the case, we hold that under the facts presented, the trial court was justified in concluding that the petitioners derive substantial revenue from goods used or consumed in this State."

We granted certiorari, 440 U.S. 907 (1979), to consider an important constitutional question with respect to state-court jurisdiction and to resolve a conflict between the Supreme Court of Oklahoma and the highest courts of at least four other States. We reverse.

II . . .

As has long been settled, and as we reaffirm today, a state court may exercise personal jurisdiction over a nonresident defendant only so long as there exist "minimum contacts" between the defendant and the forum State. *International Shoe Co. v. Washington,* supra, at 324. The concept of minimum contacts, in turn, can be seen to perform two related, but distinguishable, functions. It protects the defendant against the burdens of litigating in a distant or inconvenient forum. And it acts to ensure that the States through their courts, do not reach out beyond the limits imposed on them by their status as coequal sovereigns in a federal system.

The protection against inconvenient litigation is typically described in terms of "reasonableness" or "fairness." We have said that the defendant's contacts with the forum State must be such that maintenance of the suit "does not offend 'traditional notions of fair play and substantial justice.'" *International Shoe Co. v. Washington,* supra, at 316, quoting *Milliken v. Meyer,* 311 U.S. 457, 463 (1940). The relationship between the defendant and the forum must be such that it is "reasonable . . . to require the corporation to defend the particular suit which is brought there." 326 U.S., at 317. Implicit in this emphasis on reasonableness is the understanding that the burden on the defendant, while always a primary concern, will in an appropriate case be considered in light of other relevant factors, including the forum State's interest in adjudicating the dispute, see *McGee v. International Life Ins. Co.,* 355 U.S. 220, 223 (1957); the plaintiff's interest in obtaining convenient and effective relief, see *Kulko v. Superior Court,* supra, 436 U.S., at 92, at least when that interest is not adequately protected by the plaintiff's power to choose the forum, cf. *Shaffer v. Heitner,* 433 U.S. 186, 211, n. 37 (1977); the interstate judicial system's interest in obtaining the most efficient resolution of controversies; and the shared interest of the several States in furthering fundamental substantive social policies, see *Kulko v. Superior Court,* supra, 436 U.S., at 93, 98.

The limits imposed on state jurisdiction by the Due Process Clause, in its role as a guarantor against inconvenient litigation, have been substantially relaxed over the years. As we noted in *McGee v. International Life Ins. Co.,* supra, 355 U.S., at 222–223, this trend is largely attributable to a fundamental transformation in the American economy:

> "Today many commercial transactions touch two or more States and may involve parties separated by the full continent. With this increasing nationalization of commerce has come a great increase in the amount of business conducted by mail across state lines. At the same time modern transportation and communication have made it much less burdensome for a party sued to defend himself in a State where he engages in economic activity."

The historical developments noted in *McGee,* of course, have only accelerated in the generation since that case was decided.

Nevertheless, we have never accepted the proposition that state lines are irrelevant for jurisdictional purposes, nor could we and remain faithful to the principles of interstate federalism embodied in the Constitution. The economic interdependence of the States was foreseen and desired by the Framers. In the Commerce Clause, they provided that the Nation was to be a common market, a "free trade unit" in which the States are debarred from acting as separable economic entities. * * * But the Framers also intended that the States retain many essential attributes of sovereignty, including, in particular, the sovereign power to try causes in their courts. The sovereignty of each State, in turn, implied a limitation on the sovereignty of all of its sister States—a limitation express or implicit in both the original scheme of the Constitution and the Fourteenth Amendment.

Hence, even while abandoning the shibboleth that "[t]he authority of every tribunal is necessarily restricted by the territorial limits of the State in which it is established," *Pennoyer v. Neff,* supra, 95 U.S., at 720, we emphasized that the reasonableness of asserting jurisdiction over the defendant must be assessed "in the context of our federal system of government," *International Shoe Co. v. Washington,* supra, 326 U.S., at 317, and stressed that the Due Process Clause ensures, not only fairness, but also the "orderly administration of the laws," id., at 319. . .

Thus, the Due Process Clause "does not contemplate that a state may make binding a judgment *in personam* against an individual or corporate defendant with which the state has no contacts, ties, or relations." *International Shoe Co. v. Washington,* supra, at 319. Even if the defendant would suffer minimal or no inconvenience from being forced to litigate before the tribunals of another State; even if the forum State has a strong interest in applying its law to the controversy; even if the forum State is the most convenient location for litigation, the Due Process Clause, acting as an instrument of interstate federalism, may sometimes act to divest the State of its power to render a valid judgment. *Hanson v. Denckla,* supra, 357 U.S., at 251, 254.

III

Applying these principles to the case at hand, we find in the record before us a total absence of those affiliating circumstances that are a necessary predicate to any exercise of state-court jurisdiction. Petitioners carry on no activity whatsoever in Oklahoma. They close no sales and perform no services there. They avail themselves of none of the privileges and benefits of Oklahoma law. They solicit no business there either through salespersons or through advertising reasonably calculated to reach the State. Nor does the record show that they regularly sell cars at wholesale or retail to Oklahoma customers or residents or that they indirectly, through others, serve or seek to serve the Oklahoma market. In short, respondents seek to base jurisdiction on one, isolated occurrence and whatever inferences can be drawn therefrom: the fortuitous circumstance that a single Audi automobile, sold in New York to New York residents, happened to suffer an accident while passing through Oklahoma.

It is argued, however, that because an automobile is mobile by its very design and purpose it was "foreseeable" that the Robinsons' Audi would cause injury in Oklahoma. Yet "foreseeability" alone has never been a sufficient benchmark for personal jurisdiction under the Due Process Clause. In *Hanson v. Denckla,* supra, it was no doubt foreseeable that the settlor of a Delaware trust would subsequently move to Florida and seek to exercise a power of appointment there; yet we held that Florida courts could not constitutionally exercise jurisdiction over a Delaware trust that had no other contacts with the forum State. . .

This is not to say, of course, that foreseeability is wholly irrelevant. But the foreseeability that is critical to due process analysis is not the mere likelihood that a product will find its way into the forum State. Rather, it is that the defendant's conduct and connection with the forum State are such that he should reasonably anticipate being haled into court there. * * * The Due Process Clause, by ensuring the "orderly administration of the laws," *International Shoe Co. v. Washington,* 326 U.S., at 319, gives a degree of predictability to the legal system that allows potential defendants to structure their primary conduct with some minimum assurance as to where that conduct will and will not render them liable to suit.

When a corporation "purposefully avails itself of the privilege of conducting activities within the forum State," *Hanson v. Denckla,* supra, at 253, it has clear notice that it is subject to suit there, and can act to alleviate the risk of burdensome litigation by procuring insurance, passing the expected costs on to customers, or, if the risks are too great, severing its connection with the State. Hence if the sale of a product of a manufacturer or distributor such as Audi or Volkswagen is not simply an isolated occurrence, but arises from the efforts of the manufacturer or distributor to serve directly or indirectly, the market for its product in other States, it is not unreasonable to subject it to suit in one of those States if its allegedly defective merchandise has there been the source of injury to its owner or to others. The forum State does not exceed its powers under the Due Process Clause if it asserts personal jurisdiction over a corporation that delivers its products into the stream of commerce with the expectation that they will be purchased by consumers in the forum State. * * *

But there is no such or similar basis for Oklahoma jurisdiction over World-Wide or Seaway in this case. Seaway's sales are made in Massena, N.Y. World-Wide's market, although substantially larger, is limited to dealers in New York, New Jersey, and Connecticut. There is no evidence of record that any automobiles distributed by World-Wide are sold to retail customers outside this tri-State area. It is foreseeable that the purchasers of automobiles sold by World-Wide and Seaway may take them to Oklahoma. But the mere "unilateral activity of those who claim some relationship with a nonresident defendant cannot satisfy the requirement of contact with the forum State." *Hanson v. Denckla,* supra, at 326.

In a variant on the previous argument, it is contended that jurisdiction can be supported by the fact that petitioners earn substantial revenue from goods used in Oklahoma. The Oklahoma Supreme Court so found, 585 P.2d, at 354–355, drawing the inference that because one automobile sold by petitioners had been used in Oklahoma, others might have been used there also. While this inference seems less than compelling on the facts of the instant case, we need not question the Court's factual findings in order to reject its reasoning.

This argument seems to make the point that the purchase of automobiles in New York, from which the petitioners earn substantial revenue, would not occur *but for* the fact that the automobiles are capable of use in distant States like Oklahoma. Respondents observe that the very purpose of an automobile is to travel, and that travel of automobiles sold by petitioners is facilitated by an extensive chain of Volkswagen service centers throughout the Country, including some in Oklahoma. However, financial benefits accruing to the defendant from a collateral relation to the forum State will not support jurisdiction if they do not stem from a constitutionally cognizable contact with that State. See *Kulko v. Superior Court,* supra, 436 U.S., at 94–95. In our view, whatever marginal revenue petitioners may receive by virtue of the fact that their products are capable of use in Oklahoma is far too attenuated a contact to justify that State's exercise of *in personam* jurisdiction over them. . .

Reversed.

MR. JUSTICE BRENNAN, dissenting.

[B]ecause I believe that the Court reads *International Shoe* and its progeny too narrowly, and because I believe that the standards enunciated by those cases may already be obsolete as constitutional boundaries, I dissent.

The Court's opinions* focus tightly on the existence of contacts between the forum and the defendant. In so doing, they accord too little weight to the strength of the forum State's interest in the case and fail to explore whether there would be any actual inconvenience to the defendant. The essential inquiry in locating the constitutional limits on state-court jurisdiction over absent defendants is whether the particular exercise of jurisdiction offends "traditional notions of fair play and substantial justice." *International Shoe,* supra. * * * The clear focus in *International Shoe* was on fairness and reasonableness. * * * The Court specifically declined to establish a mechanical test based on the quantum of contacts between a State and the defendant. . . The existence of contacts, so long as there were some, was merely one way of giving content to the determination of fairness and reasonableness.

Surely *International Shoe* contemplated that the significance of the contacts necessary to support jurisdiction would diminish if some other consideration helped establish that jurisdiction would be fair and reasonable. The interests of the State and other parties in proceeding with the case in a particular forum are such considerations. *McGee v. International Life Insurance Co.,* 355 U.S. 220, 223 (1957), for instance, accorded great importance to a State's "manifest interest in providing effective means of redress" for its citizens. * * *

Another consideration is the actual burden a defendant must bear in defending the suit in the forum. *McGee,* supra. Because lesser burdens reduce the unfairness to the defendant, jurisdiction may be justified despite less significant contacts. The burden, of course, must be of constitutional dimension. Due process limits on jurisdiction do not protect a defendant from all inconvenience of travel, *McGee,* supra, at 224, and it would not be sensible to make the constitutional rule turn solely on the number of miles the defendant must travel to the courtroom. Instead, the constitutionally significant "burden" to be analyzed relates to the mobility of the defendant's defense. For instance, if having to travel to a foreign forum would hamper the defense because witnesses or evidence or the defendant himself were immobile, or if there were a disproportionately large number of witnesses or amount of evidence that would have to be transported at the defendant's expense, or if being away from home for the

* Justice Brennan's dissenting opinion dealt with a companion case, *Rush v. Savchuk,* 444 U.S. 320 (1980), as well as with *World-Wide Volkswagen Corp. v. Woodson.*

duration of the trial would work some special hardship on the defendant, then the Constitution would require special consideration for the defendant's interests. . .

[In this case, the] interest of the forum State and its connection to the litigation is strong. The automobile accident underlying the litigation occurred in Oklahoma. The plaintiffs were hospitalized in Oklahoma when they brought suit. Essential witnesses and evidence were in Oklahoma. * * * The State has a legitimate interest in enforcing its laws designed to keep its highway system safe, and the trial can proceed at least as efficiently in Oklahoma as anywhere else.

The petitioners are not unconnected with the forum. Although both sell automobiles within limited sales territories, each sold the automobile which in fact was driven to Oklahoma where it was involved in an accident. It may be true, as the Court suggests, that each sincerely intended to limit its commercial impact to the limited territory, and that each intended to accept the benefits and protection of the laws only of those States within the territory. But obviously these were unrealistic hopes that cannot be treated as an automatic constitutional shield. . .

The Court accepts that a State may exercise jurisdiction over a distributor which "serves" that State "indirectly" by "deliver[ing] its products into the stream of commerce with the expectation that they will be purchased by consumers in [other] State[s]." It is difficult to see why the Constitution should distinguish between a case involving goods which reach a distant State through a chain of distribution and a case involving goods which reach the same State because a consumer, using them as the dealer knew the customer would, took them there. In each case the seller purposefully injects the goods into the stream of commerce and those goods predictably are used in the forum State.

Furthermore, an automobile seller derives substantial benefits from States other than its own. A large part of the value of automobiles is the extensive, nationwide network of highways. Significant portions of that network have been constructed by and are maintained by the individual States, including Oklahoma. The States, through their highway programs, contribute in a very direct and important way to the value of petitioners' businesses. Additionally, a network of other related dealerships with their service departments operate throughout the country under the protection of the laws of the various States, including Oklahoma, and enhance the value of petitioners' businesses by facilitating their customers' traveling. . .

International Shoe inherited its defendant focus from *Pennoyer v. Neff*, 95 U.S. 714 (1878), and represented the last major step this Court has taken in the long process of liberalizing the doctrine of personal jurisdiction. Though its flexible approach represented a major advance, the structure of our society has changed in many significant ways since

International Shoe was decided in 1945. Justice Black, writing for the Court in *McGee v. International Life Insurance Co.,* 355 U.S. 220, 222 (1957), recognized that "a trend is clearly discernible toward expanding the permissible scope of state jurisdiction over foreign corporations and other nonresidents." . . . As the Court acknowledges, both the nationalization of commerce and the ease of transportation and communication have accelerated in the generation since 1957. The model of society on which the *International Shoe* Court based its opinion is no longer accurate. Business people, no matter how local their businesses, cannot assume that goods remain in the business' locality. Customers and goods can be anywhere else in the country usually in a matter of hours and always in a matter of a very few days. . .

The conclusion I draw is that constitutional concepts of fairness no longer require the extreme concern for defendants that was once necessary. Rather, as I wrote in dissent from *Shaffer v. Heitner,* supra, 433 U.S., at 220, minimum contacts must exist "among the *parties,* the contested transaction, and the forum State."[15] The contacts between any two of these should not be determinative. . . Assuming that a State gives a nonresident defendant adequate notice and opportunity to defend, I do not think the Due Process Clause is offended merely because the defendant has to board a plane to get to the site of the trial.

The Court . . . suggests that the defendant ought to be subject to a State's jurisdiction only if he has contacts with the State "such that he should reasonably anticipate being haled into court there." There is nothing unreasonable or unfair, however, about recognizing commercial reality. Given the tremendous mobility of goods and people, and the inability of businessmen to control where goods are taken by customers (or retailers), I do not think that the defendant should be in complete control of the geographical stretch of his amenability to suit. Jurisdiction is no longer premised on the notion that nonresident defendants have somehow impliedly consented to suit. People should understand that they are held responsible for the consequences of their actions and that in our society most actions have consequences affecting many States. When an action in fact causes injury in another State, the actor should be prepared to answer for it there unless defending in that State would be unfair for some reason other than that a State boundary must be crossed.[19]

---

[15] In some cases, the inquiry will resemble the inquiry commonly undertaken in determining which State's law to apply. That it is fair to apply a State's law to a nonresident defendant is clearly relevant in determining whether it is fair to subject the defendant to jurisdiction in that State. *Shaffer v. Heitner,* 433 U.S. 186, 225 (1977) (Brennan, J., dissenting); *Hanson v. Denckla,* 357 U.S. 235, 258 (1958) (Black, J., dissenting).

[19] One consideration that might create some unfairness would be if the choice of forum also imposed on the defendant an unfavorable substantive law which the defendant could justly have assumed would not apply.

The Reach of the Long Arm

(1) What, exactly, is the test for judicial jurisdiction after *World-Wide Volkswagen*? That is, what requirements must be satisfied by the search for relevant contacts? *McGee* looked for contacts establishing that the exercise of jurisdiction would be "reasonable" because the forum state had an interest in adjudicating the dispute and was not an unduly inconvenient place for doing so. *World-Wide Volkswagen* focuses on contacts establishing "purposeful availment" by the defendant. Does this replace the *McGee* factors or add to them? Does *World-Wide Volkswagen* establish that two cumulative requirements must be satisfied before jurisdiction can be exercised? Why weren't the factors taken into account under *McGee* adequate?

(2) Why is it important for purposes of judicial jurisdiction that the defendant have availed itself of the privilege of conducting activities within the forum state? Justice White raises the spectre of unfair surprise, observing that defendants need to know where they may be sued so they can "act to alleviate the risk of burdensome litigation." Is that persuasive? How many businesses will alter their marketing practices to avoid having to litigate in a particular state (as opposed to avoiding the application of a particular law)? Is *World-Wide Volkswagen* really a choice-of-law decision, based on the assumption that the forum will apply its own law? If so, is this the best way to handle that concern?

Can you think of a better explanation for the purposeful availment test? Is it a *quid pro quo* requirement: a state can impose the burden of having to litigate in its courts only on parties who have obtained benefits from conducting activity there? Or is the purposeful availment test best explained as an effort to limit the plaintiff's tactical advantage from having the initial choice of forum by restricting that choice to places where the defendant has some presence? Don't the kinds of contacts that satisfy the requirement vary depending on which explanation one accepts? For instance, must the contacts needed to satisfy the purposeful availment test be related to the underlying suit or can unrelated contacts (such as conducting other business in the state) also count?

(3) Compare the analysis in *World-Wide Volkswagen* with *Kulko v. Superior Court,* 436 U.S. 84 (1978). Ezra and Sharon Kulko lived in New York, where they had two children. The couple separated and Sharon moved to California. They agreed that the children, aged 11 and 12, would spend the school year with Ezra in New York and vacations with Sharon in California, and that Ezra would pay Sharon $3,000 a year in child support. The children soon decided that they preferred to live with their mother in California. Ezra bought the older child a ticket and acquiesced when Sharon subsequently sent the second child, Ilsa, a ticket without his knowledge. Sharon thereupon brought an action in California seeking custody and an increase in child support. The California Supreme Court upheld jurisdiction on the ground that Ezra's purchase of his daughter's airline ticket constituted a "purposeful act" outside the state that caused effects within it. The Supreme Court, in an opinion by Justice Marshall, reversed:

> We cannot accept the proposition that appellant's acquiescence in Ilsa's desire to live with her mother conferred jurisdiction over appellant in the California courts in this action. A father who agrees, in the interests of family harmony and his children's preferences, to allow them to spend more time in California than was required under a separation agreement can hardly be said to have "purposefully availed himself" of the "benefits and protection" of California's laws. . .
>
> The circumstances in this case clearly render "unreasonable" California's assertion of personal jurisdiction. There is no claim that appellant has visited physical injury on either property or persons within the State of California. * * * The cause of action herein asserted arises, not from defendant's commercial transactions in interstate commerce, but rather from his personal, domestic relations. It thus cannot be said that appellant has sought a commercial benefit from solicitation of business from a resident of California that could reasonably render him liable to suit in state court. . .

Appellee argued that it was reasonable for California to assert jurisdiction because of the state's interest in the welfare of its minors. The Court responded: "These interests are unquestionably important. But while the presence of the children and one parent in California arguably might favor application of California law in a lawsuit in New York, the fact that California may be the 'center of gravity' for choice-of-law purposes does not mean that California has personal jurisdiction over the defendant."

Should commercial transactions be analyzed differently from domestic relations for purposes of judicial jurisdiction? Would the result be different if Kulko sent his ex-wife a potted plant and (unknown to him) it carried a disease that caused injury to plants in California? Would there have been jurisdiction if, in addition to sending his children to live in California, Kulko had transacted unrelated business in the state?

(4) The Court in *World-Wide Volkswagen* suggests that Oklahoma law could constitutionally be applied, and in *Kulko* the Court makes a similar suggestion with respect to California law. These suggestions echo *Hanson v. Denckla,* supra p. 446, which stated that jurisdiction would not necessarily follow from the arguable applicability of Florida law. Why can't a state exercise jurisdiction whenever it may apply its own law? Isn't it a bit hollow to say that a state's law can constitutionally be applied but to deny that state's courts jurisdiction to apply it?

The Court in *Hanson* emphasized that the trustee had no contacts with the forum state, and in *World-Wide Volkswagen* that the assertion of jurisdiction would frustrate legitimate expectations. If so, shouldn't these considerations be equally determinative of choice of law? Is there any reason to impose a higher threshold of expectation upon the jurisdictional issue than upon choice of law? Isn't choice of law likely to be the more significant of the two issues? See Silberman, Shaffer v. Heitner: *The End of an Era,* 53 N.Y.U.L.Rev. 33, 88 (1978): "To believe that a defendant's contacts with the forum state should be stronger under the due process clause for jurisdictional purposes than for choice of law purposes is to believe that the accused is more concerned with where he will be hanged than whether."

But is it really a question of stronger or weaker contacts? We have also seen cases in which a court that had jurisdiction could not apply its own law. Recall, for example, *Phillips Petroleum Co. v. Shutts,* 472 U.S. 797 (1985), supra p. 383. Might it simply be that the contacts required by due process are *different* for jurisdiction than for choice of law because the nature of the burden imposed is different? What is the difference? Cf. Maier & McCoy, *A Unifying Theory for Judicial Jurisdiction and Choice of Law,* 39 Am.J.Comp.L. 249 (1991) (arguing that choice of jurisdiction is necessarily a choice-of-law decision and should therefore be determined entirely by choice-of-law considerations).

(5) The approach to judicial jurisdiction in *McGee* arguably favors plaintiffs. By the same token, the approach in *World-Wide Volkswagen* appears to favor defendants. This will not always be a problem, for in many cases there may be states where both parties can conveniently litigate. In cases like *World-Wide Volkswagen* and *Kulko,* however, we have to favor one party or the other: in *World-Wide Volkswagen,* either the plaintiff must come to New York or the defendants must come to Oklahoma; in *Kulko,* either the plaintiff must come to New York or the defendant must come to California. Why does the Court favor defendants? Why not balance instead, choosing in each case the forum that seems more convenient on balance (taking into account the interests of the states and the courts in addition to those of the parties)? One might argue that, because jurisdiction is a preliminary question unrelated to the merits, there are strong policy arguments favoring rules that are easily administered. But is that really true? As a practical matter, doesn't the choice of forum have significant consequences for the merits? Besides, how well do *Kulko* and *World-Wide Volkswagen* fare on this score? And, again, even if we want simple rules, why favor the defendant?

(6) Much of the discussion in *World-Wide Volkswagen* deals with issues of state sovereignty and federalism. What do these issues have to do with due process? Two years after *World-Wide Volkswagen,* Justice White revisited the sovereignty issue. In *Insurance Corp. of Ireland v. Compagnie des Bauxites de Guinee,* 456 U.S. 694 (1982), the Court held that a federal court could order discovery to determine its jurisdiction and could uphold jurisdiction as a sanction for failure to comply with the court's order. In the course of his opinion for the Court, Justice White dropped the following footnote:

> It is true that we have stated that the requirement of personal jurisdiction, as applied to state courts, reflects an element of federalism and the character of state sovereignty vis-a-vis other States. . . The restriction on state sovereign power described in *World-Wide Volkswagen Corp.,* however, must be seen as ultimately a function of the individual liberty interest preserved by the Due Process Clause. That clause is the only source of the personal jurisdiction requirement and the Clause itself makes no mention of federalism concerns. Furthermore, if the federalism concept operated as an independent restriction on the sovereign power of the court, it would not be possible to waive the personal jurisdiction requirement: Individual actions cannot change the powers of sovereignty, although the individual can subject himself to powers from which he may otherwise be protected.

Id. at 702–03 n.10. Why is due process the only source of constitutional limitations on personal jurisdiction? In choice of law, we saw that the Full Faith and Credit Clause prohibits an uninterested state from applying its own law and thereby subordinating the interests of another state. Why doesn't full faith and credit similarly prohibit an uninterested state from exercising jurisdiction (in which case the court would presumably dismiss or transfer the case)? Does reliance on full faith and credit answer the Court's concern about waiver, or is there some reason to treat jurisdiction as less waivable than ordinary questions of choice of law?

Does this footnote alter the test for judicial jurisdiction? Put another way, does it matter whether the sovereignty limitation operates independently or as a function of protecting individual liberty? For that matter, does it matter whether we find its origin in the Due Process Clause or the Full Faith and Credit Clause? Or is there some reason to disregard sovereignty concerns when it comes to judicial jurisdiction?

Consider whether the following case sheds light on these questions.

J. MCINTYRE MACHINERY V. NICASTRO

564 U.S. 873 (2011).

JUSTICE KENNEDY announced the judgment of the Court and delivered an opinion, in which THE CHIEF JUSTICE, JUSTICE SCALIA, and JUSTICE THOMAS join.

Whether a person or entity is subject to the jurisdiction of a state court despite not having been present in the State either at the time of suit or at the time of the alleged injury, and despite not having consented to the exercise of jurisdiction, is a question that arises with great frequency in the routine course of litigation. The rules and standards for determining when a State does or does not have jurisdiction over an absent party have been unclear because of decades-old questions left open in *Asahi Metal Industry Co. v. Superior Court of Cal., Solano Cty.,* 480 U.S. 102, 107 (1987).

Here, the Supreme Court of New Jersey, relying in part on *Asahi,* held that New Jersey's courts can exercise jurisdiction over a foreign manufacturer of a product so long as the manufacturer "knows or reasonably should know that its products are distributed through a nationwide distribution system that might lead to those products being sold in any of the fifty states." Applying that test, the court concluded that a British manufacturer of scrap metal machines was subject to jurisdiction in New Jersey, even though at no time had it advertised in, sent goods to, or in any relevant sense targeted the State.

That decision cannot be sustained. Although the New Jersey Supreme Court issued an extensive opinion with careful attention to this Court's cases and to its own precedent, the "stream of commerce" metaphor carried the decision far afield. Due process protects the defendant's right not to be coerced except by lawful judicial power. As a general rule, the exercise of judicial power is not lawful unless the defendant "purposefully avails itself of the privilege of conducting activities within the forum State, thus invoking the benefits and protections of its laws." *Hanson v. Denckla,* 357 U.S. 235, 253 (1958). There may be exceptions, say, for instance, in cases involving an intentional tort. But the general rule is applicable in this products-liability case, and the so-called "stream-of-commerce" doctrine cannot displace it.

I

This case arises from a products-liability suit filed in New Jersey state court. Robert Nicastro seriously injured his hand while using a metal-shearing machine manufactured by J. McIntyre Machinery, Ltd. (J. McIntyre). The accident occurred in New Jersey, but the machine was manufactured in England, where J. McIntyre is incorporated and operates. The question here is whether the New Jersey courts have jurisdiction over J. McIntyre, notwithstanding the fact that the company at no time either marketed goods in the State or shipped them there. Nicastro was a plaintiff in the New Jersey trial court and is the respondent here; J. McIntyre was a defendant and is now the petitioner.

At oral argument in this Court, Nicastro's counsel stressed three primary facts in defense of New Jersey's assertion of jurisdiction over J. McIntyre.

First, an independent company agreed to sell J. McIntyre's machines in the United States. J. McIntyre itself did not sell its machines to buyers in this country beyond the U.S. distributor, and there is no allegation that the distributor was under J. McIntyre's control.

Second, J. McIntyre officials attended annual conventions for the scrap recycling industry to advertise J. McIntyre's machines alongside the distributor. The conventions took place in various States, but never in New Jersey.

Third, no more than four machines (the record suggests only one), including the machine that caused the injuries that are the basis for this suit, ended up in New Jersey.

In addition to these facts emphasized by petitioner, the New Jersey Supreme Court noted that J. McIntyre held both United States and European patents on its recycling technology. * * * It also noted that the U.S. distributor "structured [its] advertising and sales efforts in accordance with" J. McIntyre's "direction and guidance whenever possible," and that "at least some of the machines were sold on consignment to" the distributor. * * *

In light of these facts, the New Jersey Supreme Court concluded that New Jersey courts could exercise jurisdiction over petitioner without contravention of the Due Process Clause. Jurisdiction was proper, in that court's view, because the injury occurred in New Jersey; because petitioner knew or reasonably should have known "that its products are distributed through a nationwide distribution system that might lead to those products being sold in any of the fifty states"; and because petitioner failed to "take some reasonable step to prevent the distribution of its products in this State." * * *

Both the New Jersey Supreme Court's holding and its account of what it called "[t]he stream-of-commerce doctrine of jurisdiction," * * * were incorrect, however. This Court's *Asahi* decision may be responsible in part for that court's error regarding the stream of commerce, and this case presents an opportunity to provide greater clarity.

II

The Due Process Clause protects an individual's right to be deprived of life, liberty, or property only by the exercise of lawful power. * * * This is no less true with respect to the power of a sovereign to resolve disputes through judicial process than with respect to the power of a sovereign to prescribe rules of conduct for those within its sphere. * * * As a general rule, neither statute nor judicial decree may bind strangers to the State. * * *

A court may subject a defendant to judgment only when the defendant has sufficient contacts with the sovereign "such that the maintenance of the suit does not offend 'traditional notions of fair play and substantial justice.'" *International Shoe Co. v. Washington,* 326 U.S. 310, 316 (1945). Freeform notions of fundamental fairness divorced from traditional practice cannot transform a judgment rendered in the absence of authority into law. As a general rule, the sovereign's exercise of power requires some act by which the defendant "purposefully avails itself of the privilege of conducting activities within the forum State, thus invoking the benefits and protections of its laws," *Hanson,* 357 U.S., at 253, though in some cases, as with an intentional tort, the defendant might well fall within the State's authority by reason of his attempt to obstruct its laws. In products-liability cases like this one, it is the defendant's purposeful availment that makes jurisdiction consistent with "traditional notions of fair play and substantial justice."

A person may submit to a State's authority in a number of ways. There is, of course, explicit consent. * * * Presence within a State at the time suit commences through service of process is another example. Citizenship or domicile—or, by analogy, incorporation or principal place of business for corporations—also indicates general submission to a State's powers. Each of these examples reveals circumstances, or a course of conduct, from which it is proper to infer an intention to benefit from and thus an intention to submit to the laws of the forum State. These examples support exercise of the general jurisdiction of the State's courts and allow the State to resolve both matters that originate within the State and those based on activities and events elsewhere. By contrast, those who live or operate primarily outside a State have a due process right not to be subjected to judgment in its courts as a general matter.

There is also a more limited form of submission to a State's authority for disputes that "arise out of or are connected with the activities within the state." *International Shoe Co., supra,* at 319. Where a defendant "purposefully avails itself of the privilege of conducting activities within the forum State, thus invoking the benefits and protections of its laws," *Hanson, supra,* at 253, it submits to the judicial power of an otherwise foreign sovereign to the extent that power is exercised in connection with the defendant's activities touching on the State. In other words, submission through contact with and activity directed at a sovereign may justify specific jurisdiction "in a suit arising out of or related to the defendant's contacts with the forum." * * *

The imprecision arising from *Asahi,* for the most part, results from its statement of the relation between jurisdiction and the "stream of commerce." The stream of commerce, like other metaphors, has its deficiencies as well as its utility. It refers to the movement of goods from manufacturers through distributors to consumers, yet beyond that descriptive purpose its meaning is far from exact. This Court has stated that a defendant's placing goods into the stream of commerce "with the expectation that they will be purchased by consumers within the forum State" may indicate purposeful availment. *World-Wide Volkswagen Corp. v. Woodson,* 444 U.S. 286, 298 (1980) (finding that expectation lacking). But that statement does not amend the general rule of personal jurisdiction. It merely observes that a defendant may in an appropriate case be subject to jurisdiction without entering the forum—itself an unexceptional proposition—as where manufacturers or distributors "seek to serve" a given State's market. The principal inquiry in cases of this sort is whether the defendant's activities manifest an intention to submit to the power of a sovereign. In other words, the defendant must "purposefully avai[l] itself of the privilege of conducting activities within the forum State, thus invoking the benefits and protections of its laws." * * * Sometimes a defendant does so by sending its goods rather than its agents. The defendant's transmission of goods permits the exercise of jurisdiction only where the defendant can be said to have targeted the forum; as a general rule, it is not enough that the defendant might have predicted that its goods will reach the forum State.

In *Asahi,* an opinion by Justice Brennan for four Justices outlined a different approach. It discarded the central concept of sovereign authority in favor of considerations of fairness and foreseeability. As that concurrence contended, "jurisdiction premised on the placement of a product into the stream of commerce [without more] is consistent with the Due Process Clause," for "[a]s long as a participant in this process is aware that the final product is being marketed in the forum State, the possibility of a lawsuit there cannot come as a surprise." * * * It was the premise of the concurring opinion that the defendant's ability to anticipate suit renders the assertion of jurisdiction fair. In this way, the opinion made foreseeability the touchstone of jurisdiction.

The standard set forth in Justice Brennan's concurrence was rejected in an opinion written by Justice O'Connor; but the relevant part of that opinion, too, commanded the assent of only four Justices, not a majority of the Court. That opinion stated: "The 'substantial connection' between the defendant and the forum State necessary for a finding of minimum contacts must come about by an action of the defendant purposefully directed toward the forum State. The placement of a product into the stream of commerce, without more, is not an act of the defendant purposefully directed toward the forum State." * * *

Since *Asahi* was decided, the courts have sought to reconcile the competing opinions. But Justice Brennan's concurrence, advocating a rule based on general notions of fairness and foreseeability, is inconsistent with the premises of lawful judicial power. This Court's precedents make clear that it is the defendant's actions, not his expectations, that empower a State's courts to subject him to judgment.

The conclusion that jurisdiction is in the first instance a question of authority rather than fairness explains, for example, why the principal opinion in *Burnham v. Superior Court*, 495 U.S. 604 (1990), "conducted no independent inquiry into the desirability or fairness" of the rule that service of process within a State suffices to establish jurisdiction over an otherwise foreign defendant. * * * As that opinion explained, "[t]he view developed early that each State had the power to hale before its courts any individual who could be found within its borders." * * * Furthermore, were general fairness considerations the touchstone of jurisdiction, a lack of purposeful availment might be excused where carefully crafted judicial procedures could otherwise protect the defendant's interests, or where the plaintiff would suffer substantial hardship if forced to litigate in a foreign forum. That such considerations have not been deemed controlling is instructive. * * *

The conclusion that the authority to subject a defendant to judgment depends on purposeful availment, consistent with Justice O'Connor's opinion in *Asahi,* does not by itself resolve many difficult questions of jurisdiction that will arise in particular cases. The defendant's conduct and the economic realities of the market the defendant seeks to serve will differ across cases, and judicial exposition will, in common-law fashion, clarify the contours of that principle.

III

In this case, petitioner directed marketing and sales efforts at the United States. [Perhaps Congress could authorize jurisdiction in appropriate courts, but we need not address that issue, nor speculate about what law would apply in such a case.] A sovereign's legislative authority to regulate conduct may present considerations different from those presented by its authority to subject a defendant to judgment in its courts. Here the question concerns the authority of a New Jersey state court to exercise jurisdiction, so it is petitioner's purposeful contacts with New Jersey, not with the United States, that alone are relevant.

Respondent has not established that J. McIntyre engaged in conduct purposefully directed at New Jersey. Recall that respondent's claim of jurisdiction centers on three facts: The distributor agreed to sell J. McIntyre's machines in the United States; J. McIntyre officials attended trade shows in several States but not in New Jersey; and up to four machines ended up in New Jersey. The British manufacturer had no office in New Jersey; it neither paid taxes nor owned property there; and it neither advertised in, nor sent any employees to, the State. Indeed, after discovery the trial court found that the "defendant does not have a single contact with New Jersey short of the machine in question ending up in this state." * * * These facts may reveal an intent to serve the U.S. market, but they do not show that J. McIntyre purposefully availed itself of the New Jersey market. . .

* * *

Due process protects petitioner's right to be subject only to lawful authority. At no time did petitioner engage in any activities in New Jersey that reveal an intent to invoke or benefit from the protection of its laws. New Jersey is without power to adjudge the rights and liabilities of J. McIntyre, and its exercise of jurisdiction would violate due process. The contrary judgment of the New Jersey Supreme Court is

Reversed.

JUSTICE BREYER, with whom JUSTICE ALITO joins, concurring in the judgment.

In my view, the outcome of this case is determined by our precedents. . . . None of our precedents finds that a single isolated sale, even if accompanied by the kind of sales effort indicated here, is sufficient. . .

Here, the relevant facts found by the New Jersey Supreme Court show no "regular . . . flow" or "regular course" of sales in New Jersey; and there is no "something more," such as special state-related design, advertising, advice, marketing, or anything else. Mr. Nicastro, who here bears the burden of proving jurisdiction, has shown no specific effort by the British Manufacturer to sell in New Jersey. He has introduced no list of potential New Jersey customers who might, for example, have regularly attended trade shows. And he has not otherwise shown that the British Manufacturer "purposefully avail[ed] itself of the privilege of conducting activities" within New Jersey, or that it delivered its goods in the stream of commerce "with the expectation that they will be purchased" by New Jersey users. * * *

Accordingly, on the record present here, resolving this case requires no more than adhering to our precedents. . . .

The plurality seems to state strict rules that limit jurisdiction where a defendant does not "inten[d] to submit to the power of a sovereign" and cannot "be said to have targeted the forum." But what do those standards mean when a company targets the world by selling products from its Web site? And does it matter if, instead of shipping the products directly, a company consigns the products through an intermediary (say, Amazon.com) who then receives and fulfills the orders? And what if the company markets its products through popup advertisements that it knows will be viewed in a forum? Those issues have serious commercial consequences but are totally absent in this case.

But though I do not agree with the plurality's seemingly strict no-jurisdiction rule, I am not persuaded by the absolute approach adopted by the New Jersey Supreme Court and urged by respondent and his *amici*. Under that view, a producer is subject to jurisdiction for a products-liability action so long as it "knows or reasonably should know that its products are distributed through a nationwide distribution system that *might* lead to those products being sold in any of the fifty states." * * * In the context of this case, I cannot agree.

For one thing, to adopt this view would abandon the heretofore accepted inquiry of whether, focusing upon the relationship between "the defendant, the *forum,* and the litigation," it is fair, in light of the defendant's contacts *with that forum,* to subject the defendant to suit there. * * * It would ordinarily rest jurisdiction instead upon no more than the occurrence of a product-based accident in the forum State. But this Court has rejected the notion that a defendant's amenability to suit "travel[s] with the chattel." * * *

For another, I cannot reconcile so automatic a rule with the constitutional demand for "minimum contacts" and "purposefu[l] avail[ment]," each of which rest upon a particular notion of defendant-focused fairness. * * * A rule like the New Jersey Supreme Court's would permit every State to assert jurisdiction in a products-liability suit against any domestic manufacturer who sells its products (made anywhere in the United States) to a national distributor, no matter how large or small the manufacturer, no matter how distant the forum, and no matter how few the number of items that end up in the particular forum at issue. What might appear fair in the case of a large manufacturer which specifically seeks, or expects, an equal-sized distributor to sell its product in a distant State might seem unfair in the case of a small manufacturer (say, an Appalachian potter) who sells his product (cups and saucers) exclusively to a large distributor, who resells a single item (a coffee mug) to a buyer from a distant State (Hawaii). I know too little about the range of these or in-between possibilities to abandon in favor of the more absolute rule what has previously been this Court's less absolute approach.

Further, the fact that the defendant is a foreign, rather than a domestic, manufacturer makes the basic fairness of an absolute rule yet more uncertain. I am again less certain than is the New Jersey Supreme Court that the nature of international commerce has changed so significantly as to require a new approach to personal jurisdiction. . .

At a minimum, I would not work such a change to the law in the way either the plurality or the New Jersey Supreme Court suggests without a better understanding of the relevant contemporary commercial circumstances. . .

Accordingly, though I agree with the plurality as to the outcome of this case, I concur only in the judgment of that opinion and not its reasoning.

JUSTICE GINSBURG, with whom JUSTICE SOTOMAYOR and JUSTICE KAGAN join, dissenting.

A foreign industrialist seeks to develop a market in the United States for machines it manufactures. It hopes to derive substantial revenue from sales it makes to United States purchasers. Where in the United States buyers reside does not matter to this manufacturer. Its goal is simply to sell as much as it can, wherever it can. It excludes no region or State from the market it wishes to reach. But, all things considered, it prefers to avoid products liability litigation in the United States. To that end, it engages a U.S. distributor to ship its machines stateside. Has it succeeded in escaping personal jurisdiction in a State where one of its products is sold and causes injury or even death to a local user?

Under this Court's pathmarking precedent in *International Shoe Co. v. Washington,* 326 U.S. 310 (1945), and subsequent decisions, one would expect the answer to be unequivocally, "No." But instead, six Justices of this Court, in divergent opinions, tell us that the manufacturer has avoided the jurisdiction of our state courts, except perhaps in States where its products are sold in sizeable quantities. Inconceivable as it may have seemed yesterday, the splintered majority today "turn[s] the clock back to the days before modern long-arm statutes when a manufacturer, to avoid being haled into court where a user is injured, need only Pilate-like wash its hands of a product by having independent distributors market it." * * *

A few points on which there should be no genuine debate bear statement at the outset. First, all agree, McIntyre UK surely is not subject to general (all-purpose) jurisdiction in New Jersey courts, for that foreign-country corporation is hardly "at home" in New Jersey. * * * The question, rather, is one of specific jurisdiction, which turns on an "affiliatio[n] between the forum and the underlying controversy." * * *

Second, no issue of the fair and reasonable allocation of adjudicatory authority among States of the United States is present in this case. New Jersey's exercise of personal jurisdiction over a foreign manufacturer whose dangerous product caused a workplace injury in New Jersey does not tread on the domain, or diminish the sovereignty, of any sister State. Indeed, among States of the United States, the State in which the injury occurred would seem most suitable for litigation of a products liability tort claim.

Third, the constitutional limits on a state court's adjudicatory authority derive from considerations of due process, not state sovereignty. . .

Finally, in *International Shoe* itself, and decisions thereafter, the Court has made plain that legal fictions, notably "presence" and "implied consent," should be discarded, for they conceal the actual bases on which jurisdiction rests. * * *

Whatever the state of academic debate over the role of consent in modern jurisdictional doctrines, the plurality's notion that consent is the animating concept draws no support from controlling decisions of this Court. Quite the contrary, the Court has explained, a forum can exercise jurisdiction when its contacts with the controversy are sufficient; invocation of a fictitious consent, the Court has repeatedly said, is unnecessary and unhelpful. * * *

When industrial accidents happen, a long-arm statute in the State where the injury occurs generally permits assertion of jurisdiction, upon giving proper notice, over the foreign manufacturer. . .

The modern approach to jurisdiction over corporations and other legal entities, ushered in by *International Shoe,* gave prime place to reason and fairness. Is it not fair and reasonable, given the mode of trading of which this case is an example, to require the international seller to defend at the place its products cause injury? Do not litigational convenience and choice-of-law considerations point in that direction? On what measure of reason and fairness can it be considered undue to require McIntyre UK to defend in New Jersey as an incident of its efforts to develop a market for its industrial machines anywhere and everywhere in the United States?[12] Is not the burden on McIntyre UK to defend in New Jersey fair, *i.e.,* a reasonable cost of transacting business internationally, in comparison to the burden on Nicastro to go to Nottingham, England to gain recompense for an injury he sustained using McIntyre's product at his workplace in Saddle Brook, New Jersey?

McIntyre UK dealt with the United States as a single market. Like most foreign manufacturers, it was concerned not with the prospect of suit in State X as opposed to State Y, but rather with its subjection to suit anywhere in the United States. * * * As a McIntyre UK officer wrote in an e-mail to McIntyre America: "American law—who needs it?!" * * * If McIntyre UK is answerable in the United States at all, is it not "perfectly

[12] The plurality suggests that the Due Process Clause might permit a federal district court in New Jersey, sitting in diversity and applying New Jersey law, to adjudicate McIntyre UK's liability to Nicastro. * * * In other words, McIntyre UK might be compelled to bear the burden of traveling to New Jersey and defending itself there under New Jersey's products liability law, but would be entitled to federal adjudication of Nicastro's state-law claim. I see no basis in the Due Process Clause for such a curious limitation.

appropriate to permit the exercise of that jurisdiction . . . at the place of injury"? * * *

The Court's judgment also puts United States plaintiffs at a disadvantage in comparison to similarly situated complainants elsewhere in the world. Of particular note, within the European Union, in which the United Kingdom is a participant, the jurisdiction New Jersey would have exercised is not at all exceptional. The European Regulation on Jurisdiction and the Recognition and Enforcement of Judgments provides for the exercise of specific jurisdiction "in matters relating to tort . . . in the courts for the place where the harmful event occurred." The European Court of Justice has interpreted this prescription to authorize jurisdiction either where the harmful act occurred or at the place of injury. * * *

The commentators who gave names to what we now call "general jurisdiction" and "specific jurisdiction" anticipated that when the latter achieves its full growth, considerations of litigational convenience and the respective situations of the parties would determine when it is appropriate to subject a defendant to trial in the plaintiff's community. See von Mehren & Trautman, Jurisdiction to Adjudicate: A Suggested Analysis, 79 Harv. L.Rev. 1121, 1166–79 (1966). Litigational considerations include "the convenience of witnesses and the ease of ascertaining the governing law." * * * As to the parties, courts would differently appraise two situations: (1) cases involving a substantially local plaintiff, like Nicastro, injured by the activity of a defendant engaged in interstate or international trade; and (2) cases in which the defendant is a natural or legal person whose economic activities and legal involvements are largely home-based, *i.e.,* entities without designs to gain substantial revenue from sales in distant markets. * * * [C]ourts presented with von Mehren and Trautman's first scenario—a local plaintiff injured by the activity of a manufacturer seeking to exploit a multistate or global market—have repeatedly confirmed that jurisdiction is appropriately exercised by courts of the place where the product was sold and caused injury.

* * *

For the reasons stated, I would hold McIntyre UK answerable in New Jersey for the harm Nicastro suffered at his workplace in that State using McIntyre UK's shearing machine. While I dissent from the Court's judgment, I take heart that the plurality opinion does not speak for the Court, for that opinion would take a giant step away from the "notions of fair play and substantial justice" underlying *International Shoe.*

Global Distribution and Purposeful Availment

(1) As *Nicastro* notes, considerable confusion followed the Court's decision in *Asahi Metal Industry Co. v. Superior Court*, 480 U.S. 102 (1987). *World-Wide Volkswagen* rejected the notion that a defendant could be held liable merely because it was foreseeable that a product might be taken to the forum state by a purchaser. But what if the product is being sold there? In *Asahi,* Justice O'Connor wrote an opinion for four Justices arguing that a defendant must have done something to "indicate an intent or purpose to serve the market in the forum State." Justice Brennan, also writing for four Justices, believed that "awareness that the stream of commerce may or will sweep the product into the forum state" should be enough.

Nicastro was expected to resolve this issue, but again neither position received the support of five Justices. What should the test be? Why, exactly, should a corporate defendant that seeks to sell its products everywhere in the United States not reasonably expect that it might be sued in a state where its product causes harm to one of that state's residents? Should the personal jurisdiction analysis take into account the inconvenience to the plaintiff and potential witnesses of litigating in a distant forum? Does your answer depend on the theory underlying the purposeful availment requirement?

(2) With respect to sales in the forum state, we can divide defendants into four categories: 1) those who intended the sales and took steps to achieve them; 2) those who knew or should have known that sales might occur but did nothing to promote them; 3) those who did not know sales would occur but took no steps to prevent them; and 4) those who did not want sales in the forum state and did what they could to prevent them. The *Nicastro* dispute is about the treatment of defendants in category 2. Is one answer right for all such defendants, or does the test need further refinement based on size and business practices?

(3) All the *Nicastro* Justices seem to agree that jurisdiction is proper over defendants in category 1. But what about the business (like McIntyre) that targets the United States generally, but no particular state? Justice Ginsburg reads the plurality opinion to suggest that the Due Process Clause shields such a defendant from suit in any state court but permits suit in a federal court, located (of course) in some state and applying that state's law. Would this require amendment of current Federal Rule of Civil Procedure 4(k)(1)(A)? Does it make sense in terms of convenience, foreseeability, or submission to authority?

The plurality reasons that a defendant is subject to specific jurisdiction only when its actions "manifest an intention to submit to the power of a sovereign." What sorts of actions manifest such an intention? Is it sensible to suppose that a U.K. manufacturer intends to submit to the authority of New Jersey in particular when it seeks to distribute its products throughout the United States? Justice Breyer, for his part, concludes that jurisdiction was improper in *Nicastro* because the case involved a "single isolated sale." How much activity beyond a single sale ought to be required?

(4) Should the constitutional test for adjudicatory jurisdiction be different in mass tort cases? *In re DES Cases,* 789 F.Supp. 552 (E.D.N.Y. 1992), was a suit brought by plaintiffs exposed *in utero* to diethylstilbestrol (DES) against many of the companies that manufactured or sold the drug. One of the defendants moved to dismiss for lack of jurisdiction, arguing that it had never produced or sold any DES in New York. The court upheld jurisdiction. Conceding that the Supreme Court's jurisdiction cases required the existence of a "territorial nexus" as well as a "state interest," Judge Weinstein observed that none of these cases involved a mass tort situation. "The territorial nexus doctrine," he argued, "is a particularly inadequate mechanism for protecting mass producers from undue litigation burdens." According to Weinstein, (1) lack of a territorial nexus "is often no indication of inconvenience"; (2) defendants are already protected by the law of venue and *forum non conveniens;* (3) the development of transportation and communications technology has caused the country to "shrink"; (4) mass tort suits typically involve corporations, which hire local counsel to appear for them; and (5) the aggregation of defendants in a mass tort creates economies of scale that lessen the costs and inconvenience. Furthermore:

> While the need for territorial nexus-based protections of defendants is arguably least pressing in mass torts, the continued reliance on such protections creates significant obstacles to their resolution. This is particularly evident in a case such as the instant one, where New York substantive law empowers the plaintiffs to bring in all industry participants to achieve a full and economical resolution of their lawsuits [on a market share theory], yet jurisdictional law may prevent the very result envisioned by the state's substantive, remedial and procedural laws.

The court therefore eliminated the requirement of a territorial nexus in mass tort cases and held that a prima facie case for jurisdiction exists if the forum state has "an appreciable interest" in the litigation in the sense that its resolution would affect "policies expressed in the substantive, procedural or remedial laws of the forum." Jurisdiction may be exercised unless a particular defendant "is unable to mount a defense in the forum state without suffering relatively substantial hardship."

Are you persuaded by Judge Weinstein's arguments for modifying the due process test in mass tort cases? Weren't all his arguments except the one about economies of scale already made and rejected by the Supreme Court? Is this new argument persuasive? And even if due process requires only that the forum have an interest to exercise adjudicatory jurisdiction, what interest does New York have in DES sales made outside New York to citizens of other states?

(5) As Justice Breyer notes in his *Nicastro* concurrence, marketing over the Internet may pose unique jurisdictional questions. What kinds of Internet activity should subject a defendant to the jurisdiction of a state with which it has no other contacts? In cases based on the operation of websites, some courts have tried to decide whether the defendant has reached out to the forum by assessing the level of "interactivity" of the website.

As the case caption suggests, *Cybersell, Inc. v. Cybersell, Inc.*, 130 F.3d 414 (9th Cir. 1997) was a trademark infringement action. An Arizona corporation organized to provide Internet marketing and advertising services ("Cybersell AZ") brought an action against a Florida corporation formed by a business school student and his father to provide similar services ("Cybersell FL"). The Ninth Circuit's analysis follows:

> Courts that have addressed interactive sites have looked to the "level of interactivity and commercial nature of the exchange of information that occurs on the Web site" to determine if sufficient contacts exist to warrant the exercise of jurisdiction. . . .
>
> [S]o far as we are aware, no court has ever held that an Internet advertisement alone is sufficient to subject the advertiser to jurisdiction in the plaintiff's home state. * * * Rather, in each, there has been "something more" to indicate that the defendant purposefully (albeit electronically) directed his activity in a substantial way to the forum state. . . .
>
> In sum, the common thread . . . is that "the likelihood that personal jurisdiction can be constitutionally exercised is directly proportionate to the nature and quality of commercial activity that an entity conducts over the Internet." * * *
>
> Here, Cybersell FL has conducted no commercial activity over the Internet in Arizona. All that it did was post an essentially passive home page on the web, using the name "CyberSell," which Cybersell AZ was in the process of registering as a federal service mark. While there is no question that anyone, anywhere could access that home page and thereby learn about the services offered, we cannot see how from that fact alone it can be inferred that Cybersell FL deliberately directed its merchandising efforts toward Arizona residents.
>
> Cybersell FL did nothing to encourage people in Arizona to access its site, and there is no evidence that any part of its business (let alone a continuous part of its business) was sought or achieved in Arizona. To the contrary, it appears to be an operation where

> business was primarily generated by the personal contacts of one of its founders. While those contacts are not entirely local, they aren't in Arizona either. No Arizonan except for Cybersell AZ "hit" Cybersell FL's web site. There is no evidence that any Arizona resident signed up for Cybersell FL's web construction services. It entered into no contracts in Arizona, made no sales in Arizona, received no telephone calls from Arizona, earned no income from Arizona, and sent no messages over the Internet to Arizona. The only message it received over the Internet from Arizona was from Cybersell AZ. Cybersell FL did not have an "800" number, let alone a toll-free number that also used the "Cybersell" name. The interactivity of its web page is limited to receiving the browser's name and address and an indication of interest-signing up for the service is not an option, nor did anyone from Arizona do so. No money changed hands on the Internet from (or through) Arizona. In short, Cybersell FL has done no act and has consummated no transaction, nor has it performed any act by which it purposefully availed itself of the privilege of conducting activities, in Arizona, thereby invoking the benefits and protections of Arizona law.
>
> We therefore hold that Cybersell FL's contacts are insufficient to establish "purposeful availment." . . .

Is "interactivity" the right test for purposeful availment? Aren't all websites interactive nowadays? What if an interactive site belongs to a local newspaper with no out-of-state subscribers? See *Young v. New Haven Advocate*, 315 F.3d 256 (4th Cir. 2002) (finding that Virginia could not exercise jurisdiction over the New Haven Advocate for a libel suit by the warden of a Virginia prison based on articles posted on the Advocate's website). But see *Janmark, Inc. v. Reidy*, 132 F.3d 1200, 1202 (7th Cir. 1997) ("there can be no serious doubt . . . that the state in which the victim of a tort suffers the injury may entertain a suit against the accused tortfeasor"); *Tamburo v. Dworkin*, 601 F.3d 693, 707 (7th Cir. 2010) ("Tortious acts aimed at a target in the forum state and undertaken for the express purpose of causing injury there" suffice to show purposeful availment by website).

For contrasting discussions of how the Internet ought to affect doctrines of personal jurisdiction, see Trammell & Bambauer, *Personal Jurisdiction and the "Interwebs,"* 100 Cornell L. Rev. 1129 (2015) (arguing that purely virtual conduct should not be enough to subject defendants to jurisdiction in a particular forum); Kleven, Note, *Minimum Virtual Contacts: A Framework for Specific Jurisdiction in Cyberspace*, 116 Mich. L. Rev. 785 (2018) (arguing that jurisdiction should be proper when (1) the defendant engages in sophisticated or continuous virtual conduct that causes harm to the plaintiff in the forum and (2) exercising jurisdiction over the defendant would be reasonable).

(6) Does intentional harm to a forum resident always suffice to create jurisdiction over the defendant? A unanimous Court said no in *Walden v. Fiore*, 571 U.S. 277 (2014). In *Walden*, a drug enforcement agent working at the Atlanta airport seized $97,000 in cash from travelers headed to Las Vegas. The travelers later sued in district court in Nevada, arguing that personal jurisdiction was proper because the officer knew his conduct would affect persons with a "significant connection" to Nevada. The Court rejected jurisdiction, holding that "it is the defendant, not the plaintiff or third parties, who must create contacts with the forum State." *Id.* at 1126.

What if the defendant's conduct injures many plaintiffs where they live, some of whom are residents of the forum and some not? Can the forum entertain the claims of the nonresident plaintiffs? In *Bristol-Myers Squibb Co. v. Superior Court of Cal., San Francisco Cty.*, 137 S.Ct. 1773 (2017), 678 plaintiffs, of whom 86 were California residents, sued a drug manufacturer in California state court, alleging that the blood thinner Plavix had harmed their health. The Court relied on *Walden* to reject jurisdiction, holding that the harms caused to California residents were irrelevant to jurisdiction over the nonresidents' claims. The Court distinguished *Phillips Petroleum Co. v. Shutts*, 472 U.S. 797 (1985), p. 383 supra, because the personal jurisdiction question in that case was whether entertaining nonresidents' claims violated the due process rights of the nonresident *plaintiffs*, not those of the defendant. 137 S. Ct. at 1782–83.

(7) Quoting *International Shoe*, the Court in *Nicastro* reaffirms that specific jurisdiction is founded on the plaintiff's injuries that "arise out of or are connected with the [defendant's] activities within the state." (Other cases use the formulation "arise out of or relate to.") Does this formulation imply that the defendant's conduct must *cause* the plaintiff's injury? Lower courts generally held that it does, dividing only on the question of what kind of causal relationship was required. See, *e.g.*, *Mass. Sch. of Law at Andover, Inc. v. Am. Bar Ass'n*, 142 F.3d 26, 35 (1st Cir. 1998) (defendant's contacts with the forum must constitute both the cause in fact and the proximate cause of the injury); *Doe v. Am. Nat'l Red Cross*, 112 F.3d 1048, 1051 n.7 (9th Cir. 1997) (only but-for causation is required); *O'Connor v. Sandy Lane Hotel Co.*, 496 F.3d 312, 323 (3d Cir. 2007) ("specific jurisdiction requires a closer and more direct causal connection than that provided by the but-for test"). The Supreme Court finally weighed in on this issue in the following case.

FORD MOTOR CO. V. MONTANA EIGHTH JUDICIAL DISTRICT COURT

141 S. Ct. 1017 (2021).

JUSTICE KAGAN delivered the opinion of the Court. . . .

Ford is a global auto company. It is incorporated in Delaware and headquartered in Michigan. But its business is everywhere. Ford markets, sells, and services its products across the United States and overseas. . . . Ford also encourages a resale market for its products: Almost all its dealerships buy and sell used Fords, as well as selling new ones. To enhance its brand and increase its sales, Ford engages in wide-ranging promotional activities, including television, print, online, and direct-mail advertisements. . . . And Ford's own network of dealers offers an array of maintenance and repair services, thus fostering an ongoing relationship between Ford and its customers.

Accidents involving two of Ford's vehicles—a 1996 Explorer and a 1994 Crown Victoria—are at the heart of the suits before us. One case comes from Montana. Markkaya Gullett was driving her Explorer near her home in the State when the tread separated from a rear tire. The vehicle spun out, rolled into a ditch, and came to rest upside down. Gullett died at the scene of the crash. The representative of her estate sued Ford in Montana state court, bringing claims for a design defect, failure to warn, and negligence. The second case comes from Minnesota. Adam Bandemer was a passenger in his friend's Crown Victoria, traveling on a rural road in the State to a favorite ice-fishing spot. When his friend rear-ended a snowplow, this car too landed in a ditch. Bandemer's air bag failed to deploy, and he suffered serious brain damage. He sued Ford in Minnesota state court, asserting products-liability, negligence, and breach-of-warranty claims.

Ford moved to dismiss the two suits for lack of personal jurisdiction, on basically identical grounds. According to Ford, the state court (whether in Montana or Minnesota) had jurisdiction only if the company's conduct in the State had given rise to the plaintiff's claims. And that causal link existed, Ford continued, only if the company had designed, manufactured, or—most likely—sold in the State the particular vehicle involved in the accident. In neither suit could the plaintiff make that showing. Ford had designed the Explorer and Crown Victoria in Michigan, and it had manufactured the cars in (respectively) Kentucky and Canada. Still more, the company had originally sold the cars at issue outside the forum States—the Explorer in Washington, the Crown Victoria in North Dakota. Only later resales and relocations by consumers had brought the vehicles to Montana and Minnesota. That meant, in Ford's view, that the courts of those States could not decide the suits. . . .

Ford contends that our jurisdictional rules prevent Montana's and Minnesota's courts from deciding these two suits. In making that argument, Ford does not contest that it does substantial business in Montana and Minnesota—that it actively seeks to serve the market for automobiles and related products in those States. Or to put that concession in more doctrinal terms, Ford agrees that it has "purposefully avail[ed] itself of the privilege of conducting activities" in both places. Ford's claim is instead that those activities do not sufficiently connect to the suits, even though the resident-plaintiffs allege that Ford cars malfunctioned in the forum States. In Ford's view, the needed link must be causal in nature: Jurisdiction attaches "only if the defendant's forum conduct *gave rise* to the plaintiff's claims." And that rule reduces, Ford thinks, to locating specific jurisdiction in the State where Ford sold the car in question, or else the States where Ford designed and manufactured the vehicle. On that view, the place of accident and injury is immaterial. So (Ford says) Montana's and Minnesota's courts have no power over these cases.

But Ford's causation-only approach finds no support in this Court's requirement of a "connection" between a plaintiff's suit and a defendant's activities. That rule indeed serves to narrow the class of claims over which a state court may exercise specific jurisdiction. But not quite so far as Ford wants. None of our precedents has suggested that only a strict causal relationship between the defendant's in-state activity and the litigation will do. [Our] most common formulation of the rule demands that the suit "arise out of *or relate to* the defendant's contacts with the forum." The first half of that standard asks about causation; but the back half, after the "or," contemplates that some relationships will support jurisdiction without a causal showing. That does not mean anything goes. In the sphere of specific jurisdiction, the phrase "relate to" incorporates real limits, as it must to adequately protect defendants foreign to a forum. But again, we have never framed the specific jurisdiction inquiry as always requiring proof of causation—*i.e.,* proof that the plaintiff's claim came about because of the defendant's in-state conduct.

And indeed, this Court has stated that specific jurisdiction attaches in cases identical to the ones here—when a company like Ford serves a market for a product in the forum State and the product malfunctions there. In *World-Wide Volkswagen*, the Court held that an Oklahoma court could not assert jurisdiction over a New York car dealer just because a car it sold later caught fire in Oklahoma. But in so doing, we contrasted the dealer's position to that of two other defendants—Audi, the car's manufacturer, and Volkswagen, the car's nationwide importer (neither of which contested jurisdiction). [If] Audi and Volkswagen's business deliberately extended into Oklahoma (among other States), then Oklahoma's courts could hold the companies accountable for a car's catching fire there—even though the vehicle had been designed and made overseas and sold in New York.... Our conclusion in *World-Wide*

Volkswagen—though, as Ford notes, technically "dicta"—has appeared and reappeared in many cases since. . . .

To see why Ford is subject to jurisdiction in these cases . . ., consider first the business that the company regularly conducts in Montana and Minnesota. Small wonder that Ford has here conceded "purposeful availment" of the two States' markets. By every means imaginable—among them, billboards, TV and radio spots, print ads, and direct mail—Ford urges Montanans and Minnesotans to buy its vehicles, including (at all relevant times) Explorers and Crown Victorias. Ford cars—again including those two models—are available for sale, whether new or used, throughout the States, at 36 dealerships in Montana and 84 in Minnesota. And apart from sales, Ford works hard to foster ongoing connections to its cars' owners. The company's dealers in Montana and Minnesota (as elsewhere) regularly maintain and repair Ford cars, including those whose warranties have long since expired. And the company distributes replacement parts both to its own dealers and to independent auto shops in the two States. Those activities, too, make Ford money. And by making it easier to own a Ford, they encourage Montanans and Minnesotans to become lifelong Ford drivers.

Now turn to how all this Montana- and Minnesota-based conduct relates to the claims in these cases, brought by state residents in Montana's and Minnesota's courts. Each plaintiff's suit, of course, arises from a car accident in one of those States. In each complaint, the resident-plaintiff alleges that a defective Ford vehicle—an Explorer in one, a Crown Victoria in the other—caused the crash and resulting harm. And as just described, Ford had advertised, sold, and serviced those two car models in both States for many years. (Contrast a case, which we do not address, in which Ford marketed the models in only a different State or region.) In other words, Ford had systematically served a market in Montana and Minnesota for the very vehicles that the plaintiffs allege malfunctioned and injured them in those States. So there is a strong "relationship among the defendant, the forum, and the litigation"—the "essential foundation" of specific jurisdiction. . . .

The only complication here, pressed by Ford, is that the company sold the specific cars involved in these crashes outside the forum States, with consumers later selling them to the States' residents. Because that is so, Ford argues, the plaintiffs' claims "would be precisely the same if Ford had never done anything in Montana and Minnesota." Of course, that argument merely restates Ford's demand for an exclusively causal test of connection—which we have already shown is inconsistent with our caselaw. And . . . in any event, . . . the owners of these cars might never have bought them, and so these suits might never have arisen, except for Ford's contacts with their home States. Those contacts might turn any resident of Montana or Minnesota into a Ford owner—even when he buys his car from out of state. He may make that purchase because he saw ads for the car in local media. And he may take into account a raft of Ford's in-state activities designed to make driving a Ford convenient there: that Ford dealers stand ready to service the car; that other auto shops have ample supplies of Ford parts; and that Ford fosters an active resale market for its old models. The plaintiffs here did not in fact establish, or even allege, such causal links. Nor should jurisdiction in cases like these ride on the exact reasons for an individual plaintiff's purchase, or on his ability to present persuasive evidence about them. But the possibilities listed above—created by the reach of Ford's Montana and Minnesota contacts—underscore the aptness of finding jurisdiction here, even though the cars at issue were first sold out of state.

For related reasons, allowing jurisdiction in these cases treats Ford fairly, as this Court's precedents explain. In conducting so much business in Montana and Minnesota, Ford "enjoys the benefits and protection of [their] laws"—the enforcement of contracts, the defense of property, the resulting formation of effective markets. *International Shoe*, 326 U.S. at 319. All that assistance to Ford's in-state business creates reciprocal obligations—most relevant here, that the car models Ford so extensively markets in Montana and Minnesota be safe for their citizens to use there. Thus our repeated conclusion: A state court's enforcement of that commitment, enmeshed as it is with Ford's government-protected in-state business, can "hardly be said to be undue." *Ibid.* And as *World-Wide Volkswagen* described, it cannot be thought surprising either. An automaker regularly marketing a vehicle in a State, the Court said, has "clear notice" that it will be subject to jurisdiction in the State's courts when the product malfunctions there (regardless where it was first sold). 444 U.S., at 297. Precisely because that exercise of jurisdiction is so reasonable, it is also predictable—and thus allows Ford to "structure [its] primary conduct" to lessen or even avoid the costs of state-court litigation. *Ibid.*

Finally, principles of "interstate federalism" support jurisdiction over these suits in Montana and Minnesota. Those States have significant interests at stake—"providing [their] residents with a convenient forum for redressing injuries inflicted by out-of-state actors," as well as enforcing their own safety regulations. *Burger King Corp. v. Rudzewicz*, 471 U.S. 462, 473 (1985). Consider, next to those, the interests of the States of first sale (Washington and North Dakota)—which Ford's proposed rule would make the most likely forums. For each of those States, the suit involves all out-of-state parties, an out-of-state accident, and out-of-state injuries; the suit's only connection with the State is that a former owner once (many years earlier) bought the car there. In other words, there is a less significant "relationship among the defendant, the forum, and the litigation." So by channeling these suits to Washington and North Dakota, Ford's regime would undermine, rather than promote, what the company calls the Due Process Clause's "jurisdiction-allocating function."

Ford mainly relies for its rule on two of our recent decisions—*Bristol-Myers* and *Walden*. But those precedents stand for nothing like the principle Ford derives from them. If anything, they reinforce all we have said about why Montana's and Minnesota's courts can decide these cases.

In [*Bristol-Myers*], non-resident plaintiffs brought claims in California state court against Bristol-Myers Squibb, the manufacturer of a nationally marketed prescription drug called Plavix. . . . We found jurisdiction improper in *Bristol-Myers* because the forum State, and the defendant's activities there, lacked any connection to the plaintiffs' claims. The plaintiffs, the Court explained, were not residents of California. They had not been prescribed Plavix in California. They had not ingested Plavix in California. And they had not sustained their injuries in California. In short, the plaintiffs were engaged in forum-shopping—suing in California because it was thought plaintiff-friendly, even though their cases had no tie to the State. That is not at all true of the cases before us. . . .

Ford falls back on *Walden* as its last resort. In that case, a Georgia police officer working at an Atlanta airport searched, and seized money from, two Nevada residents before they embarked on a flight to Las Vegas. The victims of the search sued the officer in Nevada, arguing that their alleged injury (their inability to use the seized money) occurred in [that] State. . . . But *Walden* has precious little to do with the cases before us. In *Walden*, only the plaintiffs had any contacts with the State of Nevada; the defendant-officer had never taken any act to "form[ ] a contact" of his own. But here, Ford has a veritable truckload of contacts with Montana and Minnesota, as it admits. The only issue is whether those contacts are related enough to the plaintiffs' suits. As to that issue, so what if (as *Walden* held) the place of a plaintiff's injury and residence cannot create a defendant's contact with the forum State? Those places still may be relevant in assessing the link between the defendant's forum contacts and the plaintiff's suit—including its assertions of who was injured where. . . .

JUSTICE BARRETT took no part in the consideration or decision of these cases.

JUSTICE ALITO, concurring in the judgment.

These cases can and should be decided without any alteration or refinement of our case law on specific personal jurisdiction. To be sure, for the reasons outlined in JUSTICE GORSUCH's thoughtful opinion, there are grounds for questioning the standard that the Court adopted in *International Shoe Co. v. Washington*, 326 U.S. 310 (1945). And there are also reasons to wonder whether the case law we have developed since that time is well suited for the way in which business is now conducted. But there is nothing distinctively 21st century about the question in the cases now before us, and the answer to that question is settled by our case law. . .

Ford . . . asks us to adopt an unprecedented rule under which a defendant's contacts with the forum State must be proven to have been a but-for cause of the tort plaintiff 's injury. The Court properly rejects that argument, and I agree with the main thrust of the Court's opinion. My only quibble is with the new gloss that the Court puts on our case law. Several of our opinions have said that a plaintiff's claims "must arise out of or relate to the defendant's contacts" with the forum. The Court parses this phrase "as though we were dealing with language of a statute," and because this phrase is cast in the disjunctive, the Court recognizes a new category of cases in which personal jurisdiction is permitted: those in which the claims do not "arise out of" (i.e., are not caused by) the defendant's contacts but nevertheless sufficiently "relate to" those contacts in some undefined way.

This innovation is unnecessary and, in my view, unwise. To say that the Constitution does not require the kind of proof of causation that Ford would demand—what the majority describes as a "strict causal relationship"—is not to say that no causal link of any kind is needed. And here, there is a sufficient link. It is reasonable to infer that the vehicles in question here would never have been on the roads in Minnesota and Montana if they were some totally unknown brand that had never been advertised in those States, was not sold in those States, would not be familiar to mechanics in those States, and could not have been easily repaired with parts available in those States. The whole point of those activities was to put more Fords (including those in question here) on Minnesota and Montana roads. The common-sense relationship between Ford's activities and these suits, in other words, is causal in a broad sense of the concept, and personal jurisdiction can rest on this type of link without strict proof of the type Ford would require. When "arise out of" is understood in this way, it is apparent that "arise out of" and "relate to" overlap and are not really two discrete grounds for jurisdiction. The phrase "arise out of or relate to" is simply a way of restating the basic "minimum contacts" standard adopted in *International Shoe*. . . .

JUSTICE GORSUCH, with whom JUSTICE THOMAS joins, concurring in the judgment.

. . . Until now, many lower courts have proceeded on the premise that specific jurisdiction requires two things. First, the defendant must "purposefully avail" itself of the chance to do business in a State. Second, the plaintiff's suit must "arise out of or relate to" the defendant's in-state activities. Typically, courts have read this second phrase as a unit requiring at least a but-for causal link between the defendant's local activities and the plaintiff 's injuries. As every first year law student learns, a but-for causation test isn't the most demanding. At a high level of abstraction, one might say any event in the world would not have happened "but for" events far and long removed.

Now, though, the Court pivots away from this understanding. Focusing on the phrase "arise out of or relate to" that so often appears in our cases, the majority asks us to parse those words "as though we were dealing with language of a statute." *Reiter v. Sonotone Corp.*, 442 U.S. 330, 341 (1979). In particular, the majority zeros in on the disjunctive conjunction "or," and proceeds to build its entire opinion around that linguistic feature. The majority admits that "arise out of" may connote causation. But, it argues, "relate to" is an independent clause that does not.

Where this leaves us is far from clear. For a case to "relate to" the defendant's forum contacts, the majority says, it is enough if an "affiliation" or "relationship" or "connection" exists between them. But what does this assortment of nouns *mean*? Loosed from any causation standard, we are left to guess. The majority promises that its new test "does not mean anything goes," but that hardly tells us what does. In some cases, the new test may prove more forgiving than the old causation rule. But it's hard not to wonder whether it may also sometimes turn out to be more demanding. Unclear too is whether, in cases like that, the majority would treat causation and "affiliation" as alternative routes to specific jurisdiction, or whether it would deny jurisdiction outright. . . .

Not only does the majority's new test risk adding new layers of confusion to our personal jurisdiction jurisprudence. The whole project seems unnecessary. Immediately after disavowing any need for a causal link between the defendant's forum activities and the plaintiffs' injuries, the majority proceeds to admit that such a link may be present here. The majority stresses that the Montana and Minnesota plaintiffs before us "might" have purchased their cars because of Ford's activities in their home States. . . .

With the old *International Shoe* dichotomy looking increasingly uncertain, it's hard not to ask how we got here and where we might be headed.

Before *International Shoe*, it seems due process was usually understood to guarantee that only a court of competent jurisdiction could deprive a defendant of his life, liberty, or property. In turn, a court's competency normally depended on the defendant's presence in, or consent to, the sovereign's jurisdiction. But once a plaintiff was able to "tag" the defendant with process in the jurisdiction, that State's courts were generally thought competent to render judgment on any claim against the defendant, whether it involved events inside or outside the State. *Pennoyer v. Neff*, 95 U.S. 714, 733 (1878); *Burnham v. Superior Court of Cal., County of Marin*, 495 U.S. 604, 610–611 (1990); J. Story, Commentaries on the Conflict of Laws 912–913 (3d ed. 1846).[2] . . .

Unsurprisingly, corporations soon looked for ways around rules like these. No one, after all, has ever liked greeting the process server. For centuries, individuals facing imminent suit sought to avoid it by fleeing the court's territorial jurisdiction. But this tactic proved "too crude for the American business genius," and it held some obvious disadvantages. See Jackson, What Price "Due Process," 5 N. Y. L. Rev. 435, 436 (1927). Corporations wanted to retain the privilege of sending their personnel and products to other jurisdictions where they lacked a charter to do business. At the same time, when confronted with lawsuits in the second forum, they sought to hide behind their foreign charters and deny their presence. Really, their strategy was to do business without being seen to do business. *Id.*, at 438 ("No longer is the foreign corporation confronted with the problem 'to be or not to be'—it can both be and not be!"). . . .

In many ways, *International Shoe* sought to start over. . . . In place of nearly everything that had come before, the Court sought to build a new test focused on "traditional notions of fair play and substantial justice." *International Shoe*, 326 U.S. at 316.

It was a heady promise. But it is unclear how far it has really taken us. Even today, this Court usually considers corporations "at home" and thus subject to general jurisdiction in only one or two States. All in a world where global conglomerates boast of their many "headquarters." The Court has issued these restrictive rulings, too, even though *individual* defendants remain subject to the old "tag" rule, allowing them to be sued on any claim anywhere they can be found. *Burnham*, 495 U.S., at 610–611. Nearly 80 years removed from *International Shoe*, it seems corporations continue to receive special jurisdictional protections in the name of the Constitution. Less clear is why.

Maybe, too, *International Shoe* just doesn't work quite as well as it once did. For a period, its specific jurisdiction test might have seemed a reasonable new substitute for assessing corporate "presence," a way to identify those out-of-state corporations that were simply pretending to be absent from jurisdictions where they were really transacting business. When a company "purposefully availed" itself of the benefits of another State's market in the 1940s, it often involved sending in agents, advertising in local media, or developing a network of on-the-ground dealers, much as

[2] Some disagree that due process requires even this much. Recent scholarship, for example, contends *Pennoyer*'s territorial account of sovereign power is mostly right, but the rules it embodies are not "fixed in constitutional amber"—that is, Congress might be able to change them. Sachs, *Pennoyer* Was Right, 95 Texas L. Rev. 1249, 1255 (2017). Others suggest that fights over personal jurisdiction would be more sensibly waged under the Full Faith and Credit Clause. Jackson, Full Faith and Credit—The Lawyer's Clause of the Constitution, 45 Colum. L. Rev. 1, 3 (1945). Whether these theories are right or wrong, they at least seek to answer the right question—what the Constitution as originally understood requires, not what nine judges consider "fair" and "just."

Ford did in these cases. But, today, even an individual retiree carving wooden decoys in Maine can "purposefully avail" himself of the chance to do business across the continent after drawing online orders to his e-Bay "store" thanks to Internet advertising with global reach. . . .

If that is the logic at play here, I cannot help but wonder if we are destined to return where we began. . . . But maybe all we have done since is struggle for new words to express the old ideas. Perhaps, too, none of this should come as a surprise. New technologies and new schemes to evade the process server will always be with us. But if our concern is with "*traditional* notions of fair play and substantial justice," not just our personal and idiosyncratic impressions of those things, perhaps we will always wind up asking variations of the same questions. . . .

The real struggle here isn't with settling on the right outcome in these cases, but with making sense of our personal jurisdiction jurisprudence and *International Shoe*'s increasingly doubtful dichotomy. On those scores, I readily admit that I finish these cases with even more questions than I had at the start. Hopefully, future litigants and lower courts will help us face these tangles and sort out a responsible way to address the challenges posed by our changing economy in light of the Constitution's text and the lessons of history.

———

The Role of Causation in Specific Jurisdiction

(1) What test, exactly, does the Court adopt in place of Ford's proposed causation-based test to determine whether the plaintiff's lawsuit is sufficiently related to the defendant's activity in the forum state? All agree that Ford purposefully availed itself of the laws of Minnesota and Montana by marketing its cars there, but the Court isn't especially clear about how the accidents in these cases "arise out of or relate to" its conduct in those states, considering that the cars involved were manufactured and sold elsewhere. Does Justice Kagan ever provide a definition of "relate to" (as opposed to "arise out of")?

Is the Court collapsing the "arise out of or relate to" requirement and the purposeful availment requirement into a single test? At the very least, it seems clear that the same activities directed at the forum by the defendant can suffice to meet both requirements. But those activities, it would seem, need not have a close connection to the facts that form the basis of the plaintiff's claims on the merits. Note that the Court never invokes *International Shoe*'s "fair play and substantial justice" formulation, which ordinarily involves an analysis of the forum's state interest, the balance of convenience to the parties, the efficiency of litigating in the forum, and the shared substantive policies of the several states. Instead, the Court asks whether there is a "strong relationship among the defendant, the forum, and the litigation." That relationship is present here, unlike in *Bristol-Myers* or *Walden*, in part because the forum has an interest in providing its residents with a convenient venue to redress injuries inflicted by out-of-state actors. (Won't this interest always be in play when the plaintiff is a resident of the forum?)

Or is the key factor simply that Ford's marketing efforts made it more likely that the plaintiffs would buy its cars—but if so, isn't that (as the concurring justices suggest) just the but-for test in a different guise?

(2) Perhaps, unlike the local dealership in *World-Wide Volkswagen* or the individual police officer in *Walden*, a corporation acting nationwide such as Ford should simply expect to be haled into court in any state where its products cause injury. Is there anything wrong with that, either from a fairness or a state sovereignty perspective? Has the majority in *Ford Motor Co.* signed on to a version of Justice Brennan's "stream of commerce" theory from his concurrence in *Asahi*? Even under a stream of commerce theory, though, doesn't a car arguably leave the stream of commerce once it is purchased by an individual consumer?

(3) The Court, citing Ford's brief, alludes to the Due Process Clause's "jurisdiction-allocating function." What does that mean? Why is the allocation of judicial power among states a concern of the Due Process Clause? Perhaps this function should handled, if at all, by the Full Faith and Credit Clause. As Justice Gorsuch notes, Robert Jackson made that argument in *Full Faith and Credit—The Lawyer's Clause of the Constitution*, 45 Colum. L. Rev. 1, 3 (1945). Justice Gorsuch also cites Professor Sachs, who maintains that personal jurisdiction isn't controlled directly by the Constitution at all but by general common law—which in turn is subject to Congress's authority under the Full Faith and Credit Clause. See Sachs, *Pennoyer Was Right*, 95 Tex. L. Rev. 1249 (2017). Would this be a better solution?

(4) Justice Gorsuch's concurrence argues for a wholesale reappraisal of the *International Shoe* framework. Do you agree that this framework is increasingly obsolete in an era of multinational conglomerates and Internet advertising? If so, what should replace it? Does Justice Gorsuch offer any clues?

Until now, the major modern cases we have seen—*World-Wide Volkswagen*, *Asahi*, *Nicastro*, and *Ford Motor Co.*—have involved products liability tort claims. Does the personal jurisdiction analysis differ when the underlying claim involves a consensual transaction? The following case explores this issue.

BURGER KING CORP. V. RUDZEWICZ

471 U.S. 462 (1985).

JUSTICE BRENNAN delivered the opinion of the Court.

The State of Florida's long-arm statute extends jurisdiction to "[a]ny person, whether or not a citizen or resident of this state," who, *inter alia,* "[b]reach[es] a contract in this state by failing to perform acts required by the contract to be performed in this state," so long as the cause of action arises from the alleged contractual breach. Fla.Stat. § 48.193(1)(g) (Supp.1984). The United States District Court for the Southern District of Florida, sitting in diversity, relied on this provision in exercising personal jurisdiction over a Michigan resident who allegedly had breached a franchise agreement with a Florida corporation by failing to make required payments in Florida. The question presented is whether this exercise of long-arm jurisdiction offended "traditional conception[s] of fair play and substantial justice" embodied in the Due Process Clause of the Fourteenth Amendment. *International Shoe Co. v. Washington,* 326 U.S. 310, 320 (1945).

Burger King Corporation is a Florida corporation whose principal offices are in Miami. It is one of the world's largest restaurant organizations, with over 3,000 outlets in the 50 States, the Commonwealth of Puerto Rico, and 8 foreign nations. Burger King conducts approximately 80% of its business through a franchise operation that the company styles the "Burger King System"—"a comprehensive restaurant format and operating system for the sale of uniform and quality food products." Burger King licenses its franchisees to use its trademarks and service marks for a period of 20 years and leases standardized restaurant facilities to them for the same term. . . By permitting franchisees to tap into Burger King's established national reputation and to benefit from proven procedures for dispensing standardized fare, this system enables them to go into the restaurant business with significantly lowered barriers to entry.

In exchange for these benefits, franchisees pay Burger King an initial $40,000 franchise fee and commit themselves to payment of monthly royalties, advertising and sales promotion fees, and rent computed in part from monthly gross sales. Franchisees also agree to submit to the national organization's exacting regulation of virtually every conceivable aspect of their operations. . .

Burger King oversees its franchise system through a two-tiered administrative structure. The governing contracts provide that the franchise relationship is established in Miami and governed by Florida law, and call for payment of all required fees and forwarding of all relevant notices to the Miami headquarters. The Miami headquarters sets policy and works directly with its franchisees in attempting to resolve major problems. Day-to-day monitoring of franchisees, however, is conducted through a network of 10 district offices which in turn report to the Miami headquarters.

Rudzewicz and MacShara jointly applied for a franchise to Burger King's Birmingham, Michigan district office in the autumn of 1978. Their application was forwarded to Burger King's Miami headquarters, which entered into a preliminary agreement with them in February 1979. During the ensuing four months it was agreed that Rudzewicz and MacShara would assume operation of an existing facility in Drayton Plains, Michigan. MacShara attended the prescribed management courses in Miami during this period, and the franchisees purchased $165,000 worth of restaurant equipment from Burger King's Davmor Industries division in Miami. Even before the final agreements were signed, however, the parties began to disagree over site-development fees, building design, computation of monthly rent, and whether the franchisees would be able to assign their liabilities to a corporation they had formed. During these disputes Rudzewicz and MacShara negotiated both with the Birmingham district office and with the Miami headquarters. With some misgivings, Rudzewicz and MacShara finally obtained limited concessions from the Miami headquarters, signed the final agreements, and commenced operations in June 1979. By signing the final agreements, Rudzewicz obligated himself personally to payments exceeding $1 million over the 20-year franchise relationship.

The Drayton Plains facility apparently enjoyed steady business during the summer of 1979, but patronage declined after a recession began later that year. Rudzewicz and MacShara soon fell far behind in their monthly payments to Miami. Headquarters sent notices of default, and an extended period of negotiations began among the franchisees, the Birmingham district office, and the Miami headquarters. After several Burger King officials in Miami had engaged in prolonged but ultimately unsuccessful negotiations with the franchisees by mail and by telephone, headquarters terminated the franchise and ordered Rudzewicz and MacShara to vacate the premises. They refused and continued to occupy and operate the facility as a Burger King restaurant.

Burger King commenced the instant action in the United States District Court for the Southern District of Florida in May 1981. . . Burger King alleged that Rudzewicz and MacShara had breached their franchise obligations "within [the jurisdiction of] this district court" by failing to make the required payments "at plaintiff's place of business in Miami, Dade County, Florida". . . Burger King sought damages, injunctive relief, and costs and attorney's fees. Rudzewicz and MacShara entered special appearances and argued, *inter alia,* that because they were Michigan residents and because Burger King's claim did not "arise" within the Southern District of Florida, the District Court lacked personal jurisdiction over them. The District Court denied their motions after a hearing, holding that, pursuant to Florida's long-arm statute, "a nonresident Burger King franchisee is subject to the personal jurisdiction of this Court in actions arising out of its franchise agreements." . . .

After a 3-day bench trial, the court again concluded that it had "jurisdiction over the subject matter and the parties to this cause." Finding that Rudzewicz and MacShara had breached their franchise agreements with Burger King. . ., the court entered judgment against them, jointly and severally, for $228,875 in contract damages. . .

Rudzewicz appealed to the Court of Appeals for the Eleventh Circuit. A divided panel of that Circuit reversed the judgment, concluding that the District Court could not properly exercise personal jurisdiction over Rudzewicz. . .

[On certiorari, the Supreme Court reversed.]

The Due Process Clause protects an individual's liberty interest in not being subject to the binding judgments of a forum with which he has established no meaningful "contacts, ties, or relations." *International Shoe Co. v. Washington,* 326 U.S., at 319. By requiring that individuals have "fair warning that a particular activity may subject [them] to the jurisdiction of a foreign sovereign," *Shaffer v. Heitner,* 433 U.S. 186, 218 (1977) (Stevens, J., concurring in judgment), the Due Process Clause "gives a degree of predictability to the legal system that allows potential defendants to structure their primary conduct with some minimum assurance as to where that conduct will and will not render them liable to suit," *World-Wide Volkswagen Corp. v. Woodson,* 444 U.S. 286, 297 (1980).

Where a forum seeks to assert specific jurisdiction over an out-of-state defendant who has not consented to suit there, this "fair warning" requirement is satisfied if the defendant has "purposefully directed" his activities at residents of the forum, *Keeton v. Hustler Magazine, Inc.,* 465 U.S. 770, 774 (1984), and the litigation results from alleged injuries that "arise out of or relate to" those activities, *Helicopteros Nacionales de Colombia, S.A. v. Hall,* 466 U.S. 408, 412 (1984). . .

We have noted several reasons why a forum legitimately may exercise personal jurisdiction over a nonresident who "purposefully directs" his activities toward forum residents. A State generally has a "manifest interest" in providing its residents with a convenient forum for redressing injuries inflicted by out-of-state actors. * * * Moreover, where individuals "purposefully derive benefit" from their interstate activities, *Kulko v. California Superior Court,* 436 U.S. 84, 96 (1978), it may well be unfair to allow them to escape having to account in other States for consequences that arise proximately from such activities; the Due Process Clause may not readily be wielded as a territorial shield to avoid interstate obligations that have been voluntarily assumed. And because "modern transportation and communications have made it much less burdensome for a party sued to defend himself in a State where he engages in economic activity," it usually will not be unfair to subject him to the burdens of litigating in another forum for disputes relating to such activity. *McGee v. International Life Insurance Co., supra,* 355 U.S., at 223.

Notwithstanding these considerations, the constitutional touchstone remains whether the defendant purposefully established "minimum contacts" in the forum State. *International Shoe Co. v. Washington, supra,* 326 U.S., at 316. Although it has been argued that foreseeability of causing *injury* in another State should be sufficient to establish such contacts there when policy considerations so require, the Court has consistently held that this kind of foreseeability is not a "sufficient benchmark" for exercising personal jurisdiction. *World-Wide Volkswagen Corp. v. Woodson,* 444 U.S., at 295. Instead, "the foreseeability that is critical to due process analysis . . . is that the defendant's conduct and connection with the forum State are such that he should reasonably anticipate being haled into court there." In defining when it is that a potential defendant should "reasonably anticipate" out-of-state litigation, the Court frequently has drawn from the reasoning of *Hanson v. Denckla,* 357 U.S. 235, 253 (1958):

> "The unilateral activity of those who claim some relationship with a nonresident defendant cannot satisfy the requirement of contact with the forum State. The application of that rule will vary with the quality and nature of the defendant's activity, but it is essential in each case that there be some act by which the defendant purposefully avails itself of the privilege of conducting activities within the forum State, thus invoking the benefits and protections of its laws."

This "purposeful availment" requirement ensures that a defendant will not be haled into a jurisdiction solely as a result of "random," "fortuitous," or "attenuated" contacts, *Keeton v. Hustler Magazine, Inc., supra,* 465 U.S., at 780; *World-Wide Volkswagen Corp. v. Woodson,* 444 U.S., at 299, or of the "unilateral activity of another party or a third person." *Helicopteros Nacionales de Colombia, S.A. v. Hall, supra,* 466 U.S., at 417. Jurisdiction is proper, however, where the contacts proximately result from actions by the defendant *himself* that create a "substantial connection" with the forum State. *McGee v. International Life Insurance Co.,* 355 U.S., at 223, see also *Kulko v. California Superior Court, supra,* 436 U.S., at 94, n.7.[18] Thus where the defendant "deliberately" has engaged

[18] So long as it creates a "substantial connection" with the forum, even a single act can support jurisdiction. *McGee v. International Life Insurance Co.,* 355 U.S. 220, 223 (1957). The Court has noted, however, that "some single or occasional acts" related to the forum may not be sufficient to establish jurisdiction if "their nature and quality and the circumstances of their commission" create only an "attenuated" affiliation with the forum. *International Shoe Co. v. Washington,* 326 U.S. 310, 318 (1945); *World-Wide Volkswagen Corp. v. Woodson,* 444 U.S., at 299. This distinction derives from the belief that, with respect to this category of "isolated" acts, the reasonable foreseeability of litigation in the forum is substantially diminished.

in significant activities within a State, *Keeton v. Hustler Magazine, Inc.*, 465 U.S., at 780 or has created "continuing obligations" between himself and residents of the forum, *Travelers Health Assn. v. Virginia,* 339 U.S., at 648, he manifestly has availed himself of the privilege of conducting business there, and because his activities are shielded by "the benefits and protections" of the forum's laws it is presumptively not unreasonable to require him to submit to the burdens of litigation in that forum as well.

Jurisdiction in these circumstances may not be avoided merely because the defendant did not *physically* enter the forum State. Although territorial presence frequently will enhance a potential defendant's affiliation with a State and reinforce the reasonable foreseeability of suit there, it is an inescapable fact of modern commercial life that a substantial amount of business is transacted solely by mail and wire communications across state lines, thus obviating the need for physical presence within a State in which business is conducted. So long as a commercial actor's efforts are "purposefully directed" toward residents of another State, we have consistently rejected the notion that an absence of physical contacts can defeat personal jurisdiction there. * * *

Once it has been decided that a defendant purposefully established minimum contacts within the forum State, these contacts may be considered in light of other factors to determine whether the assertion of personal jurisdiction would comport with "fair play and substantial justice." *International Shoe Co. v. Washington,* 326 U.S., at 320. Thus courts in "appropriate case[s]" may evaluate "the burden on the defendant," "the forum State's interest in adjudicating the dispute," "the plaintiff's interest in obtaining convenient and effective relief," "the interstate judicial system's interest in obtaining the most efficient resolution of controversies," and the "shared interest of the several States in furthering fundamental substantive social policies." *World-Wide Volkswagen Corp. v. Woodson, supra,* 444 U.S., at 292. These considerations sometimes serve to establish the reasonableness of jurisdiction upon a lesser showing of minimum contacts than would otherwise be required. * * * On the other hand, where a defendant who purposefully has directed his activities at forum residents seeks to defeat jurisdiction, he must present a compelling case that the presence of some other considerations would render jurisdiction unreasonable. Most such considerations usually may be accommodated through means short of finding jurisdiction unconstitutional. For example, the potential clash of the forum's law with the "fundamental substantive social policies" of another State may be accommodated through application of the forum's choice-of-law rules. Similarly, a defendant claiming substantial inconvenience may seek a change of venue. Nevertheless, minimum requirements inherent in the concept of "fair play and substantial justice" may defeat the reasonableness of jurisdiction even if the defendant has purposefully engaged in forum activities. . .

Applying these principles to the case at hand, we believe there is substantial record evidence supporting the District Court's conclusion that the assertion of personal jurisdiction over Rudzewicz in Florida for the alleged breach of his franchise agreement did not offend due process. At the outset, we note a continued division among lower courts respecting whether and to what extent a contract can constitute a "contact" for purposes of due process analysis. If the question is whether an individual's contract with an out-of-state party *alone* can automatically establish sufficient minimum contacts in the other party's home forum, we believe the answer clearly is that it cannot. . . [W]e have emphasized the need for a "highly realistic" approach that recognizes that a "contract" is "ordinarily but an intermediate step serving to tie up prior business negotiations with future consequences which themselves are the real object of the business transaction." * * * It is these factors—prior negotiations and contemplated future consequences, along with the terms of the contract and the parties' actual course of dealing—that must be evaluated in determining whether the defendant purposefully established minimum contacts within the forum.

In this case, no physical ties to Florida can be attributed to Rudzewicz other than MacShara's brief training course in Miami. Rudzewicz did not maintain offices in Florida and, for all that appears from the record, has never even visited there. Yet this franchise dispute grew directly out of "a contract which had a *substantial* connection with that State." *McGee v. International Life Insurance Co.,* 355 U.S., at 223. Eschewing the option of operating an independent local enterprise, Rudzewicz deliberately "reach[ed] out beyond" Michigan and negotiated with a Florida corporation for the purchase of a long-term franchise and the manifold benefits that would derive from affiliation with a nationwide organization. * * * Upon approval, he entered into a carefully structured 20-year relationship that envisioned continuing and wide-reaching contacts with Burger King in Florida. In light of Rudzewicz's voluntary acceptance of the long-term and exacting regulation of his business from Burger King's Miami headquarters, the "quality and nature" of his relationship to the company in Florida can in no sense be viewed as "random," "fortuitous," or "attenuated." * * * Rudzewicz's refusal to make the contractually required payments in Miami, and his continued use of Burger King's trademarks and confidential business information after his termination, caused foreseeable injuries to the corporation in Florida. . .

The Court of Appeals concluded, however, that in light of the supervision emanating from Burger King's district office in Birmingham, Rudzewicz reasonably believed that "the Michigan office was for all intents and purposes the embodiment of Burger King" and that he therefore had no "reason to anticipate a Burger King suit outside of Michigan." This reasoning overlooks substantial record evidence indicating that Rudzewicz most certainly knew that he was affiliating himself with an enterprise based primarily in Florida. The contract documents themselves emphasize that Burger King's operations are conducted and supervised from the Miami headquarters, that all relevant notices and payments must be sent there, and that the agreements were made in and enforced from Miami. Moreover, the parties' actual course of dealing repeatedly confirmed that decisionmaking authority was vested in the Miami headquarters and that the district office served largely as an intermediate link between the headquarters and the franchisees. . . Throughout these disputes, the Miami headquarters and the Michigan franchisees carried on a continuous course of direct communications by mail and by telephone, and it was the Miami headquarters that made the key negotiating decisions out of which the instant litigation arose.

Moreover, we believe the Court of Appeals gave insufficient weight to provisions in the various franchise documents providing that all disputes would be governed by Florida law. The franchise agreement, for example, stated:

> "This Agreement shall become valid when executed and accepted by BKC at Miami, Florida; it shall be deemed made and entered into in the State of Florida and shall be governed and construed under and in accordance with the laws of the State of Florida. The choice of law designation does not require that all suits concerning this Agreement be filed in Florida."

The Court of Appeals reasoned that choice-of-law provisions are irrelevant to the question of personal jurisdiction, relying on *Hanson v. Denckla* for the proposition that "the center of gravity for choice-of-law purposes does not necessarily confer the sovereign prerogative to assert jurisdiction." This reasoning misperceives the import of the quoted proposition. The Court in *Hanson* and subsequent cases has emphasized that choice-of-law *analysis*—which focuses on all elements of a transaction, and not simply on the defendant's conduct—is distinct from minimum-contacts jurisdictional analysis—which focuses at the threshold solely on the defendant's purposeful connection to the forum. Nothing in our cases, however, suggests that a choice-of-law *provision* should be ignored in considering whether a defendant has "purposefully invoked the benefits and protections of a State's laws" for jurisdictional purposes. Although such a provision standing alone would be insufficient to confer jurisdiction, we believe that, when combined with the 20-year interdependent relationship Rudzewicz established with Burger King's Miami headquarters, it reinforced his deliberate affiliation with the forum State and the reasonable foreseeability of possible litigation there. . .[24]

Nor has Rudzewicz pointed to other factors that can be said persuasively to outweigh the considerations discussed above and to establish the *unconstitutionality* of Florida's assertion of jurisdiction. We cannot conclude that Florida had no "legitimate interest in holding [Rudzewicz] answerable on a claim related to" the contacts he had established in that State. * * *[25] Moreover, although Rudzewicz has argued at some length that Michigan's Franchise Investment Law, Mich.Comp.Laws § 445.1501 *et seq.* (1979), governs many aspects of this franchise relationship, he has not demonstrated how Michigan's acknowledged interest might possibly render jurisdiction in Florida *unconstitutional.*

Notwithstanding these considerations, the Court of Appeals apparently believed that it was necessary to reject jurisdiction in this case as a prophylactic measure, reasoning that an affirmance of the District Court's judgment would result in the exercise of jurisdiction over "out-of-state consumers to collect payments due on modest personal purchases" and would "sow the seeds of default judgments against franchisees owing smaller debts." We share the Court of Appeals' broader concerns and therefore reject any talismanic jurisdictional formulas; "the facts of each case must [always] be weighed" in determining whether personal jurisdiction would comport with "fair play and substantial justice." *Kulko v. California Superior Court,* 436 U.S., at 92. . . Because Rudzewicz established a substantial and continuing relationship with Burger King's Miami headquarters, received fair notice from the contract documents and the course of dealing that he might be subject to suit in Florida, and has failed to demonstrate how jurisdiction in that forum would otherwise be fundamentally unfair, we conclude that the District Court's exercise of jurisdiction . . . did not offend due process. . .

JUSTICE STEVENS, with whom JUSTICE WHITE joins, dissenting.

---

[24] In addition, the franchise agreement's disclaimer that the "choice of law designation does not *require* that all suits concerning this Agreement be filed in Florida," reasonably should have suggested to Rudzewicz that by negative implication such suits *could* be filed there.

The lease also provided for binding arbitration in Miami of certain condemnation disputes, [a provision that] should have made it apparent to the franchisees that they were dealing directly with the Miami headquarters and that the Birmingham district office was *not* "for all intents and purposes the embodiment of Burger King."

[25] [R]udzewicz contends that Florida's interest in providing a convenient forum is negligible given the company's size and ability to conduct litigation anywhere in the country. We disagree. Absent compelling considerations, a defendant who has purposefully derived commercial benefit from his affiliations in a forum may not defeat jurisdiction there simply because of his adversary's greater net wealth.

In my opinion there is a significant element of unfairness in requiring a franchisee to defend a case of this kind in the forum chosen by the franchisor. . .

[The opinion below is] more persuasive than what this Court has written today:

> "Nothing in the course of negotiations gave Rudzewicz reason to anticipate a Burger King suit outside of Michigan. The only face-to-face or even oral contact Rudzewicz had with Burger King throughout months of protracted negotiations was with representatives of the Michigan office. Burger King had the Michigan office interview Rudzewicz and MacShara, appraise their application, discuss price terms, recommend the site which the defendants finally agreed to, and attend the final closing ceremony. There is no evidence that Rudzewicz ever negotiated with anyone in Miami or even sent mail there during negotiations. He maintained no staff in the state of Florida, and as far as the record reveals, he has never even visited the state. . .
>
> "Given that the office in Rudzewicz' home state conducted all of the negotiations and wholly supervised the contract, we believe that he had reason to assume that the state of the supervisory office would be the same state in which Burger King would file suit. Rudzewicz lacked fair notice that the distant corporate headquarters which insulated itself from direct dealings with him would later seek to assert jurisdiction over him in the courts of its own home state. . .
>
> "We discern a characteristic disparity of bargaining power in the facts of this case. There is no indication that Rudzewicz had any latitude to negotiate a reduced rent or franchise fee in exchange for the added risk of suit in Florida. He signed a standard form contract whose terms were non-negotiable and which appeared in some respects to vary from the more favorable terms agreed to in earlier discussions. . ."

Jurisdiction in Contract Cases

(1) As noted above, *Burger King* is the first of the modern cases to focus on jurisdictional limits in consensual transactions. Is the Court's analysis consistent with *World-Wide Volkswagen*? Justice Brennan says there must be "minimum contacts" showing purposeful availment, but does this requirement serve the same purpose in his analysis as in *World-Wide Volkswagen* and *Kulko*? And what do you make of the Court's suggestion that the nature of the contacts required to show purposeful availment varies depending on other factors, such as convenience and state interest? Are we back to balancing and *McGee*?

What had Rudzewicz done to avail himself of the privilege of conducting activity in Florida? The Court says that making a contract with a party from Florida is not enough, standing alone, to give Florida jurisdiction. But what else is there here? Justice Brennan urges that Rudzewicz "deliberately 'reach[ed] out beyond' Michigan" by negotiating with a Florida corporation. What does that mean other than that Rudzewicz made a contract with a party from Florida? Besides, isn't it Burger King that reached out beyond Florida to negotiate with Rudzewicz? See *Conn v. Whitmore,* 9 Utah 2d 250, 255, 342 P.2d 871, 874 (1959) (holding that Illinois had no jurisdiction because "it was the plaintiff resident of Illinois who proselytized for business in Utah"). After *Burger King,* does the home state of every party to a contract have jurisdiction, at least if the parties negotiated by phone or mail from their respective home bases?

Justice Brennan also relies on the choice-of-law clause in the contract. Is *that* what is meant by "purposefully availing" oneself of the benefits of a state? If the contract called for Alaska law, could Burger King have sued in Alaska? Is reliance on choice-of-law considerations consistent with the Court's earlier disclaimers of a connection between jurisdiction and choice of law?

(2) Can you reconcile *Burger King* with *Kulko*? If Rudzewicz has availed himself of the benefits of Florida by making this contract with Burger King, why hadn't Kulko done the same by sending his children to California? Is there any reason to treat contract and tort cases differently when it comes to jurisdiction?

(3) Isn't there something grossly unfair about allowing Burger King to force franchisees to litigate in Florida? Justice Brennan says that considerations like the relative wealth of the defendant should have no bearing on jurisdiction. Do you agree? What about substantive considerations, like unequal bargaining power in form contract situations? See Carrington & Martin, *Substantive Interests and the Jurisdiction of State Courts,* 66 Mich.L.Rev. 227 (1967).

The Court of Appeals noted its concern that if Burger King could obtain jurisdiction at home on these facts, so could any company doing interstate business, assuring easy default judgments in many cases involving small transactions. Is the Court's answer persuasive? By choosing Maine law in its sales contract, can L.L. Bean sue anyone who buys from its mail order catalogue in Maine (where L.L. Bean is headquartered)?

(4) The choice-of-law clause in Burger King's franchise agreement specifically stated that suit did not have to be brought in Florida. Would the case have been easier if the contract had limited the choice of forum? See *National Equipment Rental v. Szukhent,* 375 U.S. 311 (1964) (upholding a contract provision requiring appointment of an agent in the state to receive service of process); *M/S Bremen v. Zapata Off-Shore Co.,* 407 U.S. 1 (1972) (enforcing a clause requiring suit between American and German corporations to be brought in England even though this would result in application of a law less favorable to the plaintiff); *Carnival Cruise Lines, Inc. v. Shute,* 499 U.S. 585 (1991) (enforcing a choice-of-forum clause printed on a ticket purchased in Washington by a plaintiff from Washington for a trip from Mexico to California and requiring suit to be brought in Florida, where defendant's headquarters was located). Are there any limits on the parties' power to select a forum by contract? Should the decision whether to enforce a choice-of-forum clause take into account effects on the applicable law?

(5) To what extent should substantive policy considerations relating to other constitutional provisions, such as the Commerce Clause or the First Amendment, influence a determination of due process limits on state-court jurisdiction? In *Scanapico v. Richmond, F. & P. R. Co.,* 439 F.2d 17 (2d Cir. 1970), the court recognized that the Commerce Clause might invalidate an exercise of personal jurisdiction on the ground that it imposed an unreasonable burden on interstate commerce, but found no such burden in the particular case. Id. at 25–28 (Friendly, J., on reconsideration in banc). See also Clermont, *Restating Territorial Jurisdiction and Venue for State and Federal Courts,* 66 Cornell L.Rev. 411, 452 (1981).

For a brief period in the 1960s it seemed that a First Amendment policy in favor of the free flow of information throughout the country might increase the level of minimum contacts necessary to sustain a state's exercise of judicial power. In *New York Times v. Connor,* 365 F.2d 567, 572 (5th Cir. 1966), the court concluded that "First Amendment considerations surrounding the law of libel required a greater showing of contact to satisfy the due process clause than is necessary in asserting jurisdiction over other types of tortious activity." A relatively small circulation of the New York Times in Mississippi did not subject it to a defamation action there because "local juries incensed by the out-of-state newspaper's coverage of local events"—the notorious activities of Birmingham Police Commissioner "Bull" Connor during the height of the civil rights struggle—could not be relied upon to reach fair results. But the result went the other way with a somewhat larger circulation in Louisiana of a national magazine. *Curtis Pub. Co. v. Golino,* 383 F.2d 586 (5th Cir. 1967).

The Supreme Court later put to rest notions that the First Amendment is an independent limitation on state-court jurisdiction or even a factor in the "reasonableness" calculus surrounding jurisdiction. In *Calder v. Jones,* 465 U.S. 783 (1984), two Florida newspaper reporters were held subject to suit in California in a defamation action arising out of intentional conduct in Florida designed to cause emotional harm to the plaintiff in California. Justice Rehnquist stated:

> We . . . reject the suggestion that First Amendment concerns enter into the jurisdictional analysis. The infusion of such considerations would needlessly complicate an already imprecise inquiry. . . [T]he potential chill on protected First Amendment activity stemming from libel and defamation actions is already taken into account in the constitutional limitations on the substantive law governing such suits.

Id. at 790.

The point was made even more emphatically in *Keeton v. Hustler Magazine, Inc.*, 465 U.S. 770 (1984), a case in which a New York plaintiff brought her defamation suit in New Hampshire solely because the statute of limitations had expired everywhere else. Despite the blatant forum-shopping and the fact that fewer than 15,000 copies of *Hustler* were sold each month in New Hampshire, the Court upheld jurisdiction. The Court stated: "[w]e reject categorically the suggestion that invisible radiations from the First Amendment may defeat jurisdiction otherwise proper under the Due Process Clause." Id. at 780 n. 12. A jury later returned a substantial verdict for the plaintiff against *Hustler*.

SECTION 2. GENERAL JURISDICTION

DAIMLER AG V. BAUMAN

571 U.S. 117 (2014).

JUSTICE GINSBURG delivered the opinion of the Court.

This case concerns the authority of a court in the United States to entertain a claim brought by foreign plaintiffs against a foreign defendant based on events occurring entirely outside the United States. The litigation commenced in 2004, when twenty-two Argentinian residents filed a complaint in the United States District Court for the Northern District of California against DaimlerChrysler Aktiengesellschaft (Daimler), a German public stock company, headquartered in Stuttgart, that manufactures Mercedes-Benz vehicles in Germany. The complaint alleged that during Argentina's 1976–1983 "Dirty War," Daimler's Argentinian subsidiary, Mercedes-Benz Argentina (MB Argentina) collaborated with state security forces to kidnap, detain, torture, and kill certain MB Argentina workers, among them, plaintiffs or persons closely related to plaintiffs. Damages for the alleged human-rights violations were sought from Daimler under the laws of the United States, California, and Argentina. Jurisdiction over the lawsuit was predicated on the California contacts of Mercedes-Benz USA, LLC (MBUSA), a subsidiary of Daimler incorporated in Delaware with its principal place of business in New Jersey. MBUSA distributes Daimler-manufactured vehicles to independent dealerships throughout the United States, including California.

The question presented is whether the Due Process Clause of the Fourteenth Amendment precludes the District Court from exercising jurisdiction over Daimler in this case, given the absence of any California connection to the atrocities, perpetrators, or victims described in the complaint. Plaintiffs invoked the court's general or all-purpose jurisdiction. California, they urge, is a place where Daimler may be sued on any and all claims against it, wherever in the world the claims may arise. . . Exercises of personal jurisdiction so exorbitant, we hold, are barred by due process constraints on the assertion of adjudicatory authority.

In *Goodyear Dunlop Tires Operations, S.A. v. Brown,* 564 U.S. 915 (2011), we addressed the distinction between general or all-purpose jurisdiction, and specific or conduct-linked jurisdiction. As to the former, we held that a court may assert jurisdiction over a foreign corporation "to hear any and all claims against [it]" only when the corporation's affiliations with the State in which suit is brought are so constant and pervasive "as to render [it] essentially at home in the forum State." Instructed by *Goodyear*, we conclude Daimler is not "at home" in California, and cannot be sued there for injuries plaintiffs attribute to MB Argentina's conduct in Argentina. . .

MBUSA, an indirect subsidiary of Daimler, is a Delaware limited liability corporation. MBUSA serves as Daimler's exclusive importer and distributor in the United States, purchasing Mercedes-Benz automobiles from Daimler in Germany, then importing those vehicles, and ultimately distributing them to independent dealerships located throughout the Nation. Although MBUSA's principal place of business is in New Jersey, MBUSA has multiple California-based facilities, including a regional office in Costa Mesa, a Vehicle Preparation Center in Carson, and a Classic Center in Irvine. According to the record developed below, MBUSA is the largest supplier of luxury vehicles to the California market. In particular, over 10% of all sales of new vehicles in the United States take place in California, and MBUSA's California sales account for 2.4% of Daimler's worldwide sales. . .

Federal courts ordinarily follow state law in determining the bounds of their jurisdiction over persons. See Fed. Rule Civ. Proc. 4(k)(1)(A) (service of process is effective to establish personal jurisdiction over a defendant "who is subject to the jurisdiction of a court of general jurisdiction in the state where the district court is located"). . . California's long-arm statute allows the exercise of personal jurisdiction to the full extent permissible under the U.S. Constitution. We therefore inquire whether the Ninth Circuit's holding comports with the limits imposed by federal due process. See, e.g., *Burger King Corp. v. Rudzewicz,* 471 U.S. 462, 464 (1985). . .

International Shoe's conception of "fair play and substantial justice" presaged the development of two categories of personal jurisdiction. The first category is represented by *International Shoe* itself, a case in which the in-state activities of the corporate defendant "ha[d] not only been continuous and systematic, but also g[a]ve rise to the liabilities sued on.". . . Adjudicatory authority of this order, in which the suit "aris[es] out of or relate[s] to the defendant's contacts with the forum," *Helicopteros Nacionales de Colombia, S.A. v. Hall,* 466 U.S. 408, 414, n. 8 (1984), is today called "specific jurisdiction."

International Shoe distinguished between, on the one hand, exercises of specific jurisdiction, as just described, and on the other, situations where a foreign corporation's "continuous corporate operations within a state [are] so substantial and of such a nature as to justify suit against it on causes of action arising from dealings entirely distinct from those activities." As we have since explained, "[a] court may assert general jurisdiction over foreign (sister-state or foreign-country) corporations to hear any and all claims against them when their affiliations with the State are so 'continuous and systematic' as to render them essentially at home in the forum State." * * *

Since *International Shoe,* "specific jurisdiction has become the centerpiece of modern jurisdiction theory, while general jurisdiction [has played] a reduced role." * * * *International Shoe*'s momentous departure from *Pennoyer*'s rigidly territorial focus, we have noted, unleashed a rapid expansion of tribunals' ability to hear claims against out-of-state defendants when the episode-in-suit occurred in the forum or the defendant purposefully availed itself of the forum. Our subsequent decisions have continued to bear out the prediction that "specific jurisdiction will come into sharper relief and form a considerably more significant part of the scene." * * *

Our post-*International Shoe* opinions on general jurisdiction, by comparison, are few. "[The Court's] 1952 decision in *Perkins v. Benguet Consol. Mining Co.* remains the textbook case of general jurisdiction appropriately exercised over a foreign corporation that has not consented to suit in the forum." *Goodyear,* 131 S. Ct., at 2856 * * *. The defendant in *Perkins,* Benguet, was a company incorporated under the laws of the Philippines, where it operated gold and silver mines. Benguet ceased its mining operations during the Japanese occupation of the Philippines in World War II; its president moved to Ohio, where he kept an office, maintained the company's files, and oversaw the company's activities. * * * The plaintiff, an Ohio resident, sued Benguet on a claim that neither arose in Ohio nor related to the corporation's activities in that State. We held that the Ohio courts could exercise general jurisdiction over Benguet without offending due process. That was so, we later noted, because "Ohio was the corporation's principal, if temporary, place of business." * * *

The next case on point, *Helicopteros,* 466 U.S. 408, arose from a helicopter crash in Peru. Four U.S. citizens perished in that accident; their survivors and representatives brought suit in Texas state court against the helicopter's owner and operator, a Colombian corporation. That company's contacts with Texas were confined to "sending its chief executive officer to Houston for a contract-negotiation session; accepting into its New York bank account checks drawn on a Houston bank; purchasing helicopters, equipment, and training services from [a Texas-based helicopter company] for substantial sums; and sending personnel to [Texas] for training." *Id.*, at 416. Notably, those contacts bore no apparent relationship to the accident that gave rise to the suit. We held that the company's Texas connections did not resemble the "continuous and systematic general business contacts . . . found to exist in *Perkins*." "[M]ere purchases, even if occurring at regular intervals," we clarified, "are not enough to warrant a State's assertion of in personam jurisdiction over a nonresident corporation in a cause of action not related to those purchase transactions." *Id.*, at 418.

Most recently, in *Goodyear*, we answered the question: "Are foreign subsidiaries of a United States parent corporation amenable to suit in state court on claims unrelated to any activity of the subsidiaries in the forum State?" 131 S. Ct., at 2850. That case arose from a bus accident outside Paris that killed two boys from North Carolina. The boys' parents brought a wrongful-death suit in North Carolina state court alleging that the bus's tire was defectively manufactured. The complaint named as defendants not only The Goodyear Tire and Rubber Company (Goodyear), an Ohio corporation, but also Goodyear's Turkish, French, and Luxembourgian subsidiaries. Those foreign subsidiaries, which manufactured tires for sale in Europe and Asia, lacked any affiliation with North Carolina. A small percentage of tires manufactured by the foreign subsidiaries were distributed in North Carolina, however, and on that ground, the North Carolina Court of Appeals held the subsidiaries amenable to the general jurisdiction of North Carolina courts.

We reversed, observing that the North Carolina court's analysis "elided the essential difference between case-specific and all-purpose (general) jurisdiction." 131 S. Ct., at 2855. Although the placement of a product into the stream of commerce "may bolster an affiliation germane to specific jurisdiction," we explained, such contacts "do not warrant a determination that, based on those ties, the forum has general jurisdiction over a defendant." *Id.*, at 2857. As *International Shoe* itself teaches, a corporation's "continuous activity of some sorts within a state is not enough to support the demand that the corporation be amenable to suits unrelated to that activity." 326 U.S., at 318. Because Goodyear's foreign subsidiaries were "in no sense at home in North Carolina," we held, those subsidiaries could not be required to submit to the general jurisdiction of that State's courts. 131 S. Ct., at 2857. See also *J. McIntyre Machinery, Ltd. v. Nicastro,* 131 S.Ct. 2780, 2797–2798 (2011) (Ginsburg, J., dissenting) (noting unanimous agreement that a foreign manufacturer, which engaged an independent U.S.-based distributor to sell its machines throughout the United States, could not be exposed to all-purpose jurisdiction in New Jersey courts based on those contacts).

As is evident from *Perkins, Helicopteros,* and *Goodyear,* general and specific jurisdiction have followed markedly different trajectories post-*International Shoe.* Specific jurisdiction has been cut loose from *Pennoyer's* sway, but we have declined to stretch general jurisdiction beyond limits traditionally recognized. As this Court has increasingly trained on the "relationship among the defendant, the forum, and the litigation," *Shaffer,* 433 U.S., at 204, i.e., specific jurisdiction, general jurisdiction has come to occupy a less dominant place in the contemporary scheme.

With this background, we turn directly to the question whether Daimler's affiliations with California are sufficient to subject it to the general (all-purpose) personal jurisdiction of that State's courts. . .

In sustaining the exercise of general jurisdiction over Daimler, the Ninth Circuit relied on an agency theory, determining that MBUSA acted as Daimler's agent for jurisdictional purposes and then attributing MBUSA's California contacts to Daimler. . .

Even if we were to assume that MBUSA is at home in California, and further to assume MBUSA's contacts are imputable to Daimler, there would still be no basis to subject Daimler to general jurisdiction in California, for Daimler's slim contacts with the State hardly render it at home there.

Goodyear made clear that only a limited set of affiliations with a forum will render a defendant amenable to all-purpose jurisdiction there. "For an individual, the paradigm forum for the exercise of general jurisdiction is the individual's domicile; for a corporation, it is an equivalent place, one in which the corporation is fairly regarded as at home." * * * With respect to a corporation, the place of incorporation and principal place of business are "paradig[m] . . . bases for general jurisdiction." * * * Those affiliations have the virtue of being unique—that is, each ordinarily indicates only one place—as well as easily ascertainable. * * * These bases afford plaintiffs recourse to at least one clear and certain forum in which a corporate defendant may be sued on any and all claims.

Goodyear did not hold that a corporation may be subject to general jurisdiction only in a forum where it is incorporated or has its principal place of business; it simply typed those places paradigm all-purpose forums. Plaintiffs would have us look beyond the exemplar bases *Goodyear* identified, and approve the exercise of general jurisdiction in every State in which a corporation "engages in a substantial, continuous, and systematic course of business." That formulation, we hold, is unacceptably grasping.

As noted, the words "continuous and systematic" were used in *International Shoe* to describe instances in which the exercise of specific jurisdiction would be appropriate. * * * Turning to all-purpose jurisdiction, in contrast, *International Shoe* speaks of "instances in which the continuous corporate operations within a state [are] so substantial and of such a nature as to justify suit . . . on causes of action arising from dealings entirely distinct from those activities." *Id.*, at 318 (emphasis added). Accordingly, the inquiry under *Goodyear* is not whether a foreign corporation's in-forum contacts can be said to be in some sense "continuous and systematic," it is whether that corporation's "affiliations with the State are so 'continuous and systematic' as to render [it] essentially at home in the forum State." 131 S. Ct., at 2851.[19]

Here, neither Daimler nor MBUSA is incorporated in California, nor does either entity have its principal place of business there. If Daimler's California activities sufficed to allow adjudication of this Argentina-rooted case in California, the same global reach would presumably be available in every other State in which MBUSA's sales are sizable. Such exorbitant exercises of all-purpose jurisdiction would scarcely permit out-of-state defendants "to structure their primary conduct with some minimum assurance as to where that conduct will and will not render them liable to suit." *Burger King,* 471 U.S., at 472.

It was therefore error for the Ninth Circuit to conclude that Daimler, even with MBUSA's contacts attributed to it, was at home in California, and hence subject to suit there on claims by foreign plaintiffs having nothing to do with anything that occurred or had its principal impact in California.[20]

---

[19] We do not foreclose the possibility that in an exceptional case, * * * a corporation's operations in a forum other than its formal place of incorporation or principal place of business may be so substantial and of such a nature as to render the corporation at home in that State. But this case presents no occasion to explore that question, because Daimler's activities in California plainly do not approach that level. It is one thing to hold a corporation answerable for operations in the forum State, quite another to expose it to suit on claims having no connection whatever to the forum State.

[20] To clarify in light of JUSTICE SOTOMAYOR's opinion concurring in the judgment, the general jurisdiction inquiry does not "focu[s] solely on the magnitude of the defendant's in-state contacts." General jurisdiction instead calls for an appraisal of a corporation's activities in their entirety, nationwide and worldwide. A corporation that operates in many places can scarcely be deemed at home in all of them. Otherwise, "at home" would be synonymous with "doing business" tests framed before specific jurisdiction evolved in the United States. * * * Nothing in *International Shoe* and its progeny suggests that "a particular quantum of local activity" should give a State authority over a "far larger quantum of . . . activity" having no connection to any in-state activity. . .

Finally, the transnational context of this dispute bears attention. The Court of Appeals emphasized, as supportive of the exercise of general jurisdiction, plaintiffs' assertion of claims under the Alien Tort Statute (ATS) and the Torture Victim Protection Act of 1991 (TVPA). Recent decisions of this Court, however, have rendered plaintiffs' ATS and TVPA claims infirm. See *Kiobel v. Royal Dutch Petroleum Co.,* 133 S. Ct. 1659, 1669 (2013) (presumption against extraterritorial application controls claims under the ATS); *Mohamad v. Palestinian Authority,* 132 S. Ct. 1702, 1705 (2012) (only natural persons are subject to liability under the TVPA).

The Ninth Circuit, moreover, paid little heed to the risks to international comity its expansive view of general jurisdiction posed. Other nations do not share the uninhibited approach to personal jurisdiction advanced by the Court of Appeals in this case. In the European Union, for example, a corporation may generally be sued in the nation in which it is "domiciled," a term defined to refer only to the location of the corporation's "statutory seat," "central administration," or "principal place of business." European Parliament and Council Reg. 1215/2012, Arts. 4(1), and 63(1), 2012 O.J. (L. 351) 7, 18. * * * The Solicitor General informs us, in this regard, that "foreign governments' objections to some domestic courts' expansive views of general jurisdiction have in the past impeded negotiations of international agreements on the reciprocal recognition and enforcement of judgments." * * * Considerations of international rapport thus reinforce our determination that subjecting Daimler to the general jurisdiction of courts in California would not accord with the "fair play and substantial justice" due process demands. *International Shoe,* 326 U.S., at 316. * * *

JUSTICE SOTOMAYOR, concurring in the judgment.

I agree with the Court's conclusion that the Due Process Clause prohibits the exercise of personal jurisdiction over Daimler in light of the unique circumstances of this case. I concur only in the judgment, however, because I cannot agree with the path the Court takes to arrive at that result.

. . . In recent years, Americans have grown accustomed to the concept of multinational corporations that are supposedly "too big to fail"; today the Court deems Daimler "too big for general jurisdiction."

. . . [T]he Court's focus on Daimler's operations outside of California ignores the lodestar of our personal jurisdiction jurisprudence: A State may subject a defendant to the burden of suit if the defendant has sufficiently taken advantage of the State's laws and protections through its contacts in the State; whether the defendant has contacts elsewhere is immaterial. . .

Until today, our precedents had established a straightforward test for general jurisdiction: Does the defendant have "continuous corporate operations within a state" that are "so substantial and of such a nature as to justify suit against it on causes of action arising from dealings entirely distinct from those activities"? *International Shoe Co. v. Washington,* 326 U.S. 310, 318 (1945) * * *. In every case where we have applied this test, we have focused solely on the magnitude of the defendant's in-state contacts, not the relative magnitude of those contacts in comparison to the defendant's contacts with other States. . .

This approach follows from the touchstone principle of due process in this field, the concept of reciprocal fairness. When a corporation chooses to invoke the benefits and protections of a State in which it operates, the State acquires the authority to subject the company to suit in its courts. See *International Shoe,* 326 U.S., at 319 ("[T]o the extent that a corporation exercises the privilege of conducting activities within a state, it enjoys the benefits and protection of the laws of that state" such that an "obligatio[n] arise[s]" to respond there to suit); *J. McIntyre Machinery, Ltd. v. Nicastro,* 131 S. Ct. 2780, 2796–2797 (2011) (plurality opinion) (same principle for general jurisdiction). The majority's focus on the extent of a corporate defendant's out-of-forum contacts is untethered from this rationale. After all, the degree to which a company intentionally benefits from a forum State depends on its interactions with that State, not its interactions elsewhere.

. . . Had the majority applied our settled approach, it would have had little trouble concluding that Daimler's California contacts rise to the requisite level, given the majority's assumption that MBUSA's contacts may be attributed to Daimler and given Daimler's concession that those contacts render MBUSA "at home" in California. Our cases have long stated the rule that a defendant's contacts with a forum State must be continuous, substantial, and systematic in order for the defendant to be subject to that State's general jurisdiction. * * * We offered additional guidance in *Goodyear*, adding the phrase "essentially at home" to our prior formulation of the rule. * * *

Under this standard, Daimler's concession that MBUSA is subject to general jurisdiction in California (a concession the Court accepts) should be dispositive. For if MBUSA's California contacts are so substantial and the resulting benefits to MBUSA so significant as to make MBUSA "at home" in California, the same must be true of Daimler when MBUSA's contacts and benefits are viewed as its own. . .

The majority characterizes this result as "exorbitant," but in reality it is an inevitable consequence of the rule of due process we set forth nearly 70 years ago, that there are "instances in which [a company's] continuous corporate operations within a state" are "so substantial and of such a nature as to justify suit against it on causes of action arising from dealings entirely distinct from those activities," *International Shoe,* 326 U.S., at 318. In the era of *International Shoe,* it was rare for a corporation to have such substantial nationwide contacts that it would be subject to general jurisdiction in a large number of States. Today, that circumstance is less rare. But that is as it should be. What has changed since *International Shoe* is not the due process principle of fundamental fairness but rather the nature of the global economy. Just as it was fair to say in the 1940's that an out-of-state company could enjoy the benefits of a forum State enough to make it "essentially at home" in the State, it is fair to say today that a multinational conglomerate can enjoy such extensive benefits in multiple forum States that it is "essentially at home" in each one.

In any event, to the extent the majority is concerned with the modern-day consequences of *International Shoe*'s conception of personal jurisdiction, there remain other judicial doctrines available to mitigate any resulting unfairness to large corporate defendants. Here, for instance, the reasonableness prong may afford petitioner relief. In other cases, a defendant can assert the doctrine of forum non conveniens if a given State is a highly inconvenient place to litigate a dispute. * * * In still other cases, the federal change of venue statute can provide protection. See 28 U.S.C. § 1404(a) (permitting transfers to other districts "[f]or the convenience of parties and witnesses" and "in the interests of justice"). And to the degree that the majority worries these doctrines are not enough to protect the economic interests of multinational businesses (or that our longstanding approach to general jurisdiction poses "risks to international comity"), the task of weighing those policy concerns belongs ultimately to legislators, who may amend state and federal long-arm statutes in accordance with the democratic process. Unfortunately, the majority short circuits that process by enshrining today's narrow rule of general jurisdiction as a matter of constitutional law. . .

Jurisdiction over "Unrelated" Causes of Action

(1) The terms "general" and "specific" jurisdiction were first coined by Professors von Mehren and Trautman in their influential article, *Jurisdiction to Adjudicate: A Suggested Analysis,* 79 Harv.L.Rev. 1121 (1966). Attempting to make sense of the decisions after *International Shoe,* they suggested that courts distinguish between two broad categories of adjudicatory jurisdiction: "specific" jurisdiction, or jurisdiction to adjudicate a particular controversy because of connections between that controversy and the forum; and "general" jurisdiction, or jurisdiction to adjudicate any controversy involving a particular defendant because of connections between that defendant and the forum.

Under *Pennoyer,* all adjudicatory jurisdiction was general in that the power of the court depended entirely on the presence of the defendant or the defendant's property in the state and was not affected by the character of the suit: if the defendant was served or had property attached in the state, its courts could adjudicate any claim against that defendant. *International Shoe* appeared to change all that, shifting the focus from presence at the time of service to fairness in light of the relationship between the claim and the defendant's forum contacts. But the opinion in *International Shoe* recognized that courts could sometimes exercise jurisdiction on a claim unrelated to the defendant's forum contacts: "There have been instances in which the continuous corporate operations within a state were thought so substantial and of such a nature as to justify suit against it on causes of action arising from dealings entirely distinct from those activities." 326 U.S. at 318. Because jurisdiction in *International Shoe* was based directly on the defendant's forum activities, however, the Court did not elaborate, leaving the scope of general jurisdiction to future cases.

(2) As noted in *Daimler*, the Supreme Court first addressed the question of jurisdiction over a cause of action unrelated to the defendant's forum contacts in *Perkins v. Benguet Consol. Mining Co.,* 342 U.S. 437 (1952). Perkins, a nonresident of Ohio, brought suit in Ohio to recover unpaid dividends and damages caused by the company's failure to issue her stock certificates. Although Benguet was located in the Philippines, the Japanese occupation and disruption of the immediate post-war years forced the company to move its operations to Ohio. Because Perkins's claims did not relate to any activities of the corporation in Ohio, the state court found that due process prohibited it from exercising jurisdiction. The Supreme Court reversed. "The essence of the issue . . . at the constitutional level," the Court explained, "is one of general fairness to the corporation." Following the "realistic reasoning" of *International Shoe,* the Court upheld jurisdiction:

> During [the Japanese occupation] the president, who was also the general manager and principal stockholder of the company, returned to his home in Clermont County, Ohio. There he maintained an office in which he conducted his personal affairs and did many things on behalf of the company. He kept there office files of the company. He carried on there correspondence relating to the business of the company and to its employees. He drew and distributed there salary checks on behalf of the company, both in his own favor as president and in favor of two company secretaries who worked there with him. He used and maintained in Clermont County, Ohio, two active bank accounts carrying substantial balances of company funds. A bank in Hamilton County, Ohio, acted as transfer agent for the stock of the company. Several directors' meetings were held at his office or home in Clermont County. From that office he supervised policies dealing with the rehabilitation of the corporation's properties in

> the Philippines and he dispatched funds to cover purchases of machinery for such rehabilitation. Thus he carried on in Ohio a continuous and systematic supervision of the necessarily limited wartime activities of the company. He there discharged his duties as president and general manager, both during the occupation of the company's properties by the Japanese and immediately thereafter. While no mining properties in Ohio were owned or operated by the company, many of its wartime activities were directed from Ohio and were being given the personal attention of its president in that State at the time he was served with summons.

In *Helicopteros Nacionales de Colombia, S.A. v. Hall,* 466 U.S. 408 (1984), the Court rejected an attempt by Texas to exercise general jurisdiction over a Colombian corporation that purchased helicopters from Texas and trained its personnel there.

Do *Goodyear* and *Daimler* break any new ground relative to these cases? Are they unduly formalistic in suggesting that a defendant must be "at home" in a state to be subject to the general jurisdiction of its courts? Or is the concept of general (as opposed to specific) jurisdiction inherently formalistic? How much influence do you think the Court's practical concerns about international comity had on the result in *Daimler*?

(3) Why should a state ever be able to make a defendant litigate an issue as to which the state has no interest or connection? How do the nature or pervasiveness of a defendant's contacts with a state give the forum an appropriate interest in exercising adjudicatory jurisdiction? Is general jurisdiction analogous to assertions of interest based on residence or domicile in choice of law? If a defendant has sufficient contacts with a forum state to create general jurisdiction, does that give the state an interest in applying its own law? Conversely, should an interest in applying its law or providing a forum for its domiciliaries count in favor of allowing a state to exercise general jurisdiction? Would *Allstate v. Hague* allow *Goodyear* to be decided under North Carolina law?

(4) Academic commentators have sought to explain general jurisdiction. Echoing an argument made earlier by von Mehren and Trautman, Professor Twitchell suggests that general jurisdiction is justified to ensure that there is always at least one forum in which a plaintiff can sue. Twitchell, *The Myth of General Jurisdiction,* 101 Harv.L.Rev. 610, 665–66 (1988). Twitchell offers a number of reasons why we cannot rely on specific jurisdiction alone to serve this purpose, including that this would require courts to engage in complex specific jurisdiction analysis in every case, and that the recognition of general jurisdiction in international law would create complex problems concerning recognition of judgments.

Professor Richman, in contrast, interprets general jurisdiction as simply a manifestation of the *International Shoe* test of fairness: just as a few, strongly related contacts may make it fair to exercise jurisdiction, so, too, may a sufficiently large quantum of unrelated contacts. Richman, *Review Essay (Part II, A Sliding Scale to Supplement the Distinction Between General and Specific Jurisdiction),* 72 Cal.L.Rev. 1328 (1984). According to Richman:

> To encompass all the proper cases, the general/specific jurisdiction dichotomy must be supplemented by a *sliding scale* model of the relationship between the two key variables: the extent of the defendant's forum contacts on the one hand and the proximity of the connection between those contacts and the plaintiff's claim on the other. As the quantity and quality of the defendant's forum contacts increase, a weaker connection between the plaintiff's claim and those contacts is permissible; as the quantity and quality of the defendant's forum contacts decrease, a stronger connection between the plaintiff's claim and those contacts is required. The concepts of general jurisdiction and specific jurisdiction are simply the two opposite ends of this sliding scale.

Id. at 1345. Richman discusses *Helicopteros* as a case which satisfies neither the specific nor the general jurisdiction paradigm, but in which jurisdiction should be upheld because it is a "near-miss" on both. But why should unrelated contacts count at all? And if they do count, why do they count less than related contacts?

Beginning with these questions, Professor Brilmayer argues that the distinction between specific and general jurisdiction must be understood in terms of sovereignty. Brilmayer, *How Contacts Count: Due Process Limitations on State Court Jurisdiction,* 1980 Sup. Ct. Rev. 77. Specific jurisdiction, Brilmayer reasons, reflects the power of a state to govern what occurs or has effects within its territory. General jurisdiction, in contrast, reflects the power of a state to exercise authority over members of its political community. She explains:

> The two bases of jurisdiction [general and specific] therefore constitute alternative aspects of a State's sovereignty, namely, self-government and territoriality. Systematic unrelated activity, such as domicile, incorporation, or doing business, suggests that the person or corporate entity is enough of an "insider" that he may safely be relegated to the State's political processes. Related contacts suggest a regulatory and territorial justification. . . These two bases are independent threshold tests, so that a greater quantum of unrelated activity does not compensate for attenuated related contacts.

Id. at 87–88.

Which of these explanations is most persuasive? Which is most consistent with the cases?

(5) The kinds of contacts that suffice to justify an exercise of general jurisdiction obviously change with the underlying justification for the power. For example, because Professor Twitchell believes that general jurisdiction is desirable to assure plaintiffs access to one definite forum, she would confine it to a defendant's "home base." Professor Brilmayer, in contrast, would allow the exercise of general jurisdiction whenever the defendant's systematic contacts with the forum give it sufficient access to the state's political process to justify treatment as an "insider." Professor Richman, of course, would leave such questions to case-by-case analysis. What should the test for general jurisdiction be?

(a) *Natural persons.* Should a person's domicile have general jurisdiction over him or her? In *Milliken v. Meyer,* 311 U.S. 457, 462–63 (1940), the Court held that domicile was enough to bring an absent defendant within the state's jurisdiction, noting: "The state which accords him privileges and affords protection to him and his property by virtue of his domicile may also exact reciprocal duties." But why exactly is this duty reciprocal? What if the domicile is only technical and the person resides elsewhere? See Restatement (Second) of Conflict of Laws § 29, Reporter's Note at 124 (even technical domicile is adequate for jurisdiction). Would it be better to focus on residence instead of domicile? What if the defendant has more than one residence? Should a seasonal home suffice? See von Mehren & Trautman, 79 Harv.L.Rev. at 1178–79 ("For an individual, the sole community where it is fair to require him to litigate any cause of action is his habitual residence").

What about states other than those in which a person is domiciled or resides? Can a state, for example, assert general jurisdiction over someone who transacts a lot of business in the state? In *ABKCO Indus., Inc. v. Lennon,* 85 Misc.2d 465, 377 N.Y.S.2d 362 (1975), a former manager of the Beatles sued members of the group for breach of contract. Jurisdiction over Richard Starkey (aka Ringo Starr) was based on his extensive recording and composing activities in the state even though these activities were unrelated to ABKCO's claim. Is this proper? Doesn't your answer depend on the underlying theory of general jurisdiction?

(b) *Corporations.* Should a corporation always be suable in its state of incorporation? Or is corporate headquarters the relevant place? According to Professor Twitchell:

> Because a corporation's headquarters is the functional equivalent of an individual defendant's domicile, home base jurisdiction should be available wherever the corporation is headquartered. Jurisdiction at the place of incorporation, at first glance, seems less justifiable. . . However, because identifying a corporation's

> headquarters has proven difficult in other contexts, courts wishing to provide a uniform home base where the plaintiff is assured of a trial without the expense of threshold jurisdiction litigation should retain the place of incorporation as an alternative basis for general jurisdiction.

101 Harv.L.Rev. at 669–70. Is this analysis consistent with the cases? Why isn't the appropriate forum for general jurisdiction the corporation's principal place of business? Once again, doesn't your answer depend on the underlying theory of general jurisdiction?

Determining jurisdiction in cases involving related corporations has proven particularly troubling. Note that the Supreme Court dodged this issue in *Daimler*, holding that Daimler was not subject to general jurisdiction in California even if MBUSA's activities were attributed to it. In *Delagi v. Volkswagenwerk AG,* 29 N.Y.2d 426, 328 N.Y.S.2d 653, 278 N.E.2d 895 (1972), a New Yorker who was injured in Germany in a car made and bought in Germany sued the manufacturer in New York. The plaintiff argued that the defendant was "engaged in a systematic and regular course of business" in New York through its wholly owned subsidiary, Volkswagen of America, Inc., a New Jersey corporation and the exclusive American importer of Volkswagen automobiles. The Court disagreed: neither the German parent nor its American subsidiary was qualified to do business in New York or had an office or place of business there; all Volkswagens distributed in New York were actually sold through independent and separately-owned wholesale distributors who took title at the water's edge.

Compare this result with the same court's earlier decision in *Frummer v. Hilton Hotels Int'l, Inc.,* 19 N.Y.2d 533, 281 N.Y.S.2d 41, 227 N.E.2d 851 (1967). A New York tourist who fell and injured himself while taking a shower in the London Hilton sued the hotel (an English corporation) in New York. Jurisdiction was upheld on the basis of the activities of the Hilton Reservations Service, a separate corporation. Although the two corporations were separate, their interlocking ownership and the London corporation's reliance on business generated from New York persuaded the court that an agency relationship existed, thus justifying jurisdiction.

(c) *Internet activity.* What about defendants whose activity is conducted primarily over the Internet? A defendant that maintains a store in a state and sells goods to state residents will at some point create sufficiently "continuous and systematic" contacts to support general jurisdiction. What if the store is a "virtual" store—i.e., a website on which state residents make purchases? What volume of business should be required to support general jurisdiction in such a case? See *Gator.com Corp. v. L.L. Bean, Inc.*, 341 F.3d 1072 (9th Cir. 2003) (finding that California may exercise general jurisdiction over L.L. Bean), reh'g granted,

366 F.3d 789 (9th Cir. 2004), reh'g dismissed as moot due to settlement, 398 F.3d 1125 (9th Cir. 2005).

The operator of a "virtual store" is at least shipping goods into a state. But the nature of the defendant's business might be such that it involves much less in the way of actual physical interaction. An online brokerage, for instance, can execute customers' trades and provide account information and required disclosures without sending them any physical objects at all. In *Gorman v. Ameritrade Holding Corp.*, 293 F.3d 506 (D.C. Cir. 2002), the D.C. Circuit found that Ameritrade's provision of such services to D.C. residents sufficed to subject it to general jurisdiction in D.C. (Ameritrade protested in vain that its activities took place "in the borderless environment of cyberspace.") Is this a good idea? In *Why General Personal Jurisdiction over "Virtual Stores" is a Bad Idea,* 27 Quinnipiac L. Rev. 625 (2009), James Pielemeier argues it is not. Does *Gorman* survive *Daimler*?

(6) Whatever test one employs, the ability to distinguish between general and specific jurisdiction turns on whether a forum's contacts are "related" to the cause of action or not. What is the test for this relation? Professor Brilmayer argued that specific jurisdiction should be based on contacts that were relevant under the substantive law. 1980 Sup.Ct.Rev. at 82. In other words, the contact must be something that could be alleged as part of a well-pleaded complaint: that a defendant does business in the state would "count" in this sense only if something about this business was essential to the plaintiff's substantive cause of action. While a few courts have adopted this approach, see, e.g., *State ex rel. La Manufacture Francaise Des Pneumatiques Michelin v. Wells,* 294 Or. 296, 657 P.2d 207 (1982), other courts reject legal relevance in favor of a looser approach. Thus, a number of courts have held that if the legal violation occurred "in the wake of" or was "made possible by" local acts, these acts are "related" for purposes of specific jurisdiction. See, e.g., *Lanier v. American Bd. of Endodontics,* 843 F.2d 901 (6th Cir. 1988); *In re Oil Spill by Amoco Cadiz,* 699 F.2d 909 (7th Cir. 1983). See also *In-Flight Devices Corp. v. Van Dusen Air, Inc.,* 466 F.2d 220 (6th Cir. 1972) (defendant's local conduct was "necessarily the very soil from which the action for breach grew"). Does *Goodyear* clarify the issue?

Professors Twitchell and Brilmayer debate this issue in Brilmayer, *Related Contacts and Personal Jurisdiction,* 101 Harv.L.Rev. 1444 (1988), and Twitchell, *A Rejoinder to Professor Brilmayer,* 101 Harv.L.Rev. 1465 (1988).

(7) The Court applied *Daimler* in *BNSF Railway Co. v. Tyrrell,* 137 S.Ct. 1549 (2017). A North Dakota resident and the administrator of a South Dakota decedent's estate sued a railroad in Montana state court under the Federal Employers' Liability Act (FELA), 45 U.S.C. § 51 *et seq.*, which makes railroads liable for on-the-job injuries. Neither employee was injured in Montana. The Court held, first, that § 56 of FELA, which authorizes actions concurrently in federal and state courts "in the district . . . in which the defendant shall be doing business at the time of commencing such action," addresses venue and subject-matter jurisdiction, not personal jurisdiction. It then held that a Montana rule of civil procedure providing for personal jurisdiction over "persons found" in the state was unconstitutional insofar as it purported to authorize general jurisdiction over the railroad, which was not incorporated in Montana, did not have its principal place of business there, and was not so heavily engaged in activity in Montana "as to render it essentially at home in that State." 137 S.Ct. at 1559 (internal quotation marks omitted). Once again, Justice Sotomayor dissented for herself alone.

Have *Goodyear*, *Daimler*, and *BNSF* whittled the acceptable exercise of general jurisdiction over corporations down to the precise facts of *Perkins v. Benguet Consol. Mining Co.*?

SECTION 3. ATTACHMENT JURISDICTION

SHAFFER V. HEITNER

433 U.S. 186 (1977).

MR. JUSTICE MARSHALL delivered the opinion of the Court.

The controversy in this case concerns the constitutionality of a Delaware statute that allows a court of that State to take jurisdiction of a lawsuit by sequestering any property of the defendant that happens to be located in Delaware. Appellants contend that the sequestration statute as applied in this case violates the Due Process Clause of the Fourteenth Amendment both because it permits the state courts to exercise jurisdiction despite the absence of sufficient contacts among the defendants, the litigation, and the State of Delaware and because it authorizes the deprivation of defendants' property without providing adequate procedural safeguards. We find it necessary to consider only the first of these contentions.

I

Appellee Heitner, a nonresident of Delaware, is the owner of one share of stock in the Greyhound Corp., a business incorporated under the laws of Delaware with its principal place of business in Phoenix, Ariz. On May 22, 1974 he filed a shareholder's derivative suit in the Court of Chancery for New Castle County, Del., in which he named as defendants Greyhound . . . and 28 present or former officers or directors of [Greyhound]. In essence, Heitner alleged that the individual defendants had violated their duties to Greyhound by causing it . . . to engage in actions that resulted in the corporation's being held liable for substantial damages in a private antitrust suit and a large fine in a criminal contempt action. The activities which led to these penalties took place in Oregon.

Simultaneously with his complaint, Heitner filed a motion for an order of sequestration of the Delaware property of the individual defendants pursuant to Del.Code Ann., Tit. 10, § 366 (1975).[4] This motion was accompanied by a supporting affidavit of counsel which stated that the individual defendants were nonresidents of Delaware. . . The requested sequestration order was signed the day the motion was filed. Pursuant to that order, the sequestrator "seized" approximately 82,000 shares of Greyhound common stock belonging to 19 of the defendants [of a then market value of about $1.2 million], and options belonging to another 2 defendants. These seizures were accomplished by placing "stop transfer" orders or their equivalents on the books of the Greyhound Corp. So far as the record shows, none of the certificates representing the seized property was physically present in Delaware. The stock was considered to be in Delaware, and so subject to seizure, by virtue of Del.Code Ann., Tit. 8, § 169 (1975), which makes Delaware the situs of ownership of all stock in Delaware corporations.

All 28 defendants were notified of the initiation of the suit by certified mail directed to their last known addresses and by publication in a New Castle County newspaper. The 21 defendants whose property was seized (hereafter referred to as appellants) responded by entering a special appearance for the purpose of moving to quash service of process and to vacate the sequestration order. They contended that the *ex parte* sequestration procedure did not accord them due process of law and that the property seized was not capable of attachment in Delaware. In addition, appellants asserted that under the rule of *International Shoe Co. v. Washington,* 326 U.S. 310 (1945), they did not have sufficient contacts with Delaware to sustain the jurisdiction of that State's courts.

---

[4] Section 366 provides:

"(a) If it appears in any complaint filed in the Court of Chancery that the defendant or any one or more of the defendants is a nonresident of the State, the Court may make an order directing such nonresident defendant or defendants to appear by a day certain to be designated. . . . The Court may compel the appearance of the defendant by the seizure of all or any part of his property, which property may be sold under the order of the Court to pay the demand of the plaintiff, if the defendant does not appear, or otherwise defaults. Any defendant whose property shall have been so seized and who shall have entered a general appearance in the cause may, upon notice to the plaintiff, petition the Court for an order releasing such property or any part thereof from the seizure. . . . If such petition shall not be granted, or if no such petition shall be filed, such property shall remain subject to seizure and may be sold to satisfy any judgment entered in the cause. The Court may at any time release such property or any part thereof upon the giving of sufficient security. . . .

The Court of Chancery rejected these arguments [holding, *inter alia,*] that the statutory Delaware situs of the stock provided a sufficient basis for the exercise of *quasi in rem* jurisdiction by a Delaware court.

On appeal, the Delaware Supreme Court affirmed the judgment of the Court of Chancery. *Greyhound Corp. v. Heitner,* 361 A.2d 225 (1976). . .

Appellants' claim that the Delaware courts did not have jurisdiction to adjudicate this action received . . . cursory treatment. The court's analysis of the jurisdictional issue is contained in two paragraphs:

> "There are significant constitutional questions at issue here but we say at once that we do not deem the rule of *International Shoe* to be one of them. . . The reason, of course, is that jurisdiction under § 366 remains . . . *quasi in rem* founded on the presence of capital stock here, not on prior contact by defendants with this forum. Under 8 Del.C. § 169 the 'situs of the ownership of the capital stock of all corporations existing under the laws of this State [is] in this State,' and that provides the initial basis for jurisdiction. Delaware may constitutionally establish situs of such shares here, . . . it has done so and the presence thereof provides the foundation for § 366 in this case. . .
>
> "We hold that seizure of the Greyhound shares is not invalid because plaintiff has failed to meet the prior contacts tests of *International Shoe.*" 361 A.2d, at 229.

We noted probable jurisdiction. 429 U.S. 813.[12] We reverse.

II

The Delaware courts rejected appellants' jurisdictional challenge by noting that this suit was brought as a *quasi in rem* proceeding. Since *quasi in rem* jurisdiction is traditionally based on attachment or seizure of property present in the jurisdiction, not on contacts between the defendant and the State, the courts considered appellants' claimed lack of contacts with Delaware to be unimportant. This categorical analysis assumes the continued soundness of the conceptual structure founded on the century-old case of *Pennoyer v. Neff,* 95 U.S. 714 (1878). . .

From our perspective, the importance of *Pennoyer* is not its result, but the fact that its principles and corollaries derived from them became the basic elements of the constitutional doctrine governing state-court jurisdiction. See, e.g., Hazard, A General Theory of State-Court Jurisdiction, 1965 Sup.Ct.Rev. 241 (hereafter Hazard). As we have noted,

[12] Under Delaware law, defendants whose property has been sequestered must enter a general appearance, thus subjecting themselves to *in personam* liability, before they can defend on the merits. See *Greyhound Corp. v. Heitner,* 361 A.2d 225, 235–236 (1976). Thus, if the judgment below were considered not to be an appealable final judgment, 28 U.S.C. § 1257(2), appellants would have the choice of suffering a default judgment or entering a general appearance and defending on the merits. . . .

under *Pennoyer* state authority to adjudicate was based on the jurisdiction's power over either persons or property. This fundamental concept is embodied in the very vocabulary which we use to describe judgments. If a court's jurisdiction is based on its authority over the defendant's person, the action and judgment are denominated "*in personam*" and can impose a personal obligation on the defendant in favor of the plaintiff. If jurisdiction is based on the court's power over property within its territory, the action is called "*in rem*" or "*quasi in rem.*" The effect of a judgment in such a case is limited to the property that supports jurisdiction and does not impose a personal liability on the property owner, since he is not before the court.[17] In *Pennoyer's* terms, the owner is affected only "indirectly" by an *in rem* judgment adverse to his interest in the property subject to the court's disposition. . .

The *Pennoyer* rules generally favored nonresident defendants by making them harder to sue. This advantage was reduced, however, by the ability of a resident plaintiff to satisfy a claim against a nonresident defendant by bringing into court any property of the defendant located in the plaintiff's State. * * *

[The Court then discussed the evolution of due process limits on state court jurisdiction through *International Shoe.*] Thus, the relationship among the defendant, the forum, and the litigation, rather than the mutually exclusive sovereignty of the States on which the rules of *Pennoyer* rest, became the central concern of the inquiry into personal jurisdiction. The immediate effect of this departure from *Pennoyer's* conceptual apparatus was to increase the ability of the state courts to obtain personal jurisdiction over nonresident defendants. * * *

No equally dramatic change has occurred in the law governing jurisdiction *in rem.* There have, however, been intimations that the collapse of the *in personam* wing of *Pennoyer* has not left that decision unweakened as a foundation for *in rem* jurisdiction. Well-reasoned lower court opinions have questioned the proposition that the presence of property in a State gives that State jurisdiction to adjudicate rights to the property regardless of the relationship of the underlying dispute and the property owner to the forum. * * * The overwhelming majority of commentators have also rejected *Pennoyer's* premise that a proceeding "against" property is not a proceeding against the owners of that property.

---

17 "A judgment *in rem* affects the interests of all persons in designated property. A judgment *quasi in rem* affects the interests of particular persons in designated property. The latter is of two types. In one the plaintiff is seeking to secure a pre-existing claim in the subject property and to extinguish or establish the nonexistence of similar interests of particular persons. In the other the plaintiff seeks to apply what he concedes to be the property of the defendant to the satisfaction of a claim against him. Restatement, Judgments, 5–9." *Hanson v. Denckla,* 357 U.S. 235, 246 n. 12 (1958).

As did the Court in *Hanson,* we will for convenience generally use the term "*in rem*" in place of "*in rem* and *quasi in rem.*"

Accordingly, they urge that the "traditional notions of fair play and substantial justice" that govern a State's power to adjudicate *in personam* should also govern its power to adjudicate personal rights to property located in the State. * * *

Although this Court has not addressed this argument directly, we have held that property cannot be subjected to a court's judgment unless reasonable and appropriate efforts have been made to give the property owners actual notice of the action. * * * *Mullane v. Central Hanover Bank & Trust Co.,* 339 U.S. 306 (1950). This conclusion recognizes, contrary to *Pennoyer,* that an adverse judgment *in rem* directly affects the property owner by divesting him of his rights in the property before the court. * * * Moreover, in *Mullane* we held that Fourteenth Amendment rights cannot depend on the classification of an action as *in rem* or *in personam,* since that is

> "a classification for which the standards are so elusive and confused generally and which, being primarily for state courts to define, may and do vary from state to state." 339 U.S., at 312.

It is clear, therefore, that the law of state-court jurisdiction no longer stands securely on the foundation established in *Pennoyer.* We think that the time is ripe to consider whether the standard of fairness and substantial justice set forth in *International Shoe* should be held to govern actions *in rem* as well as *in personam.*

III

The case for applying to jurisdiction *in rem* the same test of "fair play and substantial justice" as governs assertions of jurisdiction *in personam* is simple and straightforward. It is premised on recognition that "[t]he phrase, 'judicial jurisdiction over a thing,' is a customary elliptical way of referring to jurisdiction over the interests of persons in a thing." Restatement (Second) of Conflict of Laws § 56, Introductory Note (1971) (hereafter Restatement). This recognition leads to the conclusion that in order to justify an exercise of jurisdiction *in rem,* the basis for jurisdiction must be sufficient to justify exercising "jurisdiction over the interests of persons in a thing."[23] The standard for determining whether an exercise of jurisdiction over the interests of persons is consistent with the Due Process Clause is the minimum-contacts standard elucidated in *International Shoe.*

This argument, of course, does not ignore the fact that the presence of property in a State may bear on the existence of jurisdiction by providing contacts among the forum State, the defendant, and the litigation. For example, when claims to the property itself are the source of the underlying

[23] It is true that the potential liability of a defendant in an *in rem* action is limited by the value of the property, but that limitation does not affect the argument. The fairness of subjecting a defendant to state-court jurisdiction does not depend on the size of the claim being litigated. * * *

controversy between the plaintiff and the defendant,[24] it would be unusual for the State where the property is located not to have jurisdiction. In such cases, the defendant's claim to property located in the State would normally indicate that he expected to benefit from the State's protection of his interest. The State's strong interests in assuring the marketability of property within its borders and in providing a procedure for peaceful resolution of disputes about the possession of that property would also support jurisdiction, as would the likelihood that important records and witnesses will be found in the State. The presence of property may also favor jurisdiction in cases, such as suits for injury suffered on the land of an absentee owner, where the defendant's ownership of the property is conceded but the cause of action is otherwise related to rights and duties growing out of that ownership.

It appears, therefore, that jurisdiction over many types of actions which now are or might be brought *in rem* would not be affected by a holding that any assertion of state-court jurisdiction must satisfy the *International Shoe* standard. For the type of *quasi in rem* action typified by . . . the present case, however, accepting the proposed analysis would result in significant change. These are cases where the property which now serves as the basis for state-court jurisdiction is completely unrelated to the plaintiff's cause of action. Thus, although the presence of the defendant's property in a State might suggest the existence of other ties among the defendant, the State, and the litigation, the presence of the property alone would not support the State's jurisdiction. If those other ties did not exist, cases over which the State is now thought to have jurisdiction could not be brought in that forum.

Since acceptance of the *International Shoe* test would most affect this class of cases, we examine the arguments against adopting that standard as they relate to this category of litigation. Before doing so, however, we note that this type of case also presents the clearest illustration of the argument in favor of assessing assertions of jurisdiction by a single standard. For in cases such as . . . this one, the only role played by the property is to provide the basis for bringing the defendant into court. Indeed, the express purpose of the Delaware sequestration procedure is to compel the defendant to enter a personal appearance.[33] In such cases, if a direct assertion of personal jurisdiction over the defendant would violate the Constitution, it would seem that an indirect assertion of that jurisdiction should be equally impermissible.

The primary rationale for treating the presence of property as a sufficient basis for jurisdiction to adjudicate claims over which the State

[24] This category includes true *in rem* actions and the first type of *quasi in rem* proceedings.

[33] This purpose is emphasized by Delaware's refusal to allow any defense on the merits unless the defendant enters a general appearance, thus submitting to full *in personam* liability. . . .

would not have jurisdiction if *International Shoe* applied is that a wrongdoer

> "should not be able to avoid payment of his obligations by the expedient of removing his assets to a place where he is not subject to an in personam suit." Restatement § 66, Comment a.

This justification, however, does not explain why jurisdiction should be recognized without regard to whether the property is present in the State because of an effort to avoid the owner's obligations. Nor does it support jurisdiction to adjudicate the underlying claim. At most, it suggests that a State in which property is located should have jurisdiction to attach that property, by use of proper procedures, as security for a judgment being sought in a forum where the litigation can be maintained consistently with *International Shoe*. * * * Moreover, we know of nothing to justify the assumption that a debtor can avoid paying his obligations by removing his property to a State in which his creditor cannot obtain personal jurisdiction over him. The Full Faith and Credit Clause, after all, makes the valid *in personam* judgment of one State enforceable in all other States.[36]

It might also be suggested that allowing *in rem* jurisdiction avoids the uncertainty inherent in the *International Shoe* standard and assures a plaintiff of a forum.[37] * * * We believe, however, that the fairness standard of *International Shoe* can be easily applied in the vast majority of cases. Moreover, when the existence of jurisdiction in a particular forum under *International Shoe* is unclear, the cost of simplifying the litigation by avoiding the jurisdictional question may be the sacrifice of "fair play and substantial justice." That cost is too high.

We are left, then, to consider the significance of the long history of jurisdiction based solely on the presence of property in a State. Although the theory that territorial power is both essential to and sufficient for jurisdiction has been undermined, we have never held that the presence of property in a State does not automatically confer jurisdiction over the owner's interest in that property. This history must be considered as supporting the proposition that jurisdiction based solely on the presence of property satisfies the demands of due process, but it is not decisive. "[T]raditional notions of fair play and substantial justice" can be as readily offended by the perpetuation of ancient forms that are no longer justified as by the adoption of new procedures that are inconsistent with the basic values of our constitutional heritage. Cf. *Sniadach v. Family Finance*

---

[36] Once it has been determined by a court of competent jurisdiction that the defendant is a debtor of the plaintiff, there would seem to be no unfairness in allowing an action to realize on that debt in a State where the defendant has property, whether or not that State would have jurisdiction to determine the existence of the debt as an original matter.

[37] This case does not raise, and we therefore do not consider, the question whether the presence of a defendant's property in a State is a sufficient basis for jurisdiction when no other forum is available to the plaintiff.

Corp., 395 U.S., at 340; *Wolf v. Colorado*, 338 U.S. 25, 27 (1949). The fiction that an assertion of jurisdiction over property is anything but an assertion of jurisdiction over the owner of the property supports an ancient form without substantial modern justification. Its continued acceptance would serve only to allow state-court jurisdiction that is fundamentally unfair to the defendant.

We therefore conclude that all assertions of state-court jurisdiction must be evaluated according to the standards set forth in *International Shoe* and its progeny.

IV

The Delaware courts based their assertion of jurisdiction in this case solely on the statutory presence of appellants' property in Delaware. Yet that property is not the subject matter of this litigation, nor is the underlying cause of action related to the property. Appellants' holdings in Greyhound do not, therefore, provide contacts with Delaware sufficient to support the jurisdiction of that State's courts over appellants. If it exists, that jurisdiction must have some other foundation.

Appellee Heitner did not allege and does not now claim that appellants have ever set foot in Delaware. Nor does he identify any act related to his cause of action as having taken place in Delaware. Nevertheless, he contends that appellants' positions as directors and officers of a corporation chartered in Delaware provide sufficient "contacts, ties, or relations," *International Shoe Co. v. Washington*, 326 U.S., at 319, with that State to give its courts jurisdiction over appellants in this stockholder's derivative action. This argument is based primarily on what Heitner asserts to be the strong interest of Delaware in supervising the management of a Delaware corporation. That interest is said to derive from the role of Delaware law in establishing the corporation and defining the obligations owed to it by its officers and directors. In order to protect this interest, appellee concludes, Delaware's courts must have jurisdiction over corporate fiduciaries such as appellants.

This argument is undercut by the failure of the Delaware Legislature to assert the state interest appellee finds so compelling. Delaware law bases jurisdiction, not on appellants' status as corporate fiduciaries, but rather on the presence of their property in the State. Although the sequestration procedure used here may be most frequently used in derivative suits against officers and directors, the authorizing statute evinces no specific concern with such actions. Sequestration can be used in any suit against a nonresident * * * and reaches corporate fiduciaries only if they happen to own interests in a Delaware corporation, or other property in the State. But as Heitner's failure to secure jurisdiction over seven of the defendants named in his complaint demonstrates, there is no necessary relationship between holding a position as a corporate fiduciary and owning stock or other interests in the corporation. If Delaware perceived its interest in securing jurisdiction over corporate fiduciaries to be as great as Heitner suggests, we would expect it to have enacted a statute more clearly designed to protect that interest.

Moreover, even if Heitner's assessment of the importance of Delaware's interest is accepted, his argument fails to demonstrate that Delaware is a fair forum for this litigation. The interest appellee has identified may support the application of Delaware law to resolve any controversy over appellants' actions in their capacities as officers and directors. But we have rejected the argument that if a State's law can properly be applied to a dispute, its courts necessarily have jurisdiction over the parties to that dispute.

> "[The State] does not acquire . . . jurisdiction by being the 'center of gravity' of the controversy, or the most convenient location for litigation. The issue is personal jurisdiction, not choice of law. It is resolved in this case by considering the acts of the [appellants]." *Hanson v. Denckla,* 357 U.S. 235, 254 (1958).

Appellee suggests that by accepting positions as officers or directors of a Delaware corporation, appellants performed the acts required by *Hanson v. Denckla.* He notes that Delaware law provides substantial benefits to corporate officers and directors, and that these benefits were at least in part the incentive for appellants to assume their positions. It is, he says, "only fair and just" to require appellants, in return for these benefits, to respond in the State of Delaware when they are accused of misusing their power.

But like Heitner's first argument, this line of reasoning establishes only that it is appropriate for Delaware law to govern the obligations of appellants to Greyhound and its stockholders. It does not demonstrate that appellants have "purposefully avail[ed themselves] of the privilege of conducting activities within the forum State," *Hanson v. Denckla,* supra, at 253, in a way that would justify bringing them before a Delaware tribunal. Appellants have simply had nothing to do with the State of Delaware. Moreover, appellants had no reason to expect to be haled before a Delaware court. Delaware, unlike some States, has not enacted a statute that treats acceptance of a directorship as consent to jurisdiction in the State. And "[i]t strains reason . . . to suggest that anyone buying securities in a corporation formed in Delaware 'impliedly consents' to subject himself to Delaware's . . . jurisdiction on any cause of action." Appellants, who were not required to acquire interests in Greyhound in order to hold their positions, did not by acquiring those interests surrender their right to be brought to judgment only in States with which they had had "minimum contacts."

The Due Process Clause "does not contemplate that a state may make binding a judgment . . . against an individual or corporate defendant with which the state has no contacts, ties, or relations." *International Shoe Co. v. Washington,* 326 U.S., at 319.

Delaware's assertion of jurisdiction over appellants in this case is inconsistent with that constitutional limitation on state power. The judgment of the Delaware Supreme Court must, therefore, be reversed.

MR. JUSTICE POWELL, concurring. . .

I would explicitly reserve judgment . . . on whether the ownership of some forms of property whose situs is indisputably and permanently located within a State may, without more, provide the contacts necessary to subject a defendant to jurisdiction within the State to the extent of the value of the property. In the case of real property, in particular, preservation of the common-law concept of *quasi in rem* jurisdiction arguably would avoid the uncertainty of the general *International Shoe* standard without significant cost to " 'traditional notions of fair play and substantial justice.' " Id., at 316, quoting *Milliken v. Meyer,* 311 U.S. 457, 463 (1940).

Subject to the foregoing reservation, I join the opinion of the Court.

MR. JUSTICE STEVENS, concurring in the judgment. . .

The [Due Process] requirement of fair notice . . . includes fair warning that a particular activity may subject a person to the jurisdiction of a foreign sovereign. If I visit another State, or acquire real estate or open a bank account in it, I knowingly assume some risk that the State will exercise its power over my property or my person while there. My contact with the State, though minimal, gives rise to predictable risks.

Perhaps the same consequences should flow from the purchase of stock of a corporation organized under the laws of a foreign nation, because to some limited extent one's property and affairs then become subject to the laws of the nation of domicile of the corporation. As a matter of international law, that suggestion might be acceptable because a foreign investment is sufficiently unusual to make it appropriate to require the investor to study the ramifications of his decision. But a purchase of securities in the domestic market is an entirely different matter.

One who purchases shares of stock on the open market can hardly be expected to know that he has thereby become subject to suit in a forum remote from his residence and unrelated to the transaction. As a practical matter, the Delaware sequestration statute creates an unacceptable risk of judgment without notice. Unlike the 49 other States, Delaware treats the place of incorporation as the situs of the stock, even though both the owner and the custodian of the shares are elsewhere. Moreover, Delaware denies the defendant the opportunity to defend the merits of the suit unless he subjects himself to the unlimited jurisdiction of the court. Thus, it coerces a defendant either to submit to personal jurisdiction in a forum which could not otherwise obtain such jurisdiction or to lose the securities which have been attached. If its procedure were upheld, Delaware would, in effect, impose a duty of inquiry on every purchaser of securities in the national market. For unless the purchaser ascertains both the State of incorporation of the company whose shares he is buying, and also the idiosyncrasies of its law, he may be assuming an unknown risk of litigation. I therefore agree with the Court that on the record before us no adequate basis for jurisdiction exists and that the Delaware statute is unconstitutional on its face. . .

MR. JUSTICE BRENNAN, concurring in part and dissenting in part.

I join Parts I-III of the Court's opinion. I fully agree that the minimum-contacts analysis developed in *International Shoe Co. v. Washington,* 326 U.S. 310 (1945), represents a far more sensible construct for the exercise of state-court jurisdiction than the patchwork of legal and factual fictions that has been generated from the decision in *Pennoyer v. Neff,* 95 U.S. 714 (1878). It is precisely because the inquiry into minimum contacts is now of such overriding importance, however, that I must respectfully dissent from Part IV of the Court's opinion. . .

While evidence derived through discovery might satisfy me that minimum contacts are lacking in a given case, I am convinced that as a general rule a state forum has jurisdiction to adjudicate a shareholder derivative action centering on the conduct and policies of the directors and officers of a corporation chartered by that State. Unlike the Court, I therefore would not foreclose Delaware from asserting jurisdiction over appellants were it persuaded to do so on the basis of minimum contacts.

[The] chartering State has an unusually powerful interest in insuring the availability of a convenient forum for litigating claims involving a possible multiplicity of defendant fiduciaries and for vindicating the State's substantive policies regarding the management of its domestic corporations. I believe that our cases fairly establish that the State's valid substantive interests are important considerations in assessing whether it constitutionally may claim jurisdiction over a given cause of action.

In this instance, Delaware can point to at least three interrelated public policies that are furthered by its assertion of jurisdiction. First, the State has a substantial interest in providing restitution for its local corporations that allegedly have been victimized by fiduciary misconduct, even if the managerial decisions occurred outside the State. . . Second, state courts have legitimately read their jurisdiction expansively when a cause of action centers in an area in which the forum State possesses a manifest regulatory interest. E.g., *McGee v. International Life Ins. Co.,* 355 U.S. 220 (1957) (insurance regulation); *Travelers Health Ass'n v. Virginia,* 339 U.S. 643 (1950) (blue sky laws). . . Finally, a State like Delaware has a recognized interest in affording a convenient forum for supervising and overseeing the affairs of an entity that is purely the creation of that State's law. For example, even following our decision in *International Shoe,* New York courts were permitted to exercise complete judicial authority over nonresident beneficiaries of a trust created under state law, even though, unlike appellants here, the beneficiaries personally entered into no association whatsoever with New York. *Mullane v. Central Hanover Bank & Trust Co.,* 339 U.S. 306, 313 (1950) * * *. I, of course, am not suggesting that Delaware's varied interests would justify its acceptance of jurisdiction over any transaction touching upon the affairs of its domestic corporations. But a derivative action which raises allegations of abuses of the basic management of an institution whose existence is created by the State and whose powers and duties are defined by state law fundamentally implicates the public policies of that forum.

To be sure, the Court is not blind to these considerations. It notes that the State's interests "may support the application of Delaware law to resolve any controversy over appellants' actions in their capacities as officers and directors." But this, the Court argues, pertains to choice of law, not jurisdiction. I recognize that the jurisdictional and choice-of-law inquiries are not identical. *Hanson v. Denckla,* 357 U.S. 235, 254 (1958). But I would not compartmentalize thinking in this area quite so rigidly as it seems to me the Court does today, for both inquiries "are often closely related and to a substantial degree depend upon similar considerations." Id., at 258 (Black, J., dissenting). In either case an important linchpin is the extent of contacts between the controversy, the parties, and the forum State. While constitutional limitations on the choice of law are by no means settled, see, e.g., *Home Ins. Co. v. Dick,* 281 U.S. 397 (1930), important considerations certainly include the expectancies of the parties and the fairness of governing the defendants' acts and behavior by rules of conduct created by a given jurisdiction. See, e.g., Restatement (Second) of Conflict of Laws § 6 (1971) (hereafter Restatement). These same factors bear upon the propriety of a State's exercising jurisdiction over a legal dispute. At the minimum, the decision that it is fair to bind a defendant by a State's laws and rules should prove to be highly relevant to the fairness of permitting that same State to accept jurisdiction for adjudicating the controversy.

Furthermore, I believe that practical considerations argue in favor of seeking to bridge the distance between the choice-of-law and jurisdictional inquiries. Even when a court would apply the law of a different forum, as a general rule it will feel less knowledgeable and comfortable in interpretation, and less interested in fostering the policies of that foreign jurisdiction, than would the courts established by the State that provides the applicable law. * * * Obviously, such choice-of-law problems cannot entirely be avoided in a diverse legal system such as our own. Nonetheless, when a suitor seeks to lodge a suit in a State with a substantial interest in seeking its own law applied to the transaction in question, we could wisely act to minimize conflicts, confusion, and uncertainty by adopting a liberal view of jurisdiction, unless considerations of fairness or efficiency strongly point in the opposite direction. . .

The Seductive "In Rem" Label

(1) Traditional thinking divided the universe of lawsuits between two great boxes labeled "in personam" and "in rem." Suits to determine personal obligations were generally in personam; personal jurisdiction over the defendant was both necessary and sufficient to permit the court to act (aside from some special problems concerning such matters as land and divorce, see pp. 604–609, 657–713, infra). Suits to determine interests in property, however, were said to be in rem; because each state had power over property within its borders, personal jurisdiction over persons affected was neither necessary for jurisdiction over local assets nor sufficient to give jurisdiction over assets in other states.

It is not hard to see, as the Court observed in *Shaffer,* that the stated distinction between in rem and in personam proceedings is less than airtight: An action to determine rights to property affects the rights of people, and an action to impose a personal obligation, if the judgment is enforced, will affect property. Arbitrarily or not, however, various classes of suits were placed in one or the other box. In rem actions were then further divided between pure in rem proceedings, in which the interests of "the whole world" were adjudicated (e.g., land-registration or forfeiture proceedings) and "quasi in rem" proceedings, in which a judgment affected the interests only of particular persons in the property. Quasi-in-rem actions were then divided still further into two types: type 1 actions, in which the object was to settle some dispute over rights and interests in the property itself; and type 2 actions, in which the dispute was unrelated to the property, which was simply attached for purposes of jurisdiction and to satisfy a judgment against the defendant. Actions of partition or to quiet title are type 1; *Shaffer* was a quasi-in-rem type 2 action.

(2) Because quasi-in-rem jurisdiction was based on power over property within the state, the court could not enter a deficiency judgment when the obligation exceeded the value of the property; and for the same reason the judgment usually could not be pleaded as res judicata or collateral estoppel in a later action on the same claim. In some states, moreover—not in all—a defendant whose property had been attached could appear to protect his interest by contesting the merits of the claim without subjecting himself to a judgment in personam. Delaware law did not permit a limited appearance in *Shaffer*. Should the Court have taken the narrower ground that the limited appearance was constitutionally required?

(3) *Shaffer* goes to great lengths to reject the old jurisdictional categories. Why? Wasn't the problem really that the common law attempted to treat intangible property, which has no "situs" as such, as if it were tangible? To what extent is *Shaffer* driven by the arbitrariness of attributing a Delaware situs to shares of stock in a Delaware corporation? Couldn't the Court have retained the common law for tangible property, while ruling more narrowly that, because intangible property (like a debt or stock) represents a personal obligation, it should be subsumed within the rules for in personam jurisdiction? Justice Powell suggests something along these lines, writing separately to say that in rem jurisdiction should be preserved for "property whose situs is indisputably and permanently located within a state." Why didn't the Court follow his lead?

(4) Does *Shaffer* have any effect on pure in rem actions? Under the *Pennoyer*-based conceptual system, the effect of a judgment (i.e., whether or not it is limited to the disposition of specific property) depended upon whether the court had power over a person (in personam jurisdiction) or his or her property (in rem jurisdiction). Now that a court must establish both power and reasonableness to exercise jurisdiction, should in rem jurisdiction be eliminated entirely? Or are there situations where a court should limit the stakes to the disposition of attached property even if the defendant's relation to the forum justifies *in personam* jurisdiction?

(5) Does *Shaffer* have any effect on quasi-in-rem type 1 actions? The enforcement of security interests in land, such as mortgage foreclosure, may occur in a quasi-in-rem proceeding in the state where the land is located even though the creditor, debtor, and the agreement are centered elsewhere. Presumably the *Shaffer* test is satisfied because the defendant debtor has sought the benefits of forum law to protect his or her property and the claim is related to that property. But since the contacts with the forum are so limited, isn't the forum's power confined to disposition of the property, not including an in personam judgment for a deficiency? If the chattel was removed to the forum by a third person, not the debtor, would the forum even have quasi-in-rem jurisdiction?

(6) Is there anything left, after *Shaffer,* of quasi-in-rem type 2 jurisdiction? Professor Smit argues that precisely because the stakes are more limited, a lower level of contacts should be required when property is present in the forum. Smit, *The Enduring Utility of In Rem Rules,* 43 Brook. L. Rev. 600 (1977). Is property in the state a special kind of contact if jurisdiction is limited to it? Would the result in *Kulko*, supra p. 458, have been different if Kulko had had a bank account in a California bank and his ex-wife had limited her claim for additional child support to the amount in that account? In *Feder v. Turkish Airlines,* 441 F.Supp. 1273 (S.D.N.Y. 1977), the plaintiff brought a wrongful death suit stemming from an accident in Turkey. Quasi-in-rem jurisdiction was upheld based on the attachment of a New York bank account established by the airline to pay for aircraft parts and components. The bank account was the airline's only contact with the forum. The court distinguished *Shaffer,* explaining that "[t]he attachment in this case arises from a commercial bank account which [defendant] voluntarily opened in New York for the furtherance of its business. It is not necessary that the property attached be related to the underlying cause of action; jurisdiction *quasi in rem,* at least in the second of its two manifestations, requires no such showing." Is that right?

(7) The Anticybersquatting Consumer Protection Act ("ACPA"), 15 U.S.C. § 1125(d), took effect on November 29, 1999. The ACPA creates a cause of action against individuals who register domain names that are "identical or confusingly similar to or dilutive of" protected trademarks. This in personam action permits damages, as well as other remedies such as cancellation or forfeiture of the domain name. But because registration can be done under aliases, making in personam actions difficult, the ACPA also allows an in rem action "against a domain name in the judicial district in which the domain name registrar, domain name registry, or other domain name authority . . . is located. . ." 15 U.S.C. § 1125(d)(2). This action allows only forfeiture or cancellation of the domain name as a remedy and is permitted only if the plaintiff "is not able to obtain in personam jurisdiction" over the defendant, or "through due diligence was not able to find" him. Id.

Is the maintenance of an in rem action where in personam jurisdiction is lacking constitutional under *Shaffer*? In *Caesars World, Inc. v. Caesars-Palace.Com,* 112 F.Supp. 2d 502, 504 (E.D.Va. 2000), the court characterized *Shaffer* as limited to "in rem proceedings where the underlying cause of action is unrelated to property which is located in the forum state."

(8) Two Indiana residents are involved in a single-car accident in Indiana. The passenger subsequently moves to Minnesota, where he sues the driver. The driver has no contacts with Minnesota, but the passenger obtains jurisdiction by attaching the obligation of the driver's insurance company (which does business in Minnesota). In *Seider v. Roth,* 17 N.Y.2d 111, 269 N.Y.S.2d 99, 216 N.E.2d 312 (1966), the New York court held that the contractual obligation of an insurance company to its insured under a liability policy was a debt subject to attachment under state law if the insurer did business in the state. This rule was widely followed until 1980, when the Supreme Court applied minimum contacts analysis and held it unconstitutional. *Rush v. Savchuk,* 444 U.S. 320 (1980). Was *Rush* obvious after *Shaffer*? The Court reasoned that the insurance policy was not "the subject matter of the case . . . nor . . . related to the operative facts of the negligence action." But who was the real party-in-interest? Could the plaintiff have brought a direct action against the insurer in Minnesota (assuming that Minnesota allowed such claims)? If so (the answer is not at all obvious, is it?), how is such an action different from a suit in which the plaintiff sues the policyholder but only to the extent of the policy? Or is this just lawyer's talk inasmuch as any layperson would say that a defendant who is named as a party, who must cooperate in the defense of an action, and who is accused of wrongdoing has an important stake in the case?

(9) What is the effect of *Shaffer* upon in rem admiralty proceedings in the federal courts? Admiralty proceedings customarily begin with seizure of a ship or its cargo; admiralty even indulges in the fiction that the ship itself is the wrongdoer or obligor and its seizure at the outset is a means of enforcing the shipowner's obligations. Since ships are migratory by sea, an admiralty proceeding may be commenced in any port of call. In *Amoco Overseas Oil Co. v. Compagnie Nationale Algerienne,* 605 F.2d 648, 655 (2d Cir. 1979), a maritime attachment in New York was upheld over *Shaffer* objections because the property was related to the controversy, there was no other forum in the United States, and the admiralty jurisdiction of the "peripatetic" "perpetrators of maritime injury" involved separate constitutional policies and expectations: "[M]aritime actors must reasonably expect to be sued where their property may be found." Subsequent cases go both ways on this question.

(10) In the cases so far considered, foreign attachment has been a means of obtaining jurisdiction to adjudicate the merits of the plaintiff's claim. There are two situations, however, in which foreign attachment serves quite different purposes.

The first is that in which the plaintiff has already obtained a judgment in one state and seeks to enforce it against unrelated property located in another state. Were you surprised by the dictum in footnote 36 of *Shaffer* suggesting that the presence of property by itself is a sufficient basis for an action to enforce a judgment? What is the basis for distinguishing such a case from *Shaffer* itself? Does it matter what kind of property is involved? Suppose it is the obligation of a peripatetic debtor. Does it matter if the defendant did not appear in the first action and wishes to argue that the court rendering the judgment had no jurisdiction? Is the apparent judgment exception predicated on the Full Faith and Credit Clause and therefore limited to sister-state judgments?

(11) In other cases property in the forum state is attached *before* a judgment is obtained elsewhere, as security to satisfy any judgment that may be obtained. Such a case was *Carolina Power & Light Co. v. Uranex,* 451 F.Supp. 1044 (N.D. Cal. 1977), in which a North Carolina utility sought to garnish a debt owed by a California corporation to the French defendant. An $85 million dispute involving breach of a contract for the sale of uranium concentrates was in arbitration in New York, but the defendant had no other assets in the United States. The court upheld the attachment for purposes of securing payment of a New York arbitration award even though it concluded that defendant's contacts with California were not sufficient under *Shaffer* to permit an adjudication of the underlying claim.

Is the court's distinction sound? The California court did not adjudicate the claim, but it did deprive the defendant of the temporary use of its property. After *World-Wide* and *Shaffer,* how can that be done without minimum contacts? Or was the presence of the debtor a sufficient contact for this limited purpose? Is there any reason to distinguish between attaching property to satisfy an existing judgment and attaching it before judgment as security?

Shaffer and In Personam Jurisdiction

(1) The implications of *Shaffer* for quasi-in-rem jurisdiction are explored in the previous notes. The focus here shifts to its in personam aspect: Even if Delaware cannot predicate jurisdiction on the seizure of the stock of a Delaware corporation, why don't its other contacts with the litigation justify the assertion of jurisdiction? Why, for example, weren't the defendants' activities as officers or directors of a Delaware corporation as significant a contact as the insurer's correspondence with its California customer in *McGee*? Can you reconcile the result in *Shaffer* with *Burger King*?

(2) Should Delaware corporation law apply to govern the obligations of officers and directors of Greyhound Corporation in *Shaffer*? Note that Greyhound is not a "pseudo-foreign corporation"—one carrying on all or most of its activities in one state although technically incorporated in another. Its business is nationwide, its stock is traded on national exchanges, and its activities relate to most or all states. The events giving rise to Heitner's derivative suit relate to Arizona, where Greyhound has its principal headquarters; to California, where some of its principal officers reside and where the affairs of a subsidiary are managed; and to Oregon, where the actions of Greyhound and its subsidiary violated the rights under the antitrust laws of the competing bus line. In the absence of a federal corporation law, is Delaware law the only possible choice? See Ratner & Schwartz, *The Impact of* Shaffer v. Heitner *on the Substantive Law of Corporations,* 45 Brook. L. Rev. 641 (1979).

The *Shaffer* majority assumes that Delaware law applies and yet concludes that Delaware's interest in supervising the management of a Delaware corporation does not justify jurisdiction. As we saw above, the question whether a state with sufficient contacts to apply its law should also be able to exercise jurisdiction is troubling enough, supra p. 446. Ratner & Schwartz point out its particularly difficult consequences in the context of corporation law given the unique role played by Delaware: If

Delaware law applies, "it makes sense to have that law interpreted in a consistent and knowledgeable manner—obviously, the courts best qualified to do this are the courts of Delaware." If Delaware courts cannot determine the largely judge-made law governing fiduciary duties of corporate management, "the 'Delaware' law on the subject would consist largely of a quest by courts in other states to determine what the Delaware Supreme Court would say on a subject on which that court would seldom have a chance to speak at all." 45 Brook. L. Rev. at 649–50.

(3) The Court in *Shaffer* emphasized that Delaware "has not enacted a statute that treats acceptance of a directorship as consent to jurisdiction in the State." Why should the existence of such a statute make any constitutional difference? Suppose Delaware enacted a statute stating that the state would exercise jurisdiction "to the full extent permitted by the Constitution." Would there be jurisdiction over the directors? Isn't the point of the *International Shoe* line of cases that a forum can exercise jurisdiction when its contacts are sufficient and that the invocation of a fictitious consent is then unnecessary and irrelevant?

Within thirteen days after the decision in *Shaffer,* Delaware enacted a long-arm statute asserting jurisdiction over nonresident officers and directors appointed or continuing to serve after stated subsequent dates in any action for violation of fiduciary duties. Del.Code tit. 10, § 3114 (Supp.1978). Is the statute constitutional under *Shaffer*? Its validity was upheld in *Armstrong v. Pomerance,* 423 A.2d 174 (Del. 1980), a shareholder's derivative suit against nonresident directors appointed since the effective date of the statute. Although the contact of the directors with Delaware was "limited to their acceptance of directorships in a Delaware corporation," this alone justified the exercise of jurisdiction:

> The defendants accepted their directorship with explicit statutory notice . . . that they could be haled into the Delaware Courts to answer for alleged breaches of the duties imposed on them by the very laws which empowered them to act in their corporate capacities. . . Moreover, the defendants, by purposefully availing themselves of the privilege of becoming directors of a Delaware corporation, have thereby accepted significant benefits and protections under the laws of this State. . .

423 A.2d at 176 (1980). Do you agree? Are we started on a new round of fictitious consent?

Ratner & Schwartz report that Greyhound Corporation, shortly after the enactment of the Delaware long-arm provision, sought and obtained the approval of its shareholders to reincorporate in Arizona. A major reason was that "it would be an unreasonable burden upon directors, not resident in Delaware, several of whom reside in Arizona and California, to be required to journey to Delaware to defend a case there when they have no contact with that state." Ratner & Schwartz, 45 Brook. L. Rev. at 653–54.

SECTION 4. TRANSIENT JURISDICTION

BURNHAM V. SUPERIOR COURT OF CALIFORNIA

495 U.S. 604 (1990).

JUSTICE SCALIA announced the judgment of the Court and delivered an opinion in which THE CHIEF JUSTICE and JUSTICE KENNEDY join, and in which JUSTICE WHITE joins with respect to Parts I, II-A, II-B, and II-C.

The question presented is whether the Due Process Clause of the Fourteenth Amendment denies California courts jurisdiction over a nonresident, who was personally served with process while temporarily in that State, in a suit unrelated to his activities in the State.

I

Petitioner Dennis Burnham married Francie Burnham in 1976, in West Virginia. In 1977 the couple moved to New Jersey, where their two children were born. In July 1987 the Burnhams decided to separate. They agreed that Mrs. Burnham, who intended to move to California, would take custody of the children. Shortly before Mrs. Burnham departed for California that same month, she and petitioner agreed that she would file for divorce on grounds of "irreconcilable differences."

In October 1987, petitioner filed for divorce in New Jersey state court on grounds of "desertion." Petitioner did not, however, obtain an issuance of summons against his wife, and did not attempt to serve her with process. Mrs. Burnham, after unsuccessfully demanding that petitioner adhere to their prior agreement to submit to an "irreconcilable differences" divorce, brought suit for divorce in California state court in early January 1988.

In late January, petitioner visited southern California on business, after which he went north to visit his children in the San Francisco Bay area, where his wife resided. He took the older child to San Francisco for the weekend. Upon returning the child to Mrs. Burnham's home on January 24, 1988, petitioner was served with a California court summons and a copy of Mrs. Burnham's divorce petition. He then returned to New Jersey.

Later that year, petitioner made a special appearance in the California Superior Court, moving to quash the service of process on the ground that the court lacked personal jurisdiction over him because his only contacts with California were a few short visits to the State for the purposes of conducting business and visiting his children. The Superior Court denied the motion, and the California Court of Appeal denied mandamus relief, rejecting petitioner's contention that the Due Process Clause prohibited

California courts from asserting jurisdiction over him because he lacked "minimum contacts" with the State. The court held it to be "a valid jurisdictional predicate for *in personam* jurisdiction" that the "defendant [was] present in the forum state and personally served with process." We granted certiorari.

II

A . . .

To determine whether the assertion of personal jurisdiction is consistent with due process, we have long relied on the principles traditionally followed by American courts in marking out the territorial limits of each State's authority. . . In what has become the classic expression of the criterion, we said in *International Shoe Co. v. Washington,* 326 U.S. 310 (1945), that a State court's assertion of personal jurisdiction satisfies the Due Process Clause if it does not violate " 'traditional notions of fair play and substantial justice.' " *Id.,* at 316.

Since *International Shoe,* we have only been called upon to decide whether these "traditional notions" permit States to exercise jurisdiction over absent defendants in a manner that deviates from the rules of jurisdiction applied in the 19th century. We have held such deviations permissible, but only with respect to suits arising out of the absent defendant's contacts with the state. * * * The question we must decide today is whether due process requires a similar connection between the litigation and the defendant's contacts with the State in cases where the defendant is physically present in the State at the time process is served upon him.

B

Among the most firmly established principles of personal jurisdiction in American tradition is that the courts of a State have jurisdiction over nonresidents who are physically present in the State. The view developed early that each State had the power to hale before its courts any individual who could be found within its borders, and that once having acquired jurisdiction over such a person by properly serving him with process, the State could retain jurisdiction to enter judgment against him, no matter how fleeting his visit. That view had antecedents in English common-law practice, which sometimes allowed "transitory" actions, arising out of events outside the country, to be maintained against seemingly nonresident defendants who were present in England. * * * Justice Story believed the principle, which he traced to Roman origins, to be firmly grounded in English tradition: "[B]y the common law[,] personal actions, being transitory, may be brought in any place, where the party defendant may be found," for "every nation may . . . rightfully exercise jurisdiction over all persons within its domains." J. Story, Commentaries on the Conflict of Laws 554, 543 (1846). * * *

Recent scholarship has suggested that English tradition was not as clear as Story thought * * *. Accurate or not, however, judging by the evidence of contemporaneous or near-contemporaneous decisions one must conclude that Story's understanding was shared by American courts at the crucial time for present purposes: 1868, when the Fourteenth Amendment was adopted. . .

Decisions in the courts of many States in the 19th and early 20th centuries held that personal service upon a physically present defendant sufficed to confer jurisdiction, without regard to whether the defendant was only briefly in the State or whether the cause of action was related to his activities there. * * * Although research has not revealed a case deciding the issue in every State's courts, that appears to be because the issue was so well settled that it went unlitigated. See R. Leflar, American Conflicts Law § 24, p. 43 (1968). Opinions from the courts of other States announced the rule in dictum. * * * Particularly striking is the fact that, as far as we have been able to determine, *not one* American case from the period (or, for that matter, not one American case until 1978) held, or even suggested, that in-state personal service on an individual was insufficient to confer personal jurisdiction. Commentators were also seemingly unanimous on the rule. * * *

This American jurisdictional practice is moreover, not merely old; it is continuing. It remains the practice of, not only a substantial number of the States, but as far as we are aware *all* the States and the federal government—if one disregards (as one must for this purpose) the few opinions since 1978 that have erroneously said, on grounds similar to those that petitioner presses here, that this Court's due-process decisions render the practice unconstitutional. * * * We do not know of a single State or federal statute, or a single judicial decision resting upon State law, that has abandoned in-State service as a basis of jurisdiction. Many recent cases reaffirm it. * * *

C

Despite this formidable body of precedent, petitioner contends, in reliance on our decisions applying the *International Shoe* standard, that in the absence of "continuous and systematic" contacts with the forum, a nonresident defendant can be subjected to judgment only as to matters that arise out of or relate to his contacts with forum. This argument rests on a thorough misunderstanding of our cases.

The view of most courts in the 19th century was that a court simply could not exercise *in personam* jurisdiction over a nonresident who had not been personally served with process in the forum. * * * *Pennoyer v. Neff,* while renowned for its statement of the principle that the Fourteenth Amendment prohibits such an exercise of jurisdiction, in fact set that forth only as dictum, and decided the case (which involved a judgment rendered more than two years before the Fourteenth Amendment's ratification) under "well-established principles of public law." 95 U.S., at 722. Those principles, embodied in the Due Process Clause, required (we said) that when proceedings "involv[e] merely a determination of the personal liability of the defendant, he must be brought within [the court's] jurisdiction by service of process within the State, or his voluntary appearance." *Id.,* at 733. We invoked that rule in a series of subsequent cases, as either a matter of due process or a "fundamental principl[e] of jurisprudence" * * *.

Later years, however, saw the weakening of the *Pennoyer* rule. In the late 19th and early 20th centuries, changes in the technology of transportation and communication, and the tremendous growth of interstate business activity, led to an "inevitable relaxation of the strict limits on state jurisdiction" over nonresident individuals and corporations. *Hanson v. Denckla,* 357 U.S. 235, 260 (1958) (Black, J., dissenting). . . Our opinion in *International Shoe* cast [the various legal fictions developed to expand *Pennoyer*] aside, and made explicit the underlying basis of these decisions: due process does not necessarily *require* the States to adhere to the unbending territorial limits on jurisdiction set forth in *Pennoyer*. Subsequent cases have derived from the *International Shoe* standard the general rule that a State may dispense with in-forum personal service on nonresident defendants in suits arising out of their activities in the State. * * * As *International Shoe* suggests, the defendant's litigation-related "minimum contacts" may take the place of physical presence as the basis for jurisdiction. . .

Nothing in *International Shoe* or the cases that have followed it, however, offers support for the very different proposition petitioner seeks to establish today: that a defendant's presence in the forum is not only unnecessary to validate novel, non-traditional assertions of jurisdiction, but is itself no longer sufficient to establish jurisdiction. That proposition is unfaithful to both elementary logic and the foundations of our due process jurisprudence. The distinction between what is needed to support novel procedures and what is needed to sustain traditional ones is fundamental, as we observed over a century ago:

> "[A] process of law, which is not otherwise forbidden, must be taken to be due process of law, if it can show the sanction of settled usage both in England and in this country; but it by no means follows that nothing else can be due process of law. . . [That which], in substance, has been immemorially the actual law of the land . . . therefor[e] is due process of law. But to hold that such a characteristic is essential to due process of law, would be to deny every quality of the law but its age, and to render it incapable of progress or improvement. It would be to stamp upon our jurisprudence the unchangeableness attributed to the laws of the

> Medes and Persians." *Hurtado v. California,* 110 U.S. 516, 528–529 (1884).

The short of the matter is that jurisdiction based on physical presence alone constitutes due process because it is one of the continuing traditions of our legal system that define the due process standard of "traditional notions of fair play and substantial justice." That standard was developed by *analogy* to "physical presence," and it would be perverse to say it could now be turned against that touchstone of jurisdiction.

D

Petitioner's strongest argument, though we ultimately reject it, relies upon our decision in *Shaffer v. Heitner,* 433 U.S. 186 (1977). In that case, a Delaware court hearing a shareholder's derivative suit against a corporation's directors secured jurisdiction *quasi in rem* by sequestering the out-of-State defendants' stock in the company, the situs of which was Delaware under Delaware law. Reasoning that Delaware's sequestration procedure was simply a mechanism to compel the absent defendants to appear in a suit to determine their personal rights and obligations, we concluded that the normal rules we had developed under *International Shoe* for jurisdiction over suits against absent defendants should apply—viz., Delaware could not hear the suit because the defendants' sole contact with the State (ownership of property there) was unrelated to the lawsuit. * * *

It goes too far to say, as petitioner contends, that *Shaffer* compels the conclusion that a State lacks jurisdiction over an individual unless the litigation arises out of his activities in the State. *Shaffer,* like *International Shoe,* involved jurisdiction over an *absent defendant,* and its stands for nothing more than the proposition that when the "minimum contact" that is a substitute for physical presence consists of property ownership it must, like other minimum contacts, be related to the litigation. Petitioner wrenches out of its context our statement in *Shaffer* that "all assertions of state-court jurisdiction must be evaluated according to the standards set forth in *International Shoe* and its progeny," 433 U.S., at 212. When read together with the two sentences that preceded it, the meaning of this statement becomes clear:

> "The fiction that an assertion of jurisdiction over property is anything but an assertion of jurisdiction over the owner of the property supports an ancient form without substantial modern justification. Its continued acceptance would serve only to allow state-court jurisdiction that is fundamentally unfair to the defendant.
>
> "We *therefore conclude* that all assertions of state-court jurisdiction must be evaluated according to the standards set

> forth in *International Shoe* and its progeny." *Ibid.* (emphasis added).

Shaffer was saying, in other words, not that all bases for the assertion of *in personam* jurisdiction (including, presumably, in-state service) must be treated alike and subjected to the "minimum contacts" analysis of *International Shoe;* but rather that *quasi in rem* jurisdiction, that fictional "ancient form," and *in personam* jurisdiction, are really one and the same and must be treated alike—leading to the conclusion that *quasi in rem* jurisdiction, i.e., that form of *in personam* jurisdiction based upon a "property ownership" contact and by definition unaccompanied by personal, in-state service, must satisfy the litigation-relatedness requirement of *International Shoe.* The logic of *Shaffer*'s holding—which places all suits against absent nonresidents on the same constitutional footing, regardless of whether a separate Latin label is attached to one particular basis of contact—does not compel the conclusion that physically present defendants must be treated identically to absent ones. As we have demonstrated at length, our tradition has treated the two classes of defendants quite differently, and it is unreasonable to read *Shaffer* as casually obliterating that distinction. *International Shoe* confined its "minimum contacts" requirement to situations in which the defendant "be not present within the territory of the forum," and nothing in *Shaffer* expands that requirement beyond that.

It is fair to say, however, that while our holding today does not contradict *Shaffer,* our basic approach to the due process question is different. We have conducted no independent inquiry into the desirability or fairness of the prevailing in-state service rule, leaving that judgment to the legislatures that are free to amend it; for our purposes, its validation is its pedigree, as the phrase "*traditional notions* of fair play and substantial justice" makes clear. *Shaffer* did conduct such an independent inquiry, asserting that " 'traditional notions of fair play and substantial justice' can be as readily offended by the perpetuation of ancient forms that are no longer justified as by the adoption of new procedures that are inconsistent with the basic values of our constitutional heritage." 433 U.S., at 212. Perhaps that assertion can be sustained when the "perpetuation of ancient forms" is engaged in by only a very small minority of the States. Where however, as in the present case, a jurisdictional principle is both firmly approved by tradition and still favored, it is impossible to imagine what standard we could appeal to for the judgment that it is "no longer justified." While in no way receding from or casting doubt upon the holding of *Shaffer* or any other case, we reaffirm today our time-honored approach. * * * For new procedures, hitherto unknown, the Due Process Clause requires analysis to determine whether "traditional notions of fair play and substantial justice" have been offended. *International Shoe,* 326 U.S., at 316. But a doctrine of personal jurisdiction that dates back to the adoption of the Fourteenth Amendment and is still generally observed unquestionably meets that standard. . .

Because the Due Process Clause does not prohibit the California courts from exercising jurisdiction over petitioner based on the fact of in-state service of process, the judgment is affirmed.

JUSTICE WHITE, concurring in part and concurring in the judgment. . .

The rule allowing jurisdiction to be obtained over a non-resident by personal service in the forum state, without more, has been and is so widely accepted throughout this country that I could not possibly strike it down, whether on its face or as applied in this case, on the ground that it denies due process of law guaranteed by the Fourteenth Amendment. Although the Court has the authority under the Amendment to examine even traditionally accepted procedures and declare them invalid, *e.g., Shaffer v. Heitner,* 433 U.S. 186 (1977), there has been no showing here or elsewhere that as a general proposition the rule is so arbitrary and lacking in common sense in so many instances that it should be held violative of Due Process in every case. Furthermore, until such a showing is made, which would be difficult indeed, claims in individual cases that the rule would operate unfairly as applied to the particular non-resident involved need not be entertained. At least this would be the case where presence in the forum state is intentional, which would almost always be the fact. Otherwise, there would be endless, fact-specific litigation in the trial and appellate courts, including this one. Here, personal service in California, without more, is enough, and I agree that the judgment should be affirmed.

JUSTICE BRENNAN, with whom JUSTICE MARSHALL, JUSTICE BLACKMUN, and JUSTICE O'CONNOR join, concurring in the judgment.

I agree with Justice SCALIA that the Due Process Clause of the Fourteenth Amendment generally permits a state court to exercise jurisdiction over a defendant if he is served with process while voluntarily present in the forum State. I do not perceive the need, however, to decide that a jurisdictional rule that "has been immemorially the actual law of the land" * * * automatically comports with due process simply by virtue of its "pedigree." Although I agree that history is an important factor in establishing whether a jurisdictional rule satisfies due process requirements, I cannot agree that it is the *only* factor such that all traditional rules of jurisdiction are, *ipso facto,* forever constitutional. Unlike JUSTICE SCALIA, I would undertake an "independent inquiry into the . . . fairness of the prevailing in-state service rule." * * * I therefore concur only in the judgment.

I

I believe that the approach adopted by Justice SCALIA's opinion today—reliance solely on historical pedigree—is foreclosed by our decisions in *International Shoe Co. v. Washington,* 326 U.S. 310 (1945), and *Shaffer v. Heitner,* 433 U.S. 186 (1977)... The critical insight of *Shaffer* is that all rules of jurisdiction, even ancient ones, must satisfy contemporary notions of due process. No longer were we content to limit our jurisdictional analysis to pronouncements that "[t]he foundation of jurisdiction is physical power," * * * and that "every State possesses exclusive jurisdiction and sovereignty over persons and property within its territory." *Pennoyer v. Neff,* 95 U.S. 714, 722 (1878). While acknowledging that "history must be considered as supporting the proposition that jurisdiction based solely on the presence of property satisfie[d] the demands of due process," we found that this factor could not be "decisive." 433 U.S., at 211–212. We recognized that " '[t]raditional notions of fair play and substantial justice' can be as readily offended by the perpetuation of ancient forms that are no longer justified as by the adoption of new procedures that are inconsistent with the basic values of our constitutional heritage." *Id.,* at 212 (citations omitted). I agree with this approach and continue to believe that "the minimum-contacts analysis developed in *International Shoe* . . . represents a far more sensible construct for the exercise of state-court jurisdiction than the patchwork of legal and factual fictions that has been generated from the decision in *Pennoyer v. Neff.*" *Id.,* at 219 (BRENNAN, J., concurring in part and dissenting in part).

While our *holding* in *Shaffer* may have been limited to *quasi in rem* jurisdiction, our mode of analysis was not. Indeed, that we were willing in *Shaffer* to examine anew the appropriateness of the *quasi in rem* rule—until that time dutifully accepted by American courts for at least a century—demonstrates that we did not believe that the "pedigree" of a jurisdictional practice was dispositive in deciding whether it was consistent with due process... If we could discard an "ancient form without substantial modern justification" in *Shaffer, supra,* 433 U.S., at 212, we can do so again. Lower courts, commentators, and the American Law Institute all have interpreted *International Shoe* and *Shaffer* to mean that *every* assertion of state-court jurisdiction, even one pursuant to a "traditional" rule such as transient jurisdiction, must comport with contemporary notions of due process. Notwithstanding the nimble gymnastics of Justice SCALIA's opinion today, it is not faithful to our decision in *Shaffer.*

II

Tradition, though alone not dispositive, is of course *relevant* to the question whether the rule of transient jurisdiction is consistent with due process. Tradition is salient not in the sense that practices of the past are automatically reasonable today; indeed, under such a standard, the legitimacy of transient jurisdiction would be called into question because the rule's historical "pedigree" is a matter of intense debate...

Rather, I find the historical background relevant because, however murky the jurisprudential origins of transient jurisdiction, the fact that American courts have announced the rule for perhaps a century (first in dicta, more recently in holdings) provides a defendant voluntarily present in a particular State *today* "clear notice that [he] is subject to suit" in the forum. *World-Wide Volkswagen Corp. v. Woodson,* 444 U.S. 286, 297 (1980). Regardless of whether Justice Story's account of the rule's genesis is mythical, our common understanding *now,* fortified by a century of judicial practice, is that jurisdiction is often a function of geography. The transient rule is consistent with reasonable expectations and is entitled to a strong presumption that it comports with due process. "If I visit another State, . . . I knowingly assume some risk that the State will exercise its power over my property or my person while there. My contact with the State, though minimal, gives rise to predictable risks." *Shaffer,* 433 U.S. at 218 (STEVENS, J. concurring in judgment). * * * Thus, proposed revisions to the Restatement (Second) of Conflict of Laws § 28, p. 39 (1986), provide that "[a] state has power to exercise judicial jurisdiction over an individual who is present within its territory unless the individual's relationship to the state is so attenuated as to make the exercise of such jurisdiction unreasonable."

By visiting the forum State, a transient defendant actually "avail[s]" himself * * * of significant benefits provided by the State. His health and safety are guaranteed by the State's police, fire, and emergency medical services; he is free to travel on the State's roads and waterways; he likely enjoys the fruits of the State's economy as well. Moreover, the Privileges and Immunities Clause of Article IV prevents a state government from discriminating against a transient defendant by denying him the protections of its law or the right of access to its courts. * * * Subject only to the doctrine of *forum non conveniens,* an out-of-state plaintiff may use state courts in all circumstances in which those courts would be available to state citizens. Without transient jurisdiction, an asymmetry would arise: a transient would have the full benefit of the power of the forum State's courts as a plaintiff while retaining immunity from their authority as a defendant. * * *

The potential burdens on a transient defendant are slight. "[M]odern transportation and communications have made it much less burdensome for a party sued to defend himself" in a State outside his place of residence. * * * That the defendant has already journeyed at least once before to the forum—as evidenced by the fact that he was served with process there—is an indication that suit in the forum likely would not be prohibitively inconvenient. Finally, any burdens that do arise can be ameliorated by a variety of procedural devices.[13] For these reasons, as a rule the exercise of

[13] For example, in the federal system, a transient defendant can avoid protracted litigation of a spurious suit through a motion to dismiss for failure to state a claim or though a motion for

personal jurisdiction over a defendant based on his voluntary presence in the forum will satisfy the requirements of due process.

In this case, it is undisputed that petitioner was served with process while voluntarily and knowingly in the State of California. I therefore concur in the judgment.

JUSTICE STEVENS, concurring in the judgment.

As I explained in my separate writing, I did not join the Court's opinion in *Shaffer v. Heitner,* 433 U.S. 186 (1977), because I was concerned by its unnecessarily broad reach. *Id.,* at 217–219, 97 S.Ct., at 2586–2588 (opinion concurring in judgment). The same concern prevents me from joining either Justice SCALIA's or Justice BRENNAN's opinion in this case. For me, it is sufficient to note that the historical evidence and consensus identified by Justice SCALIA, the considerations of fairness identified by Justice BRENNAN, and the common sense displayed by Justice WHITE, all combine to demonstrate that this is, indeed, a very easy case.* Accordingly, I agree that the judgment should be affirmed.

Playing Tag

(1) The facts of *Burnham* are extremely close to those of *Kulko,* supra p. 458, except that Burnham was physically served while present in California. Yet the Justices agree unanimously that there is jurisdiction on these facts. Are you surprised? Apart from upholding the constitutionality of "tag" jurisdiction, as it is sometimes called, what does *Burnham* stand for? Four justices sign each of the two main opinions. Do the White and Stevens concurrences clarify matters?

(2) What do you make of Justice Scalia's opinion? His basic point is that ongoing traditions do not suddenly become unconstitutional and that their evolution should be entrusted to state legislatures. But can legislatures be trusted on this question? Justice Brennan suggests in a footnote that reliance on state legislatures may be misplaced because "States have little incentive to limit rules such as transient jurisdiction that make it *easier* for their own citizens to sue out-of-state defendants. . . The reasoning of Justice Scalia's opinion today is strikingly oblivious to the *raison d'être* of various constitutional doctrines designed to protect out-of-

summary judgment. Fed.Rules Civ.Proc., 12(b)(6) and 56. He can use relatively inexpensive methods of discovery, such as oral deposition by telephone (Rule 30(b)(7)), deposition upon written questions (Rule 31), interrogatories (Rule 33), and requests for admission (Rule 36), while enjoying protection from harassment (Rule 26(c)), and possibly obtaining costs and attorney's fees for some of the work involved (Rule 37(a)(4), (b)–(d)). Moreover, a change of venue may be possible. 28 U.S.C. § 1404. In state court, many of the same procedural protections are available, as is the doctrine of *forum non conveniens,* under which the suit may be dismissed. * * *

* Perhaps the adage about hard cases making bad law should be revised to cover easy cases.

staters, such as the Art. IV Privileges and Immunities Clause and the Commerce Clause." 495 U.S. at 639, n.14. Justice Scalia responds in the battle of footnotes that "[t]he notion that the Constitution, through some penumbra emanating from the Privileges and Immunities Clause and the Commerce Clause, establishes this Court as a Platonic check upon the society's greedy adherence to its traditions can only be described as imperious." Id. at 627, n.5. Is the choice really between letting the Court freely impose its arbitrary preferences and trusting democracy? Can one defend a narrower role for judicial intervention where, for structural reasons like those identified by Justice Brennan, we cannot trust the ordinary political process? Is Justice Scalia's argument limited to the Due Process Clause or is he making a more general claim about the role of tradition in constitutional decisionmaking? What implications would such an approach have had for cases dealing with problems like school desegregation, police beatings, malapportioned legislatures, denial of counsel to criminal defendants, school prayer, women's rights, etc.?

At one point in his opinion, Justice Scalia declares the proposition that due process prohibits transient jurisdiction "unfaithful to both elementary logic and the foundations of our due process jurisprudence." Putting aside the question of tradition and due process, what is the "elementary logic" behind transient jurisdiction? Given the understanding of jurisdiction developed in the 50 years since *International Shoe,* what sense does it make to say that a party can be made to defend an action solely because he or she was in the forum state when served? In *Grace v. MacArthur,* 170 F.Supp. 442 (E.D. Ark. 1959), Arkansas plaintiffs sued an Illinois defendant for breach of contract. The defendant was served on a commercial flight from Tennessee to Texas when the plane was over Arkansas. No other contacts with Arkansas were recited by the court in upholding jurisdiction. Is that result really compelled by "elementary logic"?

(3) Does Justice Scalia successfully distinguish *Shaffer v. Heitner*? How can he say that the justices in *Shaffer* saw the case as involving nothing more than a form of in personam jurisdiction? And why would it matter if they did, given Justice Scalia's approach? Whatever label one uses, didn't *Shaffer* hold unconstitutional a practice with a long historical pedigree that was still practiced in every state? According to one commentator, Justice Scalia's effort to distinguish *Shaffer* "is, at best, a *non sequitur* and, at worst, intellectually dishonest." Stein, Burnham *and the Death of Theory in the Law of Personal Jurisdiction,* 22 Rutgers L.J. 597, 602 (1991). In a subsequent case involving punitive damages, Justice Scalia made the same point about the role of tradition in due process jurisprudence, but this time he stated forthrightly that *Shaffer* was wrongly decided. *Pacific Mut. Life Ins. Co. v. Haslip,* 499 U.S. 1, 36 (1991) (Scalia, J., concurring in the judgment).

(4) Is Justice Brennan's opinion any better? In a portion of the plurality opinion that has been edited out, Justice Scalia takes issue with many of Justice Brennan's arguments. Three days of enjoying the benefits of travel and police protection in California, Justice Scalia writes, "strike us as powerfully inadequate to establish, as an abstract matter, that it is 'fair' for California to decree the ownership of all Mr. Burnham's worldly goods acquired during the ten years of his marriage, and the custody over his children." 495 U.S. at 623. More important, Justice Brennan's arguments in no way depend on the fact that Burnham was served while in California; rather, the same result would seem to follow if Burnham were served after returning to New Jersey. Id. at 624. Is Justice Brennan simply arguing (without openly saying so) that *Kulko* should be overruled? Is he obliterating the line between general and specific jurisdiction? And what do you think of Justice Brennan's argument that the fact "[t]hat the defendant has already journeyed at least once before to the forum—as evidenced by the fact that he was served with process there—is an indication that suit in the forum likely would not be prohibitively inconvenient"? Is the real explanation that Justice Brennan doesn't believe in *any* constitutional limitations on state court jurisdiction?

(5) What do the separate concurrences of Justices White and Stevens add? Justice White says that transient jurisdiction has not been shown to be arbitrary in every case and that "until such a showing is made . . . claims in individual cases that the rule would operate unfairly as applied to the particular non-resident involved need not be entertained." Why should the fact that the rule survives an attack on its facial constitutionality prevent claims that it is unconstitutional as applied?

(6) Does *Burnham* resuscitate all the traditional bases for jurisdiction—consent, doing business, and the like? Is Professor Borchers right that *Burnham* signals the end of constitutional limits on jurisdiction? Borchers, *The Death of the Constitutional Law of Personal Jurisdiction: From* Pennoyer *to* Burnham *and Back Again,* 24 U.C.Davis L.Rev. 19, 87 (1990). Borchers approves of this result, arguing that state court jurisdiction should be regulated by interstate compact or federal legislation. But why should the applicability of laws respecting jurisdiction be treated differently, for constitutional purposes, than any other choice-of-law question?

(7) The footnote at the end of Justice Stevens's concurrence suggests revising the adage about hard cases to cover easy cases. How should it read? That (at least in the present Supreme Court) *both* hard cases *and* easy cases make bad law?

A NOTE ON COMPARATIVE JURISDICTION[*]

A. The European Convention on Jurisdiction and the Enforcement of Judgments

In 1968, the original Common Market countries entered into a treaty which adopted a system of rules setting forth required and prohibited bases of jurisdiction for domiciliaries of Member States. As between Member States, the Convention rules replaced the jurisdictional rules of the individual States under national law. It did not affect purely domestic litigation. In 1971, a separate Protocol conferred authority upon the European Court of Justice to provide rulings on questions that arose under the Brussels Convention, thereby creating a supranational tribunal. In 1988, a parallel Convention—the Lugano Convention—adopted the jurisdiction and enforcement provisions of the Brussels Convention for the member states of the European Free Trade Association, but without review by the European court. The Brussels/Lugano Conventions were superseded in 2001 by EU Regulation 44/2001 and then in 2012 by Regulation 1215/2012, which are substantially similar.

The jurisdictional provisions of Regulation 1215 fall into two basic categories: jurisdiction that is required and jurisdiction that is prohibited. An important goal of the Regulation was to limit the number of fora in which any given case could be brought.

The "required" bases of jurisdiction under the Regulation provide some interesting contrasts with U.S. law. With respect to the category of "general jurisdiction," Article 4 provides jurisdiction over a defendant sued in his state of domicile. The domicile of an entity other than an individual is defined as the "seat" of the company, or the location of its central administration or principal place of business (Article 63). In addition, Article 17 permits jurisdiction over suits arising from consumer contracts based on the agreement of the parties, and Article 26 confers jurisdiction on "a court of a Member State before which a defendant enters an appearance." Because jurisdiction is prohibited unless conferred by the Regulation, there is no general "doing business" jurisdiction for unrelated claims.

When it comes to specific grants of jurisdiction, the provisions of Regulation 1215 resemble U.S. long-arm statutes in certain respects. Referred to as "special jurisdiction," the provisions set forth rules for contracts and torts, and more detailed rules for matters relating the insurance and consumer contracts. Contract claims under the Regulation can be brought "in the courts for the place of performance of the obligation in question" (Art. 7(1)). For tort claims, the Regulation provides jurisdiction in the courts of the State "where the harmful event occurred" (Art. 5(2)). In *Bier v. Mines de Potasse d'Alsace S.A.*, [1976] ECR 1735 (1977), Dutch plaintiffs were injured in the Netherlands by French defendants who dumped chemicals into tributaries of the Rhine in France. The European Court of Justice held that, under the "harmful event"

[*] The following note is drawn from Silberman, Stein & Wolff, Civil Procedure: Theory and Practice (3d ed. 2009).

provision, jurisdiction existed either where the harmful act occurred (France) or at the place of injury (the Netherlands).

In a later case involving damages suffered as the result of a libelous newspaper publication, the European Court found that the plaintiff could recover full damages only if suit were brought in the place where the publisher was located; if suit were brought in a State where the publication was merely distributed, jurisdiction was limited to recovery of the harm suffered in that State. See *Shevill v. Press Alliance,* [1995] ECR I–415. Compare the approach of the European Court of Justice in *Shevill* with that of the Supreme Court of the United States in *Keeton v. Hustler Magazine, Inc.,* 465 U.S. 770 (1984), supra p. 498.

Note that the jurisdiction rules of Regulation 1215 are directed to the relationship between the controversy and the forum rather than, as in the United States, between the individual defendant and the forum state. Thus, jurisdiction in a case like *World-Wide Volkswagen v. Woodson,* 444 U.S. 286 (1980), supra p. 449, would have been sustained under the Regulation.

A broad, catch-all provision of Regulation 1215 confers jurisdiction over a "dispute arising out of the operations of a branch, agency or other establishment, in the courts for the place in which the branch, agency or other establishment is situated." (Art. 7(5)). This provision would permit jurisdiction over a claim against a corporation in the place where a branch office is located but only if the claim "arises out of" the activities of that branch. As noted above, general jurisdiction over a corporation other than at its "seat" (usually the place of incorporation or its headquarters) is not permitted under the Regulation. Is this restriction on jurisdiction wise? What policies underlie the choice made by the Regulation to ignore the broader type of general jurisdiction accepted in American jurisprudence?

In other areas, Regulation 1215 contains more expansive jurisdictional provisions than exist under United States law. Article 8(1) of the Regulation, for example, authorizes jurisdiction over all defendants where any one defendant is domiciled. In most cases, the court also has jurisdiction over any third-party defendants brought into the litigation (Art. 8(2)). What accounts for the absence of similar jurisdictional rules in the United States?

With respect to matters relating to insurance under Regulation 1215, an insurer may be sued in either its state of domicile or, if the insured is domiciled in a Contracting State, in the insured's domicile. (Art. 11). Would you favor such a rule in the United States as between states of the United States? How about in the international context?

The discussion so far has emphasized jurisdictional bases that must be asserted by Contracting States under Regulation 1215. European States have not generally imposed constitutional limitations under domestic law like those that characterize jurisdiction in the United States. However, Article 5 of the Regulation expressly prohibits Member States from asserting jurisdiction against defendants domiciled in Contracting States on a variety of grounds that would otherwise be permissible under national law. Among the "outlawed" grounds are "tag" jurisdiction, seizure of property, and nationality of the plaintiff.

B. Other International Initiatives

The United States has no international treaty on jurisdiction or recognition of judgments with any other country. In 1993, the Hague Conference on Private International Law undertook to negotiate a worldwide Convention on Jurisdiction and the Recognition of Foreign Judgments. The 1999 Draft Hague Convention was, to a substantial extent, modeled on the Brussels Convention. It set forth rules on judicial jurisdiction, which must be adhered to by parties to the Convention; it also provided that civil judgments rendered in one Convention State against a person habitually resident in another Convention State would be recognized in all other Convention States, subject to a narrow list of defenses, and provided the court that rendered the judgment had jurisdiction over the defendant according to an agreed standard.

These efforts have not resulted in a general global convention on jurisdiction but did lead in 2005 to the Hague Choice of Court Convention, which requires courts in signatory nations to uphold choice-of-court agreements between parties in civil litigation and to recognize the resulting judgments. Proceedings in other courts must be stayed unless the chosen court denies jurisdiction. The 2005 convention covers the European Union, Denmark, Mexico, Singapore, and the United Kingdom. The U.S. has signed the convention but not ratified it.

In addition, the Hague Convention on the Recognition and Enforcement of Foreign Judgments in Civil or Commercial Matters was finally adopted in July 2019. This convention is discussed infra Chapter 8, Section 4.

C. The Restatement of Foreign Relations Law

The Restatement (Third) of Foreign Relations Law (1987) offers an international law standard for jurisdiction in § 421, Jurisdiction to Adjudicate. It provides:

(1) A state may exercise jurisdiction through its courts to adjudicate with respect to a person or thing if the relationship of the state to the person or thing is such as to make the exercise of jurisdiction reasonable.

(2) In general, a state's exercise of jurisdiction to adjudicate with respect to a person or thing is reasonable if, at the time jurisdiction is asserted:

(a) the person or thing is present in the territory of the state, other than transitorily;

(b) the person, if a natural person, is domiciled in the state;

(c) the person, if a natural person, is resident in the state;

(d) the person, if a natural person, is a national of the state;

(e) the person, if a corporation or comparable juridical person, is organized pursuant to the law of the state;

(f) a ship, aircraft or other vehicle to which the adjudication relates is registered under the laws of the state;

(g) the person, whether natural or juridical, has consented to the exercise of jurisdiction;

(h) the person, whether natural or juridical, regularly carries on business in the state;

(i) the person, whether natural or juridical, had carried on activity in the state, but only in respect of such activity;

(j) the person, whether natural or juridical, had carried on outside the state an activity having a substantial, direct, and foreseeable effect within the state, but only in respect of such activity; or

(k) the thing that is the subject of adjudication is owned, possessed, or used in the state, but only in respect of a claim reasonably connected with that thing.

(3) A defense of lack of jurisdiction is generally waived by any appearance by or on behalf of a person or thing (whether as plaintiff, defendant, or third party), if the appearance is for a purpose that does not include a challenge to the exercise of jurisdiction.

Is this more like the U.S. approach or the European?

SECTION 5. FORUM NON CONVENIENS

PIPER AIRCRAFT V. REYNO

454 U.S. 235 (1981).

JUSTICE MARSHALL delivered the opinion of the Court.

. . .

I

A

In July 1976, a small commercial aircraft crashed in the Scottish highlands during the course of a charter flight from Blackpool to Perth. The pilot and five passengers were killed instantly. The decedents were all Scottish subjects and residents, as are their heirs and next of kin. There were no eyewitnesses to the accident. At the time of the crash the plane was subject to Scottish air traffic control.

The aircraft, a twin-engine Piper Aztec, was manufactured in Pennsylvania by petitioner Piper Aircraft Co. (Piper). The propellers were manufactured in Ohio by petitioner Hartzell Propeller, Inc. (Hartzell). At the time of the crash the aircraft was registered in Great Britain and was owned and maintained by Air Navigation and Trading Co., Ltd. (Air

Navigation). It was operated by McDonald Aviation, Ltd. (McDonald), a Scottish air taxi service. Both Air Navigation and McDonald were organized in the United Kingdom. The wreckage of the plane is now in a hangar in Farnsborough, England. . . .

In July 1977, a California probate court appointed respondent Gaynell Reyno administratrix of the estates of the five passengers. Reyno is not related to and does not know any of the decedents or their survivors; she was a legal secretary to the attorney who filed this lawsuit. Several days after her appointment, Reyno commenced separate wrongful-death actions against Piper and Hartzell in the Superior Court of California, claiming negligence and strict liability. Air Navigation, McDonald, and the estate of the pilot are not parties to this litigation. The survivors of the five passengers whose estates are represented by Reyno filed a separate action in the United Kingdom against Air Navigation, McDonald, and the pilot's estate. Reyno candidly admits that the action against Piper and Hartzell was filed in the United States because its laws regarding liability, capacity to sue, and damages are more favorable to her position than are those of Scotland. Scottish law does not recognize strict liability in tort. Moreover, it permits wrongful-death actions only when brought by a decedent's relatives. The relatives may sue only for "loss of support and society."

On petitioners' motion, the suit was removed to the United States District Court for the Central District of California [and then transferred] to the United States District Court for the Middle District of Pennsylvania, pursuant to 28 U.S.C. § 1404(a).[4]

B

In May 1978, after the suit had been transferred, both Hartzell and Piper moved to dismiss the action on the ground of *forum non conveniens*. The District Court granted these motions in October 1979. It relied on the balancing test set forth by this Court in *Gulf Oil Corp. v. Gilbert*, 330 U.S. 501 (1947) [where] the Court stated that a plaintiff's choice of forum should rarely be disturbed. However, when an alternative forum has jurisdiction to hear the case, and when trial in the chosen forum would "establish . . . oppressiveness and vexation to a defendant . . . out of all proportion to plaintiff's convenience," or when the "chosen forum [is] inappropriate because of considerations affecting the court's own administrative and legal problems," the court may, in the exercise of its sound discretion, dismiss the case. * * * To guide trial court discretion, the Court provided a list of "private interest factors" affecting the convenience of the litigants,

[4] Section 1404(a) provides: "For the convenience of parties and witnesses, in the interest of justice, a district court may transfer any civil action to any other district or division where it might have been brought."

and a list of "public interest factors" affecting the convenience of the forum.[6] * * *

C

On appeal, the United States Court of Appeals for the Third Circuit reversed and remanded for trial. The decision to reverse appears to be based on two alternative grounds. First, the Court held that the District Court abused its discretion in conducting the *Gilbert* analysis. Second, the Court held that dismissal is never appropriate where the law of the alternative forum is less favorable to the plaintiff.

The Court of Appeals began its review of the District Court's *Gilbert* analysis by noting that the plaintiff's choice of forum deserved substantial weight, even though the real parties in interest are nonresidents. It then rejected the District Court's balancing of the private interests. It found that Piper and Hartzell had failed adequately to support their claim that key witnesses would be unavailable if trial were held in the United States: they had never specified the witnesses they would call and the testimony these witnesses would provide. The Court of Appeals gave little weight to the fact that Piper and Hartzell would not be able to implead potential Scottish third-party defendants, reasoning that this difficulty would be "burdensome" but not "unfair" * * *. Finally, the court stated that resolution of the suit would not be significantly aided by familiarity with Scottish topography, or by viewing the wreckage.

The Court of Appeals also rejected the District Court's analysis of the public interest factors. It found that the District Court gave undue emphasis to the application of Scottish law: "the mere fact that the court is called upon to determine and apply foreign law does not present a legal problem of the sort which would justify the dismissal of a case otherwise properly before the court." * * * In any event, it believed that Scottish law need not be applied. After conducting its own choice-of-law analysis, the Court of Appeals determined that American law would govern the actions against both Piper and Hartzell. The same choice-of-law analysis apparently led it to conclude that Pennsylvania and Ohio, rather than Scotland, are the jurisdictions with the greatest policy interests in the dispute, and that all other public interest factors favored trial in the United States. . . .

---

[6] The factors pertaining to the private interests of the litigants included the "relative ease of access to sources of proof; availability of compulsory process for attendance of unwilling, and the cost of obtaining attendance of willing, witnesses; possibility of view of premises, if view would be appropriate to the action; and all other practical problems that make trial of a case easy, expeditious and inexpensive." *Gilbert*, 330 U.S., at 508. The public factors bearing on the question included the administrative difficulties flowing from court congestion; the "local interest in having localized controversies decided at home"; the interest in having the trial of a diversity case in a forum that is at home with the law that must govern the action; the avoidance of unnecessary problems in conflict of laws, or in the application of foreign law; and the unfairness of burdening citizens in an unrelated forum with jury duty. *Id.*, at 509.

In this opinion, we begin by considering whether the Court of Appeals properly held that the possibility of an unfavorable change in law automatically bars dismissal. Part II, *infra*. Since we conclude that the Court of Appeals erred, we then consider its review of the District Court's *Gilbert* analysis to determine whether dismissal was otherwise appropriate. Part III, *infra*. . .

II

The Court of Appeals erred in holding that plaintiffs may defeat a motion to dismiss on the ground of *forum non conveniens* merely by showing that the substantive law that would be applied in the alternative forum is less favorable to the plaintiffs than that of the present forum. The possibility of a change in substantive law should ordinarily not be given conclusive or even substantial weight in the *forum non conveniens* inquiry. . .

Under *Gilbert*, dismissal will ordinarily be appropriate where trial in the plaintiff's chosen forum imposes a heavy burden on the defendant or the court, and where the plaintiff is unable to offer any specific reasons of convenience supporting his choice. If substantial weight were given to the possibility of an unfavorable change in law, however, dismissal might be barred even where trial in the chosen forum was plainly inconvenient.

The Court of Appeals' decision is inconsistent with this Court's earlier *forum non conveniens* decisions in another respect. Those decisions have repeatedly emphasized the need to retain flexibility. . . If central emphasis were placed on any one factor, the *forum non conveniens* doctrine would lose much of the very flexibility that makes it so valuable.

In fact, if conclusive or substantial weight were given to the possibility of a change in law, the *forum non conveniens* doctrine would become virtually useless. Jurisdiction and venue requirements are often easily satisfied. As a result, many plaintiffs are able to choose from among several forums. Ordinarily, these plaintiffs will select that forum whose choice-of-law rules are most advantageous. Thus, if the possibility of an unfavorable change in substantive law is given substantial weight in the *forum non conveniens* inquiry, dismissal would rarely be proper. . . .

The Court of Appeals' approach is not only inconsistent with the purpose of the *forum non conveniens* doctrine, but also poses substantial practical problems. If the possibility of a change in law were given substantial weight, deciding motions to dismiss on the ground of *forum non conveniens* would become quite difficult. Choice-of-law analysis would become extremely important, and the courts would frequently be required to interpret the law of foreign jurisdictions. First, the trial court would have to determine what law would apply if the case were tried in the chosen forum, and what law would apply if the case were tried in the alternative forum. It would then have to compare the rights, remedies, and procedures available under the law that would be applied in each forum. Dismissal would be appropriate only if the court concluded that the law applied by the alternative forum is as favorable to the plaintiff as that of the chosen forum. The doctrine of *forum non conveniens*, however, is designed in part to help courts avoid conducting complex exercises in comparative law. . .

Upholding the decision of the Court of Appeals would result in other practical problems. At least where the foreign plaintiff named an American manufacturer as defendant, a court could not dismiss the case on grounds of *forum non conveniens* where dismissal might lead to an unfavorable change in law. The American courts, which are already extremely attractive to foreign plaintiffs, would become even more attractive. The flow of litigation into the United States would increase and further congest already crowded courts.

The Court of Appeals based its decision, at least in part, on an analogy between dismissals on grounds of *forum non conveniens* and transfers between federal courts pursuant to § 1404(a). In *Van Dusen v. Barrack*, 376 U.S. 612 (1964), this Court ruled that a § 1404(a) transfer should not result in a change in the applicable law. Relying on dictum in an earlier Third Circuit opinion interpreting *Van Dusen,* the court below held that that principle is also applicable to a dismissal on *forum non conveniens* grounds. * * * However, § 1404(a) transfers are different than dismissals on the ground of *forum non conveniens*.

Congress enacted § 1404(a) to permit change of venue between federal courts. Although the statute was drafted in accordance with the doctrine of *forum non conveniens,* * * * it was intended to be a revision rather than a codification of the common law. * * * District courts were given more discretion to transfer under § 1404(a) than they had to dismiss on grounds of *forum non conveniens*. * * *

The reasoning employed in *Van Dusen v. Barrack* is simply inapplicable to dismissals on grounds of *forum non conveniens*. That case did not discuss the common-law doctrine. Rather, it focused on "the construction and application" of § 1404(a). * * * Emphasizing the remedial purpose of the statute, *Barrack* concluded that Congress could not have intended a transfer to be accompanied by a change in law.* * * The statute was designed as a "federal housekeeping measure," allowing easy change of venue within a unified federal system. * * * The Court feared that if a change in venue were accompanied by a change in law, forum-shopping parties would take unfair advantage of the relaxed standards for transfer. The rule was necessary to ensure the just and efficient operation of the statute.

We do not hold that the possibility of an unfavorable change in law should *never* be a relevant consideration in a *forum non conveniens* inquiry. Of course, if the remedy provided by the alternative forum is so clearly inadequate or unsatisfactory that it is no remedy at all, the unfavorable change in law may be given substantial weight; the district court may conclude that dismissal would not be in the interests of justice.[22] In these cases, however, the remedies that would be provided by the Scottish courts do not fall within this category. Although the relatives of the decedents may not be able to rely on a strict liability theory, and although their potential damages award may be smaller, there is no danger that they will be deprived of any remedy or treated unfairly.

III

The Court of Appeals also erred in rejecting the District Court's *Gilbert* analysis. . .

A

The District Court acknowledged that there is ordinarily a strong presumption in favor of the plaintiff's choice of forum, which may be overcome only when the private and public interest factors clearly point towards trial in the alternative forum. It held, however, that the presumption applies with less force when the plaintiff or real parties in interest are foreign.

The District Court's distinction between resident or citizen plaintiffs and foreign plaintiffs is fully justified. . . When the home forum has been chosen, it is reasonable to assume that this choice is convenient. When the plaintiff is foreign, however, this assumption is much less reasonable. Because the central purpose of any *forum non conveniens* inquiry is to ensure that the trial is convenient, a foreign plaintiff's choice deserves less deference.[24]

B

The *forum non conveniens* determination is committed to the sound discretion of the trial court. It may be reversed only when there has been a clear abuse of discretion; where the court has considered all relevant public and private interest factors, and where its balancing of these factors is reasonable, its decision deserves substantial deference. * * * . . .

---

[22] At the outset of any *forum non conveniens* inquiry, the court must determine whether there exists an alternative forum. Ordinarily, this requirement will be satisfied when the defendant is "amenable to process" in the other jurisdiction. * * * In rare circumstances, however, where the remedy offered by the other forum is clearly unsatisfactory, the other forum may not be an adequate alternative, and the initial requirement may not be satisfied. Thus, for example, dismissal would not be appropriate where the alternative forum does not permit litigation of the subject matter of the dispute. * * *

[24] . . . Respondent argues that since plaintiffs will ordinarily file suit in the jurisdiction that offers the most favorable law, establishing a strong presumption in favor of both home and foreign plaintiffs will ensure that defendants will always be held to the highest possible standard of accountability for their purported wrongdoing. However, the deference accorded a plaintiff's choice of forum has never been intended to guarantee that the plaintiff will be able to select the law that will govern the case. * * *

(1)

In analyzing the private interest factors, the District Court stated that the connections with Scotland are "overwhelming." * * * This characterization may be somewhat exaggerated. Particularly with respect to the question of relative ease of access to sources of proof, the private interests point in both directions. As respondent emphasizes, records concerning the design, manufacture, and testing of the propeller and plane are located in the United States. She would have greater access to sources of proof relevant to her strict liability and negligence theories if trial were held here.[25] However, the District Court did not act unreasonably in concluding that fewer evidentiary problems would be posed if the trial were held in Scotland. A large proportion of the relevant evidence is located in Great Britain.

The Court of Appeals found that the problems of proof could not be given any weight because Piper and Hartzell failed to describe with specificity the evidence they would not be able to obtain if trial were held in the United States. It suggested that defendants seeking *forum non conveniens* dismissal must submit affidavits identifying the witnesses they would call and the testimony these witnesses would provide if the trial were held in the alternative forum. Such detail is not necessary. Piper and Hartzell have moved for dismissal precisely because many crucial witnesses are located beyond the reach of compulsory process, and thus are difficult to identify or interview. Requiring extensive investigation would defeat the purpose of their motion. Of course, defendants must provide enough information to enable the District Court to balance the parties' interests. Our examination of the record convinces us that sufficient information was provided here. Both Piper and Hartzell submitted affidavits describing the evidentiary problems they would face if the trial were held in the United States.

The District Court correctly concluded that the problems posed by the inability to implead potential third-party defendants clearly supported holding the trial in Scotland. Joinder of the pilot's estate, Air Navigation, and McDonald is crucial to the presentation of petitioners' defense. If Piper and Hartzell can show that the accident was caused not by a design defect, but rather by the negligence of the pilot, the plane's owners, or the charter company, they will be relieved of all liability. It is true, of course, that if Hartzell and Piper were found liable after a trial in the United States, they could institute an action for indemnity or contribution against these parties in Scotland. It would be far more convenient, however, to resolve all claims in one trial. . .

---

[25] In the future, where similar problems are presented, district courts might dismiss subject to the condition that defendant corporations agree to provide the records relevant to the plaintiff's claims.

(2)

The District Court's review of the factors relating to the public interest was also reasonable. . .

Scotland has a very strong interest in this litigation. The accident occurred in its airspace. All of the decedents were Scottish. Apart from Piper and Hartzell, all potential plaintiffs and defendants are either Scottish or English. As we stated in *Gilbert,* there is "a local interest in having localized controversies decided at home." * * * Respondent argues that American citizens have an interest in ensuring that American manufacturers are deterred from producing defective products, and that additional deterrence might be obtained if Piper and Hartzell were tried in the United States, where they could be sued on the basis of both negligence and strict liability. However, the incremental deterrence that would be gained if this trial were held in an American court is likely to be insignificant. The American interest in this accident is simply not sufficient to justify the enormous commitment of judicial time and resources that would inevitably be required if the case were to be tried here.

IV

The Court of Appeals erred in holding that the possibility of an unfavorable change in law bars dismissal on the ground of *forum non conveniens*. It also erred in rejecting the District Court's *Gilbert* analysis. The District Court properly decided that the presumption in favor of the respondent's forum choice applied with less than maximum force because the real parties in interest are foreign. It did not act unreasonably in deciding that the private interests pointed towards trial in Scotland. Nor did it act unreasonably in deciding that the public interests favored trial in Scotland. Thus, the judgment of the Court of Appeals is

Reversed.

JUSTICE POWELL took no part in the decision of these cases.

JUSTICE O'CONNOR took no part in the consideration or decision of these cases.

JUSTICE WHITE, concurring in part and dissenting in part.

I join Parts I and II of the Court's opinion. However, like JUSTICE BRENNAN and JUSTICE STEVENS, I would not proceed to deal with the issues addressed in Part III. To that extent, I am in dissent.

JUSTICE STEVENS, with whom JUSTICE BRENNAN joins, dissenting.

. . . I agree that [the question of whether a motion to dismiss on forum non conveniens grounds should be denied whenever the law of the alternate forum is less favorable to recovery] should be answered in the negative. Having decided that question, I would simply remand the case to the Court of Appeals for further consideration of the question whether the District

Court correctly decided that Pennsylvania was not a convenient forum in which to litigate a claim against a Pennsylvania company that a plane was defectively designed and manufactured in Pennsylvania.

Piper and the Inconvenient Forum

(1) Why should a court ever decline to hear a case over which it has jurisdiction? Given that the due process analysis already requires that the exercise of jurisdiction be "reasonable," why is a separate *forum non conveniens* doctrine necessary?

(2) Given the existence of 28 U.S.C. § 1404(a), federal courts may dismiss on *forum non conveniens* grounds only if the alternate forum is a foreign court. See *American Dredging Co. v. Miller*, 510 U.S. 443, 449 n.2 (1994) ("As a consequence [of the enactment of § 1404(a)], the federal doctrine of *forum non conveniens* has continuing application only in cases where the alternative forum is abroad."). As we saw in the discussion of *Ferens*, supra p. 391, and as *Piper* notes, when a district court transfers an action under § 1404(a), the transferee court must apply the same law the transferor court would have. What purpose does this rule serve? An analogous rule is of course impossible in the *forum non conveniens* context, since a court dismissing an action has no power to direct some other court to apply a particular law, but does it suggest that the prospect of the plaintiff's being forced to litigate under less favorable law should be relevant to a forum non conveniens analysis? Is it relevant to this question that *forum non conveniens* motions are brought only by defendants, while both sides can move for transfer under § 1404(a)? Why should plaintiffs be able to move for such a transfer anyway?

(3) Look at the factors set forth in footnote 6 of *Piper*. Does the Court explain how to weigh them against each other? Could a *forum non conveniens* dismissal ever raise issues of unconstitutional discrimination under *Hughes v. Fetter* (supra p. 414)? Under *Austin v. New Hampshire* (supra pp. 432–433)? In *Douglas v. New York, N.H. & H.R. Co.*, 279 U.S. 377 (1929), the Court rejected a privileges and immunities challenge to a New York statute that gave New York courts discretion to dismiss nonresidents' (but not residents') suits against foreign corporations doing business in the state. "There are manifest reasons," the Court observed, "for preferring residents in access to often overcrowded Courts, both in convenience and in the fact that broadly speaking it is they who pay for maintaining the Courts concerned."

Is that the Court's explanation for greater deference to a citizen's forum choice in *Piper*? Or is the idea that the distinction is between plaintiffs who have selected their home court and those who have not? Does it matter?

CHAPTER 5

RECOGNITION OF JUDGMENTS

■ ■ ■

Res Judicata: Domestic Policies of Finality

The effects of a domestic judgment on subsequent litigation in the same state differ in detail from state to state, but the major features of this largely judge-created law are very similar throughout the United States. The underlying policies are everywhere the same: to minimize the judicial energy devoted to individual cases, establish certainty and respect for court judgments, and protect the party relying on the prior adjudication from vexatious litigation. Moreover, the trend in the United States has long been toward increased finality. Without attempting a detailed survey of the law of res judicata, a few comments may refresh the student's recollection of matters examined in first-year procedure courses.

An attack on a judgment may be either *direct* or *collateral*. A timely appeal to a higher court in the same jurisdiction is the most obvious method of direct attack. In addition, procedural rules normally empower the court rendering a judgment to set it aside for stated reasons. Rule 59 of the Federal Rules of Civil Procedure, for example, authorizes the court to grant a new trial for limited reasons and for a limited period of time (motions must be made within ten days after entry of judgment); and Rule 60 provides more limited grounds (such as fraud, newly discovered evidence, and the like) and a somewhat less limited time period for relieving a party of a final judgment.

A judgment may also be collaterally attacked in subsequent litigation that raises an issue concerning the binding effect of earlier litigation. The problem is frequently referred to as that of *res judicata,* but that slippery term is often limited to the effect of a judgment on a subsequent case involving the same cause of action. *Collateral estoppel* was for many years the accepted term for the body of law governing the effect in a later litigation of findings made in an earlier adjudicatory contest involving a different cause of action but some of the same issues. These older terms are now employed more or less interchangeably with a set of newer ones incorporated in Restatement (Second) of Judgments (1982): *claim preclusion* and *issue preclusion.*

The binding effect of a prior judgment in the state in which it was rendered is largely a question of local law, though this law is heavily influenced by common-law developments elsewhere and by federal law (constitutional, statutory, and judicially created) dealing with the effect of one state's judgment in litigation in another state. A brief summary of generally accepted principles will provide a foundation for the question which is the focus of these materials, namely, collateral attacks in the state and federal courts of a sister state.

Claim preclusion precludes further suits upon the same cause of action after a final judgment. The original claim is said to be "barred" by a judgment for the defendant and "merged" in one for the plaintiff. These principles forbid relitigation of matters actually decided, on the ground that there is no assurance that a second decision will be more correct than the first. Further, policies against the fragmentation of litigation into several lawsuits when one will suffice often preclude a party from raising issues that could have been, but were not, litigated in the first suit. Judgments resulting from in rem or quasi in rem proceedings may have a more limited effect, reducing the amount due but not extinguishing the underlying claim. There are also some equitable exceptions to the merger rule, such as that an original judgment is not merged in a second judgment rendered in an action to enforce it; the plaintiff may bring suit on either the original or the second judgment until he or she obtains satisfaction.

Issue preclusion deals with situations in which issues determined in previous litigation were "(1) litigated by the parties; (2) determined by the tribunal; and (3) necessarily so determined." F. James, G. Hazard & J. Leubsdorf, Civil Procedure 607 (4th ed. 1992). If the judgment is not "on the merits" (e.g., a dismissal for want of jurisdiction), the claim may be brought again, but matters actually decided will be foreclosed by the principle of "direct estoppel." Similarly, collateral estoppel gives preclusive effect to essential findings necessarily determined in an earlier litigation in a subsequent litigation on another cause of action between the same parties. Issue preclusion is thus both broader and narrower than claim preclusion: broader since the cause of action need not be the same; narrower since issue preclusion extends only to essential issues of fact that have been actually litigated and determined. A default judgment is illustrative; it may preclude a subsequent suit involving the same claim, but it has no issue-preclusive effect because no actual contest over facts occurs when a case is terminated by default.

It should be apparent that, in effect, rules of res judicata serve to define local policies concerning the desirable scope of lawsuits. That is, rules against "splitting a cause of action" are really rules of compulsory joinder of claims, enforced by precluding subsequent assertion of the omitted claim. It is thus obviously important how a state defines the scope of a "claim" or "cause of action" for these purposes. Various tests have been suggested and used:

> Among the most common are that the cause of action is the same if: (a) the same principles of substantive and procedural law are applicable to both actions, (b) the same right is alleged to be infringed by the same wrong in both actions, (c) the judgment sought in the second action would infringe rights established in the first, (d) the same evidence would support both actions, or (e) the operative facts are the same in both actions.

Note, *Developments in the Law: Res Judicata,* 65 Harv.L.Rev. 818, 824–25 (1952). In general, the modern trend has been away from tests based on conceptualistic legal definitions and toward a more fact-based pragmatic approach.

Both claim preclusion and issue preclusion require some identity of parties. The traditional position, still followed when it comes to claim preclusion, requires that the parties to the former and current litigations be identical or in *privity*. The privity concept includes not only formally represented parties, but also hidden parties (those who are in control of litigation although not formal parties) and parties whose connection is so close that it is fair to bind them by the former judgment. Examples are successors to property interests, beneficiaries and their fiduciaries, and indemnitors and indemnitees.

Some years ago party identity or privity was also required for issue preclusion (collateral estoppel). The so-called doctrine of mutuality prevented use of a fact or issue determination by a person who would not have been bound by the determination in the earlier litigation had it been decided the other way. Recently, however, the requirement of mutuality has been relaxed, and many state courts, as well as the federal courts, now allow nonmutual issue preclusion in some situations. Thus, if P-1 has litigated and won a determination that D was negligent in a particular situation, P-2 may be permitted to take advantage of this finding in a subsequent suit against D arising out of the same occurrence or raising the same issue. The party against whom the finding is used must have been a party or in privity with a party to the previous litigation, and the issue must have been fairly and fully litigated; but the person subsequently using the finding is relieved from the requirement that he or she would have been precluded by an adverse determination.

The application of issue preclusion involves many difficult questions of analysis and policy: What issues are sufficiently important in the first litigation so that it is fair to impose on the parties (or one of them) the risk that a finding will be conclusive in subsequent litigation that may or may not be foreseeable at the time of the first case? When has a question been litigated? Is the preclusive effect of litigation affected by the limited jurisdiction of the court (e.g., a small claims court)? If mutuality does not exist (i.e., when the other party would not be bound if the finding went the other way), is it fair to bind the losing party to earlier litigation?

Full Faith and Credit to Judgments

(1) The Constitution of the United States, Art. IV, § 1 (1789):

> Full Faith and Credit shall be given in each State to the public Acts, Records, and Judicial Proceedings of every other State. And the Congress may by general Laws prescribe the Manner in which such Acts, Records and Proceedings shall be proved, and the Effect thereof.

This clause was implemented in a statute passed by the First Congress in 1790 which is now codified (as amended) at 28 U.S.C. § 1738 and which provides, in relevant part:

> The records and judicial proceedings of any court of any . . . State, Territory or Possession [of the United States] . . . , or copies thereof, so authenticated, shall have the same full faith and credit in every court within the United States and its Territories and Possessions as they have by law or usage in the courts of such State, Territory of Possession from which they are taken.

(2) Reese & Johnson, *The Scope of Full Faith and Credit to Judgments,* 49 Colum.L.Rev. 153–55 (1949):

> The historical background [of full faith and credit] is meager. One year before the Continental Congress began its sessions, the Province of Massachusetts, impelled by the problem created by "negligent and evil minded" judgment debtors who sought to escape the force of a local judgment by the simple expedient of leaving the jurisdiction, passed a statute providing in essence that the merits of a claim embodied in the judgment of a sister colony should not be subject to reexamination when sued upon in the local courts. The Articles of Confederation prescribed that "full faith and credit" should be accorded state judgments but there is no mention in the records of the Continental Congress either of the purpose of the enactment or of the meaning which the framers attached to its words. The clause as it finally appeared in the Federal Constitution was broadened to include not only "records and judicial proceedings" but also "public acts." Furthermore, it contained explicit authorization for legislative implementation by providing that Congress "may . . . prescribe . . . the Effect thereof."
>
> These were significant changes. Yet the framers apparently showed little interest in the clause and their debate of the issue is

summed up in a few pages of the *Records of the Convention.* This casual attitude is nicely shown by the brief floor explanation of its meaning: "Mr. Wilson and Docr. Johnson supposed the meaning to be that Judgments in one State should be the ground of actions in other States, and that acts of the Legislatures should be included, for the sake of Acts of insolvency." Madison added in a short passage in *The Federalist* that he thought the clause would be "particularly beneficial on the borders of contiguous states, where the effects liable to justice may be suddenly and secretly translated in any stage of the process, within a foreign jurisdiction." The real improvement of the clause over its Confederation counterpart, he thought, lay in the power given to Congress, for, he said, without that body's declaration the clause was without real meaning.

(3) The Full Faith and Credit Clause puts national sanction behind state policies with respect to the effect of a judgment. In requiring federal courts to respect state judgments (*Davis v. Davis,* 305 U.S. 32, 40 (1938)), and in requiring respect for judgments of territories and possessions, § 1738 has gone beyond the authorizing grant of the Full Faith Clause, but both requirements seem amply justified as necessary and proper to the creation of federal and territorial courts under Articles III and IV. Notice the interesting omission from the statute of any provision for state-court respect for the judgments of federal courts within the United States proper. The Supreme Court has nonetheless managed to hold that state courts are required to respect federal judgments by relying on language in the statute referring to judgments of courts in any "country" under United States jurisdiction. *Dupasseur v. Rochereau,* 88 U.S. (21 Wall.) 130, 134 (1875); *Metcalf v. Watertown,* 153 U.S. 671 (1894). See also *Stoll v. Gottlieb,* 305 U.S. 165 (1938); and *Hancock Nat. Bank v. Farnum,* 176 U.S. 640 (1900). This peculiar statutory handle was omitted in the 1948 version. In *Semtek International Inc. v. Lockheed Martin Corp.,* 531 U.S. 497 (2001), the Supreme Court held that the preclusive effect of a federal-court judgment in state court was a matter of federal common law—but that the federal common law parallels whatever preclusion rules would be applied by the courts of state in which the federal court that rendered the judgment sits. For a fuller discussion of *Semtek,* see infra pp. 873–879.

The classic full faith and credit cases involve attempts to enforce the judgments of one state in the courts of another. The following cases are illustrative.

FAUNTLEROY V. LUM*

210 U.S. 230 (1908).

[The State of Mississippi made it a crime to gamble in futures, and its courts were forbidden to enforce any contract in violation of the prohibition. Two residents of Mississippi made contracts in that State which were performed there, and which violated the prohibition. The parties submitted their dispute to arbitration, and the prevailing party sued in a state court in Mississippi to recover on the arbitration award. After the court was made aware of the prohibited nature of the transactions, the plaintiff dismissed the case. Subsequently, the party in whose favor the award had been made brought an action in Missouri, and succeeded in getting personal service upon the other citizen of Mississippi, the latter being temporarily in Missouri. Rejecting evidence offered by the defendant to show that the transactions were illegal under the laws of Mississippi, the Missouri court submitted the case to a jury, with an instruction to find for the plaintiff if they believed that the award had been made as alleged. A verdict and judgment went in favor of the plaintiff. The judgment was then assigned by the plaintiff to his attorney, who sued on it in a Mississippi court, where the prohibitory statutes of the State were pleaded as a defense. Ultimately the case went to the Supreme Court of Mississippi, where it was decided that the Missouri judgment was not required, under the Full Faith and Credit Clause, to be enforced in Mississippi, as it concerned transactions which had taken place exclusively in Mississippi, between residents of that State, which were in violation of laws embodying the public policy of that State, and to give effect to which would be enforcing transactions which the courts of Mississippi had no authority to enforce.]

MR. JUSTICE HOLMES delivered the opinion of the court. . .

The main argument urged by the defendant to sustain the judgment below is addressed to the jurisdiction of the Mississippi courts.

The laws of Mississippi make dealing in futures a misdemeanor, and provide that contracts of that sort, made without intent to deliver the commodity or to pay the price, "shall not be enforced by any court." Annotated Code of 1892, §§ 1120, 1121, 2117. The defendant contends that this language deprives the Mississippi courts of jurisdiction, and that the case is like *Anglo-American Provision Co. v. Davis Provision Co.*, 191 U.S. 373. There the New York statutes refused to provide a court into which a foreign corporation could come, except upon causes of action arising within the State, etc., and it was held that the State of New York was under no constitutional obligation to give jurisdiction to its Supreme Court against its will. One question is whether that decision is in point.

---

* The statement of facts is adapted from the dissenting opinion of Justice White, 210 U.S. at 238–39.

No doubt it sometimes may be difficult to decide whether certain words in a statute are directed to jurisdiction or to merits, but the distinction between the two is plain. One goes to the power, the other only to the duty of the court. Under the common law it is the duty of a court of general jurisdiction not to enter a judgment upon a parol promise made without consideration; but it has power to do it, and, if it does, the judgment is unimpeachable, unless reversed. Yet a statute could be framed that would make the power, that is, the jurisdiction of the court dependent upon whether there was a consideration or not. Whether a given statute is intended simply to establish a rule of substantive law, and thus to define the duty of the court, or is meant to limit its power, is a question of construction and common sense. When it affects a court of general jurisdiction and deals with a matter upon which that court must pass, we naturally are slow to read ambiguous words, as meaning to leave the judgment open to dispute, or as intended to do more than to fix the rule by which the court should decide.

The case quoted concerned a statute plainly dealing with the authority and jurisdiction of the New York court. The statute now before us seems to us only to lay down a rule of decision. The Mississippi court in which this action was brought is a court of general jurisdiction and would have to decide upon the validity of the bar, if the suit upon the award or upon the original cause of action had been brought there. The words "shall not be enforced by any court" are simply another, possibly less emphatic, way of saying that an action shall not be brought to enforce such contracts. As suggested by the counsel for the plaintiff in error, no one would say that the words of the Mississippi statute of frauds, "An action shall not be brought whereby to charge a defendant," Code 1892, § 4225, go to the jurisdiction of the court. . . We regard this question as open under the decisions below, and we have expressed our opinion upon it independent of the effect of the judgment, although it might be that, even if jurisdiction of the original cause of action was withdrawn, it remained with regard to a suit upon a judgment based upon an award, whether the judgment or award was conclusive or not. But it might be held that the law as to jurisdiction in one case followed the law in the other, and therefore we proceed at once to the further question, whether the illegality of the original cause of action in Mississippi can be relied upon there as a ground for denying a recovery upon a judgment of another State.

The doctrine laid down by Chief Justice Marshall was "that the judgment of a state court should have the same credit, validity, and effect in every other court in the United States, which it had in the State where it was pronounced, and that whatever pleas would be good to a suit thereon in such State, and none others, could be pleaded in any other court of the United States." *Hampton v. McConnel,* 3 Wheat. 234. There is no doubt that this quotation was supposed to be an accurate statement of the law as late as *Christmas v. Russell,* 5 Wall. 290, where an attempt of Mississippi, by statute, to go behind judgments recovered in other States was declared void, and it was held that such judgments could not be impeached even for fraud. . .

We assume that the statement of Chief Justice Marshall is correct. It is confirmed by the Act of May 26, 1790, c. 11, 1 Stat. 122 . . . [now 28 U.S.C. § 1738], providing that the said records and judicial proceedings "shall have such faith and credit given to them in every court within the United States, as they have by law or usage in the courts of the State from whence the said records are or shall be taken." . . . Whether the award would or would not have been conclusive, and whether the ruling of the Missouri court upon that matter was right or wrong, there can be no question that the judgment was conclusive in Missouri on the validity of the cause of action. *Pitts v. Fugate,* 41 Missouri, 405 * * *. A judgment is conclusive as to all the media concludendi, *United States v. California & Oregon Land Co.,* 192 U.S. 355; and it needs no authority to show that it cannot be impeached either in or out of the State by showing that it was based upon a mistake of law. Of course a want of jurisdiction over either the person or the subject-matter might be shown. *Andrews v. Andrews,* 188 U.S. 14; *Clarke v. Clarke,* 178 U.S. 186. But as the jurisdiction of the Missouri court is not open to dispute the judgment cannot be impeached in Mississippi even if it went upon a misapprehension of the Mississippi law. * * *

We feel no apprehensions that painful or humiliating consequences will follow upon our decision. No court would give judgment for a plaintiff unless it believed that the facts were a cause of action by the law determining their effect. Mistakes will be rare. In this case the Missouri court no doubt supposed that the award was binding by the law of Mississippi. If it was mistaken it made a natural mistake. The validity of its judgment, even in Mississippi, is, as we believe, the result of the Constitution as it always has been understood, and is not a matter to arouse the susceptibilities of the States, all of which are equally concerned in the question and equally on both sides.

Judgment reversed.

MR. JUSTICE WHITE, with whom concurred MR. JUSTICE HARLAN, MR. JUSTICE MCKENNA and MR. JUSTICE DAY, dissenting. . .

Although not wishing in the slightest degree to weaken the operation of the due faith and credit clause as interpreted and applied from the beginning, it to me seems that this ruling so enlarges that clause as to cause it to obliterate all state lines, since the effect will be to endow each State with authority to overthrow the public policy and criminal statutes of the others, thereby depriving all of their lawful authority. . .

[U]nder the rules of comity recognized at the time of the adoption of the Constitution, and which at this time universally prevail, no sovereignty was or is under the slightest moral obligation to give effect to a judgment of a court of another sovereignty, when to do so would compel the State in which the judgment was sought to be executed to enforce an illegal and prohibited contract, when both the contract and all the acts done in connection with its performance had taken place in the latter State. This seems to me conclusive of this case, since both in treatises of authoritative writers (Story, Conflict of Law § 609), and by repeated adjudications of this court it has been settled that the purpose of the due faith and credit clause was not to confer any new power, but simply to make obligatory that duty which, when the Constitution was adopted rested, as has been said, in comity alone. . .

In addition to the considerations just stated, in my opinion this case is controlled by *Anglo-Am. Prov. Co. v. Davis Prov. Co., No. 1,* supra, cited in the opinion of the court. . . [I]n considering the very language found in the statute here in question as contained in a prior statute of the same nature, the Supreme Court of the State held (*Lemonius v. Mayer,* 71 Mississippi, 514), "that by the second section of the act of 1882 the complainants were denied access to the courts of this State to enforce their demand . . . for the money advanced for the purchase of the 'futures' in cotton." The want of power in the courts of Mississippi under the local statute is therefore foreclosed in this court by the construction given to the statute by the state court of last resort. . .

No special reference has been made by me to the arbitration, because that is assumed by me to be negligible. If the cause of action was open for inquiry for the purpose of deciding whether the Missouri court had jurisdiction to render a judgment entitled to be enforced in another State, the arbitration is of no consequence. The violation of law in Mississippi could not be cured by seeking to arbitrate in that State in order to fix the sum of the fruits of the illegal acts. The ancient maxims that something cannot be made out of nothing, and that which is void for reasons of public policy cannot be made valid by confirmation or acquiescence, seem to my mind decisive.

I therefore dissent.

YARBOROUGH V. YARBOROUGH

290 U.S. 202 (1933).

[Mr. and Ms. Yarborough and their daughter Sadie lived together in Georgia until 1927, when Mr. Yarborough brought suit for divorce and Ms. Yarborough cross-claimed for divorce, custody of Sadie, and support. The Georgia court decreed a divorce, awarded custody of Sadie to Ms. Yarborough, and provided for Sadie's maintenance and support by ordering Mr. Yarborough to pay $1,750 to her grandfather as her trustee. Sadie was not a party to the Georgia proceeding; nor was a guardian ad litem appointed to represent her interests. Sadie then went to South Carolina to live with her grandfather. In 1930, Sadie, then sixteen years of age, brought suit in South Carolina to require her father to make provision for her education and maintenance. She alleged "that she is now ready for college and is without funds and, unless the defendant makes provision for her, will be denied the necessities of life and an education, and will be dependent upon the charity of others." Property of Mr. Yarborough in South Carolina was attached; and somewhat later he was served personally in South Carolina. The South Carolina court, over Yarborough's objection that the Georgia decree relieved him of all obligation to provide for Sadie's support and must be given full faith and credit in South Carolina, ordered Yarborough to pay $50 monthly for Sadie's education and support.]

MR. JUSTICE BRANDEIS delivered the opinion of the Court. . .

By the law of Georgia, it is the duty of the father to provide for the maintenance and education of his child until maturity. . . If the father fails to make such provision, any person (including a divorced wife) who furnishes necessaries of life to his minor child may recover from him therefor, unless precluded by the terms of the decree in the divorce suit or otherwise. In case of total divorce, the court is authorized to make, by its decree, final or permanent provision for the maintenance and education of children during minority, and thus fix the extent of the father's obligation. But, even if the decree for total divorce fails to include a provision for the support of minor children, they cannot maintain in their own names, or by guardian ad litem, or by next friend, an independent suit for an allowance for education and maintenance.

First. It was contended below in the trial court, and there held, that the provision of the decree of the Georgia court directing the payment to R.D. Blowers, trustee, of $1,750 to be "expended by him in his discretion for the benefit of the minor child, including her education, support, maintenance, medical attention and other necessary items of expenditure," was not intended to relieve the father from all further liability to support Sadie. This contention appears to have been abandoned. It is clear that Mrs. Yarborough, her husband, and the court intended that this provision should absolve Sadie's father from further obligation to support her. . .

Third. It is contended that the Georgia decree is not binding upon Sadie, because she was not a formal party to the suit, was not served with process, and no guardian ad litem was appointed for her therein. . . The provision which the Georgia law makes of permanent alimony for the child during minority is a legal incident of the divorce proceeding. As that suit embraces within its scope the disposition and care of minor children, jurisdiction over the parents confers eo ipso jurisdiction over the minor's custody and support. Hence, by the Georgia law, a consent (or other) decree in a divorce suit fixing permanent alimony for a minor child is binding upon it, although the child was not served with process, was not made a formal party to the suit, and no guardian ad litem was appointed therein.

Fourth. It is contended that the order for permanent alimony is not binding upon Sadie because she was not a resident of Georgia at the time it was entered. Being a minor, Sadie's domicile was Georgia, that of her father; and her domicile continued to be in Georgia until entry of the judgment in question... Mrs. Yarborough filed a cross-bill, as well as an answer; and in the cross-bill prayed "that provision for permanent alimony be made for the" support and education of Sadie. Thus the court acquired complete jurisdiction of the marriage status and, as an incident, power to finally determine the extent of her father's obligation to support his minor child.

Fifth. The fact that Sadie has become a resident of South Carolina does not impair the finality of the judgment. South Carolina thereby acquired the jurisdiction to determine her status and the incidents of that status. Upon residents of that state it could impose duties for her benefit. Doubtless, it might have imposed upon her grandfather who was resident there a duty to support Sadie. But the mere fact of Sadie's residence in South Carolina does not give that state the power to impose such a duty upon the father who is not a resident and who long has been domiciled in Georgia. He has fulfilled the duty which he owes her by the law of his domicile and the judgment of its court. Upon that judgment he is entitled to rely. It was settled by *Sistare v. Sistare,* 218 U.S. 1, that the full faith and credit clause applies to an unalterable decree of alimony for a divorced wife. The clause applies, likewise, to an unalterable decree of alimony for a minor child. We need not consider whether South Carolina would have power to require the father, if he were domiciled there, to make further provision for the support, maintenance, or education of his daughter.

Reversed.

MR. JUSTICE STONE.

I think the judgment should be affirmed...

For present purposes we may take it that the Georgia decree, as the statutes and decisions of the state declare, is unalterable and, as pronounced, is effective to govern the rights of the parties in Georgia. But there is nothing [in] the decree itself or in the history of the proceedings which led to it to suggest that it was rendered with any purpose or intent to regulate or control the relationship of parent and child, or the duties which flow from it, in places outside the state of Georgia where they might later come to reside... But, if we are to read the decree as though it contained a clause, in terms, restricting the power of any other state in which the minor might come to reside, to make provision for her support, then, in the absence of some law of Congress requiring it, I am not persuaded that the full faith and credit clause gives sanction to such control by one state of the internal affairs of another.

Congress has said that the public records and the judicial proceedings of each state are to be given such faith and credit in other states as is accorded to them in the state "from which they are taken." * * * But this broad language has never been applied without limitations. See *M'Elmoyle v. Cohen,* 13 Pet. 312. Between the prohibition of the due process clause, acting upon the courts of the state from which such proceedings may be taken, and the mandate of the full faith and credit clause, acting upon the state to which they may be taken, there is an area which federal authority has not occupied. As this Court has often recognized, there are many judgments which need not be given the same force and effect abroad which they have at home, and there are some, though valid in the state where rendered, to which the full faith and credit clause gives no force elsewhere. In the assertion of rights, defined by a judgment of one state, within the territory of another there is often an inescapable conflict of interest of the two states, and there comes a point beyond which the imposition of the will of one state beyond its own borders involves a forbidden infringement of some legitimate domestic interest of the other. That point may vary with the circumstances of the case, and, in the absence of provisions more specific than the general terms of the congressional enactment, this Court must determine for itself the extent to which one state may qualify or deny rights claimed under proceedings or records of other states.

More than once this Court has approved the doctrine that a state need give no effect to judgments for conviction of crime or for penalties procured in a sister state. See *Wisconsin v. Pelican Insurance Co.,* 127 U.S. 265; *Huntington v. Attrill,* 146 U.S. 657, 675 * * *. And the intervention of a sister state's judgment will not overcome a local policy against allowing to foreign corporations the use of local courts in settling foreign disputes. *Anglo-American Provision Co. v. Davis Provision Co.,* 191 U.S. 373. Compare *Kenney v. Supreme Lodge of the World,* 252 U.S. 411. The state of matrimonial domicile may preserve to its own resident his rights in the marriage status where another state has sought to terminate it, without acquiring jurisdiction of his person, *Haddock v. Haddock,* 201 U.S. 562, even though terminated within the other state. Cf. *Maynard v. Hill,* 125 U.S. 190. . . The interest of a state in controlling all the legal incidents of real property located within its boundaries is deemed so complete and so vital to the exercise of its sovereign powers of government within its own territory as to exclude any control over them by the statutes or judgments of other states.

It would be going further than this Court has been willing to go in any decision to say that the power of a state to pass judgment upon the sanity of its own citizen could be foreclosed by an earlier judgment of the court of some other state dealing with the same subject-matter. Cf. *Gasquet v. Fenner,* 247 U.S. 16.

Similarly it has been almost uniformly recognized that a divorce decree which by its terms or by operation of law forbids remarriage of one or both of the parties can have no effect outside the state which rendered it. Jurisdictional requirements being satisfied, the decree is effective to end the marriage for all states, but enforcement of its prohibition against remarriage in another state, even though the parties do not take up their residence there, would infringe upon the interest which every state has to maintain the stability of a union entered into according to the laws of the place of celebration. . .

The maintenance and support of children domiciled within a state, like their education and custody, is a subject in which government itself is deemed to have a peculiar interest and concern. Their tender years, their inability to provide for themselves, the importance to the state that its future citizens should be clothed, nourished, and suitably educated, are considerations which lead all civilized countries to assume some control over the maintenance of minors. The states very generally make some provision from their own resources for the maintenance and support of orphans or destitute children, but, in order that children may not become public charges, the duty of maintenance is one imposed primarily upon the parents, according to the needs of the child and their ability to meet those needs. . . The measure of the duty is the need of the child and the ability of the parent to meet those needs at the very time when performance of the duty is invoked. Hence it is no answer in such a suit that at some earlier time provision was made for the child, which is no longer available or suitable because of his greater needs, or because of the increased financial ability of the parent to provide for them, or that the child may be maintained from other sources.

In view of the universality of these principles, it comes as a surprise that any state, merely because it has made some provision for the support of a child, should, either by statute or judicial decree, so tie its own hand as to foreclose all future inquiry into the duty of maintenance however affected by changed conditions.

Even though the Constitution does not deny to Georgia the power to indulge in such a policy for itself, it by no means follows that it gives to Georgia the privilege of prescribing that policy for other states in which the child comes to live. South Carolina has adopted a different policy. It imposes on the father or his property located within the state the duty to support his minor child domiciled there. . .

[I]t would not seem open to serious question that every state has an interest in securing the maintenance and support of minor children residing within its own territory so complete and so vital to the performance of its functions as a government that no other state could set limits upon it. Of that interest, South Carolina is the sole mistress within her own territory. * * * Even though we might appraise it more lightly than does South Carolina, it is not for us to say that a state is not free, within constitutional limitations, to regard that interest as fully as important and as completely within the realm of state power as the legal incidents of land located within its boundaries, or of a marriage relationship, wherever entered into but of which it is the domicile, or its power to pass upon the sanity of its own residents, notwithstanding the earlier pronouncements of the courts of other states. . .

Here the Georgia decree did not end the relationship of parent and child, as a decree of divorce may end the marriage relationship. Had the infant continued to reside in Georgia, and had she sought in the courts of South Carolina to compel the application of property of her father, found there, to her further maintenance and support, full faith and credit to the Georgia decree applied to its own domiciled resident might have required the denial of any relief. * * * But, when she became a domiciled resident of South Carolina, a new interest came into being, the interest of the state of South Carolina as a measure of self-preservation to secure the adequate protection and maintenance of helpless members of its own community and its prospective citizens. That interest was distinct from any which Georgia could conclusively regulate or control by its judgment, even though rendered while the child was domiciled in Georgia. The present decision extends the operation of the full faith and credit clause beyond its proper function of affording protection to the domestic interests of Georgia, and makes it an instrument for encroachment by Georgia upon the domestic concerns of South Carolina.

MR. JUSTICE CARDOZO concurs in this opinion.

Judgments and the Interest of the Forum

(1) A state's laws reflect the decisions of that state's lawmakers about how to treat certain transactions and relations. A judgment of the state's court can be seen to represent essentially the same thing, only applied in a more focused way to a particular set of facts. Judicial judgments, on this view, reflect declarations of policy—"applied policy" may be more accurate—waiting for compliance or enforcement.

As in the ordinary choice-of-law context, moreover, a state's judgments reflecting what that state's law and policy require in a particular case may come into conflict with the law and policy of another state. A problem then arises if a lawsuit is brought in the second state and the first state's judgment is presented: how should the judgment be treated? As *Fauntleroy v. Lum* and *Yarborough* make clear, in terms of constitutional requirements, the answer in the judgment context is very different from the answer in the ordinary choice-of-law context. The question is, why? In *Fauntleroy,* for example, Mississippi obviously could have applied its own law to the case were there no Missouri judgment. Indeed, isn't it plain that the Missouri court in upholding the futures contract denied full faith and credit to Mississippi law, and by refusing to apply the law of the only interested state, deprived the defendant of property without due process of law? Why, then, was Mississippi required by full faith and credit to respect the Missouri judgment?

(2) Note that the question whether a judgment is entitled to any recognition at all is distinct from the question whether that judgment should be treated the same as it would be treated by a court in the rendering state. Whereas the Mississippi court in *Fauntleroy* simply ignored the Missouri judgment, the question in *Yarborough* was whether the South Carolina court could give the Georgia judgment the same effect it would give another South Carolina judgment (in which case modification was allowed) or whether it had to treat the judgment as a Georgia court would. Why should the Full Faith and Credit Clause be interpreted to require another court to apply the res judicata law of the rendering state? Why isn't it enough for the second state to recognize the foreign judgment as a judgment and apply its own law of res judicata? Does the rule adopted in *Fauntleroy* and *Yarborough* serve the purpose of the Full Faith and Credit Clause to minimize interstate friction? What about the concerns expressed in the dissents of Justices White and Stone, to wit, that requiring recognition in the circumstances of these cases will exacerbate such tensions? Does either Justice Holmes or Justice Brandeis adequately answer this charge?

What is the "rendering state" for a federal court exercising diversity jurisdiction? In *Semtek International Inc. v. Lockheed Martin Corp.,* 531 U.S. 497 (2001), the Supreme Court decided that federal law should determine the preclusive effect of such judgments—but that the federal law should ordinarily incorporate the preclusion rules of the state in which the court sits. Is this a sensible compromise? For more on *Semtek,* see infra pp. 873–879.

(3) Justice Stone's dissenting opinion in *Yarborough* has had many admirers. Relying primarily on Stone's views, Restatement (Second) of Conflict of Laws § 103, comment b (1971), states:

> Regard must be had in a federal nation for the needs of each individual State. Almost invariably, the federal policy of full faith and credit will outweigh any interest that a State may have in not recognizing or enforcing a sister State judgment. So, for example, full faith and credit requires that a valid judgment rendered in a

> State of the United States be recognized and enforced in a sister State even though action on the original claim could not have been maintained in the sister State because contrary to its strong public policy (see § 117). There will be extremely rare occasions, however, when recognition of a sister State judgment would require too large a sacrifice by a State of its interests in a matter with which it is primarily concerned. On these extremely rare occasions, the policy embodied in full faith and credit will give way before the national policy that requires protection of the dignity and of the fundamental interests of each individual State. So, full faith and credit does not require a State to recognize a sister State injunction against suit in its courts on the ground that it is an inconvenient forum. This is because a State, subject to jurisdictional limitations, should be permitted to decide for itself, and without dictation from another State, what cases its courts will hear. . . Likewise, it may be that full faith and credit is not owed a sister State custody decree on the ground that a court should be free to disregard such a decree when this is required by the best interests of the child.

See also Reese & Johnson, *The Scope of Full Faith and Credit to Judgments,* 49 Colum.L.Rev. 153, 164, 171 (1949): "[I]t seems entirely reasonable to suppose that from time to time cases will arise where the very nature of our federal government demands that the national policy of res judicata should give way before the peculiar interests of a single state."

Do you agree that there is an exception to full faith and credit, even a limited one, where recognition of a sister-state judgment "would involve an improper infringement of the interests" of a second state? Isn't that precisely what *Yarborough* rejects? See Ehrenzweig, *The Second Conflicts Restatement: A Last Appeal for Its Withdrawal,* 113 U.Pa.L.Rev. 1230, 1240 (1965):

> There is . . . no authority whatsoever for the startling proposition that [quoting an earlier version of the Second Restatement § 103] "a judgment rendered in one State of the United States need not be recognized or enforced in a sister State if such recognition or enforcement . . . would involve an improper infringement of the interests of the sister State."

But isn't the appropriate question why we don't allow courts as much freedom to apply their law to judgments as we do to pre-judgment questions of choice of law? Recall that it was Justice Stone, the dissenter in *Yarborough,* who wrote the opinion for the Court in *Pacific Employers* holding that an interested state could always apply its own law. Why does he soften his position here? And why does the Court retreat even further, to a rule requiring even an interested state to apply another state's res judicata law? If this result is compelled by the plain language of 28 U.S.C. § 1738, then why not the same result for choice of law, since the statute refers without distinction to "Acts, records, and judicial proceedings"?

Can the Court's rule be justified along the lines advocated by Professor Kramer in the choice-of-law context, supra p. 207, namely, that it will systematically advance the shared interests of all states in the finality of judgments? Why won't a rule allowing each state to apply its own res judicata law do this equally well?

(4) Can a judgment be given *greater* effect than the rendering state requires? In *Hart v. American Airlines, Inc.,* 61 Misc.2d 41, 304 N.Y.S.2d 810 (Sup. Ct. 1969), defendant's plane crashed in Kentucky, resulting in the death of 58 out of the 62 persons aboard. Multiple wrongful death suits were filed in various states. The first to reach judgment was brought in Texas by the widow of a passenger; it resulted in a verdict in favor of the plaintiff. The personal representative of a New Jersey victim of the same crash whose suit, along with that of several New York residents, was part of the *Hart* litigation pending in New York moved for summary judgment, urging the court to apply New York law, which no longer required mutuality on the issue of collateral estoppel, rather than Texas law, which did require mutuality. The New York court denied the motion for summary judgment.

Subsequently, two New York plaintiffs in the *Hart* matter also moved for summary judgment against the airline, making the same argument. The defendant responded that the Full Faith and Credit Clause prohibited the New York court from giving the judgment preclusive effect because Texas still required mutuality and the plaintiffs would not have been bound had the Texas judgment gone the other way. Noting that New York no longer required mutuality, the court applied collateral estoppel:

> This is not a situation where the judgment, as such, of the Texas court is sought to be enforced. What is here involved is a policy determination by our courts that "One who has had his day in court should not be permitted to litigate the question anew" * * *, and, further, refusal "to tolerate a condition where, on relatively the same set of facts, one fact-finder, be it court or jury" may find a party liable while another exonerates him leading to the "inconsistent results which are always a blemish on a judicial system" * * *. It is in order to carry out these policy determinations in the disposition of cases in this jurisdiction that an evidentiary use is being made of a particular determination made in the Texas action.

Faced with the argument that it had ruled the other way on the motion made by the New Jersey plaintiff, the court responded:

> . . . Contrary to defendant's assertions, the controlling factor in the *Hart* decision was the non-domiciliary status of the plaintiffs therein involved and the unwillingness of the court to apply the New York law of collateral estoppel with respect to a Texas determination on behalf of "non-domiciliary dependents of a deceased non-domiciliary 'bread-winner' " having no significant contacts with New York. . . [That result] does not, as defendant argues, preclude the application of the New York doctrine of collateral estoppel in an action brought by New York dependents of deceased New York residents.

Citing *Kilberg v. Northeast Airlines*, see supra p. 58, the court relied on New York's approach to choice of law to conclude that "[t]he state of Texas has no legitimate interest in imposing its rules on collateral estoppel upon these New York residents and a holding that permits such result would indeed constitute the 'anachronistic treatment' warned against in *Kilberg*. The fact that the plaintiffs herein involved are New York domiciliaries, as were their decedents, sufficiently establishes this state's superior interest in the issue of collateral estoppel."

An Illinois court reached the same conclusion in *Finley v. Kesling,* 105 Ill.App.3d 1, 60 Ill.Dec. 874, 433 N.E.2d 1112 (1982), but the Delaware chancery court found that applying collateral estoppel under these circumstances "is clearly at variance with the purpose and spirit of the full faith and credit clause." *Columbia Casualty Co. v. Playtex FP, Inc.,* 584 A.2d 1214 (Del.1991). What purpose of the clause is violated if a judgment is given greater effect than it would have in the state where it was rendered? See generally Shreve, *Judgments From a Choice-of-Law Perspective,* 40 Am.J.Comp.L. 985 (1992).

Note that this problem may arise in a variety of situations. In addition to mutuality, res judicata principles differ from state to state on such matters as the definition of privity, the scope of a cause of action, the requirements for compulsory counterclaims, and more. How should these issues be treated? Is the answer that the Constitution gives national sanction to any reasonable policy of foreclosing further litigation? Are there due process difficulties with giving a foreign judgment greater effect than it was meant to have in the rendering state? Did the decision in *Hart* based on the different residence of the parties violate either the Equal Protection Clause or the Privileges and Immunities Clause? See the section on unconstitutional discrimination in choice of law in Chapter 3, supra pp. 426–436.

(5) Some statutes apply to individuals against whom certain kinds of judgments have been rendered. Do foreign judgments qualify? In *Small v. United States*, 544 U.S. 385 (2005), the Supreme Court held that foreign convictions do not count for the purposes of 18 U.S.C. § 922(g), which prohibits the possession of firearms by persons convicted "in any court" of a crime punishable by more than one year in prison. Foreign laws might prohibit conduct that the U.S. permits, the Court reasoned, and foreign proceedings might not conform to U.S. notions of fairness.

In *State v. Menard*, 888 A.2d 57 (R.I. 2005), the Rhode Island Supreme Court considered a similar Rhode Island statute that prohibited firearm possession by anyone convicted "in this state or elsewhere of a crime of violence," defined to include "first and second degree arson." The defendant had been convicted of "class 4 felony arson" in Arizona, in a judgment that characterized the offense as "not of a dangerous nature." The trial court dismissed the indictment on the grounds that under Arizona law, the conviction was not for a crime of violence. The Supreme Court reversed, reasoning that the characterization of the conviction was a matter of Rhode Island law and that the elements of Arizona class 4 felony arson were similar to Rhode Island second degree arson.

Is this a constitutional issue in the interstate context, or just a question of statutory interpretation? Courts tend to assume the latter, though the *Menard* court did drop a footnote rejecting the defendant's full faith and credit argument on the grounds that "full faith and credit does not automatically compel a forum state to subordinate its own statutory policy to a conflicting public act of another state." Are there any limits on how a statute can treat foreign judgments as compared to local ones? Does it matter that these judgments are criminal convictions? (See note 8(b) infra.)

(6) Suppose that Mr. Yarborough as well as Sadie had moved to South Carolina to live. Would the Georgia judgment be entitled to less credit under these circumstances? If so, why?

In *Elkind v. Byck*, 68 Cal.2d 453, 67 Cal.Rptr. 404, 439 P.2d 316 (1968), the court held that California could award additional support for a New York child notwithstanding a prior Georgia decree providing for payments by the father out of a lump-sum settlement. *Yarborough*, the court stated, did not stand in the way because the father had moved from Georgia to California and because Georgia had subsequently adopted the Uniform Reciprocal Enforcement of Support Act, "which expressly reserved to the state of the obligor's residence the power to apply its law of support notwithstanding the decree." Justice Traynor noted that "by the adoption of the Reciprocal Support legislation in almost all states, the Federal system now espouses the principle that no state may freeze the obligations flowing from the continuing relationship of parent and child."

Does Traynor's ploy still work? The Uniform Reciprocal Enforcement of Support Act (URESA) and its revised version (RURESA) were both replaced in 1992 by the Uniform Interstate Family Support Act (UIFSA), which had been adopted in all fifty states and the District of Columbia by

1998. One of UIFSA's major accomplishments—described in the Comment to § 205 as "the cornerstone of the Act"—is to provide that the state that entered the initial child support order (the "issuing" state) maintains continuing exclusive jurisdiction ("CEJ") to modify its support orders. A state called upon to enforce the order (the "responding" state) applies the law of the issuing state. In situations like *Elkind*, where none of the parties continues to reside in the issuing state (Georgia), the petitioner and the child reside in another state (New York), and the respondent resides in or is subject to personal jurisdiction in a state where the order is registered (California), Georgia loses its CEJ unless all the parties agree that Georgia may continue to modify its order. (Why would they want to do that?) Otherwise, under § 611, upon consent of all parties, California may modify the order. It may not, however, expand the duration of child support established by the initial order: the obligor's fulfillment of the duty of support set in that order "precludes imposition of a further obligation of support" by California. Does this mean that *Elkind* is no longer good law? For further discussion of UIFSA, see Notes (1)(b) and (2) infra pp. 613–615.

(7) In *Kovacs v. Brewer,* 356 U.S. 604 (1958), a New York divorce decree awarded custody of a child to her paternal grandfather; the New York court later modified its decree to grant custody to the child's mother, who sued to enforce her rights in North Carolina. The North Carolina court held the child's welfare required that her grandfather be allowed to keep her, and the mother invoked the Constitution. The Supreme Court remanded the case for clarification:

> Whatever effect the Full Faith and Credit Clause may have with respect to custody decrees, it is clear, as the Court stated in *Halvey,* "that the State of the forum has at least as much leeway to disregard the judgment, to qualify it, or to depart from it as does the State where it was rendered."

356 U.S. at 607. New York, it was conceded, would modify the decree if changed circumstances were shown; if the North Carolina decree was based upon such a showing, there was no denial of full faith. This point is fundamental both in the sense that it seems obvious and in the sense that it should not be overlooked.

But why did the Court hedge with respect to the applicability of the Constitution to custody decrees? Justice Frankfurter minced no words in his dissent:

> [W]hen courts are confronted with the responsibility of determining the proper custody of children, a more important consideration asserts itself to which regard for curbing litigious strife is subordinated—namely, the welfare of the child. . . [B]oth the underlying purpose of the Full Faith and Credit Clause and the nature of the decrees militate strongly against a

constitutionally enforced requirement of respect to foreign custody decrees.

356 U.S. at 611–13. Can this argument be reconciled with *Fauntleroy* and *Yarborough*?

(8) Despite murmurings derived from the dissenting opinion in *Yarborough,* it seems clear that *Fauntleroy* and *Yarborough,* taken together, establish that a state cannot invoke its own interest or public policy against a sister-state judgment. But what of other defenses against foreign judgments traditionally available in the international community, such as fraud in the procurement of a judgment and the enforcement of penal or governmental claims?

(a) *Fraud.* Under some circumstances, fraud, duress, and coercion may be grounds for collateral attack upon a judgment in the rendering state. Restatement (Second) Judgments § 70 (1982). But in the famous case of *Christmas v. Russell,* 72 U.S. (5 Wall.) 290 (1866), the Supreme Court held that fraud was no defense to a suit upon a sister-state judgment because it could not be raised collaterally in the judgment state. Invoking the principle of *Kovacs v. Brewer,* lower court decisions commonly permit attack on the basis of fraud when the judgment state would do so. For the common distinction permitting attacks on domestic judgments if the fraud is "extrinsic" ("going to the opportunity to appear and defend") but not if it is "intrinsic" (e.g., perjury as to the merits) see H. Goodrich, Handbook of the Conflict of Laws 397 (4th ed. 1964). But are there due-process limits to the power of a state, even with respect to domestic judgments, to foreclose issues of fraud that could not have been raised in the original proceeding? And isn't the sole justification for *Fauntleroy's* extreme command of deference on the part of an interested state the existence of a reasonable opportunity to object in the first suit? See generally Restatement (Second) of Conflict of Laws § 115 (1971).

(b) *Penal and governmental claims.* For many years it was assumed that sister-state judgments based on penal and governmental claims need not be given full faith and credit. A statement in *Wisconsin v. Pelican Ins. Co.,* 127 U.S. 265 (1888), was thought to support the proposition, but the case did not involve the effect of a sister-state judgment in the courts of another state. *Pelican* was an attempt by Wisconsin to invoke the original jurisdiction of the United States Supreme Court to enforce a penalty against a foreign insurance company that had failed to meet Wisconsin requirements; holding that the controversy was not of a "civil nature" as required in the First Judiciary Act, the Court sensibly and understandably (why?) declined to make the original jurisdiction available for this purpose. *Huntington v. Attrill,* 146 U.S. 657 (1892), summarized supra p. 86, the leading case discussing the traditional rule against enforcing foreign "penal" claims, was a suit on a sister-state judgment, and the Court assumed that the penal exception was available whether or not the cause of action had been reduced to judgment. The Court, however, gave a restrictive definition to the penal category and actually held that Maryland was required to enforce the New York judgment in question.

These elderly cases continue to be cited for the proposition that a sister-state judgment based upon a penal or governmental claim need not be recognized in our federal system. Isn't this proposition untenable after *Fauntleroy* and *Yarborough*? Indeed, don't even the flimsy arguments against enforcing sister-state penal laws evaporate once the claim has been reduced to judgment? See pp. 85–87 supra.

In *Milwaukee County v. M.E. White Co.*, 296 U.S. 268 (1935), the Supreme Court held that a state could not constitutionally refuse to respect a sister-state judgment for taxes. The command of the full faith and credit clause, said Justice Stone, may have its exceptions: "[T]here may be limits to the extent to which the policy of one state . . . may be subordinated to the policy of another." 296 U.S., at 273. The Court assumed without deciding that penal judgments, and tax claims not reduced to judgment, need not be respected; but concluded:

> We can perceive no greater possibility of embarrassment in litigating the validity of a judgment for taxes and enforcing it than any other for the payment of money. . . In the circumstances here disclosed no state can be said to have a legitimate policy against payment of its neighbor's taxes, the obligation of which has been judicially established. . . In numerous cases this Court has held that credit must be given to the judgment of another state although the forum would not be required to entertain the suit on which the judgment was founded.

296 U.S., at 276–77.

The question of attacking a judgment for lack of jurisdiction in the rendering court is considered at pp. 589–597 infra.

THOMAS V. WASHINGTON GAS LIGHT CO.

448 U.S. 261 (1980).

MR. JUSTICE STEVENS announced the judgment of the Court and delivered an opinion in which MR. JUSTICE BRENNAN, MR. JUSTICE STEWART, and MR. JUSTICE BLACKMUN join. . .

Petitioner is a resident of the District of Columbia and was hired by respondent in the District of Columbia. During the year that he was employed by respondent, he worked primarily in the District but also worked in Virginia and Maryland. He sustained a back injury while at work in Arlington, Va., on January 22, 1971. Two weeks later he entered into an "Industrial Commission of Virginia Memorandum of Agreement as to Payment of Compensation" providing for benefits of $62 per week. Several weeks later the Virginia Industrial Commission approved the agreement and issued its award directing that payments continue "during incapacity," subject to various contingencies and changes set forth in the Virginia statute.

In 1974, petitioner notified the Department of Labor of his intention to seek compensation under the District of Columbia Act. Respondent opposed the claim primarily on the ground that since, as a matter of Virginia law, the Virginia award excluded any other recovery "at common law or otherwise" on account of the injury in Virginia, the District of Columbia's obligation to give that award full faith and credit precluded a second, supplemental award in the District.

The administrative law judge agreed with respondent that the Virginia award must be given res judicata effect in the District to the extent that it was res judicata in Virginia. He held, however, that the Virginia award, by its terms, did not preclude a further award of compensation in Virginia. Moreover, he construed the statutory prohibition against additional recovery "at common law or otherwise" as merely covering "common law and other remedies under Virginia law." After the taking of medical evidence, petitioner was awarded permanent total disability benefits payable from the date of his injury with a credit for the amounts previously paid under the Virginia award.

The Benefits Review Board upheld the award. Its order, however, was reversed by the United States Court of Appeals for the Fourth Circuit, which squarely held that a "second and separate proceeding in another jurisdiction upon the same injury after a prior recovery in another State [is] precluded by the Full Faith and Credit Clause." We granted certiorari * * * and now reverse.

I

Respondent contends that the District of Columbia was without power to award petitioner additional compensation because of the Full Faith and Credit Clause of the Constitution or, more precisely, because of the federal statute implementing that Clause. An analysis of this contention must begin with two decisions from the 1940's that are almost directly on point: *Magnolia Petroleum Co. v. Hunt,* 320 U.S. 430, and *Industrial Comm'n of Wisconsin v. McCartin,* 330 U.S. 622.

In *Magnolia,* a case relied on heavily both by respondent and the Court of Appeals, the employer hired a Louisiana worker in Louisiana. The employee was later injured during the course of his employment in Texas. A tenuous majority held that Louisiana was not permitted to award the injured worker supplementary compensation under the Louisiana Act after he had already obtained a recovery from the Texas Industrial Accident Board:

> "Respondent was free to pursue his remedy in either state but, having chosen to seek it in Texas, where the award was res judicata, the full faith and credit clause precludes him from again seeking a remedy in Louisiana upon the same grounds." 320 U.S., at 444.

Little more than three years later, the Court severely curtailed the impact of *Magnolia*. In *McCartin,* the employer and the worker both resided in Illinois and entered into an employment contract there for work to be performed in Wisconsin. The employee was injured in the course of that employment. . . [T]he employer and the employee executed a contract for payment of a specific sum in full settlement of the employee's right under Illinois law. The contract expressly provided, however, that it would "not affect any rights that applicant may have under the Workmen's Compensation Act of the State of Wisconsin." 330 U.S., at 624. The employee then obtained a supplemental award from the Wisconsin Industrial Commission; but the Wisconsin state courts vacated it under felt compulsion of the intervening decision in *Magnolia.*

This Court reversed, holding without dissent that *Magnolia* was not controlling[:] "[o]nly some unmistakable language by a state legislature or judiciary would warrant our accepting . . . a construction" that a workmen's compensation statute "is designed to preclude any recovery by proceedings brought in another state." Id., at 627–28. The Illinois statute, which the Court held not to contain the "unmistakable language" required to preclude a supplemental award in Wisconsin, broadly provided:

> "No common law or statutory right to recover damages for injury or death sustained by any employe while engaged in the line of his duty as such employe, other than the compensation herein provided, shall be available to any employe who is covered by the provisions of this act. . ." 330 U.S., at 622.

The Virginia Workmen's Compensation Act's exclusive remedy provision is not exactly the same as Illinois'; but it contains no "unmistakable language" directed at precluding a supplemental compensation award in another State that was not also in the Illinois Act. Consequently, *McCartin* by its terms, rather than the earlier *Magnolia* decision, is controlling as between the two precedents. . .

II

[I]n the Court's haste to retreat from *Magnolia,* it fashioned a rule that clashes with normally accepted full faith and credit principles. It has long been the law that "the judgment of a state court should have the same credit, validity, and effect, in every other court in the United States, which it had in the state where it was pronounced." *Hampton v. McConnel,* 3 Wheat. 234, 235 (Marshall, C.J.). See also *Mills v. Duryee,* 7 Cranch 481, 484 (Story, J.). This rule, if not compelled by the Full Faith and Credit

Clause itself, is surely required by 28 U.S.C. § 1738, which provides that the "Acts, records and judicial proceedings . . . [of any State] shall have the same full faith and credit in every court within the United States . . . as they have by law or usage in the courts of [the] State . . . from which they are taken." Thus, in effect, by virtue of the full faith and credit obligations of the several States, a State is permitted to determine the extraterritorial effect of its judgment; but it may only do so indirectly by prescribing the effect of its judgments within the State.

The *McCartin* rule, however, focusing as it does on the extraterritorial intent of the rendering State, is fundamentally different. It authorizes a State, by drafting or construing its legislation in "unmistakable language," directly to determine the extraterritorial effect of its workmen's compensation awards. An authorization to a state legislature of this character is inconsistent with the rule established in *Pacific Employers Ins. Co. v. Industrial Acc. Comm'n,* 306 U.S. 493, 502.

"This Court must determine for itself how far the full faith and credit clause compels the qualification or denial of rights asserted under the laws of one state, that of the forum, by the statute of another state."

It follows inescapably that the *McCartin* "unmistakable language" rule represents an unwarranted delegation to the States of this Court's responsibility for the final arbitration of full faith and credit questions. The Full Faith and Credit Clause "is one of the provisions incorporated into the Constitution by its framers for the purpose of transforming an aggregation of independent, sovereign States into a nation." *Sherrer v. Sherrer,* 334 U.S. 343, 355. To vest the power of determining the extraterritorial effect of a State's own laws and judgments in the State itself risks the very kind of parochial entrenchment on the interests of other States that it was the purpose of the Full Faith and Credit Clause and other provisions of Art. IV of the Constitution to prevent. * * *

Thus, a re-examination of *McCartin's* unmistakable language test reinforces our tentative conclusion that it does not provide an acceptable basis on which to distinguish *Magnolia.* But if we reject that test, we must decide whether to overrule either *Magnolia* or *McCartin*. . .

[Part III of the opinion considered *Magnolia* in light of *stare decisis,* concluding that since *McCartin* had virtually eliminated *Magnolia's* operative effect, no rights or expectations had been created in reliance upon it.]

IV

Three different state interests are affected by the potential conflict between Virginia and the District of Columbia. Virginia has a valid interest in placing a limit on the potential liability of companies that transact business within its borders. Both jurisdictions have a valid interest in the welfare of the injured employee—Virginia because the injury occurred within that State, and the District because the injured party was employed and resided there. And finally, Virginia has an interest in having the integrity of its formal determinations of contested issues respected by other sovereigns.

The conflict between the first two interests was resolved in *Alaska Packers Association v. Industrial Accident Commission,* 294 U.S. 532, and a series of later cases. [The opinion summarized the holdings in *Alaska Packers,* supra p. 360, and *Pacific Employers Ins. Co. v. Industrial Acc. Comm'n,* 306 U.S. 493 (1939), supra p. 364.]

The principle that the Full Faith and Credit Clause does not require a State to subordinate its own compensation policies to those of another State has been consistently applied in more recent cases. *Carroll v. Lanza,* 349 U.S. 408; *Crider v. Zurich,* 380 U.S. 39; *Nevada v. Hall, supra,* 440 U.S., at 421–424. Indeed, in the *Nevada* case the Court not only rejected the contention that California was required to respect a statutory limitation on the defendant's liability, but did so in a case in which the defendant was the sovereign State itself asserting, alternatively, an immunity from any liability in the courts of California.

It is thus perfectly clear that petitioner could have sought a compensation award in the first instance either in Virginia, the State in which the injury occurred, * * * or in the District of Columbia, where petitioner resided, his employer was principally located and the employment relation was formed * * *. And as those cases underscore, compensation could have been sought under either compensation scheme even if one statute or the other purported to confer an exclusive remedy on petitioner. Thus, for all practical purposes, respondent and its insurer would have had to measure their potential liability exposure by the more generous of the two workmen's compensation schemes in any event. It follows that a State's interest in limiting the potential liability of businesses within the State is not of controlling importance.

It is also manifest that the interest in providing adequate compensation to the injured worker would be fully served by the allowance of successive awards. In this respect the two jurisdictions share a common interest and there is no danger of significant conflict.

The ultimate issue, therefore, is whether Virginia's interest in the integrity of its tribunal's determinations forecloses a second proceeding to obtain a supplemental award in the District of Columbia. We return to the Court's prior resolution of this question in *Magnolia.*

The majority opinion in *Magnolia* took the position that the case called for a straightforward application of full faith and credit law: the worker's injury gave rise to a cause of action; relief was granted by the Texas Industrial Accident Board; that award precluded any further relief in

Texas; and further relief was therefore precluded elsewhere as well. The majority relied heavily on *Chicago, R.I. & P.R. Co. v. Schendel,* 270 U.S. 611, for the propositions that a workmen's compensation award stands on the same footing as a court judgment, and that a compensation award under one State's law is a bar to a second award under another State's law. * * *

But *Schendel* did not compel the result in *Magnolia*. . . In *Schendel,* the Court held that an Iowa state compensation award, which was grounded in a contested factual finding that the deceased railroad employee was engaged in intrastate commerce, precluded a subsequent claim under the Federal Employers' Liability Act brought in the Minnesota state courts, which would have required a finding that the employee was engaged in interstate commerce. *Schendel* therefore involved the unexceptionable full faith and credit principle that resolution of factual matters underlying a judgment must be given the same res judicata effect in the forum State as they have in the rendering State. . .

In contrast, neither *Magnolia* nor this case concerns a second State's contrary resolution of a factual matter determined in the first State's proceedings. Unlike the situation in *Schendel,* which involved two mutually exclusive remedies, compensation could be obtained under either Virginia's or the District's workmen's compensation statutes on the basis of the same set of facts. A supplemental award gives full effect to the facts determined by the first award and also allows full credit for payments pursuant to the earlier award. There is neither inconsistency nor double recovery.

We are also persuaded that *Magnolia's* reliance on *Schendel* for the proposition that workmen's compensation awards stand on the same footing as court judgments was unwarranted. To be sure, as was held in *Schendel,* the factfindings of state administrative tribunals are entitled to the same res judicata effect in the second State as findings by a court. But the critical differences between a court of general jurisdiction and an administrative agency with limited statutory authority forecloses the conclusion that constitutional rules applicable to court judgments are necessarily applicable to workmen's compensation awards.

A final judgment entered by a court of general jurisdiction normally establishes not only the measure of the plaintiff's rights but also the limits of the defendant's liability. A traditional application of res judicata principles enables either party to claim the benefit of the judgment insofar as it resolved issues the court had jurisdiction to decide. Although a Virginia court is free to recognize the perhaps paramount interests of another State by choosing to apply that State's law in a particular case, the Industrial Commission of Virginia does not have that power. Its jurisdiction is limited to questions arising under the Virginia Workmen's

Compensation Act. See Va.Code § 65.1–92 (1973). Typically, a workmen's compensation tribunal may only apply its own State's law.[28] In this case, the Virginia Commission could and did establish the full measure of petitioner's rights under Virginia law, but it neither could nor purported to determine his rights under the law of the District of Columbia. Full faith and credit must be given to the determination that the Virginia Commission had the authority to make; but by a parity of reasoning, full faith and credit need not be given to determinations that it had no power to make. Since it was not requested, and had no authority, to pass on petitioner's rights under District of Columbia law, there can be no constitutional objection to a fresh adjudication of those rights.

It is true, of course, that after Virginia entered its award, that State had an interest in preserving the integrity of what it had done. And it is squarely within the purpose of the Full Faith and Credit Clause, as explained in *Pacific Employers,* supra, 306 U.S., at 501, "to preserve rights acquired or confirmed under the public acts" of Virginia by requiring other States to recognize their validity. Thus, Virginia had an interest in having respondent pay petitioner the amounts specified in its award. Allowing a supplementary recovery in the District does not conflict with that interest.

As we have already noted, Virginia also has a separate interest in placing a ceiling on the potential liability of companies that transact business within the State. But past cases have established that that interest is not strong enough to prevent other States with overlapping jurisdiction over particular injuries from giving effect to their more generous compensation policies when the employee selects the most favorable forum in the first instance. Thus, the only situations in which the *Magnolia* rule would tend to serve that interest are those in which an injured workman has either been constrained by circumstances to seek relief in the less generous forum or has simply made an ill-advised choice of his first forum.

But in neither of those cases is there any reason to give extra weight to the first State's interest in placing a ceiling on the employer's liability than it otherwise would have had. For neither the first nor the second State

---

[28] See 4 A. Larson, Workmen's Compensation Law, § 86.40, at 16–44 (1980); Cheatham, supra, 44 Colum.L.Rev., at 344. The reason for this is the special nature of a workmen's compensation remedy. It is not merely a grant of a lump sum award at the end of an extended adversarial proceeding. See 4 A. Larson, supra, § 84.20, at 16–9:

> "[A] highly developed compensation system does far more than that. It stays with the claimant from the moment of the accident to the time he is fully restored to normal earning capacity. This may involve supervising an ongoing rehabilitation program, perhaps changing or extending it, perhaps providing, repairing, and replacing prosthetic devices, and supplying vocational rehabilitation. Apart from rehabilitation, optimum compensation administration may require reopening of the award from time to time for change of condition or for other reasons. . . . "

Thus, a workmen's compensation remedy is potentially quite different from the application of a particular State's law to a transitory cause of action based on fault. . . .

has any overriding interest in requiring an injured employee to proceed with special caution when first asserting his claim. . .

We therefore would hold that a State has no legitimate interest within the context of our federal system in preventing another State from granting a supplemental compensation award when that second State would have had the power to apply its workmen's compensation law in the first instance. The Full Faith and Credit Clause should not be construed to preclude successive workmen's compensation awards. Accordingly, *Magnolia Petroleum Co. v. Hunt* should be overruled.

The judgment of the Court of Appeals is reversed.

MR. JUSTICE WHITE, with whom THE CHIEF JUSTICE and MR. JUSTICE POWELL join, concurring in the judgment.

I agree that the judgment of the Court of Appeals should be reversed, but I am unable to join in the reasoning by which the plurality reaches that result. . .

The plurality contends that unlike courts of general jurisdiction, workmen's compensation tribunals generally have no power to apply the law of another State and thus cannot determine the rights of the parties thereunder. Yet I see no reason why a judgment should not be entitled to full res judicata effect under the Full Faith and Credit Clause merely because the rendering tribunal was obligated to apply the law of the forum—provided, of course, as was certainly the case here, that the forum could constitutionally apply its law. The plurality's analysis seems to grant state legislatures the power to delimit the scope of a cause of action for federal full faith and credit purposes merely by enacting choice of law rules binding on the State's workmen's compensation tribunals. . .

As a matter of logic, the plurality's analysis would seemingly apply to many everyday tort actions. I see no difference for full faith and credit purposes between a statute which lays down a forum-favoring choice of law rule and a common-law doctrine stating the same principle. Hence when a court, having power in the abstract to apply the law of another State, determines by application of the forum's choice of law rules to apply the substantive law of the forum, I would think that under the plurality's analysis the judgment would not determine rights arising under the law of some other State. . .

One purpose of the Full Faith and Credit Clause is to bring an end to litigation. . . The plurality's opinion is at odds with this principle of finality. . . It seems to me grossly unfair that the plaintiff, having the initial choice of the forum, should be given the additional advantage of a second adjudication should his choice prove disappointing. Defendants, on the other hand, would no longer be assured that the judgment of the first forum is conclusive as to their obligations, and would face the prospect of burdensome and multiple litigation based on the same operative facts. Such litigation would also impose added strain on an already overworked judicial system. . .

I would not overrule either *Magnolia* or *McCartin.* To my mind, Chief Justice Stone's opinion in *Magnolia* states the sounder doctrine; as noted, I do not see any overriding differences between workmen's compensation awards and court judgments that justify different treatment for the two. However, *McCartin* has been on the books for over 30 years and has been widely interpreted by state and federal courts as substantially limiting *Magnolia.* Unlike the plurality's opinion, *McCartin* is not subject to the objection that its principles are applicable outside the workmen's compensation area. Although I find *McCartin* to rest on questionable foundations, I am not now prepared to overrule it. And I agree with the plurality that *McCartin,* rather than *Magnolia,* is controlling as between the two precedents since the Virginia Workmen's Compensation Act lacks the "unmistakable language" which *McCartin* requires if a workmen's compensation award is to preclude a subsequent award in another State. I therefore concur in the judgment.

MR. JUSTICE REHNQUIST, with whom MR. JUSTICE MARSHALL joins, dissenting.

This is clearly a case where the whole is less than the sum of its parts. In choosing between two admittedly inconsistent precedents, *Magnolia Petroleum Co. v. Hunt,* 320 U.S. 430 (1943), and *Industrial Comm'n of Wisconsin v. McCartin,* 330 U.S. 622 (1947), six of us agree that the latter decision, *McCartin,* is analytically indefensible. The remaining three Members of the Court concede that it "rest[s] on questionable foundations." Nevertheless, when the smoke clears, it is *Magnolia* rather than *McCartin* that the plurality suggests should be overruled. Because I believe that *Magnolia* was correctly decided, and because I fear that the rule proposed by the plurality is both ill-considered and ill-defined, I dissent. . .

I . . . agree completely with the plurality's ultimate conclusion that the rule announced in *McCartin* "represents an unwarranted delegation to the States of this Court's responsibility for the final arbitration of full faith and credit questions."

One might suppose that, having destroyed *McCartin's ratio decidendi,* the plurality would return to the eminently defensible position adopted in *Magnolia.* . . The plurality instead . . . sets out in search of a new rationale to support the result reached in *McCartin,* [asserting] that Virginia's interest in limiting the liability of businesses operating within its borders can never outweigh the District of Columbia's interest in protecting its residents. In support of this proposition it cites *Alaska Packers* and *Pacific Employers.* Both of those cases, however, involved the degree of faith and credit to be afforded *statutes* of one State by the courts of another State.

The present case involves an enforceable *judgment* entered by Virginia after adjudicatory proceedings. In *Magnolia* Mr. Chief Justice Stone, who authored *both Alaska Packers* and *Pacific Employers,* distinguished those two decisions for precisely this reason. . . This distinction, which has also been overlooked by the plurality here, makes perfect sense, since Virginia surely has a stronger interest in limiting an employer's liability to a fixed amount when that employer has already been haled before a Virginia tribunal and adjudged liable than when the employer simply claims the benefit of a Virginia statute in a proceeding brought in another State.

In a similar vein, the plurality completely ignores any interest that Virginia might assert in the finality of its adjudications. While workmen's compensation awards may be "non-final" in the sense that they are subject to continuing supervision and modification, Virginia nevertheless has a cognizable interest in requiring persons who avail themselves of its statutory remedy to eschew other alternative remedies that might be available to them. Otherwise, as apparently is the result here, Virginia's efforts and expense on an applicant's behalf are wasted when that applicant obtains a duplicative remedy in another State. . .

In further support of its novel rule, the plurality attempts to distinguish the judgment entered in this case from one entered by a "court of general jurisdiction." Specifically, the plurality points out that the Industrial Commission of Virginia, unlike a state court of general jurisdiction, was limited by statute to consideration of Virginia law. According to the plurality, because the Commission "was not requested, and had no authority, to pass on petitioner's rights under District of Columbia law, there can be no constitutional objection to a fresh adjudication of those rights."

This argument might have some force if petitioner had somehow had Virginia law thrust upon him against his will. In this case, however, petitioner was free to choose the applicable law simply by choosing the forum in which he filed his initial claim. . .

The Full Faith and Credit Clause did not allot to this Court the task of "balancing" interests where the "public Acts, Records, and judicial Proceedings" of a State were involved. It simply directed that they be given the "Full Faith and Credit" that the Court today denies to those of Virginia. I would affirm the judgment of the court below.

Limitations on Full Faith and Credit

(1) Does *Thomas* undermine the "nationally unifying force" of the full faith and credit clause? Does it create an exception based on the interest or public policy of the state in which the judgment is sought to be enforced? If so, is the exception limited to the workers' compensation field? The *Thomas* case is discussed in Sterk, *Full Faith and Credit, More or Less, to Judgments: Doubts About* Thomas v. Washington Gas Light Co., 69 Geo.L.J. 1329 (1981).

(2) Was the proceeding before the Virginia Industrial Commission in *Thomas* a "judicial proceeding" within the meaning of the Full Faith and Credit Clause and the implementing statute? All members of the Court in *Thomas* assume that it was, although Chief Justice Stone in *Magnolia* was equivocal on the question, stating that whether the Texas administrative proceeding in that case "be regarded as a 'judicial proceeding,' or its award as a 'record' . . . the result is the same" since both are entitled to full faith and credit. 320 U.S. at 443. In any event, administrative awards and orders today are treated the same as judgments if the agency is empowered to adjudicate, its procedures comply with the essential elements of adjudication, and its actions are conclusive where made. See Restatement (Second) Judgments § 83(i) (1982). What about licensing proceedings? Marriages? Administrative tax determinations? Arbitration awards? In *Dean Witter Reynolds, Inc. v. Byrd,* 470 U.S. 213 (1985), the Court discussed the issue preclusive effects of a state court arbitration, required under the Federal Arbitration Act, upon a pending federal claim involving the same situation. According to the Court, neither full faith and credit nor a judicially-fashioned rule of preclusion required that preclusive effect be given to unappealed arbitration proceedings, because an arbitration without court review was not a judicial proceeding.

(3) Six justices in *Thomas* conclude that *McCartin* is an erroneous interpretation of 28 U.S.C. § 1738 (and of the Full Faith and Credit Clause?) because it permits a state to determine directly the extraterritorial effect of a judgment. Is that a correct reading of the case? Wasn't the implication of *McCartin* that Illinois had not intended to bar a claim under Wisconsin law *anywhere*? On the other hand, given the language of the Illinois statute at issue in *McCartin,* isn't that interpretation absurd?

Assuming the plurality has read *McCartin* correctly, why should the Full Faith and Credit Clause prohibit Illinois from permitting other states to give Illinois judgments *less* effect than they would be given in Illinois? Shouldn't state policies that defer to the interests of sister states be encouraged rather than overridden? What "nationally unifying policy" denies an injured worker additional benefits that *no state* wants to withhold?

(4) Does the plurality opinion undermine *all* adjudications in which the tribunal lacks authority under its law to apply the law of another state? In fields as disparate as wrongful death and divorce, state law often forecloses the choice-of-law question: if the court has jurisdiction, it must apply forum law. Is the preclusive effect of judgments in these situations now limited to facts actually litigated?

What about Justice White's observation that, under the plurality opinion, it should not matter whether the court which rendered a judgment was foreclosed from applying another state's law as a matter of jurisdiction or by its own choice-of-law rules? Is *Yarborough* overruled because the Georgia court had to apply Georgia law under the applicable choice-of-law rules?

What does any of this have to do with the state's finality interests anyway? Once a party has come to a state and invoked the time and assistance of its tribunals, shouldn't that foreclose further litigation? Indeed, given the considerations described by Justice Stevens in footnote 28, aren't the state's finality interests especially strong in this context? Or are you persuaded by Justice Stevens's argument that the plaintiff's initial choice of forum may have been ill-informed or necessitated by difficult conditions? Wasn't the plaintiff in *Yarborough* in an even worse position?

(5) What is the law respecting full faith and credit for workers' compensation awards after *Thomas*? Six justices agree that *McCartin* is overruled, but only the four justices in the plurality were prepared to overrule *Magnolia*. Justices White and Powell and Chief Justice Burger cast the deciding votes to allow a supplemental award on the ground that they would follow *McCartin*. Is this position still tenable? If not, does *Magnolia* still control despite the result in *Thomas*? How would you vote?

DURFEE V. DUKE

375 U.S. 106 (1963).

MR. JUSTICE STEWART delivered the opinion of the Court. . .

In 1956 the petitioners brought an action against the respondent in a Nebraska court to quiet title to certain bottom land situated on the Missouri River. The main channel of that river forms the boundary between the States of Nebraska and Missouri. The Nebraska court had jurisdiction over the subject matter of the controversy only if the land in question was in Nebraska. Whether the land was Nebraska land depended entirely upon a factual question—whether a shift in the river's course had been caused by avulsion or accretion. The respondent appeared in the Nebraska court and through counsel fully litigated the issues, explicitly contesting the court's jurisdiction over the subject matter of the controversy.[4] After a hearing the court found the issues in favor of the petitioners and ordered that title to the land be quieted in them. The

[4] This is, therefore, not a case in which a party, although afforded an opportunity to contest subject-matter jurisdiction, did not litigate the issue. Cf. *Chicot County Drainage Dist. v. Baxter State Bank*, 308 U.S. 371.

respondent appealed, and the Supreme Court of Nebraska affirmed the judgment after a trial *de novo* on the record made in the lower court. The State Supreme Court specifically found that the rule of avulsion was applicable, that the land in question was in Nebraska, that the Nebraska courts therefore had jurisdiction of the subject matter of the litigation, and that title to the land was in the petitioners. *Durfee v. Keiffer,* 168 Neb. 272, 95 N.W.2d 618. The respondent did not petition this Court for a writ of certiorari to review that judgment.

Two months later the respondent filed a suit against the petitioners in a Missouri court to quiet title to the same land. Her complaint alleged that the land was in Missouri. The suit was removed to a Federal District Court by reason of diversity of citizenship. The District Court after hearing evidence expressed the view that the land was in Missouri, but held that all the issues had been adjudicated and determined in the Nebraska litigation, and that the judgment of the Nebraska Supreme Court was res judicata and "is now binding upon this court." The Court of Appeals reversed. 308 F.2d 209. . .

It is not questioned that the Nebraska courts would give full res judicata effect to the Nebraska judgment quieting title in the petitioners.[6] It is the respondent's position, however, that whatever effect the Nebraska courts might give to the Nebraska judgment, the federal court in Missouri was free independently to determine whether the Nebraska court in fact had jurisdiction over the subject matter, i.e., whether the land in question was actually in Nebraska.

In support of this position the respondent relies upon the many decisions of this Court which have held that a judgment of a court in one State is conclusive upon the merits in a court in another State only if the court in the first State had power to pass on the merits—had jurisdiction, that is, to render the judgment. As Mr. Justice Bradley stated the doctrine in the leading case of *Thompson v. Whitman,* 18 Wall. 457, "we think it clear that the jurisdiction of the court by which a judgment is rendered in any State may be questioned in a collateral proceeding in another State, notwithstanding the provision of the fourth article of the Constitution and the law of 1790, and notwithstanding the averments contained in the record of the judgment itself." 18 Wall., at 469. The principle has been restated and applied in a variety of contexts.

However, while it is established that a court in one State, when asked to give effect to the judgment of a court in another State, may

---

[6] The Nebraska Supreme Court has clearly postulated the relevant law of the State: "This court adheres to the rule that if a court is one competent to decide whether or not the facts in any given proceeding confer jurisdiction, decides that it has jurisdiction, then its judgments entered within the scope of the subject matter over which its authority extends in proceedings following the lawful allegation of circumstances requiring the exercise of its jurisdiction, are not subject to collateral attack but conclusive against all the world unless reversed on appeal or avoided for error or fraud in a direct proceeding." * * *

constitutionally inquire into the foreign court's jurisdiction to render that judgment, the modern decisions of this Court have carefully delineated the permissible scope of such an inquiry. From these decisions there emerges the general rule that a judgment is entitled to full faith and credit—even as to questions of jurisdiction—when the second court's inquiry discloses that those questions have been fully and fairly litigated and finally decided in the court which rendered the original judgment.

With respect to questions of jurisdiction over the person, this principle was unambiguously established in *Baldwin v. Iowa State Traveling Men's Ass'n,* 283 U.S. 522. There it was held that a federal court in Iowa must give binding effect to the judgment of a federal court in Missouri despite the claim that the original court did not have jurisdiction over the defendant's person, once it was shown to the court in Iowa that that question had been fully litigated in the Missouri forum. "Public policy," said the Court, "dictates that there be an end of litigation; that those who have contested an issue shall be bound by the result of the contest; and that matters once tried shall be considered forever settled as between the parties. We see no reason why this doctrine should not apply in every case where one voluntarily appears, presents his case and is fully heard, and why he should not, in the absence of fraud, be thereafter concluded by the judgment of the tribunal to which he has submitted his cause." 283 U.S., at 525–526.

Following the *Baldwin* case, this Court soon made clear in a series of decisions that the general rule is no different when the claim is made that the original forum did not have jurisdiction over the subject matter. *Davis v. Davis,* 305 U.S. 32; *Stoll v. Gottlieb,* 305 U.S. 165; *Treinies v. Sunshine Mining Co.,* 308 U.S. 66; *Sherrer v. Sherrer,* 334 U.S. 343. In each of these cases the claim was made that a court, when asked to enforce the judgment of another forum, was free to retry the question of that forum's jurisdiction over the subject matter. In each case this Court held that since the question of subject-matter jurisdiction had been fully litigated in the original forum, the issue could not be retried in a subsequent action between the parties. . .

The reasons for such a rule are apparent. In the words of the Court's opinion in *Stoll v. Gottlieb,* supra, "We see no reason why a court in the absence of an allegation of fraud in obtaining the judgment, should examine again the question whether the court making the earlier determination on an actual contest over jurisdiction between the parties, did have jurisdiction of the subject matter of the litigation. . . Courts to determine the rights of parties are an integral part of our system of government. It is just as important that there should be a place to end as that there should be a place to begin litigation. After a party has his day in court, with opportunity to present his evidence and his view of the law, a collateral attack upon the decision as to jurisdiction there rendered merely retries the issue previously determined. There is no reason to expect that the second decision will be more satisfactory than the first." 305 U.S., at 172.

To be sure, the general rule of finality of jurisdictional determinations is not without exceptions. Doctrines of federal pre-emption or sovereign immunity may in some contexts be controlling. *Kalb v. Feuerstein,* 308 U.S. 433; *United States v. United States Fidelity & Guaranty Co.,* 309 U.S. 506.[12] But no such overriding considerations are present here. While this Court has not before had occasion to consider the applicability of the rule of *Davis, Stoll, Treinies,* and *Sherrer* to a case involving real property, we can discern no reason why the rule should not be fully applicable.

It is argued that an exception to this rule of jurisdictional finality should be made with respect to cases involving real property because of this Court's emphatic expressions of the doctrine that courts of one State are completely without jurisdiction directly to affect title to land in other States. This argument is wide of the mark. Courts of one State are equally without jurisdiction to dissolve the marriages of those domiciled in other States. But the location of land, like the domicile of a party to a divorce action, is a matter "to be resolved by judicial determination." *Sherrer v. Sherrer,* 334 U.S., at 349. The question remains whether, once the matter has been fully litigated and judicially determined, it can be retried in another State in litigation between the same parties. Upon the reason and authority of the cases we have discussed, it is clear that the answer must be in the negative. . .

MR. JUSTICE BLACK, concurring. . .

I concur in today's reversal of the Court of Appeals' judgment, but with the understanding that we are not deciding the question whether the respondent would continue to be bound by the Nebraska judgment should it later be authoritatively decided, either in an original proceeding between

---

[12] It is to be noted, however, that in neither of these cases had the jurisdictional issues actually been litigated in the first forum.

The restatement of Conflict of Laws recognizes the possibility of such exceptions:

"Where a court has jurisdiction over the parties and determines that it has jurisdiction over the subject matter, the parties cannot collaterally attack the judgment on the ground that the court did not have jurisdiction over the subject matter, unless the policy underlying the doctrine of res judicata is outweighed by the policy against permitting the court to act beyond its jurisdiction. Among the factors appropriate to be considered in determining that collateral attack should be permitted are that

"(a) the lack of jurisdiction over the subject matter was clear;

"(b) the determination as to jurisdiction depended upon a question of law rather than of fact;

"(c) the court was one of limited and not of general jurisdiction;

"(d) the question of jurisdiction was not actually litigated;

"(e) the policy against the court's acting beyond its jurisdiction is strong."

Restatement, *Conflict of Laws,* § 451(2) (Supp.1948). See Restatement, *Judgments,* § 10 (1942).

the States in this Court or by a compact between the two States under Art. I, § 10, that the disputed tract is in Missouri.

The Foreclosure of Jurisdictional Issues

(1) Do the considerations that underlie res judicata generally—respect for judicial action, elimination of vexation and expense to the parties, and conservation of judicial energy—apply to jurisdictional issues? The notion that questions of "jurisdiction" are special is ancient in the law: how can a court without power determine anything? Does *Durfee* hold that a court always has jurisdiction to determine its own jurisdiction? Is that right? Cf. *Bell v. Hood,* 327 U.S. 678 (1946).

(2) Foreclosure of jurisdictional issues is most obvious where the alleged defect is one of personal jurisdiction. Parties may consent to the exercise of jurisdiction over them; and good judicial administration requires that such objections be raised and decided at the outset. If the defendant believes that the court has no jurisdiction over his person, he must say so immediately if he appears in the case at all; if he does not object immediately, he waives his objection. If he makes a special appearance to raise the jurisdictional question and it is decided against him, he cannot then—without suffering adverse consequences—pick up his marbles and go home. Is there any reason—other than the unlikely one that the state where the judgment was rendered would permit a collateral attack—not to make the issue of personal jurisdiction res judicata?

A defendant is universally allowed to attack a judgment collaterally for want of personal jurisdiction if he has made no appearance at all. Why? Does the principle of finality suggest he should be required to make his objection during the initial suit instead of reopening a default judgment? Or would such a rule substantially impair the defendant's constitutional right not to be sued in a forum with which he has no connections by requiring him to go there to present his objection? Notice how the answer to this question may depend upon whether the real vice of having to defend in an inappropriate forum is litigation convenience, choice of law, or something else. Isn't it an indispensable hypothesis of res judicata that the defendant be given a reasonable opportunity to litigate the issue before it is foreclosed?

(3) Foreclosure of collateral attack upon issues of subject-matter jurisdiction is a more complex problem, largely because of the common principle that questions regarding subject-matter jurisdiction cannot be waived. Why can't they?

Durfee v. Duke, if the Court's understanding of the case is right, presents the clearest situation for precluding litigation of subject-matter jurisdiction, for the issue had been vigorously contested in the earlier proceeding. Even when subject-matter jurisdiction has been fully litigated, however, there is authority that certain issues of subject-matter jurisdiction may not be foreclosed. In *Kalb v. Feuerstein,* 308 U.S. 433 (1940), a farmer had lost his farm through state foreclosure proceedings while a petition was pending under section 75 of the Bankruptcy Act (the Frazier-Lemke Act), which deprived state courts of jurisdiction. The Court stated in dictum that collateral attack on the foreclosure judgment would have been permitted even if the issue had been contested in state court, because Congress had expressed a strong policy that would be thwarted by an impermissible exercise of jurisdiction. Has this dictum been superseded by *Durfee,* or are there still subject-matter-jurisdiction policies so strong that they survive an actual contest?

(4) If *Durfee* had been decided the other way, how would finality ever be achieved? See Currie, *Full Faith and Credit, Chiefly to Judgments: A Role for Congress,* 1964 Sup.Ct.Rev. 89, 105:

> If there are critics of the [*Durfee*] decision, I trust they will explain how the impasse that would have been created by the opposite result could be resolved. There would then be two inconsistent, final judgments. It is not hard to visualize the embarrassment that would ensue if the victors should invoke the aid of their respective law enforcement officers.

And what about Justice Black's concurrence in *Durfee*? Suppose the attorneys general of Missouri and Nebraska, as part of a larger settlement in an original suit in the Supreme Court of boundary disputes between the two states, entered a consent decree inconsistent with the *Durfee* result. Can private rights already fixed by court decree be destroyed by such a proceeding?

(5) What is the impact of *Durfee* upon cases in which subject-matter jurisdiction was not fully litigated in the initial proceeding? Notice the myriad variations of this problem: The parties may have tried the case on the merits without realizing that jurisdiction was lacking. The defendant may have conceded, erroneously, that there was jurisdiction. The parties may have concealed a known defect from the court for reasons of their own. The defendant may not have appeared at all. The record may affirmatively indicate the lack of jurisdiction, or it may contain formal jurisdictional recitals prepared by one or both parties, or it may be entirely silent on the question.

Chicot County Drainage Dist. v. Baxter State Bank, 308 U.S. 371 (1940), held that explicit litigation of the jurisdictional issue was unnecessary. A federal district court approved a readjustment plan that had the effect of cancelling certain bonds. The court exercised jurisdiction pursuant to a federal statute which the Supreme Court later held unconstitutional in an action involving different parties. In *Chicot* the Court held that the judgment was res judicata against participating bondholders in a second action in the same district court, despite the fact that the issue of constitutionality had not been raised or litigated in the first case.

> The remaining question is simply whether respondents having failed to raise the question in the proceeding to which they were parties and in which they could have raised it and had it finally determined, were privileged to remain quiet and raise it in a subsequent suit. Such a view is contrary to the well-settled principle that res judicata may be pleaded as a bar, not only as respects matters actually presented to sustain or defeat the right asserted in the earlier proceeding, "but also as respects any other available matter which might have been presented to that end."

308 U.S. at 378. See also *Sherrer v. Sherrer,* 334 U.S. 343 (1948), infra p. 682, in which subject-matter jurisdiction was held foreclosed in a divorce situation although the defendant's opposition to jurisdiction in the initial case had been rather tepid; *Coe v. Coe,* 334 U.S. 378 (1948), reaching the same result when jurisdiction had been conceded.

Can the *Chicot* decision be reconciled with *Kalb v. Feuerstein,* 308 U.S. 433 (1940), supra note (3), in which collateral attack was permitted? Observe that both cases were decided during the same Term. See also *United States v. United States Fidelity & Guar. Co.,* 309 U.S. 506 (1940), allowing a collateral attack upon a judgment against the United States on the ground of sovereign immunity. The issue had not been raised in the original suit, but Government attorneys had no power to waive the jurisdictional defect, and the immunity doctrine was held to outweigh the policy underlying res judicata.

Restatement (Second) of Conflict of Laws § 97, see comments *c* and *d* (1971), suggests a balancing test to determine whether collateral attack on subject-matter jurisdiction should be allowed:

> [D]ue process does not prevent a State from impinging on the interests of a sister State by application of a rule that parties who were subject to the personal jurisdiction of the court cannot collaterally attack the judgment for lack of jurisdiction. . .
>
> [A] State for policy reasons, [however,] may permit parties who are subject to the jurisdiction of the court to attack a judgment collaterally for lack of jurisdiction over a thing or status or of competence over the subject matter of the controversy.
>
> Whether a party should be permitted to attack the judgment collaterally is a question of weighing the policy underlying the rules of res judicata against the policy prohibiting a court from

> exceeding the powers conferred upon it. Important factors to be considered in determining whether there are sufficient grounds of public policy for denying the judgment the effect of res judicata are (1) whether the lack of jurisdiction or of competence . . . is clear or doubtful, (2) whether the determination as to jurisdiction or competence depends upon questions of fact or of law, (3) whether the court is one of general or of limited jurisdiction, (4) whether the question of jurisdiction or of competence was actually litigated and (5) the strength of the policy underlying the denial of competence to the court.

(6) The Court in *Durfee* quotes *Thompson v. Whitman,* 85 U.S. (18 Wall.) 457 (1873), for the proposition that a court that is called upon to enforce a foreign judgment may always inquire into the jurisdiction of the court which rendered that judgment. *Durfee* and the other cases discussed in these notes suggest that this rule has been considerably weakened. But has it been abandoned? Don't questions of jurisdiction still receive special treatment? Should they?

(7) *Treinies v. Sunshine Mining Co.,* 308 U.S. 66 (1939), concerned title to Sunshine Mining stock that had been the subject of a disputed division of a decedent's estate by her beneficiaries. The Washington probate court rejected the contention that it lacked jurisdiction and held that the stock belonged to John Pelkes. An Idaho court, in a second suit between the same parties, held that it belonged to Katherine Mason, ignoring the Washington judgment because it found the Washington court lacked jurisdiction. When Pelkes started a third suit in Washington, the beleaguered company filed a bill of interpleader against both Pelkes and Mason in federal court to find out who owned its stock. Both claimants invoked the Full Faith and Credit Clause, and the Supreme Court held the Idaho judgment entitled to respect:

> The contention of petitioner in the interpleader proceedings that the Idaho court did not have jurisdiction of the stock controversy because that controversy was in the exclusive jurisdiction of the Washington probate court must fall, because of the Idaho decision that the Washington probate court did not have exclusive jurisdiction. This is true even though the question of the Washington jurisdiction had been actually litigated and decided in favor of Pelkes in the Washington proceedings. . . As the Idaho District Court was a court of general jurisdiction, its conclusions are unassailable collaterally except for fraud or lack of jurisdiction. . . One trial of an issue is enough. . .

308 U.S. at 76–78.

But if the Idaho court's finding upholding its own jurisdiction was entitled to full faith, why wasn't the Washington court's finding that it had jurisdiction? Idaho denied full faith to the Washington judgment, didn't it? Does the Full Faith and Credit Clause require that the issue of full faith not be raised collaterally?

See also Restatement (Second) of Judgments § 15 (1980):

> *Inconsistent Judgments.* When in two actions inconsistent final judgments are rendered, it is the later, not the earlier, judgment that is accorded conclusive effect in a third action under the rules of res judicata.

Can you justify this "last-in-time" rule?

CLARKE V. CLARKE

178 U.S. 186 (1900).

[Ms. Clarke died, owning real estate in Connecticut. She bequeathed Connecticut real estate in three equal shares to her husband and to her two daughters. All parties lived in South Carolina. One of the daughters (Julia) died shortly thereafter, and Mr. Clarke, as executor for his wife and trustee for the surviving daughter Nancy, sued in South Carolina to obtain a construction of his wife's will. Nancy was represented by a guardian ad litem. The South Carolina court held the will worked an equitable conversion of Ms. Clarke's real estate into personalty and authorized the executor to sell it.

[Mr. Clarke then sued in Connecticut as administrator of his deceased daughter Julia, seeking instructions as to the disposition of her share of the Connecticut property. Under Connecticut law the entire share passed to Julia's surviving sister Nancy; South Carolina law would divide it between Nancy and her father. The Connecticut courts applied Connecticut law, awarding the land to the sister, and the father went to the Supreme Court.]

MR. JUSTICE WHITE . . . delivered the opinion of the court.

The Supreme Court of Errors of Connecticut held that the will of Julia H. Clarke, wife of the plaintiff in error, did not at the time of her death work an equitable conversion into personalty of the real estate situated in the State of Connecticut, and, consequently, that though personal property might be governed by the law of the domicil, real estate within Connecticut was controlled by the law of Connecticut, and hence that Nancy B. Clarke, as surviving sister of Julia Clarke, inherited, under the laws of Connecticut, to the exclusion of the father, the interest of the deceased sister Julia in the real estate in Connecticut which had passed to Julia by the will of her mother. It is assigned as error that in so deciding the Connecticut court refused full faith and credit to the decree of the courts of South Carolina, wherein it was adjudged that the will of Mrs. Clarke had the effect of converting her real estate, *wherever situated,* into personalty;

the deduction being that as under the South Carolina decision the real estate situated in Connecticut became personal property, it was the duty of the Connecticut court to have decided that the land passed by the law of South Carolina and not according to the law of Connecticut, and hence, that instead of treating the daughter Nancy as the owner of the whole of the real estate, it should have recognized the father as having a half interest therein. . .

It is a doctrine firmly established that the law of a State in which land is situated controls and governs its transmission by will or its passage in case of intestacy. . .

It is conceded that, had the will been presented to the courts of Connecticut in the first instance and rights been asserted under it, the operative force of its provisions upon real estate in Connecticut would have been within the control of such courts. But it is said a different rule must be applied where the will has been presented to a South Carolina court and a construction has been there given to it; for, in such a case, not the will but the decree of the South Carolina court, construing the will, is the measure of the rights of the parties, as to real estate in Connecticut. . . This is but to contend that what cannot be done directly can be accomplished by indirection, and that the fundamental principle which gives to a sovereignty an exclusive jurisdiction over the land within its borders is in legal effect dependent upon the non-existence of a decree of a court of another sovereignty determining the status of such land. Manifestly, however, an authority cannot be said to be exclusive, or even to exist at all, where its exercise may be thus frustrated at any time. . .

The courts of the domicil of Mrs. Clarke could properly be called upon to construe her will so far as it affected property which was within or might properly come under the jurisdiction of those tribunals. If, however, by the law as enforced in Connecticut, land in Connecticut owned by Mrs. Clarke at her decease was real estate for all purposes, despite the provisions contained in her will, that land was a subject-matter not directly amenable to the jurisdiction of the courts of another State, however much those courts might indirectly affect and operate upon it in controversies, where the court, by reason of its jurisdiction over persons and the nature of the controversy, might coerce the execution of a conveyance of or other instrument incumbering such land.

And the cogency of the reasons just given is further demonstrated by considering the case from another though somewhat similar aspect. The decree of the South Carolina court, which, it is contended, had the effect of converting real estate situated in Connecticut into personal property, was not one rendered between persons who were sui juris. Nancy B. Clarke, one of the parties to the suit in South Carolina, and whom the Connecticut court has held inherited, to the exclusion of the father, under the laws of

Connecticut, the whole of the real estate belonging to her sister, was a minor. She was therefore incompetent, in the proceedings in South Carolina, to stand in judgment for the purpose of depriving herself of the rights which belonged to her under the law of Connecticut as to the real estate within that State. Neither the executor or trustee under the will, or the guardian ad litem, or any other person assuming to represent the minor in South Carolina, had authority to act for her *quo ad* her interest in real estate beyond the jurisdiction of the South Carolina court, and which was situated in Connecticut.

It cannot be doubted that the courts of a State where real estate is situated have the exclusive right to appoint a guardian of a nonresident minor, and vest in such guardian the exclusive control and management of land belonging to said minor, situated within the State. . .

[T]he argument relied on must rest upon the false assumption that an exclusive power which confessedly exists in the courts of one jurisdiction may be wholly destroyed or rendered nugatory by the action of the courts of another jurisdiction in whom is vested no authority whatever on the subject. . .

[N]o violation of the constitutional requirement that full faith and credit must be given in one State to the judgments and decrees of the courts of another State, was brought about, as the decree of the South Carolina court, in the particular under consideration, was not entitled to be followed by the courts of Connecticut, by reason of a want of jurisdiction in the court of South Carolina over the particular subject-matter which was sought to be concluded in Connecticut by such decree. * * *

Judgment affirmed.

FALL V. EASTIN

215 U.S. 1 (1909).

MR. JUSTICE MCKENNA delivered the opinion of the court.

The question in this case is whether a deed to land situate in Nebraska, made by a commissioner under the decree of a court of the State of Washington in an action for divorce, must be recognized in Nebraska under the due faith and credit clause of the Constitution of the United States.

The action was begun in Hamilton County, Nebraska, in 1897, to quiet title to the land . . . and to cancel a deed executed therefor to defendant in error, Elizabeth Eastin.

Plaintiff alleged the following facts: She and E.W. Fall, who was a defendant in the trial court, were married in Indiana in 1876. Subsequently they went to Nebraska, and while living there, "by their joint efforts, accumulations and earnings, acquired jointly and by the same conveyance" the land in controversy. In 1889 they removed to the State of Washington, and continued to reside there as husband and wife until January, 1895, when they separated. On the twenty-seventh of February, 1895, her husband, she and he then being residents of King County, Washington, brought suit against her for divorce in the Superior Court of that county. He alleged in his complaint . . . that he was the owner of the land in controversy, it being, as he alleged, "his separate property, purchased by money received from his parents." . . . Plaintiff appeared in the action by answer and cross complaint. . .

She further alleges that a decree was entered granting her a divorce and setting apart to her the land in controversy as her own separate property forever, free and unencumbered from any claim of the plaintiff thereto, and that he was ordered and directed by the court to convey all his right, title and interest in and to the land within five days from the date of the decree.

She also alleges the execution of the deed to her by the commissioner appointed by the court, the execution and recording of [a separate deed by her husband] to defendant; that the deed [was] made without consideration and for the purpose of defrauding her, and . . . cast a cloud upon her title derived by her under the decree of divorce and the commissioner's deed. She prays that her title be quieted and that the [defendant's] deed . . . be declared null and void.

A decree was passed in favor of plaintiff, which was affirmed by the Supreme Court. *Fall v. Fall,* 75 Neb. 104, 106 N.W. 412. A rehearing was granted and the decree was reversed, Judge Sedgwick, who delivered the first opinion, dissenting. . .

The full faith and credit clause of the Constitution of the United States is invoked by plaintiff to sustain the deed executed under the decree of the court of the State of Washington. The argument in support of this is that the Washington court, having had jurisdiction of the parties and the subject-matter, in determination of the equities between the parties to the lands in controversy, decreed a conveyance to be made to her. . .

[T]he ultimate question is, What is the effect of the decree upon the land and of the deed executed under it? The Supreme Court of the State concedes, as we understand its opinion, the jurisdiction in the Washington court to render the decree. The court said (75 Neb. 104, 128):

> "We think there can be no doubt that where a court of chancery has by its decree ordered and directed persons properly within its jurisdiction to do or refrain from doing a certain act, it may compel obedience to this decree by appropriate proceedings, and that any action taken by reason of such compulsion is valid and effectual wherever it may be assailed. In the instant case, if Fall had obeyed

the order of the Washington court and made a deed of conveyance to his wife of the Nebraska land, even under the threat of contempt proceedings, or after duress by imprisonment, the title thereby conveyed to Mrs. Fall would have been of equal weight and dignity with that which he himself possessed at the time of the execution of the deed."

But Fall, not having executed a deed, the court's conclusion was, to quote its language, that "neither the decree nor the commissioner's deed conferred any right or title upon her." This conclusion was deduced, not only from the absence of power generally of the courts of one State over lands situate in another, but also from the laws of Nebraska providing for the disposition of real estate in divorce proceedings. The court said (75 Neb. at 133):

"... In *Cizek v. Cizek,* ... it was held that that portion of the decree which set off the homestead to the wife was absolutely void and subject to collateral attack, for the reason that no jurisdiction was given to the District Court in a divorce proceeding to award the husband's real estate to the wife in fee as alimony..."

The territorial limitation of the jurisdiction of courts of a State over property in another State has a limited exception in the jurisdiction of a court of equity, but it is an exception well defined. A court of equity having authority to act upon the person may indirectly act upon real estate in another State, through the instrumentality of this authority over the person...

Whether the doctrine that a decree of a court rendered in consummation of equities, or the deed of a master under it, will not convey title, and that the deed of a party coerced by the decree will have such effect is illogical or inconsequential, we need not inquire nor consider whether the other view would not more completely fulfill the Constitution of the United States, and that whatever may be done between the parties in one State may be adjudged to be done by the courts of another, and that the decree might be regarded to have the same legal effect as the act of the party which was ordered to be done...

But, however plausibly the contrary view may be sustained, we think that the doctrine that the court, not having jurisdiction of the res, cannot affect it by its decree, nor by a deed made by a master in accordance with the decree, is firmly established. [W]hen the subject-matter of a suit in a court of equity is within another State or country, but the parties within the jurisdiction of the court, the suit may be maintained and remedies granted which may directly affect and operate upon the person of the defendant and not upon the subject-matter, although the subject-matter is referred to in the decree, and the defendant is ordered to do or refrain from certain acts toward it, and it is thus ultimately but *indirectly* affected by the relief granted. In such case the decree is not of itself legal title, nor does it transfer the legal title. It must be executed by the party, and obedience is compelled by proceedings in the nature of contempt, attachment or sequestration. On the other hand, where the suit is strictly local, the subject-matter is specific property, and the relief when granted is such that it *must* act directly upon the subject-matter, and not upon the person of the defendant, the jurisdiction must be exercised in the State where the subject-matter is situated. * * *

This doctrine is entirely consistent with the provision of the Constitution of the United States, which requires a judgment in any State to be given full faith and credit in the courts of every other State. This provision does not extend the jurisdiction of the courts of one State to property situated in another, but only makes the judgment rendered conclusive on the merits of the claim or subject-matter of the suit. "It does not carry with it into another State the efficacy of a judgment upon property or persons, to be enforced by execution. To give it the force of a judgment in another State it must become a judgment there; and can only be executed in the latter as its laws permit." *M'Elmoyle v. Cohen,* 13 Pet. 312.

Plaintiff seems to contend for a greater efficacy for a decree in equity affecting real property than is given to a judgment at law for the recovery of money simply. The case of *Burnley v. Stevenson,* 24 Ohio St. 474, 478, in a sense sustains her. The action was brought in one of the courts of Ohio for the recovery of the possession of certain lands. The defendant set up in defense a conveyance for the same lands made by a master commissioner, in accordance with a decree of a court in Kentucky in a suit for specific performance of a contract concerning the lands. The defendant in *Burnley v. Stevenson* claimed title under the master's deed. The court declared the principle that a court of equity, having the parties before it, could enforce specific performance of a contract for lands situate in another jurisdiction by compelling the parties to make a conveyance of them, but said that it did not follow that the court could "make its own decree to operate as such conveyance." And it was decided that the decree could not have such effect, and as it could not, it was "clear that a deed executed by a master, under the direction of the court," could "have no greater effect" . . . and the master's deed, the court said, "must, therefore, be regarded as a nullity." . . .

The court . . . concluded that as the decree had the effect in Kentucky of determining the equities of the parties to the land in Ohio, the courts of the latter State "must accord to it the same effect" in obedience to the due faith and credit clause of the Constitution of the United States. "True," the court observed, "the courts of this State cannot enforce the performance of that decree, by compelling the conveyance through its process of attachment, but when pleaded in our courts as a cause of action, or as a ground of defense, it must be regarded as conclusive of all the rights and equities which were adjudicated and settled therein, unless it be impeached for fraud. . ."

There is . . . much temptation in the facts of this case to follow the ruling of the Supreme Court of Ohio. As we have seen, the husband of the plaintiff brought suit against her in Washington for divorce, and, attempting to avail himself of the laws of Washington, prayed also that the land now in controversy be awarded to him. She appeared in the action, and, submitting to the jurisdiction which he had invoked, made counter-charges and prayers for relief. She established her charges, she was granted a divorce, and the land decreed to her. He, then, to defeat the decree and in fraud of her rights, conveyed the land to the defendant in this suit. This is the finding of the trial court. It is not questioned by the Supreme Court, but as the ruling of the latter court, that the decree in Washington gave no such equities as could be recognized in Nebraska as justifying an action to quiet title does not offend the Constitution of the United States, we are constrained to affirm its judgment.

MR. JUSTICE HARLAN and MR. JUSTICE BREWER dissent.

MR. JUSTICE HOLMES, concurring specially.

I am not prepared to dissent from the judgment of the court, but my reasons are different from those that have been stated.

The real question concerns the effect of the Washington decree. As between the parties to it that decree established in Washington a personal obligation of the husband to convey to his former wife. A personal obligation goes with the person. If the husband had made a contract, valid by the law of Washington, to do the same thing, I think there is no doubt that the contract would have been binding in Nebraska. * * * So I conceive that a Washington decree for the specific performance of such a contract would be entitled to full faith and credit as between the parties in Nebraska. But it does not matter to its constitutional effect what the ground of the decree may be, whether a contract or something else. . . A personal decree is equally within the jurisdiction of a court having the person within its power, whatever its ground and whatever it orders the defendant to do. Therefore I think that this decree was entitled to full faith and credit in Nebraska.

But the Nebraska court carefully avoids saying that the decree would not be binding between the original parties had the husband been before the court. The ground on which it goes is that to allow the judgment to affect the conscience of purchasers would be giving it an effect in rem. It treats the case as standing on the same footing as that of an innocent purchaser. Now if the court saw fit to deny the effect of a judgment upon privies in title, or if it considered the defendant an innocent purchaser, I do not see what we have to do with its decision, however wrong. I do not see why it is not within the power of the State to do away with equity or with the equitable doctrine as to purchasers with notice if it sees fit. Still less do I see how a mistake as to notice could give us jurisdiction. If the judgment binds the defendant it is not by its own operation, even with the Constitution behind it, but by the obligation imposed by equity upon a purchaser with notice. The ground of decision below was that there was no such obligation. The decision, even if wrong, did not deny to the Washington decree its full effect. * * *

The Land Taboo

(1) Viewed simply as a choice-of-law matter, isn't it arguable that Connecticut had no legitimate interest in awarding the land in *Clarke* to a South Carolina child instead of to her South Carolina father, and therefore that the application of Connecticut law was unconstitutional? See Baxter, *Choice of Law and the Federal System,* 16 Stan. L. Rev. 1, 15–17 (1963):

> [T]he need for improvement of choice criteria [in property cases] is acute. The historical reason for the traditional situs reference—legal acquiescence in the de facto power of the situs state to effectuate its policies—has no relevance to our federal system. Like other arbitrary choice rules, the situs rule defeats maximum realization by each state of the policies underlying its internal laws. Rules of law can be justified only by reference to their impact on the interests of people. Property, unlike those who have interests in it, does not care about its ownership or the marketability of its title. These remarks are obvious to the point of banality; it should be equally obvious that the situs choice rule is defective on its face because the relationships relevant for choice criteria are those between sovereigns and people, not those between sovereigns and property.
>
> It does not follow, of course, that the situs of property should never control. Persons who live in the vicinity of the property are the intended beneficiaries of many property laws, such as the laws of nuisance, and the location of the property and hence of those people often should control the applicability of those laws. . .

(2) Even if the Constitution permits or indeed requires the application of Connecticut law in *Clarke,* isn't the decision beastly hard to reconcile with *Fauntleroy v. Lum*? Why should there be a special rule for collateral attacks on judgments respecting the disposition of real property? Or is *Clarke* best explained as a case involving collateral attack on the jurisdiction of the rendering court? Is *Clarke* overruled by *Durfee v. Duke*?

(3) What earthly reason was there for the holding in *Clarke* that a South Carolina court lacked jurisdiction to determine conflicting claims of South Carolina residents to Connecticut land? What happened to the policy of transitoriness expressed in *Hughes v. Fetter,* 341 U.S. 609 (1951), supra p. 414, and in *Tennessee Coal, Iron & R.R. Co. v. George,* 233 U.S. 354 (1914), supra p. 422?

Lurking behind this part of *Clarke* is the principle of *Livingston v. Jefferson,* 15 F.Cas. 660 (C.C.D.Va. 1811), in which a court including Chief Justice Marshall held that an action for trespass to Louisiana land was "local" and could not be maintained outside Louisiana. This tenacious rule was rejected outright in 1952 by the Arkansas Supreme Court in an outstanding opinion by Judge George Rose Smith upholding jurisdiction in Arkansas over a claim for damage caused by insecticide sprayed on Missouri land. The origin of the rule was in thirteenth-century England, where "all actions had to be brought where the cause of action arose, because the members of the jury were required to be neighbors who would know something of the litigants and of the dispute as well," and the three reasons given for the survival of the rule in trespass cases were unpersuasive as applied to states within a federal system. First, although Arkansas judges might be in no position to investigate questions respecting Russian or Chinese law, "[i]n our library we have the statutes and decisions of every other State, and it seldom takes more than a few hours to find the answer to a particular question." Besides, this consideration was not rigidly adhered to, for "American courts do not hesitate to pass upon an out-of-state title when the issue arises in a transitory action" such as for damages for nonperformance of a contract to sell land. Second, it would be unreasonable in a country without internal border controls to expect the plaintiff to pursue his remedy before the defendant leaves the jurisdiction. Finally, "there is an understandable reluctance to subject one's own citizens to suits by aliens, especially if the other jurisdiction would provide no redress if the situation were reversed," but "[w]e do not feel compelled to provide a sanctuary in Arkansas for those who have willfully and wrongfully destroyed property, torn down houses, uprooted crops, polluted streams, and inflicted other injuries upon innocent landowners in our sister States." "The truth is," the court concluded, "that the majority rule has no basis in logic or equity and rests solely upon English cases that were decided before America was discovered and in circumstances that are not even comparable to those existing in our Union. . . We prefer to afford this litigant his day in court." *Reasor-Hill Corp. v. Harrison,* 220 Ark. 521, 523–26, 249 S.W.2d 994, 995–96 (1952).

In federal court, the local action doctrine has been repealed, at least as to venue, by the Jurisdiction and Venue Clarification Act of 2011, 28 U.S.C.A. § 1391(a)(2), which provides that "the proper venue for a civil action shall be determined without regard to whether the action is local or transitory in nature." But see, *e.g.*, *Boaz Legacy, L.P. v. Roberts*, 628 F. App'x 318, 319 (5th Cir. 2016) (holding that "the subject matter jurisdiction of the federal courts is limited by the local action doctrine," under which "a local action involving real property can only be brought within the territorial boundaries of the state where the land is located") (citation omitted).

The Restatement (Second) of Conflict of Laws § 87, comment a (1971), would permit actions for harm done to land in another state:

> Such an action does not seek to affect title to foreign land, as would a bill to quiet title, nor does it require official action in the state where the land lies, as would a suit in which the plaintiff asks that the defendant be removed from the land and he himself placed in possession.

As suggested by this explanation, the Restatement believes that an action of "trespass to try title," which is essentially one "for the recovery of possession of land," should be maintainable only at the situs. Id., comment d. Why? Does this mean South Carolina still could not determine the claims of Nancy Clarke and her father? In any event, even if many states continue to recognize the local action doctrine as a matter of state law, why should it be imported into the Full Faith and Credit Clause to deny recognition to judgments rendered in states that have rejected it?

(4) *Fall v. Eastin* was a subject of lasting controversy. Did the Court hold that the Washington decree was valid insofar as it directed Fall to convey the property but that the Washington commissioner's deed was invalid? Isn't this distinction absurd? Any Nebraska policy against allowing ownership of local land to be affected by foreign courts is impaired as much by Fall's deed as by the commissioner's. Brainerd Currie defended the distinction at least in terms of full faith if not also of jurisdiction:

> The plight of a Nebraska lawyer examining a title, when he encounters on the record a conveyance by a commissioner appointed by a foreign court, is one which readily arouses sympathetic understanding. His problem, in such a suppositious case, would be to inquire fully into the unfamiliar powers of the foreign court; to examine the record of the proceedings leading to the decree; and perhaps to disentangle nice distinctions under the full faith and credit clause. It may well be said that a state could hardly tolerate such complexities.

Currie, *Full Faith and Credit to Foreign Land Decrees,* 21 U. Chi. L. Rev. 620, 639–40 (1954). But doesn't the point about "nice distinctions under the full faith and credit clause" beg the question, which is whether such distinctions are justifiable? Won't the scope of inquiry into the validity of a commissioner's deed be significantly narrowed by the principle of *Durfee v. Duke*? And why wouldn't a deed executed by Fall himself pursuant to the Washington decree be subject to exactly the same inquiry? For, as Currie emphasizes elsewhere in the same article, if the decree is invalid Fall's deed is voidable for duress. 21 U. Chi. L. Rev. at 629.

(5) If, as the Court several times conceded, the Washington court had jurisdiction to order Fall to convey the property to his wife, why wasn't the Washington decree given full faith and credit? Did the Supreme Court hold that it was not entitled to full faith? In her emphasis upon the commissioner's deed the plaintiff seems not to have asked the Nebraska court to enforce the decree itself (which may explain the Court's offended statement that she asked greater effect for the foreign decree than would be accorded a foreign money judgment, which must be sued upon before execution). What result if she had done so? See *Rozan v. Rozan,* 49 Cal.2d 322, 330–32, 317 P.2d 11, 15–16 (1957) (Traynor, J.), upholding California jurisdiction to order a conveyance of North Dakota land and concluding that its decree would be entitled to full faith and credit: "*Fall v. Eastin* . . . did not hold otherwise. In that case the Washington decree directly affected title to land in Nebraska."

(6) Short of overruling *Fauntleroy v. Lum,* supra p. 562, is there any reason why a valid Washington decree ordering a Nebraska conveyance should not be given full faith and credit? Is there some Nebraska policy at stake that is stronger than the Mississippi policy involved in *Fauntleroy*? Doesn't the willingness of Nebraska to recognize a deed executed under the duress of a foreign decree demonstrate that no significant policy would be infringed by recognizing the decree? And even if a state did not recognize such a deed (Currie, 21 U. Chi. L. Rev. at 628–29, says all states recognize them), "are we to believe that a statute defining the jurisdiction of Nebraska courts in divorce cases expresses Nebraska's policy of matrimonial support pertaining to *couples domiciled in Washington*?" Id. at 637. See *McElreath v. McElreath,* 162 Tex. 190, 194, 345 S.W.2d 722, 724 (1961), leaving open the full-faith issue and enforcing on the basis of "comity" an Oklahoma decree ordering a conveyance of Texas property that would not have been proper under Texas law: "Texas public policy does not relate to and is not concerned with the settlement by Oklahoma courts of marital property problems which arise between Oklahoma citizens. Article 4638 establishes a policy governing Texas courts in cases involving divorce and property rights based upon the marital laws of this State."

(7) If a foreign land decree is not entitled to full faith and credit, does its recognition on a comity basis deprive the losing party of property without due process of law? See Currie, 21 U. Chi. L. Rev. at 666: "Speaking very generally, there is ground for a preliminary inference that under our Constitution there exists a dichotomy: either a judgment is rendered without jurisdiction, in which case due process of law would be denied by holding it conclusive; or it is rendered with jurisdiction, in which case it is entitled to full faith and credit." At least one state court has been persuaded that it could not recognize a foreign land decree, *Sharp v. Sharp,* 65 Okla. 76, 79, 166 P. 175, 178 (1916), although *Fall v. Eastin* seems to have foreclosed this conclusion by explicitly upholding the jurisdiction of the foreign court.

(8) Professor Currie's article concluded with a word of advice for attorneys seeking not to be trapped by *Fall v. Eastin:*

> The decree . . . should purport to do no more than exercise the jurisdiction which is acknowledged; it should, upon appropriate findings of fact and of law, order the defendant to make a conveyance, and no more. Nothing whatever is to be gained by framing it in terms which purport to affect the title directly, or which call for the appointment of a commissioner to convey. Such terms . . . are an invitation to the court at the situs, and to the Supreme Court, to invoke hornbook principles in support of a holding that the foreign court had no jurisdiction to do what it did, and they are sure to arouse fears as to the effect of recognition on the recording system at the situs. . .
>
> The theory on which relief is claimed at the situs is at least equally important. Consistently with the reasoning on which recognition is demanded, the plaintiff must scrupulously avoid any prayer for relief predicated on the assumption that he has acquired legal title by virtue of the foreign decree. Thus, to bring an action of ejectment, or to rely on the foreign decree in defense to a possessory action in a state in which law and equity powers are kept separate, is the worst possible exercise of judgment. . .
>
> An action to remove the defendant's claim as a cloud on the plaintiff's title, if that remedy is otherwise available, is a tempting possibility, but is probably not advisable. In the first place, a holding that such a remedy is available only to one having a legal interest would provide an adequate non-federal ground for the refusal of relief, precluding review by the Supreme Court of the question under the full faith and credit clause. Moreover, even if the situs state gives the holder of an equitable title standing to invoke the remedy, the unsuccessful resort to that mode of relief in the *Fall* case stands as a warning that courts may shy away from any position resting on the contention that the foreign decree is a source of "title" of any kind. . .
>
> A procedure which would be strictly in conformity with the theory on which conclusive effect is claimed for the foreign decree would be to bring, at the situs, an action to effectuate the foreign decree, or to carry it into effect. . . Nevertheless, enthusiasm for the view that such a remedy has long been available should not

blind one to the unwisdom of staking the whole case on that general proposition. . .

[T]he ideal action to secure the benefits of the decree at the situs would be framed as one to enforce, or execute, the decree; and, in the alternative, to secure a declaration of the rights of the parties pursuant to the decree, with supplemental relief; and, also in the alternative, to enforce the original cause of action—if there is one—with the decree operating as res judicata.

Currie, 21 U. Chi. L. Rev. at 672–76.

WORTHLEY V. WORTHLEY

44 Cal.2d 465, 283 P.2d 19 (1955).

[The Worthleys were married in New Jersey in 1943 and lived there together until they separated in 1946. In a New Jersey action for separate maintenance in which her husband participated, Ms. Worthley obtained a decree ordering him to pay $9 a week for her support. Mr. Worthley left New Jersey in 1947 and refused to make any further payments under the support order after a date in mid-1948.]

TRAYNOR, JUSTICE. . . On November 16, 1951, plaintiff commenced this action in the Superior Court of Los Angeles County, the county of defendant's present residence. She alleged that the New Jersey decree "has become final and has never been vacated, modified, or set aside" and that defendant is delinquent in his payments thereunder in the amount of $1,089. She seeks a judgment for the accrued arrearages and asks that the New Jersey decree be established as a California decree and that defendant be ordered to pay her $9 a week until further order of the court. . .

Since the New Jersey decree is both prospectively and retroactively modifiable, N.J.S.A. § 2A:34–23, we are not constitutionally bound to enforce defendant's obligations under it. *Sistare v. Sistare,* 218 U.S. 1; *Lynde v. Lynde,* 181 U.S. 183; *Barber v. Barber,* 21 How. 582.* Nor are we bound *not* to enforce them. *People ex rel. Halvey v. Halvey,* 330 U.S. 610, 615 * * *. The United States Supreme Court has held, however, that if such obligations are enforced in this state, at least as to accrued arrearages, due process requires that the defendant be afforded an opportunity to litigate

* In recent cases the United States Supreme Court has expressly reserved judgment on the question of full faith and credit to modifiable judgments and decrees, see, *Barber v. Barber,* 323 U.S. 77, 81; *Griffin v. Griffin,* 327 U.S. 220, 234; but see, *People ex rel. Halvey v. Halvey,* 330 U.S. 610, 615, and the late Mr. Justice Jackson, a foremost expounder of the law of full faith and credit in recent years, forcefully declared that modifiable alimony and support decrees are within the scope of that clause: "Neither the full faith and credit clause of the Constitution nor the Act of Congress implementing it says anything about final judgments or, for that matter, about any judgments. Both require that full faith and credit be given to 'judicial proceedings' without limitation as to finality. Upon recognition of the broad meaning of that term much may someday depend." Concurring opinion, *Barber v. Barber,* 323 U.S. 77, 87.

the question of modification. *Griffin v. Griffin,* 327 U.S. 220, 233–234 * * *. It has also clearly indicated that as to either prospective or retroactive enforcement of such obligations, this state "has at least as much leeway to disregard the judgment, to qualify it, or to depart from it as does the State where it was rendered." *People ex rel. Halvey v. Halvey,* supra, 330 U.S. 610, 615.

In *Biewend v. Biewend,* 17 Cal.2d 108, 113–114, 109 P.2d 701, 704, it was held that the California courts will recognize and give prospective enforcement to a foreign alimony decree, even though it is subject to modification under the law of the state where it was originally rendered, by establishing it "as the decree of the California court with the same force and effect as if it had been entered in this state, including punishment for contempt if the defendant fails to comply. * * *" Similar holdings in reference to both alimony and support decrees have repeatedly been made by the District Courts of Appeal * * * and by the courts of other states * * *. It was stated in the *Biewend* case, however, that the Missouri decree would be established as a decree of the California courts "until such time as the Missouri court modifies its decree." 17 Cal.2d 108, 114, 109 P.2d 701, 705. On reconsideration we have concluded, for reasons that appear below, that this statement was erroneous insofar as it implied that the California courts will not try the issue of modification on its merits, and that the courts of this state should undertake to try such issues.

The District Court of Appeal for the Third Appellate District in a recent case has prospectively modified a support obligation created in a Nevada decree. *Starr v. Starr,* supra, 121 Cal.App.2d 633, 263 P.2d 675. . . The court concluded that if the California courts could modify the custody rights created in the Nevada decree, there was no reason why the support obligation created in the same decree could not also be modified. Similarly, the courts of a number of other states have affirmed their willingness to undertake prospective modification of alimony and support obligations created in sister-state decrees. * * *

Although the question of retroactive modification has been seldom litigated, the United States Supreme Court has expressed its approval of the proposition that actions to enforce retroactively modifiable decrees should be tried in a forum that has personal jurisdiction over both parties, and that in the trial of such actions the defendant must be afforded an opportunity to set up any mitigating defenses that would be available to him if the suit were brought in the state where the alimony or support decree was originally rendered. *Griffin v. Griffin,* 327 U.S. 220, 233–234 * * *. The same rule has been expressed by the Supreme Court of New Jersey. * * *

It is suggested that . . . we should follow certain sister-state decisions holding that alimony and support obligations created by a prospectively and retroactively modifiable decree are enforceable only in the state in which the decree was rendered. The policy implicit in those decisions is that a modifiable duty of support in one state "is of no special interest to other states and . . . is not enforceable elsewhere under principles of Conflict of Laws." Restatement, Conflict of Laws, § 458, comment *a*. This policy was rejected by this court in the *Biewend* case * * *, and by the Legislature of this state in enacting the Uniform Reciprocal Enforcement of Support Act. Code Civ.Proc. §§ 1650–1690. . .

Moreover, there is no valid reason, in a case in which both parties are before the court, why the California courts should refuse to hear a plaintiff's prayer for enforcement of a modifiable sister-state decree and the defendant's plea for modification of his obligations thereunder. If the accrued installments are modified retroactively, the judgment for a liquidated sum entered after such modification will be final and thus will be entitled to full faith and credit in all other states. *Magnolia Petroleum Co. v. Hunt,* 320 U.S. 430, 438–439, and cases cited. If the installments are modified prospectively, the issues thus determined will be res judicata so long as the circumstances of the parties remain unchanged. * * * Moreover, the interests of neither party would be served by requiring the plaintiff to return to the state of rendition and reduce her claim for accrued installments to a money judgment. In the present case, for example, defendant, a domiciliary of this state, would have to travel 3,000 miles from his home, family, and job to secure a modification of plaintiff's allegedly stale claim and to protect his interests in any proceeding for the enforcement of his support obligation that she might institute in New Jersey. If defendant is unable to afford the time or money to travel to New Jersey to make an effective appearance in plaintiff's proceedings in that state, his substantive defenses to plaintiff's claims will be foreclosed. By the same token, unless plaintiff elected to proceed under the Uniform Reciprocal Enforcement of Support Act, which has been adopted in New Jersey, * * * defendant's failure to pay the installments as they came due would force her constantly to relitigate his obligation to support. Repeated suits for arrearages would have to be brought in New Jersey as installments accrued, to be followed by repeated actions in California to enforce the New Jersey judgments for accrued installments, with the net result that the costs of litigation and the dilatoriness of the recovery would substantially reduce the value of the support to which plaintiff is entitled.

Furthermore, there is no merit to the contention that as a matter of practical convenience the issue of modification should be tried in the courts of the state where the support decree was originally rendered. Proof of changed circumstances in support cases is no more difficult than in custody cases and, as noted above, a California court that has jurisdiction of the subject matter must undertake to adjudicate a plea for modification of custody rights established by a sister-state decree. *Sampsell v. Superior*

Court, 32 Cal.2d 763, 197 P.2d 739. Moreover, in most states the problem of modification is dealt with according to general equitable principles, and the law of the state in which the support obligation originated can be judicially noticed, * * * and applied by the California courts.

Accordingly, we hold that foreign-created alimony and support obligations are enforceable in this state. In an action to enforce a modifiable support obligation, either party may tender and litigate any plea for modification that could be presented to the courts of the state where the alimony or support decree was originally rendered.

The judgment is reversed.

SPENCE, J.

I dissent. . .

[T]he New Jersey judgment which plaintiff seeks to enforce in California is modifiable retroactively, as well as prospectively, under the law of New Jersey; but the majority opinion nevertheless requires its enforcement and modification by the courts of this state. This will result in confusion worse confounded, as the courts of each of several states, including New Jersey, might be called upon to modify the same decree, both retroactively as well as prospectively. In my opinion, the New Jersey decree, until made final by the courts of that state, is based upon shifting sands, which furnish no firm foundation upon which to predicate a judgment in any other jurisdiction. . .

Non-Final Decrees

(1) The *Worthley* case deals with several related and troublesome problems in the application of the full faith and credit requirement: the treatment of decrees that lack finality or are subject to modification or to continuing supervision.

(a) *Lack of finality.* A judgment lacks finality if further judicial action by the court rendering the judgment is required to resolve the matter litigated. To the extent that issues remain subject to final determination, they are not res judicata either in the state of rendition or elsewhere. The local law of the rendering state determines whether a judgment is "final." Appeals, stays, interlocutory orders, and retention of jurisdiction may affect the "finality" of a judgment.

Whether pendency of an appeal precludes a judgment being considered as "final" depends upon the law of the state rendering the judgment. In *Paine v. Schenectady Ins. Co.,* 11 R.I. 411 (1876), the leading case on the subject, there were conflicting judgments in Rhode Island and New York, with an appeal taken from each. In Rhode Island an appeal had the effect of vacating the judgment; in New York an appeal did not vacate the judgment, which was considered as final until reversed. Despite the fact that the Rhode Island case reached judgment first, the Rhode Island court held on appeal that New York's final judgment was conclusive upon it.

(b) *Modifiability.* Orders for the support of a spouse or child ordinarily remain subject to modification by the rendering court in the light of events that may occur in the future. Suppose that a New Jersey wife obtains a valid order from a New Jersey court directing the husband to pay her $2,000 per month. At some later time he leaves New Jersey for the supposedly pleasanter climes of California. At any point in time the wife has claims for (1) past unpaid installments, and (2) present and future support. If the past unpaid installments are reduced in the rendering state to a judgment for a fixed, unmodifiable amount, that judgment must be enforced by sister states. *Lynde v. Lynde,* 181 U.S. 183 (1901). The local law of the state of rendition determines whether the judgment is modifiable, and "every reasonable implication must be resorted to against the existence of" a power to modify accrued installments of alimony "in the absence of clear language manifesting an intention to confer it." *Sistare v. Sistare,* 218 U.S. 1, 22 (1910); *Barber v. Barber,* 323 U.S. 77 (1944).

To date the Supreme Court has not explicitly required enforcement of sister-state judgments, whether for past due installments or for future installments, that remain subject to modification in the state of rendition. But why should the absconding husband or father be able to shield himself behind a supposed limitation of full faith and credit? Presumably the reasons are that the litigation of changed circumstances and other factors affecting modification impose a burden on the forum that is far greater than that of the ordinary money judgment; the rendering court is in the best position to exercise the discretion involved in supervising the continuing relationship between the parties; and that if both the rendering court and the forum undertake to supervise or to modify, unseemly conflict between them may result. How valid are these arguments?

The problem of conflicting state support orders has been resolved legislatively by the Uniform Interstate Family Support Act (UIFSA), which was promulgated in 1992 and amended most recently in 2008. The Act has been adopted in all fifty states and the District of Columbia. UIFSA treats the modification of spousal support orders and child support orders differently. Section 211 of the Act provides that a state having jurisdiction over the parties which enters a spousal support order (the "issuing" state) has "continuing, exclusive jurisdiction to modify the spousal-support order throughout the existence of the support obligation." Its order may not be modified by any other state. An issuing state which enters a child-support order, by contrast, may lose its continuing exclusive jurisdiction to modify the order under § 205 if, at the time the request for modification is filed, it is not the residence of the obligor, the individual obligee, or the child for whose benefit the support order was issued. (Those parties, may, however, consent to have the issuing state continue to exercise modification jurisdiction. Why do you suppose the parties would choose this option?) Is this legislative approach superior to leaving the issue of conflicting orders to be resolved by adjudication under the Full Faith and Credit clause?

(2) Prior to UIFSA, when a forum decided to enforce a modifiable spousal or child support order, it was unclear what state's law should be applied to the substantive question of whether the order should be increased or decreased. Assuming the forum decides to enforce a modifiable alimony or child support decree of a sister state, what law should be applied to the question of whether the order should be increased or decreased? The law of the rendering state, as suggested by Justice Traynor in *Worthley*? The law of the forum? The law of the present domicile of the supporting spouse? Of the supported spouse or child? This matter was reexamined in light of *Worthley* in *Petersen v. Petersen,* 24 Cal.App.3d 201, 100 Cal.Rptr. 822 (1972), where modification of an Illinois decree ordering the husband to pay $450 per month for the support of each of three children was sought in California. At the time of modification, the wife had remarried and was living in Seattle, Washington; the husband had also remarried and was living in California with his wife and their child; and two of the three children of the original marriage were attending college. The husband sought a reduction in the order from $450 to $300 per month based on his increased expenses in maintaining his new family; the wife sought to retain the original order and to enforce arrearages. The husband urged that since the Illinois judgment had been established as a California judgment for purposes of enforcement, California law should provide the standard for modification; the wife relied on Illinois law to determine whether a change of circumstances had occurred since the original order. Both cited *Worthley.*

The court thought that *Worthley* supported the husband, not the wife: the rendering state should not be allowed to "freeze" the obligations of the parent to his child, nor, by extension, the standard by which those obligations are measured. In *Petersen,* neither party retained any connection with the rendering state. California, where both parties were before the court and where the supporting spouse was residing, "can best exercise its discretion by utilizing its familiarity with living costs in California, and apply the California standard * * *." 24 Cal.App.3d at 206, 100 Cal.Rptr. at 825. On the facts, however, application of the California standard resulted in retention of the original Illinois order of $450 per month: while the husband's expenses had increased, so had his income; and the wife had established that the children's expenses were higher than at the time of the original decree.

The *Worthley-Petersen* approach, while commendably expanding the voluntary recognition of non-final support orders, also resulted in multiple orders with potentially conflicting or overlapping terms. UIFSA seeks to replace this multiple-order system with a one-order approach whereby only one existing order is to be enforced prospectively. When enforcement in another state is sought, the order is registered in a court of the responding state, which applies the law of the issuing state to determine the merits of the dispute. In UIFSA's eyes, the resulting order never becomes an order of the responding state. The issuing state retains ultimate responsibility for enforcement and final resolution of the obligor's compliance with all aspects of the order. Recognizing that, because of earlier practice under the now-replaced URESA and its revised version, RURESA, more than one order may be outstanding when enforcement is sought, UIFSA provides rules of priority to enable the responding court to determine which order is "controlling." These rules give highest priority to an order issued by the child's current home state, then to the most recent order, and finally to an order issued by the forum. Is this approach, attractive in theory as it is, likely to prove more workable than the earlier multiple-order system?

(3) UIFSA also offers a solution to the problem of providing support for deserted dependents. It provides both for the enforcement of a previously granted support order and for an original claim of support. UIFSA authorizes a streamlined way of assessing and collecting support. Instead of being required to obtain an order in the state of their residence (the "initiating" state) and sending it on for enforcement to the state where the obligor may be found (the "responding" state), the dependents (e.g., a deserted wife and/or children) may file an interstate proceeding in the responding state to establish, enforce, or modify a support order. In the case of an original claim for support, the responding state becomes the "issuing" state and its law governs the nature, extent, amount, and duration of current payments under a registered support order. Its order must be enforced in other states, including the initiating state.

(4) Injunctions against suit in another state on the ground that the other state is an inconvenient forum present a troublesome and unsettled problem. In *James v. Grand Trunk Western R.R.,* 14 Ill.2d 356, 152 N.E.2d 858 (1958), a Michigan plaintiff brought suit in Illinois under the Michigan wrongful-death statute, to recover for an accident that had occurred in Michigan. A Michigan court enjoined the prosecution of the Illinois action, but the Illinois court refused to respect the injunction and issued a counter-order enjoining the railroad from enforcing its Michigan injunction:

> [W]hile we quite agree with defendant's repeated assertion that a court of equity has power to restrain persons within its jurisdiction from instituting or proceeding with foreign actions (*Cole v. Cunningham,* 133 U.S. 107), . . . this jurisdiction has followed the overwhelming judicial opinion that neither the full-faith-and-credit clause nor rules of comity require compulsory recognition of such injunctions so as to abate or preclude the disposition of the pending case. . .

> [T]he Michigan injunction was apparently issued pursuant to the policy of the State embodied in a Michigan venue statute restricting venue in suits against railroads to the county in which plaintiff resides, if the railroad lines traverse that county. . . [S]imilar statutes confining transitory actions to the state of plaintiff's residence have been held unconstitutional. * * * *Tennessee Coal, Iron & Railroad Co. v. George,* 233 U.S. 354. [I]f statutes prohibiting or circumscribing the export of causes of action may not be given extraterritorial effect, it is hard to see why an equity decree should be entitled to any greater recognition. . .
>
> [I]f Illinois were not the appropriate forum to try this, or any other transitory action, the defense of *forum non conveniens* could be interposed, and, if meritorious, the Illinois court would dismiss the case. However, this court need not, and will not, countenance having its right to try cases, of which it has proper jurisdiction, determined by the courts of other States, through their injunctive process. . .

14 Ill.2d at 363–64, 366–67, 372, 152 N.E.2d, at 862, 864, 867. But aren't both the argument of forum jurisdictional policy and the notion that a judgment need be given no greater effect than a foreign statute foreclosed by *Fauntleroy v. Lum*?

The problems become very sticky when an anti-suit injunction is combined with the last-in-time rule of the *Treinies* case, noted at p. 596, supra. Suppose a New Jersey court enjoins the defendant from further pursuit of duplicative litigation in New York. Despite a succession of restraining orders, the defendant continues to press the New York litigation and the New York court, which also has personal jurisdiction over the parties, ignores the New Jersey decree and reaches judgment first. Did the New York court violate the constitutional command? Once it has done so, is New Jersey bound by the New York judgment under the last-in-time rule? And, even if it is bound, may New Jersey punish the defendant for contempt of its order while accepting New York's disposition of the merits as definitive? See *Joffe v. Joffe,* 384 F.2d 632 (3d Cir.1967), refusing to enjoin 50 N.J. 265, 234 A.2d 232 (1967), which is discussed in Ginsburg, *Judgments in Search of Full Faith and Credit: The Last-in-Time Rule for Conflicting Judgments,* 82 Harv.L.Rev. 798, 823–30 (1969). Professor Ginsburg recommends federal legislation delineating the circumstances in which anti-suit injunctions may issue with nationwide effect, and prohibition of them in all others. Absent congressional solution, she concludes that the New York judgment should disarm New Jersey from continuing the fray. Do you agree?

Professor (now Justice) Ginsburg had a chance to address interstate recognition and enforcement of injunctive judgments in the following case.

BAKER V. GENERAL MOTORS CORPORATION

522 U.S. 222 (1998).

JUSTICE GINSBURG delivered the opinion of the Court.

[Ronald Elwell was employed in the Engineering Analysis Group of General Motors from 1959 until 1989, often assisting the company in product liability actions. Sometime after 1987, the Elwell-GM employment relationship soured, leading to prolonged and acrimonious negotiations over Elwell's retirement. In May, 1991, Elwell appeared as a witness for the plaintiffs in a product liability action filed against GM in Georgia; in June, Elwell sued GM in Michigan state court, alleging wrongful discharge and other contract and tort claims. GM counterclaimed, charging breach of fiduciary duty based on Elwell's testimony in the Georgia case.

[GM and Elwell settled their dispute in August, 1992. In return for an undisclosed sum of money, Elwell agreed to the entry of a permanent injunction that, among other things, forbade him from "testifying, without the prior written consent of General Motors Corporation, either upon deposition or at trial, as an expert witness, or as a witness of any kind, and from consulting with attorneys or their agents in any litigation already filed, or to be filed in the future, involving General Motors Corporation."

[Apart from a specific allowance for the pending Georgia litigation, the Michigan injunction was unlimited. In their separate settlement agreement, however, Elwell and GM included a qualification stating that, if Elwell were ordered to testify by a court, it would "in no way form a basis for an action in violation of the Permanent Injunction or this Agreement." In the years that followed, Elwell began selling his services as a witness against GM, avoiding the Michigan decree by arranging up front for the plaintiffs to have his testimony subpoenaed. Although Michigan courts refused on several occasions either to modify the decree or to permit Elwell to testify, courts outside Michigan ruled otherwise and Elwell began regularly appearing as a witness against GM.

[In the meantime, Kenneth and Steven Baker commenced a wrongful death action against GM in a Missouri federal court, seeking to recover for the death of their mother in an automobile accident. The Bakers subpoenaed Elwell, and GM objected on the ground that the Michigan injunction barred both his deposition and his testimony at trial. The District Court allowed Elwell to testify, ruling that (1) blocking Elwell's testimony would violate Missouri's "public policy"; and (2) because a Michigan court could modify the decree, so too could a Missouri court. The plaintiffs recovered $11.3 million in damages, and GM appealed. The Court of Appeals for the Eighth Circuit reversed, holding that Elwell should not have been permitted to testify. The appeals court explained that any Missouri public policy in favor of allowing the testimony was counterbalanced by an "equally strong public policy in favor of full faith and credit." As for the power to modify, the panel observed that Michigan courts had already declined to do so, emphasizing that the Bakers' suit was precisely the kind at which the injunction was aimed.

[The Supreme Court granted certiorari "to decide whether the full faith and credit requirement stops the Bakers, who were not parties to the Michigan proceeding, from obtaining Elwell's testimony in their Missouri wrongful death action."]

II

A . . .

The animating purpose of the full faith and credit command, as this Court explained in *Milwaukee County v. M.E. White Co.*, 296 U.S. 268 (1935), "was to alter the status of the several states as independent foreign sovereignties, each free to ignore obligations created under the laws or by the judicial proceedings of the others, and to make them integral parts of a single nation throughout which a remedy upon a just obligation might be demanded as of right, irrespective of the state of its origin." Id., at 277. See also *Estin v. Estin*, 334 U.S. 541, 546 (1948) (the Full Faith and Credit Clause "substituted a command for the earlier principles of comity and thus basically altered the status of the States as independent sovereigns").

Our precedent differentiates the credit owed to laws (legislative measures and common law) and to judgments. "In numerous cases this Court has held that credit must be given to the judgment of another state although the forum would not be required to entertain the suit on which the judgment was founded." *Milwaukee County*, 296 U.S., at 277. The Full Faith and Credit Clause does not compel "a state to substitute the statutes of other states for its own statutes dealing with a subject matter concerning which it is competent to legislate." *Pacific Employers Ins. Co. v. Industrial Accident Comm'n*, 306 U.S. 493, 501 (1939); see *Phillips Petroleum Co. v. Shutts*, 472 U.S. 797, 818–819 (1985). Regarding judgments, however, the full faith and credit obligation is exacting. A final judgment in one State, if rendered by a court with adjudicatory authority over the subject matter and persons governed by the judgment, qualifies for recognition throughout the land. For claim and issue preclusion (res judicata) purposes, in other words, the judgment of the rendering State gains nationwide force. See, e.g., *Matsushita Elec. Industrial Co. v. Epstein*, 516 U.S. 367, 373 (1996); *Kremer v. Chemical Constr. Corp.*, 456 U.S. 461, 485 (1982) * * *.

A court may be guided by the forum State's "public policy" in determining the law applicable to a controversy. See *Nevada v. Hall*, 440 U.S. 410, 421–424 (1979). But our decisions support no roving "public policy exception" to the full faith and credit due judgments. See *Estin*, 334 U.S., at 546 (Full Faith and Credit Clause "ordered submission . . . even to hostile policies reflected in the judgment of another State, because the practical operation of the federal system, which the Constitution designed, demanded it."); *Fauntleroy v. Lum*, 210 U.S. 230, 237 (1908) (judgment of Missouri court entitled to full faith and credit in Mississippi even if Missouri judgment rested on a misapprehension of Mississippi law). In assuming the existence of a ubiquitous "public policy exception" permitting one State to resist recognition of another State's judgment, the District Court in the Bakers' wrongful-death action misread our precedent. "The full faith and credit clause is one of the provisions incorporated into the Constitution by its framers for the purpose of transforming an aggregation of independent, sovereign States into a nation." *Sherrer v. Sherrer*, 334 U.S. 343, 355 (1948). We are "aware of [no] considerations of local policy or law which could rightly be deemed to impair the force and effect which the full faith and credit clause and the Act of Congress require to be given to [a money] judgment outside the state of its rendition." *Magnolia Petroleum Co. v. Hunt*, 320 U.S. 430, 438 (1943).

The Court has never placed equity decrees outside the full faith and credit domain. Equity decrees for the payment of money have long been considered equivalent to judgments at law entitled to nationwide recognition. See, e.g., *Barber v. Barber*, 323 U.S. 77 (1944) (unconditional adjudication of petitioner's right to recover a sum of money is entitled to full faith and credit); see also A. Ehrenzweig, Conflict of Laws § 51, p. 182 (rev. ed.1962) (describing as "indefensible" the old doctrine that an equity decree, because it does not "merge" the claim into the judgment, does not qualify for recognition). We see no reason why the preclusive effects of an adjudication on parties and those "in privity" with them, i.e., claim preclusion and issue preclusion (res judicata and collateral estoppel),[7] should differ depending solely upon the type of relief sought in a civil action. Cf. *Barber*, 323 U.S., at 87 (Jackson, J., concurring) (Full Faith and Credit Clause and its implementing statute speak not of "judgments" but of " 'judicial proceedings' without limitation"); Fed. Rule Civ. Proc. 2 (providing for "one form of action to be known as 'civil action,' " in lieu of discretely labeled actions at law and suits in equity).

Full faith and credit, however, does not mean that States must adopt the practices of other States regarding the time, manner, and mechanisms for enforcing judgments. Enforcement measures do not travel with the sister state judgment as preclusive effects do; such measures remain subject to the even-handed control of forum law. See *McElmoyle ex rel. Bailey v. Cohen*, 13 Pet. 312, 325 (1839) (judgment may be enforced only as "laws [of enforcing forum] may permit"); see also Restatement (Second) of Conflict of Laws § 99 (1969) ("The local law of the forum determines the methods by which a judgment of another state is enforced.").

---

[7] See * * * 18 Charles A. Wright, Arthur R. Miller, & Edward H. Cooper, Federal Practice and Procedure § 4467, p. 635 (1981) (Although "[a] second state need not directly enforce an injunction entered by another state . . . [it] may often be required to honor the issue preclusion effects of the first judgment.").

Orders commanding action or inaction have been denied enforcement in a sister State when they purported to accomplish an official act within the exclusive province of that other State or interfered with litigation over which the ordering State had no authority. Thus, a sister State's decree concerning land ownership in another State has been held ineffective to transfer title, see *Fall v. Eastin*, 215 U.S. 1 (1909), although such a decree may indeed preclusively adjudicate the rights and obligations running between the parties to the foreign litigation, see, e.g., *Robertson v. Howard*, 229 U.S. 254, 261 (1913) ("[I]t may not be doubted that a court of equity in one State in a proper case could compel a defendant before it to convey property situated in another State."). And antisuit injunctions regarding litigation elsewhere, even if compatible with due process as a direction constraining parties to the decree, see *Cole v. Cunningham*, 133 U.S. 107 (1890), in fact have not controlled the second court's actions regarding litigation in that court. See, e.g., *James v. Grand Trunk Western R. Co.*, 14 Ill.2d 356, 372, 152 N.E.2d 858, 867 (1958); see also E. Scoles & P. Hay, Conflict of Laws § 24.21, p. 981 (2d ed.1992) (observing that antisuit injunction "does not address, and thus has no preclusive effect on, the merits of the litigation [in the second forum]").[9] Sanctions for violations of an injunction, in any event, are generally administered by the court that issued the injunction. * * *

B

With these background principles in view, we turn to the dimensions of the order GM relies upon to stop Elwell's testimony. Specifically, we take up the question: What matters did the Michigan injunction legitimately conclude?

As earlier recounted, the parties before the Michigan County Court, Elwell and GM, submitted an agreed-upon injunction, which the presiding judge signed. While no issue was joined, expressly litigated, and determined in the Michigan proceeding,[11] that order is claim preclusive

[9] This Court has held it impermissible for a state court to enjoin a party from proceeding in a federal court, see *Donovan v. Dallas*, 377 U.S. 408 (1964), but has not yet ruled on the credit due to a state court injunction barring a party from maintaining litigation in another State, see Ginsburg, Judgments in Search of Full Faith and Credit: The Last-in-Time Rule for Conflicting Judgments, 82 Harv. L.Rev. 798, 823 (1969); see also Reese, Full Faith and Credit to Foreign Equity Decrees, 42 Iowa L.Rev. 183, 198 (1957) (urging that, although this Court "has not yet had occasion to determine [the issue],. . . . full faith and credit does not require dismissal of an action whose prosecution has been enjoined," for to hold otherwise "would mean in effect that the courts of one state can control what goes on in the courts of another"). State courts that have dealt with the question have, in the main, regarded antisuit injunctions as outside the full faith and credit ambit. See id., at 823, and n. 99; see also id., at 828–829 ("The current state of the law, permitting [an antisuit] injunction to issue but not compelling any deference outside the rendering state, may be the most reasonable compromise between . . . extreme alternatives," i.e., "[a] general rule of respect for antisuit injunctions running between state courts," or "a general rule denying the states authority to issue injunctions directed at proceedings in other states").

[11] In no event, we have observed, can issue preclusion be invoked against one who did not participate in the prior adjudication. * * * Thus, JUSTICE KENNEDY emphasizes the obvious in noting that the Michigan judgment has no preclusive effect on the Bakers, for they were not parties

between Elwell and GM. Elwell's claim for wrongful discharge and his related contract and tort claims have "merged in the judgment," and he cannot sue again to recover more. * * * Similarly, GM cannot sue Elwell elsewhere on the counterclaim GM asserted in Michigan. * * *

Michigan's judgment, however, cannot reach beyond the Elwell-GM controversy to control proceedings against GM brought in other States, by other parties, asserting claims the merits of which Michigan has not considered. Michigan has no power over those parties, and no basis for commanding them to become intervenors in the Elwell-GM dispute. See *Martin v. Wilks,* 490 U.S. 755, 761–763 (1989). Most essentially, Michigan lacks authority to control courts elsewhere by precluding them, in actions brought by strangers to the Michigan litigation, from determining for themselves what witnesses are competent to testify and what evidence is relevant and admissible in their search for the truth. See Restatement (Second) of Conflict of Laws, §§ 137–139 (1969 and rev. 1988) (forum's own law governs witness competence and grounds for excluding evidence) * * *.

As the District Court recognized, Michigan's decree could operate against Elwell to preclude him from volunteering his testimony. * * * But a Michigan court cannot, by entering the injunction to which Elwell and GM stipulated, dictate to a court in another jurisdiction that evidence relevant in the Bakers' case—a controversy to which Michigan is foreign—shall be inadmissible. This conclusion creates no general exception to the full faith and credit command, and surely does not permit a State to refuse to honor a sister state judgment based on the forum's choice of law or policy preferences. Rather, we simply recognize that, just as the mechanisms for enforcing a judgment do not travel with the judgment itself for purposes of Full Faith and Credit, see *McElmoyle ex rel. Bailey v. Cohen,* 13 Pet. 312 (1839); see also Restatement (Second) of Conflict of Laws § 99, and just as one State's judgment cannot automatically transfer title to land in another State, see *Fall v. Eastin,* 215 U.S. 1 (1909), similarly the Michigan decree cannot determine evidentiary issues in a lawsuit brought by parties who were not subject to the jurisdiction of the Michigan court. Cf. *United States v. Nixon,* 418 U.S. 683, 710 (1974) ("[E]xceptions to the demand for every man's evidence are not lightly created nor expansively construed, for they are in derogation of the search for truth.").[12] . . .

---

to the Michigan litigation. * * * Such an observation misses the thrust of GM's argument. GM readily acknowledges "the commonplace rule that a person may not be bound by a judgment in personam in a case to which he was not made a party." * * * But, GM adds, the Michigan decree does not bind the Bakers; it binds Elwell only. Most forcibly, GM insists that the Bakers cannot object to the binding effect GM seeks for the Michigan judgment because the Bakers have no constitutionally protected interest in obtaining the testimony of a particular witness. * * * Given this argument, it is clear that issue preclusion principles, standing alone, cannot resolve the controversy GM presents.

[12] JUSTICE KENNEDY inexplicably reads into our decision a sweeping exception to full faith and credit based solely on "the integrity of Missouri's judicial processes." * * * The Michigan judgment is not entitled to full faith and credit, we have endeavored to make plain, because it

In line with its recognition of the interference potential of the consent decree, GM provided in the settlement agreement that, if another court ordered Elwell to testify, his testimony would "in no way" render him vulnerable to suit in Michigan for violation of the injunction or agreement. * * * The Eighth Circuit regarded this settlement agreement provision as merely a concession by GM that "some courts might fail to extend full faith and credit to the [Michigan] injunction." * * * As we have explained, however, Michigan's power does not reach into a Missouri courtroom to displace the forum's own determination whether to admit or exclude evidence relevant in the Bakers' wrongful-death case before it. In that light, we see no altruism in GM's agreement not to institute contempt or breach-of-contract proceedings against Elwell in Michigan for giving subpoenaed testimony elsewhere. Rather, we find it telling that GM ruled out resort to the court that entered the injunction, for injunctions are ordinarily enforced by the enjoining court, not by a surrogate tribunal.

In sum, Michigan has no authority to shield a witness from another jurisdiction's subpoena power in a case involving persons and causes outside Michigan's governance. Recognition, under full faith and credit, is owed to dispositions Michigan has authority to order. But a Michigan decree cannot command obedience elsewhere on a matter the Michigan court lacks authority to resolve. * * *

JUSTICE SCALIA, concurring in the judgment.

I agree with the Court that enforcement measures do not travel with sister-state judgments as preclusive effects do. It has long been established that "the judgment of a state Court cannot be enforced out of the state by an execution issued within it." *McElmoyle ex rel. Bailey v. Cohen*, 13 Pet. 312, 325 (1839). To recite that principle is to decide this case.

General Motors asked a District Court in Missouri to *enforce* a Michigan injunction. The Missouri court was no more obliged to enforce the Michigan injunction by preventing Elwell from presenting his testimony than it was obliged to enforce it by holding Elwell in contempt. The Full Faith and Credit Clause " 'did not make the judgments of other States domestic judgments to all intents and purposes, but only gave a general validity, faith, and credit to them, *as evidence*. No execution can issue upon such judgments without a new suit in the tribunals of other States.' " *Thompson v. Whitman*, 18 Wall. 457, 462–463 (1873) (emphasis added) (quoting J. Story, Conflict of Laws § 609). A judgment or decree of one State, to be sure, may be grounds for an action (or a defense to one) in another. But the Clause and its implementing statute "establish a rule of

impermissibly interferes with Missouri's control of litigation brought by parties who were not before the Michigan court. Thus, JUSTICE KENNEDY's hypothetical misses the mark. If the Bakers had been parties to the Michigan proceedings and had actually litigated the privileged character of Elwell's testimony, the Bakers would of course be precluded from relitigating that issue in Missouri. * * *

evidence, rather than of jurisdiction. While they make the record of a judgment, rendered after due notice in one State, conclusive evidence in the courts of another State, or of the United States, of the matter adjudged, they do not affect the jurisdiction, either of the court in which the judgment is rendered, or of the court in which it is offered in evidence. Judgments recovered in one State of the Union, when proved in the courts of another government, whether state or national, within the United States, differ from judgments recovered in a foreign country in no other respect than in not being reexaminable on their merits, nor impeachable for fraud in obtaining them, if rendered by a court having jurisdiction of the cause and of the parties." *Wisconsin v. Pelican Ins. Co.*, 127 U.S. 265, 291–292 (1888).

The judgment that General Motors obtained in Michigan " 'does not carry with it, into another State, the efficacy of a judgment upon property or persons, to be enforced by execution. To give it the force of a judgment in another State, it must be made a judgment there; and can only be executed in the latter as its laws may permit.' " *Lynde v. Lynde*, 181 U.S. 183 (1901) (quoting *McElmoyle*, supra, 13 Pet. at 325). * * *

Because neither the Full Faith and Credit Clause nor its implementing statute requires Missouri to execute the injunction issued by the courts of Michigan, I concur in the judgment.

JUSTICE KENNEDY, with whom JUSTICES O'CONNOR and THOMAS join, concurring in the judgment.

I concur in the judgment. In my view the case is controlled by well-settled full faith and credit principles which render the majority's extended analysis unnecessary and, with all due respect, problematic in some degree. . .

I

The majority, of course, is correct to hold that when a judgment is presented to the courts of a second State it may not be denied enforcement based upon some disagreement with the laws of the State of rendition. . . We have often recognized the second State's obligation to give effect to another State's judgments even when the law underlying those judgments contravenes the public policy of the second State. * * *

My concern is that the majority, having stated the principle, proceeds to disregard it by announcing two broad exceptions. First, the majority would allow courts outside the issuing State to decline to enforce those judgments "purport[ing] to accomplish an official act within the exclusive province of [a sister] State." * * * Second, the basic rule of full faith and credit is said not to cover injunctions "interfer[ing] with litigation over which the ordering State had no authority." * * * The exceptions the majority recognizes are neither consistent with its rejection of a public policy exception to full faith and credit nor in accord with established rules implementing the Full Faith and Credit Clause. As employed to resolve this case, furthermore, the exceptions to full faith and credit have a potential for disrupting judgments, and this ought to give us considerable pause.

Our decisions have been careful not to foreclose all effect for the types of injunctions the majority would place outside the ambit of full faith and credit. These authorities seem to be disregarded by today's holding. For example, the majority chooses to discuss the extent to which courts may compel the conveyance of property in other jurisdictions. That subject has proven to be quite difficult. Some of our cases uphold actions by state courts affecting land outside their territorial reach. * * * Nor have we undertaken before today to announce an exception which denies full faith and credit based on the principle that the prior judgment interferes with litigation pending in another jurisdiction. * * * As a general matter, there is disagreement among the state courts as to their duty to recognize decrees enjoining proceedings in other courts. * * *

Subjects which are at once so fundamental and so delicate as these ought to be addressed only in a case necessarily requiring their discussion, and even then with caution lest we announce rules which will not be sound in later application. . . Even if some qualification of full faith and credit were required where the judicial processes of a second State are sought to be controlled in their procedural and institutional aspects, the Court's discussion does not provide sufficient guidance on how this exception should be construed in light of our precedents. The majority's broad review of these matters does not articulate the rationale underlying its conclusions. In the absence of more elaboration, it is unclear what it is about the particular injunction here that renders it undeserving of full faith and credit. The Court's reliance upon unidentified principles to justify omitting certain types of injunctions from the doctrine's application leaves its decision in uneasy tension with its own rejection of a broad public policy exception to full faith and credit.

The following example illustrates the uncertainty surrounding the majority's approach. Suppose the Bakers had anticipated the need for Elwell's testimony in Missouri and had appeared in a Michigan court to litigate the privileged character of the testimony it sought to elicit. Assume further the law on privilege were the same in both jurisdictions. If Elwell, GM, and the Bakers were before the Michigan court and Michigan law gave its own injunction preclusive effect, the Bakers could not relitigate the point, if general principles of issue preclusion control. Perhaps the argument can be made, as the majority appears to say, that the integrity of Missouri's judicial processes demands a rule allowing relitigation of the issue; but, for the reasons given below, we need not confront this interesting question. . .

II

In the case before us, of course, the Bakers were neither parties to the earlier litigation nor subject to the jurisdiction of the Michigan courts. The majority pays scant attention to this circumstance, which becomes critical. The beginning point of full faith and credit analysis requires a determination of the effect the judgment has in the courts of the issuing State. In our most recent full faith and credit cases, we have said that determining the force and effect of a judgment should be the first step in our analysis. * * * A conclusion that the issuing State would not give the prior judgment preclusive effect ends the inquiry, making it unnecessary to determine the existence of any exceptions to full faith and credit. * * * We cannot decline to inquire into these state-law questions when the inquiry will obviate new extensions or exceptions to full faith and credit. * * *

If we honor the undoubted principle that courts need give a prior judgment no more force or effect that the issuing State gives it, the case before us is resolved. Here the Court of Appeals and both parties in their arguments before our Court seemed to embrace the assumption that Michigan would apply the full force of its judgment to the Bakers. Michigan law does not appear to support the assumption.

The simple fact is that the Bakers were not parties to the Michigan proceedings, and nothing indicates Michigan would make the novel assertion that its earlier injunction binds the Bakers or any other party not then before it or subject to its jurisdiction. . .

The opinion of the Court of Appeals suggests the Michigan court which issued the injunction intended to bind third parties in litigation in other States. * * * The question, however, is not what a trial court intended in a particular case but the preclusive effect its judgment has under the controlling legal principles of its own State. . . The fact that other Michigan trial courts refused to reconsider the injunction but instead required litigants to return to the trial court which issued it in the first place sheds little light on the substance of issue preclusion law in Michigan. In construing state law, we must determine how the highest court of the State would decide an issue. * * *

In this case, moreover, those Michigan trial courts which declined to modify the injunction did not appear to base their rulings on preclusion law. They relied instead on Michigan Court Rule 2.613(B), which directs parties wishing to modify an injunction to present their arguments to the court which entered it. * * * Rule 2.613(B) is a procedural rule based on comity concerns, not a preclusion rule. It reflects Michigan's determination that, within the State of Michigan itself, respect for the issuing court and judicial resources are best preserved by allowing the issuing court to determine whether the injunction should apply to further proceedings. As a procedural rule, it is not binding on courts of another State by virtue of full faith and credit. * * *

Under Michigan law, the burden of persuasion rests on the party raising preclusion as a defense. * * * In light of these doctrines and the absence of contrary authority, one cannot conclude that GM has carried its burden of showing that Michigan courts would bind the Bakers to the terms of the earlier injunction prohibiting Elwell from testifying. . .

Although inconsistent on this point, GM disavows its desire to issue preclude the Bakers, claiming "the only party being 'bound' to the injunction is Elwell." * * * This is difficult to accept because in assessing the preclusive reach of a judgment we look to its practical effect. * * * Despite its disclaimer, GM seeks to alter the course of the suit between it and the Bakers by preventing the Bakers from litigating the admissibility of Elwell's testimony. . .

In all events, determining as a threshold matter the extent to which Michigan law gives preclusive effect to the injunction eliminates the need to decide whether full faith and credit applies to equitable decrees as a general matter or the extent to which the general rules of full faith and credit are subject to exceptions. Michigan law would not seek to bind the Bakers to the injunction and that suffices to resolve the case. For these reasons, I concur in the judgment.

Equitable Decrees and the Obligation to Enforce Sister-State Judgments

(1) The Court rejects petitioners' suggestion that injunctions and other equity decrees are excluded from the constitutional requirement to give full faith and credit. That it took until 1998 to settle this question once and for all may seem surprising. 28 U.S.C. § 1738 refers to "judicial proceedings" without limitation, implying that decrees of all types are included. Are the purposes of the Full Faith and Credit Clause less applicable or pressing when relief is equitable than when it consists of an award of damages? Criticizing the proposition that equity is different, Professor Ehrenzweig long ago observed:

> The early conception of equity courts as acting only upon the person and his conscience, has yielded gradually to equity's expanding power over rights in rem and to the formal abolition of many distinctions between law and equity. The conflicts rule that an equity decree is a mere procedural device not "merging" the claim, and thus not entitled to recognition, is a relic of the old doctrine and now generally considered as indefensible.

> Remaining conflicts problems are closely associated with such differences as may exist between the enforcement procedures of the rendering state and the forum—every state being entitled to its own. The analysis of the case law must distinguish, therefore, among the various types of decrees.

A. Ehrenzweig, A Treatise on the Conflict of Laws 182–83 (1962); see also Price, *Full Faith and Credit and the Equity Conflict,* 84 Va. L. Rev. 747, 793–829 (1998).

Declaratory judgments, which are now authorized in virtually all states as well as in the federal courts, 28 U.S.C. §§ 2201–02, also fall within the parameters of the Full Faith and Credit Clause. In general, declaratory judgments are conclusive as to the matters declared, but in most states they do not stand in the way of further relief (e.g., a plaintiff who wins a declaratory judgment may then seek damages on the same claim). See Restatement (Second) of Judgments § 33 (1982); Shapiro, *State Courts and Federal Declaratory Judgments,* 74 Nw. U. L. Rev. 759 (1979).

The Court in *Baker* paid no attention to the fact that the underlying injunction was based on a settlement between Elwell and General Motors, rather than the result of a fully litigated judgment on the merits. Should this matter to the full faith and credit inquiry? See Price, *Full Faith and Credit and the Equity Conflict,* 84 Va. L. Rev. at 768–73 (yes, because consent decrees are more like contracts for this purpose).

(2) Ehrenzweig intimates that uncertainty about the applicability of full faith and credit to equity decrees may possibly have been caused by confusion arising from the distinction between questions of recognition and questions of enforcement. Speaking of this latter distinction, the Second Restatement of Conflict of Laws explains:

> A foreign judgment may be entitled to two forms of respect, namely, recognition and enforcement... [A] judgment is recognized to the extent that it is given the same effect with respect to the parties, the subject matter of the action and the issues involved that it has in the state where it was rendered. Some judgments ... entitle the plaintiff to affirmative relief. When this relief is granted, the judgment is said to be enforced.

Restatement (Second) of Conflict of Laws, introductory note at 302. Enforcement questions, as the Court in *Baker* notes, "do not travel with the sister state judgment as preclusive effects do" but instead "remain subject to the even-handed control of forum law." See also id. at § 99; *Lynde v. Lynde*, 181 U.S. 183, 187 (1901). This is because the judgment of one state is not immediately enforceable in another state but must instead be made the basis for a lawsuit in the second state. The Full Faith and Credit Clause then requires the second state to recognize the judgment according to the preclusion law of the state that rendered it, with the result that the second state issues its own judgment to the same effect as the first one. See R. Leflar, L. McDougal & R. Felix, American Conflicts Law § 78 (4th ed. 1986). The details of enforcing this new judgment are treated as a matter of procedure, governed by forum law. Because injunctions, by definition, call for some form of affirmative action from the court (in the form of an order to do or not do something), the rule respecting the applicability of forum law to enforcement measures may have mistakenly been thought applicable to equity decrees generally.

(3) What limits, if any, exist on a state's power to apply its own "procedural" rules in enforcing another state's judgment? Is this problem different from the substance/procedure problem in choice of law? See supra pp. 54–65, 390–392. Consider the following examples:

(a) In *McElmoyle v. Cohen*, 38 U.S. (13 Pet.) 312, 326–27 (1839), the Supreme Court held that a state could apply its own statute of limitations on judgments to bar a suit upon a sister-state judgment that would not have been barred in the rendering state. The Constitution, said the Court, makes a foreign judgment "conclusive" as to "the merits" of the claim, but it does not forbid "a plea not denying the judgment, but which resists it upon the ground of a release, payment, or a presumption of payment from the lapse of time, whether such a presumption be raised by the common-law prescription, or by a statute of limitation." Because a plea of limitation is "a plea to the remedy," the Court continued, "the lex fori must prevail." Do you agree?

McElmoyle was reaffirmed in *Watkins v. Conway*, 385 U.S. 188 (1966), which allowed Georgia to apply its statute of limitations requiring suits on foreign judgments to be brought within five years. A further question was involved in *Watkins*: Georgia would have applied a longer limitation period to a domestic judgment, and it was argued that this discriminatory treatment of foreign judgments violated both the Full Faith and Credit and the Equal Protection Clauses. Language in *McElmoyle* seeming to permit such discrimination was dismissed as "dictum" by the *Watkins* Court, which added, "[i]f appellant's analysis of the purpose and effect of the [Georgia] statute were correct, we might well agree that it violates the Federal Constitution." Id. at 189. There was no need to decide the question, however, because examining the overall Georgia scheme revealed that there was no actual discrimination. Id. at 189–91. Suppose this were not true: is there any argument for allowing a state to discriminate in the time allowed to sue on a foreign versus a domestic judgment?

Compare *Union Nat'l Bank v. Lamb*, 337 U.S. 38 (1949), in which petitioner was awarded a judgment by a Colorado court in 1927, which it then revived in Colorado in 1945. The Missouri Supreme Court refused to recognize the revived judgment on the ground that it could no longer be revived under Missouri law. The U.S. Supreme Court reversed, finding "no room for an exception" to the Full Faith and Credit Clause where "the clash of policies relates to revived judgments rather than to the nature of the underlying claim as in *Fauntleroy v. Lum.*" The Court rejected respondent's argument that the revivor served merely to extend the statute of limitations on an action to enforce the judgment, a matter properly governed by forum law under *McElmoyle.* According to Justice Douglas, "[c]ases of limitations against a cause of action on a judgment, *McElmoyle v. Cohen,* 13 Pet. 312, involve different considerations" because they "do not undermine the integrity of the judgment on which suit is brought." Because the Colorado and Missouri courts in *Lamb* were both clear that the revived judgment was a new Colorado judgment, the Missouri court was required by full faith and credit to treat it as such.

Is there more than a verbal distinction between a Colorado judgment revived after ten years and one on which Colorado permits suit to be brought for more than ten years?

(b) May a state refuse to recognize a sister-state judgment by withdrawing jurisdiction in whole or in part from its courts? In *Anglo-American Provision Co. v. Davis Provision Co.,* 191 U.S. 373 (1903), New York refused to entertain a suit on a foreign corporation's judgment against another foreign corporation based on a foreign cause of action. The Supreme Court approved in an opinion written by Justice Holmes:

> [The Full Faith and Credit Clause] establishes a rule of evidence rather than of jurisdiction. . . If the plaintiff can find a court into which it has a right to come, then the effect of the judgment is fixed by the Constitution and the act in pursuance of it which Congress has passed. * * * But the Constitution does not require the state to provide such a court. . .

191 U.S., at 374. Seventeen years later, in *Kenney v. Supreme Lodge,* 252 U.S. 411 (1920), an Illinois court refused to entertain a suit based on an Alabama wrongful-death judgment because of a state law forbidding actions for deaths occurring outside the state. The Supreme Court reversed, in another opinion by Justice Holmes. The *Anglo-American* case, he said, "is sufficiently explained without more by the views about foreign corporations that had prevailed unquestioned since *Bank of Augusta v. Earle,* 13 Pet. 519, 589–91 [stating that a corporation did not 'exist' outside its state of incorporation]." 252 U.S., at 414. "Moreover," the Court continued:

> no doubt there is truth in the proposition that the Constitution does not require the State to furnish a Court. But it is also true that there are limits to the power of exclusion and . . . the fact that here the original cause of action could not have been maintained in Illinois is not an answer to a suit upon the judgment. . . [T]his being true, it is plain that a State cannot escape its constitutional

> obligation by the simple device of denying jurisdiction in such cases to courts otherwise competent.

Id. at 414–15. Does *Kenney* overrule *Anglo-American* or are the cases distinguishable? Does the eclipse of *Bank of Augusta v. Earle* mean that New York would be required to entertain an action like that in *Anglo-American* today? Or is there room after *Kenney* for forum non conveniens as applied to suits on foreign judgments? Can you state the rule or principle governing when a state can deny jurisdiction over a suit based on a foreign judgment? Cf. *Hughes v. Fetter*, 341 U.S. 609 (1951), supra p. 414; and *Testa v. Katt*, 330 U.S. 386 (1947), infra p. 919.

Problems that formerly arose due to discrepancies in the details of enforcement law in different states are eased today by the adoption in 47 states and the District of Columbia of the Revised Uniform Enforcement of Foreign Judgments Act, 13 U.L.A. 149 (1964); see id. at 13 (Supp. 1997) (table listing adoptions).

(4) Why does Justice Ginsburg mention the distinction between recognition and enforcement in her opinion for the Court in *Baker*? Does it follow that, just because the forum can apply its own law as to the mode and form of enforcement, it can refuse to enforce the judgment of a sister state altogether? In *Sistare v. Sistare*, 218 U.S. 1 (1910), the Court said:

> [A]s pointed out in *Lynde v. Lynde*, although mere modes of execution provided by the laws of a State in which a judgment is rendered are not, by operation of the full faith and credit clause, obligatory upon courts of another State in which the judgment is sought to be enforced, nevertheless if the judgment be an enforceable judgment in the State where rendered the duty to give effect to it in another State clearly results from the full faith and credit clause, although the modes of procedure to enforce the collection may not be the same in both States.

Id. at 26. That being so, was not the Missouri court in *Baker* obliged to enforce the Michigan injunction, albeit by whatever procedures Missouri provides for enforcing injunctions? Or is Justice Ginsburg saying that full faith and credit extends only to questions of recognition (i.e., preclusion) and that there is no obligation to enforce at all?

What justification, if any, could there be for holding full faith and credit inapplicable to matters of enforcement? Noting that, as of the time it was written, the Supreme Court had not yet addressed this question, the Second Restatement observed:

> It may well be that the Supreme Court, when presented with the question, will hold that enforcement of [decrees ordering affirmative relief] is required by full faith and credit. In support of such a position, reliance may be placed upon the language of

> the full faith and credit clause . . . and its implementing statute [which appear to require that decrees of all types] be given the same measure of respect as judgments for the payment of money. In further support of such a position, reliance can also be placed on the fact that a majority of State courts have enforced sister State judgments ordering the conveyance of land.

Restatement (Second) of Conflict of Laws, § 102, comment *c* at 307–08. On the other hand, and "[i]n opposition to these arguments," the Second Restatement offered an assertion from its 1934 predecessor to the effect that, because issuing an injunction is a matter of discretion, a decision by one court will not "exclude the use of discretion by the second court." Id. But is this anything more than the rule that a second court has as much discretion to alter or modify a judgment as the court that rendered it? See supra pp. 612–614. Why should the fact of discretion be grounds to ignore altogether a judgment that would be enforced by the court that issued it?

(5) Justice Kennedy reads Justice Ginsburg's opinion more narrowly to recognize a general rule requiring enforcement subject to "two broad exceptions"—one for orders that "purport[ ] to accomplish an official act within the exclusive province of [a sister] State," the other for orders that "interfere[ ] with litigation over which the ordering State had no authority." Is this a fair reading? Does either exception help to decide whether GM should be able to enforce its injunction against Elwell?

Examining the authorities cited by the Court, it turns out that the "exception" for judgments purporting to accomplish an "official act" within another state's exclusive province is nothing more than the familiar "land taboo." See supra pp. 604–609. Why do you think Justice Ginsburg dressed it up in this more general language? Are there other sorts of "official acts" that might be denied recognition? What might these be? Cf. *Williams v. North Carolina II*, 325 U.S. 226 (1945) (allowing North Carolina to ignore a Nevada divorce decree), infra p. 677.

The only example Justice Ginsburg offers of her second "exception" (orders improperly interfering with litigation) is the antisuit injunction. Is this a fair example? According to Justice Ginsburg, antisuit injunctions "in fact have not controlled the second court's actions regarding litigation in that court," a statement she supports by citing a state court and a treatise. She adds in footnote 9 that "[s]tate courts that have dealt with the question have, in the main, regarded antisuit injunctions as outside the full faith and credit ambit." Unlike her first example, Justice Ginsburg cites no Supreme Court authority, for the simple reason that the Supreme Court had never spoken to the issue. Has it done so now?

Should antisuit injunctions be excluded from the requirements of the Full Faith and Credit Clause? Why is a final judgment enjoining litigation different from any other final judgment? If the injunction is improper, the solution is to appeal; if a second state can ignore another state's injunction, will this not put parties in an impossible position, in which courts from different states may have directly conflicting decrees? Cf. *GTE Sylvania, Inc. v. Consumers Union*, 445 U.S. 375, 386 (1980). As then-Professor Ginsburg observed:

> A general rule of respect for antisuit injunctions running between state courts would take the problem out of the limbo between the due process clause and the full faith and credit clause in which it now flounders. State courts on the receiving end of such injunctions have not found this a palatable solution, but it would be consistent with the generally strict line the Supreme Court has taken on full faith and credit to judgments.

Ginsburg, *Judgments in Search of Full Faith and Credit: The Last-in-Time Rule for Conflicting Judgments*, 82 Harv. L. Rev. 798, 828 (1969). Did Justice Ginsburg change her mind, or does the Court's language leave the question of antisuit injunctions unresolved? If so, what examples are there of this second "exception"?

(6) If neither exception controls GM's case, then what is the basis for the Court's decision? At one point in her opinion, Justice Ginsburg says that Michigan's judgment "cannot reach beyond the Elwell-GM controversy to control proceedings against GM brought in other States, by other parties, asserting claims the merits of which Michigan has not considered." Why not? Petitioners argued that it would violate due process to permit the Elwell-GM decree to bind the Bakers, who were not parties to the Michigan action. But the Court rejects that argument in footnote 11, acknowledging GM's counter that the Bakers were not being formally bound. What is the problem, then? Consider the following possibilities:

(a) The Court says that "Michigan has no power over [the Bakers], and no basis for commanding them to become intervenors in the Elwell-GM dispute," citing *Martin v. Wilks*, 490 U.S. 755 (1989). In *Martin*, two consent decrees were entered between the City of Birmingham and African-American plaintiffs alleging race discrimination in the hiring and promoting of firefighters. A group of white firefighters filed a separate suit, complaining that the affirmative action called for in these decrees violated their rights under federal law. The trial court ruled that this claim was an improper collateral attack on the consent decrees, and the Supreme Court reversed, holding that the white firefighters could not be barred by a decree entered in an action to which they had not been parties and that nothing in Fed. R. Civ. Proc. 24 required them to intervene. What does the fact that Rule 24 does not require mandatory intervention have to do with the dispute in *Baker*?

(b) Is the Court articulating a general rule against permitting the judgment in one case to affect parties in another? If the basis for such a rule were the Due Process Clause, even a Michigan court could not enforce the Elwell-GM decree if that would affect some new claimant against GM. But the Court never mentions due process, and judgments routinely affect third parties in ways that limit legal interests they would otherwise possess. Is the Court saying instead that the Full Faith and Credit Clause does not require one state to enforce another state's judgments if that would affect third parties in its courts? Why not?

In *Morris v. Jones*, 329 U.S. 545 (1947), Morris sued Chicago Lloyds in Missouri for malicious prosecution and false arrest. While his action was pending, Chicago Lloyds filed for bankruptcy in Illinois. Jones's predecessor was appointed "statutory liquidator," and the Illinois court issued an order staying all suits against the company. Morris had notice of this order but continued to prosecute his claim in Missouri anyway. Counsel for Chicago Lloyds withdrew, explaining that the company's assets were now in the hands of the liquidator, who was not made a party. The Missouri court subsequently issued a default judgment in favor of Morris, which he made the basis for his claim in the Illinois bankruptcy proceedings. The Supreme Court held that the Illinois bankruptcy court must recognize Morris's judgment. Because the Missouri court's determination of the validity and amount of Morris's claim was "final and conclusive," it could not "be challenged or retried in the Illinois proceedings." 329 U.S., at 551–52. Justice Frankfurter protested in dissent that this was unfair to the other creditors, none of whom were parties in the Missouri action and all of whom were being deprived of their right to question Morris's claim to a portion of the assets. How are the Bakers in a position different from the other creditors in *Morris*?

Might the size of any effect be relevant? The Court in *Morris* observed in dictum that "[i]f this were a situation where Missouri's policy would result in dismemberment of the Illinois estate so that Illinois creditors would go begging, Illinois would have such a large interest at stake as to prevent it." 329 U.S., at 554. Does such an exception make sense? Would it apply to the Bakers' case?

(c) Or is there some special concern when the effect is on a third party's procedural rights in litigation? Why should this be treated differently? The Court cites *United States v. Nixon*, 418 U.S. 683, 710 (1974), to the effect that "exceptions to the demand for every man's evidence are not lightly created." Yet the ability of parties to adduce even non-privileged testimony is restricted for a multitude of extrinsic policy considerations. See, e.g., Fed. R. Evid. 403 (cumulative evidence excluded to save time); Fed. R. Evid. 407 (evidence of subsequent remedial measures excluded to encourage improvements); Fed. R. Evid. 408 (evidence of settlement discussions excluded to encourage settlement). If the Bakers' right to use evidence can be limited for reasons such as these, why not when needed to recognize and enforce a sister state's judgment? Is the right to call the witnesses of one's choice weightier than this constitutional consideration? Does it matter that Elwell was being called as an expert rather than a factual witness?

Professor Earl Maltz reads the Court's opinion as a return to First Restatement thinking, in particular the creation of bright-line rules based on formalistic theories of state power. *Baker,* Maltz writes, is best understood as doing something similar:

> [T]he *Baker* majority relied upon what might be described as a pure power theory of the Full Faith and Credit Clause. The pure power theory readily accepts the premise that a state court has authority to issue binding judgments on substantive matters generally, as well as those affecting the personal rights and obligations of the parties. At the same time, however, the pure power theory contends that state courts lack power over both the procedures employed by other state courts and the ultimate status of land in other jurisdictions.

Maltz, *The Full Faith and Credit Clause and the First Restatement: The Place of* Baker v. General Motors Corp. *in Choice of Law Theory*, 73 Tul. L. Rev. 305, 310 (1998). Is this a good explanation of what the Court was up to in *Baker*?

(7) Justice Scalia concurs in the judgment on the ground that Missouri was not obliged to enforce a Michigan judgment that had not first been converted to a Missouri judgment. But what if it had been so converted? Suppose, for example, that as soon as it learned the Bakers were planning to subpoena Elwell, GM had filed an action against Elwell in Missouri, based on the Michigan decree, seeking a declaration that Elwell could not testify against GM without its permission. If granted, the Missouri court hearing the Bakers' case presumably would have been required to prevent Elwell from testifying. But this just pushes the question back a step, forcing us to ask whether a Missouri court would have been obliged to grant GM's request for a declaratory judgment had it made one. What do you think Justice Scalia would say?

Consider the following plausible, if wicked, scenario: GM learns that the Bakers plan to subpoena Elwell and files an action in Missouri seeking a declaratory judgment. The Missouri court consolidates GM's action with that of the Bakers. GM moves for summary judgment on its claim based on the Michigan decree, and on the very same day, the Bakers move for an order compelling Elwell to testify. Whose motion should the court grant and why?

ALLEN V. MCCURRY

449 U.S. 90 (1980).

JUSTICE STEWART delivered the opinion of the Court.

Acting on an informant's tip that McCurry was dealing in heroin, police officers Allen and Jacobsmeyer went to McCurry's home in St. Louis, Missouri. McCurry fired at them, seriously wounding both. A gun battle then ensued, culminating later in McCurry's surrender. Other officers then entered and searched the house. McCurry was convicted of possessing heroin and assault with intent to kill in a Missouri state court. At a pretrial suppression hearing, the state court excluded evidence seized from bureau drawers and from auto tires on the porch of his house, but admitted evidence seized in plain view. Thereafter, McCurry brought this suit under 42 U.S.C. § 1983 against Allen and Jacobsmeyer, claiming an unconstitutional search and seizure. The district court granted summary judgment for the defendants, finding that McCurry was precluded from relitigating the search and seizure question already decided against him in the state court. The court of appeals reversed, ruling that preclusion did not apply because federal habeas corpus was not available to review the merits of the unlawful search, since the state courts had afforded "an opportunity for a full and fair litigation of that claim."

II

The federal courts have traditionally adhered to the related doctrines of res judicata and collateral estoppel. . . As this Court and other courts have often recognized, res judicata and collateral estoppel relieve parties of the cost and vexation of multiple lawsuits, conserve judicial resources, and, by preventing inconsistent decisions, encourage reliance on adjudication. * * *

In recent years, this Court has reaffirmed the benefits of collateral estoppel in particular, finding the policies underlying it to apply in contexts not formerly recognized at common law. Thus, the Court has eliminated the requirement of mutuality in applying collateral estoppel to bar relitigation of issues decided earlier in federal court suits, *Blonder-Tongue Laboratories, Inc. v. University of Illinois Foundation,* 402 U.S. 313, and has allowed a litigant who was not a party to a federal case to use collateral estoppel "offensively" in a new federal suit against the party who lost on the decided issue in the first case, *Parklane Hosiery Co. v. Shore,* 439 U.S. 322. But one general limitation the Court has repeatedly recognized is that the concept of collateral estoppel cannot apply when the party against whom the earlier decision is asserted did not have a "full and fair opportunity" to litigate that issue in the earlier case. *Montana v. United States,* supra, 440 U.S., at 153; *Blonder-Tongue Laboratories, Inc. v. University of Illinois Foundation,* supra, 402 U.S., at 328–329.

The federal courts generally have also consistently accorded preclusive effect to issues decided by state courts. *E.g., Montana v. United States,* supra; *Angel v. Bullington,* 330 U.S. 183. Thus, res judicata and collateral estoppel not only reduce unnecessary litigation and foster reliance on adjudication, but also promote the comity between state and federal courts that has been recognized as a bulwark of the federal system. See *Younger v. Harris,* 401 U.S. 37, 43–45.

Indeed, though the federal courts may look to the common law or to the policies supporting res judicata and collateral estoppel in assessing the preclusive effect of decisions of other federal courts, Congress has specifically required all federal courts to give preclusive effect to state-court judgments whenever the courts of the State from which the judgments emerged would do so:

> "The . . . judicial proceedings of any court of any State . . . shall have the same full faith and credit in every court within the United States and its Territories and Possessions as they have by law or usage in the courts of such State. . ."

28 U.S.C. § 1738 (1976) * * *. It is against this background that we examine the relationship of § 1983 and collateral estoppel, and the decision of the Court of Appeals in this case.

III

This Court has never directly decided whether the rules of res judicata and collateral estoppel are generally applicable to § 1983 actions. But in *Preiser v. Rodriguez,* 411 U.S. 475, 497, the Court noted with implicit approval the view of other federal courts that res judicata principles fully apply to civil rights suits brought under that statute. * * * And the virtually unanimous view of the Court of Appeals since *Preiser* has been that § 1983 presents no categorical bar to the application of res judicata and collateral estoppel concepts. These federal appellate court decisions have spoken with little explanation or citation in assuming the compatibility of § 1983 and rules of preclusion, but the statute and its legislative history clearly support the courts' decisions.

Because the requirement of mutuality of estoppel was still alive in the federal courts until well into this century, * * * the drafters of the 1871 Civil Rights Act, of which § 1983 is a part, may have had less reason to concern themselves with rules of preclusion than a modern Congress would. Nevertheless, in 1871 res judicata and collateral estoppel could certainly have applied in federal suits following state-court litigation between the same parties or their privies, and nothing in the language of § 1983 remotely expresses any congressional intent to contravene the common law rules of preclusion or to repeal the express statutory requirements of the predecessor of 28 U.S.C. § 1738. Section 1983 creates a new federal cause of action.[11] It says nothing about the preclusive effect of state-court judgments.

Moreover, the legislative history of § 1983 does not in any clear way suggest that Congress intended to repeal or restrict the traditional doctrines of preclusion. The main goal of the Act was to override the corrupting influence of the Ku Klux Klan and its sympathizers on the governments and law enforcement agencies of the Southern States, see *Monroe v. Pape,* 365 U.S. 167, 174, and of course the debates show that one strong motive behind its enactment was grave congressional concern that the state courts had been deficient in protecting federal rights. *Mitchum v. Foster,* 407 U.S. 225, 241–242; *Monroe v. Pape,* supra, 365 U.S., at 180. But in the context of the legislative history as a whole, this congressional concern lends only the most equivocal support to any argument that, in cases where the state courts have recognized the constitutional claims asserted and provided fair procedures for determining them, Congress intended to override § 1738 or the common-law rules of collateral estoppel and res judicata. Since repeals by implication are disfavored, *Radzanower v. Touche Ross & Co.,* 426 U.S. 148, 154, much clearer support than this would be required to hold that § 1738 and the traditional rules of preclusion are not applicable to § 1983 suits.

As the Court has understood the history of the legislation, Congress realized that in enacting § 1983 it was altering the balance of judicial power between the state and federal courts. See *Mitchum v. Foster,* supra, 407 U.S., at 241. But in doing so, Congress was adding to the jurisdiction of the federal courts, not subtracting from that of the state courts. See *Monroe v. Pape,* supra, 365 U.S., at 183 ("The federal remedy is supplementary to the state remedy. . ."). The debates contain several references to the concurrent jurisdiction of the state courts over federal questions, and numerous suggestions that the state courts would retain their established jurisdiction so that they could, when the then current political passions abated, demonstrate a new sensitivity to federal rights.

To the extent that it did intend to change the balance of power over federal questions between the state and federal courts, the 42d Congress was acting in a way thoroughly consistent with the doctrines of preclusion. In reviewing the legislative history of § 1983 in *Monroe v. Pape,* supra, the Court inferred that Congress had intended a federal remedy in three

[11] "Every person who, under color of any statute, ordinance, regulation, custom, or usage, of any State or Territory, subjects, or causes to be subjected, any citizen of the United States or other person within the jurisdiction thereof to the deprivation of any rights, privileges, or immunities secured by the Constitution and laws, shall be liable to the party injured in an action at law, suit in equity, or other proper proceeding for redress." 42 U.S.C. § 1983 (1976).

It has been argued that, since there remains little federal common law after *Erie R.R. Co. v. Tompkins,* 304 U.S. 64, to hold that the creation of a federal cause of action by itself does away with the rules of preclusion would take away almost all meaning from § 1738. Currie, Res Judicata: The Neglected Defense, 45 Univ.Chi.L.Rev. 317, 328 (1978).

circumstances: where state substantive law was facially unconstitutional, where state procedural law was inadequate to allow full litigation of a constitutional claim, and where state procedural law, though adequate in theory, was inadequate in practice. 365 U.S., at 173–174. In short, the federal courts could step in where the state courts were unable or unwilling to protect federal rights. Id., at 176. This understanding of § 1983 might well support an exception to res judicata and collateral estoppel where state law did not provide fair procedures for the litigation of constitutional claims, or where a state court failed to even acknowledge the existence of the constitutional principle on which a litigant based his claim. Such an exception, however, would be essentially the same as the important general limit on rules of preclusion that already exists: Collateral estoppel does not apply where the party against whom an earlier court decision is asserted did not have a full and fair opportunity to litigate the claim or issue decided by the first court... But the Court's view of § 1983 in *Monroe* lends no strength to any argument that Congress intended to allow relitigation of federal issues decided after a full and fair hearing in a state court simply because the state court's decision may have been erroneous...

The actual basis of the Court of Appeals' holding appears to be a generally framed principle that every person asserting a federal right is entitled to one unencumbered opportunity to litigate that right in a federal district court, regardless of the legal posture in which the federal claim arises. But the authority for this principle is difficult to discern. It cannot lie in the Constitution, which makes no such guarantee, but leaves the scope of the jurisdiction of the federal district courts to the wisdom of Congress. And no such authority is to be found in § 1983 itself...

The Court of Appeals erred in holding that McCurry's inability to obtain federal habeas corpus relief upon his Fourth Amendment claim renders the doctrine of collateral estoppel inapplicable to his § 1983 suit. Accordingly, the judgment is reversed, and the case is remanded to the Court of Appeals for proceedings consistent with this opinion.

[JUSTICE BLACKMUN, joined by JUSTICES BRENNAN and MARSHALL, dissented, arguing that the legislative history of 42 U.S.C. § 1983 and federal policies underlying its enforcement outweighed the policies supporting issue preclusion. "Congress deliberately opened the federal courts to individual citizens in response to the States' failure to provide justice in their own courts... [F]ederal oversight of constitutional determinations through the federal courts [is] necessary to ensure the effective enforcement of constitutional rights." "A state criminal defendant cannot be held to have chosen 'voluntarily' to litigate his Fourth Amendment claim" when defending a serious criminal charge. "The criminal defendant is an involuntary litigant in the state tribunal, and against him all the forces of the State are arrayed. To force him to a choice between forgoing either a potential defense or a federal forum for hearing his constitutional civil claim is fundamentally unfair."]

State Judgments in Federal Courts

(1) Whether a federal statute creating a new federal remedy displaces 28 U.S.C. § 1738 involves an examination of statutory language and purpose. The importance of *Allen v. McCurry,* however, goes beyond its interpretation of a major federal statute, since it suggests a general clear statement principle against inferring exceptions to the operation of § 1738 absent strong evidence of congressional intent in a statute's language or legislative history. Is the Court correct in its interpretation of 42 U.S.C. § 1983? It is one thing, as Justice Blackmun states, to bind a federal litigant who has chosen to sue first in a state court and has lost on the merits; it is quite another to bind him when he was dragged into the state court as an unwilling defendant. Is it consistent with § 1983 to deprive the plaintiff of his choice of a federal forum? Note that in other situations involving successive litigation, full faith and credit operates to bind defendants as well as plaintiffs.

(2) Justice Blackmun's dissent in *Allen v. McCurry* contends that, since the premise of § 1983 is that state courts do not provide an adequate opportunity for the vindication of federal rights, giving a state-court judgment preclusive effect would undermine the statutory principle. If so, why wouldn't the same argument extend to all situations in which Congress has created a federal cause of action or an alternative federal forum, since "[a]ll grants of federal jurisdiction are based upon some perceived inadequacy of state courts"? D. Currie, *Res Judicata: The Neglected Defense,* 45 U. Chi. L. Rev. 317, 328 (1978). Or can Blackmun's argument be limited to situations in which mistrust of state courts is especially great, such as § 1983 cases charging state officers with denying federal rights? Note that in most situations (e.g., § 1983 actions, FELA cases, diversity cases) Congress does not oust state courts but provides for concurrent federal-court jurisdiction. Is the inference that Congress intended a repeal by implication of 28 U.S.C. § 1738 more plausible in situations of exclusive federal jurisdiction (e.g., patent and antitrust suits)? See *Lyons v. Westinghouse Elec. Corp.,* 222 F.2d 184 (2d Cir. 1955) (state-court litigation of an antitrust defense not binding in later federal-court action seeking affirmative antitrust relief). Professor Currie thought not. See 45 U. Chi. L. Rev. at 347–48.

(3) Subsequent cases have explored the interplay of § 1738 and federal law: In *Kremer v. Chemical Const. Corp.,* 456 U.S. 461 (1982), the Court bound a federal court to give preclusive effect to a state court decision affirming a state administrative agency's rejection of an employment discrimination claim. Thus, § 1738 has the effect of trumping arguments that a federal employment discrimination claim should receive special treatment. In *Migra v. Warren City Sch. Dist. Bd. of Educ.*, 465 U.S. 75 (1984), the Court extended the holding in *Allen v. McCurry* from issue preclusion to claim preclusion.

Subsequent cases have raised some trickier problems. In *Marrese v. American Acad. of Orthopaedic Surgeons*, 470 U.S. 373 (1985), plaintiffs sued the Academy on the ground that denying their applications violated the common law right of association. They lost and subsequently filed a federal antitrust suit. The district court denied the Academy's motion to dismiss for res judicata, observing that jurisdiction over Sherman Act claims is exclusively federal and reasoning that claim preclusion should not extend to a cause of action that could not be brought in the first proceeding. The court of appeals disagreed and reversed. On certiorari, the Supreme Court vacated the judgment and remanded, holding that § 1738 required the federal court to look first to state law. The Court acknowledged that, because federal jurisdiction was exclusive, there probably was no state law respecting the effect of a prior state judgment on a federal antitrust claim. Nevertheless, the Court explained, federal courts might find guidance in general principles of state law:

> If state preclusion law includes [a] requirement of prior jurisdictional competency, which is generally true, a state judgment will not have claim preclusive effect on a cause of action within the exclusive jurisdiction of the federal courts. Even in the event that a party asserting the affirmative defense of claim preclusion can show that state preclusion rules in some circumstances bar a claim outside the jurisdiction of the court that rendered the initial judgment, the federal court should first consider whether the application of the state rules would bar the particular federal claim.
>
> Reference to state preclusion law may make it unnecessary to determine if the federal court, as an exception to § 1738, should refuse to give preclusive effect to a state court judgment. The issue whether there is an exception to § 1738 arises only if state law indicates that litigation of a particular claim or issue should be barred in the subsequent federal proceeding.

Does it make sense to talk about state law on a question the state has no power to rule on? What result if state preclusion law bars claims that could not have been raised in the earlier proceeding? Is a federal court bound to follow this rule? Wouldn't it simply lead parties straight to federal court with both federal and (pendent) state law claims? Why should a state be able to determine the preclusive effect of its judgment on claims it could not have entertained?

Concurring in the judgment, Chief Justice Burger made clear his view that the plaintiffs should be barred by their failure to raise a *state* law antitrust claim that was essentially identical to the federal claim:

> If state law provides a cause of action that is virtually identical with a federal statutory cause of action, a plaintiff suing in state court is able to rely on the same theory of the case and obtain the same remedy as would be available in federal court, even when the plaintiff cannot expressly invoke the federal statute because it is within the exclusive jurisdiction of the federal courts. In this situation, the jurisdictional competency requirement is effectively satisfied. Therefore, the fact that state law recognizes the jurisdictional competency requirement does not necessarily imply that a state court judgment has no claim to preclusive effect on a cause of action within exclusive federal jurisdiction.

Do you agree? Is Chief Justice Burger saying that the plaintiff should be precluded even if state law does not bar the claim? Can this position be squared with § 1738?

In *Parsons Steel, Inc. v. First Alabama Bank,* 474 U.S. 518 (1986), Parsons Steel sued the bank in state court for fraud and in federal court for violating the Bank Holding Company Act. The federal court ruled in favor of the bank, which then moved to dismiss the state action on res judicata grounds. The state court denied this motion and submitted the case to the jury, resulting in an award of $4 million in damages. At that point, the bank returned to the federal court and asked it to enjoin the state proceedings under the Anti-Injunction Act, 28 U.S.C. § 2283. This act generally prohibits federal courts from enjoining state proceedings but permits such injunctions in a number of situations, including when necessary "to protect or effectuate [a federal court's] judgments." The district judge granted an injunction under this so-called relitigation exception. The Supreme Court reversed, holding that, in deciding whether an injunction was appropriate under § 2283, the federal court was bound by § 1738 to follow the state court's determination that the initial federal judgment was not res judicata:

> We believe that the Anti-Injunction Act and the Full Faith and Credit Act can be construed consistently, simply by limiting the relitigation exception of the Anti-Injunction Act to those situations in which the state court has not yet ruled on the merits of the res judicata issue. Once the state court has finally rejected a claim of res judicata, then the Full Faith and Credit Act becomes applicable and federal courts must turn to state law to determine the preclusive effect of the state court's decision.

Is this interpretation sensible? Doesn't the relitigation exception to the Anti-Injunction Act reflect congressional mistrust of the treatment of federal judgments by state courts? Will the Court's decision in *Parsons Steel* increase or decrease the number of anti-suit injunctions issued by federal courts? What would you do after this decision if you were in the bank's position?

(4) Suppose McCurry had not raised or litigated the search-and-seizure question in the Missouri court. Could he then litigate in his § 1983 case an issue he deliberately or inadvertently failed to raise in the criminal prosecution? The Court in *Allen* expressly reserved this question in a footnote. Restatement (Second) of Judgments § 85 (1982), implies that he could, while Professor David Currie argues that preclusion is appropriate: "Whenever there will be a large overlap of issues or evidence if two trials are held, it is wasteful to society and harassing to the adversary to have more than one. . ." Currie, 45 U. Chi. L. Rev. at 337. Currie argues that both issue preclusion and claim preclusion should be applied if two conditions are satisfied: "the party to be precluded had adequate opportunity to litigate the matter in the earlier proceeding and . . . the matter is closely enough related to the original controversy." Id. at 342.

> Forfeiture of legal rights for failure to assert them at the appropriate time is no novel phenomenon. It is the very foundation of statutes of limitations and of time limits on the filing of appeals. . . Even in habeas corpus, where the overwhelming interest of remedying unlawful restrictions on personal liberty might be thought to outweigh ordinary considerations of judicial efficiency, the Court has recently returned to the view that a failure to assert a constitutional objection within the time prescribed by state law precludes raising it in federal court. Res judicata policy demands no less.

Id. at 337–38. Should the tactical decisions of a criminal defendant be interfered with by concern for preserving a subsequent civil suit? If a defendant like McCurry feels that raising the Fourth Amendment will not help his criminal defense, should we nonetheless force him to do so at the cost of sacrificing potential recovery in a § 1983 claim?

In *Haring v. Prosise,* 462 U.S. 306 (1983), the Court seemed to follow the Restatement's approach. A § 1983 claimant had pleaded guilty to a charge of manufacturing a controlled substance in an earlier state criminal proceeding. The guilty plea prevented him from contesting a Fourth Amendment claim regarding the legality of the search which uncovered the controlled substance. The Court held that the guilty plea was not a "waiver" of any Fourth Amendment claims, which Prosise now sought to raise in his § 1983 action.

(5) If 28 U.S.C. § 1738 has not been displaced, doesn't it refer this question to the res judicata law of the state rendering the judgment? Why doesn't the Court in *Allen v. McCurry* discuss Missouri res judicata law?

(6) Is a state-court judgment preclusive even when affirmative state litigation is required to ripen a federal constitutional claim? In *San Remo Hotel, L.P. v. City & Cty. of San Francisco*, 545 U.S. 323 (2005), hotel operators brought state-law claims against the city and county of San Francisco, unsuccessfully arguing that an ordinance assessing a fee for converting residential rooms to tourist rooms effected a taking of property without just compensation. Because the Supreme Court had held in *Williamson County Regional Planning Comm'n v. Hamilton Bank of Johnson City*, 473 U.S. 172 (1985), that federal takings claims are not ripe until a state court has denied a claim for just compensation, the plaintiffs argued, full faith and credit to the state-court judgment would deprive them of a meaningful federal forum. *San Remo*, 545 U.S. at 338. The Supreme Court disagreed, treating the case as a straightforward application of *Allen v. McCurry*: "The relevant question in such cases is not whether the plaintiff has been afforded access to a federal forum; rather, the question is whether the state court actually decided an issue of fact or law that was necessary to its judgment." *Id.* at 342.

The specific holding of *San Remo* was obviated by *Knick v. Township of Scott*, 139 S.Ct. 2162 (2019). The Court reasoned that *Williamson County* and *San Remo*, taken together, sprung a "preclusion trap": "The takings plaintiff thus finds himself in a Catch-22: He cannot go to federal court without going to state court first; but if he goes to state court and loses, his claim will be barred in federal court. The federal claim dies aborning." *Id.* at 2167. The Court's solution was to overrule *Williamson County* and permit landowners to bring claims in federal court under § 1983 as soon as the uncompensated taking occurs. Should the Court have overruled *San Remo* instead? Or, perhaps better yet, waited for Congress to do so under its Full Faith and Credit Clause authority? *Id.* at 2189–90 (Kagan, J., dissenting).

Congressional Implementation of the Full Faith and Credit Clause

(1) The congressional power to implement the Full Faith and Credit Clause by "prescrib[ing] . . . the Effect" of sister-state judgments has been little utilized. A number of commentators have suggested that some of the problems studied in this chapter could be eliminated by wise congressional use of this authority. Professor Brainerd Currie, for example, urged this course:

> The implementing statute is, indeed, a helpful clarification of national policy; but one has only to recall the cases on recognition of divorce decrees [see infra Chapter 6] to appreciate that it falls far short of providing clear guidance for solving all problems. It is

> a vastly oversimplified provision, such as one might draft if the only purpose were to insure that a simple money judgment shall be enforceable by action in any state. As applied to other types of judgments, it leaves unsolved problems that Congress has power to solve. . . Because that responsibility has been only imperfectly discharged, the Court is often without guidance as to what national policy is, or is embarrassed by an oversimplified declaration of national policy that cannot easily be reconciled with rather clear national interests. It is not unreasonable to suggest that Congress should address itself to some of these problems, on a selective basis, and thus relieve the Court to some extent from the strains and tensions induced by the necessity of performing an essentially political function.

Currie, *Full Faith and Credit, Chiefly to Judgments: A Role for Congress,* 1964 Sup. Ct. Rev. 89, 90. See also Stephen E. Sachs, *Full Faith and Credit in the Early Congress*, 95 Va. L. Rev. 1201 (2009) (arguing that the implementing statute's central purpose was to declare the mode of authentication, not the effect, of sister-state judgments, and that Congress retained broad power under the Full Faith and Credit Clause to determine the latter).

Do you agree that Congress could contribute materially to the solution of full-faith problems respecting sister-state judgments? What suggestions for legislative action would you propose? A few enactments, including an Act of Congress, 28 U.S.C. § 1738A (1980) (the Parental Kidnapping Prevention Act—"PKPA"), and those parts of a widely adopted uniform act dealing with the vexing interstate problem of child support decrees, 28 U.S.C. § 1738B (1997) (the Uniform Interstate Family Support Act—"UIFSA"), are discussed in detail in Chapter 6, infra.

(2) From the beginning, the language of the full-faith statute has not been taken as requiring immediate enforcement of a sister-state judgment:

> [T]he judgment is made a debt of record, not examinable upon its merits; but it does not carry with it, into another State, the efficacy of a judgment upon property or persons, to be enforced by execution. To give it the force of a judgment in another State, it must be made a judgment there; and can only be executed in the latter as its laws may permit.

McElmoyle v. Cohen, 38 U.S. (13 Pet.) 312, 325 (1839), supra, p. 628. Even though the range of defenses to a sister-state judgment is strictly limited, this procedure has long been criticized as costly, time-consuming, and unnecessary. See Cook, *The Powers of Congress Under the Full Faith and Credit Clause,* 28 Yale L. J. 421 (1919).

Congress has provided, in 28 U.S.C. § 1963, for the registration of federal-court judgments in other federal districts, permitting execution without further litigation. This statute is limited to actions "for the recovery of money or property" and thus has been held inapplicable to an injunction, *Stiller v. Hardman,* 324 F.2d 626 (2d Cir. 1963); but the court added that the injunction operates nationwide by its own force and therefore that registration was unnecessary. Should Congress enact a similar provision for state-court judgments?

Almost all of the states have gone part way toward this goal by adopting the Uniform Enforcement of Foreign Judgments Act, 9A U.L.A. 474, which in effect provides a summary judicial procedure for suing upon a foreign judgment, but which in addition authorizes levy upon local property even before the new judgment is obtained. A revised version of the uniform act, promulgated in 1964, 9A U.L.A. 488, goes even further in providing that after a sister-state judgment is filed with the court and notice of it has been mailed to judgment debtor, the judgment shall have "the same effect" as a domestic judgment.

(3) Full faith to "judicial proceedings" has not thus far been thought to preclude the filing of a second suit on a cause that is pending in another state; credit must be given only to final judgments. Should Congress extend the full faith requirement to combat litigation of the same cause in several states at once?

(4) Does § 1738 preempt the authority of federal courts to fashion federal common-law rules of preclusion? The statute obviously does not displace federal common law with respect to federal decisions (why?), but what about decisions at the state level? That question was presented in *University of Tennessee v. Elliott,* 478 U.S. 788 (1986). Elliott, an employee of the University's Agricultural Extension Service, was told that he was being discharged for various infractions. Elliott requested an administrative hearing under state law to contest his termination, and he also filed a federal lawsuit under Title VII and § 1983 alleging that the discharge was racially motivated. After hearing extensive evidence, the state Administrative Law Judge found no racial motivation, but he ruled that termination was too severe a sanction and that Elliott should be transferred to a different position. Elliott appealed this ruling to University officials, who upheld the ALJ's determination. Rather than seek review in the state court, Elliott returned to federal court to pursue his civil rights claims, but the district court held these claims precluded by the state proceedings. The court of appeals reversed on the ground that unreviewed determinations by state administrative agencies are not entitled to full faith and credit under § 1738. The Supreme Court agreed, observing that "because § 1738 antedates the development of administrative agencies" it cannot represent a congressional determination about the preclusive effect to be given such proceedings. But, the Court added, citing decisions establishing the preclusive effect of federal judgments, "we have frequently fashioned federal common-law rules of preclusion in the absence of a governing statute." The Court went on to find that plaintiff's Title VII claim was not precluded but that his § 1983 claim was indeed barred.

MATSUSHITA ELECTRIC INDUSTRIAL CO. V. EPSTEIN

516 U.S. 367 (1996).

JUSTICE THOMAS delivered the opinion of the Court.

This case presents the question whether a federal court may withhold full faith and credit from a state-court judgment approving a class-action settlement simply because the settlement releases claims within the exclusive jurisdiction of the federal courts. The answer is no. Absent a partial repeal of the Full Faith and Credit Act, 28 U.S.C. § 1738, by another federal statute, a federal court must give the judgment the same effect that it would have in the courts of the State in which it was rendered.

I

In 1990, petitioner Matsushita Electric Industrial Co. made a tender offer for the common stock of MCA, Inc., a Delaware corporation. The tender offer not only resulted in Matsushita's acquisition of MCA, but also precipitated two lawsuits on behalf of the holders of MCA's common stock. First, a class action was filed in the Delaware Court of Chancery against MCA and its directors for breach of fiduciary duty in failing to maximize shareholder value. The complaint was later amended to state additional claims against MCA's directors for, *inter alia*, waste of corporate assets by exposing MCA to liability under the federal securities laws. In addition, Matsushita was added as a defendant and was accused of conspiring with MCA's directors to violate Delaware law. The Delaware suit was based purely on state-law claims.

While the state class action was pending, the instant suit was filed in Federal District Court in California. The complaint named Matsushita as a defendant and alleged that Matsushita's tender offer violated Securities Exchange Commission (SEC) Rules 10b–3 and 14d–10. . . Section 27 of the Exchange Act confers exclusive jurisdiction upon the federal courts for suits brought to enforce the Act or rules and regulations promulgated thereunder. * * * The District Court declined to certify the class, entered summary judgment for Matsushita, and dismissed the case. The plaintiffs appealed to the Court of Appeals for the Ninth Circuit.

After the federal plaintiffs filed their notice of appeal but before the Ninth Circuit handed down a decision, the parties to the Delaware suit negotiated a settlement. . . As required by Delaware Chancery Rule 23, which is modeled on Federal Rule of Civil Procedure 23, the Chancery Court certified the class for purposes of settlement and approved a notice of the proposed settlement. The notice informed the class members of their right to request exclusion from the settlement class and to appear and present argument at a scheduled hearing to determine the fairness of the settlement. In particular, the notice stated that "[b]y filing a valid Request for Exclusion, a member of the Settlement Class will not be precluded by the Settlement from individually seeking to pursue the claims alleged in the . . . California Federal Actions, . . . or any other claim relating to the events at issue in the Delaware Actions." * * * Two such notices were mailed to the class members and the notice was also published in the national edition of the Wall Street Journal. The Chancery Court then held a hearing. After argument from several objectors, the Court found the class representation adequate and the settlement fair.

The order and final judgment of the Chancery Court incorporated the terms of the settlement agreement, providing:

> "All claims, rights and causes of action (state or federal, including but not limited to claims arising under the federal securities law, any rules or regulations promulgated thereunder, or otherwise), whether known or unknown that are, could have been or might in the future be asserted by any of the plaintiffs or any member of the Settlement Class *(other than those who have validly requested exclusion therefrom)*, . . . in connection with or that arise now or hereafter out of the Merger Agreement, the Tender Offer, the Distribution Agreement, the Capital Contribution Agreement, the employee compensation arrangements, the Tender Agreements, the Initial Proposed Settlement, this Settlement . . . *and including without limitation the claims asserted in the California Federal Actions* . . . are hereby compromised, settled, released and discharged with prejudice by virtue of the proceedings herein and this Order and Final Judgment." * * *

The judgment also stated that the notice met all the requirements of due process. The Delaware Supreme Court affirmed. *In re MCA, Inc., Shareholders Litigation*, 633 A.2d 370 (1993) (judgment order).

Respondents were members of both the state and federal plaintiff classes. Following issuance of the notice of proposed settlement of the Delaware litigation, respondents neither opted out of the settlement class nor appeared at the hearing to contest the settlement or the representation of the class. On appeal in the Ninth Circuit, petitioner Matsushita invoked the Delaware judgment as a bar to further prosecution of that action under the Full Faith and Credit Act, 28 U.S.C. § 1738.

The Ninth Circuit rejected petitioner's argument, ruling that § 1738 did not apply. *Epstein v. MCA, Inc.*, 50 F.3d 644, 661–666 (1995). Instead, the Court of Appeals fashioned a test under which the preclusive force of a state court settlement judgment is limited to those claims that "could . . . have been extinguished by the issue preclusive effect of an adjudication of the state claims." Id., at 665. The lower courts have taken varying approaches to determining the preclusive effect of a state court judgment, entered in a class or derivative action, that provides for the release of exclusively federal claims. We granted certiorari to clarify this important area of federal law.

II

The Full Faith and Credit Act . . . directs all courts to treat a state court judgment with the same respect that it would receive in the courts of the rendering state. Federal courts may not "employ their own rules . . . in determining the effect of state judgments," but must "accept the rules chosen by the State from which the judgment is taken." *Kremer v. Chemical Constr. Corp.*, 456 U.S. 461, 481–482 (1982). Because the Court of Appeals failed to follow the dictates of the Act, we reverse.

A

The state court judgment in this case differs in two respects from the judgments that we have previously considered in our cases under the Full Faith and Credit Act. As respondents and the Court of Appeals stressed, the judgment was the product of a class action and incorporated a settlement agreement releasing claims within the exclusive jurisdiction of the federal courts. Though respondents urge "the irrelevance of section 1738 to this litigation," * * * we do not think that either of these features exempts the judgment from the operation of § 1738.

That the judgment at issue is the result of a class action, rather than a suit brought by an individual, does not undermine the initial applicability of § 1738. The judgment of a state court in a class action is plainly the product of a "judicial proceeding" within the meaning of § 1738. * * * Therefore, a judgment entered in a class action, like any other judgment entered in a state judicial proceeding, is presumptively entitled to full faith and credit under the express terms of the Act.

Further, § 1738 is not irrelevant simply because the judgment in question might work to bar the litigation of exclusively federal claims. Our decision in *Marrese v. American Academy of Orthopaedic Surgeons*, 470 U.S. 373 (1985) [supra p. 640], made clear that where § 1738 is raised as a defense in a subsequent suit, the fact that an allegedly precluded "claim is within the exclusive jurisdiction of the federal courts *does not necessarily make § 1738 inapplicable.*" *Id.*, at 380 (emphasis added). In so holding, we relied primarily on *Kremer v. Chemical Constr. Corp., supra*, which held, without deciding whether Title VII claims are exclusively federal, that state court proceedings may be issue preclusive in Title VII suits in federal court. *Kremer*, we said, "implies that absent an exception to § 1738, state law determines at least the . . . preclusive effect of a prior state judgment in a subsequent action involving a claim within the exclusive jurisdiction of the federal courts." *Marrese*, 470 U.S., at 381. Accordingly, we decided that "a state court judgment may in some circumstances have preclusive effect in a subsequent action within the exclusive jurisdiction of the federal courts." *Id.*, at 380. . .

In accord with these precedents, we conclude that § 1738 is generally applicable in cases in which the state court judgment at issue incorporates a class action settlement releasing claims solely within the jurisdiction of the federal courts.

B

Marrese provides the analytical framework for deciding whether the Delaware court's judgment precludes this exclusively federal action. When faced with a state court judgment relating to an exclusively federal claim, a federal court must first look to the law of the rendering State to ascertain the effect of the judgment. * * * If state law indicates that the particular claim or issue would be barred from litigation in a court of that state, then the federal court must next decide whether, "as an exception to § 1738," it "should refuse to give preclusive effect to [the] state court judgment." *Id.*, at 383. * * *

1

We observed in *Marrese* that the inquiry into state law would not always yield a direct answer. Usually, "a state court will not have occasion to address the specific question whether a state judgment has issue or claim preclusive effect in a later action that can be brought only in federal court." 470 U.S., at 381–382. Where a judicially approved settlement is under consideration, a federal court may consequently find guidance from general state law on the preclusive force of settlement judgments. * * * Here, in addition to providing rules regarding the preclusive force of class-action settlement judgments in subsequent suits in state court, the Delaware courts have also spoken to the particular effect of such judgments in federal court.

Delaware has traditionally treated the impact of settlement judgments on subsequent litigation in state court as a question of claim preclusion. Early cases suggested that Delaware courts would not afford claim preclusive effect to a settlement releasing claims that could not have been presented in the trial court. * * * As the Court of Chancery has perceived, however, "the . . . inquiry [was] modified in regard to class actions," * * * by the Delaware Supreme Court's decision in *Nottingham Partners v. Dana*, 564 A.2d 1089 (1989).

In *Nottingham*, a class action, the Delaware Supreme Court approved a settlement that released claims then pending in federal court. In approving that settlement, the *Nottingham* Court appears to have eliminated the . . . requirement that the claims could have been raised in the suit that produced the settlement, at least with respect to class actions:

> "[I]n order to achieve a comprehensive settlement that would prevent relitigation of settled questions at the core of a class action, a court may permit the release of a claim based on the identical factual predicate as that underlying the claims in the settled class action even though the claim was not presented and might not have been presentable in the class action." 564 A.2d, at 1106 * * *.

These cases indicate that even if, as here, a claim could not have been raised in the court that rendered the settlement judgment in a class action, a Delaware court would still find that the judgment bars subsequent pursuit of the claim. . .

Given these statements of Delaware law, we think that a Delaware court would afford preclusive effect to the settlement judgment in this case, notwithstanding the fact that respondents could not have pressed their Exchange Act claims in the Court of Chancery. The claims are clearly within the scope of the release in the judgment, since the judgment specifically refers to this lawsuit. As required by Delaware Court of Chancery Rule 23, * * * the Court of Chancery found, and the Delaware Supreme Court affirmed, that the settlement was "fair, reasonable and adequate and in the best interests of the . . . Settlement class" and that notice to the class was "in full compliance with . . . the requirements of due process." * * * The Court of Chancery "further determined that the plaintiffs[,] . . . as representatives of the Settlement Class, have fairly and adequately protected the interests of the Settlement Class." * * *[5] Under Delaware Rule 23, as under Federal Rule of Civil Procedure 23, "[a]ll members of the class, whether of a plaintiff or a defendant class, are bound by the judgment entered in the action unless, in a Rule 23(b)(3) action, they make a timely election for exclusion." * * * Respondents do not deny that, as shareholders of MCA's common stock, they were part of the plaintiff class and that they never opted out; they are bound, then, by the judgment.

2

Because it appears that the settlement judgment would be res judicata under Delaware law, we proceed to the second step of the *Marrese* analysis and ask whether § 27 of the Exchange Act, which confers exclusive jurisdiction upon the federal courts for suits arising under the Act, partially repealed § 1738. Section 27 contains no express language regarding its relationship with § 1738 or the preclusive effect of related state court

[5] Apart from any discussion of Delaware law, respondents contend that the settlement proceedings did not satisfy due process because the class was inadequately represented. * * * Respondents make this claim in spite of the Chancery Court's express ruling, following argument on the issue, that the class representatives fairly and adequately protected the interests of the class. * * * We need not address the due process claim, however, because it is outside the scope of the question presented in this Court. * * * While it is true that a respondent may defend a judgment on alternative grounds, we generally do not address arguments that were not the basis for the decision below. * * *

proceedings. Thus, any modification of § 1738 by § 27 must be implied. In deciding whether § 27 impliedly created an exception to § 1738, the "general question is whether the concerns underlying a particular grant of exclusive jurisdiction justify a finding of an implied partial repeal of § 1738." *Marrese*, 470 U.S., at 386. "Resolution of this question will depend on the particular federal statute as well as the nature of the claim or issue involved in the subsequent federal action. . . [T]he primary consideration must be the intent of Congress." *Ibid.*

As an historical matter, we have seldom, if ever, held that a federal statute impliedly repealed § 1738. * * * The rarity with which we have discovered implied repeals is due to the relatively stringent standard for such findings, namely, that there be an "irreconcilable conflict" between the two federal statutes at issue. * * *

Section 27 provides that "[t]he district courts of the United States . . . shall have exclusive jurisdiction . . . of all suits in equity and actions at law brought to enforce any liability or duty created by this chapter or the rules and regulations thereunder." * * * There is no suggestion in § 27 that Congress meant for plaintiffs with Exchange Act claims to have more than one day in court to challenge the legality of a securities transaction. Though the statute plainly mandates that suits alleging violations of the Exchange Act may be maintained only in federal court, nothing in the language of § 27 "remotely expresses any congressional intent to contravene the common-law rules of preclusion or to repeal the express statutory requirements of . . . 28 U.S.C. § 1738." * * *

Nor does § 27 evince any intent to prevent litigants in state court—whether suing as individuals or as part of a class—from voluntarily releasing Exchange Act claims in judicially approved settlements. While § 27 prohibits state courts from adjudicating claims arising under the Exchange Act, it does not prohibit state courts from approving the release of Exchange Act claims in the settlement of suits over which they have properly exercised jurisdiction, *i.e.*, suits arising under state law or under federal law for which there is concurrent jurisdiction. In this case, for example, the Delaware action was not "brought to enforce" any rights or obligations under the Act. The Delaware court asserted judicial power over a complaint asserting purely state law causes of action and, after the parties agreed to settle, certified the class and approved the settlement pursuant to the requirements of Delaware Rule of Chancery 23 and the Due Process Clause. Thus, the Delaware court never trespassed upon the exclusive territory of the federal courts, but merely approved the settlement of a common-law suit pursuant to state and nonexclusive federal law. * * * While it is true that the state court assessed the general worth of the federal claims in determining the fairness of the settlement, such assessment does not amount to a judgment on the merits of the claims. * * * The Delaware court never purported to resolve the merits of the

Exchange Act claims in the course of appraising the settlement; indeed, it expressly disavowed that purpose. * * *

The legislative history of the Exchange Act elucidates no specific purpose on the part of Congress in enacting § 27. * * * We may presume, however, that Congress intended § 27 to serve at least the general purposes underlying most grants of exclusive jurisdiction: "to achieve greater uniformity of construction and more effective and expert application of that law." * * * When a state court upholds a settlement that releases claims under the Exchange Act, it threatens neither of these policies. There is no danger that state court judges who are not fully expert in federal securities law will say definitively what the Exchange Act means and enforce legal liabilities and duties thereunder. And the uniform construction of the Act is unaffected by a state court's approval of a proposed settlement because the state court does not adjudicate the Exchange Act claims but only evaluates the overall fairness of the settlement, generally by applying its own business judgment to the facts of the case. * * *

Furthermore, other provisions of the Exchange Act suggest that Congress did not intend to create an exception to § 1738 for suits alleging violations of the Act. Congress plainly contemplated the possibility of dual litigation in state and federal courts relating to securities transactions. * * * And all that Congress chose to say about the consequences of such litigation is that plaintiffs ought not obtain double recovery. * * * Congress said nothing to modify the background rule that where a state-court judgment precedes that of a federal court, the federal court must give full faith and credit to the state court judgment. * * *

Finally, precedent supports the conclusion that the concerns underlying the grant of exclusive jurisdiction in § 27 are not undermined by state-court approval of settlements releasing Exchange Act claims. We have held that state court proceedings may, in various ways, subsequently affect the litigation of exclusively federal claims without running afoul of the federal jurisdictional grant in question. In *Becher v. Contoure Laboratories, Inc.*, 279 U.S. 388 (1929) (cited in *Marrese*, 470 U.S., at 381), we held that state court findings of fact were issue preclusive in federal patent suits. We did so with full recognition that "the logical conclusion from the establishing of [the state law] claim is that Becher's patent is void." 279 U.S., at 391. *Becher* reasoned that although "decrees validating or invalidating patents belong to the Courts of the United States," that "does not give sacrosanctity to facts that may be conclusive upon the question in issue." *Ibid.* Similarly, while binding legal determinations of rights and liabilities under the Exchange Act are for federal courts only, there is nothing sacred about the approval of settlements of suits arising under state law, even where the parties agree to release exclusively federal claims. * * *

We have also held that Exchange Act claims may be resolved by arbitration rather than litigation in federal court. In *Shearson/American Express Inc. v. McMahon*, 482 U.S. 220 (1987), we found that parties to an arbitration agreement could waive the right to have their Exchange Act claims tried in federal court and agree to arbitrate the claims. * * * It follows that state court litigants ought also to be able to waive, or "release," the right to litigate Exchange Act claims in a federal forum as part of a settlement agreement. As *Shearson/American Express Inc.* demonstrates, a statute conferring exclusive federal jurisdiction for a certain class of claims does not necessarily require resolution of those claims in a federal court.

Taken together, these cases stand for the general proposition that even when exclusively federal claims are at stake, there is no "universal right to litigate a federal claim in a federal district court." * * * If class action plaintiffs wish to preserve absolutely their right to litigate exclusively federal claims in federal court, they should either opt out of the settlement class or object to the release of any exclusively federal claims. In fact, some of the plaintiffs in the Delaware class action requested exclusion from the settlement class. They are now proceeding in federal court with their federal claims, unimpeded by the Delaware judgment.

In the end, §§ 27 and 1738 "do not pose an either-or proposition." * * * They can be reconciled by reading § 1738 to mandate full faith and credit of state court judgments incorporating global settlements, provided the rendering court had jurisdiction over the underlying suit itself, and by reading § 27 to prohibit state courts from exercising jurisdiction over suits arising under the Exchange Act. * * * Congress' intent to provide an exclusive federal forum for adjudication of suits to enforce the Exchange Act is clear enough. But we can find no suggestion in § 27 that Congress meant to override the "principles of comity and repose embodied in § 1738," * * * by allowing plaintiffs with Exchange Act claims to release those claims in state court and then litigate them in federal court. We conclude that the Delaware courts would give the settlement judgment preclusive effect in a subsequent proceeding and, further, that § 27 did not effect a partial repeal of § 1738.

C

The Court of Appeals did not engage in any analysis of Delaware law pursuant to § 1738. Rather, the Court of Appeals declined to apply § 1738 on the ground that where the rendering forum lacked jurisdiction over the subject matter or the parties, full faith and credit is not required. * * * The Court of Appeals decided that the subject-matter jurisdiction exception to full faith and credit applies to this case because the Delaware court acted outside the bounds of its own jurisdiction in approving the settlement, since the settlement released exclusively federal claims. * * *

As explained above, the state court in this case clearly possessed jurisdiction over the subject matter of the underlying suit and over the defendants. Only if this were not so—for instance, if the complaint alleged violations of the Exchange Act and the Delaware court rendered a judgment on the merits of those claims—would the exception to § 1738 for lack of subject-matter jurisdiction apply. Where, as here, the rendering court in fact had subject-matter jurisdiction, the subject-matter jurisdiction exception to full faith and credit is simply inapposite. In such a case, the relevance of a federal statute that provides for exclusive federal jurisdiction is not to the state court's possession of jurisdiction *per se*, but to the existence of a partial repeal of § 1738.[8]

* * *

The judgment of the Court of Appeals is reversed and remanded for proceedings consistent with this opinion.

[JUSTICES STEVENS, GINSBURG, and SOUTER concurred in part and dissented in part, agreeing with the Court's basic analysis but arguing that the question of Delaware law should be addressed by the court of appeals in the first instance and pointing out that the issue of adequate representation in the Delaware action remains open on remand.]

Settlement and Claim Preclusion

(1) The Court's opinion makes it seem as if the major issue in *Matsushita* is whether § 27 of the Exchange Act impliedly repeals § 1738. Are you surprised that no implied repeal is found? In *Marrese*, the Court said that if state law purports to bar a claim, the federal court should ask whether there is an applicable "exception" to § 1738. Do you think the *Marrese* Court was thinking primarily about implied repeals?

(2) Are you satisfied with the Court's explanation that the subject matter jurisdiction exception to full faith and credit "is simply inapposite" because the underlying suit was based on state law and so within the jurisdiction of the Delaware court? Certainly this was true when the complaint was filed, but didn't the state court exercise jurisdiction over the federal claim when it entered the settlement as a consent decree? If Justice Thomas is right that the Delaware court never asserted jurisdiction to adjudicate the federal claims, why isn't the issue contract enforcement rather than *res judicata*? It makes a difference, doesn't it? Do you need a

[8] *Kalb v. Feuerstein*, 308 U.S. 433 (1940), is not to the contrary. In that case, the federal statute at issue expressly prohibited certain common-law actions from being either instituted or maintained in state court. * * * Thus, by merely entertaining a common-law foreclosure suit, over which it otherwise would have had jurisdiction, the state court violated the terms of the Act. That is not the situation here, where there is no contention that just by entertaining the class action the Delaware court acted in violation of federal law.

court with jurisdiction to adjudicate a claim in order to release that claim? Do you need a court at all?

(3) Do you agree with the Court that none of the policies underlying the grant of exclusive jurisdiction in § 27 are affected by allowing claim preclusion when parties settle because the state court does not "say definitively what the Exchange Act means and enforce legal liabilities and duties thereunder"? Then why not also allow state courts to approve settlements, with claim preclusive effect, even where the complaint explicitly alleges claims under the federal securities laws? Is an exception to full faith and credit made for judgments rendered by courts lacking subject matter jurisdiction in order to deter them from improperly asserting jurisdiction, or does the exception reflect other concerns as well? Besides, how could the Delaware court determine whether the settlement was fair without interpreting the federal act and evaluating the strength of the federal claims?

(4) In *Marrese*, the plaintiffs brought an action in state court on state law grounds and lost. They subsequently filed a federal action under the Sherman Act, which makes federal jurisdiction exclusive. The Supreme Court found it unnecessary to decide whether the state judgment was preclusive under § 1738, because it was not clear that the action was preclusive even under state law. Suppose it was clear and that state law was preclusive. What result after *Matsushita*?

(5) The Court suggests that parties in the federal action could have preserved their claim by opting out of the Delaware settlement. Note, however, that the state and federal suits were both class actions. That being so, is this a realistic option? Can the federal class representative opt out for the entire class? If not, how, as a practical matter, can the federal action be maintained?

(6) The Court says in footnote 5 that it need not decide whether the plaintiffs in the federal class action can challenge the issue of adequate representation. In her dissent, Justice Ginsburg argued that the issue was open on remand. Unlike subject matter jurisdiction, the question of adequate representation was litigated in the state court. Why, then, isn't relitigation of this issue not also foreclosed under § 1738?

(7) *Matsushita* also raises some interesting questions about the authority of class representatives. In settling an action, a plaintiff trades its property in a cause of action for some form of financial or injunctive compensation. In a class action, class representatives and their attorneys are given authority to dispose of this property on behalf of class members who are not themselves present. In theory, absentee class members are protected by (1) the requirements that class representatives be typical and that attorneys for the class provide adequate representation; (2) the right to notice and (in certain cases) an opportunity to opt out; and (3) the court's duty to hold a fairness hearing before approving a settlement. How reliable do you think these protections are in practice?

In *Matsushita*, class representatives who were given authority to settle state law claims negotiated a settlement that also disposed of federal claims they could not have litigated because these were outside the jurisdiction of the state court. The question thus posed is whether class representatives should be given authority to trade property other than the claims included in the complaint. Suppose, for example, that the proposed settlement provided that class members would surrender their state law claims and also give their cars to the defendants. Should compliance with the usual requirements for approving a class action settlement be sufficient to allay further concern? Wouldn't it be safer, as a matter of either due process or rule interpretation, to restrict the settlement authority of class representatives to claims they are empowered to litigate on behalf of class members? For discussion of these and other issues, see Kahan & Silberman, *Matsushita and Beyond: The Role of State Courts in Class Actions Involving Exclusive Federal Claims,* 1996 Sup. Ct. Rev. 219. For a discussion of the effect of class judgments on non-class claims, see Wolff, *Preclusion in Class Action Litigation*, 105 Colum L. Rev. 717 (2005).

CHAPTER 6

SPECIAL PROBLEMS IN FAMILY LAW

■ ■ ■

SECTION 1. DIVORCE

Introductory Note

Before the Second World War, most American states allowed divorce only upon fault-based grounds like adultery or cruelty. Moreover, if both spouses were guilty of marital fault, the doctrine of recrimination meant that neither could get a divorce. These prevailing laws often made divorce legally impossible without cooperation between the spouses—a strategy that lent itself both to blackmail and uncertainty, since the property settlement agreements produced in this way often were contingent on withholding a valid defense to the action and thus were subject to attack on grounds of fraud.

By the 1940s, divorce seekers had discovered a promising means of escape from the need to buy freedom from a reluctant spouse: a change of locale to a state with an easy divorce law. Nevada and Florida stood out by offering manipulable grounds for divorce, pleasant surroundings during the required period of residence, and a family law bar attentive to the needs of unhappily married newcomers. It soon became clear, however, that a major drawback of this kind of individual forum-shopping was the difficulty of upholding the decree against jurisdictional attack by the stay-at-home spouse. Once it turned out that consent was still the safest strategy, both in domestic and foreign divorces, choice of law became the determinative consideration. The practice of migratory divorce flourished under the protection of the United States Supreme Court until the no-fault divorce revolution that swept the country in the 1970s and 1980s made evasion of local law unnecessary in most cases. If time is of the essence, however, migratory divorce may remain attractive.

The divorce cases afford an opportunity for quick review of the interrelating concepts of jurisdiction, choice of law, and respect for foreign judgments, the more so as they diverge sharply in several respects from ordinary practice. Jurisdiction over the defendant seems neither necessary nor sufficient to empower a court to hear a divorce case. Foreign law is virtually never considered. Foreign judgments are collaterally attacked on the basis of a lack of domicile, which usually relates to choice of law. Yet traditional principles foreclosing litigation of jurisdictional issues are applied at least as strictly in divorce cases as elsewhere, despite the frequent absence of truly adversary proceedings. For many judges divorce litigation stretches to the ultimate the great principle that they are to decide according to law and not to sympathy; the cases in this chapter both challenge doctrines firmly established outside the divorce arena and invite inquiry into whether the courts have dealt justifiably in treating or in refusing to treat divorce cases differently.

The decisions essentially raise two general problems, which are considered separately: The first is the protection of the rights of an absent spouse, and the second is the protection of the home state's interest in preserving the marriage.

A. EX PARTE DIVORCE

WILLIAMS V. NORTH CAROLINA [I]

317 U.S. 287 (1942).

MR. JUSTICE DOUGLAS delivered the opinion of the Court.

Petitioners were tried and convicted of bigamous cohabitation under § 4342 of the North Carolina Code, 1939, and each was sentenced for a term of years to a state prison. The judgment of conviction was affirmed by the Supreme Court of North Carolina. 220 N.C. 445, 17 S.E.2d 769. The case is here on certiorari.

Petitioner Williams was married to Carrie Wyke in 1916 in North Carolina and lived with her there until May, 1940. Petitioner Hendrix was married to Thomas Hendrix in 1920 in North Carolina and lived with him there until May, 1940. At that time petitioners went to Las Vegas, Nevada and on June 26, 1940, each filed a divorce action in the Nevada court. The defendants in those divorce actions entered no appearance nor were they served with process in Nevada. In the case of defendant Thomas Hendrix, service by publication was had by publication of the summons in a Las Vegas newspaper and by mailing a copy of the summons and complaint to his last post office address. In the case of defendant Carrie Williams, a North Carolina sheriff delivered to her in North Carolina a copy of the summons and complaint. A decree of divorce was granted petitioner Williams by the Nevada court on August 26, 1940, on the grounds of extreme cruelty, the court finding that "the plaintiff has been and now is a bona fide and continuous resident of the County of Clark, State of Nevada, and had been such resident for more than six weeks immediately preceding the commencement of this action in the manner prescribed by law". The Nevada court granted petitioner Hendrix a divorce on October 4, 1940, on the grounds of wilful neglect and extreme cruelty and made the same finding as to this petitioner's bona fide residence in Nevada as it made in the case of Williams. Petitioners were married to each other in Nevada on October 4, 1940. Thereafter they returned to North Carolina where they lived together until the indictment was returned. Petitioners pleaded not guilty and offered in evidence exemplified copies of the Nevada proceedings, contending that the divorce decrees and the Nevada marriage were valid in North Carolina as well as in Nevada. The State contended that since neither of the defendants in the Nevada actions was served in Nevada nor entered an appearance there, the Nevada decrees would not be recognized as valid in North Carolina. On this issue the court charged the jury in substance that a Nevada divorce decree based on substituted service where the defendant made no appearance would not be recognized in North Carolina. . . The State further contended that petitioners went to Nevada not to establish a bona fide residence but solely for the purpose of taking advantage of the laws of that State to obtain a divorce through fraud upon that court. On that issue the court charged the jury that . . . the defendants had the burden of satisfying the jury, but not beyond a reasonable doubt, of the bona fides of their residence in Nevada for the required time. Petitioners excepted to these charges. The Supreme Court of North Carolina in affirming the judgment held that North Carolina was not required to recognize the Nevada decrees under the full faith and credit clause of the Constitution (Art. IV, § 1) by reason of *Haddock v. Haddock,* 201 U.S. 562. . .

The *Haddock* case involved a suit for separation and alimony brought in New York by the wife on personal service of the husband. The husband pleaded in defense a divorce decree obtained by him in Connecticut where he had established a separate domicil. This Court held that New York, the matrimonial domicil where the wife still resided, need not give full faith and credit to the Connecticut decree, since it was obtained by the husband who wrongfully left his wife in the matrimonial domicil, service on her having been obtained by publication and she not having entered an appearance in the action. But we do not agree with the theory of the *Haddock* case that, so far as the marital status of the parties is concerned, a decree of divorce granted under such circumstances by one state need not be given full faith and credit in another. . .

Chief Justice Marshall stated in *Hampton v. M'Connel,* 3 Wheat. 234, 235, that "the judgment of a state court should have the same credit, validity, and effect, in every other court in the United States, which it had in the state where it was pronounced, and that whatever pleas would be good to a suit thereon in such state, and none others, could be pleaded in any other court in the United States." That view has survived substantially intact. *Fauntleroy v. Lum,* 210 U.S. 230. . . Thus even though the cause of action could not be entertained in the state of the forum either because it had been barred by the local statute of limitations or contravened local policy, the judgment thereon obtained in a sister state is entitled to full faith and credit. See *Christmas v. Russell,* 5 Wall. 290; *Fauntleroy v. Lum,* supra * * *. Some exceptions have been engrafted on the rule laid down by Chief Justice Marshall. But as stated by Mr. Justice Brandeis in *Broderick v. Rosner,* 294 U.S. 629, 642, "the room left for the play of conflicting policies is a narrow one." So far as *judgments* are concerned the decisions,[5] as distinguished from dicta,[6] show that the actual exceptions have been few and far between, apart from *Haddock v. Haddock.* For this Court has been reluctant to admit exceptions in case of *judgments* rendered by the courts of a sister state, since the "very purpose" of Art. IV, § 1 was "to alter the status of the several states as independent foreign sovereignties, each free to ignore obligations created under the laws or by the judicial proceedings of the others, and to make them integral parts of a single nation." . . .

This Court, to be sure, has recognized that in case of *statutes,* "the extrastate effect of which Congress has not prescribed", some "accommodation of the conflicting interests of the two states" is necessary. *Alaska Packers Ass'n v. Industrial Accident Comm.,* 294 U.S. 532, 547. But that principle would come into play only in case the Nevada decrees were assailed on the ground that Nevada must give full faith and credit in its divorce proceedings to the divorce statutes of North Carolina. Even then, it would be of no avail here. For as stated in the *Alaska Packers* case, "Prima facie every state is entitled to enforce in its own courts its own statutes, lawfully enacted. One who challenges that right, because of the force given to a conflicting statute of another state by the full faith and credit clause, assumes the burden of showing, upon some rational basis, that of the conflicting interests involved those of the foreign state are superior to those of the forum." Id., 294 U.S. at pages 547, 548. It is difficult to perceive how North Carolina could be said to have an interest in Nevada's domiciliaries superior to the interest of Nevada. Nor is there any authority which lends support to the view that the full faith and credit clause compels the courts of one state to subordinate the local policy of that state, as respects its domiciliaries, to the statutes of any other state. . .

Moreover, *Haddock v. Haddock* is not based on the contrary theory. Nor did it hold that a decree of divorce granted by the courts of one state need not be given full faith and credit in another if the grounds for the divorce would not be recognized by the courts of the forum. It does not purport to challenge or disturb the rule, earlier established by *Christmas v. Russell,* supra, and subsequently fortified by *Fauntleroy v. Lum,* supra,

[5] *Fall v. Eastin,* 215 U.S. 1; *Olmsted v. Olmsted,* 216 U.S. 386; *Hood v. McGehee,* 237 U.S. 611. These decisions refuse to require courts of one state to allow acts or judgments of another to control the disposition or devolution of realty in the former. They seem to rest on the doctrine that the state where the land is located is "sole mistress" of its rules of real property. . . .

[6] It has been repeatedly stated that the full faith and credit clause does not require one state to enforce the penal laws of another. . . .

But the question of whether a judgment based on a penalty is entitled to full faith and credit was reserved in *Milwaukee County v. M.E. White Co.,* 296 U.S. 268, 279. . . .

that even though the cause of action could not have been entertained in the state of the forum, a judgment obtained thereon in a sister state is entitled to full faith and credit. For the majority opinion in the *Haddock* case accepted both *Cheever v. Wilson,* 9 Wall. 108, and *Atherton v. Atherton,* 181 U.S. 155. *Cheever v. Wilson* held that a decree of divorce granted by a state in which one spouse was domiciled and which had personal jurisdiction over the other was as conclusive in other states as it was in the state where it was obtained. *Atherton v. Atherton* held that full faith and credit must be given a decree of divorce granted by the state of the matrimonial domicil on constructive service against the other spouse who was a non-resident of that state. The decisive difference between those cases and *Haddock v. Haddock* was said to be that in the latter the state granting the divorce had no jurisdiction over the absent spouse, since it was not the state of the matrimonial domicil, but the place where the husband had acquired a separate domicil after having wrongfully left his wife. This Court accordingly classified *Haddock v. Haddock* with that group of cases which hold that when the courts of one state do not have jurisdiction either of the subject matter or of the person of the defendant, the courts of another state are not required by virtue of the full faith and credit clause to enforce the judgment. But such differences in result between *Haddock v. Haddock* and the cases which preceded it rest on distinctions which in our view are immaterial, so far as the full faith and credit clause and the supporting legislation are concerned.

The historical view that a proceeding for a divorce was a proceeding in rem (2 Bishop, Marriage & Divorce, 4th Ed., § 164) was rejected by the *Haddock* case. We likewise agree that it does not aid in the solution of the problem presented by this case to label these proceedings as proceedings in rem. Such a suit, however, is not a mere in personam action. Domicil of the plaintiff, immaterial to jurisdiction in a personal action, is recognized in the *Haddock* case and elsewhere (Beale, Conflict of Laws, § 110.1) as essential in order to give the court jurisdiction which will entitle the divorce decree to extraterritorial effect, at least when the defendant has neither been personally served nor entered an appearance. The findings made in the divorce decrees in the instant case must be treated on the issue before us as meeting those requirements. For it seems clear that the provision of the Nevada statute that a plaintiff in this type of case must "reside" in the State for the required period requires him to have a domicil as distinguished from a mere residence in the state. . . Hence the decrees in this case, like other divorce decrees, are more than in personam judgments. They involve the marital status of the parties. Domicil creates a relationship to the state which is adequate for numerous exercises of state power. . . Each state as a sovereign has a rightful and legitimate concern in the marital status of persons domiciled within its borders. The marriage relation creates problems of large social importance. Protection of offspring, property interests, and the enforcement of marital responsibilities are but a few of the commanding problems in the field of domestic relations with which the state must deal. Thus it is plain that each state by virtue of its command over its domiciliaries and its large interest in the institution of marriage can alter within its own borders the marriage status of the spouse domiciled there, even though the other spouse is absent. There is no constitutional barrier if the form and nature of the substituted service . . . meet the requirements of due process. . . Accordingly it was admitted in the *Haddock* case that the divorce decree, though not recognized in New York, was binding on both spouses in Connecticut where granted. . . It therefore follows that, if the Nevada decrees are taken at their full face value (as they must be on the phase of the case with which we are presently concerned), they were wholly effective to change in that state the marital status of the petitioners and each of the other spouses by the North Carolina marriages. Apart from the requirements of procedural due process . . . not challenged here by North Carolina, no reason based on the Federal Constitution has been advanced for the contrary conclusion. But the concession that the decrees were effective in Nevada makes more compelling the reasons for rejection of the theory and result of the *Haddock* case.

This Court stated in *Atherton v. Atherton,* supra, 181 U.S. at page 162, that "A husband without a wife, or a wife without a husband, is unknown to the law." But if one is lawfully divorced and remarried in Nevada and still married to the first spouse in North Carolina, an even more complicated and serious condition would be realized. . . Under the circumstances of this case, a man would have two wives, a wife two husbands. The reality of a sentence to prison proves that that is no mere play on words. Each would be a bigamist for living in one state with the only one with whom the other state would permit him lawfully to live. Children of the second marriage would be bastards in one state but legitimate in the other. And all that would flow from the legalistic notion that where one spouse is wrongfully deserted he retains power over the matrimonial domicil so that the domicil of the other spouse follows him wherever he may go, while if he is to blame, he retains no such power. . .

It is objected, however, that if such divorce decrees must be given full faith and credit, a substantial dilution of the sovereignty of other states will be effected. For it is pointed out that under such a rule one state's policy of strict control over the institution of marriage could be thwarted by the decree of a more lax state. But such an objection goes to the application of the full faith and credit clause to many situations. It is an objection in varying degrees of intensity to the enforcement of a judgment of a sister state based on a cause of action which could not be enforced in the state of the forum. Mississippi's policy against gambling transactions was overriden in *Fauntleroy v. Lum,* supra, when a Missouri judgment based on such a Mississippi contract was enforced by this Court. Such is part of the price of our federal system.

This Court, of course, is the final arbiter when the question is raised as to what is a permissible limitation on the full faith and credit clause... But the question for us is a limited one. In the first place, we repeat that in this case we must assume that petitioners had a bona fide domicil in Nevada, not that the Nevada domicil was a sham... In the second place, the question as to what is a permissible limitation on the full faith and credit clause does not involve a decision on our part as to which state policy on divorce is the more desirable one. It does not involve selection of a rule which will encourage on the one hand or discourage on the other the practice of divorce. That choice in the realm of morals and religion rests with the legislatures of the states. Our own views as to the marriage institution and the avenues of escape which some states have created are immaterial. It is a Constitution which we are expounding—a Constitution which in no small measure brings separate sovereign states into an integrated whole through the medium of the full faith and credit clause. Within the limits of her political power North Carolina may, of course, enforce her own policy regarding the marriage relation—an institution more basic in our civilization than any other. But society also has an interest in the avoidance of polygamous marriages . . . and in the protection of innocent offspring of marriages deemed legitimate in other jurisdictions. And other states have an equally legitimate concern in the status of persons domiciled there as respects the institution of marriage. So when a court of one state acting in accord with the requirements of procedural due process alters the marital status of one domiciled in that state by granting him a divorce from his absent spouse, we cannot say its decree should be excepted from the full faith and credit clause merely because its enforcement or recognition in another state would conflict with the policy of the latter...

Haddock v. Haddock is overruled. The judgment is reversed and the cause is remanded to the Supreme Court of North Carolina for proceedings not inconsistent with this opinion...

MR. JUSTICE FRANKFURTER, concurring. I join in the opinion of the Court but think it appropriate to add a few words...

It is indisputable that the Nevada decrees here, like the Connecticut decree in the *Haddock* case, were valid and binding in the state where they were rendered... In denying constitutional sanction to such a valid judgment outside the state which rendered it, the *Haddock* decision made an arbitrary break with the past and created distinctions incompatible with the rôle of this Court in enforcing the Full Faith and Credit Clause. Freed from the hopeless refinements introduced by that case, the question before us is simply whether the Nevada decrees were rendered under circumstances that would make them binding against the absent spouses in the state where they were rendered. North Carolina did not challenge the power of Nevada to declare the marital status of persons found to be Nevada residents. North Carolina chose instead to disrespect the consequences of Nevada's exertion of such power. . .

Our occasional pronouncements upon the requirements of the Full Faith and Credit Clause doubtless have little effect upon divorces. Be this as it may, a court is likely to lose its way if it strays outside the modest bounds of its own special competence and turns the duty of adjudicating only the legal phases of a broad social problem into an opportunity for formulating judgments of social policy quite beyond its competence as well as its authority.

MR. JUSTICE JACKSON, dissenting.

I cannot join in exerting the judicial power of the Federal Government to compel the State of North Carolina to subordinate its own law to the Nevada divorce decrees. The Court's decision to do so . . . nullifies the power of each state to protect its own citizens against the dissolution of their marriages by the courts of other states which have an easier system of divorce.

* * *

The opinion concedes that Nevada's judgment could not be forced upon North Carolina in absence of personal service if a divorce proceeding were an action *in personam*. In other words, settled family relationships may be destroyed by a procedure that we would not recognize if the suit were one to collect a grocery bill. . .

It does not seem consistent with our legal system that one who has these continuing rights should be deprived of them without a hearing. Neither does it seem that he or she should be summoned by mail, publication, or otherwise to a remote jurisdiction chosen by the other party and there be obliged to submit marital rights to adjudication under a state policy at odds with that of the state under which the marriage was contracted and the matrimonial domicile was established.

Marriage is often dealt with as a contract. Of course a personal judgment could not be rendered against an absent party on a cause of action arising out of an ordinary commercial contract, without personal service of process. I see no reason why the marriage contract, if such it be considered, should be discriminated against, nor why a party to a marriage contract should be more vulnerable to a foreign judgment without process than a party to any other contract. I agree that the marriage contract is different, but I should think the difference would be in its favor. . .

To hold that the Nevada judgments were not binding in North Carolina because they were rendered without jurisdiction over the North

Carolina spouses, it is not necessary to hold that they were without any conceivable validity. It may be, and probably is, true that Nevada has sufficient interest in the lives of those who sojourn there to free them and their spouses to take new spouses without incurring criminal penalties under Nevada law. I know of nothing in our Constitution that requires Nevada to adhere to traditional concepts of bigamous unions or the legitimacy of the fruit thereof. And the control of a state over property within its borders is so complete that I suppose that Nevada could effectively deal with it in the name of divorce as completely as in any other. But it is quite a different thing to say that Nevada can dissolve the marriages of North Carolinians and dictate the incidence of the bigamy statutes of North Carolina by which North Carolina has sought to protect her own interests as well as theirs. In this case there is no conceivable basis of jurisdiction in the Nevada court over the absent spouses, and, a fortiori, over North Carolina herself. I cannot but think that in its preoccupation with the full faith and credit clause the Court has slighted the due process clause.

Ex Parte Divorce

(1) An "ex parte" divorce is one rendered by a court in the absence of the defendant and without personal jurisdiction over him. Before *Williams I* the understanding was that full faith was required only to those ex parte divorces granted in the state of "matrimonial domicile," and not to those granted in a state to which the plaintiff had moved alone without changing the marital domicile. Many states, however, recognized decrees of the latter type as a matter of comity; *Haddock v. Haddock,* 201 U.S. 562 (1906), merely held (in the context of a claim for support by the non-participating spouse) that the matrimonial domicile was not required by the Constitution to do so. Moreover, if the absent spouse made a personal appearance in the state of the plaintiff's alleged domicile, the decree was entitled to full faith and credit.

(2) It is easy enough to agree with Justice Douglas that a judgment valid in Nevada must be recognized in North Carolina. But notice how he glossed over the critical question whether the decree was valid at all. Is there any answer to Justice Jackson's charge that "settled family relationships may [now] be destroyed by a procedure that we would not recognize if the suit were one to collect a grocery bill"? Isn't the absent spouse's interest in marital status worthy of due-process protection? Although Nevada's interest in the marital status of Nevada domiciliaries may justify the choice of Nevada law, does it justify an assertion of jurisdiction affecting the interests of nonresidents? Isn't *Williams I* inconsistent with the principle of *Hanson v. Denckla,* 357 U.S. 235, 253

(1958), supra, p. 446, that even an interested state may not assert jurisdiction over defendants who have not voluntarily related themselves in some substantial manner to that state? If *Hanson* and *Williams I* are in conflict, which principle should prevail?

(3) Would bigamy prosecutions, even if available, be an effective deterrent to illegal divorces? The persistence of North Carolina in pursuing O.B. Williams and his Nevada playmate, Lillie Hendrix, is partially explained by the fact that their brief sojourn in Nevada was preceded and followed by longtime residence in a small town in North Carolina, where O.B. operated a store in which Lillie's husband was employed as a clerk. Apparently the reappearance in Granite Falls, N.C. of the two as purported husband and wife only a few short months after their simultaneous departure for the Alamo Motor Court in Las Vegas (leaving behind two spouses and four children) raised more than a few eyebrows. How often, however, will a busy prosecutor be inclined to vindicate a state's interest with the drastic remedy of a bigamy prosecution? Don't the harshness of the bigamy alternative and the unlikelihood of its use support an argument that collateral attack should be available to interested private persons? Isn't it obvious that the interest of North Carolina should not be sacrificed to a Nevada proceeding in which, as one wit has put it, the absconding spouses "litigate by day and copulate by night, *inter sese* and *pendente lite*?" Adams & Adams, *Ethical Problems in Advising Migratory Divorce,* 16 Hastings L.J. 60, 100 (1964). For a wonderfully entertaining discussion of the *Williams* litigation and migratory divorce in general, see Powell, *And Repent At Leisure,* 58 Harv.L.Rev. 930 (1945).

ESTIN V. ESTIN

334 U.S. 541 (1948).

MR. JUSTICE DOUGLAS delivered the opinion of the Court.

This case, here on certiorari to the Court of Appeals of New York, presents an important question under the Full Faith and Credit Clause of the Constitution. Article IV, § 1. It is whether a New York decree awarding respondent $180 per month for her maintenance and support in a separation proceeding survived a Nevada divorce decree which subsequently was granted petitioner.

The parties were married in 1937 and lived together in New York until 1942 when the husband left the wife. There was no issue of the marriage. In 1943 she brought an action against him for a separation. He entered a general appearance. The court, finding that he had abandoned her, granted her a decree of separation and awarded her $180 per month as permanent alimony. In January 1944 he went to Nevada where in 1945 he instituted an action for divorce. She was notified of the action by constructive service but entered no appearance in it. In May 1945, the Nevada court, finding that petitioner had been a bona fide resident of Nevada since January 30, 1944, granted him an absolute divorce "on the ground of three years continual separation, without cohabitation." The Nevada decree made no provision for alimony, though the Nevada court had been advised of the New York decree.

Prior to that time petitioner had made payments of alimony under the New York decree. After entry of the Nevada decree he ceased paying. Thereupon respondent sued in New York for a supplementary judgment for the amount of the arrears. Petitioner appeared in the action and moved to eliminate the alimony provisions of the separation decree by reason of the Nevada decree. The Supreme Court denied the motion and granted respondent judgment for the arrears. . . The judgment was affirmed . . . by the Court of Appeals. 296 N.Y. 308, 73 N.E.2d 113.

We held in *Williams v. North Carolina,* 317 U.S. 287, that a divorce decree granted by a State to one of its domiciliaries is entitled to full faith and credit in a bigamy prosecution brought in another State, even though the other spouse was given notice of the divorce proceeding only through constructive service. . .

Petitioner's argument . . . is that the tail must go with the hide—that since by the Nevada decree, recognized in New York, he and respondent are no longer husband and wife, no legal incidence of the marriage remains. . .

The difficulty with that argument is that the highest court in New York has held in this case that a support order can survive divorce and that this one has survived petitioner's divorce. That conclusion is binding on us, except as it conflicts with the Full Faith and Credit Clause. . . The only question for us is whether New York is powerless to make such a ruling in view of the Nevada decree.

We can put to one side the case where the wife was personally served or where she appears in the divorce proceedings. . . The only service on her in this case was by publication and she made no appearance in the Nevada proceeding. The requirements of procedural due process were satisfied and the domicile of the husband in Nevada was foundation for a decree effecting a change in the marital capacity of both parties in all the other States of the Union, as well as in Nevada. *Williams v. North Carolina,* 317 U.S. 287. But the fact that marital capacity was changed does not mean that every other legal incident of the marriage was necessarily affected.

Although the point was not adjudicated in *Barber v. Barber,* 21 How. 582, 588, the Court in that case recognized that while a divorce decree obtained in Wisconsin by a husband from his absent wife might dissolve the vinculum of the marriage, it did not mean that he was freed from payment of alimony under an earlier separation decree granted by New York. An absolutist might quarrel with the result and demand a rule that once a divorce is granted, the whole of the marriage relation is dissolved, leaving no roots or tendrils of any kind. But there are few areas of the law in black and white. The greys are dominant and even among them the shades are innumerable. For the eternal problem of the law is one of making accommodations between conflicting interests. This is why most legal problems end as questions of degree. That is true of the present problem under the Full Faith and Credit Clause. The question involves important considerations both of law and of policy which it is essential to state.

The situations where a judgment of one State has been denied full faith and credit in another State, because its enforcement would contravene the latter's policy, have been few and far between. . . The fact that the requirements of full faith and credit, so far as judgments are concerned, are exacting, if not inexorable . . ., does not mean, however, that the State of the domicile of one spouse may, through the use of constructive service, enter a decree that changes every legal incidence of the marriage relationship.

Marital status involves the regularity and integrity of the marriage relation. It affects the legitimacy of the offspring of marriage. It is the basis of criminal laws, as the bigamy prosecution in *Williams v. North Carolina* dramatically illustrates. The State has a considerable interest in preventing bigamous marriages and in protecting the offspring of marriages from being bastardized. The interest of the State extends to its domiciliaries. The State should have the power to guard its interest in them by changing or altering their marital status and by protecting them in that changed status throughout the farthest reaches of the nation. For a person domiciled in one State should not be allowed to suffer the penalties of bigamy for living outside the State with the only one which the State of his domicile recognizes as his lawful wife. And children born of the only marriage which is lawful in the State of his domicile should not carry the stigma of bastardy when they move elsewhere. These are matters of legitimate concern to the State of the domicile. They entitle the State of the domicile to bring in the absent spouse through constructive service. In no other way could the State of the domicile have and maintain effective control of the marital status of its domiciliaries.

Those are the considerations that have long permitted the State of the matrimonial domicile to change the marital status of the parties by an ex parte divorce proceeding. . . But those considerations have little relevancy here. In this case New York evinced a concern with this broken marriage when both parties were domiciled in New York and before Nevada had any concern with it. New York was rightly concerned lest the abandoned spouse be left impoverished and perhaps become a public charge. The problem of her livelihood and support is plainly a matter in which her community had a legitimate interest. The New York court, having jurisdiction over both parties, undertook to protect her by granting her a judgment of permanent alimony. Nevada, however, apparently follows the rule that dissolution of the marriage puts an end to a support order. . . But the question is whether Nevada could under any circumstances adjudicate rights of respondent under the New York judgment when she was not personally served or did not appear in the proceeding. *Bassett v. Bassett,* 9 Cir., 141 F.2d 954, held that Nevada could not. We agree with that view.

The New York judgment is a property interest of respondent, created by New York in a proceeding in which both parties were present. It imposed obligations on petitioner and granted rights to respondent. The property interest which it created was an intangible, jurisdiction over which cannot be exerted through control over a physical thing. Jurisdiction over an intangible can indeed only arise from control or power over the persons whose relationships are the source of the rights and obligations. Cf. *Curry v. McCanless,* 307 U.S. 357, 366.

Jurisdiction over a debtor is sufficient to give the State of his domicile some control over the debt which he owes. . . But we are aware of no power which the State of domicile of the debtor has to determine the personal rights of the creditor in the intangible unless the creditor has been personally served or appears in the proceeding. The existence of any such power has been repeatedly denied. *Pennoyer v. Neff,* 95 U.S. 714; *Hart v. Sansom,* 110 U.S. 151; *New York Life Ins. Co. v. Dunlevy,* 241 U.S. 518.

We know of no source of power which would take the present case out of that category. The Nevada decree that is said to wipe out respondent's claim for alimony under the New York judgment is nothing less than an attempt by Nevada to restrain respondent from asserting her claim under that judgment. That is an attempt to exercise an in personam jurisdiction over a person not before the court. That may not be done. Since Nevada had no power to adjudicate respondent's rights in the New York judgment, New York need not give full faith and credit to that phase of Nevada's judgment. A judgment of a court having no jurisdiction to render it is not entitled to the full faith and credit which the Constitution and statute of the United States demand. . .

The result in this situation is to make the divorce divisible—to give effect to the Nevada decree insofar as it affects marital status and to make it ineffective on the issue of alimony. It accommodates the interests of both Nevada and New York in this broken marriage by restricting each State to the matters of her dominant concern.

Since Nevada had no jurisdiction to alter respondent's rights in the New York judgment, we do not reach the further question whether in any event that judgment would be entitled to full faith and credit in Nevada. . . And it will be time enough to consider the effect of any discrimination shown to out-of-state ex parte divorces when a State makes that its policy.

Affirmed.

MR. JUSTICE FRANKFURTER, dissenting. . .

Nevada did not purport, so far as the record discloses, to rule on the survival of the New York separate maintenance decree. Nevada merely established a change in status. It was for New York to determine the effect, with reference to its own law, of that change in status. If it was the law of New York that divorce put an end to its separate maintenance decree, the respondent's decree would have been terminated not by the Nevada divorce but by the consequences, under the New York law, of a change in status, even though brought about by Nevada. Similarly, Nevada could not adjudicate rights in New York realty, but, if New York law provided for dower, a Nevada divorce might or might not terminate a dower interest in New York realty depending on whether or not New York treated dower rights as extinguished by divorce.

If the Nevada decree, insofar as it affected the New York separate maintenance decree, were violative of due process, New York of course would not have to give effect to it. It could not do so even if it wished. If the Nevada decree involved a violation of due process there is an end of the matter and other complicated issues need not be considered! It would not matter whether New York had a special interest in preventing its residents from becoming public charges, or whether New York treated maintenance decrees as surviving a valid divorce.

Accordingly, the crucial issue, as I see it, is whether New York has held that *no* "ex parte" divorce decree could terminate a prior New York separate maintenance decree, or whether it has decided merely that no "ex parte" divorce decree of another State could. The opinion of the Court of Appeals leaves this crucial issue in doubt. . . New York may legitimately decline to allow any "ex parte" divorce to dissolve its prior separate maintenance decree, but it may not, consistently with *Williams v. North Carolina*, 317 U.S. 287, discriminate against a Nevada decree granted to one there domiciled, and afford it less effect than it gives to a decree of its own with similar jurisdictional foundation. I cannot be sure which it has done. . .

I would therefore remand the case to the New York Court of Appeals for clarification of its rationale. . .

MR. JUSTICE JACKSON, dissenting.

If there is one thing that the people are entitled to expect from their lawmakers, it is rules of law that will enable individuals to tell whether they are married and, if so, to whom. Today many people who have simply lived in more than one state do not know, and the most learned lawyer cannot advise them with any confidence. The uncertainties that result are not merely technical, nor are they trivial; they affect fundamental rights and relations such as the lawfulness of their cohabitation, their children's legitimacy, their title to property, and even whether they are law-abiding persons or criminals. In a society as mobile and nomadic as ours, such uncertainties affect large numbers of people and create a social problem of some magnitude. It is therefore important that, whatever we do, we shall not add to the confusion. I think that this decision does just that. . .

The New York judgment of separation is based on the premise that the parties remain husband and wife, though estranged, and hence the obligation of support, incident to marriage, continues. The Nevada decree is based on the contrary premise that the marriage no longer exists and so obligations dependent on it have ceased.

The Court reaches the Solomon-like conclusion that the Nevada decree is half good and half bad under the full faith and credit clause. It is good to free the husband from the marriage; it is not good to free him from its incidental obligations. Assuming the judgment to be one which the Constitution requires to be recognized at all, I do not see how we can square this decision with the command that it be given full faith and credit. For reasons which I stated in dissenting in *Williams v. North Carolina,* 317 U.S. 287, I would not give standing under the clause to constructive service divorces obtained on short residence. But if we are to hold this divorce good, I do not see how it can be less good than a divorce would be if rendered by the courts of New York.

As I understand New York law, if, after a decree of separation and alimony, the husband had obtained a New York divorce against his wife, it would terminate her right to alimony. If the Nevada judgment is to have full faith and credit, I think it must have the same effect that a similar New York decree would have. I do not see how we can hold that it must be accepted for some purposes and not for others, that he is free of his former marriage but still may be jailed as he may in New York, for not paying the maintenance of a woman whom the Court is compelled to consider as no longer his wife.

Divisible Divorce

(1) The concept of "divisible divorce," first suggested by Justice Douglas in a concurring opinion in *Esenwein v. Pennsylvania ex rel. Esenwein,* 325 U.S. 279, 281 (1945), commanded a majority of the Court in *Estin v. Estin.* Does divisible divorce rest upon the ground that the state of marital domicile, since it has the dominant interest insofar as the economic aspects of the marriage are involved, need not give full faith and credit to these incidents of an out-of-state ex parte divorce decree? Or upon the ground that the prior New York judgment created a property interest in the wife that could not be destroyed elsewhere without personal jurisdiction over her?

(2) Would the result in *Estin* have been the same if the wife's claim for support had not been reduced to judgment in New York prior to the Nevada divorce proceeding? This question was decided in *Vanderbilt v. Vanderbilt,* 354 U.S. 416 (1957), in which a California couple separated in California. The wife moved to New York, while the husband went to Nevada and obtained an ex parte divorce decree that made no provision for alimony payments to the wife. Thereafter, the wife filed suit for support in New York, sequestering the husband's property located there. New York entered a support order regardless of the fact that the marriage had been terminated. The Supreme Court, over dissents by Justices Frankfurter and Harlan, affirmed the New York award, reasoning that Nevada could not terminate the wife's right to support in the absence of personal jurisdiction over her. As a jurisdictional matter, did the wife's sequestration proceeding survive *Shaffer* v. *Heitner*?

(3) The Court faced Justice Frankfurter's dower hypothetical in *Simons v. Miami Beach First Nat'l Bank,* 381 U.S. 81 (1965). Following a New York separation decree awarded to his wife in 1946, Sol Simons moved to Florida in 1951 and obtained an ex parte divorce decree there in 1952. He died in Florida in 1960. His former wife claimed dower under Florida law, arguing that *Estin* dictated that the Florida courts give effect to the New York separation decree, which inherently preserved her dower rights. The Supreme Court in an opinion by Justice Brennan affirmed the judgment of a Florida court dismissing her action after trial. He reasoned in part that:

> The short answer to this contention is that the only obligation imposed on Sol Simons by the New York decree, and the only rights granted petitioner under it, concerned monthly alimony for petitioner's support. Unlike the ex-husband in *Estin,* Sol Simons made the support payments called for by the separate maintenance decree notwithstanding his ex parte divorce. In making these payments until his death he complied with the full measure of the New York decree; when he died there was consequently nothing left of the New York decree for Florida to dishonor.
>
> This conclusion embodies our judgment that there is nothing in the New York decree itself that can be construed as creating or preserving any interest in the nature of or in lieu of dower in any property of the decedent, wherever located. Petitioner refers us to no New York law that treats such a decree as having that effect, or, for that matter, to any New York law that has such an effect irrespective of the existence of the decree. We think it clear that

the burden of showing this rested upon petitioner. . . It follows that insofar as petitioner's argument rests on rights created by the New York decree or by New York law, the denial of her dower by the Florida courts was not a violation of the Full Faith and Credit Clause. Cf. *Armstrong v. Armstrong,* 350 U.S. 568.

Insofar as petitioner argues that since she was not subject to the jurisdiction of the Florida divorce court its decree could not extinguish any dower right existing under Florida law, *Vanderbilt v. Vanderbilt,* 354 U.S. 416, 418, the answer is that under Florida law no dower right survived the decree. The Supreme Court of Florida has said that dower rights in Florida property, being inchoate, are extinguished by a divorce decree predicated upon substituted or constructive service. *Pawley v. Pawley,* Fla., 46 So.2d 464.

It follows that the Florida courts transgressed no constitutional bounds in denying petitioner dower in her ex-husband's Florida estate.

Is *Simons* inconsistent with *Vanderbilt*? Justice Harlan argued that *Simons* made a "partial retreat" from *Vanderbilt* because Florida was "allowed to turn property rights on its ex parte decree." Justices Black and Douglas, concurring, disputed that interpretation, arguing instead that Mrs. Simons's Florida dower rights "simply never came into existence," because she was not Mr. Simons's widow when he died. Who has it right? Why does it matter?

(4) The tension between *Estin, Vanderbilt,* and *Simons* reappeared in the context of pension rights in *Kahn v. Kahn,* 801 F.Supp. 1237 (S.D.N.Y. 1992). Miriam and Alfred Kahn were married in 1949. During the marriage, he was employed as a professor at Columbia University. One of the fringe benefits of his employment was a TIAA-CREF retirement annuity. In 1974, he sought to divorce his wife in New York, but failed to prove the ground of cruel and inhuman treatment. He was, however, ordered to pay Miriam $500 per week in spousal support. Thereafter, he moved to New Jersey and obtained an ex parte no-fault divorce in 1979. Ten years later, he retired, and elected to receive annuity benefits under a single life option. Miriam, arguing that the New Jersey divorce judgment did not affect her legal rights as a spouse to share in Alfred's pension, sought to require him to elect a joint and survivor annuity option pursuant to the Employee Retirement Income Security Act of 1974 (ERISA) as amended by the Retirement Equity Act of 1984 (REA). Alfred invoked *Simons,* arguing that Miriam's right to demand a joint and survivor option never came into existence because she was no longer his spouse when REA became effective; Miriam relied on *Estin,* arguing that New Jersey lacked personal jurisdiction over her and its decree could not terminate her property rights. Who was right? The court agreed with Alfred: the New Jersey ex parte decree, by severing the marital bond, had affected Miriam's status as a current spouse. It followed under *Simons* that her spousal right under ERISA/REA to compel him to choose a joint and survivor option did not survive the New Jersey decree. Does this ruling correctly interpret *Simons*? Does it sustain Justice Harlan's or Justice Black's view of the effect of *Simons* on *Vanderbilt*?

(5) In *May v. Anderson,* 345 U.S. 528 (1953), the Court's attempt to apply the divisible divorce doctrine to the question of child custody was marred by the lack of a clear holding. The case involved a couple who had lived in Wisconsin with their children during the marriage. After marital difficulties arose, they agreed in December of 1946 that the wife and children would go to Ohio to think matters over. On New Year's Day, the wife informed her husband that she did not intend to return, and he filed suit in Wisconsin a few days later seeking both a divorce and custody of the children. The wife was served personally in Ohio, but did not appear in the Wisconsin proceeding, which resulted in a divorce and an award of custody to the husband with reasonable visitation to the wife. Thereafter, the husband went to Ohio and brought the children back to Wisconsin, where they remained between 1947 and 1951. On July 1, 1951, the father permitted the children to visit their mother in Ohio. This time, when he demanded their return, she refused to give them up. The father filed a petition for habeas corpus in the Probate Court of Columbiana County, Ohio. Under Ohio procedure, that writ tests only the immediate right to possession of the children, neither affording the opportunity for modification of a prior decree nor for an initial determination of the future custody of children. Ultimately, the Probate Court decided that it was obliged by the Full Faith and Credit Clause to accept the Wisconsin decree as binding on the mother.

The Supreme Court, by a 5-to-3 vote, reversed. The flavor of Justice Burton's opinion is captured in the following paragraphs:

> Separated as our issue is from that of the future interests of the children, we have before us the elemental question whether a court of a state, where a mother is neither domiciled, resident nor present, may cut off her immediate right to the care, custody, management and companionship of her minor children without having jurisdiction over her in personam. Rights far more precious to appellant than property rights will be cut off if she is to be bound by the Wisconsin award of custody.
>
> "[I]t is now too well settled to be open to further dispute that the 'full faith and credit' clause and the act of Congress passed pursuant to it do not entitle a judgment in personam to extraterritorial effect if it be made to appear that it was rendered

> without jurisdiction over the person sought to be bound." *Baker v. Baker, Eccles & Co.*, 242 U.S. 394, 401, and see 403; *Thompson v. Whitman,* 18 Wall. 457; *D'Arcy v. Ketchum,* 11 How. 165.
>
> In *Estin v. Estin,* supra, and *Kreiger v. Kreiger,* supra, this Court upheld the validity of a Nevada divorce obtained ex parte by a husband, resident in Nevada, insofar as it dissolved the bonds of matrimony. At the same time, we held Nevada powerless to cut off, in that proceeding, a spouse's right to financial support under the prior decree of another state. In the instant case, we recognize that a mother's right to custody of her children is a personal right entitled to at least as much protection as her right to alimony.
>
> In the instant case, the Ohio courts gave weight to appellee's contention that the Wisconsin award of custody binds appellant because, at the time it was issued, her children had a technical domicile in Wisconsin, although they were neither resident nor present there. We find it unnecessary to determine the children's legal domicile because, even if it be with their father, that does not give Wisconsin, certainly as against Ohio, the personal jurisdiction that it must have in order to deprive their mother of her personal right to their immediate possession.

345 U.S., at 533–34.

Justice Frankfurter, who said he joined Justice Burton's "opinion of the Court," added a concurring opinion purporting to explain it. Justice Frankfurter's concurrence reads in part as follows:

> What is decided—the only thing the Court decides—is that the Full Faith and Credit Clause does not require Ohio, in disposing of the custody of children in Ohio, to accept, in the circumstances before us, the disposition made by Wisconsin. The Ohio Supreme Court felt itself so bound. This Court does not decide that Ohio would be precluded from recognizing, as a matter of local law, the disposition made by the Wisconsin court. For Ohio to give respect to the Wisconsin decree would not offend the Due Process Clause. Ohio is no more precluded from doing so than a court of Ontario or Manitoba would be, were the mother to bring the children into one of these provinces. . . [T]he child's welfare in a custody case has such a claim upon the State that its responsibility is obviously not to be foreclosed by a prior adjudication reflecting another State's discharge of its responsibility at another time. . .

345 U.S., at 535–36.

Justice Jackson, dissenting, warned that

> I fear this decision will author new confusions. The interpretative concurrence, if it be a true interpretation, seems to reduce the law

> of custody to a rule of seize-and-run. I would affirm the decision of the Ohio courts that they should respect the judgment of the Wisconsin court, until it or some other court with equal or better claims to jurisdiction shall modify it.

345 U.S., at 539, 542.

Could Wisconsin have constitutionally asserted jurisdiction over the mother based on her former domicile there or on the basis of her substantial contacts with the state? Does Justice Burton explain why personal jurisdiction over a leave-taking parent is essential to resolve the question of the children's future custody? Is there anything to be said for Justice Frankfurter's position that Ohio need not respect the Wisconsin decree even if it was valid and enforceable in Wisconsin?

As Justices Jackson and Reed feared, *May v. Anderson* created chaos in the area of interstate child custody litigation. The Uniform Child Custody Jurisdiction Act (UCCJA) was drafted to provide stability for children caught in the morass of migratory divorce. That Act has now been replaced by the Uniform Child Custody Jurisdiction and Enforcement Act (UCCJEA). Both Uniform Acts, and the federal statute, the Parental Kidnapping Prevention Act (PKPA), are discussed infra at pp. 713–752.

(6) Does the divisible-divorce doctrine ameliorate or eliminate the harshness of *Williams I* in terminating the marriage of a stay-at-home spouse? See D. Currie, *Suitcase Divorce in the Conflict of Laws:* Simons, Rosenstiel, *and* Borax, 34 U. Chi. L. Rev. 26, 29 (1966):

> . . . In the light of *Estin, Vanderbilt,* and *May,* it is arguable that the absent spouses in *Williams I* were not injured by the Nevada divorces. Their rights to claim custody or support were unaffected, and their 'marriages' existed in name only; divorce or no, the state does not force unwilling people to live together. Thus, the divorces served Nevada's interest in freeing the Nevada spouses from impediments to remarriage, and arguably did not inflict substantial harm on the stay-at-home defendants.

But *Simons* destroys this argument, doesn't it? Does *Simons* therefore demonstrate that *Williams I* was wrong?

(7) Support and custody, at issue in the cases before *Simons,* could have been sought, at the cost of inconvenience, in the divorcing court; but Mrs. Simons, it might be argued, was not disadvantaged by the remoteness of the Florida forum because she could not have got dower even if she had appeared. Is it an answer to point out that, had she appeared, she might have protected her dower interest by arguing against the divorce itself? That she was disadvantaged by being subjected to lenient Florida divorce law, in that she could have kept her marital status, and therefore her expectancy, absent Florida jurisdiction, simply by remaining in New York?

B. DIVORCE BY CONSENT

WILLIAMS V. NORTH CAROLINA [II]

325 U.S. 226 (1945).

MR. JUSTICE FRANKFURTER delivered the opinion of the Court.

This case is here to review judgments of the Supreme Court of North Carolina, affirming convictions for bigamous cohabitation, assailed on the ground that full faith and credit, as required by the Constitution of the United States, was not accorded divorces decreed by one of the courts of Nevada. *Williams v. North Carolina,* 317 U.S. 287, decided an earlier aspect of the controversy. It was there held that a divorce granted by Nevada, on a finding that one spouse was domiciled in Nevada, must be respected in North Carolina, where Nevada's finding of domicil was not questioned though the other spouse had neither appeared nor been served with process in Nevada and though recognition of such a divorce offended the policy of North Carolina. The record then before us did not present the question whether North Carolina had the power "to refuse full faith and credit to Nevada divorce decrees because, contrary to the findings of the Nevada court, North Carolina finds that no bona fide domicil was acquired in Nevada." *Williams v. North Carolina,* supra, 317 U.S. at page 302. This is the precise issue which has emerged after retrial of the cause following our reversal. Its obvious importance brought the case here. * * *

The implications of the Full Faith and Credit Clause, Article IV, Section 1 of the Constitution, first received the sharp analysis of this Court in *Thompson v. Whitman,* 18 Wall. 457. Theretofore, uncritical notions about the scope of that Clause had been expressed in the early case of *Mills v. Duryee,* 7 Cranch 481. The "doctrine" of that case, as restated in another early case, was that "the judgment of a state court should have the same credit, validity, and effect in every other court in the United States, which it had in the state where it was pronounced." *Hampton v. McConnel,* 3 Wheat. 234, 235. This utterance, when put to the test, as it was in *Thompson v. Whitman,* supra, was found to be too loose. *Thompson v. Whitman* made it clear that the doctrine of *Mills v. Duryee* comes into operation only when, in the language of Kent, "the jurisdiction of the court in another state is not impeached, either as to the subject matter or the person." Only then is "the record of the judgment . . . entitled to full faith and credit." . . .

Under our system of law, judicial power to grant a divorce—jurisdiction, strictly speaking—is founded on domicil. *Bell v. Bell,* 181 U.S. 175; *Andrews v. Andrews,* 188 U.S. 14. The framers of the Constitution were familiar with this jurisdictional prerequisite, and since 1789 neither this Court nor any other court in the English-speaking world has questioned it. Domicil implies a nexus between person and place of such permanence as to control the creation of legal relations and responsibilities of the utmost significance. The domicil of one spouse within a State gives power to that State, we have held, to dissolve a marriage wheresoever contracted. In view of *Williams v. North Carolina,* supra, the jurisdictional requirement of domicil is freed from confusing refinements about "matrimonial domicil", see *Davis v. Davis,* 305 U.S. 32, 41, and the like. Divorce, like marriage, is of concern not merely to the immediate parties. It affects personal rights of the deepest significance. It also touches basic interests of society. Since divorce, like marriage, creates a new status, every consideration of policy makes it desirable that the effect should be the same wherever the question arises.

It is one thing to reopen an issue that has been settled after appropriate opportunity to present their contentions has been afforded to all who had an interest in its adjudication. This applies also to jurisdictional questions. After a contest these cannot be relitigated as between the parties. *Forsyth v. Hammond,* 166 U.S. 506, 517; *Chicago Life Ins. Co. v. Cherry,* 244 U.S. 25, 30; *Davis v. Davis,* supra. But those not parties to a litigation ought not to be foreclosed by the interested actions of others; especially not a State which is concerned with the vindication of its own social policy and has no means, certainly no effective means, to protect that interest against the selfish action of those outside its borders. The State of domiciliary origin should not be bound by an unfounded, even if not collusive, recital in the record of a court of another State. As to the truth or existence of a fact, like that of domicil, upon which depends the power to exert judicial authority, a State not a party to the exertion of such judicial authority in another State but seriously affected by it has a right, when asserting its own unquestioned authority, to ascertain the truth or existence of that crucial fact.[6]

These considerations of policy are equally applicable whether power was assumed by the court of the first State or claimed after inquiry. This may lead, no doubt, to conflicting determinations of what judicial power is founded upon. Such conflict is inherent in the practical application of the concept of domicil in the context of our federal system.[7] . . . What was said in *Worcester County Trust Co. v. Riley* . . . is pertinent here. "Neither the Fourteenth Amendment nor the full faith and credit clause . . . requires uniformity in the decisions of the courts of different states as to the place of domicil, where the exertion of state power is dependent upon domicil within its boundaries." 302 U.S. 292, 299. If a finding by the court of one State that domicil in another State has been abandoned were conclusive upon the old domiciliary State, the policy of each State in matters of most

---

[6] We have not here a situation where a State disregards the adjudication of another State on the issue of domicil squarely litigated in a truly adversary proceeding.

[7] Since an appeal to the Full Faith and Credit Clause raises questions arising under the Constitution of the United States, the proper criteria for ascertaining domicil, should these be in dispute, become matters for federal determination. * * *

intimate concern could be subverted by the policy of every other State. This Court has long ago denied the existence of such destructive power. The issue has a far reach. For domicil is the foundation of probate jurisdiction precisely as it is that of divorce. . .

Although it is now settled that a suit for divorce is not an ordinary adversary proceeding, it does not promote analysis, as was recently pointed out, to label divorce proceedings as actions in rem. *Williams v. North Carolina,* supra, 317 U.S. at page 297. But insofar as a divorce decree partakes of some of the characteristics of a decree in rem, it is misleading to say that all the world is party to a proceeding in rem. . .

All the world is not party to a divorce proceeding. What is true is that all the world need not be present before a court granting the decree and yet it must be respected by the other forty-seven States provided—and it is a big proviso—the conditions for the exercise of power by the divorce-decreeing court are validly established whenever that judgment is elsewhere called into question. In short, the decree of divorce is a conclusive adjudication of everything except the jurisdictional facts upon which it is founded, and domicil is a jurisdictional fact. To permit the necessary finding of domicil by one State to foreclose all States in the protection of their social institutions would be intolerable.

But to endow each State with controlling authority to nullify the power of a sister State to grant a divorce based upon a finding that one spouse had acquired a new domicil within the divorcing State would, in the proper functioning of our federal system, be equally indefensible. No State court can assume comprehensive attention to the various and potentially conflicting interests that several States may have in the institutional aspects of marriage. The necessary accommodation between the right of one State to safeguard its interest in the family relation of its own people and the power of another State to grant divorces can be left to neither State.

The problem is to reconcile the reciprocal respect to be accorded by the members of the Union to their adjudications with due regard for another most important aspect of our federalism whereby "the domestic relations of husband and wife . . . were matters reserved to the States." . . . The rights that belong to all the States and the obligations which membership in the Union imposes upon all, are made effective because this Court is open to consider claims, such as this case presents, that the courts of one State have not given the full faith and credit to the judgment of a sister State that is required by Art. IV, § 1 of the Constitution.

But the discharge of this duty does not make of this Court a court of probate and divorce. Neither a rational system of law nor hard practicality calls for our independent determination, in reviewing the judgment of a State court, of that rather elusive relation between person and place which establishes domicil. . . The challenged judgment must, however, satisfy our scrutiny that the reciprocal duty of respect owed by the States to one another's adjudications has been fairly discharged, and has not been evaded under the guise of finding an absence of domicil and therefore a want of power in the court rendering the judgment.

What is immediately before us is the judgment of the Supreme Court of North Carolina, 224 N.C. 183, 29 S.E.2d 744. We have authority to upset it only if there is want of foundation for the conclusion that that Court reached. The conclusion it reached turns on its finding that the spouses who obtained the Nevada decrees were not domiciled there. The fact that the Nevada court found that they were domiciled there is entitled to respect, and more. The burden of undermining the verity which the Nevada decrees import rests heavily upon the assailant. But simply because the Nevada court found that it had power to award a divorce decree cannot, we have seen, foreclose reexamination by another State. Otherwise, as was pointed out long ago, a court's record would establish its power and the power would be proved by the record. Such circular reasoning would give one State a control over all the other States which the Full Faith and Credit Clause certainly did not confer. *Thompson v. Whitman,* supra. If this Court finds that proper weight was accorded to the claims of power by the court of one State in rendering a judgment the validity of which is pleaded in defense in another State, that the burden of overcoming such respect by disproof of the substratum of fact—here domicil—on which such power alone can rest was properly charged against the party challenging the legitimacy of the judgment, that such issue of fact was left for fair determination by appropriate procedure, and that a finding adverse to the necessary foundation for any valid sister-State judgment was amply supported in evidence, we cannot upset the judgment before us. And we cannot do so even if we also found in the record of the court of original judgment warrant for its finding that it had jurisdiction. If it is a matter turning on local law, great deference is owed by the courts of one State to what a court of another State has done. . . But when we are dealing as here with an historic notion common to all English-speaking courts, that of domicil, we should not find a want of deference to a sister State on the part of a court of another State which finds an absence of domicil where such a conclusion is warranted by the record.

When this case was first here, North Carolina did not challenge the finding of the Nevada court that petitioners had acquired domicils in Nevada. . . Upon retrial, however, the existence of domicil in Nevada became the decisive issue. The judgments of conviction now under review bring before us a record which may be fairly summarized by saying that the petitioners left North Carolina for the purpose of getting divorces from their respective spouses in Nevada and as soon as each had done so and married one another they left Nevada and returned to North Carolina to live there together as man and wife. Against the charge of bigamous cohabitation under § 14–183 of the North Carolina General Statutes, petitioners stood on their Nevada divorces and offered exemplified copies of the Nevada proceedings. The trial judge charged that the State had the burden of proving beyond a reasonable doubt that (1) each petitioner was lawfully married to one person; (2) thereafter each petitioner contracted a second marriage with another person living outside North Carolina; (3) the spouses of petitioners were living at the time of this second marriage; (4) petitioners cohabited with one another in North Carolina after the second marriage. The burden, it was charged, then devolved upon petitioners "to satisfy the trial jury, not beyond a reasonable doubt nor by the greater weight of the evidence, but simply to satisfy" the jury from all the evidence, that petitioners were domiciled in Nevada at the time they obtained their divorces. The court further charged that "the recitation" of bona fide domicil in the Nevada decree was "prima facie evidence" sufficient to warrant a finding of domicil in Nevada but not compelling "such an inference". If the jury found, as they were told, that petitioners had domicils in North Carolina and went to Nevada "simply and solely for the purpose of obtaining" divorces, intending to return to North Carolina on obtaining them, they never lost their North Carolina domicils nor acquired new domicils in Nevada. Domicil, the jury was instructed, was that place where a person "has voluntarily fixed his abode . . . not for a mere special or temporary purpose, but with a present intention of making it his home, either permanently or for an indefinite or unlimited length of time."

The scales of justice must not be unfairly weighted by a State when full faith and credit is claimed for a sister-State judgment. But North Carolina has not so dealt with the Nevada decrees. She has not raised unfair barriers to their recognition. North Carolina did not fail in appreciation or application of federal standards of full faith and credit. Appropriate weight was given to the finding of domicil in the Nevada decrees, and that finding was allowed to be overturned only by relevant standards of proof. There is nothing to suggest that the issue was not fairly submitted to the jury and that it was not fairly assessed on cogent evidence. . .

In seeking a decree of divorce outside the State in which he has theretofore maintained his marriage, a person is necessarily involved in the legal situation created by our federal system whereby one State can grant a divorce of validity in other States only if the applicant has a bona fide domicil in the State of the court purporting to dissolve a prior legal marriage. The petitioners therefore assumed the risk that this Court would find that North Carolina justifiably concluded that they had not been domiciled in Nevada. . . A man's fate often depends, as for instance in the enforcement of the Sherman Law, on far greater risks that he will estimate "rightly, that is, as the jury subsequently estimates it, some matter of degree. If his judgment is wrong, not only may he incur a fine or a short imprisonment, as here; he may incur the penalty of death." . . . Mistaken notions about one's legal rights are not sufficient to bar prosecution for crime.

We conclude that North Carolina was not required to yield her State policy because a Nevada court found that petitioners were domiciled in Nevada when it granted them decrees of divorce. North Carolina was entitled to find, as she did, that they did not acquire domicils in Nevada and that the Nevada court was therefore without power to liberate the petitioners from amenability to the laws of North Carolina governing domestic relations. And, as was said in connection with another aspect of the Full Faith and Credit Clause, our conclusion "is not a matter to arouse the susceptibilities of the states, all of which are equally concerned in the question and equally on both sides." *Fauntleroy v. Lum,* 210 U.S. 230, 238.

As for the suggestion that *Williams v. North Carolina,* supra, foreclosed the Supreme Court of North Carolina from ordering a second trial upon the issue of domicil, it suffices to refer to our opinion in the earlier case.

Affirmed.

[JUSTICE MURPHY, joined by CHIEF JUSTICE STONE and JUSTICE JACKSON, concurred in the Court's opinion and added that Nevada had "unquestioned authority, consistent with procedural due process, to grant divorces on whatever basis it seems fit to all who meet its statutory requirements" and to "give to its divorce decrees absolute and binding finality within the confines of its borders."

[JUSTICES BLACK, DOUGLAS, and RUTLEDGE dissented, the last stressing that the Court had not declared the divorces void in Nevada, so that the remarriage was legal in one state and illegal in another.]

SHERRER V. SHERRER*

334 U.S. 343 (1948).

[The petitioner and respondent in *Sherrer v. Sherrer* were married in New Jersey in 1930, and moved to Monterey, Massachusetts, in 1932, where they lived together until 1944. They had two children. There was evidence that their relationship became less than harmonious towards the end of this period, that Mrs. Sherrer was troubled by a sinus infection and had been advised by a physician to go to Florida, and that she consulted a Massachusetts attorney about divorce before leaving. In March, 1944, she told Sherrer that she wished to take a trip to Florida for a month's rest and wanted to take the children along. She later testified that she had intended even then to go to Florida to stay, but had lied in order to obtain her

* The statement of facts is taken from the dissenting opinion of Justice Frankfurter, 334 U.S. at 371–73.

husband's consent. His consent and the necessary funds were forthcoming. On April 3, 1944, Mrs. Sherrer and the children left for Florida, taking along a suitcase and a small bag, but leaving behind a trunk, some housedresses, and much of the children's clothing. They arrived the following day. She rented an apartment in St. Petersburg, which they occupied for about three weeks, then moved into a furnished cottage and later into another furnished cottage.

[About a week after Mrs. Sherrer's departure, one Phelps, who had previously been at least an acquaintance of hers, knowing that she had gone to St. Petersburg, went there, met her soon after, and saw her frequently. On April 20, she wrote to her husband that she did not care to go back to him, and returned the money for train fare which he had sent. She sent her older daughter to school and took a job as a waitress. Phelps found employment in a lumber yard.

[Florida law permits institution of proceedings for divorce after ninety days' bona fide residence in the State. On July 6, ninety-three days after her arrival in the State, Mrs. Sherrer consulted a Florida attorney, had the necessary papers drawn up, and filed a libel for divorce the same day. Sherrer, receiving notice by mail, retained Florida counsel, who entered a general appearance and filed an answer, which denied Mrs. Sherrer's allegations as to residence. The case was set for hearing on November 14. On November 9, Sherrer arrived on the scene. He and his wife entered into a stipulation, subject to the approval of the court, providing for custody of the children in him during the school year and in her during summer vacations. At the hearing, Sherrer's attorney was present, and Sherrer remained in a side room. The attorney did not cross-examine Mrs. Sherrer or offer evidence as to either jurisdiction or the merits, other than the stipulation regarding custody of the children. Sherrer was called into the courtroom and questioned as to his ability to look after the children during the school year. The hearing was closed, the decree being held up pending filing of a deposition by Mrs. Sherrer. On November 19, Sherrer returned to Massachusetts with the children. On November 29, the deposition was filed and the decree entered. On December 1, the petitioner married Phelps and the couple took up residence in the cottage which she and the children had previously occupied.

[There they remained until early in February, 1945, when they returned to Massachusetts, staying for a few days at Westfield and then returning to Monterey. Phelps' father lived in Westfield, and Phelps testified that his father's critical illness occasioned their return. A few days later, Phelps was served with papers in a $15,000 alienation of affections action brought by Sherrer. He testified that the pendency of this action was the reason for his remaining in Massachusetts even after his father's health had become less critical. The trial was set many months ahead, but Phelps and the petitioner did not return to Florida. Rent on the Florida cottage for a month following their departure was paid, but this may have been required, as it was paid on a monthly basis. Some personal belongings were left behind there. Later, the landlord was informed that Phelps and the petitioner would not continue renting the cottage, and still later they asked that their belongings be sent to Monterey.

[Sherrer had meanwhile moved out of the house which he and the petitioner had formerly lived in, which they owned together. Phelps and the petitioner moved in, and did not return to Florida. On June 28, 1945, a petition was filed by Sherrer in the Berkshire County Probate Court for a decree setting forth that his wife had deserted him and that he was living apart from her for justifiable cause. A statute provided that such a decree would empower a husband to convey realty free of dower rights. Mass.Gen.Laws c. 209, § 36 (1932). The Probate Court found that Mrs. Sherrer had not gone to Florida to make it her permanent home but with the intention of meeting Phelps, divorcing Sherrer, marrying Phelps, and returning to Massachusetts. These findings were upheld by the Supreme Judicial Court of the State.]

CHIEF JUSTICE VINSON delivered the opinion of the Court.

We granted certiorari in this case and in *Coe v. Coe,* 334 U.S. 378, to consider the contention of petitioners that Massachusetts has failed to accord full faith and credit to decrees of divorce rendered by courts of sister States...

At the outset, it should be observed that the proceedings in the Florida court prior to the entry of the decree of divorce were in no way inconsistent with the requirements of procedural due process... It is clear that respondent was afforded his day in court with respect to every issue involved in the litigation, including the jurisdictional issue of petitioner's domicile. Under such circumstances, there is nothing in the concept of due process which demands that a defendant be afforded a second opportunity to litigate the existence of jurisdictional facts. *Chicago Life Insurance Co. v. Cherry,* 244 U.S. 25; *Baldwin v. Iowa State Traveling Men's Association,* 283 U.S. 522.

It should also be observed that there has been no suggestion that under the law of Florida, the decree of divorce in question is in any respect invalid or could successfully be subjected to the type of attack permitted by the Massachusetts court. The implicit assumption underlying the position taken by respondent and the Massachusetts court is that this case involves a decree of divorce valid and final in the State which rendered it; and we so assume.

That the jurisdiction of the Florida court to enter a valid decree of divorce was dependent upon petitioner's domicile in that State is not disputed. This requirement was recognized by the Florida court which rendered the divorce decree, and the principle has been given frequent application in decisions of the State Supreme Court. But whether or not petitioner was domiciled in Florida at the time the divorce was granted was a matter to be resolved by judicial determination. Here, unlike the situation presented in *Williams v. North Carolina [II]*, 325 U.S. 226, the finding of the requisite jurisdictional facts was made in proceedings in which the defendant appeared and participated. The question with which we are confronted, therefore, is whether such a finding made under the circumstances presented by this case may, consistent with the requirements of full faith and credit, be subjected to collateral attack in the courts of a sister State in a suit brought by the defendant in the original proceedings. . .

We believe that the decision of this Court in . . . *Davis* [*v. Davis*, 305 U.S. 32] and those in related situations are clearly indicative of the result to be reached here. Those cases stand for the proposition that the requirements of full faith and credit bar a defendant from collaterally attacking a divorce decree on jurisdictional grounds in the courts of a sister State where there has been participation by the defendant in the divorce proceedings, where the defendant has been accorded full opportunity to contest the jurisdictional issues, and where the decree is not susceptible to such collateral attack in the courts of the State which rendered the decree.

Applying these principles to this case, we hold that the Massachusetts courts erred in permitting the Florida divorce decree to be subjected to attack on the ground that petitioner was not domiciled in Florida at the time the decree was entered. Respondent participated in the Florida proceedings by entering a general appearance, filing pleadings placing in issue the very matters he sought subsequently to contest in the Massachusetts courts, personally appearing before the Florida court and giving testimony in the case, and by retaining attorneys who represented him throughout the entire proceedings. It has not been contended that respondent was given less than a full opportunity to contest the issue of petitioner's domicile or any other issue relevant to the litigation. . . If respondent failed to take advantage of the opportunities afforded him, the responsibility is his own. We do not believe that the dereliction of a defendant under such circumstances should be permitted to provide a basis for subsequent attack in the courts of a sister State on a decree valid in the State in which it was rendered. . .

It is urged further, however, that because we are dealing with litigation involving the dissolution of the marital relation, a different result is demanded from that which might properly be reached if this case were concerned with other types of litigation. It is pointed out that under the Constitution, the regulation and control of marital and family relationships are reserved to the States. It is urged, and properly so, that the regulation of the incidents of the marital relation involves the exercise by the States of powers of the most vital importance. Finally, it is contended that a recognition of the importance to the States of such powers demands that the requirements of full faith and credit be viewed in such a light as to permit an attack upon a divorce decree granted by a court of a sister State under the circumstances of this case even where the attack is initiated in a suit brought by the defendant in the original proceedings.

But the recognition of the importance of a State's power to determine the incidents of basic social relationships into which its domiciliaries enter does not resolve the issues of this case. . . This is, rather, a case involving inconsistent assertions of power by courts of two States of the Federal Union and thus presents considerations which go beyond the interests of local policy, however vital. . . The full faith and credit clause is one of the provisions incorporated into the Constitution by its framers for the purpose of transforming an aggregation of independent, sovereign States into a nation. If in its application local policy must at times be required to give way, such "is part of the price of our federal system." *Williams v. North Carolina [I]*, 317 U.S. 287, 302.

This is not to say that in no case may an area be recognized in which reasonable accommodations of interest may properly be made. But as this Court has heretofore made clear, that area is of limited extent. We believe that in permitting an attack on the Florida divorce decree which again put in issue petitioner's Florida domicile and in refusing to recognize the validity of that decree, the Massachusetts courts have asserted a power which cannot be reconciled with the requirements of due faith and credit. We believe that assurances that such a power will be exercised sparingly and wisely render it no less repugnant to the constitutional commands.

It is one thing to recognize as permissible the judicial reexamination of findings of jurisdictional fact where such findings have been made by a court of a sister State which has entered a divorce decree in ex parte proceedings. It is quite another thing to hold that the vital rights and interests involved in divorce litigation may be held in suspense pending the scrutiny by courts of sister States of findings of jurisdictional fact made by a competent court in proceedings conducted in a manner consistent with the highest requirements of due process and in which the defendant has participated. We do not conceive it to be in accord with the purposes of the full faith and credit requirement to hold that a judgment rendered under the circumstances of this case may be required to run the gauntlet of such collateral attack in the courts of sister States before its validity outside of the State which rendered it is established or rejected. That vital interests are involved in divorce litigation indicates to us that it is a matter of greater rather than lesser importance that there should be a place to end such litigation. And where a decree of divorce is rendered by a competent court under the circumstances of this case, the obligation of full faith and credit requires that such litigation should end in the courts of the State in which the judgment was rendered.

Reversed.

MR. JUSTICE FRANKFURTER, with whom MR. JUSTICE MURPHY concurs, dissenting. . .*

It would certainly have been easier if from the beginning the Full Faith and Credit Clause had been construed to mean that the assumption of jurisdiction by the courts of a State would be conclusive, so that every other State would have to respect it. But such certainly has not been the law since 1873. *Thompson v. Whitman,* 18 Wall. 457. Nor was it the law when this Court last considered the divorce problem, in 1945. *Williams v. North Carolina,* 325 U.S. 226. A State that is asked to enforce the action of another State may appropriately ascertain whether that other State has power to do what it purported to do. And if the enforcing State has an interest under our Constitution in regard to the subject-matter that is vital and intimate, it should not be within the power of private parties to foreclose that interest by their private arrangement. . .

If the marriage contract were no different from a contract to sell an automobile, the parties thereto might well be permitted to bargain away all interests involved, in or out of court. But the State has an interest in the family relations of its citizens vastly different from the interest it has in an ordinary commercial transaction. That interest cannot be bartered or bargained away by the immediate parties to the controversy by a default or an arranged contest in a proceeding for divorce in a State to which the parties are strangers. Therefore, the constitutional power of a State to determine the marriage status of two of its citizens should not be deemed foreclosed by a proceeding between the parties in another State, even though in other types of controversy considerations making it desirable to put an end to litigation might foreclose the parties themselves from reopening the dispute. . .

Nowhere in the United States, not even in the States which grant divorces most freely, may a husband and wife rescind their marriage at will as they might a commercial contract. Even if one thought that such a view of the institution of marriage was socially desirable, it could scarcely be held that such a personal view was incorporated into the Constitution or into the law for the enforcement of the Full Faith and Credit Clause enacted by the First Congress. . .

Massachusetts has a right to define the terms on which it will grant divorces, and to refuse to recognize divorces granted by other States to parties who at the time are still Massachusetts domiciliaries. Has it not also the right to frustrate evasion of its policies by those of its permanent residents who leave the State to change their spouses rather than to change

* This was also a dissent to a companion case, *Coe v. Coe,* 334 U.S. 378 (1948).

their homes, merely because they go through a lukewarm or feigned contest over jurisdiction?

The nub of the *Williams* decision was that the State of domicile has an independent interest in the marital status of its citizens that neither they nor any other State with which they may have a transitory connection may abrogate against its will. Its interest is not less because both parties to the marital relationship instead of one sought to evade its laws. In the *Williams* case, it was not the interest of Mrs. Williams, or that of Mr. Hendrix, that North Carolina asserted. It was the interest of the people of North Carolina. The same is true here of the interest of Massachusetts.[9] While the State's interest may be expressed in criminal prosecutions, with itself formally a party as in the *Williams* case, the State also expresses its sovereign power when it speaks through its courts in a civil litigation between private parties. Cf. *Shelley v. Kraemer,* 334 U.S. 1. . .

[If] the doctrine of res judicata as to jurisdictional facts in controversies involving exclusively private interests as infused into the Full Faith and Credit Clause is applied to divorce decrees so as to foreclose subsequent inquiry into jurisdiction, there is neither logic nor reason nor practical desirability in not taking the entire doctrine over. Res judicata forecloses relitigation if there has been an opportunity to litigate once, whether or not it has been availed of, or carried as far as possible. *Cromwell v. County of Sac,* 94 U.S. 351; *Chicot County Drainage Dist. v. Baxter State Bank,* 308 U.S. 371. And it applies to questions of jurisdiction of subject matter as well as to that of persons. *Stoll v. Gottlieb,* 305 U.S. 165; *Treinies v. Sunshine Mining Co.,* 308 U.S. 66. Why should it not apply where there has been a wasted opportunity to litigate, but should apply where the form of a contest has been gone through?[16] Or if more than form is required, how

---

[9] The result of the assertion of the State's interest may be a windfall to a party who has sought to bargain his or her rights away and now seeks to renege on the agreement. This fact, however, should scarcely be allowed to stand in the way of the assertion by the State of its paramount concern in the matter. Such an unexpected windfall to a party, who by ethical standards may be regarded as undeserving, is a frequent consequence of findings of lack of jurisdiction. See Holmes, C.J., in *Andrews v. Andrews,* 176 Mass. 92, 96, 57 N.E. 333.

[16] It is by no means clear that the issue before the Massachusetts courts in either of these cases was or could have been litigated in Florida or Nevada. All that the Florida or Nevada courts could have determined was whether the jurisdictional requisites of State law and of the due process clause of the Constitution, Amend. 14, were met. And if a direct attack on these decrees had been made in this Court, all that we could have decided would have been the due process point. A divorce may satisfy due process requirements, and be valid where rendered, and still lack the jurisdictional requisites for full faith and credit to be mandatory. Compare *Williams v. North Carolina,* 317 U.S. 287, 307 (concurring opinion), with *Williams v. North Carolina,* 325 U.S. 226. This is true even though the Florida and Nevada courts appear to characterize the jurisdictional prerequisites under their respective laws as domicile, *Wade v. Wade,* 93 Fla. 1004, 1007, 113 So. 374; *Latterner v. Latterner,* 51 Nev. 285, 274 P. 194; since we may be unwilling to apply as loose a test of "domicile," in determining whether extra-state enforcement is mandatory, as those States might properly choose to use in determining what divorces might be granted and effective within their own borders. Thus, at no point in the proceedings in Florida or Nevada in the instant cases was there an opportunity to litigate whether Mrs. Sherrer or Mr. Coe had acquired Florida or Nevada domicile, respectively, sufficient to entitle their divorces to extraterritorial recognition.

much of a contest must it be? Must the contest be bellicose or may it be pacific? Must it be fierce or may it be tepid? Must there be a cloud of witnesses to negative the testimony of the plaintiff, or may a single doubter be enough? Certainly if the considerations that establish res judicata as between private litigants in the ordinary situations apply to the validity of a divorce against the public policy of the State of domicile, it cannot make a rational difference that the question of domicile is contested with bad feeling rather than amicably adjusted. The essence of the matter is that through the device of a consent decree a policy of vital concern to States should not be allowed to be defied with the sanction of this Court. If perchance the Court leaves open the right of a State to prove fraud in the ordinary sense—namely, that a mock contest was won by prearrangement—the claim falls that today's decision will substantially restrict the area of uncertainty as to the validity of divorces. If the Court seeks to avoid this result by holding that a party to a feigned legal contest cannot question in his home State the good faith behind an adjudication of domicile in another State, such holding is bound to encourage fraud and collusion still further. . .

Jurisdiction to Divorce and Collateral Attack on Migratory Divorce Decrees

(1) Is there any doubt that by applying Nevada law to divorce the parties in the *Williams* cases on grounds not recognized in North Carolina the Nevada courts denied full faith to North Carolina law and deprived the stay-at-home defendants of liberty or property without due process? See generally Chapter 3, supra. How long a stay in Nevada would be required to give Nevada an interest in divorcing the plaintiffs?

(2) If domicile is a jurisdictional prerequisite, whose law determines what constitutes domicile? The divorcing state? The second state? A uniform federal law developed by the Supreme Court? If the law of the divorcing state is controlling, within what limits may Nevada or other states be free to reshape that concept for their own purposes? Did the *Williams* cases decide these questions?

(3) Why did the Court in *Williams II* say Nevada lacked jurisdiction? Did Justice Frankfurter mean that the prerequisite for ex parte jurisdiction in *Williams I* was lacking? Did he also mean that Nevada could not have heard the case even if the defendants had voluntarily appeared and North Carolina law had been applied? See infra note (4). Was the "jurisdictional" language in *Williams II* justified or necessitated in order to avoid the holding of *Fauntleroy v. Lum,* supra, p. 562, that an unconstitutional choice of law cannot be the basis of collateral attack on a judgment? Observe that the policy underlying the *Fauntleroy* decision—

namely, that the adversary nature of a contract dispute and the availability of direct Supreme Court review gave substantial assurance that the laws of the interested state would be respected—has no application in the typical bilateral divorce case, in which both plaintiff and defendant are doing their level best to frustrate the home state's interest.

(4) In 1953, the Virgin Islands made a bid for the United States migratory divorce business by amending its Divorce Law to provide that:

> Notwithstanding the provisions of sections 8 and 9 hereof, if the plaintiff is within the district at the time of the filing of the complaint and has been continuously for six weeks immediately prior thereto, this shall be prima facie evidence of domicile, and where the defendant has been personally served within the district or enters a general appearance in the action, then the Court shall have jurisdiction of the action and of the parties thereto without further reference to domicile or to the place where the marriage was solemnized or the cause of action arose.

This bold attempt to remove domicile (and with it, the obligatory perjured testimony concerning intent) from divorce jurisdiction was invalidated by the Third Circuit in *Alton* v. *Alton*, 207 F.2d 667 (3d Cir. 1953), vacated as moot, 347 U.S. 610 (1954). Judge Goodrich rested the holding on two grounds: lack of authority under the Virgin Islands Organic Act to pass legislation granting divorces to persons domiciled elsewhere, and violation of the due process clause. He conceded the novelty of the latter holding in the following paragraphs:

> We think that adherence to the domiciliary requirement is necessary if our states are really to have control over the domestic relations of their citizens. The instant case would be typical. In the Virgin Islands incompatibility of temperament constitutes grounds for divorce. In Connecticut it does not. We take it that it is all very well for the Virgin Islands to provide for whatever matrimonial regime it pleases for people who live there. But the same privilege should be afforded to those who control affairs in Connecticut.
>
> Our conclusion is that the second part of this statute conflicts with the due process clause of the Fifth Amendment and the Organic Act. Domestic relations are a matter of concern to the state where a person is domiciled. An attempt by another jurisdiction to affect the relation of a foreign domiciliary is unconstitutional even though both parties are in court and neither one raises the question. The question may well be asked as to what the lack of due process is. The defendant is not complaining. Nevertheless, if the jurisdiction for divorce continues to be based on domicile, as we think it does, we believe it to be lack of due process for one

> state to take to itself the readjustment of domestic relations between those domiciled elsewhere. The Supreme Court has in a number of cases used the due process clause to correct states which have passed beyond what that court has considered proper choice-of-law rules. . .

Id., at 677. Judge Hastie disagreed with the court's conclusion that the Constitution mandated domicile as the basis for divorce jurisdiction, and suggested that the real problem was choice of law (id. at 685):

> But once the power to decide the case is based merely upon personal jurisdiction a court must decide as a separate question upon what basis, if any, the local substantive law of divorce can properly be applied to determine whether the plaintiff is entitled to the relief sought. In this case, if it should appear that Mr. and Mrs. Alton were both domiciled in Connecticut at the time of suit in the Virgin Islands and that their estrangement had resulted from conduct in the matrimonial home state, it may well be that under correct application of conflict of laws doctrine, and even under the due process clause, it is encumbent upon the Virgin Islands, lacking connection with the subject matter, to apply the divorce law of some state that has such connection, here Connecticut. Cf. *Hartford Accident & Indemnity Co. v. Delta & Pine Land Co.,* 1934, 292 U.S. 143; *Home Ins. Co. v. Dick,* 1930, 281 U.S. 397.
>
> Of course such a solution would be a novelty in divorce procedure. But the entire situation presented by this statute is very unusual. . . Accordingly, I do no more than point out that this choice of law question would have to be considered if the court's power to decide this case depended upon personal jurisdiction and that basis of jurisdiction were sustained, as I believe it should be. . .

(5) How can the statements in *Williams II* and the holding in *Alton* that domicile is requisite to divorce jurisdiction be reconciled with the constitutional policy favoring transitory actions enunciated by the Supreme Court in *Hughes v. Fetter,* 341 U.S. 609 (1951), supra, p. 414, and in *Tennessee Coal, Iron & R.R. Co. v. George,* 233 U.S. 354 (1914), supra, p. 422? Are not the interests of the domicile state amply protected by the constitutional requirement that the disinterested forum apply the law of the only interested state? See *Home Ins. Co. v. Dick,* 281 U.S. 397 (1930), supra, p. 351.

Does divorce litigation exhibit the characteristics that have caused the jurisdiction of an enacting sovereign to be exclusive in other classes of cases? See D. Currie, *Suitcase Divorce in the Conflict of Laws:* Simons, Rosenstiel, *and* Borax, 34 U. Chi. L. Rev. 26, 50–51 (1966):

> [T]he case for keeping litigation at home is strengthened when, as under the federal labor laws and most workmen's compensation laws, the general courts of the enacting sovereign are also excluded in order to promote uniform and expert enforcement; when, as in criminal sentencing, the effectuation of vital policy is entrusted in large part to the discretion of knowledgeable and sympathetic judges; when, as in maritime in rem and limitation suits and bankruptcy, the controversy is made both difficult and important by the presence of multiple parties; when, as in state habeas for federal prisoners, there is thought to be substantial hostility in other jurisdictions toward important policies of the enacting sovereign; or when, as the ALI has suggested is the case with patents, copyright, and antitrust, the sovereign has an interest that is "more important than the wishes of the parties." In general it may be said that the case for exclusive jurisdiction is at its height when error is unusually likely or unusually serious.

Should not the court in *Alton* at least have inquired whether or not the assertion of Virgin Islands jurisdiction would have frustrated Connecticut policy?

(6) State courts have upheld divorces rendered on a basis other than that of domicile. See, e.g., *Lauterbach v. Lauterbach,* 392 P.2d 24 (Alaska 1964); *Wallace v. Wallace,* 63 N.M. 414, 320 P.2d 1020 (1958); *Wood v. Wood,* 159 Tex. 350, 320 S.W.2d 807 (1959). Most of these cases, however, involve people—military personnel, students, government employees—who in fact have established a substantial connection with the divorcing state albeit not one of technical domicile. The divorcing state is providing a forum for persons in whom it has an interest, and it has invariably applied its own law. May a state, as a general matter not limited to these specific situations, divorce on the basis of a finding of local "residence" for a period of 3 months? Abandonment of the domicile requirement by such a statute, designed to eliminate the perjury practiced in other states, was upheld in *Wheat v. Wheat,* 229 Ark. 842, 318 S.W.2d 793 (1958). But is there no place for a disinterested forum to divorce people on the basis of foreign law in order to obviate the inconvenience of their litigating at their distant home?

(7) In the *Alton* case, who was deprived of life, liberty or property without due process of law? Ms. Alton, who sought the divorce? Mr. Alton, who appeared and did not contest the divorce? The State of Connecticut? Mr. Justice Clark, dissenting in *Granville-Smith v. Granville-Smith,* 349 U.S. 1, 26 (1955), declared that "neither of the Granville-Smiths claim that they have been deprived of life, liberty or property without due process of law. While the State has an interest in the marital relationship, certainly this interest does not come within the protection of the Due Process Clause." If that is so, is a Virgin Islands consent divorce entitled to full faith and credit elsewhere? Or can it be valid in the Virgin Islands but not entitled to respect in Connecticut?

(8) Did *Sherrer* really apply established principles or extend them? In precluding collateral attack on the jurisdictional issue *Sherrer* relied on three prior decisions in all of which the issue had been hotly contested in the initial proceedings. In *Baldwin v. Iowa State Traveling Men's Ass'n,* 283 U.S. 522 (1931), involving collateral attack on a federal judgment for lack of personal jurisdiction of a foreign corporation, the corporation had made a special appearance to litigate the jurisdictional question. In *Stoll v. Gottlieb,* 305 U.S. 165 (1938), the party attacking a prior judgment of a federal bankruptcy court had actually litigated the question of subject-matter jurisdiction. Similarly in *Davis v. Davis,* 305 U.S. 32 (1938), the only one of the three cases involving collateral attack in a divorce context, the parties had engaged in a true contest on the question of whether the husband was domiciled in the divorcing state.

Isn't there a vital difference between a real contest and the merely formal opposition in *Sherrer,* the defendant's consent to jurisdiction in *Coe v. Coe,* 334 U.S. 378 (1948), a companion case to *Sherrer,* and the "full opportunity to contest the jurisdictional issues" in *Johnson v. Muelberger,* 340 U.S. 581 (1951), infra note (10)? Notice the apparently conflicting decisions in *Chicot County Drainage Dist. v. Baxter State Bank,* 308 U.S. 371 (1940), and in *Kalb v. Feuerstein,* 308 U.S. 433 (1940), discussed supra p. 594, respecting collateral attack upon jurisdictional issues after a failure to raise them in non-divorce proceedings. Would *Johnson* be followed in a non-divorce case? Would *Sherrer*?

(9) Does the nature of divorce proceedings suggest that collateral attack should be more or less restricted than in other litigation? Notice Justice Frankfurter's argument, dissenting in *Sherrer,* that in divorce, unlike most private litigation, the parties cannot be relied upon to assert the interests of their home state. Indeed, in *Sherrer* and in many of the other cases in this chapter, the parties are embarked upon an effort to circumvent and frustrate the interest of their domicile. Notice how thoroughly any protection given to the home state by the jurisdiction theory was destroyed by application of "established" res judicata principles in *Sherrer.*

(10) Matters became even more dubious in *Johnson v. Muelberger,* 340 U.S. 581 (1951), where the Court held that a since-deceased husband's appearance in his second wife's Florida divorce proceeding precluded his daughter from collateral attack upon the resulting judgment even though the wife had not complied with Florida's jurisdictional ninety-day residence requirement. A Florida judge ruled that collateral attack was precluded because the husband had "had full opportunity to contest the jurisdictional issues" in the Florida court, and had chosen not to do so. After marrying a third time, the father died leaving his entire estate to his daughter, offspring of his first marriage. Her interest in attacking the Florida decree was to prevent the third wife from asserting her rights as surviving spouse to take against the will. The Supreme Court concluded that since Florida would not permit collateral attack by the daughter, the full faith and credit clause prevented New York from granting her that option.

Even if *Sherrer* is viewed as a logical extension of traditional res judicata principles, can *Johnson v. Muelberger* be defended? Does the notion that an in rem proceeding is binding on the whole world prevent an interested person who was neither notified nor given an opportunity to litigate from ever asserting that the court lacked jurisdiction over the res? Does *Johnson v. Muelberger* overrule *Thompson v. Whitman,* 85 U.S. (18 Wall.) 457 (1874)?

Does the *Johnson* holding rest on the ground that Florida considers children to be in privity with their parents for purposes of divorce? Or on the ground that Florida views the child as not having a sufficient interest to attack the divorce decree? Or both? Perhaps notions of privity are properly viewed as part of Florida's law of res judicata, which New York must respect; but is the concept of standing or party interest part of the law of res judicata? The daughter in *Johnson v. Muelberger* was asserting a property interest in a New York estate under New York law. Why can't New York apply its own concept of standing to determine whether her interest is a sufficient one? Why doesn't it violate due process for Florida to cut off the daughter's claims without notice or opportunity to litigate? Would the result be different if the daughter's property rights existed at the time of the divorce (did they?) rather than arising out of the father's subsequent death?

(11) Would Nevada be required by *Sherrer*'s res judicata principle to set aside the divorces that North Carolina refused to recognize in the *Williams* cases? In *Colby v. Colby,* 78 Nev. 150, 369 P.2d 1019 (1962), the Nevada court said no. An ex parte Nevada divorce had there been declared "void" by a Maryland court for want of domicile; distinguishing the issue of extrastate recognition from that of validity at home, the Nevada court refused to vacate the divorce. Does *Williams II* support this holding? If *Colby* is right, then *Williams II* abandoned the only really good point made in *Williams I:* that the validity of a divorce must be the same in every state. *Sherrer* settles the question, doesn't it? Which way? See Justice Frankfurter's dissenting footnote 16, protesting that the issue litigated in Florida was not the same as that raised in Massachusetts.

(12) If some states were eager to attract the migratory divorce business, others seemed bent on discouraging it. Lengthy residence requirements are an effective deterrent, but they also impair the ability of new bona fide residents to obtain access to the courts. In *Sosna v. Iowa,*

419 U.S. 393 (1975), the Supreme Court upheld Iowa's one-year residence requirement against plaintiff's claim that the law violated her constitutional right to travel and that it denied her an opportunity to make an individual showing of bona fide residence. Justice Rehnquist distinguished the state's interest in regulating divorce, with its attendant problems of determining property rights and the custody and support of children, from its less significant concern with budgetary considerations or administrative convenience advanced in earlier cases to deny newcomers prompt access to welfare benefits (*Shapiro v. Thompson,* 394 U.S. 618 (1969)), the voting booth (*Dunn v. Blumstein,* 405 U.S. 330 (1972)), or medical treatment (*Memorial Hospital v. Maricopa County,* 415 U.S. 250 (1974)). The divorce plaintiff, he argued, was merely delayed in her access to the courts, and was not "irretrievably foreclosed from obtaining some part of what she sought," as were the litigants in the cited cases. Rehnquist added that the residence requirement would tend to protect Iowa from becoming a "divorce mill for unhappy spouses" as well as to provide a "greater safeguard against collateral attack than would a requirement of bona fide residence alone." Do you agree with these arguments?

Justices Marshall and Brennan, in dissent, asserted that "the right to obtain a divorce is of sufficient importance that its denial to recent immigrants constitutes a penalty on interstate travel" in violation of *Shapiro.* They were unimpressed by the argument that plaintiff had been merely delayed, rather than foreclosed from part of her relief, noting that "[t]he year's wait prevents remarriage and locks both partners into what may be an intolerable, destructive relationship." Finally, the dissenters argued that Iowa's interests in avoiding migratory divorces and protecting its decrees against collateral attack "would adequately be protected by a simple requirement of domicile—physical presence plus intent to remain—which would remove the rigid one-year barrier while permitting the State to restrict the availability of its divorce process to citizens who are genuinely its own." Does your consideration of *Alton* lead you to accept this latter suggestion?

(13) Arizona, Arkansas, and Louisiana have laws allowing couples to enter a "covenant marriage," which is designed to be harder to dissolve than an ordinary marriage. In Louisiana, for instance, a covenant marriage may be terminated by divorce only if specified grounds are met, and then only "subsequent to the parties obtaining counseling." La. Rev. Stat. Ann. 9:307(A). In *Blackburn v. Blackburn,* 180 So. 3d 16 (Ala. Civ. App. 2015), an Alabama appellate court faced the question whether a couple who had obtained a covenant marriage in Louisiana and then moved to Alabama could be divorced under Alabama law. (The husband sought an Alabama divorce and the wife defended by seeking to enforce the covenant marriage contract.) The court said yes, relying on *Williams II* and Section 285 of the Second Restatement for the proposition that divorce is governed by the law of the domiciliary state. 180 So. 3d at 18–19. What result in *Blackburn* if the husband had moved to Alabama on his own and sought an ex parte divorce?

C. SAME-SEX DIVORCE AND DISSOLUTION

The rise of same-sex marriage and civil unions in the 21st century created a new set of conflicts among state laws. The Supreme Court eliminated interstate conflict over the validity of same-sex marriages in *Obergefell v. Hodges*, 576 U.S. 644 (2015), which held that state laws restricting marriage to one man and one woman violate the Due Process and Equal Protection Clauses of the Fourteenth Amendment. As the Court recognized, "if States are required by the Constitution to issue marriage licenses to same-sex couples, the justifications for refusing to recognize those marriages performed elsewhere are undermined. * * * The Court, in this decision, holds same-sex couples may exercise the fundamental right to marry in all States. It follows that the Court also must hold—and it now does hold—that there is no lawful basis for a State to refuse to recognize a lawful same-sex marriage performed in another State on the ground of its same-sex character." *Id.* at 678–679.

Although the legal validity of same-sex marriage is (presumably) now settled, difficult issues remain concerning same-sex divorce and the dissolution of same-sex civil unions and domestic partnerships, as the following materials illustrate. These issues continue to test the limits of jurisdiction, recognition of judgments, and choice of law, much as migratory divorce did in the mid-20th century.

CHAMBERS V. ORMISTON

935 A.2d 956 (R.I. 2007).

JUSTICE ROBINSON for the Court.

The Family Court . . . has certified the following question to this Court:

"May the Family Court properly recognize, for the purpose of entertaining a divorce petition, the marriage of two persons of the same sex who were purportedly married in another state?"

For the reasons set forth herein, it is our opinion that the certified question must be answered in the negative.

Facts and Travel

On May 26, 2004, Rhode Island residents Margaret Chambers and Cassandra Ormiston traveled to Massachusetts and applied for a marriage license in that state. After Ms. Chambers and Ms. Ormiston received a marriage license, a Massachusetts justice of the peace performed a marriage ceremony in Fall River, Massachusetts. The couple thereafter returned to Rhode Island, where they resided together until they decided to seek to dissolve in this state the relationship that Massachusetts deems to be a marriage and that had been solemnized by the Massachusetts justice of the peace.

On October 23, 2006, Ms. Chambers filed a petition for divorce in the Family Court, and on October 27 of that year Ms. Ormiston filed an answer and counterclaim. Thereafter, on December 11, 2006, the Chief Judge of the Family Court certified to this Court a question as to whether or not the Family Court has subject matter jurisdiction to grant a petition for divorce with respect to a same-sex couple. . .

Introduction

Upon contemplating the question certified by the Family Court, it became clear to us that the precise issue we must decide is ultimately the following: What is the meaning of the word "marriage" within the Rhode Island statute that empowers the Family Court to grant divorces—or, stated even more precisely, what did the word mean at the time that the members of the General Assembly enacted the statute? It is imperative that we direct our attention to the meaning of this statutory term at that point in time. . .

II. The Meaning of the Word "Marriage" in G.L. 1956 § 8–10–3(a)

The issue before us is rather narrow, and it can be decided entirely on the statutory level: Does G.L. 1956 § 8–10–3(a), the statute authorizing the Family Court to "hear and determine all petitions for divorce from the bond of marriage," empower that court to grant a divorce to the instant parties, who are described in the certified question as "two persons of the same sex who were purportedly married in another state?"

When we are called upon to decide what the General Assembly intended when it enacted a particular statute, we always begin with the principle that "[t]he plain statutory language is the best indicator of legislative intent." . . .

It is clear to us that in this instance we are *not* confronted with an ambiguous statute. Therefore we simply must determine what the words in this statute were intended to mean. Once we have done so, our interpretive task is at an end and our role is simply to apply the statute as written. . .

In carrying out the process of determining the meaning of the words employed by an enacting legislature, reference to contemporaneous dictionaries is appropriate and often helpful. . .

With respect to the case at hand, there is absolutely no reason to believe that, when the act creating the Family Court became law in 1961, the legislators understood the word marriage to refer to any state other than "the state of being united to a person of the opposite sex." The quoted words are the definition of marriage that is set forth in the 1961 edition of Webster's Third New International Dictionary of the English Language. *Id.* at 1384. Similarly, the American College Dictionary, published in 1955, defines marriage as "the legal union of a man with a woman for life." *Id.* at 746. Likewise, Funk & Wagnalls Standard College Dictionary, published in 1963, defines marriage as, "[t]he state of being married; a legal contract entered into by a man and a woman, to live together as husband and wife." *Id.* at 829. In each case, the primary dictionary definition of marriage refers only to a union between a man and a woman.

It is pertinent to note that Chief Justice Margaret Marshall, writing in 2003 for the plurality in *Goodridge v. Department of Public Health,* 440 Mass. 309, 798 N.E.2d 941 (2003), expressly acknowledged that the decision of the Supreme Judicial Court in that case "*marks a significant change in the definition of marriage* as it has been inherited from the common law, and understood by many societies for centuries." *Id.* at 965 (emphasis added).

As we understand the language of the existing divorce statute, it does not constitute "express language conferring subject-matter jurisdiction upon the Family Court" whereby it could entertain a divorce petition involving two persons of the same sex. *See State v. Kenney,* 523 A.2d 853, 854 (R.I. 1987) (noting that the powers of the Family Court are "strictly limited to those conferred by the Legislature."). Moreover, "[i]n the absence of a clear legislative intent to the contrary, such jurisdiction cannot be inferred." *State v. Zittel,* 94 R.I. 325, 330, 180 A.2d 455, 458 (1962); *see also Kenney,* 523 A.2d at 854.[14]

We have concluded that § 8–10–3(a) is unambiguous, and we have ascertained its plain meaning by looking to the meaning of the word "marriage" at the time of the statute's enactment in 1961—some forty-six years ago. Once having arrived at that plain meaning,[15] our role is to apply it to the situation at hand. *DiCicco,* 707 A.2d at 253. The plain meaning of the word "marriage" in § 8–10–3(a) indicates to us that the Family Court is without jurisdiction to entertain the instant petition for divorce.

---

[14] Both parties argue in their briefs that the common law concept of "comity" requires us to recognize their status as married for the purpose of granting them a divorce. It is our view, however, that considerations of comity (a largely discretionary and somewhat amorphous concept) do not come into play if the court lacks jurisdiction over the case before it. We have also concluded that, because our ruling as to the Family Court's lack of jurisdiction ends our inquiry, the Full Faith and Credit Clause of the United States Constitution is not relevant to these proceedings. Similarly, we have no occasion to address the applicability *vel non* of the Defense of Marriage Act, 28 U.S.C. § 1738C (2000).

[15] The plain meaning rule need not be adhered to when it would bring about "an absurd result." *Kaya v. Partington,* 681 A.2d 256, 261 (R.I.1996). Our reading of the divorce statute, however, does not produce an absurd result, but simply one that is less broad than some would prefer. It is now the role of the General Assembly to decide, if it chooses to do so, whether there should be a broader divorce statute.

* * *

A Final Consideration

We know that sometimes our decisions result in palpable hardship to the persons affected by them. It is, however, a fundamental principle of jurisprudence that a court has no power to grant relief in the absence of jurisdiction, as is true in the instant case. Ours is not a policy-making branch of the government. We are cognizant of the fact that this observation may be cold comfort to the parties before us. But, if there is to be a remedy to this predicament, fashioning such a remedy would fall within the province of the General Assembly.

Conclusion

* * *

For the reasons set forth in this opinion, the question certified by the Family Court must be answered in the negative.

SUTTELL, J., with whom GOLDBERG, J., joins, dissenting.

Because we firmly believe that our statutory law does not bar the doors of the Family Court to Rhode Island citizens desiring a judicial determination of their marital status, we respectfully dissent.

We are in complete agreement with the majority on one critical point, however. The legal recognition that ought to be afforded same-sex marriages for any particular purpose is fundamentally a question of public policy, more appropriately determined by the General Assembly after full and robust public debate. If the courts are called upon to resolve any issue involving the validity of such a marriage, they must, of course, do so, but only when presented with an actual controversy by parties having adverse interests. . . Such is not the situation with the case at bar. Neither one of the parties is contesting the legal validity of the marriage performed in the Commonwealth of Massachusetts. Both plaintiff and defendant have filed a complaint and counterclaim, respectively, seeking to terminate that relationship in the Rhode Island Family Court. Both parties have satisfied the applicable domicile and residence requirements and they have filed a certified marriage certificate from a sister sovereign state attesting to the existence of their marriage. We believe that is sufficient to invoke the authority of the Family Court to entertain their divorce petitions.

At the outset we think it essential to note that the certified question presented to this Court is extremely narrow in scope. It requires only that this Court consider whether the Family Court may recognize a same-sex marriage for the limited purpose of entertaining a divorce petition. Thus, the question of whether such a marriage is entitled to recognition in Rhode Island for any other purpose is one this Court need not and should not answer. Clearly, the certified question does not implicate the eligibility *vel non* of same-sex couples to marry under Rhode Island marriage licensing laws.

The issue presented to this Court by the certified question is by its very terms limited to the divorce context. To answer the question, the dissenting justices perceive no need to consult forty-six-year-old editions of standard dictionaries. A brief survey of current dictionaries reveals that the same definition of the word "marriage" predominates today as it did when the Family Court Act was enacted in 1961. Nevertheless, the majority, in our opinion, overlooks the one central and unassailable fact upon which the certified question is predicated. On May 26, 2004, Ms. Chambers and Ms. Ormiston (the parties) were lawfully married under the laws of the Commonwealth of Massachusetts.

As we discuss below, the Family Court has been granted authority to hear and decide their complaint and counterclaim for divorce whether or not their marriage is determined to be legally valid in Rhode Island. We would answer the certified question in the affirmative, therefore, based on the plain language of the statutory grant of jurisdiction to the Family Court. In addition, we believe such jurisdiction to be consistent with Rhode Island's domestic relations jurisprudence in 1961, when the Family Court Act was enacted, as it is today.

* * *

Family Court Jurisdiction

The Family Court is a statutory court and is vested with jurisdiction "to hear and determine all petitions for divorce from the bond of marriage and from bed and board." G.L. 1956 8–10–3(a). Without question, Ms. Chambers and Ms. Ormiston are in, subject to, and/or entitled to the benefits of the bond of marriage, at least in the Commonwealth of Massachusetts, as well as any other jurisdiction that recognizes their marriage. They now wish to dissolve that bond and return to the status of single persons. Unless one or both of them establish the domicile and residency requirements of another jurisdiction, however, the Rhode Island Family Court is the only forum available to them to terminate their marriage. Moreover, because the parties are citizens of Rhode Island it is solely within the sovereign authority of Rhode Island to determine and/or alter their marital status by granting or denying their divorce complaint and counterclaim. That, in our opinion, is precisely the relief available to them under the plain and ordinary language of § 8–10–3. . .

In this case, it cannot be gainsaid that the parties are married for all legal purposes under the laws of the Commonwealth of Massachusetts. We, the dissenting justices, discern no impediment in the language of § 8–10–3 that precludes the Family Court from entertaining their petition for divorce from the bond of their Massachusetts marriage. The subject-matter jurisdiction of the Family Court does not turn on the gender of the parties; rather it turns on their status as a married couple.

* * *

We would answer the certified question therefore in the affirmative. Such an answer in our opinion not only is compelled by the plain and ordinary meaning of the statutory language, but also is consistent with the policies and purposes of the Family Court Act by providing Rhode Island citizens a means of dissolving their marriage and judicially determining their marital status. In addition, we believe it to be consistent with the expectations of those Rhode Island residents who have in good faith entered into same-sex marriages in Massachusetts. We do not mean to suggest, however, that the Family Court is precluded from adjudicating the validity of the marriage if one of the parties alleges the marriage is void or voidable. We agree rather with the Governor, the Attorney General and several other amici curiae that this Court should answer the certified question in the affirmative without determining the legal validity of the underlying marriage. The parties in this case have not challenged the marriage, and therefore the issue of voidness is not properly before the Court. Moreover, we do not think it proper for the Court, on the state of this record, to attempt to determine whether same-sex marriage is "strongly against the public policy of this jurisdiction." *See Ex parte Chace*, 26 R.I. at 356, 58 A. at 980. The resolution of that issue resides in the State House and not the courthouse. In the case at bar, therefore, we would remand to the Family Court for further proceedings on the plaintiff's complaint and the defendant's counterclaim.

Recognition and Dissolution of Civil Unions, Domestic Partnerships, and Same-Sex Marriages

(1) Did Rhode Island violate *Hughes v. Fetter*, supra p. 414, by closing the doors of its Family Court to the Chambers-Ormiston petition for the dissolution of their Massachusetts marriage? Note that, like the parties in *Hughes*, the two women were domiciled in the state that refused to provide a forum to hear their case. Does it matter that, unlike a suit for wrongful death, a petition for divorce is not a transitory cause of action? Which way does that cut? At the time of their marriage, the Massachusetts 1913 "marriage evasion" statute, Mass. G.L. c. 207, §§ 11, 12, would have prevented their marriage if they were seeking to evade a Rhode Island law making same-sex marriages "void." Their marriage was possible in Massachusetts only because a Massachusetts court had determined that it would not have been "void" in Rhode Island, see *Cote-Whitacre v. Department of Public Health*, 2006 WL 3208758 (Mass. Super. 2006), *on remand from Cote-Whitacre v. Department of Public Health*, 446 Mass. 350,

844 N.E.2d 623 (2006), holding that Rhode Island had no "constitutional amendment, statute, or controlling appellate decision . . . that explicitly deems void or otherwise expressly forbids same-sex marriage."

Does the fact that the Rhode Island Family Court was a court of "limited" jurisdiction make a difference? In *C.M. v. C.C.*, 21 Misc.3d 926, 930, 867 N.Y.S.2d 884, 888 (2008), the Supreme Court of New York County distinguished *Ormiston* on the ground that, unlike the Rhode Island Family Court, it is "a court of general jurisdiction and has the power to grant a divorce even if the marriage [which was celebrated in Massachusetts] could not lawfully occur in this State." The Massachusetts Superior Court in *Cote-Whitacre*, by the way, had ruled that New York same-sex couples could not marry in Massachusetts because their marriages were "prohibited" in New York under *Hernandez v. Robles*, 7 N.Y.3d 338, 821 N.Y.S.2d 770, 855 N.E.2d 1 (2006). The parties in *C.M.*, however, were married before *Hernandez* was decided, and the Superior Court subsequently identified that date as the point at which New Yorkers were prohibited from marrying in Massachusetts. The Massachusetts legislature repealed the marriage evasion statute in July 2008, Mass. St., 2008, c. 216, § 1, making such determinations unnecessary. And the New York Legislature enacted a law permitting same-sex marriages in 2011, thus removing any future conflict between the marriage policies of the two states.

(2) What do you make of the dissent's argument that the "narrow" question presented in *Ormiston* required "only that this Court consider whether the Family Court may recognize a same-sex marriage for the limited purpose of entertaining a divorce petition," not that it decide the broader question of "whether such a marriage is entitled to recognition in Rhode Island for any other purpose"? How can any court grant a divorce if there is no marriage to dissolve? Recall that the U.S. Supreme Court has consistently held in the migratory divorce cases, supra pp. 657–696, that the domicile of one party is required to give the court subject-matter jurisdiction. Is the existence of a valid marriage between the parties also an essential prerequisite for subject-matter jurisdiction? If it is, does the dissent's observation that "[w]ithout question, Ms. Chambers and Ms. Ormiston are in, subject to, and/or entitled to the benefits of the bond of marriage, at least in the Commonwealth of Massachusetts, as well as any other jurisdiction that recognizes their marriage" satisfy that requirement?

(3) Why couldn't the Rhode Island court have recognized the right conferred on same-sex couples by Massachusetts to seek the termination of their Massachusetts marriage by divorce on appropriate grounds without recognizing the validity of the marriage for all purposes? The distinction between the validity of the marital status and the recognition of its incidents is well-established in the law of marriage. See supra p. 41 note (2). Why doesn't this distinction extend to dissolution as an incident of a marriage, a civil union, or a domestic partnership, when that benefit is conferred by the law of the place where the relationship was entered into? Professor Kay argues that it does. In discussing the case of *Rosengarten v. Downes*, 71 Conn.App. 372, 802 A.2d 170, *appeal granted*, 261 Conn. 936, 806 A.2d 1066, *appeal dismissed as moot* (2002), where the Connecticut intermediate appellate court affirmed the trial court's order dismissing (on its own motion) Glen Rosengarten's petition for the dissolution of his Vermont civil union for lack of subject-matter jurisdiction, she pointed out that "[i]f the court had focused on the question of divorce, and if it had kept clearly in mind that plaintiff did not ask to be allowed to cohabit in Connecticut with his partner in the Vermont civil union but rather to be freed of any such obligation, and—most significantly—if it had been able to put aside its obvious concern that to recognize the civil union for purposes of dissolution might require it in future cases to recognize such unions for all purposes, it might have reached a different conclusion." H.H. Kay, *Same-Sex Divorce in the Conflict of Laws*, 15 King's College L.J. 63, 71, 89 (2005).

(4) Why didn't Margaret Chambers and Cassandra Ormiston file their action for divorce in Massachusetts, where their marriage was certainly valid since it was performed there according to Massachusetts law? Could it have been because one of them would have had to become domiciled in Massachusetts in order to establish subject-matter jurisdiction over the divorce in that state? Under Massachusetts law, establishing domicile would have meant being a resident of the state for at least one year prior to commencing the proceeding, and testifying to an intent to remain there indefinitely. See *Williams v. North Carolina II*, supra p. 677. Opposite-sex couples do not have this problem: if they leave home to be married in a romantic honeymoon destination, such as Niagara Falls, New York, and return home to settle down, they can be divorced at home since they could easily satisfy both aspects of subject-matter jurisdiction: domicile and a marriage recognized as valid in their home state.

Is there an easy legislative fix for the conundrum facing same-sex couples? The California Legislature attempted to fashion a solution in Cal. Fam. Code § 299(d) of the Domestic Partner Rights and Responsibilities Act of 2003 (eff. January 1, 2005). That section confers subject-matter jurisdiction on superior courts "over all proceedings relating to the dissolution of domestic partnerships" and specifies that the process "shall follow the same procedures . . . as apply to the dissolution of marriage . . . except that, in accordance with the consent acknowledged by domestic partners in the Declaration of Domestic Partnership form, proceedings for dissolution . . . of a domestic partnership registered in this state may be filed in the superior courts of this state even if neither domestic partner is a resident of, or maintains a domicile in, the state at the time the proceedings are filed." Does this provision, which attempts to substitute consent for the requirement of domicile as a jurisdictional basis for dissolution of a domestic partnership, violate the Federal Due Process Clause? If it is constitutional as applied to dissolution of domestic partnerships—which have been held not to be "marriages" in California, see In re Marriage Cases, 43 Cal.4th 757, 782–83, 183 P.3d 384, 400–01 (2008)—is it also constitutional as applied to divorces?

(5) The subject-matter jurisdiction question addressed in *Chambers* has gone both ways in subsequent decisions from other states. In *In the Matter of the Marriage of J.B. and H.B.*, 326 S.W.3d 654 (Tex.App. 2010), the state appellate court reviewed a district court order upholding its jurisdiction to grant a divorce to two Massachusetts men who had been validly married in Massachusetts and subsequently relocated to Texas in 2008. The district court rested its decision on the U.S. Constitution, finding that Texas's provisions limiting marriage to opposite-sex couples violated the Equal Protection Clause. *Obergefell*, of course, later established this point, but does it follow that the Texas court was obliged to assert jurisdiction? The decision touched a nerve in the Texas culture wars: Attorney General Greg Abbott intervened in the divorce proceeding in January 2009 and vowed to appeal the order "to defend the traditional definition of marriage that was approved by the Texas voters." See James C. McKinley, Jr., *Texas Battle on Gay Marriage Looms,* New York Times, Oct. 3, 2009, at A13. Abbott's strategy was successful. The appellate court reversed the district court's order and remanded the matter with instructions to dismiss the case for lack of subject-matter jurisdiction.

The court relied on § 6.204(b) of the Texas Family Code, which prohibited the state and its subdivisions from giving any effect to a "right or claim to any legal protection, benefit, or responsibility asserted as a result of" a same-sex marriage. "In order to comply with this statutory provision and accord appellee's same-sex divorce petition no legal effect at all," the appellate court reasoned, "the trial court must not address the merits. In other words, the court must dismiss for lack of subject-matter jurisdiction." 326 S.W.3d at 665. Was this a sound interpretation of § 6.204(b)? So interpreted, doesn't the statute plainly violate *Obergefell*?

The Supreme Court of Wyoming, on the other hand, unanimously determined that there was subject-matter jurisdiction over a divorce sought by two Wyoming women who had been validly married in Canada. *Christiansen* v. *Christiansen*, 253 P.2d 153 (Wyo. 2011). Although a Wyoming statute defined marriage as a contract between a man and a woman, the court read that statute narrowly to prevent a same-sex couple from entering into a marital contract in Wyoming, and relied on Wyo. Stat. Ann. § 20–1–111, which provides that "[a]ll marriage contracts which are valid by the laws of the country in which contracted are valid in this state." Recognizing the Canadian marriage would not violate Wyoming public policy, the court concluded, especially as it was for the purpose of dissolution.

Which court had it right, Texas or Wyoming? Is it relevant that the Texas court was dealing with the dissolution of a Massachusetts marriage, while the Wyoming court had before it a Canadian marriage? Did the presence of a request for a division of community property—a form of property holding that arises only between parties to a valid marriage—influence the Texas court's decision? Wyoming is not a community property state, but even common law states are authorized to make awards of property acquired during a marriage as well as to order spousal support. No such claims appear to have been asserted by either party in *Christensen*. Did that fact make the Wyoming Court's task easier?

(6) Many same-sex couples entered into civil unions or domestic partnerships when same-sex marriages were not lawful in their states of domicile. Can a person who entered into one of these relationships get married in another state without dissolving the status it did create? The Supreme Judicial Court of Massachusetts was faced with this question in *Elia-Warnken v. Elia*, 972 N.E.2d 17 (Mass. 2012). In that case, the plaintiff had entered into a civil union in Vermont. His civil union had not been dissolved, nor had his partner died, prior to the time he married the defendant in Massachusetts. After the plaintiff filed for divorce, the defendant moved to dismiss the divorce action on the ground that the Massachusetts marriage was polygamous and void.

The Supreme Judicial Court of Massachusetts held that it would recognize plaintiff's Vermont civil union "as the equivalent of marriage in the Commonwealth," thus making his subsequent marriage to defendant void. It noted that the Vermont Supreme Court had held in *Baker v. State*, 744 A.2d 864 (1999), that same-sex couples could not be deprived of the statutory benefits and protections given to married opposite-sex couples under the "common benefits" clause of the Vermont constitution. The Vermont court deferred to the legislature to fix the problem, and it responded in 2000 by enacting the first civil union statute in the United States. Between 2000 and 2009, legal marriage for opposite-sex couples and civil unions for same-sex couples existed side by side in Vermont.

In 2009, the Vermont legislature repealed parts of the civil union statute and redefined the civil marriage statute to permit same-sex couples to marry, effective September 1, 2009. The statute also removed civil unions as an option for same-sex couples after its effective date. It did not, however, convert existing civil unions into marriages. Parties to preexisting civil unions continue to enjoy the same rights, privileges and obligations that had been conferred by civil unions prior to September 1, 2009. In addition, they were permitted to marry each other if they chose, but if they did so and later decided to end their relationship, they were required to obtain *both* a dissolution of their civil union *and* a divorce. Finally, they were forbidden to enter into a marriage with a different person unless their civil union had been dissolved.

The Massachusetts Court invoked the doctrine of comity to justify its holding:

> Here, the initial question is whether we should extend recognition to the plaintiff's civil union in the same manner as we would an out-of-State marriage under principles of comity.
>
> We define marriage as "the voluntary union of two persons as spouses, to the exclusion of all others." . . . This is the relationship established by Vermont civil unions. . . By that definition alone, a Vermont civil union is the functional equivalent of a marriage.
>
> It is true that the law establishing civil unions in Vermont stated that such unions had a "status" different from marriage. . . However, the intent of the Vermont Legislature "in enacting the civil union laws was to create legal equality between relationships based on civil unions and those based on marriage." . . . A civil union required a legal decree to solemnize, and a legal decree is required to dissolve it, just as in a marriage. . . All of the laws concerning divorce, e.g., property division, spousal maintenance, and child custody, apply equally to civil unions. . .

Elia-Warnken, 972 N.E.2d at 20–21.

Has the Supreme Judicial Court of Massachusetts done what Vermont refused to do: treat a party to an existing civil union as married? If so, has it denied Full Faith and Credit to the Vermont statutes? What was plaintiff's status in Vermont after this decision? Were he and his first partner married there? If they decide to terminate their status, should they file for a dissolution of their civil union, a divorce to end their marriage, or both?

(7) Is marriage a "public act," "record," or "judicial proceeding" entitled to recognition under the Full Faith and Credit Clause? Once Massachusetts became the first state to permit same-sex couples to marry in 2003, *see Goodridge* v. *Department of Public Health*, 798 N.E.2d 941 (Mass. 2003), the question assumed a practical, as well as a theoretical, importance. Professor Borchers argued that "the Clause has almost nothing to say" about recognition of sister-state marriages, pointing out that unlike divorce, marriage is not a "judicial proceeding" and the only relevant "public act" is the sister-state statute or common-law decision conferring or withholding the right to marry. As to that, he read *Baker* v. *General Motors*, supra p. 617, to confirm settled law that "differentiates the credit owed to laws (legislative measures and common law) and to judgments." See Borchers, Baker v. General Motors: *Implications for*

Interjurisdictional Recognition of Non-Traditional Marriages, 32 Creighton L. Rev. 147, 172, 175 (1998). Professor Grossman agreed, pointing out that "the historical practice and precedent for over 200 years has been to decide questions of marriage recognition without invoking full faith and credit principles to supply the answer." See Grossman, *Resurrecting Comity: Revisiting the Problem of Non-Uniform Marriage Laws*, 84 Ore. L. Rev. 433, 454 (2005).

In *Cote-Whitacre*, supra Note (1), the Supreme Judicial Court of Massachusetts refused to invalidate its 1913 statute denying marriage licenses to nonresidents whose marriage would be prohibited in their home states. The Court divided 3–3–1. A plurality found it "rational" for the commonwealth to hope that if it extends comity to the differing laws of sister states, they in turn "will correspondingly respect the laws of Massachusetts and recognize same-sex marriages of Massachusetts couples lawfully celebrated in this commonwealth." 844 N.E.2d at 645. How likely is that? A different plurality preferred to base its similar conclusion on grounds of federalism rather than comity: Massachusetts has a "concern for the integrity of its own laws" that may rationally be furthered by limiting same-sex marriages to Massachusetts residents. A dissenter objected that the "neutral principle" announced in *Goodridge* "forecloses application of other States' discriminatory marriage laws in the commonwealth, because such discrimination is against our public policy." Id., 844 N.E.2d at 664. Who had the better of this argument?

Citing *Hughes v. Fetter*, supra p. 414, Professor Kramer contends that the Full Faith and Credit Clause prohibits "a state's refusal to apply another state's law, otherwise applicable under forum choice-of-law rules, on the ground that it promotes a policy the forum finds repugnant." See Kramer, *Same-Sex Marriage, Conflict of Laws, and the Unconstitutional Public Policy Exception*, 106 Yale L.J. 1965, 1987–90 (1997). Does *Hughes* stand for that proposition?

Professor Reppy argues on historical grounds that the relevant Full Faith and Credit provision is the "records" designation. The issuance of a marriage license, he claims, "involves creating a 'record' under the Clause and 28 U.S.C. § 1739, which implements the records prong of the constitutional Clause." See Reppy, *The Framework of Full Faith and Credit and Interstate Recognition of Same-Sex Marriages*, 3 Ave Maria L.Rev. 393, 401 (2005). A similar argument was rejected *Wilson* v. *Ake*, 354 F.Supp.2d 1298 (D. Fla. 2005), *appeal dismissed with prejudice on joint motion of parties* (No. 04–14362, 11th Cir. 2005), a proceeding by a lesbian couple married in Massachusetts to obtain recognition of their marriage license in Florida, on the ground that the Clause does not "enable one state to legislate for the other or to project its laws across state lines so as to preclude the other from prescribing for itself the legal consequences of acts within it." Does Kramer's argument mean that *Wilson* was wrongly decided? Why do you suppose the parties dismissed the appeal?

(8) What other interstate issues arise from same-sex relationships? (Interstate child custody questions are considered in Section 2, infra.) In *V.L. v. E.L.*, 577 U.S. 404 (2016), E.L. raised her three biological children together with V.L., her same-sex partner. A Georgia court entered an adoption decree allowing V.L. to adopt the children and recognizing both women as their legal parents. After V.L. and E.L. ended their relationship while living in Alabama, V.L. alleged that E.L. had denied her access to the children and interfered with her ability to exercise her parental rights. She asked an Alabama court to register the Georgia adoption judgment and award her custody or visitation rights. The Alabama court entered an order awarding V.L. scheduled visitation with the children. The Alabama Supreme Court reversed, holding that Alabama courts were not required to give full faith and credit to the Georgia judgment. The U.S. Supreme Court summarily reversed:

> Under Georgia law, as relevant here, "[t]he superior courts of the several counties shall have exclusive jurisdiction in all matters of adoption." That provision on its face gave the Georgia Superior Court subject-matter jurisdiction to hear and decide the adoption petition at issue here. The Superior Court resolved that matter by entering a final judgment that made V.L. the legal adoptive parent of the children. Whatever the merits of that judgment, it was within the statutory grant of jurisdiction over "all matters of adoption." The Georgia court thus had the "adjudicatory authority over the subject matter" required to entitle its judgment to full faith and credit. *Baker v. General Motors Corp.*, 522 U.S. at 233.
>
> The Alabama Supreme Court reached a different result by relying on Ga. Code Ann. § 19–8–5(a). That statute states (as relevant here) that "a child who has any living parent or guardian may be adopted by a third party . . . only if each such living parent and each such guardian has voluntarily and in writing surrendered all of his or her rights to such child." The Alabama Supreme Court concluded that this provision prohibited the Georgia Superior Court from allowing V.L. to adopt the children while also allowing E.L. to keep her existing parental rights. It further concluded that this provision went not to the merits but to the Georgia court's subject-matter jurisdiction. In reaching that crucial second conclusion, the Alabama Supreme Court seems to have relied solely on the fact that the right to adoption under Georgia law is purely statutory, and "[t]he requirements of Georgia's adoptions statutes are mandatory and must be strictly construed in favor of the natural parents."

That analysis is not consistent with this Court's controlling precedent. Where a judgment indicates on its face that it was rendered by a court of competent jurisdiction, such jurisdiction " 'is to be presumed unless disproved.' " * * * There is nothing here to rebut that presumption. The Georgia statute on which the Alabama Supreme Court relied, Ga.Code Ann. § 19–8–5(a), does not speak in jurisdictional terms; for instance, it does not say that a Georgia court "shall have jurisdiction to enter an adoption decree" only if each existing parent or guardian has surrendered his or her parental rights. Neither the Georgia Supreme Court nor any Georgia appellate court, moreover, has construed § 19–8–5(a) as jurisdictional. * * *

Section 19–8–5(a) does not become jurisdictional just because it is "mandatory" and "must be strictly construed." * * * This Court "has long rejected the notion that all mandatory prescriptions, however emphatic, are properly typed jurisdictional." * * *

As Justice Holmes observed more than a century ago, "it sometimes may be difficult to decide whether certain words in a statute are directed to jurisdiction or to merits." *Fauntleroy v. Lum,* 210 U.S. 230, 234–235 (1908). In such cases, especially where the Full Faith and Credit Clause is concerned, a court must be "slow to read ambiguous words, as meaning to leave the judgment open to dispute, or as intended to do more than fix the rule by which the court should decide." *Id.,* at 235. That time-honored rule controls here. The Georgia judgment appears on its face to have been issued by a court with jurisdiction, and there is no established Georgia law to the contrary. It follows that the Alabama Supreme Court erred in refusing to grant that judgment full faith and credit.

Does the Supreme Court's *per curiam* decision in *V.L. v. E.L.* rest on the determination that the Alabama court erred in construing the Georgia statute as not jurisdictional? Isn't that a state-law issue?

In *Davenport v. Little-Bowser*, 269 Va. 546, 611 S.E.2d 366 (2005), three same-sex couples adopted four children through proceedings in the District of Columbia and New York. All four children had been born in Virginia, and the adoptive parents applied to the Virginia State Registrar for the issuance of new birth certificates containing the names of the child and both adoptive parents. The Registrar refused to issue the new certificates, and its refusal was sustained by the trial court on two grounds: first, that the Virginia birth certificate form provided spaces for listing only the names of a mother and a father, not the names of two mothers or two fathers; and second, that to issue a new certificate would compel the recognition of a status that Virginia does not accord to its own citizens. On appeal, a 5–2 majority of the Virginia Supreme Court reversed, stressing the limited nature of petitioners' requests:

> At the outset it is important to state what this case is not about. There was much discussion in the trial court, and some before this Court, concerning homosexual marriage. This case is about issuing birth certificates under the provisions of Virginia law; it is not about homosexual marriage, nor is it about "same-sex" relationships, nor is it about adoption policy in Virginia. . . .
>
> We need not address federal constitutional or statutory issues in this case because we hold that a proper interpretation of Code § 32.1–261 requires that the Registrar issue a new certificate of birth listing both of the adoptive parents in each of the cases before us.

Id., 269 Va. at 552, 557, 611 S.E.2d at 369, 372. The two dissenters emphasized that the Virginia statute relied on by the majority required only that the Registrar issue a new certificate "on the form in use at the time of [the adoptive child's] birth," and that form contained spaces only for the names of a mother and a father. Why couldn't the Rhode Island court in *Chambers* have done what the Virginia court did in *Little-Bowser*?

(9) Oklahoma enacted the following amendment to its adoption statute in 2004 to prohibit recognition of adoptions by same-sex couples performed outside the state: "This state, or any of its agencies, or any court of this state, shall not recognize an adoption by more than one individual of the same sex from any other state or foreign jurisdiction." Okla. Stat. Ann. tit. 10, § 7501–1.4 (West Supp. 2004). The statute was challenged immediately by several gay and lesbian couples who had adopted children in other states and who lived in, or wished to travel to, Oklahoma with their children, claiming that it violates the Full Faith and Credit Clause, the Equal Protection Clause, and infringes on their fundamental right to travel. The district court ruled for the plaintiffs, citing *Baker v. General Motors Corp.*, supra p. 617, in support of its holding that "regardless of whether the adoption decrees of other states are contrary to the public policy of Oklahoma, because they are judgments, not laws, they are entitled to full faith and credit." *Finstuen v. Edmondson*, 497 F.Supp.2d 1295, 1306 (W.D. Okla. 2006), *aff'd in part and rev'd in part*, 496 F.3d 1139, 1156 (10th Cir. 2007) (stating that "[w]e hold today that final adoption orders and decrees are judgments that are entitled to recognition by all other states under the Full Faith and Credit Clause. Therefore, Oklahoma's adoption amendment is unconstitutional in its refusal to recognize final adoption decrees of other states that permit adoption by same-sex couples.")

To like effect is *Embry v. Ryan*, 11 So.3d 408 (Fla. App. 2009). Two women lived together as a couple in the state of Washington, where one of them gave birth to a child whom the other soon adopted. Subsequently, the family moved to Florida where the two women decided to separate in 2004. They entered into an agreement providing for custody of the child, visitation, and property settlement in Florida. When the relationship soured, the adoptive filed a petition seeking a determination of parental responsibility, contact and support. A Florida statute provides that adoption judgments validly entered by "a court of any other jurisdiction within or without the United States, shall be recognized in this state, and the rights and obligations of the parties on matters within the jurisdiction of this state shall be determined as though the judgment were issued by a court of this state." § 63.192, Fla. Stat. The Florida Court of Appeal observed that, even though Florida does not authorize adoptions by same-sex couples, § 63.192 requires that Embry "must be given the same rights as any other adoptive person in Florida." Citing *Baker* as the Oklahoma court had done, the appellate court held that "regardless of whether the trial court believed that the Washington adoption violated a clearly established public policy in Florida, it was improper for the trial court to refuse to give the Washington judgment full faith and credit." *Id.*, 11 So.3d at 410.

On remand, the biological mother argued that recognition of the adoption did not require "ratification and affirmation of a private contract regarding child custody entered into in the context of a same sex domestic partnership, a relationship which is simply not recognized for any purpose under Florida law." Judge Fulmer, specially concurring, characterized it as urging "a distinction between recognition and enforcement of a judgment" and pointed out that it lacked merit because § 63.192 meant that the same-sex nature of the relationship was irrelevant. *Id.*, 11 So.3d at 411.

(10) Is the argument based on *Baker* valid? It was rejected by the district court but accepted by the Fifth Circuit en banc in *Adar v. Smith*, 591 F.Supp.2d 857, 862–64 (E.D. La. 2008), *rev'd*, 639 F.3d 146 (5th Cir. 2011), a case in which the district court had required the Louisiana State Registrar to recognize the New York adoption of a child born in Louisiana by two unmarried gay men who resided with the child in California. Responding to the Registrar's objection that she was not permitted by Louisiana law to enforce the sister-state judgment by issuing a new birth certificate listing the names of "two unmarried persons on a joint birth certificate," the district court acknowledged that, under *Baker*, enforcement measures remain "subject to the even-handed control of the forum's law." It pointed out, however, that the "plain language" of the relevant Louisiana statute "specifically directs the Registrar to make a new record upon receipt of the adoption decree, and no limitations or restrictions are present within the language of the statute." The Fifth Circuit, however, thought otherwise. Quoting *Baker*, it reasoned:

> The states' duty to "recognize" sister state judgments, however, does not compel states to "adopt the practices of other States regarding the time, manner, and mechanisms for enforcing judgments." . . . Rather, enforcement of judgments is "subject to the evenhanded control of forum law." "Evenhanded" means only that the state executes a sister state judgment in the same way that it would execute judgments in the forum court.
>
> In this case, the Registrar has not refused to recognize the *validity* of the New York adoption decree. The Registrar concedes that the parental relationship of Adar and Smith with Infant J cannot be revisited in its courts. That question is not at issue. The Registrar in fact offered to comply with Louisiana law and reissue a birth certificate showing one of the unmarried adults as the adoptive parent. The Registrar acknowledged that even though she would not issue the requested birth certificate with both names, the Registrar recognizes Appellees as the legal parents of their adopted child. And the Appellees apparently agree, admitting that birth certificates are merely "identity documents that *evidence* . . . the existing parent-child relationships, but do not create them." Appellees affirm that "the child at the center of this case" is already "legally adopted—and nothing that happens in this case will change that." In sum, no right created by the New York adoption order (i.e., right to custody, parental control, etc.) has been frustrated, as nothing in the order entitles Appellees to a particular type of birth certificate.

639 F.3d at 159. The Fifth Circuit went on to review other U.S. Supreme Court cases applying the Full Faith and Credit clause, including *Broderick v. Rosner,* supra p. 418, *Estin v. Estin,* supra p. 666, and *Fall v. Eastin,* supra p. 599, in which it found support for the proposition that "the Court has never required the enforcement of every right which has ripened into a judgment of another state or has been conferred by its statutes." Returning finally to *Baker*, it concluded that

> The Court continues to maintain a stark distinction between recognition and enforcement of judgments under the full faith and credit clause, as *Baker* confirms. The Court held that a Michigan injunction barring a former General Motors employee from testifying against GM could not control proceedings against GM brought in other states. . . .
>
> Similarly, the New York adoption decree cannot compel within Louisiana "an official act within the exclusive province" of that state. The full faith and credit clause emphatically "did not make the judgments of other States domestic judgments to all

> intents and purposes." . . . Rather, the adoption decree "can only be executed in [Louisiana] as its laws may permit." . . .

639 F.3d at 160 (citations omitted). Do you agree that *Baker* controls the outcome in *Adar*? How much leeway does *Baker*'s "stark distinction between recognition and enforcement of judgments under the full faith and credit clause" confer on the recognizing court? Is it significant that the adoptive parents in *Adar* were not married? Presumably the Louisiana Registrar would also deny a revised birth certificate showing both names to an unmarried opposite-sex adoptive couple. Would the case have been harder if the two men had been validly married at the time they applied for a revised birth certificate? One commentator who has analyzed both *Finstuen* and *Adar* argued that *Adar* had failed to apply the Full Faith and Credit clause properly and concluded with a plea to the U.S. Supreme Court to resolve the current conflict between the Tenth and Fifth Circuits by endorsing *Finstuen*. See Note, *Having Faith in Full Faith and Credit:* Finstuen, Adar, *and the Quest for Interstate Same-Sex Parental Recognition,* 98 Iowa L. Rev. 365 (2012).

For other variants of the distinction between recognition and enforcement of judgments in child custody litigation, see infra pp. 738–746.

SECTION 2. CHILD CUSTODY

A. INTERSTATE CHILD CUSTODY

1. Subject-Matter Jurisdiction

WELCH-DODEN V. ROBERTS

202 Ariz. 201, 42 P.3d 1166 (App. 2002).

BARKER, JUDGE.

This opinion resolves a statutory conflict in the meaning of "home state" as that phrase is used to determine initial jurisdiction between competing states in child custody disputes under Arizona's newly adopted Uniform Child Custody Jurisdiction and Enforcement Act ("UCCJEA"). Ariz.Rev.Stat. ("A.R.S.") §§ 25–1001 to –1067 (Supp.2001). This opinion also addresses other issues concerning the implementation of the UCCJEA.

This special action arises from the trial court's dismissal of a petition for dissolution of marriage, with a minor child, due to lack of jurisdiction.[1]

[1] The entire petition was dismissed. The trial court could have retained jurisdiction as to the dissolution of the marriage, even without jurisdiction over the child. A.R.S. §§ 25–311, 25–312 (2000); *Schilz v. Superior Court,* 144 Ariz. 65, 68, 695 P.2d 1103, 1106 (1985) ("Jurisdiction over the divorce does not necessarily imply jurisdiction over related proceedings."). Whether the dissolution itself should have been dismissed has not been presented in this special action and, therefore, is not addressed. *See Carrillo v. State,* 169 Ariz. 126, 132, 817 P.2d 493, 499 (App.1991).

Melissa Welch-Doden ("mother") and Terry Welch-Doden ("father") were married in Arizona in November 1996. After being unable to secure employment in Arizona, mother and father moved to Oklahoma. Their child was born in Oklahoma on April 28, 1999.

After the child was born, mother and child moved back and forth between Arizona and Oklahoma. Mother claims that she, along with her husband and the child, intended to resume their residence in Arizona. She was traveling back and forth between the two states to research employment opportunities and living expenses in Arizona. On her last return to Arizona, mother claims that she was waiting for father to join her. When he did not, she filed for divorce and custody.

The timetable of the child's residence since birth until the filing of the petition is as follows: Oklahoma from birth on April 28, 1999 and for the next seven and one-half months (April 1999–December 1999); Arizona for three months (December 1999–March 2000); Oklahoma for six months (March 2000–September 2000); Arizona for the four months prior to the filing of the petition (September 2000–January 25, 2001). At all times, the child was with mother.

Mother filed for dissolution and custody on January 25, 2001 in Arizona. On February 8, 2001, two days after being served with notice of the Arizona petition, father filed a petition for divorce and custody in Oklahoma. . .

On March 7, 2001, father appeared specially in Arizona to move to dismiss the Arizona petition for lack of jurisdiction. . . .

After hearing from both sides and conferring with the Oklahoma trial judge, the trial judge ruled that Oklahoma had home state jurisdiction pursuant to UCCJEA. The trial judge determined Oklahoma had been the child's home state *within* the six months before the petition was filed (but not the home state *for* the six-month period immediately prior to the filing). Accordingly, the trial court found that Oklahoma was entitled to jurisdiction. This was so even though the trial judge determined that the first petition filed was mother's Arizona petition.

The trial judge dismissed the Arizona action and also denied mother's motion for reconsideration. In subsequent proceedings in Oklahoma, the Oklahoma trial judge granted father's decree of divorce and awarded custody to father on September 5, 2001. The net effect of these rulings was that the child, who resided with mother in Arizona, was to be placed in the custody of father in Oklahoma. . . .

We consider several issues: First, does the UCCJEA provide that home state jurisdiction is based on a child residing in a state (a) for a six-month period *immediately prior* to the filing of a custody petition, or (b) for a six-month period that is completed *at any time within* six months of the filing?

Second, if a state has home state jurisdiction, does home state jurisdiction then become pre-eminent, thereby precluding a court without home state jurisdiction from considering the child's best interests for jurisdictional purposes?

And finally, does a state with home state jurisdiction have jurisdictional priority when a petition in another state was filed first-in-time?

All of the issues pertain to the question of jurisdiction to make an *initial* custody determination. There is a separate (but intertwined) statutory scheme for *continuing* jurisdiction after an initial custody determination in compliance with the UCCJEA has been made. A.R.S. § 25–1032. Section 25–1031 is the statutory starting place for determining initial jurisdiction.[5] In summary, subsection B makes it clear that Arizona *only* has jurisdiction pursuant to subsection A. A.R.S. § 25–1031(B) ("Subsection A of this section is the *exclusive* jurisdictional basis.") (emphasis added). Subsection A, paragraph (1) provides for Arizona to have jurisdiction when Arizona qualifies as a home state. . . If a state is the "home state" under this paragraph, it has jurisdiction. There is no further factual inquiry on the *jurisdictional* issue. Paragraphs (2)–(4) of subsection A provide the circumstances whereby Arizona may have jurisdiction when it does *not* qualify as the home state. Paragraph 2, in particular, requires the court to consider whether the child has a significant connection to the state (as well as other factors) before jurisdiction may be found. Subsection

---

[5] A.R.S. § 25–1031 provides in full as follows:

A. Except as otherwise provided in § 25–1034, a court of this State has jurisdiction to make an initial child custody determination only if any of the following is true:

1. This state is the home state of the child on the date of the commencement of the proceeding, or was the home state of the child within six months before the commencement of the proceeding and the child is absent from this state but a parent or person acting as a parent continues to live in this state.

2. A court of another state does not have jurisdiction under paragraph 1 or a court of the home state of the child has declined to exercise jurisdiction on the ground that this state is the more appropriate forum under § 25–1037 or 25–1038 and both of the following are true:

(a) The child and the child's parents, or the child and at least one parent or a person acting as a parent, have a significant connection with this state other than mere physical presence.

(b) Substantial evidence is available in this state concerning the child's care, protection, training and personal relationships.

3. All courts having jurisdiction under paragraph 1 or 2 have declined to exercise jurisdiction on the ground that a court of this state is the more appropriate forum to determine the custody of the child under § 25–1037 or 25–1038.

4. A court of any other state would not have jurisdiction under the criteria specified in paragraph 1, 2 or 3.

B. Subsection A of this section is the exclusive jurisdictional basis for making a child custody determination by a court of this state

C. Physical presence of or personal jurisdiction over a party or a child is not necessary or sufficient to make a child custody determination.

C clarifies that the presence of the child is neither necessary nor sufficient to establish jurisdiction. . .

In considering § 25–1031 as it relates to the present case, we must also take into account the statutory definition of "home state." Section 25–1002(7)(a) defines "home state" as follows:

> In this chapter, unless the context otherwise requires . . . "[h]ome state" means: The state in which a child lived with a parent or a person acting as a parent for *at least six consecutive months immediately before the commencement of a child custody proceeding,* including any period during which that person is temporarily absent from that state.

A.R.S. § 25–1002(7)(a) (emphasis added). It is the application of this definition of "home state" to § 25–1031(A)(1) that creates the statutory conflict.

Specifically, under § 25–1031(A)(1), a state has jurisdiction if the "home state" qualifier is met under either one of two elements:

> This state is the [1] home state of the child *on the date of the commencement of the proceeding,* or [2] was the home state of the child *within six months before the commencement* of the proceeding and the child is absent from this state but a parent or person acting as a parent continues to live in this state. A.R.S. § 25–1031(A)(1) (emphasis added).

The definition of "home state" under § 25–1002(7)(a) provides, however, that a state is a "home state" *only* when "a child lived with a parent . . . for at least six consecutive months *immediately before* the commencement of a child custody proceeding."[7] (Emphasis added.)

Thus, applying literally the definition of "home state" from § 25–1002(7)(a) to element one of § 25–1031(A)(1) renders superfluous the language in § 25–1031(A)(1) that says jurisdiction lies when a state is the home state "on the date of the commencement of the proceeding." That latter phrase merely restates what is already required by the definition of "home state" in § 25–1002(7)(a).

Element two of § 25–1031(A)(1) poses a more significant problem in statutory construction when the home state definition from § 25–1002(7)(a) is applied: the two statutes directly conflict. Element two of § 25–1031(A)(1) provides that a state has jurisdiction if it is the "home state . . . *within six months before*" the commencement of the child custody proceeding. Section 25–1002(7)(a), as noted above, requires that in order to be a "home state" at all, a child must have lived in a state for six consecutive months "immediately before" the child custody proceeding. Thus, if a child's

[7] We note that there are exceptions when a child is "temporarily absent from that state." A.R.S. § 25–1002(7)(a). That provision is not at issue here.

home state two months before a proceeding was commenced is different from the state to which a child has permanently moved (and in which the proceeding was commenced), § 25–1002(7)(a) would indicate there is no home state at all. Initial jurisdiction would then be determined based on substantial connections to the state and other factors under § 25–1031(A)(2). On the other hand, under the same facts, element two of § 25–1031(A)(1) would declare the *prior state* the home state because it was the home state *within* six months of the filing. Initial jurisdiction would then be in the prior state regardless of any significant connections to the state in which the filing was made.

The statutory conflict between element two of § 25–1031(A)(1) and § 25–1002(7)(a) is directly at issue here. The child lived in Oklahoma for six consecutive months ending in September 2000. The child then resided in Arizona for the next four months, immediately before the petition was filed in January 2001. Thus, under father's (and the trial judge's) reading of the statute, Oklahoma is the home state as a matter of law under element two of § 25–1031(A)(1). Oklahoma, under this view, was the home state (from March to September 2000) *within* six months of the filing of the petition in January 2001 and thus has initial jurisdiction.

Under mother's reading of the statute, however, neither Oklahoma nor Arizona is the home state as neither state meets the requirement of § 25–1002(7)(a) that the child live in the state "for at least six consecutive months *immediately before the commencement*" of the proceeding. Under that scenario, Oklahoma does not have initial jurisdiction. The trial court would be required to hold a hearing to determine whether there were significant connections with Arizona and other factors per § 25–1031(A)(2), to determine whether Arizona should have initial jurisdiction. Thus, depending upon how one resolves the conflict between these competing interpretations, the outcome may differ.

* * *

To appropriately resolve the conflict here, it is critical to examine the stated purposes behind the changes in home state jurisdiction brought about by the UCCJEA.

The precursor to the UCCJEA was the Uniform Child Custody Jurisdiction Act ("UCCJA"). It was developed in 1968 by the National Conference of Commissioners on Uniform State Laws and adopted by Arizona in 1978. . . The stated purposes of the UCCJA were to avoid jurisdictional competition and conflict, promote cooperation between states, discourage the use of the interstate system to continue custody controversies, deter abductions, avoid relitigation in different states, and facilitate enforcement of custody decrees between states. . .

All fifty states, the District of Columbia and the Virgin Islands adopted the UCCJA. . . However, many states departed from its original text, and subsequent litigation produced substantial inconsistencies in interpretation among state courts—defeating the goals of a uniform interstate jurisdictional act. . .

In particular, prior to the adoption of the UCCJEA, the UCCJA provided four separate bases to take initial jurisdiction in child custody disputes. Those bases included (1) domicile or home state, (2) significant connections to the state and a consideration of the child's relationships, training, care and protection, (3) the child's best interests, and (4) emergency.

The original drafters of the UCCJA had assumed that home state jurisdiction was the most appropriate factor in demonstrating the best interests of the child. . . They also thought that a state should be able to proceed without delay and, therefore, should find jurisdiction on any acceptable basis. Thus, the drafters included the four separate bases for jurisdiction. However, state courts were split as to whether the four bases were equal or whether home state was preferred . . . These conflicts created an unworkable and non-uniform interstate act.

Additionally, in 1981 a significant federal statute was passed by the United States Congress. That statute, the Parental Kidnapping Prevention Act ("PKPA"), 28 U.S.C. § 1738A, was aimed at interstate custody problems that continued to exist after the adoption of the UCCJA. . . It mandated states to apply full faith and credit to interstate custody decisions. Importantly, it did not allow for full faith and credit on the four bases as set forth in the UCCJA. 28 U.S.C. § 1738A(c)(2). Instead, enforceability[9] under the PKPA was based on the priority of home-state jurisdiction:

> A child custody or visitation determination made by a court of a State is consistent with the provisions of this section *only if such State* (i) *is the home State* of the child on the date of the commencement of the proceeding, *or* (ii) *had been the child's home State within six months* before the date of the commencement of the proceeding and the child is absent from such State because of his removal or retention by a contestant or for other reasons, and a contestant continues to live in such State.

28 U.S.C. § 1738A(c)(2)(A) (emphasis added).

In 1997, the National Conference of Commissioners on Uniform State Laws, which had authored the UCCJA, drafted the UCCJEA. The main purposes for revising the UCCJA were uniformity and the need to avoid

[9] "PKPA only governs enforceability of one state's custody order in another state. . . . [It] 'does not purport to control jurisdiction to issue an initial order.' " *In re Jorgensen,* 627 N.W.2d 550, 559 (Iowa 2001) (citation omitted).

disputes between competing jurisdictions. . . Arizona adopted the UCCJEA effective January 1, 2001. . .

The UCCJEA drafters dealt specifically with the conflict created by differing jurisdictions taking contrary views of the four bases of jurisdiction. They reconciled the jurisdictional provisions of the UCCJA with the PKPA. . . The drafters made it clear that the new act was to give priority to a finding of home state jurisdiction over any other jurisdictional provisions.

Furthermore, the UCCJEA completely eliminates a determination of "best interests" of a child from the jurisdictional inquiry. . . These changes advance a more efficient and "bright line" jurisdictional rule consistent with the UCCJEA's purpose. . . The UCCJEA specifically seeks to avoid a judicial analysis of substantive issues in the determination of jurisdiction. Additionally, as noted above, the statutory text of § 25–1031(A) allows consideration of other substantive factors *only* if no state qualifies as a "home state."

It is clear from the drafters' intent that the UCCJEA should be construed to promote one of its primary purposes: avoiding the jurisdictional competition and conflict that flows from hearings in competing states when each state substantively reviews subjective factors (such as "best interests") for purposes of determining initial jurisdiction. With this fundamental purpose in mind, when there is a statutory conflict in the application of home state jurisdiction, the conflict should be resolved to strengthen (rather than dilute) the certainty of home state jurisdiction. This course is consistent with the UCCJEA's statutory purpose.

Given the fundamental purpose of the UCCJEA to establish the certainty of home state jurisdiction, it is clear to us that § 25–1031(A)(1) acts to enlarge and modify the definition of home state under § 25–1002(7)(a). We hold that "home state" for purposes of determining initial jurisdiction under § 25–1031(A)(1) is not limited to the time period of "six consecutive months immediately before the commencement of a child custody proceeding [.]" A.R.S. § 25–1002(7)(a). Instead, the applicable time period to determine "home state" in such circumstances is "within six months before the commencement of the [child custody] proceeding." A.R.S. § 25–1031(A)(1). This interpretation promotes the priority of home state jurisdiction that the drafters specifically intended. To adopt the reading that mother supports would result in narrowing home state jurisdiction. It would increase the number of potentially conflicting jurisdictional disputes in competing jurisdictions. This is contrary to the UCCJEA's purpose.

Even though the UCCJEA is a uniform act, which has been adopted by twenty-seven states and introduced in nine states, we have found no cases that construe the statutory conflict at issue. While not discussing the conflict, other states have ruled in a manner that is consistent with the interpretation we adopt here. *E.g., In re McCoy,* 52 S.W.3d 297, 303–04 (Tex. App. 2001) (finding that Texas was not the children's home state at any time during the six months prior to the filing of the suit); *Nesa v. Baten,* 736 N.Y.S.2d 173, 174 (N.Y.A.D. 2002) ("New York had not been the children's home state at the time of commencement of the custody proceeding or within the preceding six months.").

* * *

Thus, we conclude that the trial court did not err in rejecting mother's position and concluding that Oklahoma had home state jurisdiction. . .

* * *

Second, mother argues that the equitable issues presented in a case such as this one (child having always been with mother; mother and child having significant connections in Arizona; mother and child having lived in Arizona for the four months prior to filing) or in a hypothetical case (child lives five months and 29 days in one state, but the prior six months in another resulting in home state jurisdiction in the prior case) require a hearing to consider the child's best interests. Mother's argument does not consider that the UCCJEA expressly provides for a factual hearing *in the home state* in which that state may decline to exercise its jurisdiction and allow another jurisdiction to proceed . . . This hearing may include a "best interests" determination.

The drafters of the UCCJEA expressly recognized—and sought to eliminate—the jurisdictional disputes that resulted when "best interests" was used to determine initial jurisdiction. That language and inquiry, present in the previously enacted UCCJA, was intentionally omitted from the newly-drafted UCCJEA. The drafters stated:

> The *"best interest" language* in the jurisdictional sections of the UCCJA was *not intended to be an invitation to address the merits of the custody dispute in the jurisdictional determination* or to otherwise provide that "best interests" considerations should override jurisdictional determinations or provide an additional jurisdictional basis.
>
> [This draft] eliminates the term "best interests" in order to clearly distinguish between the jurisdictional standards and the substantive standards relating to custody and visitation of children.

9 U.L.A. at 651–652 (emphasis added).

Thus, the "best interests" analysis does not take place in determining jurisdiction. "Best interests" may be fully explored and considered in the context of a request under A.R.S. § 25–1037.[15] That provision expressly

[15] The full text of A.R.S. § 25–1037 reads as follows:

allows for the court having home state jurisdiction to consider "all relevant factors" in determining whether the home state is an "inconvenient forum" such that jurisdiction should be elsewhere. A.R.S. § 25–1037(B).

The issue of an inconvenient forum "may be raised on motion of a party, the court's own motion or request of another court." A.R.S. § 25–1037(A). Any such request, however, must be pursued in Oklahoma rather than Arizona, as Oklahoma has home state jurisdiction pursuant to A.R.S. § 25–1031(A)(1). This is critical: To allow the state without home state jurisdiction to conduct the hearing would lead to the jurisdictional competition the drafters sought to avoid. Thus the equitable arguments that mother wishes to pursue are not eliminated, but are merely re-directed to the home state. If she chooses, mother can ask the Oklahoma court to relinquish jurisdiction.

Accordingly, mother's argument that the trial judge erred in not considering the "best interests" of the child, when dealing with a jurisdictional question under § 25–1031(A)(1), is wrong. The trial judge correctly determined that this was an issue for the Oklahoma court.

Mother also argues, relying on A.R.S. § 25–1036(A), that Arizona should have jurisdiction as her filing was first-in-time. This argument fails as well. A.R.S. § 25–1036 provides in pertinent part as follows:

> [A] court of this State *shall not exercise its jurisdiction under this article if,* at the time of the commencement of the proceeding, *a*

A. A court of this state that has jurisdiction under this chapter to make a child custody determination may decline to exercise its jurisdiction at any time if it determines that it is an inconvenient forum under the circumstances and that a court of another state is a more appropriate forum. The issue of inconvenient forum may be raised on motion of a party, the court's own motion or request of another court.

B. Before determining whether it is an inconvenient forum, a court of this state shall consider whether it is appropriate for a court of another state to exercise jurisdiction. For this purpose, the court shall allow the parties to submit information and shall consider all relevant factors including:

1. Whether domestic violence has occurred and is likely to continue in the future and which state could best protect the parties and the child.
2. The length of time the child has resided outside this state.
3. The distance between the court in this state and the court in the state that would assume jurisdiction.
4. The relative financial circumstances of the parties.
5. Any agreement of the parties as to which state should assume jurisdiction.
6. The nature and location of the evidence required to resolve the pending litigation, including testimony of the child.
7. The ability of the court of each state to decide the issue expeditiously and the procedures necessary to present the evidence.
8. The familiarity of the court of each state with the facts and issues in the pending litigation.

C. If a court of this state determines that it is an inconvenient forum and that a court of another state is a more appropriate forum, it shall stay the proceedings on condition that a child custody proceeding be promptly commenced in another designated state and may impose any other condition the court considers just and proper.

> *proceeding concerning the custody of the child has been commenced* in a court of another state having jurisdiction substantially in conformity with this chapter[.]

Id. (emphasis added). Oklahoma has a similar provision. Okla. Stat. Ann. tit. 43, § 551–206(A) (Supp.2000).

Mother's argument is that this provision mandates jurisdiction in Arizona as the filing was first-in-time. What mother ignores is that the first-in-time filing must be in a state "having jurisdiction substantially in conformity with this chapter." A.R.S. § 25–1036(A); *see also* Okla. Stat. Ann. tit. 43, § 551–206(A). Because Oklahoma had home state jurisdiction, Arizona did not have jurisdiction "substantially in conformity with this chapter." Thus, the first-in-time filing granted mother no rights. The trial court did not err by rejecting mother's request that a first-in-time filing conferred initial jurisdiction upon the Arizona Court.

For the foregoing reasons, the trial court did not err in determining that it was without jurisdiction to consider mother's child custody request. Therefore, we deny mother's requested relief.

THOMPSON, P.J. and LANKFORD, J., concurring.

The "Interstate Child"

(1) The mobility of American families, coupled with the lack of finality of child custody decrees, means that every domestic divorce case involving children is a potential interstate nightmare. In *Sampsell v. Superior Court,* 32 Cal.2d 763, 197 P.2d 739 (1948), Justice Traynor clearly recognized that, as long as the United States Supreme Court's view of full faith and credit allowed other states "at least as much leeway to disregard the judgment, to qualify it, or to depart from it" as the rendering state enjoyed (*New York ex rel. Halvey v. Halvey,* 330 U.S. 610, 619 (1947)), the critical point in interstate custody cases was to obtain control over the power to modify as well as the power to make the initial award. To achieve this goal, Traynor's concept of "concurrent jurisdiction" announced in *Sampsell* would have located jurisdiction to award custody or to modify it in several states: that where the child is domiciled, is physically present, or where there is personal jurisdiction over the parents. Conflict among these overlapping jurisdictions was to be avoided by a decent respect for the judgment of other states. This view was endorsed by Professor Currie, *Full Faith and Credit, Chiefly to Judgments: A Role for Congress,* 1964 Sup.Ct.Rev. 89, 109–118, and ultimately adopted by Restatement (Second) of Conflict of Laws § 79 (1971).

(2) But doesn't the *Sampsell* approach merely encourage the losing parent to remove the child to another jurisdiction and start over again? This concern formed the basis of the Uniform Child Custody Jurisdiction Act (UCCJA), which was promulgated in 1968. Professor Brigitte Bodenheimer, the Reporter, explained its structure as follows:

> The basic scheme of the Act is simple. First, one court in the country assumes full responsibility for custody of a particular child. Second, for this purpose a court is selected which has access to as much relevant information about the child and family in the state as possible. Third, other essential evidence, which is inevitably out-of-state in the case of an interstate child, is channelled into the first court which might be called the "custody court." Fourth, other states abide by the decision of the custody court and enforce it in their territory, if necessary. Fifth, adjustments in visitation and other ancillary provisions of the decree, and custody changes, if any, are as a rule made by the original custody court. Sixth, if the child and his family no longer have appreciable ties with the state of the original court, a new custody court is selected to take the place of the original one for purposes of adjustments and modifications, and pertinent information is channelled from the prior to the subsequent custody court.
>
> * * *
>
> Every section of the Act is to be applied in the light of its basic purposes, as expressed in section 1, to discourage continuing controversies over child custody in the interest of stability of home environment for the child, to deter child abductions and similar practices employed to obtain custody awards, and to promote mutual interstate judicial assistance in custody cases.

Bodenheimer, *The Uniform Child Custody Jurisdiction Act: A Legislative Remedy for Children Caught in the Conflict of Laws,* 22 Vand.L.Rev. 1207, 1218–19 (1969). The UCCJA was adopted in all states and the District of Columbia.

(3) As *Welch-Doden* points out, however, in practice the UCCJA did not operate as smoothly as the drafters had hoped. Given the opportunity to pick and choose among the four bases of jurisdiction it provided, many courts were unwilling to defer to a court in another state. A notable exception was provided by the New York Court of Appeals, which resolved an incipient conflict between the parties' marital home (New York) where the husband continued to reside and their summer home (Connecticut) where the wife had moved with the three children and filed a proceeding for dissolution of the marriage, child custody, and child support by observing that "given the pendency of the Connecticut action, the question with which the court should have been concerned was not whether New York was the most appropriate forum . . . [but] rather . . . whether Connecticut was 'exercising jurisdiction in conformity' with [the Act]." *Vanneck v. Vanneck*, 49 N.Y.2d 602, 609–10 (1980).

This uncertainty among the Act's jurisdictional provisions was addressed first by Congress, which enacted the Parental Kidnapping Prevention Act (PKPA), 28 U.S.C.A. § 1738A, in 1980 to give priority to the "home state" of the child, a choice that was subsequently accepted by the Commissioners and embodied in the Uniform Child Custody Jurisdiction and Enforcement Act (UCCJEA), promulgated in 1997 to replace the UCCJA. Did the PKPA also confer jurisdiction on the federal courts to determine as an initial matter which state court may proceed under the Act, or, if there are conflicting state decisions, to determine which is valid? In *Thompson* v. *Thompson*, 484 U.S. 174, 187 (1988), the Court gave limited scope to the Act, reasoning that "the context, language and history of PKPA together make out a conclusive case against inferring a cause of action in federal court to determine which of two conflicting state custody decrees is valid," adding that "ultimate review remains available in this Court for truly intractable jurisdictional deadlocks." The PKPA also makes available the use of the Federal Parent Locator Service for discovering the whereabouts of parents who have abducted their children. The UCCJEA has been enacted in 49 states (only Massachusetts had not enacted it as of 2021), the District of Columbia, and the U.S. Virgin Islands. It is usefully discussed in Hoff, *The ABC's of the UCCJEA: Interstate Child-Custody Practice Under the New Act*, 32 Fam. L.Q. 267 (1998), and Spector, *Uniform Child-Custody Jurisdiction and Enforcement Act (with Prefatory Note and Comments)*, 32 Fam. L.Q. 303 (1998).

(4) Neither the UCCJA nor the UCCJEA requires that the forum state have personal jurisdiction over both parents. Instead, both rely on notice and an opportunity to be heard. The choice was a deliberate one: Professor Bodenheimer conceded that Justice Burton's plurality opinion in *May v. Anderson*, 345 U.S. 528 (1953), supra p. 674, "caused the Commissioners some headaches," during the drafting process of the UCCJA because they believed that "no workable interstate custody law could . . . be built with or around" Burton's due process rationale. Bodenheimer, 22 Vand.L.Rev. at 1232–33. Instead, they chose to rely on Justice Frankfurter's concurrence, which they understood to mean that other states are "*authorized*" to recognize the forum's custody decision as binding without in personam jurisdiction over the absent parent. How sound was this decision? Is it consistent with due process to permit the parent in State A to assert jurisdiction over the custody issue, and thereby over the interests of the parent in State B, simply by giving notice of the proceedings and an opportunity to appear and be heard? Professor Ratner argued that jurisdiction based on the "established home" notion is just as consistent with due process as the earlier tests of jurisdiction based on the child's domicile or physical presence had been. Moreover, he urged,

> A child's residence at an established home constitutes a kind of parental "activity" in that state probably sufficient to provide the minimum contact necessary to subject an absent parent to the custody jurisdiction without offending traditional notions of fair play and substantial justice.

Ratner, *Child Custody in a Federal System,* 62 Mich.L.Rev. 795, 826 (1964). Do you agree with this interpretation of what *International Shoe Co. v. Washington* and its progeny, supra Chapter 4, require? The UCCJEA provides in section 201(c) that "physical presence of, or personal jurisdiction over, a party or a child is not necessary or sufficient to make a child-custody determination," and the Comment invokes Frankfurter's *May v. Anderson* concurrence just as the Commentary to section 12 of the UCCJA had done. Thus the matter remains an open question.

The Second Restatement took the position in section 79 of its 1988 Revisions that the PKPA's Full Faith and Credit mandate has settled the jurisdiction question with respect to the UCCJA (and presumably the UCCJEA as well). Its Comment states flatly that "[a] decree entitled to full faith and credit must necessarily have been rendered with judicial jurisdiction." Does this analysis dispose of any problems posed by *May v. Anderson*?

Is it possible that the critics have overstated the problem? The issue in *May v. Anderson* was the effect to be given the Wisconsin decree in an Ohio habeas corpus petition: a proceeding which tests only the naked legal right to "immediate possession" of the child's person. Is that the same thing as the recognition of a child custody determination in an interstate proceeding? See H.H. Kay, *Adoption in the Conflict of Laws: The UAA, Not the UCCJA, Is the Answer*, 84 Calif. L. Rev. 703, 736–39 (1996), observing that despite Burton's characterization the Wisconsin decree did not "cut off" the mother's right to custody: indeed, she was awarded visitation with the children. That she did not exercise those rights in Wisconsin does not mean she surrendered them. When the father returned the children to Ohio in 1951, she retained her visitation rights subject only to his rights as their primary custodian under the Wisconsin decree. Had he chosen to seek enforcement of the Wisconsin decree in Ohio upon the mother's refusal to return the children, it would have been open to her to seek modification of the decree in her favor, presumably because the circumstances had changed during the four and a half years since the original decree was entered. He decided not to take that risk, opting instead for the more limited habeas corpus proceeding which did not permit determination of the children's future placement. Viewed in that light, Burton's opinion may be read to say only that Wisconsin could not permanently deprive the mother of her legal rights as a parent without personal jurisdiction over her. Frankfurter's concurrence, in turn, can then be read as a corrective to Justice Jackson's overly broad reading of the plurality opinion which charged that it seemed "to reduce the law of custody to a rule of seize-and-run." The UCCJA did not mention the termination of parental rights, so it did not need to resolve that conflict among the Justices. The UCCJEA, however, does cover proceedings for the termination of parental rights in which child custody issues may arise, see Section 102, and so the Due Process jurisdictional question may yet need to be addressed.

(5) Is an interstate adoption a "child custody proceeding" subject to the Act? The UCCJEA commendably ends the confusion created by some courts that mistakenly had applied the UCCJA to interstate adoptions. Section 103 expressly provides that the UCCJEA "does not govern an adoption proceeding." The reasons why become clear through a comparison of the structure of child custody and adoption proceedings. A typical interstate adoption case did not fit the structure of the UCCJA. For one thing, since the adoptive infant is typically removed from the biological parent or parents shortly after birth to be placed with the prospective adoptive parents who live in another state, the child may have no home state. (Do you see why not?) For another thing, an adoption decree is a final judgment. As such, it is entitled to full faith and credit. Unlike a custody determination, which is not final so long as the child remains a minor, an adoption decree is not subject to modification. Thus there is no danger of inconsistent or overlapping determinations.

(6) Both the UCCJA and the UCCJEA permit a court to exercise emergency jurisdiction when the child is present in the state and in need of protection. By and large, courts construed the UCCJA provision narrowly. See *Martin v. Martin,* 45 N.Y.2d 739, 741 (1978) ("If their mother is an unfit parent, that is a matter for the Florida courts to decide."). See also *Marriage of Schwander,* 79 Cal.App.3d 1013 (1978) (California declines to exercise emergency jurisdiction over children being hidden within the state by paternal grandmother and defers to Illinois, which had awarded custody to the mother).

The UCCJEA renamed this source of jurisdiction "Temporary Emergency Jurisdiction" in § 204, and provided that it may be exercised when the child is present in the state and has been abandoned or is in need of protection from threatened mistreatment or abuse. For an example of such a case, see *In re Jaheim B.*, 169 Cal.App.4th 1343, 87 Cal.Rptr.3d 504 (2008), holding that California could exercise temporary emergency jurisdiction over a two-year-old boy whose homeless mother abandoned him outside the home of her relatives in San Diego and whose father was in prison in Alabama serving a sentence until 2028. The court rejected the father's argument that California should not exercise emergency jurisdiction because Florida was Jaheim's "home state." It found that

Jaheim had lived in Florida with his mother during the first two years of his life and had moved with her to California where they had lived for five months with her aunt and uncle until she left him alone there, telling a social worker that she could not "handle" him anymore and did not want him around her when she was out making money "in other ways" than regular employment. The San Diego court communicated with a court in Dade County, Florida, as authorized by UCCJEA § 110, and learned that no child custody proceeding was pending in Florida. It concluded that Jaheim had no "home state" at the time the San Diego County Health and Human Services Agency filed a dependency petition.

Was this conclusion correct? If so, when will California's emergency jurisdiction expire? His father proposed that Jaheim be placed with one of his relatives so that the boy could visit his father in prison; his mother did not participate in supervised visits with her son during his detention. The appellate court concluded that "[o]nce the court detained Jaheim and declared him a dependent and removed him from parental custody, 'its temporary emergency jurisdiction ripened into permanent jurisdiction and California became [his] home state.' " This conclusion is supported by the language of § 204(b) of the UCCJEA, which provides that if no child custody proceeding has been or is commenced, an order made pursuant to the exercise of temporary emergency jurisdiction becomes a final determination, if the court so provides, and the issuing state becomes the home state of the child.

(7) *Welch-Doden* addresses several important issues affecting the interpretation of the UCCJEA. Does it resolve them correctly?

(a) *Home state jurisdiction.* As the court points out, the child had lived with the mother and father in Oklahoma for the six-month period between March 2000 and September 2000, when the mother removed the child to Arizona and filed her divorce and custody proceeding there on January 25, 2001. Under the UCCJA, a state had home state jurisdiction if the state "is the domicile or the home state of the child at the time of commencement of the proceeding or had been the child's domicile or home state within six months before commencement of the proceeding and the child is absent from this state because of his removal or retention by a person claiming his custody or for other reasons, and a parent or person acting as a parent continues to live in this state." The PKPA dropped the UCCJA's reference to "domicile" and substituted the word "contestant" for the phrases "a person claiming his custody" and "a parent or person acting as a parent." It provided that a state had home state jurisdiction if "(A) such State (i) is the home State of the child on the date of the commencement of the proceeding, or (ii) had been the child's home State within six months before the date of the commencement of the proceeding and the child is absent from such State because of his removal or retention by a contestant or for other reasons, and a contestant continues to live in such State."

The UCCJEA drafters did not adopt the term "contestant," deeming it too expansive since it would, for example, cover grandparents who had a right under state law to seek visitation with the child following the death of a parent. They also decided against specifying as the reason for the child's absence from the home state "his removal or retention by a person claiming his custody." Instead, they rephrased subsection (ii) to read that the home state "was the home state of the child within six months before the commencement of the proceeding and the child is absent from this state but a parent or person acting as a parent continues to live in this state."

How do the facts of *Welch-Doden* play out under these various phrasings of the standard? Under all three versions, Arizona is eliminated as the child's home state under subsection (i) because the child had not lived there for six consecutive months on January 25, 2001, the date when the mother commenced her proceedings. The only question is whether Oklahoma qualifies as the home state because it had been the child's home state until four months before the date of commencement of the Arizona proceedings. The answer is clearest under the UCCJA and the PKPA: the mother (who is both "a person claiming . . . custody" and a "contestant") removed the child from Oklahoma and took him to Arizona. Her actions do not, therefore, affect Oklahoma's status as the child's home state. Does the UCCJEA's elimination of the language "because of his removal or retention" undercut Oklahoma's claim? Oklahoma is still the state "where a parent or person acting as a parent continues to live": isn't that sufficient?

Do you agree with *Welch-Doden* that a statutory conflict exists in the UCCJEA between the home state definition and the home state jurisdictional basis? If there is such a conflict, did the court resolve it correctly? The Montana Supreme Court thinks so; it followed *Welch-Doden*'s lead in *Stephens v. Fourth Judicial Dist. Ct.*, 331 Mont. 40, 128 P.3d 1026 (2006), where Brenda and Jesse were married in Montana on November 5, 1999, and lived there with their two children until they moved to Arkansas sometime in 2002. They returned to Montana in the spring of 2005, apparently intending to remain there permanently. Early in August 2005, however, Brenda returned to Arkansas with the children. Jesse filed for divorce and custody of the children in Montana on August 10, 2005. Brenda objected that Montana lacked subject-matter jurisdiction over the custody dispute because Arkansas was the children's "home state" within six months of the filing of the suit. Jesse argued that Arkansas lost home-state status when the entire family left to return to Montana, which meant that the children had no "home state" at the time he filed his petition on August 10, 2005. Citing *Welch-Doden*, the Montana court agreed with Brenda:

> Under the definition of "home state," no state other than Arkansas could become the "home state" of the minor children for the six months after May 1, 2005. Jesse filed a petition for dissolution on August 10, 2005. A child's home state is determined at the time an action commences. The children had not lived in Montana with a parent or person acting as a parent for at least six consecutive months immediately before Jesse filed this action in Montana in August. Montana could not acquire "home state" status under the UCCJEA until November, 2005, at the earliest.
>
> Brenda removed the children from Montana in August 2005, thereby stopping the six-month clock needed to establish Montana as the "home state' for purposes of jurisdiction under the UCCJEA. . . Thus, Arkansas was the children's "home state' under the UCCJEA when the family came to Montana in May 2005, and remained their "home state" when they returned to Arkansas in August 2005.

Stephens, 331 Mont., at 45–46; 128 P.3d, at 1030.

(b) *Best interests.* Do you agree that consideration of the best interests of the child has no relevance to the determination of jurisdiction under the UCCJEA? Did its elimination from the prior UCCJA provision increase the chances that the jurisdiction provisions will receive a more uniform application? How realistic is the court's assumption that the home state will undertake a best interests inquiry to determine whether it should decline to exercise its jurisdiction? Examine the factors listed in footnote 15 of the court's opinion. Are they the right factors? What is the relevance of "the relative financial circumstances of the parties"? Are the factors listed in order of priority? Do they give so much discretion to the court as to weaken the possibility of uniformity?

(c) *Time of filing.* Does the court correctly refuse to apply the first-in-time rule? How long can the existence of a home state prevent a court in a state that meets the "significant connection" standard from assuming jurisdiction? If the mother had delayed commencing her Arizona proceeding for two more months, would Arizona have become the child's "home state"? Presumably the father could prevent that outcome by filing a custody proceeding in Oklahoma before six months had expired. If he failed to do so, would he have conceded home state jurisdiction to Arizona?

(d) *Divorce jurisdiction. Welch-Doden* correctly points out in footnote 1 that the Arizona court could have retained jurisdiction over the dissolution proceeding, even though it could not decide the child custody question. What sense would that have made in terms of judicial economy? Does the UCCJEA mean that the Florida court in *Sherrer*, supra p. 682, could not have decided the custody issue because the mother and children had lived there for only ninety-one days before she filed suit for divorce? So long as all parties are before the court, why shouldn't child custody be a transitory proceeding like the other issues at stake in a migratory consent divorce? Have the Commissioners, by substituting subject-matter jurisdiction over the custody question for personal jurisdiction over the absent parent, actually created a "divisible divorce" doctrine of their own that permits the state of plaintiff's domicile to terminate the marriage, but requires that the home state be given priority to decide the custody issue?

What happens if a mother, father, and their two-year old son have lived together in State A for two years and the mother is three months pregnant when she leaves for Nevada, taking her son with her? Assume that she stays in Nevada for the mandatory six weeks before obtaining an ex parte divorce, and then immediately departs for California where she and her son move in with her parents. Meanwhile, the left-behind father filed for divorce in State A two weeks after the mother left home, seeking a divorce and custody of their son and the unborn child. The parties' second child, a daughter, is born in California four and a half months after the mother arrived there. Which state—or states—can exercise home state jurisdiction over the custody issue? See *Waltenburg v. Waltenburg*, 270 S.W.3d 308 (Tex.App. 2008), reversing the trial court's judgment deferring to the father's Arizona divorce and custody suit filed on March 21, 2006, four days after his pregnant wife had arrived in Texas, even though the parties' child was not born until April 7, 2006. The mother filed suit for divorce and custody in Texas when the child was four and a half months old. The Texas appellate court held that the Texas court should not have deferred to the Arizona court, because it was not exercising jurisdiction "substantially in conformity" with the Act, reasoning that the UCCJEA does not apply to unborn children. Was its decision correct?

The Texas court went on to hold that "immediately upon [the child's] birth in Texas, Texas became his home state, thus precluding the Arizona court from exercising jurisdiction over Father's custody decision." *Id.* at 318. This result is in accord with the UCCJEA provision that the "home state" of a child less than six months old is "the state in which the child lived from birth with a parent."

Consider *Gutierrez v. Gutierrez*, 921 A.2d 153 (Me. 2007), where the parties had two children (a daughter born in 2002 and a son born in 2004) and two homes: a summer home in Maine and a "primary" home in St. Croix, U.S. Virgin Islands (considered a state for UCCJEA purposes). The mother filed for divorce and custody of the children in Maine on March 16, 2006, alleging that she had begun living in the summer home with the children on June 15, 2005. The father filed a motion to dismiss, alleging that Maine lacked jurisdiction both over the divorce and the child custody proceedings. He argued that, regardless of where the mother was *domiciled*, she had not "*resided* in Maine in good faith for six months before filing the complaint" as required by the divorce statute, nor was Maine the home state of either child "on the date of the commencement of the proceeding or . . . *within* six months" of that date as required by the UCCJEA, and the children's home state, the Virgin Islands, had not declined jurisdiction. The mother rejoined that the Virgin Islands could not be the home state of the son because he had never lived there for six consecutive months, and that Maine had a "significant connection" with him. The trial court agreed with the father and dismissed the mother's proceeding for lack of jurisdiction. The Supreme Judicial Court of Maine affirmed, noting that "the trouble with [the mother's] argument regarding the son is that even if Maine could exercise jurisdiction over a parental rights determination, it would not make sense to do so, given that it cannot exercise jurisdiction over the divorce and a child custody determination of the daughter." 921 A.2d. at 158. Do you agree that this outcome is a sensible one? Suppose that, all other facts remaining the same, the son had been born in Maine on August 15, 2005: would it then be possible for the Maine court to reach the same result as to the exercise of its home state jurisdiction over him? What evidence would be present in the Virgin Islands concerning his custody?

2. Modification Jurisdiction

BRANDT V. BRANDT

2012 CO 3, 268 P.3d 406.

HOBBS, J.

I. . .

¶ 5 Petitioner Christine Brandt and Respondent George Brandt were divorced in Montgomery County, Maryland, on May 25, 2006. [The parties agreed that they would have joint custody of their child, C.B., with Christine Brandt having primary physical custody. George was at the time an active duty member of the Army, having just returned from a tour of duty in Iraq. From 2006 to 2008, the parties lived in Maryland and shared custody of C.B.]

¶ 6 In 2008, the Army transferred George Brandt to Fort Carson, Colorado Springs, Colorado. The parties divided time with C.B. equally during the summer of 2008, and C.B. returned to Maryland for the 2008–09 school year. George Brandt served at Fort Carson until 2010 when he retired, remarried, and settled with his new wife in Littleton, Colorado.

¶ 7 Christine Brandt was commissioned into the Army in 2009, serving in the Nursing Corps. Following training, she was stationed at Fort Hood, Texas, where she moved with C.B. from Maryland in March of that year. C.B.'s 2009 summer was also split between his parents. Christine Brandt was deployed to Iraq on active duty in April 2010. The parties mutually agreed that, while she was in Iraq, C.B. would live with George Brandt in

Colorado. Christine Brandt returned from Iraq on October 10, 2010, and was reassigned to Fort Hood, Texas. She and George Brandt agreed to let C.B. complete the remainder of the 2010–11 school year in Colorado at which point George Brandt would return C.B. to Christine Brandt.

¶ 8 On April 26, 2011, Christine Brandt received military orders to return to Maryland and finish her active duty in a non-deployable position at Fort Meade. . . As previously agreed between the parties, C.B. returned on May 22, 2011, to live with Christine Brandt, who was still at Fort Hood.

¶ 9 Meanwhile, on May 6, 2011, George Brandt filed a petition in the Arapahoe County district court [Colorado] to register the Maryland custody order pursuant to section 14–13–305, C.R.S. (2011), and to request that the court assume jurisdiction to modify the custody order . . . On May 25, the district court entered its order registering the Maryland decree and assuming jurisdiction to modify it ("May 25 Order"). The court based its assumption of modification jurisdiction on the fact that C.B. had resided in Colorado for more than one year and neither Christine Brandt nor George Brandt nor their child "currently reside[d]" in Maryland. . .

¶ 11 On June 20, Christine Brandt traveled back to Texas to out-process from Fort Hood, during which time she left C.B. in Maryland with his maternal grandmother. At some time during the next week, C.B. and his grandmother traveled to Pennsylvania. George Brandt, with the help of local law enforcement, exercised the Colorado writ, taking C.B. into his physical custody and returning to Colorado, where C.B. has resided with him since June 26 [2010].

¶ 12 In the meantime, Christine Brandt obtained counsel in Colorado and, on June 22, filed a motion for reconsideration and motion to dismiss the May 25 Order. She also filed an emergency motion for a telephone conference in Maryland, pursuant to which Judge Quirk in Montgomery County, Maryland held three teleconferences with Judge Russell in Arapahoe County during which both parties were represented by counsel.

¶ 13 On July 29, during the final teleconference, our district court said that: (1) Maryland had lost exclusive continuing jurisdiction due to Christine Brandt's presence in Texas, not Maryland; (2) under the UCCJEA, the preferred forum is where a child has lived for six months; and (3) Colorado was the most convenient forum to hear this case. Judge Quirk explicitly disagreed and reiterated his position from earlier teleconferences that Maryland retained exclusive continuing jurisdiction over the custody order:

> [I]t would still be my decision that continuing exclusive jurisdiction is proper here because residence, quite frankly, within the meaning of our Maryland law, of Ms. Brandt has never been anywhere but Maryland, and has continued here, and there is a

connection. That connection exists, as well as the connection of the child to Maryland.

¶ 14 The Maryland judge lamented that both states were now asserting jurisdiction, the very result the legislatures in both states had intended to avoid in enacting the uniform statute.

¶ 15 Christine Brandt petitioned us for a rule to show cause, which we issued. She claims that the district court erred in finding that she no longer resided in Maryland for purposes of determining modification jurisdiction under the UCCJEA. George Brandt argues that the district court properly assumed jurisdiction to modify the Maryland child custody order. George Brandt's motion to modify the child custody order awaits our decision.

II.

¶ 16 We hold that the district court erred by failing to apply the appropriate standard of review when assuming jurisdiction to modify Maryland's child custody order. The operative statutory term "presently reside" is not equivalent to "currently reside" or "physical presence," the two notions upon which the trial court incorrectly assumed jurisdiction. Instead, "presently reside" necessitates an inquiry broader than "technical domicile" into the totality of the circumstances that make up domicile—that is, a person's permanent home to which he or she intends to return to and remain. The appropriate legal standard to be applied in determining whether the issuing state lost exclusive continuing jurisdiction based on non-residency involves application of a totality of the circumstances test. Factors to be weighed in making the residency determination, a mixed question of fact and law, include but are not limited to the length and reasons for the parents' and the child's absence from the issuing state; their intent in departing from the state and returning to it; reserve and active military assignments affecting one or both parents; where they maintain a home, car, driver's license, job, professional licensure, and voting registration; where they pay state taxes; the issuing state's determination of residency based on the facts and the issuing state's law; and any other circumstances demonstrated by evidence in the case. The party asserting that the issuing state has lost exclusive continuing jurisdiction bears the burden of proof.

B. The UCCJEA . . .

2. Exclusive Continuing Jurisdiction

¶ 25 Once a state enters an initial child custody determination, that state has exclusive jurisdiction to modify the determination provided that initial jurisdiction was proper. . .

¶ 26 It is clear from the statute that only a court of the issuing state can decide that it has lost jurisdiction due to the erosion of a "significant connection" between the child and the state. . . However, it is equally clear that a court in either the issuing state or any other state may divest the issuing state of jurisdiction by making a determination that the child and both parents do not "presently reside" there. . .

¶ 27 Thus, although a child's home state may change within the meaning of the UCCJEA provision regarding jurisdiction to enter an initial custody order, the issuing state nevertheless may not be divested of continuing jurisdiction by any other state unless no party presently resides in the issuing state. . .

3. Modification

¶ 28 A state may modify the custody order of another state only if it would have jurisdiction to make an initial determination, and either:

> (a) The court of the [issuing] state determines that it no longer has exclusive continuing jurisdiction . . . or that a court of the [new] state would be a more convenient forum . . . ; *or*
>
> (b) A court of the [issuing] state or a court of the [new] state determines that the child, the child's parents, and any person acting as a parent *do not presently reside* in the [issuing] state.

§ 14–13–203(1)(a)–(b) (emphasis added). The issue of modification thus tracks the issue of exclusive continuing jurisdiction: the new state may modify only if it has jurisdiction to make an initial custody order, *and* if the issuing state decides that it has lost exclusive continuing jurisdiction pursuant to section 14–13–202 or either state determines that no party presently resides in the issuing state. The issuing state may also decline to exercise its jurisdiction on the grounds that the new state would be a more convenient forum to hear a modification proceeding. . . If a new state enters a modification order, that state then assumes exclusive continuing jurisdiction over determinations of child custody. . .

4. The Appropriate Procedure for Determining Where the Parents and the Child "Presently Reside"

¶ 32 The UCCJEA required a "clear end-point to the decree state's jurisdiction. . . Therefore, it is imperative that an out-of-state court tasked with enforcing a custody order has a clear factual record, either by stipulation or from the taking of evidence, on which to assess whether jurisdiction was properly asserted by the court which entered the order.

¶ 33 A plaintiff typically "bears the burden of proving that the trial court has jurisdiction to hear the case." . . . Because, under the UCCJEA, a new state may not modify an out-of-state child custody order unless it properly finds that the issuing state has been divested of jurisdiction (or declined to exercise it), the parent petitioning the new state to assume jurisdiction bears the burden of proving, not only that the new state would have jurisdiction to enter an initial child custody order, but that the issuing state has lost or declined to exercise jurisdiction as well.

¶ 34 Communication between the courts . . . is exceedingly beneficial in this type of proceeding. Inter-court communication facilitates an understanding between sister states regarding whether the issuing state has lost jurisdiction . . . , or declined to exercise jurisdiction in favor of a more convenient forum. . . Such communication alerts the issuing state to a potential loss of exclusive continuing jurisdiction, based on residence, before the new state assumes jurisdiction to modify the issuing state's child custody order. It also alerts the new state to any pending actions in the issuing state and helps to develop a factual record in the matter of jurisdiction.

¶ 35 We therefore determine that, before a court of this state may assume jurisdiction to modify an out-of-state custody order, the court must communicate with the issuing state [and] conduct a hearing at which both sides are allowed to present evidence if there is a factual dispute on the residency issue, with the burden of proof being on the parent who has petitioned for the court to assume jurisdiction, following which the district court in our state makes its findings of fact, conclusions of law, and order. . .

¶ 37 We first stress that, for purposes of modification jurisdiction, only the state that originally entered the custody order may decide that another forum would be more convenient. . . Second, while the UCCJEA for some purposes does prioritize the "home state" . . ., this preference pertains only to jurisdiction to enter an initial child custody order, not jurisdiction to modify an order that has already been entered by another state. "Home state" preference at the modification stage would defeat the purposes of exclusive continuing jurisdiction, which are to ensure that custody orders, once entered, are as stable as possible and to discourage parents from establishing new "home states" for their children so as to re-litigate the issue of custody in a friendlier forum. *See Thompson,* 484 U.S. at 180 (discussing the congressional intent behind the PKPA, with which the UCCJEA provision is meant to be consistent).

¶ 38 Absent action by Maryland disclaiming exclusive continuing jurisdiction or declining to exercise it, the only basis for Colorado to divest Maryland of jurisdiction is to determine that "the child, the child's parents, and any person acting as a parent do not presently reside" there. . .

¶ 39 Unfortunately, [the official] comment 2 to section 14–13–202 has confused construction of the operative statutory term "presently reside" and has led to a split among states in applying the act. This comment states, in part:

> Continuing jurisdiction is lost when the child, the child's parents, and any person acting as a parent no longer reside in the original decree State. . . It is the intention of this Act that [the phrase, 'do

> not presently reside'] means that the named persons *no longer continue to actually live within the State*. . . [W]hen the child, the parents, and all persons acting as parents *physically leave the state to live elsewhere,* the exclusive continuing jurisdiction ceases.
>
> The phrase "do not presently reside" is *not used in the sense of technical domicile.* The fact that the original determination State still considers one parent a domiciliary does not prevent it from losing exclusive, continuing jurisdiction after the child, the parents, and all persons acting as parents have moved from the state.

§ 14–13–202, cmt. 2 (emphasis added). Based on this commentary, some states take the view that a person resides only where physically present when a petition for assumption of modification jurisdiction is filed . . .

¶ 41 However, cases from other jurisdictions disagree that "presently reside" means only physical presence. In 2009, a California court of appeal found that the relevant question under the UCCJEA was "not whether Husband 'resided' in Pakistan, but whether he *stopped* residing in California." *In re Marriage of Nurie,* 98 Cal.Rptr.3d at 219 [where California was the original decree state and Pakistan was the modification state]. Additionally, the court rejected the wife's construction of the word "presently":

> Wife insists that the term "presently" must be given effect in the statute, and that it means continuing jurisdiction may be lost based on where the parties are "actually living" regardless of their volition or intent. *We perceive a different significance to the word "presently,"* namely that the determination of relocation must be made during the period of nonresidence in the decree state.

Id. (emphasis added). The court concluded that, because it is well established that a party may have more than one residence, the husband could have "presently resided" in Pakistan at the time the Pakistan court asserted jurisdiction while "still maintaining a 'present residence' in California." *Id.* at 220. The court held that, since the husband maintained a functioning home, car, telephones, and fax in California and was employed there, he continued to "presently reside" there. *Id.* Thus, California (the issuing state) retained jurisdiction. *Id.* . .

¶ 43 We agree that, for UCCJEA purposes, the term "presently reside" does not equal "technical domicile.". . . The reference to "technical" domicile suggests that "presently reside" means something other than meeting the technical requirements of domicile for specific purposes, including, for example, the obligation to pay state taxes. Instead, "presently reside" necessitates a broader inquiry into the totality of the circumstances that make up domicile—that is, a person's permanent home to which he or she intends to return to and remain. *Black's Law Dictionary* at 558 (9th ed. 2009). . .

¶ 45 The statutory language of sections 14–13–202(1)(b) and –203(1)(b) is clear that, before a new state can divest the issuing state of jurisdiction, the new state must "*determine*[ ] that the child, the child's parents, and any person acting as a parent *do not presently reside*" in the issuing state. (Emphasis added). This statutory requirement for determination is consistent with the UCCJEA's emphasis on the primacy of exclusive continuing jurisdiction as a means to ensure the stability of custody orders and to discourage parental kidnapping. To hold that the term "presently reside" means only physical presence would undercut the actual statutory language and purpose that centers on exclusive continuing jurisdiction remaining in the issuing state unless that jurisdiction has been clearly divested, enabling the new state to assume jurisdiction. . .

¶ 47 In sum, we decline to adopt an interpretation of the statutory term "presently reside" which is confined only to "physical presence within the borders of the state whose jurisdiction is at issue."

C. Application to this Case

¶ 48 In the case before us, residency is a hotly contested issue. Christine Brandt alleges that she has constantly maintained a home, driver's license, nursing license, and voting registration in Maryland and pays Maryland state taxes. Indeed, under both federal and Colorado law, she cannot gain or lose residence for purposes of taxation and voting registration by virtue of her service in the armed forces. 50 U.S.C.A. app. §§ 571(a), 595(a) (West 2009); § 1–2–103, C.R.S. (2011). Moreover, she received her orders to transfer back to Maryland on April 26, ten days *before* George Brandt filed the May 6 Petition. At that point, she contends, her return to Maryland was not just a matter of her intention; it was certain to occur.

¶ 49 The portion of the May 25 Order divesting Maryland of jurisdiction reads, in its entirety, as follows: "the Court finds that neither the child nor the child's parents currently reside[9] in Maryland and the child has resided in Colorado for more than a year before the filing of the petition. As a result, this Court assumes jurisdiction for purposes of modifying the Maryland child-custody determination."

¶ 50 While George Brandt argues that he and the child have significant contacts with Colorado, it is clear that the district court did not have the benefit of the legal test we articulate in this opinion. Its order assuming jurisdiction to modify Maryland's custody decree cannot stand because that order appears to be based solely on Christine Brandt being

[9] The district court's use of the phrase "currently reside" departs from the statutory term "presently reside."

out of Maryland on military assignment. The UCCJEA provision allowing Colorado to divest Maryland of jurisdiction based on where the parties "presently reside" should not be interpreted to allow one parent to re-litigate the issue of custody simply by winning the race to the courthouse when the other parent is absent from the issuing state. . .

III.

¶ 52 Accordingly, we make our rule absolute, vacate the district court's order assuming jurisdiction, and return this case to the district court for further proceedings consistent with this opinion.

MILLER-JENKINS V. MILLER-JENKINS

180 Vt. 441, 912 A.2d 951 (2006).

DOOLEY, J.

¶ 1. Lisa Miller-Jenkins appeals a family court decision finding her expartner, Janet Miller-Jenkins, to be a parent of their three-year-old child conceived via artificial insemination. On appeal, Lisa contests three family court decisions. First, she appeals the decision by the Vermont family court that found both her and Janet to be legal parents of their child [hereinafter IMJ], and awarded Lisa temporary legal and physical rights and responsibilities of the child and Janet temporary parent-child contact. Second, Lisa appeals the family court's refusal to give full faith and credit to a Virginia court order, issued after the Vermont court's temporary custody and visitation order, that was contrary to the Vermont decree and that precluded Janet's visitation rights. Finally, Lisa appeals an order of contempt issued by the family court based on her failure to abide by the temporary visitation order.

¶ 2. We granted interlocutory appeal to address the validity of these orders. We conclude the civil union between Lisa and Janet was valid and the family court had jurisdiction to dissolve the union. Further, we decide that the family court had exclusive jurisdiction to issue the temporary custody and visitation order under both the Uniform Child Custody Jurisdiction Act (UCCJA), 15 V.S.A. §§ 1031–1051, and the Parental Kidnapping Prevention Act (PKPA), 28 U.S.C. § 1738A (2000). We affirm the family court's determination that Janet is a parent of IMJ, the resulting visitation order, and the order of contempt issued against Lisa for her failure to abide by the visitation order.

¶ 3. Lisa and Janet lived together in Virginia for several years in the late 1990's. In December 2000, the parties traveled to Vermont and entered into a civil union. In 2001, while Lisa and Janet were still a couple, Lisa began to receive artificial insemination from sperm provided by an anonymous donor. Janet participated in the decision that Lisa become impregnated and helped select the anonymous donor. In April 2002, Lisa gave birth to IMJ, with Janet present in the delivery room. Lisa, Janet, and IMJ lived in Virginia until IMJ was approximately four months old and then moved together to Vermont around August of 2002. The parties lived together with IMJ in Vermont until the fall of 2003, when they decided to separate. After the separation, in September 2003, Lisa moved to Virginia with IMJ.

¶ 4. On November 24, 2003, Lisa filed a petition to dissolve the civil union in the Vermont family court in Rutland. In her complaint, Lisa listed IMJ as the "biological or adoptive child[ ] of the civil union." Lisa requested that the court award her custodial rights and award Janet parent-child contact. The family court issued a temporary order on parental rights and responsibilities on June 17, 2004. This order awarded Lisa temporary legal and physical responsibility for IMJ, and awarded Janet parent-child contact for two weekends in June, one weekend in July, and the third full week of each month, beginning in August 2004. The family court also ordered Lisa to permit Janet to have telephone contact with IMJ once daily.

¶ 5. Although Lisa permitted the first court ordered parent-child-contact weekend, she did not allow Janet to have parent-child contact after that date, nor did she allow Janet to have telephone contact with IMJ, as the family court had ordered. In fact, Lisa has not allowed Janet to have any contact with IMJ other than during that first weekend. Meanwhile, on July 1, 2004, after the Vermont court had already filed its temporary custody and visitation order and parentage decision, Lisa filed a petition in the Frederick County Virginia Circuit Court and asked that court to establish IMJ's parentage.

¶ 6. In response, on July 19, 2004, the Vermont court reaffirmed its "jurisdiction over this case including all parent-child contact issues," stated that it would not "defer to a different State that would preclude the parties from a remedy," and made clear that the temporary order for parent-child contact was to be followed. It added that "[f]ailure of the custodial parent to allow contact will result in an immediate hearing on the need to change custody."

¶ 7. Although the Vermont and Virginia courts consulted by telephone, an interstate parental-rights contest ensued. On September 2, 2004, the Vermont court found Lisa in contempt for willful refusal to comply with the temporary visitation order. On September 9, the Virginia court held it had jurisdiction to determine the parentage and parental rights of IMJ and that any claims of Janet to parental status were "based on rights under Vermont's civil union laws that are null and void under Va.Code § 20–45.3." On October 15, the Virginia court followed with a parentage order finding Lisa to be the "sole biological and natural parent" of IMJ and holding that Janet has no "claims of parentage or visitation rights over" IMJ. That order is on appeal to the Virginia Court of Appeals.

¶ 8. On November 17, 2004, the Vermont court found that both Lisa and Janet had parental interests in IMJ and set the case for a final hearing on parental rights, property, and child support. Thereafter, on December 21, 2004, the Vermont court issued a ruling refusing to give full faith and credit to the Virginia parentage decision. Lisa appealed both of these decisions, as well as the decision finding her in contempt.

¶ 9. This case is, at base, an interstate jurisdictional dispute over visitation with a child. Lisa argues here that the Vermont family court should have given full faith and credit to the Virginia court's custody and parentage decision, which determined Janet had no parentage or visitation rights with respect to IMJ. The family court rejected this argument because it concluded the Virginia decision did not comport with the PKPA, "which was designed for the very purpose of eliminating jurisdictional battles between states with conflicting jurisdictional provisions in child custody disputes." The Vermont court determined it had exercised jurisdiction consistent with the requirements of the PKPA and had continuing jurisdiction at the time Lisa's action was filed in Virginia. Therefore, it further concluded the Virginia court was prohibited from exercising jurisdiction by the PKPA, and the Vermont court had no obligation to give full faith and credit to the conflicting Virginia decision.

¶ 10. In analyzing Lisa's arguments, we note that she does not contest that if she and Janet were a validly married heterosexual couple, the family court's PKPA analysis would be correct. Because of her tacit acceptance of the family court's analysis with regard to jurisdiction under the PKPA, we provide only a summary description of why we believe that the family court was correct.

¶ 11. The purpose of the PKPA is to determine when one state must give full faith and credit to a child custody determination of another state, such that the new state cannot thereafter act inconsistently with the original custody determination. *Thompson v. Thompson,* 484 U.S. 174, 181 (1988). The PKPA follows on, and includes many of the provisions of, the Uniform Child Custody Jurisdiction Act (UCCJA), adopted in Vermont as 15 V.S.A. §§ 1031–1051. These acts were adopted to respond to "a growing public concern over the fact that thousands of children are shifted from state to state and from one family to another every year while their parents or other persons battle over their custody in the courts of several states." National Conference of Commissioners on Uniform State Laws, Uniform Child Custody Jurisdiction Act, Prefatory Note (1968). The PKPA embodies preferences "to leave jurisdiction in the state which rendered the original decree[,] . . . to promote the best interests of the child[,] . . . [and to] discourage[ ] interstate abduction and other unilateral removals of children for the purpose of obtaining a favorable custody decree." . . .

¶ 12. The PKPA applies equally to a visitation determination, requiring states to enforce "any custody determination or visitation determination made consistently with the provisions of this section by a court of another State." Because the first custody and visitation determination with respect to IMJ was made by the Vermont court, we must first examine whether that court exercised jurisdiction "consistently with the provisions of" the PKPA . . . If it did, and if it continued to have jurisdiction when Lisa filed her proceeding in the Virginia court, the Virginia court was without jurisdiction to modify the Vermont order.

¶ 13. In order for a Vermont court to exercise jurisdiction consistent with the PKPA, it must have jurisdiction under Vermont law, and meet one of four conditions. . . In this case, it met the condition that Vermont "had been the child's home State within six months before the date of the commencement of the proceeding and the child is absent from such State because of his removal or retention by a contestant or for other reasons, and a contestant continues to live in such State." For purposes of this provision, "home State" is defined to mean "the State in which, immediately preceding the time involved, the child lived with his parents, a parent, or a person acting as parent, for at least six consecutive months." Because Vermont had been IMJ's home state within six months before Lisa filed her dissolution petition in November 2003, Lisa had removed IMJ from Vermont, and Janet lived in Vermont on the date the dissolution proceeding was commenced, the requirements of subsection (A)(ii) were met. . .

¶ 14. The PKPA also requires that the court have jurisdiction under Vermont law. Whether local jurisdiction is present is determined by the UCCJA. . . For the exact reason that the Vermont proceeding met the PKPA condition discussed above, it met the identically-worded provision of the UCCJA. . . Thus, the family court had jurisdiction under Vermont law as required by [the PKPA].

¶ 15. Because the Vermont dissolution proceeding was still pending in July 2004, when Lisa filed her action in the Virginia court, and the Vermont proceeding was consistent with the PKPA, the Virginia court lacked jurisdiction pursuant to § 1738A(g) of the PKPA. That section specified that the court could not exercise jurisdiction over a proceeding to determine the custody of, or visitation with, IMJ while the Vermont proceeding was pending. The Virginia court violated this section by exercising jurisdiction over the case filed by Lisa.

¶ 16. Because the Vermont court had issued a temporary custody and visitation order, the Virginia court was also governed by § 1738A(h) of the PKPA. That section prohibited the Virginia court from modifying the Vermont court's order unless the Vermont court "no longer [had] jurisdiction to modify such determination" or had "declined to exercise jurisdiction to modify such determination." Since the Vermont court continued to exercise jurisdiction over the Vermont proceeding, the Virginia court could have modified the order only if the Vermont court had lost its initial jurisdiction. Under the PKPA, a court that had initial jurisdiction to issue a custody or visitation order continues to have jurisdiction as long as it continues to have jurisdiction under state law and one of the contestants remains a resident of the state... The latter requirement is met because Janet continues to reside in Vermont...

¶ 18. The Vermont court had continuing jurisdiction over the matter of Janet's visitation with IMJ. Therefore, the Virginia order extinguishing Janet's visitation right was issued in violation of § 1738A(h) of the PKPA. The Vermont court was not required to give full faith and credit to the Virginia order issued in violation of the PKPA.

¶ 19. Lisa ... argues that the Virginia proceeding is a parentage action, and the PKPA does not apply to parentage actions...

¶ 21. [W]e reject the argument that the PKPA is inapplicable. The PKPA applies to custody or visitation determinations. 28 U.S.C. § 1738A(a). It defines a "custody determination" as "a judgment, decree, or other order of a court providing for the custody of a child, and includes permanent and temporary orders, and initial orders and modifications." It defines a visitation determination in nearly identical terms. Lisa's dissolution petition to the Rutland Family Court sought a custody determination, and the court's temporary order included a temporary determination of both custody and visitation. Lisa's parentage petition in the Virginia court sought a determination that Janet had no parental rights, and the Virginia court issued a temporary order requiring Janet's visitation to be supervised and then a permanent order that Janet had no right to visit IMJ. Plainly, the Virginia court decisions included visitation determinations as the term is defined in the PKPA. Just as plainly, the PKPA applied to those decisions...

¶ 72. In conclusion, the family court properly assumed jurisdiction of the action to dissolve the civil union between Lisa and Janet. The civil union was not void. The court properly found that it had jurisdiction to issue a temporary order providing Janet visitation with IMJ, and it was not required to recognize and enforce a conflicting decision of the Virginia court. Finally, the record supports the family court's decision that Lisa is in contempt of court for willfully violating the temporary visitation order.

Affirmed and remanded.

MILLER-JENKINS V. MILLER-JENKINS

49 Va.App. 88, 637 S.E.2d 330 (2006).

WILLIS, JR., JUDGE.

Janet Miller-Jenkins ("Janet") appeals the October 15, 2004 "Final Order of Parentage" of the Circuit Court of Frederick County ("trial court"). In that order, the trial court held (1) that Lisa Miller-Jenkins ("Lisa") is "the sole biological and natural parent of" IMJ, a minor, (2) that Lisa "solely has the legal rights, privileges, duties and obligations as parent hereby established for the health, safety, and welfare of" IMJ, and (3) that neither Janet "nor any other person has any claims of parentage or visitation rights over" IMJ.

On appeal, Janet contends the trial court erred (1) in failing to recognize that the federal Parental Kidnapping Prevention Act ("PKPA"), 28 U.S.C. § 1738A, barred its exercise of jurisdiction, (2) in holding that the Virginia Uniform Child Custody Jurisdiction and Enforcement Act ("UCCJEA"), Code § 20–146.1 *et seq.*, permitted it to exercise jurisdiction, and (3) in refusing to enforce the June 17, 2004 custody order of the Rutland County, Vermont Family Court ("Vermont court").

We hold that the trial court erred in failing to recognize that the PKPA barred its exercise of jurisdiction. Accordingly, we vacate the orders of the trial court and remand this case with instruction to grant full faith and credit to the custody and visitation orders of the Vermont court.

II. ANALYSIS

A. *The PKPA*

1. *Statutory History and Analysis. . .*

[I]t is well settled that the PKPA preempts any conflicting state law. *See Meade v. Meade,* 812 F.2d 1473, 1476 (4th Cir. 1987) ("The PKPA quite simply preempts conflicting state court methods for ascertaining custody jurisdiction."). . .

Pursuant to Vt. Stat. Ann. tit. 15, § 1206, Lisa filed a "Complaint for Civil Union Dissolution" with the Vermont court on November 24, 2003. By doing so, she placed before the Vermont court the issues of the parties' legal and physical "rights and responsibilities" concerning IMJ and "suitable parent/child contact." In Vermont, the term "parental rights and responsibilities" means "the rights and responsibilities related to a child's physical living arrangements, parent child contact, education, medical and dental care, religion, travel and any other matter involving a child's welfare and upbringing." Vt. Stat. Ann. tit. 15, 664(1). And the term "parent child contact" means "the right of a parent who does not have physical responsibility to have visitation with the child." Vt. Stat. Ann. tit. 15, 664(2).

At its threshold, the PKPA requires that a court making a child custody or visitation determination have "jurisdiction under the law of such State." 28 U.S.C. § 1738A(c)(1). The Vermont Supreme Court held that the Vermont court had jurisdiction under the laws of Vermont over the case initiated by Lisa's complaint. *See* Vt. Stat. Ann. tit. 15, 1206. We are bound by that holding. *See* 28 U.S.C. 1738A(a) and (g). . .

Because the Vermont court acquired jurisdiction over the issues of custody and visitation, subsections (g) and (h) of the PKPA governed the trial court's ability to entertain Lisa's petition. . .

The proceeding in the Vermont court was pending when Lisa filed her petition in the trial court. The Vermont court was then exercising its jurisdiction under Vermont law and consistently with the provisions of the PKPA. Thus, subsection (g) applied. The Vermont court, by virtue of its June 17, 2004 and July 19, 2004 orders, continued to exercise jurisdiction, giving application to subsection (h). Therefore, under a "plain meaning" statutory analysis, the trial court lacked authority to exercise jurisdiction based upon Lisa's custody and visitation action in Virginia or to modify the custody and visitation orders of the Vermont court.

2. Lisa's Position

Lisa posits three arguments why the PKPA did not preclude the trial court from exercising jurisdiction over her petition.

a. Application of Vermont Law

First, Lisa argues that "to the extent the Vermont order constitutes a visitation determination, the Virginia court properly exercised jurisdiction because the Vermont order was not properly made." Specifically, Lisa contends the Vermont court could not grant "parent child contact" to Janet because it did not first determine that Janet was a parent. The Vermont Supreme Court rejected this argument. Furthermore, Lisa makes this contention despite the fact that she alleged in her "Complaint for Civil Union Dissolution" that IMJ was "the biological or adoptive child[ ] of said civil union," and despite the fact that the Vermont court in its June 17, 2004 order specifically found that IMJ was "the minor child of the parties."

Lisa cites no authority, and we know of none, that permits us to rule that the supreme court of another state incorrectly interpreted its own law. The contrary is well established. . .

b. Custody or Visitation Determination

Second, Lisa argues: "Even if the Vermont court properly made an initial custody determination within the meaning of the PKPA, the Virginia court properly exercised jurisdiction over the parentage action filed in Virginia." Specifically, Lisa contends the Virginia parentage action is not a custody or visitation determination per the PKPA. Yet, Lisa's petition to the trial court prays that she be adjudicated as having "sole parental rights" over IMJ and that Janet's claim to "parental rights" be adjudged "nugatory, void, illegal and/or unenforceable."

Lisa's complaint in the Vermont court asserted that IMJ was "the biological or adoptive" child of the civil union. She asked that court to award Janet "suitable parent/child contact" and to "award payment of suitable child support money." She thus submitted the determination of IMJ's parentage to the jurisdiction of the Vermont court. Its resolution of that issue has been affirmed by the Vermont Supreme Court and is final.

Whatever semantical machinations are involved, any common understanding of the term "parental rights" includes the right to custody . . .

c. DOMA and the MAA

Third, . . . Lisa argues that DOMA, enacted in 1996, effectively trumps the PKPA, enacted in 1980, thus enabling the trial court to exercise jurisdiction over Lisa's petition. We disagree.

Lisa cites no authority holding that either the plain wording of DOMA or its legislative history was intended to affect or partially repeal the PKPA. Therefore, any Congressional intent to repeal must be by implication. However, "[r]epeal by implication is not favored and the firmly established principle of law is that where two statutes are in apparent conflict, it is the duty of the court, if it be reasonably possible, to give to them such a construction as will give force and effect to each."

We do not read the two statutes to conflict. They can be reconciled. . .

Nothing in the wording or the legislative history of DOMA indicates that it was designed to affect the PKPA and related custody and visitation determinations. Simply put, DOMA allows a state to deny recognition to same-sex marriage entered into in another state. This case does not place before us the question whether Virginia recognizes the civil union entered into by the parties in Vermont. Rather, the only question before us is whether, considering the PKPA, Virginia can deny full faith and credit to the orders of the Vermont court regarding IMJ's custody and visitation. It cannot. The law of Vermont granted the Vermont court jurisdiction to render those decisions. By filing her complaint in Vermont, Lisa invoked the jurisdiction of the Vermont court. She placed herself and the child before that court and laid before it the assertions and prayers that formed the bases of its orders. By operation of the PKPA, her choice of forum precluded the courts of this Commonwealth from entertaining countervailing assertions and prayers.

Lisa argues that the MAA [Marriage Affirmation Act: Virginia's constitutional ballot amendment] forbade the trial court to extend full faith and credit to the orders of the Vermont court. The MAA reads:

> A civil union, partnership contract or other arrangement between persons of the same sex purporting to bestow the privileges or obligations of marriage is prohibited. Any such civil union, partnership contract or other arrangement entered into by persons of the same sex in another state or jurisdiction shall be void in all respects in Virginia and any contractual rights created thereby shall be void and unenforceable.

Code § 20–45.3.

We need not, and do not, decide whether the MAA applies to this case. If it does, it is preempted by the PKPA. *See, e.g., Meade,* 812 F.2d at 1476 (PKPA preempts conflicting state law).

B. *The UCCJEA*

Janet also contends the trial court erred in holding that the UCCJEA permitted it to exercise jurisdiction in this case. Having determined that the PKPA is the controlling law in this matter and that the PKPA preempts conflicting state law, we need not address that issue.

III. CONCLUSION

We hold that the trial court erred in failing to recognize that the PKPA prevented its exercise of jurisdiction and required it to give full faith and credit to the custody and visitation orders of the Vermont court. By so holding, we do not address whether Virginia law recognizes or endorses same-sex unions entered into in another state or jurisdiction. We do not comment on the constitutionality, viability or breadth of the UCCJEA and the MAA. We do not consider the merits of the rulings of the Vermont court. Those questions are not before us. The issue before us is the narrow one of jurisdiction. By filing her complaint in Vermont, Lisa invoked the jurisdiction of the courts of Vermont and subjected herself and the child to that jurisdiction. The PKPA forbids her prosecution of this action in the courts of this Commonwealth. Accordingly, we vacate the orders of the trial court and remand this matter to the trial court with instruction to extend full faith and credit to the custody and visitation orders of the Vermont court.

Vacated and remanded.

"Continuing, Exclusive Jurisdiction"

(1) When modification of an initial award is at issue, neither the UCCJA nor the UCCJEA permits concurrent jurisdiction. The court that made the original award retains continuing, exclusive jurisdiction to modify its order unless it has, in the interim, lost jurisdiction or has declined to exercise its jurisdiction. Do you agree with Justice Hobbs that

Christine Brandt "presently resided" in the issuing state, Maryland, even though she was away from that state on military service for a continuous period from March 2009 until June 8, 2011?

How does his definition of "current residence" differ from "technical domicile," the standard rejected by the official comment to section 14–13–202, discussed in paragraph 39 of the *Brandt* opinion? Consider *Ravenel v. Dekle*, 265 S.C. 364, 218 S.E.2d 521 (1975), involving the question whether Charles D. Ravenel had been "a citizen and resident" of South Carolina "for five years next preceding the day of election" and thus qualified to run for Governor in 1974. The facts showed that Ravenel was born in South Carolina in 1938, and lived in Charleston with his parents until he graduated from high school in 1956. He then left the state for fifteen and a half years to obtain an education between 1956 and 1964 and to work in investment banking between 1964 and 1972. He stated that he visited South Carolina four or five times a year, including one trip to obtain a marriage license in 1963 and presumably to be married there. He and his wife and children lived in a cooperative apartment in New York; their children were baptized in South Carolina. He registered to vote in New York, and voted there in five elections between 1968 and 1971. He paid New York City income taxes in 1969–71 and filed federal income tax returns for those years showing a New York address. He joined private clubs in New York City and a country club in Connecticut, taking resident memberships. He registered his automobile in Connecticut. After his return to South Carolina in 1972, Ravenel registered to vote on September 12, 1972, and paid South Carolina state income taxes in 1973 (as well as late South Carolina returns for the years 1969–1971, paying the late filing penalties).

The South Carolina Supreme Court thus set out Ravenel's position:

> [H]e has at all times since birth been a citizen and resident of South Carolina. He submits that his fifteen-and-one-half-year absence from September, 1956 until March 20, 1972, was of a temporary nature and for the purpose of attending school and procuring training desirable and necessary for the avocation which he intended to pursue and in which he is now engaged in South Carolina. His . . . testimony [is] as follows:
>
>> "I had a great interest in securing the best possible training that I could get in the field that I wanted to work in and that was finance and I went to the place where that training was the best, and that place was on Wall Street and I intended to go to Wall Street and work until I secured what I thought was complete training, never planning to maintain a permanent presence in New York City."

Under the *Brandt* analysis, where was Ravenel "technically domiciled" in 1969 (five years before the 1974 election)? In what state was he a "citizen and resident"? In what state was he "presently residing"? Are there different answers to those questions? The South Carolina court took refuge in holding that, even if Ravenel had been "domiciled" in South Carolina in 1969, the words "citizen" and "resident" are not the same, and that the constitutional term "resident" referred to "actual physical presence in the state." Since Ravenel clearly could not satisfy that test, he was ineligible to hold the office of Governor.

Suppose Ravenel and his wife had been divorced in New York in 1968, and that she was awarded custody of their children. Suppose, further, that after the divorce, she moved to Connecticut and he remained in New York until he returned to South Carolina on March 20, 1972. If, with the mother's consent, he brought the children to South Carolina in 1973 to visit their grandparents, and then filed an action seeking modification of the New York custody decree in a South Carolina court, would South Carolina have jurisdiction under the UCCJEA? On what basis? Do you think Justice Hobbs would say that Ravenel was "presently residing" in South Carolina all along? Even if your answer to that question is "yes," (is it?) does that factor permit South Carolina to assume modification jurisdiction? Does New York retain continuing exclusive jurisdiction? Or has Connecticut acquired jurisdiction over the modification question? How? Suppose both Ravenel and his wife file separate petitions with the New York court requesting it to relinquish jurisdiction in favor of their respective present residences: should the New York court do so? In favor of which state?

(2) Not all courts have been as faithful to the language and purpose of the UCCJEA as the *Brandt* court was. *Grahm v. Superior Court*, 132 Cal.App.4th 1193 (2005), is a typical example of the confusion among judges about the modification provision. *Grahm* involved a couple who divorced in California in October 2003. The court awarded joint custody of their twin daughters, aged two, to both parties with physical custody to mother. With the father's consent, the mother and the twins moved to New York in September while the father remained in California and exercised his right to visit with the children.

Four months later, the mother applied for an order in the New York court to modify custody. The New York court dismissed her motion on the ground that it lacked jurisdiction. The mother appealed the dismissal, and the New York appellate court affirmed. Following this proceeding, the father continued to seek relief on visitation issues in California, including make-up visitation time and a request to take the children on a cruise. He subsequently filed a motion to modify custody, requesting sole legal custody and primary physical custody of the twins.

The trial court declined to exercise jurisdiction, stating that it would defer to the New York court "because that's where I think the evidence is." 132 Cal.App.4th at 1196. The appellate court concluded:

> [T]he original state retains continuing exclusive jurisdiction as long as the parent who is exercising visitation rights still lives in that state and the relationship between that parent and the child has not deteriorated to the point at which the exercise of jurisdiction would be unreasonable.

Id. at 1197–98. Why did the trial court judge think the father was required to seek modification of the custody order in New York, when the California court had issued the initial custody order and the father continued to reside there and to be involved with the child?

(3) If *Grahm* doesn't resolve your doubts about the intractability of the modification problem, take a closer look at *In re Marriage of Nurie*, 176 Cal.App.4th 478 (2009), cited by the Colorado Supreme Court in *Brandt* at ¶ 41. The California appellate court described the case as "an acrimonious six-year international custody battle, in which lawyers on two continents seemingly have left no stone unturned, while the parties themselves have left no rock unhurled." *Id.* at 484. The court held that California—as the state which had initial home state jurisdiction and had granted custody to the father, who continued to reside there with the child—had "continuing, exclusive jurisdiction" over the matter. The case featured a wrongful retention of the child by the mother while on a visit with him to Pakistan, the native country of both parties. She claimed that the father, allegedly aided by three armed accomplices, had wrongfully abducted the child from her and brought him back to California in violation of an order entered by a Pakistani court prohibiting the child's removal from the country. Relying on the "unclean hands" section of the UCCJEA, the mother argued that the California court was required to relinquish jurisdiction "if [it] has jurisdiction under this part because a person seeking to invoke its jurisdiction has engaged in unjustifiable conduct. . ." Affirming the trial court's rejection of that argument, the appellate court explained:

> In this case, California was Son's home state at the time the Dissolution Action was filed and had assumed jurisdiction long before the alleged kidnapping. Since California did not acquire jurisdiction "because" of the alleged kidnapping, section 3428 [UCCJEA § 208], by its terms, does not apply.

176 Cal.App.4th at 512. It went on to uphold the trial court's refusal to relinquish its continuing, exclusive jurisdiction in favor of Pakistan given that the father, a naturalized U.S. citizen, had no plans to leave his home and place of employment in California.

The UCCJEA was not designed to provide a remedy in cases of international child abduction. The Hague Convention on the Civil Aspects of International Child Abduction, explored in the next section, was designed for that purpose. The Hague Convention was not available, however, in *Nurie* because Pakistan has not become a party to it. The UCCJEA, on the other hand, treats foreign countries as if they were states of the United States.

(4) Perhaps seeking to soften the impact of its decision on the mother, the *Welch-Doden* court observed that "[i]f she chooses, mother can ask the Oklahoma court to relinquish jurisdiction." Ask she certainly can, but why would the Oklahoma court grant her request when it is the home state and the father continues to live there? If the Oklahoma court had decided to award custody to the mother and visitation to the father, and mother and child had settled in Arizona, where would the home state be six months later if father remained in Oklahoma and exercised his visitation rights? Does *Grahm* resolve this question? Which parent's relinquishment petition might it support in the *Ravenel* hypothetical, supra note (1)?

(5) The *Miller-Jenkins* cases were the first to raise the application of the UCCJEA and the PKPA to same-sex parents. Did the high courts of Vermont and Virginia correctly resolve the full faith and credit question?

The Vermont family court issued its order in 2007, dissolving the parties' civil union, dividing their property, and awarding physical and legal custody of the child to Lisa with "parenting time" to Janet on alternating weekends in Virginia and Vermont. Lisa appealed this order to the Vermont Supreme Court, which affirmed it in all respects. The Supreme Court denied certiorari.

Thus, after Lisa's repeated losses in the highest courts of both Vermont and Virginia, followed by repeated denials of certiorari by the United States Supreme Court, it might appear that the full faith and credit issues in this interstate child custody matter had been resolved against her. The case, however, was by no means over. Lisa was repeatedly held in contempt for her refusal to abide by the Vermont family court's orders requiring visitation. Each time she violated another visitation order, and Janet obtained another contempt citation, Lisa appealed the decision. This ongoing litigation was made possible because the parties were each represented by organizations dedicated to vindicating the justice of their conflicting causes.

(6) In a brief in support of its motion appealing a decision of the Virginia Circuit Court that had directed the trial court to register and enforce the Vermont order granting parenting rights to Janet, Lisa relied on Justice Ginsburg's distinction in *Baker v. General Motors Corp.*, 522 U.S. 222 (1998), supra p. 617, between the "recognition" exacted for sister-state judgments in terms of issue and claim preclusion and the "mechanisms used for their enforcement," which are subject to the "even-handed control of forum law." Why was that distinction relevant? Because,

Lisa argued, Virginia's Constitutional Marriage Affirmation Amendment prevented the state from enforcing Janet's asserted parental rights, which arose from a civil union between two people of the same sex. *Baker* also observed that "our decisions support no roving 'public policy exception' to the full faith and credit due judgments," citing *Fauntleroy v. Lum*, 210 U.S. 230 (1908). Does that observation doom Lisa's argument? Is her argument still admissible after *Obergefell*?

(7) Would Janet be in a stronger position to refute Lisa's enforcement arguments if she had adopted the parties' daughter, thus giving her an unmodifiable final judgment, rather than placing sole reliance on the Vermont court's modifiable child custody determination under the civil union statute to ensure her parental rights? Could an adoption judgment be enforced more easily under the Full Faith and Credit Clause, or would it similarly be subject to the recognition-enforcement distinction? Recall *Adar v. Smith*, discussed supra pp. 711–713 note (10), where the Louisiana Registrar was willing to recognize the validity of an adoption by an unmarried same-sex couple, but unwilling to issue a revised birth certificate showing two unmarried persons, whether gay or straight, as parents of the child. In Justice Ginsburg's words in *Baker*, is the issuance of such a birth certificate "an official act within the exclusive province of [Louisiana]?" Did the Full Faith and Credit clause require the issuance of a revised birth certificate?

(8) The Vermont court ordered Lisa to relinquish custody of their daughter to Janet in Falls Church, Virginia, on January 1, 2010. By then, however, Lisa and the child were no longer in the United States. What had ensued in September 2009 is perhaps the most bizarre episode in this protracted case: with the help of an Amish-Mennonite pastor, Kenneth L. Miller (no relation to Lisa Miller), they had driven to Buffalo, then crossed the Canadian border in a taxi over the Rainbow Bridge at Niagara Falls, where, disguised in Mennonite dresses and scarves, they boarded a flight that took them to Mexico and ultimately to Nicaragua where they were last reported seen in April 2011. Pastor Miller's sect, the Beachy Amish-Mennonites, regard homosexual behavior as a sin.

The pastor was apprehended, tried and convicted by a federal jury in 2012 of abetting international parental kidnapping. Eric Eckholm, "Virginia Pastor Sentenced for Aiding Parental Kidnapping," The New York Times, March 5, 2013, at A18. In 2016, Philip Zodhiates, a direct-mail entrepreneur with ties to Lisa's counsel, was convicted of international kidnapping in connection with the incident. See Phil Fairbanks, "Pastor gets probation for aiding in same-sex kidnapping case," The Buffalo News, March 23, 2017.

In 2012, Janet filed a RICO action in federal court in Vermont on behalf of the child, Isabella, against Pastor Miller, Zodhiates, Lisa, and several others who she alleged helped Lisa and Isabella flee the country. Isabella turned 18 in April 2020. In February 2021, she filed an affidavit in the RICO action seeking to remove her name from the lawsuit and stating that she had been "happy, safe, healthy and . . . well cared for" in Nicaragua. "All the attorneys who purport to represent me and my wishes are acting contrary to my wishes and desires and in [a] way to further a cause that is the exact opposite of what my desires and wishes as their client in fact are," she attested. Meanwhile, in January 2021, Lisa returned to the United States and was arrested on international parental kidnapping charges. Wilson Ring, "Now-adult in same-sex custody battle seeks removal from suit," Associated Press, February 10, 2021.

B. INTERNATIONAL ABDUCTION OF CHILDREN

1. Scope of the Convention: Availability of the Return Remedy

ABBOTT V. ABBOTT

560 U.S. 1 (2010).

JUSTICE KENNEDY delivered the opinion of the Court.

This case presents . . . a question of interpretation under the Hague Convention on the Civil Aspects of International Child Abduction . . . The question is whether a parent has a "righ[t] of custody" by reason of that parent's *ne exeat* right: the authority to consent before the other parent may take the child to another country.

I

Timothy Abbott and Jacquelyn Vaye Abbott married in England in 1992. He is a British citizen, and she is a citizen of the United States. Mr. Abbott's astronomy profession took the couple to Hawaii, where their son A.J.A. was born in 1995. The Abbotts moved to La Serena, Chile, in 2002. There was marital discord, and the parents separated in March 2003. The Chilean courts granted the mother daily care and control of the child, while awarding the father "direct and regular" visitation rights, including visitation every other weekend and for the whole month of February each year.

Chilean law conferred upon Mr. Abbott what is commonly known as a *ne exeat* right: a right to consent before Ms. Abbott could take A.J.A. out of Chile. See Minors Law 16,618, art. 49 (Chile) (granting a *ne exeat* right to any parent with visitation rights). In effect a *ne exeat* right imposes a duty on one parent that is a right in the other. After Mr. Abbott obtained a British passport for A.J.A., Ms. Abbott grew concerned that Mr. Abbott would take the boy to Britain. She sought and obtained a "*ne exeat* of the minor" order from the Chilean family court, prohibiting the boy from being taken out of Chile.

In August 2005, while proceedings before the Chilean court were pending, the mother removed the boy from Chile without permission from either the father or the court. A private investigator located the mother and the child in Texas. In February 2006, the mother filed for divorce in Texas state court. Part of the relief she sought was a modification of the father's rights, including full power in her to determine the boy's place of residence and an order limiting the father to supervised visitation in Texas. This litigation remains pending.

Mr. Abbott brought an action in Texas state court, asking for visitation rights and an order requiring Ms. Abbott to show cause why the court should not allow Mr. Abbott to return to Chile with A.J.A. In February 2006, the court denied Mr. Abbott's requested relief but granted him "liberal periods of possession" of A.J.A. throughout February 2006, provided Mr. Abbott remained in Texas.

In May 2006, Mr. Abbott filed the instant action in the United States District Court for the Western District of Texas. He sought an order requiring his son's return to Chile pursuant to the Convention and enforcement provisions of the ICARA. In July 2007, after holding a bench trial during which only Mr. Abbott testified, the District Court denied relief. The court held that the father's *ne exeat* right did not constitute a right of custody under the Convention and, as a result, that the return remedy was not authorized.

The United States Court of Appeals for the Fifth Circuit affirmed on the same rationale. The court held the father possessed no rights of custody under the Convention because his *ne exeat* right was only "a veto right over his son's departure from Chile." 542 F.3d 1081, 1087 (2008). The court expressed substantial agreement with the Court of Appeals for the Second Circuit in *Croll v. Croll*, 229 F.3d 133 (2000). Relying on American dictionary definitions of "custody" and noting that *ne exeat* rights cannot be "actually exercised" within the meaning of the Convention, *Croll* held that *ne exeat* rights are not rights of custody. A dissenting opinion in *Croll* was filed by then-Judge Sotomayor. The dissent maintained that a *ne exeat* right is a right of custody because it "provides a parent with decisionmaking authority regarding a child's international relocation."

II

The Convention was adopted in 1980 in response to the problem of international child abductions during domestic disputes. The Convention seeks "to secure the prompt return of children wrongfully removed to or retained in any Contracting State," and "to ensure that rights of custody and of access under the law of one Contracting State are effectively respected in the other Contracting States."

The provisions of the Convention of most relevance at the outset of this discussion are as follows:

"Article 3: The removal or the retention of the child is to be considered wrongful where—

"*a* it is in breach of rights of custody attributed to a person, an institution or any other body, either jointly or alone, under the law of the State in which the child was habitually resident immediately before the removal or retention; and

"*b* at the time of removal or retention those rights were actually exercised, either jointly or alone, or would have been so exercised but for the removal or retention.

. . .

"Article 5: For the purposes of this Convention—

"*a* 'rights of custody' shall include rights relating to the care of the person of the child and, in particular, the right to determine the child's place of residence;

"*b* 'rights of access' shall include the right to take a child for a limited period of time to a place other than the child's habitual residence.

. . .

"Article 12: Where a child has been wrongfully removed or retained in terms of Article 3 . . . the authority concerned shall order the return of the child forthwith."

The Convention's central operating feature is the return remedy. When a child under the age of 16 has been wrongfully removed or retained, the country to which the child has been brought must "order the return of the child forthwith," unless certain exceptions apply. A removal is "wrongful" where the child was removed in violation of "rights of custody." . . . A return remedy does not alter the pre-abduction allocation of custody rights but leaves custodial decisions to the courts of the country of habitual residence. The Convention also recognizes "rights of access," but offers no return remedy for a breach of those rights.

The United States has implemented the Convention through the ICARA. The statute authorizes a person who seeks a child's return to file a petition in state or federal court and instructs that the court "shall decide the case in accordance with the Convention." If the child in question has been "wrongfully removed or retained within the meaning of the Convention," the child shall be "promptly returned," unless an exception is applicable . . .

III

As the parties agree, the Convention applies to this dispute. A.J.A. is under 16 years old; he was a habitual resident of Chile; and both Chile and the United States are contracting states. The question is whether A.J.A. was "wrongfully removed" from Chile, in other words, whether he was removed in violation of a right of custody. This Court's inquiry is shaped by the text of the Convention; the views of the United States Department of State; decisions addressing the meaning of "rights of custody" in courts of other contracting states; and the purposes of the Convention. After considering these sources, the Court determines that Mr. Abbott's *ne exeat* right is a right of custody under the Convention.

A

. . . This Court consults Chilean law to determine the content of Mr. Abbott's right, while following the Convention's text and structure to decide whether the right at issue is a "righ[t] of custody."

Chilean law granted Mr. Abbott a joint right to decide his child's country of residence, otherwise known as a *ne exeat* right. Minors Law 16,618, art. 49 (Chile) provides that "[o]nce the court has decreed" that one of the parents has visitation rights, that parent's "authorization . . . shall also be required" before the child may be taken out of the country, subject to court override only where authorization "cannot be granted or is denied without good reason." Mr. Abbott has "direct and regular" visitation rights and it follows from Chilean law, that he has a shared right to determine his son's country of residence under this provision. . .

The Convention recognizes that custody rights can be decreed jointly or alone; and Mr. Abbott's joint right to determine his son's country of residence is best classified as a joint right of custody, as the Convention defines that term. The Convention defines "rights of custody" to "include rights relating to the care of the person of the child and, in particular, the right to determine the child's place of residence." Mr. Abbott's *ne exeat* right gives him both the joint "right to determine the child's place of residence" and joint "rights relating to the care of the person of the child."

Mr. Abbott's joint right to decide A.J.A.'s country of residence allows him to "determine the child's place of residence." The phrase "place of residence" encompasses the child's country of residence, especially in light of the Convention's explicit purpose to prevent wrongful removal across international borders. And even if "place of residence" refers only to the child's street address within a country, a *ne exeat* right still entitles Mr. Abbott to "determine" that place. "[D]etermine" can mean "[t]o fix conclusively or authoritatively," Webster's New International Dictionary 711 (2d ed.1954) (2d definition), but it can also mean "[t]o set bounds or limits to," *ibid.* (1st definition), which is what Mr. Abbott's *ne exeat* right allows by ensuring that A.J.A. cannot live at any street addresses outside of Chile. It follows that the Convention's protection of a parent's custodial "right to determine the child's place of residence" includes a *ne exeat* right.

Mr. Abbott's joint right to determine A.J.A.'s country of residence also gives him "rights relating to the care of the person of the child." Few decisions are as significant as the language the child speaks, the identity he finds, or the culture and traditions she will come to absorb. These factors, so essential to self-definition, are linked in an inextricable way to the child's country of residence. One need only consider the different childhoods an adolescent will experience if he or she grows up in the United States, Chile, Germany, or North Korea, to understand how choosing a child's country of residence is a right "relating to the care of the person of the child." The Court of Appeals described Mr. Abbott's right to take part in making this decision as a mere "veto," but even by that truncated description, the father has an essential role in deciding the boy's country of residence. For example, Mr. Abbott could condition his consent to a change in country on A.J.A.'s moving to a city outside Chile where Mr. Abbott could obtain an astronomy position, thus allowing the father to have continued contact with the boy.

That a *ne exeat* right does not fit within traditional notions of physical custody is beside the point. The Convention defines "rights of custody," and it is that definition that a court must consult. This uniform, text-based approach ensures international consistency in interpreting the Convention. It forecloses courts from relying on definitions of custody confined by local law usage, definitions that may undermine recognition of custodial arrangements in other countries or in different legal traditions, including the civil-law tradition. And, in any case, our own legal system has adopted conceptions of custody that accord with the Convention's broad definition. Joint legal custody, in which one parent cares for the child while the other has joint decisionmaking authority concerning the child's welfare, has become increasingly common. . .

Ms. Abbott gets the analysis backwards in claiming that a *ne exeat* right is not a right of custody because the Convention requires that any right of custody must be capable of exercise. The Convention protects rights of custody when "at the time of removal or retention those rights were actually exercised, either jointly or alone, or would have been so exercised but for the removal or retention." In cases like this one, a *ne exeat* right is by its nature inchoate and so has no operative force except when the other parent seeks to remove the child from the country. If that occurs, the parent can exercise the *ne exeat* right by declining consent to the exit or placing conditions to ensure the move will be in the child's best interests. When one parent removes the child without seeking the *ne exeat* holder's consent, it is an instance where the right would have been "exercised but for the removal or retention."

The Court of Appeals' conclusion that a breach of a *ne exeat* right does not give rise to a return remedy would render the Convention meaningless in many cases where it is most needed. The Convention provides a return remedy when a parent takes a child across international borders in violation of a right of custody. The Convention provides no return remedy when a parent removes a child in violation of a right of access but requires contracting states "to promote the peaceful enjoyment of access rights." For example, a court may force the custodial parent to pay the travel costs of visitation, or make other provisions for the noncustodial parent to visit his or her child. . . But unlike rights of access, *ne exeat* rights can only be honored with a return remedy because these rights depend on the child's location being the country of habitual residence. . .

Ms. Abbott argues that the *ne exeat* order in this case cannot create a right of custody because it merely protects a court's jurisdiction over the child. Even if this argument were correct, it would not be dispositive. Ms. Abbott contends the Chilean court's *ne exeat* order contains no parental consent provision and so awards the father no rights, custodial or otherwise. . . Even a *ne exeat* order issued to protect a court's jurisdiction pending issuance of further decrees is consistent with allowing a parent to object to the child's removal from the country. This Court need not decide the status of *ne exeat* orders lacking parental consent provisions, however; for here . . . Mr. Abbott's rights derive not from the order but from Minors Law 16,618. That law requires the father's consent before the mother can remove the boy from Chile, subject only to the equitable power family courts retain to override any joint custodial arrangements in times of disagreement. . . The consent provision in Minors Law 16,618 confers upon the father the joint right to determine his child's country of residence. This is a right of custody under the Convention.

B

This Court's conclusion that Mr. Abbott possesses a right of custody under the Convention is supported and informed by the State Department's view on the issue. The United States has endorsed the view that *ne exeat* rights are rights of custody. In its brief before this Court the United States advises that "the Department of State, whose Office of Children's Issues serves as the Central Authority for the United States under the Convention, has long understood the Convention as including *ne exeat* rights among the protected 'rights of custody.' " . . . There is no reason to doubt that this well-established canon of deference is appropriate here. The Executive is well informed concerning the diplomatic consequences resulting from this Court's interpretation of "rights of custody," including the likely reaction of other contracting states and the impact on the State Department's ability to reclaim children abducted from this country.

C

This Court's conclusion that *ne exeat* rights are rights of custody is further informed by the views of other contracting states. In interpreting any treaty, "[t]he 'opinions of our sister signatories' . . . are 'entitled to considerable weight.' " The principle applies with special force here, for Congress has directed that "uniform international interpretation of the Convention" is part of the Convention's framework.

A review of the international case law confirms broad acceptance of the rule that *ne exeat* rights are rights of custody. [The Court cited cases from Britain, Israel, Austria, South Africa, Germany, Australia and Scotland.]. . .

It is true that some courts have stated a contrary view, or at least a more restrictive one. [The Court cited cases from Canada and France.]. . .

Scholars agree that there is an emerging international consensus that *ne exeat* rights are rights of custody, even if that view was not generally formulated when the Convention was drafted in 1980. At that time, joint custodial arrangements were unknown in many of the contracting states, and the status of *ne exeat* rights was not yet well understood. . . Since 1980, however, joint custodial arrangements have become more common. And, within this framework, most contracting states and scholars now recognize that *ne exeat* rights are rights of custody. . .

D

Adopting the view that the Convention provides a return remedy for violations of *ne exeat* rights accords with its objects and purposes. The Convention is based on the principle that the best interests of the child are well served when decisions regarding custody rights are made in the country of habitual residence. Ordering a return remedy does not alter the existing allocation of custody rights, but does allow the courts of the home country to decide what is in the child's best interests. It is the Convention's premise that courts in contracting states will make this determination in a responsible manner.

Custody decisions are often difficult. Judges must strive always to avoid a common tendency to prefer their own society and culture, a tendency that ought not interfere with objective consideration of all the factors that should be weighed in determining the best interests of the child. This judicial neutrality is presumed from the mandate of the Convention, which affirms that the contracting states are "[f]irmly convinced that the interests of children are of paramount importance in matters relating to their custody." International law serves a high purpose when it underwrites the determination by nations to rely upon their domestic courts to enforce just laws by legitimate and fair proceedings.

To interpret the Convention to permit an abducting parent to avoid a return remedy, even when the other parent holds a *ne exeat* right, would run counter to the Convention's purpose of deterring child abductions by parents who attempt to find a friendlier forum for deciding custodial disputes. Ms. Abbott removed A.J.A. from Chile while Mr. Abbott's request to enhance his relationship with his son was still pending before Chilean courts. After she landed in Texas, the mother asked the state court to diminish or eliminate the father's custodial and visitation rights. The Convention should not be interpreted to permit a parent to select which country will adjudicate these questions by bringing the child to a different country, in violation of a *ne exeat* right. Denying a return remedy for the violation of such rights would "legitimize the very action—removal of the child—that the home country, through its custody order [or other provision of law], sought to prevent" and would allow "parents to undermine the very purpose of the Convention." *Croll*, 229 F.3d, at 147 (Sotomayor, J., dissenting). This Court should be most reluctant to adopt an interpretation that gives an abducting parent an advantage by coming here to avoid a return remedy that is granted, for instance, in the United Kingdom, Israel, Germany, and South Africa.

Requiring a return remedy in cases like this one helps deter child abductions and respects the Convention's purpose to prevent harms resulting from abductions. An abduction can have devastating consequences for a child. "Some child psychologists believe that the trauma children suffer from these abductions is one of the worst forms of child abuse." A child abducted by one parent is separated from the second parent and the child's support system. Studies have shown that separation by abduction can cause psychological problems ranging from depression and acute stress disorder to posttraumatic stress disorder and identity-formation issues. . .

IV

While a parent possessing a *ne exeat* right has a right of custody and may seek a return remedy, a return order is not automatic. Return is not required if the abducting parent can establish that a Convention exception applies. One exception states return of the child is not required when "there is a grave risk that his or her return would expose the child to physical or psychological harm or otherwise place the child in an intolerable situation." Art. 13*(b)*. If, for example, Ms. Abbott could demonstrate that returning to Chile would put her own safety at grave risk, the court could consider whether this is sufficient to show that the child too would suffer "psychological harm" or be placed "in an intolerable situation." * * * The Convention also allows courts to decline to order removal if the child objects, if the child has reached a sufficient "age and degree of maturity at which it is appropriate to take account of its views." Art. 13*(b)*. The proper interpretation and application of these and other exceptions are not before this Court. These matters may be addressed on remand.

* * *

The judgment of the Court of Appeals is reversed, and the case is remanded for further proceedings consistent with this opinion.

It is so ordered.

JUSTICE STEVENS, with whom JUSTICE THOMAS and JUSTICE BREYER join, dissenting.

Petitioner Timothy Abbott, the father of A.J.A., has no authority to decide whether his son undergoes a particular medical procedure; whether his son attends a school field trip; whether and in what manner his son has a religious upbringing; or whether his son can play a videogame before he completes his homework. These are all rights and responsibilities of A.J.A.'s mother, respondent Jacquelyn Abbott. It is she who received sole custody, or "daily care and control," of A.J.A. when the expatriate couple divorced while living in Chile in 2004. Mr. Abbott possesses only visitation rights.

On Ms. Abbott's custodial rights, Chilean law placed a restriction: She was not to travel with her son outside of Chile without either Mr. Abbott's or the court's consent. Put differently, Mr. Abbott had the opportunity to veto Ms. Abbott's decision to remove A.J.A. from Chile unless a Chilean court overrode that veto. The restriction on A.J.A.'s and Ms. Abbott's travel was an automatic, default provision of Chilean law operative upon the award of visitation rights under Article 48 of Chile's Minors Law. . . It is this travel restriction—also known as a *ne exeat* clause—that the Court today declares is a "righ[t] of custody" within the meaning of the Hague Convention on the Civil Aspects of International Child Abduction.

Because the Court concludes that this travel restriction constitutes a right of custody, and because Ms. Abbott indisputably violated the restriction when she took A.J.A. from Chile without either Mr. Abbott's or the court's permission, Mr. Abbott is now entitled to the return of A.J.A. to Chile under the terms of the Convention. Thus, absent a finding of an exception to the Convention's powerful return remedy, and even if the return is contrary to the child's best interests, an American court *must* now order the return of A.J.A. to Mr. Abbott, who has no legal authority over A.J.A., based solely on his possessing a limited veto power over Ms. Abbott's ability to take A.J.A. from Chile. As I shall explain, use of the Convention's return remedy under these circumstances is contrary to the Convention's text and purpose.

I

When the drafters of the Convention gathered in 1980, they sought an international solution to an emerging problem: transborder child abductions perpetrated by noncustodial parents "to establish artificial jurisdictional links . . . with a view to obtaining custody of a child." . . . The drafters' primary concern was to remedy abuses by noncustodial parents who attempt to circumvent adverse custody decrees (*e.g.,* those granting sole custodial rights to the other parent) by seeking a more favorable judgment in a second nation's family court system.

The drafters determined that when a *noncustodial* parent abducts a child across international borders, the best remedy is return of that child to his or her country of habitual residence—or, in other words, the best remedy is return of the child to his or her *custodial* parent. The drafters concluded that the same remedy should not follow, however, when a *custodial* parent takes a child from his or her country of habitual residence in breach of the other parent's visitation rights, or "rights of access" in the Convention's parlance. The distinction between rights of custody and rights of access, therefore, is critically important to the Convention's scheme and purpose. It defines the scope of the available Convention remedies. . .

Article 3 of the Convention provides that the removal or retention of a child is "wrongful," and thus in violation of the Convention, only when the removal "is in breach of the rights of custody." The fact that a removal may be "wrongful" in the sense that it violates domestic law or violates only "rights of access" does not make it "wrongful" within the meaning of the Convention.

Only when a removal is "wrongful" under Article 3 may the parent who possesses custody rights force the child's return to the country of habitual residence under the Convention's remedial procedures. . . For those removals that frustrate a noncustodial parent's "rights of access," the Convention provides that the noncustodial parent may file an application "to make arrangements for organizing or securing the effective exercise of rights of access"; but he may not force the child's return. A parent without "rights of custody," therefore, does not have the power granted by Article 3 to compel the child's return to his or her country of habitual residence. His rights are limited to those set forth in Article 21.

II

Mr. Abbott, claiming "rights of custody" by virtue of the travel restriction Chilean law places on Ms. Abbott, seeks the return of A.J.A. to Chile. Such relief is warranted only if A.J.A.'s removal was "wrongful" within the meaning of the Convention; as such, it must have been "in breach of [Mr. Abbott's] rights of custody."[2] Art. 3. Putting aside the effect of the travel restriction, it is undisputed that Ms. Abbott possesses "rights of custody" over A.J.A. while Mr. Abbott would possess "rights of access," as those terms are used in the Convention. The only issue in this case, therefore, is whether Mr. Abbott also possesses "rights of custody" within

[2] Indisputably, Ms. Abbott's removal of A.J. A. from Chile was wrongful in the generic sense of the word. She violated Chilean law when she took A.J. A. to Texas because she sought neither Mr. Abbott's permission nor the court's authorization before doing so. She violated both the existing "*ne exeat*" order imposed by judicial decree in the couple's custody dispute, as well as Chilean statutory law defining the access rights of noncustodial parents. . . The removal was illegal, then, but it was only wrongful within the meaning of the Convention if it was in breach of Mr. Abbott's rights of custody. Unfortunately, I fear the Court's preoccupation with deterring parental misconduct—even, potentially, at the sake of the best interests of the child—has caused it to minimize this important distinction.

the meaning of the Convention by virtue of the travel restriction, or *ne exeat* clause,[3] that Chilean law imposes on Ms. Abbott. In other words, the question is whether the "right" of one parent to veto the other parent's decision to remove a child from the country, subject to judicial override, belongs in the category of "rights relating to the care of the person of the child and, in particular, the right to determine the child's place of residence." In my judgment, it clearly does not, and I need look no further than to the Convention's text to explain why. . .

Rights relating to the care of the child. The Court concludes that the veto power Mr. Abbott has over Ms. Abbott's travel plans is equivalent to those rights "relating to the care of the person of the child." This is so, the Court tells us, because Mr. Abbott has a limited power to keep A.J.A. within Chile's bounds and, therefore, indirectly to influence "the language the child speaks, the identity he finds, or the culture and traditions she will come to absorb." It is not nearly as self-evident as the Court assumes that Mr. Abbott's veto power carries with it any ability to decide the language A.J.A. speaks or the cultural experiences he will have. A.J.A.'s mere presence in Chile does not determine any number of issues, including: whether A.J.A. learns Spanish while there; whether he attends an American school or a British school or a local school; whether he participates in sports; whether he is raised Catholic or Jewish or Buddhist or atheist; whether he eats a vegetarian diet; and on and on. The travel restriction does *not* confer upon Mr. Abbott affirmative power to make any number of decisions that are vital to A.J.A.'s physical, psychological, and cultural development. To say that a limited power to veto a child's travel plans confers, also, a right "relating to the care" of that child devalues the great wealth of decisions a custodial parent makes on a daily basis to attend to a child's needs and development.

The Court's interpretation depends entirely on a broad reading of the phrase "relating to" in the Convention's definition of "rights of custody." It is, undeniably, broad language. But, as the Court reads the term, it is so broad as to be utterly unhelpful in interpreting what "rights of custody" means. . . I suppose it could be said that Mr. Abbott's ability to decide whether A.J.A. spends the night with one of his friends during a Saturday visit is also a "right relating to the care of the child." Taken in the abstract—and to its most absurd—*any* decision on behalf of a child could be construed as a right "relating to" the care of a child.

Such a view of the text obliterates the careful distinction the drafters drew between the rights of custody and the rights of access. Undoubtedly, they were aware of the concept of joint custody. . . But just because rights

[3] The Court repeatedly refers to "*ne exeat* rights," as if the single travel restriction at issue in this case were on a par with the multiple rights commonly exercised by custodial parents. Chile's statutory *ne exeat* provision is better characterized as a restriction on the travel of both the minor and the custodial parent than as a bundle of "rights" possessed by the noncustodial parent.

of custody can be shared by two parents, it does not follow that the drafters intended this limited veto power to be a right of custody. And yet this, it seems, is how the Court understands the case: Because the drafters intended to account for joint custodial arrangements, they intended for *this* travel restriction to be joint custody because it could be said, in some abstract sense, to relate to care of the child. I fail to understand how the Court's reading is faithful to the Convention's text and purpose, given that the text expressly contemplates two distinct classes of parental rights. Today's decision converts every noncustodial parent with access rights—at least in Chile—into a custodial parent for purposes of the Convention. . .

The right to determine the child's place of residence. The Court also concludes that Mr. Abbott's veto power satisfies the Convention's definition of custodial rights because it is, in the Court's view, a "right to determine the child's place of residence." I disagree with the Court's assessment of the significance and meaning of this phrase, both on its face and within the context of the Convention's other provisions. . .

The drafters . . . intended the "right to determine the child's place of residence" to be an "example" of what the Convention means by "care of the person of the child." It is indicative of the "substance" of what it means to be a custodial parent. The definition is not, as the Court would have it, one stick in the bundle that may be parsed as a singular "righ[t] of custody"; rather, it is a shorthand method to assess what types of rights a parent may have. The parent responsible for determining where and with whom a child resides, the drafters assumed, would likely *also* be the parent who has the responsibility to "care" for the child. . .

The Court's reading of this text depends on its substitution of the word "country" for the word "place." Such a substitution is not illogical, of course, in light of the Convention's international focus. See *Croll v. Croll,* 229 F.3d 133, 147, 148 (C.A.2 2000) (Sotomayor, J., dissenting) (reading "place of residence" to mean "authority over the child's more specific living arrangements" "ignores the basic international character of the Hague Convention"). But it is inconsistent with the Convention's text and purpose.

. . . I would give "place of residence" the location-specific meaning its plain text connotes, irrespective of the fact that this Convention concerns international abduction. The right described by the Convention is the right to decide, conclusively, where a child's home will be. And this makes a good deal of sense. The child lives with the parent who has custodial rights or, in the language of the Convention, "care of the person of the child," . . . The child's home—his or her "place of residence"—is fixed by the custody arrangement. This comports too with the Convention's decision to privilege the rights of custodians over the rights of those parents with only visitation rights.

Understanding the effect of a travel restriction. So, the question we confront is whether a travel restriction on one parent's right to embark on international travel with his or her child creates in the other parent a "right to determine the child's place of residence" or the ability "to fix conclusively" the child's "physical" "home." Before answering this question, it is important to understand the nature of the travel restriction we must classify. [Justice Stevens's discussion of Chilean law is omitted.]

. . . By virtue of the restriction Chilean law places on Ms. Abbott's movement, Mr. Abbott has no "right to determine [A.J.A.'s] place of residence." He cannot "conclusively" "fix," "settle," or "determine" the place where A.J.A. "actually lives or has his home." True, the travel restriction bestows upon the noncustodial parent a limited power to prevent his child from leaving the country without his permission, but it does not grant an affirmative power to fix or set the location of the child's home. Mr. Abbott has no power whatever to determine where A.J.A. actually lives within the nearly 300,000 square miles that compose Chile. Even more important, Mr. Abbott has no power whatever to select another country in which A.J.A. would live, were Mr. Abbott's work to take him to another country altogether. In sum, a right to object to a proposed departure gives a parent far less authority than a right to determine where the child shall reside. Moreover, the right to determine where to live within a country, as well as what country to live in, is far broader than the limited right to object to a child's travel abroad.

In my view, the "right" Mr. Abbott has by virtue of the travel restriction is therefore best understood as relating to his "rights of access," as the Convention defines that term—and not as a standalone "righ[t] of custody," as the Court defines it. Chile's statutory travel restriction provision is plainly ancillary to the access rights the Chilean family court granted to him as the noncustodial parent. By its terms, the obligation on the custodial parent to seek the other parent's permission before removing the child from Chile only operates upon the award of *visitation rights;* it has nothing to do with *custody rights.* And it operates automatically to facilitate the noncustodial parent's ability to access the child and to exercise his visitation rights. In the best of all possible circumstances, Mr. Abbott's limited veto power assures him relatively easy access to A.J.A. so that he may continue a meaningful relationship with his son. But this power, standing alone, does not transform him into a *custodian* for purposes of the Convention's return remedy. Instead, it authorizes him, pursuant to Article 21, to seek assistance from this country in carrying out the Chilean family court's visitation order. . .

IV

[I]n my view, the Convention's language is plain and that language precludes the result the Court reaches. . . In these circumstances, the "clear import of treaty language controls" the decision. To support its reading of the text, however, the Court turns to authority we utilize to aid us in interpreting ambiguous treaty text: the position of the Executive Branch and authorities from foreign jurisdictions that have confronted the question before the Court. Were I to agree with the Court that it is necessary turn to these sources to resolve the question before us, I would not afford them the weight the Court does in this case.

Views of the Department of State. Without discussing precisely why, we have afforded "great weight" to "the meaning given [treaties] by the departments of government particularly charged with their negotiation and enforcement." * * * We have awarded "great weight" to the views of a particular government department even when the views expressed by the department are newly memorialized, and even when the views appear contrary to those expressed by the department at the time of the treaty's signing and negotiation, In this case, it appears that both are true: The Department of State's position, which supports the Court's conclusion, is newly memorialized, and is possibly inconsistent with the Department's earlier position.

Putting aside any concerns arising from the fact that the Department's views are newly memorialized and changing, I would not in this case abdicate our responsibility to interpret the Convention's language. This does not seem to be a matter in which deference to the Executive on matters of foreign policy would avoid international conflict; . . . the State Department has made no such argument. Nor is this a case in which the Executive's understanding of the treaty's drafting history is particularly rich or illuminating. . .

Instead, the Department offers us little more than its own reading of the treaty's text. Its view is informed by no unique vantage it has, whether as the entity responsible for enforcing the Convention in this country or as a participating drafter. . . I see no reason, therefore, to replace our understanding of the Convention's text with that of the Executive Branch.

Views of foreign jurisdictions. The Court believes that the views of our sister signatories to the Convention deserve special attention when, in a case like this, "Congress has directed that 'uniform international interpretation' of the Convention is part of the Convention's framework." . . . This may well be correct, but we should not substitute the judgment of other courts for our own. . . And the handful of foreign decisions the Court cites, . . . provide insufficient reason to depart from my understanding of the meaning of the Convention, an understanding shared by many U.S. Courts of Appeals. . .

I also fail to see the international consensus—let alone the "broad acceptance"—that the Court finds among those varied decisions from foreign courts that have considered the effect of a similar travel restriction within the Convention's remedial scheme. The various decisions of the international courts are, at best, in equipoise. Indeed, the Court recognizes that courts in Canada and France have concluded that travel restrictions are not "rights of custody" within the meaning of the Convention. . .

In sum, the decisions relied upon by the Court and Mr. Abbott from our sister signatories do not convince me that we should refrain from a straightforward textual analysis in this case in order to make way for a "uniform international interpretation" of the Convention. . . There is no present uniformity sufficiently substantial to justify departing from our independent judgment on the Convention's text and purpose and the drafters' intent.

V

At bottom, the Convention aims to protect the best interests of the child . . . Recognizing that not all removals in violation of the laws of the country of habitual residence are contrary to a child's best interests, the Convention provides a powerful but limited return remedy. The judgment of the Convention's drafters was that breaches of access rights, while significant (and thus expressly protected by Article 21), are secondary to protecting the child's interest in maintaining an existing custodial relationship.

Today, the Court has upended the considered judgment of the Convention's drafters in favor of protecting the rights of noncustodial parents. In my view, the bright-line rule the Court adopts today is particularly unwise in the context of a treaty intended to govern disputes affecting the welfare of children.

I, therefore, respectfully dissent.

The Hague Abduction Convention

(1) The problem of children subjected to international abduction by their parents is addressed by the Hague Convention on the Civil Aspects of International Child Abduction, which was finalized on October 24, 1980, and is one of four Hague Conventions devoted to children. See Ann Laquer Estin, *Families Across Borders: The Hague Children's Conventions and the Case for International Family Law in the United States*, 62 Fla.L.Rev. 47 (2010). The United States became a signatory to the Convention in 1988. It is implemented in the U.S. by the International Child Abduction Remedies Act, 42 U.S.C. §§ 11601–11610 (1988) (ICARA). The Convention has been adopted in about eighty-five countries. It applies to children under the age of 16 who have been wrongfully removed from their country of habitual residence or wrongfully retained outside that country. If proceedings are commenced within a period of less than one year from the date of wrongful removal or retention, Article 12(1) requires the prompt return of the child ("the judicial or administrative authority concerned shall order the return of the child forthwith") to the country of habitual residence. The Convention is not intended to provide a forum for adjudicating the question of child custody on the merits. Instead, as Professor Linda Silberman has aptly put it, "the Abduction Convention operates as a mechanism for cooperation to deter and remedy parental abduction internationally." Silberman, *Interpreting the Hague Abduction Convention: In Search of a Global Jurisprudence,* 38 U.C. Davis L. Rev. 1049, 1059 (2005) (providing a useful overview of the Convention at pp. 1053–57). In 2002, the Hague Abduction Convention was supplemented by the Hague Convention on the Protection of Children, which operates as a jurisdiction and judgments convention for international custody decisions. See Silberman, *The 1996 Hague Convention on the Protection of Children: Should the United States Join?*, 34 Fam.L.Q. 239 (2000).

The text of the Convention, with accompanying legal analysis, is set out in 51 Fed. Reg. 10494–10516 (March 26, 1986). See generally, P. Beaumont & P. McEleavy, THE HAGUE CONVENTION ON INTERNATIONAL CHILD ABDUCTION (1999); Silberman, *Hague International Child Abduction Convention: A Progress Report,* 57 L. & Contemp. Probs. 209 (1994); Bruch, *The Central Authority's Role Under the Hague Child Abduction Convention: A Friend in Deed,* 28 Fam.L.Q. 35 (1994).

(2) *Abbott* addressed the *ne exeat* issue in the first case under the Hague Convention to reach the Supreme Court. Justice Sonia Sotomayor had previously faced the question as a Circuit Judge when she dissented in *Croll*, discussed supra p. 753, arguing that a *ne exeat* order constituted a "right of custody" under the Convention. She reasoned that the order conferred upon the father (and the Hong Kong court, which could approve the child's relocation) "significant decisionmaking power: absent an order of the Hong Kong court to the contrary, he can require that [the child] remain in Hong Kong or, alternatively, he can use his veto power as leverage to influence [the mother's] selection of the destination country." *Croll,* 229 F.3d at 145 (Sotomayor, J., dissenting). She added:

> The Hague Convention provides a remedy not when a parent moves the child from city to suburb or from home to boarding school, but when he or she transports the child across national borders. In light of the international context, the term "place of residence," as used in the Convention, logically contemplates decisions regarding international relocation. Accordingly, the right to choose the country in which a child lives, like the authority over the child's more specific living arrangements, constitutes a "right to determine the child's place of residence"

> under Article 5, and thus a "right of custody" under the Convention.

Id., at 148 (Sotomayor, J., dissenting). How did the *Abbott* majority resolve this issue? What were Justice Stevens's reasons for disagreeing? What turns on the result?

(3) Professors Silberman and Bruch disagree on the question of whether *ne exeat* clauses confer custody rights on the non-custodial parent. Silberman argues (38 U.C. Davis L. Rev. at 1070, supra note (1)) that "[w]hen one looks to the debates during the negotiations, it is clear that the negotiators intended that a parent with a right to restrict relocation was to be included in the Article 5 definition of who held 'rights of custody'." Bruch points out that "[*n*]*e exeat* orders guarantee convenient access by permitting the noncustodial parent to say something about where a child may *not* live—perhaps not out of a local jurisdiction or perhaps not abroad, depending on their terms. They do not, however, permit the noncustodial parent to designate affirmatively in which house, or on which street, or even in which locale a child *will* live—the express power to determine the child's residence that Article 5 states constitutes a right of custody for Convention purposes." Bruch, *The Unmet Needs of Domestic Violence Victims and Their Children in Hague Child Abduction Convention Cases*, 35 Fam. L.Q. 529, 539–40 (2004). How did the *Abbott* majority and dissent deal with these points?

(4) Bruch's position was supported by an *amicus curiae* brief filed in *Abbott* by two official delegates to the Hague who had participated in the negotiation and drafting of the Convention: Lawrence H. Stotter, a practicing attorney in California and a matrimonial specialist, who represented the United States, and Matti Savolainen, who represented Finland. Both were among the five members of the Drafting Committee, which was charged with preparing the final written draft of the Convention. Their brief stated that both of them "have strong and clear recollections of the intent of the drafters at the time that the Hague Convention was negotiated and finalized." That recollection is that "[t]he Drafters did not intend that a *ne exeat* order would confer a right of custody." Brief of Lawrence H. Stotter and Matti Savolainen as *Amicus Curiae* in Support of Respondent 2–3 (2009). How significant is that? Does Justice Kennedy's observation that an "emerging international consensus" now exists that "*ne exeat* rights are rights of custody, even if that view was not generally formulated when the Convention was drafted in 1980" adequately address the matter?

(5) What do you make of Justice Stevens's emphasis in part I of his dissenting opinion on the attitudes of the drafters toward removal by custodial versus noncustodial parents? Why did the drafters decide not to provide the remedy of return to a noncustodial parent whose visitation rights had been impeded by a custodial parent's removal of the child? Does *Abbott* change that result?

(6) What weight should be given to Justice Kennedy's observation about the impact of the child's residence on identity formation? Even if A.J.A. is returned to Chile, will he experience the life of a typical Chilean child? His father is British, his mother American, and the length of his domicile in Chile is dependent on his father's career moves as an astronomer. Wouldn't similar questions arise as to most children born of mixed-nationality parents? If so, what weight, if any, should identity formation be given in the interpretation of the return remedy?

A Right of Re-Return?

Abbott involved a wrongful removal. Subsequently, the Supreme Court decided a wrongful retention case, *Chafin v. Chafin*, 568 U.S. 165 (2013), and announced a novel "right of re-return" under the Convention. *Chafin* involved a military family in which the father was from the United States and the mother was from Great Britain. They met and married in Germany while Sergeant Chafin was stationed there and their daughter was born there in January 2007. In August 2007, mother and child moved to Scotland by agreement while father was deployed to Afghanistan. In February 2010, the family was reunited in Alabama. Mother, who held a British passport, entered the U.S. on a 90-day tourist visa. After repeated separations and reconciliations, the parties agreed that their marriage was over.

The mother expected to return to Scotland with the child in May, but the father had control of the child's U.K. and U.S. passports and refused to turn them over to the mother. Instead, he filed a petition for divorce in an Alabama state court. At the father's request, and because she was unwilling to leave the United States without her daughter, the mother overstayed her visa. She was arrested on a charge of domestic violence (subsequently dismissed by the prosecutor) after she allegedly threatened the father with a knife. While she was being held on that charge, the authorities learned that she was in the United States illegally. She was turned over to the U.S. Immigration and Customs Enforcement (ICE), which detained her in a deportation center for two months. She was deported to Scotland (without the child, who remained with father) by ICE in February 2011. She filed a return request in Scotland, followed by a petition in federal court in Alabama alleging father's wrongful retention of their daughter and seeking a return remedy pursuant to the Hague Convention.

The district court judge ruled that Scotland was the child's habitual residence, and issued an order in October 2011 requiring the father to return the child to the mother with the child's passports that same day, and permitting the mother to return to Scotland immediately with the child. The father requested and was denied a stay of the return order, but he did not seek a temporary stay of the district court's order from the Eleventh Circuit pending appeal. After the mother and child had returned to Scotland, the father perfected his appeal and the Eleventh Circuit held the case to be moot because, in its view, once the child had been returned to the foreign country of its habitual residence, the district court "became powerless" to grant relief.

Meanwhile, the Alabama state court had stayed the father's divorce proceeding pending the outcome of the Hague petition case in the federal court. In 2012, the Alabama Supreme Court ruled that the state court could proceed with the divorce but not with the custody matter. Was its decision correct? The father's theory of the case was that if he was able to establish that the child's habitual residence was in Alabama from February 2010 until October 2011, he would be able to obtain the child's return to Alabama and reopen the custody proceeding in the Alabama state court, which he contended has jurisdiction under the UCCJEA. How do you assess his claim?

The Supreme Court reversed the judgment of the Eleventh Circuit:

> The Hague Convention mandates the prompt return of children to their countries of habitual residence. But such return does not render this case moot; there is a live dispute between the parties over where their child will be raised, and there is a possibility of effectual relief for the prevailing parent. The courts below therefore continue to have jurisdiction to adjudicate the merits of the parties' respective claim.

568 U.S. at 180.

The mother objected both that "the District Court lacks the authority to issue a re-return order either under the Convention or pursuant to its inherent equitable powers" and that "even if the habitual residence ruling were reversed and the District Court were to issue a re-return order, that relief would be ineffectual because Scotland would simply ignore it." *Id.* at 174. To these points, the Court ruled that mother's argument "confuses mootness with the merits," going on to note that

> even if Scotland were to ignore a U.S. re-return order, or decline to assist in enforcing it, this case would not be moot. The U.S. courts continue to have personal jurisdiction over Ms. Chafin, may command her to take action even outside the United States, and may back up any such command with sanctions * * *. No law of physics prevents [the child's] return from Scotland, * * * and Ms.

> Chafin might decide to comply with an order against her and return [the child] to the United States, *see, e.g., Larbie v. Larbie,* 690 F.3d 295, 303–304 (C.A.5 2012) (mother who had taken child to United Kingdom complied with Texas court sanctions order and order to return child to United States for trial). After all, the consequence of compliance presumably would not be relinquishment of custody rights, but simply custody proceedings in a different forum.

Id. at 174–75. What do you make of these considerations? Examine particularly the Court's last sentence: doesn't it beg the question? If the "different forum" it refers to is Alabama, that assumes the District Court on remand would now find that Alabama is the child's habitual residence. If so, the conflict between Scotland and Alabama that the Convention was drafted to avoid would be invited, right? Justice Ginsburg, concurring, found that prospect "unsettling":

> As the Court's opinion explains, the Eleventh Circuit erred in holding that the child's removal to Scotland rendered further adjudication in the U.S. meaningless. Reversal of the District Court's return order, I agree, could provide Mr. Chafin with meaningful relief. A determination that the child's habitual residence was Alabama, not Scotland, would open the way for an order directing Ms. Chafin to "re-return" the child to the United States and for Mr. Chafin to seek a custody adjudication in an Alabama state court. But that prospect is unsettling. "[S]huttling children back and forth between parents and across international borders may be detrimental to those children" whose welfare led the Contracting States to draw up the Convention * * *. And the advent of rival custody proceedings in Scotland and Alabama is just what the Convention aimed to stave off.

Id. at 182 (Ginsburg, J., concurring). Justice Ginsburg went on to discuss the "management of Convention hearings and appeals in England and Wales," where "[t]o pursue an appeal from a return order . . . leave must be obtained from the first instance judge or the Court of Appeal. . . . Although an appeal does not trigger an automatic stay, . . . if leave to appeal is granted, we are informed, a stay is ordinarily ordered by the court that granted leave. . . . Appeals are then fast-tracked with a target of six weeks for disposition." Id. at 183–84. She compared the U.S. treatment of *Chafin*:

> Lynne Chafin filed her petition for a return order in May 2011. [The child] was then four years old. [She] is now six and uncertainty still lingers about the proper forum for adjudication of her parents' custody dispute. Protraction so marked is hardly consonant with the Convention's objectives. On remand, the Court rightly instructs, the Court of Appeals should decide the case "as

> expeditiously as possible." For future cases, rulemakers and legislators might pay sustained attention to the means by which the United States can best serve the Convention's aims: "to secure the prompt return of children wrongfully removed or retained in" this Nation; and "to ensure that rights of custody . . . under the law of one Contracting State are effectively respected in the other Contracting States." Art.1, Treaty Doc., at 7.

Id. at 185 (Ginsburg, J., concurring).

The Court subsequently denied certiorari in *Larbie*. Does its treatment of *Larbie* in *Chafin* amount to an endorsement of the *Larbie* approach? As the Court pointed in *Chafin*, "[i]n a recently issued decision from the Family Division of the High Court of Justice of England and Wales, a judge of that court rejected the 'concept of automatic re-return of a child in response to the overturn of [a] Hague order.' *DL v. EL,* [2013] EWHC 49, ¶ 59 (Judgt. of Jan. 17). The judge in that case did not ignore the pertinent re-return order—issued by the District Court in *Larbie*—but did not consider it binding in light of the proceedings in England." 568 U.S. at 174 n.1.

A complete statement of the English judge's conclusions reported in ¶59 of *DL v. EL* reads as follows:

> 59. F's second set of Hague proceedings, issued promptly after these events on 20 September 2012, must therefore founder at the outset, because it follows that:
>
> > a) The reversal of the Hague order by the appeal court cannot of itself amount to a 'mandate' that KL be returned to Texas, a territory of which he had by that time ceased to be a habitual resident.
> >
> > b) The order of 29 August 2012, assuming the judge had the jurisdiction to make it in terms of Texas law and procedure, is nevertheless ineffectual so far as the London court is concerned, because this court at the time of that order was seised of proceedings concerning KL's welfare and residence (custody) in order to determine counter-applications launched in October 2011 (by M) and March 2012 (by F)—albeit that those applications became and for the moment remain stayed during the pendency of the Hague proceedings.
> >
> > c) The English court rather than the Texan court therefore validly has jurisdiction in relation to welfare issues concerning KL.
> >
> > d) Without intending disrespect to the Texan court, the English court should not order KL's return to Texas save on a basis determined by his welfare.

> e) The concept of automatic re-return of a child in response to the overturn of the Hague order pursuant to which he came here is unsupported by law or principle, and would in this case be deeply inimical to KL's best interests, interests which become this court's paramount concern once F's Hague applications fall away, as I determine they now do.

Which Court has the better of this argument? Should there be a "re-return" remedy?

Habitual Residence of Infants

(1) Is an agreement between the parents necessary to establish the habitual residence of a child? In *Monasky v. Taglieri*, 140 S. Ct. 719 (2020), the Supreme Court said no. The parties were married in the U.S. and relocated to Italy, where their daughter was born. The mother asserted that the father had become physically abusive and "forced himself upon [her] multiple times," and that she feared for her life. *Id.* at 724. The mother removed her two-month-old daughter from Italy and they moved in with her parents in Ohio. An Italian court granted the father's ex parte request to terminate the mother's parental rights, and the father petitioned a federal district court in Ohio for return under the Hague Convention. *Id.* After a four-day bench trial, the district court agreed with the father that Italy was the child's habitual residence. The Sixth Circuit affirmed, rejecting the mother's argument that she and the father "never had a 'meeting of the minds' about their child's future home." *Id.* at 725 (citation omitted).

The Supreme Court affirmed. Writing for the Court, Justice Ginsburg began by noting that the Convention does not define "habitual residence" and makes no mention of an agreement between the parents. *Id.* at 726. Moreover, the Convention's explanatory report places an emphasis on "the family and social environment in which [the child's] life has developed" and treats habitual residence as "a question of pure fact, differing in that respect from domicile." *Id.* at 726, 727. Finally, high courts in other signatories to the Convention agree that an actual agreement is not needed. *Id.* at 727–28. Thus, the Court concluded, "[t]here are no categorical requirements for establishing a child's habitual residence—least of all an actual-agreement requirement for infants." *Id.* at 728.

Instead, habitual residence depends on the totality of the facts pointing to the country where the child is "at home," including

> "a change in geography combined with the passage of an appreciable period of time," "age of the child," "immigration status of child and parent," "academic activities," "social engagements,"

> "participation in sports programs and excursions," "meaningful connections with the people and places in the child's new country," "language proficiency," and "location of personal belongings."

Id. at 727 n.3 (quoting Federal Judicial Center, J. Garbolino, The 1980 Hague Convention on the Civil Aspects of International Child Abduction: A Guide for Judges 67–68 (2d ed. 2015)). Trial courts, the Court held, should receive deference when making this fact-intensive determination, subject only to a clear-error standard of review. *Id.* at 730–31. The Court rejected the mother's argument that a bright-line rule was needed to deter abduction: "When all the circumstances are in play, would-be abductors should find it more, not less, difficult to manipulate the reality on the ground, thus impeding them from forging artificial jurisdictional links . . . with a view to obtaining custody of a child." *Id.* at 729 (citation omitted).

Does the *Monasky* decision do too little to protect mothers who attempt to flee with their infant children from domestic violence? The Court acknowledges the problem but doubts "that imposing a categorical actual-agreement requirement is an appropriate solution, for it would leave many infants without a habitual residence, and therefore outside the Convention's domain." *Id.* at 729. In any event, the Court continues, the solution lies in the Hague Convention's Article 13(b), which provides an exception to the right of return if the child would thereby be exposed to "physical or psychological harm" or an "intolerable situation." After you read about the Article 13(b) exception, infra Section 2.B.2, consider whether you find the Court's response adequate. (Note that the district court in *Monasky*, while finding the mother's allegations of abuse "deeply troubling," rejected her Article 13(b) defense because it found no evidence that the father had abused the child or disregarded her well-being. *Id.*)

(2) Compare the treatment an infant's "habitual residence" under the Convention with the definition of an infant's "home state" under Section 102(7) of the UCCJEA. There, a child's home state is derived from the place where the child "has continuously lived with a parent or a person acting as a parent" for six months. In the case of a child less than six months of age, the Act provides that the home state is "the State in which the child lived from birth with any of the persons mentioned." Does *Monasky* in effect align the Convention with the UCCJEA for infants under six months of age?

(3) As *Monasky* exemplifies, the Convention uses terms that may be unfamiliar in many countries. For example, what is a child's "habitual residence"? Is that term synonymous with "domicile" or, perhaps, "home state"? What constitutes a "wrongful" removal or retention under the Convention? What are "custody rights"? Only rights awarded by a court? Or pre-decretal rights arising from the parent-child relationship? Are visitation rights that permit a parent to have access to the child "custody rights"? What about an order prohibiting a parent from removing the child from the court's jurisdiction without permission of the other parent and/or a court (known as a *ne exeat* clause)? Whose law determines these issues?

Professor Silberman points out that the Convention is a multilateral treaty that is enforced and interpreted by the national courts of each adopting country. 38 U.C. Davis L. Rev. at 1062–72. Yet its effectiveness depends on a common judicial understanding of these terms. How easy is that to achieve? Compare *Whallon v. Lynn*, 230 F.3d 450 (1st Cir. 2000), with *Croll v. Croll*, 229 F.3d 133 (2d Cir. 2000). *Whallon* applied the Mexican doctrine of "patria potestas" to recognize the custodial right of an unmarried father to request the return of his five-year-old daughter whose mother had taken her from Mexico to the United States without his consent. Although this doctrine was unknown in the U.S., the court examined Mexican sources to determine its scope. In *Croll*, the court consulted Webster's Third and Black's Law Dictionary to determine the meaning of a *ne exeat* clause used in the decree of a Hong Kong court. Which court got the interpretive process right?

Concurring in *Monasky*, Justice Thomas complained that the majority strayed from the "plain meaning of the treaty's text," resorting to extratextual sources such as explanatory reports and decisions by courts in other signatory nations. *Monasky*, 140 S. Ct. at 732 (Thomas, J., concurring). "Because the [foreign] decisions are not contemporaneous with the treaty's passage," he wrote, "they do not necessarily provide the best evidence of the original understanding of the phrase [habitual residence]." *Id.* at 733. Quoting Justice Stevens's dissent in *Abbott*, he concluded, "By relying too heavily on the judicial decisions of the treaty's other signatories, rather than on a more thorough textual analysis, we risk being persuaded to reach the popular answer, but perhaps not the correct one. In short, 'we should not substitute the judgment of other courts for our own.' " *Id.* at 734. Is Justice Thomas's interpretive method appropriate for an international treaty?

2. Defenses to the Return Remedy

VAN DE SANDE V. VAN DE SANDE

431 F.3d 567 (7th Cir. 2005).

POSNER, CIRCUIT JUDGE.

The International Child Abduction Remedies Act, 42 U.S.C. §§ 11601 *et seq.*, implementing the Hague Convention on the Civil Aspects of International Child Abduction, T.I.A.S. No. 11,670, 1343 U.N.T.S. 89 (Oct. 25, 1980), entitles a person whose child has been abducted to the United States (usually by a parent) to petition in federal court for the return of the child. 42 U.S.C. § 11603(b). "The Convention was created to discourage abductions by parents who either lost, or would lose, a custody contest. . . The Convention drafters adopted a 'remedy of return' . . . to discourage abductions, reconnect children with their primary caretakers, and locate each custody contest in the forum where most of the relevant evidence existed. [But] while the remedy of return works well if the abductor is a non-custodial parent, it is inappropriate when the abductor is a primary caretaker who is seeking to protect herself and the children from the other parent's violence." Merle H. Weiner, "Navigating the Road Between Uniformity and Progress: The Need for Purposive Analysis of the Hague Convention on the Civil Aspects of International Child Abduction," 33 *Colum. Human Rts. L. Rev.* 275, 278–79 (2002). In such a case "the remedy [of return] puts the victim's most precious possession, her child, in close proximity to her batterer either without her protection (assuming she does not return with the child), or with her protection, thereby exposing her to further violence." Merle H. Weiner, "International Child Abduction and the Escape from Domestic Violence," 69 *Fordham L.Rev.* 593, 634 (2000); cf. 18 U.S.C. § 1204(c)(2). "A typical pattern involves a female U.S. national who has married a male foreign national and moved with her spouse to a foreign country. In most Hague cases invoking grave risk on the basis of domestic violence, the abuse begins before the transnational move. Ultimately, the victim flees with her children back to the United States in order to escape the abuse. The batterer, left behind in the country of habitual residence, then files a petition under the Hague Convention requesting return of the children to adjudicate the custody issues." Roxanne Hoegger, "What If She Leaves? Domestic Violence Cases Under the Hague Convention and the Insufficiency of the Undertakings Remedy," 18 *Berkeley Women's L.J.* 181, 187 (2003).

The present case approximates the "typical pattern" in which the remedy of return is problematic. The two children of Davy and Jennifer Van De Sande, a married but estranged couple, are habitual residents of Belgium, Davy's native country. Davy has been awarded custody of his two children by a Belgian court, but Jennifer, who is living with the children in the United States, has refused to give them up. She became an "abducter" when Davy got the custody decree, though it was ex parte. Davy brought this suit to get the children back.

An abducter has a narrow defense: Article 13(b) of the Convention excuses return if "there is a grave risk that his or her return would expose the child to physical or psychological harm or otherwise place the child in an intolerable situation." The abducter must prove this by clear and convincing evidence. 42 U.S.C. § 11603(e)(2)(A). Although Jennifer submitted affidavits setting forth the circumstances that she contends create such a risk, the district court granted summary judgment for Davy, primarily on the ground that there is no indication that the Belgian legal system cannot or will not protect the children. The only condition that the judge inserted in the order directing the return of the children to Davy is that he pay for their airfare to Belgium.

Jennifer presented six affidavits—two by her and one each by her father, her mother, her brother, and a friend. The affidavits paint a consistent and disturbing picture. According to them Davy began beating Jennifer shortly after their marriage in 1999. The beatings were frequent and serious. For example, when she was seven months pregnant with their first child, Davy slammed Jennifer's head against a wall, choked her, and pushed her toward the top of a flight of stairs, threatening to topple her down them. The beatings, which typically consisted of choking Jennifer, throwing her against a wall, and kicking her in the shins, and occurred several times a week throughout the marriage whenever the two of them were together, continued when they moved from the United States to Belgium. Davy's mother joined in beating her daughter-in-law. (The Van De Sandes' grievance against Jennifer is that she is an indifferent housekeeper.) She complained several times to the Belgian police, but they said they could do nothing unless she went to a doctor to verify her injuries; and she did not do that.

Davy's beatings of Jennifer continued after the two children were born, and were often done in their presence, which caused them to cry. The older child (born in August 2000, so 4 years old when her mother refused to return to Belgium in October 2004) would tell her father to stop, but without success. Physical abuse of the daughter by her father began when she started wetting her bed. He would spank her, and once when Jennifer entered the girl's bedroom and told Davy to stop beating their daughter he grabbed Jennifer by the throat and shoved her out of the room. Once he struck the daughter a sharp blow to the side of her head. His mother (the daughter's grandmother) struck the daughter in the head at least twice.

Davy also abused Jennifer verbally in the children's presence, calling her a "cunt," "whore," "lazy fucking bitch," and "lazy fat bitch." (He is fluent in English, as are the children.) Davy once told their daughter "Fuck mommy." And one time he picked her up, sat her on his lap, and said, "Tell Mommy she's a cunt."

In 2004, during a visit to Jennifer's parents, Jennifer told Davy that she and the children would not return to Belgium. He threatened to kill the children. He had earlier threatened to kill Jennifer. And the next day, in a conversation with Jennifer's brother, he threatened to kill "everybody." Jennifer told her father about Davy's threats, and the police were called and an officer escorted him from the house.

After he returned to Belgium without the children, the daughter stopped wetting her bed—except after her weekly phone conversation with him. It was after returning to Belgium that he obtained ex parte the order from the Belgian court awarding him custody of the children and thus providing him with the precondition to bringing this suit.

If the affidavits submitted by Jennifer are accurate, as we must assume they are, given the procedural posture of the case, Jennifer has satisfied the statutory requirement that her evidence of risk of harm to the children be clear and convincing. Cf. *Anderson v. Liberty Lobby, Inc.,* 477 U.S. 242, 255–56 (1986); *Masson v. New Yorker Magazine, Inc.,* 501 U.S. 496, 508 (1991). But is it clear and convincing evidence of a *grave* risk of harm? The district judge thought not. In reaching this conclusion, however, he was unduly influenced by the fact that most of the physical and all the verbal abuse was directed to Jennifer rather than to the children. The younger child, a boy, apparently wasn't beaten at all; the girl was spanked and hit repeatedly, but not injured; and no expert evidence of the psychological effect of Davy's conduct on either child was presented.

The judge inexplicably gave no weight to Davy's threat to kill the children. Perhaps, standing alone, such a threat could be discounted as an emotional reaction to the prospect of losing custody of them. But given Davy's propensity for violence, and the grotesque disregard for the children's welfare that he displayed by beating his wife severely and repeatedly in their presence and hurling obscene epithets at her also in their presence, it would be irresponsible to think the risk to the children less than grave. The gravity of a risk involves not only the probability of harm, but also the magnitude of the harm if the probability materializes. *Nunez-Escudero v. Tice-Menley,* 58 F.3d 374, 377 (8th Cir. 1995); cf. *United States v. Carroll Towing Co.,* 159 F.2d 169, 173 (2d Cir. 1947) (L. Hand, J.). The probability that Davy, or his mother, another person of violent temper (if the affidavits are true), would some day lose control and inflict actual physical injury on the children (or at least on the daughter) could not be thought negligible.

But against this it can be argued that the Hague Convention is really just a venue statute, designed "to deter parents from engaging in international forum shopping in custody cases." *Baxter v. Baxter,* 423 F.3d 363, 367 (3d Cir. 2005); see, e.g., *Silverman v. Silverman,* 338 F.3d 886, 899 (8th Cir. 2003). Maybe we should be asking not what the risk to the children might be in a jurisdiction that had no laws for the protection of children, but merely whether the jurisdiction of residence has adequate laws; Belgium, we can assume, does.

Friedrich v. Friedrich, 78 F.3d 1060, 1069 (6th Cir. 1996), proposed such an approach, but did so in acknowledged dictum, *id.* at 1069, since "Mrs. Friedrich alleges nothing more than adjustment problems that would attend the relocation of most children," and thus her defense of grave risk of harm failed at the threshold. *Id.* at 1067. The dictum has been repeated, e.g., *March v. Levine,* 249 F.3d 462, 471 (6th Cir. 2001); *Miller v. Miller,*

240 F.3d 392, 402 (4th Cir. 2001); *Blondin v. Dubois*, 238 F.3d 153, 162 (2d Cir. 2001), and it influenced the district court in this case, but we do not think it correct. See *Nunez-Escudero v. Tice-Menley, supra,* 58 F.3d at 377. There is a difference between the law on the books and the law as it is actually applied, and nowhere is the difference as great as in domestic relations. Because of the privacy of the family and parental control of children, most abuse of children by a parent goes undetected. *Pennsylvania v. Ritchie,* 480 U.S. 39, 60 (1987); *Coy v. Iowa,* 487 U.S. 1012, 1022 (1988) (concurring opinion). To give a father custody of children who are at great risk of harm from him, on the ground that they will be protected by the police of the father's country, would be to act on an unrealistic premise. The rendering court must satisfy itself that the children will in fact, and not just in legal theory, be protected if returned to their abuser's custody.

Moreover, to define the issue not as whether there is a grave risk of harm, but as whether the lawful custodian's country has good laws or even as whether it both has and zealously enforces such laws, disregards the language of the Convention and its implementing statute; for they say nothing about the laws in the petitioning parent's country. The omission to mention them does not seem to have been an accident—the kind of slip in draftsmanship that courts sometimes correct in the exercise of their interpretive authority. If handing over custody of a child to an abusive parent creates a grave risk of harm to the child, in the sense that the parent may with some nonnegligible probability injure the child, the child should not be handed over, however severely the law of the parent's country might punish such behavior. In such a case, any order divesting the abducting parent of custody would have to be conditioned on the child's being kept out of the custody of the abusing parent until the merits of the custody dispute between the parents could be resolved by the court in the abusive parent's country. At argument Davy's lawyer was willing to entertain the possibility that the district judge should have imposed such a condition on the order returning the children to Davy in Belgium. This concession alone requires that we remand the case to the district court for further consideration, for "in order to ameliorate any short-term harm to the child, courts in the appropriate circumstances have made return contingent upon 'undertakings' from the petitioning parent." *Feder v. Evans-Feder,* 63 F.3d 217, 226 (3d Cir. 1995); see also *Gaudin v. Remis,* 415 F.3d 1028, 1035–36 (9th Cir. 2005); *Blondin v. Dubois,* 189 F.3d 240, 248–49 (2d Cir. 1999).

But "undertakings," as an alternative to refusing to return the child, will not always do the trick. *Walsh v. Walsh,* 221 F.3d 204, 219 (1st Cir. 2000). The ex parte order that Davy obtained, granting him custody of the children, does not preclude Jennifer's challenging his custody; and we are told that in April of this year Jennifer filed such a challenge in a Belgian court but that the court has taken no action. Pending resolution of the custody dispute, prudence would require that the children if returned to

Belgium be placed in the custody of some third party in that country—obviously not Davy's mother! (assuming as we must at this stage of the litigation that she really did beat her granddaughter). Instead of remaining in their own mother's custody in the United States, the children might find themselves in a foster-care institution until the custody litigation was resolved, even though there is no suggestion that their mother is an abusive, neglectful, or otherwise unfit parent, whatever the deficiencies in her housekeeping skills.

Return plus conditions ("undertakings") can in some, maybe many, cases properly accommodate the interest in the child's welfare to the interests of the country of the child's habitual residence. Often the bulk of the evidence concerning risk of harm will be found in that country and the left-behind parent's defense to charges of abuse may be more difficult and costly to prepare and present in the country to which the abducter has fled. But in cases of child abuse the balance may shift against return plus conditions. In a comment on "undertakings" that was quoted with approval in *Danaipour v. McLarey,* 286 F.3d 1, 25 (1st Cir. 2002), the State Department has advised that "if the requested . . . court is presented with unequivocal evidence that return would cause the child a 'grave risk' of physical or psychological harm, . . . then it would seem less appropriate for the court to enter extensive undertakings than to deny the return request. The development of extensive undertakings in such a context could embroil the court in the merits of the underlying custody issues and would tend to dilute the force of the Article 13(b) exception." The court added that "undertakings are most effective when the goal is to preserve the status quo of the parties prior to the wrongful removal. This, of course, is not the goal in cases where there is evidence that the status quo was abusive." 286 F.3d at 25; see also Hoegger, *supra,* 18 *Berkeley Women's L.J.* at 196–99; Weiner, *supra,* 69 *Fordham L.Rev.* at 678–81.

Concern with comity among nations argues for a narrow interpretation of the "grave risk of harm" defense; but the safety of children is paramount. Jennifer presented at the summary judgment stage sufficient evidence of a grave risk of harm to her children, and the adequacy of conditions that would protect the children if they were returned to their father's country is sufficiently in doubt, to necessitate an evidentiary hearing in order to explore these issues fully. The hearing should be held promptly and conducted expeditiously in order to comply with the Convention's goal of expediting the return of abducted children to their country of habitual residence, Hague Convention, *supra,* Art. 11; *March v. Levine, supra,* 249 F.3d at 474, provided that the return will not expose the children to a grave risk of harm.

Reversed and Remanded.

The Scope of the Available Defenses to Return

(1) Justice Kennedy observed at the end of his opinion in *Abbott* that although the father's *ne exeat* right meant that he "has a right of custody and may seek a return remedy, a return order is not automatic." Various exceptions to the duty of prompt return are specified in the Convention, including the two contained in Article 13: one in 13(b) that "there is a grave risk that his or her return would expose the child to physical or psychological harm or otherwise place the child in an intolerable situation," and another that permits the court to refuse to order a return "if it finds that the child objects to being returned and has attained an age and degree of maturity at which it is appropriate to take account of its views."

Do these exceptions swallow the rule? How broadly should they be construed? How likely is it that the courts or administrative agencies charged with administering the Convention in the Contracting States will develop consistent interpretations? A Special Commission to Review the Operation of the Hague Convention on the Civil Aspects of International Child Abduction is in place; it meets every two years. Is it likely to help provide uniformity among the Contracting States?

(2) *Van De Sande* dealt with Article 13(b), one of the most contentious exceptions to the duty of prompt return. Does it do so correctly? What, exactly, is Judge Posner's rationale for holding that the mother had met her required burden of showing grave harm to the child by clear and convincing evidence? Why can't the Belgian courts protect the child?

(3) As Professor Linda Silberman pointed out in 2000, the identity of the most common abductors had changed over the first twenty years of the Convention's existence: it was initially thought that non-custodial fathers were and would continue to be the typical abductors of their children. Instead, it turns out that many abductors are custodial mothers, including some in "high-profile cases" who "alleged that the removal has been necessitated by domestic violence on the part of the father." Silberman, *The Hague Child Abduction Convention Turns Twenty: Gender Politics and Other Issues*, 33 J. Int'l L. & Pol. 221, 224 (2000).

Silberman's observation has only become stronger with the passage of time. By 2006, at the time of the Fifth Meeting of the Commission to Review the Convention, it had become clear that "two-thirds of abductors involved in Hague proceedings are primary caretakers, mostly mothers, and that this 'gives rise to issues which had not been foreseen by the drafters of the Convention.'" Merle H. Weiner, *Half-Truths, Mistakes, and Embarrassments: The United States Goes to the Fifth Meeting of the Special Commission to Review the Operation of the Hague Convention on the Civil Aspects of International Child Abduction*, 2008 Utah L.Rev. 221, 282 (2008). Two years later, a study prepared using 2008 figures for the Sixth Meeting of the Special Commission showed little change: "the majority,

69% of abductors were mothers, most of whom (88%) were primary or joint primary caretakers." Nigel Lowe and Victoria Stephens, *Operating the 1980 Hague Abduction Convention: The 2008 Statistics*, 41 Family Law 1216 [UK] (2011). What should follow from this fact? Weiner, who attended the two-week session of the Fifth Meeting in 2006 as an observer, came away with the conclusion that the "United States' participation was a failure of U.S. foreign policy" in part because

> The United States had an opportunity to take a leadership role in fashioning a response to [the topic of domestic violence], but instead the United States exhibited hostility to the plight of women and children fleeing for reasons of safety.

Id. at 223. Weiner went on to offer favorable commentary on suggestions discussed during the meeting for strengthening the Article 13(b) defense at pp. 283–306, while noting at p. 286 that the U.S. "opposed all efforts at the Fifth Meeting to broaden the Article 13(b) defense" and to speculate on possible explanations (but not justifications) that may have motivated the U.S. position.

(4) Judge Posner cites *Blondin v. Dubois*, 238 F.3d 153 (2d Cir. 2001) [*Blondin IV*], a high-profile international custody dispute involving a French family, where the trial court found that the father had repeatedly beaten and threatened to kill the mother, often in the presence of the children, and had threatened to kill the children as well. After seven years, the mother had had enough. Forging the father's signature to obtain U.S. passports for the children, she fled to the United States in 1997, where she and the children moved in with her brother and his family in New York. The father filed a timely petition for return of the children pursuant to the Hague Convention. The mother did not contest the court's finding that she had wrongfully removed the children from France, instead invoking the Article 13(b) defense. In *Blondin I*, 19 F.Supp.2d 123 (S.D.N.Y.1998), the trial court found that a grave risk existed and declined to order the children returned to their father's custody in France. On appeal, the Second Circuit vacated the judgment on this point and remanded the matter to enable the trial judge to consider "the full panoply of arrangements"—including those that might be made available through the cooperation of the French government—"in order to allow the courts [of France] an opportunity to adjudicate custody." *Blondin v. Dubois*, 189 F.3d 240, 242 (2d Cir. 1999) [*Blondin II*].

On remand, the trial court reiterated its finding under Article 13(b), relying in part on the expert testimony of a well-respected child psychoanalyst that Marie-Eline had suffered "an acute, severe traumatic disorder" because of the abuse she had witnessed and suffered while living in France. Dr. Solnit further testified that Marie-Eline had significantly recovered while living in "the secure environment" provided by her extended family in New York. Finally, Dr. Solnit was of the opinion that removing the children from this secure environment and returning them to France would "almost certainly" trigger a post-traumatic stress disorder that "would set them back in a very harmful way" and "would undo the benefit of the psychological and emotional roots they have established with their mother and her extended family."

On appeal, the Second Circuit accepted the trial court's finding and affirmed its order denying the father's motion for the children's prompt return to France. Noting that Dr. Solnit's testimony stood "uncontroverted" as "the only expert testimony presented on the risk of psychological harm to the children," 238 F.3d at 160, the Second Circuit concluded that "we see no basis upon which to question the District Court's finding that the children will suffer from a recurrence of traumatic stress disorder if they return to France." *Id.* at 161. The Second Circuit went on to dismiss the father's evidence concerning arrangements that he and the French government were willing to make to facilitate repatriation of the children as "essentially inapposite, as it does not purport to cast doubt on the Court's finding that *even with all of these arrangements in place*, the children face an almost certain recurrence of traumatic stress disorder on returning to France because they associate France with their father's abuse and the trauma they suffered as a result." *Id.*

(5) Has the Second Circuit in effect created a domestic violence exception to the Convention? If so, what are its limits? The Second Circuit stressed that the case presented the court "with a rare situation in which, for unexplained reasons, no evidence was presented by one party that would contradict the conclusions of an expert procured by the opposing party." *Id.* at 160. Why do you suppose the father chose not to present such evidence? The Hague Convention rests on the assumption that the courts of the country from which the child was wrongfully removed or retained provide the proper forum to resolve the underlying custody dispute. Didn't the district court, with the Second Circuit's approval, permit the mother to profit from her wrongful conduct in removing the children from France? Professor Silberman thinks so. In her view, the Second Circuit's decision "threatens the basic framework and objectives of the Child Abduction Convention" by transforming "what should be a summary Hague proceeding into a conventional custody hearing—replete with individual 'best interest' assessments and extensive psychological testimony." See Silberman, 33 Int'l L. & Pol. at 239. Do you agree? But how can a court decide whether the Article 13(b) defense applies without some factual basis to rest upon?

Lowe and Stephens, in their assessment of the global operation of the Hague Convention prepared in 2011 based on 2008 statistics, concluded that "[t]here was a significant increase in the number of applications, the proportion of returns had declined and applications took longer to resolve" compared to the 2003 report. See 41 Family Law at 1217. Does their assessment support Silberman's view?

On the other hand, Professor Weiner applauded the District Court's interpretation of Article 13(b), noting that "it is still the best avenue presently available for domestic violence victims who seek to defeat a petition and who have not been forced to go to or remain in the child's habitual residence" while warning that "[a]t best, Article 13(b) offers a piecemeal case-by-case solution, available only to women whose judges understand the link between adult-on-adult violence and harm to children, and whose judges do not blindly trust either the ability of Contracting States to protect domestic violence victims, or batterers' promises to adhere to undertakings." Weiner, *International Child Abduction and the Escape from Domestic Violence*, 69 Fordham L. Rev. 593, 662 (2000) (going on to present alternative ways of handling domestic violence cases under the Convention). Weiner expressed these opinions before the Second Circuit handed down its 2001 decision on the second appeal in *Blondin*. How do you suppose she would analyze that decision?

(6) Does *Van De Sande* follow *Blondin*'s approach to Article 13(b) in domestic abuse cases? No expert testimony was offered in *Van De Sande*; what testimony does the Seventh Circuit accept instead? Note Judge Posner's reliance on Professor Weiner's article as well as that of another domestic violence advocate, Roxanne Hoegger: has he accepted their analysis? What do you suppose Professor Silberman would say about *Van De Sande*? She believes that "the strongest claims for non-return" exist in cases where "allegations of physical and even sexual abuse of the child" are made. See Silberman, *Interpreting the Hague Abduction Convention: In Search of a Global Jurisprudence*, 38 U.C. Davis L. Rev. 1049, 1074 (2005). In cases like *Blondin* (and *Van De Sande*?) where the primary caretaker parent refuses to return with the child because she "asserts that she has been the victim of serious domestic violence or other threat and that she cannot return without danger to herself," Silberman hesitates. She recognizes that "[a]lthough the Convention only requires the return of the child and not the parent, when a child has been in the care of one parent, return without the primary caretaker potentially places a child at 'grave risk' or creates an 'intolerable situation.'" *Id.* at 1077. Is this what Judge Posner was worried about?

Silberman had earlier expressed the view that

> the social context of the Abduction Convention has changed over time, and there is new concern about the child's (and often the abductor's) welfare when return is ordered. In order to preserve the return objective of the Convention while simultaneously ensuring the safety of the child upon return, the role of safe return orders needs careful thought and creative implementation. A new

> procotol to the Convention could create the appropriate mechanisms, whether they be orders issued by the court hearing the Hague application made enforceable in the court of the State to which the child is to be returned, or the establishment of procedures for cooperation facilitating the issuance of mirror orders in both the requested and requesting States.

Silberman, *Patching Up the Abduction Convention: A Call for a New International Protocol and a Suggestion for Amendment to ICARA*, 38 Tex. Int'l L.J. 41, 55 (2003). Is this a promising approach? For her part, Weiner applauds Judge Posner's approach in *Van De Sande* to require trial courts to examine carefully whether the protections promised in undertakings will actually be forthcoming. Weiner, 2008 Utah L. Rev. at 288 n. 348.

(7) What do you think of Judge Posner's discussion of the alternative arrangements for care of the children that might be made pending a determination of the merits of the custody dispute by a Belgian court? Either the children might remain in the U.S. with their mother while she litigates the custody question in Belgium, or the children might be returned to Belgium without the mother and placed in temporary care while awaiting the outcome. Which course do you think is preferable? Note that there no suggestion that the custody dispute might be tried in a state court in the U.S. Does the UCCJEA authorize jurisdiction in the U.S. for such a determination? Section 204 permits a court to exercise "temporary emergency jurisdiction" if a child is present in the state and the child "or a sibling or parent of the child" is subjected to or threatened with "mistreatment or abuse." Section 207 permits the home state to decline to exercise its jurisdiction on the ground that it is an inconvenient forum and another state is a more appropriate forum. One of the factors the home state shall consider in making that determination is "whether domestic violence has occurred and is likely to continue in the future and which State could best protect the parties and the child." Should this remedy be read into the Hague Abduction Convention? Or ICARA?

(8) The "age and maturity" defense available under Article 13 was considered in *Felder v. Wetzel*, 696 F.3d 92 (1st Cir. 2012), a case where the mother, Claudia Felder, alleged that her 14-year-old daughter, K.W., was being wrongfully retained by her godmother and her non-custodial biological father. K.W. was living in Massachusetts with the mother's permission while attending school there, and was to return to Switzerland, her habitual residence, at the end of the school year. As that date approached, K.W. attempted suicide, apparently to avoid returning to her mother's custody, and was hospitalized on an emergency basis. After her daughter was released into the godmother's care, the mother filed a return petition in federal district court so that her treatment could be continued in Zurich.

The district court dismissed the mother's petition on the ground that the Swiss Guardianship Authority had "revoked Felder's parental custody" and had deferred to the U.S. courts to decide the matter. The First Circuit, interpreting the Swiss orders differently, reversed and remanded for further proceedings. Noting in its opinion filed September 28, 2012, that "K.W. will turn fifteen in December, 2012," the appellate court observed:

> The explanatory report on the Convention states that "it would be very difficult to accept that a child of, for example, fifteen years of age, should be returned against its will." . . . However, "[n]o part of the Hague Convention requires a court to allow the child to testify or to credit the child's views, so the decision rests within the sound decision of the trial court." . . .
>
> In carrying out these proceedings, the district court should bear in mind that Article 11 of the Hague Convention requires that '[t]he judicial or administrative authorities of Contracting States shall act expeditiously in proceedings for the return of children." At the same time, protection of the child's safety and, where appropriate, autonomy is of paramount concern, and such delay as is necessary to explore fully the ramifications of the sought return of K.W. is entirely justified under the circumstances.

Id., 696 F.3d at 101. What does that mean? Is it a direction to the district court to take evidence on whether the child is likely to make another suicide attempt if she is returned to her mother's custody in Switzerland? If so, should the district court refuse to order a return? Would a Massachusetts state court then decide whether the mother, the godmother, or the biological father should have custody? Does the Massachusetts court have jurisdiction under the UCCJEA? Can Massachusetts become a "home state" when the child's "habitual residence" in in Switzerland?

(9) Article 20 of the Hague Convention provides that "[t]he return of the child under the provisions of article 12 may be refused if this would not be permitted by the fundamental principles of the requested State relating to the protection of human rights and fundamental freedoms." While its scope is arguably broader than that of Article 13(b) since it was drafted to provide a wider "safety valve" for political refugees who resist the return of their children to the State where they were persecuted, Article 20 has not often been invoked beyond that situation and is rarely successful even there. See Weiner, *Strengthening Article 20*, 38 U.S.F. L.Rev. 701, 705–10 (2004) (attributing this relative neglect to a statement by the Reporter, commentary by the U.S. State Department, and court interpretations, all tending to suggest that the defense is extremely hard to justify). Weiner seeks to strengthen Article 20 so that it will provide a viable defense for domestic violence victims who currently lack other viable defenses. She thus summarizes her argument:

> [I]t violates fundamental principles of human rights to send a domestic violence victim's child back to a location where the mother is unsafe. This inflicts a horrific choice on the domestic violence victim: your safety or your child. She can return with her child to the child's habitual residence, but her safety and life will be at risk. Alternatively, she can choose her own safety and not return to her child's habitual residence. However, then she will be temporarily deprived of her child pending the custody contest, she will be leaving her child without her protection, and she will be increasing the risk of losing any subsequent custody contest because she will be absent from that proceeding. A court should not return a domestic violence victim's child if the mother would be faced with such an inhumane choice.

Id., at 703–04.

Are you persuaded? In a companion article, Weiner demonstrates how such an argument could be made to a United States court to defend against the child's return in such a case. See Weiner, *Using Article 20*, 38 Fam. L. Q. 583 (2004).

LOZANO V. MONTOYA ALVAREZ

572 U.S. 1 (2014).

JUSTICE THOMAS delivered the opinion of the Court.

When a parent abducts a child and flees to another country, the Hague Convention on the Civil Aspects of International Child Abduction generally requires that country to return the child immediately if the other parent requests return within one year. The question in this case is whether that 1-year period is subject to equitable tolling when the abducting parent conceals the child's location from the other parent. We hold that equitable tolling is not available.

I

To address "the problem of international child abductions during domestic disputes," *Abbott v. Abbott,* 560 U.S. 1, 8 (2010), in 1980 the Hague Conference on Private International Law adopted the Convention on the Civil Aspects of International Child Abduction (Hague Convention or Convention), T.I.A.S. No. 11670, S. Treaty Doc. No. 99–11 (Treaty Doc.). The Convention states two primary objectives: "to secure the prompt return of children wrongfully removed to or retained in any Contracting State," and "to ensure that rights of custody and of access under the law of one Contracting State are effectively respected in the other Contracting States." Art. 1, *id.,* at 7.

To those ends, the Convention's "central operating feature" is the return of the child. *Abbott,* 560 U.S., at 9. That remedy, in effect, lays venue for the ultimate custody determination in the child's country of habitual residence rather than the country to which the child is abducted. See *id.,* at 20 ("The Convention is based on the principle that the best interests of the child are well served when decisions regarding custody rights are made in the country of habitual residence").

The return remedy is not absolute. Article 13 excuses return where, for example, the left-behind parent was not "actually exercising" custody rights when the abducting parent removed the child, or where there is a "grave risk" that return would "place the child in an intolerable situation." Hague Convention, Arts. 13(a)–(b), Treaty Doc., at 10. A state may also refuse to return the child if doing so would contravene "fundamental principles . . . relating to the protection of human rights and fundamental freedoms." Art. 20, *id.*, at 11.

This case concerns another exception to the return remedy. Article 12 of the Convention states the general rule that when a court receives a petition for return within one year after the child's wrongful removal, the court "shall order the return of the child forthwith." *Id.,* at 9. Article 12 further provides that the court,

> "where the proceedings have been commenced after the expiration of the period of one year [from the date of the wrongful removal], shall also order the return of the child, unless it is demonstrated that the child is now settled in its new environment." *Ibid.*

Thus, at least in some cases, failure to file a petition for return within one year renders the return remedy unavailable.

The United States ratified the Hague Convention in 1988, and Congress implemented the Convention that same year through the International Child Abduction Remedies Act (ICARA). 102 Stat. 437, 42 U.S.C. §§ 11601–11610. That statute instructs courts to "decide the case in accordance with the Convention." § 11603(d). Echoing the Convention, ICARA further provides that "[c]hildren who are wrongfully removed . . . are to be promptly returned unless one of the narrow exceptions set forth in the Convention applies." § 11601(a)(4). Finally, ICARA requires the abducting parent to establish by a preponderance of the evidence that Article 12's exception to return applies. § 11603(e)(2)(B).

II

Diana Lucia Montoya Alvarez and Manuel Jose Lozano are the parents of the girl at the center of this dispute. Montoya Alvarez and Lozano met and began dating in London in early 2004. Montoya Alvarez gave birth to a daughter in October 2005.

Montoya Alvarez and Lozano describe their relationship in starkly different terms. Lozano stated that they were " 'very happy together,' " albeit with "normal couple problems." * * * Montoya Alvarez described a pattern of physical and emotional abuse that included multiple incidents of rape and battery. The District Court found insufficient evidence to make specific findings about domestic violence but determined that Lozano's claim that he never mistreated Montoya Alvarez was "not credible." . . .

In November 2008, when the child was just over three years old, Montoya Alvarez went to New York to visit her sister Maria. During that time, the child remained in London with Lozano and his visiting mother. When Montoya Alvarez returned on November 18, she became acutely concerned about the child's fearful behavior around Lozano. The next day, Montoya Alvarez left with the child and never returned. . .

On November 10, 2010, more than 16 months after Montoya Alvarez and the child left the United Kingdom, Lozano filed a Petition for Return of Child pursuant to the Hague Convention and ICARA, 42 U.S.C. § 11603, in the United States District Court for the Southern District of New York.

After a 2-day evidentiary hearing, the District Court denied Lozano's petition. * * * The District Court concluded that Lozano had stated a prima facie case of wrongful removal under the Hague Convention. * * * Prior to her removal, the child was a habitual resident of the United Kingdom, see Hague Convention, Art. 4, and Lozano had custody rights that he was actually exercising at the time of removal, see Arts. 3(a)–(b).

Because the petition was filed more than one year after the child's wrongful removal, however, the District Court denied the petition on the basis that the child was now settled in New York. * * * "Viewing the totality of the circumstances," the court found sufficient indicia of "stability in her family, educational, social, and most importantly, home life," * * * to conclude that the child was settled in her current environment and that repatriation would be "extremely disruptive." * * * Lozano argued that the child should be returned forthwith because the 1-year period in Article 12 should be equitably tolled during the period that Montoya Alvarez concealed the child. The court rejected that argument, holding that the 1-year period could not be extended by equitable tolling. * * *

On appeal, the Second Circuit affirmed. * * *. The Court of Appeals agreed that the 1-year period in Article 12 is not subject to equitable tolling. . .

IV

We conclude that the parties to the Hague Convention did not intend equitable tolling to apply to the 1-year period in Article 12. Unlike federal statutes of limitations, the Convention was not adopted against a shared background of equitable tolling. Even if the Convention were subject to a presumption that statutes of limitations may be tolled, the 1-year period in Article 12 is not a statute of limitations. And absent a presumption in favor of equitable tolling, nothing in the Convention warrants tolling the 1-year period.

A

First, there is no general presumption that equitable tolling applies to treaties. Congress is presumed to incorporate equitable tolling into federal statutes of limitations because equitable tolling is part of the established backdrop of American law. * * * It does not follow, however, that we can export such background principles of United States law to contexts outside their jurisprudential home.

It is particularly inappropriate to deploy this background principle of American law automatically when interpreting a treaty. "A treaty is in its nature a contract between . . . nations, not a legislative act." *Foster v. Neilson,* 2 Pet. 253, 314 (1829) (Marshall, C.J., for the Court); * * *. Even if a background principle is relevant to the interpretation of federal statutes, it has no proper role in the interpretation of treaties unless that principle is shared by the parties to "an agreement among sovereign powers." * * *

Lozano has not identified a background principle of equitable tolling that is shared by the signatories to the Hague Convention. To the contrary, Lozano concedes that in the context of the Convention, "foreign courts have failed to adopt equitable tolling . . . because they lac[k] the presumption that we [have]." Tr. of Oral Arg. 19–20. While no signatory state's court of last resort has resolved the question, intermediate courts of appeals in several states have rejected equitable tolling. See *Cannon v. Cannon,* [2004] EWCA (Civ) 1330, [2005] 1 W.L.R. 32, ¶ 51 (Eng.) (rejecting the "tolling rule" as "too crude an approach" for the Convention); [the Court also cited cases from Canada and Hong Kong]. The American presumption that federal statutes of limitations can be equitably tolled therefore does not apply to this multilateral treaty. * * *

It does not matter to this conclusion that Congress enacted a statute to implement the Hague Convention. See ICARA, 42 U.S.C. §§ 11601–11610. ICARA does not address the availability of equitable tolling. Nor does it purport to alter the Convention. . . Congress' mere enactment of implementing legislation did not somehow import background principles of American law into the treaty interpretation process, thereby altering our understanding of the treaty itself.

B

Even if the presumption in favor of equitable tolling had force outside of domestic law, we have only applied that presumption to statutes of limitations. * * * The 1-year period in Article 12 is not a statute of limitations.

As a general matter, "[s]tatutes of limitations establish the period of time within which a claimant must bring an action." * * * They characteristically embody a "policy of repose, designed to protect defendants." * * * And they foster the "elimination of stale claims, and certainty about a plaintiff's opportunity for recovery and a defendant's potential liabilities." * * *

[E]xpiration of the 1-year period in Article 12 does not eliminate the remedy the Convention affords the left-behind parent—namely, the return of the child. Before one year has elapsed, Article 12 provides that the court "shall order the return of the child forthwith." Treaty Doc., at 9. But even after that period has expired, the court "shall also order the return of the child, unless it is demonstrated that the child is now settled." *Ibid.* The continued availability of the return remedy after one year preserves the possibility of relief for the left-behind parent and prevents repose for the abducting parent. Rather than establishing any certainty about the respective rights of the parties, the expiration of the 1-year period opens the door to consideration of a third party's interests, *i.e.,* the child's interest in settlement. Because that is not the sort of interest addressed by a statute of limitations, we decline to treat the 1-year period as a statute of limitations.

C

Without a presumption of equitable tolling, the Convention does not support extending the 1-year period during concealment. Article 12 explicitly provides that the 1-year period commences on "the date of the wrongful removal or retention," and makes no provision for an extension of that period. *Id.,* at 9. Further, the practical effect of the tolling that Lozano requests would be to delay the commencement of the 1-year period until the left-behind parent discovers the child's location. Commencing the 1-year period upon discovery is the obvious alternative to the commencement date the drafters actually adopted because the subject of the Hague Convention, child abduction, is naturally associated with the sort of concealment that might justify equitable tolling under other circumstances. * * * Given that the drafters did not adopt that alternative, the natural implication is that they did not intend the 1-year period to commence on that later date. * * * We cannot revisit that choice.

Lozano contends that equitable tolling is nevertheless consistent with the purpose of the Hague Convention because it is necessary to deter child abductions. In his view, "absent equitable tolling, concealment 'probably will' result in non-return," which will in turn encourage abduction. * * *

We agree, of course, that the Convention reflects a design to discourage child abduction. But the Convention does not pursue that goal at any cost. The child's interest in choosing to remain, Art. 13, or in avoiding physical or psychological harm, Art. 13(b), may overcome the return remedy. The same is true of the child's interest in settlement. * * * We are unwilling to apply equitable tolling principles that would, in practice, rewrite the treaty. * * *

Nor is it true that an abducting parent who conceals a child's whereabouts will necessarily profit by running out the clock on the 1-year period. American courts have found as a factual matter that steps taken to promote concealment can also prevent the stable attachments that make a child "settled." * * * Other signatories to the Hague Convention have likewise recognized that concealment may be taken into account in the factual determination whether the child is settled. See, *e.g., Cannon,* [2005] 1 W.L.R., ¶¶ 52–61. * * * Equitable tolling is therefore neither required by the Convention nor the only available means to advance its objectives.

D

Finally, Lozano contends that the Hague Convention leaves room for United States courts to apply their own "common law doctrine of equitable tolling" to the 1-year period in Article 12 without regard to whether the drafters of the Convention intended equitable tolling to apply. Brief for Petitioner 25. Specifically, Lozano contends that the Convention recognizes additional sources of law that permit signatory states to return abducted children even when return is not available or required pursuant to the Convention. Article 34 of the Convention provides that "for the purpos[e] of obtaining the return of a child," the Convention "shall not restrict the application of an international instrument in force between the State of origin and the State addressed" or the application of "other law of the State addressed." Treaty Doc., at 13; see also Art. 18, *id.,* at 11 ("The provisions of this Chapter do not limit the power of a judicial or administrative authority to order the return of the child at any time"). In Lozano's view, equitable tolling principles constitute "other law" that should apply here.

That contention mistakes the nature of equitable tolling as this Court has applied it. We do not apply equitable tolling as a matter of some independent authority to reconsider the fairness of legislative judgments balancing the needs for relief and repose. * * * To the contrary, we may apply equitable tolling to the Hague Convention only if we determine that the treaty drafters so intended. * * * For the foregoing reasons, we conclude that they did not. . . .

JUSTICE ALITO, with whom JUSTICE BREYER and JUSTICE SOTOMAYOR join, concurring.

I concur fully in the opinion of the Court. I write separately to explain why courts have equitable discretion under the Hague Convention to order a child's return even after the child has become settled, and how that discretion prevents abuses that petitioner claims will follow from holding that Article 12's 1-year period may not be equitably tolled.

The Convention is designed to protect the interests of children and their parents. Much of the Convention can be understood as an attempt to balance the various interests of children and non-abducting parents when a parent abducts a child from the child's country of habitual residence.

When a child has been absent from the country of habitual residence for less than a year, the Convention conclusively presumes that the child's nascent attachment to the new country is outweighed by the non-abducting parent's interest in prompt return and the child's own interest in returning to the country from which he or she was removed just a few months previously. This is why Article 12 requires return "forthwith" if the petition for return is brought within a year of abduction, unless one of the narrow exceptions set forth in Article 13 or 20 applies. * * * But, as the Convention recognizes, at some point the child will become accustomed to the new environment, making Article 12's conclusive presumption inappropriate. Thus, if the petition for return is brought after a year has elapsed, the court must determine whether the child has become "settled" in the new country; and if this has occurred, the court need not order return. * * * As the majority recognizes, this provision of the Convention "opens the door to consideration of . . . the child's interest in settlement."

But opening the door to consideration of the child's attachment to the new country does not mean closing the door to evaluating all other interests of the child and the non-abducting parent. The fact that, after one year, a child's need for stability requires a court to take into account the child's attachment to the new country does not mean that such attachment becomes the *only* factor worth considering when evaluating a petition for return.

Nothing in Article 12 prohibits courts from taking other factors into account. To the contrary, the Convention explicitly permits them to do so. Article 18 provides that "[t]he provisions of this Chapter [including Article 12] do not limit the power of a judicial or administrative authority to order the return of the child at any time." Hague Convention, Treaty Doc., at 11. A court thus has power to order the child's return in the exercise of its sound discretion even where Article 12's obligation to order such return no longer applies. . .

Equitable discretion is . . . a far better tool than equitable tolling with which to address the dangers of concealment. Equitable tolling would require return *every* time the abducting parent conceals the child and thereby prevents the non-abducting parent from filing a return petition within a year, regardless of how settled in the new country the child has become. Thus, on petitioner's view, a court would be bound to return a 14-year-old child who was brought to the United States shortly after birth and had been concealed here ever since. By contrast, when a court exercises its equitable discretion, it may consider other factors in addition to concealment. While concealment is a significant factor and should weigh heavily in a court's analysis, in appropriate cases it can be overcome by circumstances such as the extended length of the child's residence in this country, any strong ties the child has formed here, and the child's attenuated connections to his or her former country.

In short, I believe the power of a court, in the exercise of its sound discretion, to return even a settled child prevents the inapplicability of equitable tolling to Article 12's 1-year limit from encouraging parents to flee to the United States and conceal their children here. In light of this understanding, I have no difficulty joining the opinion of the Court.

Equitable Tolling and the Hague Convention

(1) Does *Lozano* protect the interests of the child at the expense of the left-behind parent? Is it consistent with *Abbott v. Abbott* in that respect? What sources may a U.S. court properly consult to identify the purposes of an international treaty? Was the Court right that background principles of American law such as equitable tolling should not be read into treaties to which the U.S. is a signatory, or federal statutes implementing them, even if an equivalent domestic statute would be read that way?

(2) As the Court mentions, a British appellate court in *Cannon* v. *Cannon*, [2004] EWCA Civ.1330 [51], [2005] 1 WLR 32 (Eng.), had rejected the U.S. "equitable tolling" approach as "too crude" before *Lozano* was decided. *Cannon* involved a U.S. father and an Irish mother married in California in 1994. Their daughter, S, was born there the same year. In December 1998, the mother took S on an agreed holiday to Dublin, and refused to return to California. The father obtained a return order in Dublin in July 1999. The mother obeyed the order, and returned with S. to California. Immediately upon her return, however, she once again wrongfully removed the child, this time to England. Once there, the mother went into hiding with S, deliberately concealing their whereabouts from the father. Four years later, he successfully traced them to Liverpool and immediately commenced proceedings to secure S.'s return. Commenting on these facts, the English trial court judge observed:

> The concealment involved assuming new identities for both M. and S, which included, in the case of the child, elaborate and planned arrangements for her to take over the birth date as well as the name of a child who had died. In terms, therefore, of the degree of parental determination displayed to follow through the abduction and to sever the child's relationship with her father, this case is at the extreme end of the range.

Id., at [5]. He read Articles 12(2) and 18 (which provides that "the provisions of this Chapter do not limit the power of a judicial or administrative authority to order the return of the child at any time") to deprive him of any residual or discretionary authority to order a return. This judgment was reversed on appeal, with Thorpe, LJ, characterizing it as "a bold course" which "rejected all previous authority in the courts of the United Kingdom." *Id.*, at [1]. Judge Thorpe reasoned that the "settlement" issue had two components: one physical, the other emotional. Noting that "the fugitive from justice is always alert for any sign that the pursuers are closing in and equally in a state of mental and physical readiness to move on before the approaching arrest" *id.*, at [56], he showed how this mental state might affect the child: "A very young child must take its emotional and psychological state in large measure from that of the sole carer. An older child will be consciously or unconsciously enmeshed in the sole carer's web of deceit and subterfuge." *Id.*, at [57]. These considerations led him to agree with Counsel that "it will be very difficult indeed for a person who has hidden a child away to demonstrate that it is settled in its new environment and thus overcome the real obligation to order a return." *Id.*, at [52].

(3) Do you agree with Justice Alito that "[e]quitable discretion is . . . a far better tool than equitable tolling with which to address the dangers of concealment"? In *Lozano*, in addition to asking for equitable tolling, the father argued that the child's illegal immigration status made the "settled" defense unavailable as a matter of law. The Second Circuit, in a part of its decision the Supreme Court did not review, rejected that argument and adopted instead a multi-factor test in which the child's immigration status was one among seven factors to be considered by the trial court in making the "settled" determination:

> (1) the age of the child; (2) the stability of the child's residence in the new environment; (3) whether the child attends school or day care consistently; (4) whether the child attends church [or participates in other community or extracurricular school activities]; (5) the respondent's employment and financial stability; (6) whether the child has friends and relatives in the new area; and (7) the immigration status of the child and the respondent.

697 F.3d at 57. Are these the right factors? Does their adjudication turn the Hague Convention into a custody decision on the merits? The Second Circuit acknowledged the problem, but concluded that "[a]lthough one of the primary objectives of the Convention is to ensure the 'prompt return' of abducted children without reaching the merits of underlying custody disputes, . . . the settled exception recognizes that there may come a point at which 'repatriation might not be in [the child's] best interest.' " *Id.* at 56. For this proposition, the Second Circuit cited its own prior holding in

Blondin IV, discussed supra p. 782, note (4). On this point, is *Lozano* subject to the criticisms made earlier of *Blondin* that such cases transform what was intended to be a summary procedure into a trial on the merits?

(4) The United States has not designated a "specialized" court to have exclusive jurisdiction over Hague Convention cases. Should it do so? If so, should it be a federal court established under Article III, § 1 of the Constitution, like (for example) the federal Court of Claims and the Court of International Trade? Or should each state establish a specialized court of its own? Although the state courts have primary jurisdiction in cases under the PKPA (see *Thompson v. Thompson*, 484 U.S. 174 (1988), declining federal jurisdiction under the PKPA), the federal and state courts have concurrent jurisdiction both under the UCCJEA and ICARA to hear Hague Convention cases. If a specialized court is to be established, should the state courts be preferred because of their greater expertise in family law and child custody matters? Or should the federal courts get the nod because the Hague Convention is a treaty, and governed by federal law? See Weiner, 2008 Utah L.Rev. at 238 (supra p. 781, note (3)), concluding that Congress has the "constitutional authority to amend ICARA and divest state courts of jurisdiction" and to "go even further and consolidate jurisdiction in a single federal court." Would you support such a congressional enactment? If so, would you want to permit that court to decline to exercise its jurisdiction in an appropriate case? What might be an example of such a case?

(5) The Hague Abduction Convention applies only between states which are parties to its terms ("contracting" states). If a child is removed from its habitual residence and taken to a non-contracting state, the Convention affords no relief to the left-behind parent. Congress enacted the International Parental Kidnapping Crime Act ("IPKCA") in 1993 to remedy this problem. IPKCA prohibits a person from removing a child from the United States or retaining a child (who has been in the United States) outside the United States, "with intent to obstruct the lawful exercise of parental rights." The Act imposes penalties of a fine or imprisonment for not more than three years, or both. 18 U.S.C. § 1204 (1993). Pastor Kenneth L. Miller, who assisted Lisa Miller (one of the parties in the *Miller-Jenkins* litigation, supra pp. 738–746) in fleeing to Nicaragua with her daughter, Isabella, was convicted under this statute.

Section 1204(c) provides the following defenses:

(c) It shall be an affirmative defense under this section that—

(1) the defendant acted within the provisions of a valid court order granting the defendant legal custody or visitation rights and that order was obtained pursuant to the Uniform Child Custody Jurisdiction Act or the Uniform Child Custody

Jurisdiction and Enforcement Act and was in effect at the time of the offense;

(2) the defendant was fleeing an incidence or pattern of domestic violence;

(3) the defendant had physical custody of the child pursuant to a court order granting legal custody or visitation rights and failed to return the child as a result of circumstances beyond the defendant's control, and the defendant notified or made reasonable attempts to notify the other parent or lawful custodian of the child of such circumstances within 24 hours after the visitation period had expired and returned the child as soon as possible.

How do the Hague Abduction Convention and IPKCA fit together? Section 1204(d) of IPKCA provides that it "does not detract" from the Convention. In *United States v. Amer*, 110 F.3d 873, 882 (2d Cir. 1997), the Second Circuit referred to this subsection and also pointed to a "Sense of Congress" resolution accompanying IPKCA which indicates that the Hague Convention, in cases where it is applicable, should be "the option of first choice for a parent who seeks the return of a child who has been removed from the parent." IPKCA takes over if the Convention does not apply, and "closes the gap left open by the unfortunate fact that few countries have signed on to the Convention." Consistent with this interpretation, the court held that the defenses contained within the Convention do not apply to IPKCA cases. Thus an Egyptian father who had removed the children from the family home in Queens, New York, without their mother's knowledge or consent and flown with them to Egypt was unable to invoke the 13(b) defense available under the Convention. Was this the right result? Note that IPKCA contains an explicit defense available in cases of domestic violence. Should a similar defense be incorporated into ICARA?

SECTION 3. DECEDENTS' ESTATES

(1) It is textbook law that the death of an individual with assets in more than one jurisdiction gives rise to more than one administration: "Administration in each state, whether principal or ancillary, is separate and complete in itself. Legally each local administration is wholly independent of the others. . ." R. Leflar, Conflict of Laws 374 (1959). It was said at common law, for example, that an executor or administrator could neither sue nor be sued outside the state of his appointment.

This philosophy reached what may have been its zenith (or nadir) in *Ingersoll v. Coram*, 211 U.S. 335 (1908). A New York lawyer's Montana administrator had lost on the merits a Montana suit to collect a fee for services rendered by the decedent. His Massachusetts administratrix was thereafter permitted to sue for the same fee in Massachusetts despite the plea of res judicata, on the ground that there was no privity between administrators appointed in different states.

(2) The common-law rule precluding suits against foreign executors or administrators often had the effect, for example, in nonresident-motorist cases, of denying the plaintiff a forum that modern jurisdictional principles make clearly appropriate when the defendant is alive. One argument for this result was that the administrator's authority extended only to assets in the appointing state, over which no other state could exercise in rem jurisdiction. But it seemed odd to call a personal-injury action "in rem"; and after *Shaffer v. Heitner,* supra p. 513, the in rem label should no longer be determinative. In modern terms the foreign administrator is likely to have no contacts of his own with the forum state; but so long as he is sued only for acts of the decedent, and no attempt is made to hold him personally liable, he has nothing to lose by being sued there. The beneficiaries of the estate do have something to lose; does *World-Wide Volkswagen,* supra p. 449, imply that the decedent's contacts cannot be attributed to them or to the representative?

The most serious policy argument for the rule forbidding suits against foreign representatives was that it promoted the interest of the appointing state in administering estates efficiently and equitably in a single proceeding. See McDowell, Foreign Personal Representatives 86, 121 (1957). The principal fear, however, seems to have been that suits outside the appointing court might interfere with pro-rata distribution or subject the representative to conflicting orders; and these objections could be met by requiring the plaintiff to present his judgment, conclusive on the merits, as a claim in the estate proceeding. In a comparable situation involving a liquidator appointed for an insolvent Illinois association the Supreme Court held a Missouri judgment entitled to full faith and credit: "[P]roof and allowance of claims are matters distinct from distribution of assets. . . The establishment of the existence and amount of a claim against the debtor in no way disturbs the possession of the liquidator court, in no way affects title to the property, and does not necessarily involve a determination of what priority the claim should have." *Morris v. Jones,* 329 U.S. 545 (1947).

(3) Legislatures responded to the inconvenience and unfairness of the common-law rule in two principal ways: by providing generally that foreign representatives had capacity to be sued like anyone else, and by authorizing long-arm jurisdiction over them. It took judges a little while to get used to the idea; the statutes were sometimes construed away or held unconstitutional. E.g., *New Mexico ex rel. Scott v. Zinn,* 74 N.M. 224, 392 P.2d 417 (1964); *Knoop v. Anderson,* 71 F.Supp. 832 (N.D. Iowa 1947). By 1966, however, it was possible to report that "two-thirds of the state legislatures and the Congress to boot [legislating for the District of Columbia], have no sympathy" for the common-law rule, D. Currie, *The*

Multiple Personality of the Dead: Executors, Administrators, and the Conflict of Laws, 33 U.Chi.L.Rev. 429, 439–44 (1966); *Hayden v. Wheeler,* 33 Ill.2d 110, 210 N.E.2d 495 (1965), construing a long-arm reference to the "personal representative" to include one appointed elsewhere and noting the court's inability to see any reason why the death of a nonresident driver should destroy jurisdiction, seems to represent the modern view.

(4) The converse common-law rule preventing suits by the foreign administrator was riddled with exceptions undermining its asserted policy of keeping assets within the forum state for the benefit of local creditors. For example, *Hare v. O'Brien,* 233 Pa. 330, 82 A. 475 (1912), allowed a foreign representative to sue on a judgment, on the incredible ground that the claim belonged to him personally. Moreover, the Supreme Court held in *Blake v. McClung,* 172 U.S. 239 (1898), that in any event the Privileges and Immunities Clause of Article IV forbade a state to prefer its own citizens in distributing an insolvent estate. A number of states have done away with the common-law rule, see McDowell, supra note (2), at 67–75; but the Uniform Probate Code, 8 U.L.A. 1 (2010), adopted in eighteen states, still does not permit a foreign representative to sue if there is a local one (§§ 4–204, 4–205). It does make a judgment against one representative binding on another (§ 4–401).

(5) Why isn't the refusal to permit a foreign representative to sue a denial of full faith and credit to the decree that appointed him? Why doesn't it offend the national policy favoring transitory actions the Supreme Court found in the Full Faith and Credit Clause in *Hughes v. Fetter,* supra p. 414?

Kansas at one time attempted to give its courts "exclusive jurisdiction to determine the devolution of property by will or by descent of all persons who are residents of Kansas at the time of death as to real property located in Kansas and tangible or intangible property wherever located." G.S.1955 Supp. 59–303. Except for foreign land, this law would have created a universal executor or administrator with power to sue or be sued anywhere, subject to ordinary limitations, eliminating most of the difficulties of the vestiges of the old principle of separate administrations. But the state supreme court held the statute unconstitutional: property located elsewhere was within exclusive control of the situs. *In re De Lano's Estate,* 181 Kan. 729, 315 P.2d 611 (1957). On the other hand, as early as 1912 the United States Supreme Court had held that a Minnesota decree appointing a statutory successor to an insolvent Minnesota corporation was entitled to full faith and credit in Wisconsin, and that the successor was therefore entitled to sue in that state to enforce the obligations of Wisconsin shareholders. *Converse v. Hamilton,* 224 U.S. 243 (1912). Why shouldn't this pattern be followed in the case of a decedent's estate?

(6) The federal courts have adopted limitations on their jurisdiction to protect them against hearing certain family law and decedent's estates matters. Thus, the Supreme Court, in dictum, "disclaimed altogether any jurisdiction in the courts of the United States upon the subject of divorce," even when the parties are of diverse citizenship. See *Barber v. Barber*, 62 U.S. (21 How.) 582, 584 (1859). And federal courts will not probate a will or issue letters of administration, for to do so would interfere with the power of the states over "matters of strict probate." See *Sutton v. English*, 246 U.S. 199, 205 (1918). Line-drawing in these cases, however, is no less difficult than in other areas we have encountered. Recognizing this problem, the Supreme Court "reined in" the domestic relations exception in *Ankenbrandt v. Richards*, 504 U.S. 689 (1992), holding that it did not oust a federal court of diversity jurisdiction in tort cases, even when the claim was brought by an ex-wife against her ex-husband for sexual and physical abuse of their daughters. Grounding the derivation of the "domestic relations exception" in Congress' original provision for diversity jurisdiction, the Judiciary Act of 1789, the Court stressed that only "divorce, alimony, and child custody decrees" remain outside federal jurisdictional bounds. *Id.*, at 703, 704.

In *Marshall v. Marshall*, 547 U.S. 293 (2006), the Court similarly revisited, clarified, and narrowed the "probate exception." It held that the exception did not prevent a federal bankruptcy court from adjudicating the claims of Vickie Lynn Marshall (a.k.a. Anna Nicole Smith), widow of Texas oilman J. Howard Marshall II, that her husband's son, E. Pierce Marshall, had defrauded her of an inter vivos gift worth approximately $500 million that she expected to receive from the decedent. She and J. Howard Marshall met in 1991, when she was 24 years old and working as a topless dancer. They married and, shortly thereafter, he died of a heart attack at the age of 90, leaving an estate estimated to be worth approximately $1.6 billion. The bankruptcy court, whose order was affirmed by the federal district court, held for the widow. The Texas probate court, where the will was being probated, had held for the son following a five-month jury trial. The Ninth Circuit held that all federal courts, including bankruptcy courts, are bound by the probate exemption. Accordingly, it vacated the district court's final judgment and remanded with instructions to dismiss the widow's claims for lack of jurisdiction.

The Supreme Court reversed the Ninth Circuit in a unanimous opinion by Justice Ginsburg, who pointed out that Vickie's counterclaim in the Bankruptcy Court "alleges a widely recognized tort" of the kind often addressed by trial courts in both state and federal courts. The Court rephrased the probate exception, stating that it

> reserves to state probate courts the probate or annulment of a will and the administration of a decedent's estate; it also precludes federal courts from endeavoring to dispose of property that is in the custody of a state probate court. But it does not bar federal

courts from adjudicating matters outside those confines and otherwise within federal jurisdiction.

The Court also rejected the Ninth Circuit's determination that the Bankruptcy Court was bound by the Texas Probate Court's ruling that it had exclusive jurisdiction over all of Vickie's claims against E. Pierce Marshall. Citing *Tennessee Coal, Iron & R.R. Co. v. George*, supra p. 422, Justice Ginsburg pointed out that "[w]e have long recognized that 'a State cannot create a transitory cause of action and at the same time destroy the right to sue on that transitory cause of action in any court having jurisdiction.' " *Id.*, 547 U.S. at 311–12.

The case was remanded for further proceedings, with the Court cautioning that several issues remained open, including the matter of whether Vickie's counterclaim was a "core" bankruptcy proceeding, and the validity of E. Pierce's arguments concerning claim and issue preclusion between the Texas probate court and the federal courts. On remand, these issues assumed controlling significance. The Ninth Circuit held that the bankruptcy court lacked jurisdiction to enter a final judgment on Vickie's counterclaim because it was "for personal injury, was not related to the bankruptcy estate because she had obtained her discharge, and it was not 'core'." *In re Marshall*, 600 F.3d 1037, 1069 (2010), *aff'd, Stern v. Marshall*, 564 U.S. 462 (2011). (By the time the case reached the Supreme Court a second time, both of the original parties had died, and the matter was being litigated by their respective estates.)

In a 5–4 decision by Chief Justice Roberts, the Court held that (1) Vickie's counterclaim was a "core" bankruptcy proceeding under the 1984 Bankruptcy Act, §§ 157(b)(1)–(2); but (2) § 157(b)(2)(C), which made all "counterclaims by the estate against persons filing claims against the estate" core bankruptcy proceedings, violated Article III of the Constitution. It did so by permitting non-core proceedings to be decided by non-Article III bankruptcy court judges, who do not have life tenure, and whose salaries are not protected against being diminished. The proper course for the bankruptcy court to follow would have been to make proposed findings of fact and conclusions of law and transmit those to the federal district court which alone was empowered to enter final judgment on the counterclaim. The Supreme Court further held that the findings of the Texas probate court that J. Howard Marshall had not intended to make a gift to his widow from assets that passed through either his will or his living trust were entitled to preclusive effect in the district court. Justice Breyer dissented, joined by Justices Ginsburg, Sotomayor, and Kagan, arguing that the congressional delegation of adjudicatory authority over compulsory counterclaims to a bankruptcy court does not violate "any constitutional separation of powers principle related to Article III."

How far does *Stern* go? Does it prevent bankruptcy courts from entertaining jury trials on issues of state law unrelated to the "core" bankruptcy claim? The possibilities are explored in *Note, Stern v. Marshall: How Anna Nicole Smith Almost Stripped Bankruptcy Courts of Jury Trials,* 98 Iowa. L. Rev. 337 (2012).

(7) Other conflict-of-laws problems that may arise in the administration of decedents' estates have been considered at various points in this book. The traditional choice-of-law rules for determining succession to movable and immovable property by intestate succession or by will were studied in Chapter 1 supra, pp. 28–33. Statutory choice-of-law rules governing the execution of wills were discussed in Chapter 2 at pp. 97–100, supra. The problem of the foreign land decree, considered in Chapter 5 at pp. 589–609, supra, often arises in estate administration. See generally Ester & Scoles, *Estate Planning and Conflict of Law,* 24 Ohio St.L.J. 270 (1963); Scoles, *Conflict of Laws in Estate Planning,* 9 U.Fla.L.Rev. 398 (1956).

CHAPTER 7

CONFLICTS BETWEEN FEDERAL AND STATE LAW

■ ■ ■

SECTION 1. FEDERAL QUESTION JURISDICTION

OSBORN V. BANK OF THE UNITED STATES

22 U.S. (9 Wheat.) 738 (1824).

[In *McCulloch v. Maryland*, 17 U.S. (4 Wheat.) 316 (1819), the Supreme Court affirmed the power of Congress to incorporate a national bank and denied the power of the states to tax it. Undaunted, Ohio made clear its intention to enforce a tax of $50,000 on each branch of the Bank of the United States. The Bank went to federal court and obtained a temporary injunction to restrain the state auditor from collecting the tax. The auditor violated the injunction by forcibly invading the bank and taking $120,475. Federal commissioners responded by imprisoning the state treasurer and taking his keys. The federal court that issued the injunction ordered the state officials to return all the money taken from the Bank. They appealed, arguing that the court lacked subject-matter jurisdiction.]

MR. CHIEF JUSTICE MARSHALL delivered the opinion of the Court. . .

The appellants contest the jurisdiction of the court on two grounds: 1st. That the act of Congress has not given it. 2d. That, under the constitution, Congress cannot give it.

1. The first part of the objection depends entirely on the language of the act. The words are, that the bank shall be "made able and capable in law,"—"to sue and be sued, plead and be impleaded, answer and be answered, defend and be defended, in all state courts having competent jurisdiction, and in any circuit court of the United States."

These words seem to the court to admit of but one interpretation; they cannot be made plainer by explanation. They give, expressly, the right "to sue and be sued," "in every circuit court of the United States," and it would be difficult to substitute other terms which would be more direct and appropriate for the purpose. . .

2. We will now consider the constitutionality of the clause in the act of incorporation, which authorizes the bank to sue in the federal courts. In support of this clause, it is said, that the legislative, executive and judicial powers of every well-constructed government, are co-extensive with each other; that is, they are potentially co-extensive. The executive department may constitutionally execute every law which the legislature may constitutionally make, and the judicial department may receive from the legislature the power of construing every such law. All governments which are not extremely defective in their organization, must possess, within themselves, the means of expounding, as well as enforcing, their own laws. If we examine the constitution of the United States, we find that its framers kept this great political principle in view. The . . . 3d article declares, "that the judicial power shall extend to all cases in law and equity, arising under this constitution, the laws of the United States, and treaties made, or which shall be made, under their authority." This clause enables the judicial department to receive jurisdiction to the full extent of the constitution, laws and treaties of the United States, when any question respecting them shall assume such a form that the judicial power is capable of acting on it. . .

The suit of the Bank of the United States v. Osborn and others, is a case, and the question is, whether it arises under a law of the United States? The appellants contend, that it does not, because several questions may arise in it, which depend on the general principles of the law, not on any act of Congress. If this were sufficient to withdraw a case from the jurisdiction of the federal Courts, almost every case, although involving the construction of a law, would be withdrawn; and a clause in the constitution, relating to a subject of vital importance to the government, and expressed in the most comprehensive terms, would be construed to mean almost nothing. There is scarcely any case, every part of which depends on the constitution, laws or treaties of the United States. The questions, whether the fact alleged as the foundation of the action, be real or fictitious; whether the conduct of the plaintiff has been such as to entitle him to maintain his action; whether his right is barred; whether he has received satisfaction, or has in any manner released his claims, are questions, some or all of which may occur, in almost every case; and if their existence be sufficient to arrest the jurisdiction of the court, words which seem intended to be as extensive as the constitution, laws and treaties of the Union—which seem designed to give the courts of the government the construction of all its acts, so far as they affect the rights of individuals—would be reduced to almost nothing.

In those cases in which original jurisdiction is given to the Supreme Court, the judicial power of the United States cannot be exercised in its appellate form. In every other case, the power is to be exercised in its original or appellate form, or both, as the wisdom of Congress may direct. . . Original jurisdiction, so far as the constitution gives a rule, is co-extensive with the judicial power. We find, in the constitution, no prohibition to its exercise, in every case in which the judicial power can be exercised. It would be a very bold construction, to say, that this power could be applied in its appellate form only, to the most important class of cases to which it is applicable. The constitution establishes the Supreme Court, and defines its jurisdiction. It enumerates cases in which its jurisdiction is original and exclusive; and then defines that which is appellate, but does not insinuate, that in any such case, the power cannot be exercised in its original form, by courts of original jurisdiction. It is not insinuated, that the judicial power, in cases depending on the character of the cause, cannot be exercised, in the first instance, in the Courts of the Union, but must first be exercised in the tribunals of the State; tribunals over which the government of the Union has no adequate control, and which may be closed to any claim asserted under a law of the United States. We perceive, then, no ground on which the proposition can be maintained, that Congress is incapable of giving the Circuit Courts original jurisdiction, in any case to which the appellate jurisdiction extends.

We ask, then, if it can be sufficient to exclude this jurisdiction, that the case involves questions depending on general principles? A cause may depend on several questions of fact and law. Some of these may depend on the construction of a law of the United States; others on principles unconnected with that law. If it be a sufficient foundation for jurisdiction, that the title or right set up by the party, may be defeated by one construction of the constitution or law of the United States, and sustained by the opposite construction, provided the facts necessary to support the action be made out, then all the other questions must be decided as incidental to this, which gives that jurisdiction. Those other questions cannot arrest the proceedings. Under this construction, the judicial power of the Union extends, effectively and beneficially, to that most important class of cases, which depend on the character of the cause. On the opposite construction, the judicial power never can be extended to a whole case, as expressed by the constitution, but to those parts of cases only which present the particular question involving the construction of the constitution or the law. We say, it never can be extended to the whole case, because, if the circumstance that other points are involved in it, shall disable Congress from authorizing the Courts of the Union to take jurisdiction of the original cause, it equally disables Congress from authorizing those courts to take jurisdiction of the whole cause, on an appeal, and thus will be restricted to a single question in that cause; and words obviously intended to secure to those who claim rights under the constitution, laws or treaties of the United States, a trial in the federal Courts, will be restricted to the insecure remedy of an appeal, upon an insulated point, after it has received that shape against his will. We think, then, that when a question to which the judicial power of the Union is extended by the constitution, forms an ingredient of the original cause, it is in the power of Congress to give the

Circuit Courts jurisdiction of that cause, although other questions of act or of law may be involved in it.

The case of the Bank is, we think, a very strong case of this description. The charter of incorporation not only creates it, but gives it every faculty which it possesses. The power to acquire rights of any description, to transact business of any description, to make contracts of any description, to sue on those contracts, is given and measured by its charter, and that charter is a law of the United States. This being can acquire no right, make no contract, bring no suit, which is not authorized by a law of the United States. It is not only itself the mere creature of a law, but all its actions and all its rights are dependent on the same law. Can a being, thus constituted, have a case which does not arise literally, as well as substantially, under the law?

Take the case of a contract, which is put as the strongest against the Bank. When a Bank sues, the first question which presents itself, and which lies at the foundation of the cause, is, has this legal entity a right to sue? Has it a right to come, not into this Court particularly, but into any Court? This depends on a law of the United States. The next question is, has this being a right to make this particular contract? If this question be decided in the negative, the cause is determined against the plaintiff; and this question, too, depends entirely on a law of the United States. These are important questions, and they exist in every possible case. The right to sue, if decided once, is decided forever; but the power of Congress was exercised antecedently to the first decision on the right, and if it was constitutional then, it cannot cease to be so, because the particular question is decided. It may be revived at the will of the party, and most probably would be renewed, were the tribunal to be changed. But the question respecting the right to make a particular contract, or to acquire a particular property, or to sue on account of a particular injury, belongs to every particular case, and may be renewed in every case. The question forms an original ingredient in every cause. Whether it be, in fact, relied on or not, in the defence, it is still a part of the cause, and may be relied on. The right of the plaintiff to sue cannot depend on the defence which the defendant may choose to set up. His right to sue is anterior to that defence, and must depend on the state of things when the action is brought. The question which the case involved, then, must determine its character, whether those questions be made in the cause or not.

The appellants say, that the case arises on the contract; but the validity of the contract depends on a law of the United States, and the plaintiff is compelled, in every case, to show its validity. The case arises emphatically under the law; the act of Congress is its foundation. The contract could never have been made, but under the authority of that act. The act itself is the first ingredient in the case—is its origin—is that from which every other part arises. That other questions may also arise, as the execution of the contract, or its performance, cannot change the case, or give it any other origin than the charter of incorporation. The action still originates in, and is sustained by, that charter.

It is said, that a clear distinction exists between the party and the cause; that the party may originate under a law with which the cause has no connection; and that Congress may with the same propriety, give a naturalized citizen, who is the mere creature of law, a right to sue in the courts of the United States, as give the right to the Bank. This distinction is not denied; and if the act of Congress was a simple act of incorporation, and contained nothing more, it might be entitled to great consideration. But the act does not stop with incorporating the Bank. It proceeds to bestow upon the being it has made, all the faculties and capacities which that being possesses. Every act of the Bank grows out of this law, and is tested by it. To use the language of the constitution, every act of the bank arises out of this law. A naturalized citizen is, indeed, made a citizen under an act of Congress, but the act does not proceed to give, to regulate, or to prescribe his capacities. He becomes a member of the society, possessing all the rights of a native citizen, and standing, in the view of the constitution, on the footing of a native. The constitution does not authorize Congress to enlarge or abridge those rights. The simple power of the national legislature is, to prescribe a uniform rule of naturalization, and the exercise of this power exhausts it, so far as respect the individual. The constitution then takes him up, and, among other rights, extends to him the capacity of suing in the Courts of the United States, precisely under the same circumstances under which a native might sue. . .

Upon the best consideration we have been able to bestow on this subject, we are of opinion, that the clause in the act of incorporation, enabling the bank to sue in the courts of the United States, is consistent with the constitution, and to be obeyed in all courts.

[Turning to the merits, the Court upheld the judgment in favor of the Bank except for an award of interest.]

MR. JUSTICE JOHNSON [dissenting]. . .

I have very little doubt, that the public mind will be easily reconciled to the decision of the Court here rendered: for, whether necessary or unnecessary, originally, a state of things has now grown up, in some of the states, which renders all the protection necessary, that the general government can give to this Bank. The policy of the decision is obvious, that is, if the Bank is to be sustained; and few will bestow upon its legal correctness, the reflection that it is necessary to test it by the constitution and laws, under which it is rendered.

The Bank of the United States is now identified with the administration of the national government. It is an immense machine economically and beneficially applied to the fiscal transactions of the nation. Attempts have been made to dispense with it, and they have failed; serious and very weighty doubts have been entertained of its constitutionality, but they have been abandoned; and it is now become the functionary that collects, the depository that holds, the vehicle that transports, the guard that protects, and the agent that distributes and pays away, the millions that pass annually through the national treasury; and all this, not only without expense to the government, but after paying a large *bonus,* and sustaining actual annual losses to a large amount; furnishing the only possible means of embodying the most ample security for so immense a charge.

Had its effects, however, and the views of its framers, been confined exclusively to its fiscal uses, it is more than probable, that this suit, and the laws in which it originated, would never have had existence. But it is well known, that with the object was combined another, of a very general, and not less important character. The expiration of the charter of the former Bank, led to State creations of banks; each new bank increased the facilities of creating others; and the necessities of the general government, both to make use of the state banks for their deposits, and to borrow largely of all who would lend to them, produced that rage for multiplying banks, which, aided by the emoluments derived to the States in their creation, and the many individual incentives which they developed, soon inundated the country with new description of bills of credit, against which, it was obvious, that the provisions of the constitution opposed no adequate inhibition. A specie-paying Bank, with an overwhelming capital, and the whole aid of the government deposits, presented the only resource to which the government could resort, to restore that power over the currency of the country, which the framers of the constitution evidently intended to give to Congress alone. But this necessarily involved a restraint upon individual cupidity, and the exercise of state power; and in the nature of things, it was hardly possible, for the mighty effort necessary to put down an evil, spread so wide, and arrived to such maturity, to be made, without embodying against it an immense moneyed combination, which could not fail of making its influence to be felt, wherever its claimances could reach, or its industry and wealth be brought to operate.

I believe, that the good sense of a people, who know that they govern themselves, and feel that they have no interests distinct from those of their government, would readily concede to the Bank, thus circumstanced, some, if not all the rights here contended for. But I cannot persuade myself, that they have been conceded in the extent which this decision affirms. Whatever might be proper to be done by an amendment of the constitution, this Court is only, at present, expounding its existing provisions. In the present instance, I cannot persuade myself, that the constitution sanctions the vesting of the right of action in this bank, in cases in which the privilege is exclusively personal, or in any case, merely on the ground that a question might possibly be raised in it, involving the constitution, or constitutionality of a law of the United States.

When laws were heretofore passed for raising a revenue by a duty on stamped paper, the tax was quietly acquiesced in, notwithstanding it entrenched so closely on the questionable power of the States over the law of contracts; but had the same law which declared void contracts not written upon stamped paper, declared, that every person holding such paper should be entitled to bring his action "in any Circuit Court" of the United States, it is confidently believed, that there could have been but one opinion on the constitutionality of such a provision. The whole jurisdiction over contracts, might thus have been taken from the State Courts, and conferred upon those of the United States. Nor would the evil have rested there; by a similar exercise of power, imposing a stamp on deeds, generally, jurisdiction over the territory of the State, whoever might be parties, even between citizens of the same state—jurisdiction of suits instituted for the recovery of legacies or distributive portions of intestates' estates—jurisdiction, in fact, over almost every possible case, might be transferred to the Courts of the United States. Wills might be required to be executed on stamped paper; taxes may be, and have been, imposed upon legacies and distributions, and in all such cases, there is not only a possibility, but a probability, that a question may arise, involving the constitutionality, construction, & c., of a law of the United States. If the circumstance, that the questions which the case involves, are to determine its character, whether those questions be made in the case or not, then, every case here alluded to, may as well be transferred to the jurisdiction of the United States, as those to which this Bank is a party. But still further, as was justly insisted in argument, there is not a tract of land of the United States, acquired under laws of the United States, whatever be the number of mesne transfers that it may have undergone, over which the jurisdiction of the Courts of the United States might not be extended by Congress, upon the very principle on which the right of suit in this bank is here maintained. Nor is the case of the alien, put in argument, at all inapplicable. The one acquires its character of individual property, as the other does his political existence, under a law of the United States; and there is not a suit which may be instituted to recover the one, nor an action of ejectment to be brought by the other, in which a right acquired under a law of the United States, does not lie as essentially at the basis of the right of action, as in the suits brought by this Bank. . .

And here I must observe, that I altogether misunderstood the counsel, who argued the cause for the plaintiff in error, if any of them contended against the jurisdiction, on the ground, that the cause involved questions depending on general principles. No one can question, that the Court which has jurisdiction of the principal question, must exercise jurisdiction over every question. Neither did I understand them as denying, that if Congress could confer on the Circuit Courts appellate, they could confer original jurisdiction. The argument went to deny the right to assume jurisdiction on a mere hypothesis. It was one of description, identity, definition; they contended, that until a question involving the construction or administration of the laws of the United States did actually arise, the *casus federis* was not presented, on which the constitution authorized the government to take to itself the jurisdiction of the cause. . .

And this doctrine has my hearty concurrence in its general application. A very simple case may be stated, to illustrate its bearing on the question of jurisdiction between the two governments. By virtue of treaties with Great Britain, aliens holding lands were exempted from alien disabilities, and made capable of holding, aliening and transmitting their estates, in common with natives. But why should the claimants of such lands, to all eternity, be vested with the privilege of bringing an original suit in the courts of the United States? It is true, a question might be made, upon the effect of the treaty, on the rights claimed by or through the alien; but until that question does arise, nay, until a decision against the right takes place, what end has the United States to subserve, in claiming jurisdiction of the cause? . . .

Efforts have been made to fix the precise sense of the constitution, when it vests jurisdiction in the general government, in "cases arising under the laws of the United States." To me, the question appears susceptible of a very simple solution; that all depends upon the identity of the case supposed; according to which idea, a case may be such, in its very existence, or may become such in its progress. An action may "live, move and have its being," in a law of the United States; such is that given for the violation of a patent-right, and four or five different actions given by this act of incorporation; particularly that against the president and directors for over-issuing; in all of which cases, the plaintiff must count upon the law itself as the ground of his action. And of the other description, would have been an action of trespass, in this case, had remedy been sought for an actual levy of the tax imposed. [Many such cases] have occurred in this Court, in which the suit, in its form, was such as occur in ordinary cases, but in which the pleadings or evidence raised the question on the law or constitution of the United States. In this class of cases, the occurrence of a question makes the case, and transfers it, as provided for under the 25th section of the Judiciary Act, to the jurisdiction of the United States. . . But until the plaintiff can control the defendant in his pleadings, I see no practical mode of determining when the case does occur, otherwise than by permitting the cause to advance, until the case for which the constitution provides shall actually arise. If it never occurs, there can be nothing to complain of; and such are the provisions of the 25th section. The cause might be transferred to the Circuit Court before an adjudication takes place; but I can perceive no earlier stage at which it can possibly be predicated of such a case, that it is one within the constitution; nor any possible necessity for transferring it then, or until the Court has acted upon it to the prejudice of the claims of the United States. It is not, therefore, because Congress may not vest an *original* jurisdiction, where they can constitutionally vest in the circuit courts *appellate* jurisdiction, that I object to this general grant of the right to sue; but because the peculiar nature of this jurisdiction is such as to render it impossible to exercise it, in a strictly original form, and because the principle of a possible occurrence of a question, as a ground of jurisdiction, is transcending the bounds of the constitution, and placing it on a ground which will admit of an enormous accession, if not an unlimited assumption, of jurisdiction. . .

Federal Questions and Federal Interests

(1) Dissenting in *Textile Workers Union v. Lincoln Mills,* 353 U.S. 448 (1957), Justice Frankfurter observed that the "litigation-provoking problem" with respect to the scope of federal question jurisdiction "has been the degree to which federal law must be in the forefront of the case and not collateral, peripheral or remote." This was not the issue in *Osborn* itself, of course, for the Bank's claim was that the state's effort to tax it violated the Constitution as interpreted in *McCulloch v. Maryland.* The more difficult question—the "case of a contract," which Chief Justice Marshall describes as "the strongest against the Bank"—was presented in a companion case, *Bank of the United States v. Planters' Bank of Georgia,* 22 U.S. (9 Wheat.) 904 (1824). The Bank of the United States purchased notes issued by a state bank, which then refused to honor them. The national bank sued for payment, and the state bank argued that the federal court lacked jurisdiction. That question, said the Court, "was fully considered" and disposed of in *Osborn.*

(2) There is very little in *Osborn* about the language of Article III. Why? Why shouldn't we say, for example, that the suit in *Planters' Bank* "arises under" state law because state law forms the basis for the plaintiff's claim? Chief Justice Marshall relies in part on the argument that, except for the original jurisdiction of the Supreme Court, the appellate and original jurisdiction of the federal courts are co-extensive. But isn't the difference that appellate jurisdiction is exercised only after a federal issue has been raised and litigated? Does this argument actually support Justice Johnson's position?

(3) What, exactly, are the constitutional limits on federal question jurisdiction under *Osborn*? In his *Lincoln Mills* dissent, Justice Frankfurter says *Osborn* is generally understood to hold that

> federal jurisdiction under the "arising" clause of the Constitution, though limited to cases involving potential federal questions, has such flexibility that Congress may confer it whenever there exists in the background some federal proposition that might be challenged, despite the remoteness of the likelihood of actual presentation of such a federal question.

353 U.S. at 471. Is this an accurate statement of the holding in *Osborn*? Aren't there potential federal questions in every litigation—if nothing else, questions as to the constitutionality of the governing state law? Was Justice Johnson right to protest that the result of *Osborn* was to make every case one arising under federal law?

In addition to *Osborn,* Justice Frankfurter relied for his description on several subsequent cases applying Chief Justice Marshall's opinion. The *Pacific Railroad Removal Cases,* 115 U.S. 1 (1885), involved state law tort and contract claims against railroads chartered by the United States. Relying on *Osborn,* the Supreme Court held that the defendants could remove these cases to federal court, explaining that "the corporations now before us, not only derive their existence, but their powers, their functions, their duties, and a large portion of their resources, from those [chartering] acts, and, by virtue thereof sustain important relations to the Government of the United States." Similarly, in *Schumacher v. Beeler,* 293 U.S. 367 (1934), the Court upheld a provision of the Bankruptcy Act of 1926 that conferred federal jurisdiction over controversies brought by a bankruptcy trustee on behalf of the debtor's estate. This might include, for example, a tort action based on an accident occurring prior to the bankruptcy, which, if successful, would bring money into the estate. See also *Williams v. Austrian,* 331 U.S. 642 (1947).

Do these cases support Justice Frankfurter's broad restatement of the holding in *Osborn*? Were they rightly decided?

(4) The Court has, at various times, said that the Constitution's grant of federal question jurisdiction is designed to (a) advance the uniform interpretation and implementation of federal law; (b) avoid or minimize the effects of state court hostility to federal law; and (c) provide a forum that specializes in federal law and is therefore more likely to apply that law correctly. See, e.g., *Merrell Dow Pharmaceuticals Inc. v. Thompson,* 478 U.S. 804, 826 (1986) (Brennan, J., dissenting). Do these purposes help define the proper scope of federal question jurisdiction? Aren't these concerns adequately protected by Justice Johnson's approach, which authorizes federal jurisdiction if the need to litigate a federal issue is apparent when suit is filed or if a federal issue emerges in the course of the litigation (at which point removal may be allowed)? What is Chief Justice Marshall afraid of? Is it that jurisdiction should be settled at the outset? Or is he concerned that hostile state courts may subvert federal law *indirectly* by distorting *state* law when protection is sought by the holder of a federal right? How might this happen in the *Planters' Bank* case? In the *Pacific Railroad Removal Cases*? In *Schumacher v. Beeler*? Does this suggest a reading of *Osborn* that is narrower than Justice Frankfurter's?

(5) Professor Wechsler once suggested that, under *Osborn,* Congress could confer federal jurisdiction over a case if it could have gone farther and prescribed federal substantive law for that case. Wechsler, *Federal Jurisdiction and the Revision of the Judicial Code,* 13 Law & Contemp. Probs. 216, 224–25 (1948). Justice Frankfurter criticized this theory of "protective jurisdiction" in his *Lincoln Mills* dissent:

> Surely the technical restrictions of Article III are not met or respected by a beguiling phrase that the greater power here must necessarily include the lesser. In the compromise of federal and state interests leading to distribution of jealously guarded judicial power in a federal system, * * * it is obvious that very different considerations apply to cases involving questions of federal law and those turning solely on state law. . . [U]nder the theory of "protective jurisdiction," . . . every contract or tort arising out of a contract affecting commerce might be a potential cause of action in the federal courts, even though only state law was involved in the decision of the case. At least in *Osborn* and the bankruptcy cases, a substantive federal law was present somewhere in the background.

Isn't this right? Isn't there a difference between conferring jurisdiction because a federal interest Congress created may be threatened, and conferring jurisdiction because Congress could have created a federal interest?

(6) Justice Frankfurter went on to argue that *Osborn* should no longer be followed:

> Marshall's holding was undoubtedly influenced by his fear that the bank might suffer hostile treatment in the state courts that could not be remedied by an appeal on an isolated federal question. There is nothing in Article III that affirmatively supports the view that original jurisdiction over federal question cases must extend to every case in which there is the potentiality of appellate jurisdiction. We also have become familiar with removal procedures that could be adapted to alleviate any remaining fears by providing for removal to a federal court whenever a federal question was raised. In view of these developments, we would not be justified in perpetuating a principle that permits assertion of original federal jurisdiction on the remote possibility of presentation of a federal question.

Do you agree? Mightn't there still be circumstances in which the concerns underlying *Osborn* are present?

(7) A more recent brush with the problem posed by *Osborn* came in *Verlinden B.V. v. Central Bank of Nigeria,* 461 U.S. 480 (1983). The Foreign Sovereign Immunities Act (FSIA) generally confirms the immunity of foreign nations from suit in state or federal court. It makes a number of exceptions, however, including one for cases involving commercial activities or specified torts. In 28 U.S.C. § 1330(a), Congress conferred federal jurisdiction over nonjury civil actions in which a foreign nation is not immune. The Supreme Court upheld the constitutionality of this grant of jurisdiction, reasoning that the FSIA "codifies the standards governing foreign immunity as an aspect of substantive federal law" and that therefore "every action against a foreign sovereign necessarily involves application of a body of substantive federal law, and accordingly 'arises under' federal law within the meaning of Article III." What federal interest is protected by exercising jurisdiction when immunity is not an issue? Should the Court have held § 1330(a) unconstitutional?

LOUISVILLE & NASHVILLE R. CO. V. MOTTLEY

211 U.S. 149 (1908).

[In 1871, the Mottleys were injured in a train collision while riding on defendant's train. They signed an agreement releasing the railroad from liability in exchange for free passes to ride defendant's trains as long as they lived. The defendant honored this contract until 1907, when it repudiated the agreement on the ground that Congress had passed a statute forbidding railroads to give free passes. The Mottleys brought suit in federal court and obtained a decree ordering specific performance. The railroad appealed to the Supreme Court.]

MR. JUSTICE MOODY, after making the foregoing statement, delivered the opinion of the Court.

Two questions of law . . . have been argued before us. They are, first, whether that part of the act of Congress of June 29, 1906 (34 Stat. 584), which forbids the giving of free passes or the collection of any different compensation for transportation of passengers than that specified in the tariff filed, makes it unlawful to perform a contract for transportation of persons, who in good faith, before the passage of the act, had accepted such contract in satisfaction of a valid cause of action against the railroad; and, second, whether the statute, if it should be construed to render such a contract unlawful, is in violation of the Fifth Amendment of the Constitution of the United States. We do not deem it necessary, however, to consider either of these questions, because, in our opinion, the court below was without jurisdiction of the cause. Neither party has questioned that jurisdiction, but it is the duty of this court to see to it that the jurisdiction of the Circuit Court, which is defined and limited by statute, is not exceeded. This duty we have frequently performed of our own motion. * * *

There was no diversity of citizenship and it is not and cannot be suggested that there was any ground of jurisdiction, except that the case was a "suit ... arising under the Constitution and laws of the United States." It is the settled interpretation of these words, as used in this statute, conferring jurisdiction, that a suit arises under the Constitution and laws of the United States only when the plaintiff's statement of his own cause of action shows that it is based upon those laws or that Constitution. It is not enough that the plaintiff alleges some anticipated defense to his cause of action and asserts that the defense is invalidated by some provision of the Constitution of the United States. Although such allegations show that very likely, in the course of the litigation, a question under the Constitution would arise, they do not show that the suit, that is, the plaintiff's original cause of action, arises under the Constitution. In *Tennessee v. Union & Planters' Bank*, 152 U.S. 454, the plaintiff, the State of Tennessee, brought suit in the Circuit Court of the United States to recover from the defendant certain taxes alleged to be due under the laws of the State. The plaintiff alleged that the defendant claimed an immunity from the taxation by virtue of its charter, and that therefore the tax was void, because in violation of the provision of the Constitution of the United States, which forbids any State from passing a law impairing the obligation of contracts. The cause was held to be beyond the jurisdiction of the Circuit Court, the court saying, by Mr. Justice Gray (p. 464), "a suggestion of one party, that the other will or may set up a claim under the Constitution or laws of the United States, does not make the suit one arising under that Constitution or those laws." . . .

The interpretation of the act which we have stated was first announced in *Metcalf v. Watertown*, 128 U.S. 586, and has since been repeated and applied in [citing 17 cases]. The application of this rule to the case at bar is decisive against the jurisdiction of the Circuit Court.

The Well Pleaded Complaint Rule

(1) Is there federal jurisdiction under *Mottley* in a case like *Planters' Bank*? The statute conferring jurisdiction—currently 28 U.S.C. § 1331—uses the same language as Article III, conferring jurisdiction over all civil actions "arising under" federal law. This statute was enacted in 1875 without substantial debate, but what legislative history exists suggests that Congress thought it was conferring jurisdiction to the full extent permitted by the Constitution. See F. Frankfurter & J. Landis, The Business of the Supreme Court 65–69 (1928). That being so, what basis is there for reading the statute to confer less jurisdiction than Article III allows?

(2) *Mottley*'s interpretation of § 1331 is known as the "well pleaded complaint rule," because it makes federal question jurisdiction turn on whether one of the essential elements of a plaintiff's claim raises a federal issue. It is, in other words, a pleading rule; and because the elements of a claim are defined by the sovereign that creates it, if the plaintiff asserts a state cause of action, federal jurisdiction will turn on how the state defines the elements of that claim.

In any event, the critical point is that, under *Mottley,* federal jurisdiction depends on the plaintiff's claim and is to be determined "upon the face of the complaint unaided by the answer. . ." *Gully v. First National Bank,* 299 U.S. 109, 112–13 (1936). One reason this is critical is because, since 1887, defendants have been allowed to remove a case to federal court only if the plaintiff could have filed there in the first place; removal is not allowed on the ground that the defendant has a federal defense, but requires that there be a federal element in the plaintiff's claim. 28 U.S.C. § 1441(a), (b).

(3) Is *Mottley* consistent with the goals of federal jurisdiction to advance uniformity, avoid state court hostility, and provide expertise in the interpretation of federal law? Aren't these objectives equally at stake when a federal issue is presented by the defendant? What other purpose might be served by drawing a line between federal questions raised in the complaint and federal questions raised in the answer or reply?

Consider the problem in choice-of-law terms: It is easy to determine jurisdiction in cases raising only state law issues or federal law issues; these are, in effect, "false conflicts" in terms of jurisdiction. The difficulty arises in mixed cases, which both state and federal courts have an interest in adjudicating. If adopted as a statutory rule, *Osborn* would sweep all these mixed cases—or "true conflicts"—into federal court. Can *Mottley* be understood as a choice-of-law rule for jurisdiction, apportioning the mixed cases to retain those most suited for federal adjudication in federal court while leaving to the states cases best suited for adjudication there? How well does it serve this purpose? Why are cases in which the federal issue is part of the plaintiff's claim better suited for federal adjudication than those in which the federal issue is raised by the defendant? Are such issues more likely to be reached? Are they more likely to be important in the litigation? Can you come up with a better rule? How important is the problem of administrability in this context? How well does the *Mottley* rule do on this score?

(4) Can you square this understanding of the well pleaded complaint rule with the provision for removal? Consider Professor Wechsler's criticism of § 1441(a):

> Though the plaintiff who puts forth the federal claim is content to seek its vindication in the state tribunals, the defendant may insist upon an initial federal forum. When, on the other hand, the plaintiffs' reliance is on state law and the defendant claims a federal defense, neither party may remove. . . It would, it seems to me, be far more logical to shape the rule precisely in reverse, granting removal to defendants when they claim a federal defense against the plaintiff's state-created claim and to the plaintiff when, as the issues have developed, he relies by way of replication on assertion of a federal right. . . The reason for providing the initial federal forum is fear that state courts will view the federal right ungenerously. That reason is quite plainly absent in the only situation where, apart from federal officers, removal now obtains: the case where the *defendant* may remove because the *plaintiff's* case is federal.

Wechsler, *Federal Jurisdiction and the Revision of the Judicial Code,* 13 Law & Contemp. Probs. 216, 233–34 (1948). Aren't there reasons for allowing a defendant to remove when a federal issue is raised by plaintiff that are independent of the plaintiff's interest? But then why not add defense removal? Consider the following argument by Judge Posner:

> It would be a serious mistake to make all cases in which a federal defense was asserted removable as a matter of right. In many the federal defense would have little merit—would, indeed, have been concocted purely to confer federal jurisdiction—yet this fact might be impossible to determine, with any confidence, without having a trial before the trial. Of course, frivolous federal claims are also a problem when only plaintiffs can use them to get into federal court, but a less serious problem. If the plaintiff gets thrown out of federal court because his claim is frivolous, and must start over in state court, he has lost time; and the loss may be fatal if meanwhile the statute of limitations has run. But the defendant may be delighted to see the plaintiff's case thrown out of federal court when the court discovers that the federal defense is frivolous. This is why it would not be a complete answer to . . . give the district court discretion to remand the case back to the state court.

R. Posner, The Federal Courts: Crisis and Reform 190–91 (1985).

(5) One should not leave the subject of the well pleaded complaint rule without noting that its administration in practice has required some complex refinements. The creation of a declaratory judgment remedy, for example, threatened to expand federal jurisdiction by allowing parties who would otherwise be defendants to initiate an action by converting what would have been their defense into the basis of a claim for declaratory relief. Thus, in *Skelly Oil Co. v. Phillips Petroleum Co.*, 339 U.S. 667 (1950), Skelly agreed to sell gas to Phillips, which would in turn sell to a third party. Skelly was allowed to cancel the contract, however, if federal regulators had not approved the third party's purchase by a particular date. A dispute arose over whether the third party had obtained timely approval, and Phillips brought a federal action for a declaration that the contract was still in force. Reasoning that the Declaratory Judgment Act was not intended to expand federal jurisdiction, the Supreme Court held that the trial court should unravel the declaratory judgment action and determine whether there would have been federal jurisdiction over the lawsuit that would otherwise have been filed. Without the Declaratory Judgment Act, the Court found, Skelly would have cancelled and Phillips would have sued to enforce the contract—in which case the federal question would have been raised by Skelly as a defense. There was, therefore, no jurisdiction under *Mottley*. See also *Franchise Tax Bd. v. Construction Laborers Vacation Trust*, 463 U.S. 1 (1983) (extending *Skelly* to actions brought under state declaratory judgment laws).

In another interesting case, *Avco Corp. v. Aero Lodge*, 390 U.S. 557 (1968), the Supreme Court allowed a defendant to remove a state court action to enforce the no-strike clause of a collective bargaining agreement even though the only federal issue raised by the parties was the defendant's preemption defense. In *Franchise Tax Board*, the Court limited this holding, explaining that "preemption removal" is proper only where the "preemptive force [of federal law] is so powerful" that "any complaint that comes within the scope of the federal cause of action necessarily 'arises under' federal law." 463 U.S. at 23–24. In other words, where Congress has manifested an especially strong desire to preempt state law, the usual rule that plaintiff is master of the complaint may be displaced and the court may find that the plaintiff's claim is "really" federal. Unfortunately, the Court failed to make clear exactly how one knows whether this condition is satisfied.

GRABLE & SONS METAL PRODUCTS, INC. V. DARUE ENGINEERING & MANUFACTURING

545 U.S. 308 (2005).

JUSTICE SOUTER delivered the opinion of the Court.

The question is whether want of a federal cause of action to try claims of title to land obtained at a federal tax sale precludes removal to federal court of a state action with non-diverse parties raising a disputed issue of federal title law. We answer no, and hold that the national interest in providing a federal forum for federal tax litigation is sufficiently substantial to support the exercise of federal question jurisdiction over the disputed issue on removal, which would not distort any division of labor between the state and federal courts, provided or assumed by Congress.

I

In 1994, the Internal Revenue Service seized Michigan real property belonging to petitioner Grable & Sons Metal Products, Inc., to satisfy Grable's federal tax delinquency. Title 26 U.S.C. § 6335 required the IRS to give notice of the seizure, and there is no dispute that Grable received actual notice by certified mail before the IRS sold the property to respondent Darue Engineering & Manufacturing. Although Grable also received notice of the sale itself, it did not exercise its statutory right to redeem the property within 180 days of the sale, § 6337(b)(1), and after that period had passed, the Government gave Darue a quitclaim deed. § 6339.

Five years later, Grable brought a quiet title action in state court, claiming that Darue's record title was invalid because the IRS had failed to notify Grable of its seizure of the property in the exact manner required by § 6335(a), which provides that written notice must be "given by the Secretary to the owner of the property [or] left at his usual place of abode or business." Grable said that the statute required personal service, not service by certified mail.

Darue removed the case to Federal District Court as presenting a federal question, because the claim of title depended on the interpretation of the notice statute in the federal tax law. The District Court declined to remand the case at Grable's behest after finding that the "claim does pose a significant question of federal law," * * * and ruling that Grable's lack of a federal right of action to enforce its claim against Darue did not bar the exercise of federal jurisdiction. On the merits, the court granted summary judgment to Darue, holding that although § 6335 by its terms required personal service, substantial compliance with the statute was enough. * * *

The Court of Appeals for the Sixth Circuit affirmed. * * * On the jurisdictional question, the panel thought it sufficed that the title claim raised an issue of federal law that had to be resolved, and implicated a substantial federal interest (in construing federal tax law). The court went on to affirm the District Court's judgment on the merits. We granted certiorari on the jurisdictional question alone, * * * to resolve a split within the Courts of Appeals on whether *Merrell Dow Pharmaceuticals Inc. v. Thompson,* 478 U.S. 804 (1986), always requires a federal cause of action as a condition for exercising federal-question jurisdiction. We now affirm.

II

Darue was entitled to remove the quiet title action if Grable could have brought it in federal district court originally * * * as a civil action "arising under the Constitution, laws, or treaties of the United States," [28 U.S.C.]

§ 1331. This provision for federal-question jurisdiction is invoked by and large by plaintiffs pleading a cause of action created by federal law (*e.g.*, claims under 42 U.S.C. § 1983). There is, however, another longstanding, if less frequently encountered, variety of federal "arising under" jurisdiction, this Court having recognized for nearly 100 years that in certain cases federal question jurisdiction will lie over state-law claims that implicate significant federal issues. * * * The doctrine captures the commonsense notion that a federal court ought to be able to hear claims recognized under state law that nonetheless turn on substantial questions of federal law, and thus justify resort to the experience, solicitude, and hope of uniformity that a federal forum offers on federal issues. * * *

The classic example is *Smith v. Kansas City Title & Trust Co.*, 255 U.S. 180 (1921), a suit by a shareholder claiming that the defendant corporation could not lawfully buy certain bonds of the National Government because their issuance was unconstitutional. Although Missouri law provided the cause of action, the Court recognized federal-question jurisdiction because the principal issue in the case was the federal constitutionality of the bond issue. *Smith* thus held, in a somewhat generous statement of the scope of the doctrine, that a state-law claim could give rise to federal-question jurisdiction so long as it "appears from the [complaint] that the right to relief depends upon the construction or application of [federal law]." *Id.*, at 199.

The *Smith* statement has been subject to some trimming to fit earlier and later cases recognizing the vitality of the basic doctrine, but shying away from the expansive view that mere need to apply federal law in a state-law claim will suffice to open the "arising under" door. As early as 1912, this Court had confined federal-question jurisdiction over state-law claims to those that "really and substantially involv[e] a dispute or controversy respecting the validity, construction or effect of [federal] law." *Shulthis v. McDougal,* 225 U.S. 561, 569 (1912). This limitation was the ancestor of Justice Cardozo's later explanation that a request to exercise federal-question jurisdiction over a state action calls for a "common-sense accommodation of judgment to [the] kaleidoscopic situations" that present a federal issue, in "a selective process which picks the substantial causes out of the web and lays the other ones aside." * * * It has in fact become a constant refrain in such cases that federal jurisdiction demands not only a contested federal issue, but a substantial one, indicating a serious federal interest in claiming the advantages thought to be inherent in a federal forum. *E.g., Chicago v. International College of Surgeons,* 522 U.S. 156, 164 (1997); *Merrell Dow, supra,* at 814, and n. 12; *Franchise Tax Bd. of Cal. v. Construction Laborers Vacation Trust for Southern Cal.,* 463 U.S. 1, 28 (1983).

But even when the state action discloses a contested and substantial federal question, the exercise of federal jurisdiction is subject to a possible veto. For the federal issue will ultimately qualify for a federal forum only if federal jurisdiction is consistent with congressional judgment about the sound division of labor between state and federal courts governing the application of § 1331. Thus, *Franchise Tax Bd.* explained that the appropriateness of a federal forum to hear an embedded issue could be evaluated only after considering the "welter of issues regarding the interrelation of federal and state authority and the proper management of the federal judicial system." *Id.*, at 8. Because arising-under jurisdiction to hear a state-law claim always raises the possibility of upsetting the state-federal line drawn (or at least assumed) by Congress, the presence of a disputed federal issue and the ostensible importance of a federal forum are never necessarily dispositive; there must always be an assessment of any disruptive portent in exercising federal jurisdiction. See also *Merrell Dow, supra,* at 810.

These considerations have kept us from stating a "single, precise, all-embracing" test for jurisdiction over federal issues embedded in state-law claims between nondiverse parties. * * * We have not kept them out simply because they appeared in state raiment, as Justice Holmes would have done, see *Smith, supra,* at 214 (dissenting opinion), but neither have we treated "federal issue" as a password opening federal courts to any state action embracing a point of federal law. Instead, the question is, does a state-law claim necessarily raise a stated federal issue, actually disputed and substantial, which a federal forum may entertain without disturbing any congressionally approved balance of federal and state judicial responsibilities.

III

A

This case warrants federal jurisdiction. Grable's state complaint must specify "the facts establishing the superiority of [its] claim," * * * and Grable has premised its superior title claim on a failure by the IRS to give it adequate notice, as defined by federal law. Whether Grable was given notice within the meaning of the federal statute is thus an essential element of its quiet title claim, and the meaning of the federal statute is actually in dispute; it appears to be the only legal or factual issue contested in the case. The meaning of the federal tax provision is an important issue of federal law that sensibly belongs in a federal court. The Government has a strong interest in the "prompt and certain collection of delinquent taxes," * * * and the ability of the IRS to satisfy its claims from the property of delinquents requires clear terms of notice to allow buyers like Darue to satisfy themselves that the Service has touched the bases necessary for good title. The Government thus has a direct interest in the availability of a federal forum to vindicate its own administrative action, and buyers (as well as tax delinquents) may find it valuable to come before judges used to federal tax matters. Finally, because it will be the rare state title case that raises a contested matter of federal law, federal jurisdiction to resolve genuine disagreement over federal tax title provisions will portend only a microscopic effect on the federal-state division of labor. * * *

B

Merrell Dow Pharmaceuticals Inc. v. Thompson, 478 U.S. 804 (1986), on which Grable rests its position, is not to the contrary. *Merrell Dow* considered a state tort claim resting in part on the allegation that the defendant drug company had violated a federal misbranding prohibition, and was thus presumptively negligent under Ohio law. *Id.,* at 806. The Court assumed that federal law would have to be applied to resolve the claim, but after closely examining the strength of the federal interest at stake and the implications of opening the federal forum, held federal jurisdiction unavailable. Congress had not provided a private federal cause of action for violation of the federal branding requirement, and the Court found "it would . . . flout, or at least undermine, congressional intent to conclude that federal courts might nevertheless exercise federal-question jurisdiction and provide remedies for violations of that federal statute solely because the violation . . . is said to be a . . . 'proximate cause' under state law." *Id.,* at 812.

Because federal law provides for no quiet title action that could be brought against Darue, Grable argues that there can be no federal jurisdiction here, stressing some broad language in *Merrell Dow* (including the passage just quoted) that on its face supports Grable's position * * *. But an opinion is to be read as a whole, and *Merrell Dow* cannot be read whole as overturning decades of precedent, as it would have done by effectively adopting the Holmes dissent in *Smith,* see *supra,* at 5, and converting a federal cause of action from a sufficient condition for federal-question jurisdiction[5] into a necessary one.

In the first place, *Merrell Dow* disclaimed the adoption of any bright-line rule, as when the Court reiterated that "in exploring the outer reaches of § 1331, determinations about federal jurisdiction require sensitive judgments about congressional intent, judicial power, and the federal system." 478 U.S., at 810. The opinion included a lengthy footnote explaining that questions of jurisdiction over state-law claims require "careful judgments," *id.,* at 814, about the "nature of the federal interest at stake," *id.,* at 814, n. 12 (emphasis deleted). And as a final indication that it did not mean to make a federal right of action mandatory, it expressly approved the exercise of jurisdiction sustained in *Smith,* despite the want of any federal cause of action available to *Smith*'s shareholder plaintiff. 478 U.S., at 814, n. 12. *Merrell Dow* then, did not toss out, but specifically

[5] For an extremely rare exception to the sufficiency of a federal right of action, see *Shoshone Mining Co. v. Rutter,* 177 U.S. 505, 507 (1900).

retained the contextual enquiry that had been *Smith*'s hallmark for over 60 years. At the end of *Merrell Dow*, Justice Holmes was still dissenting.

Accordingly, *Merrell Dow* should be read in its entirety as treating the absence of a federal private right of action as evidence relevant to, but not dispositive of, the "sensitive judgments about congressional intent" that § 1331 requires. The absence of any federal cause of action affected *Merrell Dow*'s result two ways. The Court saw the fact as worth some consideration in the assessment of substantiality. But its primary importance emerged when the Court treated the combination of no federal cause of action and no preemption of state remedies for misbranding as an important clue to Congress's conception of the scope of jurisdiction to be exercised under § 1331. The Court saw the missing cause of action not as a missing federal door key, always required, but as a missing welcome mat, required in the circumstances, when exercising federal jurisdiction over a state misbranding action would have attracted a horde of original filings and removal cases raising other state claims with embedded federal issues. For if the federal labeling standard without a federal cause of action could get a state claim into federal court, so could any other federal standard without a federal cause of action. And that would have meant a tremendous number of cases.

One only needed to consider the treatment of federal violations generally in garden variety state tort law. "The violation of federal statutes and regulations is commonly given negligence per se effect in state tort proceedings." * * * A general rule of exercising federal jurisdiction over state claims resting on federal mislabeling and other statutory violations would thus have heralded a potentially enormous shift of traditionally state cases into federal courts. Expressing concern over the "increased volume of federal litigation," and noting the importance of adhering to "legislative intent," *Merrell Dow* thought it improbable that the Congress, having made no provision for a federal cause of action, would have meant to welcome any state-law tort case implicating federal law "solely because the violation of the federal statute is said to [create] a rebuttable presumption [of negligence] . . . under state law." 478 U.S., at 811–812 (internal quotation marks omitted). In this situation, no welcome mat meant keep out. *Merrell Dow*'s analysis thus fits within the framework of examining the importance of having a federal forum for the issue, and the consistency of such a forum with Congress's intended division of labor between state and federal courts.

As already indicated, however, a comparable analysis yields a different jurisdictional conclusion in this case. Although Congress also indicated ambivalence in this case by providing no private right of action to Grable, it is the rare state quiet title action that involves contested issues of federal law, see n. 3, *supra*. Consequently, jurisdiction over actions like Grable's would not materially affect, or threaten to affect, the normal currents of litigation. Given the absence of threatening structural consequences and the clear interest the Government, its buyers, and its delinquents have in the availability of a federal forum, there is no good reason to shirk from federal jurisdiction over the dispositive and contested federal issue at the heart of the state-law title claim.

[JUSTICE THOMAS concurred to say that while the Court correctly applied its precedents, he would be open to overruling them and adopting the rule that § 1331 jurisdiction exists only when federal law creates the cause of action, should persuasive evidence be offered that this was the original meaning of § 1331.]

State Incorporation of Federal Law (and Vice-Versa)

(1) Cases like *Smith, Merrell Dow,* and *Grable* demonstrate that, while satisfying the well pleaded complaint rule may be necessary to obtain jurisdiction under § 1331, it is not always sufficient. In each of these cases, an essential element of plaintiff's claim was federal, yet in *Merrell Dow* the Court found that there was no federal jurisdiction. What is the principle animating these decisions? Why should there ever be federal jurisdiction over a state-created cause of action? Justice Holmes wrote for the Court in *American Well Works Co. v. Layne & Bowler Co.,* 241 U.S. 257 (1916), that there was no federal jurisdiction in such cases because "[a] suit arises under the law that creates the cause of action." Five years later, the Court decided *Smith,* in which it upheld federal jurisdiction over an action to enjoin the defendant Trust Company from purchasing federal bonds on the ground that state law forbade making unlawful investments and the legislation authorizing the bonds was unconstitutional. Justice Holmes wrote a famous dissent that bears extensive quotation:

> It is evident that the cause of action arises not under any law of the United States but wholly under Missouri law. The defendant is a Missouri corporation and the right claimed is that of a stockholder to prevent the directors from doing an act, that is, making an investment alleged to be contrary to their duty. But the scope of their duty depends upon the charter of their corporation and other laws of Missouri. If those laws had authorized the investment in terms the plaintiff would have had no case, and this seems to me to make manifest what I am unable to deem even debatable, that, as I have said, the cause of action arises wholly under Missouri law. If the Missouri law authorizes or forbids the investment according to the determination of this Court upon a point under the Constitution or acts of Congress, still that point is material only because the Missouri law saw fit to make it so. The whole foundation of the duty is Missouri law,

> which at its sole will incorporated the other law as it might incorporate a document. The other law or document depends for its relevance and effect not on its own force but upon the law that took it up so I repeat once more the cause of action arises wholly from the law of the state. . . The mere adoption by a state law of a United States law as a criterion or test, when the law of the United States has no force *proprio vigore,* does not cause a case under the state law to be also a case under the law of the United States. . .

Do you agree? Suppose the state court agreed with the plaintiff that the federal bond issue was unconstitutional—perhaps because of hostility to federal law, or simply by mistake. Wouldn't that undermine Congress' objective in issuing the bonds? Isn't the purpose of federal jurisdiction under § 1331 to reduce the likelihood of such an occurrence by giving access to a federal forum? Why is it relevant to jurisdiction that the state creates (and may abolish) the remedy if the state uses federal law in a way that implicates the objective of that law?

(2) What is the federal interest in *Merrell Dow*? Was the *Merrell Dow* Court right that Congress's failure to create a private right of action, combined with its assumed indifference to the state's decision to do so, suggested that Congress did not want federal courts to hear the claim? Was Ohio's incorporation of the FDCA analogous to adopting the Federal Rules of Civil Procedure for its own courts? Or does it matter that the FDCA also applies of its own force?

Consider the following argument: There are two potential federal interests in a case like *Merrell Dow:* (1) an interest in the level of enforcement of the FDCA, and (2) an interest in the nature of the obligation imposed by the FDCA. The first interest is reflected in the choice of an enforcement scheme. Thus, Congress's decision not to create a private cause of action sets a nationwide level of enforcement that depends on the resources of the FDA. Congress's decision not to preempt a state-created private remedy (presumed for purposes of the decision in *Merrell Dow*) suggests federal indifference to the decision of a particular state to increase the level of FDCA enforcement in that state.

It does not follow, however, that Congress is equally indifferent to the nature of the obligation the state imposes. In providing this additional remedy, state courts may misconstrue the FDCA, imposing substantive obligations different from or inconsistent with those intended by Congress. The grant of federal jurisdiction in § 1331 makes a federal forum available to minimize the likelihood of such an occurrence. Consequently, if a particular state chooses to increase FDCA enforcement by creating a private cause of action, there is an independent federal interest in providing federal jurisdiction to assure that the FDCA is properly construed to do what Congress intends.

Are you persuaded? Is this federal interest adequately protected by allowing defendants to raise a defense of federal preemption?

(3) Many people read *Merrell Dow* to overrule *Smith* and adopt the rule that the existence of a federal cause of action is a prerequisite to arising-under jurisdiction. *Grable* shows that this is not the case. But what is the test after *Grable*? Justice Souter talks about "important" and "substantial" questions of federal law that are "actually in dispute," but do those criteria distinguish *Merrell Dow*? Does the fact that finding federal jurisdiction in *Merrell Dow* would have brought more cases into federal court than the finding in *Grable* do so? How about the fact that the federal issue in *Grable* is the validity of government action? Are the purposes behind the federal authorization of IRS seizures and sales at stake in Grable's suit against Darue?

(4) Is there federal jurisdiction under § 1331 in the following situations?

(a) California taxes sales of gasoline, but exempts fuel sold "to the government of the United States or any department thereof." Standard Oil Company sues for a refund of taxes paid on gasoline sold to Army Post Exchanges. The question is whether the PX is a department of the United States government. See *Standard Oil Co. v. Johnson,* 316 U.S. 481 (1942) (the Supreme Court finds that it has jurisdiction to review a state court finding).

(b) A Louisiana statute levies a tax on estates subject to federal estate tax. The question is whether a particular estate is subject to federal (and hence state) tax. See *Flournoy v. Wiener,* 321 U.S. 253 (1944) (appeal dismissed on other grounds).

(c) 28 U.S.C. § 1338(a) gives the federal courts exclusive jurisdiction over cases "arising under any Act of Congress relating to patents." Does a state-law claim alleging malpractice by a patent attorney have to be brought in federal court? In *Gunn v. Minton*, 568 U.S. 251 (2013), the Court said no. Applying *Grable*, the Court concluded that although the federal patent law issue was "necessary" to the plaintiff's case and was "actually disputed," it was not "substantial" in its effect on federal interests: no matter how this issue was resolved in the malpractice suit it would not effect the validity of the underlying patent. *Id.* at 258–64. Likewise, entertaining the patent law issue in federal court would disturb the "congressionally approved balance of federal and state judicial responsibilities" because there was no indication that Congress "meant to bar from state courts state legal malpractice claims simply because they require resolution of a hypothetical patent issue." *Id.* at 264.

(d) A state adopts the Federal Rules of Civil Procedure for its own courts and provides that state courts should follow federal interpretations of the rules. Does every procedural issue arising in civil cases now present a federal question?

(5) *Shoshone Mining Co. v. Rutter,* 177 U.S. 505 (1900). A federal statute laid down conditions for the issuance of patents for mining claims by the Commissioner of the General Land Office. The law provided for settlement of disputes between conflicting claimants in a "court of competent jurisdiction." Such disputes, the Court held, did not arise under federal law:

> A suit to enforce a right which takes its origin in the laws of the United States is not necessarily one arising under the Constitution or laws of the United States, within the meaning of the jurisdiction clauses, for if it did every action to establish title to real estate (at least in the newer States) would be such a one. . .
>
> The adverse suit . . . is "to determine the question of the right of possession." . . . By sections 2319, 2324 and 2332, Revised Statutes, it is expressly provided that this right of possession may be determined by "local customs or rules of miners in the several mining districts, so far as the same are applicable and not inconsistent with the laws of the United States;" or by "the statute of limitations for mining claims of the State or Territory where the same may be situated." So that in a given case, the right of possession may not involve any question under the Constitution or laws of the United States, but simply a determination of local rules and customs, or state statutes, or even only a mere matter of fact.

This case presents the opposite problem from cases like *Grable*: federal law incorporates state law. How does that change the analysis? Since state and local law is to govern, if claimants have access to a state or territorial court is there any further federal interest?

(6) Chief Justice Roberts has complained that, in outlining the "slim category" of cases that have their origin in state law but where federal jurisdiction is still proper, the Court does not "paint on a blank canvas. Unfortunately, the canvas looks like one that Jackson Pollock got to first." *Gunn v. Minton*, 568 U.S. 251, 258 (2013). Having looked at some of the cases, do you agree? Would borrowing from choice-of-law principles help?

SECTION 2. THE ERIE DOCTRINE

ERIE R.R. CO. V. TOMPKINS

304 U.S. 64 (1938).

MR. JUSTICE BRANDEIS delivered the opinion of the Court.

The question for decision is whether the oft-challenged doctrine of *Swift v. Tyson* shall now be disapproved.

Tompkins, a citizen of Pennsylvania, was injured on a dark night by a passing freight train of the Erie Railroad Company while walking along its right of way at Hughestown in that State. He claimed that the accident occurred through negligence in the operation, or maintenance, of the train; that he was rightfully on the premises as licensee because on a commonly used beaten footpath which ran for a short distance alongside the tracks; and that he was struck by something which looked like a door projecting from one of the moving cars. To enforce that claim he brought an action in the federal court for southern New York, which had jurisdiction because the company is a corporation of that State. It denied liability; and the case was tried by a jury.

The Erie insisted that its duty to Tompkins was no greater than that owed to a trespasser. It contended, among other things, that its duty to Tompkins, and hence its liability, should be determined in accordance with the Pennsylvania law; that under the law of Pennsylvania, as declared by its highest court, persons who use pathways along the railroad right of way—that is a longitudinal pathway as distinguished from a crossing—are to be deemed trespassers; and that the railroad is not liable for injuries to undiscovered trespassers resulting from its negligence, unless it be wanton or wilful. Tompkins denied that any such rule had been established by the decisions of the Pennsylvania courts; and contended that, since there was no statute of the State on the subject, the railroad's duty and liability is to be determined in federal courts as a matter of general law.

The trial judge refused to rule that the applicable law precluded recovery. The jury brought in a verdict of $30,000; and the judgment entered thereon was affirmed by the Circuit Court of Appeals, which held, 90 F.2d 603, 604, that it was unnecessary to consider whether the law of Pennsylvania was as contended, because the question was one not of local, but of general, law and that "upon questions of general law the federal courts are free, in absence of a local statute, to exercise their independent judgment as to what the law is; and it is well settled that the question of the responsibility of a railroad for injuries caused by its servants is one of general law. . . Where the public has made open and notorious use of a railroad right of way for a long period of time and without objection, the company owes to persons on such permissive pathway a duty of care in the operation of its trains. . . It is likewise generally recognized law that a jury may find that negligence exists toward a pedestrian using a permissive path on the railroad right of way if he is hit by some object projecting from the side of the train."

The Erie had contended that application of the Pennsylvania rule was required, among other things, by § 34 of the Federal Judiciary Act of September 24, 1789, c. 20, 28 U.S.C. § 725 [now 28 U.S.C. § 1652], which provides:

> "The laws of the several States, except where the Constitution, treaties, or statutes of the United States otherwise require or provide, shall be regarded as rules of decision in trials at common law, in the courts of the United States, in cases where they apply."

Because of the importance of the question whether the federal court was free to disregard the alleged rule of the Pennsylvania common law, we granted certiorari.

First. Swift v. Tyson, 16 Pet. 1, 18 [1842], held that federal courts exercising jurisdiction on the ground of diversity of citizenship need not, in matters of general jurisprudence, apply the unwritten law of the State as declared by its highest court; that they are free to exercise an independent judgment as to what the common law of the State is—or should be; and that, as there stated by Mr. Justice Story:

> "The true interpretation of the 34th section limited its application to state laws strictly local, that is to say, to the positive statutes of the state, and the construction thereof adopted by the local tribunals, and to rights and titles to things having a permanent locality, such as the rights and titles to real estate, and other matters immovable and intraterritorial in their nature and character. It never has been supposed by us, that the section did apply, or was intended to apply, to questions of a more general nature, not at all dependent upon local statutes or local usages of a fixed and permanent operation, as, for example, to the construction of ordinary contracts or other written instruments, and especially to questions of general commercial law, where the state tribunals are called upon to perform the like functions as ourselves, that is, to ascertain upon general reasoning and legal analogies, what is the true exposition of the contract or instrument, or what is the just rule furnished by the principles of commercial law to govern the case."

The Court in applying the rule of § 34 to equity cases, *Mason v. United States,* 260 U.S. 545, 559, said: "The statute, however, is merely declarative of the rule which would exist in the absence of the statute." The federal courts assumed, in the broad field of "general law," the power to declare rules of decision which Congress was confessedly without power to enact as statutes. Doubt was repeatedly expressed as to the correctness of the construction given § 34, and as to the soundness of the rule which it introduced. But it was the more recent research of a competent scholar, who examined the original document, which established that the construction given to it by the Court was erroneous; and that the purpose of the section was merely to make certain that, in all matters except those in which some federal law is controlling, the federal courts exercising jurisdiction in diversity in citizenship cases would apply as their rules of decision the law of the State, unwritten as well as written.[5]

Criticism of the doctrine became widespread after the decision of *Black & White Taxicab Co. v. Brown & Yellow Taxicab Co.,* 276 U.S. 518. There, Brown and Yellow, a Kentucky corporation owned by Kentuckians, and the Louisville & Nashville Railroad, also a Kentucky corporation, wished that the former should have the exclusive privileges of soliciting passenger and baggage transportation at the Bowling Green, Kentucky, railroad station; and that the Black and White, a competing Kentucky corporation, should be prevented from interfering with that privilege. Knowing that such a contract would be void under the common law of Kentucky, it was arranged that the Brown and Yellow reincorporate under the law of Tennessee, and that the contract with the railroad should be executed there. The suit was then brought by the Tennessee corporation in the federal court for western Kentucky to enjoin competition by the Black and White; an injunction issued by the District Court was sustained by the Court of Appeals; and this Court, citing many decisions in which the doctrine of *Swift v. Tyson* had been applied, affirmed the decree.

Second. Experience in applying the doctrine of *Swift v. Tyson,* had revealed its defects, political and social; and the benefits expected to flow from the rule did not accrue. Persistence of state courts in their own opinions on questions of common law prevented uniformity; and the impossibility of discovering a satisfactory line of demarcation between the province of general law and that of local law developed a new well of uncertainties.

On the other hand, the mischievous results of the doctrine had become apparent. Diversity of citizenship jurisdiction was conferred in order to prevent apprehended discrimination in state courts against those not citizens of the State. *Swift v. Tyson* introduced grave discrimination by non-citizens against citizens. It made rights enjoyed under the unwritten "general law" vary according to whether enforcement was sought in the state or in the federal court; and the privilege of selecting the court in which

[5] Charles Warren, New Light on the History of the Federal Judiciary Act of 1789 (1923), 37 Harv.L.Rev. 49, 51–52, 81–88, 108.

the right should be determined was conferred upon the non-citizen.[9] Thus, the doctrine rendered impossible equal protection of the law. In attempting to promote uniformity of law throughout the United States, the doctrine had prevented uniformity in the administration of the law of the State.

The discrimination resulting became in practice far-reaching. This resulted in part from the broad province accorded to the so-called "general law" as to which federal courts exercised an independent judgment. In addition to questions of purely commercial law, "general law" was held to include the obligations under contracts entered into and to be performed within the State; the extent to which a carrier operating within a State may stipulate for exemption from liability for his own negligence or that of his employee; the liability for torts committed within the State upon persons resident or property located there, even where the question of liability depended upon the scope of a property right conferred by the State; and the right to exemplary or punitive damages. Furthermore, state decisions construing local deeds, mineral conveyances, and even devises of real estate were disregarded. . .

The injustice and confusion incident to the doctrine of *Swift v. Tyson* have been repeatedly urged as reasons for abolishing or limiting diversity of citizenship jurisdiction. Other legislative relief has been proposed. If only a question of statutory construction were involved, we should not be prepared to abandon a doctrine so widely applied throughout nearly a century. But the unconstitutionality of the course pursued has now been made clear and compels us to do so.

Third. Except in matters governed by the Federal Constitution or by Acts of Congress, the law to be applied in any case is the law of the State. And whether the law of the State shall be declared by its Legislature in a statute or by its highest court in a decision is not a matter of federal concern. There is no federal general common law. Congress has no power to declare substantive rules of common law applicable in a State whether they be local in their nature or "general," be they commercial law or a part of the law of torts. And no clause in the Constitution purports to confer such a power upon the federal courts. As stated by Mr. Justice Field when protesting in *Baltimore & Ohio R. Co. v. Baugh,* 149 U.S. 368, 401, against ignoring the Ohio common law of fellow servant liability: ". . . Supervision over either the legislative or the judicial action of the States is in no case permissible except as to matters by the Constitution specifically authorized or delegated to the United States. Any interference with either, except as thus permitted, is an invasion of the authority of the State and, to that extent, a denial of its independence."

[9] It was even possible for a non-resident plaintiff defeated on a point of law in the highest court of a State nevertheless to win out by taking a nonsuit and renewing the controversy in the federal court. . . .

The fallacy underlying the rule declared in *Swift v. Tyson* is made clear by Mr. Justice Holmes.[23] The doctrine rests upon the assumption that there is "a transcendental body of law outside of any particular State but obligatory within it unless and until changed by statute," that federal courts have the power to use their judgment as to what the rules of common law are; and that in the federal courts "the parties are entitled to an independent judgment on matters of general law":

> "But law in the sense in which courts speak of it today does not exist without some definite authority behind it. The common law so far as it is enforced in a State, whether called common law or not, is not the common law generally but the law of that State existing by the authority of that State without regard to what it may have been in England or anywhere else. . .
>
> "[T]he authority and only authority is the State, and if that be so, the voice adopted by the State as its own [whether it be of its Legislature or of its Supreme Court] should utter the last word."

Thus the doctrine of *Swift v. Tyson* is, as Mr. Justice Holmes said, "an unconstitutional assumption of powers by courts of the United States which no lapse of time or respectable array of opinion should make us hesitate to correct." In disapproving that doctrine we do not hold unconstitutional § 34 of the Federal Judiciary Act of 1789 or any other Act of Congress. We merely declare that in applying the doctrine this Court and the lower courts have invaded rights which in our opinion are reserved by the Constitution to the several States.

Fourth. The defendant contended that by the common law of Pennsylvania as declared by its highest court in *Falchetti v. Pennsylvania R. Co.*, 307 Pa. 203, 160 A. 859, the only duty owed to the plaintiff was to refrain from wilful or wanton injury. The plaintiff denied that such is the Pennsylvania law. In support of their respective contentions the parties discussed and cited many decisions of the Supreme Court of the State. The Circuit Court of Appeals ruled that the question of liability is one of general law; and on that ground declined to decide the issue of state law. As we hold this was error, the judgment is reversed and the case remanded to it for further proceedings in conformity with our opinion.

Reversed.

[JUSTICE CARDOZO took no part in the consideration or decision of this case; and JUSTICES BUTLER and MCREYNOLDS dissented].

---

[23] *Kuhn v. Fairmont Coal Co.*, 215 U.S. 349, 370–372; *Black & White Taxicab Co. v. Brown & Yellow Taxicab Co.*, 276 U.S. 518, 532–36.

MR. JUSTICE REED [concurring in part]. . .

To decide the case now before us and to "disapprove" the doctrine of *Swift v. Tyson* requires only that we say that the words "the laws" include in their meaning the decisions of the local tribunals. As the majority opinion shows, by its reference to Mr. Warren's researches and the first quotation from Mr. Justice Holmes, that this Court is now of the view that "laws" includes "decisions," it is unnecessary to go further and declare that the "course pursued" was "unconstitutional," instead of merely erroneous.

The "unconstitutional" course referred to in the majority opinion is apparently the ruling in *Swift v. Tyson* that the supposed omission of Congress to legislate as to the effect of decisions leaves federal courts free to interpret general law for themselves. I am not at all sure whether, in the absence of federal statutory direction, federal courts would be compelled to follow state decisions. There was sufficient doubt about the matter in 1789 to induce the first Congress to legislate. No former opinions of this Court have passed upon it. Mr. Justice Holmes evidently saw nothing "unconstitutional" which required the overruling of *Swift v. Tyson,* for he said in the very opinion quoted by the majority, "I should leave *Swift v. Tyson,* undisturbed, as I indicated in *Kuhn v. Fairmont Coal Co.,* but I would not allow it to spread the assumed dominion into new fields." *Black & White Taxicab Co. v. Brown & Yellow Taxicab Co.,* 276 U.S. 518, 535. If the opinion commits this Court to the position that the Congress is without power to declare what rules of substantive law shall govern the federal courts, that conclusion also seems questionable. The line between procedural and substantive law is hazy but no one doubts federal power over procedure. *Wayman v. Southard,* 10 Wheat. 1. The Judiciary Article and the "necessary and proper" clause of Article One may fully authorize legislation, such as this section of the Judiciary Act.

In this Court, *stare decisis,* in statutory construction, is a useful rule, not an inexorable command. * * * It seems preferable to overturn an established construction of an Act of Congress, rather than, in the circumstances of this case, to interpret the Constitution. . .

The Law Applicable in Federal Courts

(1) The First Congress not only created a separate system of federal courts (why?) but provided for concurrent jurisdiction with state courts of cases "between a citizen of the State where the suit is brought, and a citizen of another State" in which the matter in dispute exceeded $500. 1 Stat. 73 (1789) (also providing for jurisdiction of suits between citizens of a state and aliens). Apart from an increase in the jurisdictional amount to $75,000, the definition of "States" to include territories, the District of Columbia, and Puerto Rico (§ 1332(d)), and the provision that a corporation shall be deemed a citizen of its "principal place of business" as well as of "any State by which it has been incorporated" (§ 1332(c)), the present statutory provisions governing diversity jurisdiction are substantially the same as those in force when *Erie* was decided.

(2) What was so bad about *Swift v. Tyson*? The problem of fraudulent manufacture of diversity jurisdiction by foreign incorporation has been cured by the 1958 enactment of § 1332(c), under which a corporation is a citizen of its principal place of business. If the trouble with *Swift* was the difficulty of distinguishing between general and local questions, weren't there less drastic solutions than overruling? Besides, is the *Erie* distinction between substance and procedure much better? See infra pp. 838–847. *Swift's* "discrimination" between domestic cases and those involving citizens of different states might be defended on the ground that interposition of federal law in the latter case serves to resolve a possible conflict between the laws of two interested states. And couldn't the forum-shopping aspect of *Swift,* thought to give the non-citizen an unfair opportunity to choose the more favorable law, have been remedied by amending the statute to permit removal by a resident defendant?

In any event, does the fact that *Swift* may have been problematic as a matter of policy justify overruling it? Shouldn't the Court have left the decision to rewrite the Rules of Decision Act to Congress? *Stare decisis* is usually at its strongest in the context of statutory interpretation. See *Kimble v. Marvel Ent., LLC,* 576 U.S. 446, 456 (2015). Indeed, according to Professor Levi, "More than any other doctrine in the field of precedent, [the doctrine of finality for the construction of a statute] has served to limit the freedom of the Court. It marks an essential difference between statutory interpretation on the one hand and case law and constitutional interpretation on the other." Levi, *An Introduction to Legal Reasoning,* 15 U.Chi.L.Rev. 501, 540 (1948). *Swift v. Tyson* presented a particularly strong case for the application of this principle: it had been on the books for almost a century, and literally thousands of decisions had been based on it. As Judge Friendly observed, "If ever Congress' reenactment of a statute or failure to alter it could fairly be taken as approving a prior judicial interpretation, the unchanged existence of Section 34 for a century after Story's construction was such a case." Friendly, *In Praise of Erie—And of the New Federal Common Law,* 39 N.Y.U.L.Rev. 383, 389–91 (1964).

(3) In the end, the decision to overrule *Swift* was made on constitutional grounds.[10] But what, exactly, was held unconstitutional, and

[10] It was once fashionable to refer to the constitutional discussion in *Erie* as "dictum." See, e.g., Clark, *State Law in the Federal Courts: The Brooding Omnipresence of* Erie v. Tompkins, 55 Yale L.J. 267, 278 (1946). Judge Friendly's answer seems conclusive: "A court's stated and, on its view, necessary basis for deciding does not become dictum because a critic would have decided on another basis." 39 N.Y.U.L.Rev. at 385–86.

why? Surely Congress has power to enact rules for determining the liability of interstate railroads to trespassers, and how can it violate state rights for the federal courts to determine the law in a field of federal concern? See *Textile Workers Union v. Lincoln Mills,* 353 U.S. 448 (1957), holding that § 301 of the Taft-Hartley Act, 29 U.S.C. § 185, which gives the federal courts jurisdiction of "suits for violation of contracts between an employer and a labor organization representing employees in an industry affecting commerce," impliedly conferred the power to create federal common law in order to enforce a congressional policy favoring enforcement of collective-bargaining agreements. Was the real difficulty in *Erie* that Congress had failed to delegate lawmaking powers to the courts in railroad-accident cases? Cf. the much-criticized *In re Debs,* 158 U.S. 564 (1895), upholding, without statutory authority, an injunction against striking railroad workers on the ground they were interfering with interstate commerce. But can't that gap be filled by Congress's supposed acquiescence in *Swift v. Tyson*?

The suggestion that the result in *Erie* turns on Congress's failure to delegate lawmaking power to the federal courts is hard to square with Justice Brandeis's statement that "Congress has no power to declare substantive rules of common law applicable in a State. . ." Why not? Can't the exercise of federal power be justified on the ground that it is "necessary and proper" to implement the grant of diversity jurisdiction in Article III, § 2? Is that what *Erie* declares unconstitutional? Why?

Note that the Supreme Court has upheld federal power to declare the law under other constitutional grants of jurisdiction, such as admiralty cases and disputes between states. See *Texas v. New Jersey,* 379 U.S. 674 (1965); *Southern Pacific Co. v. Jensen,* 244 U.S. 205 (1917). In *Jensen,* the Court said:

> Article III, § 2, of the Constitution, extends the judicial power of the United States "To all cases of admiralty and maritime jurisdiction;" and Article I, § 8, confers upon the Congress power "To make all laws which may be necessary and proper for carrying into execution the foregoing powers and all other powers vested by this Constitution in the Government of the United States or in any department or officer thereof." Considering our former opinions, it must now be accepted as settled doctrine that in consequence of these provisions Congress has paramount power to fix and determine the maritime law, which shall prevail throughout the country . . . [a]nd further, that in the absence of some controlling statute the general maritime law as accepted by the federal courts constitutes part of our national law applicable to matters within the admiralty and maritime jurisdiction. . .

> The general system of maritime law which was familiar to the lawyers and statesmen of the country when the Constitution was adopted, was most certainly intended and referred to when it was declared in that instrument that the judicial power of the United States shall extend "to all cases of admiralty and maritime jurisdiction." . . . It certainly could not have been intended to place the rules and limits of maritime law under the disposal and regulation of the several States, as that would have defeated the uniformity and consistency at which the Constitution aimed on all subjects of a commercial character affecting the intercourse of the States with each other or with foreign states.

244 U.S. at 214–15. Is *Jensen*'s argument for uniform law less persuasive in diversity than in admiralty? See D. Currie, *Federalism and the Admiralty,* 1960 Sup. Ct. Rev. 158–64:

> [A] uniform law was apparently one reason for the establishment of the admiralty jurisdiction in 1789, while the diversity jurisdiction is generally regarded as intended only to insure unbiased protection against the provincialism of state courts in the administration of their own laws in cases involving citizens of other states.

Complete the next sentence for Professor Currie: And therefore. . .

(4) Compare *Erie* with the principle discussed in Chapter 3 that a state court violates the Due Process Clause of the Fourteenth Amendment by applying its own law to a case in which it has no interest, supra pp. 351–392. On the hypothesis that diversity jurisdiction exists only to protect nonresidents from bias in the administration of state law, is the federal court in a diversity case in the same position as the Texas court in *Home Ins. Co. v. Dick,* 281 U.S. 397 (1930) (supra p. 351)? The Texas court entertains the action in order to provide a convenient forum, the federal court to provide an impartial one; in neither case has the forum sovereign any legitimate concern with the substantive law to be applied. In short, is not *Erie* an application of the principle that a disinterested forum may not frustrate the policies of an interested state? See B. Currie, Selected Essays on the Conflict of Laws at 443; Hill, *The Erie Doctrine and the Constitution,* 53 Nw.U.L.Rev. 427, 440–41 (1958); Weintraub, *The Erie Doctrine and State Conflict of Laws Rules,* 39 Ind.L.J. 228, 240 (1964).

(5) None of *Erie's* concerns about federalism and states' rights were new in 1938. On the contrary, these claims probably were taken much more seriously in the middle of the 19th century, when *Swift* was decided. Justice Story certainly was aware of the arguments, and surely he understood them. So what was he thinking when he wrote the opinion in *Swift v. Tyson*? One interpretation holds that the Supreme Court made a self-conscious grab for power to fashion a national law to protect mercantilist interests from "an uncongenial anticommercial environment often found in state courts." See M. Horowitz, The Transformation of American Law: 1780–1860 252 (1977). Is there a less cynical explanation? In the course of his *Swift* opinion, Justice Story says: "In the ordinary use of language it will hardly be contended that the decisions of Courts constitute laws. They are, at most, only evidence of what the laws are, and are not of themselves laws." 41 U.S. (16 Pet.) at 18. But if common law decisions are mere evidence, what are they evidence of? What is "the law"? And consider the following puzzles associated with the "federal common law" of *Swift v. Tyson*: a plaintiff could not make it the basis for federal question jurisdiction, and it did not preempt inconsistent state law. Why not? What is this common law that Justice Story is talking about?

The source of these anomalies may lie in the non-positivist understanding of the common law that was prevalent in the 18th and 19th centuries. The point is not that judges in these years thought that common law was "discovered" whereas today we understand that it is "made." Eighteenth-century judges understood that common law adjudication involved an exercise of creativity and will on their part. The difference was rather that this creativity was thought to be exercised in the service of principles that did not depend on the formal sanction of a particular sovereign. That is, the common law was seen as a body distinct from the positive law of any particular state, applicable until replaced by positive legislative enactment. The decisions of New York courts did not make "New York common law" because there was no such thing. There was only the general common law, and this could be determined equally well by any judge—including a federal judge. According to Professor Kramer, this understanding helps clarify the treatment of so-called federal common law:

> The peculiar nature of the common law authorized in *Swift v. Tyson* . . . fits comfortably in this framework: the law applied in diversity cases did not preempt inconsistent state law or confer federal jurisdiction because it was not "federal" law at all; it was merely the federal judge's interpretation of the principles constituting the distinct field of the common law. *Erie's* real significance is that it represents the Supreme Court's formal declaration that this view of the common law (with all its implications for our understanding of law in general) is dead, a victim of positivism and realism.

Kramer, *The Lawmaking Power of the Federal Courts,* 12 Pace L.Rev. 263, 283 (1992).

On this view, the critical development in the years after *Swift v. Tyson* was the emergence of positivism and the idea that no law—including common law—exists without the backing of a particular sovereign. See Lessig, *Erie-Effects of Volume 110: An Essay on Context in Interpretive*

Theory, 110 Harv. L. Rev. 1785, 1789–95 (1997). Justice Holmes made the point in his famous dissent in *Black & White Taxicab & Transfer Co.,* 276 U.S. at 533–34:

> The fallacy and illusion that I think exist [behind *Swift v. Tyson*] consist in supposing that there is this outside thing to be found. Law is a word used with different meanings, but law in the sense in which courts think of it today does not exist without some definite authority behind it. The common law so far as it is enforced in a State, whether called common law or not, is not the common law generally but the law of that State existing by the authority of that State without regard to what it may have been in England or anywhere else.

Does this suggest that *Swift*'s interpretation of the Rules of Decision Act was correct, not only as a matter of statutory construction but also in constitutional terms? Scholars have suggested that the answer is yes—and that Justice Brandeis's reliance on Professor Warren's article was in fact misplaced. See, e.g., Fletcher, *The General Common Law and Section 34 of the Judiciary Act of 1789: The Example of Marine Insurance,* 97 Harv.L.Rev. 1513 (1984). But see Goldsmith & Walt, Erie *and the Irrelevance of Legal Positivism,* 84 Va. L. Rev. 673 (1998) (arguing that there is no necessary connection between *Erie* and the rise of legal positivism as an historical, conceptual, or normative matter). So was *Erie* wrong? Or do changes in our jurisprudential framework justify changing our constitutional understandings? Recall Justice Scalia's opinions in *Sun Oil v. Wortman,* 486 U.S. 717 (1988), supra p. 391, and *Burnham v. Superior Court,* 495 U.S. 604 (1990), supra p. 531, both suggesting that ongoing constitutional practices remain constitutional: would Justice Scalia overrule *Erie*?

(6) Considerable ink has been spilled on the question of how a federal court is to ascertain state law. Is the problem different from or more difficult than the problem of determining another state's law in an ordinary choice-of-law case?

GUARANTY TRUST CO. OF NEW YORK V. YORK

326 U.S. 99 (1945).

MR. JUSTICE FRANKFURTER delivered the opinion of the Court.

[Guaranty Trust, trustee to enforce the rights of noteholders of Van Sweringen Corp., was also a substantial creditor of related corporations. In 1931, Guaranty Trust agreed to exchange some of the notes for Van Sweringen stock in order to reduce Van Sweringen's debt and strengthen its financial position. In 1942, York, donee of a noteholder who had rejected the purchase offer, sued in equity in a New York federal court. York alleged that Guaranty Trust was acting to protect its own interests in accepting the offer and had failed to disclose its self-interest when sponsoring it. The court of appeals held a New York statute of limitations inapplicable and found that the action was not barred by laches.]

In exercising their jurisdiction on the ground of diversity of citizenship, the federal courts, in the long course of their history, have not differentiated in their regard for State law between actions at law and suits in equity. Although § 34 of the Judiciary Act of 1789 * * * directed that the "laws of the several States . . . shall be regarded as rules of decision in trials of common law . . . ," this was deemed, consistently for over a hundred years, to be merely declaratory of what would in any event have governed the federal courts and therefore was equally applicable to equity suits.

Partly because the States in the early days varied greatly in the manner in which equitable relief was afforded and in the extent to which it was available, * * * Congress provided that "the forms and modes of proceeding in suits . . . of equity" would conform to the settled uses of courts of equity. Section 2, 1 Stat. 275, 276 * * *. But this enactment gave the federal courts no power that they would not have had in any event when courts were given "cognizance," by the first Judiciary Act, of suits "in equity." . . . In giving federal courts "cognizance" of equity suits in cases of diversity jurisdiction, Congress never gave, nor did the federal courts ever claim, the power to deny substantive rights created by state law or to create substantive rights denied by State law.

This does not mean that whatever equitable remedy is available in a State court must be available in a diversity suit in a federal court, or conversely, that a federal court may not afford an equitable remedy not available in a State court. Equitable relief in a federal court is of course subject to restrictions: the suit must be within the traditional scope of equity as historically evolved in the English Court of Chancery * * *; a plain, adequate and complete remedy at law must be wanting, § 16, 1 Stat. 73, 82 * * *; explicit Congressional curtailment of equity powers must be respected, see, e.g., Norris-LaGuardia Act, 47 Stat. 70, 29 U.S.C. § 101 et seq.; the constitutional right to trial by jury cannot be evaded * * *. That a State may authorize its courts to give equitable relief unhampered by any or all such restrictions cannot remove these fetters from the federal courts. * * * State law cannot define the remedies which a federal court must give simply because a federal court in diversity jurisdiction is available as an alternative tribunal to the State's courts. Contrariwise, a federal court may afford an equitable remedy for a substantive right recognized by a State even though a State court cannot give it. Whatever contradiction or confusion may be produced by a medley of judicial phrases severed from their environment, the body of adjudications concerning equitable relief in diversity cases leaves no doubt that the federal courts enforced State-created substantive rights if the mode of proceeding and remedy were consonant with the traditional body of equitable remedies, practice and procedure, and in so doing they were enforcing rights created by the States and not arising under any inherent or statutory federal law.

Inevitably, therefore, the principle of *Erie R. Co. v. Tompkins,* an action at law, was promptly applied to a suit in equity. *Ruhlin v. New York Life Ins. Co.,* 304 U.S. 202.

And so this case reduces itself to the narrow question whether, when no recovery could be had in a State court because the action is barred by the statute of limitations, a federal court in equity can take cognizance of the suit because there is diversity of citizenship between the parties. Is the outlawry, according to State law, of a claim created by the States a matter of "substantive rights" to be respected by a federal court of equity when that court's jurisdiction is dependent on the fact that there is a State-created right, or is such statute of "a mere remedial character," * * * which a federal court may disregard?

Matters of "substance" and matters of "procedure" are much talked about in the books as though they defined a great divide cutting across the whole domain of law. But, of course, "substance" and "procedure" are the same key-words to very different problems. Neither "substance" nor "procedure" represents the same invariants. Each implies different variables depending upon the particular problem for which it is used. * * * And the different problems are only distantly related at best, for the terms are in common use in connection with situations turning on such different considerations as those that are relevant to questions pertaining to *ex post facto* legislation, the impairment of the obligations of contract, the enforcement of federal rights in the State courts and the multitudinous phases of the conflict of laws. * * *

Here we are dealing with a right to recover derived not from the United States but from one of the States. When, because the plaintiff happens to be a non-resident, such a right is enforceable in a federal as well as in a State court, the forms and mode of enforcing the right may at times, naturally enough, vary because the two judicial systems are not identical. But since a federal court adjudicating a State-created right solely because of the diversity of citizenship of the parties is for that purpose, in effect, only another court of the State, it cannot afford recovery if the right to recover is made unavailable by the State nor can it substantially affect the enforcement of the right as given by the State.

And so the question is not whether a statute of limitations is deemed a matter of "procedure" in some sense. The question is whether such a statute concerns merely the manner and the means by which a right to recover, as recognized by the State, is enforced, or whether such statutory limitation is a matter of substance in the aspect that alone is relevant to our problem, namely, does it significantly affect the result of a litigation for a federal court to disregard a law of a State that would be controlling in an action upon the same claim by the same parties in a State court?

It is therefore immaterial whether statutes of limitation are characterized either as "substantive" or "procedural" in State court opinions in any use of those terms unrelated to the specific issue before us. *Erie R. Co. v. Tompkins* was not an endeavor to formulate scientific legal terminology. It expressed a policy that touches vitally the proper distribution of judicial power between State and federal courts. In essence, the intent of that decision was to insure that, in all cases where a federal court is exercising jurisdiction solely because of the diversity of citizenship of the parties, the outcome of the litigation in the federal court should be substantially the same, so far as legal rules determine the outcome of a litigation, as it would be if tried in a State court. The nub of the policy that underlies *Erie R. Co. v. Tompkins* is that for the same transaction the accident of a suit by a non-resident litigant in a federal court instead of in a State court a block away should not lead to a substantially different result. And so, putting to one side abstractions regarding "substance" and "procedure," we have held that in diversity cases the federal courts must follow the law of the State as to burden of proof, *Cities Service Oil Co. v. Dunlap,* 308 U.S. 208, as to conflict of laws, *Klaxon Co. v. Stentor Co.,* 313 U.S. 487, as to contributory negligence, *Palmer v. Hoffman,* 318 U.S. 109, 117. . .

Plainly enough, a statute that would completely bar recovery in a suit if brought in a State court bears on a State-created right vitally and not merely formally or negligibly. As to consequences that so intimately affect recovery or non-recovery a federal court in a diversity case should follow State law. . .

[E]ven before *Erie R. Co. v. Tompkins,* federal courts relied on statutes of limitations of the States in which they sat. In suits at law State limitations statutes were held to be "rules of decision" within § 34 of the Judiciary Act of 1789 and as such applied in "trials at common law." * * * While there was talk of freedom of equity from such State statutes of limitations, the cases generally refused recovery where suit was barred in a like situation in the State courts, even if only by way of analogy. . .

Diversity jurisdiction is founded on assurance to non-resident litigants of courts free from susceptibility to potential local bias. The Framers of the Constitution, according to Marshall, entertained "apprehensions" lest distant suitors be subjected to local bias in State courts, or, at least, viewed with "indulgence the possible fears and apprehensions" of such suitors. *Bank of the United States v. Deveaux,* 5 Cranch 61, 87. And so Congress afforded out-of-State litigants another tribunal, not another body of law. The operation of a double system of conflicting laws in the same State is plainly hostile to the reign of law. Certainly, the fortuitous circumstance of residence out of a State of one of the parties to a litigation ought not to give rise to a discrimination against others equally concerned but locally resident. The source of substantive rights enforced by a federal court under diversity jurisdiction, it cannot be said too often, is the law of the States. Whenever that law is authoritatively declared by a State, whether its voice be the legislature or its highest court, such law ought to govern in litigation founded on that law, whether the forum of application is a State or a federal court and whether the remedies be sought at law or may be had in equity. . .

The judgment is reversed and the case is remanded for proceedings not inconsistent with this opinion. . .

Outcome Determinativeness

(1) How is the judge to determine whether applying a particular federal rule rather than its state law counterpart will "significantly affect the result of a litigation"? Isn't *any* rule potentially outcome determinative in this sense inasmuch as failure to comply may result in dismissal or other sanctions? And why is outcome determinativeness relevant anyway? Does your answer to this question help define the scope of the test?

(2) Several years after *Guaranty Trust,* the Supreme Court sought to clarify its meaning in a trio of cases.

(a) The question in *Ragan v. Merchants Transfer & Warehouse Co.,* 337 U.S. 530 (1949), was whether to apply Fed.R.Civ.Proc. 3 to toll a state statute of limitations. Under Rule 3, suit is commenced when the complaint is filed. Under Kansas law, however, the limitations period continued to run until service was made on the defendant. Although the plaintiff in *Ragan* filed his complaint before the 2-year Kansas statute of limitations had run, he did not serve the defendant until afterwards. The Supreme Court held that state law applied to determine when the statute was tolled.

(b) In *Woods v. Interstate Realty Co.,* 337 U.S. 535 (1949), the Court held that a Tennessee corporation that had not qualified to do business in Mississippi could not maintain a diversity action in a Mississippi federal court if its failure to qualify barred it from suing in the state courts.

(c) In *Cohen v. Beneficial Industrial Loan Corp.,* 337 U.S. 541 (1949), the Court held that a federal court must apply a New Jersey statute requiring the plaintiff in a shareholder derivative suit to post bond as security for expenses even though the federal rules imposed no such requirement.

Do these cases help clarify the test of *Guaranty Trust*? Do they seem rightly decided?

(3) Is the *Guaranty Trust* test constitutionally required? Could Congress, for example, enact a 5-year statute of limitations to govern diversity cases in federal court? If so, then why wasn't the case controlled by the statute instructing federal courts to apply traditional equity rules (still in force to the extent it was not displaced by the Federal Rules of Civil Procedure)? If *Guaranty Trust* is based on an interpretation of the Rules of Decision Act, is it a sensible reading of the statute?

BYRD V. BLUE RIDGE RURAL ELEC. CO-OP., INC.

356 U.S. 525 (1958).

MR. JUSTICE BRENNAN delivered the opinion of the Court. . .

[Byrd was an employee of R.H. Bouligny, Inc., which had contracted to construct new power lines for the Blue Ridge Rural Electric Cooperative. He brought a diversity action against Blue Ridge for personal injuries suffered while connecting power lines to one of the new substations, but the Court of Appeals set aside a judgment in his favor on the ground that he was a "statutory employee" of Blue Ridge and therefore his sole remedy was workmen's compensation. The Supreme Court held that the Court of Appeals had erred in directing the entry of a judgment for the defendant without giving the plaintiff an opportunity to introduce evidence pertinent to the new test of "statutory employee" laid down by the Court of Appeals; it went on to discuss a problem of choosing between federal and state law:]

A question is also presented as to whether on remand the factual issue is to be decided by the judge or by the jury. The respondent argues on the basis of the decision of the Supreme Court of South Carolina in *Adams v. Davison-Paxon Co.,* 230 S.C. 532, 96 S.E.2d 566, that the issue of immunity should be decided by the judge and not by the jury. That was a negligence action brought in the state trial court against a store owner by an employee of an independent contractor who operated the store's millinery department. The trial judge denied the store owner's motion for a directed verdict made upon the ground that § 72–111 barred the plaintiff's action. The jury returned a verdict for the plaintiff. The South Carolina Supreme Court reversed, holding that it was for the judge and not the jury to decide on the evidence whether the owner was a statutory employer, and that the store owner had sustained his defense. . .

The respondent argues that this state-court decision governs the present diversity case and "divests the jury of its normal function" to decide the disputed fact question of the respondent's immunity under § 72–111. This is to contend that the federal court is bound under *Erie R. Co. v. Tompkins,* 304 U.S. 64, to follow the state court's holding to secure uniform enforcement of the immunity created by the State.

First. It was decided in *Erie R. Co. v. Tompkins* that the federal courts in diversity cases must respect the definition of state-created rights and obligations by the state courts. We must, therefore, first examine the rule in *Adams v. Davison-Paxon Co.* to determine whether it is bound up with these rights and obligations in such a way that its application in the federal court is required. * * *

The Workmen's Compensation Act is administered in South Carolina by its Industrial Commission. The South Carolina courts hold that, on judicial review of actions of the Commission under § 72–111, the question whether the claim of an injured workman is within the Commission's jurisdiction is a matter of law for decision by the court, which makes its own findings of fact relating to that jurisdiction. The South Carolina Supreme Court states no reasons in *Adams v. Davison-Paxon Co.* why, although the jury decides all other factual issues raised by the cause of action and defenses, the jury is displaced as to the factual issue raised by the affirmative defense under § 72–111. The decisions cited to support the holding . . . are concerned solely with defining the scope and method of judicial review of the Industrial Commission. A State may, of course, distribute the functions of its judicial machinery as it sees fit. The decisions relied upon, however, furnish no reason for selecting the judge rather than the jury to decide this single affirmative defense in the negligence action. They simply reflect a policy, cf. *Crowell v. Benson,* 285 U.S. 22, that administrative determination of "jurisdictional facts" should not be final but subject to judicial review. The conclusion is inescapable that the *Adams* holding is grounded in the practical consideration that the question had theretofore come before the South Carolina courts from the Industrial Commission and the courts had become accustomed to deciding the factual issue of immunity without the aid of juries. We find nothing to suggest that this rule was announced as an integral part of the special relationship created by the statute. Thus the requirement appears to be merely a form and mode of enforcing the immunity, *Guaranty Trust Co. v. York,* 326 U.S. 99, 108, and not a rule intended to be bound up with the definition of the rights and obligations of the parties. . .

Second. But cases following *Erie* have evinced a broader policy to the effect that the federal courts should conform as near as may be—in the absence of other considerations—to state rules even of form and mode where the state rules may bear substantially on the question whether the litigation would come out one way in the federal court and another way in the state court if the federal court failed to apply a particular local rule. E.g., *Guaranty Trust Co. v. York,* supra; *Bernhardt v. Polygraphic Co.,* 350 U.S. 198. Concededly the nature of the tribunal which tries issues may be important in the enforcement of the parcel of rights making up a cause of action or defense, and bear significantly upon achievement of uniform enforcement of the right. It may well be that in the instant personal-injury case the outcome would be substantially affected by whether the issue of immunity is decided by a judge or a jury. Therefore, were "outcome" the only consideration, a strong case might appear for saying that the federal court should follow the state practice.

But there are affirmative countervailing considerations at work here. The federal system is an independent system for administering justice to litigants who properly invoke its jurisdiction. An essential characteristic of that system is the manner in which, in civil common-law actions, it distributes trial functions between judge and jury and, under the influence—if not the command[10]—of the Seventh Amendment, assigns the decisions of disputed questions of fact to the jury. *Jacob v. New York,* 315 U.S. 752. The policy of uniform enforcement of state-created rights and obligations . . . cannot in every case exact compliance with a state rule—not bound up with rights and obligations—which disrupts the federal system of allocating functions between judge and jury. *Herron v. Southern Pacific Co.,* 283 U.S. 91. Thus the inquiry here is whether the federal policy favoring jury decisions of disputed fact questions should yield to the state rule in the interest of furthering the objective that the litigation should not come out one way in the federal court and another way in the state court.

We think that in the circumstances of this case the federal court should not follow the state rule. It cannot be gainsaid that there is a strong federal policy against allowing state rules to disrupt the judge-jury relationship in the federal courts. In *Herron v. Southern Pacific Co.,* supra, the trial judge in a personal-injury negligence action brought in the District Court for Arizona on diversity grounds directed a verdict for the defendant when it appeared as a matter of law that the plaintiff was guilty of contributory negligence. The federal judge refused to be bound by a provision of the Arizona Constitution which made the jury the sole arbiter of the question of contributory negligence. This Court sustained the action of the trial judge, holding that "state laws cannot alter the essential character or function of a federal court" because that function "is not in any sense a local matter, and state statutes which would interfere with the appropriate performance of that function are not binding upon the federal court under either the Conformity Act or the 'Rules of Decision' Act." Id., at 94. Perhaps even more clearly in light of the influence of the Seventh Amendment, the function assigned to the jury "is an essential factor in the process for which the Federal Constitution provides." Id., at 95. Concededly the *Herron* case was decided before *Erie R. Co. v. Tompkins,* but even when *Swift v. Tyson,* 16 Pet. 1., was governing law and allowed federal courts sitting in diversity cases to disregard state decisional law, it was never thought that state statutes or constitutions were similarly to be disregarded. *Green v. Neal's Lessee,* 6 Pet. 291. Yet *Herron* held that state statutes and constitutional

[10] Our conclusion makes unnecessary the consideration of—and we intimate no view upon—the constitutional question whether the right of jury trial protected in federal courts by the Seventh Amendment embraces the factual issue of statutory immunity when asserted, as here, as an affirmative defense in a common-law negligence action.

provisions could not disrupt or alter the essential character or function of a federal court.

Third. We have discussed the problem upon the assumption that the outcome of the litigation may be substantially affected by whether the issue of immunity is decided by a judge or a jury. But clearly there is not present here the certainty that a different result would follow, cf. *Guaranty Trust Co. of New York v. York,* supra, or even the strong possibility that this would be the case, cf. *Bernhardt v. Polygraphic Co.,* supra. There are factors present here which might reduce that possibility. The trial judge in the federal system has powers denied the judges of many States to comment on the weight of evidence and credibility of witnesses, and discretion to grant a new trial if the verdict appears to him to be against the weight of the evidence. We do not think the likelihood of a different result is so strong as to require the federal practice of jury determination of disputed factual issues to yield to the state rule in the interest of uniformity of outcome. . .

Reversed and remanded.

MR. JUSTICE WHITTAKER, concurring in part and dissenting in part. . .

The Federal District Court, in this diversity case, is bound to follow the substantive South Carolina law that would be applied if the trial were to be held in a South Carolina court, in which State the Federal District Court sits. *Erie R. Co. v. Tompkins,* 304 U.S. 64. A Federal District Court sitting in South Carolina may not legally reach a substantially different result than would have been reached upon a trial of the same case "in a State court a block away." *Guaranty Trust Co. v. York,* 326 U.S. 99, 109. . .

Inasmuch as the law of South Carolina, as construed by its highest court, requires its courts—not juries—to determine whether jurisdiction over the subject matter of cases like this is vested in its Industrial Commission, and inasmuch as the Court's opinion concedes "that in the instant personal-injury case the outcome would be substantially affected by whether the issue of immunity is decided by a judge or a jury," it follows that in this diversity case the jurisdictional issue must be determined by the judge—not by the jury. . .

[JUSTICES FRANKFURTER and HARLAN, dissenting, argued that there should be no new trial and did not reach the choice-of-law problem.]

Byrd Balancing

(1) What are the "affirmative countervailing considerations" referred to in the second section of Justice Brennan's opinion? How can these interests be legitimate in light of *Erie*'s conclusion that there are no federal interests in a diversity case? Or is that too broad a statement of *Erie*?

What, exactly, are these countervailing considerations being balanced against? The state's interest in having its procedural rule applied? A federal interest in securing uniform results and preventing forum shopping? What is the source of such an interest? How is it to be measured?

(2) In the first section of his opinion, Justice Brennan draws a distinction between "a form and mode of enforcing the immunity" and "a rule intended to be bound up with the definition of the rights and obligations of the parties." What is this all about? Does it reintroduce the procedure/substance distinction that Justice Frankfurter was at such pains to put aside in *Guaranty Trust*? Why? If the state rule is "bound up with the definition of the rights and obligations of the parties," should the federal court still balance? Why or why not?

(3) In the opinion's final section, Justice Brennan suggests that the choice between a bench trial and a jury trial may not be outcome determinative after all. Do you agree? If you were a lawyer, wouldn't this choice affect your litigating strategy?

HANNA V. PLUMER

380 U.S. 460 (1965).

CHIEF JUSTICE WARREN delivered the opinion of the Court. . .

[An Ohio resident brought a diversity action against the executor of a deceased Massachusetts resident in the United States District Court for the District of Massachusetts for injuries arising out of an automobile accident in South Carolina. A copy of the summons was left with the defendant's wife in compliance with Rule 4(d)(1) of the Federal Rules of Civil Procedure, which provides that "service shall be made . . . upon an individual . . . by delivering a copy of the summons and of the complaint to him personally or by leaving copies thereof at his dwelling house . . . with some person of suitable age and discretion then residing therein. . ." Defendant contended that the action should be dismissed on the basis of a Massachusetts statute that required in-hand service of process to an executor or administrator. The district court's dismissal of the action was affirmed by the court of appeals on the ground that manner of service of process was a "substantive" rather than "procedural" issue within the meaning of the *Erie* doctrine and was therefore governed by state law.]

We conclude that the adoption of Rule 4(d)(1), designed to control service of process in diversity actions, neither exceeded the congressional mandate embodied in the Rules Enabling Act nor transgressed constitutional bounds, and that the Rule is therefore the standard against which the District Court should have measured the adequacy of the service. Accordingly, we reverse the decision of the Court of Appeals.

The Rules Enabling Act, 28 U.S.C. § 2072 (1958 ed.), provides, in pertinent part:

> "The Supreme Court shall have the power to prescribe, by general rules, the forms of process, writs, pleadings, and motions, and the practice and procedure of the district courts of the United States in civil actions.
>
> "Such rules shall not abridge, enlarge or modify any substantive right and shall preserve the right of trial by jury. . ."

Under the cases construing the scope of the Enabling Act, Rule 4(d)(1) clearly passes muster. Prescribing the manner in which a defendant is to be notified that a suit has been instituted against him, it relates to the "practice and procedure of the district courts." * * * "The test must be whether a rule really regulates procedure,—the judicial process for enforcing rights and duties recognized by substantive law and for justly administering remedy and redress for disregard or infraction of them." *Sibbach v. Wilson & Co.,* 312 U.S. 1, 14. In *Mississippi Pub. Corp. v. Murphree,* 326 U.S. 438, this Court upheld Rule 4(f), which permits service of a summons anywhere within the State (and not merely the district) in which a district court sits:

> "We think that Rule 4(f) is in harmony with the Enabling Act. . . Undoubtedly most alterations of the rules of practice and procedure may and often do affect the rights of litigants. Congress' prohibition of any alteration of substantive rights of litigants was obviously not addressed to such incidental effects as necessarily attend the adoption of the prescribed new rules of procedure upon the rights of litigants who, agreeably to rules of practice and procedure, have been brought before a court authorized to determine their rights. . ."

Thus were there no conflicting state procedure, Rule 4(d)(1) would clearly control. . .

Respondent, by placing primary reliance on *York* and *Ragan,* suggests that the *Erie* doctrine acts as a check on the Federal Rules of Civil Procedure, that despite the clear command of Rule 4(d)(1), *Erie* and its progeny demand the application of the Massachusetts rule. Reduced to essentials, the argument is: (1) *Erie,* as refined in *York,* demands that federal courts apply state law whenever application of federal law in its stead will alter the outcome of the case. (2) In this case, a determination that the Massachusetts service requirements obtain will result in immediate victory for respondent. If, on the other hand, it should be held that Rule 4(d)(1) is applicable, the litigation will continue, with possible victory for petitioner. (3) Therefore, *Erie* demands application of the Massachusetts rule. The syllogism possesses an appealing simplicity, but is for several reasons invalid.

In the first place, it is doubtful that, even if there were no Federal Rule making it clear that in-hand service is not required in diversity actions, the *Erie* rule would have obligated the District Court to follow the Massachusetts procedure. "Outcome-determination" analysis was never intended to serve as a talisman. *Byrd v. Blue Ridge Cooperative,* 356 U.S. 525, 537. Indeed, the message of *York* itself is that choices between state and federal law are to be made not by application of any automatic, "litmus paper" criterion, but rather by reference to the policies underlying the *Erie* rule. * * *

The *Erie* rule is rooted in part in a realization that it would be unfair for the character or result of a litigation materially to differ because the suit had been brought in a federal court. . . *Swift v. Tyson* introduced grave discrimination by non-citizens against citizens. . . Thus, the doctrine rendered impossible equal protection of the law. *Erie R. Co. v. Tompkins.* * * *

The decision was also in part a reaction to the practice of "forum-shopping" which had grown up in response to the rule of *Swift v. Tyson.* * * * That the *York* test was an attempt to effectuate these policies is demonstrated by the fact that the opinion framed the inquiry in terms of "substantial" variations between state and federal litigation. * * * Not only are nonsubstantial, or trivial, variations not likely to raise the sort of equal protection problems which troubled the Court in *Erie;* they are also unlikely to influence the choice of a forum. The "outcome-determination" test therefore cannot be read without reference to the twin aims of the *Erie* rule: discouragement of forum-shopping and avoidance of inequitable administration of the laws.

The difference between the conclusion that the Massachusetts rule is applicable, and the conclusion that it is not, is of course at this point "outcome-determinative" in the sense that if we hold the state rule to apply, respondent prevails, whereas if we hold that Rule 4(d)(1) governs, the litigation will continue. But in this sense *every* procedural variation is "outcome-determinative." . . . Though choice of the federal or state rule will at this point have a marked effect upon the outcome of the litigation, the difference between the two rules would be of scant, if any, relevance to the choice of a forum. Petitioner, in choosing her forum, was not presented with a situation where application of the state rule would wholly bar recovery; rather, adherence to the state rule would have resulted only in altering the way in which process was served. Moreover, it is difficult to argue that permitting service of defendant's wife to take the place of in-hand service of defendant himself alters the mode of enforcement of state-created rights in a fashion sufficiently "substantial" to raise the sort of equal protection problems to which the *Erie* opinion alluded.

There is, however, a more fundamental flaw in respondent's syllogism: the incorrect assumption that the rule of *Erie R. Co. v. Tompkins* constitutes the appropriate test of the validity and therefore the applicability of a Federal Rule of Civil Procedure. The *Erie* rule has never been invoked to void a Federal Rule. It is true that there have been cases where this Court has held applicable a state rule in the face of an argument that the situation was governed by one of the Federal Rules. But the holding of each such case was not that *Erie* commanded displacement of a Federal Rule by an inconsistent state rule, but rather that the scope of the Federal Rule was not as broad as the losing party urged, and therefore, there being no Federal Rule which covered the point in dispute, *Erie* commanded the enforcement of state law.

"Respondent contends, in the first place, that the charge was correct because of the fact that Rule 8(c) of the Rules of Civil Procedure makes contributory negligence an affirmative defense. We do not agree. Rule 8(c) covers only the manner of pleading. The question of the burden of establishing contributory negligence is a question of local law which federal courts in diversity of citizenship cases . . . must apply." *Palmer v. Hoffman,* 318 U.S. 109, 117.[12] (Here, of course, the clash is unavoidable; Rule 4(d)(1) says—implicitly, but with unmistakable clarity—that in-hand service is not required in federal courts.) At the same time, in cases adjudicating the validity of Federal Rules, we have not applied the *York* rule or other refinements of *Erie,* but have to this day continued to decide questions concerning the scope of the Enabling Act and the constitutionality of specific Federal Rules in light of the distinction set forth in *Sibbach.* * * *

Nor has the development of two separate lines of cases been inadvertent. . . When a situation is covered by one of the Federal Rules, the question facing the court is a far cry from the typical, relatively unguided *Erie* choice: the court has been instructed to apply the Federal Rule, and can refuse to do so only if the Advisory Committee, this Court and Congress erred in their prima facie judgment that the Rule in question transgresses neither the terms of the Enabling Act nor constitutional restrictions.

We are reminded by the *Erie* opinion that neither Congress nor the federal courts can, under the guise of formulating rules of decision for federal courts, fashion rules which are not supported by a grant of federal authority contained in Article I or some other section of the Constitution; in such areas state law must govern because there can be no other law. But the opinion in *Erie,* which involved no Federal Rule and dealt with a

[12] To the same effect, see *Ragan v. Merchants Transfer Co.,* 337 U.S. 530; *Cohen v. Beneficial Loan Corp.,* 337 U.S. 541 at 556; id. at 557 (Douglas, J., dissenting); cf. *Bernhardt v. Polygraphic Co.,* 350 U.S. 198 at 201–202; see generally *Iovino v. Waterson,* 274 F.2d 41, at 47–48.

question which was "substantive" in every traditional sense (whether the railroad owed a duty of care to Tompkins as a trespasser or a licensee), surely neither said nor implied that measures like Rule 4(d)(1) are unconstitutional. For the constitutional provision for a federal court system (augmented by the Necessary and Proper Clause) carries with it congressional power to make rules governing the practice and pleading in those courts, which in turn includes a power to regulate matters which, though falling within the uncertain area between substance and procedure, are rationally capable of classification as either. . .

Thus, though a court, in measuring a Federal Rule against the standards contained in the Enabling Act and the Constitution, need not wholly blind itself to the degree to which the Rule makes the character and result of the federal litigation stray from the course it would follow in state courts, *Sibbach v. Wilson & Co.*, supra, at 13–14, it cannot be forgotten that the *Erie* rule, and the guidelines suggested in *York,* were created to serve another purpose altogether. To hold that a Federal Rule of Civil Procedure must cease to function whenever it alters the mode of enforcing state-created rights would be to disembowel either the Constitution's grant of power over federal procedure or Congress' attempt to exercise that power in the Enabling Act. Rule 4(d)(1) is valid and controls the instant case.

Reversed.

MR. JUSTICE BLACK concurs in the result.

MR. JUSTICE HARLAN, concurring. . .

Erie was something more than an opinion which worried about "forum-shopping and avoidance of inequitable administration of the laws," * * * although to be sure these were important elements of the decision. I have always regarded that decision as one of the modern cornerstones of our federalism, expressing policies that profoundly touch the allocation of judicial power between the state and federal systems. *Erie* recognized that there should not be two conflicting systems of law controlling the primary activity of citizens, for such alternative governing authority must necessarily give rise to a debilitating uncertainty in the planning of everyday affairs.[1] And it recognized that the scheme of our Constitution envisions an allocation of law-making functions between state and federal legislative processes which is undercut if the federal judiciary can make substantive law affecting state affairs beyond the bounds of congressional legislative powers in this regard. . .

To my mind the proper line of approach in determining whether to apply a state or a federal rule, whether "substantive" or "procedural," is to stay close to basic principles by inquiring if the choice of rule would

[1] Since the rules involved in the present case are parallel rather than conflicting, this first rationale does not come into play here.

substantially affect those primary decisions respecting human conduct which our constitutional system leaves to state regulation. If so, *Erie* and the Constitution require that the state rule prevail, even in the face of a conflicting federal rule. . .

So long as a reasonable man could characterize any duly adopted federal rule as "procedural," the Court, unless I misapprehend what is said, would have it apply no matter how seriously it frustrated a State's substantive regulation of the primary conduct and affairs of its citizens. Since the members of the Advisory Committee, the Judicial Conference, and this Court who formulated the Federal Rules are presumably reasonable men, it follows that the integrity of the Federal Rules is absolute. Whereas the unadulterated outcome and forum-shopping tests may err too far toward honoring state rules, I submit that the Court's "arguably procedural, *ergo* constitutional" test moves too fast and far in the other direction. . .

It remains to apply what has been said to the present case. . . The evident intent of [the Massachusetts] statute is to permit an executor to distribute the estate which he is administering without fear that further liabilities may be outstanding for which he could be held personally liable. If the Federal District Court in Massachusetts applies Rule 4(d)(1) [it] would mean simply that an executor would have to check at his own house or at the federal courthouse as well as the registry of probate before he could distribute the estate with impunity. As this does not seem enough to give rise to any real impingement on the vitality of the state policy which the Massachusetts rule is intended to serve, I concur in the judgment of the Court.

Erie and the Federal Rules of Civil Procedure

(1) Was the court in *Hanna* justified in placing so much emphasis on the existence of a Federal Rule of Civil Procedure? See Fed.R.Civ.P. 1 ("These rules govern the procedure in the United States District Courts in all suits of a civil nature. . ."); 28 U.S.C. § 2072 (the Rules Enabling Act: "All laws in conflict with such rules shall be of no further force or effect"); 28 U.S.C. § 1652 (state laws are rules of decision "except where the Constitution or treaties of the United States or Acts of Congress otherwise require or provide"); U.S. Constitution, Article VI ("This Constitution, and the Laws of the United States which shall be made in pursuance thereof . . . shall be the supreme Law of the Land"). But before this massive engine of federal supremacy can get under way the Rule must pass two tests: It must be constitutional, and it must be within the authority given the Court by the Enabling Act.

Is the grant of rule making authority as broad as the power of Congress in diversity cases?

"The test" of whether a judicially promulgated rule is proper under the Rules Enabling Act, said the Court in *Sibbach v. Wilson & Co.,* 312 U.S. 1, 14 (1941), "must be whether a rule really regulates procedure—the judicial process for enforcing rights and duties recognized by substantive law and for justly administering remedy and redress for disregard or infraction of them." Doesn't that seem too broad? Suppose the Supreme Court were to promulgate a rule that was procedural in form as a pretext for achieving substantive ends? Or, more realistically, suppose the Court's rules have both substantive and procedural objectives? The Rules Enabling Act also provides that the rules "shall not abridge, enlarge or modify any substantive right." Doesn't that limit the rule making power beyond asking whether the rules "really regulate procedure"?

In *The Irrepressible Myth of* Erie, 87 Harv.L.Rev. 693, 718–38 (1974), Dean Ely argues that the *Sibbach* test wholly ignores this statutory requirement; he would strike down (even in a federal-question case?) any rule that offended "substantive" state policy, i.e., a policy not simply "designed to make the process of litigation a fair and efficient mechanism for the resolution of disputes." Is it clear that the "substantive right" prohibition is not merely a means of emphasizing the limitation to matters of procedure? See generally Burbank, *The Rules Enabling Act of 1934,* 130 U.Pa.L.Rev. 1015 (1982).

(2) Can every rule that is validly promulgated under the Rules Enabling Act be applied in a diversity case? What about the constitutional concerns expressed in *Erie*? Or were these concerns already put to rest in *Byrd*?

Are there any constitutional limits on the use of federal rules of procedure in diversity cases? Could the federal courts, for example, apply a statute of limitations longer than that of the state whose law created the right of action? Cf. *Sun Oil Co. v. Wortman,* 486 U.S. 717 (1988), supra p. 391. If the purpose of diversity jurisdiction is simply to protect an out-of-state party from potential state court bias, is there ever an interest in providing a federal forum when the state courts are closed? What about interpleader, where the justification for federal jurisdiction is that in many cases no state can constitutionally provide a forum? See also *Allstate Ins. Co. v. Charneski,* 286 F.2d 238 (7th Cir.1960) (concerning the availability of a declaratory judgment).

(3) Even apart from the Constitution, do you agree with *Hanna*'s interpretation of the Rules Enabling Act? What about the concerns for uniformity and forum shopping reflected in the Rules of Decision Act? What purpose of the Rules Enabling Act is served by interpreting it to displace state rules of procedure in diversity cases? *Hanna* suggests that this is necessary to achieve the Rules Enabling Act's goal of providing uniform federal rules of procedure. Is that goal present in diversity cases? Wasn't Congress concerned with creating one system of procedure to ensure uniform enforcement of federal law across districts in federal question cases? In diversity cases, isn't the objective of uniformity between state and federal courts of paramount importance?

(4) The Civil Rules do not answer every procedural question, and neither federal statutes nor rules adopted by the district courts themselves fill all the gaps. What is a court to do when none of these sources provides an answer? Do *Guaranty Trust* and *Byrd* remain applicable? Are state procedural rules "rules of decision" whose application § 1652 demands?[11]

(5) *Hanna* does not dispense with the necessity for construing the federal rule. In *Hanna* itself, however, the Court concluded that a clash between the applicable federal and state rules was "inevitable." Do you agree? Was the clash in *Hanna* more inevitable than in *Palmer v. Hoffman,* which involved Rule 8(c) and is discussed in *Hanna*? Is the degree to which application of a federal rule would frustrate state policy relevant to the question of construction?

WALKER V. ARMCO STEEL CORP.

446 U.S. 740 (1980).

JUSTICE MARSHALL delivered the opinion for a unanimous Court.

This case presents the issue whether in a diversity action the federal court should follow state law or, alternatively, Rule 3 of the Federal Rules of Civil Procedure in determining when an action is commenced for the purpose of tolling the state statute of limitations.

I

According to the allegations of the complaint, petitioner, a carpenter, was injured on August 22, 1975, in Oklahoma City, Okla., while pounding a Sheffield nail into a cement wall. Respondent was the manufacturer of the nail. Petitioner claimed that the nail contained a defect which caused its head to shatter and strike him in the right eye, resulting in permanent injuries. The defect was allegedly caused by respondent's negligence in manufacture and design.

Petitioner is a resident of Oklahoma, and respondent is a foreign corporation having its principal place of business in a State other than Oklahoma. Since there was diversity of citizenship, petitioner brought suit

[11] That Congress did not think the Rules of Decision Act embraced all procedural matters was strongly suggested by the contemporaneous enactment of a separate statute providing that "the forms of writs and executions . . . and modes of process" in federal common-law actions conform to those of the States (1 Stat. 93, 94 (1789)). The successor to this conformity provision disappeared with the adoption of the Federal Rules of Civil Procedure in 1938.

in the United States District Court for the Western District of Oklahoma. The complaint was filed on August 19, 1977. Although summons was issued that same day, service of process was not made on respondent's authorized service agent until December 1, 1977. On January 5, 1978, respondent filed a motion to dismiss the complaint on the ground that the action was barred by the applicable Oklahoma statute of limitations. Although the complaint had been filed within the 2-year statute of limitations, * * * state law does not deem the action "commenced" for purposes of the statute of limitations until service of the summons on the defendant, Okla.Stat., Tit. 12, § 97 (1971). If the complaint is filed within the limitations period, however, the action is deemed to have commenced from the date of filing if the plaintiff serves the defendant within 60 days, even though that service may occur outside the limitations period. In this case, service was not effectuated until long after this 60-day period had expired. Petitioner in his reply brief to the motion to dismiss admitted that his case would be foreclosed in state court, but he argued that Rule 3 of the Federal Rules of Civil Procedure governs the manner in which an action is commenced in federal court for all purposes, including the tolling of the state statute of limitations.

The District Court dismissed the complaint as barred by the Oklahoma statute of limitations. The court concluded that Okla.Stat., Tit. 12, § 97 (1971) was "an integral part of the Oklahoma statute of limitations," and therefore under *Ragan v. Merchants Transfer & Warehouse Co.,* 337 U.S. 530 (1949), state law applied. The court rejected the argument that *Ragan* had been implicitly overruled in *Hanna v. Plumer,* 380 U.S. 460 (1965). . . The United States Court of Appeals for the Tenth Circuit affirmed. That court concluded that Okla.Stat., Tit. 12, § 97 (1971), was in "direct conflict" with Rule 3. However, the Oklahoma statute was "indistinguishable" from the statute involved in *Ragan,* and the court felt itself "constrained" to follow *Ragan.*

We granted certiorari because of a conflict among the Courts of Appeals. We now affirm.

II

The question whether state or federal law should apply on various issues arising in an action based on state law which has been brought in federal court under diversity of citizenship jurisdiction has troubled this Court for many years. [The Court discussed *Guaranty Trust Co. v. York,* 326 U.S. 99 (1945), supra p. 838, emphasizing its focus on whether not applying state law could substantially affect the outcome.]

The decision in *York* led logically to our holding in *Ragan v. Merchants Transfer & Warehouse Co., supra.* In *Ragan,* the plaintiff had filed his complaint in federal court on September 4, 1945, pursuant to Rule 3 of the Federal Rules of Civil Procedure. The accident from which the claim arose had occurred on October 1, 1943. Service was made on the defendant on

December 28, 1945. The applicable statute of limitations supplied by Kansas law was two years. Kansas had an additional statute [regarding tolling that was essentially identical to the Oklahoma statute at issue here]. The defendant moved for summary judgment on the ground that the Kansas statute of limitations barred the action since service had not been made within either the 2-year period or the 60-day period. It was conceded that had the case been brought in Kansas state court it would have been barred. Nonetheless, the District Court held that the statute had been tolled by the filing of the complaint. The Court of Appeals reversed. . .

We affirmed, relying on *Erie* and *York*. "We cannot give [the cause of action] longer life in the federal court than it would have had in the state court without adding something to the cause of action. We may not do that consistently with *Erie R. Co. v. Tompkins*." 337 U.S., at 533–534. We rejected the argument that Rule 3 of the Federal Rules of Civil Procedure governed the manner in which an action was commenced in federal court for purposes of tolling the state statute of limitations. Instead, we held that the service of summons statute controlled because it was an integral part of the state statute of limitations, and under *York,* that statute of limitations was part of the state-law cause of action.

Ragan was not our last pronouncement in this difficult area, however. In 1965 we decided *Hanna v. Plumer,* 380 U.S. 460, holding that in a civil action where federal jurisdiction was based upon diversity of citizenship, Rule 4(d)(1) of the Federal Rules of Civil Procedure, rather than state law, governed the manner in which process was served. . . The Court in *Hanna* . . . concluded that the *Erie* doctrine was simply not the appropriate test of the validity and applicability of one of the Federal Rules of Civil Procedure:

"The *Erie* rule has never been invoked to void a Federal Rule. It is true that there have been cases where this Court had held applicable a state rule in the face of an argument that the situation was governed by one of the Federal Rules. But the holding of each such case was not that *Erie* commanded displacement of a Federal Rule by an inconsistent state rule, but rather that the scope of the Federal Rule was not as broad as the losing party urged, and therefore, there being no Federal Rule which covered the point in dispute, *Erie* commanded the enforcement of state law." 380 U.S., at 470.

The Court cited *Ragan* as one of the examples of this proposition, 380 U.S., at 470, n. 12. The Court explained that where the Federal Rule was clearly applicable, as in *Hanna,* the test was whether the Rule was within the scope of the Rules Enabling Act, 28 U.S.C. § 2072, and if so, within a constitutional grant of power such as the Necessary and Proper Clause of Art. I.

III

The present case is indistinguishable from *Ragan*. The statutes in both cases require service of process to toll the statute of limitations, and in fact the predecessor to the Oklahoma statute in this case was derived from the predecessor to the Kansas statute in *Ragan*. * * * Here, as in *Ragan*, the complaint was filed in federal court under diversity jurisdiction within the 2-year statute of limitations, but service of process did not occur until after the 2-year period and the 60-day service period had run. In both cases the suit would concededly have been barred in the applicable state court, and in both instances the state service statute was held to be an integral part of the statute of limitations by the lower court more familiar than we with state law. Accordingly, as the Court of Appeals held below, the instant action is barred by the statute of limitations unless *Ragan* is no longer good law.

Petitioner argues that the analysis and holding of *Ragan* did not survive our decision in *Hanna*.[8] Petitioner's position is that Okla.Stat., Tit. 12, § 97 (1971), is in direct conflict with the Federal Rule. Under *Hanna*, petitioner contends, the appropriate question is whether Rule 3 is within the scope of the Rules Enabling Act and, if so, within the constitutional power of Congress. In petitioner's view, the Federal Rule is to be applied unless it violates one of those two restrictions. . .

We note at the outset that the doctrine of *stare decisis* weighs heavily against petitioner in this case. Petitioner seeks to have us overrule our decision in *Ragan*. . . This Court in *Hanna* distinguished *Ragan* rather than overruled it, and for good reason. Application of the *Hanna* analysis is premised on a "direct collision" between the Federal Rule and the state law. In *Hanna* itself the "clash" between Rule 4(d)(1) and the state in-hand service requirement was "unavoidable." The first question must therefore be whether the scope of the Federal Rule in fact is sufficiently broad to control the issue before the Court. It is only if that question is answered affirmatively that the *Hanna* analysis applies.[9]

As has already been noted, we recognized in *Hanna* that the present case is an instance where "the scope of the Federal Rule [is] not as broad as the losing party urge[s], and therefore, there being no Federal Rule which cover[s] the point in dispute, *Erie* command[s] the enforcement of state law." Rule 3 simply states that "[a] civil action is commenced by filing a complaint with the court." There is no indication that the Rule was

---

[8] Mr. Justice Harlan in his concurring opinion in *Hanna* concluded that *Ragan* was no longer good law. 380 U.S., at 474–478. * * *

[9] This is not to suggest that the Federal Rules of Civil Procedure are to be narrowly construed in order to avoid a "direct collision" with state law. The Federal Rules should be given their plain meaning. If a direct collision with state law arises from the plain meaning, then the analysis developed in *Hanna v. Plumer* applies.

intended to toll a state statute of limitations,[10] much less that it purported to displace state tolling rules for purposes of state statutes of limitations. In our view, in diversity actions[11] Rule 3 governs the date from which various timing requirements of the Federal Rules begin to run, but does not affect state statutes of limitations.* * *

In contrast to Rule 3, the Oklahoma statute is a statement of a substantive decision by that State that actual service on, and accordingly actual notice by, the defendant is an integral part of the several policies served by the statute of limitations. * * * The statute of limitations establishes a deadline after which the defendant may legitimately have peace of mind; it also recognizes that after a certain period of time it is unfair to require the defendant to attempt to piece together his defense to an old claim. A requirement of actual service promotes both of those functions of the statute... As such, the service rule must be considered part and parcel of the statute of limitations. Rule 3 does not replace such policy determinations found in state law. Rule 3 and Okla.Stat., Tit. 12, § 97 (1971), can exist side by side, therefore, each controlling its own intended sphere of coverage without conflict.

Since there is no direct conflict between the Federal Rule and the state law, the *Hanna* analysis does not apply. Instead, the policies behind *Erie* and *Ragan* control the issue... [A]lthough in this case failure to apply the state service law might not create any problem of forum shopping, the result would be an "inequitable administration" of the law. *Hanna v. Plumer,* 380 U.S., at 468. There is simply no reason why, in the absence of a controlling federal rule, an action based on state law which concededly

---

[10] "Rule 3 simply provides that an action is commenced by filing the complaint and has as its primary purpose the measuring of time periods that begin running from the date of commencement; the rule does not state that filing tolls the statute of limitations." 4 C. Wright & A. Miller, Federal Practice and Procedure § 1057, p. 191 (1969) (footnote omitted).

The Note of the Advisory Committee on the Rules states:

"When a Federal or State statute of limitations is pleaded as a defense, a question may arise under this rule whether the mere filing of the complaint stops the running of the statute, or whether any further step is required, such as, service of the summons and complaint or their delivery to the marshal for service. The answer to this question may depend on whether it is competent for the Supreme Court, exercising the power to make rules of procedure without affecting substantive rights, to vary the operation of statutes of limitations. The requirement of Rule 4(a) that the clerk shall forthwith issue the summons and deliver it to the marshal for service will reduce the chances of such a question arising." 28 U.S.C.App., pp. 394–395.

This Note establishes that the Advisory Committee predicted the problem which arose in *Ragan* and arises again in the instant case. It does not indicate, however, that Rule 3 was *intended* to serve as a tolling provision for statute of limitations purposes; it only suggests that the Advisory Committee thought the Rule *might* have that effect.

[11] The Court suggested in *Ragan* that in suits to enforce rights under a federal statute Rule 3 means that filing of the complaint tolls the applicable statute of limitations. 337 U.S., at 533, distinguishing *Bomar v. Keyes,* 162 F.2d 136, 140–141 (CA2) (1947). * * * See also *Walko Corp. v. Burger Chef Systems, Inc.,* 554 F.2d, at 1167, n. 19 (D.C.Cir.); 4 Wright & *Miller, supra,* § 1056, and authorities collected therein. We do not here address the role of Rule 3 as a tolling provision for a statute of limitations, whether set by federal law or borrowed from state law, if the cause of action is based on federal law.

would be barred in the state courts by the state statute of limitations should proceed through litigation to judgment in federal court solely because of the fortuity that there is diversity of citizenship between the litigants. The policies underlying diversity jurisdiction do not support such a distinction between state and federal plaintiffs, and *Erie* and its progeny do not permit it.

The judgment of the Court of Appeals is affirmed.

Interpreting Rules of Procedure

(1) Rule 3 states that "[a] civil action is commenced by filing a complaint with the court," but does not specify for what purposes. Two arguments were thus available for the Court in *Walker* to find that Rule 3 did not operate to toll the Oklahoma statute of limitations. First, the Court could have held that Rule 3 applied only to start time periods in other Federal Rules of Civil Procedure, tolling neither state nor federal statutes of limitations. Alternatively, the Court could find that Rule 3 tolled federal but not state statutes of limitations.

Which argument is more persuasive? Which does the Court make in *Walker*? Note that there was abundant authority, cited in footnote 11 of the Court's opinion (including a dictum in *Ragan*), suggesting that Rule 3 did operate to toll federal statutes of limitations. *Walker* reserves this question, holding that, even if Rule 3 governs federal statutes of limitations, it does not apply to state statutes. But if Rule 3 does not toll federal statutes of limitations, what does?

(2) Can you reconcile the Court's interpretation of Rule 3 in *Walker* with its interpretation of Rule 4 in *Hanna*? Rule 4 says simply that service may be made by leaving a copy of the summons and complaint at the defendant's home; it does not qualify this permission in any way or say anything about federal question cases or diversity cases. Therefore, the *Hanna* Court concluded, Rule 4 says "implicitly, but with unmistakable clarity" that in-hand service is not required in either type of case. Rule 3 is equally plain: it says simply that an action is commenced in federal court by filing the complaint. Yet the *Walker* Court assumes, contrary to the apparent intent of the Advisory Note (quoted in footnote 10), that Rule 3 may toll federal but not state statutes of limitations. Why is Rule 4 read broadly, making a clash with state law "unavoidable," while Rule 3 is read to incorporate an implied exception for state statutes? Is the difference that Oklahoma's tolling provision serves a substantive purpose while the Massachusetts service rule in *Hanna* is purely procedural in nature? And what do you make of the statement in footnote 9 that Federal Rules are not "to be narrowly construed in order to avoid a 'direct collision' with state law"? Isn't that exactly what the Court does in *Walker*?

Which approach to interpreting Federal Rules of Civil Procedure makes more sense: *Hanna*'s or *Walker*'s?

(3) *Walker* is not the final word on interpreting the federal rules. In *Burlington Northern Ry. v. Woods,* 480 U.S. 1 (1987), Woods was awarded damages in an Alabama federal district court. After the verdict was affirmed on appeal, the court of appeals assessed a penalty (10% of the damages) prescribed by Alabama law for unsuccessful appeals of money judgments. Burlington Northern objected, arguing that under Federal Rule of Appellate Procedure 38 penalties were appropriate only if the appellate court found the appeal frivolous. The Supreme Court held that Rule 38 governed. Writing for a unanimous Court, Justice Marshall reasoned:

> In *Hanna* . . . we set forth the appropriate test for resolving conflicts between state law and Federal Rules. The initial step is to determine whether, when fairly construed, the scope of Federal Rule 38 is "sufficiently broad" to cause a "direct collision" with the state law or, implicitly, to "control the issue" before the court, thereby leaving no room for the operation of that law. . . The rule must then be applied if it represents a valid exercise of Congress' rule-making authority, which originates in the Constitution and has been bestowed on this Court by the Rules Enabling Act. . .
>
> Rule 38 affords a Court of Appeals plenary discretion to assess "just damages" in order to penalize an appellant who takes a frivolous appeal and to compensate the injured appellee for the delay and added expense of defending the District Court's judgment. Thus, the Rule's discretionary mode of operation unmistakably conflicts with the mandatory provision of Alabama's affirmance penalty statute. Moreover, the purposes underlying the Rule are sufficiently co-extensive with the asserted purposes of the Alabama statute to indicate that the Rule occupies the statute's field of operation so as to preclude its application in federal diversity actions.
>
> Petitioner nevertheless argues that, because Alabama has a similar Appellate Rule which may be applied in state court alongside the affirmance penalty statute, . . . a federal court sitting in diversity could impose the mandatory penalty and likewise remain free to exercise its discretionary authority under Federal Rule 38. This argument, however, ignores the significant possibility that a Court of Appeals may, in any given case, find a limited justification for imposing penalties in an amount *less than 10%* of the lower court's judgment. Federal Rule 38 adopts a case-by-case approach to identifying and deterring frivolous appeals;

> the Alabama statute precludes any exercise of discretion within its scope of operation. Whatever circumscriptive effect the mandatory affirmance penalty statute may have on the state court's exercise of discretion under Alabama's Rule 38, that Rule provides no authority for defining the scope of discretion allowed under Federal Rule 38.

Can you reconcile this analysis with *Walker*? (Note that both opinions were written by Justice Marshall for a unanimous Court.) Is the Alabama penalty substantive or procedural? What purpose is served by interpreting Rule 38 to displace this Alabama rule in a diversity case?

(4) What law determines the effect of a forum selection clause in federal court? In *Stewart Organization, Inc. v. Ricoh Corp.*, 487 U.S. 22 (1988), Stewart contracted to market Ricoh copiers; the agreement included a forum selection clause requiring disputes on the contract to be litigated in New York. Business relations soured, and Stewart sued Ricoh for breach of contract in an Alabama federal district court. Ricoh moved to transfer the case to New York under 28 U.S.C. § 1404(a). The district judge denied the motion, holding that the question of transfer was governed by Alabama law and that Alabama disfavored forum selection clauses. In yet another opinion by Justice Marshall, the Supreme Court held that § 1404(a) governed. According to the Court, "when the federal law sought to be applied is a congressional statute, the first and chief question . . . is whether the statute is sufficiently broad to control the issue before the Court. . . This question involves a straightforward exercise in statutory interpretation to determine if the statute covers the point in dispute." At that point, the Court dropped the following footnote:

> Our cases at times have referred to the question at this stage of the analysis as an inquiry into whether there is a "direct collision" between state and federal law. * * * Logic indicates, however, and a careful reading of the relevant passages confirms, that this language is not meant to mandate that federal law and state law be perfectly co-extensive and equally applicable to the issue at hand; rather, the "direct collision" language, at least where the applicability of a federal statute is at issue, expresses the requirement that the federal statute be sufficiently broad to cover the point in dispute.

If the federal statute covers the point in dispute, however, and if it is constitutional, then under *Hanna* "that is the end of the matter" and a federal court must apply federal law.

Rather than contest the constitutionality of § 1404(a), Ricoh argued that the court could enforce both state and federal law. The Supreme Court disagreed:

> It is true that § 1404(a) and Alabama's putative policy regarding forum-selection clauses are not perfectly coextensive. Section 1404(a) directs a District Court to take account of factors other than those that bear solely on the parties' private ordering of their affairs. . . It is conceivable in a particular case, for example, that because of these factors a District Court acting under § 1404(a) would refuse to transfer a case notwithstanding the counterweight of a forum-selection clause, whereas the coordinate state rule might dictate the opposite result. . . But this potential conflict in fact frames an additional argument for the supremacy of federal law. Congress has directed that multiple considerations govern transfer within the federal court system, and a state policy focusing on a single concern or subset of the factors identified in § 1404(a) would defeat that command. Its application would impoverish the flexible and multifaceted analysis that Congress intended to govern motions to transfer within the federal system. The forum-selection clause, which represents the parties' agreement as to the most proper forum, should receive neither dispositive consideration (as respondent might have it) nor no consideration (as Alabama might have it), but rather the consideration which Congress provided in § 1404(a).

The Court therefore remanded the case; only Justice Scalia dissented.

In *Atlantic Maritime Construction Co. v. District Court*, 571 U.S. 49, 64 (2013), the Court offered more clarity about the weight that should be given to a valid forum selection clause in the § 1404(a) analysis: a valid clause "should control except in unusual cases." But which law should be used to determine validity: federal law, or the law governing the contract? The circuits are split and scholars disagree. See Roosevelt & Jones, *Adrift on* Erie: *Characterizing Forum-Selection Clauses*, 52 Akron L. Rev. 297 (2018). And is there any way to enforce a forum selection clause other than a motion under § 1404(a)? See Sachs, *The Forum Selection Defense*, 10 Duke J. Const. L. & Pub. Pol'y 1 (2015) (suggesting motion to dismiss or for summary judgment).

GASPERINI V. CENTER FOR HUMANITIES, INC.

518 U.S. 415 (1996).

JUSTICE GINSBURG delivered the opinion of the Court.

Under the law of New York, appellate courts are empowered to review the size of jury verdicts and to order new trials when the jury's award "deviates materially from what would be reasonable compensation." N.Y. Civ. Prac. Law and Rules (CPLR) § 5501(c) (McKinney 1995). Under the Seventh Amendment, which governs proceedings in federal court, but not in state court, "the right of trial by jury shall be preserved, and no fact tried by a jury, shall be otherwise re-examined in any Court of the United States, than according to the rules of the common law." The compatibility of these provisions, in an action based on New York law but tried in federal court by reason of the parties' diverse citizenship, is the issue we confront in this case. We hold that New York's law controlling compensation awards for excessiveness or inadequacy can be given effect, without detriment to the Seventh Amendment, if the review standard set out in CPLR § 5501(c) is applied by the federal trial court judge, with appellate control of the trial court's ruling limited to review for "abuse of discretion."

I

Petitioner William Gasperini, a journalist for CBS News and the Christian Science Monitor, began reporting on events in Central America in 1984. He earned his living primarily in radio and print media and only occasionally sold his photographic work. During the course of his seven-year stint in Central America, Gasperini took over 5,000 slide transparencies, depicting active war zones, political leaders, and scenes from daily life. In 1990, Gasperini agreed to supply his original color transparencies to The Center for Humanities, Inc. (Center) for use in an educational videotape, Conflict in Central America. Gasperini selected 300 of his slides for the Center; its videotape included 110 of them. The Center agreed to return the original transparencies, but upon the completion of the project, it could not find them.

Gasperini commenced suit in the United States District Court for the Southern District of New York, invoking the court's diversity jurisdiction pursuant to 28 U.S.C. § 1332. He alleged several state-law claims for relief, including breach of contract, conversion, and negligence. The Center conceded liability for the lost transparencies and the issue of damages was tried before a jury.

At trial, Gasperini's expert witness testified that the "industry standard" within the photographic publishing community valued a lost transparency at $1,500. This industry standard, the expert explained, represented the average license fee a commercial photograph could earn over the full course of the photographer's copyright, *i.e.*, in Gasperini's case, his lifetime plus 50 years. Gasperini estimated that his earnings from photography totaled just over $10,000 for the period from 1984 through 1993. He also testified that he intended to produce a book containing his best photographs from Central America.

After a three-day trial, the jury awarded Gasperini $450,000 in compensatory damages. This sum, the jury foreperson announced, "is [$]1500 each, for 300 slides." Moving for a new trial under Federal Rule of Civil Procedure 59, the Center attacked the verdict on various grounds, including excessiveness. Without comment, the District Court denied the motion.

The Court of Appeals for the Second Circuit vacated the judgment entered on the jury's verdict. 66 F.3d 427 (1995). Mindful that New York law governed the controversy, the Court of Appeals endeavored to apply CPLR § 5501(c), which instructs that, when a jury returns an itemized verdict, as the jury did in this case, the New York Appellate Division "shall determine that an award is excessive or inadequate if it deviates materially from what would be reasonable compensation." The Second Circuit's application of § 5501(c) as a check on the size of the jury's verdict followed Circuit precedent elaborated two weeks earlier in *Consorti v. Armstrong World Industries, Inc.*, 64 F.3d 781, superseded, 72 F.3d 1003 (1995). Surveying Appellate Division decisions that reviewed damage awards for lost transparencies, the Second Circuit concluded that testimony on industry standard alone was insufficient to justify a verdict; prime among other factors warranting consideration were the uniqueness of the slides' subject matter and the photographer's earning level.

Guided by Appellate Division rulings, the Second Circuit held that the $450,000 verdict "materially deviates from what is reasonable compensation." * * * Some of Gasperini's transparencies, the Second Circuit recognized, were unique, notably those capturing combat situations in which Gasperini was the only photographer present. * * * But others "depicted either generic scenes or events at which other professional photojournalists were present." * * * No more than 50 slides merited a $1,500 award, the court concluded, after "[g]iving Gasperini every benefit of the doubt." * * * Absent evidence showing significant earnings from photographic endeavors or concrete plans to publish a book, the court further determined, any damage award above $100 each for the remaining slides would be excessive. Remittiturs "presen[t] difficult problems for appellate courts," the Second Circuit acknowledged, for court of appeals judges review the evidence from "a cold paper record." * * * Nevertheless, the Second Circuit set aside the $450,000 verdict and ordered a new trial, unless Gasperini agreed to an award of $100,000.

This case presents an important question regarding the standard a federal court uses to measure the alleged excessiveness of a jury's verdict in an action for damages based on state law. We therefore granted certiorari.

II

Before 1986, state and federal courts in New York generally invoked the same judge-made formulation in responding to excessiveness attacks on jury verdicts: courts would not disturb an award unless the amount was so exorbitant that it "shocked the conscience of the court." . . .

In both state and federal courts, trial judges made the excessiveness assessment in the first instance, and appellate judges ordinarily deferred to the trial court's judgment. * * *

In 1986, as part of a series of tort reform measures, New York codified a standard for judicial review of the size of jury awards. Placed in CPLR § 5501(c), the prescription reads:

> "In reviewing a money judgment . . . in which it is contended that the award is excessive or inadequate and that a new trial should have been granted unless a stipulation is entered to a different award, the appellate division shall determine that an award is excessive or inadequate if it deviates materially from what would be reasonable compensation."

As stated in Legislative Findings and Declarations accompanying New York's adoption of the "deviates materially" formulation, the lawmakers found the "shock the conscience" test an insufficient check on damage awards; the legislature therefore installed a standard "invit[ing] more careful appellate scrutiny." At the same time, the legislature instructed the Appellate Division . . . to state the reasons for the court's rulings on the size of verdicts, and the factors the court considered in complying with § 5501(c). In his signing statement, then-Governor Mario Cuomo emphasized that the CPLR amendments were meant to ratchet up the review standard: "This will assure greater scrutiny of the amount of verdicts and promote greater stability in the tort system and greater fairness for similarly situated defendants throughout the State." * * *

New York state-court opinions confirm that § 5501(c)'s "deviates materially" standard calls for closer surveillance than "shock the conscience" oversight. * * *

Although phrased as a direction to New York's intermediate appellate courts, § 5501(c)'s "deviates materially" standard, as construed by New York's courts, instructs state trial judges as well. * * * Application of § 5501(c) at the trial level is key to this case.

To determine whether an award "deviates materially from what would be reasonable compensation," New York state courts look to awards approved in similar cases. * * * Under New York's former "shock the conscience" test, courts also referred to analogous cases. * * * The "deviates materially" standard, however, in design and operation, influences outcomes by tightening the range of tolerable awards. * * *

III

In cases like Gasperini's, in which New York law governs the claims for relief, does New York law also supply the test for federal court review of the size of the verdict? The Center answers yes. The "deviates materially" standard, it argues, is a substantive standard that must be applied by federal appellate courts in diversity cases. The Second Circuit agreed. * * * Gasperini, emphasizing that § 5501(c) trains on the New York Appellate Division, characterizes the provision as procedural, an allocation of decisionmaking authority regarding damages, not a hard cap on the amount recoverable. Correctly comprehended, Gasperini urges, § 5501(c)'s direction to the Appellate Division cannot be given effect by federal appellate courts without violating the Seventh Amendment's re-examination clause.

As the parties' arguments suggest, CPLR § 5501(c), appraised under *Erie R. Co. v. Tompkins*, 304 U.S. 64 (1938), and decisions in *Erie*'s path, is both "substantive" and "procedural": "substantive" in that § 5501(c)'s "deviates materially" standard controls how much a plaintiff can be awarded; "procedural" in that § 5501(c) assigns decisionmaking authority to New York's Appellate Division. Parallel application of § 5501(c) at the federal appellate level would be out of sync with the federal system's division of trial and appellate court functions, an allocation weighted by the Seventh Amendment. The dispositive question, therefore, is whether federal courts can give effect to the substantive thrust of § 5501(c) without untoward alteration of the federal scheme for the trial and decision of civil cases.

A . . .

Classification of a law as "substantive" or "procedural" for *Erie* purposes is sometimes a challenging endeavor.[7] *Guaranty Trust Co. v. York*, 326 U.S. 99 (1945), an early interpretation of *Erie*, propounded an "outcome-determination" test: "[D]oes it significantly affect the result of a litigation for a federal court to disregard a law of a State that would be controlling in an action upon the same claim by the same parties in a State court?" 326 U.S., at 109. . . A later pathmarking case, qualifying *Guaranty Trust*, explained that the "outcome-determination" test must not be applied mechanically to sweep in all manner of variations; instead, its application must be guided by "the twin aims of the *Erie* rule: discouragement of forum-shopping and avoidance of inequitable administration of the laws." *Hanna v. Plumer*, 380 U.S. 460, 468 (1965).

Informed by these decisions, we address the question whether New York's "deviates materially" standard, codified in CPLR § 5501(c), is outcome-affective in this sense: Would "application of the [standard] . . . have so important an effect upon the fortunes of one or both of the litigants that failure to [apply] it would [unfairly discriminate against citizens of the forum State, or] be likely to cause a plaintiff to choose the federal court"? *Id.*, at 468, n. 9.

---

[7] Concerning matters covered by the Federal Rules of Civil Procedure, the characterization question is usually unproblematic: It is settled that if the Rule in point is consonant with the Rules Enabling Act, 28 U.S.C. § 2072, and the Constitution, the Federal Rule applies regardless of contrary state law. See *Hanna v. Plumer*, 380 U.S. 460, 469–474 (1965); *Burlington Northern R. Co. v. Woods*, 480 U.S. 1, 4–5 (1987). Federal courts have interpreted the Federal Rules, however, with sensitivity to important state interests and regulatory policies. See, *e.g.*, *Walker v. Armco Steel Corp.*, 446 U.S. 740, 750–752 (1980) * * *.

We start from a point the parties do not debate. Gasperini acknowledges that a statutory cap on damages would supply substantive law for *Erie* purposes. * * * Although CPLR § 5501(c) is less readily classified, it was designed to provide an analogous control. . .

[New York law instructs the court to review verdicts more closely, to engage in more rigorous comparative evaluations, and to state its reasons for altering a verdict.] We think it a fair conclusion that CPLR § 5501(c) differs from a statutory cap principally "in that the maximum amount recoverable is not set by statute, but rather is determined by case law." * * * In sum, § 5501(c) contains a procedural instruction, but the State's objective is manifestly substantive. * * *

It thus appears that if federal courts ignore the change in the New York standard and persist in applying the "shock the conscience" test to damage awards on claims governed by New York law, " 'substantial' variations between state and federal [money judgments]" may be expected. * * * We therefore agree with the Second Circuit that New York's check on excessive damages implicates what we have called *Erie*'s "twin aims." Just as the *Erie* principle precludes a federal court from giving a state-created claim "longer life . . . than [the claim] would have had in the state court," * * * so *Erie* precludes a recovery in federal court significantly larger than the recovery that would have been tolerated in state court.

B

CPLR § 5501(c), as earlier noted, is phrased as a direction to the New York Appellate Division. Acting essentially as a surrogate for a New York appellate forum, the Court of Appeals reviewed Gasperini's award to determine if it "deviate[d] materially" from damage awards the Appellate Division permitted in similar circumstances. . . Gasperini urges that the provision shifts fact-finding responsibility from the jury and the trial judge to the appellate court. Assigning such responsibility to an appellate court, he maintains, is incompatible with the Seventh Amendment's re-examination clause, and therefore, Gasperini concludes, § 5501(c) cannot be given effect in federal court. Although we reach a different conclusion than Gasperini, we agree that the Second Circuit did not attend to "[a]n essential characteristic of [the federal-court] system," *Byrd v. Blue Ridge Rural Elec. Cooperative, Inc.*, 356 U.S. 525, 537 (1958), when it used § 5501(c) as "the standard for [federal] appellate review," *Consorti*, 72 F.3d, at 1013 * * *.

That "essential characteristic" was described in *Byrd*, a diversity suit for negligence in which a pivotal issue of fact would have been tried by a judge were the case in state court. The *Byrd* Court held that, despite the state practice, the plaintiff was entitled to a jury trial in federal court. In so ruling, the Court said that the *Guaranty Trust* "outcome-determination" test was an insufficient guide in cases presenting countervailing federal interests. * * * The Court described the countervailing federal interests present in *Byrd* this way:

> "The federal system is an independent system for administering justice to litigants who properly invoke its jurisdiction. An essential characteristic of that system is the manner in which, in civil common-law actions, it distributes trial functions between judge and jury and, under the influence—if not the command—of the Seventh Amendment, assigns the decisions of disputed questions of fact to the jury." * * *

The Seventh Amendment, which governs proceedings in federal court, but not in state court, bears not only on the allocation of trial functions between judge and jury, the issue in *Byrd*; it also controls the allocation of authority to review verdicts, the issue of concern here. . .

Byrd involved the first clause of the Amendment, the "trial by jury" clause. This case involves the second, the "re-examination" clause. In keeping with the historic understanding, the re-examination clause does not inhibit the authority of trial judges to grant new trials "for any of the reasons for which new trials have heretofore been granted in actions at law in the courts of the United States." Fed. Rule Civ. Proc. 59(a). That authority is large. * * * "The trial judge in the federal system," we have reaffirmed, "has . . . discretion to grant a new trial if the verdict appears to [the judge] to be against the weight of the evidence." * * * This discretion includes overturning verdicts for excessiveness and ordering a new trial without qualification, or conditioned on the verdict winner's refusal to agree to a reduction (remittitur). See *Dimick v. Schiedt*, 293 U.S. 474, 486–487 (1935) (recognizing that remittitur withstands Seventh Amendment attack, but rejecting additur as unconstitutional).

In contrast, appellate review of a federal trial court's denial of a motion to set aside a jury's verdict as excessive is a relatively late, and less secure, development. [The Court then held that nothing in the Seventh Amendment precludes appellate review of the trial judge's ruling on a motion to set aside a jury verdict as excessive.]

C

In *Byrd*, the Court faced a one-or-the-other choice: trial by judge as in state court, or trial by jury according to the federal practice. In the case before us, a choice of that order is not required, for the principal state and federal interests can be accommodated. The Second Circuit correctly recognized that when New York substantive law governs a claim for relief, New York law and decisions guide the allowable damages. * * * But that court did not take into account the characteristic of the federal-court system that caused us to reaffirm: "The proper role of the trial and appellate courts in the federal system in reviewing the size of jury verdicts is . . . a matter of federal law." * * *.

New York's dominant interest can be respected, without disrupting the federal system, once it is recognized that the federal district court is capable of performing the checking function, *i.e.*, that court can apply the State's "deviates materially" standard in line with New York case law evolving under CPLR § 5501(c).[22] We recall, in this regard, that the "deviates materially" standard serves as the guide to be applied in trial as well as appellate courts in New York.

Within the federal system, practical reasons combine with Seventh Amendment constraints to lodge in the district court, not the court of appeals, primary responsibility for application of § 5501(c)'s "deviates materially" check. Trial judges have the "unique opportunity to consider the evidence in the living courtroom context," * * * while appellate judges see only the "cold paper record," * * *.

District court applications of the "deviates materially" standard would be subject to appellate review under the standard the Circuits now employ when inadequacy or excessiveness is asserted on appeal: abuse of discretion. * * * In light of *Erie*'s doctrine, the federal appeals court must be guided by the damage-control standard state law supplies, but as the Second Circuit itself has said: "If we reverse, it must be because of an abuse of discretion. . . The very nature of the problem counsels restraint. . . We must give the benefit of every doubt to the judgment of the trial judge." * * *

IV

It does not appear that the District Court checked the jury's verdict against the relevant New York decisions demanding more than "industry standard" testimony to support an award of the size the jury returned in this case. As the Court of Appeals recognized, * * * the uniqueness of the photographs and the plaintiff's earnings as photographer—past and reasonably projected—are factors relevant to appraisal of the award. * * * Accordingly, we vacate the judgment of the Court of Appeals and instruct that court to remand the case to the District Court so that the trial judge, revisiting his ruling on the new trial motion, may test the jury's verdict against CLPR § 5501(c)'s "deviates materially" standard.

[JUSTICE STEVENS dissented, arguing that the decision of the court of appeals should be affirmed because "there is no reason to suppose that [it] has reached a conclusion with which the District Court could permissibly

[22] JUSTICE SCALIA finds in Federal Rule of Civil Procedure 59 a "federal standard" for new trial motions in "direct collision" with, and "leaving no room for the operation of," a state law like CPLR § 5501(c). * * * The relevant prescription, Rule 59(a), has remained unchanged since the adoption of the Federal Rules by this Court in 1937. * * * Rule 59(a) is as encompassing as it is uncontroversial. It is indeed "Hornbook" law that a most usual ground for a Rule 59 motion is that "the damages are excessive." * * * Whether damages are excessive for the claim-in-suit must be governed by some law. And there is no candidate for that governance other than the law that gives rise to the claim for relief—here, the law of New York.

disagree on remand. . ." He also disagreed that the Seventh Amendment has any bearing on how a federal appellate court reviews the district court in a diversity case. *Byrd* dealt only with the Amendment's first clause, requiring trial by jury, and not with the re-examination clause. Moreover, "[t]he majority's persuasive demonstration that New York law sets forth a substantive limitation on the size of jury awards seems to refute the contention that New York has merely asked appellate courts to reexamine facts. The majority's analysis would thus seem to undermine the conclusion that the Reexamination Clause is relevant to this case." Justice Stevens went on to conclude:

> My disagreement is tempered, however, because the majority carefully avoids defining too strictly the abuse of discretion standard it announces. To the extent that the majority relies only on "practical reasons" for its conclusion that the Court of Appeals should give some weight to the District Court's assessment in determining whether state substantive law has been properly applied, I do not disagree with its analysis. . .
>
> In the end, therefore, my disagreement with the label that the majority attaches to the standard of appellate review should not obscure the far more fundamental point on which we agree. Whatever influence the Seventh Amendment may be said to exert, *Erie* requires federal appellate courts sitting in diversity to apply "the damage control standard state law supplies."]

JUSTICE SCALIA, with whom THE CHIEF JUSTICE and JUSTICE THOMAS join, dissenting.

[JUSTICE SCALIA first dissents from the Court's holding that the Seventh Amendment permits appellate review of a trial judge's decision to set aside a verdict as excessive.]

II . . .

The Court also directs that the case be remanded to the District Court, so that it may "test the jury's verdict against CPLR § 5501(c)'s 'deviates materially' standard." This disposition contradicts the principle that "[t]he proper role of the trial and appellate courts in the federal system in reviewing the size of jury verdicts is . . . a matter of federal law." * * *

The Court acknowledges that state procedural rules cannot, as a general matter, be permitted to interfere with the allocation of functions in the federal court system. . . But changing the standard by which trial judges review jury verdicts *does* disrupt the federal system, and is plainly inconsistent with "the strong federal policy against allowing state rules to disrupt the judge-jury relationship in federal court." *Byrd v. Blue Ridge Rural Elec. Cooperative, Inc.*, 356 U.S. 525, 538 (1958). The Court's opinion does not even acknowledge, let alone address, this dislocation. . .

The Court [says that state law should apply] at least where the state rule that governs "whether a new trial or remittitur should be ordered" is characterized as "substantive" in nature. That, at any rate, is the reason the Court asserts for giving § 5501(c) dispositive effect. The objective of that provision, the Court states, "is manifestly substantive," since it operates to "contro[l] how much a plaintiff can be awarded" by "tightening the range of tolerable awards." Although "less readily classified" as substantive than "a statutory cap on damages," it nonetheless "was designed to provide an analogous control," by making a new trial mandatory when the award "deviat[es] materially" from what is reasonable.

I do not see how this can be so. It seems to me quite wrong to regard this provision as a "substantive" rule for *Erie* purposes. The "analog[y]" to "a statutory cap on damages" fails utterly. There is an absolutely fundamental distinction between a *rule of law* such as that, which would ordinarily be imposed upon the jury in the trial court's instructions, and a *rule of review*, which simply determines how closely the jury verdict will be scrutinized for compliance with the instructions. A tighter standard for reviewing jury determinations can no more plausibly be called a "substantive" disposition than can a tighter appellate standard for reviewing trial-court determinations. The one, like the other, provides additional assurance *that the law has been complied with*; but the other, like the one, *leaves the law unchanged.*

The Court commits the classic *Erie* mistake of regarding whatever changes the outcome as substantive. That is not the only factor to be considered. See *Byrd*, 356 U.S., at 537. . . Outcome-determination "was never intended to serve as a talisman," *Hanna v. Plumer*, 380 U.S. 460, 466–467 (1965), and does not have the power to convert the most classic elements of the process of assuring that the law is observed into the substantive law itself. The right to have a jury make the findings of fact, for example, is generally thought to favor plaintiffs, and that advantage is often thought significant enough to be the basis for forum selection. But no one would argue that *Erie* confers a right to a jury in federal court wherever state courts would provide it; or that, were it not for the Seventh Amendment, *Erie* would require federal courts to dispense with the jury whenever state courts do so.

In any event, the Court exaggerates the difference that the state standard will make. It concludes that different outcomes are likely to ensue depending on whether the law being applied is the state "deviates materially" standard of § 5501(c) or the "shocks the conscience" standard. [But the standard applied by the federal courts has varied considerably at the district court level. It is therefore] at least highly questionable whether the consistent outcome differential claimed by the Court even exists. What seems to me far more likely to produce forum-shopping is the consistent difference between the state and federal *appellate* standards, which the Court leaves untouched. . .

To say that application of § 5501(c) in place of the federal standard will not consistently produce disparate results is not to suggest that the decision the Court has made today is not a momentous one. The *principle* that the state standard governs is of great importance, since it bears the potential to destroy the uniformity of federal practice and the integrity of the federal court system. Under the Court's view, a state rule that directed courts "to determine that an award is excessive or inadequate if it deviates *in any degree* from *the proper measure of compensation*" would have to be applied in federal courts, effectively requiring federal judges to determine the amount of damages *de novo,* and effectively taking the matter away from the jury entirely. * * * Or consider a state rule that allowed the defendant a second trial on damages, with judgment ultimately in the amount of the lesser of two jury awards. * * * Under the reasoning of the Court's opinion, even such a rule as that would have to be applied in the federal courts.

The foregoing describes why I think the Court's *Erie* analysis is flawed. But in my view, one does not even reach the *Erie* question in this case. The standard to be applied by a district court in ruling on a motion for a new trial is set forth in Rule 59 of the Federal Rules of Civil Procedure, which provides that "[a] new trial may be granted . . . for any of the reasons for which new trials have heretofore been granted in actions at law *in the courts of the United States*" (emphasis added). That is undeniably a federal standard. . . Assuming (as we have no reason to question) that this is a correct interpretation of what Rule 59 requires, it is undeniable that the federal rule is " 'sufficiently broad' to cause a 'direct collision' with the state law or, implicitly, to 'control the issue' before the court, thereby leaving no room for the operation of that law." *Burlington Northern R. Co. v. Woods,* 480 U.S. 1, 4–5 (1987). It is simply not possible to give controlling effect both to the federal standard and the state standard in reviewing the jury's award. That being so, the court has no choice but to apply the Federal Rule, which is an exercise of what we have called Congress's "power to regulate matters which, though falling within the uncertain area between substance and procedure, are rationally capable of classification as either," *Hanna,* 380 U.S., at 472. . .

Byrd Redux

(1) What test does the Court apply in this case? Is the choice between the state and federal rules in this case difficult because it is outcome determinative? Or is the critical factor that the state rule is substantive?

Or must the state rule be both substantive and outcome determinative before the *Erie* question becomes close?

Justice Scalia says the New York rule is not substantive because it is a "rule of review" rather than a "rule of law." What does that mean? Is this a purely formal test? Scalia accuses the majority of mistakenly treating as substantive for *Erie* purposes anything that changes the outcome. Is that what the Court does, or does the majority's test of substance turn on a law's purpose? But, then, how does the substance/procedure inquiry relate to the question of outcome determinativeness?

(2) What is the relationship between this case and *Hanna, Burlington Northern*, and *Ricoh*? In those cases, the Court held that federal law applies so long as it is (a) legitimate and (b) broad enough to cover the point in dispute. The federal rule at issue in *Gasperini* is unquestionably legitimate (otherwise what standard would govern review of jury verdicts in federal question cases?), and it is obviously broad enough to cover the point in dispute. So why doesn't it apply?

(3) The Court relies on *Byrd* for its analysis and conclusion. But what distinguishes *Byrd* from *Hanna, Burlington Northern*, and *Ricoh*? Is the critical distinction that the rule at issue here is a matter of federal common law? Justice Scalia argues that Rule 59 commands using the federal standard. If he is wrong (is he?), why should that make a difference? Or is *Byrd* applicable only in cases involving the right to trial by jury? Does that make sense?

What role, if any, does the Seventh Amendment actually play in this case?

(4) The Court reaches its Solomonic conclusion by balancing state and federal interests. Is this the sort of balancing contemplated by *Byrd*? Does the result make sense? Note how the Court takes a New York standard written for state appellate judges and extended for convenience to state trial courts and holds that it should be applied by federal trial courts but not federal appellate courts. Isn't this a funny way of respecting state interests? The problem of balancing state and federal interests in this context is examined in Bauer, *The* Erie *Doctrine Revisited: How a Conflicts Perspective Can Aid the Analysis,* 74 Notre Dame L. Rev. 1235, 1281–99 (1999).

SEMTEK INTERNATIONAL INC. V. LOCKHEED MARTIN CORP.

531 U.S. 497 (2001).

JUSTICE SCALIA delivered the opinion of the Court.

This case presents the question whether the claim-preclusive effect of a federal judgment dismissing a diversity action on statute-of-limitations grounds is determined by the law of the State in which the federal court sits.

I

[Semtek sued Lockheed for breach of contract and various business torts in California state court. Lockheed removed the action to the Federal District Court, which dismissed Semtek's complaint under California's 2-year statute of limitations; the court specified in its order that Semtek's claims were dismissed "in [their] entirety on the merits and with prejudice." After this decision was affirmed on appeal, Semtek filed the same action in Maryland, which has a longer statute of limitations. Lockheed's effort to remove the action failed, as the company was a citizen of Maryland for purposes of diversity jurisdiction, but the Maryland trial court granted Lockheed's motion to dismiss for res judicata. Semtek appealed, arguing that a California state court would not have accorded claim-preclusive effect to a statute-of-limitations dismissal by one of its own courts. The Maryland appeals court affirmed the dismissal, holding that the res judicata effect of a federal diversity judgment is a matter of federal law and that the judgment was preclusive. The U.S. Supreme Court granted certiorari.]

II

Petitioner contends that the outcome of this case is controlled by *Dupasseur v. Rochereau,* 21 Wall. 130, 135 (1875), which held that the res judicata effect of a federal diversity judgment "is such as would belong to judgments of the State courts rendered under similar circumstances," and may not be accorded any "higher sanctity or effect." Since, petitioner argues, the dismissal of an action on statute-of-limitations grounds by a California state court would not be claim preclusive, it follows that the similar dismissal of this diversity action by the California federal court cannot be claim preclusive. While we agree that this would be the result demanded by *Dupasseur,* the case is not dispositive because it was decided under the Conformity Act of 1872, 17 Stat. 196, which required federal courts to apply the procedural law of the forum State in nonequity cases. That arguably affected the outcome of the case. * * *

Respondent, for its part, contends that the outcome of this case is controlled by Federal Rule of Civil Procedure 41(b), which provides as follows:

> "Involuntary Dismissal: Effect Thereof. For failure of the plaintiff to prosecute or to comply with these rules or any order of court, a defendant may move for dismissal of an action or of any claim against the defendant. Unless the court in its order for dismissal otherwise specifies, a dismissal under this subdivision and any dismissal not provided for in this rule, other than a dismissal for lack of jurisdiction, for improper venue, or for failure to join a

> party under Rule 19, operates as an adjudication upon the merits."

Since the dismissal here did not "otherwise specif[y]" (indeed, it specifically stated that it was "on the merits"), and did not pertain to the excepted subjects of jurisdiction, venue, or joinder, it follows, respondent contends, that the dismissal "is entitled to claim preclusive effect." * * *

Implicit in this reasoning is the unstated minor premise that all judgments denominated "on the merits" are entitled to claim-preclusive effect. That premise is not necessarily valid. The original connotation of an "on the merits" adjudication is one that actually "pass[es] directly on the substance of [a particular] claim" before the court. Restatement [(Second) of Judgments] § 19, Comment a, at 161. That connotation remains common to every jurisdiction of which we are aware. See *ibid.* ("The prototyp[ical] [judgment on the merits is] one in which the merits of [a party's] claim are in fact adjudicated [for or] against the [party] after trial of the substantive issues"). And it is, we think, the meaning intended in those many statements to the effect that a judgment "on the merits" triggers the doctrine of res judicata or claim preclusion. See, *e.g., Parklane Hosiery Co. v. Shore,* 439 U.S. 322, 326, n. 5 (1979) ("Under the doctrine of res judicata, a judgment on the merits in a prior suit bars a second suit involving the same parties or their privies based on the same cause of action"); *Goddard v. Security Title Ins. & Guarantee Co.,* 14 Cal.2d 47, 51, 92 P.2d 804, 806 (1939) ("[A] final judgment, rendered upon the merits by a court having jurisdiction of the cause . . . is a complete bar to a new suit between [the parties or their privies] on the same cause of action").

But over the years the meaning of the term "judgment on the merits" "has gradually undergone change," R. Marcus, M. Redish, & E. Sherman, Civil Procedure: A Modern Approach 1140–1141 (3d ed. 2000), and it has come to be applied to some judgments (such as the one involved here) that do not pass upon the substantive merits of a claim and hence do not (in many jurisdictions) entail claim-preclusive effect. Compare, *e.g., Western Coal & Mining Co. v. Jones,* 27 Cal.2d 819, 826, 167 P.2d 719, 724 (1946), and *Koch v. Rodlin Enterprises, Inc.,* 223 Cal.App.3d 1591, 1596, 273 Cal.Rptr. 438, 441 (1990), with *Plaut v. Spendthrift Farm, Inc.,* 514 U.S. 211, 228 (1995) (statute of limitations); *Goddard, supra,* at 50–51, 92 P.2d, at 806–807, and *Allston v. Incorporated Village of Rockville Centre,* 25 App.Div.2d 545, 546, 267 N.Y.S.2d 564, 565–566 (1966), with *Federated Department Stores, Inc. v. Moitie,* 452 U.S. 394, 399, n. 3 (1981) (demurrer or failure to state a claim). * * * That is why the Restatement of Judgments has abandoned the use of the term—"because of its possibly misleading connotations," Restatement § 19, Comment a, at 161.

In short, it is no longer true that a judgment "on the merits" is necessarily a judgment entitled to claim-preclusive effect; and there are a number of reasons for believing that the phrase "adjudication upon the merits" does not bear that meaning in Rule 41(b). To begin with, Rule 41(b) sets forth nothing more than a default rule for determining the import of a dismissal (a dismissal is "upon the merits," with the three stated exceptions, unless the court "otherwise specifies"). This would be a highly peculiar context in which to announce a federally prescribed rule on the complex question of claim preclusion, saying in effect, "All federal dismissals (with three specified exceptions) preclude suit elsewhere, unless the court otherwise specifies." And even apart from the purely default character of Rule 41(b), it would be peculiar to find a rule governing the effect that must be accorded federal judgments by other courts ensconced in rules governing the internal procedures of the rendering court itself. Indeed, such a rule would arguably violate the jurisdictional limitation of the Rules Enabling Act: that the Rules "shall not abridge, enlarge or modify any substantive right," 28 U.S.C. § 2072(b). * * * In the present case, for example, if California law left petitioner free to sue on this claim in Maryland even after the California statute of limitations had expired, the federal court's extinguishment of that right (through Rule 41(b)'s mandated claim-preclusive effect of its judgment) would seem to violate this limitation.

Moreover, as so interpreted, the Rule would in many cases violate the federalism principle of *Erie R. Co. v. Tompkins*, 304 U.S. 64, 78–80 (1938), by engendering " 'substantial' variations [in outcomes] between state and federal litigation" which would "[l]ikely . . . influence the choice of a forum," *Hanna v. Plumer,* 380 U.S. 460, 467–468 (1965). See also *Guaranty Trust Co. v. York,* 326 U.S. 99, 108–110 (1945). Cf. *Walker v. Armco Steel Corp.,* 446 U.S. 740, 748–753 (1980). With regard to the claim-preclusion issue involved in the present case, for example, the traditional rule is that expiration of the applicable statute of limitations merely bars the remedy and does not extinguish the substantive right, so that dismissal on that ground does not have claim-preclusive effect in other jurisdictions with longer, unexpired limitation periods. * * * Out-of-state defendants sued on stale claims in California and in other States adhering to this traditional rule would systematically remove state-law suits brought against them to federal court—where, unless otherwise specified, a statute-of-limitations dismissal would bar suit everywhere. . .

We think the key to a more reasonable interpretation of the meaning of "operates as an adjudication upon the merits" in Rule 41(b) is to be found in Rule 41(a), which, in discussing the effect of voluntary dismissal by the plaintiff, makes clear that an "adjudication upon the merits" is the opposite of a "dismissal without prejudice":

> "Unless otherwise stated in the notice of dismissal or stipulation, the dismissal is without prejudice, except that a notice of dismissal operates as an adjudication upon the merits when filed

> by a plaintiff who has once dismissed in any court of the United States or of any state an action based on or including the same claim."

* * * The primary meaning of "dismissal without prejudice," we think, is dismissal without barring the defendant from returning later, to the same court, with the same underlying claim. That will also ordinarily (though not always) have the consequence of not barring the claim from other courts, but its primary meaning relates to the dismissing court itself. . .

We think, then, that the effect of the "adjudication upon the merits" default provision of Rule 41(b)—and, presumably, of the explicit order in the present case that used the language of that default provision—is simply that, unlike a dismissal "without prejudice," the dismissal in the present case barred refiling of the same claim in the United States District Court for the Central District of California. That is undoubtedly a necessary condition, but it is not a sufficient one, for claim-preclusive effect in other courts.[12]

III

Having concluded that the claim-preclusive effect, in Maryland, of this California federal diversity judgment is dictated neither by *Dupasseur v. Rochereau,* as petitioner contends, nor by Rule 41(b), as respondent contends, we turn to consideration of what determines the issue. Neither the Full Faith and Credit Clause, U.S. Const., Art. IV, § 1, nor the full faith and credit statute, 28 U.S.C. § 1738, addresses the question. By their terms they govern the effects to be given only to state-court judgments (and, in the case of the statute, to judgments by courts of territories and possessions). And no other federal textual provision, neither of the Constitution nor of any statute, addresses the claim-preclusive effect of a judgment in a federal diversity action.

It is also true, however, that no federal textual provision addresses the claim-preclusive effect of a federal-court judgment in a federal-question case, yet we have long held that States cannot give those judgments merely whatever effect they would give their own judgments, but must accord them the effect that this Court prescribes. * * * The reasoning of that line of cases suggests, moreover, that even when States are allowed to give federal judgments (notably, judgments in diversity cases) no more than the effect accorded to state judgments, that disposition is by direction of this Court, which has the last word on the claim-preclusive effect of all federal

[12] We do not decide whether, in a diversity case, a federal court's "dismissal upon the merits" (in the sense we have described), under circumstances where a state court would decree only a "dismissal without prejudice," abridges a "substantive right" and thus exceeds the authorization of the Rules Enabling Act. We think the situation will present itself more rarely than would the arguable violation of the Act that would ensue from interpreting Rule 41(b) as a rule of claim preclusion; and if it is a violation, can be more easily dealt with on direct appeal.

judgments. . . In short, federal common law governs the claim-preclusive effect of a dismissal by a federal court sitting in diversity. * * *

It is left to us, then, to determine the appropriate federal rule. And despite the sea change that has occurred in the background law since *Dupasseur* was decided—not only repeal of the Conformity Act but also the watershed decision of this Court in *Erie*—we think the result decreed by *Dupasseur* continues to be correct for diversity cases. Since state, rather than federal, substantive law is at issue there is no need for a uniform federal rule. And indeed, nationwide uniformity in the substance of the matter is better served by having the same claim-preclusive rule (the state rule) apply whether the dismissal has been ordered by a state or a federal court. This is, it seems to us, a classic case for adopting, as the federally prescribed rule of decision, the law that would be applied by state courts in the State in which the federal diversity court sits. See *Gasperini v. Center for Humanities, Inc.,* 518 U.S. 415, 429–431 (1996); *Walker v. Armco Steel Corp.,* 446 U.S., at 752–753; * * *. As we have alluded to above, any other rule would produce the sort of "forum-shopping . . . and . . . inequitable administration of the laws" that *Erie* seeks to avoid, *Hanna,* 380 U.S., at 468, since filing in, or removing to, federal court would be encouraged by the divergent effects that the litigants would anticipate from likely grounds of dismissal. See *Guaranty Trust Co. v. York,* 326 U.S., at 109–110.

This federal reference to state law will not obtain, of course, in situations in which the state law is incompatible with federal interests. If, for example, state law did not accord claim-preclusive effect to dismissals for willful violation of discovery orders, federal courts' interest in the integrity of their own processes might justify a contrary federal rule. No such conflict with potential federal interests exists in the present case. Dismissal of this state cause of action was decreed by the California federal court only because the California statute of limitations so required; and there is no conceivable federal interest in giving that time bar more effect in other courts than the California courts themselves would impose. . . The judgment is reversed, and the case remanded for further proceedings not inconsistent with this opinion.

Erie and Preclusion

(1) The usual rule has been to apply the preclusion law of the forum, even when a case is governed by the substantive law of another sovereign. This is true in both the interstate and international context. Why not here? If your answer is "federalism," what specifically does that mean? Why are federal courts *less* sovereign than other courts when it comes to rules governing the effects of their judgments? For commentary on *Semtek,* see, e.g., Burbank, Semtek, *Forum Shopping, and Federal Common Law,* 77

Notre Dame L. Rev. 1027 (2002); Woolley, *The Sources of Federal Preclusion Law after* Semtek, 72 U. Cin. L. Rev. 527 (2003).

(2) How persuasive is the Court's argument for reading Rule 41 more narrowly than its language suggests? The phrase "on the merits" traditionally was understood to mean "claim preclusive." This was its universal meaning when Rule 41 was adopted, and there is no hint, either then or in later rule amendments, that the phrase was meant to have any other meaning. Justice Scalia cites a subsequent trend in some state courts to deny preclusive effect to certain judgments (typically statute-of-limitations dismissals or demurrers) while still describing these as "on the merits." What does that have to do with the interpretation of Rule 41? Are you surprised to see such arguments in an opinion authored by Justice Scalia?

Why does the Court stretch so far to give the rule this narrow reading?

(3) What do you make of the Court's use of authority? Consider the following:

(a) Justice Scalia suggests that, if Rule 41 did govern the preclusive effect of a federal judgment, it "would arguably violate the jurisdictional limitation of the Rules Enabling Act" that federal rules not "abridge, enlarge, or modify any substantive right." In footnote 2 of the opinion, he reserves the question whether even the narrow reading of Rule 41 might go too far to satisfy the Rules Enabling Act. But what about *Sibbach v. Wilson & Co.,* 312 U.S. 1 (1941), supra p. 853? Is the Court hinting that *Sibbach* should be overturned or limited? Is that a good or a bad idea?

(b) Justice Scalia further suggests that, if Rule 41 governed the preclusive effect of a diversity judgment, it would violate "the federalism principle" of *Erie* itself, and he cites *Hanna v. Plumer* and *Guaranty Trust Co. v. York* for support. Is *Guaranty Trust* still good law? Wasn't the whole point of *Hanna* that *Erie*'s principle and its concern for forum shopping are *inapplicable* in cases under the Rules Enabling Act? Is the Court trying to signal a revision in the law, or did the Justices just not read the cases carefully?

(c) *Walker v. Armco Steel Co.* is cited repeatedly. Is *Semtek* just a reprise of *Walker*, with the Court construing a rule narrowly so as not to displace state substantive law absent a clear statement to the contrary? Then what about *Ricoh* and *Burlington Northern*? Are these still good law? Can you reconcile the cases?

(4) Why doesn't federal common law pose the same problems, especially with respect to the *Erie* principle? Has the Court avoided this difficulty by having federal common law incorporate state law? These issues are addressed infra pp. 895–907.

SHADY GROVE ORTHOPEDIC ASSOCIATES, P.A. V. ALLSTATE INSURANCE CO.

559 U.S. 393 (2010).

JUSTICE SCALIA announced the judgment of the Court and delivered the opinion of the Court with respect to Parts I and II-A, an opinion with respect to Parts II-B and II-D, in which THE CHIEF JUSTICE, JUSTICE THOMAS, and JUSTICE SOTOMAYOR join, and an opinion with respect to Part II-C, in which THE CHIEF JUSTICE and JUSTICE THOMAS join.

New York law prohibits class actions in suits seeking penalties or statutory minimum damages. * * * We consider whether this precludes a federal district court sitting in diversity from entertaining a class action under Federal Rule of Civil Procedure 23. * * *

I

[Shady Grove provided care to a woman injured in an automobile accident. It submitted a claim for benefits under her insurance to Allstate. New York law required Allstate to pay a valid claim within 30 days, and if not to pay statutory interest on the overdue benefits at two percent per month. Allstate paid late and refused to pay the interest. Alleging that this was Allstate's routine practice, Shady Grove sought to certify a class of all those to whom Allstate owed interest. New York Civil Practice Law § 901(b) prohibits suits to recover statutory damages from proceeding as class actions. The lower courts found that this restriction was a substantive limit not in conflict with Federal Rule of Civil Procedure 23, which sets out the requirements for class certification in federal court.]

II

The framework for our decision is familiar. We must first determine whether Rule 23 answers the question in dispute. * * * If it does, it governs—New York's law notwithstanding—unless it exceeds statutory authorization or Congress's rulemaking power. * * * We do not wade into *Erie*'s murky waters unless the federal rule is inapplicable or invalid.* * *.

A

The question in dispute is whether Shady Grove's suit may proceed as a class action. Rule 23 provides an answer. It states that "[a] class action may be maintained" if two conditions are met: The suit must satisfy the criteria set forth in subdivision (a) (*i.e.,* numerosity, commonality, typicality, and adequacy of representation), and it also must fit into one of the three categories described in subdivision (b). Fed. Rule Civ. Proc. 23(b). By its terms this creates a categorical rule entitling a plaintiff whose suit meets the specified criteria to pursue his claim as a class action. . . Because § 901(b) attempts to answer the same question—*i.e.,* it states that Shady Grove's suit "may *not* be maintained as a class action" (emphasis added) because of the relief it seeks—it cannot apply in diversity suits unless Rule 23 is ultra vires.

The dissent argues that § 901(b) has nothing to do with whether Shady Grove may maintain its suit as a class action, but affects only the *remedy* it may obtain if it wins. * * * Whereas "Rule 23 governs procedural aspects of class litigation" by "prescrib[ing] the considerations relevant to class certification and postcertification proceedings," § 901(b) addresses only "the size of a monetary award a class plaintiff may pursue." * * * Accordingly, the dissent says, Rule 23 and New York's law may coexist in peace.

We need not decide whether a state law that limits the remedies available in an existing class action would conflict with Rule 23; that is not what § 901(b) does. By its terms, the provision precludes a plaintiff from "maintain[ing]" a class action seeking statutory penalties. Unlike a law that sets a ceiling on damages (or puts other remedies out of reach) in properly filed class actions, § 901(b) says nothing about what remedies a court may award; it prevents the class actions it covers from coming into existence at all.[4] Consequently, a court bound by § 901(b) could not certify a class action seeking both statutory penalties and other remedies even if it announces in advance that it will refuse to award the penalties in the event the plaintiffs prevail; to do so would violate the statute's clear prohibition on "maintain[ing]" such suits as class actions. . . .

The dissent all but admits that the literal terms of § 901(b) address the same subject as Rule 23—*i.e.,* whether a class action may be maintained—but insists the provision's *purpose* is to restrict only remedies. * * * Unlike Rule 23, designed to further procedural fairness and efficiency, § 901(b) (we are told) "responds to an entirely different concern": the fear that allowing statutory damages to be awarded on a class-wide basis would "produce overkill." * * * The dissent reaches this conclusion on the basis of (1) constituent concern recorded in the law's bill jacket; (2) a commentary suggesting that the Legislature "apparently fear[ed]" that combining class actions and statutory penalties "could result in annihilating punishment of the defendant." * * *

This evidence of the New York Legislature's purpose is pretty sparse. But even accepting the dissent's account of the Legislature's objective at face value, it cannot override the statute's clear text. Even if its aim is to restrict the remedy a plaintiff can obtain, § 901(b) achieves that end by limiting a plaintiff's power to maintain a class action. The manner in which the law "could have been written" has no bearing; what matters is the law

4 Contrary to the dissent's implication, we express no view as to whether state laws that set a ceiling on damages recoverable in a single suit * * * are pre-empted. Whether or not those laws conflict with Rule 23, § 901(b) does conflict because it addresses not the remedy, but the procedural right to maintain a class action. . . .

the Legislature *did* enact. We cannot rewrite that to reflect our perception of legislative purpose. . .

The dissent's approach of determining whether state and federal rules conflict based on the subjective intentions of the state legislature is an enterprise destined to produce "confusion worse confounded." * * *It would mean, to begin with, that one State's statute could survive pre-emption (and accordingly affect the procedures in federal court) while another State's identical law would not, merely because its authors had different aspirations. It would also mean that district courts would have to discern, in every diversity case, the purpose behind any putatively pre-empted state procedural rule, even if its text squarely conflicts with federal law. That task will often prove arduous. Many laws further more than one aim, and the aim of others may be impossible to discern. Moreover, to the extent the dissent's purpose-driven approach depends on its characterization of § 901(b)'s aims as substantive, it would apply to many state rules ostensibly addressed to procedure. . .

But while the dissent does indeed artificially narrow the scope of § 901(b) by finding that it pursues only substantive policies, that is not the central difficulty of the dissent's position. The central difficulty is that even artificial narrowing cannot render § 901(b) compatible with Rule 23. *Whatever* the policies they pursue, they flatly contradict each other. Allstate asserts (and the dissent implies) that we can (and must) *interpret* Rule 23 in a manner that avoids overstepping its authorizing statute. . . If the Rule were susceptible of two meanings—one that would violate § 2072(b) and another that would not—we would agree. * * * But it is not. Rule 23 unambiguously authorizes *any* plaintiff, in *any* federal civil proceeding, to maintain a class action if the Rule's prerequisites are met. We cannot contort its text, even to avert a collision with state law that might render it invalid. . . What the dissent's approach achieves is not the avoiding of a "conflict between Rule 23 and § 901(b)," but rather the invalidation of Rule 23 (pursuant to § 2072(b) of the Rules Enabling Act) to the extent that it conflicts with the substantive policies of § 901. There is no other way to reach the dissent's destination. We must therefore confront head-on whether Rule 23 falls within the statutory authorization.

B

Erie involved the constitutional power of federal courts to supplant state law with judge-made rules. In that context, it made no difference whether the rule was technically one of substance or procedure; the touchstone was whether it "significantly affect[s] the result of a litigation." * * * That is not the test for either the constitutionality or the statutory validity of a Federal Rule of Procedure. Congress has undoubted power to supplant state law, and undoubted power to prescribe rules for the courts it has created, so long as those rules regulate matters "rationally capable of classification" as procedure. * * * In the Rules Enabling Act, Congress authorized this Court to promulgate rules of procedure subject to its review, 28 U.S.C. § 2072(a), but with the limitation that those rules "shall not abridge, enlarge or modify any substantive right," § 2072(b).

We have long held that this limitation means that the Rule must "really regulat[e] procedure,—the judicial process for enforcing rights and duties recognized by substantive law and for justly administering remedy and redress for disregard or infraction of them." * * * The test is not whether the rule affects a litigant's substantive rights; most procedural rules do. * * * What matters is what the rule itself regulates: If it governs only "the manner and the means" by which the litigants' rights are "enforced," it is valid; if it alters "the rules of decision by which [the] court will adjudicate [those] rights," it is not. * * *

Applying that test, we have rejected every statutory challenge to a Federal Rule that has come before us. . . [W]e think it obvious that rules allowing multiple claims (and claims by or against multiple parties) to be litigated together are also valid. . .

Allstate argues that Rule 23 violates § 2072(b) because the state law it displaces, § 901(b), creates a right that the Federal Rule abridges—namely, a "substantive right . . . not to be subjected to aggregated class-action liability" in a single suit. . . [However,] the substantive nature of New York's law, or its substantive purpose, *makes no difference*. A Federal Rule of Procedure is not valid in some jurisdictions and invalid in others—or valid in some cases and invalid in others—depending upon whether its effect is to frustrate a state substantive law (or a state procedural law enacted for substantive purposes). . .

Hanna unmistakably expressed the same understanding that compliance of a Federal Rule with the Enabling Act is to be assessed by consulting the Rule itself, and not its effects in individual applications:

> "[T]he court has been instructed to apply the Federal Rule, and can refuse to do so only if the Advisory Committee, this Court, and Congress erred in their prima facie judgment that the Rule in question transgresses neither the terms of the Enabling Act nor constitutional restrictions." * * *

In sum, it is not the substantive or procedural nature or purpose of the affected state law that matters, but the substantive or procedural nature of the Federal Rule. We have held since *Sibbach,* and reaffirmed repeatedly, that the validity of a Federal Rule depends entirely upon whether it regulates procedure. * * * If it does, it is authorized by § 2072 and is valid in all jurisdictions, with respect to all claims, regardless of its incidental effect upon state-created rights. . . .

D

We must acknowledge the reality that keeping the federal-court door open to class actions that cannot proceed in state court will produce forum shopping. That is unacceptable when it comes as the consequence of judge-made rules created to fill supposed "gaps" in positive federal law. * * * For where neither the Constitution, a treaty, nor a statute provides the rule of decision or authorizes a federal court to supply one, "state law must govern because there can be no other law." * * * But divergence from state law, with the attendant consequence of forum shopping, is the inevitable (indeed, one might say the intended) result of a uniform system of federal procedure. Congress itself has created the possibility that the same case may follow a different course if filed in federal instead of state court. * * * The short of the matter is that a Federal Rule governing procedure is valid whether or not it alters the outcome of the case in a way that induces forum shopping. To hold otherwise would be to "disembowel either the Constitution's grant of power over federal procedure" or Congress's exercise of it. * * *

* * *

The judgment of the Court of Appeals is reversed, and the case is remanded for further proceedings.

It is so ordered.

[JUSTICE STEVENS concurred in part and concurred in the judgment. He believed that the "shall not abridge" language of § 2072(b) requires a Federal Rule of Civil Procedure to accommodate state substantive law, stating that "federal rules cannot displace a State's definition of its own rights or remedies." However, he believed that the New York law was procedural and thus could be displaced by Rule 23.]

JUSTICE GINSBURG, with whom JUSTICE KENNEDY, JUSTICE BREYER, and JUSTICE ALITO join, dissenting.

The Court today approves Shady Grove's attempt to transform a $500 case into a $5,000,000 award, although the State creating the right to recover has proscribed this alchemy. If Shady Grove had filed suit in New York state court, the 2% interest payment authorized by New York Ins. Law Ann. § 5106(a) (West 2009) as a penalty for overdue benefits would, by Shady Grove's own measure, amount to no more than $500. By instead filing in federal court based on the parties' diverse citizenship and requesting class certification, Shady Grove hopes to recover, for the class, statutory damages of more than $5,000,000. The New York Legislature has barred this remedy, instructing that, unless specifically permitted, "an action to recover a penalty, or minimum measure of recovery created or imposed by statute may not be maintained as a class action." * * * The Court nevertheless holds that Federal Rule of Civil Procedure 23, which prescribes procedures for the conduct of class actions in federal courts, preempts the application of § 901(b) in diversity suits.

The Court reads Rule 23 relentlessly to override New York's restriction on the availability of statutory damages. Our decisions, however, caution us to ask, before undermining state legislation: Is this conflict really necessary? Cf. Traynor, *Is This Conflict Really Necessary?* 37 Tex. L.Rev. 657 (1959). Had the Court engaged in that inquiry, it would not have read Rule 23 to collide with New York's legitimate interest in keeping certain monetary awards reasonably bounded. I would continue to interpret Federal Rules with awareness of, and sensitivity to, important state regulatory policies. Because today's judgment radically departs from that course, I dissent.

I

A

[Parts A and B of Justice Ginsburg's opinion set out the *Erie* framework and argue that earlier cases "have avoided immoderate interpretations of the Federal Rules that would trench on state prerogatives without serving any countervailing federal interest."]

C

Our decisions instruct over and over again that, in the adjudication of diversity cases, state interests—whether advanced in a statute, *e.g., Cohen,* or a procedural rule, *e.g., Gasperini*—warrant our respectful consideration. Yet today, the Court gives no quarter to New York's limitation on statutory damages and requires the lower courts to thwart the regulatory policy at stake: To prevent excessive damages, New York's law controls the penalty to which a defendant may be exposed in a single suit. . .

D

Shady Grove contends—and the Court today agrees—that Rule 23 unavoidably preempts New York's prohibition on the recovery of statutory damages in class actions. The Federal Rule, the Court emphasizes, states that Shady Grove's suit "may be" maintained as a class action, which conflicts with § 901(b)'s instruction that it "may not" so proceed. * * * Accordingly, the Court insists, § 901(b) "cannot apply in diversity suits unless Rule 23 is ultra vires." *Ibid.* Concluding that Rule 23 does not violate the Rules Enabling Act, the Court holds that the federal provision controls Shady Grove's ability to seek, on behalf of a class, a statutory penalty of over $5,000,000. * * * The Court, I am convinced, finds conflict where none is necessary. Mindful of the history behind § 901(b)'s enactment, the thrust of our precedent, and the substantive-rights limitation in the Rules Enabling Act, I conclude, as did the Second Circuit and every District Court to have considered the question in any detail that Rule 23 does not collide with § 901(b). As the Second Circuit well understood, Rule 23 prescribes the considerations relevant to class certification and postcertification proceedings—but it does not command that a particular remedy be available when a party sues in a representative capacity. Section 901(b), in contrast, trains on that latter issue. Sensibly read, Rule 23 governs procedural aspects of class litigation, but allows state law to control the size of a monetary award a class plaintiff may pursue.

In other words, Rule 23 describes a method of enforcing a claim for relief, while § 901(b) defines the dimensions of the claim itself. In this regard, it is immaterial that § 901(b) bars statutory penalties in wholesale, rather than retail, fashion. The New York Legislature could have embedded the limitation in every provision creating a cause of action for which a penalty is authorized; § 901(b) operates as shorthand to the same effect. It is as much a part of the delineation of the claim for relief as it would be were it included claim by claim in the New York Code. The Court single-mindedly focuses on whether a suit "may" or "may not" be maintained as a class action. Putting the question that way, the Court does not home in on the reason *why*. Rule 23 authorizes class treatment for suits satisfying its prerequisites because the class mechanism generally affords a fair and efficient way to aggregate claims for adjudication. Section 901(b) responds to an entirely different concern; it does not allow class members to recover statutory damages because the New York Legislature considered the result of adjudicating such claims en masse to be exorbitant. The fair and efficient *conduct* of class litigation is the legitimate concern of Rule 23; the *remedy* for an infraction of state law, however, is the legitimate concern of the State's lawmakers and not of the federal rulemakers. * * *

Suppose, for example, that a State, wishing to cap damages in class actions at $1,000,000, enacted a statute providing that "a suit to recover more than $1,000,000 may not be maintained as a class action." Under the Court's reasoning—which attributes dispositive significance to the words "may not be maintained"—Rule 23 would preempt this provision, nevermind that Congress, by authorizing the promulgation of rules of procedure for federal courts, surely did not intend to displace state-created ceilings on damages. The Court suggests that the analysis might differ if the statute "limit[ed] the remedies available in an existing class action," *ante* at 1439, such that Rule 23 might not conflict with a state statute prescribing that "no more than $1,000,000 may be recovered in a class action." There is no real difference in the purpose and intended effect of these two hypothetical statutes. The notion that one directly impinges on Rule 23's domain, while the other does not, fundamentally misperceives the office of Rule 23. The absence of an inevitable collision between Rule 23 and § 901(b) becomes evident once it is comprehended that a federal court sitting in diversity can accord due respect to both state and federal prescriptions. Plaintiffs seeking to vindicate claims for which the State has provided a statutory penalty may pursue relief through a class action if they forgo statutory damages and instead seek actual damages or injunctive or declaratory relief; any putative class member who objects can opt out and pursue actual damages, if available, and the statutory penalty in an individual action.* * * In this manner, the Second Circuit explained, "Rule 23's procedural requirements for class actions can be applied along with the substantive requirement of CPLR 901(b)." * * * In sum, while phrased as responsive to the question whether certain class actions may begin, § 901(b) is unmistakably aimed at controlling how those actions must end. On that remedial issue, Rule 23 is silent.

Any doubt whether Rule 23 leaves § 901(b) in control of the remedial issue at the core of this case should be dispelled by our *Erie* jurisprudence, including *Hanna,* which counsels us to read Federal Rules moderately and cautions against stretching a rule to cover every situation it could conceivably reach. The Court states that "[t]here is no reason . . . to read Rule 23 as addressing only whether claims made eligible for class treatment by some *other* law should be certified as class actions." To the contrary, *Palmer, Ragan, Cohen, Walker, Gasperini,* and *Semtek* provide good reason to look to the law that creates the right to recover. That is plainly so on a more accurate statement of what is at stake: Is there any reason to read Rule 23 as authorizing a claim for relief when the State that created the remedy disallows its pursuit on behalf of a class? None at all is the answer our federal system should give. . . .

By finding a conflict without considering whether Rule 23 rationally should be read to avoid any collision, the Court unwisely and unnecessarily retreats from the federalism principles undergirding *Erie*. Had the Court reflected on the respect for state regulatory interests endorsed in our decisions, it would have found no cause to interpret Rule 23 so woodenly—and every reason not to do so. Cf. Traynor, 37 Tex. L.Rev., at 669 ("It is bad enough for courts to prattle unintelligibly about choice of law, but unforgiveable when inquiry might have revealed that there was no real conflict.").

II

[Justice Ginsburg goes on to ask whether failure to apply the state rule would cause a plaintiff to choose federal court and concludes that it would.]

* * *

I would continue to approach *Erie* questions in a manner mindful of the purposes underlying the Rules of Decision Act and the Rules Enabling Act, faithful to precedent, and respectful of important state interests. I would therefore hold that the New York Legislature's limitation on the recovery of statutory damages applies in this case, and would affirm the Second Circuit's judgment.

Erie and Class Actions

(1) *Unilateralism and multilateralism.* Justice Ginsburg urges the Court to consider both state and federal interests and decide whether they conflict. Justice Scalia's approach by contrast looks only to the scope of the federal rule. Is Justice Ginsburg's approach more sensible? Is it consistent with *Hanna* and the Supremacy Clause?

(2) Is this conflict really necessary? What interest does the federal government have in allowing a class action when New York would not? Does it depend on why New York would not allow it?

(3) *The limits of unilateralism.* Justice Scalia and the rest of the plurality believe that a Federal Rule must be given effect unless it is invalid. Justice Ginsburg and the four dissenters believe that the language of § 2072(b) requires a court to look at state law in order to decide whether applying a Federal Rule would impermissibly enlarge, abridge, or modify a state law right. Justice Stevens sides with the dissent on this issue but deems the New York law procedural. Is the Stevens/Ginsburg position consistent with *Sibbach*? What should lower courts do going forward?

(4) Suppose the New York legislature had drafted a particular statutory cause of action to award statutory damages and explicitly noted that because multiplication could lead to annihilative liability, those damages would not be recoverable in a class action. The dissent and Justice Stevens clearly believe that such a statute would prevent recovery of statutory damages in a class action in federal court. Does the Scalia plurality disagree? If not, is this case just about how to construe a particular state statute?

SECTION 3. ERIE AND CHOICE OF LAW

KLAXON CO. V. STENTOR ELEC. MFG. CO.

313 U.S. 487 (1941).

MR. JUSTICE REED delivered the opinion of the Court.

The principal question in this case is whether in diversity cases the federal courts must follow conflict of laws rules prevailing in the states in which they sit. . .

In 1918, respondent, a New York corporation, transferred its entire business to petitioner, a Delaware corporation. Petitioner contracted to use its best efforts to further the manufacture and sale of certain patented devices covered by the agreement, and respondent was to have a share of petitioner's profits. The agreement was executed in New York, the assets were transferred there, and petitioner began performance there although later it moved its operations to other states. Respondent was voluntarily dissolved under New York law in 1919. Ten years later it instituted this action in the United States District Court for the District of Delaware, alleging that petitioner had failed to perform its agreement to use its best efforts. Jurisdiction rested on diversity of citizenship. In 1939 respondent recovered a jury verdict of $100,000, upon which judgment was entered. Respondent then moved to correct the judgment by adding interest at the rate of six percent from June 1, 1929, the date the action had been brought. The basis of the motion was the provision in § 480 of the New York Civil Practice Act directing that in contract actions interest be added to the principal sum "whether theretofore liquidated or unliquidated." The District Court granted the motion, taking the view that the rights of the parties were governed by New York law and that under New York law the addition of such interest was mandatory. 30 F.Supp. 425, 431. The Circuit Court of Appeals affirmed, 115 F.2d 268, and we granted certiorari, limited to the question whether § 480 of the New York Civil Practice Act is applicable to an action in the federal court in Delaware. 312 U.S. 674.

The Circuit Court of Appeals was of the view that under New York law the right to interest before verdict under § 480 went to the substance of the obligation, and that proper construction of the contract in suit fixed New York as the place of performance. It then concluded that § 480 was applicable to the case because "it is clear by what we think is undoubtedly the better view of the law that the rules for ascertaining the measure of damages are not a matter of procedure at all, but are matters of substance which should be settled by reference to the law of the appropriate state according to the type of case being tried in the forum. The measure of damages for breach of a contract is determined by the law of the place of performance; Restatement, Conflict of Laws § 413." The court referred also to § 418 of the Restatement, which makes interest part of the damages to be determined by the law of the place of performance. Application of the New York statute apparently followed from the court's independent determination of the "better view" without regard to Delaware law, for no Delaware decision or statute was cited or discussed.

We are of opinion that the prohibition declared in *Erie R. Co. v. Tompkins,* 304 U.S. 64, against such independent determinations by the federal courts, extends to the field of conflict of laws. The conflict of laws rules to be applied by the federal court in Delaware must conform to those prevailing in Delaware's state courts. Otherwise, the accident of diversity of citizenship would constantly disturb equal administration of justice in co-ordinate state and federal courts sitting side by side. See *Erie R. Co. v. Tompkins,* supra, 304 U.S. at 74–77. Any other ruling would do violence to the principle of uniformity within a state, upon which the *Tompkins* decision is based. Whatever lack of uniformity this may produce between federal courts in different states is attributable to our federal system, which leaves to a state, within the limits permitted by the Constitution, the right to pursue local policies diverging from those of its neighbors. It is not for the federal courts to thwart such local policies by enforcing an independent "general law" of conflict of laws. Subject only to review by this Court on any federal question that may arise, Delaware is free to determine whether a given matter is to be governed by the law of the forum or some other law. * * * This Court's views are not the decisive factor in determining the applicable conflicts rule. * * * And the proper function of the Delaware federal court is to ascertain what the state law is, not what it ought to be. . .

Accordingly, the judgment is reversed and the case remanded to the Circuit Court of Appeals for decision in conformity with the law of Delaware.

Reversed.

The Choice Among Conflicting State Laws Under *Erie*

(1) The problem presented in *Klaxon* can be approached on a number of different levels. First, in regard to forum shopping: Was the Court justified in viewing disuniformity between courts in a single state as more serious than disuniformity between federal courts? Professor Cavers said yes, arguing that as a practical matter "forum-shopping across the courthouse square . . . is a much greater risk than forum shopping across state lines," because the latter requires employment of out-of-state counsel "who might lack the first lawyer's own background knowledge of the controversy and who certainly would share in the fees." ALI, Study of the Division of Jurisdiction Between State and Federal Courts 159 (Tent. Draft No. 1, 1963).

Might it be added that, however unfortunate it may be that the federal courts cannot wipe out disuniformity among the states, the worst thing they could do would be to create additional disuniformity themselves?

(2) Professors Hart and Wechsler were sharply critical of *Klaxon*. The greatness of *Erie*, they maintained, was that by destroying the separate federal common law that decision made it easier for people to predict the legal consequences of their actions, and, therefore, to plan their conduct with assurance. Since everyone agreed in *Erie* that Pennsylvania law would govern absent *Swift v. Tyson*, the possibility of a contrary federal law was disruptive. *Klaxon*, in their view, was a step backward from this position; for when there is doubt as to which state's law applies, a federal choice-of-law doctrine would promote *Erie's* principle of assuring a predictable uniform result. See R. Fallon, D. Meltzer & D. Shapiro, Hart and Wechsler's The Federal Courts and the Federal System 591–97 (7th ed. 2015).

Do you agree? (Professors Fallon, Meltzer, and Shapiro present the Hart and Wechsler critique with some skepticism.) How likely do you think it is that the federal courts will develop uniform choice-of-law doctrine? See Cavers, ALI Study at 165, 183–90. How likely is it that federal choice-of-law doctrine will provide predictable results? Note in this regard that, where federal choice-of-law rules have been developed, the federal courts have strongly favored the Second Restatement's "most significant relationship" test. See, e.g., *Liu v. Republic of China,* 892 F.2d 1419 (9th Cir. 1989) (choice of law to determine sovereign immunity under Foreign Sovereign Immunities Act). Is this a step forward? And consider 28 U.S.C. § 1441(b), which prohibits removal of a diversity case by a resident defendant. In many cases this would give the plaintiff under the Hart-Wechsler argument an irremediable choice between federal and state conflicts principles, and it was precisely this incomplete availability of removal that made *Swift v. Tyson* such an obstacle to predictability. Note finally the difficulty in some cases of predicting at the planning stage whether all parties to a potential suit will be diverse and whether the jurisdictional minimum amount will be satisfied. See Hill, *The Erie Doctrine and the Constitution,* 53 Nw.U.L.Rev. 427, 561 (1958).

The criticism of *Klaxon* continues. See, e.g., Fruehwald, *Choice of Law in Federal Courts: A Reevaluation,* 37 Brandeis L.J. 21, 36–44 (1999); Mark D. Rosen, *Choice-of-Law as Non-Constitutional Federal Law,* 99 Minn. L. Rev. 1017 (2015) (arguing that choice of law is inherently federal, even when done by state courts); Allan Erbsen, *Erie's Four Functions: Reframing Choice of Law in Federal Courts,* 89 Notre Dame L. Rev. 579, 645 (2013) (arguing that Klaxon is "thoroughly muddled: it creates federal law under the guise of adopting state law based on an irrelevant fear of applying general law"). For a less negative view, see Roosevelt, *Choice of Law in Federal Courts: From* Erie *and* Klaxon *to CAFA and* Shady Grove, 106 Nw. L. Rev. 1 (2012).

(3) If removal were always available, a federal conflicts doctrine might possibly enhance predictability. Moreover, it has been argued that *Klaxon* is unfortunate because the federal courts, free from parochial loyalties, are in an ideal position to resolve conflicts between the states. See, e.g., Hart, *The Relations Between State and Federal Law,* 54 Colum.L.Rev. 489, 515 (1954). But is either the active promotion of predictability or the development of choice-of-law rules within the purpose of the diversity grant as defined in *Erie, York,* and succeeding decisions? Doesn't the notion that the diversity court sits only to provide an unbiased forum suggest, as *Klaxon* in effect held, that (apart from bias, and subject to countervailing policies respecting the administration of federal courts) the case should be decided as it would have been if there were no federal courts?

(4) If the basis and effect of *Erie* are that the diversity court is a disinterested forum, should it not, like other disinterested courts, make its own choice of laws? See Hill, *The Erie Doctrine and the Constitution,* 53 Nw.U.L.Rev. 427, 545 (1958). Or is this question one more appropriately addressed to the state courts and legislatures that would apply *their* choice-of-law rules in these cases?

(5) The discussion of *Klaxon* up to this point has assumed that the conflict of laws is an independent system of rules applied without regard to the content of the substantive law. But isn't the whole point of modern choice-of-law analysis that selecting an applicable law is merely part of the ordinary process of interpreting laws to define the elements of a claim or defense? Is there anything more substantive than that?

Does it follow that *Klaxon* is constitutionally *required*? Recall the notes on renvoi in Section 6 of Chapter 2. If a state wrongful death statute applies "to deaths caused within this state," would it be constitutionally acceptable for a federal court to apply it to a death caused out of state? If not, why should the result be different because the state has adopted a territorial restriction as a matter of choice of law?

This reasoning suggests an argument that federal courts must follow the restrictions that state choice-of-law rules place on the scope of state law; otherwise they are not really applying state law. (Essentially the same argument, based on the Full Faith and Credit Clause, can be made with respect to state courts. How has it fared in that context?) What does it suggest about adherence to state choice-of-law rules that resolve conflicts between state laws? See Roosevelt, *Resolving Renvoi: The Bewitchment of Our Intelligence by Means of Language,* 80 Notre Dame L. Rev. 1821, 1857–64, 1872–74 (2005).

Does the *Klaxon* Court think that its decision is constitutionally required? It depicts the case as an extension of *Erie*, but does the extension rest on the constitutional element of *Erie*, or its policy arguments?

Note that nothing in the Constitution requires Congress to establish federal districts along state borders. Suppose that Congress established federal districts spanning more than one state: whose choice-of-law rules should these courts apply in diversity cases? Could this be determined without federal choice-of-law rules? Could it be determined on the basis of the location of the courthouse?

(6) *Griffin v. McCoach,* 313 U.S. 498 (1941), applied *Klaxon* unblinkingly to an interpleader case in a Texas federal court, although some of the parties were non-residents who could not have been sued in a state court in Texas. Consider also the problem of which state's choice-of-law doctrine to follow if federal service of process is made beyond the limits of state jurisdiction in an impleader case as authorized by Rule 4, or if a state law claim is pendent to a federal claim for which nationwide service is provided. What sense does it make to apply the law of a state in whose courts the action could never have been brought?

(7) *Van Dusen v. Barrack,* 376 U.S. 612 (1964). Numerous actions arising from a Massachusetts plane crash were filed in federal court in Pennsylvania. The plaintiffs argued that transferring the actions to Massachusetts would not serve the "interest of justice," as required by 28 U.S.C. § 1404(a), because it might diminish their recovery: Massachusetts limited wrongful-death damages to $20,000, and the federal court there was more likely than its Pennsylvania counterpart to apply Massachusetts law. Approving transfer, the Court rejected the premise of the plaintiffs' argument: "[I]n cases such as the present, where the defendants seek transfer, the transferee district court must . . . apply the state law that would have been applied if there had been no change of venue." Though "a superficial reading" of prior statements that federal courts should "apply the laws 'of the states in which they sit' " might suggest the opposite conclusion, the essence of *Erie* was that "the accident of a suit by a non-resident litigant in a federal court instead of in a State court a block away, should not lead to a substantially different result" (quoting *Guaranty Trust Co. v. York,* supra p. 838). Thus *Erie* forbade "a result in federal court which could not have been achieved in the courts of the State where the action was filed. . . The legislative history of § 1404(a) certainly does not justify the rather startling conclusion that one might 'get a change of law as a bonus for a change of venue.' "

Ferens v. John Deere Co., 494 U.S. 516 (1990), applied the same reasoning to reach the same result in a case in which the *plaintiff* requested a transfer. Injured in an accident on his farm in Pennsylvania, Ferens filed suit in Mississippi federal court to take advantage of that state's six-year statute of limitations. Ferens then had the case transferred back to Pennsylvania, where it was too late to sue. Absent the transfer, wrote Justice Kennedy for the majority, the Mississippi limitation period would have applied; and, as *Van Dusen* had said, the transfer statute was not intended to affect the outcome of the case.

Writing for four dissenters, Justice Scalia argued that the logic of *Van Dusen* required the opposite result:

> [J]ust as it is unlikely that Congress, in enacting § 1404(a), meant to provide the defendant with a vehicle by which to manipulate in his favor the substantive law to be applied in a diversity case, so too is it unlikely that Congress meant to provide the *plaintiff* with a vehicle by which to appropriate the law of a distant and inconvenient forum in which he does not intend to litigate, and to carry that prize back to the State in which he wishes to try the case.

But might there not be cases in which a plaintiff seeks a transfer for good reasons? Isn't the real problem in *Ferens* that Justice Scalia's opinion for the Court in *Sun Oil Co. v. Wortman,* supra p. 391, allows Mississippi to apply its longer statute of limitations to a case in which it has no interest?

Does the *Ferens* rule defeat a contrary forum-selection clause in the parties' contract? In *Atl. Marine Const. Co. v. U.S. Dist. Court for W. Dist. of Texas,* 571 U.S. 49 (2013), the Court said no: "[W]hen a party bound by a forum-selection clause flouts its contractual obligation and files suit in a different forum, a § 1404(a) transfer of venue will not carry with it the original venue's choice-of-law rules." *Id.* at 64–65.

Van Dusen and *Ferens* were diversity cases. Should they govern the transfer of a federal statutory claim that borrows state limitations law? Compare *In re Korean Air Lines Disaster of Sept. 1, 1983,* 829 F.2d 1171 (D.C. Cir. 1987) (*Van Dusen* does not apply) and *Newton v. Thomason,* 22 F.3d 1455 (9th Cir. 1994) (same), with *Eckstein v. Balcor Film Investors,* 8 F.3d 1121 (7th Cir. 1993) (*Van Dusen* and *Ferens* apply). See Norwood, *Double Forum Shopping and the Extension of* Ferens *to Federal Claims That Borrow State Limitations Periods,* 44 Emory L.J. 501 (1995).

(8) As discussed supra pp. 309–318, federal multidistrict litigation (MDL) has become a commonplace mechanism for adjudicating mass product liability claims. Under *Van Dusen* and *Ferens,* when a case is filed in a proper venue and transferred to an MDL court, that court must apply the choice-of-law rules that would have applied in the original venue. See, *e.g., Chang v. Baxter Healthcare Corp.,* 599 F.3d 728, 732 (7th Cir. 2010) ("When a diversity case is transferred by the multidistrict litigation panel, the law applied is that of the jurisdiction from which the case was transferred. . ."). Increasingly, however, defendants waive their objections to venue and personal jurisdiction and allow plaintiffs to file claims directly in the MDL court. See, *e.g., In re Vioxx Prods. Liab. Litig.,* 478 F. Supp. 2d 897, 904 (E.D. La. 2007). In such cases, there is no original venue to look to—so which choice-of-law rules should the MDL court apply?

Under a literal reading of *Klaxon* the MDL court would apply the choice-of-law rules of the state in which it sits. But, to the extent *Klaxon* reflects the notion that choice-of-law rules express substantive policy decisions about the scope of state law, this solution seems odd: what interest does the MDL court have? Can the MDL court devise its own choice-of-law rules as a matter of federal common law, say, always applying the law of the state where the plaintiff was injured, or where the product was purchased? (Is the MDL forum a version of Currie's "disinterested third state"? Recall that Currie argued such cases should be dismissed on *forum non conveniens* grounds; see supra, p. 182.) Professor Bradt argues instead that the MDL court should apply the choice-of-law rules of an otherwise proper forum that the plaintiff elects at the outset of the case.

Bradt, *The Shortest Distance: Direct Filing and Choice of Law in Multidistrict Litigation*, 88 Notre Dame L. Rev. 759 (2012). Is this an attractive solution? Is it consistent with *Klaxon*?

SECTION 4. FEDERAL COMMON LAW

CLEARFIELD TRUST CO. V. UNITED STATES

318 U.S. 363 (1943).

MR. JUSTICE DOUGLAS delivered the opinion of the Court.

On April 28, 1936, a check was drawn on the Treasurer of the United States through the Federal Reserve Bank of Philadelphia to the order of Clair A. Barner in the amount of $24.20 . . . for services rendered by Barner to the Works Progress Administration. . . Some unknown person obtained it in a mysterious manner . . . , endorsed the check in the name of Barner and transferred it to J.C. Penney Co. in exchange for cash and merchandise. Barner never authorized the endorsement nor participated in the proceeds of the check. J.C. Penney Co. endorsed the check over to the Clearfield Trust Co. which . . . endorsed it as follows: "Pay to the order of Federal Reserve Bank of Philadelphia, Prior Endorsements Guaranteed."[1] . . . Neither the Clearfield Trust Co. nor J.C. Penney Co. had any knowledge or suspicion of the forgery. . . On or before May 10, 1936, Barner advised the timekeeper and the foreman of the W.P.A. project on which he was employed that he had not received the check. . . No notice was given the Clearfield Trust Co. or J.C. Penney Co. of the forgery until January 12, 1937. . . The first notice received by Clearfield Trust Co. that the United States was asking reimbursement was on August 31, 1937.

This suit was instituted in 1939 by the United States against the Clearfield Trust Co., the jurisdiction of the federal District Court being invoked pursuant to the provisions of § 24(1) of the Judicial Code [now 28 U.S.C. § 1345]. The cause of action was based on the express guaranty of prior endorsements made by the Clearfield Trust Co. . . The District Court held that the rights of the parties were to be determined by the law of Pennsylvania and that since the United States unreasonably delayed in giving notice of the forgery to the Clearfield Trust Co., it was barred from recovery. . . [T]he Circuit Court of Appeals reversed.

We agree with the Circuit Court of Appeals that the rule of *Erie R. Co. v. Tompkins,* 304 U.S. 64, does not apply to this action. The rights and duties of the United States on commercial paper which it issues are governed by federal rather than local law. When the United States disburses its funds or pays its debts, it is exercising a constitutional

---

[1] Guarantee of all prior indorsements on presentment for payment of such a check to Federal Reserve banks or member bank depositories is required by Treasury Regulations. * * *

function or power. This check was issued for services performed under the Federal Emergency Relief Act of 1935, 49 Stat. 115. The authority to issue the check had its origin in the Constitution and the statutes of the United States and was in no way dependent on the laws of Pennsylvania or of any other state. Cf. *Board of Commissioners v. United States,* 308 U.S. 343; *Royal Indemnity Co. v. United States,* 313 U.S. 289. The duties imposed upon the United States and the rights acquired by it as a result of the issuance find their roots in the same federal sources.[2] Cf. *Deitrick v. Greaney,* 309 U.S. 190; *D'Oench, Duhme & Co. v. Federal Deposit Ins. Corp.,* 315 U.S. 447. In absence of an applicable Act of Congress it is for the federal courts to fashion the governing rule of law according to their own standards. . .

In our choice of the applicable federal rule we have occasionally selected state law. See *Royal Indemnity Co. v. United States,* supra. But reasons which may make state law at times the appropriate federal rule are singularly inappropriate here. The issuance of commercial paper by the United States is on a vast scale and transactions in that paper from issuance to payment will commonly occur in several states. The application of state law, even without the conflict of laws rules of the forum, would subject the rights and duties of the United States to exceptional uncertainty. It would lead to great diversity in results by making identical transactions subject to the vagaries of the laws of the several states. The desirability of a uniform rule is plain. And while the federal law merchant developed for about a century under the regime of *Swift v. Tyson,* 16 Pet. 1, represented general commercial law rather than a choice of a federal rule designed to protect a federal right, it nevertheless stands as a convenient source of reference for fashioning federal rules applicable to these federal questions. . .

[The Court held that the United States was not barred because Clearfield had not shown that the delay in giving notice caused it injury.]

BANK OF AMERICA V. PARNELL

352 U.S. 29 (1956).

MR. JUSTICE FRANKFURTER delivered the opinion of the Court.

Petitioner, alleging diversity of citizenship, brought suit in the District Court for the Western District of Pennsylvania alleging that in September and October 1948 two individual defendants, Parnell and Rocco, and two corporate defendants, the First National Bank in Indiana and the Federal

---

[2] Various Treasury Regulations govern the payment and endorsement of government checks and warrants and the reimbursement of the Treasurer of the United States by Federal Reserve banks and member bank depositories on payment of checks or warrants bearing a forged endorsement. * * * Forgery of the check was an offense against the United States. * * *

Reserve Bank of Cleveland, had converted 73 Home Owners' Loan Corporation bonds which belonged to petitioner. . .

At the trial it appeared that these bonds were bearer bonds with payment guaranteed by the United States. They carried interest coupons calling for semi-annual payment. They were due to mature May 1, 1952, but pursuant to their terms, had been called on or about May 1, 1944. On May 2, 1944, the bonds disappeared while petitioner was getting them ready for presentation to the Federal Reserve Bank for payment. In 1948 they were presented to the First National Bank for payment by Parnell on behalf of Rocco. The First National Bank forwarded them to the Federal Reserve Bank of Cleveland. It cashed them and paid the First National Bank, which issued cashier's checks to Parnell. Parnell then turned the proceeds over to Rocco less a fee—there was conflicting testimony as to whether the fee was nominal or substantial.

The principal issue at the trial was whether the respondents took the bonds in good faith, without knowledge or notice of the defect in title. On this issue the trial judge charged: ". . . the two defendants, Parnell and the bank, . . . have the burden of showing that they acted innocently, honestly, and in good faith. . ." The jury brought in verdicts for petitioner. . . [T]he Court of Appeals . . . considered our decision in *Clearfield Trust Co. v. United States,* 318 U.S. 363, controlling and held that federal law placed the burden of proof on petitioner to show notice and lack of good faith on the part of respondents. The court further found that there was no evidence of bad faith by the First National Bank since the bonds were not "overdue" as a matter of federal law when presented to it and therefore directed entry of judgment for it. The court found that there was evidence of bad faith on the part of Parnell but ordered a new trial because of the erroneous instructions. . .

The Court of Appeals misconceived the nature of this litigation in holding that the *Clearfield Trust* case controlled. . .

Securities issued by the Government generate immediate interests of the Government. These were dealt with in *Clearfield Trust* and in *National Metropolitan Bank v. United States,* 323 U.S. 454. But they also radiate interests in transactions between private parties. The present litigation is purely between private parties and does not touch the rights and duties of the United States. The only possible interest of the United States in a situation like the one here, exclusively involving the transfer of Government paper between private persons, is that the floating of securities of the United States might somehow or other be adversely affected by the local rule of a particular State regarding the liability of a converter. This is far too speculative, far too remote a possibility to justify the application of federal law to transactions essentially of local concern.

We do not mean to imply that litigation with respect to Government paper necessarily precludes the presence of a federal interest, to be governed by federal law, in all situations merely because it is a suit between private parties, or that it is beyond the range of federal legislation to deal comprehensively with Government paper. We do not of course foreclose such judicial or legislative action in appropriate situations by concluding that this controversy over burden of proof and good faith represents too essentially a private transaction not to be dealt with by the local law of Pennsylvania where the transactions took place. Federal law of course governs the interpretation of the nature of the rights and obligations created by the Government bonds themselves. A decision with respect to the "overdueness" of the bonds is therefore a matter of federal law, which, in view of our holding, we need not elucidate. . .

Reversed and remanded.

MR. JUSTICE BLACK and MR. JUSTICE DOUGLAS, dissenting.

We believe that the "federal law merchant," which *Clearfield Trust Co. v. United States,* 318 U.S. 363, 367, held applicable to transactions in the commercial paper of the United States should be applicable to all transactions in that paper. . . Not until today has a distinction been drawn between suits by the United States on that paper and suits by other parties to it. But the Court does not stop there. Because this is "essentially a private transaction," it is to be governed by local law. Yet the nature of the rights and obligations created by commercial paper of the United States Government is said to be controlled by federal law. Thus, federal law is to govern some portion of a dispute between private parties, while that portion of the dispute which is "essentially of local concern" is to be governed by local law. The uncertainties which inhere in such a dichotomy are obvious. * * *

The virtue of a uniform law governing bonds, notes, and other paper issued by the United States is that it provides a certain and definite guide to the rights of all parties rather than subjecting them to the vagaries of the laws of many States. . . If the rule of the *Clearfield Trust* case is to be abandoned as to some parties, it should be abandoned as to all and we should start afresh on this problem.

BANCO NACIONAL DE CUBA V. SABBATINO

376 U.S. 398 (1964).

MR. JUSTICE HARLAN delivered the opinion of the Court. . .

[Relations between the United States and Fidel Castro's revolutionary regime in Cuba grew increasingly strained in 1960. In July of that year, responding to a U.S. reduction of Cuba's quota for sugar imports into the United States, Cuba nationalized the property of U.S. nationals in Cuba.

Among the expropriated property was sugar belonging to Compania Azucarera Vertientes (CAV), a Cuban corporation owned largely by U.S. residents. CAV had contracted to sell this sugar to Farr, Whitlock & Co., an American commodities broker. After the sugar was nationalized, however, Farr, Whitlock entered into a second contract to buy the sugar from the Cuban government. Farr, Whitlock shipped the sugar and received payment, but rather than pay the Cuban government, it turned the proceeds over to CAV's receiver, Sabbatino. Cuba assigned its rights under the second contract to Banco Nacional de Cuba, which filed suit in federal district court. The defendants argued that Cuba never had any right to the sugar because the Cuban expropriation violated international law.

[The district court ruled in favor of the defendants, disregarding the expropriation decree on the ground that it was retaliatory, discriminatory, and confiscatory; the court of appeals affirmed. The question before the Supreme Court was whether to reverse this ruling under the "act-of-state" doctrine, which provides that "the courts of one country will not sit in judgment on the acts of the government of another done within its own territory." The Court first held that application of the act-of-state doctrine—which would require the trial court to accept the validity of Cuba's expropriation—was compelled neither by international law nor by the Constitution.]

The act of state doctrine does, however, have "constitutional" underpinnings. It arises out of the basic relationships between branches of government in a system of separation of powers. It concerns the competency of dissimilar institutions to make and implement particular kinds of decisions in the area of international relations. The doctrine as formulated in past decisions expresses the strong sense of the Judicial Branch that its engagement in the task of passing on the validity of foreign acts of state may hinder rather than further this country's pursuit of goals both for itself and for the community of nations as a whole in the international sphere. Many commentators disagree with this view. . . Whatever considerations are thought to predominate, it is plain that the problems involved are uniquely federal in nature. If federal authority, in this instance this Court, orders the field of judicial competence in this area for the federal courts, and the state courts are left free to formulate their own rules, the purposes behind the doctrine could be as effectively undermined as if there had been no federal pronouncement on the subject. . .

[A]n issue concerned with a basic choice regarding the competence and function of the Judiciary and the National Executive in ordering our relationships with other members of the international community must be treated exclusively as an aspect of federal law.[23] It seems fair to assume that the Court did not have rules like the act of state doctrine in mind when it decided *Erie R. Co. v. Tompkins.* Soon thereafter, Professor Philip C. Jessup, now a judge of the International Court of Justice, recognized the potential dangers were *Erie* extended to legal problems affecting international relations.[24] He cautioned that rules of international law should not be left to divergent and perhaps parochial state interpretations. His basic rationale is equally applicable to the act of state doctrine. . .

We are not without other precedent for a determination that federal law governs; there are enclaves of federal judge-made law which bind the States. A national body of federal-court-built law has been held to have been contemplated by § 301 of the Labor Management Relations Act, *Textile Workers Union of America v. Lincoln Mills,* 353 U.S. 448. Principles formulated by federal judicial law have been thought by this Court to be necessary to protect uniquely federal interests, *D'Oench, Duhme & Co. v. Federal Deposit Ins. Corp.,* 315 U.S. 447; *Clearfield Trust Co. v. United States,* 318 U.S. 363. Of course the federal interest guarded in all these cases is one the ultimate statement of which is derived from a federal statute. Perhaps more directly in point are the bodies of law applied between States over boundaries and in regard to the apportionment of interstate waters.

In *Hinderlider v. La Plata River Ditch Co.,* 304 U.S. 92, 110, in an opinion handed down the same day as *Erie* and by the same author, Mr. Justice Brandeis, the Court declared, "For whether the water of an interstate stream must be apportioned between the two States is a question of 'federal common law' upon which neither the statutes nor the decisions of either State can be conclusive." Although the suit was between two private litigants and the relevant States could not be made parties, the Court considered itself free to determine the effect of an interstate compact regulating water apportionment. The decision implies that no State can undermine the federal interest in equitably apportioned interstate waters even if it deals with private parties. This would not mean that, absent a compact, the apportionment scheme could not be changed judicially or by Congress, but only that apportionment is a matter of federal law. * * * The problems surrounding the act of state doctrine are, albeit for different reasons, as intrinsically federal as are those involved in water apportionment or boundary disputes. The consideration supporting exclusion of state authority here are much like those which led the Court in *United States v. California,* 332 U.S. 19, to hold that the Federal Government possessed paramount rights in submerged lands though

---

[23] At least this is true when the Court limits the scope of judicial inquiry. We need not now consider whether a state court might, in certain circumstances, adhere to a more restrictive view concerning the scope of examination of foreign acts than that required by this Court.

[24] The Doctrine of Erie Railroad v. Tompkins Applied to International Law, 33 Am.J.Int'l L. 740 (1939).

within the three-mile limit of coastal States. We conclude that the scope of the act of state doctrine must be determined according to federal law.[25]

[Because a challenge to the Cuban decree would "be likely to give offense to the expropriating country" and "could seriously interfere with negotiations being carried on by the Executive Branch," the Court held the decree could not be challenged. Justice White, in dissent, did not dispute the conclusion that the issue was one of federal law. The act-of-state doctrine is considered in greater detail infra pp. 1055–1072.]

Federal Common Law and Incorporation of State Law

(1) Friendly, *In Praise of Erie—And of the New Federal Common Law*, 39 N.Y.U.L.Rev. 383, 407, 421 (1964):

> By focusing judicial attention on the nature of the right being enforced, *Erie* caused the principle of a specialized federal common law, binding in all courts because of its source, to develop within a quarter century into a powerful unifying force. . . The Supreme Court, in the years since *Erie,* has been forging a new centripetal tool incalculably useful to our federal system. It has employed a variety of techniques—spontaneous generation as in the cases of government contracts or interstate controversies, implication of a private federal cause of action from a statute providing other sanctions, construing a jurisdictional grant as a command to fashion federal law, and the normal judicial filling of statutory interstices.

(2) What was the source of authority for the creation of federal common law in *Clearfield* and in *Sabbatino*? As those opinions demonstrate, the Supreme Court has not always been very explicit on this question. An obvious possibility in *Clearfield* would have been to hold that the grant of jurisdiction over cases to which the United States is a party—like those in admiralty cases and suits between states, see supra p. 835, and unlike the diversity grant—gives the federal courts lawmaking powers. Some lower courts have so indicated, e.g., *Tri-State Ins. Co. v. United States,* 340 F.2d 542, 544 (8th Cir. 1965); *RFC v. United Distillers Products Corp.*, 229 F.2d 665, 666 (2d Cir. 1956), but the Supreme Court seems never to have said so. Alexander Hamilton was cryptic as to the reasons for this grant of jurisdiction: "Controversies between the nation and its members or citizens, can only be properly referred to the national tribunals. Any

---

[25] Various constitutional and statutory provisions indirectly support this determination, see U.S. Const., Art. I, § 8, cls. 3, 10; Art. II, §§ 2, 3; Art. III, § 2; 28 U.S.C. §§ 1251(a)(2), (b)(1), (b)(3), 1332(a)(2), 1333, 1350–1351, by reflecting a concern for uniformity in this country's dealings with foreign nations and indicating a desire to give matters of international significance to the jurisdiction of federal institutions. * * *

other plan would be contrary to reason, to precedent, and to decorum." *The Federalist,* No. 80. Do you suppose the framers of Article III meant only to protect the Government from bias in the administration of state law, and to leave the definition of its rights to the states in the absence of congressional action?

In other cases the courts have inferred common lawmaking authority from federal statutes. For example, in *Textile Workers v. Lincoln Mills,* 353 U.S. 448 (1957), the Supreme Court held that the purposes of the Taft-Hartley Act demanded a federal judge-made law governing the enforcement of collective-bargaining agreements, although the statute spoke only of jurisdiction; and in *J.I. Case Co. v. Borak,* 377 U.S. 426 (1964), the Court held that violation of rules promulgated under § 14(a) of the Securities Act, 15 U.S.C. § 78n(a) (misleading proxy solicitations), gave rise to private claims governed by federal law. There is no constitutional objection to a congressional grant of common-law power, is there? Compare the doctrines limiting delegation of congressional powers to the executive, *A.L.A. Schechter Poultry Corp. v. United States,* 295 U.S. 495 (1935), and to the states, *Knickerbocker Ice Co. v. Stewart,* 253 U.S. 149 (1920). Is it fair to say that the Court in *Clearfield* based its lawmaking authority on statutes and regulations adopted under the money powers of Congress? Can *Sabbatino* be explained in this fashion? Note the attempt in footnote 25 of the opinion to suggest a statutory or constitutional source.

Is *Sabbatino* best understood as an example of what Judge Friendly calls "spontaneous generation"?[1] Do federal courts have the constitutional authority to make such law after *Erie*? In *United States v. Standard Oil Co.,* 332 U.S. 301, 307 (1947), the Court held that the government's right to recover for injuries to a soldier was a matter of federal common law, explaining:

> [T]he matter in issue is neither primarily one of state interest nor exclusively for determination by state law within the spirit and purpose of the *Erie* decision. . . [*Erie*'s] object and effect were . . . to bring federal judicial power under subjection to state authority in matters essentially of local interest and state control. Conversely there was no purpose or effect for broadening state power over matters essentially of federal character.

Does this mean that federal courts could use Congress's commerce power to create a federal common law of injuries to trespassers upon interstate

---

[1] Judge Friendly cites two cases for this technique, *Priebe & Sons, Inc. v. United States,* 332 U.S. 407 (1947), and *Hinderlider v. La Plata River and Cherry Creek Ditch Co.,* 304 U.S. 92 (1938). Though the Court did not specify the basis for creating federal common law in either decision, both fit easily into the traditional pattern. *Priebe* applied federal common law to determine the validity of a liquidated damages clause in a government contract authorized by federal law, in a case to which the United States was a party. *Hinderlider* required the Court to determine water rights under an interstate compact approved by Congress (making matters of construction federal questions).

railroads? Is this theory contrary to the Rules of Decision Act? Is *Sabbatino*? See also Kramer, *The Lawmaking Power of the Federal Courts,* 12 Pace L. Rev. 263 (1992) (arguing that, as a matter of separation of powers, federal courts can make common law on any subject which the Constitution allows the federal government to regulate, but that federalism concerns require the courts to wait for Congress to take the first step with respect to matters within the concurrent jurisdiction of the states; *Sabbatino* was thus properly decided because the Constitution preempts state authority over international relations).

The questions posed in this note underscore the important point that the *Erie* doctrine is not limited to diversity cases; even in a federal-question case, some issues may be governed by state law.

(3) Friendly, *In Praise of Erie—And of the New Federal Common Law,* 39 N.Y.U. L. Rev. 383, 410 (1964):

> *Clearfield* decided not one issue but two. The first, to which most of the opinion was devoted and on which it is undeniably sound, is that the right of the United States to recover for conversion of a Government check is a federal right, so that the courts of the United States may formulate a rule of decision. The second, over which the Supreme Court jumped rather quickly and not altogether convincingly, is whether, having this opportunity, the federal courts should adopt a uniform nation-wide rule or should follow state law. . . [T]he question persists why it is more important that federal fiscal officials rather than Pennsylvanians dealing in commercial paper should have the solace of uniformity. The issue that must be determined in each instance is what heed Congress intended to have paid to state law in an area where no heed need constitutionally be paid—more realistically, in Gray's famous phrase, "to guess what it would have intended on a point not present to its mind, if the point had been present."

Suppose that after the Supreme Court's decision in *Clearfield* the bank sued J.C. Penney, its endorser, to make good its loss. Does *Parnell* mean that in the bank's action the issue of late notice is governed by state law? Would that be tolerable?

Notice that in both *Clearfield* and *Parnell* the Court approached the choice-of-law problem without regard to whether state law favored the plaintiff or the defendant, or to the purpose of the law. What do you think of that?

(4) Further evidence of the difficulty of predicting when the Supreme Court will resort to federal common law is afforded by decisions concerning torts affecting the Government. Rather early it was established that the United States could sue for trespass although no federal statute said so: "As an owner of property in almost every state of the Union, they [the

United States] have the same right to have it protected by the local laws that other persons have." *Cotton v. United States,* 52 U.S. (11 How.) 229, 231 (1850). And, still during the era of *Swift v. Tyson,* the Court held that the measure of damages for the conversion of oil from federal land was a "local" matter governed by state law. *Mason v. United States,* 260 U.S. 545 (1923). Moreover, the Federal Tort Claims Act, 28 U.S.C. § 1346(b), enacted in 1946, explicitly makes the tort liability of the United States dependent in the main upon "the law of the place where the act or omission occurred," and in 1963 the Supreme Court squarely held that the liability of a federal officer in tort, if any, had to be based upon state law. *Wheeldin v. Wheeler,* 373 U.S. 647, 652 (1963). Yet in *Howard v. Lyons,* 360 U.S. 593 (1959), a diversity case, the court held that the extent of the privilege accorded federal officers for official statements "allegedly defamatory under state law" was a matter of federal law:

> The authority of a federal officer to act derives from federal sources, and the rule which recognizes a privilege under appropriate circumstances as to statements made in the course of duty is one designed to promote the effective functioning of the Federal Government. No subject could be one of more peculiarly federal concern, and it would deny the very considerations which give the rule of privilege its being to leave determination of its extent to the vagaries of the laws of the several States. *Cf. Clearfield Trust Co. v. United States,* 318 U.S. 363. We hold that the validity of petitioner's claim of absolute privilege must be judged by federal standards, to be formulated by the courts in the absence of legislative action by Congress.

360 U.S. at 597.

What sense is there in the distinction between *Howard* and *Wheeldin*? In *Boyle v. United Technologies Corp.,* 487 U.S. 500 (1988), the Court held that military suppliers have a federal common law immunity in tort actions brought by injured soldiers and their families. Boyle, a Marine helicopter copilot, was killed when a helicopter built by United Technologies crashed during a training exercise. Boyle's father sued, alleging that the helicopter's escape-hatch was defective, and a jury awarded $725,000. The court of appeals reversed on the ground that United Technologies satisfied the requirements of a federal common law "military contractor" defense. This defense extends the government's immunity to private suppliers if (1) the United States approved "reasonably precise" specifications in the contract; (2) the equipment conformed to those specifications; and (3) the supplier warned the United States about dangers in the use of the equipment that were known to the supplier but not to the United States. In affirming, the Supreme Court explained that

> a few areas, involving "uniquely federal interests," * * * are so committed by the Constitution and laws of the United States to federal control that state law is pre-empted and replaced, where necessary, by federal law of a content prescribed (absent explicit statutory directive) by the courts—so-called "federal common law."

The dispute in *Boyle,* the Court continued, "borders upon" two areas previously found to involve such interests: contract disputes in which the United States is a party (because holding United Technologies liable would affect future military procurement contracts), and tort suits against federal officials for actions in the course of their duty (because the government's interest is the same whether its business is carried out by employees or by independent contractors). The Court added that state law should not be displaced unless its use would undermine federal interests, but found that "[h]ere, the state-imposed duty of care that is the asserted basis of the contractor's liability (specifically, the duty to equip helicopters with the sort of escape-hatch mechanism petitioner claims was necessary) is precisely contrary to the duty imposed by the Government contract (the duty to manufacture and deliver helicopters with the sort of escape-hatch mechanism shown by the specifications)."

(5) Does the Alien Tort Statute, 28 U.S.C. § 1350, authorize federal courts to a recognize private cause of action for violations of the law of nations? The statute, which was enacted in 1789, uses wholly jurisdictional language: "The district courts shall have original jurisdiction of any civil action by an alien for a tort only, committed in violation of the law of nations or a treaty of the United States." In *Sosa v. Alvarez-Machain,* 542 U.S. 692 (2004), the Court assumed "that the First Congress understood that the district courts would recognize private causes of action for certain torts in violation of the law of nations, though we have found no basis to suspect Congress had any examples in mind beyond those torts corresponding to Blackstone's three primary offenses: violation of safe conducts, infringement of the rights of ambassadors, and piracy." *Id.* at 724. As to whether courts could recognize causes of action beyond these narrow categories, the Court had this to say:

> [T]he judicial power should be exercised on the understanding that the door is still ajar subject to vigilant doorkeeping, and thus open to a narrow class of international norms today. *Erie* did not in terms bar any judicial recognition of new substantive rules, no matter what the circumstances, and post-*Erie* understanding has identified limited enclaves in which federal courts may derive some substantive law in a common law way.

Id. at 729. Is this an accurate statement of the current status of federal common law? What is the basis for judicial law-making under the Alien

Tort Statute? See *Nestle USA, Inc. v. Doe*, 141 S. Ct. 1931, 1942 (2021) (Gorsuch, J., concurring) ("nothing in the statute's terse terms obviously authorizes federal courts to invent new causes of action on their own").

(6) A classic statement of the relationship between state and federal law is found in Fallon, et al., Hart and Wechsler's The Federal Courts and the Federal System 488–89 (7th ed. 2015):

> Federal law is generally interstitial in its nature. It rarely occupies a legal field completely, totally excluding all participation by the legal systems of the states. . . It builds upon legal relationships established by the states, altering or supplanting them only so far as necessary for the special purpose. Congress acts, in short, against the background of the total *corpus juris* of the states in much the way that a state legislature acts against the background of the common law, assumed to govern unless changed by legislation. That this is so was partially affirmed in [the Rules of Decision Act].

Sometimes, as in the Tort Claims Act (supra note (4)), Congress expressly incorporates state law to determine federal rights. In other cases, federal statutes have been held to refer to state law although they were silent on the question. See, for example, *De Sylva v. Ballentine,* 351 U.S. 570, 580–82 (1956), in which the Court (speaking through Justice Harlan) looked to state law in holding that a child born out of wedlock came within the statutory provision for renewal of a copyright by the "children" of a deceased author:

> The scope of a federal right is, of course, a federal question, but that does not mean that its content is not to be determined by state, rather than federal law. * * * This is especially true where a statute deals with a familial relationship; there is no federal law of domestic relations, which is primarily a matter of state concern.

In *Kamen v. Kemper Fin. Servs., Inc.,* 500 U.S. 90 (1991), the Court was called upon to define the contours of a demand requirement in a shareholders derivative action founded on the Investment Company Act (ICA). While noting that "[b]ecause the ICA is a federal statute, any common law rule necessary to effectuate a private cause of action under that statute is necessarily federal," the Court said that there was a presumption in favor of incorporating state law. Preemptive federal common law should be created "only when the scheme in question evidences a distinct need for nationwide legal standards, * * * or when express provisions in analogous statutory schemes embody congressional policy choices readily applicable to the issue at hand." This presumption is "particularly strong" in areas like corporate law, where "private parties have entered legal relationships with the expectation that their rights and obligations would be governed by state law standards." Consequently, the

Court held, the trial court should have used state law, which included a futility exception to the requirement.

Similar reasoning featured in the Court's unanimous opinion in *Rodriguez v. FDIC*, 140 S. Ct. 713, 717 (2020), which rejected the use of federal common law to determine how a consolidated corporate tax refund should be distributed among members of a group that files a consolidated tax return. "[S]tate law," said the Court, "is well equipped to handle disputes involving corporate property rights. That cases like the one now before us happen to involve corporate property rights in the context of a federal bankruptcy and a tax dispute doesn't change much." *Id.* at 719.

Is this the same reasoning Justice Scalia employed in *Semtek*? How exactly can one tell whether there is a "distinct need for need for nationwide legal standards"?

(7) The Foreign Sovereign Immunities Act, 28 U.S.C. § 1330, provides the exclusive basis for federal jurisdiction over claims against a foreign state when an exception to sovereign immunity exists. In such cases, the foreign state is to be held liable "in the same manner and to the same extent as a private individual." 28 U.S.C. § 1606. Which choice-of-law rules should govern these cases, if the substantive claim arises under state law? Departing from other courts of appeals, the Ninth Circuit held that a federal common law of choice of law applies. *Cassirer v. Thyssen-Bornemisza Collection Foundation*, 862 F.3d 951, 961 (9th Cir. 2017). The Supreme Court granted certiorari, 142 S.Ct. 55 (2021). Does the reasoning of *Klaxon* suggest that the Ninth Circuit is wrong? Or are these cases analogous to *Semtek*—and in which case, what result?

(8) To what extent does the Rules of Decision Act dictate the answer to the cases discussed in these notes?

SECTION 5. PREEMPTION AND SUPREMACY

Closely related to the question of whether a federal statute authorizes the creation of federal common law is the question of whether a federal statute preempts state law. In cases of clear conflict between substantive state law and substantive federal law, no difficulty arises. Article VI of the Constitution makes federal law "the supreme Law of the Land" and provides that "the Judges in every State shall be bound thereby." But not all supremacy issues present themselves in such simple fashion. This section first considers how the Court goes about determining whether a conflict exists. It then considers two supremacy-related problems involving the litigation of federal claims in state court: cases in which a state court declines to exercise jurisdiction over a federal claim and those in which a state court applies state procedural rules that undermine federal substantive rights (what has been called a "reverse-*Erie*" problem).

A. PREEMPTION

ENGLISH V. GENERAL ELECTRIC CO.

496 U.S. 72 (1990).

JUSTICE BLACKMUN delivered the opinion of the Court. . .

I

Petitioner Vera M. English was employed from 1972 to 1984 as a laboratory technician at the nuclear-fuels production facility operated by respondent General Electric Company (GE) in Wilmington, N.C. In February 1984, petitioner complained to GE's management and to the Nuclear Regulatory Commission (NRC) about several perceived violations of nuclear-safety standards at the facility, including the failure of her co-workers to clean up radioactive material spills in the laboratory.

[Frustrated by the company's lack of response, English dramatized her concerns by deliberately not cleaning a contaminated table, instead outlining the spill with red tape to make it conspicuous. A few days later she called her supervisor's attention to the fact that the spill had still not been cleaned. For this she was disciplined and, some months later, fired.]

In August, petitioner filed a complaint with the Secretary of Labor charging GE with violating § 210(a) of the Energy Reorganization Act of 1974 * * * which makes it unlawful for an employer in the nuclear industry to

"discharge any employee or otherwise discriminate against any employee with respect to his compensation, terms, conditions, or privileges of employment because the employee . . .

"(1) commenced, caused to be commenced, or is about to commence or cause to be commenced a proceeding under this Act or the Atomic Energy Act of 1954, as amended, or a proceeding for the administration or enforcement of any requirement imposed under this Act or the Atomic Energy Act of 1954, as amended;

"(2) testified or is about to testify in any such proceeding or;

"(3) assisted or participated or is about to assist or participate in any manner in such a proceeding . . . or in any other action to carry out the purposes of this Act or the Atomic Energy Act of 1954, as amended."

. . .

The Secretary, however, dismissed the complaint as untimely because it had not been filed, as required by § 210(b)(1), within 30 days after the May 15 notice of the company's final decision.

In March 1987, petitioner filed a diversity action against GE in the United States District Court for the Eastern District of North Carolina.

Petitioner in four counts raised two claims, one for wrongful discharge and one for intentional infliction of emotional distress. With respect to the latter, petitioner alleged that she was suffering from severe depression and emotional harm as a result of GE's "extreme and outrageous conduct." . . . Petitioner sought punitive as well as compensatory damages.

Although the District Court concluded that petitioner had stated a valid claim for intentional infliction of emotional distress under North Carolina law, it nonetheless granted GE's motion to dismiss. * * * The court did not accept GE's argument that petitioner's claim fell within the field of nuclear safety, a field that, according to GE, had been completely pre-empted by the Federal Government. The court held, however, that petitioner's claim was pre-empted because it conflicted with three particular aspects of § 210: (1) a provision that bars recovery under the section to any employee who "deliberately causes a violation of any requirement of [the Energy Reorganization Act,] or of the Atomic Energy Act," § 210(g); (2) the absence of any provision generally authorizing the Secretary to award exemplary or punitive damages; and (3) the provisions requiring that a whistleblower invoking the statute file an administrative complaint within 30 days after the violation occurs, and that the Secretary resolve the complaint within 90 days after its filing. See § 210(b)(1) and (b)(2)(A). In the court's view, Congress enacted this scheme to foreclose all remedies to whistle-blowers who themselves violate nuclear-safety requirements, to limit exemplary damages awards against the nuclear industry, and to guarantee speedy resolution of allegations of nuclear-safety violations-goals the court found incompatible with the broader remedies petitioner sought under state tort law.

The United States Court of Appeals for the Fourth Circuit affirmed. . .

II

A

The sole question for our resolution is whether the Federal Government has pre-empted petitioner's state-law tort claim for intentional infliction of emotional distress. Our cases have established that state law is pre-empted under the Supremacy Clause, * * *, in three circumstances. First, Congress can define explicitly the extent to which its enactments pre-empt state law. * * * Pre-emption fundamentally is a question of congressional intent * * * and when Congress has made its intent known through explicit statutory language, the courts' task is an easy one.

Second, in the absence of explicit statutory language, state law is pre-empted where it regulates conduct in a field that Congress intended the Federal Government to occupy exclusively. Such an intent may be inferred from a "scheme of federal regulation . . . so pervasive as to make reasonable the inference that Congress left no room for the States to supplement it," or where an Act of Congress "touch[es] a field in which the federal interest is so dominant that the federal system will be assumed to preclude enforcement of state laws on the same subject." * * * Although this Court has not hesitated to draw an inference of field pre-emption where it is supported by the federal statutory and regulatory schemes, it has emphasized: "Where . . . the field which Congress is said to have pre-empted" includes areas that have "been traditionally occupied by the States," congressional intent to supersede state laws must be "clear and manifest." * * *

Finally, state law is pre-empted to the extent that it actually conflicts with federal law. Thus, the Court has found pre-emption where it is impossible for a private party to comply with both state and federal requirements, * * *, or where state law "stands as an obstacle to the accomplishment and execution of the full purposes and objectives of Congress." * * *[5]

It is undisputed that Congress has not explicitly pre-empted petitioner's state-law tort action by inserting specific pre-emptive language into any of its enactments governing the nuclear industry. The District Court and apparently the Court of Appeals did not rest their decisions on a field pre-emption rationale either, but rather on what they considered an actual tension between petitioner's cause of action and the congressional goals reflected in § 210. In this Court, respondent seeks to defend the judgment both on the lower courts' rationale and on the alternative ground that petitioner's tort claim is located within a field reserved for federal regulation—the field of nuclear safety. Before turning to the specific aspects of § 210 on which the lower courts based their decisions, we address the field pre-emption question.

B

This is not the first case in which the Court has had occasion to consider the extent to which Congress has pre-empted the field of nuclear safety. In *Pacific Gas & Electric Co. v. State Energy Resources Conservation and Development Comm'n*, 461 U.S. 190 (1983), the Court carefully analyzed the congressional enactments relating to the nuclear industry in order to decide whether a California law that conditioned the construction of a nuclear powerplant on a state agency's approval of the plant's nuclear-waste storage and disposal facilities fell within a pre-empted field. Although we need not repeat all of that analysis here, we summarize briefly the Court's discussion of the actions Congress has taken in the nuclear realm and the conclusions it drew from these actions.

---

[5] By referring to these three categories, we should not be taken to mean that they are rigidly distinct. Indeed, field pre-emption may be understood as a species of conflict pre-emption: A state law that falls within a pre-empted field conflicts with Congress' intent (either express or plainly implied) to exclude state regulation. Nevertheless, because we previously have adverted to the three-category framework, we invoke and apply it here.

[The Court here described the evolution of the regulatory framework.]

After reviewing the relevant statutory provisions and legislative history, the Court in Pacific Gas concluded that "the Federal Government has occupied the entire field of nuclear safety concerns, except the limited powers expressly ceded to the States." * * * Although we ultimately determined that the California statute at issue there did not fall within the pre-empted field, we made clear our view that Congress intended that only "the Federal Government should regulate the radiological safety aspects involved in the construction and operation of a nuclear plant." * * * In the present dispute, respondent and petitioner disagree as to whether petitioner's tort action falls within the boundaries of the pre-empted field referred to in Pacific Gas.

Respondent maintains that the pre-empted field of "nuclear safety" is a large one, and that § 210 is an integral part of it. Specifically, respondent contends that because the Federal Government is better able to promote nuclear safety if whistleblowers pursue the federal remedy, *the whole area* marked off by § 210 should be considered part of the pre-empted field identified in *Pacific Gas.* Accordingly, respondent argues that all state-law remedies for conduct that is covered by § 210 are pre-empted by Congress' decision to have the Federal Government exclusively regulate the field of nuclear safety.

Petitioner and the United States as *amicus curiae,* on their part, contend that petitioner's claim for intentional infliction of emotional distress is not pre-empted because the Court made clear in *Pacific Gas* that state laws supported by nonsafety rationales do not lie within the pre-empted field. They argue that since the state tort of intentional infliction of emotional distress is supported by a nonsafety rationale—namely, the State's "substantial interest in protecting its citizens from the kind of abuse of which [petitioner] complain[s]" * * *—petitioner's cause of action must be allowed to go forward.

We think both arguments are somewhat wide of the mark. With respect to respondent's contention, we find no "clear and manifest" intent on the part of Congress, in enacting § 210, to pre-empt all state tort laws that *traditionally* have been available to those persons who, like petitioner, allege outrageous conduct at the hands of an employer. Indeed, acceptance of respondent's argument would require us to conclude that Congress has displaced not only state tort law, which is at issue in this case, but also state *criminal* law, to the extent that such criminal law is applied to retaliatory conduct occurring at the site of a nuclear employer. For example, if an employer were to retaliate against a nuclear whistleblower by hiring thugs to assault the employee on the job (conduct literally covered by § 210), respondent's position would imply that the state criminal law prohibiting such conduct is within the pre-empted field. We simply cannot believe that Congress intended that result. Instead, we think the District Court was essentially correct in observing that while § 210 obviously bears some relation to the field of nuclear safety, its "paramount" purpose was the protection of employees. * * * Accordingly, we see no basis for respondent's contention that all state-law claims arising from conduct covered by the section are necessarily included in the pre-empted field.

Nor, however, can we accept petitioner's position, or the reading of *Pacific Gas* on which it is based. It is true that the holding in that case was premised, in part, on the conclusion that the California ban on nuclear construction was not motivated by safety concerns. Indeed, the majority of the Court suggested that a "state moratorium on nuclear construction grounded in safety concerns falls squarely within the prohibited field." * * * In other words, the Court defined the pre-empted field, in part, by reference to the motivation behind the state law. This approach to defining the field had some support in the text of the 1959 amendments to the Atomic Energy Act, which provided, among other things, that "[n]othing in this section shall be construed to affect the authority of any State or local agency to regulate activities *for purposes other than protection against radiation hazards.*" * * * But the Court did not suggest that a finding of safety motivation was *necessary* to place a state law within the pre-empted field. On the contrary, it took great pains to make clear that state regulation of matters directly affecting the radiological safety of nuclear-plant construction and operation, "even if enacted out of nonsafety concerns, would nevertheless [infringe upon] the NRC's exclusive authority." * * * Thus, even as the Court suggested that part of the pre-empted field is defined by reference to the purpose of the state law in question, it made clear that another part of the field is defined by the state law's actual effect on nuclear safety.

Because it is clear that the state tort law at issue here is not motivated by safety concerns, the former portion of the field argument is not relevant. The real issue, then, is whether petitioner's tort claim is so related to the "radiological safety aspects involved in the . . . operation of a nuclear [facility]" * * * that it falls within the pre-empted field. In addressing this issue, we must bear in mind that not every state law that in some remote way may affect the nuclear safety decisions made by those who build and run nuclear facilities can be said to fall within the pre-empted field. We have no doubt, for instance, that the application of state minimum wage and child labor laws to employees at nuclear facilities would not be pre-empted, even though these laws could be said to affect tangentially some of the resource allocation decisions that might have a bearing on radiological safety. Instead, for a state law to fall within the pre-empted zone, it must have some direct and substantial effect on the decisions made by those who build or operate nuclear facilities concerning radiological safety levels. We recognize that the claim for intentional infliction of emotional distress at issue here may have some effect on these decisions, because liability for claims like petitioner's will attach additional consequences to retaliatory conduct by employers. As employers find retaliation more costly, they will be forced to deal with complaints by whistle-blowers by other means, including altering radiological safety policies. Nevertheless, we believe that this effect is neither direct nor substantial enough to place petitioner's claim in the pre-empted field.

C

We now turn to the question whether, as the lower courts concluded, petitioner's claim conflicts with particular aspects of § 210. On its face, the section does no more than grant a federal administrative remedy to employees in one industry against one type of employer discrimination-retaliation for whistle-blowing. Ordinarily, the mere existence of a federal regulatory or enforcement scheme, even one as detailed as § 210, does not by itself imply pre-emption of state remedies. The Court has observed: "Undoubtedly, every subject that merits congressional legislation is, by definition, a subject of national concern. That cannot mean, however, that every federal statute ousts all related state law. . . Instead, we must look for special features warranting pre-emption." * * * Here, the District Court identified three "special features" of § 210 that it believed were incompatible with petitioner's claim.

The District Court relied first on § 210(g), which provides that "Subsection (a) of this section [the prohibition on employer retaliation] shall not apply" where an employee "deliberately causes a violation of any requirement of this Act or of the Atomic Energy Act." According to the District Court and respondent, this section reflects a congressional desire to preclude *all* relief, including state remedies, to a whistle-blower who deliberately commits a safety violation referred to in § 210(g). Permitting any state-law claim based on whistle-blowing retaliation, the court reasoned, would frustrate this congressional objective. We do not agree. As an initial matter, we note that the text of § 210(g) specifically limits its applicability to the remedy provided by § 210(a) and does not suggest that it bars state-law tort actions. Nor does the legislative history of § 210 reveal a clear congressional purpose to supplant state-law causes of action that might afford broader relief. Indeed, the only explanation for any of the statute's remedial limitations is the Committee Report's statement that employees who deliberately violate nuclear-safety requirements would be denied protection under § 210(g) "[i]n order to avoid abuse of the protection afforded *under this section*." * * *

The District Court also relied on the absence in § 210 of general authorization for the Secretary to award exemplary damages against employers who engage in retaliatory conduct. The District Court concluded, and respondent now argues, that this absence implies a congressional intent to bar a state action, like petitioner's, that permits such an award. As the District Court put it, § 210 reflects "an informed judgment [by Congress] that in no circumstances should a nuclear whistler blower receive punitive damages when fired or discriminated against because of his or her safety complaints." * * * We believe the District Court and respondent have read too much into Congress' decision not to authorize exemplary damages for most § 210 violations. First, even with respect to actions brought under § 210, the District Court was incorrect in stating that "in no circumstances" will a nuclear whistle-blower receive punitive damages; § 210(d) authorizes a district court to award exemplary damages in enforcement proceedings brought by the Secretary. Moreover, and more importantly, we think the District Court failed to follow this Court's teaching that "[o]rdinarily, state causes of action are not pre-empted solely because they impose liability over and above that authorized by federal law." * * * Absent some specific suggestion in the text or legislative history of § 210, which we are unable to find, we cannot conclude that Congress intended to pre-empt all state actions that permit the recovery of exemplary damages.

Finally, we address the District Court's holding that the expeditious time-frames provided by Congress for the processing of § 210 claims reflect a congressional decision that no whistle-blower should be able to recover under any other law after the time for filing under § 210 has expired. The District Court reasoned, and respondent agrees, that if a state-law remedy is available after the time for filing a § 210 complaint has run, a whistle-blower will have less incentive to bring a § 210 complaint. As a result, the argument runs, federal regulatory agencies will remain unaware of some safety violations and retaliatory behavior and will thus be unable to ensure radiological safety at nuclear facilities. We cannot deny that there is some force to this argument, but we do not believe that the problem is as great as respondent suggests.

First, many, if not most, retaliatory incidents come about as a response to safety complaints that employees register with federal regulatory agencies. The Federal Government thus is already aware of these safety violations, whether or not the employee invokes the remedial provisions of § 210. Also, we are not so sure as respondent seems to be that employees will forgo their § 210 options and rely solely on state remedies for retaliation. Such a prospect is simply too speculative a basis on which to rest a finding of pre-emption. The Court has observed repeatedly that pre-emption is ordinarily not to be implied absent an "actual conflict." * * * The "teaching of this Court's decisions . . . enjoin[s] seeking out conflicts between state and federal regulation where none clearly exists." * * *

Preemption of State Law

(1) As *English* notes, there are three different kinds of preemption. "Express preemption" occurs when a statute explicitly states that certain kinds of state claims are preempted. Express preemption analysis is not always as easy as *English* suggests. Some statutes preempt state "standards" or "requirements" that are not identical to federal standards, and the question of which, if any, common-law actions are preempted has proved difficult. In *Riegel v. Medtronic, Inc.*, 552 U.S. 312 (2008), for example, the Court construed Congress's use of the word "requirement[s]" in the preemption clause of Medical Device Amendments of 1976 ("MDA"), 21 U.S.C. § 360k(a), to mean that premarket approval of a medical device by the Food and Drug Administration ("FDA") preempted state common-law actions alleging that the device was defectively designed, labeled, or manufactured. In dissent, Justice Ginsburg read "requirement[s]" as referring solely to state statutes and regulatory enactments. Complicating the matter further, Congress may include a "saving clause" indicating an intent not to preempt certain claims; figuring out where preemption ends and saving begins is often no easy task. See, e.g., *Geier v. American Honda Motor Co.*, 529 U.S. 861 (2000) (interpreting preemption and saving clauses of National Traffic and Motor Vehicle Safety Act).

"Field preemption" occurs when the court decides that a federal regulatory scheme is so comprehensive that any state supplementation would be an interference, or that the federal interest in an area of law is so dominant as to preclude state involvement. Here again, difficult questions arise with respect to the definition of the exclusively federal field. May a state make it a misdemeanor for aliens to fail to carry an alien registration document? In *Arizona v. United States*, 567 U.S. 387, 400–03 (2012), the Supreme Court said yes, on the grounds that Congress had occupied the field of alien registration, including on matters of enforcement. On the other hand, the Court upheld another provision of the same law, which required state officers to make a reasonable attempt to ascertain the immigration status of any person they stop or detain if they have reasonable suspicion that the person is an alien unlawfully present in the United States? *Id.* at 411–15. Why was this provision not in the preempted field?

Last, "implied conflict preemption" occurs when, despite the absence of express or field preemption, enforcement of a state law would conflict with federal law. Conflict may be obvious—if it is impossible to comply with both state and federal law—or it may be more subtle, if the state law "stands as an obstacle to the accomplishment and execution of the full purposes and objectives of Congress." *Hines v. Davidowitz*, 312 U.S. 52, 67 (1941).

Are all these variants of preemption applications of a single principle? What is that principle?

(2) The choice-of-law analogs to express and field preemption may not be obvious. (Is an express preemption clause a statutory solution to a choice-of-law problem?). The analysis that goes into implied conflict preemption, however, looks very much like interest analysis: the court examines the policy behind the federal law to see if enforcement of the state law would frustrate that policy. See Davis, *On Preemption, Congressional Intent, and Conflict of Laws*, 66 U. Pitt. L. Rev. 181 (2004). If there is a conflict, it is of course resolved in favor of federal law, and this too looks like a particular solution (here, constitutionally prescribed) to a true conflict. But if there is no conflict, the result is that *both* state and federal law are given effect. Why is that? Is there any analog in the choice-of-law theories we have seen? Should there be?

(3) For examples of implied conflict preemption analysis, consider the following cases:

(a) *Geier v. American Honda Motor Co.*, 529 U.S. 861 (2000). Alexis Geier was injured when her 1987 Honda Accord struck a tree. She sued Honda under District of Columbia tort law, claiming that the car was defectively designed because it lacked a driver's side airbag. Honda argued that the design defect claim was preempted by the National Motor Vehicle Safety Act and Federal Motor Vehicle Safety Standard 208, promulgated under the Act. After concluding that common law tort suits were neither expressly preempted by the Act's preemption clause nor expressly preserved by its saving clause, the Court considered implied preemption.

Safety Standard 208 required manufacturers to equip at least 10% of their 1987 vehicles with passive restraints (at the time chiefly either airbags or auto-locking seatbelts) meeting a specified performance standard. Geier argued that this represented a federal minimum requirement, reflecting the conclusion that airbags were desirable, and was therefore not inconsistent with a state tort rule providing that an absence of airbags constituted defective design. By a 5–4 vote, the Supreme Court disagreed. It noted that the Department of Transportation had considered and rejected a rule making airbags the only acceptable form of passive restraint, based on fear of a backlash inspired by public perceptions of airbag safety risks. The Court reasoned that the choice to allow a mix of devices through the performance standard was intended to build public confidence in airbags and to allow the industry the opportunity to develop cheaper and more effective alternatives. A state tort rule effectively requiring airbags "would have presented an obstacle to the variety and mix of devices that the federal regulation sought."

(b) *Sprietsma v. Mercury Marine*, 537 U.S. 51 (2002). Jeanne Sprietsma was killed when she fell from a boat and was struck by its outboard motor. Her husband sued the manufacturer under Illinois tort law, arguing that the motor was unreasonably dangerous because it did not include a propeller guard. Defendant Mercury Marine asserted that this design defect theory was preempted by the Federal Boat Safety Act. The implied preemption argument relied on the fact that the Coast Guard, empowered to issue safety standards by the Act, had considered and rejected a propeller guard requirement, and the theory that a diversity of state requirements enforced through common law would frustrate the federal interest in uniformity.

A unanimous Supreme Court rejected both theories. The Court reasoned that although a federal decision not to regulate can sometimes indicate a conclusion that no state regulation is appropriate, the Coast Guard's explanation of its decision (that no "universally acceptable" propeller guard existed) did not mean that a propeller guard would not have been appropriate for the type of motor involved in the accident. As for the second theory, the Court granted that uniformity was "one of the FBSA's main goals" and "important to the industry," but found that it was "not unyielding" and did not justify the displacement of state tort remedies that compensate victims and "serve the Act's more prominent objective, emphasized by its title, of promoting boating safety."

Following *Geier* and *Sprietsma*, how easy do you think it is to decide whether a federal decision not to impose a particular requirement implies a judgment that the requirement is undesirable? In each case, the Court identified a number of purposes behind the federal action. In *Geier*, the Department of Transportation sought to reduce the risk of injury in individual accidents (something that studies suggested airbags achieved quite well), but also to allow the auto industry the opportunity to explore different devices and to phase in passive restraints gradually. In *Sprietsma*, the Federal Boating Safety Act was designed to promote uniformity of requirements (so that manufacturers need not worry about divergent or inconsistent state standards) and also boating safety. How easy is it to rank these goals, as the Court does explicitly in *Sprietsma* and implicitly in *Geier*? Are the Court's hierarchies consistent?

Compare the questions that the Court confronted in these cases to the questions a court performing interest analysis must decide, and recall the criticisms of interest analysis from Chapter 2, Section 3. Does considering implied conflict preemption make ascertaining the purpose of state laws seem less problematic?

(4) In *Wyeth v. Levine*, 555 U.S. 555, 587, 588 (2009), Justice Thomas wrote in a concurring opinion:

> I have become increasingly skeptical of this Court's "purposes and objectives" pre-emption jurisprudence. Under this approach, the Court routinely invalidates state laws based on perceived conflicts

> with broad federal policy objectives, legislative history, or generalized notions of congressional purposes that are not embodied within the text of federal law. . . . Congressional and agency musings, however, do not satisfy the Article I, § 7, requirements for enactment of federal law and, therefore, do not pre-empt state law under the Supremacy Clause.

Do you agree? Is Justice Thomas launching a challenge to entire project of purposive statutory interpretation that lies at the heart of interest analysis, or is his critique limited to implied conflict preemption?

(5) Is there a relationship between choice of law at the state level and federal preemption? Professors O'Connor and Ribstein think there should be. Noting that preemption is often defended as necessary to provide uniform rules to stimulate interstate and international trade, they argue that

> a federal substantive law is but one means to achieve that goal. Sometimes clarity can be obtained through state laws subject to coordinated choice-of-law approaches. This latter possibility promotes a healthy federalism because the benefits of state law—experimentation, jurisdictional competition, and diverse options—can be retained. In such circumstances, courts should be reluctant to conclude that state laws are preempted. Where, however, sovereign authority over state laws is uncoordinated, either as a functional or a formal matter, then courts should place a thumb on the scale in favor of preemption of state law.

Erin O'Hara O'Connor & Larry E. Ribstein, *Preemption and Choice-of-Law Coordination*, 111 Mich. L. Rev. 647, 712–13 (2013).

Do you agree that courts facing questions of federal preemption should first ask whether (some? all?) states have coordinated their choice-of-law rules?

(6) Can state-federal conflicts tell us anything about choice of law more generally? Professor Roosevelt argues that the existence of a constitutionally required resolution for conflicts between state and federal law reveals the extent to which choice of law should be understood as involving clashes of substantive rights rather than a procedural choice between laws. See Roosevelt, *The Myth of Choice of Law: Rethinking Conflicts*, 97 Mich. L. Rev. 2448, 2493–98 (1999). Consider this argument as you read the cases that follow.

B. SUPREMACY

"Discrimination" Against Federal Law

TESTA V. KATT

330 U.S. 386 (1947).

MR. JUSTICE BLACK delivered the opinion of the Court.

Section 205(e) of the Emergency Price Control Act provides that a buyer of goods at above the prescribed ceiling price may sue the seller "in any court of competent jurisdiction" for not more than three times the amount of the overcharge plus costs and a reasonable attorney's fee. Section 205(c) provides that federal district courts shall have jurisdiction of such suits "concurrently with State and Territorial courts." Such a suit under § 205(e) must be brought "in the district or county in which the defendant resides or has a place of business. . ."

The respondent was in the automobile business in Providence, Providence County, Rhode Island. In 1944 he sold an automobile to petitioner Testa, who also resides in Providence, for $1100, $210 above the ceiling price. The petitioner later filed this suit against respondent in the State District Court in Providence. Recovery was sought under § 205(e). The court awarded a judgment of treble damages and costs to petitioner. On appeal to the State Superior Court, where the trial was *de novo,* the petitioner was again awarded judgment, but only for the amount of the overcharge plus attorney's fees. Pending appeal from this judgment, the Price Administrator was allowed to intervene. On appeal, the State Supreme Court reversed, 71 R.I. 472, 47 A.2d 312. It interpreted § 205(e) to be "a penal statute in the international sense." It held that an action for violation of § 205(e) could not be maintained in the courts of that State. The State Supreme Court rested its holding on its earlier decision in *Robinson v. Norato,* 71 R.I. 256, 43 A.2d 467 (1945), in which it had reasoned that: A state need not enforce the penal laws of a government which is foreign in the international sense; § 205(e) is treated by Rhode Island as penal in that sense; the United States is "foreign" to the State in the "private international" as distinguished from the "public international" sense; hence Rhode Island courts, though their jurisdiction is adequate to enforce similar Rhode Island "penal" statutes, need not enforce § 205(e). Whether state courts may decline to enforce federal laws on these grounds is a question of great importance. For this reason, and because the Rhode Island Supreme Court's holding was alleged to conflict with this Court's previous holding in *Mondou v. New York, N.H. & H.R. Co.,* 223 U.S. 1, we granted certiorari. 329 U.S. 703.

For the purposes of this case, we assume, without deciding that § 205(e) is a penal statute in the "public international," "private international," or any other sense. So far as the question of whether the Rhode Island courts properly declined to try this action, it makes no difference into which of these categories the Rhode Island court chose to place the statute which Congress has passed. For we cannot accept the basic premise on which the Rhode Island Supreme Court held that it has no more obligation to enforce a valid penal law of the United States than it has to enforce a penal law of another state or a foreign country. Such a broad assumption flies in the face of the fact that the States of the Union constitute a nation. It disregards the purpose and effect of Article VI of the Constitution which provides: "This Constitution, and the Laws of the United States which shall be made in Pursuance thereof; and all Treaties made, or which shall be made, under the Authority of the United States, shall be the supreme Law of the Land; and the Judges in every State shall be bound thereby, any Thing in the Constitution or Laws of any State to the Contrary notwithstanding."

It cannot be assumed, the supremacy clause considered, that the responsibilities of a state to enforce the laws of a sister state are identical with its responsibilities to enforce federal laws. Such an assumption represents an erroneous evaluation of the statutes of Congress and the prior decisions of this Court in their historic setting. Those decisions establish that state courts do not bear the same relation to the United States that they do to foreign countries. The first Congress that convened after the Constitution was adopted conferred jurisdiction upon the state courts to enforce important federal civil laws, and succeeding Congresses conferred on the states jurisdiction over federal crimes and actions for penalties and forfeitures.

Enforcement of federal laws by state courts did not go unchallenged. Violent public controversies existed throughout the first part of the Nineteenth Century until the 1860's concerning the extent of the constitutional supremacy of the Federal Government. During that period there were instances in which this Court and state courts broadly questioned the power and duty of state courts to exercise their jurisdiction to enforce United States civil and penal statutes or the power of the Federal Government to require them to do so. But after the fundamental issues over the extent of federal supremacy had been resolved by war, this Court took occasion in 1876 to review the phase of the controversy concerning the relationship of state courts to the Federal Government. *Claflin v. Houseman*, 93 U.S. 130. The opinion of a unanimous court in that case was strongly buttressed by historic references and persuasive reasoning. It repudiated the assumption that federal laws can be considered by the states as though they were laws emanating from a foreign sovereign. Its teaching is that the Constitution and the laws passed pursuant to it are the supreme laws of the land, binding alike upon states, courts and the people, "any Thing in the Constitution or Laws of any State to the Contrary notwithstanding." It asserted that the obligation of states to enforce these federal laws is not lessened by reason of the form in which they are cast or the remedy which they provide. And the Court stated that "If an act of Congress gives a penalty to a party aggrieved, without specifying a remedy for its enforcement, there is no reason why it should not be enforced, if not provided otherwise by some act of Congress, by a proper action in a State court." Id. at 137. . .

[The Court was presented with another case testing the duty of state courts to enforce federal law in *Mondou v. New York, N.H. & H.R. Co.*, 223 U.S. 1 (1912).] The precise question in the *Mondou* case was whether rights arising under the Federal Employers' Liability Act, 36 Stat. 291, could "be enforced, as of right, in the courts of the States when their jurisdiction, as fixed by local laws, is adequate to the occasion. . ." Id. at 46. The Supreme Court of Connecticut had decided that they could not. Except for the penalty feature, the factors it considered and its reasoning were strikingly similar to that on which the Rhode Island Supreme Court declined to enforce the federal law here involved. But this Court held that the Connecticut court could not decline to entertain the action. The contention that enforcement of the congressionally created right was contrary to Connecticut policy was answered as follows:

> "The suggestion that the act of Congress is not in harmony with the policy of the State, and therefore that the courts of the State are free to decline jurisdiction, is quite inadmissible, because it presupposes what in legal contemplation does not exist. When Congress, in the exertion of the power confided to it by the Constitution, adopted that act, it spoke for all the people and all the States, and thereby established a policy for all. That policy is as much the policy of Connecticut as if the act had emanated from its own legislature, and should be respected accordingly in the courts of the State." *Mondou v. New York, N.H. & H.R. Co.*, supra at 57.

So here, the fact that Rhode Island has an established policy against enforcement by its courts of statutes of other states and the United States which it deems penal, cannot be accepted as a "valid excuse." Cf. *Douglas v. New York, N.H. & H.R. Co.*, 279 U.S. 377, 388. For the policy of the federal Act is the prevailing policy in every state. . .

The Rhode Island court in its *Robinson* decision, on which it relies, cites cases of this Court which have held that states are not required by the full faith and credit clause of the Constitution to enforce judgments of the courts of other states based on claims arising out of penal statutes. But those holdings have no relevance here, for this case raises no full faith and credit question. Nor need we consider in this case prior decisions to the effect that federal courts are not required to enforce state penal laws.

Compare *Wisconsin v. Pelican Ins. Co.,* 127 U.S. 265, with *Massachusetts v. Missouri,* 308 U.S. 1, 20. For whatever consideration they may be entitled to in the field in which they are relevant, those decisions did not bring before us our instant problem of the effect of the supremacy clause on the relation of federal laws to state courts. Our question concerns only the right of a state to deny enforcement to claims growing out of a valid federal law.

It is conceded that this same type of claim arising under Rhode Island law would be enforced by that State's courts. Its courts have enforced claims for double damages growing out of the Fair Labor Standards Act. Thus the Rhode Island courts have jurisdiction adequate and appropriate under established local law to adjudicate this action. Under these circumstances the State courts are not free to refuse enforcement of petitioners' claim. See *McKnett v. St. Louis & S.F.R. Co.,* 292 U.S. 230; and compare *Herb v. Pitcairn,* 324 U.S. 117, 325 U.S. 77. The case is reversed and the cause is remanded for proceedings not inconsistent with this opinion.

HOWLETT V. ROSE

496 U.S. 356 (1990).

JUSTICE STEVENS delivered the opinion of the Court.

Section 1 of the Civil Rights Act of 1871, Rev.Stat. § 1979, now codified as 42 U.S.C. § 1983, creates a remedy for violations of federal rights committed by persons acting under color of state law. State courts as well as federal courts have jurisdiction over § 1983 cases. The question in this case is whether a state-law defense of "sovereign immunity" is available to a school board otherwise subject to suit in a Florida court even though such a defense would not be available if the action had been brought in a federal forum.

Petitioner, a former high school student, filed a complaint in the Circuit Court for Pinellas County, Florida, naming the School Board of Pinellas County and three school officials as defendants. He alleged that an assistant principal made an illegal search of his car while it was parked on school premises and that he was wrongfully suspended from regular classes for five days. Contending that the search and subsequent suspension violated rights under the Fourth and Fourteenth Amendments of the Federal Constitution and under similar provisions of the State Constitution, he prayed for damages and an order expunging any reference to the suspension from the school records.

[The Florida courts dismissed the suit on the following rationale:] "[W]hen a section 1983 action is brought in *state* court, the sole question to be decided on the basis of *state* law is whether the state has waived its common law sovereign immunity to the extent necessary to allow a section

1983 action in state court. . . Florida has not so waived its sovereign immunity." * * *

. . . Florida has extended absolute immunity from suit not only to the State and its arms but also to municipalities, counties, and school districts that might otherwise be subject to suit under § 1983 in federal court. That holding raises the concern that the state court may be evading federal law and discriminating against federal causes of action. The adequacy of the state-law ground to support a judgment precluding litigation of the federal claim is itself a federal question which we review *de novo*. * * *

Federal law is enforceable in state courts not because Congress has determined that federal courts would otherwise be burdened or that state courts might provide a more convenient forum—although both might well be true—but because the Constitution and laws passed pursuant to it are as much laws in the States as laws passed by the state legislature. The Supremacy Clause makes those laws "the supreme Law of the Land," and charges state courts with a coordinate responsibility to enforce that law according to their regular modes of procedure. "The laws of the United States are laws in the several States, and just as much binding on the citizens and courts thereof as the State laws are. . . The two together form one system of jurisprudence, which constitutes the law of the land for the State; and the courts of the two jurisdictions are not foreign to each other, nor to be treated by each other as such, but as courts of the same country, having jurisdiction partly different and partly concurrent." * * * . . .

Three corollaries follow from the proposition that "federal" law is part of the "Law of the Land" in the State:

1. A state court may not deny a federal right, when the parties and controversy are properly before it, in the absence of "valid excuse." . . .

2. An excuse that is inconsistent with or violates federal law is not a valid excuse: The Supremacy Clause forbids state courts to dissociate themselves from federal law because of disagreement with its content or a refusal to recognize the superior authority of its source. . .

3. When a state court refuses jurisdiction because of a neutral state rule regarding the administration of the courts, we must act with utmost caution before deciding that it is obligated to entertain the claim. * * * The requirement that a state court of competent jurisdiction treat federal law as the law of the land does not necessarily include within it a requirement that the State create a court competent to hear the case in which the federal claim is presented. The general rule, "bottomed deeply in belief in the importance of state control of state judicial procedure, is that federal law takes the state courts as it finds them." * * *. The States thus have great latitude to establish the structure and jurisdiction of their own courts. * * * In addition, States may apply their own neutral procedural rules to federal claims, unless those rules are pre-empted by federal law. * * *

These principles are fundamental to a system of federalism in which the state courts share responsibility for the application and enforcement of federal law. [The Court here discusses *Mondou* and *Testa*.]

The parties disagree as to the proper characterization of the District Court of Appeal's decision. Petitioner argues that the court adopted a substantive rule of decision that state agencies are not subject to liability under § 1983. Respondents, stressing the court's language that it had not "opened its own courts for federal actions against the state," * * * argue that the case simply involves the court's refusal to take cognizance of § 1983 actions against state defendants. We conclude that whether the question is framed in pre-emption terms, as petitioner would have it, or in the obligation to assume jurisdiction over a "federal" cause of action, as respondents would have it, the Florida court's refusal to entertain one discrete category of § 1983 claims, when the court entertains similar state-law actions against state defendants, violates the Supremacy Clause.

If the District Court of Appeal meant to hold that governmental entities subject to § 1983 liability enjoy an immunity over and above those already provided in § 1983, that holding directly violates federal law. The elements of, and the defenses to, a federal cause of action are defined by federal law. . .

Federal law makes governmental defendants that are not arms of the State, such as municipalities, liable for their constitutional violations. * * * Florida law, as interpreted by the District Court of Appeal, would make all such defendants absolutely immune from liability under the federal statute. To the extent that the Florida law of sovereign immunity reflects a substantive disagreement with the extent to which governmental entities should be held liable for their constitutional violations, that disagreement cannot override the dictates of federal law. . .

If, on the other hand, the District Court of Appeal meant that § 1983 claims are excluded from the category of tort claims that the Circuit Court could hear against a school board, its holding was no less violative of federal law. * * * . . . The State of Florida has constituted the Circuit Court for Pinellas County as a court of general jurisdiction. It exercises jurisdiction over tort claims by private citizens against state entities (including school boards), of the size and type of petitioner's claim here, and it can enter judgment against them. That court also exercises jurisdiction over § 1983 actions against individual officers and is fully competent to provide the remedies the federal statute requires.* * * . . .

Respondents have offered no neutral or valid excuse for the Circuit Court's refusal to hear § 1983 actions against state entities. The Circuit Court would have had jurisdiction if the defendant were an individual officer and the action were based on § 1983. It would also have had jurisdiction over the defendant school board if the action were based on established state common law or statutory law. A state policy that permits actions against state agencies for the failure of their officials to adequately police a parking lot and for the negligence of such officers in arresting a person on a roadside, but yet declines jurisdiction over federal actions for constitutional violations by the same persons can be based only on the rationale that such persons should not be held liable for § 1983 violations in the courts of the State. That reason, whether presented in terms of direct disagreement with substantive federal law or simple refusal to take cognizance of the federal cause of action, flatly violates the Supremacy Clause.

Supremacy and Discrimination

(1) Granted that a valid federal statute requiring state courts to entertain federal actions is paramount under the supremacy clause, where does Congress get power to impose such a requirement? Justice Frankfurter protested (too late?) that "neither Congress nor the British Parliament nor the Vermont Legislature has power to confer jurisdiction upon the New York courts." *Brown v. Gerdes,* 321 U.S. 178, 188 (1944) (concurring opinion). See Sandalow, Henry v. Mississippi *and the Adequate State Ground: Proposals for a Revised Doctrine,* 1965 Sup.Ct.Rev. 187, 207 n. 84, finding congressional authority in the Necessary and Proper Clause and suggesting the additional possibility of an inference from "the fact that Article III permits, but does not require, establishment of federal courts inferior to the Supreme Court."

Assuming that Congress has the power to require state-court jurisdiction, was the Court right in *Mondou* and *Testa* in holding that Congress had not left the states a choice in the matter? See Sandalow, 1965 Sup.Ct.Rev. at 206–07:

> [I]t is difficult to perceive the federal interest that justifies so substantial an intrusion upon the power of the states to determine the purposes to be served by agencies of state government. . . In both *Mondou* and *Testa* a federal court was open to the plaintiff, so that a decision sustaining the refusal to adjudicate would in no way have interfered with the vindication of federal rights. . . Federal policy was substantive, that recovery should be permitted under specified circumstances. State policy, on the other hand, was concerned only with the use to be made of state courts, a matter not touched by the federal policy. . . In the absence of a declaration by Congress that state courts must enforce rights that Congress has created, there appears to be no substantial reason why the Supreme Court should impose such an obligation.

Has Professor Sandalow overlooked the significance of 28 U.S.C. § 1445(a), forbidding removal of FELA actions filed in state courts? Or does § 1445(a) merely evidence congressional expectation that state courts will exercise jurisdiction and an intention that, if these courts are willing to do so, plaintiffs should be able to choose their forum?

(2) The state courts' duty to enforce federal law has not been absolute. In *Douglas v. New York, N.H. & H.R.R.,* 279 U.S. 377 (1929), the Court upheld a state court's refusal to entertain an FELA action on the basis of a statute construed to allow discretionary dismissal of actions by non-residents against foreign corporations doing business in the State:

> It may very well be that if the Supreme Court of New York were given no discretion, being otherwise competent, it would be subject to a duty. But there is nothing in the Act of Congress that purports to force a duty upon such Courts as against an otherwise valid excuse. [Citing *Mondou.*]

279 U.S. at 387–88. See also *Missouri ex rel. Southern Ry. v. Mayfield,* 340 U.S. 1 (1950), reaffirming *Douglas* and explaining for the state courts on remand that forum non conveniens, if applied without discrimination against federal rights, is a "valid excuse."

Does this mean that a state court is free to close its doors to an FELA claim on the basis of an expired local statute of limitations? Cf. *Wells v. Simonds Abrasive Co.,* 345 U.S. 514 (1953), supra p. 421, permitting a court of one state to apply a local statute of limitations to defeat a cause of action created by another state, despite the policy of the Full Faith and Credit Clause favoring enforcement of foreign rights. Notice, moreover, that the case supposed is not simply the converse of *Guaranty Trust Co. v. York,* 326 U.S. 99 (1945), supra p. 838, for that case held that a disinterested federal court could not enlarge the relevant limitation period, not that such a court could not protect its docket by applying its own *shorter* limitation period. Nevertheless the Supreme Court has long held that a state court cannot dismiss an action based on the FELA before the expiration of the federal limitation period. *Engel v. Davenport,* 271 U.S. 33 (1926) (Jones Act, which incorporates FELA in seamen's actions); *McAllister v. Magnolia Petroleum Co.,* 357 U.S. 221 (1958) (unseaworthiness claim joined to Jones Act count); see *Burnett v. New York Central R.R.,* 380 U.S. 424 (1965) (FELA limitation tolled as a matter of federal law during pendency of a state-court action later dismissed for improper venue).

Should these holdings be extended to all federal limitation statutes, or do they reflect some peculiarly plaintiff-oriented policy of the FELA? Notice further that in the case of a state limitation period *longer* than that of the FELA the state is not, as is a federal diversity court, disinterested; the holding that the state court cannot entertain an action in that case, *Atlantic Coast Line R.R. v. Burnette,* 239 U.S. 199 (1915), must be explained in relation to the general preemption of additional state remedies for railroad plaintiffs, rather than by a lack of state concern.

(3) Professor Sandalow observes that *Mondou* is usually read as holding "only that a state must enforce a federally created right if it enforces analogous forum-created rights" but finds the reasoning of the opinion broader:

> Federal policy is the same whatever lines the state has drawn in defining the jurisdiction of its courts over local claims. If the state may not assert a policy at variance with that expressed by the federal law, adjudication of the claim would seem to be required even in the absence of discrimination since, insofar as the local jurisdictional rule prevents adjudication, it is to that extent, under the reasoning of *Mondou,* inconsistent with the policy underlying the federal claim.

1965 Sup.Ct.Rev. at 205. But would you like to see *Mondou* extended to forbid a reasonable dismissal on grounds of forum non conveniens? Is it not appropriate, in considering whether federal policy requires state court jurisdiction, to consider the strength of the state policy against hearing the action? To what extent does *Testa* undermine the teaching of the earlier cases that a state may have a "valid excuse" for refusing to entertain a federal claim? Compare the decisions respecting an adequate state ground for purposes of Supreme Court review, e.g., *Henry v. Mississippi,* 379 U.S. 443 (1965).

(4) Why can't state courts, as in *Testa* and *Mondou,* apply choice-of-law rules, such as the rule against enforcing foreign penal statutes or the public policy exception, that lead them to refuse to enforce a federal law? Because this frustrates the federal purpose, in violation of the Supremacy Clause, or because federal law is not foreign and federal policy is ipso facto state policy? Does it matter which rationale we adopt? Could both be true?

What about a choice-of-law rule that led the court to choose state law instead of federal law? Can you think of a choice-of-law approach that would produce this result? Why would this be impermissible?

(5) In *Howlett,* the Court considered two possible descriptions of what the state courts were doing: adopting a substantive rule that school boards were immune from suit under § 1983, or excluding such claims from the trial court's jurisdiction. Which is correct? Can you imagine a case in which the outcome would depend on the description?

(6) What are the limits on the principle of *Testa* and *Howlett*? Could a state traffic court be forced to hear a FELA or § 1983 claim? Would *Howlett* come out the same way if Florida had stripped all its trial courts of jurisdiction to hear *any* claims against school boards? Is discrimination the issue, or supremacy?

In *Haywood v. Drown*, 556 U.S. 729 (2009), the Court rejected a New York statute that stripped the state's trial courts of jurisdiction over inmates' damages actions against corrections officials and substituted an action against the state in the New York court of claims. The statute applied equally to claims under federal and state law. This was still not a valid excuse, wrote Justice Stevens. Equality of treatment is "the beginning, not the end" of the analysis, and states may not withhold jurisdiction based on substantive disagreement. How can a court decide when that is the motivation?

(7) If Congress expressly vests state courts with jurisdiction to entertain a federal cause of action but remains silent as to whether federal courts may do so as well, what result? In *Mims v. Arrow Fin. Servs., LLC*, 565 U.S. 368 (2012), a unanimous Court held that general federal-question jurisdiction under 28 U.S.C. § 1331 continues to lie unless "overcome by an explicit statutory directive, by unmistakable implication from legislative history, or by a clear incompatibility between state-court jurisdiction and federal interests." *Id.* at 378 (citation omitted). Why should the presumption be in favor of concurrent jurisdiction?

Federal Law in State Courts: Reverse *Erie*

DICE V. AKRON, CANTON & YOUNGSTOWN R.R.

342 U.S. 359 (1952).

Opinion of the Court by MR. JUSTICE BLACK. . .

Petitioner, a railroad fireman, was seriously injured when an engine in which he was riding jumped the track. Alleging that his injuries were due to respondent's negligence, he brought this action for damages under the Federal Employers' Liability Act, 35 Stat. 65, 45 U.S.C. § 51 et seq., in an Ohio court of common pleas. Respondent's defenses were (1) a denial of negligence and (2) a written document signed by petitioner purporting to release respondent in full for $924.63. Petitioner admitted that he had signed several receipts for payments made him in connection with his injuries but denied that he had made a full and complete settlement of all his claims. He alleged that the purported release was void because he had signed it relying on respondent's deliberately false statement that the document was nothing more than a mere receipt for back wages.

After both parties had introduced considerable evidence the jury found in favor of petitioner and awarded him a $25,000 verdict. The trial judge later entered judgment notwithstanding the verdict. In doing so he reappraised the evidence as to fraud, found that petitioner had been "guilty of supine negligence" in failing to read the release, and accordingly held that the facts did not "sustain either in law or equity the allegations of fraud by clear, unequivocal and convincing evidence."[1] This judgment notwithstanding the verdict was reversed by the Court of Appeals of Summit County, Ohio, on the ground that under federal law, which controlled, the jury's verdict must stand because there was ample evidence to support its finding of fraud. The Ohio Supreme Court, one judge dissenting, reversed the Court of Appeals' judgment and sustained the trial court's action, holding that: (1) Ohio, not federal, law governed; (2) under that law petitioner, a man of ordinary intelligence who could read, was bound by the release even though he had been induced to sign it by the deliberately false statement that it was only a receipt for back wages; and (3) under controlling Ohio law factual issues as to fraud in the execution of this release were properly decided by the judge rather than by the jury. 155 Ohio St. 185, 98 N.E.2d 301. We granted certiorari because the decision of the Supreme Court of Ohio appeared to deviate from previous decisions of this Court that federal law governs cases arising under the Federal Employers' Liability Act. 342 U.S. 811.

First. . . Validity of releases under the Federal Employers' Liability Act raises a federal question to be determined by federal rather than state law. . . Manifestly the federal rights affording relief to injured railroad employees under a federally declared standard could be defeated if states were permitted to have the final say as to what defenses could and could not be properly interposed to suits under the Act. Moreover, only if federal law controls can the federal Act be given that uniform application throughout the country essential to effectuate its purposes. . .

Second. . . The correct federal rule is that . . . a release of rights under the Act is void when the employee is induced to sign it by the deliberately false and material statements of the railroad's authorized representatives made to deceive the employee as to the contents of the release. The trial court's charge to the jury correctly stated this rule of law.

Third. Ohio provides and has here accorded petitioner the usual jury trial of factual issues relating to negligence. But Ohio treats factual questions of fraudulent releases differently. It permits the judge trying a negligence case to resolve all factual questions of fraud "other than fraud in the factum." The factual issue of fraud is thus split into fragments, some to be determined by the judge, others by the jury.

It is contended that since a state may consistently with the Federal Constitution provide for trial of cases under the Act by a nonunanimous verdict, *Minneapolis & St. Louis R. Co. v. Bombolis*, 241 U.S. 211, Ohio may lawfully eliminate trial by jury as to one phase of fraud while allowing

---

[1] The trial judge had charged the jury that petitioner's claim of fraud must be sustained "by clear and convincing evidence," but since the verdict was for petitioner, he does not here challenge this charge as imposing too heavy a burden under controlling federal law.

jury trial as to all other issues raised. The *Bombolis* case might be more in point had Ohio abolished trial by jury in all negligence cases including those arising under the federal Act. But Ohio has not done this. It has provided jury trials for cases arising under the federal Act but seeks to single out one phase of the question of fraudulent releases for determination by a judge rather than by a jury. Compare *Testa v. Katt,* 330 U.S. 386.

We had previously held that "The right to trial by jury is 'a basic and fundamental feature of our system of federal jurisprudence' " and that it is "part and parcel of the remedy afforded railroad workers under the Employers' Liability Act." *Bailey v. Central Vermont R. Co.,* 319 U.S. 350, 354. We also recognized in that case that to deprive railroad workers of the benefit of a jury trial where there is evidence to support negligence "is to take away a goodly portion of the relief which Congress has afforded them." It follows that the right to trial by jury is too substantial a part of the rights accorded by the Act to permit it to be classified as a mere "local rule of procedure" for denial in the manner that Ohio has here used. *Brown v. Western R. Co.,* 338 U.S. 294.

The trial judge and the Ohio Supreme Court erred in holding that petitioner's rights were to be determined by Ohio law and in taking away petitioner's verdict when the issues of fraud had been submitted to the jury on conflicting evidence and determined in petitioner's favor. . . The cause is reversed and remanded. . .

MR. JUSTICE FRANKFURTER, whom MR. JUSTICE REED, MR. JUSTICE JACKSON and MR. JUSTICE BURTON join, concurring for reversal but dissenting from the Court's opinion. . .

It has been settled ever since the Second Employers' Liability Cases [*Mondou v. New York, N.H. & H.R. Co.*], 223 U.S. 1, that no State which gives its courts jurisdiction over common law actions for negligence may deny access to its courts for a negligence action founded on the Federal Employers' Liability Act. Nor may a State discriminate disadvantageously against actions for negligence under the Federal Act as compared with local causes of action in negligence. *McKnett v. St. Louis & S.F.R. Co.,* 292 U.S. 230, 234; *Missouri ex rel. Southern R. Co. v. Mayfield,* 340 U.S. 1, 4. Conversely, however, simply because there is concurrent jurisdiction in Federal and State courts over actions under the Employers' Liability Act, a State is under no duty to treat actions arising under that Act differently from the way it adjudicates local actions for negligence, so far as the mechanics of litigation, the forms in which law is administered, are concerned. This surely covers the distribution of functions as between judge and jury in the determination of the issues in a negligence case.

In 1916 the Court decided without dissent that States in entertaining actions under the Federal Employers' Liability Act need not provide a jury system other than that established for local negligence actions. States are not compelled to provide the jury required of Federal courts by the Seventh Amendment. *Minneapolis & St. L.R. Co. v. Bombolis,* 241 U.S. 211. . .

Ohio and her sister States with a similar division of functions between law and equity are not trying to evade their duty under the Federal Employers' Liability Act; nor are they trying to make it more difficult for railroad workers to recover, than for those suing under local law. The States merely exercise a preference in adhering to historic ways of dealing with a claim of fraud; they prefer the traditional way of making unavailable through equity an otherwise valid defense. The state judges and local lawyers who must administer the Federal Employers' Liability Act in State courts are trained in the ways of local practice; it multiplies the difficulties and confuses the administration of justice to require, on purely theoretical grounds, a hybrid of State and Federal practice in the State courts as to a single class of cases. Nothing in the Employers' Liability Act or in the judicial enforcement of the Act for over forty years forces such judicial hybridization upon the States. The fact that Congress authorized actions under the Federal Employers' Liability Act to be brought in State as well as in Federal courts seems a strange basis for the inference that Congress overrode State procedural arrangements controlling all other negligence suits in a State, by imposing upon State courts to which plaintiffs choose to go the rules prevailing in the Federal courts regarding juries. Such an inference is admissible, so it seems to me, only on the theory that Congress included as part of the right created by the Employers' Liability Act an assumed likelihood that trying all issues to juries is more favorable to plaintiffs. At least, if a plaintiff's right to have all issues decided by a jury rather than the court is "part and parcel of the remedy afforded railroad workers under the Employers' Liability Act," the *Bombolis* case should be overruled explicitly instead of left as a derelict bound to occasion collisions on the waters of the law. . .

The judgment of the Ohio Supreme Court must be reversed for it applied the State rule as to validity of releases. . . Moreover, we cannot say with confidence that the Ohio trial judge applied the Federal standard correctly. . . [W]e would return the case for further proceedings on the sole question of fraud in the release.

State-Court Enforcement of Federal Law

(1) If a state court does entertain an action based on federal law, as in *Dice,* is the applicability of state procedural laws governed by the same considerations that determine the use of federal procedure in diversity cases? See *Central Vermont Ry. v. White,* 238 U.S. 507 (1915) (burden of proof respecting contributory negligence is federal question); *Brady v.*

Southern Ry., 320 U.S. 476 (1943) (sufficiency of evidence to sustain verdict also federal question). Indeed the bulk of the Supreme Court's decisions reversing state courts in FELA cases have been concerned with the sufficiency of the evidence. Is there any doubt that to permit state law to govern these issues would threaten substantial federal policies? See also *Garrett v. Moore-McCormack Co.*, 317 U.S. 239 (1942), holding that federal law governs the burden of proof respecting fraud in the inducement of a release from liability to a seaman under both the Jones Act and the general maritime law.

Is it correct to say that the question in a case like *Dice* is the extent to which state interests in the efficient administration of state courts should be allowed to impinge upon federal policy? Two differences between this situation and that of *Erie* suggest themselves: First, in any direct conflict federal law must prevail in either case under the Supremacy Clause; second, the states are not without interests in the merits of the litigation as are diversity courts under *Erie.*

(2) Is it possible to reconcile *Dice* with the decisions holding that federal law governs the division of function between judge and jury in diversity cases? E.g., *Byrd v. Blue Ridge Rural Electric Co-op.*, 356 U.S. 525 (1958), supra p. 843. If, as *Hanna* and subsequent cases appear to hold, the housekeeping interests of the federal courts may override even substantive state policies, why is it necessary to ignore a similar state housekeeping interest in *Dice*? Must the Supremacy Clause operate automatically and blindly?

(3) Is it possible to reconcile *Dice* and the decisions in note (1) with *Bombolis* and its companion cases, cited in *Dice,* allowing a state court to empanel a jury of seven or to accept a less-than-unanimous verdict in an FELA case? The Seventh Amendment, discussed at length in *Bombolis,* was surely a red herring, for the issue in all these cases is the policy of the federal statute. Is trial to a judge more likely to frustrate federal policy than trial to a seven-person jury or to a jury that need not be unanimous? If a state abolished civil juries altogether, would it be permitted to try FELA cases to the judge? Would it be permitted to refuse to entertain FELA actions on the ground of inconvenience if federal law forbade a judge trial?

(4) See also *Brown v. Western Ry.*, 338 U.S. 294 (1949), in which a state court had dismissed, with prejudice to any further state proceeding, an FELA complaint found insufficient to state a claim under a local rule construing allegations "most strongly against the pleader." Reversing, the Supreme Court said that "strict local rules of pleading cannot be used to impose unnecessary burdens upon rights of recovery authorized by federal laws" and that it was the duty of the Court "to construe the allegations of this complaint ourselves in order to determine whether petitioner has been denied a right of trial granted him by Congress." The state court, wrote Justice Black, "has decided as a matter of law that no inference of railroad negligence could be drawn from the facts alleged," which included negligently leaving clinkers beside the tracks; but "these allegations are sufficient," the Court concluded, "to permit introduction of evidence from which a jury might infer that petitioner's injuries were due to the railroad's negligence in failing to provide a reasonably safe place to work." 338 U.S., at 297–98. Justices Frankfurter and Jackson dissented, comparing the issue to that raised by application of the federal procedure rules in a diversity case. How would this issue be resolved in a diversity case after *Hanna v. Plumer,* 380 U.S. 460 (1965), supra p. 847?

If all that was involved in *Brown v. Western Ry.* was the proper form of words to use in a pleading, should the state rule be allowed to apply, in the interest of simplifying the state courts' job, because the matter is within the control of the plaintiff's lawyer and has no effect on primary conduct? Or is there an applicable federal policy of protecting plaintiffs against dismissals based upon the inexactness of their attorneys' language? Is the decision better explained as passing not upon the technicalities of pleading but upon the minimum proof required in an FELA action? See *Norfolk & W. Ry. v. Liepelt,* 444 U.S. 490 (1980), requiring a state trial judge in an FELA case to instruct the jury in accord with federal practice that a damage award would not be subject to federal income tax. "[Q]uestions concerning the measure of damages in an FELA action," said the Court, "are federal in character;" and the purpose of the federal rule was to prevent "the jury from inflating the award and thus overcompensating the plaintiff on the basis of an erroneous assumption that the judgment will be taxable." The dissent found no federal interest implicated: "This issue truly can be characterized as one of the 'ordinary incidents of state procedure.' "

CHAPTER 8

INTERNATIONAL CONFLICTS

■ ■ ■

SECTION 1. THE SCOPE OF LEGISLATIVE JURISDICTION

A. BASES FOR JURISDICTION UNDER INTERNATIONAL LAW

UNITED STATES V. YUNIS

681 F.Supp. 896 (D.D.C.1988).

BARRINGTON D. PARKER, DISTRICT JUDGE. Defendant's motion to dismiss, presenting interesting and novel legal issues, challenges the authority for and the limits to which the United States government may extend its prosecutorial arm over certain crimes allegedly committed by a nonresident alien on foreign soil. . .

I

Background

This criminal proceeding and indictment arise from the hijacking of a Jordanian civil aircraft, Royal Jordanian Airlines ("ALIA") Flight 402, on June 11, and 12, 1985. [The defendant is charged with violating the Hostage Taking Act, 18 U.S.C. § 1203, and the Destruction of Aircraft Act, 18 U.S.C. § 32.] There is no dispute that the only nexus to the United States was the presence of several American nationals on board the flight. The airplane was registered in Jordan, flew the Jordanian flag and never landed on American soil or flew over American airspace.

On the morning of June 11, the aircraft was positioned at the Beirut International Airport, Beirut, Lebanon, for a scheduled departure to Amman, Jordan. As the 50–60 passengers boarded, several Arab men, one allegedly the defendant, stormed the plane and ordered the pilot to fly to Tunis, Tunisia where a meeting of the Arab League Conference was underway. The airplane departed from Beirut with all passengers, including the Americans, held hostage. [Landing privileges were denied in several Mideast nations, and approximately 30 hours later] the hijackers were forced to return to Beirut, their point of initial departure.

After landing, the hostages were directed to exit the aircraft. The hijackers then called an impromptu press conference and the defendant Yunis allegedly read a speech, which he originally intended to give to the delegates of the Arab League Conference then meeting in Tunis. Following the speech, the hijackers blew up the Jordanian aircraft, quickly left the scene and vanished into the Beirut landscape.

Between June 11 and 12, 1985, ALIA flight 402 never landed on or flew over American space. Its flightpath was limited to an area within and around the Mediterranean Sea. Based on the absence of any nexus to United States territory, Yunis has moved to dismiss the entire indictment, arguing that no United States federal court has jurisdiction to prosecute a foreign national for crimes committed in foreign airspace and on foreign soil. He further claims that the presence of the American nationals on board the aircraft is an insufficient basis for exercising jurisdiction under principles of international law.

Defendant's motion raises several threshold inquiries: whether or not there is a basis for jurisdiction under international law, and if so, whether Congress intended to and had authority to extend jurisdiction of our federal courts over criminal offenses and events which were committed and occurred overseas and out of the territorial jurisdiction of such courts.

II.

ANALYSIS

A. JURISDICTION UNDER INTERNATIONAL LAW

The parties agree that there are five traditional bases of jurisdiction over extra-territorial crimes under international law:

> *Territorial,* wherein jurisdiction is based on the place where the offense is committed;
>
> *National,* wherein jurisdiction is based on the nationality of the offender;
>
> *Protective,* wherein jurisdiction is based on whether the national interest is injured;
>
> *Universal,* wherein jurisdiction is conferred in any forum that obtains physical custody of the perpetrator of certain offenses considered particularly heinous and harmful to humanity;
>
> *Passive personal,* wherein jurisdiction is based on the nationality of the victim.

These general principles were developed in 1935 by a Harvard Research Project in an effort to codify principles of jurisdiction under international law. *See Harvard Research in International Law, Jurisdiction with Respect to Crime,* 29 Am.J.Int'l L. 435, 445 (Supp.1935).

Most courts, including our Court of Appeals, have adopted the Harvard Research designations on jurisdiction. * * * Several reputable treatises have also recognized the principles. * * *

The Universal and the Passive Personal principle appear to offer potential bases for asserting jurisdiction over the hostage-taking and aircraft piracy charges against Yunis. However, his counsel argues that the Universal principle is not applicable because neither hostage-taking nor aircraft piracy are heinous crimes encompassed by the doctrine. He urges further, that the United States does not recognize Passive Personal as a legitimate source of jurisdiction. The government flatly disagrees and maintains that jurisdiction is appropriate under both.

1. Universal Principle

The Universal principle recognizes that certain offenses are so heinous and so widely condemned that "any state if it captures the offender may prosecute and punish that person on behalf of the world community regardless of the nationality of the offender or victim or where the crime was committed." M. Bassiouni, II International Criminal Law, Ch. 6 at 298 (ed. 1986). The crucial question for purposes of defendant's motion is how crimes are classified as "heinous" and whether aircraft piracy and hostage taking fit into this category.

Those crimes that are condemned by the world community and subject to prosecution under the Universal principal are often a matter of international conventions or treaties. * * *

Both offenses are the subject of international agreements. A majority of states in the world community including Lebanon, have signed three treaties condemning aircraft piracy: The Tokyo Convention, The Hague Convention, and the Montreal Convention. The Hague and the Montreal Conventions explicitly rely on the principle of Universal jurisdiction in mandating that all . . . "contracting states . . . of which the alleged offender is found, . . . shall, be obliged, *without exception whatsoever and whether or not the offense was committed in its territory,* to submit the case to its competent authorities for the purpose of prosecution." Hague Convention Art. 7; Montreal Convention Art. 7 (emphasis added). These two provisions together demonstrate the international community's strong commitment to punish aircraft hijackers irrespective of where the hijacking occurred.

The global community has also joined together and [through the United Nations] adopted the International Convention for the Taking of Hostages, an agreement which condemns and criminalizes the offense of hostage taking. Like the conventions denouncing aircraft piracy, this treaty requires signatory states to prosecute any alleged offenders "present in its territory."

In light of the global efforts to punish aircraft piracy and hostage taking, international legal scholars unanimously agree that these crimes fit within the category of heinous crimes for purposes of asserting universal jurisdiction. * * * In The Restatement (Revised) of Foreign Relations Law of the United States, a source heavily relied upon by the defendant, aircraft hijacking is specifically identified as a universal crime over which all states should exercise jurisdiction.

Our Circuit has cited the Restatement with approval and determined that the Universal principle, standing alone, provides sufficient basis for asserting jurisdiction over an alleged offender. * * * Therefore, under recognized principles of international law, and the law of this Circuit, there is clear authority to assert jurisdiction over Yunis for the offenses of aircraft piracy and hostage taking.

2. Passive Personal Principle

This principle authorizes states to assert jurisdiction over offenses committed against their citizens abroad. It recognizes that each state has a legitimate interest in protecting the safety of its citizens when they journey outside national boundaries. Because American nationals were on board the Jordanian aircraft, the government contends that the Court may exercise jurisdiction over Yunis under this principle. Defendant argues that this theory of jurisdiction is neither recognized by the international community nor the United States and is an insufficient basis for sustaining jurisdiction over Yunis.

Although many international legal scholars agree that the principle is the most controversial of the five sources of jurisdiction, they also agree that the international community recognizes its legitimacy. . . More importantly, the international community explicitly approved of the principle as a basis for asserting jurisdiction over hostage takers. As noted above, the Hostage Taking Convention set forth certain mandatory sources of jurisdiction. But it also gave each signatory country discretion to exercise extraterritorial jurisdiction when the offense was committed "with respect to a hostage who is a national of that state if that state considers it appropriate." Art. 5(a)(d). Therefore, even if there are doubts regarding the international community's acceptance, there can be no doubt concerning the application of this principle to the offense of hostage taking, an offense for which Yunis is charged. * * *

Defendant's counsel correctly notes that the Passive Personal principle traditionally has been an anathema to United States lawmakers. But his reliance on the Restatement (Revised) of Foreign Relations Laws for the claim that the United States can never invoke the principle is misplaced. In the past, the United States has protested any assertion of such jurisdiction for fear that it could lead to indefinite criminal liability for its own citizens. This objection was based on the belief that foreigners visiting the United States should comply with our laws and should not be permitted to carry their laws with them. Otherwise Americans would face criminal prosecutions for actions unknown to them as illegal.[10] However, in the most recent draft of the Restatement, the authors noted that the theory "has been increasingly accepted when applied to terrorist and other organized attacks on a state's nationals by reason of their nationality, or to assassinations of a state's ambassadors, or government officials." Restatement (Revised) § 402, comment g (Tent. Draft No. 6). * * * The authors retreated from their wholesale rejection of the principle, recognizing that perpetrators of crimes unanimously condemned by members of the international community, should be aware of the illegality of their actions.[11] Therefore, qualified application of the doctrine to serious and universally condemned crimes will not raise the specter of unlimited and unexpected criminal liability.

Thus the Universal and Passive Personality principles, together provide ample grounds for this Court to assert jurisdiction over Yunis. In fact, reliance on both strengthens the basis for asserting jurisdiction. Not only is the United States acting on behalf of the world community to punish alleged offenders of crimes that threaten the very foundations of world order, but the United States has its own interest in protecting its nationals.[14]

[The court went on to find that Congress had asserted legislative jurisdiction in the relevant statutes. The Hostage Taking Act, 18 U.S.C. § 1203, explicitly conferred jurisdiction over offenders who seized or detained United States nationals anywhere. The Destruction of Aircraft

---

[10] The case most widely cited for the United States' rejection of the passive personality principle is known as the *Cutting* case, 1887 For.Rel. 751 (1888), reported in 2 J.B. Moore International Law Digest 232–40 (1906). In that case, the Secretary of State protested the Mexican authority's assertion of jurisdiction over an American national seized while traveling in Mexico. The American was prosecuted for writing an article in a Texas newspaper criticizing a Mexican national. The Mexican authorities indicted him for criminal libel.

[11] While it might be too much to expect the average citizen to be familiar with all of the criminal laws of every country, it is not unrealistic to assume that he would realize that committing a terrorist act might subject him to foreign prosecution. See Note, Bringing the Terrorist to Justice, 11 Cornell Int'l L.J. 71 (1978).

[14] The government also argues that a third doctrine, the Protective principle, offers grounds for asserting jurisdiction over Yunis. Because this principle gives states wide latitude in defining the parameters of their jurisdiction, the international community has strictly construed the reach of this doctrine to those offenses posing a direct, specific threat to national security. * * *

Recently, some academicians have urged a more liberal interpretation of the protective principle when applied to terroristic activities. Given "the increase in the number of terroristic threats against United States nationals abroad, there can be no doubt that the United States has significant security and protective interests at stake." Paust, Federal Jurisdiction over Extraterritorial Acts of Terrorism, 23 Va. J. of Int'l Law 191, 210 (1983).

In this case, the hijackers never made any demands upon the United States government nor directly threatened its security. Indeed, it was almost happenstance that three American nationals were on board the aircraft. Given the regional focus of the hijacking, a court would have to adopt an expansive view of the principle to assert jurisdiction over Yunis. Since jurisdiction is available under the universality and passive personality principle, there is no reason to reach out and rely on the protective principle as well.

Act, 18 U.S.C. § 32(b), similarly authorized prosecutions over anyone who commits an offense if the offender "is later found in the United States." The court dismissed charges under 18 U.S.C. § 32(a), however, finding that this statute applied only to aircraft that were destroyed on a flight over the United States or originating or terminating here.]

The Limits of Legislative Jurisdiction in International Law

(1) In international as in domestic law, "jurisdiction" denotes the competence of a nation to act. The exercise of different kinds of governmental power is identified by different adjectival references. According to § 401 of the Restatement (Third) of the Foreign Relations Law of the United States (1987) [hereafter Third Restatement], international law regulates (a) *jurisdiction to prescribe,* i.e., the power of a nation to apply its substantive law to particular persons or events; (b) *jurisdiction to adjudicate,* i.e., the power of a nation to subject persons or things to the process of its courts or administrative tribunals; and (c) *jurisdiction to enforce,* i.e., the power of a nation to compel compliance or punish noncompliance with its laws, whether through judicial or nonjudicial action. The actual significance of these labels is questionable, since limits in all three contexts are based on the same theory, but international lawyers place great stock in using the separate terms. This section deals primarily with jurisdiction to prescribe, also known as legislative jurisdiction.

(2) Legislative jurisdiction was long defined in international law exclusively in territorial terms. When it first emerged in the 16th century, territoriality served the important political purpose of justifying local control as the hold of the Papacy and the Holy Roman Empire weakened in medieval Europe. The territorial principle was formally established in the Peace of Westphalia of 1648, which ended the bloody Thirty Years War.

By the early 20th century, the notion of territoriality as the exclusive basis of jurisdictional competence had come to seem increasingly implausible. (Can you explain why?) The pathbreaking case was *S.S. Lotus (France v. Turkey)*, 1927 PCIJ, ser. A, No. 10. A French steamer collided with a Turkish vessel on the high seas, killing both crew members and passengers. The French ship put into port in Turkey, and Turkish officials arrested, tried, and convicted a French naval officer for criminal negligence. France brought an action in the Permanent Court of International Justice protesting this exercise of jurisdiction on the ground that only the flag state of the vessel on which acts were taken had jurisdiction to punish those acts. The court upheld Turkish jurisdiction. On its facts, the case did not require a dramatic departure from existing principles of territoriality. Although the Turkish law under which the

French officer was prosecuted asserted protective jurisdiction (punishing even acts of foreigners committed abroad if these injured a Turkish national), the court was able to sidestep this problem on the ground that the effects of the negligence were felt in Turkish territory since it was a Turkish flag ship that sank. This "effects doctrine" (or "objective territorial principle," as it is sometimes called)[13] had already achieved limited recognition in the cases. Rather than stop there, however, the court gave a much broader statement of the scope of jurisdiction in international law:

> Far from laying down a general prohibition to the effect that States may not extend the application of their laws and the jurisdiction of their courts to persons, property or acts outside their territory, [international law] leaves them in this respect a wide measure of discretion which is only limited in certain cases by prohibitive rules; as regards other cases, every State remains free to adopt the principles which it regards as best and most suitable.

Building on this concept, the *Harvard Research in International Law,* cited in *Yunis,* identified the five principles discussed in Judge Parker's opinion as adequate to support the exercise of legislative jurisdiction.

What is the source of these principles? Do they reflect a single theory of sovereignty or several different theories? Or do they rest on custom and convention?

(3) The territorial principle remains the most common basis for exercising jurisdiction. According to the Third Restatement, ch. 4, Introductory Note at 237, "[t]erritoriality and nationality remain the principal bases of jurisdiction to prescribe." As between the two, moreover, "[t]erritoriality is considered the normal, and nationality an exceptional, basis for the exercise of jurisdiction." Id. § 402, comment b.

The "effects doctrine," which provided the basis for the actual holding in the *Lotus* case, is generally treated as an aspect of territoriality, and a state may regulate activity occurring outside the state if that activity has or is intended to have effects within it. Some applications of this principle have nevertheless proved controversial. Thus, while shooting or sending libelous publications across a boundary is generally not problematic, disputes have arisen over efforts to regulate economic or commercial activity abroad on the ground that it affects domestic markets. The extraterritorial application of U.S. antitrust laws on this basis has caused friction between the United States and its trading partners. Indeed, some nations have enacted "blocking statutes" to impede the enforcement of U.S.

---

[13] 'Effects jurisdiction is sometimes called 'objective jurisdiction,' since it is the object of conduct that is its realm. It is thus distinguished from 'subjective jurisdiction,' another term for territorial jurisdiction, where what is encompassed is the subject or the actor responsible for conduct." M. Janis, An Introduction to International Law 326 (3d ed. 1999).

antitrust laws, such as England's Protection of Trading Interests Act, which prevents the recovery of "multiple damages" awards and authorizes British officials to forbid compliance with U.S. discovery orders. See G. Born & D. Westin, International Civil Litigation in United States Courts 584–87 (3d ed. 1996). The tables may be turning, however, for Europe's growing economic power has led to increasing acceptance of effects-based jurisdiction within the European Community. In response, the United States agreed to coordinate antitrust policy with the EC. See US/EC Agreement on Antitrust Cooperation and Coordination, 61 BNA Antitrust & Trade Reg. Rep. 382 (Sept. 26, 1991). In any event, many authorities argue that such problems can be minimized by allowing legislative jurisdiction only if effects are "substantial," while others would confine the effects doctrine to a much narrower category of cases. See, e.g., Third Restatement § 402 comment d; I. Brownlie, Principles of Public International Law 313 (5th ed. 1998).

Does the effects doctrine need to be confined? Should limits be imposed as a matter of jurisdictional competence or should these be left to be resolved as a matter of discretion and agreement among nations? It matters, doesn't it? Compare the problem to the distinction between limits imposed on the legislative jurisdiction of states of the United States by the Constitution and those left to be resolved as a matter of ordinary policy. The issue of self-imposed restraints is considered infra pp. 948–982.

(4) The nationality principle is the most widely accepted alternative basis for exercising legislative jurisdiction, and this principle was used even during the heyday of territoriality. See Bartolus, The Conflict of Laws 51 (J. Beale trans. 1914). See also *Blackmer v. United States,* 284 U.S. 421 (1932), upholding service of a subpoena on a United States citizen in France on the ground that "[b]y virtue of the obligations of citizenship, the United States retained its authority over him, and he was bound by its laws made applicable to him in a foreign country." The United States has relied on this principle only sparingly, but some countries provide that their nationals may be prosecuted for all crimes (or all serious crimes) wherever committed. See Henkin, Pugh, Schacter & Smit, International Law 1061 (3d ed. 1993) (citing French, German, Indian, and English provisions). According to Third Restatement § 402 comment e, international law "has increasingly recognized the right of the state to exercise jurisdiction on the basis of domicile or residence in regard to 'private law' matters such as the law of wills and succession, divorce and family rights, and, in some cases, liability for damages for injury." An example of a U.S. law that does rely on the nationality principle is the Prosecutorial Remedies and Other Tools to End the Exploitation of Children Today Act of 2003 (PROTECT Act), 18 U.S.C. § 2243, which imposes criminal penalties on U.S. citizens who travel to foreign countries to engage in sex with minors. In *United States v. Clark,* 435 F.3d 1100 (9th Cir. 2006), the Act was upheld as consistent with international law and as a valid exercise of Congress's power under the Foreign Commerce Clause. But see *United States v. Al-Maliki,* 787 F.3d 784 (6th Cir. 2015) (expressing doubt that the Foreign Commerce Clause extends so far).

(5) The other three bases for exercising jurisdiction to prescribe are more controversial and hence less frequently employed.

(a) *The Protective Principle.* The protective principle recognizes jurisdiction if a national interest is injured. As noted in *Yunis,* because states could abuse this principle by defining their interests broadly, it has been strictly construed to cover only "offenses directed against the security of the state or other offenses threatening the integrity of governmental functions that are generally recognized as crimes by developed legal systems, e.g., espionage, counterfeiting of the state's seal or currency, falsification of official documents, as well as perjury before consular officials, and conspiracy to violate the immigration or customs laws." Third Restatement § 402 comment f. See, e.g., *United States v. Pizzarusso,* 388 F.2d 8 (2d Cir. 1968), in which an alien was prosecuted for knowingly making false statements in Canada on a U.S. visa application. Another reason for construing the protective principle narrowly is to prevent it from being used to punish acts that are specifically protected as civil liberties in the state where they occur (such as political expression).

The protective principle is related to, but should be distinguished from, the effects doctrine. The latter principle permits a state to protect *private* interests from *actual* injury, while the former allows a nation to protect *governmental* interests from the *threat* of harm.

The *Yunis* court says it need not rely on this principle to uphold jurisdiction. Could it have done so?

(b) *The Passive Personality Principle.* Under this principle a state claims jurisdiction over acts committed abroad solely because they injure a national of the state. The passive personality principle is reflected, for example, in a provision of the French Civil Code that gives French courts jurisdiction over persons anywhere who are legally responsible to French nationals, even with respect to obligations incurred outside France. French Civil Code, art. 14. See also *United States v. Benitez,* 741 F.2d 1312, 1316 (11th Cir. 1984) ("The nationality of the victims, who are United States government agents, clearly supports jurisdiction.")

The passive personality principle was argued in the *Lotus* case, but a majority of the court refused to rule on its validity. Most commentators agree that the passive personality principle "is the least justifiable, as a general principle, of the various bases of jurisdiction." I. Brownlie at 306. As noted in *Yunis,* however, while the passive personality principle is not generally recognized in customary international law, "it is increasingly accepted as applied to terrorist and other organized attacks on a state's nationals by reason of their nationality, or to assassination of a state's diplomatic representatives or other officials." Third Restatement § 402 comment g.

(c) *The Universality Principle.* The universality principle confers jurisdiction on any state that obtains custody of an offender. It is based on recognition that all states require authority to punish certain acts that are dangerous to the international community as a whole wherever they occur. Universal jurisdiction has traditionally been asserted over the crime of piracy. See *United States v. Smith,* 18 U.S. (5 Wheat.) 153, 161 (1820). After World War II, commentators argued that the universality principle should be extended to perpetrators of genocide, and the Israeli government relied on this principle to justify the trial (though not the kidnapping) of Adolf Eichmann. As *Yunis* demonstrates, the universality principle has more recently been extended to include air piracy and some forms of international terrorism. In *Filartiga v. Pena-Irala,* 630 F.2d 876, 890 (2d Cir. 1980), the court explained that "the torturer has become—like the pirate and slave trader before him—*hostis humani generis,* an enemy of all mankind." See also *Demjanjuk v. Petrovsky,* 776 F.2d 571, 582–83 (6th Cir. 1985), holding that Israel had universal jurisdiction over a Nazi war criminal even though his crimes were committed before Israel was a state:

> [N]either the nationality of the accused or the victim(s), nor the location of the crime is significant. The underlying assumption is that the crimes are offenses against the law of nations or against humanity and that the prosecuting nation is acting for all nations. This being so, Israel or any other nation, regardless of its status in 1942 or 1943, may undertake to vindicate the interest of all nations by seeking to punish the perpetrators of such crimes.

In recognizing the universality principle, *Yunis* relies on its acceptance in formal international treaties and conventions. Could jurisdiction ever be asserted on this basis without such conventions? What other crimes or acts ought to be encompassed? Consider *United States v. Yousef,* 327 F.3d 56 (2d Cir. 2003), holding that "customary international law currently does not provide for the prosecution of 'terrorist' acts under the universality principle, in part due to the failure of States to achieve anything like consensus on the definition of terrorism."

The Permissible Scope of U.S. Law

(1) The critical case in the United States expanding legislative jurisdiction beyond territoriality was *United States v. Aluminum Co. of America (Alcoa),* 148 F.2d 416 (2d Cir. 1945). Like the *Lotus* case, *Alcoa* involved recognition of the effects doctrine. A group of foreign corporations formed a cartel to regulate competition in the aluminum industry. No acts in furtherance of this combination occurred in the United States, though American companies bought and sold aluminum from cartel members. In an opinion by Learned Hand, the court interpreted the Sherman Act to apply to agreements intended to affect and affecting United States commerce. "[A]ny state," Judge Hand wrote, "may impose liabilities, even upon persons not within its allegiance, for conduct outside its borders that has consequences within its borders that the state reprehends. . ."

The scope of jurisdiction to prescribe in the United States is set forth in the Third Restatement:

§ 402. Bases of Jurisdiction to Prescribe

Subject to § 403, a state has jurisdiction to prescribe with respect to

(1) (a) conduct that, wholly or in substantial part, takes place within its territory;

(b) the status of persons, or interests in things, present within its territory;

(c) conduct outside its territory that has or is intended to have substantial effect within its territory;

(2) the activities, interests, status, or relations of its nationals outside as well as within its territory;

(3) certain conduct outside its territory by persons not its nationals that is directed against the security of the state or against a limited class of other state interests.

Section 403, discussed infra pp. 992–993, instructs the court to apply a balancing test when another nation could also apply its law; § 402 thus establishes the outer boundaries of jurisdiction to prescribe in the United States. Does § 402 reflect all five of the bases discussed in *Yunis*? Does it recognize the universality principle? How about the passive personality principle?

The Fourth Restatement of Foreign Relations Law, published in 2018, maintains the Third Restatement's bases of prescriptive jurisdiction while adding the following two bases: first, "certain conduct outside its territory that harms its nationals," and second, "certain offenses of universal concern, such as piracy, slavery, forced labor, trafficking in persons, recruitment of child soldiers, torture, extrajudicial killing, genocide, and certain acts of terrorism, even if no specific connection exists between the United States and the persons or conduct being regulated." Restatement (Fourth) of the Foreign Relations Law of the United States § 402(d), (f) (2018). In other words, § 402 reflects all five of the bases discussed in *Yunis*, as is confirmed by §§ 408–413 of the Fourth Restatement. Is this an improvement?

(2) What is the source of these limits in United States law? It is well settled that if Congress enacts legislation contrary to public international law, United States courts must disregard international law and apply the domestic statute. See *Head Money Cases,* 112 U.S. 580, 598–99 (1884); *Whitney v. Robertson,* 124 U.S. 190, 194 (1888). It does not follow that international law is irrelevant, for courts generally presume that Congress does not intend to run afoul of international law unless it has clearly said so. *Murray v. Schooner Charming Betsy,* 6 U.S. (2 Cranch) 64, 118 (1804); Third Restatement § 114. Are there other limits on the extraterritorial application of United States law? Does the Constitution constrain Congress in the multinational context? See Brilmayer & Norchi, *Federal Extraterritoriality and Fifth Amendment Due Process,* 105 Harv. L. Rev. 1217 (1992).

(3) Compare the limits imposed on the legislative jurisdiction of the United States under international law with those imposed on the states under the United States Constitution (discussed in Chapter 3). Is the scope of jurisdiction in international law broader or narrower? Could a state apply its law on the basis of the passive personality principle? How about the universality or protective principle? Should the scope of legislative jurisdiction in international law be broader or less broad?

(4) What about state legislative jurisdiction in the international context? Judicial analyses of this issue tend to track the Supreme Court's due process cases from *Dick* and *Delta Pine* to *Allstate* and *Shutts.* In *Gerling Global Reinsurance Corp. of Am. v. Gallagher*, 267 F.3d 1228 (11th Cir. 2001), the court struck down Florida's Holocaust Victim Insurance Act, which required insurers doing business in Florida to provide information about and pay the claims of insured Holocaust victims, on the grounds that it sought to regulate transactions with insufficient contacts to Florida. The Ninth Circuit disagreed in *Gerling Global Reinsurance Corp. of Am. v. Low*, 296 F.3d 832 (9th Cir. 2002), upholding the analogous California statute against a due process challenge. Should there be some counterpart to the domestic full faith and credit analysis? Does the *Allstate* merger moot the issue? Or are there other doctrines that can do the work of full faith and credit?

The Supreme Court reversed *Low* on the grounds that the California statute interfered with the President's conduct of foreign affairs and was therefore preempted. *American Insurance Ass'n v. Garamendi*, 539 U.S. 396 (2003). See also, e.g., *Crosby v. National Foreign Trade Council*, 530 U.S. 363 (2000) (finding Massachusetts statute that barred state entities from doing business with Burma preempted by federal foreign affairs power). In *Steinberg v. International Commission on Holocaust Era Insurance Claims*, 133 Cal.App.4th 689, 34 Cal.Rptr.3d 944 (App. 2005), the plaintiffs sought to avoid *Garamendi* on the ground that their class was limited to policyholders and heirs whose claims were rejected by Generali, an Italian company not subject to the executive agreements signed with Germany and Austria. The court rejected the argument as "irrelevant," noting that "[i]t is not the executive agreements themselves which dictated the result in *Garamendi,* but the policy reflected in them, a policy which extends to claims against Generali." *Id.* at 952.

(5) What status should customary international law have in the domestic courts of the United States? Chief Justice Marshall said in *The Nereide,* 13 U.S. (9 Cranch) 388, 423 (1815), that "the Court is bound by the law of nations which is a part of the law of the land"—a sentiment subsequent Courts have reiterated from time to time. See *The Paquete Habana,* 175 U.S. 677, 700 (1900) (customary international law is part of "our law"); *Banco Nacional de Cuba v. Sabbatino,* 376 U.S. 398 (1964) (rules regarding foreign relations and international law "must be treated exclusively as an aspect of federal law.") Such statements have been understood by most commentators to mean that customary international law is federal common law. See Brilmayer, *Federalism, State Authority, and the Preemptive Power of International Law,* 1994 Sup. Ct. Rev. 295; Koh, *Is International Law Really State Law?,* 111 Harv. L. Rev. 1824 (1998).

Does it therefore follow that customary international law preempts inconsistent state law? As Professor Brilmayer points out, state courts typically ignore customary international law norms when it comes to jurisdiction or choice of law, routinely exercising jurisdiction or applying their own law in circumstances inconsistent with these norms. Brilmayer, 1994 Sup. Ct. Rev. at 295–300. Should they be permitted to do so? Brilmayer thinks not—together with most international law scholars. As federal common law, they say, customary international norms both provide a basis for federal jurisdiction and displace inconsistent state rules. See *id.*; Koh, 111 Harv. L. Rev. at 1830–60; Henkin, *International Law as Law in the United States,* 82 Mich. L. Rev. 1555 (1984).

The stakes in this debate are not confined to choice of law and jurisdiction, but raise questions about the applicability of various human rights norms that have developed in international law since World War II. See Third Restatement § 702 & comment *a* (listing rights while observing that "[t]he list is not necessarily complete, and is not closed"). Emphasizing (1) that the nature of federal common law changed after *Erie,* and (2) that the range of issues encompassed by international law has become vastly larger in recent decades, Professors Curtis Bradley and Jack Goldsmith reject the argument that customary international law should be treated as federal common law. Such rules may be described as "federal common law" in the sense of providing background norms for interpreting federal statutes, they say, but principles of federalism and the protection of state interests require denying international law the status of true federal law absent express adoption by statute. Bradley & Goldsmith, *Customary*

International Law as Federal Common Law: A Critique of the Modern Position, 110 Harv. L. Rev. 815 (1997); Bradley & Goldsmith, *Federal Courts and the Incorporation of International Law,* 111 Harv. L. Rev. 2260 (1998). Their position has been strenuously criticized. See Koh, supra; Goodman & Jinks, Filartiga*'s Firm Footing: International Human Rights and Federal Common Law,* 66 Fordham L. Rev. 463 (1997); Neuman, *Sense and Nonsense About Customary International Law: A Response to Professor Bradley and Goldsmith,* 66 Fordham L. Rev. 371 (1997); Stephens, *The Law of Our Land: Customary International Law as Federal Law After* Erie, 66 Fordham L. Rev. 393 (1997).

B. FEDERAL STATUTES

Ascertaining the Scope of Federal Law

MORRISON V. NATIONAL AUSTRALIA BANK LTD.

561 U.S. 247 (2010).

JUSTICE SCALIA delivered the opinion of the Court.

We decide whether § 10(b) of the Securities Exchange Act of 1934 provides a cause of action to foreign plaintiffs suing foreign and American defendants for misconduct in connection with securities traded on foreign exchanges.

I

[The plaintiffs were three Australian citizens who bought stock in National Australia Bank ("National"), the largest bank in Australia. National's stock was traded on the Australian Stock Exchange and other foreign securities exchanges, but not on any U.S. exchange. (The New York Stock Exchange did, however, list National's American Depository Receipts, which afford exposure to National's stock.) In 1998, National bought a mortgage servicing company headquartered in Florida [HomeSide]. According to the plaintiffs, this company misrepresented its financial condition and National, though aware of the misrepresentations, did nothing to correct them until years later, when it announced it was writing down the value of the company. National's shares then declined and the plaintiffs sued in the Southern District of New York, alleging violations of §§ 10(b) and 20(a) of the Securities and Exchange Act of 1934 and SEC Rule 10b–5. The District Court dismissed for lack of subject-matter jurisdiction on the grounds that the alleged fraud had only a minimal connection with the United States and the Second Circuit affirmed. The Supreme Court first noted that the jurisdictional disposition was erroneous: "to ask what conduct § 10(b) reaches is to ask what conduct § 10(b) prohibits, which is a merits question." It then addressed the merits.]

III

A

It is a "longstanding principle of American law 'that legislation of Congress, unless a contrary intent appears, is meant to apply only within the territorial jurisdiction of the United States.'" *EEOC v. Arabian American Oil Co.,* 499 U.S. 244 (1991) *(Aramco)* (quoting *Foley Bros., Inc. v. Filardo,* 336 U.S. 281, 285 (1949)). This principle represents a canon of construction, or a presumption about a statute's meaning, rather than a limit upon Congress's power to legislate. It rests on the perception that Congress ordinarily legislates with respect to domestic, not foreign matters. Thus, "unless there is the affirmative intention of the Congress clearly expressed" to give a statute extraterritorial effect, "we must presume it is primarily concerned with domestic conditions." *Aramco, supra,* at 248 (internal quotation marks omitted). The canon or presumption applies regardless of whether there is a risk of conflict between the American statute and a foreign law. When a statute gives no clear indication of an extraterritorial application, it has none.

Despite this principle of interpretation, long and often recited in our opinions, the Second Circuit believed that, because the Exchange Act is silent as to the extraterritorial application of § 10(b), it was left to the court to "discern" whether Congress would have wanted the statute to apply. * * * This disregard of the presumption against extraterritoriality did not originate with the Court of Appeals panel in this case. It has been repeated over many decades by various courts of appeals in determining the application of the Exchange Act, and § 10(b) in particular, to fraudulent schemes that involve conduct and effects abroad. That has produced a collection of tests for divining what Congress would have wanted, complex in formulation and unpredictable in application.

The Second Circuit . . . later formalized [its decisions] into (1) an "effects test," "whether the wrongful conduct had a substantial effect in the United States or upon United States citizens," and (2) a "conduct test," "whether the wrongful conduct occurred in the United States." *SEC v. Berger,* 322 F.3d 187, 192–193 (2d Cir. 2003). These became the north star of the Second Circuit's § 10(b) jurisprudence, pointing the way to what Congress would have wished. Indeed, the Second Circuit declined to keep its two tests distinct on the ground that "an admixture or combination of the two often gives a better picture of whether there is sufficient United States involvement to justify the exercise of jurisdiction by an American court." *Itoba Ltd. v. Lep Group PLC,* 54 F.3d 118, 122 (1995). . .

As they developed, these tests were not easy to administer. The conduct test was held to apply differently depending on whether the harmed investors were Americans or foreigners: When the alleged damages consisted of losses to American investors abroad, it was enough that acts "of material importance" performed in the United States "significantly contributed" to that result; whereas those acts must have "directly caused" the result when losses to foreigners abroad were at issue. * * * And "merely preparatory activities in the United States" did not suffice "to trigger application of the securities laws for injury to foreigners located abroad." * * * This required the court to distinguish between mere preparation and using the United States as a "base" for fraudulent activities in other countries. * * * But merely satisfying the conduct test was sometimes insufficient without " 'some additional factor tipping the scales' " in favor of the application of American law. District courts have noted the difficulty of applying such vague formulations. There is no more damning indictment of the "conduct" and "effects" tests than the Second Circuit's own declaration that "the presence or absence of any single factor which was considered significant in other cases . . . is not necessarily dispositive in future cases."

Other Circuits embraced the Second Circuit's approach, though not its precise application. Like the Second Circuit, they described their decisions regarding the extraterritorial application of § 10(b) as essentially resolving matters of policy. While applying the same fundamental methodology of balancing interests and arriving at what seemed the best policy, they produced a proliferation of vaguely related variations on the "conduct" and "effects" tests. . .

Commentators have criticized the unpredictable and inconsistent application of § 10(b) to transnational cases. * * * Some have challenged the premise underlying the Courts of Appeals' approach, namely that Congress did not consider the extraterritorial application of § 10(b) (thereby leaving it open to the courts, supposedly, to determine what Congress would have wanted). * * * Others, more fundamentally, have noted that using congressional silence as a justification for judge-made rules violates the traditional principle that silence means no extraterritorial application.

The criticisms seem to us justified. The results of judicial-speculation-made-law—divining what Congress would have wanted if it had thought of the situation before the court—demonstrate the wisdom of the presumption against extraterritoriality. Rather than guess anew in each case, we apply the presumption in all cases, preserving a stable background against which Congress can legislate with predictable effects. . .

B

Rule 10b–5, the regulation under which petitioners have brought suit, . . . was promulgated under § 10(b), and "does not extend beyond conduct encompassed by § 10(b)'s prohibition." Therefore, if § 10(b) is not extraterritorial, neither is Rule 10b–5.

On its face, § 10(b) contains nothing to suggest it applies abroad:

> "It shall be unlawful for any person, directly or indirectly, by the use of any means or instrumentality of interstate commerce or of the mails, or of any facility of any national securities exchange . . . [t]o use or employ, in connection with the purchase or sale of any security registered on a national securities exchange or any security not so registered, . . . any manipulative or deceptive device or contrivance in contravention of such rules and regulations as the [Securities and Exchange] Commission may prescribe. . ." 15 U.S.C. 78j(b).

Petitioners and the Solicitor General contend, however, that three things indicate that § 10(b) or the Exchange Act in general has at least some extraterritorial application.

First, they point to the definition of "interstate commerce," a term used in § 10(b), which includes "trade, commerce, transportation, or communication . . . between any foreign country and any State." 15 U.S.C. § 78c(a)(17). But "we have repeatedly held that even statutes that contain broad language in their definitions of 'commerce' that expressly refer to '*foreign* commerce' do not apply abroad." * * * The general reference to foreign commerce in the definition of "interstate commerce" does not defeat the presumption against extraterritoriality. . .

Petitioners and the Solicitor General next point out that Congress, in describing the purposes of the Exchange Act, observed that the "prices established and offered in such transactions are generally disseminated and quoted throughout the United States and foreign countries." 15 U.S.C. § 78b(2). The antecedent of "such transactions," however, is found in the first sentence of the section, which declares that "transactions in securities as commonly conducted upon securities exchanges and over-the-counter markets are affected with a national public interest." § 78b. Nothing suggests that this *national* public interest pertains to transactions conducted upon *foreign* exchanges and markets. The fleeting reference to the dissemination and quotation abroad of the prices of securities traded in domestic exchanges and markets cannot overcome the presumption against extraterritoriality.

[The Court also considered and rejected an argument based on § 30(b) of the Exchange Act, 15 U.S.C. § 78dd(b), which exempts foreign transactions that do not violate regulations promulgated by the Securities and Exchange Commission "to prevent . . . evasion of [the Act]."]

The concurrence claims we have impermissibly narrowed the inquiry in evaluating whether a statute applies abroad, citing for that point the dissent in *Aramco*. But we do not say, as the concurrence seems to think, that the presumption against extraterritoriality is a "clear statement rule," if by that is meant a requirement that a statute say "this law applies abroad." Assuredly context can be consulted as well. But whatever sources of statutory meaning one consults to give "the most faithful reading" of the text, there is no clear indication of extraterritoriality here. The concurrence does not even try to refute that conclusion, but merely puts forward the same (at best) uncertain indications relied upon by petitioners and the Solicitor General. As the opinion *for the Court* in *Aramco* (which we prefer to the dissent) shows, those uncertain indications do not suffice.[8]

In short, there is no affirmative indication in the Exchange Act that § 10(b) applies extraterritorially, and we therefore conclude that it does not.

IV

A

Petitioners argue that the conclusion that § 10(b) does not apply extraterritorially does not resolve this case. They contend that they seek no more than domestic application anyway, since Florida is where HomeSide and its senior executives engaged in the deceptive conduct of manipulating HomeSide's financial models; their complaint also alleged that Race and Hughes made misleading public statements there. This is less an answer to the presumption against extraterritorial application than it is an assertion—a quite valid assertion—that that presumption here (as often) is not self-evidently dispositive, but its application requires further analysis. For it is a rare case of prohibited extraterritorial application that lacks *all* contact with the territory of the United States. But the presumption against extraterritorial application would be a craven watchdog indeed if it retreated to its kennel whenever *some* domestic activity is involved in the case. The concurrence seems to imagine just such a timid sentinel, but our cases are to the contrary. In *Aramco,* for example, the Title VII plaintiff had been hired in Houston, and was an American citizen. * * * The Court concluded, however, that neither that territorial event nor that relationship was the "focus" of congressional concern, * * * but rather domestic employment. * * *

Applying the same mode of analysis here, we think that the focus of the Exchange Act is not upon the place where the deception originated, but upon purchases and sales of securities in the United States. Section 10(b) does not punish deceptive conduct, but only deceptive conduct "in connection with the purchase or sale of any security registered on a national securities exchange or any security not so registered." 15 U.S.C. § 78j(b). Those purchase-and-sale transactions are the objects of the statute's solicitude. It is those transactions that the statute seeks to

8 The concurrence notes that, post-*Aramco,* Congress provided explicitly for extraterritorial application of Title VII, the statute at issue in *Aramco.* * * * All this shows is that Congress knows how to give a statute explicit extraterritorial effect—and how to limit that effect to particular applications, which is what the cited amendment did. See Civil Rights Act of 1991, § 109, 105 Stat. 1077.

"regulate"; it is parties or prospective parties to those transactions that the statute seeks to "protec[t]." And it is in our view only transactions in securities listed on domestic exchanges, and domestic transactions in other securities, to which § 10(b) applies. . .

The primacy of the domestic exchange is suggested by the very prologue of the Exchange Act, which sets forth as its object "[t]o provide for the regulation of securities exchanges . . . operating in interstate and foreign commerce and through the mails, to prevent inequitable and unfair practices on such exchanges. . ." * * * We know of no one who thought that the Act was intended to "regulat[e]" *foreign* securities exchanges—or indeed who even believed that under established principles of international law Congress had the power to do so. The Act's registration requirements apply only to securities listed on national securities exchanges.

. . .

The same focus on domestic transactions is evident in the Securities Act of 1933, enacted by the same Congress as the Exchange Act, and forming part of the same comprehensive regulation of securities trading. That legislation makes it unlawful to sell a security, through a prospectus or otherwise, making use of "any means or instruments of transportation or communication in interstate commerce or of the mails," unless a registration statement is in effect. * * * The Commission has interpreted that requirement "not to include . . . sales that occur outside the United States." * * *.

Finally, we reject the notion that the Exchange Act reaches conduct in this country affecting exchanges or transactions abroad for the same reason that *Aramco* rejected overseas application of Title VII to all domestically concluded employment contracts or all employment contracts with American employers: The probability of incompatibility with the applicable laws of other countries is so obvious that if Congress intended such foreign application "it would have addressed the subject of conflicts with foreign laws and procedures." * * * Like the United States, foreign countries regulate their domestic securities exchanges and securities transactions occurring within their territorial jurisdiction. And the regulation of other countries often differs from ours as to what constitutes fraud, what disclosures must be made, what damages are recoverable, what discovery is available in litigation, what individual actions may be joined in a single suit, what attorney's fees are recoverable, and many other matters. * * * The Commonwealth of Australia, the United Kingdom of Great Britain and Northern Ireland, and the Republic of France have filed *amicus* briefs in this case. So have (separately or jointly) such international and foreign organizations as the International Chamber of Commerce, the Swiss Bankers Association, the Federation of German Industries, the French Business Confederation, the Institute of International Bankers, the

European Banking Federation, the Australian Bankers' Association, and the Association Francaise des Entreprises Privées. They all complain of the interference with foreign securities regulation that application of § 10(b) abroad would produce, and urge the adoption of a clear test that will avoid that consequence. The transactional test we have adopted—whether the purchase or sale is made in the United States, or involves a security listed on a domestic exchange—meets that requirement.

B

The Solicitor General suggests a different test, which petitioners also endorse: "[A] transnational securities fraud violates [§] 10(b) when the fraud involves significant conduct in the United States that is material to the fraud's success." * * *. Neither the Solicitor General nor petitioners provide any textual support for this test. The Solicitor General sets forth a number of purposes such a test would serve: achieving a high standard of business ethics in the securities industry, ensuring honest securities markets and thereby promoting investor confidence, and preventing the United States from becoming a "Barbary Coast" for malefactors perpetrating frauds in foreign markets. * * *. But it provides no textual support for the last of these purposes, or for the first two as applied to the foreign securities industry and securities markets abroad. It is our function to give the statute the effect its language suggests, however modest that may be; not to extend it to admirable purposes it might be used to achieve.

If, moreover, one is to be attracted by the desirable consequences of the "significant and material conduct" test, one should also be repulsed by its adverse consequences. While there is no reason to believe that the United States has become the Barbary Coast for those perpetrating frauds on foreign securities markets, some fear that it has become the Shangri-La of class-action litigation for lawyers representing those allegedly cheated in foreign securities markets.

The Solicitor General points out that the "significant and material conduct" test is in accord with prevailing notions of international comity. If so, that proves that *if* the United States asserted prescriptive jurisdiction pursuant to the "significant and material conduct" test it would not violate customary international law; but it in no way tends to prove that that is what Congress has done.

* * *

Section 10(b) reaches the use of a manipulative or deceptive device or contrivance only in connection with the purchase or sale of a security listed on an American stock exchange, and the purchase or sale of any other security in the United States. This case involves no securities listed on a domestic exchange, and all aspects of the purchases complained of by those petitioners who still have live claims occurred outside the United States.

Petitioners have therefore failed to state a claim on which relief can be granted. We affirm the dismissal of petitioners' complaint on this ground.

It is so ordered.

JUSTICE SOTOMAYOR took no part in the consideration or decision of this case.

[JUSTICE BREYER concurred.]

JUSTICE STEVENS, with whom JUSTICE GINSBURG joins, concurring in the judgment.

While I agree that petitioners have failed to state a claim on which relief can be granted, my reasoning differs from the Court's. I would adhere to the general approach that has been the law in the Second Circuit, and most of the rest of the country, for nearly four decades.

I

The text and history of § 10(b) are famously opaque on the question of when, exactly, transnational securities frauds fall within the statute's compass. As those types of frauds became more common in the latter half of the 20th century, the federal courts were increasingly called upon to wrestle with that question. The Court of Appeals for the Second Circuit, located in the Nation's financial center, led the effort. . . Relying on opinions by Judge Henry Friendly, the Second Circuit eventually settled on a conduct-and-effects test. This test asks "(1) whether the wrongful conduct occurred in the United States, and (2) whether the wrongful conduct had a substantial effect in the United States or upon United States citizens." * * * Numerous cases flesh out the proper application of each prong.

The Second Circuit's test became the "north star" of § 10(b) jurisprudence not just regionally but nationally as well. With minor variations, other courts converged on the same basic approach.* * * Neither Congress nor the Securities Exchange Commission (Commission) acted to change the law. To the contrary, the Commission largely adopted the Second Circuit's position in its own adjudications.

In light of this history, the Court's critique of the decision below for applying "judge-made rules" is quite misplaced. This entire area of law is replete with judge-made rules, which give concrete meaning to Congress' general commands. . .

The development of § 10(b) law was hardly an instance of judicial usurpation. Congress invited an expansive role for judicial elaboration when it crafted such an open-ended statute in 1934. And both Congress and the Commission subsequently affirmed that role when they left intact the relevant statutory and regulatory language, respectively, throughout all the years that followed. Unlike certain other domains of securities law, this is "a case in which Congress has enacted a regulatory statute and then has accepted, over a long period of time, broad judicial authority to define substantive standards of conduct and liability," and much else besides.

This Court has not shied away from acknowledging that authority. We have consistently confirmed that, in applying § 10(b) and Rule 10b–5, courts may need "to flesh out the portions of the law with respect to which neither the congressional enactment nor the administrative regulations offer conclusive guidance." * * * And we have unanimously "recogniz[ed] a judicial authority to shape . . . the 10b–5 cause of action," for that is a task "Congress has left to us." Indeed, we have unanimously endorsed the Second Circuit's basic interpretive approach to § 10(b)—ridiculed by the Court today—of striving to "divin[e] what Congress would have wanted." "Our task," we have said, is "to attempt to infer how the 1934 Congress would have addressed the issue."

Thus, while the Court devotes a considerable amount of attention to the development of the case law, it draws the wrong conclusions. The Second Circuit refined its test over several decades and dozens of cases, with the tacit approval of Congress and the Commission and with the general assent of its sister Circuits. That history is a reason we should give additional weight to the Second Circuit's "judge-made" doctrine, not a reason to denigrate it. "The longstanding acceptance by the courts, coupled with Congress' failure to reject [its] reasonable interpretation of the wording of § 10(b), . . . argues significantly in favor of acceptance of the [Second Circuit] rule by this Court."

II

The Court's other main critique of the Second Circuit's approach—apart from what the Court views as its excessive reliance on functional considerations and reconstructed congressional intent—is that the Second Circuit has "disregard[ed]" the presumption against extraterritoriality. It is the Court, however, that misapplies the presumption, in two main respects.

First, the Court seeks to transform the presumption from a flexible rule of thumb into something more like a clear statement rule. We have been here before. In the case on which the Court primarily relies, *EEOC v. Arabian American Oil Co.*, 499 U.S. 244 (1991) *(Aramco)*, Chief Justice Rehnquist's majority opinion included a sentence that appeared to make the same move. * * * Justice Marshall, in dissent, vigorously objected. * * *

Yet even *Aramco*—surely the most extreme application of the presumption against extraterritoriality in my time on the Court[6]—contained numerous passages suggesting that the presumption may be

[6] And also one of the most short lived. See Civil Rights Act of 1991, § 109, 105 Stat. 1077 (repudiating *Aramco*).

overcome without a clear directive. * * * And our cases both before and after *Aramco* make perfectly clear that the Court continues to give effect to "*all available evidence* about the meaning" of a provision when considering its extraterritorial application, lest we defy Congress' will. * * * Contrary to Justice Scalia's personal view of statutory interpretation, that evidence legitimately encompasses more than the enacted text. Hence, while the Court's dictum that "[w]hen a statute gives no clear indication of an extraterritorial application, it has none," makes for a nice catchphrase, the point is overstated. The presumption against extraterritoriality can be useful as a theory of congressional purpose, a tool for managing international conflict, a background norm, a tiebreaker. It does not relieve courts of their duty to give statutes the most faithful reading possible.

Second, and more fundamentally, the Court errs in suggesting that the presumption against extraterritoriality is fatal to the Second Circuit's test. For even if the presumption really were a clear statement . . . rule, it would have only marginal relevance to this case.

It is true, of course, that "this Court ordinarily construes ambiguous statutes to avoid unreasonable interference with the sovereign authority of other nations," *F. Hoffmann-La Roche Ltd. v. Empagran S. A.,* 542 U.S. 155, 164 (2004), and that, absent contrary evidence, we presume "Congress is primarily concerned with domestic conditions," *Foley Bros., Inc. v. Filardo,* 336 U.S. 281, 285 (1949). Accordingly, the presumption against extraterritoriality "provides a sound basis for concluding that Section 10(b) does not apply when a securities fraud with no effects in the United States is hatched and executed entirely outside this country.* * * But that is just about all it provides a sound basis for concluding. And the conclusion is not very illuminating, because no party to the litigation disputes it. No one contends that § 10(b) applies to wholly foreign frauds.

Rather, the real question in this case is how much, and what kinds of, *domestic* contacts are sufficient to trigger application of § 10(b). In developing its conduct-and-effects test, the Second Circuit endeavored to derive a solution from the Exchange Act's text, structure, history, and purpose. Judge Friendly and his colleagues were well aware that United States courts "cannot and should not expend [their] resources resolving cases that do not affect Americans or involve fraud emanating from America."

The question just stated does not admit of an easy answer. The text of the Exchange Act indicates that § 10(b) extends to at least some activities with an international component, but, again, it is not pellucid as to which ones. The Second Circuit draws the line as follows: § 10(b) extends to transnational frauds "only when substantial acts in furtherance of the fraud were committed within the United States," * * * or when the fraud was " 'intended to produce' " and did produce " 'detrimental effects within' " the United States. * * *

This approach is consistent with the understanding shared by most scholars that Congress, in passing the Exchange Act, "expected U.S. securities laws to apply to certain international transactions or conduct." It is also consistent with the traditional understanding, regnant in the 1930's as it is now, that the presumption against extraterritoriality does not apply "when the conduct [at issue] occurs within the United States," and has lesser force when "the failure to extend the scope of the statute to a foreign setting will result in adverse effects within the United States." And it strikes a reasonable balance between the goals of "preventing the export of fraud from America," protecting shareholders, enhancing investor confidence, and deterring corporate misconduct, on the one hand, and conserving United States resources and limiting conflict with foreign law, on the other.* * *

Thus, while § 10(b) may not give any "clear indication" on its face as to how it should apply to transnational securities frauds, it does give strong clues that it should cover at least some of them. And in my view, the Second Circuit has done the best job of discerning what sorts of transnational frauds Congress meant in 1934—and still means today—to regulate. I do not take issue with the Court for beginning its inquiry with the statutory text, rather than the doctrine in the Courts of Appeals. I take issue with the Court for beginning *and ending* its inquiry with the statutory text, when the text does not speak with geographic precision, and for dismissing the long pedigree of, and the persuasive account of congressional intent embodied in, the Second Circuit's rule.

Repudiating the Second Circuit's approach in its entirety, the Court establishes a novel rule that will foreclose private parties from bringing § 10(b) actions whenever the relevant securities were purchased or sold abroad and are not listed on a domestic exchange.[12] The real motor of the Court's opinion, it seems, is not the presumption against extraterritoriality but rather the Court's belief that transactions on domestic exchanges are "the focus of the Exchange Act" and "the objects of [its] solicitude." In reality, however, it is the "public interest" and "the interests of investors" that are the objects of the statute's solicitude. And while the clarity and simplicity of the Court's test may have some salutary consequences, like all bright-line rules it also has drawbacks.

Imagine, for example, an American investor who buys shares in a company listed only on an overseas exchange. That company has a major

---

[12] The Court's opinion does not, however, foreclose the Commission from bringing enforcement actions in additional circumstances, as no issue concerning the Commission's authority is presented by this case. The Commission's enforcement proceedings not only differ from private § 10(b) actions in numerous potentially relevant respects, but they also pose a lesser threat to international comity. * * *

American subsidiary with executives based in New York City; and it was in New York City that the executives masterminded and implemented a massive deception which artificially inflated the stock price—and which will, upon its disclosure, cause the price to plummet. Or, imagine that those same executives go knocking on doors in Manhattan and convince an unsophisticated retiree, on the basis of material misrepresentations, to invest her life savings in the company's doomed securities. Both of these investors would, under the Court's new test, be barred from seeking relief under § 10(b).

The oddity of that result should give pause. For in walling off such individuals from § 10(b), the Court narrows the provision's reach to a degree that would surprise and alarm generations of American investors—and, I am convinced, the Congress that passed the Exchange Act. Indeed, the Court's rule turns § 10(b) jurisprudence (and the presumption against extraterritoriality) on its head, by withdrawing the statute's application from cases in which there is *both* substantial wrongful conduct that occurred in the United States *and* a substantial injurious effect on United States markets and citizens.

III

In my judgment, if petitioners' allegations of fraudulent misconduct that took place in Florida are true, then respondents may have violated § 10(b), and could potentially be held accountable in an enforcement proceeding brought by the Commission. But it does not follow that shareholders who have failed to allege that the bulk or the heart of the fraud occurred in the United States, or that the fraud had an adverse impact on American investors or markets, may maintain a private action to recover damages they suffered abroad. Some cases involving foreign securities transactions have extensive links to, and ramifications for, this country; this case has Australia written all over it. Accordingly, for essentially the reasons stated in the Court of Appeals' opinion, I would affirm its judgment.

The Court instead elects to upend a significant area of securities law based on a plausible, but hardly decisive, construction of the statutory text. In so doing, it pays short shrift to the United States' interest in remedying frauds that transpire on American soil or harm American citizens, as well as to the accumulated wisdom and experience of the lower courts. I happen to agree with the result the Court reaches in this case. But "I respectfully dissent," once again, "from the Court's continuing campaign to render the private cause of action under § 10(b) toothless."

The Evolution of the Presumption Against Extraterritoriality

(1) *A page of history.* The "presumption against extraterritoriality" made its first formal appearance in *American Banana Co. v. United Fruit Co.,* 213 U.S. 347 (1909). Costa Rica invaded Panama, allegedly at the behest of the United Fruit Company, which was seeking to monopolize the Central American banana trade. Costa Rican soldiers seized a plantation owned by the American Banana Company and conveyed it to one Astua, who promptly sold it to United Fruit. American Banana brought an antitrust action against United Fruit in New York, basing its claim on these as well as more conventional anticompetitive acts. The complaint was dismissed, and the case made its way by writ of error to the Supreme Court. Writing for the Court, Justice Holmes observed: "It is obvious that, however stated, the plaintiff's case depends on several rather startling propositions. In the first place, the acts causing the damage were done, so far as appears, outside the jurisdiction of the United States and within that of other states. It is surprising to hear it argued that they were governed by the act of Congress." The surprise, Holmes continued, came from the fact that

> the general and almost universal rule is that the character of an act as lawful or unlawful must be determined wholly by the law of the country where the act is done. *Slater v. Mexican National R.R. Co.,* 194 U.S. 120, 126. This principle was carried to an extreme in *Milliken v. Pratt,* 125 Mass. 374. For another jurisdiction, if it should happen to lay hold of the actor, to treat him according to its own notions rather than those of the place where he did the acts, not only would be unjust, but would be an interference with the authority of another sovereign, contrary to the comity of nations, which the other states concerned justly might resent.

These considerations, Holmes concluded, "would lead in case of doubt to a construction of any statute as intended to be confined in its operation and effect to the territorial limits over which the lawmaker has general and legitimate power." 213 U.S. at 355–57.

How would you characterize the analysis in this opinion? Isn't Holmes merely following the narrow territorial conception of legislative jurisdiction that prevailed in the late 19th and early 20th centuries? Does the result turn on the fact that the case is international rather than interstate?

(2) *American Banana*'s narrow interpretation of the antitrust laws was not long-lived. In several subsequent cases involving acts committed partly in the United States and partly abroad, the Court applied U.S. antitrust law while speaking the language of effects. See, e.g., *Thomsen v. Cayser,* 243 U.S. 66, 88 (1917) ("the combination affected the foreign commerce of this country and was put into operation here"); *United States v. Sisal Sales Corp.,* 274 U.S. 268, 276 (1927) (defendants' acts here and abroad created liability because they "brought about forbidden results within the United States"). None of the results in these cases actually turned on the effects doctrine because in each case some of the conduct constituting the conspiracy had occurred in the United States. But these dicta provided Learned Hand with the authority he needed in *Alcoa* to apply the Sherman Act to a conspiracy committed entirely abroad on the ground that its effects were felt in the United States. *United States v. Aluminum Co. of America,* 148 F.2d 416 (2d Cir. 1945), discussed supra p. 944.

The problem with *Alcoa's* expansive interpretation of the antitrust laws was that foreign acts deliberately affecting United States commerce often were intended also to affect foreign commerce—sometimes with the approval or even the encouragement of foreign governments. *Alcoa* thus brought about precisely what the presumption against territoriality was designed to prevent: conflicts with foreign nations that caused tension in international relations. To avoid these problems, courts in subsequent cases moderated the effects doctrine by recognizing that deference to foreign law may sometimes be appropriate despite effects in the United States. The leading decision is *Timberlane Lumber Co. v. Bank of America,* 549 F.2d 597 (9th Cir. 1976), where the court explained:

> The effects test by itself is incomplete because it fails to consider other nations' interests. Nor does it expressly take into account the full nature of the relationship between the actors and this country. . . [Courts must therefore ask the question] which is unique to the international setting of whether the interests of, and links to, the United States—including the magnitude of the effects on American foreign commerce—are sufficiently strong, vis-a-vis those of other nations, to justify an assertion of extraterritorial authority. . .
>
> The elements to be weighed [in making this inquiry] include the degree of conflict with foreign law or policy, the nationality or allegiance of the parties and the locations or principal places of business of corporations, the extent to which enforcement by either state can be expected to achieve compliance, the relative significance of effects on the United States as compared with those elsewhere, the extent to which there is explicit purpose to harm or affect American commerce, the foreseeability of such effect, and the relative importance to the violations charged of conduct within the United States as compared with conduct abroad. A court evaluating these factors should identify the potential degree of conflict if American authority is asserted. . . Having assessed the conflict, the court should then determine whether in the face of it the contacts and interests of the United States are sufficient to support the exercise of extraterritorial jurisdiction.

See also *Mannington Mills, Inc. v. Congoleum Corp.*, 595 F.2d 1287, 1297–98 (3d Cir. 1979). Do the *Timberlane* factors reflect mandatory or discretionary limits on the scope of American antitrust law? Could Congress overrule this decision?

These developments in antitrust law were confined to the lower courts during this period. Thus, while both *Alcoa* and *Timberlane* acquired a sort of quasi-Supreme Court status and in the process became a cornerstone of American antitrust policy,[1] the Supreme Court did not actually endorse Judge Hand's interpretation of the Sherman Act. The Supreme Court did, however, apply *Alcoa*'s reasoning to the Lanham Act. In *Steele v. Bulova Watch Co.*, 344 U.S. 280 (1952), Bulova alleged that Steele was making and selling watches stamped with its name. Steele defended on the ground that he produced the watches in Mexico. The Court held that Bulova could state a claim, holding that "[u]nlawful effects in this country . . . are often decisive" and that American law may therefore be applied if the particular facts reveal no conflict with foreign law. Noting that Steele's mark had already been nullified in Mexican proceedings, the Court added that "there is thus no conflict which might afford petitioner a pretext that such relief would impugn foreign law."

(3) Other cases in this period also depart from the presumption against extraterritoriality. *Vermilya-Brown Co. v. Connell*, 335 U.S. 377 (1948), involved the applicability of the Fair Labor Standards Act on an American army base located on land leased from England. The Act regulated commerce among the states, defined to include "any Territory or possession of the United States." The question was whether the leased base was a "possession"—a question made difficult, the Court observed, by the fact that possession is "not a word of art, descriptive of a recognized geographical or governmental entity." The Court nonetheless applied the Act, explaining:

> [O]ur duty as a Court is to construe the word "possession" as our judgment instructs us the lawmakers, within constitutional limits, would have done had they acted at the time of the legislation with the present situation in mind. . . It depends on the purpose of the statute. Where as here the purpose is to regulate labor relations in an area vital to our national life, it seems reasonable to interpret its provisions to have force where the nation has sole power, rather than to limit the coverage to sovereignty.

---

1 In the case of *Alcoa*, this is due not only to its place as the critical opinion establishing effects-based jurisdiction, but also because the case was referred to the Second Circuit by the Supreme Court for lack of a quorum. See *Alcoa*, 148 F.2d at 421. The *Timberlane* factors, for their part, were officially endorsed by the Justice Department. U.S. Dept. of Justice, Antitrust Enforcement Guidelines for International Operations (1988).

More striking are the Court's decisions in *Lauritzen v. Larsen,* 345 U.S. 571 (1953), and *Romero v. International Terminal Operating Co.,* 358 U.S. 354 (1959), both involving the extraterritorial scope of the Jones Act. These cases should have been easy. The Jones Act merely extends the Federal Employer's Liability Act (FELA) to seamen, and the Court had already ruled in *New York Central R.R. v. Chisholm,* 268 U.S. 29 (1925), based on the presumption against extraterritoriality, that the FELA applies only to injuries in the United States. In *Lauritzen* and *Romero,* the Court acknowledged *Chisholm* and then ignored it.

In *Lauritzen,* a Danish seaman injured on a Danish ship while in port in Cuba sued for compensation, basing his claim on the fact that he joined the crew in New York. Justice Jackson began by observing that reading the unqualified language of the Jones Act literally would produce needless conflict with other nations. The question was, what limits should the Court read into the law? Rather than rely on a presumption against extraterritoriality, Justice Jackson reasoned:

> Maritime law, like our municipal law, has attempted to avoid or resolve conflicts between competing laws by ascertaining and valuing points of contact between the transaction and the states or governments whose competing laws are involved. The criteria, in general, appear to be arrived at from weighing of the significance of one or more connecting factors between the shipping transaction regulated and the national interest served by the assertion of authority.

After careful consideration of the relevant contacts, including the place of wrong, the law of the flag, the nationality of the parties, the place of contract, and the interests of the forum, Justice Jackson found "an overwhelming preponderance" in favor of Danish law.

In *Romero,* the Court applied the "broad principles of choice of law . . . set forth in *Lauritzen*" to deny a similar claim where the injury occurred in United States waters. Rather than a presumption against extraterritoriality, which should have led to recovery under American law, the Court reasoned that "in the absence of a contrary congressional direction, we must apply those principles of choice of law that are consonant with the needs of a general federal maritime law and with due recognition of our self-regarding respect for the relevant interests of foreign nations in the regulation of maritime commerce as part of the legitimate concern of the international community." Such concerns, Justice Frankfurter explained, are distorted by "mechanical" doctrines like *lex loci delicti,* and require a more discriminating investigation into the interests of the concerned nations. On the particular facts in *Romero,* which involved a Spanish seaman injured on a Spanish ship docked in New Jersey, the Court found the shared nationality of the parties controlling: "The amount and type of recovery which a foreign seaman may receive from his foreign employer while sailing on a foreign ship should not depend on the wholly fortuitous circumstance of the place of injury."

Lauritzen and *Romero* are discussed from the choice-of-law perspective in B. Currie, Selected Essays on the Conflict of Laws ch. 7 (1963).

(4) In 1991, the presumption against extraterritoriality returned in *EEOC v. Arabian American Oil Co.,* 499 U.S. 244 (1991) (*Aramco*). The Arabian American Oil Company, a Delaware corporation, employed an American citizen named Boureslan in Saudi Arabia from 1980 until 1984, when he was discharged. He sued, alleging discrimination on the grounds of race, religion, and national origin, in violation of Title VII of the Civil Rights Act of 1964. The Supreme Court, in an opinion by Chief Justice Rehnquist, invoked the presumption to hold that Title VII did not govern relations between American employers and American employees abroad. Boureslan and the EEOC offered various arguments in favor of such application, including the existence of an "alien exemption," which excluded the foreign employees of American employers abroad. The Court deemed this argument "plausible, but no more persuasive than that," in part because accepting the exemption as evidence of extraterritorial scope might lead the conclusion that Title VII protected the American employees of foreign employers abroad. It consequently decided to follow the presumption and dismissed the case.

Dissenting, Justice Marshall, joined by Justices Blackmun and Stevens, argued that the majority had conflated two distinct doctrines, a weak gap-filling presumption to be used when all other methods of interpretation had run out, and a clear-statement rule to operate in cases where extraterritorial application would threaten executive control over foreign affairs. The dissenting Justices found neither applicable: executive authority was not threatened by the regulation of relations between Americans abroad, and the ordinary process of interpretation led to the conclusion that Title VII was intended to operate abroad.

Does the majority opinion make sense? Is the case a true conflict or a false conflict? (Saudi Arabian labor law does include a requirement that businesses employ 75% Saudi nationals, but Boureslan's complaint asserted that he had been fired because of personal animus, not in an effort to comply with Saudi law.) Does employment of an American by a foreign employer present a different category? See generally Kramer, *Vestiges of Beale: Extraterritorial Application of American Law,* 1991 Sup. Ct. Rev. 179; G. Born, *A Reappraisal of the Extraterritorial Reach of U.S. Law,* 24 Law & Pol'y Int'l Bus. 1 (1992).

(5) Congress, already involved with other revisions to Title VII when *Aramco* was handed down, acted quickly to overturn *Aramco* and make clear that Title VII does apply to relations between American employers and employees abroad. See Civil Rights Act of 1991, § 109, Pub.L. 102–66, 105 Stat. 1071, 1076, codified at 42 U.S.C. §§ 2000e(f), 2000e–1. The reaction to *Morrison* was not as far-reaching: in § 929P of the Dodd-Frank Wall Street Reform and Consumer Protection Act of 2010, Congress amended the securities laws to extend government enforcement authority (though not the private cause of action) to extraterritorial transactions based on the conduct and effects tests rejected in *Morrison*. (Oddly, Congress did so by extending federal jurisdiction to such cases, apparently ignoring *Morrison*'s statement that the relevant issue went to the merits rather than jurisdiction.) Still, this legislative reaction suggests that the presumption against extraterritoriality failed to capture congressional preferences in *Aramco* and *Morrison*. Does that make it a bad rule? What other justifications might be offered for the presumption? That judges simply lack the power to enforce laws beyond what Congress has written? That separation of powers concerns dictate extreme judicial modesty in the international arena? That it functions as a penalty default to encourage Congress to address the issue? See Dodge, *Understanding the Presumption Against Extraterritoriality,* 16 Berkeley J. Int'l L. 85 (1998) (justifying *Aramco* while arguing that lower courts have not treated the case as a simple clear statement rule and have divided over its meaning); Bradley, *Territorial Intellectual Property Rights in an Age of Globalism,* 37 Va. J. Int'l L. 505 (1997) (defending the presumption, principally on separation of powers grounds).

(6) Justice Scalia criticizes the conduct and effects tests as difficult to administer, suggesting that the territorialist approach is a simple, bright-line rule. Deciding whether a security is listed on an American exchange should be easy enough, but something more is required to decide whether a transaction whose elements occur in multiple jurisdictions constitutes a purchase or sale "in the United States." (Indeed, as Justice Stevens suggests, the conduct and effects tests could be understood as an attempt to do just that.) In *Absolute Activist Value Master Fund Ltd. v. Ficeto*, 677 F.3d 60 (2d Cir. 2012), the Second Circuit considered several possible approaches, ultimately deciding that a purchase or sale occurs within the United States when "irrevocable liability was incurred or title was transferred" there. But is determining where *that* occurs always easy? Recall the treatment of acceptance in *Milliken v. Pratt*, supra Chapter 1.

How else might the applicability of American law in international cases be determined? One easy solution would be simply to decline to choose among conflicting laws and apply American law to any case in an American court. Would you recommend this solution?

(7) *Merits or jurisdiction?* In *Morrison*, the Court of Appeals dismissed for lack of subject-matter jurisdiction after deciding that § 10(b) did not reach the alleged conduct. Other courts, including the Supreme Court in *Aramco*, had done the same thing. The reasoning appears to be as follows: Federal jurisdiction exists when a case is to be decided under federal law. But if federal law does not apply (i.e., if the statute the plaintiff invokes does not attach consequences to the defendant's conduct), then the case cannot be decided under federal law. Hence, there is no subject-matter jurisdiction. *Morrison* holds to the contrary that in such a case the plaintiff has simply failed to state a claim. Does this point have relevance to choice of law more generally? Recall the unprovided-for case, supra Chapter 2, Section 3.C. Currie, and the court in *Erwin v. Thomas*, supra p. 170, seemed to follow a similar line of reasoning: neither state is interested (i.e., neither state's law gives the parties rights) but the case must be decided under some law, and forum law is the natural choice. Does *Morrison* suggest that the correct answer is instead that the plaintiff has failed to state a claim? See Kramer, *The Myth of the "Unprovided-For" Case*, 75 Va. L. Rev. 1045 (1989).

RJR NABISCO, INC. V. EUROPEAN COMMUNITY

579 U.S. 325 (2016).

JUSTICE ALITO delivered the opinion of the Court.

The Racketeer Influenced and Corrupt Organizations Act (RICO), 18 U.S.C. §§ 1961–1968, created four new criminal offenses involving the activities of organized criminal groups in relation to an enterprise. §§ 1962(a)–(d). RICO also created a new civil cause of action for "[a]ny person injured in his business or property by reason of a violation" of those prohibitions. § 1964(c). We are asked to decide whether RICO applies extraterritorially—that is, to events occurring and injuries suffered outside the United States.

I

A

RICO is founded on the concept of racketeering activity. The statute defines "racketeering activity" to encompass dozens of state and federal offenses, known in RICO parlance as predicates. These predicates include any act "indictable" under specified federal statutes, §§ 1961(1)(B)–(C), (E)–(G), as well as certain crimes "chargeable" under state law, § 1961(1)(A), and any offense involving bankruptcy or securities fraud or drug-related activity that is "punishable" under federal law, § 1961(1)(D). A predicate offense implicates RICO when it is part of a "pattern of racketeering activity"—a series of related predicates that together demonstrate the existence or threat of continued criminal activity. * * *

RICO's § 1962 sets forth four specific prohibitions aimed at different ways in which a pattern of racketeering activity may be used to infiltrate, control, or operate "a[n] enterprise which is engaged in, or the activities of which affect, interstate or foreign commerce." These prohibitions can be summarized as follows. Section 1962(a) makes it unlawful to invest income derived from a pattern of racketeering activity in an enterprise. Section 1962(b) makes it unlawful to acquire or maintain an interest in an enterprise through a pattern of racketeering activity. Section 1962(c) makes it unlawful for a person employed by or associated with an enterprise to conduct the enterprise's affairs through a pattern of racketeering activity. Finally, § 1962(d) makes it unlawful to conspire to violate any of the other three prohibitions.

Violations of § 1962 are subject to criminal penalties, § 1963(a), and civil proceedings to enforce those prohibitions may be brought by the Attorney General, §§ 1964(a)–(b). Separately, RICO creates a private civil cause of action that allows "[a]ny person injured in his business or property by reason of a violation of section 1962" to sue in federal district court and recover treble damages, costs, and attorney's fees. § 1964(c).

B

This case arises from allegations that petitioners—RJR Nabisco and numerous related entities (collectively RJR)—participated in a global money-laundering scheme in association with various organized crime groups. Respondents—the European Community and 26 of its member states—first sued RJR in the Eastern District of New York in 2000, alleging that RJR had violated RICO. . .

Greatly simplified, the complaint alleges a scheme in which Colombian and Russian drug traffickers smuggled narcotics into Europe and sold the drugs for euros that—through a series of transactions involving black-market money brokers, cigarette importers, and wholesalers—were used to pay for large shipments of RJR cigarettes into Europe. . .

The complaint alleges that RJR engaged in a pattern of racketeering activity consisting of numerous acts of money laundering, material support to foreign terrorist organizations, mail fraud, wire fraud, and violations of the Travel Act. . .

These violations allegedly harmed respondents in various ways, including through competitive harm to their state-owned cigarette businesses, lost tax revenue from black-market cigarette sales, harm to European financial institutions, currency instability, and increased law enforcement costs. . .

II

The question of RICO's extraterritorial application really involves two questions. First, do RICO's substantive prohibitions, contained in § 1962, apply to conduct that occurs in foreign countries? Second, does RICO's private right of action, contained in § 1964(c), apply to injuries that are suffered in foreign countries? We consider each of these questions in turn. To guide our inquiry, we begin by reviewing the law of extraterritoriality.

It is a basic premise of our legal system that, in general, "United States law governs domestically but does not rule the world." * * * This principle finds expression in a canon of statutory construction known as the presumption against extraterritoriality: Absent clearly expressed congressional intent to the contrary, federal laws will be construed to have only domestic application. *Morrison v. National Australia Bank Ltd.,* 561 U.S. 247, 255 (2010). The question is not whether we think "Congress would have wanted" a statute to apply to foreign conduct "if it had thought of the situation before the court," but whether Congress has affirmatively and unmistakably instructed that the statute will do so. *Id.,* at 261. "When a statute gives no clear indication of an extraterritorial application, it has none." *Id.,* at 255.

There are several reasons for this presumption. Most notably, it serves to avoid the international discord that can result when U.S. law is applied to conduct in foreign countries. See, *e.g., Kiobel v. Royal Dutch Petroleum Co.,* 133 S.Ct. 1659, 1663–1664 (2013); *EEOC v. Arabian American Oil Co.,* 499 U.S. 244, 248 (1991) (*Aramco*); * * *. But it also reflects the more prosaic "commonsense notion that Congress generally legislates with domestic concerns in mind." * * * We therefore apply the presumption across the board, "regardless of whether there is a risk of conflict between the American statute and a foreign law." *Morrison, supra,* at 255. . .

Morrison and *Kiobel* reflect a two-step framework for analyzing extraterritoriality issues. At the first step, we ask whether the presumption against extraterritoriality has been rebutted—that is, whether the statute gives a clear, affirmative indication that it applies extraterritorially. We must ask this question regardless of whether the statute in question regulates conduct, affords relief, or merely confers jurisdiction. If the statute is not extraterritorial, then at the second step we determine whether the case involves a domestic application of the statute, and we do this by looking to the statute's "focus." If the conduct relevant to the statute's focus occurred in the United States, then the case involves a permissible domestic application even if other conduct occurred abroad; but if the conduct relevant to the focus occurred in a foreign country, then the case involves an impermissible extraterritorial application regardless of any other conduct that occurred in U.S. territory.

What if we find at step one that a statute clearly *does* have extraterritorial effect? Neither *Morrison* nor *Kiobel* involved such a finding. But we addressed this issue in *Morrison,* explaining that it was necessary to consider § 10(b)'s "focus" only because we found that the statute does not apply extraterritorially: "If § 10(b) did apply abroad, we would not need to determine which transnational frauds it applied to; it would apply to all of them (barring some other limitation)." 561 U.S., at 267, n. 9. The scope of an extraterritorial statute thus turns on the limits Congress has (or has not) imposed on the statute's foreign application, and not on the statute's "focus."

III

With these guiding principles in mind, we first consider whether RICO's substantive prohibitions in § 1962 may apply to foreign conduct. Unlike in *Morrison* and *Kiobel*, we find that the presumption against extraterritoriality has been rebutted—but only with respect to certain applications of the statute.

A

The most obvious textual clue is that RICO defines racketeering activity to include a number of predicates that plainly apply to at least some foreign conduct. These predicates include the prohibition against engaging in monetary transactions in criminally derived property, which expressly applies, when "the defendant is a United States person," to offenses that "tak[e] place outside the United States." 18 U.S.C. § 1957(d)(2). Other examples include the prohibitions against the assassination of Government officials, * * * and the prohibition against hostage taking, which applies to conduct that "occurred outside the United States" if either the hostage or the offender is a U.S. national, if the offender is found in the United States, or if the hostage taking is done to compel action by the U.S. Government, § 1203(b). At least one predicate—the prohibition against "kill[ing] a national of the United States, while such national is outside the United States"—applies *only* to conduct occurring outside the United States. § 2332(a).

We agree with the Second Circuit that Congress's incorporation of these (and other) extraterritorial predicates into RICO gives a clear, affirmative indication that § 1962 applies to foreign racketeering activity—but only to the extent that the predicates alleged in a particular case themselves apply extraterritorially. Put another way, a pattern of racketeering activity may include or consist of offenses committed abroad in violation of a predicate statute for which the presumption against extraterritoriality has been overcome. To give a simple (albeit grim) example, a violation of § 1962 could be premised on a pattern of killings of Americans abroad in violation of § 2332(a)—a predicate that all agree applies extraterritorially—whether or not any domestic predicates are also alleged.

We emphasize the important limitation that foreign conduct must violate "a predicate statute that manifests an unmistakable congressional intent to apply extraterritorially." * * * Although a number of RICO predicates have extraterritorial effect, many do not. The inclusion of *some* extraterritorial predicates does not mean that *all* RICO predicates extend to foreign conduct. This is apparent for two reasons. First, "when a statute provides for some extraterritorial application, the presumption against extraterritoriality operates to limit that provision to its terms." *Morrison,* 561 U.S., at 265. Second, RICO defines as racketeering activity only acts that are "indictable" (or, what amounts to the same thing, "chargeable" or "punishable") under one of the statutes identified in § 1961(1). If a particular statute does not apply extraterritorially, then conduct committed abroad is not "indictable" under that statute and so cannot qualify as a predicate under RICO's plain terms.

RJR resists the conclusion that RICO's incorporation of extraterritorial predicates gives RICO commensurate extraterritorial effect. It points out that "RICO itself" does not refer to extraterritorial application; only the underlying predicate statutes do. . .

The presumption against extraterritoriality does not require us to adopt such a constricted interpretation. While the presumption can be overcome only by a clear indication of extraterritorial effect, an express statement of extraterritoriality is not essential. "Assuredly context can be consulted as well." *Morrison, supra,* at 265. Context is dispositive here. Congress has not expressly said that § 1962(c) applies to patterns of racketeering activity in foreign countries, but it has defined "racketeering activity"—and by extension a "pattern of racketeering activity"—to encompass violations of predicate statutes that *do* expressly apply extraterritorially. Short of an explicit declaration, it is hard to imagine how Congress could have more clearly indicated that it intended RICO to have (some) extraterritorial effect. This unique structure makes RICO the rare statute that clearly evidences extraterritorial effect despite lacking an express statement of extraterritoriality.

We therefore conclude that RICO applies to some foreign racketeering activity. A violation of § 1962 may be based on a pattern of racketeering that includes predicate offenses committed abroad, provided that each of those offenses violates a predicate statute that is itself extraterritorial. This fact is determinative as to § 1962(b) and § 1962(c), both of which prohibit the employment of a pattern of racketeering. Although they differ as to the end for which the pattern is employed—to acquire or maintain control of an enterprise under subsection (b), or to conduct an enterprise's affairs under subsection (c)—this difference is immaterial for extraterritoriality purposes.

[The Court declined to address Section 1962(a), which targets certain uses of *income* derived from a pattern of racketeering, and RICO's conspiracy provision, § 1962(d).]

B

RJR contends that, even if RICO may apply to foreign patterns of racketeering, the statute does not apply to foreign *enterprises*. Invoking *Morrison*'s discussion of the Exchange Act's "focus," RJR says that the "focus" of RICO is the enterprise being corrupted—not the pattern of racketeering—and that RICO's enterprise element gives no clear indication of extraterritorial effect. Accordingly, RJR reasons, RICO requires a domestic enterprise.

This argument misunderstands *Morrison*. As explained above, only at the second step of the inquiry do we consider a statute's "focus." Here, however, there is a clear indication at step one that RICO applies extraterritorially. We therefore do not proceed to the "focus" step. The *Morrison* Court's discussion of the statutory "focus" made this clear, stating that "[i]f § 10(b) did apply abroad, we would not need to determine which transnational frauds it applied to; it would apply to all of them (barring some other limitation)." 561 U.S., at 267, n. 9. The same is true here. RICO—or at least §§ 1962(b) and (c)—applies abroad, and so we do not need to determine which transnational (or wholly foreign) patterns of racketeering it applies to; it applies to all of them, regardless of whether they are connected to a "foreign" or "domestic" enterprise. This rule is, of course, subject to the important limitation that RICO covers foreign predicate offenses only to the extent that the underlying predicate statutes are extraterritorial. But within those bounds, the location of the affected enterprise does not impose an independent constraint.

It is easy to see why Congress did not limit RICO to domestic enterprises. A domestic enterprise requirement would lead to difficult line-drawing problems and counterintuitive results. It would exclude from RICO's reach foreign enterprises—whether corporations, crime rings, other associations, or individuals—that operate within the United States. Imagine, for example, that a foreign corporation has operations in the United States and that one of the corporation's managers in the United States conducts its U.S. affairs through a pattern of extortion and mail fraud. Such domestic conduct would seem to fall well within what Congress meant to capture in enacting RICO. Congress, after all, does not usually exempt foreigners acting in the United States from U.S. legal requirements. * * * Yet RJR's theory would insulate this scheme from RICO liability—both civil and criminal—because the enterprise at issue is a foreign, not domestic, corporation.

Seeking to avoid this result, RJR offers that any " 'emissaries' " a foreign enterprise sends to the United States—such as our hypothetical U.S.-based corporate manager—could be carved off and considered a "distinct domestic enterprise" under an association-in-fact theory. RJR's willingness to gerrymander the enterprise to get around its proposed domestic enterprise requirement is telling. It suggests that RJR is not really concerned about whether an enterprise is foreign or domestic, but whether the relevant conduct occurred here or abroad. And if that is the concern, then it is the pattern of racketeering activity that matters, not the enterprise. . .

Although we find that RICO imposes no domestic enterprise requirement, this does not mean that every foreign enterprise will qualify. Each of RICO's substantive prohibitions requires proof of an enterprise that is "engaged in, or the activities of which affect, interstate or foreign commerce." §§ 1962(a), (b), (c). We do not take this reference to "foreign commerce" to mean literally all commerce occurring abroad. Rather, a RICO enterprise must engage in, or affect in some significant way, commerce directly involving the United States—*e.g.,* commerce between the United States and a foreign country. Enterprises whose activities lack that anchor to U.S. commerce cannot sustain a RICO violation. . .

IV

We now turn to RICO's private right of action, on which respondents' lawsuit rests. Section 1964(c) allows "[a]ny person injured in his business or property by reason of a violation of section 1962" to sue for treble damages, costs, and attorney's fees. Irrespective of any extraterritorial application of § 1962, we conclude that § 1964(c) does not overcome the presumption against extraterritoriality. A private RICO plaintiff therefore must allege and prove a *domestic* injury to its business or property.

A

The Second Circuit thought that the presumption against extraterritoriality did not apply to § 1964(c) independently of its application to § 1962, reasoning that the presumption "is primarily concerned with the question of what *conduct* falls within a statute's purview." We rejected that view in *Kiobel,* holding that the presumption "constrain[s] courts considering causes of action" under the ATS, a " 'strictly jurisdictional' " statute that "does not directly regulate conduct or afford relief." 133 S.Ct., at 1664. We reached this conclusion even though the underlying substantive law consisted of well-established norms of international law, which by definition apply beyond this country's borders. See *id.,* at 1664–1666.

The same logic requires that we separately apply the presumption against extraterritoriality to RICO's cause of action despite our conclusion that the presumption has been overcome with respect to RICO's substantive prohibitions. "The creation of a private right of action raises issues beyond the mere consideration whether underlying primary conduct should be allowed or not, entailing, for example, a decision to permit enforcement without the check imposed by prosecutorial discretion." *Sosa v. Alvarez-Machain,* 542 U.S. 692, 727 (2004). Thus, as we have observed in other contexts, providing a private civil remedy for foreign conduct creates a potential for international friction beyond that presented by merely applying U.S. substantive law to that foreign conduct. See, *e.g., Kiobel,* 133 S.Ct., at 1665 ("Each of th[e] decisions" involved in defining a cause of action based on "conduct within the territory of another sovereign" "carries with it significant foreign policy implications").

Consider antitrust. In that context, we have observed that "[t]he application . . . of American private treble-damages remedies to anti-competitive conduct taking place abroad has generated considerable controversy" in other nations, even when those nations agree with U.S. substantive law on such things as banning price fixing. *F. Hoffmann-La Roche Ltd. v. Empagran S.A.,* 542 U.S. 155, 167 (2004). . .

We received similar warnings in *Morrison,* where France, a respondent here, informed us that "most foreign countries proscribe securities fraud" but "have made very different choices with respect to the best way to implement that proscription," such as "prefer[ring] 'state actions, not private ones' for the enforcement of law." Brief for Republic of France as *Amicus Curiae,* O.T. 2009, No. 08–1191, p. 20; * * *. Allowing foreign investors to pursue private suits in the United States, we were told, "would upset that delicate balance and offend the sovereign interests of foreign nations." *Id.,* at 26.

Allowing recovery for foreign injuries in a civil RICO action, including treble damages, presents the same danger of international friction. * * * This is not to say that friction would necessarily result in every case, or that Congress would violate international law by permitting such suits. It is to say only that there is a potential for international controversy that militates against recognizing foreign-injury claims without clear direction from Congress. Although "a risk of conflict between the American statute and a foreign law" is not a prerequisite for applying the presumption against extraterritoriality, *Morrison,* 561 U.S., at 255, where such a risk is evident, the need to enforce the presumption is at its apex.

Respondents urge that concerns about international friction are inapplicable in this case because here the plaintiffs are not foreign citizens seeking to bypass their home countries' less generous remedies but rather the foreign countries themselves. Respondents assure us that they "are satisfied that the[ir] complaint . . . comports with limitations on prescriptive jurisdiction under international law and respects the dignity of foreign sovereigns." *Ibid.* Even assuming that this is true, however, our interpretation of § 1964(c)'s injury requirement will necessarily govern suits by nongovernmental plaintiffs that are not so sensitive to foreign sovereigns' dignity. We reject the notion that we should forgo the presumption against extraterritoriality and instead permit extraterritorial suits based on a case-by-case inquiry that turns on or looks to the consent of the affected sovereign. See *Morrison, supra,* at 261 ("Rather than guess anew in each case, we apply the presumption in all cases"). Respondents suggest that we should be reluctant to permit a foreign corporation to be sued in the courts of this country for events occurring abroad if the nation of incorporation objects, but that we should discard those reservations when a foreign state sues a U.S. entity in this country under U.S. law—instead of in its own courts and under its own laws—for conduct committed on its own soil. We refuse to adopt this double standard. "After all, in the law, what is sauce for the goose is normally sauce for the gander." * * *

B

Nothing in § 1964(c) provides a clear indication that Congress intended to create a private right of action for injuries suffered outside of the United States. The statute provides a cause of action to "[a]ny person injured in his business or property" by a violation of § 1962. § 1964(c). The word "any" ordinarily connotes breadth, but it is insufficient to displace the presumption against extraterritoriality. See *Kiobel,* 133 S.Ct., at 1665–1666. The statute's reference to injury to "business or property" also does not indicate extraterritorial application. If anything, by cabining RICO's private cause of action to particular kinds of injury—excluding, for example, personal injuries—Congress signaled that the civil remedy is not coextensive with § 1962's substantive prohibitions. The rest of § 1964(c) places a limit on RICO plaintiffs' ability to rely on securities fraud to make out a claim. This too suggests that § 1964(c) is narrower in its application than § 1962, and in any event does not support extraterritoriality. . .

[The] presumption against extraterritoriality must be applied separately to both RICO's substantive prohibitions and its private right of action. It is not enough to say that a private right of action must reach abroad because the underlying law governs conduct in foreign countries. Something more is needed, and here it is absent.

Respondents contend that background legal principles allow them to sue for foreign injuries, invoking what they call the " 'traditional rule' that 'a plaintiff injured in a foreign country' could bring suit 'in American courts.' " * * * But the rule respondents invoke actually provides that a court will ordinarily "apply *foreign* law to determine the tortfeasor's liability" to "a plaintiff injured in a foreign country." * * * Respondents' argument might have force if they sought to sue RJR for violations of *their own laws* and to invoke federal diversity jurisdiction as a basis for proceeding in U.S. courts. * * * The question here, however, is not "whether a federal court has jurisdiction to entertain a cause of action provided by foreign or even international law. The question is instead whether the court has authority to recognize a cause of action *under U.S. law*" for injury suffered overseas. *Kiobel,* 133 S.Ct., at 1666 (emphasis added). As to that question, the relevant background principle is the presumption against extraterritoriality, not the "traditional rule" respondents cite.

[Next, the Court rejected the idea, put forward by JUSTICE GINSBURG in her partial dissent, that § 1964(c) should be read *in pari materia* with

§ 4 of the Clayton Act, 15 U.S.C. § 15, which provides a private right of action for injuries suffered abroad as a result of antitrust violations.]

C

Section 1964(c) requires a civil RICO plaintiff to allege and prove a domestic injury to business or property and does not allow recovery for foreign injuries. The application of this rule in any given case will not always be self-evident, as disputes may arise as to whether a particular alleged injury is "foreign" or "domestic." But we need not concern ourselves with that question in this case. As this case was being briefed before this Court, respondents filed a stipulation in the District Court waiving their damages claims for domestic injuries. The District Court accepted this waiver and dismissed those claims with prejudice. Respondents' remaining RICO damages claims therefore rest entirely on injury suffered abroad and must be dismissed.

The judgment of the United States Court of Appeals for the Second Circuit is reversed, and the case is remanded for further proceedings consistent with this opinion.

So ordered.

JUSTICE SOTOMAYOR took no part in the consideration or decision of this case.

JUSTICE GINSBURG, with whom JUSTICE BREYER and JUSTICE KAGAN join, concurring in Parts I, II, and III and dissenting from Part IV and from the judgment. . .

I would not distinguish, as the Court does, between the extraterritorial compass of a private right of action and that of the underlying proscribed conduct. Instead, I would adhere to precedent addressing RICO, linking, not separating, prohibited activities and authorized remedies. * * * . . .

RICO's private right of action, it cannot be gainsaid, expressly incorporates § 1962, whose extraterritoriality, the Court recognizes, is coextensive with the underlying predicate offenses charged. * * * The sole additional condition § 1964(c) imposes on access to relief is an injury to one's "business or property." Nothing in that condition should change the extraterritoriality assessment. . .

This very case illustrates why pinning a domestic-injury requirement onto § 1964(c) makes little sense. All defendants are U.S. corporations, headquartered in the United States, charged with a pattern of racketeering activity directed and managed from the United States, involving conduct occurring in the United States. In particular, according to the complaint, defendants received in the United States funds known to them to have been generated by illegal narcotics trafficking and terrorist activity, conduct violative of § 1956(a)(2); traveled using the facilities of interstate commerce in furtherance of unlawful activity, in violation of § 1952; provided material support to foreign terrorist organizations "in the United States and elsewhere," in violation of § 2339B; and used U.S. mails and wires in furtherance of a "scheme or artifice to defraud," in violation of §§ 1341 and 1343. In short, this case has the United States written all over it.

The Court nevertheless deems a domestic-injury requirement for private RICO plaintiffs necessary to avoid international friction. When the United States considers whether to initiate a prosecution or civil suit, the Court observes, it will take foreign-policy considerations into account, but private parties will not. It is far from clear, however, that the Court's blanket rule would ordinarily work to ward off international discord. Invoking the presumption against extraterritoriality as a bar to *any* private suit for injuries to business or property abroad, this case suggests, might spark, rather than quell, international strife. Making such litigation available to domestic but not foreign plaintiffs is hardly solicitous of international comity or respectful of foreign interests. * * * . . .

To the extent extraterritorial application of RICO could give rise to comity concerns not present in this case, those concerns can be met through doctrines that serve to block litigation in U.S. courts of cases more appropriately brought elsewhere. Where an alternative, more appropriate forum is available, the doctrine of *forum non conveniens* enables U.S. courts to refuse jurisdiction. See *Piper Aircraft Co. v. Reyno,* 454 U.S. 235 (1981) (dismissing wrongful-death action arising out of air crash in Scotland involving only Scottish victims); Restatement (Second) of Conflict of Laws § 84 (1969). Due process constraints on the exercise of general personal jurisdiction shelter foreign corporations from suit in the United States based on conduct abroad unless the corporation's "affiliations with the [forum] in which suit is brought are so constant and pervasive 'as to render it essentially at home [there].' " *Daimler AG v. Bauman,* 134 S.Ct. 746, 751, 187 L.Ed.2d 624 (2014) (quoting *Goodyear Dunlop Tires Operations, S.A. v. Brown,* 564 U.S. 915, 919 (2011); alterations omitted). These controls provide a check against civil RICO litigation with little or no connection to the United States.

The Court hems in RICO out of concern about establishing a "double standard." But today's decision does exactly that. U.S. defendants commercially engaged here and abroad would be answerable civilly to U.S. victims of their criminal activities, but foreign parties similarly injured would have no RICO remedy. " 'Sauce for the goose' " should indeed serve the gander as well. * * * I would resist reading into § 1964(c) a domestic-injury requirement Congress did not prescribe. . .

[JUSTICE BREYER's opinion concurring in part, dissenting in part, and dissenting from the judgment is omitted.]

Extraterritorial Application of Federal Statutes

(1) *Morrison* and *RJR Nabisco* lay out a two-step process for determining whether federal statutes apply in cases with international elements. The court asks first whether the presumption against extraterritoriality has been overcome; if the answer is no, the Court asks whether the case involves a permissible domestic application by looking to the statute's "focus."

What sources is a court allowed to consult at the first step? Are traditional choice-of-law tools for ascertaining the scope of a state's law relevant here? Where does the presumption of territorial scope come from? Does it borrow from Joseph Beale's premises?

What about the second step? Does it have an analogue in traditional or modern choice of law? How is a court supposed to identify a statute's "focus"? Don't statutes usually have multiple foci? And why not just ask whether the statute was meant to cover the facts of the case at bar?

(2) In *RJR Nabisco*, the Court concludes that RICO's substantive provisions apply extraterritorially but that its provision authorizing private rights of action, 18 U.S.C. § 1964(c), does not apply to injuries sustained abroad. Was Justice Ginsburg right that the Court should not have addressed the statute's cause of action and its underlying substantive proscription separately? Is Justice Alito's reasoning akin to Currie's "moderate and restrained interpretation" of forum law? Are you convinced that a broader reading would cause international friction? Is there a true conflict in *RJR Nabisco*? Is Justice Ginsburg right that there are better ways to avoid international friction?

(3) What are the implications of the Court's methodology in *Morrison* and *RJR Nabisco* for determining the extraterritorial scope of other federal laws? Should different tests or approaches be taken to determine the extraterritorial application of each U.S. law? See Dodge, *Understanding the Presumption Against Extraterritoriality,* 16 Berkeley J. Int'l L. 85, 101–12 (1998) (discussing cases in which courts apply different versions of the presumption against extraterritoriality). Courts have tended to perform a separate extraterritoriality inquiry for each federal law. These examples give a flavor of the analysis:

(a) *Federal tort claims. Flatow v. Islamic Republic of Iran,* 999 F.Supp. 1 (D.D.C.1998), involved the 1996 "anti-terrorism" amendments to the Foreign Sovereign Immunities Act, which authorize a federal cause of action to be brought against foreign nations designated as "terrorist states" by the U.S. State Department when these nations sponsor terrorist attacks against United States nationals. That the amendments were meant to apply extraterritorially was obvious. But, the court noted, with the exception of punitive damages (which were expressly provided for), the federal statute failed to supply substantive tort rules for decision. The court therefore found it necessary to conduct a choice-of-law analysis. Applying the Second Restatement, it found that the interests of the United States were stronger than those of the Palestinian Authority in the Gaza Strip. Should the court have approached the problem this way? Should it have applied the Second Restatement? Should it have applied U.S. law? (In 2008, Congress amended the FSIA again, creating an express federal cause of action for state-sponsored acts of terror. See 28 U.S.C. § 1605A; *Opati v. Republic of Sudan*, 140 S. Ct. 1601, 1606 (2020).)

The Federal Tort Claims Act (FTCA), in 28 U.S.C. § 1346(b), waives the sovereign immunity of the United States for injuries caused by its employees "under circumstances where the United States, if a private person, would be liable to the claimant in accordance with the law of the place where the act or omission occurred." Section 2680(k) of the Act excludes from the waiver "[a]ny claim arising in a foreign country." In cases where both the allegedly tortious conduct and the injury occur in a foreign country, the application of this exception is clear. But where does a claim "arise" for a cross-border tort?

The Supreme Court addressed this question in *Sosa v. Alvarez-Machain*, 542 U.S. 692 (2004). Alvarez-Machain, a Mexican resident, was suspected of participating in the torture of a Drug Enforcement Agency (DEA) employee in Mexico. The DEA hired Mexican nationals, including Sosa, to kidnap Alvarez-Machain and bring him to the U.S., where he was prosecuted for the torture. Eventually acquitted, Alvarez-Machain sued the U.S. for the Mexican kidnapping under the FTCA.

Most of the cases that found conduct within the U.S. causing injury abroad relied on what came to be called the "headquarters doctrine," a rule that allowed plaintiffs to establish that tort claims arose within the U.S. by basing them on decisions made there. *Sosa* rejected the headquarters doctrine, relying in part on the theory that Congress, legislating in 1942 against the background of territorialist choice-of-law theory, presumably assumed that a claim "arose" where the injury occurred. *Sosa* makes clear that cases relying on the headquarters doctrine to find conduct within the U.S. when an injury occurs abroad are no longer good law. Does it also overrule the cases denying recovery where foreign conduct causes U.S. injury?

(b) *The Alien Tort Statute.* In addition to bringing claims under the FTCA, the plaintiff in *Sosa* also sued under the Alien Tort Statute (ATS), which gives federal district courts jurisdiction over "any civil action by an alien for a tort only, committed in violation of the law of nations or a treaty of the United States." 28 U.S.C. § 1350. What acts might violate the law of nations? In *Sosa*, the Supreme Court offered a relatively short list—offenses against ambassadors, violations of safe conduct, and individual actions arising out of prize captures and piracy—reasoning that these claims were recognized by the First Congress, which passed the ATS as part of the Judiciary Act of 1789. Should that list be closed, or might new claims be recognized in the future? The Court pronounced that it was leaving the door "ajar subject to vigilant doorkeeping." *Sosa*, 542 U.S. at 729. Justice Scalia, concurring, argued that it should be closed, on the grounds that after *Erie* federal courts cannot fashion federal common law on the basis of a jurisdictional grant alone. See *id.* at 740–44; see also *Jesner v. Arab Bank, PLC*, 138 S. Ct. 1386 (2018) (applying *Sosa* to hold that the ATS does not provide a cause of action against foreign corporations).

The first encounter between the ATS and the presumption against extraterritoriality featured a suit by Nigerians against a multinational oil company based on human rights violations occurring in Nigeria. Writing for the majority in *Kiobel v. Royal Dutch Petroleum Co.*, 569 U.S. 108 (2013), Chief Justice Roberts took the opportunity to hold that the ATS applied only to torts occurring within the United States, with a possible exception for pirates, who "may well be a category unto themselves." *Id.* at 121. After concluding that the statute did not apply extraterritorially, the majority never proceeded to the second *Morrison/RJR Nabisco* step and identified the statute's "focus." Why not? Isn't it possible that the focus of the ATS is nongeographic—aimed, that is, at providing a forum for violations of the laws of nations, regardless of where they occur? See Dodge, *The New Presumption Against Extraterritoriality*, 133 Harv. L. Rev. 1582, 1607–08 (2020).

Justice Breyer, writing for four concurring justices in *Kiobel*, relied in part on § 403 of the Third Restatement and would have interpreted the ATS to reach 1) torts occurring on American soil; 2) torts committed by American nationals; and 3) torts substantially and adversely affecting an important American national interest, including the interest in not harboring "a torturer or other common enemy of mankind," whom he saw as "today's pirates." *Id.* at 127, 131 (Breyer, J., concurring). Justice Breyer declined to apply the *Morrison* presumption against extraterroriality, reasoning that the ATS was enacted "with 'foreign matters' in mind." *Id.* at 129. If true, does that mean the presumption should not apply, or simply that it has been overcome?

In *Nestle USA, Inc. v. Doe,* 141 S. Ct. 1931 (2021), six individuals from Mali alleged that two U.S.-based companies, Nestlé USA and Cargill, aided and abetted child slavery and human trafficking by supporting cocoa farms in Ivory Coast. Despite *Kiobel's* holding that the ATS does not apply extraterritorially, the plaintiffs argued that their claims could go forward because the companies' major operational decisions were made in the United States. *Id.* at 1935. Thus forced to address the second-step "focus" question it had avoided in *Kiobel*, the Court made clear that allegations about general corporate activity were inadequate to support domestic application of the ATS. *Id.* at 1937. A plurality of three justices went further, refusing to expand *Sosa* beyond offenses against ambassadors, violations of safe conduct, and piracy. *Id.* at 1937–40 (plurality opinion); see also 1942–43 (Gorsuch, J., concurring) (construing the ATS as a purely jurisdictional statute and calling *Sosa* into question).

Do the ATS decisions make a good case for the soundness of the *Morrison/RJR Nabisco* framework? Or is the problem that Congress never provided a substantive cause of action in the ATS, choosing instead to confer jurisdiction on the federal courts and then incorporate by reference the "law of nations"? Judge Friendly called the ATS a "legal Lohengrin" because "no one seems to know whence it came." *IIT v. Vencap, Ltd.*, 519 F.2d 1001, 1015 (2d Cir. 1975). Does that mean no one can know for sure how broadly it applies? Or can help be sought in general choice-of-law principles—which, after all, apply to many hoary common-law causes of action whose origins are similarly unclear? See generally Wuerth, *The Alien Tort Statute and Federal Common Law: A New Approach*, 85 Notre Dame L. Rev. 1931 (2010).

(c) *The bankruptcy code.* In *Maxwell Communication Corp. v. Barclays Bank*, 170 B.R. 800 (Bankr. S.D.N.Y. 1994), the court invoked the presumption against extraterritoriality and considerations of comity in refusing to allow a foreign debtor's estate to avoid a transfer to foreign banks. The decision was eventually affirmed by the Second Circuit on comity grounds alone. See *In re Maxwell Communication Corp.*, 93 F.3d 1036 (2d Cir. 1996). The Bankruptcy Court's use of the presumption against extraterritoriality was criticized in Harrison, *The Extraterritoriality of the Bankruptcy Code: Will the Borders Contain the Code?*, 12 Bankr.Dev. J. 809 (1996), and the criticism was picked up in In *re French*, 320 B.R. 78 (D. Md. 2004), where the court allowed the bankruptcy trustee for a Maryland debtor to set aside the transfer of property located in Bermuda to her U.S.-resident children. The court reasoned that the presumption did not apply "where the failure to extend the scope of the statute to a foreign setting will result in adverse effects within the United States." 320 B.R. at 82 (citations omitted). For more commentary, see Green & Benzija, *Spanning the Globe: The Intended Extraterritorial Reach of the Bankruptcy Code*, 10 Am. Bankr.Inst. L.Rev. 85 (Spring, 2002). Various statutory solutions have been proposed. See Shidlovitsky, *Adoption of Chapter 15: A Necessary Step in International Bankruptcy Reform*, 10 S.W. J. L. & Trade Am. 171 (2003–04). In 2005, Congress adopted the United Nations Commission on International Trade Law's Model Law, a largely procedural reform designed to enhance interjurisdictional cooperation, as Chapter 15 of the Bankruptcy Code.

(d) *Labor law.* The Court has generally adhered to the presumption against extraterritoriality in the labor area. The question of extraterritorial labor regulation was first raised in *Sandberg v. McDonald,* 248 U.S. 185 (1918). British sailors sued their British vessel while in an American port, seeking to have wage advances declared unlawful under the Seaman's Act of 1915. The Court easily disposed of their claim, citing *American Banana* for the proposition that, absent clear language to the contrary, the Act is presumed to cover only contracts made in the United States.

Sandberg was the first in a line of cases construing federal labor laws narrowly in accordance with the traditional rule of territoriality. *Jackson v. The Archimedes,* 275 U.S. 463 (1928), relied on *Sandberg* and *American Banana* to hold the Merchant Marine Act of 1920 inapplicable to contracts made outside the United States. *Benz v. Compania Naviera Hidalgo, S.A.,* 353 U.S. 138 (1957), relied on *Sandberg* and *Jackson* to withhold the protection of the Labor Management Relations Act from foreign seamen having a contract dispute with their foreign vessel. *McCulloch v. Sociedad Nacional,* 372 U.S. 10 (1963), relied on *Benz* in giving the same interpretation to the National Labor Relations Act. Finally, *Windward Shipping Ltd. v. American Radio Ass'n,* 415 U.S. 104 (1974), relied on *Benz* and *McCulloch* in holding that the Labor Management Relations Act does not reach contract disputes between foreign seamen and foreign employers even when American unions participate in order to protect American jobs and wages.

Other labor cases followed suit. *Foley Bros. v. Filardo,* 336 U.S. 281 (1949), relied on the presumption against extraterritoriality to deny a claim under the Eight Hour Law by American citizens working in Iraq and Iran. Justice Reed did not cite any of the cases discussed above, instead locating the presumption against extraterritoriality in *Blackmer v. United States,* 284 U.S. 421 (1932), supra p. 942, a rare case in which the presumption was deemed adequately rebutted.

(e) *Intellectual property.* Problems respecting the extraterritorial reach of laws regulating patent, copyright, and other forms of intellectual property have attracted considerable interest, in part because of the Internet's global reach. In *Kirtsaeng v. John Wiley & Sons, Inc.*, 568 U.S. 519 (2013), the Court held that the "first sale" doctrine, a limitation on copyright owner's exclusive rights codified in the Copyright Act, 17 U.S.C. § 109(a), applies to copies of copyrighted works lawfully made abroad. The statute's text, context, and common-law predecessors all pointed to a "*non*-geographical interpretation." *Id.* at 530 (emphasis in original). None of the justices cited *Morrison* or the presumption against extraterritoriality, although Justice Ginsburg noted in her dissent that the Copyright Act itself does not apply overseas. *Id.* at 562 (Ginsburg, J., dissenting). And in *Impression Prods., Inc. v. Lexmark Int'l, Inc.*, 137 S. Ct. 1523, 1536 (2017), the Court held that the exhaustion requirement under the Patent Act applied without regard to geography—again without any reference to the presumption.

Do these cases suggest that the *Morrison/RJR Nabisco* framework just doesn't apply to intellectual property statutes? Some contrary evidence can be found in *Microsoft Corp. v. AT&T Corp.*, 550 U.S. 437, 454 (2007), in which the Court cited the presumption against extraterritoriality in holding that § 271(f) of the Patent Act, 35 U.S.C. § 271(f)(1), which imposes infringement liability for supplying a patented invention's components "from the United States" for "combination" abroad, did not apply to copies of Microsoft Windows sent from the United States to a foreign manufacturer on a master disk. The Court emphasized that foreign law might strike a different balance as to patent rights. *Id.* at 455. Can these problems be solved by conventional statutory interpretation, or do we need an international regime of intellectual property rights? What should such a regime look like? See Holbrook, *Boundaries, Extraterritoriality, and Patent Infringement Damages*, 92 Notre Dame L. Rev. 1745 (2017); Burk, *Virtual Exit in the Global Information Economy*, 73 Chi.-Kent L. Rev. 943 (1998); Koren, *Copyrights in Cyberspace—Rights Without Laws?*, 73 Chi.-Kent L. Rev. 1155 (1998); Bradley, *Territorial Intellectual Property Rights in an Age of Globalism*, 37 Va. J. Int'l L. 505 (1997); Litman, *Revising Copyright Law for the Information Age*, 75 Or. L. Rev. 19 (1996).

(f) *Digital privacy.* Enacted in 1986, the Stored Communication Act (SCA), 18 U.S.C. § 2703, aims to provide privacy protection for digital records comparable to those enjoyed by physical records under the Fourth Amendment by generally requiring a warrant before the government may obtain electronic communications from a service provider. In *Matter of Warrant to Search a Certain E-Mail Acct. Controlled & Maintained by Microsoft Corp.*, 829 F.3d 197 (2d Cir. 2016), a district court issued a warrant under the SCA, directing Microsoft to seize and produce the contents of an e-mail account it maintained for a customer suspected of drug trafficking. Microsoft moved to quash the warrant on the grounds that the relevant data was stored in the "cloud" at one of its data centers in Ireland.

Applying the *Morrison/RJR Nabisco* framework, the Second Circuit first reasoned from the SCA's text and constitutional antecedents that the Act's warrant provisions did not contemplate extraterritorial application. 829 F.3d at 210–16. Turning to the second step of the *Morrison/RJR Nabisco* test, the court held that "the relevant provisions of the SCA focus on protecting the privacy of the content of a user's stored electronic communications. Although the SCA also prescribes methods under which the government may obtain access to that content for law enforcement purposes, it does so in the context of a primary emphasis on protecting user content—the 'object[ ] of the statute's solicitude." *Id.* at 217 (quoting *Morrison*). The court concluded: "Because the content subject to the

Warrant is located in, and would be seized from, the Dublin datacenter, the conduct that falls within the focus of the SCA would occur outside the United States, regardless of the customer's location and regardless of Microsoft's home in the United States." *Id.* at 221. It therefore ordered the warrant quashed.

Did the court correctly identify the statute's "focus"? As the concurring judge noted, unlike the Fourth Amendment's warrant requirement, which expressly focuses on the "place" to be searched, the SCA's warrant provision merely allows the government to require a service provider to disclose certain communications. In the case of Microsoft, wouldn't that disclosure occur in the U.S.? *Id.* at 227–28 (Lynch, J., concurring). Why should the location of the data in Ireland be dispositive, given that digital records can be fragmented and dispersed in many places? *Id.* at 228–29 (citing Orin S. Kerr, *The Next Generation Communications Privacy Act*, 162 U. Pa. L. Rev. 373, 408 (2014)). And is it so clear that the *customer's* location (in this case it was unknown) shouldn't matter?

The Supreme Court ordered the case dismissed as moot after Congress enacted the Clarifying Lawful Overseas Use of Data Act (CLOUD Act), Pub. L. 115–141 (2018), § 103(a)(1), which amends the SCA to make clear that its warrant provisions apply "regardless of whether such communication, record, or other information is located within or outside of the United States." See *United States v. Microsoft Corp.*, 138 S. Ct. 1186 (2018). Did the presumption against extraterritoriality have a salutary action-forcing effect here? Or does Congress's action suggest that the Second Circuit got it wrong?

(4) Does the *Morrison/RJR Nabisco* approach represent an improvement over the conventional choice-of-law rules that attempt to ascertain the scope of state laws? Why is there no equivalent of the presumption against extraterritoriality in modern Conflict of Laws thinking? See Restatement (Third) of the Conflict of Laws § 5.01 cmt. c (Preliminary Draft No. 7, October 2021) ("A State court following this Restatement will not apply a presumption against the extraterritorial application of its own State's laws."); Dodge, *Presumptions Against Extraterritoriality in State Law*, 53 U.C. Davis L. Rev. 1389 (2020) (finding that twenty states apply a presumption against extraterritorial application of state law while nearly as many have rejected such a presumption).

Identifying and Resolving Conflicts with Foreign Law

F. HOFFMANN-LA ROCHE V. EMPAGRAN S.A.

542 U.S. 155 (2004).

JUSTICE BREYER delivered the opinion of the Court.

The Foreign Trade Antitrust Improvements Act of 1982 (FTAIA) excludes from the Sherman Act's reach much anticompetitive conduct that causes only foreign injury. It does so by setting forth a general rule stating that the Sherman Act "shall not apply to conduct involving trade or commerce . . . with foreign nations." * * * 15 U.S.C. § 6a. It then creates exceptions to the general rule, applicable where (roughly speaking) that conduct significantly harms imports, domestic commerce, or American exporters.

We here focus upon anticompetitive price-fixing activity that is in significant part foreign, that causes some domestic antitrust injury, and that independently causes separate foreign injury. We ask two questions about the price-fixing conduct and the foreign injury that it causes. First, does that conduct fall within the FTAIA's general rule excluding the Sherman Act's application? That is to say, does the price-fixing activity constitute "conduct involving trade or commerce . . . with foreign nations"? We conclude that it does.

Second, we ask whether the conduct nonetheless falls within a domestic-injury exception to the general rule, an exception that applies (and makes the Sherman Act nonetheless applicable) where the conduct (1) has a "direct, substantial, and reasonably foreseeable effect" on domestic commerce, and (2) "such effect gives rise to a [Sherman Act] claim." §§ 6a(1)(A), (2). We conclude that the exception does not apply where the plaintiff's claim rests solely on the independent foreign harm.

To clarify: The issue before us concerns (1) significant foreign anticompetitive conduct with (2) an adverse domestic effect and (3) an independent foreign effect giving rise to the claim. In more concrete terms, this case involves vitamin sellers around the world that agreed to fix prices, leading to higher vitamin prices in the United States and independently leading to higher vitamin prices in other countries such as Ecuador. We conclude that, in this scenario, a purchaser in the United States could bring a Sherman Act claim under the FTAIA based on domestic injury, but a purchaser in Ecuador could not bring a Sherman Act claim based on foreign harm.

I

The plaintiffs in this case originally filed a class-action suit on behalf of foreign and domestic purchasers of vitamins. . . Their complaint alleged that petitioners, foreign and domestic vitamin manufacturers and distributors, had engaged in a price-fixing conspiracy, raising the price of vitamin products to customers in the United States and to customers in foreign countries.

As relevant here, petitioners moved to dismiss the suit as to the *foreign* purchasers (the respondents here), five foreign vitamin distributors located in Ukraine, Australia, Ecuador, and Panama, each of which bought vitamins from petitioners for delivery outside the United States. * * * Respondents have never asserted that they purchased any vitamins in the United States or in transactions in United States commerce, and the question presented assumes that the relevant "transactions occurr[ed] entirely outside U.S. commerce," * * * The District Court dismissed their claims. * * * It applied the FTAIA and found none of the exceptions applicable. * * * Thereafter, the *domestic* purchasers transferred their claims to another pending suit and did not take part in the subsequent appeal. * * *.

A divided panel of the Court of Appeals reversed. * * * The panel concluded that the FTAIA's general exclusionary rule applied to the case, but that its domestic-injury exception also applied. It basically read the plaintiffs' complaint to allege that the vitamin manufacturers' price-fixing conspiracy (1) had "a direct, substantial, and reasonably foreseeable effect" on ordinary domestic trade or commerce, *i.e.*, the conspiracy brought about higher domestic vitamin prices, and (2) "such effect" gave "rise to a [Sherman Act] claim," *i.e.*, an injured *domestic* customer could have brought a Sherman Act suit * * *. Those allegations, the court held, are sufficient to meet the exception's requirements. * * *.

The court assumed that the foreign effect, *i.e.*, higher prices in Ukraine, Panama, Australia, and Ecuador, was independent of the domestic effect, *i.e.*, higher domestic prices. * * * But it concluded that, in light of the FTAIA's text, legislative history, and the policy goal of deterring harmful price-fixing activity, this lack of connection does not matter. * * *

We granted certiorari to resolve a split among the Courts of Appeals about the exception's application. * * *

II

The FTAIA seeks to make clear to American exporters (and to firms doing business abroad) that the Sherman Act does not prevent them from entering into business arrangements (say, joint-selling arrangements), however anticompetitive, as long as those arrangements adversely affect only foreign markets. See H.R.Rep. No. 97–686, pp. 1–3, 9–10 (1982), U.S.Code Cong. & Admin.News 1982, 2487, 2487–2488, 2494–2495 (hereinafter House Report). It does so by removing from the Sherman Act's reach, (1) export activities and (2) other commercial activities taking place abroad, *unless* those activities adversely affect domestic commerce, imports to the United States, or exporting activities of one engaged in such activities within the United States.

The FTAIA says:

> "Sections 1 to 7 of this title [the Sherman Act] shall not apply to conduct involving trade or commerce (other than import trade or import commerce) with foreign nations unless—
>
> "(1) such conduct has a direct, substantial, and reasonably foreseeable effect—
>
> "(A) on trade or commerce which is not trade or commerce with foreign nations [*i.e.,* domestic trade or commerce], or on import trade or import commerce with foreign nations; or
>
> "(B) on export trade or export commerce with foreign nations, of a person engaged in such trade or commerce in the United States [*i.e.,* on an American export competitor]; and
>
> "(2) such effect gives rise to a claim under the provisions of sections 1 to 7 of this title, other than this section.
>
> "If sections 1 to 7 of this title apply to such conduct only because of the operation of paragraph (1)(B), then sections 1 to 7 of this title shall apply to such conduct only for injury to export business in the United States." 15 U.S.C. § 6a.

This technical language initially lays down a general rule placing *all* (nonimport) activity involving foreign commerce outside the Sherman Act's reach. It then brings such conduct back within the Sherman Act's reach *provided that* the conduct *both* (1) sufficiently affects American commerce, *i.e.,* it has a "direct, substantial, and reasonably foreseeable effect" on American domestic, import, or (certain) export commerce, *and* (2) has an effect of a kind that antitrust law considers harmful, *i.e.,* the "effect" must "giv[e] rise to a [Sherman Act] claim." §§ 6a(1), (2).

We ask here how this language applies to price-fixing activity that is in significant part foreign, that has the requisite domestic effect, and that also has independent foreign effects giving rise to the plaintiff's claim.

III

[The Court first considered and rejected an argument that the FTAIA exclusion applies only to exports, not to wholly foreign commerce.]

IV

We turn now to the basic question presented, that of the exception's application. Because the underlying antitrust action is complex, potentially raising questions not directly at issue here, we reemphasize that we base our decision upon the following: The price-fixing conduct significantly and adversely affects both customers outside the United States and customers within the United States, but the adverse foreign effect is independent of any adverse domestic effect. In these circumstances, we find that the FTAIA exception does not apply (and thus the Sherman Act does not apply) for two main reasons.

First, this Court ordinarily construes ambiguous statutes to avoid unreasonable interference with the sovereign authority of other nations. See, *e.g.,* * * * *Romero v. International Terminal Operating Co.,* 358 U.S. 354, 382–383 (1959) (application of Jones Act in maritime case); *Lauritzen v. Larsen,* 345 U.S. 571, 578 (1953) (same). This rule of construction reflects principles of customary international law—law that (we must assume) Congress ordinarily seeks to follow. See Restatement (Third) of Foreign Relations Law of the United States §§ 403(1), 403(2) (1986) (hereinafter Restatement) (limiting the unreasonable exercise of prescriptive jurisdiction with respect to a person or activity having connections with another State); *Murray v. Schooner Charming Betsy,* 2 Cranch 64, 118, 2 L.Ed. 208 (1804) ("[A]n act of congress ought never to be construed to violate the law of nations if any other possible construction remains"); *Hartford Fire Ins. Co. v. California,* 509 U.S. 764, 817 (1993) (Scalia, J., dissenting) (identifying rule of construction as derived from the principle of " 'prescriptive comity' ").

This rule of statutory construction cautions courts to assume that legislators take account of the legitimate sovereign interests of other nations when they write American laws. It thereby helps the potentially conflicting laws of different nations work together in harmony—a harmony particularly needed in today's highly interdependent commercial world.

No one denies that America's antitrust laws, when applied to foreign conduct, can interfere with a foreign nation's ability independently to regulate its own commercial affairs. But our courts have long held that application of our antitrust laws to foreign anticompetitive conduct is nonetheless reasonable, and hence consistent with principles of prescriptive comity, insofar as they reflect a legislative effort to redress *domestic* antitrust injury that foreign anticompetitive conduct has caused. See *United States v. Aluminum Co. of America,* 148 F.2d 416, 443–444 (C.A.2 1945) (L. Hand, J.); 1 P. Areeda & D. Turner, Antitrust Law ¶ 236 (1978).

But why is it reasonable to apply those laws to foreign conduct *insofar as that conduct causes independent foreign harm and that foreign harm alone gives rise to the plaintiff's claim?* Like the former case, application of those laws creates a serious risk of interference with a foreign nation's ability independently to regulate its own commercial affairs. But, unlike the former case, the justification for that interference seems insubstantial. See Restatement § 403(2) (determining reasonableness on basis of such factors as connections with regulating nation, harm to that nation's interests, extent to which other nations regulate, and the potential for conflict). Why should American law supplant, for example, Canada's or Great Britain's or Japan's own determination about how best to protect Canadian or British or Japanese customers from anticompetitive conduct engaged in significant part by Canadian or British or Japanese or other foreign companies?

We recognize that principles of comity provide Congress greater leeway when it seeks to control through legislation the actions of *American* companies, see Restatement § 402; and some of the anticompetitive price-fixing conduct alleged here took place in *America*. But the higher foreign prices of which the foreign plaintiffs here complain are not the consequence of any domestic anticompetitive conduct *that Congress sought to forbid,* for Congress did not seek to forbid any such conduct insofar as it is here relevant, *i.e.,* insofar as it is intertwined with foreign conduct that causes independent foreign harm. Rather Congress sought to *release* domestic (and foreign) anticompetitive conduct from Sherman Act constraints when that conduct causes foreign harm. Congress, of course, did make an exception where that conduct also causes domestic harm. * * * But any independent domestic harm the foreign conduct causes here has, by definition, little or nothing to do with the matter.

We thus repeat the basic question: Why is it reasonable to apply this law to conduct that is significantly foreign insofar as that conduct causes independent foreign harm and that foreign harm alone gives rise to the plaintiff's claim? We can find no good answer to the question.

The Areeda and Hovenkamp treatise notes that under the Court of Appeals' interpretation of the statute

> "a Malaysian customer could . . . maintain an action under United States law in a United States court against its own Malaysian supplier, another cartel member, simply by noting that unnamed third parties injured [in the United States] by the American [cartel member's] conduct would also have a cause of action. Effectively, the United States courts would provide worldwide subject matter jurisdiction to any foreign suitor wishing to sue its own local supplier, but unhappy with its own sovereign's provisions for private antitrust enforcement, provided that a different plaintiff had a cause of action against a different firm for injuries that were within U.S. [other-than-import] commerce. It does not seem excessively rigid to infer that Congress would not have intended that result." P. Areeda & H. Hovenkamp, Antitrust Law ¶ 273, pp. 51–52 (Supp.2003).

We agree with the comment. We can find no convincing justification for the extension of the Sherman Act's scope that it describes.

Respondents reply that many nations have adopted antitrust laws similar to our own, to the point where the practical likelihood of interference with the relevant interests of other nations is minimal. Leaving price fixing to the side, however, this Court has found to the contrary. See, *e.g., Hartford Fire,* 509 U.S., at 797–799 (noting that the alleged conduct in the London reinsurance market, while illegal under United States antitrust laws, was assumed to be perfectly consistent with British law and policy) * * *.

Regardless, even where nations agree about primary conduct, say, price fixing, they disagree dramatically about appropriate remedies. The application, for example, of American private treble-damages remedies to anticompetitive conduct taking place abroad has generated considerable controversy. * * * And several foreign nations have filed briefs here arguing that to apply our remedies would unjustifiably permit their citizens to bypass their own less generous remedial schemes, thereby upsetting a balance of competing considerations that their own domestic antitrust laws embody. * * *

These briefs add that a decision permitting independently injured foreign plaintiffs to pursue private treble-damages remedies would undermine foreign nations' own antitrust enforcement policies by diminishing foreign firms' incentive to cooperate with antitrust authorities in return for prosecutorial amnesty. * * *

Respondents alternatively argue that comity does not demand an interpretation of the FTAIA that would exclude independent foreign injury cases *across the board.* Rather, courts can take (and sometimes have taken) account of comity considerations case by case, abstaining where comity considerations so dictate. * * *

In our view, however, this approach is too complex to prove workable. The Sherman Act covers many different kinds of anticompetitive agreements. Courts would have to examine how foreign law, compared with American law, treats not only price fixing but also, say, information-sharing agreements, patent-licensing price conditions, territorial product resale limitations, and various forms of joint venture, in respect to both primary conduct and remedy. The legally and economically technical nature of that enterprise means lengthier proceedings, appeals, and more proceedings—to the point where procedural costs and delays could themselves threaten interference with a foreign nation's ability to maintain the integrity of its own antitrust enforcement system. Even in this relatively simple price-fixing case, for example, competing briefs tell us (1) that potential treble-damages liability would help enforce widespread anti-price-fixing norms (through added deterrence) and (2) the opposite, namely, that such liability would hinder antitrust enforcement (by reducing incentives to enter amnesty programs). * * * How could a court seriously interested in resolving so empirical a matter—a matter potentially related to impact on foreign interests—do so simply and expeditiously?

We conclude that principles of prescriptive comity counsel against the Court of Appeals' interpretation of the FTAIA. Where foreign anticompetitive conduct plays a significant role and where foreign injury is independent of domestic effects, Congress might have hoped that America's antitrust laws, so fundamental a component of our own economic system, would commend themselves to other nations as well. But, if America's antitrust policies could not win their own way in the international marketplace for such ideas, Congress, we must assume, would not have tried to impose them, in an act of legal imperialism, through legislative fiat.

Second, the FTAIA's language and history suggest that Congress designed the FTAIA to clarify, perhaps to limit, but not *to expand* in any significant way, the Sherman Act's scope as applied to foreign commerce. * * * And we have found no significant indication that at the time Congress wrote this statute courts would have thought the Sherman Act applicable in these circumstances. . . .

Taken together, these two sets of considerations, the one derived from comity and the other reflecting history, convince us that Congress would not have intended the FTAIA's exception to bring independently caused foreign injury within the Sherman Act's reach.

V

Respondents point to several considerations that point the other way. For one thing, the FTAIA's language speaks in terms of the Sherman Act's *applicability* to certain kinds of *conduct.* The FTAIA says that the Sherman Act applies to foreign "conduct" with a certain kind of harmful domestic effect. Why isn't that the end of the matter? How can the Sherman Act both *apply to the conduct* when one person sues but *not apply to the same conduct* when another person sues? The question of who can or cannot sue is a matter for other statutes (namely, the Clayton Act) to determine.

Moreover, the exception says that it applies if the conduct's domestic effect gives rise to "*a* claim," not to "*the plaintiff's* claim" or "*the claim at issue.*" 15 U.S.C. § 6a(2) (emphases added). The alleged conduct here did have domestic effects, and those effects were harmful enough to give rise to "a" claim. Respondents concede that this claim is not their own claim; it is someone else's claim. But, linguistically speaking, they say, that is beside the point. Nor did Congress place the relevant words "gives rise to a claim" in the FTAIA to suggest any geographical limitation; rather it did so for a here neutral reason, namely, in order to make clear that the domestic effect must be an *adverse* (as opposed to a beneficial) effect. * * *

Despite their linguistic logic, these arguments are not convincing. Linguistically speaking, a statute can apply and not apply to the same conduct, depending upon other circumstances; and those other circumstances may include the nature of the lawsuit (or of the related underlying harm). It also makes linguistic sense to read the words "a claim" as if they refer to the "plaintiff's claim" or "the claim at issue."

At most, respondents' linguistic arguments might show that respondents' reading is the more natural reading of the statutory language. But those arguments do not show that we *must* accept that reading. And that is the critical point. The considerations previously mentioned—those of comity and history—make clear that the respondents' reading is not consistent with the FTAIA's basic intent. If the statute's language reasonably permits an interpretation consistent with that intent, we should adopt it. And, for the reasons stated, we believe that the statute's language permits the reading that we give it.

Finally, respondents point to policy considerations, namely, that application of the Sherman Act in present circumstances will (through increased deterrence) help protect Americans against foreign-caused anticompetitive injury. Petitioners, however, have made important experience-backed arguments (based upon amnesty-seeking incentives) to the contrary. We cannot say whether, on balance, respondents' side of this empirically based argument or the enforcement agencies' side is correct. But we can say that the answer to the dispute is neither clear enough, nor of such likely empirical significance, that it could overcome the considerations we have previously discussed and change our conclusion.

For these reasons, we conclude that petitioners' reading of the statute's language is correct. That reading furthers the statute's basic purposes, it properly reflects considerations of comity, and it is consistent with Sherman Act history.

VI

[The Court notes that it has proceeded under the assumption that the anticompetitive conduct "independently caused foreign injury; that is, the conduct's domestic effects did not help to bring about that foreign injury." If they have preserved the argument, it adds, respondents may assert on remand that the foreign injury is not independent.]

JUSTICE O'CONNOR took no part in the consideration or decision of this case.

JUSTICE SCALIA, with whom JUSTICE THOMAS joins, concurring in the judgment.

I concur in the judgment of the Court because the language of the statute is readily susceptible of the interpretation the Court provides and because only that interpretation is consistent with the principle that statutes should be read in accord with the customary deference to the application of foreign countries' laws within their own territories.

Antitrust and Extraterritoriality

(1) The chief alternative to always applying American law in cases within its scope is to balance the interests involved in the particular case and defer to foreign law where foreign interests are paramount. This practice is endorsed in the Third Restatement of Foreign Relations Law, which provides:

§ 403. Limitations on Jurisdiction to Prescribe

(1) Even when one of the bases for jurisdiction under § 402 is present, a state may not exercise jurisdiction to prescribe law with respect to a person or activity having connections with another state when the exercise of such jurisdiction is unreasonable.

(2) Whether exercise of jurisdiction over a person or activity is unreasonable is determined by evaluating all relevant factors, including, where appropriate:

(a) the link of the activity to the territory of the regulating state, i.e., the extent to which the activity takes place within the territory, or has substantial, direct, and foreseeable effect upon or in the territory;

(b) the connections, such as nationality, residence, or economic activity, between the regulating state and the person principally responsible for the activity to be regulated, or between that state and those whom the regulation is designed to protect;

(c) the character of the activity to be regulated, the importance of the regulation to the regulating state, the extent to which other states regulate such activities, and the degree to which the desirability of such regulation is generally accepted;

(d) the existence of justified expectations that might be protected or hurt by the regulation;

(e) the importance of the regulation to the international political, legal, or economic system;

(f) the extent to which the regulation is consistent with the traditions of the international system;

(g) the extent to which another state may have an interest in regulating the activity; and

(h) the likelihood of conflict with regulation by another state.

(3) When it would not be unreasonable for each of two states to exercise jurisdiction over a person or activity, but the prescriptions by the two states are in conflict, each state has an obligation to evaluate its own as well as the other state's interest in exercising jurisdiction, in light of all the relevant factors, including those set out in Subsection (2); a state should defer to the other state if that state's interest is clearly greater.

According to the comments, the notion that exercising jurisdiction on one of the grounds in § 402 may be unlawful because it is "unreasonable" has "emerged as a principle of international law." § 403, comment a. Moreover, while some United States courts "have applied the principle of reasonableness as a requirement of comity," § 403 makes the principle of reasonableness "a rule of international law." *Id.* Does this matter?

Isn't the approach in the Third Restatement just another version of § 6 of the Restatement (Second) of Conflict of Laws, supra p. 241? Are there other alternatives? Could the methods discussed in Chapter 2 for interstate cases be used in the international context? See Dodge, *Extraterritoriality and Conflict-of-Laws Theory: An Argument for Judicial Unilateralism,* 39 Harv. Int'l L.J. 101 (1998).

(2) The Fourth Restatement of the Foreign Relations Law takes a very different approach. In § 402(2), it states that "[i]n exercising jurisdiction to prescribe, the United States takes account of the legitimate interests of other nations as a matter of prescriptive comity." What does this mean? The comments to the Fourth Restatement define comity as "deference to foreign states that international law does not mandate." *Id.* § 401 comment a. Is this an improvement over the Third Restatement, which attempts to resolve conflicts with foreign law through a rule of reasonableness conceived as flowing from international law?

In a sharp divergence from the Third Restatement, the Fourth Restatement rejects a balancing approach to resolving conflicts, asserting that "state practice does not support a requirement of case-by-case balancing to establish reasonableness as a matter of international law." *Id.* § 407, Reporters' Note 3. Instead, unlike its predecessor, the Fourth Restatement adopts a presumption against extraterritoriality that mirrors the *Morrison/RJR Nabisco* framework. *Id.* § 404. In addition, the Fourth Restatement calls for "reasonableness in interpretation" of U.S. law, *id.* § 405, with the aim of "avoid[ing] unreasonable interference with the sovereign authority of other nations," *id.* § 405, Reporters' Note 1 (quoting *Hoffmann*).

In the end, as one of its Reporters has cheerfully acknowledged, the Fourth Restatement "is unilateral—it asks only *whether* U.S. law should be applied," not *which* country's law prevails. Dodge, *Reasonableness in the Restatement (Fourth) of Foreign Relations Law,* 55 Willamette L. Rev. 521,

533 (2019). Does this approach better capture the Supreme Court's jurisprudence? Does it represent an advance compared to the Third Restatement?

(3) *Hoffmann* presents itself as a decision about the scope of U.S. law. It holds that the Sherman Act does not give plaintiffs a claim based on conduct outside the U.S. that causes injury outside the U.S. In the vocabulary of interest analysis, is *Hoffmann* a false conflict? Is it an example of Currie's suggested moderate and restrained interpretation? Is that the meaning of the canon of construction disfavoring "unreasonable interference with the sovereign authority of other nations"? For commentary on *Hoffmann,* see, e.g., Guzman, *The Case for International Antitrust,* 22 Berkeley J. Int'l L. 355 (2004); Sprigman, *Fix Prices Globally, Get Sued Locally? U.S. Jurisdiction over International Cartels,* 72 U. Chi. L. Rev. 265 (2005).

(4) When is there a conflict between U.S. and foreign law? In *Hartford Fire Ins. Co. v. California,* 509 U.S. 764 (1993), the Court considered a situation in which the Sherman Act did extend extraterritorially to prohibit conduct that Great Britain authorized. (The British government submitted a brief attesting that its law was intended to allow defendants to engage in the conduct for which plaintiffs sought to impose liability.) There was still no conflict, Justice Souter wrote for the Court, because "defendants do not argue that British law requires them to act in some fashion prohibited by the law of the United States, or claim that their compliance with the laws of both countries is otherwise impossible."

That is not the ordinary understanding of "conflict," as critics, including earlier editions of this casebook, pointed out. See Lowenfeld, *Conflict, Balancing of Interests, and the Exercise of Jurisdiction to Prescribe: Reflections on the* Insurance Antitrust Case, 89 Am. J. Int'l L. 42 (1995); Kramer, *Extraterritorial Application of American Law After the* Insurance Antitrust Case, 89 Am. J. Int'l. L. 750, 754 (1995). For an interesting set of perspectives on *Hartford,* see the collection of mock opinions written by conflicts scholars in *Conference on Jurisdiction, Justice, and Choice of Law for the 21st Century,* 29 New Eng. L. Rev. 517 (1995). (*Hoffmann* seems to back away from *Hartford* by citing Justice Scalia's dissent on the role of "prescriptive comity.") If we grant that there may be a conflict between authorization and prohibition, how should a court address it?

Would a case-by-case balancing of interests using the factors of § 403(2) be a good idea? (It would strongly resemble analysis under the Second Restatement, if that helps crystallize your views.) Does it matter that the context is international rather than interstate? Justice Breyer considers this possibility towards the end of Part IV of the opinion. He says it is too complex to be workable: "How could a court seriously interested in resolving so empirical a matter—a matter potentially related to impact on foreign interests—do so simply and expeditiously?" (Recall Currie's lament that "[n]ot even a very ponderous Brandeis brief could marshal the relevant considerations. . .") Kramer suggests that courts should balance statute-by-statute rather than case-by-case. See 89 Am. J. Int'l L. at 755. Is that what *Hoffmann* is doing?

(5) Do courts have the authority to limit the scope of statutes based on considerations like the § 403(2) factors? (Alternatively, do they have authority to resolve true conflicts in favor of foreign law on a case-by-case basis?) The *Hoffmann* respondents argued that the plain language of the FTAIA states that the Sherman Act "applies" to conduct that has a certain effect, and that should be the end of the matter. A law cannot both apply and not apply to conduct depending on who sues. Breyer responds that it can, though he does not give examples. Does choice-of-law analysis shed light on this issue? Does the matter become any clearer if we ask to whom the law gives claims or defenses, rather than whether or not it "applies"?

(6) Should the test for extraterritorial application of the antitrust laws (or any other laws, for that matter) differ in criminal cases? In *United States v. Nippon Paper Indus.*, 109 F.3d 1 (1st Cir. 1997), the United States attempted to prosecute a Japanese corporation for price-fixing that took place entirely in Japan but was targeted solely at North American markets. The trial court held that a criminal antitrust prosecution could not be based solely on extraterritorial conduct and dismissed. The court of appeals reversed. "The words of Section One have not changed since the *Hartford* Court found that they clearly evince Congress' intent to apply the Sherman Act extraterritorially," the court explained, "and it would be disingenuous of us to pretend that the words had lost their clarity simply because this is a criminal proceeding." Id. at 6. Should *Aramco*'s presumption against extraterritoriality continue to operate when it comes to criminal prosecutions? What about the rule of lenity, according to which doubts about statutory scope are resolved in favor of criminal defendants? Or might considerations of comity operate differently in the criminal context? The First Circuit brushed such considerations aside, emphasizing the seriousness of the conduct alleged and explaining:

> If the government can prove these charges, we see no tenable reason why principles of comity should shield [the defendant] from prosecution. We live in an age of international commerce, where decisions reached in one corner of the world can reverberate around the globe in less time than it takes to tell the tale. Thus, a ruling in [the defendant's] favor would create perverse incentives for those who would use nefarious means to influence markets in the United States, rewarding them for erecting as many territorial firewalls as possible between cause and effect.

Id. at 8. See Note, *The Extraterritorial Reach of the Criminal Provisions of U.S. Antitrust Laws,* 19 U. Pa. J. Int'l Econ. L. 1067 (1998).

C. THE CONSTITUTION

UNITED STATES V. VERDUGO-URQUIDEZ

494 U.S. 259 (1990).

CHIEF JUSTICE REHNQUIST delivered the opinion of the Court.

The question presented by this case is whether the Fourth Amendment applies to the search and seizure by United States agents of property that is owned by a nonresident alien and located in a foreign country. We hold that it does not.

Respondent Rene Martin Verdugo-Urquidez is a citizen and resident of Mexico. He is believed by the United States Drug Enforcement Agency (DEA) to be one of the leaders of a large and violent organization in Mexico that smuggles narcotics into the United States. Based on a complaint charging respondent with various narcotics-related offenses, the Government obtained a warrant for his arrest on August 3, 1985. . .

Following respondent's arrest, Terry Bowen, a DEA agent assigned to the Calexico DEA office, decided to arrange for searches of Verdugo-Urquidez's Mexican residences located in Mexicali and San Felipe. Bowen believed that the searches would reveal evidence related to respondent's alleged narcotics trafficking activities and his involvement in the kidnapping and torture-murder of DEA Special Agent Enrique Camarena Salazar (for which respondent subsequently has been convicted in a separate prosecution). Bowen telephoned Walter White, the Assistant Special Agent in charge of the DEA office in Mexico City, and asked him to seek authorization for the search from the Director General of the Mexican Federal Judicial Police (MFJP). After several attempts to reach high ranking Mexican officials, White eventually contacted the Director General, who authorized the searches and promised the cooperation of Mexican authorities. Thereafter, DEA agents working in concert with officers of the MFJP searched respondent's properties in Mexicali and San Felipe and seized certain documents. . .

The District Court granted respondent's motion to suppress evidence seized during the searches, concluding that the Fourth Amendment applied to the searches and that the DEA agents had failed to justify searching respondent's premises without a warrant. A divided panel of the Court of Appeals for the Ninth Circuit affirmed. It cited this Court's decision in *Reid v. Covert,* 354 U.S. 1 (1957), which held that American citizens tried by United States military authorities in a foreign country were entitled to the protections of the Fifth and Sixth Amendments, and concluded that "[t]he Constitution imposes substantive constraints on the federal government, even when it operates abroad." Relying on our decision in *INS v. Lopez-Mendoza,* 468 U.S. 1032 (1984), where a majority of Justices assumed that illegal aliens in the United States have Fourth Amendment rights, the Ninth Circuit majority found it "difficult to conclude that Verdugo-Urquidez lacks these same protections." It also observed that persons in respondent's position enjoy certain trial-related rights, and reasoned that "[i]t would be odd indeed to acknowledge that Verdugo-Urquidez is entitled to due process under the fifth amendment, and to a fair trial under the sixth amendment, . . . and deny him the protection from unreasonable searches and seizures afforded under the fourth amendment." Having concluded that the Fourth Amendment applied to the searches of respondent's properties, the court went on to decide that the searches violated the Constitution because the DEA agents failed to procure a search warrant. . .

Before analyzing the scope of the Fourth Amendment, we think it significant to note that it operates in a different manner than the Fifth Amendment, which is not at issue in this case. The privilege against self-incrimination guaranteed by the Fifth Amendment is a fundamental trial right of criminal defendants. * * * Although conduct by law enforcement officials prior to trial may ultimately impair that right, a constitutional violation occurs only at trial. * * * The Fourth Amendment functions differently. It prohibits "unreasonable searches and seizures" whether or not the evidence is sought to be used in criminal trial, and a violation of the Amendment is "fully accomplished" at the time of an unreasonable governmental intrusion. * * * For purposes of this case, therefore, if there were a constitutional violation, it occurred solely in Mexico. Whether evidence obtained from respondent's Mexican residences should be excluded at trial in the United States is a remedial question separate from the existence *vel non* of the constitutional violation. * * *

The Fourth Amendment provides that:

> "[t]he right of the people to be secure in their persons, houses, papers, and effects, against unreasonable searches and seizures, shall not be violated, and no Warrants shall issue, but upon probable cause, supported by Oath or affirmation, and particularly describing the place to be searched, and the persons or things to be seized."

That text, by contrast with the Fifth and Sixth Amendments, extends its reach only to "the people." Contrary to the suggestion of *amici curiae* that the Framers used this phrase "simply to avoid [an] awkward rhetorical redundancy," * * * "the people" seems to have been a term of art employed in select parts of the Constitution. The Preamble declares that the Constitution is ordained and established by "the People of the United States." The Second Amendment protects "the right of the people to keep and bear Arms," and the Ninth and Tenth Amendments provide that certain rights and powers are retained by and reserved to "the people." * * * While this textual exegesis is by no means conclusive, it suggests that "the people" protected by the Fourth Amendment, and by the First and Second Amendments, and to whom rights and powers are reserved in the Ninth and Tenth Amendments, refers to a class of persons who are part of a national community or who have otherwise developed sufficient connection with this country to be considered part of that community. * * * The language of these Amendments contrasts with the words "person" and "accused" used in the Fifth and Sixth Amendments regulating procedure in criminal cases.

What we know of the history of the drafting of the Fourth Amendment also suggests that its purpose was to restrict searches and seizures which might be conducted by the United States in domestic matters. . . The driving force behind the adoption of the Amendment . . . was widespread hostility among the former Colonists to the issuance of writs of assistance empowering revenue officers to search suspected places for smuggled goods, and general search warrants permitting the search of private houses, often to uncover papers that might be used to convict persons of libel. * * * The available historical data show, therefore, that the purpose of the Fourth Amendment was to protect the people of the United States against arbitrary action by their own Government; it was never suggested that the provision was intended to restrain the actions of the Federal Government against aliens outside of the United States territory.

There is likewise no indication that the Fourth Amendment was understood by contemporaries of the Framers to apply to activities of the United States directed against aliens in foreign territory or in international waters. Only seven years after the ratification of the Amendment, French interference with American commercial vessels engaged in neutral trade triggered what came to be known as the "undeclared war" with France. In an Act to "protect the Commerce of the United States" in 1798, Congress authorized President Adams to "instruct the commanders of the public armed vessels which are, or which shall be employed in the service of the United States, to subdue, seize and take any armed French vessel, which shall be found within the jurisdictional limits of the United States or elsewhere, on the high seas." [Another provision authorized private vessels to take the same action, and] these enactments resulted in scores of seizures of foreign vessels under congressional authority. * * * Some commanders were held liable by this Court for unlawful seizures because their actions were beyond the scope of the congressional grant of authority, * * * but it was never suggested that the Fourth Amendment restrained the authority of Congress or of United States agents to conduct operations such as this.

The global view taken by the Court of Appeals of the application of the Constitution is also contrary to this Court's decisions in the *Insular Cases,* which held that not every constitutional provision applies to governmental activity even where the United States has sovereign power. See, *e.g., Balzac v. Porto Rico,* 258 U.S. 298 (1922) * * *; *Dorr v. United States,* 195 U.S. 138 (1904) * * *. In *Dorr,* we declared the general rule that in an unincorporated territory—one not clearly destined for statehood—Congress was not required to adopt "a system of laws which shall include the right of trial by jury, and that *the Constitution does not, without legislation and of its own force, carry such right to territory so situated.*" 195 U.S., at 149 (emphasis added). Only "fundamental" constitutional rights are guaranteed to inhabitants of those territories. *Id.* at 148 * * *. If that is true with respect to territories ultimately governed by Congress, respondent's claim that the protections of the Fourth Amendment extend to aliens in foreign nations is even weaker. And certainly, it is not open to us in light of the *Insular Cases* to endorse the view that every constitutional provision applies wherever the United States Government exercises its power.

Indeed, we have rejected the claim that aliens are entitled to Fifth Amendment rights outside the sovereign territory of the United States. In *Johnson v. Eisentrager,* 339 U.S. 763 (1950), the Court held that enemy aliens arrested in China and imprisoned in Germany after World War II could not obtain writs of habeas corpus in our federal courts on the ground that their convictions for war crimes had violated the Fifth Amendment and other constitutional provisions. The *Eisentrager* opinion acknowledged that in some cases constitutional provisions extend beyond the citizenry; "[t]he alien . . . has been accorded a generous and ascending scale of rights as he increases his identity with our society." But our rejection of extraterritorial application of the Fifth Amendment was emphatic:

> "Such extraterritorial application of organic law would have been so significant an innovation in the practice of governments that, if intended or apprehended, it could scarcely have failed to excite contemporary comment. Not one word can be cited. No decision of this Court supports such a view. None of the learned commentators on our Constitution has even hinted at it. The practice of every modern government is opposed to it." *Id.,* at 784.

If such is true of the Fifth Amendment, which speaks in the relatively universal term of "person," it would seem even more true with respect to the Fourth Amendment, which applies only to "the people."

To support his all-encompassing view of the Fourth Amendment, respondent points to language from a plurality opinion in *Reid v. Covert,* 354 U.S. 1 (1957). *Reid* involved an attempt by Congress to subject the wives of American servicemen to trial by military tribunals without the protection of the Fifth and Sixth Amendments. The Court held that it was unconstitutional to apply the Uniform Code of Military Justice to the trials of the American women for capital crimes. Four Justices [said:]

> "The United States is entirely a creature of the Constitution. Its power and authority have no other source. It can only act in accordance with all the limitations imposed by the Constitution. When the Government reaches out to punish a *citizen* who is abroad, the shield which the Bill of Rights and other parts of the Constitution provide to protect his life and liberty should not be stripped away just because he happens to be in another land." *Id.*, at 5–6 (emphasis added; footnote omitted).

Respondent urges that we interpret this discussion to mean that federal officials are constrained by the Fourth Amendment wherever and against whomever they act. But the holding of *Reid* stands for no such sweeping proposition: it decided that United States citizens stationed abroad could invoke the protection of the Fifth and Sixth Amendments. The concurring opinions by Justices Frankfurter and Harlan in *Reid* . . . declined even to hold that United States citizens were entitled to the full range of constitutional protections in all overseas criminal prosecutions. * * * Since respondent is not a United States citizen, he can derive no comfort from the *Reid* holding.

Verdugo-Urquidez also relies on a series of cases in which we have held that aliens enjoy certain constitutional rights. * * * These cases, however, establish only that aliens receive constitutional protections when they have come within the territory of the United States and developed substantial connections with this country. * * * Respondent is an alien who has had no previous significant voluntary connection with the United States, so these cases avail him not. . .

Not only are history and case law against respondent, but as pointed out in *Johnson v. Eisentrager, supra,* the result of accepting his claim would have significant and deleterious consequences for the United States in conducting activities beyond its boundaries. The rule adopted by the Court of Appeals would apply not only to law enforcement operations abroad, but also to other foreign policy operations which might result in "searches or seizures." The United States frequently employs armed forces outside this country—over 200 times in our history—for the protection of American citizens or national security. * * * Application of the Fourth Amendment to those circumstances could significantly disrupt the ability of the political branches to respond to foreign situations involving our national interest. . . The Members of the Executive and Legislative Branches are sworn to uphold the Constitution, and they presumably desire to follow its commands. But the Court of Appeals' global view of its applicability would plunge them into a sea of uncertainty as to what might be reasonable in the way of searches and seizures conducted abroad. Indeed, the Court of Appeals held that absent exigent circumstances, United States agents could not effect a "search or seizure" for law enforcement purposes in a foreign country without first obtaining a warrant—which would be a dead letter outside the United States—from a magistrate in this country. Even if no warrant were required, American agents would have to articulate specific facts giving them probable cause to undertake a search or seizure if they wished to comply with the Fourth Amendment as conceived by the Court of Appeals. . .

For better or worse, we live in a world of nation-states in which our Government must be able to "functio[n] effectively in the company of sovereign nations." *Perez v. Brownell,* 356 U.S. 44, 57 (1958). Some who violate our laws may live outside our borders under a regime quite different from that which obtains in this country. Situations threatening to important American interests may arise half-way around the globe, situations which in view of the political branches or our Government require an American response with armed force. If there are to be restrictions on searches and seizures which occur incident to such American action, they must be imposed by the political branches through diplomatic understanding, treaty, or legislation.

The judgment of the Court of Appeals is accordingly reversed.

[Opinions by JUSTICE STEVENS, concurring in the judgment, and by JUSTICE BLACKMUN, dissenting, are omitted.]

JUSTICE KENNEDY, concurring. . .

The distinction between citizens and aliens follows from the undoubted proposition that the Constitution does not create, nor do general principles of law create, any judicial relation between our country and some undefined, limitless class of noncitizens who are beyond our territory. We should note, however, that the absence of this relation does not depend on the idea that only a limited class of persons ratified the instrument that formed our Government. Though it must be beyond dispute that persons outside the United States did not and could not assent to the Constitution, that is quite irrelevant to any construction of the powers conferred or the limitations imposed by it. . . The force of the Constitution is not confined because it was brought into being by certain persons who gave their immediate assent to its terms.

For somewhat similar reasons, I cannot place any weight on the reference to "the people" in the Fourth Amendment as a source of restricting its protections. With respect, I submit these words do not detract from its force or its reach. Given the history of our Nation's concern over warrantless and unreasonable searches, explicit recognition of "the right of the people" to Fourth Amendment protection may be interpreted to underscore the importance of the right, rather than to restrict the category of persons who may assert it. The restrictions that the United States must observe with reference to aliens beyond its territory or jurisdiction depend, as a consequence, on general principles of interpretation, not on an inquiry as to who formed the Constitution or a construction that some rights are mentioned as being those of "the people." . . .

We have not overruled either *In re Ross,* 140 U.S. 453 (1891), or the so-called *Insular Cases* * * *. These authorities . . . stand for the proposition that we must interpret constitutional protections in light of the undoubted power of the United States to take actions to assert its legitimate power and authority abroad. Justice Harlan made this observation in his opinion concurring in the judgment in *Reid v. Covert:*

> "I cannot agree with the suggestion that every provision of the Constitution must always be deemed automatically applicable to American citizens in every part of the world. For *Ross* and the *Insular Cases* do stand for an important proposition, one which seems to me a wise and necessary gloss on our Constitution. The proposition is, of course, not that the Constitution 'does not apply' overseas, but that there are provisions in the Constitution which do not *necessarily* apply in all circumstances in every foreign place. In other words, it seems to me that the basic teaching of *Ross* and the *Insular Cases* is that there is no rigid and abstract rule that Congress, as a condition precedent to exercising power over Americans overseas, must exercise it subject to all the guarantees of the Constitution, no matter what the conditions and considerations are that would make adherence impracticable and anomalous." 354 U.S., at 74.

The conditions and considerations of this case would make adherence to the Fourth Amendment's warrant requirement impracticable and anomalous. . . The absence of local judges or magistrates available to issue warrants, the differing and perhaps unascertainable conceptions of reasonableness and privacy that prevail abroad, and the need to cooperate with foreign officials all indicate that the Fourth Amendment's warrant requirement should not apply in Mexico as it does in this country. . .

I do not mean to imply, and the Court has not decided, that persons in the position of the respondent have no constitutional protection. The United States is prosecuting a foreign national in a court established under Article III, and all of the trial proceedings are governed by the Constitution. All would agree, for instance, that the dictates of the Due Process Clause of the Fifth Amendment protect the defendant. . .

JUSTICE BRENNAN, with whom JUSTICE MARSHALL joins, dissenting. . .

I

Particularly in the past decade, our Government has sought, successfully, to hold foreign nationals criminally liable under federal laws for conduct committed entirely beyond the territorial limits of the United States that nevertheless has effects in this country. Foreign nationals must now take care not to violate our drug laws, our antitrust laws, our securities laws, and a host of other federal criminal statutes. . .

The Constitution is the source of Congress' authority to criminalize conduct, whether here or abroad, and of the Executive's authority to investigate and prosecute such conduct. But the same Constitution also prescribes limits on our Government's authority to investigate, prosecute, and punish criminal conduct, whether foreign or domestic. . . The Court today creates an antilogy: the Constitution authorizes our Government to enforce our criminal laws abroad, but when Government agents exercise this authority, the Fourth Amendment does not travel with them. This cannot be. At the very least, the Fourth Amendment is an unavoidable correlative of the Government's power to enforce the criminal law.

A . . .

According to the majority, the term "the people" [in the Fourth Amendment] refers to "a class of persons who are part of a national community or who have otherwise developed sufficient connection with this country to be considered part of that community." The Court admits that "the people" extends beyond the citizenry, but leaves the precise contours of its "sufficient connection" test unclear. . .

What the majority ignores, however, is the most obvious connection between Verdugo-Urquidez and the United States: he was investigated and is being prosecuted for violations of United States law and may well spend the rest of his life in a United States prison. The "sufficient connection" is supplied not by Verdugo-Urquidez, but by the Government. Respondent is entitled to the protections of the Fourth Amendment because our Government, by investigating him and attempting to hold him accountable under United States criminal laws, has treated him as a member of our community for purposes of enforcing our laws. He has become, quite literally, one of the governed. . .

Mutuality is essential to ensure the fundamental fairness that underlies our Bill of Rights. Foreign nationals investigated and prosecuted for alleged violations of United States criminal laws are just as vulnerable to oppressive government behavior as are United States citizens investigated and prosecuted for the same alleged violations. . . [W]hen United States agents conduct unreasonable searches, whether at home or abroad, they are disregarding our Nation's values. For over 200 years, our country has considered itself the world's foremost protector of liberties. The privacy and sanctity of the home have been primary tenets of our moral, philosophical, and judicial beliefs. Our national interest is defined by those values and by the need to preserve our own commitment to a government that cannot, on mere whim, break down doors and invade the most personal of places. We exhort other nations to follow our example. How can we explain to others—and to ourselves—that these long cherished ideals are suddenly of no consequence when the door being broken belongs to a foreigner? . . .

B

In its effort to establish that respondent does not have sufficient connection to the United States to be considered one of "the people" protected by the Fourth Amendment, the Court relies on the text of the Amendment, historical evidence, and cases refusing to apply certain constitutional provisions outside the United States. None of these, however, justifies the majority's cramped interpretation of the Fourth Amendment's applicability.

[Justice Brennan argued that the Court's reliance on the phrase "the people" was misplaced because the drafting history of the Fourth Amendment suggests that its focus was "on *what* the Government can and cannot do, and *how* it may act, not *against whom* these actions may be taken." *Johnson v. Eisentrager* was inapposite because it dealt with the constitutional rights of an alien enemy in war, while the *Insular Cases* were limited to their facts by *Reid v. Covert* and dealt with the rights of an accused in a territorial court rather than in an ordinary federal court.]

C

The majority's rejection of respondent's claim to Fourth Amendment protection is apparently motivated by its fear that application of the Amendment to law enforcement searches against foreign nationals overseas "could significantly disrupt the ability of the political branches to respond to foreign situations involving our national interest." The majority's doomsday scenario—that American Armed Forces conducting a mission to protect our national security with no law enforcement objective "would have to articulate specific facts giving them probable cause to undertake a search or seizure"—is fanciful. . . Accepting respondent as one of the "governed" . . . hardly requires the Court to accept enemy aliens in wartime as among "the governed" entitled to invoke the protection of the Fourth Amendment.

Moreover, with respect to non-law-enforcement activities not directed against enemy aliens in wartime but nevertheless implicating national security, doctrinal exceptions to the general requirements of a warrant and probable cause likely would be applicable more frequently abroad, thus lessening the purported tension between the Fourth Amendment's strictures and the Executive's foreign affairs power. . . In most cases implicating foreign policy concerns in which the reasonableness of an overseas search or seizure is unclear, application of the Fourth Amendment will not interfere with the Executive's traditional prerogative in foreign affairs because a court will have occasion to decide the constitutionality of such a search only if *the Executive* decides to bring a criminal prosecution and introduce evidence seized abroad. When the Executive decides to conduct a search as part of an ongoing criminal investigation, fails to get a warrant, and then seeks to introduce the fruits of that search at trial, however, the courts must enforce the Constitution. . .

The Extraterritorial Reach of the Constitution

(1) The Constitution obviously protects citizens of the United States at home, and the Supreme Court held more than a century ago that aliens are also entitled to many constitutional protections when they are in the United States. *Wong Wing v. United States,* 163 U.S. 228 (1896) (Fifth and Sixth Amendments); *Yick Wo v. Hopkins,* 118 U.S. 356 (1886) (equal protection).[14] Aliens not present within the United States are similarly entitled to constitutional protection with respect to property located here. *Asahi Metal Indus. v. Superior Court,* 480 U.S. 102 (1987) (due process); *Russian Volunteer Fleet v. United States,* 282 U.S. 481 (1931) (takings). The current debate has thus focused primarily on the rights of persons harmed abroad by actions of the United States government. Does *Verdugo-Urquidez* resolve this debate? Does it reopen the question of the protection afforded aliens in the United States?

(2) The *Verdugo-Urquidez* Court's conclusion rests to some extent on the claim that nothing in the original Constitution suggests an intent to provide extraterritorial constitutional protection. Is its historical account persuasive? According to Professor Neuman, "the drafting of the Bill of Rights reflected inattention to the problematics of government action abroad rather than a conscious effort to design entitlements solely for application within the territory." Neuman, *Whose Constitution?,* 100 Yale L.J. 909, 980 (1991). Does that surprise you? Even if the Court is right, what weight should it have given to subsequent developments, both within the United States and in international law, in thinking about legislative jurisdiction?

(3) What kind of connection is required to make someone one of "the people" for purposes of Fourth Amendment protection? If "the people" means citizens, why are aliens protected when they are in the United States? And why is Verdugo-Urquidez entitled to the protections of the

[14] Note, however, that in the deportation area the Supreme Court has upheld federal power to deport without the protections of the criminal process. *Fong Yue Ting v. United States,* 149 U.S. 698 (1893); Aleinikoff, *Federal Regulation of Aliens and the Constitution,* 83 Am.J.Int'l L. 862 (1989).

Fifth Amendment when he is tried? Conversely, if constitutional protections are defined territorially, how do you explain the result in *Reid*?

To what extent does Chief Justice Rehnquist's opinion rely on the theory that the Constitution reflects a compact between the citizens of the United States and its government? Even assuming the validity of such a theory, does it follow that aliens are unprotected? Consider Madison's response in his 1800 Report on the Virginia Resolves: "To this reasoning, also, it might be answered that, although aliens are not parties to the Constitution, it does not follow that the Constitution has vested in Congress an absolute power over them. The parties to the Constitution may have granted, or retained, or modified, the power over aliens, without regard to that particular consideration." Shouldn't the Bill of Rights be understood as a set of restrictions imposed by the American people on what their government officials can do regardless of the identity of the person acted upon? Cf. L. Brilmayer, Justifying International Acts (1991) (arguing that a nation cannot rely on different theories of sovereignty to justify treating insiders and outsiders differently); Roosevelt, *Guantanamo and the Conflict of Laws:* Rasul *and Beyond*, 153 U. Pa. L. Rev. 2017 (2005) (describing different theories of extraterritorial application of the Constitution).

Can you articulate the conception of constitutional protection in multinational cases that underlies the majority opinion? Is "realpolitik" the best explanation for this result?

(4) Justice Kennedy provides Chief Justice Rehnquist with the fifth vote in *Verdugo*. Is his analysis consistent with that of the Chief Justice? Why is adherence to the Fourth Amendment's warrant requirement "impracticable and anomalous"? Won't requiring American agents to submit their evidence to a magistrate or judge still serve the purpose of the Fourth Amendment to restrain unjustified searches?

(5) Do you agree with Justice Brennan that if the United States requires compliance with American criminal laws it must also provide the protection of the Bill of Rights? Can't prescriptive and proscriptive laws have different reaches if they serve different purposes?

(6) What counts as an extraterritorial application of the Constitution? In *Verdugo-Urquidez*, the Court sensibly reasons that the relevant conduct is the search, which took place in Mexico. What if Verdugo-Urquidez confesses to U.S. agents in Mexico and then argues that his confession should be suppressed in a U.S. trial because he did not receive *Miranda* warnings? Professor Godsey argues that because "the privilege against self-incrimination is a trial right[,] . . . whether the interaction occurs within the borders of the United States or abroad becomes immaterial to the applicability of the privilege if the suspect later stands trial in the United States." Godsey, Miranda's *Final Frontier—The*

International Arena: A Critical Analysis of United States v. Bin Laden, *and a Proposal for a New* Miranda *Exception Abroad*, 51 Duke L. J. 1703, 1723–26 (2002). But is this so clear? If the Fifth Amendment does not apply to federal officers interrogating aliens abroad, why is a confession given to them any different from a confession given to a suspect's neighbors, which is admissible despite the lack of a *Miranda* warning?

(7) Can courts invalidate legislation as applied to foreign entities that work closely with U.S. entities? In *Agency for International Development v. Alliance for Open Society International, Inc.*, 140 S. Ct. 2082 (2020) ("*AOSI II*"), U.S. non-governmental organizations with foreign affiliates brought a First Amendment challenge to a federal law that conditioned aid on recipients' agreement to oppose prostitution and sex trafficking. The Court had invalidated this spending condition on compelled-speech grounds as applied to U.S. organizations in *Agency for International Development v. Alliance for Open Society International, Inc.*, 570 U.S. 205 (2013) ("*AOSI I*"). In *AOSI II*, however, the Court held that "[a]s foreign organizations operating abroad, plaintiffs' foreign affiliates possess no rights under the First Amendment," 140 S. Ct. at 2087, and declined to strike the condition as applied to the foreign affiliates. The Court rejected the plaintiffs' invitation to extend First Amendment rights to "foreign organizations that are *closely identified* with American organizations," saying that this would "enmesh the courts in difficult line-drawing exercises—how closely identified is close enough?—and leave courts without any principled basis for making those judgments." *Id.* at 2088–2089.

Writing in dissent, Justice Breyer concluded that the funding condition violated the First Amendment rights of *U.S. organizations* who happened to speak through foreign affiliates. As for the majority's line-drawing concerns, Justice Breyer stated that "the price of making difficult judgment calls is well worth paying to protect First Amendment rights." *Id.* at 2103 (Breyer, J., dissenting). How can courts resolve whether the relevant constitutional rights claimant in a case is a U.S. or a non-U.S. actor? Is this analogous to the question of whether a case has a domestic "focus" under the second step of the *Morrison*/*RJR Nabisco* test? Is it akin to asking whether a state has an interest in applying, say, a guest statute to a case in which a car was driven in one state but registered and insured in another?

Extraterritoriality and the Suspension Clause

BOUMEDIENE V. BUSH

553 U.S. 723 (2008).

JUSTICE KENNEDY delivered the opinion of the Court.

[Beginning in January 2002, U.S. authorities started transferring terrorism suspects to the naval base at Guantanamo Bay, Cuba. In *Rasul v. Bush*, 542 U.S. 466 (2004), the Court held that such detainees were entitled to file habeas petitions under 28 U.S.C. § 2241, which authorizes courts to issue the writ to those in custody "in violation of the Constitution or laws or treaties of the United States." The Court noted that the petitioners alleged that their custody was illegal and that the statute "by its terms, requires nothing more." *Rasul*, 542 U.S. at 484. It dismissed the presumption against extraterritoriality as having "no application to the operation of the habeas statute with respect to persons detained within 'the territorial jurisdiction' of the United States." *Id.* at 480 (citing *Foley Bros. v. Filardo*, 336 U.S. 281 (1949)).

[Congress responded to *Rasul* by amending the habeas statute, in the Military Commissions Act of 2006, to strip federal courts of jurisdiction to entertain habeas petitions from detained aliens who had been determined to be enemy combatants and relegate those aliens to proceedings before a Combatant Status Review Tribunal (CSRT). This constituted a suspension of the writ of habeas corpus, and in *Boumediene* the Court considered whether aliens detained at Guantanamo were entitled to the protection of the Suspension Clause, which provides that "The Privilege of the Writ of Habeas Corpus shall not be suspended, unless when in Cases of Rebellion or Invasion the public Safety may require it."]

III

In deciding the constitutional questions now presented we must determine whether petitioners are barred from seeking the writ or invoking the protections of the Suspension Clause either because of their status, *i.e.*, petitioners' designation by the Executive Branch as enemy combatants, or their physical location, *i.e.*, their presence at Guantanamo Bay. The Government contends that noncitizens designated as enemy combatants and detained in territory located outside our Nation's borders have no constitutional rights and no privilege of habeas corpus. Petitioners contend they do have cognizable constitutional rights and that Congress, in seeking to eliminate recourse to habeas corpus as a means to assert those rights, acted in violation of the Suspension Clause.

We begin with a brief account of the history and origins of the writ. Our account proceeds from two propositions. First, protection for the privilege of habeas corpus was one of the few safeguards of liberty specified in a Constitution that, at the outset, had no Bill of Rights. In the system conceived by the Framers the writ had a centrality that must inform proper interpretation of the Suspension Clause. Second, to the extent there were settled precedents or legal commentaries in 1789 regarding the extraterritorial scope of the writ or its application to enemy aliens, those authorities can be instructive for the present cases.

[The Court's historical analysis concluded that the writ was considered a vital safeguard of liberty and an important element of the separation of powers. "The separation-of-powers doctrine, and the history that influenced its design, therefore must inform the reach and purpose of the Suspension Clause." The Court also concluded that historical evidence on the availability of habeas to noncitizens detained beyond the sovereign's borders was inconclusive and did not provide a sufficient basis on which to decide the case.]

IV

Drawing from its position that at common law the writ ran only to territories over which the Crown was sovereign, the Government says the Suspension Clause affords petitioners no rights because the United States does not claim sovereignty over the place of detention.

Guantanamo Bay is not formally part of the United States. * * * And under the terms of the lease between the United States and Cuba, Cuba retains "ultimate sovereignty" over the territory while the United States exercises "complete jurisdiction and control." * * * Under the terms of the 1934 Treaty, however, Cuba effectively has no rights as a sovereign until the parties agree to modification of the 1903 Lease Agreement or the United States abandons the base. * * *.

The United States contends, nevertheless, that Guantanamo is not within its sovereign control. This was the Government's position well before the events of September 11, 2001. * * * And in other contexts the Court has held that questions of sovereignty are for the political branches to decide. * * * Even if this were a treaty interpretation case that did not involve a political question, the President's construction of the lease agreement would be entitled to great respect. * * *

We therefore do not question the Government's position that Cuba, not the United States, maintains sovereignty, in the legal and technical sense of the term, over Guantanamo Bay. * * * As we did in *Rasul*, however, we take notice of the obvious and uncontested fact that the United States, by virtue of its complete jurisdiction and control over the base, maintains de facto sovereignty over this territory. * * *

Were we to hold that the present cases turn on the political question doctrine, we would be required first to accept the Government's premise that de jure sovereignty is the touchstone of habeas corpus jurisdiction.

This premise, however, is unfounded. For the reasons indicated above, the history of common-law habeas corpus provides scant support for this proposition; and, for the reasons indicated below, that position would be inconsistent with our precedents and contrary to fundamental separation-of-powers principles.

A

The Court has discussed the issue of the Constitution's extraterritorial application on many occasions. These decisions undermine the Government's argument that, at least as applied to noncitizens, the Constitution necessarily stops where de jure sovereignty ends. . .

Fundamental questions regarding the Constitution's geographic scope first arose at the dawn of the 20th century when the Nation acquired noncontiguous Territories: Puerto Rico, Guam, and the Philippines—ceded to the United States by Spain at the conclusion of the Spanish-American War—and Hawaii—annexed by the United States in 1898. At this point Congress chose to discontinue its previous practice of extending constitutional rights to the territories by statute. * * *

In a series of opinions later known as the *Insular Cases*, the Court addressed whether the Constitution, by its own force, applies in any territory that is not a State. * * * The Court held that the Constitution has independent force in these territories, a force not contingent upon acts of legislative grace. Yet it took note of the difficulties inherent in that position.

Prior to their cession to the United States, the former Spanish colonies operated under a civil-law system, without experience in the various aspects of the Anglo-American legal tradition, for instance the use of grand and petit juries. * * * The Court thus was reluctant to risk the uncertainty and instability that could result from a rule that displaced altogether the existing legal systems in these newly acquired Territories. * * *

These considerations resulted in the doctrine of territorial incorporation, under which the Constitution applies in full in incorporated Territories surely destined for statehood but only in part in unincorporated Territories. * * * As the Court later made clear, "the real issue in the *Insular Cases* was not whether the Constitution extended to the Philippines or Porto Rico when we went there, but which of its provisions were applicable by way of limitation upon the exercise of executive and legislative power in dealing with new conditions and requirements." * * * It may well be that over time the ties between the United States and any of its unincorporated Territories strengthen in ways that are of constitutional significance. * * * But, as early as . . . 1922, the Court took for granted that even in unincorporated Territories the Government of the United States was bound to provide to noncitizen inhabitants "guaranties of certain fundamental personal rights declared in the Constitution." * * *

Yet noting the inherent practical difficulties of enforcing all constitutional provisions "always and everywhere," * * * the Court devised in the *Insular Cases* a doctrine that allowed it to use its power sparingly and where it would be most needed. This century-old doctrine informs our analysis in the present matter.

Practical considerations likewise influenced the Court's analysis a half-century later in *Reid* * * *. The petitioners there, spouses of American servicemen, lived on American military bases in England and Japan. They were charged with crimes committed in those countries and tried before military courts, consistent with executive agreements the United States had entered into with the British and Japanese governments. * * * Because the petitioners were not themselves military personnel, they argued they were entitled to trial by jury. * * *

That the petitioners in *Reid* were American citizens was a key factor in the case and was central to the plurality's conclusion that the Fifth and Sixth Amendments apply to American civilians tried outside the United States. But practical considerations, related not to the petitioners' citizenship but to the place of their confinement and trial, were relevant to each Member of the *Reid* majority. And to Justices Harlan and Frankfurter (whose votes were necessary to the Court's disposition) these considerations were the decisive factors in the case. . .

Practical considerations weighed heavily as well in *Johnson v. Eisentrager*, 339 U.S. 763 (1950), where the Court addressed whether habeas corpus jurisdiction extended to enemy aliens who had been convicted of violating the laws of war. The prisoners were detained at Landsberg Prison in Germany during the Allied Powers' postwar occupation. The Court stressed the difficulties of ordering the Government to produce the prisoners in a habeas corpus proceeding. It "would require allocation of shipping space, guarding personnel, billeting and rations" and would damage the prestige of military commanders at a sensitive time. * * * In considering these factors the Court sought to balance the constraints of military occupation with constitutional necessities. * * *

True, the Court in *Eisentrager* denied access to the writ, and it noted the prisoners "at no relevant time were within any territory over which the United States is sovereign, and [that] the scenes of their offense, their capture, their trial and their punishment were all beyond the territorial jurisdiction of any court of the United States." * * * The Government seizes upon this language as proof positive that the *Eisentrager* Court adopted a formalistic, sovereignty-based test for determining the reach of the Suspension Clause. * * * We reject this reading for three reasons.

First, we do not accept the idea that the above-quoted passage from *Eisentrager* is the only authoritative language in the opinion and that all the rest is dicta. The Court's further determinations, based on practical considerations, were integral to Part II of its opinion and came before the decision announced its holding. * * *

Second, because the United States lacked both de jure sovereignty and plenary control over Landsberg Prison, * * *, it is far from clear that the *Eisentrager* Court used the term sovereignty only in the narrow technical sense and not to connote the degree of control the military asserted over the facility. * * * The Justices who decided *Eisentrager* would have understood sovereignty as a multifaceted concept. * * * Even if we assume the *Eisentrager* Court considered the United States' lack of formal legal sovereignty over Landsberg Prison as the decisive factor in that case, its holding is not inconsistent with a functional approach to questions of extraterritoriality. The formal legal status of a given territory affects, at least to some extent, the political branches' control over that territory. De jure sovereignty is a factor that bears upon which constitutional guarantees apply there.

Third, if the Government's reading of *Eisentrager* were correct, the opinion would have marked not only a change in, but a complete repudiation of, the *Insular Cases'* (and later *Reid*'s) functional approach to questions of extraterritoriality. * * * A constricted reading of *Eisentrager* overlooks what we see as a common thread uniting the *Insular Cases*, *Eisentrager*, and *Reid*: the idea that questions of extraterritoriality turn on objective factors and practical concerns, not formalism.

B

The Government's formal sovereignty-based test raises troubling separation-of-powers concerns as well. The political history of Guantanamo illustrates the deficiencies of this approach. The United States has maintained complete and uninterrupted control of the bay for over 100 years. * * * Yet the Government's view is that the Constitution had no effect there, at least as to noncitizens, because the United States disclaimed sovereignty in the formal sense of the term. The necessary implication of the argument is that by surrendering formal sovereignty over any unincorporated territory to a third party, while at the same time entering into a lease that grants total control over the territory back to the United States, it would be possible for the political branches to govern without legal constraint.

Our basic charter cannot be contracted away like this. The Constitution grants Congress and the President the power to acquire, dispose of, and govern territory, not the power to decide when and where its terms apply. Even when the United States acts outside its borders, its powers are not "absolute and unlimited" but are subject "to such restrictions as are expressed in the Constitution." * * * Abstaining from questions involving formal sovereignty and territorial governance is one thing. To hold the political branches have the power to switch the

Constitution on or off at will is quite another. The former position reflects this Court's recognition that certain matters requiring political judgments are best left to the political branches. The latter would permit a striking anomaly in our tripartite system of government, leading to a regime in which Congress and the President, not this Court, say "what the law is." * * *

These concerns have particular bearing upon the Suspension Clause question in the cases now before us, for the writ of habeas corpus is itself an indispensable mechanism for monitoring the separation of powers. The test for determining the scope of this provision must not be subject to manipulation by those whose power it is designed to restrain.

C

As we recognized in *Rasul*, * * * the outlines of a framework for determining the reach of the Suspension Clause are suggested by the factors the Court relied upon in *Eisentrager*. * * *

Based on . . . language from *Eisentrager*, and the reasoning in our other extraterritoriality opinions, we conclude that at least three factors are relevant in determining the reach of the Suspension Clause: (1) the citizenship and status of the detainee and the adequacy of the process through which that status determination was made; (2) the nature of the sites where apprehension and then detention took place; and (3) the practical obstacles inherent in resolving the prisoner's entitlement to the writ.

Applying this framework, we note at the onset that the status of these detainees is a matter of dispute. The petitioners, like those in *Eisentrager*, are not American citizens. But the petitioners in *Eisentrager* did not contest, it seems, the Court's assertion that they were "enemy alien[s]." *Ibid.* In the instant cases, by contrast, the detainees deny they are enemy combatants. They have been afforded some process in CSRT proceedings to determine their status; but, unlike in *Eisentrager*, * * * there has been no trial by military commission for violations of the laws of war. The difference is not trivial. The records from the *Eisentrager* trials suggest that, well before the petitioners brought their case to this Court, there had been a rigorous adversarial process to test the legality of their detention. The *Eisentrager* petitioners were charged by a bill of particulars that made detailed factual allegations against them. * * * To rebut the accusations, they were entitled to representation by counsel, allowed to introduce evidence on their own behalf, and permitted to cross-examine the prosecution's witnesses. * * *

In comparison the procedural protections afforded to the detainees in the CSRT hearings are far more limited, and, we conclude, fall well short of the procedures and adversarial mechanisms that would eliminate the need for habeas corpus review. Although the detainee is assigned a

"Personal Representative" to assist him during CSRT proceedings, the Secretary of the Navy's memorandum makes clear that person is not the detainee's lawyer or even his "advocate." * * * The Government's evidence is accorded a presumption of validity. * * *. The detainee is allowed to present "reasonably available" evidence, * * *, but his ability to rebut the Government's evidence against him is limited by the circumstances of his confinement and his lack of counsel at this stage. And although the detainee can seek review of his status determination in the Court of Appeals, that review process cannot cure all defects in the earlier proceedings. * * *

As to the second factor relevant to this analysis, the detainees here are similarly situated to the *Eisentrager* petitioners in that the sites of their apprehension and detention are technically outside the sovereign territory of the United States. As noted earlier, this is a factor that weighs against finding they have rights under the Suspension Clause. But there are critical differences between Landsberg Prison, circa 1950, and the United States Naval Station at Guantanamo Bay in 2008. Unlike its present control over the naval station, the United States' control over the prison in Germany was neither absolute nor indefinite. Like all parts of occupied Germany, the prison was under the jurisdiction of the combined Allied Forces. * * * The United States was therefore answerable to its Allies for all activities occurring there. * * * The Allies had not planned a long-term occupation of Germany, nor did they intend to displace all German institutions even during the period of occupation. * * * The Court's holding in *Eisentrager* was thus consistent with the *Insular Cases*, where it had held there was no need to extend full constitutional protections to territories the United States did not intend to govern indefinitely. Guantanamo Bay, on the other hand, is no transient possession. In every practical sense Guantanamo is not abroad; it is within the constant jurisdiction of the United States. * * *

As to the third factor, we recognize, as the Court did in *Eisentrager*, that there are costs to holding the Suspension Clause applicable in a case of military detention abroad. Habeas corpus proceedings may require expenditure of funds by the Government and may divert the attention of military personnel from other pressing tasks. While we are sensitive to these concerns, we do not find them dispositive. Compliance with any judicial process requires some incremental expenditure of resources. Yet civilian courts and the Armed Forces have functioned along side each other at various points in our history. * * * The Government presents no credible arguments that the military mission at Guantanamo would be compromised if habeas corpus courts had jurisdiction to hear the detainees' claims. And in light of the plenary control the United States asserts over the base, none are apparent to us. * * *

There is no indication, furthermore, that adjudicating a habeas corpus petition would cause friction with the host government. No Cuban court has jurisdiction over American military personnel at Guantanamo or the enemy combatants detained there. While obligated to abide by the terms of the lease, the United States is, for all practical purposes, answerable to no other sovereign for its acts on the base. Were that not the case, or if the detention facility were located in an active theater of war, arguments that issuing the writ would be "impracticable or anomalous" would have more weight. * * * Under the facts presented here, however, there are few practical barriers to the running of the writ. To the extent barriers arise, habeas corpus procedures likely can be modified to address them. * * *

It is true that before today the Court has never held that noncitizens detained by our Government in territory over which another country maintains de jure sovereignty have any rights under our Constitution. But the cases before us lack any precise historical parallel. They involve individuals detained by executive order for the duration of a conflict that, if measured from September 11, 2001, to the present, is already among the longest wars in American history. * * * The detainees, moreover, are held in a territory that, while technically not part of the United States, is under the complete and total control of our Government. Under these circumstances the lack of a precedent on point is no barrier to our holding.

We hold that Art. I, § 9, cl. 2, of the Constitution has full effect at Guantanamo Bay. If the privilege of habeas corpus is to be denied to the detainees now before us, Congress must act in accordance with the requirements of the Suspension Clause. * * * This Court may not impose a de facto suspension by abstaining from these controversies. * * * The MCA does not purport to be a formal suspension of the writ; and the Government, in its submissions to us, has not argued that it is. Petitioners, therefore, are entitled to the privilege of habeas corpus to challenge the legality of their detention.

[The Court then went on the consider and reject the argument that Congress had provided an adequate alternative to habeas.

JUSTICES SOUTER, GINSBURG, and BREYER joined the KENNEDY opinion and also concurred in an opinion, written by Souter, arguing that the *Boumediene* decision should not come as a surprise.

CHIEF JUSTICE ROBERTS, joined by JUSTICES SCALIA, THOMAS, and ALITO, dissented on the grounds that Congress had provided an adequate alternative to habeas.]

JUSTICE SCALIA, with whom THE CHIEF JUSTICE, JUSTICE THOMAS, and JUSTICE ALITO join, dissenting.

Today, for the first time in our Nation's history, the Court confers a constitutional right to habeas corpus on alien enemies detained abroad by our military forces in the course of an ongoing war. . . The writ of habeas corpus does not, and never has, run in favor of aliens abroad; the Suspension Clause thus has no application, and the Court's intervention in this military matter is entirely *ultra vires*. * * *

I

[Justice Scalia argues that the majority opinion shows insufficient deference to the coordinate branches and the military, disrupts their reliance on settled law, and "will almost certainly cause more Americans to be killed."]

II

A

* * * We have frequently stated that we owe great deference to Congress's view that a law it has passed is constitutional. * * * That is especially so in the area of foreign and military affairs; "perhaps in no other area has the Court accorded Congress greater deference." * * * Indeed, we accord great deference even when the President acts alone in this area. * * *

In light of those principles of deference, the Court's conclusion that "the common law [does not] yiel[d] a definite answer to the questions before us," * * * leaves it no choice but to affirm the Court of Appeals. * * *

How, then, does the Court weave a clear constitutional prohibition out of pure interpretive equipoise? The Court resorts to "fundamental separation-of-powers principles" to interpret the Suspension Clause. * * *

That approach distorts the nature of the separation of powers and its role in the constitutional structure. The "fundamental separation-of-powers principles" that the Constitution embodies are to be derived not from some judicially imagined matrix, but from the sum total of the individual separation-of-powers provisions that the Constitution sets forth. * * * And if the understood scope of the writ of habeas corpus was "designed to restrain" (as the Court says) the actions of the Executive, the understood *limits* upon that scope were (as the Court seems not to grasp) just as much "designed to restrain" the incursions of the Third Branch. * * *

B

The Court purports to derive from our precedents a "functional" test for the extraterritorial reach of the writ, * * * which shows that the Military Commissions Act unconstitutionally restricts the scope of habeas. That is remarkable because the most pertinent of those precedents, *Johnson v. Eisentrager*, * * * conclusively establishes the opposite. * * * Like the petitioners here, the Germans claimed that their detentions violated the Constitution and international law, and sought a writ of habeas corpus. Writing for the Court, Justice Jackson held that American courts lacked habeas jurisdiction:

> "We are cited to [*sic*] no instance where a court, in this or any other country where the writ is known, has issued it on behalf of an alien enemy who, at no relevant time and in no stage of his captivity, has been within its territorial jurisdiction. Nothing in the text of the Constitution extends such a right, nor does anything in our statutes." * * *
>
> Justice Jackson then elaborated on the historical scope of the writ:
>
> "The alien, to whom the United States has been traditionally hospitable, has been accorded a generous and ascending scale of rights as he increases his identity with our society. . .
>
> "But, in extending constitutional protections beyond the citizenry, the Court has been at pains to point out that it was the alien's presence within its territorial jurisdiction that gave the Judiciary power to act." * * *

Eisentrager thus held—*held* beyond any doubt—that the Constitution does not ensure habeas for aliens held by the United States in areas over which our Government is not sovereign. . . * * *

Eisentrager mentioned practical concerns, to be sure—but not for the purpose of determining *under what circumstances* American courts could issue writs of habeas corpus for aliens abroad. It cited them to support *its holding* that the Constitution does not empower courts to issue writs of habeas corpus to aliens abroad in any circumstances. * * * *Eisentrager* nowhere mentions a "functional" test, and the notion that it is based upon such a principle is patently false. . . * * *

After transforming the *a fortiori* elements discussed above into a "functional" test, the Court is still left with the difficulty that most of those elements exist here as well with regard to all the detainees. * * * But no one looking for "functional" equivalents would put *Eisentrager* and the present cases in the same category, much less place the present cases in a preferred category. The difference between them cries out for lesser procedures in the present cases. The prisoners in *Eisentrager* were prosecuted for crimes after the cessation of hostilities; the prisoners here are enemy combatants detained during an ongoing conflict. * * *

The category of prisoner comparable to these detainees are not the *Eisentrager* criminal defendants, but the more than 400,000 prisoners of war detained in the United States alone during World War II. Not a single one was accorded the right to have his detention validated by a habeas corpus action in federal court—and that despite the fact that they were present on U.S. soil. * * * The Court's analysis produces a crazy result: Whereas those convicted and sentenced to death for war crimes are without judicial remedy, all enemy combatants detained during a war, at least insofar as they are confined in an area away from the battlefield over which the United States exercises "absolute and indefinite" control, may seek a writ of habeas corpus in federal court. And, as an even more bizarre implication from the Court's reasoning, those prisoners whom the military plans to try by full-dress Commission at a future date may file habeas petitions and secure release before their trials take place.

There is simply no support for the Court's assertion that constitutional rights extend to aliens held outside U.S. sovereign territory, * * * and *Eisentrager* could not be clearer that the privilege of habeas corpus does not extend to aliens abroad. By blatantly distorting *Eisentrager*, the Court avoids the difficulty of explaining why it should be overruled. * * * . . . It is a sad day for the rule of law when such an important constitutional precedent is discarded without an *apologia*, much less an apology.

C

What drives today's decision is neither the meaning of the Suspension Clause, nor the principles of our precedents, but rather an inflated notion of judicial supremacy. The Court says that if the extraterritorial applicability of the Suspension Clause turned on formal notions of sovereignty, "it would be possible for the political branches to govern without legal constraint" in areas beyond the sovereign territory of the United States. * * * That cannot be, the Court says, because it is the duty of this Court to say what the law is. * * *. It would be difficult to imagine a more question-begging analysis. * * * Our power "to say what the law is" is circumscribed by the limits of our statutorily and constitutionally conferred jurisdiction. * * * And that is precisely the question in these cases: whether the Constitution confers habeas jurisdiction on federal courts to decide petitioners' claims. It is both irrational and arrogant to say that the answer must be yes, because otherwise we would not be supreme. * * *

III

* * * In sum, because I conclude that the text and history of the Suspension Clause provide no basis for our jurisdiction, I would affirm the Court of Appeals even if *Eisentrager* did not govern these cases.

* * *

Today the Court warps our Constitution in a way that goes beyond the narrow issue of the reach of the Suspension Clause, invoking judicially brainstormed separation-of-powers principles to establish a manipulable "functional" test for the extraterritorial reach of habeas corpus (and, no doubt, for the extraterritorial reach of other constitutional protections as well). * * *

The Nation will live to regret what the Court has done today. I dissent.

---

(1) Controversies respecting the scope of constitutional protection in cases with foreign elements have arisen throughout American history, beginning with the Alien Acts of 1798. This legislation (enacted together with the equally infamous Sedition Act) authorized the President to deport or arrest "dangerous" aliens without a hearing on the basis of mere suspicion. Federalists defended the acts on a ground echoed in *Verdugo-Urquidez,* namely, that the Constitution protects only members of the political community that ratified it. For example, a Report to the House of Representatives recommended that the acts not be repealed:

> [T]he Constitution was made for citizens, not for aliens, who of consequence have no rights under it, but remain in the country and enjoy the benefit of the laws, not as a matter of right, but merely as a matter of favor and permission, which favor and permission may be withdrawn whenever the Government charged with the general welfare shall judge their further continuance dangerous.

9 Annals of Cong. 2987 (1799). The Republican response, in contrast, reflected an understanding of the Constitution similar to that in Justice Brennan's dissent: the Constitution is part of the law of the United States and therefore is binding wherever the United States exercises sovereignty. James Madison spelled out the implications of this understanding in his 1800 Report defending the Virginia Resolves:

> [I]t does not follow, because aliens are not parties to the Constitution, as citizens are parties to it, that whilst they actually conform to it, they have no right to its protection. Aliens are not more parties to the laws than they are parties to the Constitution; yet it will not be disputed that, as they own, on one hand, a temporary obedience, they are entitled, in return, to their protection and advantage. . . Alien friends . . . are under the municipal law, and must be tried and punished according to that law only. . . [T]he offence being committed by the individual, not by his nation,—the individual only, and not the nation, is punishable; and the punishment must be conducted according to the municipal law, not according to the law of nations.

The Alien Acts expired in June of 1800, and Republican victories in elections held that same year effectively ended this controversy without definitive resolution. But these same two views of the nature of constitutional protection were presented and debated in other controversies throughout the 19th century, the most important being the controversy over slavery in the territories. Indeed, Chief Justice Taney's opinion for the Court in *Dred Scott v. Sandford,* 60 U.S. (19 How.) 393 (1857), relies on both theories: because African Americans were not part of the "people" who adopted the Constitution, they were not entitled to constitutional protections (such as the right to sue in federal court); and because the Constitution is part of the municipal law of the United States, it binds the government wherever it acts and thus protects the right of citizens of the territories to own slaves.

The first decisive judicial test arose after the Civil War in connection with the anti-Chinese movement in California. As noted above, the Court held that resident aliens were entitled to constitutional protection. The reasoning in these opinions rejects the "membership" view of constitutional protection and treats the Constitution as law binding the government regardless of the identity of the person acted upon. Thus, in striking down a federal statute subjecting illegal immigrants to a year at hard labor without indictment or trial by jury, the Court explained:

> [I]t must be concluded that all persons within the territory of the United States are entitled to the protection guaranteed by [the fifth and sixth] amendments, and that even aliens shall not be held to answer for a capital or other infamous crime, unless on a presentment or indictment of a grand jury, nor be deprived of life, liberty or property without due process of law.

Wong Wing v. United States, 163 U.S. 228, 238 (1896).

Not surprisingly, the application of this municipal law theory in the 19th century included a territorial bias: as part of the law of the United States, the Constitution applied wherever the United States had sovereignty; but the sovereignty of the United States was defined territorially. This implicit premise was made explicit in *In re Ross,* 140 U.S. 453 (1891), which raised the question whether an American citizen being tried for murder in an American "consular" court in Japan was entitled to rights under the Fifth and Sixth Amendments. In holding that he was not, the Court explained:

> By the Constitution a government is ordained and established "for the United States of America," and not for countries outside of their limits. The guarantees it affords . . . apply only to citizens and others within the United States, or who are brought there for trial for alleged offences committed elsewhere, and not to residents or temporary sojourners abroad. The Constitution can have no operation in another country.

In the late 19th and early 20th centuries, the issue presented itself in the context of United States acquisition of distant territories populated by non-white, non-English speaking peoples. In the *Insular Cases,* discussed in *Boumediene,* the Court backed away from its earlier decisions affording full constitutional protection within the territory of the United States. In the middle of the 20th century, dealing with Americans abroad, the Court took a more generous view in *Reid v. Covert,* 354 U.S. 1 (1957), also discussed in *Boumediene.* Lower courts interpreted *Reid* broadly to confirm the constitutional rights of citizens abroad. A few courts read the opinion to require extending the same protection to aliens. See *United States v. Toscanino,* 500 F.2d 267 (2d Cir. 1974) (Fourth and Fifth Amendments); *United States v. Tiede,* 86 F.R.D. 227 (U.S.Ct. for Berlin 1979) (Sixth Amendment).

Does this history authoritatively resolve the problem presented in *Verdugo* and *Boumediene* one way or the other? Do you think the original understanding of the Suspension Clause or English habeas practice might?

(2) How do the majority and the dissent in *Boumediene* use the distinctive nature of the Constitution to support their positions? Is the problem of defining the extraterritorial scope of the Constitution different from that of defining the extraterritorial scope of a federal statute? Is it different from any question of extraterritoriality? Consider the following observation from Professor Neuman:

> To resolve the question of the proper scope of the individual rights provisions of the United States Constitution, it is useful to ask what rights in a constitution are *for,* and in particular what United States constitutional rights are for. The general question may receive different answers in different constitutional traditions, and consequently the scope of rights under different constitutions may vary.

Whose Constitution?, 100 Yale L.J. 909, 976 (1991). Isn't this essentially what interest analysts have been saying since the 1950s? But how should this be done with a provision like the Fourth Amendment? How about the Suspension Clause?

Neuman agrees with Justice Brennan in *Verdugo-Urquidez* that, insofar as an alien is being held to American criminal laws, he or she is entitled to correlative protections afforded by the Constitution. Is the content of Mexican law (or the fact that Mexican law was complied with) relevant to the decision? Although we do not know the precise content of Mexican law, it appears to be less restrictive than the Fourth Amendment. Do you think *Verdugo* is a true conflict or a false one? Might it be a case where Mexican and American law could be treated as cumulative? What about *Boumediene*?

(3) Finish the following sentence: "The Suspension Clause applies to alleged enemy combatants detained at Guantanamo Bay because ______." Does Justice Kennedy's functional analysis provide any guidelines for determining whether *other* constitutional provisions apply to detainees held abroad? How important to the Court's analysis is the fact that the Suspension Clause is a structural provision that safeguards the separation of powers by ensuring that the political branches do not usurp the independent judiciary's role in determining the lawfulness of executive custody? See Franklin, *Enemy Combatants and the Jurisdictional Fact Doctrine*, 29 Cardozo L. Rev. 1001 (2008).

Does *Boumediene*'s Suspension Clause reasoning imply that alien detainees at Guantanamo may invoke the Constitution's substantive provisions as well? The Supreme Court has dodged this question, but the D.C. Circuit took it on in *Al Hela v. Trump*, 972 F.3d 120 (D.C. Cir. 2020). Al Hela is a prominent Yemeni citizen who has been detained at Guantanamo since 2004 and is alleged to have ties with both Yemeni security services and terrorist organizations. He filed a habeas petition arguing that his detention violated the Fifth Amendment's substantive and procedural due process guarantees. A panel of the D.C. Circuit responded to these claims as follows:

> First, Al Hela argues that *Boumediene*'s extension of the Suspension Clause to Guantanamo Bay abrogated *Eisentrager* because due process rights are implied by and inextricably intertwined with access to the habeas writ. On this view, habeas is a jurisdictional vehicle for presenting substantive claims rooted in the Fifth Amendment, and *Boumediene* could not have extended one without the other. Yet the Court in *Boumediene* clearly differentiated between the Suspension and Due Process Clauses and carefully limited its holding to the Suspension Clause by noting "our opinion does not address the content of the law that governs petitioners' detention" and "holds only that petitioners before us are entitled to seek the writ." The Court also recognized the exceptional nature of its holding, recognizing "[i]t is true that before today the Court has never held that noncitizens detained by our Government in territory over which another country maintains *de jure* sovereignty have any rights under our Constitution."
>
> In *Boumediene*, the Court established for the first time that the Suspension Clause guarantees Guantanamo detainees a "meaningful opportunity" to challenge their detention before a court with "the power to order the conditional release of an individual unlawfully detained." Thus, a writ of habeas corpus provides a procedure—a "mechanism" or a "device"—that detainees may use to challenge their detention. The writ also provides a judicial remedy, namely, the power to order "conditional release" when the Executive has exceeded its recognized detention authority. . .
>
> Beyond extending the writ's procedure and remedy, however, the Supreme Court explicitly "disclaimed any intention to disturb existing law governing the extraterritorial reach of any constitutional provisions, other than the Suspension Clause."

> Second, Al Hela argues *Boumediene* established a universal three-factor test for the extraterritorial extension of constitutional rights, and that under this test we must extend the Due Process Clause of the Fifth Amendment to Guantanamo Bay. Since *Boumediene* derived the factors of its "functional test" from "pragmatic concerns" animating the *Eisentrager* decision, Al Hela maintains we should distinguish *Eisentrager* by concluding that these factors apply differently to Guantanamo Bay, Cuba, than they did to Landsberg Prison, Germany. This argument overshoots the mark. *Boumediene* did not create a new framework for lower courts to incorporate constitutional rights beyond our nation's borders.
>
> To be sure, *Boumediene* applied a "functional test" to determine when and where the Suspension Clause follows United States forces abroad. . . . But nothing in *Boumediene* suggests this functional test applies beyond the Suspension Clause. To the contrary, the Court emphasized the limited and exceptional nature of its holding, a conclusion bolstered by the fact that the Court has never applied *Boumediene*'s "functional test" to any other constitutional provision. Nor has this court applied *Boumediene* to constitutional provisions other than the Suspension Clause or extended the extraterritorial reach of the Suspension Clause beyond Guantanamo Bay.
>
> Al Hela effectively asks us to expand *Boumediene* and abrogate *Eisentrager* as well as longstanding circuit precedent. Yet *Boumediene* recognized only the availability of habeas relief to detainees in Guantanamo Bay. The "Privilege of the Writ of Habeas Corpus" is a "procedural protection" for challenging unlawful detention but does not include substantive rights. The Court addressed only the availability of the writ and specifically declined to go further. Therefore, *Eisentrager* and the cases that follow remain good law, and we have no authority to undermine or to ignore controlling decisions of the Supreme Court. Rather, lower courts "should follow the case which directly controls, leaving to [the Supreme] Court the prerogative of overruling its own decisions." . . .
>
> While we must enforce constitutional limits on the Executive Branch in this context as in any other, it would be well beyond our authority to extend or to create new constitutional limits on the conduct of wartime detention by the political branches.

973 F.3d at 140–43.

Does the *Al Hela* panel provide a principled basis for declining to extend *Boumediene* beyond the Suspension Clause? Can you think of one?

Does the availability of the Suspension Clause to detainees entail the availability of whatever substantive constitutional rights they might seek to enforce via habeas? Does this follow from the proposition that "every right, when withheld, must have a remedy, and every injury its proper redress," *Marbury v. Madison*, 5 U.S. (1 Cranch) 137, 163 (1803)? Or could the Suspension Clause, in some circumstances, be a remedy in search of a right?

Concurring in *Al Hela*, Judge Griffith argued that it was unnecessary to decide whether Guantanamo detainees have procedural due process rights, given that in his view Al Hela's claims failed under the Suspension Clause, and that the D.C. Circuit had "already afforded detainees as much protection under the Suspension Clause as we have afforded non-detainees in similar settings under the Due Process Clause." 973 F.3d at 153 (Griffith, J., concurring). Is this the same as asserting that the Constitution regulates the procedures by which the U.S. government deals with alleged enemy combatants abroad?

On April 21, 2021, the D.C. Circuit granted Al Hela's petition for rehearing *en banc*. By that time, the government had abandoned its position that detainees at Guantanamo categorically lack due process rights.

Extraterritoriality and Implied Constitutional Remedies

Can a U.S. government actor, acting in the U.S., be held liable for violating the constitutional rights of a foreign national who remains in his home country? The following tragic case explores that question.

HERNANDEZ V. MESA

140 S. Ct. 735 (2020).

JUSTICE ALITO delivered the opinion of the Court. . . .

I

. . . Sergio Adrián Hernández Güereca, a 15-year-old Mexican national, was with a group of friends in a concrete culvert that separates El Paso, Texas, from Ciudad Juarez, Mexico. The border runs through the center of the culvert, which was designed to hold the waters of the Rio Grande River but is now largely dry. Border Patrol Agent Jesus Mesa, Jr., detained one of Hernández's friends who had run onto the United States' side of the culvert. After Hernández, who was also on the United States' side, ran back across the culvert onto Mexican soil, Agent Mesa fired two shots at Hernández; one struck and killed him on the other side of the border.

Petitioners and Agent Mesa disagree about what Hernández and his friends were doing at the time of shooting. According to petitioners, they were simply playing a game, running across the culvert, touching the fence on the U.S. side, and then running back across the border. According to Agent Mesa, Hernández and his friends were involved in an illegal border crossing attempt, and they pelted him with rocks.

The shooting quickly became an international incident, with the United States and Mexico disagreeing about how the matter should be handled. On the United States' side, the Department of Justice conducted an investigation. When it finished, the Department, while expressing regret over Hernández's death, concluded that Agent Mesa had not violated Customs and Border Patrol policy or training, and it declined to bring charges or take other action against him. Mexico was not and is not satisfied with the U.S. investigation. It requested that Agent Mesa be extradited to face criminal charges in a Mexican court, a request that the United States has denied.

Petitioners, Hernández's parents, were also dissatisfied and therefore brought suit for damages in the United States District Court for the Western District of Texas. Among other claims, they sought recovery of damages under *Bivens* [*v. Six Unknown Fed. Narcotics Agents*, 403 U.S. 388 (1971)], alleging that Mesa violated Hernández's Fourth and Fifth Amendment rights. . . .

II

In *Bivens*, the Court broke new ground by holding that a person claiming to be the victim of an unlawful arrest and search could bring a Fourth Amendment claim for damages against the responsible agents even though no federal statute authorized such a claim. The Court subsequently extended *Bivens* to cover two additional constitutional claims: in *Davis v. Passman*, 442 U.S. 228 (1979), a former congressional staffer's Fifth Amendment claim of dismissal based on sex, and in *Carlson v. Green*, 446 U.S. 14 (1980), a federal prisoner's Eighth Amendment claim for failure to provide adequate medical treatment. After those decisions, however, the Court changed course.

Bivens, *Davis*, and *Carlson* were the products of an era when the Court routinely inferred "causes of action" that were "not explicit" in the text of the provision that was allegedly violated. . . . *Bivens* extended this practice to claims based on the Constitution itself.

In later years, we came to appreciate more fully the tension between this practice and the Constitution's separation of legislative and judicial power. The Constitution grants legislative power to Congress; this Court and the lower federal courts, by contrast, have only "judicial Power." Art. III, § 1. But when a court recognizes an implied claim for damages on the ground that doing so furthers the "purpose" of the law, the court risks arrogating legislative power. No law "pursues its purposes at all costs." Instead, lawmaking involves balancing interests and often demands compromise. Thus, a lawmaking body that enacts a provision that creates a right or prohibits specified conduct may not wish to pursue the provision's purpose to the extent of authorizing private suits for damages. For this reason, finding that a damages remedy is implied by a provision that makes no reference to that remedy may upset the careful balance of interests struck by the lawmakers.

This problem does not exist when a common-law court, which exercises a degree of lawmaking authority, fleshes out the remedies available for a common-law tort. Analogizing *Bivens* to the work of a common-law court, petitioners and some of their *amici* make much of the fact that common-law claims against federal officers for intentional torts were once available. But *Erie R. Co. v. Tompkins*, 304 U.S. 64, 78 (1938), held that "[t]here is no federal general common law," and therefore federal courts today cannot fashion new claims in the way that they could before 1938.

With the demise of federal general common law, a federal court's authority to recognize a damages remedy must rest at bottom on a statute enacted by Congress, and no statute expressly creates a *Bivens* remedy. Justice Harlan's *Bivens* concurrence argued that this power is inherent in the grant of federal question jurisdiction, but our later cases have demanded a clearer manifestation of congressional intent.

In both statutory and constitutional cases, our watchword is caution. For example, in *Jesner v. Arab Bank, PLC*, 138 S.Ct. 1386, 1391–1403 (2018), we expressed doubt about our authority to recognize any causes of action not expressly created by Congress. And we declined to recognize a claim against a foreign corporation under the Alien Tort Statute.

In constitutional cases, we have been at least equally reluctant to create new causes of action. We have recognized that Congress is best positioned to evaluate "whether, and the extent to which, monetary and other liabilities should be imposed upon individual officers and employees of the Federal Government" based on constitutional torts. We have stated that expansion of *Bivens* is "a 'disfavored' judicial activity," and have gone so far as to observe that if "the Court's three *Bivens* cases [had] been . . . decided today," it is doubtful that we would have reached the same result. And for almost 40 years, we have consistently rebuffed requests to add to the claims allowed under *Bivens* [citing cases].

When asked to extend *Bivens*, we engage in a two-step inquiry. We first inquire whether the request involves a claim that arises in a "new context" or involves a "new category of defendants." And our understanding of a "new context" is broad. We regard a context as "new" if it is "different in a meaningful way from previous *Bivens* cases decided by this Court."

When we find that a claim arises in a new context, we proceed to the second step and ask whether there are any "special factors that counsel hesitation" about granting the extension. If there are—that is, if we have reason to pause before applying *Bivens* in a new context or to a new class of defendants—we reject the request.

We have not attempted to "create an exhaustive list" of factors that may provide a reason not to extend *Bivens*, but we have explained that "central to [this] analysis" are "separation-of-powers principles." We thus consider the risk of interfering with the authority of the other branches, and we ask whether "there are sound reasons to think Congress might doubt the efficacy or necessity of a damages remedy," and "whether the Judiciary is well suited, absent congressional action or instruction, to consider and weigh the costs and benefits of allowing a damages action to proceed."

III

A

The *Bivens* claims in this case assuredly arise in a new context. Petitioners contend that their Fourth and Fifth Amendment claims do not involve a new context because *Bivens* and *Davis* involved claims under those same two amendments, but that argument rests on a basic misunderstanding of what our cases mean by a new context. A claim may arise in a new context even if it is based on the same constitutional provision as a claim in a case in which a damages remedy was previously recognized. And once we look beyond the constitutional provisions invoked in *Bivens*, *Davis*, and the present case, it is glaringly obvious that petitioners' claims involve a new context, *i.e.*, one that is meaningfully different. *Bivens* concerned an allegedly unconstitutional arrest and search carried out in New York City; *Davis* concerned alleged sex discrimination on Capitol Hill. There is a world of difference between those claims and petitioners' cross-border shooting claims, where "the risk of disruptive intrusion by the Judiciary into the functioning of other branches" is significant.

Because petitioners assert claims that arise in a new context, we must proceed to the next step and ask whether there are factors that counsel hesitation. As we will explain, there are multiple, related factors that raise warning flags.

B

The first is the potential effect on foreign relations. "The political branches, not the Judiciary, have the responsibility and institutional capacity to weigh foreign-policy concerns." *Jesner*, 138 S.Ct. at 1403. Indeed, we have said that "matters relating to the conduct of foreign relations . . . are so exclusively entrusted to the political branches of government as to be largely immune from judicial inquiry or interference." "Thus, unless Congress specifically has provided otherwise, courts traditionally have been reluctant to intrude upon the authority of the Executive in [these matters]." We must therefore be especially wary before allowing a *Bivens* remedy that impinges on this arena.

A cross-border shooting is by definition an international incident; it involves an event that occurs simultaneously in two countries and affects both countries' interests. Such an incident may lead to a disagreement between those countries, as happened in this case.

The United States, through the Executive Branch, which has "the lead role in foreign policy," has taken the position that this incident should be handled in a particular way—namely, that Agent Mesa should not face charges in the United States nor be extradited to stand trial in Mexico. As noted, the Executive decided not to take action against Agent Mesa because it found that he "did not act inconsistently with [Border Patrol] policy or training regarding use of force." We presume that Border Patrol policy and training incorporate both the Executive's understanding of the Fourth Amendment's prohibition of unreasonable seizures and the Executive's assessment of circumstances at the border. Thus, the Executive judged Agent Mesa's conduct by what it regards as reasonable conduct by an agent under the circumstances that Mesa faced at the time of the shooting, and based on the application of those standards, it declined to prosecute. The Executive does not want a Mexican criminal court to judge Agent Mesa's conduct by whatever standards would be applicable under Mexican law; nor does it want a jury in a *Bivens* action to apply its own understanding of what constituted reasonable conduct by a Border Patrol agent under the circumstances of this case. Such a jury determination, the Executive claims, would risk the "embarrassment of our government abroad" through "multifarious pronouncements by various departments on one question."

The Government of Mexico has taken a different view of what should be done. It has requested that Agent Mesa be extradited for criminal prosecution in a Mexican court under Mexican law, and it has supported petitioners' *Bivens* suit. In a brief filed in this Court, Mexico suggests that shootings by Border Patrol agents are a persistent problem and argues that the United States has an obligation under international law, specifically Article 6(1) of the International Covenant on Civil and Political Rights, to provide a remedy for the shooting in this case. Mexico states that it "has a responsibility to look after the well-being of its nationals" and that "it is a priority to Mexico to see that the United States provides adequate means to hold the agents accountable and to compensate the victims."

Both the United States and Mexico have legitimate and important interests that may be affected by the way in which this matter is handled. The United States has an interest in ensuring that agents assigned the difficult and important task of policing the border are held to standards and judged by procedures that satisfy United States law and do not undermine the agents' effectiveness and morale. Mexico has an interest in exercising sovereignty over its territory and in protecting and obtaining justice for its nationals. It is not our task to arbitrate between them.

In the absence of judicial intervention, the United States and Mexico would attempt to reconcile their interests through diplomacy—and that has occurred. The broad issue of violence along the border, the occurrence of crossborder shootings, and this particular matter have been addressed through diplomatic channels. In 2014, Mexico and the United States established a joint Border Violence Prevention Council, and the two countries have addressed cross-border shootings through the United States-Mexico bilateral Human Rights Dialogue. Following the Justice Department investigation in the present case, the United States reaffirmed its commitment to "work with the Mexican government within existing mechanisms and agreements to prevent future incidents."

For these reasons, petitioners' assertion that their claims have "nothing to do with the substance or conduct of U.S. foreign policy" is plainly wrong.[3]

C

[T]he issue here implicates an element of national security. One of the ways in which the Executive protects this country is by attempting to control the movement of people and goods across the border, and that is a daunting task. The United States' border with Mexico extends for 1,900 miles, and every day thousands of persons and a large volume of goods enter this country at ports of entry on the southern border. The lawful passage of people and goods in both directions across the border is beneficial to both countries.

Unfortunately, there is also a large volume of illegal cross-border traffic. During the last fiscal year, approximately 850,000 persons were apprehended attempting to enter the United States illegally from Mexico, and large quantities of drugs were smuggled across the border. In addition, powerful criminal organizations operating on both sides of the border present a serious law enforcement problem for both countries.

On the United States' side, the responsibility for attempting to prevent the illegal entry of dangerous persons and goods rests primarily with the U.S. Customs and Border Protection Agency, and one of its main responsibilities is to "detect, respond to, and interdict terrorists, drug smugglers and traffickers, human smugglers and traffickers, and other

[3] It is no answer to argue, as Mexico does, that refusing to extend *Bivens* "is what [would] negatively affect international relations." When a third party intervenes and takes sides in a dispute between two countries, one country is likely to be pleased and the other displeased. But no matter which side the third party supports, it will have injected itself into their relations.

persons who may undermine the security of the United States." 6 U.S.C. § 211(c)(5). While Border Patrol agents often work miles from the border, some, like Agent Mesa, are stationed right at the border and have the responsibility of attempting to prevent illegal entry. For these reasons, the conduct of agents positioned at the border has a clear and strong connection to national security. . .

Petitioners protest that "shooting people who are just walking down a street in Mexico" does not involve national security, but that misses the point. The question is not whether national security requires such conduct—of course, it does not—but whether the Judiciary should alter the framework established by the political branches for addressing cases in which it is alleged that lethal force was unlawfully employed by an agent at the border. . . . Since regulating the conduct of agents at the border unquestionably has national security implications, the risk of undermining border security provides reason to hesitate before extending *Bivens* into this field.

D

Our reluctance to take that step is reinforced by our survey of what Congress has done in statutes addressing related matters. We frequently "look to analogous statutes for guidance on the appropriate boundaries of judge-made causes of action." When foreign relations are implicated, it "is even more important . . . 'to look for legislative guidance before exercising innovative authority over substantive law.' " Accordingly, it is "telling" that Congress has repeatedly declined to authorize the award of damages for injury inflicted outside our borders.

A leading example is 42 U.S.C. § 1983, which permits the recovery of damages for constitutional violations by officers acting under color of *state* law. We have described *Bivens* as a "more limited" "federal analog" to § 1983. It is therefore instructive that Congress chose to make § 1983 available only to "citizen[s] of the United States or other person[s] within the jurisdiction thereof." It would be "anomalous to impute . . . a judicially implied cause of action beyond the bounds [Congress has] delineated for [a] comparable express caus[e] of action." *Blue Chip Stamps v. Manor Drug Stores*, 421 U.S. 723, 736 (1975). Thus, the limited scope of § 1983 weighs against recognition of the *Bivens* claim at issue here.

Section 1983's express limitation to the claims brought by citizens and persons subject to United States jurisdiction is especially significant, but even if this explicit limitation were lacking, we would presume that § 1983 did not apply abroad. See *RJR Nabisco, Inc. v. European Community*, 136 S.Ct. 2090, 2100 (2016) ("Absent clearly expressed congressional intent to the contrary, federal laws will be construed to have only domestic application"). We presume that statutes do not apply extraterritorially to "ensure that the Judiciary does not erroneously adopt an interpretation of

U.S. law that carries foreign policy consequences not clearly intended by the political branches." *Kiobel v. Royal Dutch Petroleum Co.*, 569 U.S. 108, 116 (2013); see also *EEOC v. Arabian American Oil Co.*, 499 U.S. 244, 248 (1991).

If this danger provides a reason for caution when Congress has enacted a statute but has not provided expressly whether it applies abroad, we have even greater reason for hesitation in deciding whether to extend a judge-made cause of action beyond our borders. "[T]he danger of unwarranted judicial interference in the conduct of foreign policy is magnified" where "the question is not what Congress has done but instead what courts may do." *Kiobel*, 569 U.S. at 116. Where Congress has not spoken at all, the likelihood of impinging on its foreign affairs authority is especially acute.

Congress's treatment of ordinary tort claims against federal officers is also revealing. As petitioners and their *amici* stress, the traditional way in which civil litigation addressed abusive conduct by federal officers was by subjecting them to liability for common-law torts. For many years, such claims could be raised in state or federal court, and this Court occasionally considered tort suits against federal officers for extraterritorial injuries. See, *e.g.*, *Mitchell v. Harmony*, 13 How. 115, 14 L.Ed. 75 (1852) (affirming award in trespass suit brought by U.S. citizen against U.S. Army officer who seized personal property in Mexico during the Mexican-American war). After *Erie*, federal common-law claims were out, but we recognized the continuing viability of state-law tort suits against federal officials as recently as *Westfall v. Erwin*, 484 U.S. 292 (1988).

In response to that decision, Congress passed the so-called Westfall Act, formally the Federal Employees Liability Reform and Tort Compensation Act of 1988, 28 U.S.C. § 2679. That Act makes the Federal Tort Claims Act (FTCA) "the exclusive remedy for most claims against Government employees arising out of their official conduct." Thus, a person injured by a federal employee may seek recovery directly from the United States under the FTCA, but the FTCA bars "[a]ny claim arising in a foreign country." § 2680(k).[10] The upshot is that claims that would otherwise permit the recovery of damages are barred if the injury occurred abroad.

Yet another example is provided by the Torture Victim Protection Act of 1991, note following 28 U.S.C. § 1350, which created a cause of action that may be brought by an alien in a U.S. court under the Alien Tort Statute, § 1350. Under the Torture Victim Protection Act, a damages action may be brought by or on behalf of a victim of torture or an extrajudicial

[10] Petitioners contend that Congress excluded claims arising abroad in order to avoid subjecting the United States to liability under foreign law, something that cannot occur under *Bivens*. But neither the legislative history recounted in *Sosa v. Alvarez-Machain*, 542 U.S. 692, 707 (2004), nor anything else offered by petitioners shows that this was the only reason for this limitation. And the fact remains that the FTCA does not permit claims for torts committed abroad, a limitation that is consistent with Congress's general practice of avoiding extraterritorial legislation. See, *e.g.*, *Kiobel v. Royal Dutch Petroleum Co.*, 569 U.S. 108, 115–116 (2013).

killing carried out by a person who acted under the authority of a foreign state. Consequently, this provision, which is often employed to seek redress for acts committed abroad, cannot be used to sue a United States officer.

These statutes form a pattern that is important for present purposes. When Congress has enacted statutes creating a damages remedy for persons injured by United States Government officers, it has taken care to preclude claims for injuries that occurred abroad.

Instead, when Congress has provided compensation for injuries suffered by aliens outside the United States, it has done so by empowering Executive Branch officials to make payments under circumstances found to be appropriate. . . . This pattern of congressional action—refraining from authorizing damages actions for injury inflicted abroad by Government officers, while providing alternative avenues for compensation in some situations—gives us further reason to hesitate about extending *Bivens* in this case.

E

In sum, this case features multiple factors that counsel hesitation about extending *Bivens,* but they can all be condensed to one concern—respect for the separation of powers. "Foreign policy and national security decisions are 'delicate, complex, and involve large elements of prophecy' for which 'the Judiciary has neither aptitude, facilities[,] nor responsibility.' " To avoid upsetting the delicate web of international relations, we typically presume that even congressionally crafted causes of action do not apply outside our borders. These concerns are only heightened when judges are asked to fashion constitutional remedies. Congress, which has authority in the field of foreign affairs, has chosen not to create liability in similar statutes, leaving the resolution of extraterritorial claims brought by foreign nationals to executive officials and the diplomatic process. . . .

[JUSTICE THOMAS, joined by JUSTICE GORSUCH, argued in concurrence that *Bivens* should be overruled.]

JUSTICE GINSBURG, with whom JUSTICE BREYER, JUSTICE SOTOMAYOR, and JUSTICE KAGAN join, dissenting.

. . . Plaintiffs' *Bivens* action arises in a setting kin to *Bivens* itself: Mesa, plaintiffs allege, acted in disregard of instructions governing his conduct and of Hernández's constitutional rights. . . . For these reasons, as Mesa acknowledged at oral argument, Hernández's parents could have maintained a *Bivens* action had the bullet hit Hernández while he was running up or down the United States side of the embankment.

The only salient difference here: the fortuity that the bullet happened to strike Hernández on the Mexican side of the embankment. But Hernández's location at the precise moment the bullet landed should not matter one whit. After all, "the purpose of *Bivens* is to deter the *officer*."

And primary conduct constrained by the Fourth Amendment is an *officer*'s unjustified resort to excessive force. Mesa's allegedly unwarranted deployment of deadly force occurred on United States soil. It scarcely makes sense for a remedy trained on deterring rogue officer conduct to turn upon a happenstance subsequent to the conduct—a bullet landing in one half of a culvert, not the other. . . .

Finally, although the bullet happened to land on the Mexican side of the culvert, the United States, as in *Bivens*, unquestionably has jurisdiction to prescribe law governing a Border Patrol agent's conduct. That prescriptive jurisdiction reaches "conduct that . . . takes place within [United States] territory." Restatement (Third) of Foreign Relations Law of the United States § 402 (1986). The place of a rogue officer's conduct "has peculiar significance" to choice of the applicable law where, as here, "the primary purpose of the tort rule involved is to deter or punish misconduct." Restatement (Second) of Conflict of Laws § 145, Comment *e*, p. 420 (1969).[1]

Even accepting, *arguendo*, that the setting in this case could be characterized as "new," there is still no good reason why Hernández's parents should face a closed courtroom door. As in *Bivens*, plaintiffs lack recourse to alternative remedies. And not one of the "special factors" the Court identifies weigh any differently based on where a bullet happens to land. . . .

The special factors featured by the Court relate, in the main, to foreign policy and national security. But . . . no policies or policymakers are challenged in this case. Plaintiffs target the rogue actions of a rank-and-file law enforcement officer acting in violation of rules controlling his office.

. . . The Court nevertheless asserts that the instant suit has a "potential effect on foreign relations" because it invites courts "to arbitrate between" the United States and Mexico. Plaintiffs, however, have brought a civil damages action, no different from one a federal court would entertain had the fatal shot hit Hernández before he reached the Mexican side of the border. True, cross-border shootings spark bilateral discussion, but so too does a range of smuggling and other border-related issues that courts routinely address "concurrently with whatever diplomacy may also be addressing them." . . .

Moreover, the Court, in this case, cannot escape a "potential effect on foreign relations" by declining to recognize a *Bivens* action. As the Mexican

---

[1] [Relocated footnote:] *United States v. Verdugo-Urquidez*, 494 U.S. 259 (1990), is not dispositive of the Fourth Amendment claim in this case. There, the Court held that the Fourth Amendment did not apply to federal agents' warrantless search of a Mexican drug trafficker's home in Mexico. *Verdugo-Urquidez*'s practical concerns, among them, that a warrant issued by a U.S. judge "would be a dead letter outside the United States," *id.*, at 274, do not bear on the complaint filed by Hernández's parents. In contrast to *Verdugo-Urquidez*, it would not be "impracticable" or "anomalous" to subject Mesa's U.S.-based conduct to Fourth Amendment scrutiny.

Government alerted the Court: "[R]efus[al] to consider [Hernández's] parents' claim on the merits . . . is what has the potential to negatively affect international relations."

Notably, recognizing a *Bivens* suit here honors our Nation's international commitments. Article 9(5) of the International Covenant on Civil and Political Rights (ICCPR) provides that "[a]nyone who has been the victim of unlawful arrest or detention shall have an enforceable right to compensation." The United States ratified the ICCPR with the "understandin[g]" that Article 9(5) "require[s] the provision of effective and enforceable mechanisms by which a victim of an unlawful arrest or detention or a miscarriage of justice may seek and, where justified, obtain compensation from either the responsible individual or the appropriate governmental entity." One fitting mechanism to obtain compensation is a *Bivens* action.

The Court also asserts, as cause for hesitation, "the risk of undermining border security." But the Court speaks with generality of the national-security involvement of Border Patrol officers. It does not home in on how a *Bivens* suit for an unjustified killing would in fact undermine security at the border. . . . Instructions regulating Border Patrol agents tell them to guard against deploying unjustified deadly force. See 8 CFR § 287.8(a)(2)(ii). Given that instruction, I do not grasp how allowing a *Bivens* action here would intrude upon the political branches' national-security prerogatives. . . .

Section 1983 actions, the Court points out, are available only to "person[s] within the jurisdiction" of the United States. 42 U.S.C. § 1983. That statute has, as its provenance, Reconstruction-era policies aiming to secure to former slaves federal rights and to ward off state and local incursion on those rights. "It is inconceivable that . . . Congress [then] thought about (and deliberately excluded liability for) cross-border incidents involving federal officials."

The FTCA is also inapposite. Its exclusion of "claim[s] arising in a foreign country," 28 U.S.C. § 2680(k), reflects "Congress's 'unwilling[ness] to subject the United States to liabilities depending upon the laws of a foreign power.'" *Sosa v. Alvarez-Machain*, 542 U.S. 692, 707 (2004). Here, however, the suit arises under U.S. law. Even as the Westfall Act amended the FTCA to make it the "exclusive" remedy for scope-of-employment claims against Government officers, § 2679(b)(1), Congress carved out an exception for *Bivens* suits, § 2679(b)(2)(A) (excepting civil claims "brought for a violation of the Constitution of the United States"). The Torture Victim Protection Act of 1991 applies exclusively to wrongdoers acting under color of *foreign* law. 28 U.S.C. § 1350 Note. The conduct of federal and state officers is outside that Act's purview.

Nor are concerns sometimes attending application of our law abroad implicated in this case. True, the Court has applied a "presumption against extraterritorial application" to statutes that do not make plain their governance beyond U.S. borders. *Kiobel v. Royal Dutch Petroleum Co.*, 569 U.S. 108, 115 (2013). But plaintiffs in this case allege a tort stemming from stateside conduct. Cf. *id.* at 124–125 (if conduct at issue "touch[es] and concern[s] the territory of the United States . . . with sufficient force," the presumption against extraterritoriality is displaced). This case scarcely resembles those in which applying "U.S. law . . . to conduct in foreign countries" might spark "international discord." *RJR Nabisco, Inc. v. European Community*, 136 S.Ct. 2090, 2100 (2016). Quite the opposite. Withholding a *Bivens* suit here threatens to exacerbate bilateral relations and in no way fosters our international commitments. . . .

According to *amici* former Customs and Border Protection officials, "the United States has not extradited a Border Patrol agent to stand trial in Mexico, and to [*amici*'s] knowledge has itself prosecuted only one agent in a cross-border shooting." These *amici* warn that, "[w]ithout the possibility of civil liability, the unlikely prospect of discipline or criminal prosecution will not provide a meaningful deterrent to abuse at the border." In short, it is all too apparent that to redress injuries like the one suffered here, it is *Bivens* or nothing. I resist the conclusion that "nothing" is the answer required in this case. . . .

---

(1) Does a U.S. officer, acting in the U.S., violate the Constitution when he shoots an innocent Mexican national standing in Mexico? The Supreme Court in *Hernandez* sidesteps this issue, but the Fifth Circuit reached it in its initial encounter with the case. Relying on *Verdugo-Urquidez*, that court held that Hernández lacked a Fourth Amendment claim because he had "no 'significant voluntary connection' to the United States." *Hernandez v. United States*, 785 F.3d 117, 119 (5th Cir. 2015) (*en banc*). As for the Fifth Amendment, the court held that Agent Mesa was protected by qualified immunity because no case had clearly established that that the amendment proscribes cross-border shootings. (The Supreme Court vacated and reversed this judgment, cautioning the Fifth Circuit to address the availability of the *Bivens* remedy before reaching the substantive constitutional questions. See *Hernandez v. Mesa*, 137 S. Ct. 2003 (2017) (per curiam).)

Were the Fifth Circuit's holdings correct as a substantive matter? Was Hernández seeking to enforce the Constitution extraterritorially? Or is Justice Ginsburg correct that under conventional choice-of-law rules (such as § 145 of the Second Restatement) the relevant act occurred in the U.S.? Even if the relevant act occurred abroad, is Justice Ginsburg right that *Verdugo-Urquidez* is distinguishable because, unlike the warrant requirement, the bar on unreasonable seizures can be enforced abroad without insuperable practical difficulties? Were practical difficulties the basis for the plurality opinion in *Verdugo-Urquidez*? For Justice Kennedy's concurrence?

If one were to apply *Boumediene*'s multi-factor approach, with its emphasis on "practical considerations," does the fact that the United States is the only country that can regulate its border agents' conduct point toward applying the Fourth Amendment here? If a *Bivens* action went forward, would there be any possibility of a conflict with Mexican law? Are the foreign relations concerns cited by the majority in *Hernandez* relevant to the substantive question of whether the Constitution applies?

(2) As the *Hernandez* Court acknowledges, federal courts in the nineteenth century sometimes awarded damages against federal officers for cross-border wrongs. Thus, the Court in *The Apollon*, 22 U.S. 362 (1824), allowed the owners of a French vessel seized in foreign waters to recover damages from federal officials. Justice Story wrote:

> It may be fit and proper for the government, in the exercise of the high discretion confided to the executive, for great public purposes, to act on a sudden emergency, or to prevent an irreparable mischief, by summary measures, which are not found in the text of the laws. Such measures are properly matters of state, and if the responsibility is taken, under justifiable circumstances, the Legislature will doubtless apply a proper indemnity. But this Court can only look to the questions, whether the laws have been violated; and if they were, justice demands, that the injured party should receive a suitable redress.

Id. at 366–67. See also, *e.g.*, *Maley v. Shattuck*, 7 U.S. 458 (1806); *Little v. Barreme*, 6 U.S. 170 (1804).

Justice Alito argues that such cases are an inadequate basis on which to premise a *Bivens* remedy because federal courts are no longer in the business, post-*Erie*, of creating general common law. Is this a persuasive response? Does it speak to the antecedent question whether cross-border seizures can violate the Constitution?

(3) The majority in *Hernandez* rests its holding on the scope of the *Bivens* remedy rather than the scope of the Constitution. Were you persuaded that there are "special factors that counsel hesitation" in extending *Bivens* to cross-border cases? How does the Court's *Bivens* analysis differ from the usual presumption against extraterritoriality as applied, for instance, to the implied Section 10(b) cause of action in *Morrison* or the private RICO cause of action in *RJR Nabisco*? Is the Court's rejection of Hernández's claim grounded in extraterritoriality concerns or in the majority's antipathy to *Bivens*?

(4) The Court finds support for its holding in Congress's decision, in the Westfall Act, to make the FTCA the exclusive statutory remedy for torts committed by federal officers and to expressly bar "[a]ny claim arising in a foreign country." Professor Fallon argues that, by preempting state law and thereby "creating a substantially broadened category of victims of constitutional lawbreaking for whom it is *Bivens* actions or nothing," Congress indicated that *Bivens* should retain broad vitality so that victims of constitutional torts are not left without a remedy. Fallon, *Bidding Farewell to Constitutional Torts*, 107 Cal. L. Rev. 933, 989 (2019). Which side got the statutory interpretation question right?

(5) Should U.S. agents acting abroad be bound by the terms of human rights treaties entered into by the United States, or are these treaties similarly limited to actions taken within the United States? See Meron, *Extraterritoriality of Human Rights Treaties,* 89 Am. J. Int'l L. 78, 80–81 (1995) ("In view of the purposes and objects of human rights treaties, there is no a priori reason to limit a state's obligation to respect human rights to its national territory.").

SECTION 2. THE EUROPEAN PERSPECTIVE[15]

MATHIAS REIMANN, CONFLICT OF LAWS IN WESTERN EUROPE: A GUIDE THROUGH THE JUNGLE

3–17 (1995).

1. The Sources of Law

Like most areas of modern Western law, European conflicts law is a medley of statutory rules, case law, and academic writings. While in theory only statutes are binding in the civil law culture (i.e., in most of Western Europe), in practice, appellate decisions are followed almost as a matter of course, and scholars wield considerable influence. Thus, in practice, the situation looks roughly like the U.S. scene, at least at first glance. Yet, an American lawyer should be aware that there are in fact significant differences. They concern the respective emphasis on the various sources of law and the conception of statutes. These differences are matters of degree but are of considerable practical relevance.

a. The Primacy of Conventions and Statutes

In contrast to her American colleague, a European conflicts lawyer seeks rules primarily in conventions and statutes; other sources take second place.

[15] We gratefully acknowledge the assistance of Mathäus Mogendorf, LL.M. candidate at the University of California, Berkeley, Law School and Jakob Hölldobler, LL.M. candidate at the University of Pennsylvania Law School, in the selection, analysis, and translation of materials in this section.

While it has, of course, long ceased to be true that Anglo-American law consists mainly of cases whereas continental law is statutory, this traditional distinction still matters. It continues to shape the view of the relative importance of legal sources in the two systems. For continental lawyers, the primacy of statutory law is assumed and is welcome, while Americans shy away from statutes and feel more at home with cases, especially, as every teacher knows, in law school.

Moreover, the traditional distinction continues to hold particularly true in conflicts law. In the United States, statutory rules on jurisdiction, choice of law, or recognition of judgments are few and of limited importance; they mostly supplement an area dominated by case law. In Western Europe, in contrast, most basic rules are legislatively enacted. It is true that there are subjects and countries where statutory conflicts law is scarce and case law reigns supreme, especially in choice of law. Yet this is the exception, not, as in the United States, the rule. . .

Not only do statutory rules govern most of European conflicts law, but they also enjoy greater respect than their counterparts in the United States. In continental Europe, statutes have since the middle ages been regarded not merely as one legal source among others but as the paramount texts and thus the unquestionable basis of all legal discourse. In the civil law tradition, law is regarded as coming primarily from the legislator, instead of from the courts, and thus in statutory form. Statutes thereby enjoy utmost respect.

This respect manifests itself in two seemingly contradictory ways: . . . On the one hand, the wording of statutes and conventions is taken very seriously. It is the point of departure of all legal analysis in Western Europe. Drafted with care and precision, statutory language is considered to provide the answers in most cases. Thus, where statutory provisions plainly apply, they decide an issue without further ado. Where they leave room for disagreement, they are the constant and most important point of reference. Gaps are filled and doubts resolved primarily by extrapolation from other parts or from the overall structure of the act. Case law and scholarly opinion may aid the interpretation, but they will, as a rule, serve a mere auxiliary function.

On the other hand, continental judges and scholars tend to read statutes broadly and to reason from them, like an American judge does from a case, by analogy. In other words, they begin with the statute's exact working, but they do not end with it. Instead, they consider the statute in order to give general guidance for similar cases, interpret it teleologically, and assume that the decision that comes closest to the spirit of the statute is normally the best. All this evinces both deference to the legislator and trust that statutory rules embody reasonable and useful principles.

b. Case Law and Scholarship

This is not to belittle the role of case law and scholarly views. Both play a significant role in European conflicts law as well. In the absence of enacted rules, case law governs whole areas. . . Yet, even here the courts rarely endorse general theories or innovate approaches. They rather go about the business of deciding cases in an unpretentious and traditional manner that strikes an American observer as uninspired, if not boring.

Academic opinion also has long held a prominent place, especially in choice of law. In contrast to the judge-made common law, the civil law has been developed largely by scholars ever since the days of the Roman emperor and particularly since the high middle ages. Even today, academic writing often precedes and thus prepares the way for both statutes and court decisions, so that the jurists' views enjoy great respect in legislatures and courts. Academic writers have an even greater impact in continental Europe than in the United States partially because the European academic literature is not nearly as preoccupied with grand theoretical issues as American conflicts scholarship, but rather is more focused on the concrete practical problems that courts face. It is thus likely to strike an American observer as rule-orientated and theoretically barren. Yet, it can also, particularly in the general parts of the great treatises, be abstract and dogmatic in the sense of being preoccupied with the definition, interpretation, and ordering of general concepts the practical importance of which is not always clear. . .

2. The Importance of Rules and the Method of Analysis

European conflict law differs from its American counterpart in its drive for clarity of concepts and precision of rules, in its ambition to reach results by logical deduction from them, and in its desire to maintain a logical coherence among them.

a. The Preference for Rules

In modern American conflicts law, both in choice of law and personal jurisdiction, the emphasis has shifted from rules and bright-line tests to approaches and multifactor analysis, i.e., to more general and open-ended methodologies. In contrast, European conflicts lawyers continue to look primarily for and to rules. In style, most European conflicts law thus reminds an American observer of a Restatement: it tends to be blackletter. This is particularly true where statutes govern, but even in case law or scholarly opinion, one is like to find unambiguously stated rules that provide for apparently clear results. . . .

Sometimes these rules build on open-ended criteria, like the "strongest connection" between an issue and a national law, and thus require comparisons or call for value judgments. Here, they remind an American lawyer of criteria such as "the most significant relationship" in a Second

Restatement. As in the Second Restatement, such general criteria are often made concrete through reference to specific factors. The employment of such open-ended criteria within conflicts rules is a more recent phenomenon in Europe. While it has, so far, affected only few, albeit important areas (mainly choice of law in contracts cases), it may indicate a trend towards greater use of general criteria. . . For the time being, however, such criteria are still the exception to the rule of using rather unambiguous factors such as nationality, domicile, and the place of certain events. Moreover, continental lawyers, feeling bound by legislative commands, on the whole tend to apply even open-ended rules more conscientiously than their American colleagues. Similarly, while exception clauses, such as public policy, are very common, they are normally not used to undermine the system of rules. Manipulation for the sake of a particular result is not unknown in Europe either, but it is less frequent, less accepted, and certainly less openly recognized.

In the continental European view, rules should ideally yield results by direct application to the facts, i.e., by logical categorization of the fact-situation under the criteria set forth by the rule. Sometimes, of course, rules provide no clear answers. Yet, in contrast to their American colleagues, Europeans assume that this is exception. Since they take rules more seriously and attribute greater authority to them than Americans, they rarely make reference to criteria outside of the rules, or at least rarely admit it. Beneath these respective attitudes lie different conceptions of the nature and function of rule generally. Since the days of Legal Realism, the American credo has become that "rules *guide*, but they do not *control* decision." The European assumption is that rules do control decisions—at least in the vast majority of cases.

b. Beyond Rules

This does not mean that interests, practical concerns, and desirability of results play no role in European conflicts law. These factors are simply considered at a different stage in the lawmaking process and in a more generalized fashion than in the United States. In the United States, they usually come into play more or less *ad hoc* when courts decide individual disputes. European conflicts law, in contrast, tends to typify and generalize them and to incorporate them into (mostly statutory) rules. As a result of having already been taken into account at the rule-making stage, they are normally not, as in the United States, open for debate in each case. . .

As a result of this orientation toward rules and preference for deductive reasoning, European conflicts law places utmost importance on precise knowledge of rules and principles, their interplay, and the technique of their application. In contrast, the ability to argue general policies, interests, or fairness plays a minor role, at least in the individual case. Consequently, an American observer will find much of European conflicts law amazingly clear and straightforward, yet suspiciously rigid and dogmatic: just as a European jurist is likely to see the American conflicts process as hopelessly confused by multifactor tests and unprincipled *ad hoc* decisions. Whatever the merits of the respective methods, an American lawyer looking at European conflicts law should accept this difference lest she underestimate the significance of rules and misunderstand the intellectual disposition of her continental colleagues.

3. The Values of the Legal Order

The prevalence of statutes and the emphasis on rules indicate already that the European values of the legal order differ from those cherished in the United States. The United States is a country of immigrants with a diverse culture and a relatively short history. As a result, American society is committed to flexibility, change, and individualism. European nations including the common law jurisdictions, in contrast, are mostly old countries with more homogenous populations and long traditions. As a result, Western European society values stability, consistency, and social welfare. Of course, the differences are matters of degree and may be diminishing, but they are still reflected in the legal culture generally, and in conflicts law in particular. As a general matter, European conflicts law is marked by comparatively greater preference for certainty, logical consistency, and stability of rules, and for predictability of results over justice in the individual case. . .

For an American conflicts lawyer dealing with transatlantic conflicts cases, the different values result in advantages as well as pitfalls.

On the one hand, the relative clarity, consistency, and stability of rules, and the emphasis on predictability of results, make European conflicts law more easily accessible to American lawyers than the more uncertain, fluctuating, and disparate American law is to her Swiss or Italian colleague. A half hour of studying the Rome [I] Convention may enable an American lawyer to understand the basics of Western European choice of law rules in contracts and to predict the outcomes of all but the very difficult cases with a high degree of certainty. In contrast, a European lawyer, after having spent half an hour on American choice of law rules, has at best understood that she better not venture any prediction.

On the other hand, the values underlying and the characteristic features shaping European conflicts law require that American lawyers change their ways of thinking and adjust to the premises and predilections of the civil law culture. If they fail to take rules seriously and to handle them carefully, if they insist on emphasizing policies and interests in individual cases, and if they disregard the goals of certainty and predictability, they are bound to misinterpret and mishandle European conflicts law. They will also alienate European colleagues as well as judges and thus, inevitably, hurt their client's case.

The European preference for rules that Reimann notes has produced two major choice-of-law regulations for the European Union. Regulation 593/2008 (Rome I) governs contractual choice of law, and Regulation 864/2007 (Rome II) governs torts. Selected provisions follow.

ROME I

CHAPTER II

UNIFORM RULES

Article 3

Freedom of choice

1. A contract shall be governed by the law chosen by the parties. The choice shall be made expressly or clearly demonstrated by the terms of the contract or the circumstances of the case. By their choice the parties can select the law applicable to the whole or to part only of the contract.

2. The parties may at any time agree to subject the contract to a law other than that which previously governed it, whether as a result of an earlier choice made under this Article or of other provisions of this Regulation. Any change in the law to be applied that is made after the conclusion of the contract shall not prejudice its formal validity under Article 11 or adversely affect the rights of third parties.

3. Where all other elements relevant to the situation at the time of the choice are located in a country other than the country whose law has been chosen, the choice of the parties shall not prejudice the application of provisions of the law of that other country which cannot be derogated from by agreement.

. . .

Article 4

Applicable law in the absence of choice

1. To the extent that the law applicable to the contract has not been chosen in accordance with Article 3 and without prejudice to Articles 5 to 8 [which provide specific rules for other particular kinds of contracts], the law governing the contract shall be determined as follows:

(a) a contract for the sale of goods shall be governed by the law of the country where the seller has his habitual residence;

(b) a contract for the provision of services shall be governed by the law of the country where the service provider has his habitual residence;

(c) a contract relating to a right *in rem* in immovable property or to a tenancy of immovable property shall be governed by the law of the country where the property is situated;

(d) notwithstanding point (c), a tenancy of immovable property concluded for temporary private use for a period of no more than six consecutive months shall be governed by the law of the country where the landlord has his habitual residence, provided that the tenant is a natural person and has his habitual residence in the same country;

(e) a franchise contract shall be governed by the law of the country where the franchisee has his habitual residence;

(f) a distribution contract shall be governed by the law of the country where the distributor has his habitual residence;

(g) a contract for the sale of goods by auction shall be governed by the law of the country where the auction takes place, if such a place can be determined;

. . .

2. Where the contract is not covered by paragraph 1 or where the elements of the contract would be covered by more than one of points (a) to (h) of paragraph 1, the contract shall be governed by the law of the country where the party required to effect the characteristic performance of the contract has his habitual residence.

3. Where it is clear from all the circumstances of the case that the contract is manifestly more closely connected with a country other than that indicated in paragraphs 1 or 2, the law of that other country shall apply.

4. Where the law applicable cannot be determined pursuant to paragraphs 1 or 2, the contract shall be governed by the law of the country with which it is most closely connected.

Article 6

Consumer contracts

1. Without prejudice to Articles 5 and 7, a contract concluded by a natural person for a purpose which can be regarded as being outside his trade or profession (the consumer) with another person acting in the exercise of his trade or profession (the professional) shall be governed by the law of the country where the consumer has his habitual residence, provided that the professional:

(a) pursues his commercial or professional activities in the country where the consumer has his habitual residence, or

(b) by any means, directs such activities to that country or to several countries including that country, and the contract falls within the scope of such activities.

2. Notwithstanding paragraph 1, the parties may choose the law applicable to a contract which fulfils the requirements of paragraph 1, in accordance with Article 3. Such a choice may not, however, have the result of depriving the consumer of the protection afforded to him by provisions that cannot be derogated from by agreement by virtue of the law which, in the absence of choice, would have been applicable on the basis of paragraph 1.

3. If the requirements in points (a) or (b) of paragraph 1 are not fulfilled, the law applicable to a contract between a consumer and a professional shall be determined pursuant to Articles 3 and 4.

. . .

Article 9

Overriding mandatory provisions

1. Overriding mandatory provisions are provisions the respect for which is regarded as crucial by a country for safeguarding its public interests, such as its political, social or economic organisation, to such an extent that they are applicable to any situation falling within their scope, irrespective of the law otherwise applicable to the contract under this Regulation.

2. Nothing in this Regulation shall restrict the application of the overriding mandatory provisions of the law of the forum.

3. Effect may be given to the overriding mandatory provisions of the law of the country where the obligations arising out of the contract have to be or have been performed, in so far as those overriding mandatory provisions render the performance of the contract unlawful. In considering whether to give effect to those provisions, regard shall be had to their nature and purpose and to the consequences of their application or non-application.

. . .

Article 13

Incapacity

In a contract concluded between persons who are in the same country, a natural person who would have capacity under the law of that country may invoke his incapacity resulting from the law of another country, only if the other party to the contract was aware of that incapacity at the time of the conclusion of the contract or was not aware thereof as a result of negligence.

CHAPTER III

OTHER PROVISIONS

. . .

Article 21

Public policy of the forum

The application of a provision of the law of any country specified by this Regulation may be refused only if such application is manifestly incompatible with the public policy (*ordre public*) of the forum.

ROME II

Chapter II

TORTS/DELICTS

Article 4

General rule

1. Unless otherwise provided for in this Regulation, the law applicable to a non-contractual obligation arising out of a tort/delict shall be the law of the country in which the damage occurs irrespective of the country in which the event giving rise to the damage occurred and irrespective of the country or countries in which the indirect consequences of that event occur.

2. However, where the person claimed to be liable and the person sustaining damage both have their habitual residence in the same country at the time when the damage occurs, the law of that country shall apply.

3. Where it is clear from all the circumstances of the case that the tort/delict is manifestly more closely connected with a country other than that indicated in paragraphs 1 or 2, the law of that other country shall apply. A manifestly closer connection with another country might be based in particular on a preexisting relationship between the parties, such as a contract, that is closely connected with the tort/delict in question.

Article 5

Product liability

1. Without prejudice to Article 4(2), the law applicable to a non-contractual obligation arising out of damage caused by a product shall be:

(a) the law of the country in which the person sustaining the damage had his or her habitual residence when the damage occurred, if the product was marketed in that country; or, failing that,

(b) the law of the country in which the product was acquired, if the product was marketed in that country; or, failing that,

(c) the law of the country in which the damage occurred, if the product was marketed in that country.

However, the law applicable shall be the law of the country in which the person claimed to be liable is habitually resident if he or she could not reasonably foresee the marketing of the product, or a product of the same type, in the country the law of which is applicable under (a), (b) or (c).

2. Where it is clear from all the circumstances of the case that the tort/delict is manifestly more closely connected with a country other than that indicated in paragraph 1, the law of that other country shall apply. A manifestly closer connection with another country might be based in particular on a pre-existing relationship between the parties, such as a contract, that is closely connected with the tort/delict in question.

. . .

CHAPTER IV

FREEDOM OF CHOICE

Article 14

Freedom of choice

1. The parties may agree to submit non-contractual obligations to the law of their choice:

(a) by an agreement entered into after the event giving rise to the damage occurred; or

(b) where all the parties are pursuing a commercial activity, also by an agreement freely negotiated before the event giving rise to the damage occurred.

The choice shall be expressed or demonstrated with reasonable certainty by the circumstances of the case and shall not prejudice the rights of third parties.

2. Where all the elements relevant to the situation at the time when the event giving rise to the damage occurs are located in a country other than the country whose law has been chosen, the choice of the parties shall not prejudice the application of provisions of the law of that other country which cannot be derogated from by agreement.

. . .

Article 16

Overriding mandatory provisions

Nothing in this Regulation shall restrict the application of the provisions of the law of the forum in a situation where they are mandatory irrespective of the law otherwise applicable to the non-contractual obligation.

Article 17

Rules of safety and conduct

In assessing the conduct of the person claimed to be liable, account shall be taken, as a matter of fact and in so far as is appropriate, of the rules of safety and conduct which were in force at the place and time of the event giving rise to the liability.

CHAPTER VI

OTHER PROVISIONS

. . .

Article 24

Exclusion of renvoi

The application of the law of any country specified by this Regulation means the application of the rules of law in force in that country other than its rules of private international law.

. . .

Article 26

Public policy of the forum

The application of a provision of the law of any country specified by this Regulation may be refused only if such application is manifestly incompatible with the public policy (*ordre public*) of the forum.

HILLSIDE (NEW MEDIA) LIMITED V. BJARTE BAASLAND

[2010] EWHC 3336 (Comm) (20 December 2010).
England and Wales High Court, Queens Bench Division, Commercial Court.

[Hillside is an English company that allowed individuals to place online bets on casino games and sporting events after opening an account. The account application required individuals to provide an address and to accept Hillside's "terms, conditions, and rules." These included the following provision:

> All sport wagers . . . are considered to be placed and received in the UK and all Conditions shall be governed by the laws of England and you irrevocably submit to the exclusive jurisdiction of the courts of England. All gaming . . . is considered to be placed and received in Gibraltar and all Conditions are governed by the laws of Gibraltar and you irrevocably submit to the exclusive jurisdiction of the courts of Gibraltar.

Customers made bets after depositing funds in a "wallet" for the account. Funds for sporting bets were held by Hillside in an account in its name at a Birmingham branch of the Royal Bank of Scotland; funds for gaming (casino) bets were held in a similar account in the name of Hillside Gibraltar. Sporting bets were processed in England and gaming bets in Gibraltar.]

[Bjarte Baasland, a Norwegian citizen, incurred large gambling losses using Hillside's services. Baasland's Norwegian lawyers wrote Hillside, threatening litigation unless Hillside mitigated his losses. The letter asserted that Norwegian law governed and rendered Hillside liable on various theories. Baasland never instituted the threatened proceedings, but Hillside filed this suit in England seeking a determination that English law applied and a declaration of non-liability under that law.]

MR. JUSTICE ANDREW SMITH:

The first submission raises issues of private international law of some complexity. It requires consideration of whether English law would govern (i) any claim that Mr Baasland might have on a contractual basis, such as an implied term in a contractual arrangement with Hillside, and (ii) any non-contractual claim that he might have. . .

[The Norwegian lawyers'] letter . . . appears to assert a tortious and non-contractual claim, and I consider first whether such a claim would be governed by English law. . .

First, the position under the Rome II Regulation: article 4 is headed "General Rule", and, so far as it is relevant, it provides as follows:

> "1 . . . the law applicable to a non-contractual obligation arising out of a tort/delict shall be the law of the country in which the damage occurs irrespective of the country in which the event giving rise to the damage occurred and the country or countries in which the indirect consequences of that event occur.
>
> 2 . . .
>
> 3. Where it is clear from all the circumstances of the case that the tort/delict is manifestly more closely connected with a country other than that indicated in paragraph 1 . . . , the law of that other country shall apply. A manifestly closer connection with another country might be based in particular on a pre-existing relationship between the parties, such as a contract, that is closely related with the tort/delict in question".
>
> This article therefore raises two questions:
>
> i) In which country did the "damage" occur? and
>
> ii) Is the tort manifestly more closely connected with a country other than that in which the damage occurred?

The damage that Mr Baasland asserted through his Norwegian lawyers was financial loss suffered through his unsuccessful gambling. . .

The question where Mr Baasland suffered immediate financial loss of this kind requires further consideration of his arrangements for placing bets. . .

When Mr Baasland first transferred funds to his "wallet", he became the creditor of a debt in respect of the funds so deposited. As funds were added to the wallet by way of further transfers or winnings from his gambling, the value of the chose in action representing the debt increased, and, because bets were placed or funds withdrawn, the value was reduced. There might be room for debate about the legal analysis of how the debt was created. There are perhaps three possibilities:

i) That there was a single contract whereby the funds were deposited in the wallet and thereafter Mr Baasland placed bets, and that under that single contract Mr Baasland had the right to require that the funds in the wallet be used in accordance with the terms on which they were deposited: that is to say, that, unless and until they were used for betting, Mr Baasland might have them repaid at any time.

ii) That there was a contract about the deposit of funds which was separate from any wagering contract, and under it the terms on which the funds were deposited were to similar effect, as far as is material, to those which I have described in (i).

iii) Thirdly, that the money was transferred to the wallet by way of a gratuitous deposit for which there was no valuable consideration. . .

Whatever the analysis, what matters for present purposes is that the deposit created a debt owed to Mr Baasland, and Mr Baasland suffered no loss simply as a result of transferring funds to the wallet. He suffered loss only when he was allowed to use those funds to place bets. At that point the loss that he suffered was that the value of the chose in action represented by the funds in the wallet was reduced, if not exhausted. This, as it seems to me, was the immediate loss that Mr Baasland suffered as a result of being allowed facilities to gamble and, as it is alleged, allowed to use the facilities without appropriate warnings, safeguards and protections.

This analysis of the position under English law . . . leads to these questions:

i) Where, as a matter of English law, was the situs of the chose in action when it was reduced in value or exhausted by bets placed by Mr Baasland?

ii) Were the arrangements whereby Mr Baasland placed bets governed by English law or by Norwegian law or by some other law?. . .

The general rule stated in Dicey, Morris & Collins in The Conflict of Laws, 14th Ed, Vol 2, Rule 120 is that "Choses in action are generally situate in the country where they are properly recoverable and enforceable". Although at common law this principle led to the general rule that (with some exceptions that are irrelevant for present purposes) debts are situate where the debtor resides (see Dicey, Morris & Collins, loc cit, at para 22–026), its application in a case such as this, where the debtor is a corporation and the case is covered by the Lugano Convention, depends, as I see it, upon the debtor's domicil. That is the primary ground on which a court takes jurisdiction under article 2 of the Lugano Convention. The domicil of a corporation is determined in accordance with section 42 of the Civil Jurisdiction and Judgments Act, 1982. It depends upon where it has its "seat", and this in turn depends upon where it was incorporated and has its registered or other official address or where its central management and control is exercised.

Hillside is domiciled in England. It is incorporated in England, has its central management and control in England, and has its registered office in England. . . [T]his analysis means that there is no basis for an argument that any claim in tort or other non-contractual claim is governed wholly or partly by Norwegian law.

I come to the question which law governs the arrangements whereby Mr Baasland placed bets. Under article 4 of the Rome Convention, subject to any express choice of law made by the parties, a contract is generally governed by the law of the country with which it is most closely connected. The parties may select a law applicable to the whole of their contract or only to a part of it.

In this case, the parties did not choose a law to govern the whole of their contract. Assuming that the Rules were incorporated into their contract, they chose that different laws should govern the "Conditions" depending upon the type of bet being considered. The scope of this provision is not clear because the evidence does not explain what the "Conditions" were or what they provided. However, on any view (i) the parties did not choose a law that governed their overall relationship or matters that were not covered by the Conditions; and (ii) they did not elect that any part of the relationship should be governed by the law of Norway.

I do not consider that, if the general rule in article 4 of the Convention is applied, it would lead to the parties' relationship being governed by the law of Norway. Article 4(2) provides that prima facie it is to be "presumed that the contract is most closely connected with the country where the party who is to effect the performance which is characteristic of the contract has, at the time of conclusion of the contract, his habitual residence, or, in the case of a body corporate or incorporate, its central administration". Dicey, Morris & Collins (loc cit) at para 33–54 submit that, in the case of a wagering contract, the party that is to effect performance that is characteristic of it is the party who offers the facility for placing wagers. I agree with that submission. Further, I would conclude in this case that, since the facilities were offered through Hillside's website, Hillside were the party whose performance is characteristic of the contract, notwithstanding that, as I see it, Hillside received only some bets as a principal contracting party and received others as an agent for an undisclosed principal. I therefore consider that the general rule in article 4 would mean that the law of England governs the overall contract. Certainly I do not think that there is any argument that under the general rule the contract is governed either wholly or in part by the law of Norway.

There are two circumstances in which the general rule in article 4 does not apply. First, article 4(5) provides that the general rule does not apply "if it appears from the circumstances as a whole that the contract is more closely connected with another country". I do not consider that this provides any possible argument that Mr Baasland's contractual arrangements were governed by the law of Norway.

Secondly, the general rule might be displaced if article [6], which deals with "Certain consumer contracts" applies. It seems likely that Mr Baasland was a consumer within the meaning of the article. If article [6] does apply, then Mr Baasland's contract was governed by the law of the country in which he has his habitual residence, which I would suppose to be Norway, provided (i) one of the conditions in article [6(2)] is satisfied and (ii) neither of the conditions in article [6(4)] applies.

There is no evidence that any of the conditions in article (2) is satisfied in this case. The only condition that I need mention is this: "if in [the country of the consumer's habitual residence] the conclusion of the contract was preceded by a specific invitation addressed to him or by advertising, and he had taken in that country all the steps necessary on his part for the conclusion of the contract". There is no evidence that there was any such invitation addressed to Mr Baasland, and, while the precise scope of the term "advertising" is not clear, I do not consider that it covers any circumstances in which goods or facilities can be found on the internet, through a search engine or in some similar way. The Guiliano-Lagarde Report indicates that there must be something more recognisable as advertising directed to publication in the country of the consumer's habitual residence. There is no evidence that the conclusion of any contract entered into by Mr Baasland was preceded by advertising. I therefore do not need to consider article [6(4)]. . .

If I had reached a different conclusion about where the damage occurred, I should have nevertheless considered that English law would govern the claim because article 4(3) of the Rome II Regulation applies. Any tort, as it seems to me, is manifestly more closely connected with

England than any other country because (i) the losses occurred by way of dealings with funds in an English bank account, (ii) they resulted from the facilities offered through a website which was owned by an English company, which was operated from England, and to which Mr Baasland might have had access from England, Norway or any other country, and (iii) the relationship was governed by a relationship of which the proper law or putative proper law is English. . .

Although some of the issues about the governing law are of some complexity, I conclude that any claim which Mr Baasland might have is probably governed by English law, and, more importantly, that there is no realistic possibility of Mr Baasland succeeding in an argument that he has a claim governed by the law of Norway. . .

I therefore grant Hillside's application for summary judgment.

European Rules and Practice

(1) Rome I recites in its preamble that "freedom to choose the applicable law should be one of the cornerstones of the system of conflict-of-law rules in matters of contractual obligations." Consistent with this theme, the basic rule set forth in Article 3 lets parties choose any law without the Second Restatement's requirement of a reasonable relation. Can that be explained as a way of accommodating competing sovereign regulatory regimes, or is it just the triumph of liberty of contract? Article 3 also allows the parties to change their choice at any time. Does that make sense?

Recall that the ALI's 2001 proposed revision to the Uniform Commercial Code endorsed a similar unrestricted choice but was rejected by states. Why do you think the members of the European Union accepted it? Might it be because the UCC required adoption at the state level, while Rome I binds almost all EU members (Denmark opted out)?

(2) Rome I includes some exceptions to its general rule. For instance, Article 3 notes that if "all other elements relevant to the situation at the time of the choice are located in a country other than the country whose law has been chosen," then that country's non-waivable provisions will apply. Thus, it expands party autonomy only in the multistate context. Does that make sense, given that no relation to the chosen law is required in the multistate context? Article 6 preserves for consumers non-waivable protections of their home law. Article 9 allows the forum to apply its own "overriding mandatory provisions," defined as provisions "the respect or which is regarded as crucial by a country for safeguarding its public interests." It further provides that the law of the country of performance will govern, if it makes performance illegal—but only, apparently, if the prohibitions amount to "overriding mandatory provisions." What do you think this means? Article 21 preserves a limited "manifestly incompatible" public policy exception.

(3) If the parties do not choose an applicable law, Article 4(1) sets out specific rules for particular kinds of contracts. Do any of these surprise you? For contracts not listed, Article 4(2) directs application of the law of the country "where the party required to effect the characteristic performance has his habitual residence." Is that a sensible choice? Article 4(3) then allows an override to the rules of both paragraphs 1 and 2 for contracts "manifestly more closely connected" with another country. If all else fails, Article 4(4) directs court to use the law of the country with which the contract "is most closely connected." Overall, how different is Rome I from the Second Restatement?

(4) Capacity to contract features in two of the cases featured in this book, *Milliken v. Pratt*, supra p. 19, and *Lilienthal v. Kaufman*, supra p. 177. How would those cases come out under Rome I Article 13? Is the rule of Article 13 preferable to the analysis performed by the American courts?

(5) The Rome II preamble recites that *lex loci delicti* "is the basic solution for non-contractual obligations in virtually all the Member States." Attempting to standardize application of this principle, Rome II deals with cross-border torts by selecting the law of the place of injury, just as Joseph Beale's "last act" rule did. Beale's justification was that a tort is not complete, and hence no obligation arises, without injury. Rome II states that choosing the law of the place of injury "strikes a fair balance between the interests of the person claimed to be liable and the person sustaining the damage and also reflects the modern approach to civil liability and the development of systems of strict liability." Is this a better explanation?

The general benefit of rules, as opposed to standards, is supposed to be that they are clear, predictable, and easy to apply. Does *Hillside* make you doubt any of those characterizations?

(6) Rome II, Article 4(1), sets out the basic rule of *lex loci*. Article 4(2) provides an exception for common domicile cases, which are to be decided under the law of common domicile. This exception does not attempt to distinguish between loss-allocating and conduct-regulating rules but applies generally. Is the distinction more trouble than it's worth? But whose speed limit should govern a car accident in Spain involving French domiciliaries? Article 17 provides that "[i]n assessing the conduct of the person claimed to be liable, account shall be taken, as a matter of fact and in so far as is appropriate, of the rules of safety and conduct which were in force at the place and time of the event giving rise to the liability." Does this reintroduce the distinction? Or is it akin to the First Restatement's exception to the last act rule for "the application of a standard of care." See supra p. 16, note 3. What does "as a matter of fact" mean?

Article 4(3) provides a general exception for cases that are "manifestly more closely connected with a country other than that indicated in paragraphs 1 or 2. . ." This echoes an earlier provision of European law, although "manifestly" has been added, presumably in an attempt to make recourse to the exception less frequent. Article 4(3) goes on to suggest by way of example that a pre-existing relationship between the parties, to which the tort is closely connected, might establish a manifestly closer connection to some other jurisdiction. The Second Restatement similarly directs courts to consider the state where the relationship between the parties is centered. Does Rome II give this factor greater weight? If so, is it deserved?

In BGH Urt. v. 19.7.2011—VI ZR 217/10, BGHZ 190, 301–314, the German Supreme Court applied the "manifestly more closely connected" exception to apply Swiss law to the tort claim of a German resident who had traveled to Switzerland for medical treatment. The patient returned to Germany and continued to take medication prescribed by the Swiss doctor; when he suffered serious side effects, he sued, alleging that the doctor had failed to adequately inform him of the risks. The court reasoned that although the injury was suffered in Germany, the doctor-patient relationship established a closer connection to Switzerland. It also noted that it would be undesirable to have the doctor-patient relationship governed by Swiss law and a related tort governed by German law. Do you agree?

Like Rome I, Rome II also has exceptions for overriding mandatory provisions of the forum (Article 16) and forum public policy (Article 26). How frequently do you think these exceptions will be invoked?

(7) Article 14 allows the parties to choose a law to govern non-contractual liability, either after or, in some cases, before the event. Does party autonomy for torts make sense?

(8) Rome II, Article 24, excludes renvoi. As far as choice of law within the EU goes, the substantive uniformity of choice of law moots the issue anyway. But what about a choice-of-law case involving, say, the United States and France? Rome I, Article 20, excludes renvoi as well. Is there any greater need for renvoi with contracts than with torts? (Recall that the Second Restatement endorses renvoi in the context of real property, § 222, comment e, and a few other circumstances.)

(9) Can you identify a theory behind Rome I and Rome II? Most Europeans believe that the American "revolution" in choice of law has been a failure and has little relevance for European practice. Do these materials support that conclusion?

SECTION 3. THE ACT OF STATE DOCTRINE

BANCO NACIONAL DE CUBA V. SABBATINO

376 U.S. 398 (1964).

[Relations between the United States and Fidel Castro's revolutionary regime in Cuba grew increasingly strained in 1960. In July of that year, responding to a U.S. reduction of Cuba's quota for sugar imports into the United States, Cuba nationalized the property of U.S. citizens in Cuba. Among the expropriated property was sugar belonging to Compania Azucarera Vertientes (CAV), a Cuban corporation owned largely by U.S. residents. CAV had contracted to sell this sugar to Farr, Whitlock & Co., an American commodities broker. After the sugar was nationalized, however, Farr, Whitlock made a second contract to buy the sugar from the Cuban government. Farr, Whitlock shipped the sugar and received payment, but rather than pay the Cuban government, it turned the proceeds over to CAV's receiver, Sabbatino. Cuba assigned its rights under the second contract to Banco Nacional de Cuba, which filed suit in federal district court. The defendants (Sabbatino and Farr, Whitlock) argued that Cuba never had any right to the sugar because the Cuban expropriation violated international law. The district court ruled in favor of the defendants and the court of appeals affirmed.]

MR. JUSTICE HARLAN delivered the opinion of the Court.

The question which brought this case here, and is now found to be the dispositive issue, is whether the so-called act of state doctrine serves to sustain petitioner's claims in this litigation. . .

IV.

The classic American statement of the act of state doctrine, which appears to have taken root in England as early as 1674 * * * and began to emerge in the jurisprudence of this country in the late eighteenth and early nineteenth centuries, * * * is found in *Underhill v. Hernandez,* 168 U.S. 250, where Chief Justice Fuller said for a unanimous Court (p. 252):

> "Every sovereign State is bound to respect the independence of every other sovereign State, and the courts of one country will not sit in judgment on the acts of the government of another done within its own territory. Redress of grievances by reason of such acts must be obtained through the means open to be availed of by sovereign powers as between themselves."

Following this precept the Court in that case refused to inquire into acts of Hernandez, a revolutionary Venezuelan military commander whose government had been later recognized by the United States, which were made the basis of a damage action in this country by Underhill, an

American citizen, who claimed that he had been unlawfully assaulted, coerced, and detained in Venezuela by Hernandez.

None of this Court's subsequent cases in which the act of state doctrine was directly or peripherally involved manifest any retreat from *Underhill.* See *American Banana Co. v. United Fruit Co.,* 213 U.S. 347; *Oetjen v. Central Leather Co.,* 246 U.S. 297; *Ricaud v. American Metal Co.,* 246 U.S. 304; *Shapleigh v. Mier,* 299 U.S. 468; * * *. On the contrary, in two of these cases, *Oetjen* and *Ricaud,* the doctrine as announced in *Underhill* was reaffirmed in unequivocal terms. . .

The outcome of this case, therefore, turns upon whether any of the contentions urged by respondents against the application of the act of state doctrine in the premises is acceptable: (1) that the doctrine does not apply to acts of state which violate international law, as is claimed to be the case here; (2) that the doctrine is inapplicable unless the Executive interposes it in a particular case; and (3) that, in any event, the doctrine may not be invoked by a foreign government plaintiff in our own courts.

V.

Preliminarily, we discuss the foundations on which we deem the act of state doctrine to rest. . . We do not believe that this doctrine is compelled either by the inherent nature of sovereign authority, as some of the earlier decisions seem to imply, see *Underhill, supra; American Banana, supra; Oetjen, supra,* or by some principle of international law. If a transaction takes place in one jurisdiction and the forum is in another, the forum does not by dismissing an action or by applying its own law purport to divest the first jurisdiction of its territorial sovereignty; it merely declines to adjudicate or makes applicable its own law to parties or property before it. The refusal of one country to enforce the penal laws of another is a typical example of an instance when a court will not entertain a cause of action arising in another jurisdiction. While historic notions of sovereign authority do bear upon the wisdom of employing the act of state doctrine, they do not dictate its existence.

That international law does not require application of the doctrine is evidenced by the practice of nations. Most of the countries rendering decisions on the subject fail to follow the rule rigidly. No international arbitral or judicial decision suggests that international law prescribes recognition of sovereign acts of governments, and apparently no claim has ever been raised before an international tribunal that failure to apply the act of state doctrine constitutes a breach of international obligation. If international law does not prescribe use of the doctrine, neither does it forbid application of the rule even if it is claimed that the act of state in question violated international law. The traditional view of international law is that it establishes substantive principles for determining whether one country has wronged another. Because of its peculiar nation-to-nation character the usual method for an individual to seek relief is to exhaust local remedies and then to repair to the executive authorities of his own state to persuade them to champion his claim in diplomacy or before an international tribunal. * * * Although it is, of course, true that the United States courts apply international law as part of our own, in appropriate circumstances * * *, the public law of nations can hardly dictate to a country which is in theory wronged how to treat that wrong within its domestic borders.

Despite the broad statement in *Oetjen* that "The conduct of the foreign relations of our Government is committed by the Constitution to the Executive and Legislative . . . Departments," * * * it cannot of course be thought that "every case or controversy which touches foreign relations lies beyond judicial cognizance." *Baker v. Carr,* 369 U.S. 186, 211. The text of the Constitution does not require the act of state doctrine; it does not irrevocably remove from the judiciary the capacity to review the validity of foreign acts of state.

The act of state doctrine does, however, have "constitutional" underpinnings. It arises out of the basic relationships between branches of government in a system of separation of powers. It concerns the competency of dissimilar institutions to make and implement particular kinds of decisions in the area of international relations. The doctrine as formulated in past decisions expresses the strong sense of the Judicial Branch that its engagement in the task of passing on the validity of foreign acts of state may hinder rather than further this country's pursuit of goals both for itself and for the community of nations as a whole in the international sphere.

[The Court went on to hold that the act of state doctrine was a matter of federal common law; this part of the opinion is reprinted supra pp. 898–901.]

VI.

If the act of state doctrine is a principle of decision binding on federal and state courts alike but compelled by neither international law nor the Constitution, its continuing vitality depends on its capacity to reflect the proper distribution of functions between the judicial and political branches of the Government on matters bearing upon foreign affairs. It should be apparent that the greater the degree of codification or consensus concerning a particular area of international law, the more appropriate it is for the judiciary to render decisions regarding it, since the courts can then focus on the application on an agreed principle to circumstances of fact rather than on the sensitive task of establishing a principle not inconsistent with the national interest or with international justice. It is also evident that some aspects of international law touch much more sharply on national nerves than do others; the less important the implications of an issue are for our foreign relations, the weaker the justification for exclusivity in the political branches. The balance of relevant considerations may also be shifted if the government which perpetrated the challenged act of state is no longer in existence, . . . for the political interest of this country may, as a result, be measurably altered. Therefore, rather than laying down or reaffirming an inflexible and all-encompassing rule in this case, we decide only that the Judicial Branch will not examine the validity of a taking of property within its own territory by a foreign sovereign government, extant and recognized by this country at the time of suit, in the absence of a treaty or other unambiguous agreement regarding controlling legal principles, even if the complaint alleges that the taking violates customary international law.

There are few if any issues in international law today on which opinion seems to be so divided as the limitations on a state's power to expropriate the property of aliens. [The Court cited differing practices and views on the question of when expropriation is permissible.]

The disagreement as to relevant international law standards reflects an even more basic divergence between the national interests of capital importing and capital exporting nations and between the social ideologies of those countries that favor state control of a considerable portion of the means of production and those that adhere to a free enterprise system. It is difficult to imagine the courts of this country embarking on adjudication in an area which touches more sensitively the practical and ideological goals of the various members of the community of nations.

When we consider the prospect of the courts characterizing foreign expropriations, however justifiably, as invalid under international law and ineffective to pass title, the wisdom of the precedents is confirmed. While each of the leading cases in this Court may be argued to be distinguishable on its facts from this one—*Underhill* because sovereign immunity provided an independent ground and *Oetjen, Ricaud,* and *Shapleigh* because there was no actual violation of international law—the plain implication of all these opinions . . . is that the act of state doctrine is applicable even if international law has been violated. . .

The possible adverse consequences of a conclusion to the contrary of that implicit in these cases is highlighted by contrasting the practices of the political branch with the limitations of the judicial process in matters of this kind. Following an expropriation of any significance, the Executive engages in diplomacy aimed to assure that United States citizens who are harmed are compensated fairly. Representing all claimants of this country, it will often be able, either by bilateral or multilateral talks, by submission to the United Nations, or by the employment of economic and political sanctions, to achieve some degree of general redress. Judicial determinations of invalidity of title can, on the other hand, have only an occasional impact, since they depend on the fortuitous circumstance of the property in question being brought into this country. Such decisions would, if the acts involved were declared invalid, often be likely to give offense to the expropriating country; since the concept of territorial sovereignty is so deep seated, any state may resent the refusal of the courts of another sovereign to accord validity to acts within its territorial borders. Piecemeal dispositions of this sort involving the probability of affront to another state could seriously interfere with negotiations being carried on by the Executive Branch and might prevent or render less favorable the terms of an agreement that could otherwise be reached. Relations with third countries which have engaged in similar expropriations would not be immune from effect.

The dangers of such adjudication are present regardless of whether the State Department has, as it did in this case, asserted that the relevant act violated international law. If the Executive Branch has undertaken negotiations with an expropriating country, but has refrained from claims of violation of the law of nations, a determination to that effect by a court might be regarded as a serious insult, while a finding of compliance with international law would greatly strengthen the bargaining hand of the other state with consequent detriment to American interests.

Even if the State Department has proclaimed the impropriety of the expropriation, the stamp of approval of its view by a judicial tribunal, however impartial, might increase any affront and the judicial decision might occur at a time, almost always well after the taking, when such an impact would be contrary to our national interest. Considerably more serious and far-reaching consequences would flow from a judicial finding that international law standards had been met if that determination flew in the face of a State Department proclamation to the contrary. When articulating principles of international law in its relations with other states, the Executive Branch speaks not only as an interpreter of generally accepted and traditional rules, as would the courts, but also as an advocate of standards it believes desirable for the community of nations and protective of national concerns. In short, whatever way the matter is cut, the possibility of conflict between the Judicial and Executive Branches could hardly be avoided. . .

Against the force of such considerations, we find respondents' countervailing arguments quite unpersuasive. Their basic contention is that the United States courts could make a significant contribution to the growth of international law, a contribution whose importance, it is said, would be magnified by the relative paucity of decisional law by international bodies. But given the fluidity of present world conditions, the effectiveness of such a patchwork approach toward the formulation of an acceptable body of law concerning state responsibility for expropriations is, to say the least, highly conjectural. Moreover, it rests upon the sanguine presupposition that the decisions of the courts of the world's major capital exporting country and principal exponent of the free enterprise system would be accepted as disinterested expressions of sound legal principle by those adhering to widely different ideologies.

It is contended that regardless of the fortuitous circumstances necessary for United States jurisdiction over a case involving a foreign act of state and the resultant isolated application to any expropriations program taken as a whole, it is the function of the courts to justly decide individual disputes before them. Perhaps the most typical act of state case involves the original owner or his assignee suing one in association with the expropriating state who has had "title" transferred to him. But it is difficult to regard the claim of the original owner, who otherwise may be recompensed through diplomatic channels, as more demanding of judicial cognizance than the claim of title by the innocent third party purchaser, who, if the property is taken from him, is without any remedy.

Respondents claim that the economic pressure resulting from the proposed exception to the act of state doctrine will materially add to the protection of United States investors. We are not convinced, even assuming the relevance of this contention. Expropriations take place for a variety of reasons, political and ideological as well as economic. When one considers the variety of means possessed by this country to make secure foreign investment, the persuasive or coercive effect of judicial invalidation of acts of expropriation dwindles in comparison. The newly independent states are in need of continuing foreign investment; the creation of a climate unfavorable to such investment by wholesale confiscations may well work to their long-run economic disadvantage. Foreign aid given to many of these countries provides a powerful lever in the hands of the political branches to ensure fair treatment of United States nationals. Ultimately the sanctions of economic embargo and the freezing of assets in this country may be employed. Any country willing to brave any or all of these consequences is unlikely to be deterred by sporadic judicial decisions directly affecting only property brought to our shores. If the political branches are willing to exercise their ample powers to effect compensation, this reflects a judgment of the national interest which the judiciary would be ill-advised to undermine directly.

It is suggested that if the act of state doctrine is applicable to violations of international law, it should only be so when the Executive Branch expressly stipulates that it does not wish the courts to pass on the question of validity. * * * We should be slow to reject the representations of the Government that such a . . . principle would work serious inroads on the maximum effectiveness of United States diplomacy. Often the State Department will wish to refrain from taking an official position, particularly at a moment that would be dictated by the development of private litigation but might be inopportune diplomatically. Adverse domestic consequences might flow from an official stand which could be assuaged, if at all, only by revealing matters best kept secret. Of course, a relevant consideration for the State Department would be the position contemplated in the court to hear the case. It is highly questionable whether the examination of validity by the judiciary should depend on an educated guess by the Executive as to probable result and, at any rate, should a prediction be wrong, the Executive might be embarrassed in its dealings with other countries. . .

However offensive to the public policy of this country and its constituent States an expropriation of this kind may be, we conclude that both the national interest and progress toward the goal of establishing the rule of law among nations are best served by maintaining intact the act of state doctrine in this realm of its application.

VII.

Finally, we must determine whether Cuba's status as a plaintiff in this case dictates a result at variance with the conclusions reached above. If the Court were to distinguish between suits brought by sovereign states and those of assignees, the rule would have little effect unless a careful examination were made in each case to determine if the private party suing had taken property in good faith. Such an inquiry would be exceptionally difficult, since the relevant transaction would almost invariably have occurred outside our borders. If such an investigation were deemed irrelevant, a state could always assign its claim. . .

Respondents offer another theory for treating the case differently because of Cuba's participation. It is claimed that the forum should simply apply its own law to all the relevant transactions. An analogy is drawn to the area of sovereign immunity, *National City Bank v. Republic of China*, 348 U.S. 356, in which, if a foreign country seek redress in our courts, counterclaims are permissible. But immunity relates to the prerogative right not to have sovereign property subject to suit; fairness has been thought to require that when the sovereign seeks recovery, it be subject to legitimate counterclaims against it. The act of state doctrine, however, although it shares with the immunity doctrine a respect for sovereign states, concerns the limits for determining the validity of an otherwise applicable rule of law. It is plain that if a recognized government sued on a contract with a United States citizen, concededly legitimate by the locus of its making, performance, and most significant contacts, the forum would not apply its own substantive law of contracts. Since the act of state doctrine reflects the desirability of presuming the relevant transaction valid, the same result follows; the forum may not apply its local law regarding foreign expropriations.

Since the act of state doctrine proscribes a challenge to the validity of the Cuban expropriation decree in this case, any counterclaim based on asserted invalidity must fail. Whether a theory of conversion or breach of contract is the proper cause of action under New York law, the presumed validity of the expropriation is unaffected. . .

The judgment of the Court of Appeals is reversed and the case is remanded to the District Court for proceedings consistent with this opinion.

W.S. KIRKPATRICK V. ENVIRONMENTAL TECTONICS CORP.

493 U.S. 400 (1990).

JUSTICE SCALIA delivered the opinion of the Court.

In this case we must decide whether the act of state doctrine bars a court in the United States from entertaining a cause of action that does not rest upon the asserted invalidity of an official act of a foreign sovereign, but that does require imputing to foreign officials an unlawful motivation (the obtaining of bribes) in the performance of such an official act.

I.

The facts as alleged in respondent's complaint are as follows: In 1981, Harry Carpenter, who was then Chairman of the Board and Chief Executive Officer of petitioner W.S. Kirkpatrick & Co., Inc. (Kirkpatrick), learned that the Republic of Nigeria was interested in contracting for the construction and equipment of an aeromedical center at Kaduna Air Force Base in Nigeria. He made arrangements with Benson "Tunde" Akindele, a Nigerian citizen, whereby Akindele would endeavor to secure the contract for Kirkpatrick. It was agreed that, in the event the contract was awarded to Kirkpatrick, Kirkpatrick would pay to two Panamanian entities controlled by Akindele a "commission" equal to 20% of the contract price, which would in turn be given as a bribe to officials of the Nigerian Government. In accordance with this plan, the contract was awarded to petitioner W.S. Kirkpatrick & Co., International (Kirkpatrick International), a wholly owned subsidiary of Kirkpatrick; Kirkpatrick paid the promised "commission" to the appointed Panamanian entities; and those funds were disbursed as bribes. All parties agree that Nigerian law prohibits both the payment and the receipt of bribes in connection with the award of a government contract.

Respondent Environmental Tectonics Corporation, International, an unsuccessful bidder for the Kaduna contract, learned of the 20% "commission" and brought the matter to the attention of the Nigerian Air Force and the United States Embassy in Lagos. Following an investigation by the Federal Bureau of Investigation, the United States Attorney for the District of New Jersey brought cases against both Kirkpatrick and Carpenter for violations of the Foreign Corrupt Practices Act of 1977 and both pleaded guilty.

Respondent then brought this civil action in the United States District Court for the District of New Jersey against Carpenter, Akindele, petitioners, and others, seeking damages under the Racketeer Influenced and Corrupt Organizations Act, the Robinson-Patman Act, and the New Jersey Anti-Racketeering Act. The defendants moved to dismiss the complaint under Rule 12(b)(6) of the Federal Rules of Civil Procedure on the ground that the action was barred by the act of state doctrine.

The District Court, having requested and received a letter expressing the views of the legal advisor to the United States Department of State as to the applicability of the act of state doctrine, treated the motion as one for summary judgment under Rule 56 of the Federal Rules of Civil Procedure, and granted the motion. . .

The Court of Appeals for the Third Circuit reversed. . . The Court of Appeals found particularly persuasive the letter to the District Court from the legal advisor to the Department of State, which had stated that in the opinion of the Department judicial inquiry into the purpose behind the act of a foreign sovereign would not produce the "unique embarrassment, and the particular interference with the conduct of foreign affairs, that may result from the judicial determination that a foreign sovereign's acts are invalid." The Court of Appeals acknowledged that "the Department's legal conclusions as to the reach of the act of state doctrine are not controlling on the courts," but concluded that "the Department's factual assessment of whether fulfillment of its responsibilities will be prejudiced by the course of civil litigation is entitled to substantial respect." . . . [A]ccordingly, it reversed the judgment of the District Court and remanded the case for trial. We granted certiorari.

II

This Court's description of the jurisprudential foundation for the act of state doctrine has undergone some evolution over the years. We once viewed the doctrine as an expression of international law, resting upon "the highest considerations of international comity and expediency," *Oetjen v. Central Leather Co.,* 246 U.S. 297, 303–304 (1918). We have more recently described it, however, as a consequence of domestic separation of powers, reflecting "the strong sense of the Judicial Branch that its engagement in the task of passing on the validity of foreign acts of state may hinder" the conduct of foreign affairs, *Banco Nacional de Cuba v. Sabbatino,* 376 U.S. 398, 423 (1964). . .

The parties have argued at length about . . . whether the purpose of the act of state doctrine would be furthered by its application in this case. We find it unnecessary, however, to pursue those inquiries, since the factual predicate for application of the act of state doctrine does not exist. Nothing in the present suit requires the court to declare invalid, and thus ineffective as "a rule of decision for the courts of this country," *Ricaud v.*

American Metal Co., 246 U.S. 304, 310 (1918), the official act of a foreign sovereign.

In every case in which we held the act of state doctrine applicable, the relief sought or the defense interposed would have required a court in the United States to declare invalid the official act of a foreign sovereign performed within its own territory. In *Underhill v. Hernandez,* 168 U.S. 250, 254 (1897), holding the defendant's detention of the plaintiff to be tortious would have required denying legal effect to "acts of a military commander representing the authority of the revolutionary party as government, which afterwards succeeded and was recognized by the United States." In *Oetjen v. Central Leather Co., supra,* and in *Ricaud v. American Metal Co., supra,* denying title to the party who claimed through purchase from Mexico would have required declaring that government's prior seizure of the property, within its own territory, legally ineffective. * * * In *Sabbatino,* upholding the defendant's claim to the funds would have required a holding that Cuba's expropriation of goods located in Havana was null and void. In the present case, by contrast, neither the claim nor any asserted defense requires a determination that Nigeria's contract with Kirkpatrick International was or was not, effective. . .

Petitioners insist, however, that the policies underlying our act of state cases—international comity, respect for the sovereignty of foreign nations on their own territory, and the avoidance of embarrassment to the Executive Branch in its conduct of foreign relations—are implicated in the present case because, as the District Court found, a determination that Nigerian officials demanded and accepted a bribe "would impugn or question the nobility of a foreign nation's motivations," and would "result in embarrassment to the sovereign or constitute interference in the conduct of foreign policy of the United States." The United States, as *amicus curiae,* favors the same approach to the act of state doctrine, though disagreeing with petitioners as to the outcome it produces in the present case. We should not, the United States urges, "attach dispositive significance to the fact that this suit involves only the 'motivation' for, rather than the 'validity' of, a foreign sovereign act," Brief for United States as *Amicus Curiae* 37, and should eschew "any rigid formula for the resolution of act of state cases generally," *id.,* at 9. In some future case, perhaps, "litigation . . . based on alleged corruption in the award of contracts or other commercially oriented activities of foreign governments could sufficiently touch on 'national nerves' that the act of state doctrine or related principles of abstention would appropriately be found to bar the suit," *id.,* at 40 (quoting *Sabbatino,* 376 U.S., at 428, 84 S.Ct., at 940), and we should therefore resolve this case on the narrowest possible ground, viz., that the letter from the legal advisor to the District Court gives sufficient indication that, "in the setting of this case," the act of state doctrine poses no bar to adjudication, *ibid.*

These urgings are deceptively similar to what we said in *Sabbatino,* where we observed that sometimes, even though the validity of the act of a foreign sovereign within its own territory is called into question, the policies underlying the act of state doctrine may not justify its application. We suggested that a sort of balancing approach could be applied—the balance shifting against application of the doctrine, for example, if the government that committed the "challenged act of state" is no longer in existence. But what is appropriate in order to avoid unquestioning judicial acceptance of the acts of foreign sovereigns is not similarly appropriate for the quite opposite purpose of expanding judicial incapacities where such acts are not directly (or even indirectly) involved. It is one thing to suggest, as we have, that the policies underlying the act of state doctrine should be considered in deciding whether despite the doctrine's technical availability, it should nonetheless not be invoked; it is something quite different to suggest that those underlying policies are a doctrine unto themselves, justifying expansion of the act of state doctrine (or, as the United States puts it, unspecified "related principles of abstention") into new and uncharted fields.

The short of the matter is this: Courts in the United States have the power, and ordinarily the obligation, to decide cases and controversies properly presented to them. The act of state doctrine does not establish an exception for cases and controversies that may embarrass foreign governments, but merely requires that, in the process of deciding, the acts of foreign sovereigns taken within their own jurisdictions shall be deemed valid. That doctrine has no application to the present case because the validity of no foreign sovereign act is at issue.

The judgment of the Court of Appeals for the Third Circuit is affirmed.

Judicial Cognizance of Foreign Acts of State

(1) Early cases applying the act-of-state doctrine, like *Underhill, Oetjen,* and *Ricaud,* treat it as a rule of comity or international law. *Sabbatino* shifts to a justification based on separation of powers. Does this matter? What is the actual holding in *Sabbatino*? How about the Court's test for applying the doctrine? Is the new test required by the shift in justification?

Sabbatino met with disapproval in Congress, which promptly enacted the so-called Second Hickenlooper Amendment. Codified at 22 U.S.C. § 2370(e)(2), the amendment provides:

> [N]o court in the United States shall decline on the ground of the federal act of state doctrine to make a determination on the merits giving effect to the principles of international law in a case in

> which a claim of title or other right to property is asserted by any party including a foreign state . . . based upon (or traced through) a confiscation or other taking . . . by an act of that state in violation of the principles of international law.

The Amendment sets forth the applicable principles of international law and provides that the act-of-state doctrine *should* apply if the President certifies that application is required by foreign policy interests of the United States.

Although the Second Hickenlooper Amendment appears to overrule *Sabbatino,* courts have confined it through interpretation to a relatively narrow class of cases. Thus, most courts hold that the Amendment applies only if the specific property directly involved in the allegedly unlawful foreign act is located in the United States. See, e.g., *Banco Nacional de Cuba v. Chase Manhattan Bank,* 658 F.2d 875, 882 n. 10 (2d Cir. 1981). More important, courts have held that the Amendment protects only a limited class of rights. In *Hunt v. Coastal States Gas Producing Co.,* 583 S.W.2d 322 (Tex. 1979), Libya had nationalized the Hunts' oil concession and contracted to sell oil to Coastal States. The Hunts' suit against Coastal States was dismissed on act-of-state grounds. According to the court, the Hickenlooper Amendment applies only to property and not to contract rights. Furthermore, because Libya was "both the place of the contract's execution and performance as well as the location of the subject matter, Libyan law governs the interpretation and construction of the rights conferred to Hunt. . ." And under Libyan law, the court concluded, the Hunts had only a contractual right. Why don't contract rights constitute "a claim of title or other right to property"?

(2) In *Federal Republic of Germany v. Philipp,* 141 S. Ct. 703 (2021), the heirs of German Jewish art dealers brought common-law property claims against Germany, alleging that in 1935 the Nazi government had unlawfully coerced the dealers into selling a valuable collection. Germany argued that it was immune from suit under the Foreign Sovereign Immunities Act (FSIA). In response, the plaintiffs relied on the FSIA's expropriation exception—written in very similar terms to the Second Hickenlooper Amendment—which denies immunity to a foreign sovereign in any case "in which rights in property taken in violation of international law are in issue." 28 U.S.C. § 1605(a)(3). The Court ruled unanimously in Germany's favor, holding that § 1605(a)(3) incorporates the so-called "domestic takings rule," which "assumes that what a country does to property belonging to its own citizens within its own borders is not the subject of international law." 141 S. Ct. at 709. In particular, the Court rejected the plaintiffs' argument that § 1605(a)(3) denies sovereign immunity when an act of domestic appropriation is part of a campaign of genocide or other human rights violations. Its narrow interpretation of the expropriation exception was bolstered, wrote Chief Justice Roberts, by the need to avoid international friction and by the idea that "United States law governs domestically but does not rule the world." *Id.* at 714 (quoting *Kiobel v. Royal Dutch Petroleum Co.*, 569 U.S. 108, 115 (2013). If Congress extended the expropriation exception, or the Second Hickenlooper Amendment, to acts of state in violation of international human rights norms, would this be an exercise of prescriptive jurisdiction justified by the universality principle?

(3) The act-of-state doctrine has been described, at different times, as an abstention rule, an application of the political question doctrine, and a rule of sovereign immunity. But can't the doctrine be understood as a straightforward principle of choice of law? If the act-of-state doctrine is a choice-of-law principle, what kind of principle is it? Courts applying the doctrine typically dismiss for lack of jurisdiction, explaining that judges should not risk interfering with foreign relations by passing on the legitimacy of the act of a foreign government, even if that act is repugnant to U.S. law. See, e.g., *International Assoc. of Machinists v. OPEC,* 649 F.2d 1354 (9th Cir. 1981). Is the act-of-state doctrine thus an exception to the public policy doctrine? Or is it analogous to the traditional exception for penal laws? Recall Learned Hand's explanation in *Moore v. Mitchell,* 30 F.2d 600 (2d Cir. 1929), supra p. 87, that courts do not enforce foreign penal laws because this "may commit the domestic state to a position which would seriously embarrass its neighbor." But isn't there a difference between refusing to enforce another state's policy, as under the penal law exception, and refusing to permit an attack on that policy, as under the act-of-state doctrine?

Not all courts applying the act-of-state doctrine dismiss solely on grounds of judicial incompetence. In many cases, judges couple a dismissal for lack of jurisdiction with firm condemnation of the foreign act of state. In *Sabbatino* itself, for example, the Court openly denounced Cuba's action as "discriminatory, arbitrary, and confiscatory" as well as "manifestly in violation of those principles of international law which have long been accepted by the free countries of the West." 376 U.S. at 402–03. See also *First National Bank of Boston v. Banco Nacional de Cuba,* 658 F.2d 895 (2d Cir. 1981). In these cases, doesn't the act-of-state doctrine look more like an *application* of the public policy exception?

In still other cases, courts refusing to permit attack on a foreign act of state actually enforce the foreign law and dismiss on the merits. See, e.g., *Galu v. Swissair,* 873 F.2d 650 (2d Cir. 1989) (applying Swiss law). In these cases, doesn't the act-of-state doctrine resemble the traditional preference for territorial rules in choice of law?

Which of these views makes the most sense? Does it matter?

(4) Consistent with earlier cases applying the act-of-state doctrine, *Sabbatino* carefully confines the doctrine to acts of a foreign nation "within its own territory." What is the rationale for this limitation? Its initial appearance in cases like *Underhill* and *Oetjen* is not surprising, since these cases were decided when the territorial principle reigned unchallenged in the courts. Does the limitation still make sense given the erosion of strict territoriality? Does it make sense given the Court's shift to a rationale based on separation of powers and avoiding embarrassment in foreign relations? Not surprisingly, courts attempting to enforce the territorial limitation have encountered the same problems of definition that arise in ordinary choice of law cases. See G. Born & D. Westin, International Civil Litigation in United States Courts 724–28 (3d ed. 1996).

(5) In most cases involving the act-of-state doctrine, the court dismisses a plaintiff's claim on the ground that the defendant's action was authorized or required by a foreign act of state. *Sabbatino* presents a more difficult problem in that the plaintiff invoked the act-of-state doctrine offensively to bar the defendants from raising a defense. Should that matter? Recall Justice Brandeis's argument in *Bradford Elec. Light Co. v. Clapper,* 286 U.S. 145, 160 (1932), supra p. 358, that the public policy doctrine could be used to bar a foreign cause of action but not a foreign defense. Is the argument applicable in *Sabbatino*? Should it have been? Does the Court's failure to distinguish between offensive and defensive uses have any implications for understanding the nature of the act-of-state doctrine?

(6) Professor Burley argues that the courts' inconsistent use of the act-of-state doctrine can be understood and justified by reference to the nature of the foreign government. Burley, *Law Among Liberal States: Liberal Internationalism and the Act of State Doctrine,* 92 Colum.L.Rev. 1907 (1992). Burley draws a distinction between liberal and non-liberal regimes, defined by whether a nation protects equality and property rights, makes law through a representative legislature, and depends primarily on a market economy. The role of the act-of-state doctrine, Burley argues, has varied—and should vary—depending on whether the other nation is liberal or not. Because the United States shares overlapping interests and approaches with other liberal states, differences in legal rules may be resolved within a "zone of law." Consequently, conflicts of laws between liberal states may be handled as an ordinary matter of choice of law: U.S. courts may balance interests or employ whatever other techniques seem appropriate to choose the applicable law, invoking the act-of-state doctrine as appropriate within the rubric of the traditional public policy exception. When it comes to non-liberal states, on the other hand, differences in fundamental outlook and approach consign the resolution of legal differences to a "zone of politics" in which adjudication is inappropriate. Conflicts in legal rules are therefore better left to political and diplomatic channels. The role of the act-of-state doctrine in this sphere is like the political question doctrine, and the court should decline jurisdiction as a way of refusing to treat the foreign act of state as law at all. In this way, Burley urges, the act-of-state doctrine may become part of a broad array of international techniques for encouraging the spread of liberal democracy.

Should courts vary the content or application of choice-of-law rules based on such considerations? Cf. Kramer, *Return of the Renvoi,* 66 N.Y.U. L. Rev. 979, 1015–28, 1038 n. 188 (1991) (arguing that, because choice-of-law rules should reflect tradeoffs among shared policies, they may differ between different states). But what is the difference between declining jurisdiction (to the act of a liberal state) on public policy grounds, and declining jurisdiction (to the act of a nonliberal state) on the ground that its acts do not qualify as law?

(7) What kinds of action qualify as "acts of state" for purposes of the act-of-state doctrine? Most cases have involved expropriations of property, and lower courts have struggled in applying *Sabbatino* to other alleged acts of state. See, e.g., *O.N.E. Shipping v. Flota Mercante Grancolombiana,* 830 F.2d 449 (2d Cir. 1987) (cargo reservation laws); *DeRoburt v. Gannett Co.,* 733 F.2d 701 (9th Cir. 1984) (receipt of loan). A few courts have held the act-of-state doctrine inapplicable to governmental acts other than the taking of property. E.g., *Mannington Mills, Inc. v. Congoleum Corp.,* 595 F.2d 1287 (3d Cir. 1979) (not applicable to foreign patent issuance); but see *Honduras Aircraft Registry v. Honduras,* 129 F.3d 543, 549–550 (11th Cir. 1997) (no "commercial activity" exception). Is there any reason to restrict the doctrine this way? How about terrorism? In *Flatow v. Islamic Republic of Iran,* 999 F.Supp. 1, 24 (D.D.C. 1998), the D.C. District Court concluded that while some violations of international law might be shielded by the act of state doctrine, "bus bombings and other acts of international terrorism" were not.

(8) Whose acts count as acts of state? In *Alfred Dunhill of London, Inc. v. Republic of Cuba,* 425 U.S. 682 (1976), Cuba confiscated the assets of businesses manufacturing Havana cigars and appointed "interventors" to take over the companies. American importers paid the interventors on accounts due from before the Cuban confiscation, and the interventors refused demands to return this money (which an American court held belonged to the original owners). In subsequent litigation, the interventors argued that their refusal to repay constituted an act of state that could not be questioned by an American court. The Supreme Court disagreed. Noting that the burden of establishing an act of state rests on the party asserting the defense, the Court reasoned that "[n]o statute, decree, order, or resolution of the Cuban Government itself was offered in evidence indicating that Cuba had repudiated its obligations in general or any class thereof or that it had as a sovereign matter determined to confiscate the amounts due three foreign importers."

Lower courts are divided over what is necessary to establish an act of state under *Dunhill.* Some courts require an unambiguous exercise of authority by senior government officials. E.g., *Remington Rand Corp. v. Business Sys.,* 830 F.2d 1260 (3d Cir. 1987). Others are willing to recognize action by any official with apparent authority to act for the state. E.g., *Bokkelen v. Grumman Aerospace Corp.,* 432 F.Supp. 329 (E.D.N.Y. 1977). All courts apparently agree that conduct plainly authorized or required by foreign law qualifies as an act of state. See Restatement (Third) of the Foreign Relations Law of United States § 443, comment i (1987). Thus, in *Galu v. Swiss Air Transport Co.,* 873 F.2d 650 (2d Cir. 1989), the plaintiff sued Swissair for cooperating with Swiss police in forcibly deporting her. The court ruled that the availability of an act-of-state defense depended on local law:

> The issue is whether the action taken against [the plaintiff] in removing her to the United States was an action that had been ordered in the exercise of the sovereign authority of Switzerland, or whether it was simply an ad hoc decision of local police officers. The burden is on defendant to establish foreign law to the extent necessary to demonstrate its entitlement to the act of state defense. Evidence of foreign law is required not to determine whether the forcible removal . . . was lawful but whether it was in fact an act of state.

If the act-of-state doctrine is triggered by the exercise of "sovereign authority," why limit it to executive action? Why isn't the enactment of a foreign statute itself an act of state requiring deference?

If the enactment of a statute may constitute an act of state, how about statutes governing relations between private parties? Here the tension between the act-of-state doctrine and the public policy exception becomes most evident: the public policy exception tells courts not to enforce foreign laws that are repugnant to forum policy; the act-of-state doctrine requires them to do so. Which approach makes more sense? So long as the court dismisses for lack of jurisdiction, does it even matter? Does it matter that the case is presented in an international rather than an interstate context?

(9) The Court in *Kirkpatrick* finds the act-of-state doctrine applicable only when the *legal validity* of a foreign act of state is challenged, and not when the *motivation* for that act is in issue. Given the policies underlying the act-of-state doctrine, especially the emphasis on not embarrassing the Executive in the conduct of foreign affairs, does this limitation make sense? Consider *Hunt v. Mobil Oil,* 550 F.2d 68, 77 (2d Cir. 1977), a suit arising from the same events as *Hunt v. Coastal States,* supra note (1). This time the Hunts brought an antitrust action against seven major oil companies, alleging that these companies conspired to prevent the Hunts from reaching a satisfactory agreement with Libya. The complaint did not name

Libya as a defendant and carefully avoided mentioning that Libya had terminated its relationship with the Hunts by nationalizing their interests. The court of appeals nonetheless dismissed on act-of-state grounds:

> The attempted transmogrification of Libya from lion to lamb undertaken here does not succeed in evading the act of state doctrine because we cannot logically separate Libya's motivation from the validity of its seizure. The American judiciary is being asked to make inquiry into the subtle and delicate issue of the policy of a foreign sovereign, a Serbonian Bog, precluded by the act of state doctrine as well as by the realities of the fact finding competence of the court in an issue of far reaching national concern.

See also *Clayco Petroleum Corp. v. Occidental Petroleum Corp.,* 712 F.2d 404 (9th Cir. 1983) ("In this case . . . the very existence of plaintiffs' claim depends upon establishing that the motivation for the sovereign act was bribery. Thus, embarrassment would result from adjudication.").

In *Kirkpatrick,* Justice Scalia rejects this reasoning on the ground that, while it makes sense to consider the policies underlying a doctrine in limiting its availability, "it is something quite different to suggest that those underlying policies are a doctrine unto themselves, justifying expansion of the act of state doctrine . . . into new and uncharted fields." But how does one know what the doctrine "is" without considering its underlying policies? Isn't that the whole point of interest analysis? What is Justice Scalia's justification for limiting the act-of-state doctrine to challenges to the legal validity of a foreign government's acts?

(10) How else might *Kirkpatrick* have been decided? The Solicitor General argued that, consistent with *Sabbatino,* the Court should balance the relevant factors to determine whether judicial resolution was appropriate. Applying that approach in *Kirkpatrick,* the SG continued, the act-of-state doctrine need not be applied: the suit was between private parties, the United States had a strong interest in enforcing its anti-corruption laws, there was no direct conflict with Nigerian law, and only commercial interests were at issue. Is this approach better?

(11) Should the applicability of the act-of-state doctrine be decided by the Executive branch? In *Bernstein v. N.V. Nederlandsche-Amerikaansche Stoomvaart-Maatschappij,* 210 F.2d 375 (2d Cir. 1954), a Jewish businessman sued to recover property seized by the Nazis during World War II. The State Department submitted a letter to the court stating that it had no objection to U.S. courts ruling on the validity of acts by Nazi officials. Based on this express executive authorization, the court found the act-of-state doctrine inapplicable.

The Supreme Court avoided ruling on the validity of this so-called *Bernstein* exception in *Sabbatino* because it read the State Department's letter to say that the Executive branch wished to take no position on the case. In *First National City Bank v. Banco Nacional de Cuba,* 406 U.S. 759 (1972), a plurality of three expressly endorsed the exception. Justice Rehnquist wrote:

> The act of state doctrine is grounded on judicial concern that application of customary principles of law to judge the acts of a foreign sovereign might frustrate the conduct of foreign relations by the political branches of the government. We conclude that where the Executive Branch, charged as it is with primary responsibility for the conduct of foreign affairs, expressly represents to the Court that application of the act of state doctrine would not advance the interests of American foreign policy, that doctrine should not be applied by the courts. . . We believe this to be no more than an application of the classical common-law maxim that "[t]he reason of the law ceasing, the law itself also ceases."

At least four Justices expressly rejected the *Bernstein* exception. Writing for himself and three other dissenters, Justice Brennan quoted Justice Harlan's statement in *Sabbatino* that "[i]t is highly questionable whether the examination of validity by the judiciary should depend on an educated guess by the Executive as to probable result and, at any rate, should a prediction be wrong, the Executive might be embarrassed in its dealings with other countries." Allowing the Executive to determine jurisdiction, Justice Brennan continued, relinquishes a judicial function to the Executive, politicizes the judiciary, fosters disrespect for the rule of law, and risks treating individual litigants unfairly. Writing separately, Justice Powell concurred with the result reached by the plurality, but agreed with Justice Brennan that *Sabbatino* had implicitly rejected the *Bernstein* exception. Justice Powell added, "I would feel uncomfortable with a doctrine which would require the judiciary to receive the Executive's permission before invoking its jurisdiction. Such a notion, in the name of the doctrine of separation of powers, seems to me to conflict with that very doctrine."

Despite its apparent rejection by five of the Justices, lower courts reacted with confusion to the Supreme Court's handling of the *Bernstein* exception. Some courts continued to apply the exception, *e.g., Occidental of Umm al Qaywayn, Inc. v. A Certain Cargo of Petroleum,* 577 F.2d 1196, 1204 (5th Cir. 1978), while other courts expressly rejected it, e.g., *Braniff Airways v. Civil Aeronautics Bd.,* 581 F.2d 846, 851 & n. 18 (D.C.Cir. 1978). Most courts adopted an intermediate position, treating the existence of a *Bernstein* letter as a significant, but not dispositive, factor in the analysis. See Restatement (Third) of Foreign Relations Law of the United States § 443, Reporter's Note 8 (1987) (citing cases).

SECTION 4. RECOGNITION OF JUDGMENTS

HILTON V. GUYOT

159 U.S. 113 (1895).

MR. JUSTICE GRAY delivered an opinion for the Court. . .

[A French court rendered judgment for over $195,000 against Hilton and Libbey, New York citizens trading in Paris, for sums due on an account with a French firm. Guyot, liquidator of the French firm, sued on the French judgment in a New York federal court. The trial court held the judgment conclusive.]

No law has any effect, of its own force, beyond the limits of the sovereignty from which its authority is derived. The extent to which the law of one nation, as put in force within its territory, whether by executive order, by legislative act, or by judicial decree, shall be allowed to operate within the dominion of another nation, depends upon what our greatest jurists have been content to call "the comity of nations." Although the phrase has been often criticized, no satisfactory substitute has been suggested.

"Comity," in the legal sense, is neither a matter of absolute obligation, on the one hand, nor of mere courtesy and good will, upon the other. But it is the recognition which one nation allows within its territory to the legislative, executive or judicial acts of another nation, having due regard both to international duty and convenience, and to the rights of its own citizens or of other persons who are under the protection of its laws. . .

In order to appreciate the weight of the various authorities cited at the bar, it is important to distinguish different kinds of judgments. Every foreign judgment, of whatever nature, in order to be entitled to any effect, must have been rendered by a court having jurisdiction of the cause, and upon regular proceedings and due notice. In alluding to different kinds of judgments, therefore, such jurisdiction, proceedings and notice will be assumed. It will also be assumed that they are untainted by fraud, the effect of which will be considered later.

A judgment in rem, adjudicating the title to a ship or other movable property within the custody of the court, is treated as valid everywhere. As said by Chief Justice Marshall: "The sentence of a competent court, proceeding in rem, is conclusive with respect to the thing itself, and operates as an absolute change of the property. By such sentence, the right of the former owner is lost, and a complete title given to the person who claims under the decree. No court of coordinate jurisdiction can examine the sentence. The question, therefore, respecting its conformity to general or municipal law can never arise, for no coordinate tribunal is capable of making the inquiry." . . .

A judgment affecting the status of persons, such as a decree confirming or dissolving a marriage, is recognized as valid in every country, unless contrary to the policy of its own law. . .

Other judgments, not strictly in rem, under which a person has been compelled to pay money, are so far conclusive that the justice of the payment cannot be impeached in another country, so as to compel him to pay it again. For instance, a judgment in foreign attachment is conclusive, as between the parties, of the right to the property or money attached. . .

The extraterritorial effect of judgments in personam, at law or in equity, may differ, according to the parties to the cause. A judgment of that kind between two citizens or residents of the country, and thereby subject to the jurisdiction in which it is rendered, may be held conclusive as between them everywhere. So, if a foreigner invokes the jurisdiction by bringing an action against a citizen, both may be held bound by a judgment in favor of either. And if a citizen sues a foreigner, and judgment is rendered in favor of the latter, both may be held equally bound. * * *

The effect to which a judgment, purely executory, rendered in favor of a citizen or resident of the country, in a suit there brought by him against a foreigner, may be entitled in an action thereon against the latter in his own country—as is the case now before us—presents a more difficult question, upon which there has been some diversity of opinion. . .

[W]e are satisfied that, where there has been opportunity for a full and fair trial abroad before a court of competent jurisdiction, conducting the trial upon regular proceedings, after due citation or voluntary appearance of the defendant, and under a system of jurisprudence likely to secure an impartial administration of justice between the citizens of its own country and those of other countries, and there is nothing to show either prejudice in the court, or in the system of laws under which it was sitting, or fraud in procuring the judgment, or any other special reason why the comity of this nation should not allow it full effect, the merits of the case should not, in an action brought in this country upon the judgment, be tried afresh, as on a new trial or an appeal, upon the mere assertion of the party that the judgment was erroneous in law or in fact. The defendants, therefore, cannot be permitted, upon that general ground, to contest the validity or the effect of the judgment sued on. But they have sought to impeach that judgment upon several other grounds, which require separate consideration.

It is objected that the appearance and litigation of the defendants in the French tribunals were not voluntary, but by legal compulsion, and therefore that the French courts never acquired such jurisdiction over the defendants, that they should be held bound by the judgment. [The Court found that the French court had personal jurisdiction of the defendants.]

It is next objected that in those courts one of the plaintiffs was permitted to testify not under oath, and was not subjected to cross-examination by the opposite party, and that the defendants were, therefore, deprived of safeguards which are by our law considered essential to secure honesty and to detect fraud in a witness; and also that documents and papers were admitted in evidence, with which the defendants had no connection, and which would not be admissible under our own system of jurisprudence. But it having been shown by the plaintiffs, and hardly denied by the defendants, that the practice followed and the method of examining witnesses were according to the law of France, we are not prepared to hold that the fact that the procedure in these respects differed from that of our own courts is, of itself, a sufficient ground for impeaching the foreign judgment. . .

When an action is brought in a court of this country, by a citizen of a foreign country against one of our own citizens, to recover a sum of money adjudged by a court of that country to be due from the defendant to the plaintiff, and the foreign judgment appears to have been rendered by a competent court, having jurisdiction of the cause and of the parties, and upon due allegations and proofs, and opportunity to defend against them, and its proceedings are according to the course of a civilized jurisprudence, and are stated in a clear and formal record, the judgment is prima facie evidence, at least, of the truth of the matter adjudged; and it should be held conclusive upon the merits tried in the foreign court, unless some special ground is shown for impeaching the judgment, as by showing that it was affected by fraud or prejudice, or that, by the principles of international law, and by the comity of our own country, it should not be given full credit and effect. . .

[I]t is unnecessary in this case to determine [whether the French judgment may be impeached for fraud] because there is a distinct and independent ground upon which we are satisfied that the comity of our nation does not require us to give conclusive effect to the judgments of the courts of France; and that ground is, the want of reciprocity, on the part of France, as to the effect to be given to the judgments of this and other foreign countries. . .

The defendants . . . alleged, and at the trial offered to prove, that . . . when the judgments of tribunals of foreign countries against the citizens of France are sued upon in the courts of France, the merits of the controversies upon which those judgments are based are examined anew, unless a treaty to the contrary effect exists between the Republic of France and the country in which such judgment is obtained (which is not the case between the Republic of France and the United States), and that the tribunals of the Republic of France give no force and effect, within the jurisdiction of that country, to the judgments duly rendered by courts of competent jurisdiction of the United States against citizens of France after proper personal service of the process of those courts has been made thereon in this country. We are of opinion that this evidence should have been admitted. . .

[T]here is hardly a civilized nation on either continent, which, by its general law, allows conclusive effect to an executory foreign judgment for the recovery of money. . . In the great majority of the countries on the continent of Europe, . . . the judgment rendered in a foreign country is allowed the same effect only as the courts of that country allow to the judgments of the country in which the judgment in question is sought to be executed. . .

The reasonable, if not the necessary, conclusion appears to us to be that judgments rendered in France, or in any other foreign country, by the laws of which our own judgments are reviewable upon the merits, are not entitled to full credit and conclusive effect when sued upon in this country, but are prima facie evidence only of the justice of the plaintiffs' claim.

In holding such a judgment, for want of reciprocity, not to be conclusive evidence of the merits of the claim, we do not proceed upon any theory of retaliation upon one person by reason of injustice done to another; but upon the broad ground that international law is founded upon mutuality and reciprocity, and that by the principles of international law recognized in most civilized nations, and by the comity of our own country, which it is our judicial duty to know and to declare, the judgment is not entitled to be considered conclusive. . .

If the judgment had been rendered in this country, . . . the French courts would not have executed or enforced it, except after examining into its merits. The very judgment now sued on would be held inconclusive in almost any other country than France. In England, and in the Colonies subject to the law of England, the fraud alleged in its procurement would be a sufficient ground for disregarding it. In the courts of nearly every other nation, it would be subject to reexamination, either merely because it was a foreign judgment, or because judgments of that nation would be reexaminable in the courts of France.

For these reasons . . . the judgment is reversed.

CHIEF JUSTICE FULLER, with whom concurred MR. JUSTICE HARLAN, MR. JUSTICE BREWER, and MR. JUSTICE JACKSON, dissenting.

[T]he doctrine of res judicata applicable to domestic judgments should be applied to foreign judgments as well, and rests on the same general ground of public policy that there should be an end of litigation. . .

I cannot yield my assent to the proposition that because by legislation and judicial decision in France that effect is not there given to judgments recovered in this country which, according to our jurisprudence, we think should be given to judgments wherever recovered (subject, of course, to the recognized exceptions), therefore we should pursue the same line of conduct as respects the judgments of French tribunals. The application of the doctrine of res judicata does not rest in discretion; and it is for the government, and not for its courts, to adopt the principle of retorsion, if deemed under any circumstances desirable or necessary. . .

Recognition of Foreign-Country Judgments

(1) Does the comity doctrine of *Hilton v. Guyot* represent a better accommodation of the relevant interests than the full faith and credit law developed by the Supreme Court? What effect would be given to foreign judgments in an ideal world? Is there any policy reason for treating foreign-country judgments differently from those of sister states?

The Second Restatement takes a compromise position on this issue:

> A valid judgment rendered in a foreign nation after a fair trial in a contested proceeding will be recognized in the United States so far as the immediate parties and the underlying cause of action are concerned.

Restatement (Second) of Conflict of Laws § 98 (1971). While a general policy in favor of recognition is stated, its application is limited to contested cases and to effects upon the immediate parties and the underlying cause of action. The reference to "fair trial" permits inquiry concerning the impartiality of the foreign court. See Peterson, *Foreign Country Judgments and the Second Restatement of Conflict of Laws,* 72 Colum.L.Rev. 220 (1972).

Professors von Mehren and Trautman in their exhaustive survey of the subject disagree in part with the Second Restatement's general policy in favor of recognition, arguing that the principles underlying domestic res-judicata practice and recognition of sister-state judgments are not readily transferable to international recognition practice. von Mehren & Trautman, *Recognition of Foreign Adjudications: A Survey and a Suggested Approach,* 81 Harv.L.Rev. 1601 (1968):

> Although federal-system practice and international practice will share certain requirements, there are sufficient differences between the two that recognition may properly be refused to a judgment from a foreign country when it should be accorded to a comparable judgment from a sister state.
>
> In the United States, full faith and credit substitutes a federal policy for individual state policies, and sister-state judgments are accorded more substantial preclusive effects than if each state were free to follow its more egocentric predilections.

> In addition, doctrinal propositions basic to our federal-system practice interact in a way that blurs distinctions essential to proper understanding of international practice. In particular, whether recognition is to be accorded tends—aside from minimal due process requirements such as a fair and orderly procedure—to become a reflex of whether the rendering court had jurisdiction, especially in view of constitutional restraints, to render a judgment effective for that community's own purposes. This blending of issues that are usually separate in international recognition practice is doctrinally attractive because of the interplay between due process and full faith and credit and reflects inherent differences between the federal and the international contexts. . . By and large, sister-state judgments are rendered by courts whose procedures and standards are similar to those of the recognizing jurisdiction and by men who, even if not known personally, are members of a national legal profession. Finally, some of the procedures and standards are defined by the Federal Constitution, and to this extent the parties can seek direct review before the Supreme Court of the United States.

81 Harv.L.Rev. at 1607. Are you persuaded?

(2) When does the reciprocity requirement of *Hilton* apply? Consider whether a French judgment would be subject to relitigation (assuming that the French court had jurisdiction) in the following cases: (a) an action between two citizens of France; (b) an action brought by an American citizen against a French national; (c) a judgment in favor of an American defendant in a suit brought against him in France by a French national; (d) a French divorce decree; (e) the disposition of a ship's cargo by a French court.

(3) Is the reciprocity position of the *Hilton* case based on a theory of retaliation? If not, then what is its justification? If so, why should courts discriminate against private litigants because of the policies of the litigants' governments?

Most commentators dislike the reciprocity requirement. The Second Restatement concedes that uniform acts, state statutes, and international arrangements often require reciprocity, but disapproves of the principle not only in the recognition of foreign country judgments (§ 98, comment e) but also in choice of law generally:

> In formulating common law rules of choice of law, the courts are rarely guided by considerations of reciprocity. Private parties . . . should not be made to suffer for the fact that the courts of the state from which they come give insufficient consideration to the interests of the state of the forum.

Restatement (Second) of Conflict of Laws § 6, comment k. See also Restatement (Third) of Foreign Relations Law § 481, comment d & Reporter's Note 1 (1987); G. Born & D. Westin, International Civil Litigation in United States Courts 951–55 (3d ed. 1996); Reese, *The Status in this Country of Judgments Rendered Abroad,* 50 Colum. L. Rev. 783, 793 (1950); Comment, *The Reciprocity Rule and Enforcement of Foreign Judgments,* 16 Colum. J. Trasnat'l L. 327, 346–48 (1977).

Courts, too, generally reject reciprocity as a condition for recognition. According to the Third Restatement of Foreign Relations Law, *Hilton's* reciprocity requirement "is no longer followed in the great majority of State and federal courts in the United States." Restatement (Third) of Foreign Relations Law § 481, comment d. In *Somportex, Ltd. v. Philadelphia Chewing Gum Corp.,* 318 F.Supp. 161 (E.D.Pa. 1970), a federal court in a diversity action predicted that Pennsylvania state courts would no longer follow *Hilton* with respect to reciprocity, explaining:

> The primary reason which has been advanced [for abandoning the reciprocity requirement] is that our legal system has adopted a policy that calls for an end to litigation. Whether or not a foreign court would recognize an American judgment is not relevant to this policy. However, it is in furtherance of that objective if litigation which was begun in a foreign court and which is presently before an American tribunal, is brought to an end. The Court finds that the concept of reciprocity is a provincial one, one which fosters decisions that do violence to the legitimate goals of comity between foreign nations.

See also *Nicol v. Tanner,* 310 Minn. 68, 256 N.W.2d 796 (1976). But doesn't requiring reciprocity put pressure on non-conforming states to adopt a more generally accepted approach? See Kramer, *Return of the Renvoi,* 66 N.Y.U. L. Rev. 979, 1021–28 (1991); L. Brilmayer, Conflict of Laws: Foundations and Future Directions ch. 4 (2d ed. 1995).

Decisions in a few states indicate that pockets of adherence to the reciprocity requirement remain. See, e.g., *Banque Libanaise Pour Le Commerce v. Khreich,* 915 F.2d 1000, 1004–06 (5th Cir. 1990); *Corporacion Salvadorena de Calzado, S.A. v. Injection Footwear Corp.,* 533 F.Supp. 290 (S.D.Fla. 1982); *Medical Arts Building v. Eralp,* 290 N.W.2d 241 (N.D. 1980); *Cannistraro v. Cannistraro,* 352 Mass. 65, 223 N.E.2d 692 (1967). If Congress adopts the statute proposed by the American Law Institute (see note 8), reciprocity will become a condition for recognition by virtue of federal law.

(4) Is a default judgment rendered by a foreign court entitled to recognition? In *Somportex Ltd. v. Philadelphia Chewing Gum Corp.,* 453 F.2d 435 (3d Cir. 1971), a Pennsylvania seller negotiated through a New York exporter with a British buyer for the sale of chewing gum in England.

In the buyer's breach-of-contract action in an English court, jurisdiction was asserted over the Pennsylvania seller under the English equivalent of our long-arm statutes. The seller, through an English solicitor, first made a "conditional appearance" to contest personal jurisdiction, then abandoned this effort and allowed a default judgment to be entered against it for the amount claimed, including loss of good will and attorneys' fees (items that were not recoverable in Pennsylvania). The Third Circuit affirmed a summary judgment for the English buyer: Under applicable Pennsylvania law the default judgment was entitled to recognition; the issue of personal jurisdiction was foreclosed since the seller had not availed itself of a full and fair opportunity to litigate that issue in the English court; and there was nothing in Pennsylvania policy against the enforcement of foreign default judgments or the recovery of good will and attorneys' fees.

One aspect of a fair proceeding is adequate notification. In *Julen v. Larson*, 25 Cal.App.3d 325, 101 Cal.Rptr. 796 (1972), the California court refused to recognize a Swiss default judgment on the ground that the defendant, who could not read German, was served in California with legal documents written in German.

(5) What defenses should be available (aside from the reciprocity problem) against the recognition of a foreign-country judgment? Are the enforcing state's standards of jurisdiction and competence of greater relevance in the international situation than they are under the full faith and credit requirement within our federal system?

Should recognition be denied to a foreign judgment on the ground that the nation whose law was applied lacked legislative jurisdiction? *Schibsby v. Westenholz* [1870] L.R. 6 Q.B. 155, involved an action in an English court to enforce a French default judgment. The plaintiff was a Dane living in France, the defendant was a Dane living in England, and the case involved an agreement made in England for the sale of Swedish oats. The French court exercised jurisdiction under the notorious Article 14 of the French Civil Code, authorizing the exercise of jurisdiction over foreigners in certain actions brought by French plaintiffs (including aliens resident in France). The English court refused to recognize a judgment rendered on this jurisdictional basis:

> Can the empire of France pass a law to bind the whole world? . . . We think . . . the answer should be, No, but every country can pass laws to bind a great many persons; and therefore the further question has to be determined, whether the defendant in the particular suit was such a person as to be bound by the judgment.

The court held that defendants who were French citizens or residents, or who were present in France "when the obligation was contracted," and plaintiffs who had invoked the jurisdiction of the French court would be bound by the French judgment, but that nonresident defendants who had neither acted in France nor owned property there would not be so bound. Is this the kind of "jurisdictional" defect that normally does, or should, lead to non-recognition? Cf. *Fauntleroy v. Lum,* 210 U.S. 230 (1908), supra p. 562.

In addition to the application of jurisdictional tests, a foreign-country judgment generally is subject to attack on the grounds that it was procured by fraud, violated local public policy, or is contrary to natural justice, a vague category that includes instances in which the foreign procedure departed rather flagrantly from American notions of fairness. See Restatement (Second) of Conflict of Laws § 98. Of these defenses, public policy is the most frequently invoked. Should there be a public policy exception for the recognition or enforcement of foreign judgments? Why here but not when it comes to the judgments of sister states?

In American courts, the First Amendment was frequently raised as a defense to foreign judgments based on laws that were not sufficiently speech-protective to meet U.S. constitutional standards. See, e.g., *Telnikoff v. Matusevitch*, 702 A.2d 230 (Md. 1997). (Whether this was a public policy defense or an actual constitutional bar to enforcement was often unclear.) In 2010, Congress enacted the Securing the Protection of our Enduring and Established Constitutional Heritage Act (the SPEECH Act). The Act prohibits both state and federal courts from recognizing or enforcing foreign defamation judgments unless the underlying law provided as much speech protection as the federal First Amendment and the law of the state in which the court is located, or the defendant would have been found liable even if the law had provided such protection. It also authorizes individuals subject to foreign defamation judgments to bring pre-enforcement declaratory actions in federal district court.

(6) The previous note examined the question whether a foreign country judgment, valid where rendered, should be tested under the different jurisdictional standards of the forum. Are there converse situations in which the forum should recognize a foreign country judgment even though it is subject to collateral attack where rendered? Consider a judgment resulting from a real contest that is subject to a technical defect in the rendering state, a defect that is not considered serious at the forum with respect to its domestic judgments. In *Pemberton v. Hughes,* [1899] 1 Ch. 781 (C.A.), the validity of the exercise of a power to appoint English property to "any woman whom [the appointee] should marry" turned on the validity of a prior uncontested Florida divorce. Mrs. Pemberton and her first husband were domiciled in Florida at the time of the divorce proceeding; but the return date fixed in the summons served on the wife gave her only nine days rather than the required ten to make an appearance. The court assumed, despite conflicting evidence on the question, that the defect would lead a Florida court to consider its decree invalid. Nevertheless, the court concluded:

> Where no substantial justice, according to English notions, is offended, all that English Courts look to is the finality of the judgment and the jurisdiction of the Court, in this sense and to this extent—namely, its competence to entertain the sort of case which it did deal with, and its competence to require the defendant to appear before it. If the Court had jurisdiction in this sense and to this extent, the Courts of this country never inquire whether the jurisdiction has been properly or improperly exercised, provided always that no substantial injustice, according to English notions, has been committed.

The other judges, in separate opinions, agreed. Would it violate due process for a court in the United States to give greater effect to a foreign judgment than it would have in the nation that rendered it?

(7) The Uniform Foreign Money-Judgments Recognition Act, 13 U.L.A. 419 (1980), adopted in 32 states as of 2021, provides that a foreign money judgment "is enforceable in the same manner as the judgment of a sister-state which is entitled to full faith and credit." Reciprocity is not required. A foreign judgment is not conclusive (i.e., may not be enforced) if the tribunal is not impartial, its procedures do not comport with due process, or if there is no jurisdiction over the defendant or subject matter. In addition, a foreign judgment need not (but may) be recognized if the defendant "did not receive notice of the proceedings in sufficient time to enable him to defend"; the judgment was obtained by fraud; the underlying claim "is repugnant to the public policy of this state"; the judgment conflicts with another final and conclusive judgment; "the proceeding in the foreign court was contrary to a [dispute-resolution] agreement between the parties"; or, "in the case of jurisdiction based on personal service, the foreign court was a seriously inconvenient forum for the trial of the action." Which of these defenses would be available against a domestic judgment? Against a sister-state judgment? The Act is discussed in Scoles & Aarnas, *The Recognition of Foreign Nation Judgments: California, Oregon, and Washington,* 57 Or.L.Rev. 377, 382–89 (1978); Homburger, *Recognition and Enforcement of Foreign Judgments,* 18 Am.J.Comp.L. 367 (1970); Kulzer, *Recognition of Foreign Country Judgments in New York: The Uniform Foreign Money-Judgments Recognition Act,* 18 Buff.L.Rev. 1 (1969). The 1962 Act was modestly revised in 2005 as the Uniform Foreign Country Money-Judgments Recognition Act and had been adopted by 28 states and the District of Columbia as of 2021.

(8) Why is the recognition of a foreign judgment a matter of state law at all? *Hilton,* a pre-*Erie* diversity case, applies the non-federal general common law of the *Swift v. Tyson* era. Post-*Erie,* in the absence of a federal statute, most state courts have applied state law and federal courts exercising diversity jurisdiction have done likewise. (In federal question cases, there is no reason to consult state law, and federal law controls. See

C. Wright, A. Miller & E. Cooper, Federal Practice and Procedure § 4473 (1981); *Phillips USA, Inc. v. Allflex USA, Inc.,* 77 F.3d 354, 358–60 (10th Cir. 1996); *Choi v. Kim,* 50 F.3d 244, 248–50 (3d Cir. 1995); Born, International Civil Litigation in United States Courts, at 1003–1005.

But is the reciprocity policy of *Hilton* so intimately related to the relations of the United States with foreign powers that federal law is controlling even in state courts? The New York Court of Appeals, in an influential early decision, argued that it is not: "[T]he question is one of private rather than public international law, of private right rather than public relations." *Johnston v. Compagnie Generale Transatlantique,* 242 N.Y. 381, 387, 152 N.E. 121, 123 (1926). Most commentators, to the contrary, have favored federal rules.

Which side has it right? See *Zschernig v. Miller,* 389 U.S. 429 (1968), in which the Court struck down an Oregon statute providing for the escheat of decedents' estates when an alien heir's country would not allow U.S. citizens reciprocal rights of inheritance. The statute, aimed primarily at Communist countries, was held to be "an [invalid] intrusion by the State into the field of foreign affairs which the Constitution entrusts to the President and the Congress." 389 U.S. at 432. See also *Banco Nacional de Cuba v. Sabbatino,* 376 U.S. 398, 425–27 (1964), supra p. 1055, and *Garamendi,* supra p. 946. The Tenth Circuit's opinion in *Phillips USA* suggests that concerns about interference with national foreign relations policy should be handled on a case-by-case basis. See 77 F.3d at 359 n.5. Is that feasible? (In a portion of the *Hoffmann* decision not reproduced above, Justice Breyer rejected the case-by-case approach as too difficult and time-consuming.) Is it consistent with choice-of-law thinking?

Even if the federal interest in the issue is not so strong as to preempt state law in the absence of federal action, Congress could enact a statute setting uniform rules. (What in the Constitution gives Congress the power to do so?) In 2006, the American Law Institute proposed such a statute. Citing *Sabbatino* and *Garamendi,* the ALI report suggests that enforcement of foreign judgments "is an aspect of the relation between the United States and the foreign state" and raises the kind of foreign relations issues that the Supreme Court has held are exclusively the province of the federal government. See ALI, *Recognition and Enforcement of Foreign Judgments: Analysis and Proposed Federal Statute* (2006).

The proposed statute excludes domestic relations and bankruptcy judgments, as well as arbitral awards. For judgments within its scope, it prescribes enforcement subject to a reciprocity requirement and several other conditions. Foreign judgments "shall not be recognized or enforced" if the foreign adjudication did not meet standards of fundamental fairness; if there is doubt about the impartiality of the rendering tribunal; if the judgment was obtained by fraud; if the substantive law on which the judgment is based is contrary to the policy of the United States or a particular state; or if jurisdiction is based on certain prohibited bases: seizure of property in the forum, except in maritime or admiralty cases, where the claim is unrelated to the property; nationality, domicile, or state of incorporation; service of process based on transitory presence within the jurisdiction; or any other "unreasonable or unfair" basis. Foreign judgments need not (but may be) recognized or enforced if the rendering court lacked subject matter jurisdiction, or its state lacked legislative jurisdiction; if the proceeding leading to the judgment was commenced after a pending U.S. proceeding involving the same parties and subject matter; if the judgment conflicts with another foreign judgment entitled to recognition; or if the judgment results from an attempt to prevent adjudication by a "more appropriate court" in the U.S. Tax and penal judgments likewise may but need not be enforced, and declaratory judgments or injunctions are not directly enforceable but may be entitled to recognition. Default judgments are entitled to recognition as long as jurisdiction and service of process were proper.

The proposed statute provides that if the foreign judgment orders payment in a foreign currency, the U.S. court enforcing the judgment may order payment in that currency or in U.S. dollars "at the exchange rate prevailing on the date of the judgment granting enforcement." What law determined in which country's currency the underlying international judgment was expressed? Is this a choice-of-law question? If so, how should it be resolved? What turns on it? See Vaughan Black, *Foreign Currency Obligations in Private International Law*, 302 *Recueil des cours* (2003) (proposing an international convention).

(9) Or should the recognition of foreign-nation judgments be handled by international treaties? In the 1970s, the United States and the United Kingdom sought to conclude a bilateral agreement on mutual recognition and enforcement of foreign judgments. The proposed convention, which is reprinted in 16 Int'l Leg.Mat. 71 (1977), would have applied broadly to judgments and orders binding where rendered, but would have excluded judgments for revenue claims, punitive damages, administrative orders and awards, and status determinations. The agreement was not ratified due to differences over the size and punitive nature of some U.S. civil judgments and the reach of U.S. judicial jurisdiction.

Treaties among other countries may also affect the recognition of U.S. judgments abroad and the enforcement against U.S. citizens in third countries of judgments predicated on a thin jurisdictional basis (e.g., Article 14 of the French Civil Code, permitting jurisdiction of noncitizens solely on the basis of the plaintiff's French nationality).

(10) As mentioned in Chapter 4, supra p. 543, the European Convention on Jurisdiction and Enforcement of Judgments (the Brussels and Lugano Conventions) establishes certain rules governing full faith and credit for judgments within the European Community. Among Member States, judgments rendered on jurisdictional grounds authorized by the Convention are entitled to recognition and enforcement in other Convention States. The court that hears the case and renders the judgment determines its own jurisdiction, and no challenge is permitted in the State where enforcement is sought, even when a judgment was obtained by default. A handful of limited defenses to recognition and enforcement are permitted, (a) public policy, (b) default judgments obtained without proper service or an opportunity to be heard, and (c) conflicts with earlier judgments.

In the absence of a Convention, recognition and enforcement of another country's judgments in many European countries, including the United Kingdom, can be difficult. Most European nations have statutes that set forth the circumstances in which a foreign judgment will or will not be enforced. A number of countries impose a reciprocity requirement, that is, enforcement and recognition depend upon showing that the courts of the country whose judgment is at issue would enforce the judgment of the requested country if the facts were reversed. In some countries, such as the United Kingdom, default judgments are generally not enforced unless the defendant was said to be "present" or if the defendant appeared or contractually consented to the jurisdiction of the foreign court. "Public policy" remains an important limitation for most countries in determining whether or not to recognize or enforce the judgment of another country.

Getting U.S. judgments recognized and enforced abroad is especially difficult. American tort damages are often regarded as "excessive" and such judgments are rarely enforced. Judgments resting on "doing business" or "tag" jurisdiction are also generally not respected. Other judgments—seen as a product of contingent fees, broad discovery, and jury verdicts—are likely to be viewed with suspicion and not enforced. See Restatement (Third) of Foreign Relations Law of the United States, Reporters' Note 6, at pp. 601–03 (1987); A. Lowenfeld, Recognition and Enforcement of Judgments, in International Litigation and the Quest for Reasonableness 109, 129–36 (1996); Wurmnest, *Recognition and Enforcement of U.S. Money Judgments in Germany*, 23 Berkeley J. Int'l L. 175 (2005).

(11) After more than two decades of negotiation, the Hague Convention on the Recognition and Enforcement of Foreign Judgments in Civil or Commercial Matters was finalized in 2019. As its name suggests, the Convention covers judgments in civil and commercial matters. According to its Article 2(1), it excludes the status and legal capacity of natural persons, family law matters, insolvency, privacy, intellectual property, and certain antitrust issues. The Convention sets forth, in Article 5(1), a disjunctive list of criteria to be used by a court in one signatory nation to determine whether a judgment from another signatory nation is eligible for recognition and enforcement. These criteria include that:

> (a) the person against whom recognition or enforcement is sought was habitually resident in the State of origin at the time that person became a party to the proceedings in the court of origin;
>
> (b) the natural person against whom recognition or enforcement is sought had their principal place of business in the State of origin at the time that person became a party to the proceedings in the court of origin and the claim on which the judgment is based arose out of the activities of that business; . . .
>
> (e) the defendant expressly consented to the jurisdiction of the court of origin in the course of the proceedings in which the judgment was given;
>
> (f) the defendant argued on the merits before the court of origin without contesting jurisdiction within the timeframe provided in the law of the State of origin, unless it is evident that an objection to jurisdiction or to the exercise of jurisdiction would not have succeeded under that law;
>
> (g) the judgment ruled on a contractual obligation and it was given by a court of the State in which performance of that obligation took place, or should have taken place, in accordance with
>
> > (i) the agreement of the parties, or
> >
> > (ii) the law applicable to the contract, in the absence of an agreed place of performance, unless the activities of the defendant in relation to the transaction clearly did not constitute a purposeful and substantial connection to that State; . . .
>
> (j) the judgment ruled on a non-contractual obligation arising from death, physical injury, damage to or loss of tangible property, and the act or omission directly causing such harm occurred in the State of origin, irrespective of where that harm occurred . . .

Article 7 provides that a recognition or enforcement may be refused if the defendant did not receive adequate notice under the laws of the nation in which recognition is sought; if the judgment was obtained by fraud; if recognition or enforcement would be "manifestly incompatible with the public policy" of the nation where it is sought; if the underlying proceedings were contrary to an agreement calling for the dispute to be resolved in another nation; if the judgment is inconsistent with a judgment between the same parties in the nation where recognition is sought; or if the judgment is inconsistent with an earlier judgment by another nation between the same parties on the same subject matter, provided that the earlier judgment fulfills the conditions for recognition.

As of September 2021, only Uruguay, Ukraine, Israel, and Costa Rica had signed the Hague Convention. How does the Convention differ from U.S. law on recognition and enforcement of judgments? Does it represent an improvement?

(12) Recognition of foreign country judgments is the subject of an enormous literature. See, e.g., G. Born & D. Westin, International Civil Litigation in United States Courts 935–86 (3d ed. 1996); E. Scoles, P. Hay, P. Borchers & S. Symeonides, Conflict of Laws 1153–87 (3d ed. 2000); Shill, *Ending Judgment Arbitrage: Jurisdictional Competition and the Enforcement of Foreign Money Judgments in the United States*, 54 Harv. Int'l L.J. 459 (2013); Coyle, *Rethinking Judgments Reciprocity*, 92 N.C. L. Rev. 1109 (2014).

APPENDIX A

THE CONSTITUTION OF THE UNITED STATES

■ ■ ■

We the People of the United States, in Order to form a more perfect Union, establish Justice, insure domestic Tranquility, provide for the common defence, promote the general Welfare, and secure the Blessings of Liberty to ourselves and our Posterity, do ordain and establish this Constitution for the United States of America.

ARTICLE I.

Section 1. All legislative Powers herein granted shall be vested in a Congress of the United States, which shall consist of a Senate and House of Representatives. . .

Section 8. The Congress shall have Power To lay and collect Taxes, Duties, Imposts and Excises, to pay the Debts and provide for the common Defence and general Welfare of the United States; but all Duties, Imposts and Excises shall be uniform throughout the United States; . . .

To borrow Money on the credit of the United States;

To regulate Commerce with foreign Nations, and among the several States and with the Indian Tribes;

To establish an uniform Rule of Naturalization, and uniform Laws on the subject of Bankruptcies throughout the United States;

To coin Money, regulate the Value thereof, and of foreign Coin, and fix the Standard of Weights and Measures;

To provide for the Punishment of counterfeiting the Securities and current Coin of the United States;

To establish Post Offices and post Roads;

To promote the Progress of Science and useful Arts, by securing for limited Times to Authors and Inventors the Exclusive Right to their respective Writings and Discoveries;

To constitute Tribunals inferior to the supreme Court;

To define and punish Piracies and Felonies committed on the high Seas, and Offences against the Law of Nations;

To declare War, grant Letters of Marque and Reprisal, and make Rules concerning Captures on Land and Water;

To raise and support Armies, but no Appropriation of Money to that Use shall be for a longer Term than two Years;

To provide and maintain a Navy;

To make Rules for the Government and Regulation of the land and naval Forces;

To provide for calling forth the Militia to execute the Laws of the Union, suppress Insurrections and repel Invasions;

To provide for organizing, arming, and disciplining, the Militia, and for governing such Part of them as may be employed in the Service of the United States, reserving to the States respectively, the Appointment of the Officers, and the Authority of training the Militia according to the discipline prescribed by Congress;

To exercise exclusive Legislation in all Cases whatsoever, over such District (not exceeding ten Miles square) as may, by Cession of particular States, and the Acceptance of Congress, become the Seat of the Government of the United States, and to exercise like Authority over all Places purchased by the Consent of the Legislature of the State in which the Same shall be, for the Erection of Forts, Magazines, Arsenals, dock-Yards, and other needful Buildings;—And

To make all Laws which shall be necessary and proper for carrying into Execution the foregoing Powers, and all other Powers vested by this Constitution in the Government of the United States, or in any Department or Officer thereof. . .

Section 10. No State shall enter into any Treaty, Alliance, or Confederation; grant Letters of Marque and Reprisal; coin Money; emit Bills of Credit; make any Thing but gold and silver Coin a Tender in Payment of Debts; pass any Bill of Attainder, ex post facto Law, or Law impairing the Obligation of Contracts, or grant any Title of Nobility. . .

ARTICLE II.

Section 1. The executive Power shall be vested in a President of the United States of America. He shall hold his Office during the Term of four Years, and, together with the Vice President, chosen for the same Term, be elected, as follows. . .

ARTICLE III.

Section 1. The judicial Power of the United States, shall be vested in one supreme Court, and in such inferior Courts as the Congress may from time to time ordain and establish. The Judges, both of the supreme and inferior Courts, shall hold their Offices during good Behaviour, and shall, at stated Times, receive for their Services, a Compensation, which shall not be diminished during their Continuance in Office.

Section 2. The judicial Power shall extend to all Cases, in Law and Equity, arising under this Constitution, the Laws of the United States, and Treaties made, or which shall be made, under their Authority;—to all Cases affecting Ambassadors, other public Ministers and Consuls;—to all Cases of admiralty and maritime Jurisdiction;—to Controversies to which the United States shall be a Party;—to Controversies between two or more States;—between a State and Citizens of another State;—between citizens of different States;—between Citizens of the same State claiming Lands under Grants of different States, and between a State, or the Citizens thereof, and foreign States, Citizens or Subjects.

In all Cases affecting Ambassadors, other public Ministers and Consuls, and those in which a State shall be Party, the supreme Court shall have original Jurisdiction. In all the other Cases before mentioned, the supreme Court shall have appellate Jurisdiction, both as to Law and Fact, with such Exceptions, and under such Regulations as the Congress shall make.

The Trial of all Crimes, except in Cases of Impeachment, shall be by Jury; and such Trial shall be held in the State where the said Crimes shall have been committed; but when not committed within any State, the Trial shall be at such Place or Places as the Congress may by Law have directed. . .

ARTICLE IV.

Section 1. Full Faith and Credit shall be given in each State to the public Acts, Records, and judicial Proceedings of every other State. And the Congress may by general Laws prescribe the Manner in which such Acts, Records and Proceedings shall be proved, and the Effect thereof.

Section 2. The Citizens of each State shall be entitled to all Privileges and Immunities of Citizens in the several States.

A Person charged in any State with Treason, Felony, or other Crime, who shall flee from Justice, and be found in another State, shall on demand of the executive Authority of the State from which he fled, be delivered up, to be removed to the State having Jurisdiction of the Crime. . .

ARTICLE VI.

. . . This Constitution, and the Laws of the United States which shall be made in Pursuance thereof; and all Treaties made, or which shall be made, under the Authority of the United States, shall be the supreme Law of the Land; and the Judges in every State shall be bound thereby, any Thing in the Constitution or Laws of any State to the Contrary notwithstanding. . .

ARTICLES IN ADDITION TO, AND AMENDMENT OF, THE CONSTITUTION OF THE UNITED STATES OF AMERICA, PROPOSED BY CONGRESS, AND RATIFIED BY THE SEVERAL STATES, PURSUANT TO THE FIFTH ARTICLE OF THE ORIGINAL CONSTITUTION.

AMENDMENT V.

No person shall be held to answer for a capital, or otherwise infamous crime, unless on a presentment or indictment of a Grand Jury, except in cases arising in the land or naval forces, or in the Militia, when in actual service in time of War or public danger; nor shall any person be subject for the same offence to be twice put in jeopardy of life or limb; nor shall be compelled in any criminal case to be a witness against himself, nor be deprived of life, liberty, or property, without due process of law; nor shall private property be taken for public use, without just compensation. . .

AMENDMENT X.

The powers not delegated to the United States by the Constitution, nor prohibited by it to the States, are reserved to the States respectively, or to the people. . .

AMENDMENT XIV.

Section 1. All persons born or naturalized in the United States, and subject to the jurisdiction thereof, are citizens of the United States and of the State wherein they reside. No State shall make or enforce any law which shall abridge the privileges or immunities of citizens of the United States; nor shall any State deprive any person of life, liberty, or property, without due process of law; nor deny to any person within its jurisdiction the equal protection of the laws. . .

Section 5. The Congress shall have power to enforce, by appropriate legislation, the provisions of this article.

APPENDIX B

TITLE 28, UNITED STATES CODE

■ ■ ■

JUDICIARY AND JUDICIAL PROCEDURE

(As Amended to January 1, 2018)

§ 1331. *Federal Question*

The district courts shall have original jurisdiction of all civil actions arising under the Constitution, laws, or treaties of the United States.

§ 1652. *State laws as rules of decision*

The laws of the several states, except where the Constitution or treaties of the United States or Acts of Congress otherwise require or provide, shall be regarded as rules of decision in civil actions in the courts of the United States, in cases where they apply.

§ 1738. *State and Territorial statutes and judicial proceedings; full faith and credit*

The Acts of the legislature of any State, Territory, or Possession of the United States, or copies thereof, shall be authenticated by affixing the seal of such State, Territory or Possession thereto.

The records and judicial proceedings of any court of any such State, Territory or Possession, or copies thereof, shall be proved or admitted in other courts within the United States and its Territories and Possessions by the attestation of the clerk and seal of the court annexed, if a seal exists, together with a certificate of a judge of the court that the said attestation is in proper form.

Such Acts, records and judicial proceedings or copies thereof, so authenticated, shall have the same full faith and credit in every court within the United States and its Territories and Possessions as they have by law or usage in the courts of such State, Territory or Possession from which they are taken.

§ 1738A. *Full faith and credit given to child custody determinations*

(a) The appropriate authorities of every State shall enforce according to its terms, and shall not modify except as provided in subsections (f), (g), and (h) of this section, any custody determination or visitation determination made consistently with the provisions of this section by a court of another State.

(b) As used in this section, the term—

(1) "child" means a person under the age of eighteen;

(2) "contestant" means a person, including a parent, who claims a right to custody or visitation of a child;

(3) "custody determination" means a judgment, decree, or other order of a court providing for the custody or visitation of a child, and includes permanent and temporary orders, and initial orders and modifications;

(4) "home State" means the State in which, immediately preceding the time involved, the child lived with his parents, a parent, or a person acting as parent, for at least six consecutive months, and in the case of a child less than six months old, the State in which the child lived from birth with any of such persons. Periods of temporary absence of any of such persons are counted as part of the six-month or other period;

(5) "modification" and "modify" refer to a custody determination which modifies, replaces, supersedes, or otherwise is made subsequent to, a prior custody determination concerning the same child, whether made by the same court or not;

(6) "person acting as a parent" means a person, other than a parent, who has physical custody of a child and who has either been awarded custody by a court or claims a right to custody;

(7) "physical custody" means actual possession and control of a child; and

(8) "State" means a State of the United States, the District of Columbia, the Commonwealth of Puerto Rico, or a territory or possession of the United States.

(9) "visitation determination" means a judgment, decree, or other order of a court providing for the visitation of a child and includes permanent and temporary orders and initial orders and modifications.

(c) A child custody determination made by a court of a State is consistent with the provisions of this section only if—

(1) such court has jurisdiction under the law of such State; and

(2) one of the following conditions is met:

(A) such State (i) is the home State of the child on the date of the commencement of the proceeding, or (ii) had been the child's home State within six months before the date of the commencement of the proceeding and the child is absent from such State because of his removal or retention by a contestant or for other reasons, and a contestant continues to live in such State;

(B) (i) it appears that no other State would have jurisdiction under subparagraph (A), and (ii) it is in the best interest of the child that a court of such State assume jurisdiction because (I) the child and his parents, or the child and at least one contestant, have a significant connection with such State other than mere physical presence in such State, and (II) there is available in such State substantial evidence concerning the child's present or future care, protection, training, and personal relationships;

(C) the child is physically present in such State and (i) the child has been abandoned, or (ii) it is necessary in an emergency to protect the child because the child, a sibling, or parent of the child has been subjected to or threatened with mistreatment or abuse;

(D) (i) it appears that no other State would have jurisdiction under subparagraph (A), (B), (C), or (E), or another State has declined to exercise jurisdiction on the ground that the State whose jurisdiction is in issue is the more appropriate forum to determine the custody of the child, and (ii) it is in the best interest of the child that such court assume jurisdiction; or

(E) the court has continuing jurisdiction pursuant to subsection (d) of this section.

(d) The jurisdiction of a court of a State which has made a child custody determination consistently with the provisions of this section continues as long as the requirement of subsection (c)(1) of this section continues to be met and such State remains the residence of the child or of any contestant.

(e) Before a child custody determination is made, reasonable notice and opportunity to be heard shall be given to the contestants, any parent whose parental rights have not been previously terminated and any person who has physical custody of a child.

(f) A court of a State may modify a determination of the custody of the same child made by a court of another State, if—

(1) it has jurisdiction to make such a child custody determination; and

(2) the court of the other State no longer has jurisdiction, or it has declined to exercise such jurisdiction to modify such determination.

(g) A court of a State shall not exercise jurisdiction in any proceeding for a custody determination commenced during the pendency of a proceeding in a court of another State where such court of that other State is exercising jurisdiction consistently with the provisions of this section to make a custody determination.

(h) A court of a State may not modify a visitation determination made by a court of another State unless the court of the other State no longer has jurisdiction to modify such determination or has declined to exercise jurisdiction to modify such determination.

§ 1738B. *Full faith and credit for child support orders.*

(a) General Rule.—The appropriate authorities of each State—

(1) shall enforce according to its terms a child support order made consistently with this section by a court of another State; and

(2) shall not seek or make a modification of such an order except in accordance with subsections (e), (f), and (i).

(b) Definitions.—In this section:

(1) The term "child" means—

(A) a person under 18 years of age; and

(B) a person 18 or more years of age with respect to whom a child support order has been issued pursuant to the laws of a State.

(2) The term "child's State" means the State in which a child resides.

(3) The term "child's home State" means the State in which a child lived with a parent or a person acting as parent for at least 6 consecutive months immediately preceding the time of filing of a petition or comparable pleading for support and, if a child is less than 6 months old, the State in which the child lived from birth with any of them. A period of temporary absence of any of them is counted as part of the 6-month period.

(4) The term "child support" means a payment of money, continuing support, or arrearages or the provision of a benefit (including payment of health insurance, child care, and educational expenses) for the support of a child.

(5) The term "child support order"—

(A) means a judgment, decree, or order of a court requiring the payment of child support in periodic amounts or in a lump sum; and

(B) includes—

(i) a permanent or temporary order; and

(ii) an initial order or a modification of an order.

(6) The term "contestant" means—

(A) a person (including a parent) who—

(i) claims a right to receive child support;

(ii) is a party to a proceeding that may result in the issuance of a child support order; or

(iii) is under a child support order; and

(B) a State or political subdivision of a State to which the right to obtain child support has been assigned.

(7) The term "court" means a court or administrative agency of a State that is authorized by State law to establish the amount of child support payable by a contestant or make a modification of a child support order.

(8) The term "modification" means a change in a child support order that affects the amount, scope, or duration of the order and modifies, replaces, supersedes, or otherwise is made subsequent to the child support order.

(9) The term "State" means a State of the United States, the District of Columbia, the Commonwealth of Puerto Rico, the territories and possessions of the United States, and Indian country (as defined in section 1151 of title 18).

(c) Requirements of Child Support Orders.—A child support order made by a court of a State is made consistently with this section if—

(1) a court that makes the order, pursuant to the laws of the State in which the court is located and subsections (e), (f), and (g)—

(A) has subject matter jurisdiction to hear the matter and enter such an order; and

(B) has personal jurisdiction over the contestants; and

(2) reasonable notice and opportunity to be heard is given to the contestants.

(d) Continuing Jurisdiction.—A court of a State that has made a child support order consistently with this section has continuing, exclusive jurisdiction over the order if the State is the child's State or the residence of any individual contestant unless the court of another State, acting in accordance with subsections (e) and (f), has made a modification of the order.

(e) Authority To Modify Orders.—A court of a State may modify a child support order issued by a court of another State if—

(1) the court has jurisdiction to make such a child support order pursuant to subsection (i); and

(2) (A) the court of the other State no longer has continuing, exclusive jurisdiction of the child support order because that State no longer is the child's State or the residence of any individual contestant and the parties have not consented in a record or open court that the tribunal of the other State may continue to exercise jurisdiction to modify its order; or

(B) each individual contestant has filed written consent with the State of continuing, exclusive jurisdiction for a court of another State to modify the order and assume continuing, exclusive jurisdiction over the order.

(f) Recognition of Child Support Orders.—If 1 or more child support orders have been issued with regard to an obligor and a child, a court shall apply the following rules in determining which order to recognize for purposes of continuing, exclusive jurisdiction and enforcement:

(1) If only 1 court has issued a child support order, the order of that court must be recognized.

(2) If 2 or more courts have issued child support orders for the same obligor and child, and only 1 of the courts would have continuing, exclusive jurisdiction under this section, the order of that court must be recognized.

(3) If 2 or more courts have issued child support orders for the same obligor and child, and more than 1 of the courts would have continuing, exclusive jurisdiction under this section, an order issued by a court in the current home State of the child must be recognized, but if an order has not been issued in the current home State of the child, the order most recently issued must be recognized.

(4) If 2 or more courts have issued child support orders for the same obligor and child, and none of the courts would have continuing, exclusive jurisdiction under this section, a court having jurisdiction over the parties shall issue a child support order, which must be recognized.

(5) The court that has issued an order recognized under this subsection is the court having continuing, exclusive jurisdiction under subsection (d).

(g) Enforcement of Modified Orders.—A court of a State that no longer has continuing, exclusive jurisdiction of a child support order may enforce the order with respect to nonmodifiable obligations and unsatisfied obligations that accrued before the date on which a modification of the order is made under subsections (e) and (f).

(h) Choice of Law.—

(1) In general.—In a proceeding to establish, modify, or enforce a child support order, the forum State's law shall apply except as provided in paragraphs (2) and (3).

(2) Law of state of issuance of order.—In interpreting a child support order including the duration of current payments and other obligations of support, a court shall apply the law of the State of the court that issued the order.

(3) Period of limitation.—In an action to enforce arrears under a child support order, a court shall apply the statute of limitation of the forum State or the State of the court that issued the order, whichever statute provides the longer period of limitation.

(i) Registration for Modification.—If there is no individual contestant or child residing in the issuing State, the party or support enforcement agency seeking to modify, or to modify and enforce, a child support order issued in another State shall register that order in a State with jurisdiction over the nonmovant for the purpose of modification.

§ 1738C. *Certain Acts, Records, and Proceedings and the Effect Thereof.*

No State, Territory, or Possession of the United States, or Indian Tribe, shall be required to give effect to any public act, record, or judicial proceeding of any other State, Territory, Possession, or Tribe respecting a relationship between persons of the same sex that is treated as a marriage under the laws of such other State, Territory, Possession, or Tribe, or a right or claim arising from such relationship.

§ 1739. *State and Territorial nonjudicial records; full faith and credit*

All nonjudicial records or books kept in any public office of any State, Territory, or Possession of the United States, or copies thereof, shall be proved or admitted in any court or office in any other State, Territory, or Possession by the attestation of the custodian of such records or books, and the seal of his office annexed, if there be a seal, together with a certificate of a judge of a court of record of the county, parish, or district in which such office may be kept, or of the Governor, or secretary of state, the chancellor or keeper of the great seal, of the State, Territory, or Possession that the said attestation is in due form and by the proper officers.

If the certificate is given by a judge, it shall be further authenticated by the clerk or prothonotary of the court, who shall certify, under his hand and the seal of his office, that such judge is duly commissioned and qualified; or, if given by such Governor, secretary, chancellor, or keeper of the great seal, it shall be under the great seal of the State, Territory, or Possession in which it is made.

Such records or books or copies thereof, so authenticated, shall have the same full faith and credit in every court and office within the United States and its Territories and Possessions as they have by law or usage in the courts or offices of the State, Territory, or Possession from which they are taken.

§ 1963. *Registration in other districts*

A judgment in an action for the recovery of money or property entered in any court of appeals, district court, bankruptcy court, or in the Court of International Trade may be registered by filing a certified copy of the judgment in any other district or, with respect to the Court of International Trade, in any judicial district, when the judgment has become final by appeal or expiration of the time for appeal or when ordered by the court that entered the judgment for good cause shown. Such a judgment entered in favor of the United States may be so registered any time after judgment is entered. A judgment so registered shall have the same effect as a judgment of the district court of the district where registered and may be enforced in like manner.

A certified copy of the satisfaction of any judgment in whole or in part may be registered in like manner in any district in which the judgment is a lien.

The procedure prescribed under this section is in addition to other procedures provided by law for the enforcement of judgments.

§ 2071. *Rule-making power generally*

(a) The Supreme Court and all courts established by Act of Congress may from time to time prescribe rules for the conduct of their business. Such rules shall be consistent with Acts of Congress and rules of practice and procedure prescribed under section 2072 of this title.

(b) Any rule prescribed by a court, other than the Supreme Court, under subsection (a) shall be prescribed only after giving appropriate public notice and an opportunity for comment. Such rule shall take effect upon the date specified by the prescribing court and shall have such effect on pending proceedings as the prescribing court may order.

(c) (1) A rule of a district court prescribed under subsection (a) shall remain in effect unless modified or abrogated by the judicial council of the relevant circuit.

(2) Any other rule prescribed by a court other than the Supreme Court under subsection (a) shall remain in effect unless modified or abrogated by the Judicial Conference. . .

(f) No rule may be prescribed by a district court other than under this section.

§ 2072. *Rules of Procedure and Evidence; power to prescribe*

(a) The Supreme Court shall have the power to prescribe general rules of practice and procedure and rules of evidence for cases in the United States district courts (including proceedings before magistrates thereof) and courts of appeals.

(b) Such rules shall not abridge, enlarge or modify any substantive right. All laws in conflict with such rules shall be of no further force or effect after such rules have taken effect.

(c) Such rules may define when a ruling of a district court is final for the purposes of appeal under section 1291 of this title.

INDEX

References are to Pages